R. Gupta's®

POPULAR MASTER GUIDE

HTET

HARYANA TEACHER ELIGIBILITY TEST

LEVEL-II (Class 6 to 8)

Social Studies

For

Trained Graduate Teacher (TGT)

by

RPH Editorial Board

2026
EDITION

RAMESH PUBLISHING HOUSE, NEW DELHI

Published by

O.P. Gupta *for* Ramesh Publishing House

Admin. Office

12-H, New Daryaganj Road, Opp. Officers' Mess,
New Delhi-110002 ✆ 23275224, 23245124

E-mail: info@rameshpublishinghouse.com

For Online Shopping: www.rameshpublishinghouse.com

Showroom

• Balaji Market, Nai Sarak, Delhi-110006 ✆ 23282525 📱 9354373464

• 4457, Nai Sarak, Delhi-110006

Book Code: R-1936

ISBN: 978-93-86845-64-1

Price: ₹ 520

Printed at: B.K. Offset, Delhi

CONTENTS

LANGUAGES

GENERAL STUDIES

Scheme of Exam

Level-2: Trained Graduate Teacher (TGT) Social Studies

There shall be only one paper. All questions will be Multiple Choice Questions (MCQs) each carrying one mark with four alternatives out of which one answer will be correct.

S.No.	Subjects	No. of Questions	Marks
1.	Child Development and Pedagogy	30	30
2.	**Languages** (Hindi 15 MCQs and English 15 MCQs)	30	30
3.	**General Studies** (Quantitative Aptitude 10 MCQs, Reasoning Ability 10 MCQs and Haryana G.K. and Awareness 10 MCQs)	30	30
4.	Subject Specific (Social Studies)	60	60
	Total	**150**	**150**

NATURE AND STANDARD OF QUESTIONS

- The test items on Child Development and Pedagogy will focus on educational psychology of teaching and learning, relevant to the age group of 11-16 years. They will focus on understanding the characteristics, needs and psychology of diverse learners, interaction with learners and the attributes and qualities of a good facilitator of learning.
- The test items for Languages (Hindi & English) will focus on the proficiencies related to the medium of instruction relevant to the age group of 11-16 years.
- The test items for Quantitative Aptitude, Reasoning Ability and Haryana G.K. and Awareness will focus on the elements of Mental and Reasoning ability and General Knowledge regarding Haryana State.
- The test items in subject specific will focus on the concepts, problem solving abilities and pedagogical understanding of the subjects. The test items shall be evenly distributed over different divisions of the syllabus of that subject as prescribed for classes VI-X by the Board of School Education Haryana.

NEGATIVE MARKING

- There shall be no negative marking.

LANGUAGE OF QUESTION PAPERS

- All questions except those concerning language subjects, will be bilingual *i.e.* Hindi and English.

Previous Years' Paper

Haryana Teacher Eligibility Test (HTET)

TGT Social Studies (Level-2), Exam 2024

(Exam held on 31-07-2025)

PART-I : CHILD DEVELOPMENT AND PEDAGOGY

1. The most appropriate group of qualities in reference of adolescent boys and girls is:

1. Ideal, Good adjustment, Self-respect
2. Abstract thinking, Reasoning, Decision-making
3. Observation, Feeling of revolt, Habit of repetition
4. Philosophy, Good adjustment, Feeling of social service

2. Who experimented on 'cat' with reference to trial and error theory of learning?

1. Pavlov 2. Skinner
3. Thorndike 4. Guilford

3. Heredity plays the greatest role in the:

1. Social Development 2. Spiritual Development
3. Physical Development 4. Cultural Development

4. Which of the following is **not** a projective method of personality measurement?

1. Association technique 2. Construction technique
3. Case study 4. Completion technique

5. Who was the exponent of the method of Insight learning?

1. Thorndike 2. Kohler
3. Davis 4. Skinner

6. "Learning takes place through a process of need reduction." The learning theory related to the statement is:

1. Insight theory
2. Operant conditioned theory
3. Conditioned response theory
4. Reinforcement theory

7. "Anything can be taught at any stage of development." Expressed by:

1. Ausubel 2. Bruner
3. Piaget 4. Gagne

8. Who postulated the Brain Storming Method for fostering and boosting creativity?

1. Myres 2. Torance
3. Osborn 4. Gordon

9. Plateau in the learning curve indicates:

1. Working conditions are favourable
2. No fatigue
3. Task is simple
4. Loss of interest

10. According to a traditional saying, 'when the fox could not reach the grapes despite all it's efforts, it said that the grapes are sour'. This is an example of:

1. Withdrawal 2. Rationalization
3. Projection 4. Regression

11. Conditioned Response Theory is given by:

1. Pavlov 2. Skinner
3. Thorndike 4. Kohler

12. ________ is **not** necessary for the education of visually impaired students.

1. Books in small letters
2. Audio cassette
3. Brail text material on the paper
4. Abacus for teaching of Mathematics

13. The concept of reformatory school is:

1. for mentally retarded children
2. for gifted children
3. for juvenile delinquent children
4. for normal children

14. Theory of Intelligence given by Spearman is:

1. One factor theory 2. Two factor theory
3. Three factor theory 4. Multi-factor theory

1. 2	**2.** 3	**3.** 3	**4.** 3	**5.** 2	**6.** 4	**7.** 2
8. 3	**9.** 4	**10.** 2	**11.** 1	**12.** 1	**13.** 3	**14.** 2

15. Tolman's theory is related to:
1. Energy system 2. Cathexes
3. Topology 4. Development stages

16. According to the need hierarchy theory of Maslow, basic need at bottom level's is considered:
1. Belongingness
2. Physiological Need
3. Self-Actualization
4. Security

17. Agraphia is:
1. In this the patient loses the ability to read.
2. In this the patient does not have the ability to express his thoughts in writing.
3. In this the patient does not have the ability to do simple addition and subtraction.
4. In this the patient is found to be unable to name the objects.

18. Kohler proved that learning is:
1. bonding of stimulus and responses.
2. the perception of different part of situation.
3. an autonomous random activity.
4. the whole situation perception.

19. The concept of 'emotional intelligence' was given by:
1. Dan Golman
2. Peter Salovay and John Mayer
3. Tolman
4. Terman

20. Following are the stages of Kohlberg's theory **except** ________.
1. Conventional 2. Pre-conventional
3. Sensori Motor 4. Post-conventional

21. "The development of child starts from the head and moves towards the feet." The given statement is related to which theory of development?
1. Principle of Development Direction
2. Principle of Development Sequence
3. Principle of Continuous Development
4. Principle of Interrelation

22. Which is **not** an appropriate statement regarding learning?
1. Learning is universal process.
2. Learning is not the change in behaviour.
3. Learning helps in adjustment.
4. Learning is transferable from one situation to another.

23. Teacher needs to create an inclusive environment in the classroom:
1. special children should be kept away from educational activities.
2. the rights and dignity of special children should be protected.
3. special children should be considered as inferior to normal children.
4. special children should be looked down upon among normal students.

24. According to Piaget, concrete operational stage is:
1. 0 to 2 years 2. 7 to 11 years
3. 11 to 12 years 4. above 12 years

25. In continuous and comprehensive evaluation, 'comprehensive' means:
1. by evaluation of all subjects
2. by evaluation of only educational field
3. by homework evaluation
4. by evaluating the development of educational and co-educational field

26. "You can make a student to sit in the class but can't force him to acquire knowledge." This statement is confirmed by which law of learning?
1. by the law of Readiness
2. by the law of Exercise
3. by the law of Disuse
4. by the law of Effect

27. Which out of the following is the process of arousing, sustaining and regulating activity?
1. Interest 2. Opinion
3. Attitude 4. Motivation

28. In which of the following, instinct does **not** match with related emotion?
1. Laughter – Amusement
2. Self-Abasement – Feeling of superiority
3. Gregariousness – Feeling of loneliness
4. Repulsion – Disgust

29. In the following who is related to modeling concept?
1. Sigmund Freud 2. Thorndike
3. Albert Bandura 4. Guilford

30. The mental age of a 6 (six) years old girl is 7.5 (seven years six months) years, her I.Q. will be:
1. 125 2. 90
3. 75 4. 140

15. 3	**16.** 2	**17.** 2	**18.** 4	**19.** 2	**20.** 3	**21.** 1	**22.** 2
23. 2	**24.** 2	**25.** 4	**26.** 1	**27.** 4	**28.** 2	**29.** 3	**30.** 1

PART-II : भाषा – हिन्दी

31. तत्सम-तद्भव शब्दों के संदर्भ में अनुपयुक्त विकल्प चुनिए :
1. गर्त - गड्ढा 2. जृम्भिका - जवाँई
3. चर्मचटक - चमगादड़ 4. परिकूट - परकोटा

32. निम्न में से 'शिक्षण-सूत्र' **नहीं** है :
1. पूर्ण से अंश की ओर 2. प्रेरणा से तर्क की ओर
3. स्थूल से सूक्ष्म की ओर 4. उपर्युक्त सभी

33. निम्न में से **असंगत** को चुनिए :
1. अं, अः – अयोगवाह ध्वनियाँ
2. ड़, ढ़ – उत्क्षिप्त ध्वनियाँ
3. श, ष, स – स्पर्श संघर्षी
4. ऐ, औ – अर्ध संवृत

34. निम्न में से प्रक्षेपित शिक्षण सहायक सामग्री **नहीं** है :
1. दूरदर्शन 2. फिल्म स्ट्रीप
3. ओवरहेड प्रोजेक्टर 4. फिल्म

35. समस्तपद एवं समास विग्रह की दृष्टि से **असंगत** विकल्प चुनिए:
1. लोकप्रिय - अधिकरण तत्पुरुष
2. पवन से चलने वाली चक्की - पनचक्की
3. नवयुवक - नव है जो युवक
4. परीक्षाभवन - परीक्षा के लिए भवन

36. किस विकल्प में विलोम-युग्म सही **नहीं** है?
1. वैमनस्य - सौमनस्य 2. अभिमानी - निरभिमानी
3. अभ्यर्थी - प्रत्यर्थी 4. स्वार्थी - निस्स्वार्थ

37. प्रत्यय की दृष्टि से **असंगत** विकल्प चुनिए :
1. ई - द्रौपदी, जानकी, वाल्मीकि
2. य - माहात्म्य, वैधव्य, पौलस्त्य
3. तर - महत्तर, वृहत्तर, दृढतर
4. एय - भागिनेय, पाथेय, वैनतेय

38. 'पर्यायवाची' की दृष्टि से **असुमेलित** को चुनिए :
1. तरंग - ऊर्मि, वीचि, कल्लोल
2. तरणि - नौका, द्रोणी, करवाल
3. तोता - रक्ततुंड, कीर, सुग्गा
4. योनि - अपत्यपथ, जन्मवर्त्म, रतिकुहर

39. **असंगत** विकल्प चुनिए :
1. समुद्र में लगने वाली आग - दावानल
2. लोक-प्रचलित बात, जिसके वक्ता का पता न हो - किंवदन्ती
3. पशुओं द्वारा जुगाली करने की प्रक्रिया - पागुर
4. जिसके पति ने दूसरा विवाह कर लिया हो - अध्यूढा

40. किस शब्द में 'कु' उपसर्ग का प्रयोग **नहीं** हुआ है
1. कुज 2. कुमार 3. कुचो 4. कुमति

41. समश्रुत भिन्नार्थक शब्द 'मनुजात - मनुजाद' का क्रमशः **सही** अर्थ चुनिए:
1. मनुष्य को खाने वाला, मनुष्य से पैदा हुआ
2. मनु उत्पन्न हुआ, अफ्रीकी निवासी
3. मनु उत्पन्न, मनुष्य को खाने वाला
4. मनुज का पुत्र, मनुज से संबंध रखने वाला

42. यण् संधि दृष्टि से **संगत** विकल्प चुनिए :
1. जात्यामान = जाती + अभिमान
2. पर्युषण = परि + ऊषण
3. वध्विच्छा = वधु + इच्छा
4. महैन्द्रजालिक = महा + ऐन्द्रजालिक

निर्देश (प्र.सं. 43 से 45 तक): *अधोलिखित गद्यांश को पढ़कर उत्तर दीजिए :*

हमें इस बात को समझना होगा कि युद्ध की अनुपस्थिति ही शांति की परिभाषा नहीं है। बुद्ध ने जिस शांतिपूर्ण समाज की परिकल्पना की थी, उसमें समानता का वह संदेश भी शामिल था, जो हमें इस बात का अहसास कराता है कि मनुष्य को मनुष्य से पृथक् दिखाने का हर प्रयास मनुष्यता का शत्रु है। ऐसे प्रत्येक प्रयास को विफल बनाना मनुष्योचित है, एक शर्त भी है मनुष्य के रूप में जीने की। हमारी चिंता यह होनी चाहिए कि हमें स्वयं को मनुष्य कैसे बनाएँ एवं कैसे मनुष्य बनाए रखें। मनुष्य बनने का अर्थ है - अपने भीतर दूसरे की पीड़ा को समझने का अहसास जगाना, अपने भीतर करुणा का वह भाव जगाना, जो हमें दूसरे से जोड़ता है। छोटे-छोटे पुल बनाने होंगे हमें दूसरे से जुड़ने के लिए—करुणा का पुल, मैत्री का पुल, समानता का पुल, विषमता मिटाने वाला पुल ______ । ऐसा समझकर ही हम मानवोचित आचरण का मंत्र अपना सकते हैं, प्रबुद्ध बन सकते हैं।

43. लेखक के अनुसार शांति की परिभाषा **नहीं** है :
1. युद्ध की अनुपस्थिति।
2. शांतिपूर्ण समाज की परिकल्पना।
3. जिसमें समानता का संदेश सम्मिलित हो।
4. स्वयं को मनुष्य बनाना।

44. लेखक के अनुसार मनुष्य बनने का क्या अर्थ है?
1. बुद्धोपदिष्ट राह का अनुगामी।
2. मनुष्य को मनुष्य से पृथक दिखाना।
3. दूसरे की पीड़ा को समझने का भाव जगाना।
4. प्रबुद्ध मानवोचित आचरण।

45. गद्यांश में प्रयुक्त पदों की व्याकरणिक विवेचना के संदर्भ में **असंगत** कथन चुनिए।
1. अनुपस्थिति - दो उपसर्ग 2. मनुष्यता - जातिवाचक संज्ञा
3. प्रत्येक - अव्ययीभाव समास 4. विषमता - व्यंजन संधि

31. 2	**32.** 2	**33.** 4	**34.** 1	**35.** 2	**36.** 3	**37.** 1	**38.** 2
39. 1	**40.** 2	**41.** 3	**42.** 2	**43.** 1	**44.** 3	**45.** 4	

PART-II : LANGUAGE – ENGLISH

46. Fill in the blank with the **correct** option:
Stress, intonation and rhythm can be taught through ________.

1. skimming
2. scanning
3. drills of various types
4. transcription

47. Which one of the following is **not** a teaching aid in developing listening skills?

1. Use of phonetic dictionary
2. Gramophones
3. Television
4. Film & film strips

48. Fill in the blank with the **correct** option:
Multimedia materials for teaching ________ are.

1. LSRW lesson
2. grammar, syntax and lexicon
3. text, image, audio, video and animation
4. phonetic, phonemic lessons

49. Complete the sentence with the **correct** option:
Multilinguistic resource ________.

1. will increase the level of learner participation
2. will decrease the level of learner participation
3. is poor compared to any standardized text-book
4. deprives the teacher's role as a facilitator

Directions (Qs. No. 50 to 59): *Read the following passage and answer the questions that follow:*

I worked for a brief while in a college in Delhi, and among my more uncomfortable memories is a language exercise, I gave a group of eight undergraduates: I asked them to imagine that they had already graduated and wanted them to write an application for a suitable job. Seven of the eight students wrote applications for the jobs of clerks. Even in one of the good universities, and in a college that had a reputation for it academic standard, the system has snuffed out all youthful ambition.

Even the highest youthful ambition in the prestigious colleges is to pass the competitive examination for appointments in the administrative services, and there are colleges that are more proud of the bureaucrats among their alumni than of any scholars, scientists or leaders of opinion. And these latter, understandably, are a small number. Students derive the meanness of their ambitions from the meanness of the goals that the colleges propose to themselves. And of the most ambitious, as well as of the least, among the students, it could be said that they think more of what society will do to or for them, than of what they would be able to do for and to society. This is an excellent apprenticeship for joining the ranks of hirelings or of the unemployed.

50. How long did the author work in a Delhi College?

1. long time
2. short time
3. three years
4. seven years

51. What exercise did the author give the students?

1. a comprehension passage
2. precis writing
3. expansion of a poem
4. a language exercise

52. Seven out of the eight students wanted to become ________.

1. scholars
2. bureaucrats
3. clerks
4. scientists

53. What according to the author is the highest ambition of students in good colleges?

1. to qualify for administrative services
2. to become leaders of opinion
3. to teach
4. to practice medicine

54. In the sentence "And these latter understandably are a small number", what does "these latter" refer to?

1. clerks, doctors & engineers
2. bureaucrats, scholars and clerks
3. scholars, scientists and leaders of opinion
4. only administrators

55. Fill in the blank with the **correct** option:
The thinking of the most ambitious and the least ambitious is ________.

1. uncommon
2. alike
3. dissimilar
4. for the society

56. Identify the statement which is **true**:

1. The college where the author worked in Delhi had a reputation for its academic standards.
2. The students, who were asked to do the language exercise were graduates.
3. All colleges produce scientists, scholars and leaders of opinion.
4. The language exercise is stored in the author's less comfortable memories.

46. 3	**47.** 1	**48.** 3	**49.** 1	**50.** 2	**51.** 4
52. 3	**53.** 1	**54.** 3	**55.** 2	**56.** 1	

57. Fill in the blank with the **correct** option:
Another word for "snuffed out" is ________.
1. smelled
2. instilled
3. encouraged
4. killed

58. Choose the opposite of "former" from the passage:
1. least 2. latter
3. already 4. most

59. Fill in the blank with the **correct** option:
"Alumni" in the passage means ________.
1. unsuccessful students 2. successful students
3. bureaucrats 4. old students

60. Which one of the following is the first step in teaching formal grammar?
1. comparison & generalization
2. collection and presentation of examples
3. application of rules
4. motivation and testing of previous knowledge

PART-III : GENERAL STUDIES

Quantitative Aptitude, Reasoning Ability and GK & Awareness

61. The square root of $\dfrac{\left(1\frac{3}{4}\right)^4 - \left(2\frac{1}{3}\right)^4}{\left(1\frac{3}{4}\right)^2 - \left(2\frac{1}{3}\right)^2}$ is equal to:
1. $2\frac{11}{12}$ 2. $2\frac{1}{12}$
3. $3\frac{11}{12}$ 4. $3\frac{1}{12}$

62. X can do a work in 6 days and Y can do same work in 8 days. With the help of Z, all three finished the work in 3 days. If they altogether got ₹ 2000 after completing the work, then Z gets:
1. ₹ 200 2. ₹ 250
3. ₹ 400 4. ₹ 500

63. Find the **odd** one:
1. Rectangle 2. Square
3. Cube 4. Triangle

64. By selling an item for ₹ 153, a man gets loss of 10%. For how much should he sell them to get profit of 20%?
1. ₹ 204 2. ₹ 214
3. ₹ 220 4. ₹ 170

65. A, B, C, D and E are sitting around a circular table facing the centre. Only A is between E and B. D is to the immediate left of B. Who is to the immediate left of C?
1. E 2. D
3. B 4. A

66. Shekhar walks 10 metres towards North. Then he walks 6 metres towards South. Then he walks 3 metres towards East. How far is he from his starting point?
1. 7 metres 2. 6 metres
3. 5 metres 4. 4 metres

67. Next term of the following number series will be:
5, 6, 9, 15, 25, ?
1. 35 2. 377
3. 40 4. 411

68. If the letters in the word CYBERNETICS are rearranged in the alphabetical order, which letter will be in the middle in order after rearrangement?
1. E 2. I 3. N 4. R

69. P is Q's sister. R is Q's mother. S is R's father. T is S's mother. How is P related to S?
1. Daughter 2. Sister
3. Grandmother 4. Granddaughter

70. If ZIP = 300 and ZAN = 400, then ZOO = ?
1. 250 2. 350 3. 200 4. 500

71. Find the missing term in the following letter series:
AYD, BVF, DRH, ?, KGL
1. FMJ 2. GMJ
3. GNJ 4. FNK

72. Sachin is shorter than Kamal, but taller than Ram. Mohan is the tallest. Arun is a little shorter than Kamal and a little taller than Sachin. Who is the second tallest among these five persons?
1. Sachin 2. Arun
3. Ram 4. Kamal

57. 4	**58.** 2	**59.** 4	**60.** 4	**61.** 1	**62.** 2	**63.** 3	**64.** 1
65. 1	**66.** 3	**67.** 3	**68.** 2	**69.** 4	**70.** 1	**71.** 2	**72.** 4

73. The diameter of a sphere whose volume is $113\frac{1}{7}$ cubic metres is:

1. 3 metres
2. 6 metres
3. 7 metres
4. 14 metres

74. If the diameter of a right circular cylinder is 28 cm and its height is 20 cm, then the total surface area is equal to:

1. 1760 cm^2
2. 1232 cm^2
3. 1496 cm^2
4. 2992 cm^2

75. The perimeter of the rhombus is 52 cm. If one of the diagonal is 24 cm, the area of the rhombus is equal to:

1. 240 cm^2
2. 120 cm^2
3. 180 cm^2
4. 90 cm^2

76. The radius and the height of right circular cone are in the ratio 5 : 12. If its volume is 314 $metre^3$, the diameter of its base is equal to (π = 3.14):

1. 10 metres
2. 5 metres
3. 20 metres
4. 15 metres

77. The value of $\sec(90°-A) - \cot A \cos(90°-A) \tan(90°-A)$ is:

1. tan A
2. cot A
3. cos A
4. sin A

78. If the height of a tower is $2\sqrt{3}$ metres and the length of its shadow is 2 metres, then the angle of elevation of sun is equal to:

1. 30°
2. 45°
3. 60°
4. 75°

79. The least number of complete years, in which a sum of money put at 20% compound interest will be more than doubled, is:

1. 2
2. 3
3. 4
4. 5

80. How many numbers from 11 to 50 are there which are exactly divisible by 7 but not by 3?

1. 3
2. 4
3. 5
4. 7

81. Who among the following received Arjuna Award of 2023?

1. Diksha Dagar
2. Vinesh Phogat
3. Babita Kumari
4. Reetika Hooda

82. Which of the following Wild Life Sanctuary is located in Panchkula?

1. Chhilchhila Sanctuary
2. Bir Shikargarh Sanctuary
3. Nahar Sanctuary
4. Kaparwas Sanctuary

83. Which of the following districts does **not** come under the Shivalik Development Agency?

1. Ambala
2. Panchkula
3. Yamuna Nagar
4. Kurukshetra

84. Per capita income of Haryana during 2023-24 on constant prices is:

1. ₹ 3,25,759
2. ₹ 1,85,490
3. ₹ 1,63,285
4. ₹ 1,04,550

85. The Chief Justice of Punjab and Haryana High Court is:

1. Justice Sheel Nagu
2. Justice Ravishankar Jha
3. Justice Ritu Bahri
4. Justice Krishna Murari

86. Identify the composition of Haryana Public Service Commission:

1. Chairman and four members
2. Chairman and three members
3. Chairman and five members
4. Chairman and six members

87. Read the following statements about Bhadanakas:

(*a*) During 12th century they were ruling over the area of Gurugram & Rewari

(*b*) They defeated Chauhan ruler Prithviraj-III.

Choose the **correct** code:

1. Only statement (*a*) is true.
2. Only statement (*b*) is true.
3. Neither statement (*a*) nor statement (*b*) is true.
4. Both the statements are true.

88. As per Mahabharata, who among the following led an expedition to Rohtak?

1. Bhishma
2. Arjuna
3. Bhim
4. Nakul

89. Which district of Haryana shares its boundaries with Seven districts of Haryana?

1. Ambala
2. Panchkula
3. Kurukshetra
4. Jind

90. The Sikh Chieftain of Ladawa who fought against British during the First-Anglo-Maratha war:

1. Gurdit Singh
2. Lal Singh
3. Bhoj Singh
4. Manohar Singh

73. 2	**74.** 4	**75.** 2	**76.** 1	**77.** 4	**78.** 3	**79.** 3	**80.** 2	**81.** 1
82. 2	**83.** 4	**84.** 2	**85.** 1	**86.** 3	**87.** 1	**88.** 4	**89.** 4	**90.** 1

PART-IV : SUBJECT KNOWLEDGE—SOCIAL STUDIES

91. During Sultanate period the Barid-e-Mumalik was:
1. Chief of the Army
2. Chief of the Intelligence Department
3. Revenue Minister
4. Chief of Cavalry

92. Which of the following was **not** an official in Mauryan Administration?
1. Antpal 2. Prashasta
3. Dronmukh 4. Nayak

93. If the demand function is pq = c, where c is constant, then which of the following statement are **correct** with respect to this demand function?

(*i*) the shape of this demand curve will be like rectangular hyperbola.

(*ii*) at all points on this demand curve e = –1

(*iii*) at all points on this demand curve total expenditure will remain the same.

(*iv*) at all points on this demand curve the product of p and q will be the same.

Use the following codes to select **correct** answer:

Codes:
1. Only (*i*) is correct
2. Only (*i*) and (*ii*) are correct
3. Only (*i*), (*ii*) and (*iii*) are correct
4. (*i*), (*ii*), (*iii*) & (*iv*) all are correct

94. Which of the following pairs is **not** correctly matched?

	Ruler		**Title**
1.	Rajadhiraj-I	–	Vijayrajendra
2.	Rajendra Chola-I	–	Shangham Tavirt
3.	Mahendravarman-I	–	Mattavilasa
4.	Narsinghvarman	–	Vatapikonda

95. In which year Right to Information Act was enacted by the Government of India?
1. October, 1986 2. August, 1999
3. January, 2014 4. October, 2005

96. In federal system of government there is:
1. Single administration
2. Distribution of Powers
3. Centralised decision-making
4. Less expenses

97. In the 2023 Global Hunger Index India ranked ______ out of the 125 countries.
1. 26 2. 37
3. 111 4. 125

98. Which of the following neighbouring countries had better performance in terms of human development than India in year 2022?
1. Bangladesh 2. Sri Lanka
3. Nepal 4. Pakistan

99. Anekantavada is related with:
1. Buddhism 2. Charvaka Philosophy
3. Jainism 4. Ajivika Sect

100. Who among the following scholars argued that "God not only created Adam as the first man, he was also the first king of the earth and present kings being his successors?
1. John Locke 2. Friedrich Engels
3. R.M. MacIver 4. Robert Filmer

101. When was National Food Security Act enacted in India?
1. 2009 2. 2015
3. 2014 4. 2013

102. The geographical shape of the earth is called:
1. Circular 2. Spheroid
3. Geoid 4. Gnomon

103. Which among the following is/are **not** correctly matched?

(*a*) Equinox – only 21st March

(*b*) Summer solstice – 21st June

(*c*) Winter solstice – 22nd December

Code:
1. (*a*), (*b*) and (*c*) 2. (*b*) and (*c*)
3. (*a*) and (*c*) 4. Only (*a*)

104. Match List-I with List-II and select the **correct** answer by using the codes given below the lists:

List-I	**List-II**
(*a*) Right to Equality	(*i*) Article 19-22
(*b*) Right to Freedom	(*ii*) Article 32
(*c*) Cultural and Educational Rights	(*iii*) Article 14-18
(*d*) Right to Constitutional Remedies	(*iv*) Article 29-30

Codes:

	(*a*)	(*b*)	(*c*)	(*d*)
1.	(*iii*)	(*i*)	(*iv*)	(*ii*)
2.	(*i*)	(*iii*)	(*iv*)	(*ii*)
3.	(*iv*)	(*iii*)	(*ii*)	(*i*)
4.	(*ii*)	(*iv*)	(*iii*)	(*i*)

91. 2	**92.** 3	**93.** 4	**94.** 2	**95.** 4	**96.** 2	**97.** 3
98. 2	**99.** 3	**100.** 4	**101.** 4	**102.** 3	**103.** 4	**104.** 1

105. Which of the following pairs is **not** correctly matched?

	Artefact		**Places where found**
1.	Bronze mirror	–	Dholavira
2.	Statue of Priest King	–	Mohanjodaro
3.	Clay model of a plough	–	Banawali
4.	Pot depicting the story of a thirsty crow	–	Kalibangan

106. Which of the following is **not** an intrusive volcanic landform?

1. Batholith
2. Caldera
3. Dyke
4. Sill

107. Who among the following scholars is **not** related to resurgence of political theory?

1. Michael Oakeshott
2. John Rawls
3. Jurgen Habermas
4. Alfred Cobban

108. The 'land of mid-night Sun' is found at/along:

1. Tropic of cancer
2. Tropic of capricorn
3. Equator
4. North of Arctic circle

109. Which of the following features is/are **true** regarding Mathura Art?

(*a*) The sculpture were made of red sano stones.

(*b*) In this style Buddha, Bodhisattavas, Jain Tirthankaras and Hindu gods & goddess have been depicted

(*c*) The large number of Jaina sculpture found at Kankali Tila in Mathura.

Code:

1. Only (*b*)
2. Only (*c*)
3. (*a*) and (*c*)
4. (*a*), (*b*) and (*c*)

110. As per the continental drif theory of Alfred Wegener which among the following is/are **correctly** matched?

(*a*) Super continent – Pangaea

(*b*) Mega ocean – Panthalassa

(*c*) Southern continental masa – Laurasia

Select the **correct** answer from the codes given below:

Code:

1. (*a*), (*b*) and (*c*)
2. (*a*) and (*c*)
3. Only (*c*)
4. (*a*) and (*b*)

111. Consider the following statements:

I. J.S. Mill in his book "On Liberty" deals with individual liberty.

II. He distinguishes between "Self regarding action" and "Other regarding action."

Which of the statements given above is/are **correct**?

1. Only (I)
2. Only (II)
3. Both (I) and (II)
4. Neither (I) nor (II)

112. Which of the following terminology is related to Nozick's theory of Justice?

1. Original Position
2. Veil of ignorance
3. Difference principle
4. Entitlement theory of justice

113. The nodal agency that undertakes the procurement, distribution and storage of foodgrain in India is:

1. State Trading Corporation
2. Food Corporation of India
3. Union Ministry of Agriculture
4. Respective, State governments

114. The temperature found at the upper limit of mesosphere is:

1. +80°C
2. –180°C
3. -100°C
4. +100°C

115. Which of the following layer of interior of earth is the liquid state?

1. Mental
2. Outer core
3. Inner core
4. Crust

116. When one moves upward from right to left on a negatively sloped straight line demand curve, then the value of price elasticity of demand:

1. remains constant
2. increases
3. decrease
4. first increases and then decreases

105. 4	**106.** 2	**107.** 4	**108.** 4	**109.** 4	**110.** 4
111. 3	**112.** 4	**113.** 2	**114.** 3	**115.** 2	**116.** 2

117. Which Article of the Constitution of India mentions the special procedure in respect of Money Bills?

1. Article 108 2. Article 109
3. Article 111 4. Article 112

118. Which statement is **false** regarding the Tripartite Struggle for the control over Kannauj?

1. The political-economic importance of Kannauj city was the reason for this conflict.
2. This conflict occurred among Pala, Gurjar Pratihar and Rashtrakuta.
3. Vatsaraja and Dharamapal were the first to initiate this conflict.
4. Ultimately the Pala rulers succeeded in this conflict.

119. Who can grant special leave to an appeal from any judgement or matter passed by any court in the territory of India?

1. Parliament
2. The President
3. Union Law Minister
4. Supreme Court

120. Who is Director General of World Trade Organization?

1. Ngozi Okonjo-Iweala
2. Robert Azevedo
3. Pascal Lamy
4. Supachai Punitch Pakdi

121. 'The sunset law' was associated with which of the following Land revenue systems?

1. Mahalwari-system
2. Rayyatwari system
3. Parmanent settlement
4. Ain-e-Dehsala system

122. By which treaty was the European Union formed?

1. Dunkirk treaty 2. Marrakesh treaty
3. Maastricht treaty 4. Bretton Woods treaty

123. Who suggested a collective security system for Asia in 1969?

1. Nikita Khrushchev 2. Leonid Brezhnev
3. Mikhail Gorbachev 4. Richard Nixon

124. 'Sargaso Sea' is located into:

1. North Atlantic Ocean
2. South Atlantic Ocean
3. South Pacific Ocean
4. Arctic Ocean

125. Read the following statements about agriculture in India & select the **correct** answer using codes given below.

According to Economic Survey of 2023-24:

(*i*) agriculture sector provides livelihood to about 42.3 percent of population.

(*ii*) the share of agriculture sector in country's GDP is 18.2 percent at current prices.

(*iii*) the average annual growth rate of agriculture sector remained at 4.18 percent at constant prices over last 5 years.

(*iv*) the productivity of Indian agriculture is highest in the world.

1. Only (*i*) is correct
2. Only (*i*) & (*ii*) are correct
3. Only (*i*), (*ii*) and (*iii*) are correct
4. (*i*), (*ii*), (*iii*) & (*iv*) all are correct

126. Suppose your principal is penalizing you deliberately. You do your best efforts to make him happy. But he deals with you as enemy. What would you do under this situation?

1. You will always abuse him
2. You will not do anything
3. You will always find fault in him
4. You will never low to his wrong will

127. Which of the following pairs is **not** correctly matched?

	Writer		**Book**
1.	Geoffrey Chaucer	–	The Canterbury Tales
2.	Leon Batista Alberti	–	On the dignity of Man
3.	Lorenzo Valla	–	On Pleasure
4.	Balthasar Castiglione	–	The Book of Courtier

128. The Act of 1872 relating to Inter-caste and Widow remarriage is known as:

1. Widow Remarriage Act
2. Inter-caste Marriage Act
3. Brahma Marriage Act
4. The Special Marriage Act

129. The sum of production in the three sectors within a country during in particular year is called:

1. GNP 2. NNP
3. GDP 4. GNI

117. 2	**118.** 4	**119.** 4	**120.** 1	**121.** 3	**122.** 3	**123.** 2
124. 1	**125.** 3	**126.** 4	**127.** 2	**128.** 3	**129.** 3	

130. When was the ASEAN Regional Forum (ARF) established?

1. 1992 2. 1993
3. 1994 4. 1995

131. Arrange the following events in chronological order.

(*a*) Puna Pact
(*b*) Ahmedabad Mill Satyagrah
(*c*) Rowlatt Satyagrah
(*d*) Gandhi-Irwin Pact

1. (*a*), (*b*), (*c*), (*d*)
2. (*b*), (*d*), (*a*), (*c*)
3. (*c*), (*d*), (*a*), (*b*)
4. (*b*), (*c*), (*d*), (*a*)

132. Who appoints the State Election Commissioner?

1. Chief Election Commissioner of India
2. President of India
3. Governor of the concerned state
4. The Legislative Assembly of the concerned State.

133. The sectors are classified into public and private sector is on the basis of:

1. Employment conditions
2. The nature of economic activity
3. Ownership of enterprise
4. Number of workers employed in the enterprise

134. Who invented the term 'Iron Law of Wages'?

1. Adam Smith
2. Ferdinand Lassalle
3. David Ricardo
4. Karl Marx

135. Which one of the following is not a Coalfield of Gondwana period of India?

1. Korba
2. Jharia
3. Ramgarh
4. Nichahom

136. Which of the following subjects is not included in the union list of the Constitution of India?

1. Atomic energy 2. Banking
3. Agriculture 4. Airways

137. Consider the following statements and choose the **correct** option.

I. After the Chinese Revolution in 1949. India was one of the first countries to recognize the communist government.

II. Atal Bihari Vajpayee became the first Indian Prime Minister after Nehru to visit China.

1. Only (I) is correct
2. Only (II) is correct
3. Both (I) and (II) are correct
4. Both (I) and (II) are not correct

138. Mandovi, Zuari and Rachol are the rivers flowing in which state in India?

1. Kerala 2. Chhattisgarh
3. Goa 4. Maharashtra

139. Which of the following statements is **not** correct about the 'Ayagar System of Vijaynagar'?

1. In this system each village was an independent unit.
2. 10 officials were appointed in each village to govern.
3. These officials were called 'Ayagar'
4. Ayagar could be sold or mortgaged their posts.

140. Match the following pairs:

Organisation	**Year of Establishment**
(*a*) Bombay Presidency Association	(*i*) 1875
(*b*) The Indian Association	(*ii*) 1870
(*c*) Poona Sarvajanik Sabha	(*iii*) 1876
(*d*) The Indian League	(*iv*) 1885

Codes:

	(*a*)	(*b*)	(*c*)	(*d*)
1.	(*i*)	(*ii*)	(*iv*)	(*iii*)
2.	(*iv*)	(*iii*)	(*ii*)	(*i*)
3.	(*i*)	(*iii*)	(*iv*)	(*ii*)
4.	(*iv*)	(*i*)	(*ii*)	(*iii*)

141. Arrange the following events of Akbar's reign in chronologics order:

(*a*) Establishment of Ibadat Khana
(*b*) Introduction of Dahsala System
(*c*) Beginning of the Mansabdari System

Codes:

1. (*a*), (*b*), (*c*) 2. (*c*), (*a*), (*b*)
3. (*c*), (*b*), (*a*) 4. (*b*), (*c*), (*a*)

142. What is rank of India in the world in the production of milk?

1. First 2. Second
3. Third 4. Fourth

130. 3	**131.** 4	**132.** 3	**133.** 3	**134.** 2	**135.** 4	**136.** 3
137. 1	**138.** 3	**139.** 2	**140.** 2	**141.** 2	**142.** 1	

143. 'Quriltais' was:
1. Mongol Military Contingents
2. A kind of tax
3. Unit of ten thousands soldiers
4. The assembly of Mongol Chieftains

144. The terms 'Parkland' or 'Bush-veld' are related with which type of climate?
1. Equatorial
2. Monsoon
3. Savanna
4. Mediterranean

145. Tropical Dry Evergreen Forests are found in :
1. Konkan Coast
2. Coromandel Coast
3. Malabar Coast
4. Utkal Plains

146. Which of the following United Nations Secretary General was awarded the Nobel Peace Prize Posthumously?
1. Dag Hammarskjöld 2. U Thant
3. Kurt Waldheim 4. Ban Ki-Moon

147. Which of the following mountains range is **not** associated with the Lesser Himalaya?
1. Dhaula Dhar 2. Pir Panjal
3. Mahabharat 4. Zanskar

148. When was Mahatma Gandhi National Rural Employment Guarantee Act, enacted?
1. 2004 2. 2005
3. 2014 4. 2019

149. Which among the following Indian state does **not** shares international border with Bangladesh?
1. Assam 2. Manipur
3. Mizoram 4. Meghalaya

150. Which among the following is **not** a major tea producing state of South India?
1. Tamil Nadu 2. Karnataka
3. Kerala 4. Goa

EXPLANATORY ANSWERS

1. During adolescence, the cognitive abilities of boys and girls develop rapidly. They begin to move beyond concrete experiences to develop abstract thinking. They use reasoning to analyze situations and gradually acquire the ability of independent decision-making. These qualities are considered most appropriate for this stage.

2. Edward Lee Thorndike conducted experiments on cats and propounded the "Trial and Error Learning Theory". In his puzzle-box experiments, he showed how the cat, after several trials and errors, learned the correct way to escape, establishing the basis of trial-and-error learning.

3. Heredity plays its greatest role in physical development. Traits such as height, weight, body structure, complexion, and other physical characteristics are largely determined by genetic factors. While environment influences social or cultural development, heredity is dominant in shaping physical growth.

4. Projective methods of personality assessment include Association techniques, Construction techniques, and Completion techniques, as they reveal unconscious aspects of personality. The Case study method, however, is a descriptive and observational method, not a projective one. Hence, this option is correct.

5. German psychologist Wolfgang Köhler was the exponent of the theory of Insight Learning. Through experiments on chimpanzees, he demonstrated that animals often solve problems suddenly by perceiving the relationships among elements in a situation, leading to the so-called "Aha experience". This approach was different from Thorndike's trial-and-error learning.

6. The statement "Learning takes place through a process of need reduction" relates to reinforcement theory. According to this view, learning occurs when a response reduces a need or drive, such as hunger or thirst. The reduction of need works as reinforcement, strengthening the behaviour and making it more likely to occur again.

7. Jerome Bruner emphasized that "anything can be taught at any stage of development, provided it is presented in an intellectually honest form". He advocated the spiral curriculum, where complex ideas can be introduced at a simple level and revisited at more advanced levels as the learner develops.

8. Alex Osborn, an advertising executive, postulated the brainstorming method as a group creativity technique. It encourages generating a large number of ideas without immediate criticism, thus fostering originality and boosting creative thinking.

9. A plateau in the learning curve indicates that progress in learning has temporarily stopped. This often happens due to loss of interest, mental fatigue, or lack of motivation, even though the learner may have the ability to progress further with renewed effort.

143. 4	**144.** 3	**145.** 2	**146.** 1	**147.** 4	**148.** 2	**149.** 2	**150.** 4

10. The saying about the fox and the grapes (from Aesop's fable) is an example of rationalization, a defense mechanism where an individual justifies failure or inability by giving acceptable but false reasons. The fox, unable to get the grapes, rationalized the situation by claiming the grapes were sour.

11. The Conditioned Response Theory was given by Ivan Pavlov. Through his classical conditioning experiments with dogs, Pavlov demonstrated how a neutral stimulus (like a bell) could become associated with an unconditioned stimulus (food) to produce a conditioned response (salivation).

12. For the education of visually impaired students, small-letter books are not useful. Instead, aids such as audio cassettes, Braille text material, and mathematical tools like the abacus are essential for effective learning.

13. Reformatory schools are specially designed for juvenile delinquents, i.e., children who are involved in crimes or socially unacceptable behaviour. These schools focus on rehabilitation, moral development, and social adjustment.

14. Charles Spearman gave the Two-Factor Theory of Intelligence. According to him, intelligence is based on a general factor (g) that influences overall mental performance and specific factors (s) related to particular abilities or tasks.

15. Edward Tolman's theory, known as purposive behaviorism, emphasized that learning is purposeful and goal-directed. He is most famously associated with the concept of cognitive maps, where rats in mazes learned to form spatial representations of their environment. This idea links his work to **topology**, i.e., the mapping of paths, routes, and spatial relations.

At the same time, Tolman also described six types of learning, one of which was **cathexis**, the learned tendency to connect specific objects with the satisfaction (or frustration) of a drive. For example, a hungry rat developing a preference for a path leading to food (positive cathexis) or avoiding a path linked to shock (negative cathexis). Thus, while his broader system included cathexis, equivalence beliefs, field expectancies, and others, the most widely recognized and exam-relevant link is with **topology** because of his cognitive map experiments.

16. In Maslow's hierarchy of needs, the most basic level is physiological needs. These include food, water, air, shelter, sleep, and other essentials for survival. Only when these are fulfilled can individuals move upward to higher needs like safety, belongingness, esteem, and finally self-actualization.

17. Agraphia is a neurological disorder where an individual loses the ability to write, despite having intact motor skills and understanding. It is usually caused by damage to specific areas of the brain such as the left parietal lobe.

18. Kohler, in his experiments with chimpanzees, showed that learning occurs through sudden insight, not mere trial-and-error. He emphasized perceiving the entire situation as a whole, leading to the sudden "Aha" moment of problem-solving.

19. The concept of emotional intelligence was first introduced by Peter Salovey and John Mayer in 1990, describing the ability to understand and manage one's own emotions as well as those of others. Daniel Goleman later popularized the term through his book in 1995, but he was not the originator.

20. Kohlberg's theory of moral development has three main levels—pre-conventional, conventional, and post-conventional—each with two stages. The *sensorimotor stage*, however, is part of Piaget's cognitive development theory, not Kohlberg's moral theory.

21. The statement "the development of a child starts from the head and moves towards the feet" explains the *cephalocaudal principle*, which is part of the principle of development direction. It shows that growth and motor control first appear in the head region and then progress downward to the arms, trunk, and legs.

22. This is not an appropriate statement. Learning is in fact defined as a relatively permanent change in behaviour or knowledge resulting from experience and practice. The other statements—universality of learning, its role in adjustment, and transferability—are correct features of learning.

23. An inclusive classroom ensures that children with special needs are given equal opportunities, respect, and dignity. They should participate in educational activities with others, without being treated as inferior or separated from normal students.

24. According to Jean Piaget's stages of cognitive development, the *concrete operational stage* spans from 7 to 11 years. During this stage, children develop logical thinking, understand concepts of conservation, and can classify and organize objects, though abstract reasoning is still limited.

25. In Continuous and Comprehensive Evaluation (CCE), "comprehensive" refers to assessing both scholastic (educational/academic) and co-scholastic (non-academic such as attitudes, values, life skills, arts, sports) aspects of development to ensure holistic evaluation of a child's progress.

26. Thorndike's law of readiness states that learning becomes effective only when a learner is mentally and physically ready to learn. The statement that one can make a student sit in the class but not force knowledge into him reflects this law—unless the child is prepared, real learning cannot take place.

27. Motivation is the process of arousing, sustaining, and regulating activity. It energizes behaviour, directs it toward a goal, and maintains it until the goal is achieved. Interest, opinion, and attitude influence learning, but motivation is the direct driving force.

28. This pair does not match correctly. Self-abasement is linked with feelings of inferiority, humility, or shame, not superiority. The other instincts and related emotions—laughter with amusement, gregariousness with loneliness, and repulsion with disgust—are properly matched.

29. The concept of modeling is associated with Albert Bandura's Social Learning Theory. He emphasized that individuals, especially children, learn by observing and imitating the behaviours of role models in their environment.

30. Intelligence Quotient (IQ) is calculated as:

$$IQ = \frac{\text{Mental Age}}{\text{Chronological Age}} \times 100$$

Here, Mental Age = 7.5 years,
Chronological Age = 6 years.

$$IQ = \frac{7.5}{6} \times 100 = 125$$

Thus, the girl's IQ is 125.

31. **जृम्भिका - जवाँई** अनुपयुक्त है। जृम्भिका (तत्सम) का तद्भव रूप जँभाई या जम्हाई है, जबकि जवाँई का तत्सम रूप जामातृ है। अतः यह युग्म गलत है। गर्त-गड्ढा, चर्मचटक-चमगादड़ और परिकूट-परकोटा सही मेल हैं।

32. **प्रेरणा से तर्क की ओर** शिक्षण-सूत्र नहीं है। शिक्षण-सूत्र जैसे "पूर्ण से अंश की ओर" और "स्थूल से सूक्ष्म की ओर" स्थापित हैं, लेकिन 'प्रेरणा से तर्क की ओर' कोई मान्य सूत्र नहीं है।

33. **ऐ, औ - अर्ध संवृत** असंगत है। स्वर वर्गीकरण में ऐ और औ अर्ध विवृत स्वर हैं, अर्ध संवृत नहीं। अन्य विकल्प जैसे अं, अः (अयोगवाह), ड़, ढ़ (उत्क्षिप्त), और श, ष, स (संघर्षी) संगत हैं।

34. **दूरदर्शन** प्रक्षेपित शिक्षण सहायक सामग्री नहीं है।

प्रक्षेपित शिक्षण सहायक सामग्री वे होती हैं जिन्हें किसी स्क्रीन पर प्रकाश स्रोत या प्रोजेक्टर की सहायता से प्रदर्शित किया जाता है। दूरदर्शन एक इलेक्ट्रॉनिक उपकरण है जो सीधे प्रसारण (Broadcast) के आधार पर चित्र और ध्वनि प्रस्तुत करता है। यह प्रक्षेपण उपकरण नहीं है, बल्कि स्वयं में दृश्य-श्रव्य सामग्री का प्रसारण माध्यम है।

- **फिल्म स्ट्रीप :** इसमें स्थिर छवियाँ होती हैं जिन्हें प्रोजेक्टर द्वारा स्क्रीन पर प्रक्षेपित किया जाता है।
- **ओवरहेड प्रोजेक्टर :** यह पारदर्शी शीट पर लिखी या छपी सामग्री को स्क्रीन पर प्रक्षेपित करता है।
- **फिल्म :** यह चलचित्र है जिसे प्रोजेक्टर की सहायता से परदे पर दिखाया जाता है।

अतः स्पष्ट है कि दिए गए विकल्पों में केवल **दूरदर्शन** अप्रक्षेपित सामग्री है।

35. पवन से चलने वाली चक्की - पनचक्की असंगत है। वास्तव में 'पनचक्की' का समास विग्रह "पानी से चलने वाली चक्की" है, न कि "पवन से चलने वाली चक्की"। अन्य विकल्प सही हैं—लोकप्रिय (लोक में प्रिय, अधिकरण तत्पुरुष), नवयुवक (नव है जो युवक, कर्मधारय), परीक्षाभवन (परीक्षा के लिए भवन, सम्प्रदान तत्पुरुष)।

36. **अभ्यर्थी - प्रत्यर्थी** सही विलोम-युग्म नहीं है।

'अभ्यर्थी' का अर्थ है याचक या उम्मीदवार, जो किसी पद या अवसर के लिए निवेदन करता है। 'प्रत्यर्थी' का अर्थ है—प्रतिद्वंदी या विरोधी, जो उसी अवसर पर प्रतिस्पर्धा में खड़ा होता है। दोनों शब्द एक ही संदर्भ में प्रयुक्त होते हैं, पर अर्थ की दृष्टि से एक-दूसरे के विपरीत नहीं हैं, इसलिए इन्हें विलोम नहीं कहा जा सकता।

- **वैमनस्य - सौमनस्य :** वैरभाव और सद्भाव के लिए यह सही विलोम है।
- **अभिमानी - निरभिमानी :** अभिमान से युक्त और अभिमान रहित - यह भी विलोम है।
- **स्वार्थी - निस्वार्थ :** स्वार्थ में लिप्त और स्वार्थ से रहित - यह भी उपयुक्त विलोम है।

अतः दिए गए विकल्पों में अनुपयुक्त विलोम-युग्म **अभ्यर्थी - प्रत्यर्थी** है।

37. **ई - द्रौपदी, जानकी, वाल्मीकि** असंगत है। 'ई' प्रत्यय से स्त्रीलिंग सूचक शब्द बनते हैं, जैसे द्रौपदी, जानकी। लेकिन 'वाल्मीकि' इसमें नहीं आता, क्योंकि यह ई प्रत्यय से नहीं बना है। बाकी विकल्प - 'य', 'तर' और 'एय' - सही उदाहरणों के साथ संगत हैं।

38. **तरणि - नौका, द्रोणी, करवाल** असुमेलित है। 'तरणि' का अर्थ सूर्य होता है, इसका पर्यायवाची आदित्य, भानु, भास्कर आदि हैं। नौका, द्रोणी और करवाल 'नाव' के पर्याय हैं, अतः यह युग्म असंगत है।

39. **समुद्र में लगने वाली आग - दावानल** असंगत है। दावानल का अर्थ है वन में लगने वाली अग्नि, न कि समुद्र में। समुद्र में लगने वाली आग को 'बड़वानल' कहा जाता है। शेष विकल्प सही हैं - लोक-प्रचलित बात जिसके वक्ता का पता न हो = किंवदन्ती, पशुओं की जुगाली = पागुर, और जिसके पति ने दूसरा विवाह कर लिया हो = अध्यूढा।

40. **कुमार** में 'कु' उपसर्ग का प्रयोग नहीं हुआ है। कुमार शब्द संस्कृत धातु से बना है और इसमें 'कु' उपसर्ग नहीं है। जबकि कुज, कुचो और कुमति में 'कु' उपसर्ग के प्रयोग से ही शब्द निर्मित हुए हैं।

41. मनुजात का अर्थ है मनु से उत्पन्न, अर्थात् मनुष्य या मानव। मनुजाद का अर्थ है मनुष्य को खाने वाला। इसमें 'आद' प्रत्यय का अर्थ है खाने वाला। इसलिए यह युग्म सही है।

42. **पर्युषण = परि + ऊषण :** यह यण संधि दृष्टि से संगत विकल्प है। यहाँ 'परि + ऊषण' में 'इ + ऊ = यू' होता है, जो यण संधि का नियम है। इस प्रकार 'परि + ऊषण' → पर्युषण' बनता है।

- जाती + अभिमान → जात्यभिमान (यह यण संधि है, लेकिन विकल्प में 'जात्यमान' लिखा है, जो गलत रूप है)।
- वधु + इच्छा → वध्विच्छा (यह यण संधि है, पर विकल्प में आधार शब्द 'वधु' को सही रूप में नहीं दिया गया है)।
- महा + ऐन्द्रजालिक → महेन्द्रजालिक (यह वृद्धि संधि है, यण संधि नहीं)।

अतः सही उत्तर है **पर्युषण = परि + ऊषण।**

43. लेखक के अनुसार शांति की परिभाषा केवल युद्ध की अनुपस्थिति नहीं है। गद्यांश में स्पष्ट कहा गया है कि बुद्ध की परिकल्पना के अनुसार शांति का अर्थ समानता के संदेश से युक्त शांतिपूर्ण समाज है। इसलिए युद्ध का न होना मात्र शांति नहीं माना जा सकता।

44. मनुष्य बनने का अर्थ है अपने भीतर करुणा और संवेदनशीलता को विकसित करना, जिससे हम दूसरों की पीड़ा को समझ सकें और उनसे जुड़ सकें।

45. **विषमता - व्यंजन संधि :** यह असंगत है। 'विषमता' शब्द 'विषम' + 'ता' से बना है, जो प्रत्यय की प्रक्रिया है, संधि नहीं। शेष विकल्प - 'अनुपस्थिति' (दो उपसर्ग), 'मनुष्यता' (जातिवाचक आधार से बना भाववाचक), और 'प्रत्येक' (अव्ययीभाव समास) - सही हैं।

46. The most suitable way to teach stress, intonation, and rhythm is through different types of drills. Drills give students repeated opportunities to practice pronunciation, intonation, and rhythm, which helps them achieve naturalness in speaking.

47. A phonetic dictionary does not help in developing listening skills. It helps in understanding pronunciation and knowing the correct phonetic transcription of words, but it does not directly develop listening ability. On the other hand, gramophones, television, and films/film strips engage both listening and viewing, thereby developing listening skills.

48. The use of multimedia materials in teaching involves various media such as text, pictures, sound, video, and animation. This integrated approach makes teaching more effective, attractive, and participatory.

49. The use of multilingual resources increases student participation. When various linguistic resources are used, learners feel connected to their mother tongue and other languages, which enhances their active participation and strengthens the learning process.

50. The author worked for a short time (a brief while) in a college in Delhi. Therefore, the correct answer is *short time*.

51. The author assigned the task of writing an application for a job after graduation as a *language exercise* for students.

52. Seven out of eight students wrote job applications for the position of *clerks*.

53. According to the author, the highest ambition of students in good colleges is to pass the competitive examination for appointment to the *Administrative Services*.

54. In the sentence "And these latter, understandably, are a small number," the phrase "these latter" refers to *scholars, scientists, and leaders of opinion*, whose number is very small.

55. According to the author, the thinking of the most ambitious and the least ambitious students is *alike*.

56. The college where the author worked in Delhi had a reputation for its academic standards: This statement is true. The passage clearly mentions that the college was well-known for its academic standards.

57. "Snuffed out" means to end or to *kill*. Therefore, the correct meaning is *killed*.

58. The antonym of "former" is "latter," and this is the word used in the passage.

59. "Alumni" means *former students* or old students of an educational institution.

60. The first stage in teaching any lesson, including formal grammar, is to prepare students and connect the new topic with their prior knowledge. This stage is called *Motivation* and *Testing of Previous Knowledge*.

- **Motivation:** Creates interest and curiosity among students about the topic.
- **Testing of Previous Knowledge:** Helps the teacher find out what the students already know, so new knowledge can be built on that foundation.

After this, the sequence of the teaching process includes:

- Collection and presentation of examples,
- Comparison and generalization,
- And finally, application of rules.

Hence, the first stage is *Motivation and Testing of Previous Knowledge*.

61. The given expression is

$$= \frac{\left(\frac{7}{4}\right)^4 - \left(\frac{7}{3}\right)^4}{\sqrt{\left(\frac{7}{4}\right)^2 - \left(\frac{7}{3}\right)^2}}$$

Using the identity $a^4 - b^4 = (a^2 - b^2)(a^2 + b^2)$, the fraction reduces to $a^2 + b^2$. Substituting $a = 7/4$, $b = 7/3$:

$$a^2 + b^2 = \left(\frac{7}{4}\right)^2 + \left(\frac{7}{3}\right)^2 = \frac{49}{16} + \frac{49}{9}$$

$$\text{Taking LCM} = \frac{441}{144} + \frac{784}{144} = \frac{1225}{144}$$

$$\text{Now,} \quad \sqrt{\frac{1225}{144}} = \frac{\sqrt{1225}}{\sqrt{144}} = \frac{35}{12} = 2\frac{11}{12}$$

62. Rates: $X = \frac{1}{6}$, $Y = \frac{1}{8}$ (work/day).

Together finish in 3 days $\Rightarrow$ rate $= 1/3$.

$$Z = \frac{1}{3} - \left(\frac{1}{6} + \frac{1}{8}\right) = \frac{1}{24}$$

In 3 days, Z does $3 \times \frac{1}{24} = \frac{1}{8}$ of work

$$\Rightarrow \quad \text{Z share} = \frac{1}{8} \times 2000 = ₹\ 250$$

63. **Cube** : It's the only 3-D solid, the others (rectangle, square, triangle) are 2-D figures.

64. SP = 153 at 10% loss

$$\Rightarrow CP = \frac{153}{0.9} = 170.$$

For 20% profit: SP = 1.2 × 170 = ₹ 204.

65. Around the circle (facing center):

"Only A is between E and B" $\Rightarrow$ order E – A – B.

"D is to the immediate left of B"

$\Rightarrow$ clockwise after B is D.

Arrangement: E $\rightarrow$ A $\rightarrow$ B $\rightarrow$ D $\rightarrow$ C (clockwise).

Immediate left of C (clockwise neighbour) is E.

66. Shekhar walks 10 m north, then 6 m south $\rightarrow$ net movement = 4 m north. Next, he walks 3 m east. His position forms a right triangle with sides 4 m (north) and 3 m (east). Distance from the start

$$= \sqrt{4^2 + 3^2} = \sqrt{25} = 5\,\text{m}.$$

67. Series: 5, 6, 9, 15, 25, ?
Differences: +1, +3, +6, +10. These are triangular numbers T_1, T_2, T_3, T_4. The next triangular number is 15. Therefore, next term = 25 + 15 = 40.

68. Rearranging "CYBERNETICS" alphabetically gives: B, C, C, E, E, I, N, R, S, T, Y.
The word has 11 letters, so the 6th letter is the middle. The 6th letter is **I**.

69. R is Q's mother. Since P is Q's sister, R is also P's mother. S is R's father, meaning S is P's grandfather. Thus, P is related to S as his granddaughter.

70. Rule → Each letter value = 27 − (alphabetical position), then sum × 10.

- ZIP: Z = 1, I = 18, P = 11
→ total 30 → 30 × 10 = 300.
- ZAN: Z = 1, A = 26, N = 13
→ total 40 → 40 × 10 = 400.
- ZOO: Z = 1, O = 12, O = 12
→ total 25 → 25 × 10 = 250.

71. The series is AYD, BVF, DRH, ?, KGL. Each letter follows its own independent sequence.

- **First letters (A, B, D, ?, K):**
Positions → A(1), B(2), D(4), ? , K(11).
Differences: +1, +2, +3, +4.
So, after D(4), we get G(7).
- **Second letters (Y, V, R, ?, G):**
Positions → Y(25), V(22), R(18), ?, G(7).
Differences: −3, −4, −5, −6.
After R(18), we get M(13).
- **Third letters (D, F, H, ?, L):**
Positions → D(4), F(6), H(8), ?, L(12).
Differences: +2 consistently.
After H(8), we get J(10).

Thus, the missing term is GMJ.

72. We arrange the five persons by height step by step.

- Given: Sachin is shorter than Kamal but taller than Ram ⇒ order so far: Ram < Sachin < Kamal.
- Mohan is the tallest ⇒ Mohan > Kamal.
- Arun is shorter than Kamal but taller than Sachin ⇒ Ram < Sachin < Arun < Kamal < Mohan.

From this order, Mohan is the tallest and Kamal is the **second tallest**.

73. Formula for the volume of a sphere:

$$V = \frac{4}{3}\pi r^3$$

It is given that the volume corresponds to a sphere of radius 3 m.

So, diameter = $2r$ = 6 m.

Thus, the correct diameter is **6 metres**.

74. Given: Diameter = 28 cm
⇒ Radius = 14 cm.; Height = 20 cm.
Total surface area of cylinder:

$$TSA = 2\pi r(h + r)$$

Substitute values:

$$TSA = 2 \times \pi \times 14 \times (20 + 14)$$
$$= 2 \times \pi \times 14 \times 34$$
$$= 952\pi = 952 \times \frac{22}{7} = 2992 \text{ cm}^2$$

So, the total surface area = 2992 cm^2.

75. Perimeter of rhombus = 52 cm
⇒ Side = 52 ÷ 4 = 13.
One diagonal = 24 cm ⇒ half of it = 12 cm.
Using Pythagoras in right triangle:

$$\left(\frac{d_2}{2}\right)^2 + 12^2 = 13^2$$
$$\left(\frac{d_2}{2}\right)^2 + 144 = 169$$
$$\left(\frac{d_2}{2}\right)^2 = 25$$
$$\Rightarrow \frac{d_2}{2} = 5 \Rightarrow d_2 = 10$$
$$\text{Area of rhombus} = \frac{d_1 \times d_2}{2} = \frac{24 \times 10}{2} = 120 \text{ cm}^2.$$

So, the required area is **120 cm^2**.

76. Let the radius of the cone be r and the height be h.
Given ratio, $r : h = 5 : 12$
⇒ $r = 5x$, $h = 12x$.

Volume of cone: $V = \frac{1}{3}\pi r^2 h$

Substituting, $V = 314$, $\pi = 3.14$:

$$314 = 1/3 \times 3.14 \times (5x)^2 \times 12x$$
$$314 = 1/3 \times 3.14 \times 25x^2 \times 12x$$
$$314 = 314x^3$$
$$\Rightarrow x^3 = 1 \Rightarrow x = 1$$

So, $r = 5x = 5$ m.
Diameter = $2r$ = 10 m.

77. Expression:

$$E = \sec(90° - A) - \cot A \cdot \cos(90° - A) \cdot \tan(90° - A)$$

Use identities:

$$\sec(90° - A) = \operatorname{cosec} A,$$
$$\cos(90° - A) = \sin A, \tan(90° - A) = \cot A.$$

So, $E = \operatorname{cosec} A - \cot A \cdot \sin A \cdot \cot A$
$= \operatorname{cosec} A - \cot^2 A \sin A$

Now, $\operatorname{cosec} A = \frac{1}{\sin A}$

$$\cot^2 A = \frac{\cos^2 A}{\sin^2 A}$$

$$E = \frac{1}{\sin A} - \frac{\cos^2 A}{\sin^2 A} . \sin A$$

$$= \frac{1}{\sin A} - \frac{\cos^2 A}{\sin A}$$

$$= \frac{1 - \cos^2 A}{\sin A} = \frac{\sin^2 A}{\sin A} = \sin A.$$

78. Height of tower = $2\sqrt{3}$ m,

Shadow = 2 m.

$$\tan \theta = \frac{\text{heigth}}{\text{shadow}}$$

$$= \frac{2\sqrt{3}}{2} = \sqrt{3}$$

So, $\theta = 60°$.

79. Compound interest formula:

$$A = P\left(1 + \frac{r}{100}\right)^n$$

Here, $r = 20\%$.

For doubling: $(1.2)^n > 2$

Check values:

$(1.2)^2 = 1.44$

$(1.2)^3 = 1.728$

$(1.2)^4 = 2.0736 > 2$

So, least $n = 4$.

80. Numbers between 11 and 50 divisible by 7: 14, 21, 28, 35, 42, 49.

Exclude those divisible by 3 also: 21, 42.

Remaining: 14, 28, 35, 49.

Count = 4.

81. Diksha Dagar, the professional golfer from Haryana, was one of the 26 athletes honoured with the Arjuna Award in 2023. This recognition was for her achievements and contributions to golf at both national and international levels. The other names listed are prominent wrestlers, but they were not in the final Arjuna Award list for 2023.

82. Bir Shikargarh Wildlife Sanctuary is situated in Panchkula district, Haryana. It is notable for its Vulture Conservation and Breeding Centre at Pinjore. By contrast, Chhilchhila Sanctuary lies in Kurukshetra, Nahar in Rewari, and Kaparwas in Jhajjar. Hence, only Bir Shikargarh matches Panchkula.

83. The Shivalik Development Agency covers the districts that fall under the Shivalik range: Ambala, Panchkula, and Yamuna Nagar. Kurukshetra lies in the plains and is not included under the Agency's jurisdiction.

84. According to Haryana's economic survey and budget estimates for 2023–24 at constant (2011–12) prices, the state's per capita income is around ₹ 1,85,490. This figure reflects income growth adjusted for inflation.

85. Justice Sheel Nagu is the present Chief Justice of the Punjab and Haryana High Court. He assumed office in July 2024 and continues to serve as the head of the High Court, which has jurisdiction over Punjab, Haryana, and Chandigarh.

86. The Haryana Public Service Commission (HPSC) is constituted with one Chairman and five Members. While the State Government has the authority to vary the strength, the most recognized and cited composition is six in total (1 Chairman + 5 Members).

87. (*a*) **True** → In the 12th century, the Bhadanakas ruled over the area around Gurugram and Rewari. Their domain extended into regions of present-day Haryana, including parts of Delhi and Bayana.

(*b*) **False** → The Bhadanakas did not defeat Prithviraj Chauhan. On the contrary, Prithviraj-III destroyed their power around 1182 CE, leading to their decline.

88. In the Mahabharata's Sabha Parva, Nakul, the Pandava prince, led the western Digvijaya campaign. He conquered Rohitaka (identified with present-day Rohtak), which was then a prosperous cattle-rich region and a center of Karttikeya worship. Hence, Nakul is credited with leading the expedition to Rohtak.

89. Jind district, often called the "Heart of Haryana" because of its central location, uniquely shares borders with seven districts: Fatehabad, Hisar, Rohtak, Sonipat, Panipat, Karnal, and Kaithal. This makes Jind the only district in Haryana with such extensive adjacency.

90. The Sikh chieftain of Ladawa who resisted the British during the First Anglo-Maratha War was **Gurdit Singh**. Historical and regional records mention Gurdit Singh as a prominent leader from Ladawa (in present-day Haryana) who stood against British forces during the late 18th century conflict. His opposition formed part of the broader resistance by local Sikh sardars against the growing influence of the East India Company in North India.

91. The Barid-e-Mumalik was the head of the intelligence and postal department during the Sultanate period. His primary duty was to collect information from different parts of the empire and report it to the Sultan. This included political developments, activities of nobles, and law-and-order conditions. He also supervised the royal correspondence system, ensuring communication across the empire was maintained effectively.

92. Dronmukh was not an official post in the Mauryan administration but rather a territorial-administrative division. According to Arthashastra, a Dronmukh comprised around 400 villages and served as a regional headquarters for administrative purposes. On the other hand, Antpal (or Anta-Mahamatta) was indeed an official responsible for guarding and managing frontier forts, Prashasta (sometimes called Prashastri) was an officer overseeing specific administrative tasks like prisons or record-keeping, and Nayak was a recognized military officer who often functioned as the City Security Chief or subordinate to the Senapati. Thus, the one that was not an official but an administrative unit is Dronmukh.

93. The given demand function is $pq = cpq = c$. This implies: (*i*) Its graph is a rectangular hyperbola since the product of pp and qq is constant. (*ii*) Elasticity of demand at all points is equal to –1, showing unitary elasticity. (*iii*) Total expenditure ($p \times qp \times q$) remains the same throughout, as it equals cc. (*iv*) By definition, the product of price and quantity is constant everywhere on this curve. Thus, all four statements hold true.

94. The given pair is incorrect. Rajadhiraj I was known as Vijayrajendra, Mahendravarman I composed *Mattavilasa Prahasana*, and Narasimhavarman was famous as Vatapikonda for defeating the Chalukyas at Vatapi. But "Shangham Tavirt" is not a historically attested title of Rajendra Chola I. He was more commonly associated with the title "Gangaikonda Chola" after his victory over the Pala kingdom and bringing the Ganga water to Tamil Nadu.

95. The Right to Information Act was passed by the Government of India in 2005 and came into full force on 12th October 2005. It gave Indian citizens the right to access information from any public authority, promoting transparency and accountability in governance. It became one of the most significant pieces of legislation empowering citizens to demand information.

96. A federal system is characterized by a clear division of powers between the central authority and the constituent units (states or provinces). Each level of government has its own jurisdiction and autonomy in certain matters, which distinguishes it from a unitary system where powers are centralized. This ensures a balance between unity and regional diversity.

97. In the Global Hunger Index 2023, India ranked 111th out of 125 countries. This ranking highlighted India's struggle with hunger and malnutrition despite economic growth. Indicators such as child stunting, child wasting, undernourishment, and child mortality contributed to this position, reflecting significant challenges in food security and nutrition.

98. Among India's neighboring countries, Sri Lanka performed better in terms of Human Development Index (HDI) in 2022. Despite facing an economic crisis, Sri Lanka maintained higher human development indicators like literacy, life expectancy, and healthcare compared to India. Bangladesh, Nepal, and Pakistan all had lower HDI values than India.

99. Anekantavada is a core doctrine of Jain philosophy. It refers to the principle of manifoldness or multiplicity of viewpoints, emphasizing that truth and reality can be perceived differently from diverse perspectives. This doctrine promotes intellectual tolerance and non-absolutism, recognizing the limitations of one-sided viewpoints.

100. Robert Filmer, an English political theorist, propounded the patriarchal theory of the state in his work *Patriarcha*. He argued that God created Adam as both the first man and the first king, and that all kings are Adam's successors. Thus, monarchs derive their authority directly from divine origin, and subjects have no right to resist them.

101. The National Food Security Act (NFSA) was enacted in 2013. It aimed to provide subsidized food grains to approximately two-thirds of India's population. Under this Act, priority households and Antyodaya Anna Yojana households are entitled to receive rice, wheat, and coarse grains at highly subsidized rates, thereby ensuring food and nutritional security.

102. The true geographical shape of the Earth is called a geoid. It represents the mean sea level of the Earth extended continuously through the continents. The geoid is an irregular but uniquely defined surface, which differs slightly from a perfect sphere or spheroid due to the uneven distribution of mass and gravitational pull across the planet.

103. Checking options:

(*a*) Equinox – only 21st March → Incorrect, because equinox occurs twice a year, around 21st March and 23rd September, when day and night are equal.

(*b*) Summer solstice – 21st June → Correct, this marks the longest day in the Northern Hemisphere.

(*c*) Winter solstice – 22nd December → Correct, this marks the shortest day in the Northern Hemisphere.

Hence, only (*a*) is not correctly matched.

104. Checking options:

(*a*) Right to Equality → Articles 14–18 (ensuring equality before law and prohibition of discrimination).

(*b*) Right to Freedom → Articles 19–22 (covering freedom of speech, movement, and protection in respect of conviction).

(*c*) Cultural and Educational Rights → Articles 29–30 (safeguarding rights of minorities to conserve culture and establish educational institutions).

(*d*) Right to Constitutional Remedies → Article 32 (empowers citizens to move to Supreme Court to enforce fundamental rights).

Hence, correct match is (*a*)-(*iii*), (*b*)-(*i*), (*c*)-(*iv*), (*d*)-(*ii*).

105. **Pot depicting the story of a thirsty crow – Kalibangan:** This pair is not correctly matched. The painted pot/jar resembling the folk tale of the thirsty crow, with a bird depicted on a tree and related motifs, was actually discovered at **Lothal (Gujarat)**, not at Kalibangan. Kalibangan, on the other hand, is notable for its fire altars and evidence of a ploughed agricultural field.

The other pairs are correct: Bronze mirrors have been found at Harappa and Mohenjodaro (not Dholavira), the famous steatite bust of the Priest King belongs to Mohenjodaro, and the clay model of a plough has been found at Banawali. Thus, the mismatched pair is the pot attributed wrongly to Kalibangan.

106. A caldera is not an intrusive volcanic landform but an extrusive one. It is a large depression formed when a volcano erupts and collapses inward, often after a massive explosive eruption. In contrast, batholiths, dykes, and sills are intrusive features formed when magma solidifies beneath the Earth's surface.

107. Alfred Cobban is not associated with the resurgence of political theory. The revival of political theory in the mid-20th century is linked to scholars like Michael Oakeshott, John Rawls, and Jürgen Habermas, who emphasized normative, philosophical, and critical dimensions of political study. Cobban, however, was primarily a historian known for his works on the French Revolution, not a theorist in this context.

108. The phenomenon of the "Land of the Midnight Sun" occurs in the high latitudes north of the Arctic Circle and south of the Antarctic Circle, where the sun remains visible at midnight during the local summer. This happens due to the tilt of the Earth's axis, which allows the polar regions to experience continuous daylight for several weeks.

109. All three statements are true regarding Mathura art: (a) Sculptures were made of spotted red sandstone (sano stones) found in the region. (b) This style depicts a wide variety of figures including the Buddha, Bodhisattvas, Jain Tirthankaras, and Hindu gods and goddesses. (c) A large number of Jain sculptures have been excavated from Kankali Tila in Mathura, showing its importance as a Jain art center as well.

110. According to Wegener's continental drift theory: *(a)* The supercontinent was called Pangaea, *(b)* the surrounding mega ocean was **Panthalassa**, but *(c)* the southern continental mass was **Gondwanaland**, not Laurasia. Laurasia referred to the northern continental block.

Therefore, only *(a)* and *(b)* are correctly matched.

111. J.S. Mill, in his famous work On *Liberty* (1859), strongly advocated individual liberty and the protection of personal freedoms against state encroachment. He distinguished between "self-regarding actions" (affecting only oneself, where society should not interfere) and "other-regarding actions" (affecting others, where society has a right to intervene).

Thus, Both statements (I) and (II) are correct.

112. Robert Nozick proposed the *Entitlement Theory of Justice* in his book *Anarchy, State, and Utopia* (1974). He argued that justice in holdings is determined by principles of acquisition, transfer, and rectification, rejecting redistributive justice. The other terms — "original position," "veil of ignorance," and "difference principle" — are part of John Rawls' theory of justice, not Nozick's.

113. The Food Corporation of India (FCI), established in 1965, is the nodal agency responsible for procurement, storage, and distribution of food grains under the Public Distribution System (PDS) and for maintaining buffer stocks. It plays a crucial role in ensuring food security in India.

114. The mesosphere extends roughly from 50 km to 80 km above the Earth's surface. Temperatures here decrease with height, and at the upper limit (the mesopause), the temperature can fall to about −100°C, making it the coldest layer of the atmosphere.

115. The Earth's interior is divided into crust, mantle, outer core, and inner core. The outer core is in a liquid state, composed mainly of molten iron and nickel. This liquid layer is responsible for generating Earth's magnetic field. The mantle and crust are solid, while the inner core, despite high temperatures, is solid due to immense pressure.

116. On a negatively sloped straight-line demand curve, price elasticity of demand is not constant. As one moves upward from right to left (towards higher price and lower quantity), elasticity increases because the percentage change in quantity demanded becomes larger relative to the percentage change in price. At the upper portion of the curve, demand is highly elastic, while at the lower portion, it is inelastic.

117. Article 109 of the Indian Constitution lays down the special procedure with respect to Money Bills. It states that a Money Bill can only be introduced in the Lok Sabha, requires the President's recommendation, and the Rajya Sabha can only make recommendations but cannot reject or amend it.

118. This statement is false. The Tripartite Struggle (8th–9th centuries CE) for the control of Kannauj was fought mainly among the Palas (Bengal), Gurjara-Pratiharas (Rajasthan/ Madhya Pradesh), and Rashtrakutas (Deccan). Vatsaraja of the Gurjara-Pratiharas and Dharmapala of the Palas were among the first major rulers involved. However, none of the dynasties achieved a permanent victory. The Pratiharas under Nagabhata II gained temporary advantage, but the struggle continued without final success for the Palas.

119. Under Article 136 of the Indian Constitution, the Supreme Court has the power to grant special leave to appeal against any judgment, decree, determination, sentence, or order in any cause or matter passed by any court or tribunal within the territory of India (except military tribunals/courts martial).

120. Ngozi Okonjo-Iweala of Nigeria is the current Director-General of the World Trade Organization (WTO). She assumed office on 1 March 2021, becoming the first woman and the first African to head the WTO.

121. The "Sunset Law" was linked with the Permanent Settlement system of Bengal introduced by Lord Cornwallis in 1793. Under this, zamindars had to deposit the land revenue to the Company treasury before sunset on the due date. Failure to do so would result in their estates being auctioned off, hence it was termed the "Sunset Law."

122. The European Union was formally established by the Maastricht Treaty, signed in 1992 and effective from 1993. This treaty expanded cooperation among European nations beyond economic integration, introducing political union, common foreign and security policy, and paving the way for the Euro currency.

123. In 1969, Soviet leader Leonid Brezhnev suggested a collective security system for Asia. His proposal was aimed at countering U.S. influence in the region and building a framework for security cooperation among Asian countries under Soviet guidance.

124. The Sargasso Sea is located in the North Atlantic Ocean. It is unique because it has no land boundaries but is defined by ocean currents. It is characterized by floating sargassum seaweed and calm blue water, lying roughly between the West Indies and the Azores.

125. Checking options:

(i) **Correct:** Agriculture provides livelihood to about 42.3% of India's population.

(ii) **Correct:** Its share in India's GDP stood at 18.2% at current prices (2023–24).

(iii) **Correct:** The average annual growth rate of the agriculture sector was 4.18% at constant prices over the last five years.

(iv) **Incorrect:** Indian agricultural productivity is not the highest in the world; countries like the USA, China, and others have higher productivity.

Therefore, Only *(i)*, *(ii)* and *(iii)* are correct.

126. The correct course in such a situation is not to stoop to wrongful demands or injustice, even if the authority figure treats you unfairly. This response reflects moral strength and self-respect, showing resilience against undue pressure while continuing to act rightly.

127. This pair is not correctly matched. The work On the Dignity of Man (Oration on the Dignity of Man) was written by Giovanni Pico della Mirandola, not Alberti. Alberti is known for works on architecture such as *De re aedificatoria*. The other pairs are correct: Chaucer authored The Canterbury Tales, Valla wrote On Pleasure, and Castiglione wrote The Book of the Courtier.

128. The Act of 1872 that legalized inter-caste and widow remarriage is known as the Brahma Marriage Act. It was later expanded to cover broader civil marriages and served as a precursor to the Special Marriage Act of 1954.

129. The sum of production in the three sectors (agriculture, industry, and services) within a country during a particular year is called Gross Domestic Product (GDP). It measures the total monetary value of goods and services produced within the country's boundaries.

130. The ASEAN Regional Forum (ARF) was established in 1994. It serves as a platform for dialogue and consultation on regional security issues in the Asia-Pacific, aiming to foster constructive engagement and promote peace and stability.

131. Arranging options:

(*b*) Ahmedabad Mill Satyagraha – 1918, Gandhi's first hunger strike in India in support of mill workers.

(*c*) Rowlatt Satyagraha – 1919, organized against the repressive Rowlatt Act.

(*d*) Gandhi–Irwin Pact – 1931, agreement ending the Civil Disobedience Movement temporarily.

(*a*) Poona Pact – 1932, agreement between Gandhi and Dr. B.R. Ambedkar regarding separate electorates for depressed classes.

Hence, the correct order is (b), (c), (d), (a).

132. The State Election Commissioner is appointed by the Governor of the respective state under Article 243K of the Constitution. This body conducts elections to Panchayats and Municipalities independently from the Election Commission of India.

133. The classification of sectors into public and private is based on ownership. Enterprises owned and managed by the government are in the public sector, while those owned by individuals or groups are in the private sector.

134. The German socialist Ferdinand Lassalle coined the term "Iron Law of Wages." He expanded on the classical economists' wage theories and argued that wages naturally tend to remain at subsistence level, as higher wages would lead to population increase and eventually push wages back down.

135. Nichahom is not a coalfield of the Gondwana period in India. The important Gondwana coalfields include Korba (Chhattisgarh), Jharia (Jharkhand), and Ramgarh (Jharkhand). Nichahom, located in Jammu & Kashmir, belongs to the Tertiary coal deposits, not Gondwana.

136. Agriculture is part of the State List (List II) in the Seventh Schedule of the Indian Constitution, giving state legislatures exclusive power to legislate on it. In contrast, subjects like atomic energy, banking, and airways are part of the Union List (List I), which fall under Parliament's exclusive jurisdiction.

137. India was among the first non-socialist countries to recognize the People's Republic of China after the 1949 Revolution, doing so on 30 December 1949. This makes Statement I correct. However, Statement II is incorrect because it was Rajiv Gandhi, not Atal Bihari Vajpayee, who became the first Indian Prime Minister after Nehru to visit China in December 1988. Vajpayee visited China much later, in 2003 as Prime Minister.

138. The Mandovi (Mhadei), Zuari, and Rachol are important rivers flowing through Goa. The Mandovi and Zuari rivers together form an extensive estuarine system, vital to Goa's economy and ecology. The port of Mormugao, located at the mouth of the Zuari, highlights the strategic importance of these rivers.

139. This is the incorrect statement. In the Ayagar system of the Vijayanagar Empire, **12 officials** (not 10) were appointed in each village to manage administration, revenue, law, and irrigation. Each village was treated as an independent administrative unit, and these hereditary officials were collectively called Ayagars. Their posts were indeed hereditary, and they could also be sold or mortgaged like property, making it a distinctive feature of this system.

140. Matching options:

- *(a)* **Bombay Presidency Association → 1885** *(iv)***:** It was established by leaders like Pherozeshah Mehta, K.T. Telang, and Badruddin Tyabji to articulate the political aspirations of western India.
- *(b)* **The Indian Association → 1876** *(iii)*: Founded by Surendranath Banerjee and Ananda Mohan Bose in Bengal, it played a significant role in mobilizing public opinion and later merged with the Indian National Congress.
- *(c)* **Poona Sarvajanik Sabha → 1870** *(ii)*. Initiated by Mahadev Govind Ranade and others, it became a key political body voicing the interests of the Deccan region.
- *(d)* **The Indian League → 1875** *(i)*. Founded by Sisir Kumar Ghosh in Calcutta, it was among the earliest associations seeking greater representation of Indians in governance.

Thus, the correct sequence is *(a)*-*(iv)*, *(b)*-*(iii)*, *(c)*-*(ii)*, *(d)*-*(i)*.

141. Arranging chronological order:

(c) Beginning of the Mansabdari System – 1571, introduced by Akbar to organize military and civil administration through ranking.

(a) Establishment of Ibadat Khana – 1575, at Fatehpur Sikri, to hold interfaith religious discussions.

(b) Introduction of Dahsala System – 1580, devised by Raja Todar Mal for revenue collection, based on the average produce of ten years.

Thus, the correct chronological order is *(c)*, *(a)*, *(b)*.

142. India ranks first in the world in milk production. The country is the largest producer and consumer of milk, contributing around 24% of global output, largely due to the success of Operation Flood and the cooperative movement led by the National Dairy Development Board.

143. A "Quriltai" (or Kurultai) was a political and military council or assembly of Mongol and Turkic chiefs where major decisions, such as the election of a new Khan or launching of military campaigns, were taken. It was an important institution in Mongol governance.

144. The terms "Parkland" or "Bush-veld" are associated with Savanna climate regions, characterized by tropical wet and dry seasons. These regions have scattered trees and extensive grasslands, typical in parts of Africa, Brazil, and Australia.

145. Tropical Dry Evergreen Forests are typically found along the Coromandel Coast of Tamil Nadu. These forests are characterized by short, evergreen trees with closed canopies and are adapted to the dry season with moisture retained from coastal influences.

146. Dag Hammarskjöld, the second Secretary-General of the United Nations, was awarded the Nobel Peace Prize posthumously in 1961 after his death in a plane crash during a peace mission in Congo. He is the only UN Secretary-General to have received this honor after death.

147. The Zanskar range is part of the Trans-Himalaya, not the Lesser Himalaya. The Lesser Himalaya, also known as Himachal, includes ranges such as Dhauladhar, Pir Panjal, and Mahabharat. Zanskar lies to the north, between the Great Himalayas and the Ladakh range.

148. The Mahatma Gandhi National Rural Employment Guarantee Act (MGNREGA) was enacted in 2005. It provides at least 100 days of guaranteed wage employment in a financial year to every rural household whose adult members volunteer for unskilled manual work.

149. Manipur does not share an international border with Bangladesh. The Indian states that share borders with Bangladesh are West Bengal, Assam, Meghalaya, Tripura, and Mizoram. Manipur shares an international border with Myanmar.

150. Goa is not a major tea-producing state in South India. The main tea-producing states in the region are Tamil Nadu (Nilgiris), Kerala (Wayanad, Idukki), and Karnataka (Chikmagalur, Kodagu). Tea cultivation is not significant in Goa.

Previous Years' Paper

Haryana Teacher Eligibility Test (HTET)

TGT Social Studies (Level-2), Exam 2023

(Exam held on 03-12-2023)

PART-I : CHILD DEVELOPMENT AND PEDAGOGY

1. According to which psychologist, the role of social and cultural factors are important in the cognitive development of children?
A. Vygotsky B. Piaget
C. Bruner D. Hull

2. Which teaching support material is **not** useful for visually impaired students?
A. Braille materials B. Talking books
C. Film strips D. Embossed map

3. The education which promotes 'learning by doing' and ensures the student's interaction with their environment to learn, that is known as:
A. Special education B. Progressive education
C. Integrated education D. Inclusive education

4. Inclusive Education means:
A. Education for socially deprived children
B. Education for disabled children
C. Education for normal and disabled children
D. Education for all children

5. Which teaching learning strategy is most useful for students in context of social learning?
A. Field trip B. Lecture
C. Experiment D. Brain storming

6. Which of the following is **not** an objective type question?
A. Matching questions
B. Analytical questions
C. Multiple choice questions
D. Blank space questions

7. Which educational intervention is **not** suitable for slow learners?
A. Acceleration
B. Remedial teaching
C. Drill work
D. Cooperative teaching method

8. When the lesson to be learned by a child is long and difficult and requires a lot of understanding, then which method of learning will be appropriate?
A. Spaced method B. Whole method
C. Massed method D. Incidental method

9. Choose the **correct** code for the approved social behaviour pattern in adolescene:
(*a*) Leadership skills (*b*) Empathy
(*c*) Ego-centrism (*d*) Stereotyping

Codes:
A. (*a*) & (*b*) B. (*b*) & (*d*)
C. (*a*), (*b*) & (*c*) D. (*a*), (*c*) & (*d*)

10. Which of the following pair is **not** correct regarding motivational theories and their proponents?

	Motivational Theories	**Proponent**
A.	Instinct theory	Atkinson
B.	Need Hierarchical theory	Maslow
C.	Drive theory	Woodworth
D.	Achievement Motivation theory	Mc'Clelland

11. Which of the following is **not** a performance test of intelligence?
A. Koh's Block Design Test
B. Alexander's Pass Along Test
C. Saguine Form Board Test
D. Stanford-Binet Test

12. Which of the following is **not** a principle of development?
A. Development is the product of heredity and environment.
B. Developmental pattern is predictable.
C. Development follows linear path.
D. Development proceeds from general to specific.

1. A	**2.** C	**3.** B	**4.** D	**5.** A	**6.** B	**7.** A	**8.** A	**9.** A	**10.** A
11. D	**12.** C								

13. According to Gagne, to what highest level of learning should a teacher strive to take students?
A. Concept learning
B. Problem solving learning
C. Rule learning
D. Discrimination learning

14. Choose the **correct** code of the following factors, which affects learning:
(*a*) Motivation
(*b*) Aptitude
(*c*) Interest
(*d*) Attention

Code:
A. (*c*) & (*d*) B. (*a*), (*b*) & (*d*)
C. (*a*) & (*c*) D. (*a*), (*b*), (*c*) & (*d*)

15. Which of the following is **not** a common characteristic of social development in adolescence?
A. Harmonious relationship with parents
B. New social grouping
C. Search for identity
D. Hero-worship

16. Which of the following factor does **not** influence the development of child under environmental factors?
A. Nutrition
B. Mental stress of the mother during pregnancy
C. Accidents
D. Endocrine glands

17. 'Law of use' and 'Law of disuse' is related with which law of learning according to Thorndike's learning theory?
A. Law of readiness
B. Law of exercise
C. Law of effect
D. Law of multiple response

18. Which of the following characteristics is **not** related to the concrete operational stage of the Cognitive Development theory propounded by Piaget?
A. Reversibility B. Serialization
C. Animism D. Conservation

19. Which teaching maxim is **not** beneficial for the learning disabled children?
A. Simple to complex
B. Abstract to concrete
C. Direct to indirect
D. Known to unknown

20. Which stages of Kohlberg's moral development theory are **not** related to level of conventional morality?
(*a*) Individualism and exchange
(*b*) Good interpersonal relations
(*c*) Maintaining the social order
(*d*) Social contracts and individual rights

Choose the **correct** code:

Code:
A. (*a*) & (*b*) B. (*b*) & (*c*)
C. (*a*) & (*d*) D. (*c*) & (*d*)

21. Which of the following laws is **not** related to heredity?
A. Law of Similarity
B. Law of Variation
C. Law of Regression
D. Law of Progression

22. Which of the following factors does **not** affect the teaching learning process?
A. Physical appearance of teacher
B. Mental health of teacher
C. Content knowledge of teacher
D. Communication skills of teacher

23. According to Moral Development theory of Piaget, adolescent period is:
A. Stage of moral realism
B. Stage of morality constraint
C. Stage of heteronomous morality
D. Stage of autonomous morality

24. Which statement is **not** correct in context of individual differences?
A. Two persons are not exactly same.
B. Individual differences are deviation in regards to characteristics.
C. Individual differences distinguish individuals in their totality.
D. Individual differences are the sole result of heredity.

25. Learning through mental processes like attention and reflection is called:
A. Imitative learning B. Motor learning
C. Cognitive learning D. Affective learning

26. Which of the following is **not** a principle of effective learning?
A. Motivation B. Individual approach
C. Passive attendance D. Feedback

13. B	**14.** D	**15.** A	**16.** D	**17.** B	**18.** C	**19.** B	**20.** C	**21.** D	**22.** A
23. D	**24.** D	**25.** C	**26.** C						

27. The **true** meaning of continuous and comprehensive evaluation is:
(*a*) Taking frequent tests
(*b*) Taking continuous tests at appropriate intervals
(*c*) To evaluate scholastic and co-scholastic both aspects
(*d*) Measuring only educational achievements

Choose the **correct** code:

Code:
A. (*b*) & (*d*) B. (*b*) & (*c*)
C. (*a*), (*b*) & (*c*) D. (*b*), (*c*) & (*d*)

28. A learning difficulty that create problem for a child to distinguish letters and words is:
A. Dysplasticia B. Dyslexia
C. Dysgraphia D. Dyscalculia

29. Which three aspects of intelligence are emphasized in the triarchic theory of Sternberg?
(*a*) Componential (*b*) Experiential
(*c*) Operational (*d*) Contextual

Choose the **correct** code:

Code:
A. (*a*), (*b*) & (*c*) B. (*b*), (*c*) & (*d*)
C. (*a*), (*b*) & (*d*) D. (*a*), (*c*) & (*d*)

30. In Pavlov's conditioning theory, which factor does **not** positively affect the conditioning between natural and artificial stimuli?
A. Appropriate timing of stimuli presentation
B. Repetition of stimuli
C. Controlled environment
D. Lack of motive

भाग-II : भाषा - हिन्दी

31. निम्न में से कौन-सा संधि शब्द अपने युग्म से सुमेलित **नहीं** है?
A. अजंत - व्यंजन संधि
B. वयोवृद्ध - विसर्ग संधि
C. महौदार्य - वृद्धि स्वर संधि
D. तेजोपुंज - गुण स्वर संधि

32. किस विकल्प के शब्दों में वार्तनिक अशुद्धि **नहीं** है?
A. सुधीजन, शताब्दी B. साधूवाद, सुरसरी
C. शूभेषी, भार्यापति D. चन्द्रमोलि, पुत्रेषणा

33. वाक्यांश के लिए एकल शब्द के संबंध में कौन-सा युग्म **असंगत** है?
A. जिसे वहन करना कठिन हो – दुर्विभाव्य
B. जिसे किसी ने न सूँघा हो – अनाघ्रात
C. कोई काम करने की इच्छा – चिकीर्षा
D. विजय प्राप्ति की तीव्र इच्छा – विजीगिषा

34. निम्न में से कौन-सा शब्द 'धनुष' का पर्यायवाची **नहीं** है?
A. चाप B. कार्मुक
C. शरासन D. कासार

35. 'नीम हकीम खतरे जान' उक्त लोकोक्ति का **सही** अर्थ है :
A. पहले स्वार्थ बाद में परमार्थ करना।
B. अल्पज्ञान खतरनाक होता है।
C. दोषी के साथ निर्दोष को सजा मिलना।
D. अत्यन्त धीरे काम चलना।

36. किस क्रमांक में 'कादंबरी-कादंबिनी' शब्द-युग्म का क्रमशः **सही** अर्थ है?
A. शराब, घटा B. कुशल, सेवक
C. विनीत, बुराई D. कुशल, पवित्र

37. संज्ञा के संबंध में कौन-सा कथन संगत **नहीं** है?
A. व्यक्तिवाचक संज्ञाओं का प्रयोग सदैव (आदरार्थक के अतिरिक्त) एकवचन में होता है।
B. देश, त्योहार, नदी उक्त व्यक्तिवाचक संज्ञा के उदाहरण हैं।
C. 'द्रव्यवाचक' तथा 'समूहवाचक', जातिवाचक संज्ञा के ही भेद माने जाते हैं।
D. 'विद्वत्ता', 'पांडित्य' उक्त यौगिक भाववाचक संज्ञा के उदाहरण हैं।

38. विलोम शब्द के संबंध में कौन-सा युग्म **असंगत** है?
A. घमण्डी - विनीत
B. चिरायु - दीर्घायु
C. तारुण्य - वार्धक्य
D. तेजस्वी - निस्तेज

39. उपसर्ग की दृष्टि से किस विकल्प का शब्द-युग्म **असंगत** है?
A. निर् - निराकरण, निरपराध
B. अनु - अनूदित, अन्वीक्षण
C. परा - परार्थ, पराश्रित
D. सु - सुदूर, सुकृत

27. B **28.** B **29.** C **30.** D **31.** D **32.** A **33.** A, D **34.** D **35.** B **36.** A
37. B **38.** B **39.** C

40. सर्वनाम के संबंध में कौन-सा युग्म संगत **नहीं** है?
A. मैंने आज व्याकरण पढ़ा - पुरुषवाचक सर्वनाम
B. कमरे में कोई हँस रहा है - अनिश्चयवाचक सर्वनाम
C. इसी ने मेरी जिंदगी बचाई थी - प्रश्नवाचक सर्वनाम
D. वह स्वयं को सुधार रहा है - निजवाचक सर्वनाम

41. तत्पुरुष समास का कौन-सा समस्तपद अपने युग्म से सही सुमेलित **नहीं** है?
A. गुरुदक्षिणा - संबंध तत्पुरुष
B. देशाटन - अधिकरण तत्पुरुष
C. रेखांकित - करण तत्पुरुष
D. देशनिर्वासित - अपादान तत्पुरुष

42. विशेषण के संबंध में कौन-सा कथन **असंगत** है?
A. जिस विकारी शब्द से संज्ञा की व्याप्ति मर्यादित होती है, उसे विशेषण कहते हैं।
B. 'भला, दानी, दुष्ट' उक्त शब्द, गुणवाचक विशेषण के उदाहरण हैं।
C. 'कक्षा में साठ छात्र पढ़ते हैं' संख्यावाचक विशेषण का उदाहरण है।
D. संकेतवाचक विशेषण में किसी वस्तु की नाप या तौल का बोध होता है।

43. निम्न में से कौन-सा शब्द 'अपत्यवाचक तद्धित प्रत्यय' से निर्मित **नहीं** है?
A. वैनतेय B. कौरव
C. वासुदेव D. वैधव्य

44. 'ग', 'ल' तथा 'ब' उक्त वर्णों का क्रमशः उच्चारण स्थान है :
A. तालु, कण्ठ, ओष्ठ B. दन्त, कण्ठ, तालु
C. कण्ठ, दन्त, ओष्ठ D. ओष्ठ, कण्ठ, तालु

45. किस विकल्प का वाक्य पूर्वकालिक क्रिया का उदाहरण **नहीं** है?
A. राम खेलकर चला गया।
B. तुम्हें ऐसा करना शोभा नहीं देता है।
C. सीता खाना बनाकर जयपुर जाएगी।
D. अध्यापक उदाहरण देकर छात्रों को पढ़ाते हैं।

PART-II : LANGUAGE – ENGLISH

46. Choose the option that gives the **correct** meaning of the given phrasal verb:

Give in
A. distribute B. deposit
C. donate D. surrender

47. Fill in the blank with the most appropriate modal auxiliary:

Your mother is seriously ill. You ______ leave for home at once. (obligation)
A. needs B. might
C. could D. must

48. Choose the **correct** preposition to fill in the blank:

He told all _______ the incident.
A. between B. among
C. beside D. about

49. Choose the most appropriate preposition to fill in the blank:

I am going home the day ______ tomorrow.
A. in B. on
C. after D. at

50. Choose the most appropriate preposition to fill in the blank:

Mohan gazed _______ the sky in the hope of rain.
A. at B. unto
C. besides D. into

51. Choose the **correct** option that gives the correct passive voice of the given sentence:

Have they done the work?
A. Have the work been done?
B. Has the work been done?
C. Had the work been done?
D. Will the work be done?

52. Choose the **correct** tense form to fill in the blank:

The Headmaster _______ to meet you.
A. want B. wants
C. is wanting D. was wanting

53. Choose the part of sentence which is **incorrect**:

(*a*) Has Sachin / (*b*) not breaked/ (*c*) the record held/ (*d*) by Bradman who made 10,000 runs in his career?
A. (*a*) B. (*b*)
C. (*c*) D. (*d*)

40. C **41.** A **42.** D **43.** D **44.** C **45.** B **46.** D **47.** D **48.** D **49.** C
50. A **51.** B **52.** B **53.** B

54. Choose the **correct** option to fill in the blank:

______ had the police reached than the thieves fled.

A. As soon as B. No sooner
C. Scarcely D. As well

55. Choose the **correct** tense form to fill in the blank:

She jumped off the train while it _______ .

A. moved B. had moved
C. has moved D. was moving

56. Change the narration to Reported speech and choose the **right** option:

I said to him, "Do you know when she will go home?"

A. I told him if he knew when she will go home?
B. I said to him that did he knew when she would go home.
C. I asked him if he knew when she would go home.
D. I said to him that did he know when will she go home?

57. Choose the **correct** option for the given one word:

Sinecure

A. one who lives by himself
B. an office with no work but high pay
C. surgery without anesthesia
D. cure by naturopathy

58. Choose the option that gives the **correct** meaning of the given phrasal verb:

Send for

A. start on a journey
B. reach to a decision
C. call someone in
D. improve

59. Choose the option that gives the **correct** meaning of the phrasal verb:

Turn out

A. to evict someone
B. to kill someone
C. to ridicule someone
D. to give legal notice to someone

60. Fill in the blank with the most appropriate meaning of the underlined idiom:

Rakesh had to deal with all his problems by himself, because he didn't want to depend on his fair weather friends.

A. Friends who come from rich family.
B. Friends who are loyal only during a time of success.
C. Friends with whom one lived in one's college time.
D. Friends who no longer live with you.

PART-III : GENERAL STUDIES

Quantitative Aptitude, Reasoning Ability and GK & Awareness

61. In a family, A is the father of X, B is the mother of Y. The sister of X and Z is Y. Which of the following statement is definitely **not** true?

A. B is the wife of A
B. B has a daughter
C. X is the son of A
D. Y is the sister of Z

62. If A walks 8 km South then turn right and walks 6 km and again turns North-East and walks 10 km. How far is A from the starting point?

A. 0 km
B. 8 km
C. 10 km
D. 12 km

63. If 10 persons can complete (2/5)th of a work in 8 days, then how many persons are required to complete the remaining work in 12 days?

A. 6 B. 8
C. 10 D. 12

64. The base of a right prism is a triangle whose perimeter is 32 cm and the inradius of the triangle is 6 cm. If the volume of the prism is 576 cc, then its height is:

A. 4 cm B. 5 cm
C. 6 cm D. 8 cm

65. If the number of diagonals of a regular polygon is 27, then the number of sides is:

A. 6 B. 9
C. 10 D. 12

54. B **55.** D **56.** C **57.** B **58.** C **59.** A **60.** B **61.** C **62.** A **63.** C
64. C **65.** B

66. In two alloys A and B, the ratio of copper and zinc is 5 : 2 and 3 : 4 respectively. 7 kg of alloy A and 21 kg of the alloy B are mixed together to form a new alloy. What will be the ratio of copper and zinc in the new alloy?

A. 1 : 2 B. 2 : 1
C. 2 : 3 D. 1 : 1

67. If 7 cosec θ – 3 cot θ = 7 where θ is in first quadrant, then the value of 7 cot θ – 3 cosec θ is equal to:

A. 3 B. 5
C. 3/7 D. 5/7

68. If an equilateral triangle ABC be inscribed in a circle, then the tangents at their vertices will form another triangle is:

A. Scalene triangle B. Isosceles triangle
C. Equilateral triangle D. Right angled triangle

69. A shopkeeper sells an article at 15% gain. Had he sold it for ₹ 18 more; he would have gained 18%. The cost price (in ₹) of the article is:

A. 600 B. 540
C. 350 D. 380

70. Find the **wrong** number in the given series:

0, 3, 9, 12, 36, 39, 42, 120, 360

A. 12 B. 39
C. 42 D. 360

71. The difference between two positive numbers is 3. If the sum of their squares is 369, then sum of the numbers is:

A. 25 B. 27
C. 31 D. 33

72. In a division sum, the divisor is 12 times the quotient and 5 times the remainder. If the remainder is 36, then the dividend is:

A. 2706 B. 2736
C. 2796 D. 2766

73. If A denotes 'divided by', B denotes 'added to', C denotes 'subtracted from' and D denotes 'multiplied by', then 20 C 12 B 8 A 2 D 6 is equal to:

A. 16 B. 18
C. 32 D. 36

74. A person covers 12 km at 3 km/hr, 18 km at 9 km/hr and 24 km at 4 km/hr. The average speed in covering the whole distance is:

A. 4 km/hr B. 4.2 km/hr
C. 4.4 km/hr D. 4.5 km/hr

75. Find the odd word from the given alternatives:

A. Violin B. Harp
C. Guitar D. Flute

76. If 16 – 4 = 2, 9 – 3 = 2, 81 – 3 = 4, then the value of 64 – 4 is:

A. 3 B. 2
C. 4 D. 6

77. The missing term of the following series is:

DBC, KIJ, QOP, __?__, ZXY

A. VUW B. USV
C. UTV D. VTU

78. If 'PROJECT' is coded as 'CEOPRT' and 'PLANE' is coded as 'ELNP' then the 'ORGANISED' will be coded as:

A. ADEGIOSR B. ADEGIROS
C. ADEGOIRS D. ADEGIORS

79. In a row of boys, A is 7th from the left and B is 12th from the right. If they interchange their positions A becomes 22nd from the left. How many total boys are there in a row?

A. 27 B. 31
C. 33 D. 34

80. A travels 8 km from East to West and turns right and travel 2 km. Now again he turn right and travel 5 km. In which direction is he now positioned with reference to starting point?

A. South-West
B. North-West
C. North-East
D. South-East

81. Who is the Chief Information Officer of Haryana?

A. Smt. Jyoti Arora
B. Dr. Jagbir Singh
C. Shri Vijay Vardhan
D. Smt. Kamaldeep Bhandari

82. In Haryana, where the Vulture Conservation Centre is located?

A. Jind B. Pinjore
C. Mahendragarh D. Ambala

83. The UPSC Chairman, who subsequently became the Governor of Haryana:

A. Dr. A.R. Kidwai
B. Shri Muzaffar Husain Berney
C. Shri B.N. Chakravarti
D. Shri Mahabir Prasad

66. D	**67.** A	**68.** C	**69.** A	**70.** C	**71.** B	**72.** B	**73.** C	**74.** D	**75.** D
76. A	**77.** D	**78.** D	**79.** C	**80.** B	**81.** C	**82.** B	**83.** A		

84. In which district of Haryana, the Khelo India Women's Archery ranking competition was organised?
A. Sonipat
B. Panipat
C. Karnal
D. Yamunanagar

85. How many Tehsils are there in Haryana?
A. 95 B. 49
C. 143 D. 74

86. The Scheme, which is being run by the Haryana government to replace paddy crop with more tradition crops is:
A. Meri Fasal Mera Byora
B. Meri Virasat
C. Mera Pani Meri Virasat
D. Hamara Dhan

87. Where in the Haryana, the National Institute of Fashion Technology is located?
A. Panipat B. Ambala
C. Panchkula D. Kurukshetra

88. Who among the following Sages of Haryana was popularly known as Puran Bhagat?
A. Baba Mast Nath B. Baba Gorakh Nath
C. Baba Chaurangi Nath D. Baba Puran Nath

89. The Morni hills of Haryana belongs to:
A. Aravalli range
B. Hindukush range
C. Outer range of Himalayas
D. Inner range of Himalayas

90. During the revolt of 1857, who among the following attacked British establishments in Rohtak?
A. Tafzal Husain B. Imam Ali
C. Mohar Singh D. Harsukh Rai

PART-IV : SUBJECT KNOWLEDGE—SOCIAL STUDIES

91. In critique of nationalism who said "Patriotism cannot be our final spiritual shelter; my refuge is humanity. I will not buy glass for the price of diamonds, and I will never allow patriotism to triumph over humanity as long as I live"?
A. Mahatma Gandhi B. Rabindranath Tagore
C. Bertrand Russell D. Aurobindo Ghosh

92. Which of the following Pratihara rulers assumed the title of "Adivaraha"?
A. Nagabhatta II B. Mihirbhoj
C. Mahipala D. Mahendrapala

93. Which of the following pairs are **correctly** matched?
(*a*) Minhaj-us-Siraj : Tabkat-i-Nasiri
(*b*) Ziauddin Barani : Tarikh-i-Firozshahi
(*c*) Amir Khusrau : Futuh-us-Salatin
(*d*) Badayuni : Muntakhab-ut-Tawarikh

Codes:
A. (*a*), (*b*), (*d*) B. (*a*), (*c*)
C. (*a*), (*b*), (*c*) D. (*a*), (*b*)

94. When there is no work to do on farms, people go to urban areas to look for jobs. This kind of unemployment is known as:
A. Structural unemployment
B. Disguised unemployment
C. Seasonal unemployment
D. Cyclical unemployment

95. Hot and dry local wind of Northern Plains of India is called:
A. Loo B. Monsoon
C. Trade Winds D. All options are wrong

96. Which of the following is called the Prime Meridian?
A. 23°30′ North B. 23°30′ South
C. 82°30′ East D. 0° Longitude

97. Which one is **not** written by Dr. Bhim Rao Ambedkar?
A. Annihilation of Caste
B. Untouchable
C. Who were the Shudras?
D. Riddles in Hinduism

98. Who described freedom as 'silence of laws'?
A. Thomas Hobbes B. Isaiah Berlin
C. Bertrand Russell D. John Locke

99. What is the name given to the full moon night?
A. Amavasya
B. Poornima
C. Both (A) & (B) are right
D. Both (A) & (B) are wrong

84. A	**85.** A	**86.** C	**87.** C	**88.** C	**89.** C	**90.** A	**91.** B	**92.** B	**93.** A
94. C	**95.** A	**96.** D	**97.** B	**98.** A	**99.** B				

100. Which of the following pairs is **not** correctly matched?

Department		**Founded by**
A. Diwan-i-Arj	:	Iltutmish
B. Diwan-i-Mustkharaj	:	Alauddin Khalji
C. Diwan-i-Kohi	:	Muhammad Bin Tughlaq
D. Diwan-i-Khairat	:	Firoz Shah Tughlaq

101. Which of the following is **true** regarding theory of representation?

(*a*) Characteristic representation believe that only people who are drawn from a particular group can genuinely articulate its interests.

(*b*) Mandate doctrine believe in popular guidance to those who exercise government power.

A. Only (*a*) B. None

C. Only (*b*) D. Both (*a*), (*b*)

102. Which of the following pairs are correctly matched?

(*a*) Ashoka : Nigrodha

(*b*) Menander : Nagasena

(*c*) Kanishka : Mahakassapa

(*d*) Harsha : Huen Tsang

Codes:

A. (*a*), (*b*), (*c*) B. (*a*), (*b*), (*d*)

C. Only (*a*), (*b*) D. (*a*), (*b*), (*c*) and (*d*)

103. Which planet does **not** have rings around it?

A. Jupiter B. Saturn

C. Uranus D. Earth

104. Water freezes at:

A. 0°C B. 5°C

C. 15°C D. 100°C

105. Which of the following is/are issued by the RBI and acts as legal tender money?

(*a*) Demand deposits

(*b*) Coins of all denomination

(*c*) Currency notes of various denominations, except one rupee note

(*d*) One rupee currency notes

Choose the **correct** option:

A. Only (*a*) and (*c*) are correct

B. Only (*b*) and (*c*) are correct

C. Only (*c*) is correct

D. Only (*d*) is correct

106. In which of the following states is the Indus Valley Civilization site "Juni-Kuran" located?

A. Gujarat B. Maharashtra

C. Uttar Pradesh D. Punjab

107. Match the following List-I with List-II and select the **correct** answer using the codes given below the list:

List-I	**List-II**
(*a*) Brihadeshwer Temple of Tanjore	(*i*) Gupta Dynasty
(*b*) Dashavatar Temple of Devgarh	(*ii*) Rashtrakuta Dynasty
(*c*) Kailash Temple of Ellora	(*iii*) Chola Dynasty
(*d*) Kandariya Mahadeva Temple of Khajuraho	(*iv*) Chandela Dynasty

Codes:

	(*a*)	(*b*)	(*c*)	(*d*)
A.	(*ii*)	(*i*)	(*iii*)	(*iv*)
B.	(*ii*)	(*iv*)	(*iii*)	(*i*)
C.	(*iii*)	(*i*)	(*ii*)	(*iv*)
D.	(*iii*)	(*ii*)	(*i*)	(*iv*)

108. Arrange the food security related programs in India in chronological order:

(*a*) Targeted Public Distribution System (TPDS)

(*b*) Antyodaya Anna Yojana

(*c*) Integrated Food Security Scheme

(*d*) Food Security Act

A. (*a*) (*b*) (*c*) (*d*) B. (*a*) (*b*) (*d*) (*c*)

C. (*d*) (*c*) (*a*) (*b*) D. (*b*) (*a*) (*c*) (*d*)

109. Who held that "The notion of sovereignty must be expunged from political theory"?

A. Lindsay B. Barkar

C. H.J. Laski D. Krabbe

110. In criticism of democracy who said "Liberal or 'thin' democracy is contributing to growing cynicism about politics and the paralysis of public institutions"?

A. Benjamin Barber

B. C. Wright Mills

C. Bernard Crick

D. J.J. Rousseau

111. Which one (Author-Books) is **not** in right combination?

A. Germaine Greer - 'The Female Eununch'

B. Simone de Beauvoir - 'Sexual Politics'

C. Betty Friedan - 'The Feminine Mystique'

D. Naomi Wolf - 'Fire with fire'

112. Major human activity in Ladakh is:

A. Tourism B. Agriculture

C. Mining D. Industry

100. A **101.** D **102.** B **103.** D **104.** A **105.** C **106.** A **107.** C **108.** B **109.** D
110. A **111.** B **112.** B

113. Which one/ones are function/power of the Security Council of UNO?

(*a*) To investigate any disputes which might lead to international friction.

(*b*) To recommend the admission of new Members.

(*c*) To bring issues threatening, the maintenance of peace and security to the attention of other United Nations organs.

A. Only (*a*) B. Only (*a*), (*c*)
C. Only (*b*), (*c*) D. Only (*a*), (*b*)

114. Identify the apex institution for rural financing in India:

A. IDBI B. NABARD
C. SIDBI D. HSCARDBL

115. Which of the following is **not** an indicator of Human Development?

A. PQLI B. HDI
C. BSE D. Per Capita Income

116. Which of the following rulers was called "Sarvakshatrantak" in Puranas?

A. Bimbisara B. Ajatashatru
C. Shishunaga D. Mahapadma Nanda

117. From Column-I and Column-II, choose the correct pair:

Column-I	Column-II
(*a*) Measurement of NI by Dadabhai Naoroji	(*i*) 1917-18
(*b*) Establishment of CSO	(*ii*) 1948
(*c*) New Economic Policy	(*iii*) 1951
(*d*) CACP	(*iv*) 1965

A. (*a*)-(*i*) B. (*b*)-(*ii*)
C. (*c*)-(*iii*) D. (*d*)-(*iv*)

118. The celestial bodies which have their own heat and light, are called as:

A. Planets
B. Stars
C. Satellites
D. All options are right

119. Match the following:

Return	Factor
(*a*) Profit	(*i*) Labour
(*b*) Rent	(*ii*) Land
(*c*) Wage	(*iii*) Capital
(*d*) Interest	(*iv*) Entrepreneurship

Codes:

	(*a*)	(*b*)	(*c*)	(*d*)
A.	(*i*)	(*ii*)	(*iii*)	(*iv*)
B.	(*iv*)	(*iii*)	(*ii*)	(*i*)
C.	(*iv*)	(*ii*)	(*i*)	(*iii*)
D.	(*i*)	(*iii*)	(*ii*)	(*iv*)

120. In which category has Haryana been in the "SDG India Index-3.0" report?

A. Achiever (100)
B. Front runner (65-99)
C. Performer (50-64)
D. Aspirant (0-49)

121. Who is the author of "Social Origins of Dictatorship and Democracy"?

A. Jennifer Gandhi
B. Barrington Moore
C. Hanna Arendt
D. Carl Schmitt

122. How many Nationalized Banks are there, in India (September, 2023)?

A. 8 B. 10
C. 12 D. 14

123. Arrange the following in correct chronological order and select the **correct** answer from the codes given below:

(*a*) Battle of Porto Novo
(*b*) Battle of Plassey
(*c*) Battle of Wandiwash
(*d*) Battle of Buxar

Codes:

A. (*b*), (*d*), (*a*), (*c*) B. (*b*), (*c*), (*d*), (*a*)
C. (*c*), (*b*), (*a*), (*d*) D. (*c*), (*a*), (*d*), (*b*)

124. Which of the following pairs is **incompatible**?

A. Kanpur : Nana Saheb
B. Lucknow : Hazrat Mahal
C. Faizabad : Maulvi Ahmad Ullah
D. Bareilly : Begum Zeenat Mahal

125. Which of the following countries established the International African Association in 1876?

A. England B. Portugal
C. Belgium D. Turkey

126. The narrow zone of contact between the land, water and air is:

A. Lithosphere B. Hydrosphere
C. Atmosphere D. Biosphere

113. D **114.** B **115.** C **116.** D **117.** D **118.** B **119.** C **120.** B **121.** B **122.** C
123. B **124.** D **125.** C **126.** D

127. What will be the elasticity of demand for a product, if it has multiple uses?
A. $e > 1$ B. $e < 1$
C. $e = 0$ D. $e = \infty$

128. Which river drains into the Arabian Sea?
A. Tapi B. Ganga
C. Kaveri D. Mahanadi

129. Who among the following was not the chairman/ member of the State Reorganization Commission formed in 1953?
A. Fazal Ali B. K.M. Munshi
C. Hridaynath Kunzru D. K.M. Pannikar

130. Who among the following contributed to the establishment of the Swaraj Party in 1923?
A. Motilal Nehru and Chittaranjan Das
B. Jawaharlal Nehru and Subhash Chandra Bose
C. Bhagat Singh and Chandra Shekhar Azad
D. Rammanohar Lohia and Jai Prakash Narayan

131. Which sentence regarding environmentalism is **not** correct?
(*a*) Arne Naess is considered as father of deep ecology.
(*b*) Murray Bookchin is the inventor of Gaia hypothesis.
(*c*) Term ecology is derived from Latin word Oikos.
A. Only (*c*) B. Only (*a*), (*c*)
C. Only (*b*), (*c*) D. All (*a*), (*b*), (*c*)

132. The states in India have been formed mainly on the basis of:
A. Religion B. Languages
C. Castes D. Culture

133. Who is the President of 78th Session of United Nation's General Assembly ?
A. M. Csaba Korosi B. Sam Kutesa
C. M. Dennis Francis D. Peter Thomson

134. Find the missing figures in given example of credit creation and choose the correct option:

Round	Deposits	Loans (80%)	Reserve Ratio (20%)
I	1000	800	(*i*)
II	800	(*ii*)	160
III	(*iii*)	512	(*iv*)
IV	512	409.6	102.4

	(*i*)	(*ii*)	(*iii*)	(*iv*)
A.	200	640	580	68
B.	200	580	580	68
C.	200	640	640	128
D.	200	580	640	128

135. Which agreement/s is/are signed between India and USA?
(*a*) Basic Exchange and Cooperation Agreement for Geospatial Intelligence (BECA).
(*b*) General Security of Military Information Agreement (GSOMIA).
(*c*) Logistics Exchange Memorandum of Agreement (LEMOA).
A. Only (*c*) B. Only (*a*), (*c*)
C. All (*a*), (*b*), (*c*) D. Only (*a*), (*b*)

136. Maps that focus on specific information, is called:
A. Thematic Map
B. Physical Map
C. Political Map
D. All options are right

137. Which is the **right** order of milestone events of UNO formation?
(*a*) Inter-Allied Declaration
(*b*) Yalta Conference
(*c*) Dumbarton Oaks Conference
A. (*a*), (*b*), (*c*) B. (*b*), (*a*), (*c*)
C. (*a*), (*c*), (*b*) D. (*c*), (*a*), (*b*)

138. What is the National Consumer Helpline (NCH) Number with the motto 'Jaago Grahak Jaago'?
A. 1800-3000-145 B. 1857
C. 2014 D. 1915

139. Which one is **not** a qualitative method of distribution maps?
A. Chorochromatic Method
B. Choroschematic Method
C. Tint Method
D. Choropleth Method

140. Which one is considered an example of 'Coalitional Presidentialism'?
A. Mexico B. South Africa
C. Brazil D. USA

141. Which gas leads to increase in global temperature?
A. CO_2 B. O_2
C. O_3 D. N_2

142. In which country the term 'Cohabitation' is used to define system of divided government?
A. France B. U.K.
C. USA D. Italy

143. Western Ghats is also known as:
A. Sahyadri B. Himadri
C. Aravalli D. Shiwalik

127. A	**128.** A	**129.** B	**130.** A	**131.** C	**132.** B	**133.** C	**134.** C	**135.** C	**136.** A
137. C	**138.** D	**139.** D	**140.** C	**141.** A	**142.** A	**143.** A			

144. Which of the following festivals was considered very important in Hampi?
A. Mahanavami B. Holi
C. Onam D. Diwali

145. Which of the following is the basis for constructing Indifference Curve (IC)?
A. Consumer's Income
B. Absolute prices of two goods
C. Relative prices of two goods
D. Consumer preference scale

146. Genghis Khan belonged to which of the following Mongol Clans?
A. Borjigid B. Khalkha
C. Bayads D. Hamnigan

147. Which is the first private sector train of India?
A. Vande Bharat
B. Tejas Express
C. Gareeb Rath
D. Rajdhani Express

148. Who among the following painted the picture titled "The Last Judgment"?
A. Leonardo da Vinci B. Michelangelo
C. Raphael D. Masaccio

149. Direct rays of the sun fall on the Tropic of Cancer on:
A. 21st March B. 21st June
C. 22nd December D. 23rd September

150. Consider the following statements:
(I) WTO (1995) was established on the basis of Dunkal proposal in place of GATT (1947).
(II) WTO has been established on the basis of an international treaty approved by the parliaments of the member countries.

Choose the **correct** option:
A. Only (I) is correct.
B. Only (II) is correct.
C. Both (I) and (II) are correct.
D. Both (I) and (II) are wrong

EXPLANATORY ANSWERS

1. (A): Lev Vygotsky emphasized the crucial role of social and cultural factors in a child's cognitive development, distinguishing his perspective from others like Piaget who focused more on individual cognitive stages. Vygotsky's sociocultural theory proposes that children learn actively and through hands-on experiences, and their learning is deeply influenced by the cultural contexts in which they grow up.

2. (C): Film strips are not suitable for visually impaired students because they rely heavily on visual content which cannot be perceived by students with visual impairments. In contrast, Braille materials, talking books, and embossed maps are specifically designed to be accessible for the visually impaired, utilizing tactile or auditory information.

3. (B): Progressive education is an educational movement emphasizing real-world experiences, problem-solving, and critical thinking. This approach encourages 'learning by doing,' where students actively engage with their environment to foster learning, reflecting the principles set out by educational reformers like John Dewey.

4. (D): Inclusive education refers to the educational model that seeks to include all children within the mainstream educational system, regardless of their physical, intellectual, social, emotional, linguistic, or other conditions.

This approach aims to provide equal opportunities for all students, not just those who are disabled or socially deprived.

5. (A): A field trip is an effective teaching-learning strategy in the context of social learning because it allows students to interact directly with the environment and engage socially with peers and guides. This hands-on experience not only enhances learning but also supports social development by fostering communication and observational skills in a real-world context. This method aligns closely with social learning theory, which emphasizes learning through observation and interaction within social settings.

6. (B): Analytical questions require detailed analysis and are typically answered in an essay or short-answer format, making them not objective. Objective type questions, like matching, multiple choice, and

144. A **145.** D **146.** A **147.** B **148.** B **149.** B **150.** C

blank space questions, require students to select or write a specific answer without requiring extended reasoning or explanation.

7. **(A):** Acceleration is not suitable for slow learners as it involves progressing through education at a faster rate than typical, which can be overwhelming for these students. Remedial teaching, drill work, and cooperative teaching methods are more beneficial as they provide additional support, practice, and collaborative learning opportunities, respectively.

8. **(A):** The spaced method is appropriate for learning long and difficult lessons as it involves breaking the learning into shorter sessions over a longer period. This method allows for better understanding and retention by providing time for reflection and assimilation of the material, as opposed to the massed method which involves cramming the information in a short time.

9. **(A):** Approved social behaviour patterns in adolescence include leadership skills and empathy. Leadership skills involve guiding others and making decisions responsibly, while empathy entails understanding and sharing the feelings of others. Ego-centrism, focusing on oneself, and stereotyping, applying generalized beliefs to individuals, are generally not seen as positive behaviours.

10. **(A):** The instinct theory is associated with William McDougall, not John Atkinson, making option A incorrect. Atkinson is known for his work on the Expectancy-Value Theory, not the Instinct Theory. Maslow's Need Hierarchical Theory, Woodworth's Drive Theory, and McClelland's Achievement Motivation Theory are correctly paired with their respective proponents.

11. **(D):** The Stanford-Binet Test is not a performance test of intelligence but a standardized IQ test that measures cognitive abilities through verbal, quantitative, and non-verbal reasoning. Performance tests of intelligence, like Koh's Block Design Test, Alexander's Pass Along Test, and Saguine Form Board Test, typically involve manipulating materials and require minimal verbal instruction, focusing instead on tasks that demonstrate practical problem-solving and spatial reasoning.

12. **(C):** Development does not necessarily follow a linear path, as this implies a fixed sequence of stages or progress that is the same for everyone. In reality, developmental patterns can vary greatly between individuals and can be influenced by numerous factors, making development multi-directional rather than strictly linear. Other listed principles, such as development being a product of heredity and environment, and developmental patterns being predictable, are generally accepted in developmental psychology.

13. **(B):** According to Robert Gagne, the highest level of learning a teacher should strive to take students to is problem-solving learning. This level involves applying rules to solve problems in new situations, which represents a higher-order cognitive skill encompassing understanding and application, beyond simple concept or rule learning.

14. **(D):** All the factors listed—motivation, aptitude, interest, and attention—affect learning. These elements are crucial as they determine how effectively an individual engages with educational content. Motivation drives effort, aptitude influences ability to understand, interest enhances engagement, and attention is necessary for effective information processing.

15. **(A):** A harmonious relationship with parents is not a common characteristic of social development in adolescence. Typically, adolescence is marked by a quest for greater independence, which can often lead to conflicts with parents as the individual seeks to establish a separate identity. Other options, such as new social groupings, a search for identity, and hero-worship, are more typically associated with adolescent social development.

16. **(D):** Endocrine glands are not an environmental but a biological factor influencing child development. These glands play a critical role in physical and hormonal development through the secretion of hormones. Environmental factors typically include elements like nutrition, the mental state of the mother during pregnancy, and accidents, which have external impacts on a child's growth and development.

17. **(B):** The 'Law of Use' and 'Law of Disuse' relate to Thorndike's Law of Exercise. According to this law, connections between stimuli and responses are strengthened through use and weakened through disuse, implying that practicing a skill improves it, whereas failing to practice leads to its decay.

18. **(C):** Animism is not a characteristic related to Piaget's concrete operational stage of cognitive development. Animism, the belief that inanimate objects have life and feelings, is more typical of the earlier preoperational stage. The concrete operational stage, however, is marked by abilities such as reversibility, serialization, and conservation, where children begin to understand logical operations and are less egocentric.

19. (B): The teaching maxim "abstract to concrete" is not typically beneficial for learning-disabled children who generally benefit more from concrete to abstract approaches. Learning-disabled students often find it easier to understand and retain information when taught from simple to complex, direct to indirect, and known to unknown, as these methods build a foundation of understanding by starting with tangible, familiar concepts.

20. (C): The stages of "Individualism and exchange" and "Social contracts and individual rights" in Kohlberg's moral development theory are not part of the conventional level of morality. These stages belong to the pre-conventional and post-conventional levels, respectively. The conventional level involves maintaining social order and good interpersonal relations, focusing on complying with laws and the expectations of others to uphold societal norms.

21. (D): The "Law of Progression" is not typically associated with heredity. Heredity laws such as the Law of Similarity, Law of Variation, and Law of Regression deal with how genetic traits are passed down and vary among individuals. The Law of Progression suggests a forward movement or development which is more general and not specifically tied to genetic inheritance.

22. (A): The physical appearance of a teacher does not fundamentally affect the teaching-learning process. While factors like the mental health of the teacher, content knowledge, and communication skills directly influence the effectiveness of teaching and the learning environment, physical appearance is not directly related to educational outcomes.

23. (D): According to Jean Piaget's theory of moral development, the adolescent period is characterized as the "Stage of Autonomous Morality".

At this stage, individuals begin to see morality as based on mutual respect and cooperation, moving beyond the earlier stages where rules are seen as unchangeable and imposed by authority.

24. (D): The statement that individual differences are solely the result of heredity is incorrect. While heredity plays a significant role, environmental factors, experiences, and personal choices also contribute substantially to individual differences. Other statements recognize the complexity and uniqueness of individual differences.

25. (C): Cognitive learning involves the use of mental processes such as attention, memory, and reflection. This type of learning is concerned with the acquisition of problem-solving abilities and understanding, rather than just the mechanical repetition of actions, distinguishing it from imitative, motor, and affective learning.

26. (C): Passive attendance is not a principle of effective learning. Effective learning principles emphasize active engagement, motivation, individualized approaches, and feedback, which are crucial for enhancing the learning experience and ensuring better educational outcomes.

27. (B): Continuous and comprehensive evaluation means evaluating both scholastic and co-scholastic aspects of a student's performance, not just through continuous tests, but also at appropriate intervals to monitor progress comprehensively. It encompasses a broader understanding of student abilities and development, beyond mere academic achievements.

28. (B): Dyslexia is a learning difficulty characterized by problems with accurate and/or fluent word recognition, poor spelling, and decoding abilities. It specifically affects the ability to distinguish letters and words, which is different from other learning difficulties like dysgraphia (writing disorders) or dyscalculia (math difficulties).

29. (C): According to Sternberg's Triarchic Theory of Intelligence, the three aspects of intelligence are Componential (analytical), Experiential (creative), and Contextual (practical). These elements encompass the ability to analyze information, use creativity to solve problems, and adapt to different environments, respectively.

30. (D): In Pavlov's conditioning theory, a lack of motive does not positively affect the conditioning between natural and artificial stimuli. Effective conditioning generally requires appropriate timing, repetition of stimuli, and a controlled environment to establish a strong association. Motivation or a relevant stimulus is often necessary to create a meaningful connection for the conditioned response.

31. (D): 'तेजोपुंज' शब्द गुण स्वर संधि का उदाहरण नहीं है। यह शब्द 'तेजस्' और 'पुंज' का समास है, न कि संधि। संधि में दो शब्दों के मिलने से उनके बीच के ध्वनियों में परिवर्तन होता है। यहाँ पर गुण स्वर संधि नहीं हुई है।

32. (A): 'सुधीजन' और 'शताब्दी' शब्दों में वर्तनी सही है। ये दोनों शब्द उचित रूप से लिखे गए हैं और इनमें किसी प्रकार की अशुद्धि नहीं है, जबकि अन्य विकल्पों में वर्तनी संबंधी गलतियाँ पाई गई हैं।

34. (D): 'कासार' शब्द 'धनुष' का पर्यायवाची नहीं है। 'धनुष' के पर्यायवाची शब्द होते हैं 'चाप', 'कार्मुक', और 'शरासन'। 'कासार' का अर्थ एक छोटा तालाब या पोखर होता है। अतः यह 'धनुष' से संबंधित नहीं है।

35. (B): 'नीम हकीम खतरे जान' लोकोक्ति का अर्थ है कि अल्पज्ञान खतरनाक होता है। यह उक्ति उन लोगों के बारे में है जिन्हें थोड़ा ज्ञान होता है और वे उसे अधिक समझते हैं, जिससे कि अक्सर गलतियां हो जाती हैं और यह खतरनाक साबित हो सकता है।

36. (A): 'कादंबरी' का अर्थ है शराब और 'कादंबिनी' का अर्थ है घटा। इस युग्म का क्रमशः सही अर्थ दिया गया है जो संस्कृत साहित्य में प्रयोग होता है। 'कादंबरी' बाणभट्ट की प्रसिद्ध कृति का नाम भी है और इसका संदर्भ शराब से है, जबकि 'कादंबिनी' बादलों की शृंखला या घटा को दर्शाता है।

37. (B): देश, त्योहार, नदी ये व्यक्तिवाचक संज्ञाओं के उदाहरण नहीं हैं, बल्कि ये जातिवाचक संज्ञा के उदाहरण हो सकते हैं। व्यक्तिवाचक संज्ञा विशेष व्यक्ति, स्थान, या वस्तु के नाम होते हैं जैसे कि राम, दिल्ली, गंगा आदि। इसलिए यह कथन संगत नहीं है।

38. (B): 'चिरायु' और 'दीर्घायु' दोनों का अर्थ है दीर्घ जीवन या लंबी आयु होना। इसलिए यह विलोम शब्द का युग्म नहीं है क्योंकि दोनों शब्दों के अर्थ समान हैं। विलोम शब्द का अर्थ होता है विपरीत अर्थ वाले शब्द।

39. (C): 'परा' उपसर्ग का प्रयोग 'परार्थ' और 'पराश्रित' जैसे शब्दों में गलत है जबकि अन्य उपसर्गों के शब्द-युग्म सही हैं।

40. (C): 'इसी ने मेरी जिंदगी बचाई थी' में 'इसी' एक निश्चयवाचक सर्वनाम है, न कि प्रश्नवाचक सर्वनाम। प्रश्नवाचक सर्वनाम वे होते हैं जो प्रश्न पूछने के लिए प्रयुक्त होते हैं जैसे कि कौन, क्या, कहाँ, आदि। इसलिए यह युग्म संगत नहीं है।

41. (A): 'गुरुदक्षिणा' वास्तव में कर्मधारय समास है, जहाँ 'गुरु' और 'दक्षिणा' दोनों शब्द स्वतंत्र अर्थ रखते हैं लेकिन संयुक्त रूप से एक विशेष प्रकार की दक्षिणा का बोध कराते हैं, जो गुरु को दी जाती है। यह संबंध तत्पुरुष समास नहीं है क्योंकि वहाँ उत्तरपद प्रधान होता है और पूर्वपद उसकी विशेषता बताता है।

42. (D): संकेतवाचक विशेषण में वस्तु की नाप, तौल, मात्रा का बोध नहीं होता है। यह परिभाषा वास्तव में परिमाणवाचक विशेषण के लिए उपयुक्त है। संकेतवाचक विशेषण उन शब्दों को कहते हैं जो किसी वस्तु की स्थिति, स्थान, या समय का बोध कराते हैं, जैसे कि 'यह', 'वह', 'यहाँ', 'वहाँ'।

43. (D): 'वैधव्य' अपत्यवाचक तद्धित प्रत्यय से निर्मित नहीं है। यह शब्द 'विधवा' से बना है, जो किसी व्यक्ति की स्थिति या अवस्था का बोध कराता है। अन्य शब्द जैसे 'वैनतेय', 'कौरव', और 'वासुदेव' व्यक्तियों के नामों से जुड़े हुए हैं और उनके पिता या पूर्वजों का संकेत देते हैं।

44. (C): 'ग', 'ल', और 'ब' का उच्चारण स्थान क्रमशः कण्ठ, दन्त, ओष्ठ है। 'ग' वर्ण का उच्चारण कण्ठ से होता है, 'ल' का दन्त से, और 'ब' का ओष्ठ से होता है। ये उच्चारण स्थान इन वर्णों के उत्पादन की स्थिति को सही ढंग से दर्शाते हैं।

45. (B): ''तुम्हें ऐसा करना शोभा नहीं देता है।'' यह वाक्य पूर्वकालिक क्रिया का उदाहरण नहीं है। पूर्वकालिक क्रियाएं वे होती हैं जहां एक क्रिया के पूरा होने के बाद दूसरी क्रिया होती है, जैसे कि अन्य विकल्पों में दिखाया गया है। यह वाक्य एक सामान्य निषेधात्मक वाक्य है जो किसी क्रिया के अनुचित होने का संकेत देता है।

46. (D): "Give in" as a phrasal verb means to yield or surrender under pressure, not to distribute, deposit, or donate. This expression is typically used when someone reluctantly agrees to something after a period of resistance. Thus, the correct answer that conveys this meaning is "surrender."

47. (D): The modal auxiliary "must" is used to express obligation or necessity. In the sentence provided, "Your mother is seriously ill. You must leave for home at once," it indicates that it is necessary or obligatory for the person to go home immediately due to the serious illness of their mother.

48. (D): The correct preposition to use when someone is conveying information about a topic is "about." The sentence "He told all about the incident" means that he provided information concerning the incident to everyone involved or present.

49. (C): The phrase "the day after tomorrow" is used to refer to the day that follows the next day. Therefore, the most appropriate preposition to use in the sentence "I am going home the day after tomorrow" is "after," which properly links the timing of the action to the day being referred to.

50. (A): When discussing the act of looking with focus or attention at something, "at" is the correct preposition. In the sentence "Mohan gazed at the sky in the hope of rain," "at" correctly describes Mohan's action of looking intently towards the sky.

51. (B): The passive voice of the sentence "Have they done the work?" is "Has the work been done?"

This transformation from active to passive voice correctly maintains the present perfect tense and agrees in number with the singular noun "work."

52. (B): The correct form of the verb to fit the sentence "The Headmaster wants to meet you" is "wants." This form agrees with the singular subject "The Headmaster" and is in the simple present tense, which is used for stating general facts or habitual actions.

53. (B): The incorrect part of the sentence is "not breaked." The correct past participle of "break" is "broken." Thus, the sentence should read, "Has Sachin not broken the record held by Bradman who made 10,000 runs in his career?"

54. (B): The expression "No sooner had the police reached than the thieves fled" is correct for describing events that occurred almost simultaneously. "No sooner" is followed by "than" to indicate that soon after one event happens, another follows immediately.

55. (D): The correct tense form for the sentence "She jumped off the train while it was moving" is "was moving." This form indicates that the action of the train (moving) was ongoing at the time she jumped off, which is best expressed using the past continuous tense.

56. (C): The original sentence is in direct speech and asks a question. When changing to reported speech, the structure needs to reflect that it's a question being relayed indirectly. The correct transformation would be, "I asked him if he knew when she would go home." This maintains the interrogative nature inside the indirect structure and properly shifts the tense from "will go" to "would go."

57. (B): "Sinecure" refers to a position that requires little to no responsibility, effort, or actual work but still offers financial compensation. This term typically applies to jobs that are given more for patronage or reward than for the purpose of actually performing duties. This option correctly describes a job with high pay and minimal responsibilities.

58. (C): "Send for" means to request someone to come to you, typically by sending a message or calling them. It's often used in contexts where assistance or presence is needed. The correct meaning in this context is "call someone in," which implies requesting someone's arrival at a location for consultation or help.

59. (A): The phrasal verb "turn out" has several meanings depending on the context, but a common one, especially when used with "someone," is to expel or evict them from a place, which fits with the general idea of forcing someone out. Therefore, "to evict someone" is the correct interpretation in this context.

60. (B): "Fair weather friends" are those who are supportive or friendly only when it is easy or beneficial to be so, particularly during good times. When challenges arise, these friends typically disappear or are not dependable. This idiom accurately describes friends who are loyal only during a time of success.

61. (C):

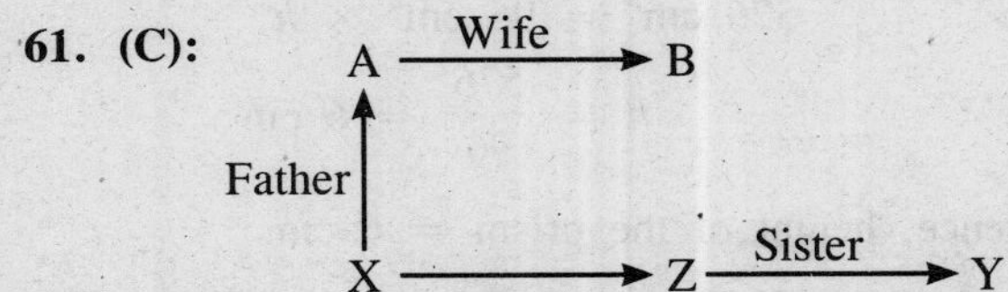

Here, option (C) 'X is the son of A' Definitely not true, because it is not sure, whether X is daughter or son.

62. (A): Here, P = Starting point,

P South
North-East 10 km
8 km
C B
6 km
← Right

PB = 8 km

BC = 6 km

CP = 10 km

$$\because \quad CP = \sqrt{PB^2 + BC^2} = \sqrt{8^2 + 6^2}$$

$$= \sqrt{64 + 36} = \sqrt{100} = 10 \text{ km}$$

A starts walking from P and finally reaches at P Therefore, A is 0 km away from starting point (P).

63. (C):

$$\because \quad \frac{m_1 d_1 h_1}{w_1} = \frac{m_2 d_2 h_2}{w_2}$$

$$\therefore \quad \frac{10 \times 8 \times h}{\frac{2}{5}} = \frac{m_2 \times 12 \times h}{\left(1 - \frac{2}{5}\right)}$$

$$\Rightarrow \quad \frac{10 \times 8}{\frac{2}{5}} = \frac{m_2 \times 12}{\frac{3}{5}}$$

$$\Rightarrow \quad \frac{10 \times 8}{2} = \frac{m_2 \times 12}{3}$$

$$\Rightarrow \quad 40 = 4m_2$$

$$\Rightarrow \quad m_2 = 10$$

Therefore, required number of persons = 10.

64. (C): Perimeter of a right prism triangle = 32 cm

Semi-perimeter, $S = \frac{32}{2} = 16$ cm

Inradius of the triangle, $r = 6$ cm

∴ Area of the right prism triangle,

$$A = Sr = 16 \times 6 = 96 \text{ cm}^2$$

∴ Volume of the prism = $A \times h$

(Where, h = height of the prism)

$\Rightarrow \quad 576 \text{ cm}^3 = 96 \text{ cm}^2 \times h$

$\therefore \quad h = \frac{576}{96} = 6$ cm

Hence, height of the prism = 6 cm.

65. (B): Given, the number of diagonals of a regular polygon = 27

$\Rightarrow \quad \frac{n(n-3)}{2} = 27$

$\Rightarrow \quad n^2 - 3n = 54$

$\Rightarrow \quad n^2 - 3n - 54 = 0$

$\Rightarrow \quad n^2 + 6n - 9n - 54 = 0$

$\Rightarrow \quad n(n + 6) - 9(n + 6) = 0$

$\Rightarrow \quad (n + 6)(n - 9) = 0$

$\Rightarrow \quad n = -6$ or $n = 9$

[$\because n \neq -6$]

Therefore, the number of sides = n = 9.

66. (D): Alloy A = 7 kg

Copper : Zinc = 5 : 2

$\therefore \quad$ Copper in A $= 7 \times \frac{5}{5+2} = 5$ kg

Zink in A $= 7 \times \frac{2}{7} = 2$ kg

and Alloy B = 21 kg

Copper : Zinc = 3 : 4

$\therefore \quad$ Copper in B $= 21 \times \frac{3}{3+4}$

$= 21 \times \frac{3}{7} = 9$ kg

Zinc in B $= 21 \times \frac{4}{7} = 12$ kg

∵ Alloy A and Alloy B are mixed together to form a new alloy

∴ Total copper in new alloy = 5 + 9 = 14 kg and total zinc in new alloy = 2 + 12 = 14 kg

Hence, the ratio of copper and zinc in the new alloy = 14 : 14 = 1 : 1.

67. (A): $7 \operatorname{cosec} \theta - 3 \cot \theta = 7$

or $\quad \cot \theta = \frac{7}{3}(\operatorname{cosec} \theta - 1)$

$\Rightarrow \quad 7 \operatorname{cosec} \theta - 7 = 3 \cot \theta$

$\Rightarrow \quad 7(\operatorname{cosec} \theta - 1) = 3 \cot \theta$

Squaring both sides

$49(\operatorname{cosec} \theta - 1)^2 = 9 \cot^2 \theta$

$\Rightarrow 49(\operatorname{cosec} \theta - 1)^2 - 9(\operatorname{cosec}^2 \theta - 1) = 0$

$\Rightarrow (\operatorname{cosec} \theta - 1)[49(\operatorname{cosec} \theta - 1) - 9(\operatorname{cosec} \theta + 1)] = 0$

$\therefore \quad \operatorname{cosec} \theta = 1$

or, $\quad 40 \operatorname{cosec} \theta - 58 = 0$

$\Rightarrow \quad \operatorname{cosec} \theta = \frac{58}{40} = \frac{29}{20}$

$\therefore \quad \cot \theta = 0$ or $\frac{21}{20}$

$\left[\cot \theta = \frac{7}{3}(\operatorname{cosec} \theta - 1)\right]$

Here, $7 \cot \theta - 3 \operatorname{cosec} \theta = 0 - 3 \times 1 = -3$

or, $\quad 7 \cot \theta - 3 \operatorname{cosec} \theta = 7 \times \frac{21}{20} - 3 \times \frac{29}{20}$

$= \frac{3}{20}(49 - 29)$

$= \frac{3}{20} \times 20 = 3$

Hence, $7 \cot \theta - 3 \operatorname{cosec} \theta = 3$

∴ Option (A) is correct.

68. (C): In a circle, if an equilateral triangle is inscribed, the tangents at the vertices will also form an equilateral triangle. This follows because the symmetry and equal angles of the inscribed equilateral triangle ensure that the angles between the tangents at each vertex are also equal, making the triangle formed by these tangents equilateral.

69. (A): Let the cost price of an article = ₹ x

Then, S.P. of an article $= \frac{115}{100}x$

According to question,

$\frac{115}{100}x + 18 = \frac{118}{100}x$

$\Rightarrow \quad \frac{118}{100}x - \frac{115}{100}x = 18$

$\Rightarrow \quad \frac{3}{100}x = 18$

$\Rightarrow \quad x = 600$

Hence, the cost price of the article = x = ₹ 600.

70. (C): 0 3 9 12 36 39 [117] 120 360

+3 ×3 +3 ×3 +3 ×3 +3 ×3

In place of 42, it should be 117.

Therefore, the wrong number in the given series = 42.

71. (B): Let two positive numbers be x and y

Then, $x - y = 3$

and $x^2 + y^2 = 369$

$\because \quad (x - y)^2 = x^2 + y^2 - 2xy$

$\therefore \quad 3^2 = 369 - 2xy$

$\Rightarrow \quad 2xy = 369 - 9$

$\Rightarrow \quad 2xy = 360$

Now, $(x + y)^2 = x^2 + y^2 + 2xy$

$= 369 + 360$

$\Rightarrow \quad (x + y)^2 = 729$

$= (27)^2$

$\therefore \quad x + y = 27$

Hence, sum of the numbers is 27.

72. (B): Given, remainder = 36

$\therefore$ Divisor = 5 × 36

= 180

and quotient = $\frac{180}{12} = 15$

Now, Divident = Divisor × Quotient + Remainder

= 180 × 15 + 36

$\Rightarrow$ Dividend = 2700 + 36 = 2736

Hence, the dividend is 2736.

73. (C): Given, A = ÷, B = +, C = –, D = ×

$\therefore$ 20 C 12 B 8 A 2 D 6

= 20 – 12 + 8 ÷ 2 × 6

= 20 – 12 + 4 × 6

= 20 – 12 + 24

= 44 – 12 = 32.

74. (D): The average speed = $\frac{\text{Total distance}}{\text{Total time}}$

$= \frac{12 + 18 + 24}{\frac{12}{3} + \frac{18}{9} + \frac{24}{4}}$

$= \frac{54}{4 + 2 + 6}$

$= \frac{54}{12} = \frac{9}{2}$

= 4.5 km/hr.

75. (D): Violin, Harp, and Guitar are string instruments where the sound is produced by the vibration of strings. Flute, however, is a woodwind instrument where sound is produced by the flow of air across an opening.

Therefore, Flute is the odd one out.

76. (A): Given, 16 – 4 = 2

$\Rightarrow \quad 16 = 4^2$

9 – 3 = 2

$\Rightarrow \quad 9 = 3^2$

81 – 3 = 4

$\Rightarrow \quad 81 = 3^4$

$\therefore$ 64 – 4 = 3

$\Rightarrow \quad 64 = 4^3$.

77. (D): Given,

–1 –1 –1 –1 –1

D B C K I J Q O P V T U Z X Y

+1 +1 +1 +1 +1

$\therefore$? = The missing term in the series = VTU.

78. (D): Given,

'P R O [J] E C T' = 'C E O P R T'
16 18 15 10 5 3 20 = 3 5 15 16 18 20

P L [A] N E = E L N P
16 12 1 14 5 = 5 12 14 16

In both cases, Middle letter is removed and remaining letters are arranged in alphabetic order.

Similarly,

O R G A [N] I S E D
15 18 7 1 14 9 19 5 4

= A D E G I O R S
1 4 5 7 9 15 18 19

Therefore, 'ORGANISED' will be coded as 'ADEGIORS'.

79. (C): Left 7th 12th Right

A B

After interchanging their position

$\therefore$ Total boys in a row = 22 + 11

= 33.

80. (B):

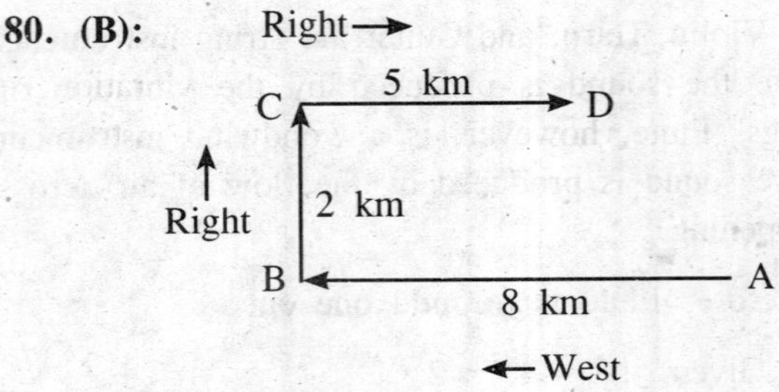

Here, Starting point = A

AB = 8 km;

BC = 2 km

CD = 5 km

Therefore, He is now in North-west positione with refrence to starting point.

81. (C): Shri Vijay Vardhan is the current Chief Information Officer of Haryana, also known as the Chief Information Commissioner. This role involves overseeing the application of the Right to Information Act within the state, ensuring transparency and accessibility of information to the public. Vijay Vardhan, with his background and experience in administrative roles, was appointed to this position to enhance the governance and information dissemination processes in Haryana.

82. (B): The Vulture Conservation Centre in Haryana is located in Pinjore. This center plays a significant role in the conservation and rehabilitation of vultures, which are critically endangered species. The efforts here are part of a broader initiative to protect these birds from extinction, addressing environmental concerns and promoting biodiversity.

83. (A): Dr. A.R. Kidwai, who served as the UPSC Chairman, later became the Governor of Haryana. His tenure in both roles highlighted his significant contributions to public administration and governance, reflecting his commitment to civil service and administrative reforms.

84. (A): The Khelo India Women's Archery ranking competition was organized in the district of Sonipat, Haryana. This event is part of the Khelo India initiative, aimed at fostering sports development and encouraging participation in sports across various levels, particularly among women in archery.

85. (A): Haryana has a total of 95 Tehsils. This administrative division is crucial for local governance and facilitates the management of resources and developmental programs at a more localized level, ensuring that administrative services are accessible to the residents of the state.

86. (C): The Haryana government runs the scheme "Mera Pani Meri Virasat" to encourage farmers to shift from water-intensive paddy crops to more traditional and less water-consuming crops. This initiative is aimed at sustainable agriculture practices, addressing water scarcity, and promoting the cultivation of crops better suited to the regional climate and soil health.

87. (C): The National Institute of Fashion Technology (NIFT) in Haryana is located in Panchkula. This institute is part of the network of fashion technology education centers across India that provide professional training and education in the field of design, technology, and management, tailored to the evolving needs of the fashion industry.

88. (C): The sage known as Puran Bhagat in Haryana was Baba Chaurangi Nath. He is revered in local folklore and religious traditions, embodying the spiritual and cultural heritage of the region. His life and teachings continue to be celebrated and have a lasting influence on the local communities.

89. (C): The Morni Hills in Haryana are part of the outer range of the Himalayas. This geographical feature is significant for its natural beauty and biodiversity, making it a popular destination for eco-tourism and nature enthusiasts. The hills provide a serene environment and are home to a variety of flora and fauna.

90. (A): During the revolt of 1857, Tafzal Husain led attacks on British establishments in Rohtak, Haryana. This participation was part of the wider Indian uprising against British colonial rule, with local leaders like Tafzal Husain playing crucial roles in mobilizing resistance and fighting for independence.

91. (B): Rabindranath Tagore, an eminent Indian poet, philosopher, and Nobel laureate, critiqued nationalism by emphasizing the superiority of humanity over patriotism. In his view, nationalism, if placed above human values, is akin to exchanging diamonds for glass—an inferior choice. He believed that true spiritual refuge lies in humanity, transcending the narrower confines of patriotism.

92. (B): Mihirbhoj, a prominent ruler of the Gurjara-Pratihara dynasty, assumed the title "Adivaraha," which means "the primeval boar," an incarnation of the Hindu god Vishnu. This title reflects Mihirbhoj's reverence for Hindu deities and his desire to establish his reign under divine protection. His reign, which lasted from the mid-9th to early 10th century, marked a period of significant military and cultural achievements, helping to consolidate and expand the Pratihara Empire.

93. (A):

(*a*) **Minhaj-us-Siraj:** Tabkat-i-Nasiri - Minhaj-us-Siraj was a 13th-century historian who authored "Tabkat-i-Nasiri," a comprehensive chronicle of Muslim rulers in India, particularly the Delhi Sultanate.

(*b*) **Ziauddin Barani:** Tarikh-i-Firozshahi - Ziauddin Barani, another eminent historian of the Delhi Sultanate, wrote "Tarikh-i-Firozshahi," documenting the history of the period, especially during the reign of Firoz Shah Tughlaq.

(*d*) **Badayuni:** Muntakhab-ut-Tawarikh - Abdul Qadir Badayuni compiled "Muntakhab-ut-Tawarikh," which is a significant historical account covering the reigns of several Mughal emperors, notably Akbar.

Amir Khusrau did not write Futuh-us-Salatin; instead, it was written by Isami.

94. (C): Seasonal unemployment occurs when people are out of work during certain seasons of the year, typically when their jobs are dependent on particular times or seasons, such as in agriculture. During off-seasons when there is no agricultural work available, these workers often migrate to urban areas seeking temporary employment until the next farming season begins.

95. (A): The "Loo" is a hot and dry wind that blows across the Northern Plains of India during the summer months, particularly from May to June. These winds originate from the desert regions and can raise temperatures significantly, often exceeding 45 degrees Celsius (113 degrees Fahrenheit).

96. (D): The Prime Meridian is an imaginary line of longitude that runs from the North Pole to the South Pole and passes through Greenwich, London. It is defined as 0 degrees longitude and serves as the starting point for measuring longitude around the globe. This meridian divides the Earth into the Eastern Hemisphere and the Western Hemisphere.

97. (B): "Untouchable" is a novel written by Mulk Raj Anand, not Dr. Bhim Rao Ambedkar. The novel portrays a day in the life of Bakha, a young Indian sweeper boy, and addresses themes of caste discrimination and social injustice in colonial India. Mulk Raj Anand, a prominent Indian writer and social activist, used the narrative to highlight the plight of the untouchables (Dalits) in society, shedding light on the harsh realities they faced.

98. (A): Thomas Hobbes, a 17th-century English philosopher, characterized freedom as the "silence of laws" in his seminal work, "Leviathan." For Hobbes, freedom was not merely the absence of external constraints but the absence of laws that could hinder an individual's actions or choices. He viewed laws as necessary for maintaining order and preventing chaos in society but believed that true freedom existed when individuals were not restrained by laws that dictated their behaviour.

99. (B): In Hindu culture, the full moon night is known as "Poornima." It is considered auspicious and holds special significance in religious and spiritual practices. Poornima occurs when the moon is completely illuminated by the Sun's rays, appearing round and bright in the night sky. It is a time for festivities, prayers, and rituals, often marked by gatherings, fasting, and offerings to deities.

100. (A): Diwan-i-Arj: Iltutmish - Diwan-i-Arj was established by Balban, not Iltutmish. It was a revenue department responsible for the assessment and collection of land revenue based on the actual produce of the land, in contrast to the fixed revenue system prevalent earlier.

101. (D):

(*a*) Characteristic representation posits that individuals can effectively represent and advocate for the interests of a particular group only if they belong to that group themselves. This theory emphasizes the importance of shared identity and experiences in accurately articulating the concerns and needs of a community or demographic.

(*b*) Mandate doctrine, on the other hand, suggests that elected representatives derive their authority and legitimacy from the mandate given to them by the electorate. According to this doctrine, representatives are expected to follow and act upon the preferences and interests expressed by the voters who elected them, thereby ensuring that government actions are guided by popular will.

102. (B):

(*a*) **Ashoka:** Nigrodha - Ashoka, the Mauryan emperor, is associated with the story of meeting the Buddhist monk Nigrodha, who reportedly converted Ashoka to Buddhism. This encounter is significant in Ashoka's personal transformation and his subsequent promotion of Buddhism across his empire.

(*b*) **Menander:** Nagasena - Menander, also known as Milinda in Buddhist texts, was a Greco-Bactrian king who ruled in northwestern India around the 2nd century BCE. He is famously associated with his philosophical dialogues with the Buddhist sage Nagasena, recorded in the text known as the Milinda Panha (Questions of Milinda).

(*d*) **Harsha:** Huen Tsang (Xuanzang) - Harsha, also known as Harshavardhana, was a 7th-century Indian emperor who ruled over North India. He is known for his patronage of Buddhism and his support for the famous Chinese Buddhist monk Huen Tsang (Xuanzang).

103. (D): Earth is the only planet that does not have rings around it. While Jupiter, Saturn, and Uranus are known for their prominent ring systems, Earth does not possess any visible rings. The rings around Jupiter, Saturn, and Uranus are composed of varying materials such as dust, rock particles, and ice, orbiting around these planets in distinct bands.

104. (A): Water freezes at 0°C under standard atmospheric pressure. This temperature marks the point where liquid water transitions into solid ice. During freezing, water molecules slow down and arrange themselves into a crystalline structure, resulting in the solidification of water.

105. (C): Currency notes of various denominations, except the one rupee note, are issued by the RBI and act as legal tender. This includes all denominations of currency notes from ₹ 2 to ₹ 500. Legal tender refers to currency that must be accepted for payment of debt or other financial obligations within a country's jurisdiction.

106. (A): Juni-Kuran, indeed, is located in Gujarat. This site in Gujarat has provided significant archaeological findings related to the Indus Valley Civilization, contributing to our understanding of their urban planning, culture, and trade networks. The site, spread over an area of roughly 410 meters by 350 meters, was strategically built on the southern shore of the Great Rann of Kutch.

107. (C):

(*a*) **Brihadeshwer Temple of Tanjore:** This magnificent temple is associated with the Chola Dynasty (*iii*). Built by Raja Raja Chola I in the 11th century, it is an architectural marvel known for its grandeur and its significant influence on Dravidian temple architecture.

(*b*) **Dashavatar Temple of Devgarh:** This temple is associated with the Gupta Dynasty (*i*). The Gupta Empire, known for its cultural and artistic achievements, patronized various temples and architectural marvels during its rule.

(*c*) **Kailash Temple of Ellora:** This temple is associated with the Rashtrakuta Dynasty (*ii*). The Rashtrakutas were prolific builders and patrons of art and architecture, contributing significantly to the development of the Ellora caves.

(*d*) **Kandariya Mahadeva Temple of Khajuraho:** This temple is associated with the Chandela Dynasty (*iv*). The Chandela rulers of central India are renowned for constructing the intricate temples of Khajuraho, famous for their exquisite sculptures and architectural finesse.

108. (B):

(*a*) **Targeted Public Distribution System (TPDS):** In June, 1997, the Government of India launched the Targeted Public Distribution System (TPDS) with focus on the poor. The goal was to give food grains to a population of people living in poverty (BPL).

(*b*) **Antyodaya Anna Yojana:** Antyodaya Anna Yojana (AAY) is one of the public distribution system schemes in India implemented from 2000. The main aim of the scheme was to provide highly subsidized food grains to the poorest of the poor families in rural and urban areas.

(*d*) **Food Security Act:** Passed in September 2013 (National Food Security Act, 2013), aiming to provide subsidized food grains to approximately two-thirds of India's population.

(*c*) **Integrated Food Security Scheme:** The Integrated Food Security Scheme, also known as the Pradhan Mantri Garib Kalyan Anna Yojana (PMGKAY), is a program that provides free food grains to eligible beneficiaries through the Targeted Public Distribution System (TPDS). The scheme was launched on January 1, 2023.

109. (D): Krabbe considered that the "notion of sovereignty must expunged from political theory". He believed that the concept of absolute power vested in the state was outdated and an obstacle to a just and peaceful world order. His concept of the "sovereignty of law" highlights his belief in a legal framework that transcends national boundaries and upholds a shared sense of right and justice.

110. (A): The statement criticizing liberal or 'thin' democracy as contributing to growing cynicism about politics and the paralysis of public institutions is attributed to Benjamin Barber. He was an American political theorist who expressed his concerns about the limitations of liberal democracy and its impact on civic engagement and governance. His works often explored the challenges and shortcomings of democratic practices in modern societies.

111. (B): Simone de Beauvoir - 'Sexual Politics': Simone de Beauvoir, a French existentialist philosopher and feminist, did not write 'Sexual Politics'. The book 'Sexual Politics' was written by Kate Millett, published in 1970. It critiques patriarchy and analyzes power dynamics in gender and sexuality, making it a significant feminist work.

112. (B): The main human activity in Ladakh is agriculture, with about 90% of the population depending on it for their livelihood. The people of Ladakh are self-supporting farmers who live in small settlements across the high desert. They grow a variety of crops based on the Indus River, including barley, wheat, buckwheat, peas, rapeseed, and beans. In warmer regions with lower altitudes, they also grow apples and apricots.

113. (D):

(*a*) **To investigate any disputes which might lead to international friction:** One of the primary functions of the UN Security Council is to investigate and mediate disputes between countries that have the potential to escalate into international conflicts? This helps in preventing conflicts from escalating and promotes peaceful resolution through diplomacy and mediation.

(*b*) **To recommend the admission of new Members:** The Security Council plays a role in recommending new member states to the United Nations. This recommendation is then sent to the General Assembly for final approval. The Security Council assesses the applications for membership based on various criteria, including adherence to the purposes and principles of the UN Charter.

114. (B): NABARD (National Bank for Agriculture and Rural Development) serves as the apex institution for rural financing in India. It was established in 1982 to promote sustainable and equitable agriculture and rural development across the country. NABARD provides credit facilities, refinance support, and developmental assistance to banks, cooperatives, and other institutions involved in rural development.

115. (C): BSE refers to the Bombay Stock Exchange, which is one of the major stock exchanges in India. It is not an indicator of Human Development. The Bombay Stock Exchange is a financial market where securities such as stocks, bonds, and derivatives are bought and sold by investors. It primarily reflects the performance and activities of the financial markets rather than social or economic indicators related to human development.

116. (D): Mahapadma Nanda, known as "Sarvakshatrantak" in the Puranas, was the founder of the Nanda Dynasty and ruled over the Magadha Empire in ancient India. The title "Sarvakshatrantak" signifies his reputation as the destroyer of all kings, highlighting his military prowess and the extent of his conquests. Under his rule, the Nanda Dynasty expanded its influence significantly, marking a notable period in ancient Indian history characterized by centralization of power and territorial expansion.

117. (D): CACP - 1965: The Commission for Agricultural Costs and Prices (CACP), set up in 1965, is a decentralized agency of the Government of India (GoI). It is an expert body that recommends the Minimum Support Prices (MSPs) by taking into consideration various factors.

118. (B): Stars are massive celestial objects primarily composed of hydrogen and helium that undergo nuclear fusion, producing immense heat and light through this process. Planets, on the other hand, do not generate their own heat and light but instead reflect the light of stars like the Sun. Satellites are celestial bodies that orbit planets or other larger bodies.

119. (C):

(*a*) **Profit - Entrepreneurship:** Profit is the return for entrepreneurship. Entrepreneurs take risks and organize the other factors of production to create goods and services. The reward they receive for their efforts and risk-taking is profit.

(*b*) **Rent - Land:** Rent is the return for land. Landowners earn rent for allowing others to use their land or property for various purposes such as farming, building structures, or mining resources.

(*c*) **Wage - Labour:** Wage is the return for labour. Workers receive wages as compensation for their time, effort, and skills provided in the production of goods and services.

(*d*) **Interest - Capital:** Interest is the return for capital. Capital refers to the financial resources or physical assets used in production. Lenders earn interest as a return on the money they loan, and investors earn interest on their invested capital.

120. (B): In the "SDG India Index-3.0" report, Haryana is categorized as a "Front runner," indicating a score between 65 and 99. This category reflects significant progress in achieving the Sustainable Development Goals (SDGs), demonstrating the state's effective efforts in areas such as health, education, gender equality, and economic growth. Being a "Front runner" suggests that Haryana is well on its way to meeting the SDG targets, showing commendable development performance compared to other states and Union Territories in India.

121. (B): "Social Origins of Dictatorship and Democracy" is a seminal work authored by Barrington Moore, published in 1966. In this book, Moore explores the social and economic conditions that lead to the development of different political regimes, including democracies, dictatorships, and fascist states. He examines the historical trajectories of countries like England, France, the United States, China, Japan, and India, analyzing how class structures and conflicts shape political outcomes.

122. (C): As of September 2023, India has 12 nationalized banks. Nationalized banks are those that were previously privately owned but were taken over by the government to ensure better financial stability and accessibility of banking services across the country. These banks play a crucial role in the Indian economy by providing financial services to a large segment of the population, particularly in rural and semi-urban areas.

123. (B):

(*b*) The Battle of Plassey was fought in north-eastern India on 23 June 1757. Troops of the British East India Company, led by Robert Clive, came up against the forces of Siraj-ud-Daulah, the last Nawab of Bengal, and his French allies.

(*c*) The Battle of Wandiwash was a battle in India between the French and the British in 1760. The battle was part of the Third Carnatic War fought between the French and British colonial empires, which itself was a part of the global Seven Years' War.

(*d*) The Battle of Buxar was fought on 22 October 1764 between the forces under the command of the British East India Company led by Hector Munro and the combined armies of Mir Qasim, the Nawab of Bengal; the Nawab of Awadh; and the Mughal King Shah Alam II.

(*a*) The Battle of Porto Novo was fought between Hyder Ali of Mysore and the British East India Company on 1 July 1781. The English were victorious and this battle put a check on the expansion of Hyder Ali.

124. (D): Bareilly: Begum Zeenat Mahal - This pair is incompatible. Begum Zeenat Mahal was associated with Delhi, not Bareilly. She was the wife of the last Mughal emperor, Bahadur Shah Zafar, and played a role in the resistance during the 1857 uprising in Delhi.

125. (C): The International African Association, established in 1876 by King Leopold II of Belgium, was initially presented as a philanthropic and scientific organization aimed at exploring and developing the interior of Africa.

However, its true motives soon became clear as it became a vehicle for Leopold's personal ambitions to acquire territory and resources in Africa.

126. (D): The biosphere includes all the zones where life exists on Earth, including the interactions between the atmosphere, hydrosphere (water bodies), and lithosphere (land). It encompasses the surface of the Earth where living organisms, including humans, plants, and animals, interact with their environments.

127. (A): If a product has multiple uses, its elasticity of demand can indeed be greater than 1 ($e > 1$). This higher elasticity indicates that changes in price are likely to have a proportionally larger effect on the quantity demanded. This is because consumers may have more alternatives or substitutes for the product, making them more responsive to changes in price.

128. (A): The Tapi River, originating in the central Indian state of Madhya Pradesh, flows westward across Maharashtra and Gujarat before draining into the Arabian Sea. It is one of the major westward-flowing rivers of peninsular India, known for its relatively short but significant course through the states it traverses.

129. (B): K.M. Munshi was not a member of the State Reorganization Commission formed in 1953. The State Reorganization Commission, formed in 1953, was tasked with the complex job of reorganizing states and territories in India based on linguistic and administrative considerations. Chaired by Fazal Ali, with members including Hridaynath Kunzru and K.M. Panikkar, the commission played a pivotal role in recommending the reorganization of states to better reflect linguistic and cultural identities.

130. (A): The Swaraj Party was founded in 1923 by Motilal Nehru and Chittaranjan Das as a faction within the Indian National Congress. Their aim was to advocate for a more assertive approach towards achieving self-government (Swaraj) in India. Dissatisfied with the Congress' non-cooperation movement, which they believed had become passive, they sought to contest elections and work within the legislative framework to push for nationalist goals.

131. (C):

(*b*) Murray Bookchin did not invent the Gaia hypothesis; it was formulated by James Lovelock and Lynn Margulis, making statement (b) incorrect.

(*c*) The term "ecology" is derived from the Greek word "oikos," not Latin, which refers to "household" or "environment," making statement (c) incorrect.

132. (B): Language has been a significant factor in the formation of states in India, particularly after the reorganization of states in 1956 and subsequently in 1960s and 1970s. This reorganization aimed to create states that corresponded to linguistic boundaries to better represent and serve the linguistic and cultural diversity of the Indian population.

133. (C): M. Dennis Francis currently serves as the President of the 78th Session of the United Nations General Assembly. He was elected to this prestigious position in June 2023. Previously, Mr. Francis held the role of Permanent Representative of Trinidad and Tobago to the United Nations, bringing a wealth of diplomatic experience to the role.

135. (C):

(*a*) **Basic Exchange and Cooperation Agreement for Geospatial Intelligence (BECA):** This agreement allows for the exchange of geospatial information, which is crucial for targeting and navigation purposes, including missile targeting. It facilitates better coordination between Indian and US armed forces during military exercises and operations.

(*b*) **General Security of Military Information Agreement (GSOMIA):** GSOMIA enables the sharing of classified military information between India and the USA. It enhances mutual trust and cooperation by allowing both countries to share sensitive defense technology and intelligence.

(*c*) **Logistics Exchange Memorandum of Agreement (LEMOA):** LEMOA facilitates logistical support and supplies between India and the USA during authorized port visits, joint exercises, and humanitarian missions. It allows both countries to use each other's facilities for refueling, replenishment, and maintenance of defense equipment.

136. (A): Thematic maps focus on specific information or themes, such as population density, climate zones, economic activities, or political boundaries. They are designed to visually represent and communicate spatial patterns and relationships related to a particular topic or theme.

137. (C):

(*a*) **Inter-Allied Declaration:** This was a joint declaration issued by the Allied powers in 1941 during World War II, affirming their commitment to the principles of collective security and post-war cooperation.

(*c*) **Dumbarton Oaks Conference:** Held in 1944; this conference laid the foundation for the establishment of the United Nations by proposing the structure and functions of the organization.

(*b*) **Yalta Conference:** Held in 1945, the Yalta Conference finalized the plans for the United Nations, including its structure and the participation of member states, paving the way for the UN Charter to be drafted and signed later in 1945.

138. (D): The National Consumer Helpline (NCH) with the motto "Jaago Grahak Jaago" has the number 1915. Jaago Grahak Jaago is a consumer awareness program launched in 2005 by the Ministry of Consumer-Government of India.

139. (D): Choropleth Method is not a qualitative method of distribution maps. It uses colors or shades to represent the magnitude or density of a statistical variable within predefined geographic regions. Darker colors typically indicate higher values, while lighter shades represent lower values, making it effective for visualizing quantitative data such as population density, income levels, or election results.

140. (C): Brazil is considered an example of coalitional presidentialism. In Brazil's political system, the president often needs to form alliances with multiple political parties to secure legislative support due to the fragmented nature of the Brazilian Congress. This coalition-building is crucial for passing legislation and implementing policies effectively, reflecting the characteristics of coalitional presidentialism.

141. (A): Carbon dioxide (CO_2) is known to contribute significantly to the greenhouse effect, which leads to an increase in global temperatures. It is a greenhouse gas that traps heat in the Earth's atmosphere, preventing it from escaping into space. Increased levels of CO_2 and other greenhouse gases due to human activities, such as burning fossil fuels and deforestation, are major contributors to global warming and climate change.

142. (A): In France, the term "cohabitation" refers to a political situation where the President of the Republic comes from a different political party than the majority of the members of the National Assembly

(Parliament). This leads to a system of divided government, where the President governs alongside a Prime Minister and cabinet from a different political party, potentially leading to tensions and challenges in governance.

143. (A): The Western Ghats, also known as Sahyadri, are a UNESCO World Heritage site and a biodiversity hotspot in India. Stretching over 1,600 kilometers along the western coast, these mountains are home to diverse flora and fauna, many of which are endemic to the region. The Ghats play a crucial role in India's climate, acting as a barrier to the monsoon winds and influencing weather patterns across the subcontinent.

144. (A): Mahanavami, also known as Navaratri, is considered a very important festival in Hampi, Karnataka. It celebrates the victory of good over evil and is marked with traditional rituals, music, dance, and religious ceremonies. In the historical context of Hampi, which was once the capital of the Vijayanagara Empire, Mahanavami would have been celebrated with great pomp and grandeur, reflecting the cultural and religious significance of the festival in the region.

145. (D): The basis for constructing an Indifference Curve (IC) is the consumer's preference scale. Indifference curves represent combinations of two goods that provide the consumer with the same level of satisfaction or utility. These curves are derived from the consumer's preferences and reflect the trade-offs they are willing to make between different goods given their utility-maximizing behaviour.

146. (A): Genghis Khan, whose birth name was Temüjin, belonged to the Borjigid clan, a prominent Mongol lineage. Rising from humble beginnings, he unified the Mongol tribes through a combination of military prowess, strategic alliances, and political acumen. Genghis Khan's leadership and military campaigns transformed the disparate Mongol tribes into a formidable empire that stretched from China to Eastern Europe, known historically as the Mongol Empire.

147. (B): Tejas Express is considered the first private sector train of India. It was introduced as part of the Indian government's initiative to allow private operators to run certain trains on the Indian Railways network. The Tejas Express operates between Lucknow and New Delhi and is known for its modern amenities and services.

148. (B): Michelangelo painted the famous fresco titled "The Last Judgment" on the altar wall of the Sistine Chapel in Vatican City. This monumental work, completed between 1536 and 1541, depicts the Second Coming of Christ and the final judgment of souls. It is renowned for its dramatic portrayal of heaven, hell, and purgatory, showcasing Michelangelo's mastery of human anatomy and emotive expression.

149. (B): On 21st June each year, the direct rays of the sun fall on the Tropic of Cancer, marking the summer solstice in the Northern Hemisphere. This day has the longest daylight hours of the year in the northern latitudes.

150. (C):

I. WTO and the Dunkel Proposal: The statement is accurate. The World Trade Organization (WTO) was established in 1995, succeeding the General Agreement on Tariffs and Trade (GATT) which had been in place since 1947. The Dunkel Text, named after Arthur Dunkel, the Director-General of GATT at the time, emerged from the Uruguay Round of trade negotiations and served as the foundation for the creation of the WTO.

II. WTO and International Treaty: This statement is also correct. The WTO was established through the Marrakesh Agreement, an international treaty signed in 1994 by 123 countries. This treaty required ratification by the national parliaments of member countries for the WTO to come into effect.

Previous Paper (Solved)

Haryana Teacher Eligibility Test (HTET)

TGT Social Studies (Level-2), Exam 2022

(Exam held on 04 December, 2022)

PART-I

Child Development and Pedagogy

Directions: *Answer the following questions by selecting the **most appropriate** option.*

1. Thematic Apperception Test is used to measure the ________ of students.
A. Intelligence B. Aptitude
C. Attitude D. Personality

2. Which of the following statement is ***correct*** about the development of children?
A. Development is a product of only hereditary.
B. Development follows a random pattern.
C. Development is a cumulative process.
D. Different aspects of development are not inter-related.

3. 'Acceleration' is an important plan for education of which type of special children?
A. Gifted B. Slow learner
C. Learning disabled D. Mentally retarded

4. Which of the following factors does ***not*** affect the teaching-learning process?
A. Teaching skill of teacher
B. Mental health of teacher
C. Subject knowledge of teacher
D. Physical appearance of teacher

5. Which of the following is ***not*** a characteristic of creativity?
A. Originality B. Flexibility
C. Rigidity D. Fluency

6. Which of the following is ***not*** a subjective method of personality assessment?
A. Interview
B. Observation
C. Autobiography
D. Word Association

7. Who propounded the Triarchic theory of Intelligence?
A. Gardner B. Guilford
C. Sternberg D. Vernan

8. 'Family and School' are the examples of which environmental system in Bronfenbrenner's Bio-ecological Model theory?
A. Macro system B. Micro system
C. Exosystem D. Chromosystem

9. Which of the following pair is ***not*** correct?

Theory Propounder		Theory
A. Piaget	–	Cognitive Development Theory
B. Bandura	–	Social Learning Theory
C. Erikson	–	Psycho-socio Development Theory
D. Vygotsky	–	Moral Development Theory

10. What is the mechanism called, through which a child tries to change his own ego to that of someone else?
A. Identification B. Rationalization
C. Sublimation D. Projection

11. Who developed the Socio-cultural theory of development?
A. Vygotsky B. Erikson
C. Kohlberg D. Bronfenbrenner

12. Which of the following is ***not*** an extrinsic motive?
A. Competing in sport for trophy
B. Doing job for salary
C. Doing social service for self-satisfaction
D. Buy one get one free

13. "Mental health is the full and harmonious functioning of the whole personality". This definition of mental health is given by whom?
A. Menninger B. Hadfield
C. Drever D. Waltin

14. 'Development proceeds in the direction of longitudinal axis (head to foot)', called:
A. Cephalic-Caudal
B. Proximodistal
C. Spiral
D. Circular

15. What type of reinforcement schedule is to reinforce each correct response of the learner, in operant conditioning?
A. Fixed interval
B. Variable interval
C. Fixed ratio
D. Continuous

16. Who propounded the 'Need of Hierarchy Theory' of Motivation?
A. Hull
B. Maslow
C. Atkinson
D. Thomson

17. Meenal is average in intelligence and low in creativity and high level in adjustment. This is an example of:
A. Inter Individual Differences
B. Intra Individual Differences
C. Observable Differences
D. Expected Differences

18. Which of the following elements is ***not*** related to Skinner's operant conditioning theory?
A. Extinction
B. Discrimination
C. Spontaneous recovery
D. Reinforcement

19. Which of the following is ***not*** the characteristic of a well-adjusted person?
A. Awareness of his own potentials and limitations
B. Respecting himself and others
C. Balanced aspirations
D. Rigidity in behaviour

20. According to Piaget's cognitive development theory, the 'ability of reversibility' develops during which developmental stage?
A. Sensory motor
B. Pre-operational
C. Concrete-operational
D. Formal-operational

21. Out of the following Psychologists, who is ***not*** related with Gestaltism?
A. Kohler B. Koffka
C. Kretschmer D. Wertheimer

22. Which of the following statement is ***not*** correct with reference to adjustment?
A. It creates imbalance.
B. It motivates to change the life as per the demand of the situation.
C. It gives ability to bring desirable changes in the conditions of environment.
D. In the absence of adjustment one is surrounded by tension an anxiety.

23. Which type of curriculum did Bruner suggest to follow for the cognitive development of children?
A. Inclusive curriculum
B. Special curriculum
C. Spiral curriculum
D. Integrated curriculum

24. Cattell's culture free test of intelligence is a type of:
A. Individual Verbal Test
B. Group Verbal Test
C. Non-Verbal Test
D. Verbal and Non-Verbal Test

25. A type of intelligence test in which the questions are similar in difficulty level but more importance is given to the time element:
A. Speed Test
B. Power Test
C. Verbal Test
D. Performance Test

26. What kind of changes does growth bring about in children?
A. Structural
B. Functional
C. Structural and functional both
D. None of these

27. Which of the following component is ***not*** the part of Guilford structure of Intellect model?
A. Operation
B. Cognition
C. Content
D. Product

28. Which of the following statement is ***not*** correct with reference to Attitude?
A. Attitude has motivational affective characteristics.
B. Attitude can range strongly positive to strongly negative.
C. Attitude have a subject-object relationship.
D. Attitude is innate and acquired both.

29. Which of the following match is ***not*** correct?

Erikson's Stages of Psycho-social Development	**Serial Number of Stages**
A. Initiative Vs Guilt	– Stage 3
B. Identity Vs Role Confusion	– Stage 5
C. Autonomy Vs Shame and Doubt	– Stage 1
D. Industry Vs Inferiority	– Stage 4

30. Which of the following is ***not*** a projective technique of personality assessment?
A. Word-association
B. Sentence completion
C. Expressive movement
D. Sociometry

PART-II

भाषा : हिन्दी

निर्देशः *निम्नलिखित प्रश्नों के उत्तर देने के लिए **सबसे उचित** विकल्प चुनिए।*

31. उच्चारण की दृष्टि से 'ग' व्यंजन की ध्वनिगत विशेषताएँ हैं :

A. कंठ्य, अघोष, महाप्राण B. कंठ्य, सघोष, महाप्राण

C. कंठ्य, सघोष, अल्पप्राण D. कंठ्य, अघोष, अल्पप्राण

32. वचन की दृष्टि से कौन-सा युग्म **सही** है?

A. दर्शन — दर्शनों

B. प्राण — प्राणों

C. नारी — नारियों

D. हस्ताक्षर — हस्ताक्षरों

33. 'गिरीश' शब्द में कौन-सी संधि है?

A. दीर्घ स्वर संधि B. गुण स्वर संधि

C. यण् स्वर संधि D. व्यंजन संधि

34. 'जाह्नवी' शब्द का पर्याय है :

A. मंदाकिनी B. कुमुदनी

C. पथगामिनी D. नलनी

35. 'सरसिज' शब्द में कौन-सा समास है?

A. कर्मधारय समास B. द्वन्द्व समास

C. अव्ययीभाव समास D. अलुक् तत्पुरुष समास

36. विलोम की दृष्टि से असंगत विकल्प चुनिए :

A. ग्रस्त — मुक्त

B. व्यष्टि — समष्टि

C. आविर्भाव — तिरोभूत

D. अर्वाचीन — प्राचीन

37. किस विकल्प में परिमाणवाचक विशेषण का प्रयोग हुआ है?

A. प्रणव पाँच किलो दूध पी गया।

B. प्रणव पाँच केले खा गया।

C. प्रणव पाँचवीं कक्षा में पढ़ता है।

D. प्रणव के साथ कुछ बच्चे खेल रहे हैं।

38. 'जिज्ञासा' का सटीक समानार्थी है :

A. उत्कंठा B. ज्ञानेप्सा

C. वांछा D. इच्छा

39. "यह आपका माहात्म्य है।" वाक्य में प्रयुक्त 'माहात्म्य' शब्द में कौन-सी संज्ञा है?

A. जातिवाचक B. भाववाचक

C. समूहवाचक D. व्यक्तिवाचक

40. "सामने जो बड़ा-सा घर दिखाई दे रहा है, वह मेरा है।" वाक्य में किस सर्वनाम का प्रयोग हुआ है?

A. पुरुषवाचक B. निजवाचक

C. निश्चयवाचक D. अनिश्चयवाचक

41. किस विकल्प में भाववाचक तद्धित प्रत्यय का प्रयोग हुआ है?

A. बुलावा B. चचेरा

C. सौजन्य D. लखेरा

42. किस शब्द में 'अन्' उपसर्ग का प्रयोग **नहीं** हुआ है?

A. अनुत्तर B. अनुपम

C. अनुद्धार D. अनुगमन

43. क्रिया की दृष्टि से असंगत विकल्प चुनिए :

A. रमेश पत्र लिखवाता है–प्रेरणार्थक क्रिया

B. बालक छत पर खड़ा है–अकर्मक क्रिया

C. अध्यापक बालक को हिंदी पढ़ा रहा है–द्विकर्मक क्रिया

D. प्रणीता जोर-जोर से हँस रही है–सकर्मक क्रिया

44. विसर्ग ध्वनि का प्रयोग किन शब्दों में होता है?

A. तत्सम शब्दों में B. देशज शब्दों में

C. तद्भव शब्दों में D. उपर्युक्त सभी शब्दों में

45. 'साध्वाचरण' शब्द का सही संधि-विच्छेद है :

A. साध्व + आचरण B. साध + आचरण

C. साधू + आचरण D. साधु + आचरण

Language : English

Directions: *Answer the following questions by selecting the **most appropriate** option.*

46. Choose the option that brings out the meaning of the underline idiom:

A lion's share of India's annual budget is for defence.

A. major share

B. minor amount

C. small

D. very little

47. Select the appropriate one word substitution for the following:

Former students of a school or college

A. Emblem B. Alumni

C. Expert D. Incharge

48. Select the ***correct*** preposition for the blank:

I shall do it _______ pleasure.

A. in B. with

C. about D. over

49. Change the Narration:

"I'm taking the children to the zoo tomorrow." She said.

A. She told that she would be taking the children to the zoo the day after
B. She said that she will take the children to the zoo the next day
C. She told that she will be taking the children to the zoo
D. She will take the children to the zoo, she said

50. Select the *correct* meaning of the underlined phrasal verb:

Who can say what will turn up next?

A. remember B. divide
C. end D. happen

51. Select the appropriate preposition for the blank:

He has not yet recovered ________ his illness.

A. over B. in
C. at D. from

52. Select the *correct* antonym of:

Gloomy

A. Praise B. Coarse
C. Cheerful D. Dismal

53. Choose the *correct* synonym of:

Genius

A. Happy B. Cheerful
C. Talented D. Comfort

54. Change the narration in Reported Speech. Choose the *right* option:

'Who has been using my typewriter?' Said Mother.

A. Mother asked who has been using her typewriter
B. Mother said who was using her typewriter
C. Mother asked who had been using her typewriter
D. Mother asked her typewriter was being used by who

55. Choose the appropriate conjunction for the blank:

I shall not go ________ I am invited.

A. and B. unless
C. but D. there

56. Choose the part of sentence that has error:

she does not (A)/ resemble to (B)/ either of (C)/ her parents (D).

A. A B. B
C. C D. D

57. Change the voice and select the *correct* option:

Somebody has put out the light.

A. The light has put out by somebody
B. The light has been put out by somebody
C. Somebody has been out to put light
D. The light is being put out by somebody

58. Select the *correct* tense form from the options given:

Peter (try) to come in quietly but his mother (hear) him

A. tried, heard
B. trying, hears
C. was trying, was hearing
D. is trying, hears

59. Select the *correct* tense form from the options given:

When I first (come) to this house, it (be) a very quiet area.

A. comes, is B. came, was
C. coming, is D. come, are

60. Change the voice from Active to Passive and select the *correct* options:

Bees make honey

A. Honey is make by bees
B. Bees are making honey
C. Honey are made by bees
D. Honey is made by bees

PART-III

General Studies : Quantitative Aptitude, Reasoning Ability and GK & Awareness

Directions: *Answer the following questions by selecting the* ***most appropriate*** *option.*

61. Find the value of:

$$\sqrt{8+2\sqrt{8+2\sqrt{8+....}}}$$

A. 8 B. 10
C. 11 D. 4

62. If each side of the square be increased by 50%, then find the percentage increase in the area:

A. 50% B. 100%
C. 125% D. 150%

63. If × stands for –, ÷ stands for +, + stands for ÷, – stands for ×, then what is the value of 15 – 5 ÷ 5 × 20 + 10?

A. 70 B. 78
C. 75 D. 73

64. By selling a commodity for ₹ 72,000, a person made a profit of 20%. What was the cost price of that commodity?
A. ₹ 60,000 B. ₹ 50,000
C. ₹ 40,000 D. ₹ 65,000

65. Which term is wrong in following series?
8, 13, 21, 32, 47, 63, 83
A. 13 B. 32
C. 47 D. 63

66. A solid cube is coloured red on a faces. It is cut into 64 smaller cube of equal size. How many small cube have no face coloured?
A. 24 B. 16
C. 8 D. 4

67. Find the next term in the following number series: 2, 7, 24, 77, 238, ...
A. 721 B. 722
C. 723 D. 733

68. Anil introduces Prashant, "He is the husband of the grand daughter of the father of my father". How is Prashant related to Anil?
A. Brother B. Brother-in-law
C. Nephew D. Son

69. Four groups of letters are given below, three of them are alike in certain way while one is different, choose the ***odd*** one:
A. STUA B. RQPA
C. MLKA D. HGFA

70. Earth is related to Axis in the same way as wheel is related to:
A. Tyre B. Car
C. Road D. Hub

71. Find the next term in the following letter series:
LXF, MTJ, NPN, OLR, ...
A. PHV B. PIU
C. PJW D. PKX

72. If A is 40 meter South-West of B, C is 40 meter South-East of B, then C is in which direction fo A?
A. East B. West
C. North-East D. South

73. The average marks obtained by 150 students was 35. If the average marks of passed students was 39 and that of the failed students was 15, find the number of students, who passed the examination:
A. 120 B. 125
C. 135 D. 140

74. If $a^x = b$, $b^y = c$ and $c^z = a$, then what is the value of xyz?
A. abc B. 1
C. $\frac{1}{abc}$ D. ab

75. Find the smallest perfect square number which is exactly divisible by 4, 5, 6, 15 and 18:
A. 800 B. 225
C. 900 D. 361

76. What is the value of $\left(\sqrt{5}\right)^{-5/2} \times \left(\sqrt{5}\right)^{-3/2}$?
A. $\frac{1}{25}$ B. $\frac{1}{125}$
C. $\frac{1}{325}$ D. $\frac{1}{625}$

77. A sum of money doubles itself in 15 years at compound interest. In how many years it will become 8 times at the same compound interest rate?
A. 30 years B. 40 years
C. 60 years D. 45 years

78. If 25 men can reap a crop in 60 days, then in how many days will 10 men reap the crop?
A. 125 days B. 92 days
C. 100 days D. 150 days

79. If $x + \frac{1}{x} = 5$, then what is the value of $x^3 + \frac{1}{x^3}$?
A. 125 B. 110
C. 115 D. 105

80. In a certain code '786' means 'Study very hard', '958' means 'Hard work pays', '645' means 'Study and work', which is the code for 'very'?
A. 8 B. 6
C. 7 D. 5

81. Percentage of posts which have been reserved for women in Panchayati Raj Institutions of Haryana:
A. 25% B. 33%
C. 66% D. 50%

82. The district, where first time in Haryana E-challan has been introduced:
A. Gurugram B. Panchkula
C. Hisar D. Rohtak

83. 'Global City Project' is being developed by:
A. HSIIDC, Govt. of Haryana
B. GMDA, Govt. of Haryana
C. HUDA, Govt. of Haryana
D. Ministry of Urban Development, Govt. of India

84. The district, where Dolomite is found:
A. Mahendragarh B. Gurugram
C. Faridabad D. Panipat

85. The award, which is given to a sport coach for excellence in coaching by the Haryana State:
A. Dronacharya award
B. Guru Vashistha award

C. Maharana Pratap award
D. Arjuna award

86. The Position of Haryana in India in respect of area is:
A. 11th B. 21st
C. 15th D. 18th

87. The place, which was visited and mentioned by Chinese traveller Yuan Chwang:
A. Agroha B. Sugh
C. Kurukshetra D. Panipat

88. The de jure head of the State Administration in Haryana is:
A. Chief Minister of the State
B. Divisional Commissioner
C. Advocate General of the State
D. Governor of the State

89. Under which scheme of Haryana Government the socio-economic data of all the families of Haryana is being created?
A. Antyoday Parivar Utthan Yojna
B. Parivar Pehchan Patra-Yojana
C. Mukhyamantri Parivar Samriddhi Yojna
D. Jan Aadhar Yojna

90. The smallest (in term of area) wild life sanctuary is:
A. Bhindawas B. Nahar
C. Saraswati D. Chhilchhila

PART-IV

Subject Knowledge—Social Studies

Directions: *Answer the following questions by selecting the most **appropriate** option.*

91. To which land revenue system was Sir Thomas Munro associated with?
A. Ryotwari System
B. Mahalwari
C. Permanent Settlement
D. Zamindari

92. In which country of the continent of Africa the Atlas Mountains does ***not*** extended?
A. Morocco B. Algeria
C. Tunisia D. Mozambique

93. Who among the following led the movement called, 'Nyaya Yudh' (Struggle for Justice) in Haryana?
A. Bansi Lal
B. Chotu Ram
C. Devi Lal
D. Bhagwat Dayal Sharma

94. Lok Prahari vs Union of India (2018) case is related to:
A. Euthanasia
B. Electoral Refcrms
C. Sexual harassment at workplace
D. Capital Punishment

95. The total number of nominated members in the Parliament of India, can be:
A. 10 B. 12
C. 14 D. 16

96. Under which of the following markets is the firm a 'price taker'?
A. Monopoly
B. Monopolistic competition
C. Perfect competition
D. Oligopoly

97. Which of the following is ***not*** matching?
A. Brazil Current – The South Atlantic Ocean
B. Humboldt Current – The North Pacific Ocean
C. Gulf Stream – The North Atlantic Ocean
D. Agulhas Current – The Indian Ocean

98. The principle of maximum social advantage was propounded by:
A. E. Lindahl B. A. Wagner
C. R.A. Musgrave D. H. Dalton

99. The election symbol of the Congress Party in the Lok Sabha elections of 1971, was:
A. A pair of bullocks carrying a yoke
B. A farmer with plough
C. A cow with suckling calf
D. An oil lamp

100. How many members were there in Nehru Committee that drafted the Constitution for India in 1928?
A. 9 B. 5
C. 7 D. 11

101. Who was the architect of Paris?
A. Baron Haussmann
B. Ebenezer Howard
C. Joseph Mathews
D. Charles Wood

102. When total utility decreases, marginal utility is:
A. Zero B. Positive
C. Negative D. None of these

103. Match List-I with List-II and select the ***correct*** answer using the codes given below the list:

List-I (Name of President Of Indian National Congress)	**List-II (Session of the Indian National Congress)**
(*a*) Ambika Charan Mazumdar	(*i*) 1924
(*b*) Dadabhai Naoroji	(*ii*) 1916
(*c*) Mahatma Gandhi	(*iii*) 1925
(*d*) Mrs. Sarojini Naidu	(*iv*) 1906

Codes:

	(*a*)	(*b*)	(*c*)	(*d*)
A.	(*i*)	(*ii*)	(*iii*)	(*iv*)
B.	(*iii*)	(*iv*)	(*i*)	(*ii*)
C.	(*ii*)	(*iv*)	(*i*)	(*iii*)
D.	(*ii*)	(*iv*)	(*iii*)	(*i*)

104. Which one of the following countries is a landlocked?
A. Bolivia
B. Peru
C. Ecuador
D. Uruguay

105. Which International Organization was established in Bretton Woods Conference?
A. UNICEF B. WHO
C. IMF D. NATO

106. All combinations on an isoquant curve signify:
A. Same level of inputs
B. Same level of output
C. Same level of satisfaction
D. Same level of income

107. "All India Anti-Untouchability League 1932" was established by:
A. Dr. Bhimrao Ambedkar
B. Mahatma Gandhi
C. Jyotiba Phule
D. Dr. Rajendra Prasad

108. Match List-I with List-II and select the ***correct*** answer using the codes given below the list:

List-I (Sea Farer)	**List-II (Countries)**
(*a*) Vasco-da-Gama	(*i*) Spain
(*b*) Christopher Columbus	(*ii*) Portugal
(*c*) Captain Cook	(*iii*) Holland
(*d*) Tasman	(*iv*) Great Britain

Codes:

	(*a*)	(*b*)	(*c*)	(*d*)
A.	(*iii*)	(*ii*)	(*i*)	(*iv*)
B.	(*ii*)	(*i*)	(*iv*)	(*iii*)
C.	(*i*)	(*iv*)	(*iii*)	(*ii*)
D.	(*iv*)	(*iii*)	(*ii*)	(*i*)

109. Disposable income is equal to:
A. Personal income – Saving
B. Personal income – Personal taxes
C. GNP – Saving
D. Consumption – Saving

110. Who propounded the "Theory of Drain of Wealth"?
A. Jawaharlal Nehru B. Lala Lajpat Rai
C. Bal Gangadhar Tilak D. Dadabhai Naoroji

111. $\frac{\Delta C}{\Delta Y}$ stands for:
A. MPC B. APC
C. MPS D. APS

112. Match List-I with List-II and select the ***correct*** answer using the codes given below the list:

List-I (Name of the Movement)	**List-II (Leader of the Movement)**
(*a*) Satyashodhak	(*i*) Jyotirao Phule
(*b*) Self Respect Movement	(*ii*) E.V. Ramasamy Naicker
(*c*) Rajahmundry Social Reform Association	(*iii*) Veeresalingam Pantulu
(*d*) Namdhari	(*iv*) Ram Singh

Codes:

	(*a*)	(*b*)	(*c*)	(*d*)
A.	(*i*)	(*ii*)	(*iii*)	(*iv*)
B.	(*ii*)	(*iv*)	(*i*)	(*iii*)
C.	(*i*)	(*iv*)	(*iii*)	(*ii*)
D.	(*ii*)	(*iv*)	(*iii*)	(*i*)

113. Which of the following is ***not*** related to macro economics?
A. General price level
B. National income
C. Theory of output and employment level
D. Consumer equilibrium

114. Election to the Constituent Assembly were held in:
A. July, 1946 B. November, 1946
C. January, 1950 D. June, 1949

115. Which of the following is ***not*** correctly matched?
A. Alluvial Soil – Uttar Pradesh
B. Black Soil – Maharashtra
C. Red and Yellow Soil – Tamil Nadu
D. Laterite Soil – Punjab

116. Who was the Chairman of the 'states committee' of the Constituent Assembly?
A. Sachchidanand Sinha
B. Dr. Rajendra Prasad
C. Dr. B.R. Ambedkar
D. Jawaharlal Nehru

117. By what name is the climate is known similar to the Savanna?
A. South Africa type
B. Brazil type
C. Sudan type
D. Western Australia type

118. Which of the following words/terminologies is/are **not** mentioned in the Constitution of India?
(*i*) Federalism
(*ii*) No confidence motion
(*iii*) Defamation
(*iv*) Incitement to an offence

Select the ***correct*** option from the codes given below:
A. Only (*i*) and (*iv*)
B. Only (*ii*) and (*iv*)
C. Only (*i*) and (*ii*)
D. Only (*ii*) and (*iii*)

119. The demand for a factor is:
A. Derived demand
B. Direct demand
C. Joint demand
D. All options are wrong

120. Which of the following is **not** included in the high clouds?
A. Cirrus
B. Cirro-Stratus
C. Strato-Cumulus
D. Cirro-Cumulus

121. The ***correct*** descending order of the height of the mountain peaks as given below is:
(*a*) Kanchanjunga
(*b*) Godwin Austen (K-2)
(*c*) Nanga Parbat
(*d*) Nandadevi
A. (*b*), (*c*), (*a*), (*d*)
B. (*b*), (*a*), (*c*), (*d*)
C. (*a*), (*b*), (*c*), (*d*)
D. (*a*), (*c*), (*d*), (*b*)

122. Aggregate supply depends on:
A. Capital
B. Level of technology
C. Labour productivity
D. All options are right

123. Which of the following statements related to National Human Rights Commission is/are ***false***?
(*i*) The commission consists of one chairman and six members.
(*ii*) This commission was constituted on 12th October, 1993.
(*iii*) This commission is in conformity with the Paris principles of October, 1991.

Codes:
A. Only (*i*)
B. Only (*ii*)
C. (*i*) and (*iii*)
D. All (*i*), (*ii*) and (*iii*)

124. The Right of the President to send messages to both the houses of Parliament is mentioned in:
A. Article 84
B. Article 87
C. Article 88(1)
D. Article 86(1)

125. Which among the following articles of Indian Constitution is related to 'The Maxim Nemo debet bis Vexari' theory?
A. Article 20(1)
B. Article 20(2)
C. Article 20(3)
D. Article 21

126. In Koppen's Climatic Classification of India the central Ganges valley is represented by:
A. Aw
B. Amw
C. Cwg
D. Bshw

127. Which of the following coal areas are located in Damodar valley?

Select the ***correct*** answer from the codes given below:
(*a*) Jharia
(*b*) Raniganj
(*c*) Singrauli
(*d*) Sohagpur

Codes:
A. (*b*), (*c*), (*d*)
B. (*b*), (*c*)
C. (*a*), (*b*)
D. (*a*), (*b*), (*c*)

128. The ***correct*** chronological order of following geological structures in India is:
A. Cudappah–Dharwar–Gondwana–Vindhyan
B. Dharwar–Cudappah–Gondwana–Vindhyan
C. Vindhyan–Gondwana–Dharwar–Cudappah
D. Dharwar–Cudappah–Vindhyan–Gondwana

129. The last ruler of the Haryank dynasty was:
A. Nagadasaka
B. Mundak
C. Aniruddha
D. Udayin

130. Which of the following is ***not*** correctly matched?

	(River)		**(Subsidiary Rivers)**
A.	Ganga	–	Ghaghara, Tons, Ken
B.	Chambal	–	Banas, Kalisindh, Shipra
C.	Damodar	–	Rihand, Tungbhadra, Manjara
D.	Brahmaputra	–	Dibang, Lohit, Dihang

131. Battle of Talikota (1565) was fought between Vijayanagar empire and:
A. Golconda
B. Bijapur
C. Ahmednagar
D. All of the above

132. Where and when was the Second Buddhist Council held?
A. Pataliputra in 250 BCE
B. Sri Lanka in 1st Century BCE
C. Vaishali in 383 BCE
D. Mandalay in 1871 CE

133. Who is considered as the Guru of Saint Mirabai?
A. Eknath B. Ravidas
C. Namdev D. Ramdas

134. Which of the following external agency is providing financial help for Delhi-Mumbai Industrial Corridor Project?
A. World Bank
B. Asian Development Bank
C. German Government
D. Government of Japan

135. The leading coastal region in Tidal power generation in India is:
A. Kerala Coast
B. Bay of Cambay
C. Bay of Mannar
D. Uttari Sarkar Coast

136. Female saint of South India, Karikkal Ammaiyar was the devotee of:
A. Vishnu B. Shiva
C. Brahma D. Krishna

137. Members of Election Commission are appointed by:
A. President B. Prime Minister
C. Parliament D. Chief Justice

138. Who was the first Finance Minister of independent India?
A. R.K.S. Chetty
B. C.D. Deshmukh
C. Morarji Desai
D. H.N. Bahuguna

139. The first Vice Chairman of Niti Aayog was:
A. Rajiv Kumar
B. Amitabh Kant
C. Arvind Panagariya
D. Raghuram Rajan

140. The measuring unit in Germany 'elle' was used to measure:
A. Cloth B. Land
C. Weight D. Density

141. Make in India Programme concern:
A. 30 Industries/Sector
B. 25 Industries/Sector
C. 20 Industries/Sector
D. 15 Industries/Sector

142. What percentage of the total number of members of Lok Sabha can be the total number of Union Council of Ministers?
A. 10 per cent B. 15 per cent
C. 20 per cent D. 25 per cent

143. The ruler of Gupta period who was an expert player of Veena:
A. Chandragupta B. Skandagupta
C. Samudragupta D. Vishnugupta

144. Match List-I with List-II and select the correct answer using the codes given below:

List-I	List-II
(*a*) Boston of the East	(*i*) Bangalore
(*b*) Cottonopolis of India	(*ii*) Ahmedabad
(*c*) Manchester of South India	(*iii*) Coimbatore
(*d*) Electronic city	(*iv*) Mumbai

Codes:

	(*a*)	(*b*)	(*c*)	(*d*)
A.	(*ii*)	(*iv*)	(*iii*)	(*i*)
B.	(*iii*)	(*ii*)	(*iv*)	(*i*)
C.	(*i*)	(*iii*)	(*ii*)	(*iv*)
D.	(*i*)	(*ii*)	(*iii*)	(*iv*)

145. At which of the following places was the national government established during the Quit India Movement?
(*i*) Tamluk
(*ii*) Satara
(*iii*) Faizpur
(*iv*) Ballia

Codes:
A. (*i*), (*ii*) and (*iv*)
B. (*i*), (*ii*), (*iii*) and (*iv*)
C. (*ii*) and (*iv*)
D. (*ii*), (*iii*) and (*iv*)

146. The number of stipulated elected MPs from Haryana is:
A. 10 B. 12
C. 20 D. 15

147. Choose the ***correct*** answer from the options given below:
A. Tehri Dam – Tons river
B. Bhakra Dam – Bhagirathi river
C. Lakhwar Dam – Vyas river
D. Srisailam Dam – Krishna river

148. When was the Bahujan Samaj Party formed under the leadership of Kanshi Ram?
A. 1986 B. 1987
C. 1989 D. 1984

149. When was World Trade Organization established?
A. 1 January, 1994
B. 1 January, 1995
C. 1 January, 1996
D. 1 January, 1997

150. According to Malthus, population increases in:
A. Geometrical progression
B. Arithmetical progression
C. Harmonic progression
D. None of these

Answers

1. (D)	**2. (C)**	**3. (A)**
4. (D)	**5. (C)**	**6. (D)**
7. (C)	**8. (B)**	**9. (D)**
10. (A)	**11. (A)**	**12. (C)**
13. (B)	**14. (A)**	**15. (D)**
16. (B)	**17. (B)**	**18. (*)**
19. (D)	**20. (C)**	**21. (C)**
22. (A)	**23. (C)**	**24. (C)**
25. (A)	**26. (A)**	**27. (B)**
28. (D)	**29. (C)**	**30. (D)**
31. (C)	**32. (C)**	**33. (A)**
34. (A)	**35. (D)**	**36. (C)**
37. (A)	**38. (B)**	**39. (B)**
40. (C)	**41. (C)**	**42. (D)**
43. (D)	**44. (A)**	**45. (D)**
46. (A)	**47. (B)**	**48. (B)**
49. (*)	**50. (D)**	**51. (D)**
52. (C)	**53. (C)**	**54. (C)**
55. (B)	**56. (B)**	**57. (B)**
58. (A)	**59. (B)**	**60. (D)**

61. (D): Let $x = \sqrt{8+2\sqrt{8+2\sqrt{8}}}$ ......

$$x^2 = 8 + 2x$$

$$\Rightarrow \quad x^2 - 2x - 8 = 0$$

$$\Rightarrow \quad (x-4)(x+2) = 0$$

$$\Rightarrow \quad x = 4$$

or $\quad x = -2$

$$\therefore \quad x = 4$$

$(\because x > 0)$

62. (C): Let each side of square = x

Area of the square = x^2

$$\text{Side increased} = x + \frac{50x}{100}$$

$$= x + \frac{x}{2} = \frac{3x}{2}$$

$$\text{Area} = \left(\frac{3x}{2}\right)^2 = \frac{9x^2}{4}$$

$$\text{Area increased} = \frac{9x^2}{4} - x^2$$

$$= \frac{5x^2}{4}$$

$$\text{\% area increased} = \frac{5x^2}{4 \times x^2} \times 100 = 125\%.$$

63. (B): $15 \times 5 + 5 - 20 \div 10$

$= 75 + 5 - 2$

$= 80 - 2$

$= 78.$

64. (A): 100 + 20 = ₹ 120

When SP ₹ 120 then C.P. = ₹ 100

When SP ₹ 72000 then C.P. = $\frac{100}{120} \times 72000$

= ₹ 60000

Hence, C.P. of the commodity = ₹ 60000.

65. (C):

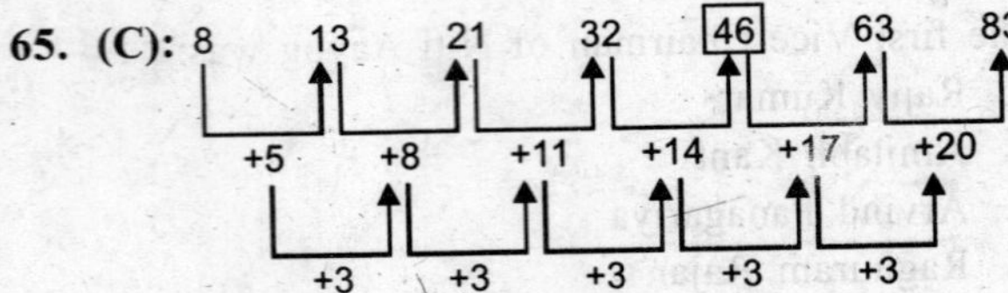

46 will come at the place of 47.

Hence, wrong number = 47.

66. (C)

67. (C): 2 7 24 77 238 723

× 3 + 1 × 3 + 3 × 3 + 5 × 3 + 7 × 3 + 9

Hence, 723 will come at the next term.

68. (B)

69. (A): First three letter of 'STUA' are in increasing order while first three letters in remaining three letter-clusters, i.e., 'RQPA', 'MLKA' and 'HGFA' are in decreasing order.

So, letter-cluster 'STUA' is odd.

70. (D): Earth is related to Axis in the same way as wheel is related to Hub.

71. (A):

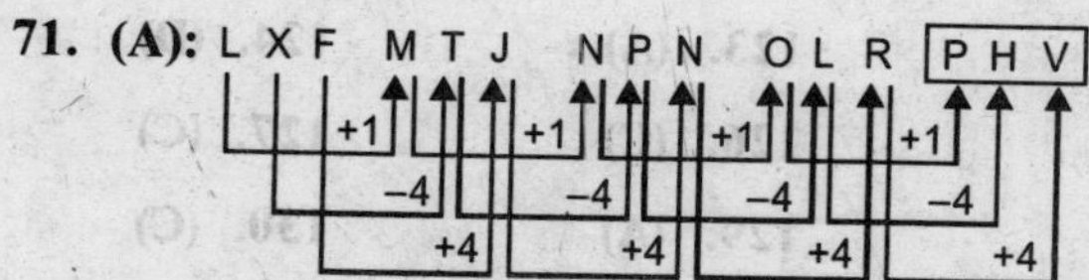

Hence, next term will be PHV.

72. (A):

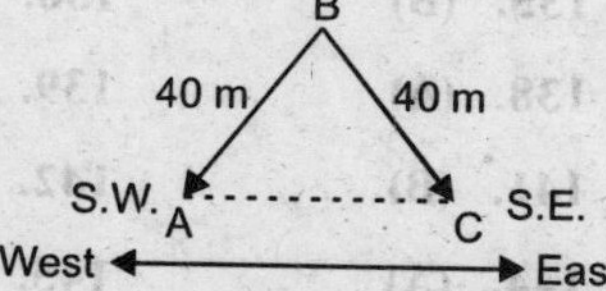

Clearly, C is in East direction of A.

73. (B): Total marks obtained by 150 students

$= 150 \times 35$

$= 5250$

Let number of passed students $= y$

$\therefore$ Number of failed students $= 150 - y$

According to the question,

Total marks of passed students $= 39y$

Total marks of failed students $= (150 - y) \times 15$

$$39y + (150 - y) \times 15 = 5250$$

$$\Rightarrow \quad 39y + 2250 - 15y = 5250$$

$$\Rightarrow \quad 24y = 3000$$

$$\Rightarrow \quad y = 125$$

Hence, number of passed students = 125.

74. (B): $\because$

$$a^x = b$$

$$b^y = c$$

and $$c^z = a$$

$$\therefore \quad a^x \times b^y \times c^z = b \times c \times a$$

$$\Rightarrow \quad (abc)^{xyz} = (abc)^1$$

$$\Rightarrow \quad xyz = 1$$

Hence, the value of $xyz = 1$.

75. (C): LCM of 4, 5, 6, 15 and 18 = 180

800 is not divided by 180

225 is not divided by 180

900 is divided by 180

Hence, 900 is the smallest perfect square number which is exactly divisible by 4, 5, 6, 15 and 18.

76. (A): The Value of $\left(\sqrt{5}\right)^{\frac{-5}{2}} \times \left(\sqrt{5}\right)^{\frac{-3}{2}}$

$$= \left(\sqrt{5}\right)^{\frac{-8}{2}}$$

$$= \left(\sqrt{5}\right)^{-4}$$

$$= (5)^{\frac{1}{2}\times -4} = (5)^{-2}$$

$$= \frac{1}{5^2} = \frac{1}{25}.$$

77. (D):

$$A = P\left(1+\frac{r}{100}\right)^t$$

$$\Rightarrow \quad 2P = P\left(1+\frac{r}{100}\right)^{15}$$

$$\frac{2P}{P} = \left(1+\frac{r}{100}\right)^{15}$$

$$\Rightarrow \quad \left(1+\frac{r}{100}\right)^{15} = 2 \qquad \ldots(i)$$

Now,

$$A = P\left(1+\frac{r}{100}\right)^t$$

$$8P = P\left(1+\frac{r}{100}\right)^t$$

$$\frac{8P}{P} = \left(1+\frac{r}{100}\right)^t$$

$$8 = \left(1+\frac{r}{100}\right)^t$$

$$\Rightarrow \quad \left(1+\frac{r}{100}\right)^t = 8 = 2^3$$

$$= \left[\left(1+\frac{r}{100}\right)^{15}\right]^3$$

$$\Rightarrow \quad \left(1+\frac{r}{100}\right)^t = \left(1+\frac{r}{100}\right)^{45}$$

Hence, $t = 45$ years.

78. (D): $\because$ 25 men can reap a crop in 60 days

$\therefore$ 1 man can reap the crop in 60×25 days

$\therefore$ 10 men can reap the same crop in

$$\frac{60 \times 25}{10} = 150 \text{ days}$$

Hence, 10 men can reap the crop in 150 days.

79. (B): $\because$ $x + \frac{1}{x} = 5$

$\therefore$ $x^3 + \frac{1}{x^3} = \left(x + \frac{1}{x}\right)^3 - 3x.\frac{1}{x}\left(x + \frac{1}{x}\right)$

$= (5)^3 - 3 \times (5)$

$= 125 - 15$

$= 110$

Hence, the value of $x^3 + \frac{1}{x^3} = 110$.

80. (C) **81.** (D) **82.** (A)
83. (A) **84.** (A) **85.** (B)
86. (B) **87.** (B) **88.** (D)
89. (B) **90.** (D) **91.** (A)
92. (D) **93.** (C) **94.** (B)
95. (B) **96.** (C) **97.** (B)
98. (D) **99.** (C) **100.** (D)
101. (A) **102.** (C) **103.** (C)
104. (A) **105.** (C) **106.** (B)
107. (B) **108.** (B) **109.** (B)
110. (D) **111.** (A) **112.** (A)
113. (D) **114.** (A) **115.** (D)
116. (D) **117.** (C) **118.** (*)
119. (A) **120.** (C) **121.** (B)
122. (D) **123.** (A) **124.** (D)
125. (B) **126.** (C) **127.** (C)
128. (D) **129.** (A) **130.** (C)
131. (D) **132.** (C) **133.** (B)
134. (D) **135.** (B) **136.** (B)
137. (A) **138.** (A) **139.** (C)
140. (A) **141.** (B) **142.** (B)
143. (C) **144.** (A) **145.** (A)
146. (D) **147.** (D) **148.** (D)
149. (B) **150.** (A)

Previous Paper (Solved)

Haryana Teacher Eligibility Test (HTET)

TGT Social Studies (Level-2), Exam 2021

(Exam held on 19 December, 2021)

PART-I

Child Development and Pedagogy

Directions: *Answer the following questions by selecting the **most appropriate** option.*

1. What is the process of releasing the hidden emotional suffocation and powers inside the children called?
A. Emotional stability
B. Emotional sensitivity
C. Emotional catharsis
D. Emotional competency

2. When a person tried to make his/her thoughts and action according to other whom he like to follow, then this kind of activity called which type of defence mechanism?
A. Identification B. Projection
C. Rationalisation D. Displacement

3. According to Jean Piaget between which age the child develops abstract reasoning?
A. 6 to 8 years B. 8 to 10 years
C. 7 to 9 years D. 11 to 14 years

4. Which one of the following is ***not*** the common speech disorder of childhood?
A. Depletion of Energy
B. Lisping
C. Slurring
D. Stuttering

5. How many cards prescribed in Rorschach Ink Block Test?
A. 12 B. 10
C. 30 D. 31

6. What is the age range of puberty stage?
A. 10 to 12 years
B. 6 to 12 years
C. 11 to 16 years
D. 8 to 10 years

7. According to 'Ross', which stage of development is known as 'Pseudo Maturity' stage?
A. Infancy B. Childhood
C. Adolescence D. Adhulthood

8. Out of the following which one is ***not*** the type of performance test of intelligence?
A. Army alpha test
B. Koh's block design test
C. The cube construction test
D. The pass along test

9. Out of the following which one characteristic ***not*** suits to gifted children?
A. Learn rapidly and easily.
B. Perform difficult mental task.
C. Knows about many things of which most of the students are unaware.
D. Much drill is required to retain what he/she has heard or read.

10. Which one of the following is the ***correct*** logical order of observational learning process according Learning Theory of Bandura?
A. Attentional → Retentional → Motivational → Production
B. Attentional → Motivational → Retentional → Production
C. Motivational → Attentional → Retentional → Production
D. Attentional → Retentional → Production → Motivational

11. Who invented sociometric technique?
A. J.E. Anderson B. J.L. Moreno
C. E.B. Hurlock D. G.S. Marmor

12. Who stated that "An individual is intelligent in proportion as he is able to carry on abstract thinking?
A. Terman B. Dearborn
C. Buckingham D. Calvin

13. Girls surpass boys physically in:
A. Infancy B. Later childhood
C. Early childhood D. Adolescence

14. Who is known as father of Educational Psychology?
A. E.L. Thorndike B. Pestalozzi
C. Herbart D. Froebel

15. Out of the following which one is the subject matter for study of Gestalt Psychologist?
A. Cognitive processes
B. Consciousness
C. Mental and behavioural processes a wholes
D. Modes and problems of existence

16. Who stated that "Personality is the sum total of innate and acquired dispositions"?
A. Mortin Prince
B. Allpórt
C. Valentine
D. Cattell

17. Out of the following which one is *wrong* characteristic of Delinquents?
A. Damaging school property
B. Bullying and mockery
C. Torturing
D. Aesthanic in constitution

18. Which of the following is the characteristic of introverted thinking type personality?
A. Realistic and Practical
B. Absorbed in his own intellectual pursuit
C. Supports theory with facts
D. Propagates his views with insistence and vehemence

19. Out of the following which one activity is *not* suitable for satisfying the instincts curiosity?
A. Awarding positions in the class or school
B. Answering the questions of the students
C. Problem solving
D. Discussion in class

20. Out of the following which one is *not* the stage of creativity prescribed by Gordon in his Synectics Technique?
A. Detachment involvement
B. Finding something similar
C. Deferment
D. Concept formation

21. Out of the following which one of the statement is *wrong* in context of characteristics of sentiments?
A. Emotions are the basis of sentiments.
B. Sentiments are innate.
C. Sentiments get older with the passage of time and they may even change their state.
D. Most of the animals do not have sentiments because of they do not have intellectual comprehension.

22. A type of thinking in which one's interpret sensation with experience is known as what?
A. Reflective thinking
B. Perceptual thinking
C. Creative thinking
D. Critical thinking

23. Out of the following which is ***correct*** sequence given by James Lange's "Theory of Emotions"?
A. Situation → Bodily disturbance → Mental state
B. Situation → Mental state → Bodily expressions
C. Situation → Bodily expressions → Mental state
D. Situation → Mental state → Bodily disturbance

24. Sometimes the children of gifted parents are born with less intelligence than their parents or vice versa, which Law of Heredity is called?
A. Law of Regression
B. Law of Selective Traits
C. Law of Maternal and Paternal Lines
D. Law of Chance

25. Which is the fourth stage of psycho-social development of an individual according to Erikson?
A. Intimacy v/s isolation
B. Identity v/s role confusion
C. Industry v/s inferiority
D. Generativity v/s stagnation

26. Which one of the following is ***false*** statement in context of Development?
A. Development involves change
B. The development pattern is unpredicatble
C. Early development is more critical than later development
D. Development is the product of maturation and learning

27. Out of the following which one is the ***wrong*** statement in context of characteristics and nature of guidance?
A. Guidance is assisting the individual to adjust himself.
B. Guidance of promotion of the growth of the individual in self-Guidance.
C. Guidance is helping the individual himself through others efforts only.
D. Guidance is assisting an individual to find his place.

28. What did Freud consider the paternal love of girls?
A. Oedipus complex
B. Electra complex
C. Narcissism
D. Feeling of dependence

29. Which is the oldest method for the study of behaviour?
A. Experimental method
B. Clinical method
C. Psycho-physical method
D. Introspection method

30. Out of the following which one is *not* the characteristic of insight?
A. Incidental
B. Response in novel situation
C. Habit strength
D. Response spontaneity

PART-II

भाषा : हिन्दी

निर्देशः *निम्नलिखित प्रश्नों के उत्तर देने के लिए* ***सबसे उचित*** *विकल्प चुनिए।*

31. किस विकल्प के सभी शब्द विदेशज हैं?
A. लाजवाब, मशीन, पवन
B. कारीगर, अतिशयोक्ति, कहानी
C. मुमकिन, अमूमन, पक्षवार
D. किस्सा, स्कूल, हमला

32. प्रत्यय की दृष्टि से किस शब्द की रचना **अनुचित** है?
A. मुरेला – एला
B. कँटीला – ईला
C. विलीन – ईन
D. ससुराल – आल

33. किस वाक्य में सर्वनाम संबंधी **अशुद्धि** है?
A. तुम्हारी पुस्तक यह नहीं वह है।
B. मैं अपना कार्य कर रहा हूँ।
C. जिसने भी खाया है, सराहा है।
D. मेरे को कुछ भी याद नहीं आ रहा।

34. किस वाक्य में परिमाणवाचक विशेषण का प्रयोग हुआ है?
A. मैं नीली कमीज नहीं पहनता।
B. इस बार बारिश में बहुत ओले गिरे।
C. खेल का मैदान लम्बा है।
D. दिनेश अच्छा गायक है।

35. विलोम शब्द की दृष्टि से **अनुचित** युग्म पहचानिए :
A. बद – नेक
B. दुश्चरित्र – निश्चरित्र
C. विस्तृत – संक्षिप्त
D. मधुर – कटु

36. किस विकल्प में 'संकेतार्थक' वाक्य है?
A. प्रियतम मेरा मित्र है।
B. यदि तुम आओ तो मैं चलूँ।
C. हो सकता है कल मौसम ठीक हो जाए।
D. राजेश अपना कमरा साफ करो।

37. निम्न में से कौन-सा शब्द 'अनु' उपसर्ग से निर्मित **नहीं** है?
A. आनुपातिक B. अनुदात्त
C. अनूदित D. अनुरंजक

38. 'विपत्ति के समय थोड़ी सहायता भी बड़ी होती है' उक्त भाव की व्यंजक लोकोक्ति चुनिए :
A. डूबते को तिनके का सहारा
B. चुपड़ी और दो-दो
C. चार दिन की चाँदनी फिर अँधेरी रात
D. आम के आम गुठलियों के दाम

39. किस भाववाचक संज्ञा का निर्माण व्यक्तिवाचक संज्ञा से हुआ है?
A. बचपन
B. कैशोर्य
C. ऐश्वर्य
D. मातृत्व

40. क्रिया के संबंध में कौन-सा युग्म **अनुचित** है?
A. भिखारी सड़क पर चिल्ला रहे थे। –अकर्मक क्रिया
B. राधा श्याम को पत्र लिखती है। –द्विकर्मक क्रिया
C. बगीचे में मोर नाच रहा है। –सकर्मक क्रिया
D. वह विद्यालय से आकर खाना खाएगा। –पूर्वकालिक क्रिया

41. पर्यायवाची शब्दों के संदर्भ में **असंगत** विकल्प चुनिए :
A. जीभ – वाचा, रसना, वाणी
B. अहंकार – दंभ, दर्प, मद
C. किरण – रश्मि, मयूख, प्रभा
D. कौआ – प्रियक, मधुदूत, अतिसौरभ

42. समास-विग्रह की दृष्टि से कौन-सा विकल्प **उचित** है?
A. हथकरघा – हाथों से चलने वाला करघा
B. भुजग – भूमि में जन्म लेने वाला
C. देशभक्ति – देश के द्वारा भक्ति
D. पशुबलि – पशु के लिए बलि

43. किस विकल्प में संधि-विच्छेद **अनुचित** है?
A. बहिरेकता = बहिः + एकता
B. आशीर्वचन = आशीः + वचन
C. रतिरंश = रतिः + रंश
D. तपश्चर्या = तपः + चर्या

44. निम्न में से किस मुहावरे का अर्थ संगत **नहीं** है?
A. नहले पर दहला मारना – करारा जवाब देना
B. बत्तीसी बंद होना – चुप हो जाना
C. सिर का पसीना पाँव तक आना – कठिन परिश्रम करना
D. थाली का बैंगन होना – सर्व सुलभ होना

45. निम्न में से किस विकल्प का कथन **गलत** है?
A. 'ऋ' का उच्चारण स्थान 'मूर्धा' है।
B. विसर्ग ध्वनि की गणना नासिक्य वर्णों में की जाती है।
C. 'य' और 'व' को अर्ध स्वर भी कहा जाता है।
D. 'ड़' और 'ढ़' उत्क्षिप्त वर्ण कहलाते हैं।

Language : English

Directions: *Answer the following questions by selecting the* ***most appropriate*** *option.*

46. Select the ***appropriate*** modal for the expression given:

Harish has annoyed his boss today. He ______ be fired soon. (probability)

A. may B. can
C. ought to D. would

47. Choose the ***correct*** tense form to fill in the blank;

Municipality has decided to ______ the overhead wires.

A. did away with
B. do away with
C. had done away with
D. had done away wtih

48. Select the ***appropriate*** modal to fill in the blank:

Trespassers ______ be punished. (legal notice)

A. shall
B. may
C. should
D. ought to

49. Select the ***appropriate*** preposition to fill in the blank:

His hut is ______ hotel Taj.

A. above
B. out
C. besides
D. beside

50. Choose the ***correct*** meaning of the underlined words:

The law and order situation will only become worse in the state due to the riots, if the government does not do something right now to <u>nip it in the bud</u>.

A. To plan in detail to stop a threat
B. To destroy the problem in the initial stage only
C. To arrest the culprits
D. To stop something harmful in the initial stage

51. Select the ***correct*** option (Phrasal Verb) for the underlined word:

She <u>rejected</u> his request to take her home.

A. turned up
B. turned down
C. turned out
D. turned off

52. Choose the ***correct*** option to fill in the blank:

This pen is both good ______ cheap.

A. as well as B. as well
C. but only D. and

53. Choose the ***correct*** option for the following:

One who wastes a lot of money is:

A. frugal B. recluse
C. prodigal D. reticent

54. Choose the part of the sentence which is ***incorrect***:

The party president made (*a*)/ Rakesh (*b*)/ a M.P. candidate (*c*)/ for the coming election. (*d*)

A. (*a*) B. (*b*)
C. (*c*) D. (*d*)

55. Select the ***correct*** option (Phrasal Verb) for the blank left in the sentence:

Cholera has ______ in this village.

A. broken out
B. broken down
C. broken up
D. broken off

56. Choose the ***correct*** meaning of the underlined words:

The hostess <u>broke the ice</u> by introducing the strangers to each other.

A. To make people relax with each other
B. To make people perplexed with each other
C. To serve welcome drink to the guests
D. To start a game of puzzle

57. Choose the ***correct*** tense form to fill in the following:

I had consulted my lawyer before I ______ the complaint.

A. did lodged
B. had lodged
C. lodge
D. lodged

58. Choose the ***appropriate*** modal to fill in the blank:

He ______ listen to the stories of his Grand Ma before he slept. (Past habit)

A. could B. shall
C. would D. might

59. Choose the part of the sentence which is ***incorrect***:

He did not (*a*)/ keep his words (*b*)/ to pick him up (*c*)/ from WTP. (*d*)

A. (*b*) B. (*c*)
C. (*d*) D. (*a*)

60. Choose the ***appropriate*** preposition to fill in the blank:

What is the time ______ your watch?

A. in B. from
C. by D. on

PART-III

General Studies : Quantitative Aptitude, Reasoning Ability and GK & Awareness

Directions: *Answer the following questions by selecting the **most appropriate** option.*

61. The sum of length, breadth and depth of a cuboid is 19 cm and its principal diagonal is $5\sqrt{5}$ cm, then its surface area is:

A. 361 cm^2 B. 286 cm^2
C. 236 cm^2 D. 340 cm^2

62. In a row of boys, A is 15th from the left and B is fourth from the right. There are three boys between A and B, C is first left of A. What is the position of C from the right?

A. 9th B. 10th
C. 12th D. 13th

63. Among five persons A, B, C, D and E, A is shorter than B but taller than E. C is the tallest. D is shorter than B but taller than A. Who among them is shortest?

A. B B. A
C. D D. E

64. A train 140 metre long is running at 60 km/hour. How much time will it take to pass a platform 260 metre long?

A. 18 sec B. 24 sec
C. 30 sec D. 32 sec

65. Two alloys are both made up of copper and tin. The ratio of copper and tin in the first alloy is 1 : 3 and in second alloy is 2 : 5. In what ratio should two alloys be mixed, to obtain a new alloy such that the ratio of copper and tin be 3 : 8?

A. 3 : 5 B. 4 : 9
C. 4 : 7 D. 3 : 8

66. If 4 men or 6 women can do a piece of work in 12 days working 7 hours a day. How many days will it take to complete a work twice as large with 10 men and 3 women working together 8 hours a day?

A. 6 B. 7
C. 8 D. 9

67. If $x = \dfrac{1}{1+\sqrt{2}}$, then the value of $x^2 + 2x + 3$ is:

A. 0 B. 1
C. 4 D. 2

68. The next term of the following letter series will be:
CAE, HFJ, MKO, RPT, _____

A. UTY B. WUY
C. VUZ D. WUZ

69. The length of a wire is 66 metre, then the number of circles of circumference 1.32 cm that can be made from the wire is:

A. 1000 B. 50
C. 500 D. 5000

70. The sum of two numbrs is 520. If the bigger number is decreased by 4% and the smaller number is increased by 12%, then the obtained numbers are equal, then smaller number is:

A. 210 B. 240
C. 270 D. 300

71. A cloth merchant on selling 33 metre of cloth obtains a profit equal to the selling price of 11 metre of cloth. The profit percentage is:

A. 11% B. 22%
C. 50% D. 40%

72. A said, "that boy is the grandson of my mother's husband. I have no brother or sister." How is the boy related to A?

A. Uncle B. Son
C. Nephew D. Cousin

73. Find the ***wrong*** number in the following series?
135, 226, 353, 552, 739

A. 353 B. 226
C. 552 D. 739

74. The difference between simple interest and the compound interest compounded annually at the rate of 12% per annum on ₹ 5000 for two years will be:

A. ₹ 72 B. ₹ 84
C. ₹ 96 D. ₹ 36

75. The perimeter of a rhombus is 100 cm and one of its diagonal is 40 cm. Then its area is:

A. 300 cm^2 B. 600 cm^2
C. 780 cm^2 D. 900 cm^2

76. Find the ***wrong*** term of the following series:
G4T, J9R, M20P, P41N, S90L

A. J9R B. M20P
C. P41N D. S90L

77. If W = 23, STRONG = 93, then WEAK is equal to:

A. 40 B. 41
C. 43 D. 44

78. If a person walks 8 km towards South then turns right and walks 8 km, again turns left and walks 10 km. In which direction is he from starting point?

A. East-South B. North-East
C. North-South D. South-West

79. If $5a + \frac{1}{3a} = 5$, then the value of $9a^2 + \frac{1}{25a^2}$ is:

A. $\frac{51}{5}$ B. $\frac{29}{5}$

C. $\frac{52}{5}$ D. $\frac{39}{5}$

80. A person walks 2 km towards East and then he turns to South and walk 1 km. Again he turns to East and walks 2 km after that he turns to North and walk 4 km. Now how far is he from his starting point?

A. 5 km B. 6 km

C. 3 km D. 4 km

81. Read the following statements about Haryana Sahitya Academy:

(*i*) The Chief Minister serves as the President of the academy.

(*ii*) 'Harigandha' is the Magazine of the academy.

Choose the ***correct*** code:

A. Only statement (*i*) is correct

B. Only statement (*ii*) is correct

C. Neither (*i*) nor (*ii*) is correct

D. Both the statements are correct

82. Where the 'Panchwati' pilgrimage site is located in Haryana?

A. In Palwal B. In Ambala

C. In Hathin D. In Ballabhgarh

83. In which district the 'Chinkara' Breeding Centre' is situated?

A. Kaithal B. Panchkula

C. Hisar D. Bhiwani

84. Match the following

Name	Place
(*a*) Birbal's Rang Mahal	(*i*) Narnaul
(*b*) Spiritual Museum	(*ii*) Gurugram
(*c*) Chor Gumbad	(*iii*) Yamunanagar
(*d*) Sohna Fort	(*iv*) Panipat

Code:

	(*a*)	(*b*)	(*c*)	(*d*)
A.	(*ii*)	(*iii*)	(*iv*)	(*i*)
B.	(*iii*)	(*iv*)	(*i*)	(*ii*)
C.	(*iv*)	(*ii*)	(*iii*)	(*i*)
D.	(*iii*)	(*ii*)	(*i*)	(*iv*)

85. How many gold medals were won by Haryana state in the '36th National Junior Athletics Championship', which was held in February, 2021?

A. 13 B. 18

C. 21 D. 24

86. Who among the following was the longest serving Governor of Haryana?

A. B.N. Chakraborty B. A.R. Kidwai

C. Jagannath Pahadia D. Kaptan Singh Solanki

87. Which of the following pair/pairs is/are ***true***?

(*i*) State Animal – Black buck

(*ii*) Saraswati Wild Life Sanctuary – Kaithal

(*iii*) Nahar Wild Life Sanctuary – Jhajjar

Choose the ***correct*** code:

A. Only (*i*) B. (*i*) and (*iii*)

C. (*i*) and (*ii*) D. Only (*iii*)

88. The hero of 1857 Revolution Abdurrahman Khan was related to:

A. Bahadurgarh B. Farrukhnagar

C. Jhajjar D. Yamunanagar

89. The amount which is given to the sports woman on the occasion of marriage under 'Mukhyamantri Vivah Shagun Yojana'?

A. ₹ 11,000 B. ₹ 21,000

C. ₹ 31,000 D. ₹ 51,000

90. The minimum number of members in the Council of Minister of Haryana can be:

A. 10 B. 12

C. 14 D. 06

PART-IV

Social Studies

Directions: *Answer the following questions by selecting the* ***most appropriate*** *option.*

91. With respect to the military system of Alauddin Khilji, which of the following statements is/are **true**?

(*i*) Alauddin Khilji raised a huge standing army.

(*ii*) Alauddin Khilji established city named 'Siri' for the soldiers.

(*iii*) Alauddin Khilji paid the soldiers in cash instead of Iqta.

Code:

A. Only (*i*) B. Only (*iii*)

C. (*i*) and (*ii*) D. (*i*), (*ii*) and (*iii*)

92. "Persons with disabilities have equal rights and that the government should make possible their full participation in society."

In which Act above provision mentioned?

A. Persons with Disabilities Act, 2015

B. Persons with Disabilities Act, 2005

C. Persons with Disabilities Act, 2016
D. Persons with Disabilities Act, 2017

93. Which of the following is not included in the 'National Food Security Mission 2007'?
A. Wheat Mission B. Rice Mission
C. Pulse Mission D. Oilseeds Mission

94. 'Make in India' is related on which of the following field?
A. Manufacturing Sector
B. Agricultural Sector
C. Service Sector
D. Education Sector

95. When Targeted Public Distribution System (TPDS) was started?
A. June, 1997 B. July, 1998
C. August, 1999 D. April, 2000

96. Which one of the following Saints was **not** associated with Naqshbandi Silsila?
A. Shah Waliullah
B. Khwaja Baqi Billah
C. Khwaja Mir Dard
D. Sheikh Sharfuddin Yahya

97. Which of the following countries prepared the 'Dawes Plan' to get Germany out of the economic crisis?
A. Britain
B. France
C. United State of America
D. Russia

98. The exponent of 'Mahalwari System' of land revenue was:
A. Captain Alexander Reed
B. Thomas Munro
C. Holt Mackenzie
D. Lord Cornwallis

99. Which one of the following is not correctly matched?

	Grassland	Regions
A.	Prairie	North America
B.	Veld	South Africa
C.	Downs	South America
D.	Steppes	Eurasia

100. Guru Gobind Singh founded Khalsa Panth in:
A. 1598 B. 1636
C. 1699 D. 1704

101. Which of the following is not an Iron ore producing area of Odisha?
A. Kudremukh B. Gurumahisani
C. Badam Pahar D. Kiriburu

102. 'Chinook' wind blows in:
A. Switzerland B. Sahara desert
C. Italy D. USA

103. The thunderstorms causes rains during April and May in Assam called:
A. Mango showers B. Loo
C. Cherry Blossoms D. Bardoli Chheerha

104. When the agreement was signed between India and Pakistan to inform about nuclear installations?
A. 31 December, 1988 B. 27 January, 1991
C. 31 December, 2020 D. 1 January, 2021

105. In which year did the 'Incident of Bloody Sunday' take place in Russia?
A. 1903 B. 1905
C. 1917 D. 1927

106. The decadal growth rate of population during 2001-2011 in India was:
A. +21.54 B. +20.54
C. +17.64 D. +18.64

107. Which of the following is **not** an Indian Multinational Corporation?
A. I.T.C. B. Zomato
C. Micromax D. Nestle

108. Which is **not** a direct challenges towards Indian Democracy?
A. Degradation of moral value
B. Danger of communalism
C. Caste system
D. All options are right

109. Who wrote the book 'The Power Elite'?
A. Wright Mills B. Mosca
C. Michels D. Pareto

110. Normal Lapse rate in troposphere is:
A. 6°C Per 1000 meter
B. 8°C Per 1000 meter
C. 6.5°C Per 1000 meter
D. 5.5°C Per 1000 meter

111. Match List-I with List-II identify the **correct** answer from code given below:

List-I	List-II
(*a*) Political Science is an Art	(*i*) Gettel
(*b*) Political Science is combination of Art, Philosophy and Science	(*ii*) Bluntschi
(*c*) Political Science is Science of State	(*iii*) Easton
(*d*) Politics authoritative allocation of value	(*iv*) Catlin

Code:

	(*a*)	(*b*)	(*c*)	(*d*)
A.	(*i*)	(*ii*)	(*iii*)	(*iv*)
B.	(*ii*)	(*iv*)	(*i*)	(*iii*)
C.	(*iii*)	(*ii*)	(*i*)	(*iv*)
D.	(*ii*)	(*iii*)	(*iv*)	(*i*)

112. Who was the Governor of R.B.I. at the time of implementation of New Economic Reforms (LPG-1991) in India?
A. Manmohan Singh B. C. Rangrajan
C. S. Venkataraman D. Amitabh Ghosh

113. Himachal Himalaya is also known as:
A. The Himadri B. The Lesser Himalaya
C. The Outer Himalaya D. The Trans Himalaya

114. Speaker of the Lok Sabha addresses his/her resignation to:
A. President of India
B. Chief Justice of India
C. Deputy Speaker of Lok Sabha
D. Vice President of India

115. Al-Biruni's 'Kitab-ul-Hind' is written in which of the following language?
A. Persian B. Arabic
C. Turkish D. Urdu

116. Which one of the following is not correctly matched with the standardization marks related to consumer protection?

A. Agmark	—	Food Products
B. Ecomark	—	Domestic Consumer Products
C. Hallmark	—	Precious Metals
D. Woolmark	—	Cotton and Silk Fabric

117. Which of the following statements is/are **true**?
(*i*) Dietrich Brandis became the country's first Inspector General of Forests during the British era.
(*ii*) The Imperial Forest Research Institute was set up at Dehradun in 1905.
(*iii*) In the Forest Act of 1878 the forests were divided into two categories.
Code:
A. Only (*i*) B. Only (*iii*)
C. (*i*), (*ii*) and (*iii*) D. (*i*) and (*ii*)

118. Who gave the scarcity centred definitions of economics?
A. Marshall B. Robbins
C. Samuelson D. Robinson

119. Which one is **not** kind of Max Weber's legitination view?
A. Legal Authority
B. Power Authority
C. Traditional Authority
D. Charismatic Authority

120. Which of the statement are true about globalization?
A. Globalization is purely economic phenomenon
B. Globalization began in 1991
C. Globalization is the same as westernization
D. Globalization is a dimensional phenomenon

121. Which one of the following is not a terrestrial planet?
A. Venus B. Mars
C. Jupiter D. Mercury

122. Which of the following is **not** cause of origin of Earthquakes?
A. Vulcanicity B. Oceanic Waves
C. Faulting D. Hydrostatic Pressure

123. Who was the third Speaker of Lok Sabha?
A. Sardar Hukum Singh
B. Shree G.S. Dhillon
C. Shree N. Sanjeeva Reddy
D. Shree Baliram Bhagat

124. The **correct** decreasing order of the following Oceans according to the area is:
A. Pacific > Indian > Atlantic > Arctic
B. Pacific > Atlantic > Indian > Arctic
C. Pacific > Atlantic > Arctic > Indian
D. Atlantic > Pacific > Indian > Arctic

125. In which article of Indian Constitution the composition of Panchayats is described?
A. Article 243 B. Article 243-A
C. Article 243-B D. Article 243-C

126. What is the sequence of improvement in the concept of economic development?
(*a*) Income
(*b*) Per Capita Income
(*c*) PQLI
(*d*) HDI

Which sequence is **correct**?
A. (*a*), (*b*), (*c*), (*d*) B. (*a*), (*c*), (*b*), (*d*)
C. (*a*), (*d*), (*b*), (*c*) D. (*b*), (*c*), (*d*), (*a*)

127. Match List-I with List-II and identify the **correct** answer from the code given below:

List-I (Committee)	**List-II** (Year)
(*a*) Ashok Mehta Committee	(*i*) 1986
(*b*) L.M. Singhvi Committee	(*ii*) 1978
(*c*) John Mathai Committee	(*iii*) 1953-54
(*d*) Santhanam Committee	(*iv*) 1963

Code:

	(*a*)	(*b*)	(*c*)	(*d*)
A.	(*i*)	(*ii*)	(*iii*)	(*iv*)
B.	(*i*)	(*iii*)	(*ii*)	(*iv*)
C.	(*ii*)	(*i*)	(*iii*)	(*iv*)
D.	(*i*)	(*ii*)	(*iv*)	(*iii*)

128. Who constitutes the Finance Commission for Panchayat to review the financial position?
A. Parliament B. Legislature
C. President D. Governor

129. Which one of the following is an violent and explosive type volcanoes?

A. Hawaiin B. Strombolian
C. Vulcanian D. Pelean

130. Which of the following is not function of Reserve Bank of India?
A. Creation of Credit
B. Credit Control
C. Monetary Policy
D. Issue of Currency Notes

131. Who decides the emoluments, allowances and privileges of Governor?
A. President
B. Comptroller and Auditor General
C. Voter
D. Parliament

132. Which of the following rulers is the builder of 'Nishumbhasudini' Devi Temple?
A. Vijayalaya Chola B. Rajraj-I
C. Rajendra-II D. Pulakeshin-II

133. 'Vetti' in the Chola period was:
A. Group of Merchants B. A sea port
C. A kind of tax D. A royal ritual

134. Which of the following comment is **inconsistent,** with respect to H.D.I.?
A. H.D.I. stands for 'Hunger Development Index', which also presented as Rank.
B. It is using purchasing power parity method.
C. Life expectancy at birth denotes average expected length of life of a person at the time of birth
D. H.D.I. includes income, health and education.

135. 'Meanders' are formed through erosion of which agent?
A. River B. Wind
C. Sea Waves D. Underground water

136. Which one of the following is **not** correctly matched?
A. Mahadandanayaka — Chief Judicial Officer
B. Nagara-Shreshthi — Chief Banker/merchant
C. Uprik — Chief Craftsman
D. Sarthavaha — Leader of the merchant caravans

137. Which economist first studied poverty in India and indicated a decrease in the percentage of rural poor between 1956-1968?
A. B.M. Dandekar B. B.S. Minhas
C. D.T. Lakkarwala D. M.S. Ahluwalia

138. The **correct** chronology of the conquests of Alauddin Khilji is:
(*i*) Conquest of Chittorgarh
(*ii*) Conquest of Gujarat
(*iii*) Conquest of Ranthambore
(*iv*) Second Campaign of Devgiri

Code:
A. (*ii*), (*iii*), (*i*), (*iv*) B. (*iii*), (*i*), (*ii*), (*iv*)
C. (*ii*), (*i*), (*iii*), (*iv*) D. (*i*), (*iv*), (*iii*), (*ii*)

139. Which one of the following mountain is **not** located in Europe?
A. Atlas B. Alps
C. Black forest D. Apennines

140. Match List-I with List-II and select the **correct** answer using code given below:

List-I (Archeological Sites)	List-II (Excavator)
(*a*) Sutkagan Dor	(*i*) George F. Dales
(*b*) Bhagwanpura	(*ii*) S.R. Rao
(*c*) Balakot	(*iii*) Aurel Stein
(*d*) Lothal	(*iv*) J.P. Joshi

Code:

	(*a*)	(*b*)	(*c*)	(*d*)
A.	(*ii*)	(*iii*)	(*i*)	(*iv*)
B.	(*iii*)	(*iv*)	(*i*)	(*ii*)
C.	(*iii*)	(*i*)	(*ii*)	(*iv*)
D.	(*iii*)	(*i*)	(*iv*)	(*ii*)

141. What is the order of contribution of different sectors to GDP of India?
A. Tertiary > Secondary > Primary
B. Tertiary > Primary > Secondary
C. Primary > Secondary > Tertiary
D. Primary > Tertiary > Secondary

142. What is the meaning of word 'sustainable development'?
A. Rapid development
B. Agricultural development
C. Industrial development
D. Economic development with environment protection

143. In which part of Indian Constitution the Union and the States Administrative Relations are mentioned?
A. Part XIX, Chapter-II
B. Part XI, Chapter-III
C. Part XI, Chapter-I
D. All options are wrong

144. From which of the following archeological sites pit-houses have been found?
A. Damdma B. Burzahom
C. Chopani Mando D. Shortugai

145. In which of the following inscriptions of Ashoka his name 'Ashoka' has been mentioned?
A. Ahraura Inscription B. Nettur Inscription
C. Bhabru Inscription D. Rupnath Inscription

146. Vice-President of India is elected by:
A. Members of all Legislatures
B. Members of Parliament

C. Only members of Rajya Sabha
D. All options are right

147. Which is the most backward state in Female literacy in India, as per census-2011?
A. Haryana B. Bihar
C. Rajasthan D. Jharkhand

148. Which one of the following is not correctly matched?
A. Tropic of Cancer — 23½° N
B. Tropic of Capricorn — 23½° S
C. Prime Meridian — 90° Eastern Longitude
D. International Date Line — 180° East and 180° West Longitude

149. Which statement is **not** true a 'HAFED':
A. 'HAFED' sands for Haryana Agricultural Farm Educational Department.
B. HAFED is the largest apex cooperative union in the state of Haryana.
C. HAFED came into existence 1 November, 1966.
D. HAFED plans to open 'Hafed Markets' in all the districts of Haryana.

150. In which Constitution Amendment the new words are added in Preamble of Indian Constitution?
A. 42nd B. 44th
C. 52nd D. 86th

Answers

1. (C)	**2. (A)**	**3. (D)**	**4. (A)**
5. (B)	**6. (C)**	**7. (B)**	**8. (A)**
9. (D)	**10. (D)**	**11. (B)**	**12. (A)**
13. (B & D)	**14. (A)**	**15. (C)**	**16. (C)**
17. (D)	**18. (B)**	**19. (A)**	**20. (B)**
21. (B)	**22. (B)**	**23. (A)**	**24. (A)**
25. (C)	**26. (B)**	**27. (C)**	**28. (B)**
29. (D)	**30. (C)**	**31. (D)**	**32. (C)**
33. (D)	**34. (B)**	**35. (B)**	**36. (B)**
37. (B)	**38. (A)**	**39. (C)**	**40. (C)**
41. (D)	**42. (A)**	**43. (C)**	**44. (D)**
45. (B)	**46. (B)**	**47. (B)**	**48. (A)**
49. (D)	**50. (D)**	**51. (B)**	**52. (D)**
53. (C)	**54. (C)**	**55. (A)**	**56. (A)**
57. (D)	**58. (C)**	**59. (A)**	**60. (C)**

61. (C): Given, $l + b + h = 19$ cm

$\Rightarrow \quad (l + b + h)^2 = (19)^2$

$\Rightarrow l^2 + b^2 + h^2 + 2(lb + bh + lh) = 361 \text{ cm}^2 \quad ...(i)$

and given, principal diagonal $= 5\sqrt{5}$ cm

$\Rightarrow \quad \sqrt{l^2 + b^2 + h^2} = 5\sqrt{5}$ cm

$\Rightarrow \quad l^2 + b^2 + h^2 = 125 \text{ cm}^2 \quad ...(ii)$

From (i) and (ii)

$125 + 2(lb + bh + lh) = 361$

$\Rightarrow \quad 2(lb + bh + lh) = 361 - 125$

$\Rightarrow \quad 2(lb + bh + lh) = 236 \text{ cm}^2$

Hence, the surface area $= 236 \text{ cm}^2$.

62. (A): Given, in a row of boys

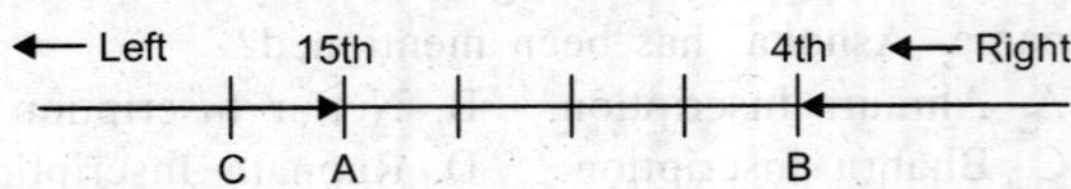

A = 15th from the left
B = 4th from the right
C = first left of A

and 3 boys between A and B

Hence, the position of C from the right $= 4 + 3 + 2 = 9$th

63. (D): Among five persons

C > B > D > A > E

Hence, E is the shortest among them.

64. (B): A train to cover distance = 140 + 260 = 400 m

and speed of the train = 60 km/hr

$$= 60 \times \frac{5}{18} \text{ m/s} = 10 \times \frac{5}{3} = \frac{50}{3} \text{ m/s}$$

∴ Train will take time to pass a platform

$$= \frac{400}{\frac{50}{3}} = \frac{400 \times 3}{50} = 24 \text{ seconds.}$$

65. (C): Let x units and y units of alloy were taken out from each alloy.

Then copper and tin in the first alloy will be $\frac{1}{4}x$ and $\frac{3}{4}x$ while in the second alloy, copper and tin will be $\frac{2}{7}y$ and $\frac{5}{7}y$ respectively.

From the question,

$$\frac{\frac{1}{4}x + \frac{2}{7}y}{\frac{3}{4}x + \frac{5}{7}y} = \frac{3}{8} \text{ or } \frac{7x + 8y}{21x + 20y} = \frac{3}{8}$$

or, $56x + 64y = 63x + 60y$

or, $7x = 4y$

or, $\frac{x}{y} = \frac{4}{7}$

Hence, $x : y = 4 : 7$.

66. (B): Here, M_1 = 6 women, d_1 = 12 days, h_1 = 7 hours, w_1 = 1 and $M_2 = 3 + 10 \times \frac{6}{4} = 3 + 15 = 18$ women, d_2 = ?, h_2 = 8 hours, w_2 = 2

[4 men = 6 women ⇒ 1 men = $\frac{6}{4}$ women]

$\because \quad \frac{M_1 d_1 h_1}{w_1} = \frac{M_2 d_2 h_2}{w_2}$

$\Rightarrow \quad \frac{6 \times 12 \times 7}{1} = \frac{18 \times d_2 \times 8}{2}$

$\Rightarrow \quad d_2 = \frac{6 \times 12 \times 7}{9 \times 8} = 7$ days.

67. (C): Given, $x = \frac{1}{1+\sqrt{2}}$

$= \frac{1}{1+\sqrt{2}} \times \frac{\sqrt{2}-1}{\sqrt{2}-1} = \frac{\sqrt{2}-1}{2-1} = \left(\sqrt{2}-1\right)$

$\therefore x^2 = \left(\sqrt{2}-1\right)^2 = 2+1-2\sqrt{2} = 3-2\sqrt{2}$

$x^2 + 2x + 3 = 3-2\sqrt{2}+2\left(\sqrt{2}-1\right)+3$

$= 3-2\sqrt{2}+2\sqrt{2}-2+3$

$= 6 - 2 = 4.$

68. (B):

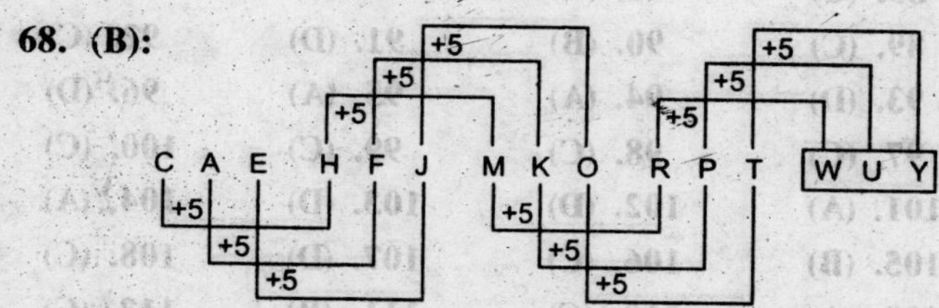

Hence, the next term = WUY.

69. (D): Given, the length of a wire = 66 m

= 66 × 100 cm = 6600 cm

∴ Circumference = 6600 cm

and circumference of small circle = 1.32 cm

∴ The required number of circumferene

$= \frac{6600}{1.32} = 5000.$

70. (B): Let the two numbers are x and $(520 - x)$

The smaller number = x, bigger number = $(520 - x)$

Then, $(520 - x) \times \frac{100-4}{100} = x \times \frac{100+12}{100}$

$\Rightarrow \quad 96(520 - x) = 112x$

$\Rightarrow 96 \times 520 - 96x = 112x$

$\Rightarrow \quad 208x = 96 \times 520$

$\Rightarrow \quad x = \frac{96 \times 520}{208}$

$\Rightarrow \quad x = \frac{40 \times 96}{16} = 40 \times 6 = 240$

Hence, the smaller number, $x = 240$.

71. (C): Let the selling price of 1 m cloth = ₹ 1

Then, the selling price of 33 m cloth = ₹ 33

∴ Profit = Selling price of 11 m cloth = ₹ 11

∴ The cost price of 33 m cloth

= 33 − 11 = ₹ 22

Hence, the profit percentage = $\frac{\text{Profit} \times 100}{\text{C.P.}}$

$= \frac{11 \times 100}{22} = 50\%.$

72. (B):

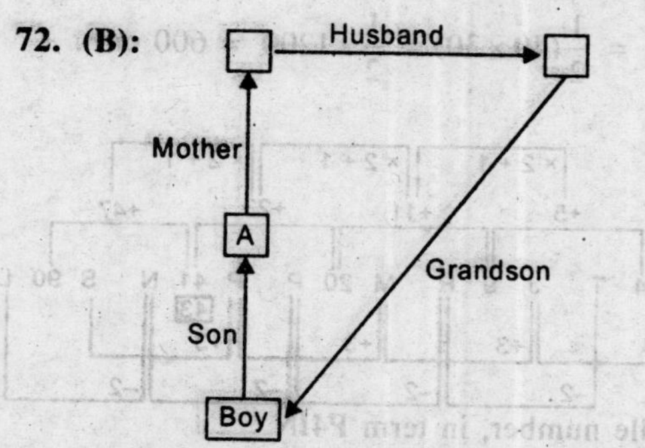

Here, The Boy is the son of A.

73. (C)

74. (A): Given, P = ₹ 5000, r = 12% p.a., t = 2 years

∴ Compound interest

$= P\left(1+\frac{r}{100}\right)^n - P = P\left[\left(1+\frac{r}{100}\right)^n - 1\right]$

$= 5000\left[\left(1+\frac{12}{100}\right)^2 - 1\right] = 5000\left[\left(\frac{28}{25}\right)^2 - 1\right]$

$= 5000\left[\frac{784}{625} - 1\right] = 5000\left[\frac{159}{625}\right]$

= 8 × 159 = ₹ 1272

and Simple interest = $\frac{Prt}{100} = \frac{5000 \times 12 \times 2}{100}$

= 50 × 24 = ₹ 1200

Hence, the required difference = C.I. = S.I.

= ₹ 1272 − ₹ 1200 = ₹ 72.

75. (B): Given, the perimeter of a rhombus = 100 cm

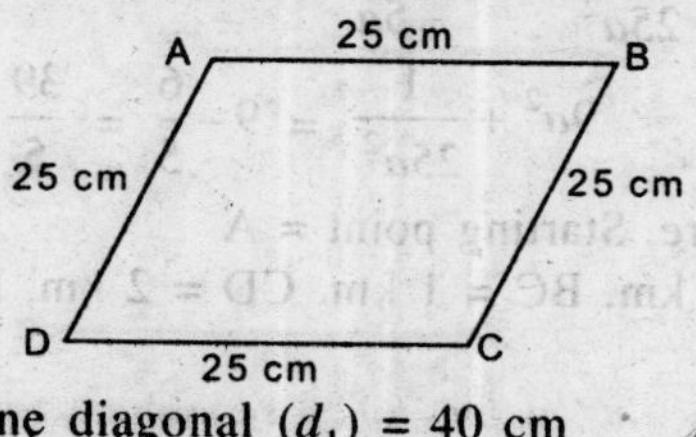

One diagonal (d_1) = 40 cm

$\left(\frac{d_1}{2}\right)^2 + \left(\frac{d_2}{2}\right)^2 = (25)^2$

$\Rightarrow \quad (20)^2 + \left(\frac{d_2}{2}\right)^2 = 625$

$\Rightarrow \quad \left(\frac{d_2}{2}\right)^2 = 625 - 400$

$\Rightarrow \quad \left(\frac{d_2}{2}\right)^2 = 225$

$\Rightarrow \quad \left(\frac{d_2}{2}\right)^2 = (15)^2$

$\Rightarrow \quad \frac{d_2}{2} = 15 \Rightarrow d^2 = 30$ cm.

$\therefore$ Area of the rhombus $= \frac{1}{2}(d_1 \times d_2)$

$= \frac{1}{2}(40 \times 30) = \frac{1}{2} \times 1200 = 600 \text{ cm}^2.$

76. (C):

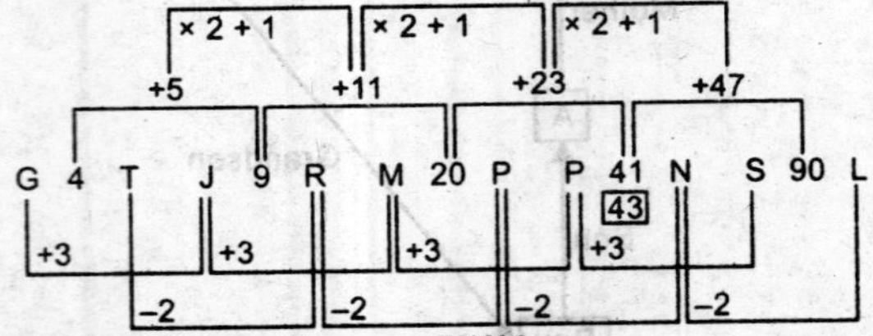

For middle number, in term P4IN
Place of 41 should be 43
Hence, the wrong term P4IN.

77. (A): Given, W = 23
STRONG = 93
$\Rightarrow$ 19 + 20 + 18 + 15 + 14 + 7 = 93
Similarly, WEAK = 23 + 5 + 1 + 11
$\Rightarrow$ WEAK = 40.

78. (D)

79. (D): Given, $5a + \frac{1}{3a} = 5$

Multiplying both by $\frac{3}{5}$

$\therefore \quad \frac{3}{5}\left(5a + \frac{1}{3a}\right) = 5 \times \frac{3}{5}$

$\Rightarrow \quad 3a + \frac{1}{5a} = 3$

Squaring both sides,

$9a^2 + \frac{1}{25a^2} + 2.3a.\frac{1}{5a} = 9$

$\Rightarrow \quad 9a^2 + \frac{1}{25a^2} = 9 - \frac{6}{5} = \frac{39}{5}.$

80. (A): Here, Starting point = A
AB = 2 km, BC = 1 km, CD = 2 km, DE = 4 km

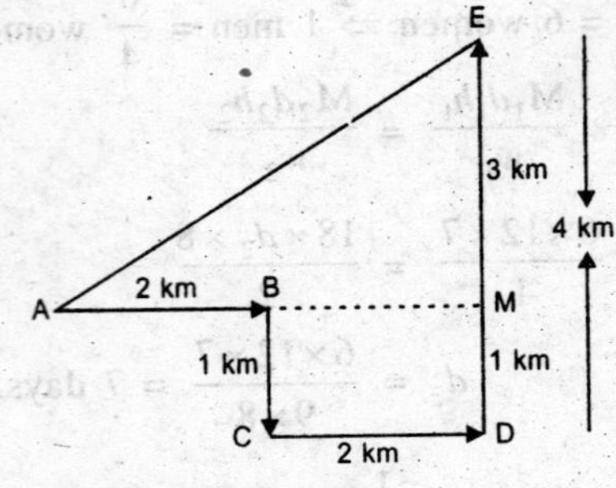

CD = BM = 2 km
BC = DM = 1 km
ME = DE – DM = 4 – 1 = 3 km
and AM = AB + BM = 2 + 2 = 4 km
$\because \quad EA^2 = ME^2 + AM^2$
$\therefore \quad EA^2 = 3^2 + 4^2 = 9 + 16 = 25 = 5^2$
$\Rightarrow \quad EA^2 = 5^2 \Rightarrow EA = 5$ km
Hence, He is 5 km far from his starting point (A).

81. (D)	**82. (A)**	**83. (D)**	**84. (B)**
85. (C)	**86. (A)**	**87. (C)**	**88. (C)**
89. (C)	**90. (B)**	**91. (D)**	**92. (C)**
93. (D)	**94. (A)**	**95. (A)**	**96. (D)**
97. (C)	**98. (C)**	**99. (C)**	**100. (C)**
101. (A)	**102. (D)**	**103. (D)**	**104. (A)**
105. (B)	**106. (C)**	**107. (D)**	**108. (C)**
109. (A)	**110. (C)**	**111. (B)**	**112. (C)**
113. (B)	**114. (C)**	**115. (B)**	**116. (D)**
117. (A)	**118. (B)**	**119. (B)**	**120. (D)**
121. (C)	**122. (B)**	**123. (A)**	**124. (B)**
125. (D)	**126. (A)**	**127. (C)**	**128. (D)**
129. (D)	**130. (A)**	**131. (D)**	**132. (A)**
133. (C)	**134. (A)**	**135. (A)**	**136. (C)**
137. (B)	**138. (A)**	**139. (A)**	**140. (B)**
141. (A)	**142. (D)**	**143. (D)**	**144. (B)**
145. (B)	**146. (B)**	**147. (B)**	**148. (C)**
149. (A)	**150. (A)**		

Previous Paper (Solved)

Haryana Teacher Eligibility Test (HTET)

TGT Social Studies (Level-2), Exam 2020

(Exam held on 3 January, 2021)

PART-I

Child Development and Pedagogy

Directions: *Answer the following questions by selecting the* ***most appropriate*** *option.*

1. Which of the following is ***not*** the main law of learning as prescribed by Thorndike?
A. Law of Exercise
B. Law of Effect
C. Law of Readiness
D. Law of Generalization

2. Who first introduced the word 'Emotional Intelligence'?
A. Fredrick and Kirk
B. Henry and Peter
C. John and Cronback
D. Mayer and Salovey

3. Which of the following approach is based on analysing the behaviour of disabled child and find out the root cause of his/her learning deficiency?
A. Psychoanalytic approach
B. Behavioural approach
C. Individualized instructional approach
D. Multisensory approach

4. Who first introduced the concept of "Latent Learning"?
A. Kurt Lewin
B. E.L. Thorndike
C. Edward Chace Tolman
D. Pavlov

5. Who was the main propounder of 'functionalism'?
A. William James B. J.B. Watson
C. Clark Hull D. Edward Tolman

6. Which of the following is example of Innate Motive?
A. Award B. Hunger
C. Punishment D. Incentives

7. In which stage of development, the sexual changes that occur in the child's body starts to appear?
A. Early childhood B. Later Adolescence
C. Adulthood D. Puberty

8. What is the other name of classical conditioning?
A. Type S conditioning
B. Type R conditioning
C. Type S-R conditioning
D. Type U conditioning

9. What is age group given by Erikson for the stage "industry vs inferiority"?
A. 6 to 11 years
B. 12 to 20 years
C. 3 to 6 years
D. 18 months to 3 years

10. Out of the following which is ***not*** correct principle of 'Development'?
A. Principle of continuity
B. Principle of individual difference
C. Principle of uniformity of pattern
D. Principle of proceeding from specific to general responses

11. Which of the 'thoughts of school' in Psychology is also called as 'Black box theory'?
A. Behaviourism B. Structuralism
C. Functionalism D. Gestaltism

12. Which of the following is ***not*** the characteristic of Good Mental Health?
A. Ability to adjust B. Emotional Maturity
C. Self-confidence D. Intolerance

13. Scale I in Cattell Culture Free Intelligence Test was prepared for whom?
A. For 8 to 12 years mental deficient person
B. For 4 to 8 years mental deficient person
C. For 12 to 15 years mental deficient person
D. For 2 to 4 years mental deficient person

14. Which of the following is the ***correct*** logical order for 'process of creativity'?
A. Insight → Preparation → Incubation → Verification
B. Preparation → Insight → Incubation → Verification
C. Preparation → Incubation → Insight → Verification
D. Preparation → Insight → Verification → Incubation

15. Which of the following terms is ***not*** related with the operant conditioning?
A. Insight
B. Reinforcement
C. Spontaneous Recovery
D. Extinction

16. Who introduces 'Learning Disable' word very first for the children suffered from various learning problems?
A. Heward B. Samuel Kirk
C. Van Riper D. Birch

17. Which of the following Psychologist is ***not*** supporter of views about "Psychology as a Science of Soul"?
A. Plato B. Aristotle
C. Descartes D. Wundt

18. In which branch of Psychology there is a scope of study of Telepathy, Rebirth etc.?
A. Physiological Psychology
B. Clinical Psychology
C. Parapsychology
D. Developmental Psychology

19. According to Jean Piaget in which stage child is able to understand Hypothesis and getting thinking ability on the basis of logical statement?
A. 0 to 2 years B. 2 to 6 years
C. 6 to 11 years D. 11 to 15 years

20. Which of the following Psychology studies about man's thinking, memory, language, perception etc.?
A. Humanist Psychology
B. Cognitive Psychology
C. Abnormal Psychology
D. Clinical Psychology

21. Which of the following is ***not*** the type of personality given by Kretschmer?
A. Athletic B. Aesthetic
C. Asthenic D. Pyknic

22. What is the age group for the moral development stage "Heteronomy Reciprocity" given by Jean Piaget?
A. 0 to 5 years B. 13 to 18 years
C. 5 to 8 years D. 11 to 13 years

23. Which of the following is ***not*** the characteristic of Learning Disabled Children?
A. Perceptual effectiveness
B. Emotional instability
C. Disorder of attention
D. Impulsivity

24. What is the I.Q. Range of severe mental retarded child?
A. 50 to 60 B. 36 to 51
C. 20 to 35 D. below 20

25. In which stage of development, interest/friendship develops towards same sexual groups?
A. 12 to 14 years B. 15 to 18 years
C. 10 to 12 years D. 19 to 21 years

26. Which of the following is ***not*** the type of Realistic thinking?
A. Convergent thinking B. Creative thinking
C. Evaluative thinking D. Autistic thinking

27. Out of the following which psychologist was ***not*** supporter of 'Humanist Psychology'?
A. Freud B. Maslow
C. Rogers D. Arthur Combs

28. Who was the propounder of 'structuralism'?
A. William James B. William West
C. Wilhelm Wundt D. Wilhelm Hunt

29. Which of the following component is ***not*** related with the 'Motivation Cycle'?
A. Need B. Drive
C. Emotion D. Incentive

30. The 'emotion of fear' associated with which basic instinct?
A. Repulsion B. Pugnacity
C. Appeal D. Escape

PART-II

भाषा : हिन्दी

निर्देशः *निम्नलिखित प्रश्नों के उत्तर देने के लिए* ***सबसे उचित*** *विकल्प चुनिए।*

31. किस वाक्य में संबंधसूचक अव्यय का प्रयोग हुआ है?
A. राधा ऊपर नाचती है।
B. अनिता राधा से मधुर गाती है।
C. राम बहुत तेज चल रहा था।
D. मोहन आजकल ज्यादा बोलता है।

32. 'अक' प्रत्यय युक्त पद ***नहीं*** है :
A. विधायक B. प्रेरक
C. निंदक D. लड़ाक

33. किस विकल्प में नित्य पुल्लिंग संज्ञा है?
A. खरगोश B. गिलहरी
C. बटेर D. कोयल

34. समास विग्रह की दृष्टि से ***अनुचित*** विकल्प चुनिए :
A. मातृभक्ति = माता के लिए भक्ति
B. वाग्वीर = वाक् (वाणी) में वीर
C. इन्द्रियजय = इन्द्रियों के लिए जय
D. जीवदया = जीवों पर दया

35. ***गलत*** समास विग्रह चुनिए :
A. दूर के लिए दर्शन = दूरदर्शन
B. दूर से आगत = दूरागत
C. पाठ के लिए शाला = पाठशाला
D. सभा के लिए मण्डप = सभामण्डप

36. नामधातु क्रिया ***नहीं*** है :
A. लतियाना
B. सजाना
C. झुठलाना
D. गलियाना

37. वर्णोच्चारण की दृष्टि से ***बेमेल*** चुनिए :
A. ओ, औ - कंठोष्ठ
B. व, फ - दन्तोष्ठ
C. द, ध - तालु
D. ठ, ड - मूर्धा

38. किस विकल्प में 'अनु' उपसर्ग का प्रयोग ***नहीं*** हुआ है?
A. अनुस्वार
B. अनुषंग
C. अनुदार
D. अनुशास्ति

39. वार्तनिक दृष्टि से ***अशुद्ध*** शब्द चुनिए :
A. तिरपन
B. अजमाइश
C. अन्त्याक्षरी
D. छिपकली

40. अनिश्चयवाचक सर्वनाम वाला वाक्य चुनिए :
A. मैं कुछ पुस्तकें लाया हूँ, इन्हें तुम रख लो।
B. दाल में कुछ काला है।
C. केवल वही तुम्हारी प्रशंसा कर सकता है।
D. वह चाहता है कि तुम सदैव आगे बढ़ो।

41. 'सु' उपसर्ग-रहित पद चुनिए :
A. सुषुप्ति
B. स्वस्थ
C. स्वल्प
D. सौष्ठव

42. किस शब्द में व्यंजन सन्धि का प्रयोग हुआ है?
A. वागीश्वर
B. धातूष्मा
C. अधमर्ण
D. पूर्णोपमा

43. संधि विच्छेद की दृष्टि से ***असंगत*** चुनिए :
A. फणि + इन्द्र = फणीन्द्र
B. सुधी + इन्द्र = सुधीन्द्र
C. अभि + इष्ट = अभीष्ट
D. रजनी + ईश = रजनीश

44. "टहलना स्वास्थ्य के लिए लाभकारी है।" वाक्य में प्रयुक्त क्रिया है :
A. प्रेरणार्थक क्रिया
B. संयुक्त क्रिया
C. रंजक क्रिया
D. क्रियार्थक संज्ञा

45. प्रत्यय की दृष्टि से ***असंगत*** विकल्प चुनिए :
A. हथ + औड़ी = हथौड़ी
B. अणु + इक = आणविक
C. साँप + ओला = सँपोला
D. भाँग + एड़ी = भँगेड़ी

Language : English

Directions: *Answer the following questions by selecting the **most appropriate** option.*

46. Choose the part of the sentence which is ***incorrect***:
(*a*) His/(*b*) new film/(*c*) is really worth/(*d*) to be seen.
A. (*a*)
B. (*b*)
C. (*c*)
D. (*d*)

47. Select the ***appropriate*** modal for the expression given:
When .... we expect you? (possibility)
A. may
B. will
C. have to
D. dare

48. Select the ***correct*** option (phrasal verb) for the underlined word:
Most of the patients respect Dr. John for his kindness.
A. pay back
B. zest for
C. make over
D. look up to

49. Choose the ***correct*** meaning of the underlined words:
The baby monkeys ran every which way.
A. up
B. straight
C. in different directions
D. down

50. Choose the ***correct*** tense form:
Nanny died last week. She .... from cancer for some time. (suffer)
A. suffering
B. is suffering
C. had been suffering
D. suffers

51. Select the ***appropriate*** modal for the expression given:
If you do that again you .... be punished. (threat)
A. may
B. shall
C. can
D. ought

52. Choose the ***correct*** option for the following:
An instrument for detecting earthquakes is:
A. A Fathometer
B. Lithoscope
C. A Seismograph
D. Cardiograph

53. Choose the ***correct*** meaning of the underlined words:
It's a pity you don't like football. But each to their own.
A. everyone has different opinions
B. everyone has similar opinions
C. each and all are same
D. each one likes football

54. Choose the ***correct*** option to fill the blank :
Immediately after the operation he could see nothing .... vague shadows.
A. as long as
B. however
C. but
D. notwithstanding

55. Select the ***correct*** option (phrasal verb) for the underlined word:

I don't know how we are going to cope with the cold during winters.

A. make up for B. put up with
C. put down D. set up

56. Select ***appropriate*** preposition to fill in the blank:

They walked .... the footpath until they came to a bridge.

A. into B. since
C. along D. in

57. Choose the ***correct*** tense form :

My car .... for the third time since I got it. (break down)

A. break down
B. has broken down
C. was broke down
D. has broken

58. Choose the part of the sentence which is ***incorrect*** :

(*a*) James/(*b*) is busy/(*c*) to prepare/(*d*) tonight's dinner.

A. (*a*) B. (*b*)
C. (*c*) D. (*d*)

59. Choose the ***correct*** option to fill the blank :

The room was empty .... for a chair in the corner.

A. except B. and
C. between D. behind

60. Select ***appropriate*** preposition to fill in the blank :

The programme was broadcasted ...... the world.

A. in B. off
C. onto D. across

PART-III

General Studies : Quantitative Aptitude, Reasoning Ability and GK & Awareness

Directions: *Answer the following questions by selecting* ***the most appropriate*** *option.*

61. Among five persons P, Q, R, S and T, T is shorter than R and S. Q is not as tall as T but taller than one person. R is shorter than one person.

Who among them is the tallest?

A. R B. Q
C. S D. P

62. Three numbers are in the ratio 2 : 3 : 4. The sum of their cubes is 33957, then the numbers are :

A. 14, 21, 28
B. 12, 18, 24
C. 8, 12, 16
D. 4, 6, 8

63. A is father of X; B is mother of Y. The sister of X and Z is Y. Which of the following statement is necessarily not true?

A. B is the mother of Z.
B. X is the sister of Z.
C. B is the wife of A.
D. Y is the son of A.

64. A person walks 1 km towards East and then he turns to South and walks 5 km. Again he turns to East and walks 2 km, after this he turns to North and walks 9 km. Now, how far is he from his starting point?

A. 4 km B. 5 km
C. 7 km D. 9 km

65. Find the next term of the following letter series :

DHL, PTX, BFJ, ...

A. CGK B. KOS
C. NRV D. OVZ

66. 12 men take 18 days to complete a job whereas 12 women in 18 days can complete $\frac{3}{4}$ part of the same job. How many days will 10 men and 8 women together take to complete the same job?

A. 6 B. $7\frac{1}{2}$
C. $13\frac{1}{2}$ D. 14

67. The radius of a sphere is doubled. What per cent of its volume is increased?

A. 200% B. 450%
C. 550% D. 700%

68. A dealer sells an article for ₹ 24 and gains as much per cent as the price of the article, then the cost price of the article is:

A. ₹ 15 B. ₹ 17
C. ₹ 18 D. ₹ 20

69. In a group of 15 people, 7 read Hindi, 8 read English and 3 read none of these language. How many people read Hindi and English both?

A. 0 B. 3
C. 4 D. 5

70. If p and q are rational numbers and $\frac{3+\sqrt{5}}{3-\sqrt{5}} = p + q\sqrt{5}$, then value of p and q are:

A. $p = \frac{2}{7}$; $q = \frac{3}{2}$ B. $p = \frac{7}{2}$; $q = \frac{2}{7}$

C. $p = \frac{7}{2}$; $q = \frac{3}{2}$ D. $p = \frac{7}{2}$; $q = \frac{7}{2}$

71. If the compound interest on a certain sum for two years at 3% p.a. be ₹ 101.50, then what would be the simple interest on the same sum for same period?

A. ₹ 50 B. ₹ 100

C. ₹ 125 D. ₹ 147

72. Find the ***missing*** term of the following letter series :

A, CD, GHI, ? , UVWXY

A. LMNO B. MNO

C. MNOP D. NOPQ

73. One angle of a quadrilateral is 108° and the remaining three angles are equal. Find each of the three equal angles :

A. 63° B. 74°

C. 84° D. 96°

74. Amit is West to Prakash and North to Sumit. Tarun is in East of Sumit. Tarun is in which direction with reference to Amit ?

A. North-West B. South

C. South-East D. North

75. If DRIVER = 12, PEDESTRIAN = 20, ACCIDENT = 16, then CAR = ?

A. 3 B. 6

C. 8 D. 16

76. Find the ***wrong*** number in the following series:

69, 55, 26, 13, 5

A. 5 B. 13

C. 26 D. 55

77. If $2^x = 4^y = 8^z$ and $\frac{1}{2x} + \frac{1}{4y} + \frac{1}{4z} = 4$, then the value of x is:

A. $\frac{7}{16}$ B. $\frac{7}{17}$

C. $\frac{7}{19}$ D. $\frac{7}{23}$

78. In a journey of 80 kms a train covers the first 60 kms at 40 km/hr. and the remaining distance at 20 km/hr. The average speed for the whole journey is:

A. 24 km/hr. B. 30 km/hr.

C. 32 km/hr. D. 36 km/hr.

79. A swimming pool, 30 m long has a depth of water 0.80 m at one end and 2.4 m at the other end. The area of the vertical cross-section of the pool along the length is:

A. 48 m^2 B. 72 m^2

C. 156 m^2 D. 192 m^2

80. Anil is standing at 16th position from the left end in a row. Vikas is at 18th position from the right end. Gopal is 11th from Anil towards the right and 3rd from Vikas towards the right end. How many persons are standing in this row?

A. 41 B. 42

C. 48 D. 49

81. Which of the following are ***true*** about the functions of HAFED?

(*i*) It procures agriculture products.

(*ii*) It markets agriculture products.

(*iii*) It supplies agriculture inputs.

Choose the ***correct*** code :

A. (*i*) and (*ii*) B. only (*i*)

C. (*i*) and (*iii*) D. (*i*), (*ii*) and (*iii*)

82. Where in Haryana 'City-forest' is being developed?

A. Murthal B. Sohna

C. Yamunanagar D. Hansi

83. 'Air Shuttle Service' has been started from which city of Haryana?

A. Hisar B. Karnal

C. Rohtak D. Ambala

84. The President of 'Haryana Sahitya Academy' is:

A. Dr. Kumud Bansal B. Sh. Manohar Lal

C. Dr. Ashok Batra D. Sh. Rana Oberoi

85. Consider the following statements about Minty Agarwal:

(*a*) Minty Agarwal, a native of Haryana, is a Squadron Leader in Indian Air Force.

(*b*) She is the first woman, who received Yudha Seva Medal.

Choose the ***correct*** answer :

A. Statement (*a*) is true

B. Statement (*b*) is true

C. Both (*a*) and (*b*) are false

D. Both (*a*) and (*b*) are true

86. Ancient Bhawani Amba Mata temple is situated in:

A. Jind B. Ambala

C. Sonipat D. Kurukshetra

87. In January 2020, which of the following Nagar Palika was raised to the status of Nagar Parishad (Municipal Council)?

A. Rania B. Jhajjar

C. Beri D. Sirsi

88. Who was the Nawab of Jhajjar during the uprising of 1857?

A. Abd-ur Rahman Khan
B. Nawab Shamsuddin
C. Sadruddin
D. Bisarat Ali

89. The original founding place of Topara Inscription of Ashoka is located in:
A. Ambala district
B. Yamunanagar district
C. Kurukshetra district
D. Kaithal district

90. Identify the rivers, which flows from Mahendragarh district:
(*i*) Ambumati (*ii*) Dohan
(*iii*) Kasavati (*iv*) Indori

Choose the ***correct*** code :
A. (*i*) and (*iii*)
B. (*ii*) and (*iii*)
C. (*i*), (*iii*) and (*iv*)
D. (*i*), (*ii*), (*iii*) and (*iv*)

PART-IV

Social Studies

Directions: *Answer the following questions by selecting the **most appropriate** option.*

91. Professor Muhammad Yunus is the founder of which one of the following banks?
A. Commercial Bank (Pakistan)
B. Co-operative Bank (India)
C. Grameen Bank (Bangladesh)
D. State Bank of India

92. Which one of the following is ***not*** correctly matched?

	Forest	Tree
A.	Monsoon	Sal
B.	Mangrove	Sundari
C.	Tropical Evergreen	Rosewood
D.	Alpine	Teak

93. Which of the following pairs of the list and contents is/are correctly matched?
(*a*) State List : Public Health, Police and Education
(*b*) Union List : Citizenship and Atomic Energy
(*c*) Concurrent List : Marriage and Civil Procedure

Select the ***correct*** answer using the codes given below:
A. Only (*a*) B. (*a*), (*b*) and (*c*)
C. Only (*b*) and (*c*) D. Only (*c*)

94. If the actual unemployment rate is below the natural rate of unemployment, it would be expected that:
A. The rate of inflation would increase
B. Wages would fall
C. Natural rate of unemployment will fall
D. Demands for goods and services will fall

95. The ***correct*** sequence of following passes in Himalaya from West towards East is:
(*a*) Banihal (*b*) Baralacha
(*c*) Bomdila (*d*) Jelep La
A. (*a*), (*c*), (*b*), (*d*) B. (*d*), (*a*), (*b*), (*c*)
C. (*b*), (*a*), (*c*), (*d*) D. (*a*), (*b*), (*d*), (*c*)

96. In which economic system do we find "Consumers' Sovereignty"?
A. Socialism B. Mixed Economy
C. Capitalism D. Communism

97. Which one of the following cities was known as 'Shiraj of East'?
A. Jaunpur B. Agra
C. Lahore D. Lakhnauti

98. Which one of the following is ***not*** a superimposed river?
A. Damodar B. Son
C. Sutlej D. Subarnarekha

99. Which Article of the constitution of India is related to the joint session of the parliament?
A. 72 B. 102
C. 108 D. 111

100. Which one of the following is ***not*** correctly matched?

	Iron ore mines	State / Region
A.	Dalli and Rajhara	Jharkhand
B.	Baba Budan hills	Karnataka
C.	Karimnagar	Telangana
D.	Noamundi and Gua	Jharkhand

101. Who published the "Human Development Report"?
A. B.M.I. B. H.D.I.
C. U.N.D.P. D. World Bank

102. As per census-2011, which state/union territory has highest percent of Muslim peoples religion in its total population?
A. Assam B. Jammu and Kashmir
C. Lakshadweep D. Kerala

103. Democracy is a system of government in which the final power rests with:
A. The mob B. The people
C. The politicians D. The civil service

104. Choose the Indian MNCs Groups:
(*a*) Infosys (*b*) Sun Pharma
(*c*) Tata Motors (*d*) Ford
A. (*a*), (*b*), (*d*) B. (*b*), (*c*), (*d*)
C. (*a*), (*c*), (*d*) D. (*a*), (*b*), (*c*)

105. In winter, western Himalaya receives maximum rainfall through:
A. South-West Monsoon
B. South-East Monsoon
C. Western Depressions
D. Convectional Rainfall

106. The Tarkunde Committee (1975) was concerned with:
A. Inclusive Development
B. Economic Reforms
C. Agriculture Reforms
D. Electoral Reforms

107. Arrange the following events of French Revolution in chronological order and choose the right answer:
(*a*) Fall of Bastille
(*b*) Formation of National Assembly
(*c*) Establishment of the French Republic
(*d*) Declaration of the Rights of man
A. (*b*), (*d*), (*a*), (*c*) B. (*a*), (*b*), (*c*), (*d*)
C. (*b*), (*a*), (*d*), (*c*) D. (*a*), (*b*), (*d*), (*c*)

108. In which session of Congress was the demand of 'Purna Swaraj' formally accepted?
A. Calcutta, 1929 B. Lahore, 1929
C. Lahore, 1930 D. Karachi, 1930

109. Which of the following is ***not*** a central problem of an economy?
A. What to produce?
B. How to produce?
C. For whom to produce?
D. Where to produce?

110. The monetary policy in India is formulated by:
A. Central Government
B. Industrial Financial Corporation of India
C. Reserve Bank of India
D. Industrial Development Bank of India

111. Theory of "Separation of power" was propounded by:
A. Aristotle B. Montesquieu
C. Carl Fedrich D. J.S. Mill

112. Which of the following are the characteristics of federal Government?
(*i*) Division of Powers
(*ii*) Supermacy of the Constitution
(*iii*) Flexible Constitution
(*iv*) Independent Judiciary
Correct option is:
A. (*i*) and (*ii*) B. (*i*), (*ii*) and (*iii*)
C. (*i*), (*ii*) and (*iv*) D. (*i*), (*ii*), (*iii*) and (*iv*)

113. Regional Rural Banks are sponsored by:
A. Nationalised Commercial Bank
B. Reserve Bank of India
C. State Government
D. Government of India

114. During period of inflation, tax rates should:
A. Increase B. Decrease
C. Remain Constant D. Fluctuate

115. NABARD stands for:
A. National Business for Accounting and Reviewing
B. National Bank for Agriculture and Rural Development
C. National Bank for Aeronautics and Radar Development
D. National Bureau for Air and Road Transport

116. Which of the following is the basic cause of cyclical unemployment?
A. A general deficiency in the demand for goods and services
B. The reluctance of workers to move to other parts of the country where work is available
C. The inability to change occupations because of lack of skills
D. Workers' ignorance of opportunities of employment

117. Which section has the provision of "Paid Leave"?
A. Unorganised Sector B. Organised Sector
C. Primary Sector D. None of these

118. W.T.O. basically promotes:
A. Financial Support B. Global Peace
C. Unilateral Trade D. Multilateral Trade

119. The editor of the first Hindi newspaper Udant Martand was:
A. Mahavir Prasad Dwivedi
B. Bharatendu Harishchandra
C. Jugal Kishore Shukla
D. Raja Shivaprasad

120. When was the New Consumer Protection Act implemented in India?
A. 1976 B. 2020
C. 1996 D. 2006

121. Which of the following was ***not*** a part of Lenin's 'April Thesis'?
A. The War be brought to an end
B. Right to vote for all
C. Land be transferred to peasants
D. The Banks be nationalized

122. The winds blow from sub tropical high pressure towards the sub polar low pressure in South-West to North-East direction are called as:
A. North-East Trade Winds
B. Westerlies (Northern Hemisphere)
C. South-East Trade Winds
D. Westerlies (Southern Hemisphere)

123. Match List-I with List-II and select the ***correct*** answer using code given below:

Grasslands	**Region/Country**
(*a*) Pustaz	(*i*) Amazon Basin
(*b*) Compos	(*ii*) Hungary
(*c*) Llanos	(*iii*) Brazilian Plateau
(*d*) Selvas	(*iv*) Orinoco Basin

Codes:

	(*a*)	(*b*)	(*c*)	(*d*)
A.	(*i*)	(*ii*)	(*iii*)	(*iv*)
B.	(*ii*)	(*i*)	(*iv*)	(*iii*)
C.	(*ii*)	(*i*)	(*iii*)	(*iv*)
D.	(*ii*)	(*iii*)	(*iv*)	(*i*)

124. In which year was Nazi Dictatorship established in Germany?
A. 1930 B. 1931
C. 1932 D. 1933

125. Two-party system is found in:
A. France
B. India
C. China
D. U.S.A. (United States of America)

126. Which of the following "Fundamental Rights" is ***not*** included under the Indian Constitution?
A. Right to Freedom
B. Right to work
C. Equality of opportunity in matters of employment
D. Right to protect one's culture

127. 'Diffused Day Light' is:
A. The solar radiation that goes into zero
B. The sun light, earth receives during dawn and twilight
C. The terrestrial radiation
D. The solar radiation received by ozone layer

128. Which one of the following is ***not*** a Metamorphic Rock?
A. Marble B. Quartzite
C. Graphite D. Gabbro

129. The Greenwich Mean Time is the local time at:
A. 180° East Meridian
B. 180° West Meridian
C. 180° East and 180° West both Meridians
D. Prime Meridian

130. Liberals of nineteenth century Europe predominantly belong to which class?
A. Ruling B. Clergy
C. Nobility D. Bourgeois

131. Which one of the following is ***not*** a Earthquake measuring scale?
A. Richter B. Mercalli
C. Rossi-Forel D. Moh

132. In which year did USA join the Second World War?
A. 1939 B. 1940
C. 1941 D. 1942

133. Who has written the book "Freedom From Fear"?
A. Lord Bryce B. Nelson Mandela
C. Aung San Su Kyi D. J.S. Mill

134. 'Sargasso Sea' is located at:
A. North Pacific Ocean
B. South Atlantic Ocean
C. North Atlantic Ocean
D. South Pacific Ocean

135. Match the List-I with List-II and choose the ***correct*** option:

List-I (Invention)	**List-II (Inventor)**
(*i*) Powerloom	(*a*) Samuel F.B. Morse
(*ii*) Telegraph	(*b*) Jethro Tull
(*iii*) Water Frame	(*c*) Edmund Cartwright
(*iv*) Seed drill	(*d*) Richard Arkwright

Codes:

	(*i*)	(*ii*)	(*iii*)	(*iv*)
A.	(*c*)	(*a*)	(*d*)	(*b*)
B.	(*d*)	(*a*)	(*b*)	(*c*)
C.	(*a*)	(*c*)	(*d*)	(*b*)
D.	(*b*)	(*a*)	(*d*)	(*c*)

136. When was Bombay declared the capital of Bombay Presidency?
A. 1801 B. 1810
C. 1819 D. 1829

137. Which one of the following cities in India is located closest to tropic of cancer?
A. Jodhpur B. Ranchi
C. Raipur D. Kolkata

138. Who painted 'Germania–Guarding the Rhine'?
A. Raphael B. Michelangelo
C. Lorenz Clasen D. Leonardo da Vinci

139. Which one of the following is ***not*** correctly matched?

Parts of the Indian Constitution		**Provision**
A. II	–	Citizenship
B. XIX	–	Amendment of the Constitution
C. V	–	The Union
D. XV	–	Elections

140. Which of the following pairs of list and contents is/are correctly matched?

(*a*) Rajni Kothari	:	Caste in Indian Politics
(*b*) Jai Prakash Narayan	:	Caste in India : Their mechanism Genesis and development
(*c*) M.N. Shriniwas	:	Caste in modern India and other Essays

Select the correct answer using the code given below:

A. (*a*) only B. (*a*), (*b*) and (*c*)
C. (*a*) and (*c*) only D. (*b*) only

141. The doctrine of the divine and absolute right of the monarch was refuted by:

A. Rousseau B. Montesquieu
C. John Locke D. Voltaire

142. Match List-I with List-II and select the ***correct*** answer using the codes given below the lists:

List-I	List-II
(*i*) Rastriya Lok Dal	(*a*) United Progressive Alliance
(*ii*) Bhartiya Janata Party	(*b*) Left Front
(*iii*) Congress Party	(*c*) National Democratic Alliance
(*iv*) Communist Party of India (Marxist)	(*d*) State Party

Codes:

	(*i*)	(*ii*)	(*iii*)	(*iv*)
A.	(*c*)	(*a*)	(*d*)	(*b*)
B.	(*d*)	(*b*)	(*a*)	(*c*)
C.	(*b*)	(*c*)	(*a*)	(*d*)
D.	(*d*)	(*c*)	(*a*)	(*b*)

143. Disposable personal income is equal to:

A. Personal income (–) personal direct taxes
B. Net National product (–) personal income
C. Net National product (–) personal income (+) transfer payments
D. Net National product (–) personal income (–) depreciation

144. Electorate means:

A. The body of voters
B. The elected representatives of people
C. The nominated members of parliament
D. The candidates who actually contest the elections

145. Forces considered as obstruction in nationalism in Europe during 19th Century were:

(*a*) Habsburg Monarchy
(*b*) The Intelligentia
(*c*) Ottoman Monarchy
(*d*) Labour Class

Choose the ***correct*** code:

A. (*a*) and (*c*) B. (*a*) and (*b*)
C. (*b*) and (*c*) D. (*a*), (*b*) and (*c*)

146. Two party system is better because:

A. It gives despotic powers to the cabinet.
B. It gives an opportunity to the opposition party to indulge in an irresponsible eroticism of government.
C. It makes smooth changes in government possible.
D. It leads to the formation of coalition government.

147. Gender divisions, we usually refer to:

A. Unequal roles assigned by the society to man and women
B. Unequal child sex ratio
C. Biological difference between men and women
D. Absence of voting rights for women in democracies

148. Choose the correct chronological order of the following events:

(*a*) Champaran Satyagraha
(*b*) Lucknow Pact
(*c*) Kheda Satyagraha
(*d*) Jallianwala Bagh Tragedy

Choose the ***correct*** code:

A. (*c*), (*a*), (*d*), (*b*) B. (*b*), (*a*), (*c*), (*d*)
C. (*b*), (*c*), (*a*), (*d*) D. (*c*), (*d*), (*a*), (*b*)

149. Who among the following early Sociologists established 'New Harmony' a cooperative community in USA?

A. Adam Smith B. Robert Owen
C. Louis Blank D. John Stuart Mill

150. Which one of the following is ***not*** correctly matched?

Volcanic mountains	Country/Place
A. Mt. Agung	Japan
B. Mt. Meyon	Philippines
C. Mt. Merapi	Indonesia
D. Mt. Cotopaxi	Ecuador

Answers

1	2	3	4	5	6	7	8	9	10
D	D	C	C	A	B	D	A	A	D
11	**12**	**13**	**14**	**15**	**16**	**17**	**18**	**19**	**20**
A	D	*	C	A	B	D	C	D	B
21	**22**	**23**	**24**	**25**	**26**	**27**	**28**	**29**	**30**
B	C	A	C	C	D	A	C	C	D
31	**32**	**33**	**34**	**35**	**36**	**37**	**38**	**39**	**40**
B	D	A	C	A	B	C	C	B	B
41	**42**	**43**	**44**	**45**	**46**	**47**	**48**	**49**	**50**
B	A	A	D	A	D	A	D	C	C

51	52	53	54	55	56	57	58	59	60
B	C	A	C	B	C	B	C	A	D
61	62	63	64	65	66	67	68	69	70
C	A	D	B	C	C	D	D	B	C
71	72	73	74	75	76	77	78	79	80
B	C	C	C	B	A	A	C	A	A
81	82	83	84	85	86	87	88	89	90
D	A	A	B	D	B	B	A	B	B
91	92	93	94	95	96	97	98	99	100
C	D	C	A	D	C	A	C	C	A
101	102	103	104	105	106	107	108	109	110
C	C	B	D	C	D	C	B	D	C
111	112	113	114	115	116	117	118	119	120
B	C	A	A	B	A	B	D	C	B
121	122	123	124	125	126	127	128	129	130
B	B	D	D	D	B	B	D	D	D
131	132	133	134	135	136	137	138	139	140
D	C	C	C	A	C	B	C	B	C
141	142	143	144	145	146	147	148	149	150
C	D	A	A	A	C	A	B	B	A

Explanatory Answers

62. Let, numbers are $2x$, $3x$ and $4x$

Then, $(2x)^3 + (3x)^3 + (4x)^3 = 33957$

$\therefore\ 8x^3 + 27x^3 + 64x^3 = 33957$

$\Rightarrow\ 99x^3 = 33957$

$x^3 = \dfrac{33957}{99}$

$= 343$

$= (7)^3$

$\therefore\ x = 7$

Hence, numbers $= 2x, 3x, 4x = 14, 21, 28.$

64.

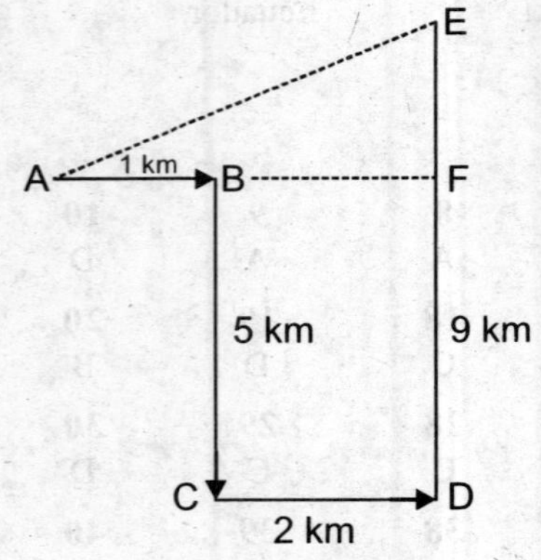

Here, starting point = A

AB = 1 km,

BC = 5 km,

CD = 2 km,

DE = 9 km

$\because$ BC = DF = 5 km

and CD = BF = 2 km

$\therefore$ FE = DE – DF

= DE – BC

= 9 – 5

= 4 km

AF = AB + BF

= 1 + 2

= 3 km

$\because\ AE^2 = (EF)^2 + (FA)^2$

$\Rightarrow\ = 4^2 + 3^2$

$\Rightarrow\ = 16 + 9$

$\Rightarrow\ = 25$

$\Rightarrow\ = 5^2$

$\therefore$ AE = 5 km

Hence, he is 5 km far from his starting point.

65.

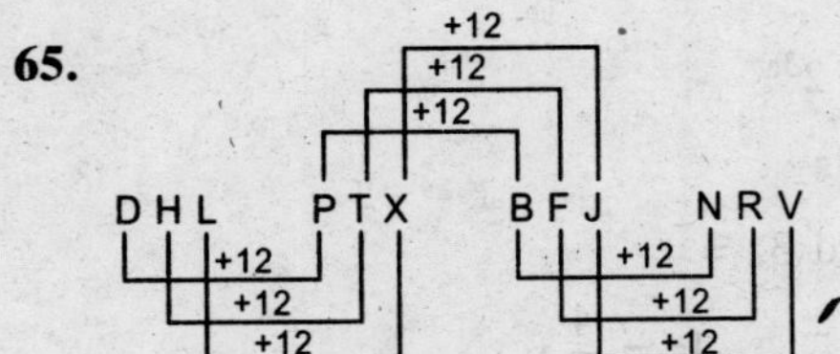

Hence, the next term of the letter series is NRV.

66. ∵ 12 men take 18 days to complete a job.

∴ 1 man's 1 day's job is $\frac{1}{18 \times 12}$

and 12 women complete $\frac{3}{4}$ part of work in 18 days.

∴ 1 women's 1 day's job is $\frac{1}{24 \times 12}$

∴ 10 men and 8 women 1 day work

$$= \frac{10}{18 \times 12} + \frac{8}{24 \times 12}$$

$$= \frac{1}{24}\left[\frac{10}{9} + \frac{8}{12}\right]$$

$$= \frac{1}{24}\left[\frac{40+24}{36}\right]$$

$$= \frac{1}{24}\left[\frac{64}{36}\right]$$

$$= \frac{8}{3 \times 36}$$

$$= \frac{2}{3 \times 9}$$

$$= \frac{2}{27}$$

Hence, required time $= \frac{27}{2}$ days

$= 13\frac{1}{2}$ days.

68. Let the cost price of the article = ₹ x

Then, Profit = Selling Price – Cost Price

∴ Profit = ₹ $24 - x$

∴ $\text{Profit \%} = \frac{\text{Profit} \times 100}{\text{Cost Price}}$

According to the question,

$$x = \frac{(24 - x) \times 100}{x}$$

∴ $x^2 = 2400x - 100x$

$\Rightarrow x^2 + 100x - 2400 = 0$

$\Rightarrow x^2 + 120x - 20x - 2400 = 0$

$\Rightarrow x(x + 120) - 20(x + 120) = 0$

$\Rightarrow (x - 20)(x + 120) = 0$

$\Rightarrow x = 20, x = -120$

Hence, cost price of the article = ₹ 20

69. Let, Hindi = H, and English = E

Then, $n(H) = 7$, $n(E) = 8$

$$n(H \cup E) = 15 - 3 = 12$$

∵ $n(H \cup E) = n(H) + n(E) - n(H \cap E)$

∴ $12 = 7 + 8 - n(H \cap E)$

$\Rightarrow n(H \cap E) = 15 - 12 = 3$

Hence, number of people read both Hindi and English

$= n(H \cap E) = 3$.

71. Let the principal = ₹ P,
Given, $r = 3\%$, Compound interest = ₹ 101.50
and $n = 2$ years

∵ Compound interest $= P\left(1 + \frac{r}{100}\right)^n - P$

$$\Rightarrow \quad 101.50 = P\left(1 + \frac{3}{100}\right)^2 - P$$

$$\Rightarrow \quad 101.50 = P\left[\left(\frac{103}{100}\right)^2 - 1\right]$$

$$\Rightarrow \quad 101.50 = P[(1.03)^2 - 1]$$

$$\Rightarrow \quad 101.50 = P[1.0609 - 1]$$

$$\Rightarrow \quad 101.50 = P[0.0609]$$

$$P = \frac{101.50}{0.0609}$$

$$= \frac{101.5000}{0.0609}$$

$$= ₹\frac{1015000}{609}$$

Then, Simple interest $= \frac{p \times r \times t}{100}$

$$= \frac{\frac{1015000}{609} \times 2 \times 3}{100}$$

$$= \frac{10150 \times 2}{203}$$

$$= \frac{20300}{203}$$

$$= 100$$

Hence, required simple interest = ₹ 100.

73. Let the value of each of the three equal angles = $x°$

Then, sum of four angles of quadrilateral = 360°

$\therefore \quad 108° + 3x = 360°$

$3x = 360 - 108$

$3x = 252$

$x = \frac{252}{3}$

$= 84°$

74. According to question,

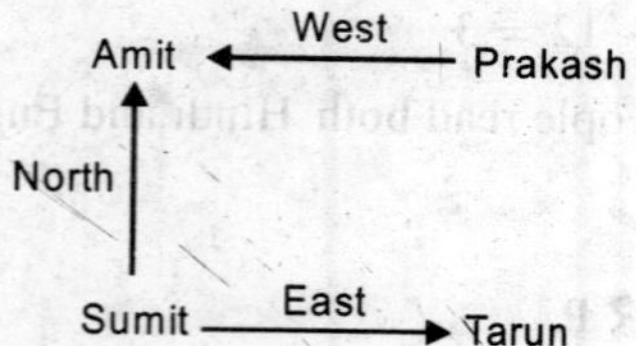

Tarun is in South-East of Amit.

75. Given,

DRIVER = 12,

PEDESTRIAN = 20

ACCIDENT = 16

$\because$ Number of alphabet in DRIVER = 6

Here, number of letters is multiplied by 2

$\therefore \quad 6 \times 2 = 12$

Similarly,

Number of alphabet in PEDESTRIAN = 10

$\therefore \quad 10 \times 2 = 20$

Number of alphabet in ACCIDENT = 8

$\therefore \quad 8 \times 2 = 16$

Similarly,

Number of alphabet in CAR = 3

$\therefore \quad 3 \times 2 = 6$

Hence, CAR = 6.

77. Given, $2^x = 4^y = 8^z$

$\Rightarrow 2^x = 4^y = 2^{3z}$

$\Rightarrow 2^x = 4^{2y} = 2^{3z}$

$\Rightarrow x = 2y = 3z$

$\therefore 4y = 2x$ and $3z = x$

$\Rightarrow \quad 4z = \frac{4}{3}x$

$\therefore \quad \frac{1}{2x} + \frac{1}{4y} + \frac{1}{4z} = 4$

$\Rightarrow \quad \frac{1}{2x} + \frac{1}{2x} + \frac{1}{\frac{4}{3}x} = 4$

$\Rightarrow \quad \frac{1}{2x} + \frac{1}{2x} + \frac{3}{4x} = 4$

$\Rightarrow \quad \frac{1}{x} + \frac{3}{4x} = 4$

$\Rightarrow \quad \frac{4+3}{4x} = 4$

$\Rightarrow \quad \frac{7}{4x} = 4$

$\Rightarrow \quad 7 = 16x$

$\Rightarrow \quad x = \frac{7}{16}$

78. Average speed for the whole journey

$= \frac{80}{\frac{60}{40} + \frac{20}{20}}$ km/hr.

$= \frac{80}{\frac{3}{2} + 1}$

$= \frac{80}{\frac{5}{2}}$

$= 80 \times \frac{2}{5}$

$= 16 \times 2$

$= 32$ km/hr.

Previous Paper (Solved)

Haryana Teacher Eligibility Test (HTET)

TGT Social Studies (Level-2), Exam 2019

(Exam held on 17 November, 2019)

PART-I

Child Development and Pedagogy

Directions: *Answer the following questions by selecting the **most appropriate** option.*

1. Out of the following which activity/area may ***not*** be considered as co-scholastic aspect of learner?
A. Social skill B. Attitude and values
C. Creative skill D. Curricular subjects

2. Out of the following which is ***not*** related with 'Cognition'?
A. Perception B. Thinking
C. Walking D. Concept formation

3. A student learns new concepts such as 'Carnivorous animal' on the basis of words known by him such as tiger, dog, lion, leopard etc. This type of learning is known as what?
A. Combinational learning
B. Subordinate learning
C. Correlative learning
D. Superordinate learning

4. "Children's understanding that their gender will not change even if they adopt the behaviour, dress, or hairstyles of the other gender". This type of children's understanding is known as what?
A. Gender identity B. Gender stability
C. Gender consistency D. Gender stereotypes

5. What is the age group of late childhood stage?
A. 2 to 6 years B. 6 to 12 years
C. 4 to 7 years D. 11 to 15 years

6. Assessment of all-round development of the child's personality is known as which type of evaluation?
A. Continuous evaluation
B. Comprehensive evaluation
C. Above (A) and (B) both
D. Neither (A) nor (B) above

7. According to Bronfrenbrener, law and customs are examples of which of the following ecological system of child?
A. Micro system B. Macro system
C. Meso system D. Exo system

8. Who was the propounder of N.D.I. motivation formula?
A. McDougall B. Hilgard
C. Blair and Jones D. Maslow

9. Out of the following which alternative shows characteristics of "Concrete Operational Stage" given by Jean Piaget?
A. Development of idea of 'cause-effect relationship' and 'object permanence' in children.
B. The child gains understanding of principles such as conservation logical thought emerges.
C. The child begins to represent the world symbolically.
D. Becomes capable of creating several forms of logical thought.

10. Out of the following which is ***not*** the other name of childhood?
A. Elementary school age
B. Smart age
C. Pre-gang age
D. Gang age

11. Who proposed "Sociocultural Theory" of cognitive development?
A. Jean Piaget B. Lev Vygotsky
C. J.S. Bruner D. Kohlberg

12. Which word was used by Thurstone for 'intelligence'?
A. Primary Mental Abilities
B. Universal Mental Abilities
C. Neutral Mental Abilities
D. Higher Mental Abilities

13. Which of the following is ***not*** a defence mechanism?
A. Identification B. Compensation
C. Rationalisation D. Association

14. Which of the following is ***not*** an element of emotional intelligence?
A. Entrepreneurial competence
B. Self-motivation
C. Empathy
D. Handling relationships

15. Characteristic of good adjustment is:
A. Tolerance
B. Lack of confidence
C. Emotional unstability
D. Irregular life habit

16. The first psychological laboratory was established by whom?
A. Galton B. Cattell
C. Pestalozzi D. Wundt

17. "Incorporation of new information into existing mental frame works" is known as what?
A. Assimilation
B. Accommodation
C. Equilibration
D. Organisation

18. For the emotional development of his pupil the teacher should:
A. Try to usurp the place of pupil's parents.
B. Develop love and affection for his pupil.
C. Take a loveable attitude towards the mischief of the pupil.
D. Show favours to few selected pupils.

19. Which is ***not*** the cause of delinquency?
A. Physical defect
B. Poverty
C. Failure
D. Proper home environment

20. A type of intelligence which is mostly visible in dancers, athletes, surgeons etc., is known as what?
A. Bodily-kinesthetic intelligence
B. Spatial intelligence
C. Logical-mathematical intelligence
D. Musical intelligence

21. 'Out of sight out of mind' is characteristic of which of the following developmental stage?
A. Sensory-motor stage
B. Pre operational stage
C. Concrete operational stage
D. Formal operational stage

22. Which is ***not*** the component of motivation?
A. Needs B. Rote Memory
C. Drives D. Incentives

23. Out of the following which is ***not*** the other name of Adolescence?
A. Transitional period of childhood and adulthood
B. Problem age
C. Stage of stress, strain and storm
D. Smart age

24. Out of the following which is ***not*** the type of group non-verbral intelligence test?
A. Army Beta test
B. Army Alpha test
C. Chicago test
D. Revence progressive matrices

25. According to Kohlberg "a stage of moral development during which individuals judge morality largely in terms of existing social norms or rules" is known as which level of morality?
A. preconventional level of morality
B. conventional level of morality
C. postconventional level of morality
D. unconventional level of morality

26. A type of learning in which students try to learn by emerging new rule through given learning material, is known as what?
A. Rote learning B. Meaningful learning
C. Reception learning D. Discovery learning

27. Out of the follwoing alternative which does ***not*** come under processes in socialization?
A. learning to behave in socially approved ways
B. playing approved social roles
C. development of social attitudes
D. egocentric behaviour

28. What is the approximate I.Q. range of 'Mangolism' meantally retarded children?
A. 20 to 25 B. below 20
C. 25 to 36 D. 36 to 51

29. Direct method of personality adjustment is:
A. Sublimation B. Projection
C. Regression D. Removing of hurdles

30. Out of the following which is fourth level of Taylor's level theory of creativity?
A. Expressive creativity B. Productive creativity
C. Innovative creativity D. Inventive creativity

PART-II

भाषा : हिन्दी

निर्देशः *निम्नलिखित प्रश्नों के उत्तर देने के लिए* ***सबसे उचित*** *विकल्प चुनिए।*

31. किस विकल्प में विसर्ग संधि का प्रयोग ***नहीं*** हुआ है?
A. तिरोधान B. शिरोधार्य
C. दीपोत्सव D. रजोभव

32. 'हेमन्त को खीर अच्छी लगती है'— वाक्य किस कारक का उदाहरण है?
A. कर्मकारक B. संबंध कारक
C. संप्रदान कारक D. अधिकरण कारक

33. एकवचन से बहुवचन बने विकल्पों में असंगत चुनिए :

A. डाकू–डाकुओं B. वधू–वधुएँ
C. तरबूजा–तरबुजाओं D. भालू–भालुओं

34. वार्तनिक दृष्टि से अशुद्ध विकल्प चुनिए :

A. दवाइयाँ B. प्राणिविज्ञान
C. वृत्यानुप्रास D. मृत्यूपरान्त

35. किस वाक्य में 'आज्ञार्थ' (विध्यर्थ) वृत्ति का प्रयोग हुआ है?

A. तुम अगर कहते तो मैं ऐसा जरूर करती।
B. सभी को अपरिग्रह की भावना रखनी चाहिए।
C. नेता को चाहिए कि वह समूह के प्रत्येक व्यक्ति का सम्मान करे।
D. मैं चाहता हूँ कि तुम भले इंसान बनो।

36. प्रत्यय की दृष्टि से असंगत विकल्प बताइए :

A. विचार + ईय = विचारणीय
B. दृश् + तव्य = द्रष्टव्य
C. वृष्णि + एय = वार्ष्णेय
D. वल्मीक + इ = बाल्मीकि

37. किस विकल्प में द्वन्द्व समास का उदाहरण ***नहीं*** है?

A. भक्ष्याभक्ष्य B. कृष्णार्जुन
C. रुद्रप्रिया D. उचितानुचित

38. स्त्रीलिंग-पुल्लिंग की दृष्टि से अनुचित विकल्प छाँटिए :

A. कुँजड़ा–कुँजड़िन B. तीतर–तीतरिन
C. धोबी–धोबिन D. पापी–पापिन

39. किस विकल्प में 'आ' उपसर्ग का प्रयोग हुआ है?

A. आत्यन्तिक B. आतिथ्य
C. आख्यायिका D. आधिपत्य

40. विलोम की दृष्टि से बेमेल को छाँटिए :

A. आर्य–अनार्य B. उर्वर–अनुर्वर
C. ऐच्छिक–अनिवार्य D. खल–दुर्जन

41. पर्यायवाची की दृष्टि से असंगत विकल्प चुनिए :

A. पक्षी– शकुंत, द्विज, नभचर
B. बैल– ऋषभ, वृषभ, अक्षधर
C. वेद– आम्नाय, आगम, आकर
D. हरिण– कुरंग, प्लवंग, सारंग

42. 'भाववाच्य' वाला विकल्प चुनिए :

A. नानी द्वारा कहानी सुनाई गई।
B. गर्मियों में रोज नहाया जाता है।
C. भारत द्वारा नया उपग्रह छोड़ा गया।
D. कोहली ने शतक लगाया।

43. निम्न में से किस विकल्प में 'कम' शब्द का विशेषणीय प्रयोग किया गया है?

A. गर्मी में 'कम' खाना चाहिए। B. आज उसने 'कम' खाना खाया।
C. 'कम' ही पढ़ पाते हैं। D. 'कम' बोलना ही श्रेयस्कर है।

44. किस वाक्य में 'निपात' का प्रयोग हुआ है?

A. राम और श्याम दिनभर से खेल रहे हैं।
B. कविता आज दिल्ली जा रही है।
C. तुम आज दिनभर सोते ही रहोगे।
D. मेरी भारी भूल थी जो उसके बहकावे में आ गया।

45. 'दुर्घटना क्या और कैसे हुई' – वाक्य में प्रयुक्त क्रिया-विशेषण का भेद इंगित कीजिए :

A. परिमाणवाचक B. कालवाचक
C. रीतिवाचक D. स्थानवाचक

Language : English

Directions: *Answer the following questions by selecting the **most appropriate** option.*

46. Choose the correct presposition.

I had not slept or eaten anything properly .... two days.

A. since B. from
C. in D. for

47. Fill in the blank with the correct option :

.... doing the cooking, I look after the garden.

A. Beside B. However
C. Besides D. Therefore

48. Choose the correct synonym for the word given below :

Gallant

A. Valiant B. Impolite
C. Rude D. Fearful

49. Choose the correct option for the underlined word.

Our parents have raised us to be a good citizen.

A. Brought up B. Brought by
C. Brought out D. Brought down

50. Choose the correct determiner.

.... knowledge is a dangerous thing.

A. The little B. Little
C. A little D. The few

51. Choose the correct form of verb.

Did you not .... about the world Atlas.

A. knew B. known
C. know D. knows

52. Choose the correct passive construction for the sentence given.

We visited the zoo of Jaipur on last Sunday.

A. Zoo of Jaipur were visited by us on last Sunday.
B. On last Sunday the zoo of Jaipur was visited by us.
C. We were visited the zoo of Jaipur on last Sunday.
D. Zoo of Jaipur was being visited on Sunday last by us.

53. Cooking is his hobby.

The underlined word is used as a :

A. Verb B. Gerund
C. Participle D. Infinitive

54. Choose the word which is spelt correctly.

A. Commited B. Committed
C. Comitteed D. Committeed

55. Fill in the blank by choosing the correct option.

The Headmaster and the Secreatry .... present in the meeting.

A. was B. were
C. was being D. were being

56. Choose the most appropriate form of Indirect speech for the given sentence.

The teacher said to Hari, "Why did you not do your homework yesterday"?

A. The teacher asked Hari why had he not done his homework the previous day?
B. The teacher asked Hari why he had not done his homework the previous day?
C. The teacher said to Hari why had he not done their homework the previous day?
D. The teacher said Hari that he had not done his homework the previous day.

57. Choose the correct antonym for the word given below:

Bankrupt

A. Penniless B. Insolvent
C. Ruined D. Solvent

58. Fill in the blank with appropriate preposition.

I paid the bill .... cash.

A. in B. at
C. for D. with

59. Choose the correct modal.

Some people .... ski better than others.

A. must B. can
C. could D. should

60. Choose the correct word for the sentence.

A man who is womanish in his habits.

A. Arsonist B. Epicure
C. Effeminate D. Fealty

PART-III

General Studies : Quantitative Aptitude, Reasoning Ability and GK & Awareness

Directions: *Answer the following questions by selecting the* ***most appropriate*** *option.*

61. Which is the correct conclusion based on given statements?

Statement:

I. All leaves are roots.
II. Some roots are branches.

Conclusion:

A. Some leaves are branches.
B. Some branches are not roots.
C. No branch is leaf.
D. Some roots are leaves.

62. Two persons depart from their office towards their houses. First person goes 8 km in north direction and second person goes 6 km in east direction and reach their houses, find out the direct distance of their Houses?

A. 10 km
B. 12 km
C. 14 km
D. 15 km

63. What will be the angle between minute end and hour end in a Clock at 7 : 20?

A. 160° B. 100°
C. 260° D. 120°

64. Complete the following Series:
WE, SG, PJ, LN, IS, ?

A. FZ B. FX
C. EY D. EX

65. In a code language GRANT is written as UOBSH, TIME is written as FNJU how is PRIDE written in that language?

A. QSJEF B. OQHCD
C. FEJSQ D. TPMED

66. Find the next term of the following letter series :
DHL, PTX, BFJ, ...

A. CGK B. KOS
C. NRV D. OVZ

67. The population of a town is 8,500. In first year it was increased by 20% and in second year again increased by 25%, then what is the total population after two years?

A. 10,950 B. 12,750
C. 11,950 D. 12,550

68. What is the difference between compound interest and simple interest on the amount of ₹ 18,000 in 2 years with the rate of 10% per year?
A. ₹ 150 B. ₹ 180
C. ₹ 210 D. ₹ 316

69. The total amount of ₹ 14,500 with simple interest in 6 years is ₹ 21,460, find out the Rate of interest per annum?
A. 4% B. 10%
C. 6% D. 8%

70. The sides of a triangular farm are 20 m, 21 m and 29 m respectively. How much will be total expenses for cutting the crop at the rate of ₹ 15 per square meter?
A. ₹ 21,00 B. ₹ 1,890
C. ₹ 3,150 D. ₹ 2,500

71. Average runs of 6 players in cricket match was 36. If one player made 16 runs, then what is the average run of remaining players?
A. 24 B. 30
C. 36 D. 40

72. Complete the following series:

24, 60, 120, 210, ?
A. 336 B. 270
C. 512 D. 500

73. The ratio of speeds, of a Bus and Car is 6 : 7. If car covers 364 km distance in 4 hours, what is the speed of Bus?
A. 60 km/h B. 72 km/h
C. 78 km/h D. 84 km/h

74. In a certain code language "go home" is written as "ta na", "sweet home" is written as "na ja", "Sweet and Sour" is written as "pa sa ja", then how "Sour" is coded as?
A. pa B. sa
C. pa or sa D. na

75. The ratio of two numbers are 3 : 5 and the addition of those numbers is 240, what is the difference of those numbers?
A. 60 B. 100
C. 120 D. 90

76. If 3/5 of 60% of a Number is 36, then the value of the number is:
A. 60 B. 100
C. 120 D. 150

77. If DRIVER = 12, PEDESTRIAN = 20, ACCIDENT = 16, then CAR = ?
A. 3 B. 6
C. 8 D. 16

78. A and B together can do a work in 15 days, if B alone can do that work in 20 days. Then how many days will A take to do same work alone?
A. 60 B. 45
C. 40 D. 30

79. Anil is standing at 16th position from the left end in a row of boys. Vikas is at 18th position from the right end. Gopal is 11th from Anil towards the right and 3rd from Vikas towards the right end. How many boys are standing in this row?
A. 41 B. 42
C. 48 D. 49

80. Which of the following is a leap year?
A. 1800 B. 1900
C. 1700 D. 2000

81. How many Administrative divisions are there in Haryana?
A. Four B. Five
C. Six D. Seven

82. The city of Haryana, which is ***not*** part of National Capital Region :
A. Gurugram B. Sonipat
C. Faridabad D. Hisar

83. Gurugram is related to which ancient Guru?
A. Ved Vyas B. Dronacharya
C. Parashuram D. Kripacharya

84. Who is the brand ambassador of 'Beti Bachao-Beti Padhao Campaign' in Haryana?
A. Anu Kumari B. Sakshi Malik
C. Kalpna Chawala D. Saina Nehwal

85. The district which does ***not*** share boundary with other states is:
A. Panipat B. Rohtak
C. Rewari D. Palwal

86. The river, which makes border between Haryana and Uttar Pradesh:
A. Yamuna B. Ganga
C. Sahibi D. Markanda

87. Where Pratap Singh revolted against the British?
A. Rohtak B. Jind
C. Ambala D. Sirsa

88. Where is the National Cancer Institute situated?
A. Sampla B. Meham
C. Badsa D. Kalanaur

89. Sohna town is famours for:
A. Historical Lake B. Historical Palace
C. Hot water Springs D. Gardens

90. State animal of Haryana is :
A. Black buck B. Asiatic Lion
C. Chinkara D. Tiger

PART-IV

Social Studies

Directions: *Answer the following questions by selecting the* ***most appropriate*** *option.*

91. Who was the Czar of Russia during October Revolution?
A. Vladimir Lenin B. Nicholas-II
C. Alexander Kerensky D. Nicholas-I

92. "Indira Sawhney and other Vs. Union of India" case is related to :
A. OBC reservation
B. Abolition of reservation of scheduled caste
C. Women protection
D. Rights of working women

93. Read the following sentence carefully :
I. The two Houses of Parliament of India do not have the same powers.
II. It is because of this reason the terminology "upper chamber" and "lower chamber" is used in Constitution of India.

Choose the correct option :
A. II is correct and I is incorrect
B. I is correct and II is incorrect
C. Both I and II are correct
D. Both I and II are incorrect

94. Which among the following is ***not*** an example of Intermountane Plateaus?
A. Tibet Plateau
B. Mexican Plateau
C. Deccan Trap
D. Plateau of Bolivia and Peru

95. Production possibilities curve is also known as :
A. Indifference Curve B. Demand Curve
C. Supply Curve D. Transformation Curve

96. What is I.C.O.R. ?

A. $\frac{\text{Change in Capital}}{\text{Change in Production}}$

B. $\frac{\text{Change in Income}}{\text{Change in Capital}}$

C. $\frac{\text{Change in Income}}{\text{Change in Consumption}}$

D. $\frac{\text{Change in Production}}{\text{Change in Capital}}$

97. Rani Laxmibai was defeated and killed in :
A. June, 1757 B. June, 1858
C. July, 1757 D. July, 1858

98. The founder of Hoa Hao Movement is:
A. Huynh Phu So B. Aung San Suu Kyi
C. Mao Zedong D. Faan Boi Chau

99. What is the difference between GNP and GDP?
A. Excess of indirect taxes over subsidies
B. Depreciation
C. Excess of subsidies over indirect taxes
D. Net factor income from abroad

100. In India the 'No-confidence' motion against the central government :
A. Can be presented either in Lok Sabha or Rajya Sabha.
B. Can be presented only in the Lok Sabha.
C. Can be presented only in the Rajya Sabha.
D. Can be presented by the largest party of the opposition in Lok Sabha.

101. Who was the founder of Swaraj Party?
A. C.R. Das B. B.R. Ambedkar
C. J.L. Nehru D. M.K. Gandhi

102. Read the following sentences carefully :
I. International Monetary Fund (IMF) is one of the biggest moneylenders for any country in the world.
II. Its all the member states have equal voting rights.
Choose the correct option :
A. I is correct and II is incorrect
B. I is incorrect and II is correct
C. Both I and II are incorrect
D. Both I and II are correct

103. In the Union Budget of India, profits from public sector undertakings are taken under :
A. Fiscal deficit B. Planned expenditure
C. Capital receipts D. Revenue receipts

104. Economic survey is published by :
A. Planning Commission
B. Indian Statistical Institute
C. RBI
D. Ministry of Finance

105. 'Kennelly-Heaviside' layer in Ionosphere is :
A. D Layer B. E Layer
C. F Layer D. G Layer

106. From the following which country was the last to adopt the Universal Adult Franchise?
A. India
B. South Africa
C. United State of America
D. Germany

107. Read the following statements carefully :

I. The Chief Election Commissioner (CEC) is appointed by the President of India.

II. The Chief Election Commissioner (CEC) is answerable to the President.

Choose the correct option :

A. Both I and II are correct
B. Both I and II are incorrect
C. I is correct and II is incorrect
D. I is incorrect and II is correct

108. 'ENSO' event is associated with :

A. Tourism B. Trade
C. Transport D. Indian Monsoon

109. What is the name of the book written by Montesquieu?

A. The Social Contract B. The Spirit of Laws
C. Das Capital D. Treatise on Tolerance

110. In which year Khilafat Movement was started?

A. 1921 B. 1918
C. 1919 D. 1920

111. In which year Nepoleon Bonaparte crowned himself as emperor of France?

A. 1801 B. 1802
C. 1803 D. 1804

112. Which of the following statement is ***incorrect***?

A. A monopolist may restrict the output and rises the price.
B. Under monopoly there is no difference between a firm and an industry.
C. Product differentiation is peculiar to monopolistic competition.
D. Commodities offered for sale under a perfect competition will be heterogeneous.

113. Where Champaran is situated?

A. Gujarat B. Uttar Pradesh
C. Bihar D. Madhya Pradesh

114. The antipode meridian of 55° West meridian is :

A. 55° East longitude
B. 125° East longitude
C. 125° West longitude
D. 155° East longitude

115. The oceanic current flowing at southernmost edge of Africa from North towards South is:

A. Agulhas B. Canarry
C. Mozambique D. Benguela

116. Whose statement is this, "I shall strive for a constitution which will release India from all thralldom and patronage .... I shall work for an India in which the poorest shall feel that it is their country"?

A. B.R. Ambedkar B. Jawaharalal Nehru
C. Dr. Rajendra Prasad D. Mahatma Gandhi

117. Match the following and select the ***correct*** answer by using ***codes*** given below :

Volcano	**Coutnry**
(*a*) Stramboli	(*i*) Tanzania
(*b*) Cotapaxi	(*ii*) Italy
(*c*) Mt. Popa	(*iii*) Equador
(*d*) Kilimanjaro	(*iv*) Myanmar

Codes :

	(*a*)	(*b*)	(*c*)	(*d*)
A.	(*i*)	(*ii*)	(*iii*)	(*iv*)
B.	(*ii*)	(*i*)	(*iii*)	(*iv*)
C.	(*ii*)	(*iii*)	(*i*)	(*iv*)
D.	(*ii*)	(*iii*)	(*iv*)	(*i*)

118. Economic planning is related to :

A. Socialist Economy
B. Mixed Economy
C. Both Socialist and Mixed Economy
D. None of these

119. Which one of the following is ***not*** matched correctly?

Landforms		**Forming Agents**
A. Cirques	—	Glaciers
B. Peniplain	—	Rivers
C. Loes	—	Wind
D. Nunatak	—	Sea waves

120. When Earth, Sun and Moon are at quadrature, which tides will occur?

A. Spring tide B. Diurnal tide
C. Mixed tide D. Neap tide

121. Match the following :

(*a*) Gurjara Pratihar	(*i*) Western Deccan
(*b*) Rashtrakutas	(*ii*) Bengal
(*c*) Palas	(*iii*) Gujarat and Rajasthan
(*d*) Cholas	(*iv*) Tamil Nadu

Codes :

	(*a*)	(*b*)	(*c*)	(*d*)
A.	(*iii*)	(*i*)	(*ii*)	(*iv*)
B.	(*i*)	(*ii*)	(*iii*)	(*iv*)
C.	(*ii*)	(*iii*)	(*i*)	(*iv*)
D.	(*iv*)	(*ii*)	(*i*)	(*iii*)

122. Which one of the following pairs is ***not*** matched correctly?

Crop		**Leading Producing State (India)**
A. Tea	—	Assam
B. Jute	—	West Bengal
C. Coffee	—	Karnataka
D. Rubber	—	Tamil Nadu

123. Which of the following is a subject of concurrent list?

A. Communications
B. Computer software
C. Police
D. Marriage

124. The basis of the creation of new states by the first State Reorganisation Commission formed after the Independence of India was :
A. Culture
B. Language
C. Religion
D. Geographical conditions

125. Find out the areas in which democratic systems have not been very successful in :
A. maintaining peace and order
B. reducing economic inequalities
C. maintaining dignity and freedom of the citizens
D. maintaining accommodation of social diversity

126. Which economist is ***not*** related to Indifference curve method?
A. Hicks B. Pareto
C. Allen D. Marshall

127. As per Census 2011, what is the ***correct***, increasing order of three lowest sex ratio States of India?
A. Haryana < Sikkim < Punjab
B. Haryana < Jammu & Kashmir < Sikkim
C. Haryana < Sikkim < Jammu & Kashmir
D. Haryana < Punjab < Sikkim

128. "Trade Cycle" is ***not*** related to :
A. Price level in economy
B. Production level
C. Employment level
D. Political party in government

129. In India, seats are kept reserved in local self governing bodies for :
A. only for scheduled castes
B. only for women
C. only for scheduled castes, scheduled tribes and women
D. scheduled castes, scheduled tribes, other backward classes and women

130. What was the name of 'Political Alliance' formed in Nepal in 2006 for the support of democracy?
A. For democracy
B. Hope
C. Seven Party Alliance
D. Democracy for peace

131. Who wrote Prayag Prashasti?
A. Harishena B. Kalhan
C. Harshavardhana D. Kalidas

132. Calculate the 'Mode'.
7, 12, 8, 5, 6, 4, 9, 10, 8, 9, 7, 9, 6, 5, 9
A. 15 B. 9
C. 5 D. 11

133. The mother of Shah Jahan was :
A. Kachhwaha Princess B. Sisodiya Princess
C. Rathore Princess D. Chauhan Princess

134. Typhoon originates at :
A. North Atlantic Ocean
B. North-West Pacific Ocean
C. South Indian Ocean
D. South Pacific Ocean

135. Who composed 'Harshacharita'?
A. Kalidas B. Harishena
C. Banbhatta D. Ravikirti

136. What is the value of price elasticity of demand for the rectangular hyperbola demand curve?
A. $e > 1$ B. $e < 1$
C. $e = 1$ D. $e = 0$

137. Raziya was the daughter of :
A. Qutubuddin Aibak B. Khizr Khan
C. Bahlol Lodi D. Shamsuddin Iltutmish

138. 'Bhur' Topography is a characteristic of :
A. The upper and middle Ganga plains
B. The Brahmaputra plains
C. Tista Plain
D. The Sundarban Delta

139. What is the highest and lowest population density of India?
A. Delhi (11297) and Arunachal Pradesh (17)
B. Delhi (9768) and Arunachal Pradesh (171)
C. Maharashtra (1122) and Nagaland (212)
D. Delhi (14444) and Nagaland (22)

140. Who wrote Kitab-ul-Hind?
A. Amir Khusrow B. Abul Fazal
C. Al-Biruni D. Amir Hasan Dehlvi

141. Which is the second rule of H.H. Gossen?
A. Law of Diminishing Marginal Utility
B. Law of Equi Marginal Utility
C. Consumer surplus
D. Law of variable proportions

142. Most of the inscription of Ashoka were written in :
A. Pali B. Hindi
C. Sanskrit D. Prakrit

143. When did the IMF start functioning?
A. 1945 B. 1946
C. 1947 D. 1948

144. The most powerful factor behind the 'Rights" is :
A. Religious traditions
B. Beliefs of political parties
C. Recognition by society
D. Emotional claims

145. Which one of the following pair is ***not*** matched correctly?

River Valley Projects		**River**
A. Shivasamudram	—	Kaveri
B. Pochampad	—	Godavari
C. Kakrapar	—	Narmada
D. Ukai	—	Tapi

146. The fundamental base of "Sexual division of labour" is :

A. Biological structure
B. Political conventions
C. Stereotype beliefs
D. Uncertain social roles

147. Match **List-I** with **List-II** and select the ***correct*** answer by using ***codes*** given below :

List-I (Forests)	**List-II (Region)**
(*a*) Mangrove	(*i*) Coromandal Coast
(*b*) Tropical evergreen	(*ii*) Ganga-Brahmaputra delta
(*c*) Tropical Dry evergreen	(*iii*) Nilgiri and Annamalai Hills
(*d*) Wet temperate	(*iv*) Western Ghats

Codes :

	(*a*)	(*b*)	(*c*)	(*d*)
A.	(*ii*)	(*iii*)	(*iv*)	(*i*)
B.	(*ii*)	(*i*)	(*iv*)	(*iii*)
C.	(*ii*)	(*iv*)	(*i*)	(*iii*)
D.	(*ii*)	(*iv*)	(*iii*)	(*i*)

148. In India, the political parties are given 'recognition' by:

A. The President
B. Parliament
C. Election Commission
D. All Party Parliamentary Committee

149. A consumer is in equilibrium when marginal utilities are :

A. Minimum B. Equal
C. Highest D. Increasing

150. 'Manikaran' (Himachal Pradesh) is known for :

A. Solar Energy B. Wind Energy
C. Geothermal Energy D. Atomic Energy

Answers

1	**2**	**3**	**4**	**5**	**6**	**7**	**8**	**9**	**10**
D	C	D	C	B	B	B	B	C	C
11	**12**	**13**	**14**	**15**	**16**	**17**	**18**	**19**	**20**
B	A	D	A	A	D	A	B	D	A
21	**22**	**23**	**24**	**25**	**26**	**27**	**28**	**29**	**30**
A	B	D	A	B	D	D	A	D	C
31	**32**	**33**	**34**	**35**	**36**	**37**	**38**	**39**	**40**
C	C	C	C	B	A	C	B	C	D
41	**42**	**43**	**44**	**45**	**46**	**47**	**48**	**49**	**50**
C	B	B	C	C	D	C	A	A	C
51	**52**	**53**	**54**	**55**	**56**	**57**	**58**	**59**	**60**
C	B	B	B	B	B	D	A	B	C
61	**62**	**63**	**64**	**65**	**66**	**67**	**68**	**69**	**70**
D	A	B	C	C	C	B	B	D	C
71	**72**	**73**	**74**	**75**	**76**	**77**	**78**	**79**	**80**
D	A	C	C	A	B	B	A	A	D
81	**82**	**83**	**84**	**85**	**86**	**87**	**88**	**89**	**90**
C	D	B	B	B	A	B	C	C	A
91	**92**	**93**	**94**	**95**	**96**	**97**	**98**	**99**	**100**
C	A	B	C	D	A	B	A	D	B
101	**102**	**103**	**104**	**105**	**106**	**107**	**108**	**109**	**110**
A	A	D	D	B	B	C	D	B	C
111	**112**	**113**	**114**	**115**	**116**	**117**	**118**	**119**	**120**
D	D	C	B	A	D	D	C	D	D
121	**122**	**123**	**124**	**125**	**126**	**127**	**128**	**129**	**130**
A	D	D	B	B	D	B	D	D	C
131	**132**	**133**	**134**	**135**	**136**	**137**	**138**	**139**	**140**
A	B	C	B	C	C	D	A	A	C
141	**142**	**143**	**144**	**145**	**146**	**147**	**148**	**149**	**150**
B	D	C	C	C	C	C	C	B	C

Explanatory Answers

61. Statement:

I. All leaves are roots.

II. Some roots are branches.

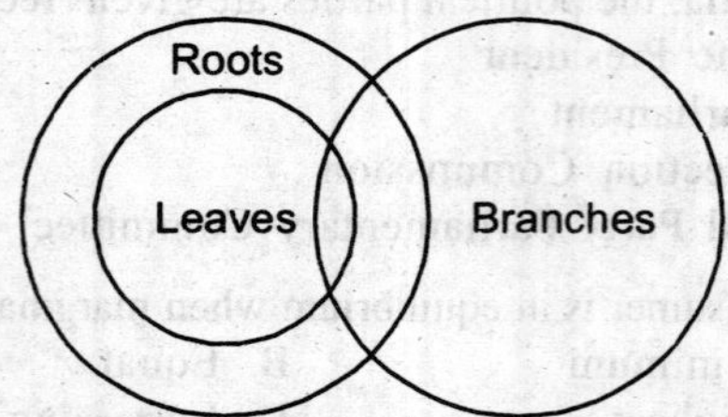

Conclusion: Some roots are leaves.

62.

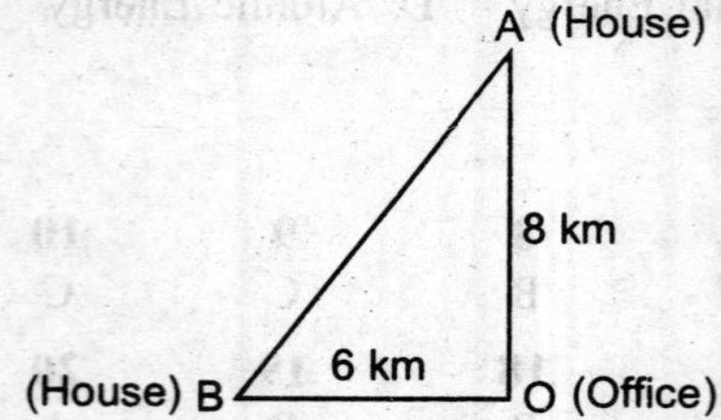

Here, OA = 8 km

OB = 6 km

Distance of their house

$$AB = \sqrt{OA^2 + OB^2}$$

$$= \sqrt{8^2 + 6^2}$$

$$= \sqrt{64 + 36}$$

$$= \sqrt{100}$$

= 10 km.

63. $\because$ 60 minutes = 360°

$\therefore$ 1 minute = 6°

The angle between minute hand and hour hand in a clock at 7 : 20.

= 16.7 minutes

= 16.7 × 6°

= 100.2°

= 100° (Approx.)

64.

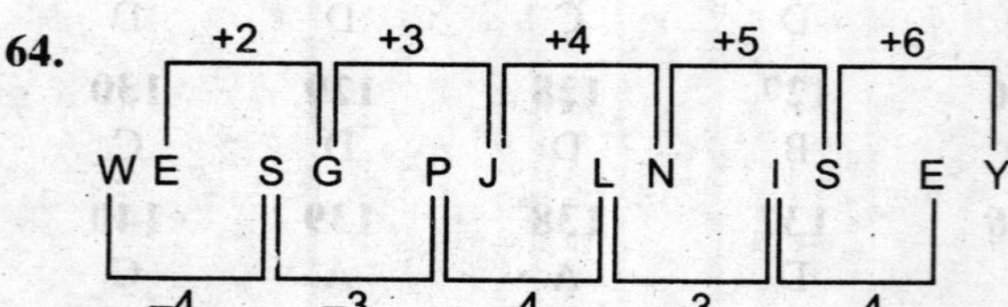

Here, next term in the series = EY.

65. As,

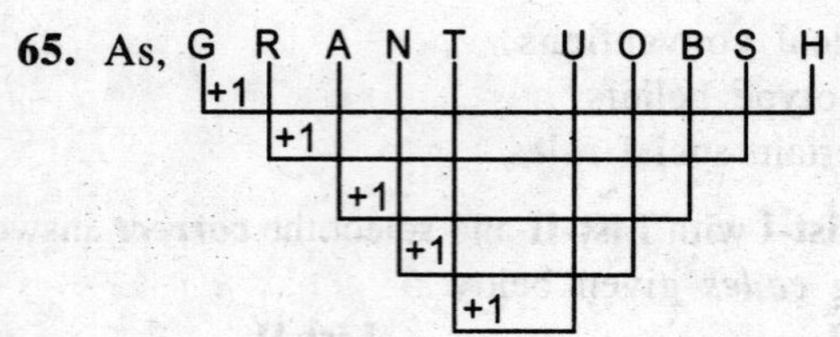

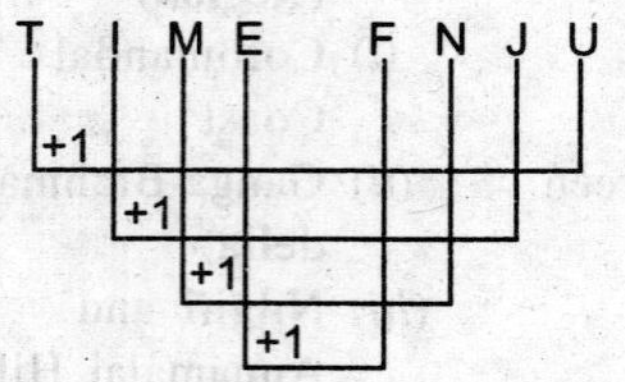

Similarly,

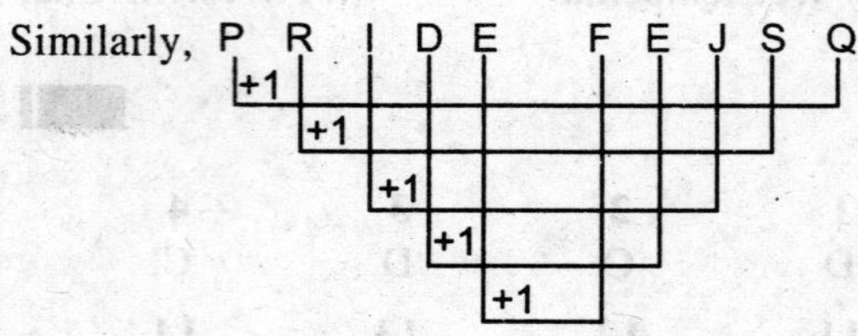

66.

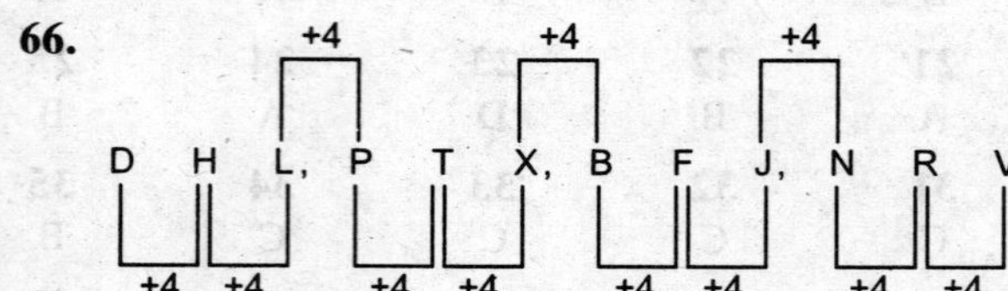

Here, next term in the letter series = NRV

67. Here, P = 8500, r_1 = 20%, r_2 = 25%

$\therefore$ The total population after two years

$$= P\left(1 + \frac{r_1}{100}\right)\left(1 + \frac{r_2}{100}\right)$$

$$= 8500\left(1 + \frac{20}{100}\right)\left(1 + \frac{25}{100}\right)$$

$$= 8500\left(1 + \frac{1}{5}\right)\left(1 + \frac{1}{4}\right)$$

$$= 8500\left(\frac{6}{5}\right)\left(\frac{5}{4}\right)$$

$$= 8500 \times \frac{3}{2}$$

= 12,750.

68. Here, P = ₹ 18000,

t = 2 years,

r = 10%

$\therefore$ Compound Interest $= P\left(1+\frac{r}{100}\right)^n - P$

$= ₹\ 18000\left(1+\frac{10}{100}\right)^2 - 18000$

$= ₹\ 18000\left[\left(1+\frac{1}{10}\right)^2 - 1\right]$

$= ₹\ 18000\left[\left(\frac{11}{10}\right)^2 - 1\right]$

$= ₹\ 18000\left[\frac{121}{100} - 1\right]$

$= ₹\ 18000 \times \frac{21}{100}$

$= ₹\ 180 \times 21$

Simple Interest $= \frac{P \times r \times t}{100}$

$= \frac{18000 \times 10 \times 2}{100}$

$= ₹\ 180 \times 20$

Hence, the difference between compound interest and simple interest

$= ₹\ 180 \times 21 - ₹\ 180 \times 20$
$= ₹\ 180\ (21 - 20)$
$= ₹\ 180.$

69. Here, P = ₹ 14,500
t = 6 years
A = ₹ 21,460

Simple interest = ₹ 21,460 – ₹ 14,500
= ₹ 6960

Rate $= \frac{\text{S.I.} \times 100}{P \times t}$

$\therefore \quad r = \frac{6960 \times 100}{14500 \times 6}$

$= \frac{6960}{145 \times 6}$

$= \frac{6960}{870}$

= 8%.

70. Let the sides of a triangular farm are

a = 20 m,
b = 21 m
and c = 29 m

Then, $s = \frac{a+b+c}{2}$

$= \frac{20+21+29}{2}$

$= \frac{70}{2}$

= 35 m

Area of a triangular farm

$= \sqrt{s(s-a)(s-b)(s-c)}$

$= \sqrt{35(35-20)(35-21)(35-29)}\ m^2$

$= \sqrt{35 \times 15 \times 14 \times 6}$

$= \sqrt{7 \times 5 \times 5 \times 3 \times 7 \times 2 \times 3 \times 2}$

$= 7 \times 5 \times 3 \times 2\ m^2$

Hence, the total expenses for cutting at the rate of ₹ 15 per m^2

= ₹ 15 × 7 × 5 × 3 × 2
= ₹ 3150.

71. The total run of 6 players in a cricket match
= 6 × 36
= 216

The total run of remaning 5 players
= 216 – 16
= 200

$\therefore$ The average run of remaining players

$= \frac{200}{5} = 40.$

72. 24, 60, 120, 210, ?

Dividing each term by 6

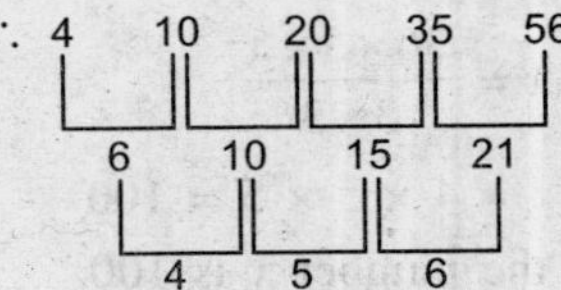

Here, next term in the given series
= 56 × 6
= 336.

73. Let the speed of a Bus and Car is $6x$ km/h and $7x$ km/h

Then, $7x \times 4 = 364$ (Speed × Time = Distance)

$\Rightarrow \quad 28x = 364$

$\Rightarrow \quad x = \frac{364}{28}$

$= \frac{52}{4} = 13$

$\therefore$ Speed of Bus = $6x$ km/h

= 6 × 13

= 78 km/h.

74. Given, code language

"go home" → "ta na"

"sweet home" → "na ja"

"sweet and sour" → "pa sa ja"

Here, "home" → "na"

"sweet" → ja

go → ta

"and sour" → "pa sa"

$\therefore$ "sour" is coded as "pa" or "sa".

75. Let the two numbers are $3x$ and $5x$

Then, $3x + 5x = 240$

$\Rightarrow$ $8x = 240$

$\Rightarrow$ $x = 30$

$\therefore$ The difference of these numbers

$= 5x - 3x$

$= 2x$

$= 2 \times 30$

$= 60.$

76. Let the number is x

Then, $\frac{3}{5}$ of 60% of $x = 36$

$\Rightarrow$ $x \times \frac{60}{100} \times \frac{3}{5} = 36$

$\Rightarrow$ $x \times \frac{3}{5} \times \frac{3}{5} = 36$

$\Rightarrow$ $x = \frac{36 \times 5 \times 5}{3 \times 3}$

$= 4 \times 5 \times 5 = 100$

Hence, the value of the number x is 100.

77. Given, DRIVER = 12

Here, number of letters is multiplied by 2

$\therefore$ 6 × 2 = 12

PEDESTRIAN = 10 × 2 = 20

ACCIDENT = 8 × 2 = 16

$\therefore$ CAR = 3 × 2 = 6.

78. (A + B)'s 1 day's work = $\frac{1}{15}$

B's 1 day's work = $\frac{1}{20}$

$\therefore$ A's 1 day's work = $\frac{1}{15} - \frac{1}{20}$

$= \frac{4-3}{60} = \frac{1}{60}$

$\therefore$ A's time = 60 days.

79.

Anil is 16th from the left.

Vikas is 18th from the right.

Gopal is 11th from Anil towards the right and 3rd from Vikas towards the right end.

$\therefore$ The Number of boys between Anil and Vikas

= 11 − 4 = 7

$\therefore$ The number of boys standing in this row

= 16 + 7 + 18

= 16 + 25 = 41.

81. Haryana is one of the 28 states in India, located in the northern part of the country. It was carved out of the former state of East Punjab on 1 November 1966 on a linguistic basis. Chandigarh is the state capital, Faridabad in National Capital Region is the most populous city of the state, and Gurugram is a leading financial hub of the NCR, with major Fortune 500 companies located in it. Haryana has 6 administrative divisions.

83. Gurgaon was historically inhabited by the Hindu people, and in early times it formed a part of an extensive kingdom ruled over by Ahir clan. In Earlier History it is told that it was the Village of guru Dronacharya who was the Teacher of Kauravas and Pandvas. During Akbar's reign, Gurugram fell within the governing regions of Delhi and Agra. As the Mughal empire started to decline, the place was torn between contending powers. By 1803 most of it came under the British rule through the treaty of Surji Arjungaon with Sindhia. The town was first occupied by the cavalry unit posted to watch the army of Begum Samru of Sirdhana. It become a Part of the district, which was divided into units called parganas. These units were given to petty chiefs for the military service rendered by them. Eventually these units came under direct control of the British, with the last major administrative change in 1836. After the revolt of 1857, it was transferred from the North-Western provinces to Punjab province. In 1861, the district, which Gurugram was a part of was rearranged into five tehsils: Gurgaon, Ferozepur Jhirka, Nuh, Palwal and Rewari (10) and the modern-day city came under the control of Gurgaon tehsil. In 1947, Gurgaon became a part of independent India and fell under the Indian state of Punjab. In 1966, the city came under the administration of Haryana with the creation of the new state.

84. The Beti Bachao, Beti Padhao (BBBP) scheme was launched on 22 January 2015 by PM Narendra Modi. It aims to address the issue of the declining child sex ratio image (CSR) and is a national initiative jointly run by the Ministry of Women and Child Development, the Ministry of Health and Family Welfare and the Ministry of Education. It initially focused multi-sector action in 100 districts throughout the country where there was a low CSR. On 26 August 2016, Olympics 2016 bronze medallist Sakshi Malik was made brand ambassador for BBBP.

86. The Yamuna is the second-largest tributary river of the Ganga and the longest tributary in India. Originating from the Yamunotri Glacier at a height of 6,387 metres on the southwestern slopes of Banderpooch peaks of the Lower Himalaya in Uttarakhand, it travels a total length of 1,376 kilometres and has a drainage system of 366,223 square kilometres, 40.2% of the entire Ganga Basin. It merges with the Ganga at Triveni Sangam, Prayagraj. which is a site of the Kumbh Mela, a Hindu festival held every 12 years. It crosses several states: Haryana and Uttar Pradesh, passing by Uttarakhand and later Delhi, and meeting its tributaries on the way, including Tons, Chambal, its longest tributary which has its own large basin, followed by Sindh, the Betwa, and Ken.

89. Sohna is a town and a municipal committee in the Gurgaon district of Haryana, India. A popular tourist weekend and conference retreat, it is on the highway from Gurgaon to Alwar near a vertical rock. Sohna is known for its hot springs and Shiva temple. Sohna tehsil is part of Ahirwal Region.

90. Black Buck, common name for an antelope, mainly is a resident of India but with other small populations in Pakistan and Nepal. The Black Buck has ringed horns that have a moderate spiral twist of three to four turns and are up to 70 cm (28 inch) long. The name Black Buck has also been applied to the sable antelope of Africa. The adult male stands about 80 cm (about 32 inch) at the shoulder and weighs 32 to 43 kg (71 to 95 lb). The body's upper parts are black; the underparts and a ring around the eyes are white. The light-brown female is usually hornless. Males are dark brown.

Previous Paper (Solved)

Haryana Teacher Eligibility Test (HTET)

TGT Social Studies (Level-2), Exam 2018*

PART-I

Child Development and Pedagogy

Directions: *Answer the following questions by selecting the **most appropriate** option.*

1. Which of the following is ***not*** true about dramatic play?
A. It is a form of active play.
B. It is known as make believe play.
C. It involve overt behaviour.
D. It is always reproductive.

2. 'Dyscalculia' is a type of :
A. Locomotor Disability
B. Learning Disability
C. Intellectual Disability
D. Visual Impairment

3. Which of the following is ***not*** true about the Broca's area of brain?
A. It is located in the left frontal lobe.
B. It supports grammatical processing.
C. It is responsible for language production.
D. It is responsible for comprehending word meaning.

4. Which of the following theory assumes that Child Development is ***not*** a continuous process?
A. Cognitive Development theory of Piaget
B. Behaviourism
C. Social learning theory
D. Ecological system theory

5. The statement 'Personality is nothing but a set of learned responses', best describe which of the following view about personality?
A. Behaviouristic view
B. Structuralist view
C. Functionalist view
D. Cognitivist view

6. Which of the following is ***not*** an example of newborn 'reflexes'?
A. Eye blink B. Sucking
C. Swimming D. Driving Car

7. Which of the following is ***not*** true about children's play?
A. The number of play activities decrease with increasing age.
B. Play becomes increasingly social with increasing age.
C. The number of playmates increases with increasing age.
D. Play become increasingly sex-appropriate with increasing age.

8. The 'Three Stratum Theory' of Intelligence was given by :
A. Piaget B. Binnet
C. Carrol D. Cattle

9. Four year old Binny started wetting her bed after her parents brings home a new baby. Which of the following type 'defense mechanism' it is?
A. Regression
B. Suppression
C. Rationalization
D. Displacement

10. Which of the following statement is ***not*** true?
A. Classical conditioning deals with voluntary behaviours.
B. Operant conditioning deals with voluntary behaviours.
C. Classical conditioning deals with involuntary behaviours.
D. In operant conditioning, 'consequences' are important in framing an association.

11. Knowing 'how to ride a bicycle' is an example of :
A. Procedural knowledge
B. Declarative knowledge
C. Explicit knowledge
D. No option is correct

12. If a child is sharing with you what he did after he got up in the morning, he is using his :

***Exam held on 06-01-2019.**

A. Semantic Memory
Γ. Sensory Register
C. Procedural Memory
D. Episodic Memory

13. Which of the following type is ***not*** a type of Intelligence, as given in Sternberg's Triarchial Theory of successful intelligence?
A. Analytical Intelligence
B. Creative Intelligence
C. Musical Intelligence
D. Practical Intelligence

14. The seat belt buzzer of a car, stops as soon as the driver put on the seat belt. It is an example of :
A. Positive Reinforcement
B. Negative Reinforcement
C. Positive Punishment
D. Negative Punishment

15. The example 'you scratch my back and I will scratch yours', indicates which type of morality as given by Piaget?
A. Beginning of Morality of Cooperation
B. Pre-conventional morality
C. Realism
D. Not related to moral concern

16. Meeta has overcome her fear of toy-snakes. However on one occasion her fear returned when she found toy-snake on her bed. Such return of fear can be termed as:
A. Stimulus Generalization
B. Stimulus Discrimination
C. Spontaneous Recovery
D. Extinction

17. Which of the following is ***not*** true about 'Zone of Proximal Development'?
A. It is related to Vygotsky's theory.
B. It sets the upper limit on what the child is capable to learn.
C. It is a range of tasks that a learner cannot perform without help of others but yet cannot perform independently.
D. It is the upper limit of a task that a learner can successfully perform independently.

18. Out of the following alternative which one is ***not*** comes under processes in socialization?
A. Learning to behave in socially approved way
B. Playing approved social roles
C. Development of social attitude
D. Approval of egocentric behaviour

19. Presentation of an unpleasant stimulus to decrease the occurrence of a response is known as:
A. Positive Reinforcement
B. Negative Reinforcement
C. Punishment
D. Motivator

20. According to Kohlberg, Good Boy/Good Girl orientation indicates
A. Pre conventional Morality
B. Post conventional Morality
C. Conventional Morality
D. Relative Morality

21. Which of the following system contains 'Parents Work Place' as per the Bronfenbrenner's Ecological Theory of Development?
A. Micro System
B. Macro System
C. Meso System
D. Exo System

22. Which of the following statement is ***not*** correct?
A. Intellectual Disability and Learning Disability are not same.
B. A child with learning disability essentially has an IQ score less than 70.
C. Intellectual Disability occurs before age 18.
D. Intellectual Disability and learning Disability both are Developmental Disability.

23. The Assessment done during or before instruction is known as:
A. Summative Assessment
B. Formative Assessment
C. Formal Assessment
D. Diagnostic Assessment

24. 'Autism' was first described by:
A. Samuel Kirk
B. Leo Kanner
C. B.F. Skinner
D. J.B. Watson

25. During the developmental period of foetus, head is well developed before his legs. This best describes which of the following tendency of development?
A. Proximo-distal
B. Cephalo-caudal
C. Uniformity
D. Integration

26. Which of the following is ***not*** a process of Cognitive Development as given by Piaget?
A. Assimilation
B. Accommodation
C. Adaptation
D. Shaping

27. Which of the following is ***not*** a type of intelligence as proposed by Gardener?
A. Musical Intelligence
B. Linguistic Intelligence
C. Logico-Mathematical Intelligence
D. Creative Intelligence

28. Which of the following is ***not*** related to the classical conditioning experiment?
A. Extinction
B. Spontaneous Recovery

C. Shaping
D. Stimulus Discrimination

29. A mother gently strokes her infant's forehead each time immediate before breast reeding. Soon, she noticed that each time the baby's forehead is stroked, he makes active sucking movement. The baby's behaviour best describes:
A. Trial and Error learning
B. Classical Conditioning
C. Operant Conditioning
D. Social Learning

30. In which of the following stage of Cognitive Development, as described by Jean Piaget, a child become capable of understanding 'Conservation'?
A. Sensory Motor Stage
B. Pre-operational Stage
C. Concrete Operational Stage
D. Formal Operational Stage

PART-II

भाषा-I: हिन्दी

निर्देशः *निम्नलिखित प्रश्नों के उत्तर देने के लिए* ***सबसे उचित*** *विकल्प चुनिए।*

31. असंगत कथन छाँटिए :
A. नापाक इरादे से की जाने वाली मंत्रणा–दित्सा
B. दोपहर से पहले का समय–पूर्वाह्न
C. जिसे देखकर रोंगटे खड़े हो जाएँ–लोमहर्षक
D. बालुका युक्त तट/भूमि–सिकता

32. किस वाक्य में सर्वनाम पदबंध का प्रयोग हुआ है?
A. मेरे रिश्तेदारों में से कोई समय पर नहीं पहुँचा।
B. रिश्तों में स्वार्थ देखने वाले युवा सान्निध्य की ऊष्मा पहचानें।
C. राम ने लंका के अत्याचारी, राक्षस-राज रावण को मार डाला।
D. पाँचवीं मंजिल से गिरा, मरेगा नहीं तो क्या जिंदा रहेगा।

33. ***अशुद्ध*** संधि वाला विकल्प चुनिए :
A. मद + उन्मत्त = मदोन्मत्त
B. विद्वत् + मुख = विद्वन्मुख
C. तत् + उपरान्त = तदोपरान्त
D. षट् + आयतन = षडायतन

34. किस विकल्प में तत्पुरुष समास ***नहीं*** है?
A. वाक्चातुर्य B. तीर्थाटन
C. अरण्यरोदन D. मीनकेतु

35. तत्सम-तद्भव की दृष्टि से ***असंगत*** विकल्प चुनिए :
A. वार्ताक – बैंगन
B. लोहमशा – लोमड़ी
C. मस्तक – माथा
D. शण्ठिका – सोंठ

36. वार्तनिक दृष्टि से ***अशुद्ध*** विकल्प चुनिए :
A. विद्वता B. गीतांजली
C. पक्षिगण D. स्वामिभक्त

37. किस वाक्य में सार्वनामिक विशेषण का प्रयोग हुआ है?
A. तुम सब आ गए; अच्छे कहाँ रह गए।
B. जो बाहर खड़ा है उसे अन्दर बुलाओ।
C. तुम छात्रों के लिए कुछ किताबें ले आओ।
D. कुछ तुम करो; कुछ मैं करूँगा।

38. निम्न में से किस विकल्प में 'गरुड' का पर्याय ***नहीं*** है?
A. अहिभोजी B. वैनतेय
C. हेरम्ब D. खगनाथ

39. 'वयोवृद्ध' शब्द में संधि है :
A. स्वर संधि B. वर्णागम संधि
C. विसर्ग संधि D. व्यंजन संधि

40. किस विकल्प में दो उपसर्गों का प्रयोग ***नहीं*** हुआ है?
A. सारोपा B. सहगामिनी
C. पुनरुद्धार D. समाधि

41. ***अशुद्ध*** वाक्य चुनिए :
A. आपसे मिलकर मुझे आनन्द का आभास हुआ।
B. मेरठ में कई दर्शनीय स्थल हैं।
C. यह छात्रवृत्ति केवल छात्राओं के लिए है।
D. मैं अपना मत स्पष्ट करना चाहता हूँ।

42. किस वाक्य में 'इच्छार्थ वृत्ति' का प्रयोग हुआ है?
A. ईश्वर तुम्हारा भला करे।
B. कृपया यह प्रकरण जाँच दीजिए।
C. लगता है इस वर्ष खूब वर्षा होगी।
D. यदि वह पढ़ता तो आज सफल हो जाता।

43. निम्न में से भाववाच्य चुनिए :
A. गर्मियों में रोज नहाया जाता है।
B. नानी द्वारा कहानी सुनाई गई।
C. कुत्ता सारी रात भौंकता है।
D. किसानों द्वारा फसल काट ली गई है।

44. निम्न में 'संकर शब्द' किस विकल्प में ***नहीं*** है?

A. विज्ञापनदाता
B. डबलरोटी
C. आमचुनाव
D. हिन्दीकरण

45. 'वह दिनभर लिखता रहा।' वाक्य में प्रयुक्त क्रिया विशेषण का भेद इंगित कीजिए :

A. कालवाचक क्रिया विशेषण
B. रीतिवाचक क्रिया विशेषण
C. स्थानवाचक क्रिया विशेषण
D. परिमाणवाचक क्रिया विशेषण

PART-II

Language-II : English

Directions: *Answer the following questions by selecting the* ***most appropriate*** *option.*

46. Choose the word which is spelt ***correctly***:

A. Disentigration B. Disintegration
C. Dissintegration D. Desintegration

47. Choose the ***correct*** word for the following expression:

One who makes maps or charts.

A. Cartoonist B. Cartographer
C. Choreographer D. Choirmaster

48. Fill in the blank with appropriate conjunction :

Grievances cannot be redressed .... they are known.

A. unless B. and
C. but D. before

49. "He wore a turban made of silk."

The underlined words are :

A. Adverb B. Adverb Phrase
C. Adjective Phrase D. Noun Phrase

50. "There is a mystery about his death and the police are looking into it."

The underlined phrasal verb means :

A. To investigate
B. To take care of
C. To look behind
D. To revise quickly

51. Fill in the blank with appropriate preposition :

We stayed .... Mumbai for five days.

A. in B. at
C. into D. by

52. *Hearing* the noise, the boy woke up :

A. Pronoun B. Noun
C. Verb D. Participle

53. Fill in the blank with the correct option :

I have not heard the .... news.

A. latest B. late
C. latter D. later

54. Choose the most appropriate modal for the blank:

When I was young, I .... climb any tree in the forest.

A. can B. must
C. may D. could

55. Fill in the blank with appropriate preposition :

We're going for a drive .... the country.

A. on B. at
C. in D. for

56. Fill in the blank by choosing the ***correct*** option :

He is .... his glasses.

A. look for B. look
C. looking for D. will look

57. Choose the ***correct*** answer from the options below :

"I took it home with me", She said.

A. She just took it home.
B. She said she had taken it home with her.
C. She said she would take it home.
D. She said she will take it home with her.

58. Choose the ***correct*** passive construction for the given sentence.

They were carrying the injured player off the field.

A. The injured player was being carried off the field.
B. The injured player will be carried off the field.
C. The injured player must be taken off the field.
D. Carry the injured player off the field.

59. Choose the ***correct*** verb for the blank from the options below :

The earth .... round the sun.

A. move B. moved
C. moves D. shall move

60. "They arrived soon-after."

The word 'after' is used as :

A. Preposition B. Adverb
C. Adjecti D. Conjunction

PART-III

General Studies : Quantitative Aptitude, Reasoning Ability and GK & Awareness

Directions: *Answer the following questions by selecting the most appropriate option.*

61. Arjun travels half of his journey by train at the speed of 120 km/hr and rest half by car at 80 km/hr. What is his average speed ?

A. 88 km/hr
B. 92 km/hr
C. 96 km/hr
D. 100 km/hr

62. If 11 oranges are bought for ₹ 10 and sold 10 oranges for ₹ 11. What is the gain in percentage?

A. 11% B. 21%
C. 25% D. 28%

63. Amulya does a piece of work in 2 days and Bindu does it in 6 days. In how many days will the two do it together?

A. 2/3 days
B. 3/2 days
C. 5/3 days
D. 3 days

64. A total of 324 coins of 20 paise and 25 paise make a sum of ₹ 71, then number of 20 paise coins is:

A. 124 B. 140
C. 200 D. 210

65. How many 6's are there in the following number series, each of which is immediately preceded by 1 or 5 and immediately followed by 3 or 9?

263756429613416391569231654321967

A. One
B. Two
C. Three
D. Four

66. If "BORN" is coded as "APQO" and "LACK" is coded as "KBBL", then "GRlD" will be coded as :

A. FSEH B. SFHE
C. FSHE D. FHSE

67. There are deer and peacocks in a zoo. By counting heads they are 80. The number of their legs is 200. How many peacocks are there?

A. 20 B. 40
C. 52 D. 60

68. Which set of numbers is like the given set?

2, 14, 16

A. 2, 7, 8
B. 2, 9, 16
C. 3, 21, 24
D. 4, 16, 18

69. Statements :

I. All players are doctors.
II. Some doctors are musicians.

Conclusions :

I. Some doctors are players as well as musicians.
II. All musicians are doctors.

Then which of the following is ***correct***?

A. Only conclusion I follows.
B. Only conclusion II follows.
C. Both conclusion I and II follow.
D. Neither conclusion I nor II follows.

70. If '+' mean '÷', '×' mean '–', '÷' mean '+' and '–' mean '×', then

16 ÷ 8 × 6 – 2 + 12 = ?

A. 22 B. 24
C. 23 D. 120

71. A is B's sister, C is B's mother, D is C's father, E is D's mother, then how is A related to D ?

A. Daughter
B. Mother
C. Grand Mother
D. Grand Father

72. Find the next term of the following series :

0, 5, 22, 57, 116, ?

A. 205 B. 216
C. 192 D. 207

73. A tank is $\frac{2}{5}$ part full. If 16 litres of water is added to the tank, it becomes $\frac{6}{7}$ part full, then total capacity of tank is :

A. 24 litres
B. 35 litres
C. 38 litres
D. 42 litres

74. What is the number of odd days in a leap year ?

A. 0 B. 1
C. 2 D. 3

75. Find the least number, when divided by 12, 15, 20 and 54, leaves in each case a remainder of 8:

A. 504 B. 540

C. 546 D. 548

76. If A's income is 40% less than that of B. How much per cent B's income is more than that of A ?

A. 25% B. 40%

C. $33\frac{1}{3}\%$ D. $66\frac{2}{3}\%$

77. Find the least number by which 294 must be multiplied to make it a perfect square.

A. 3 B. 4

C. 6 D. 12

78. If the fractions $\frac{2}{5}, \frac{3}{8}, \frac{4}{9}, \frac{5}{13}$ and $\frac{6}{11}$ are arranged in ascending order, which one will be fourth place?

A. $\frac{3}{8}$ B. $\frac{4}{9}$

C. $\frac{5}{13}$ D. $\frac{6}{11}$

79. Find the average of first seven prime numbers.

A. 8 B. 9

C. $8\frac{1}{7}$ D. $8\frac{2}{7}$

80. Find out the odd-one :

A. EJNO B. HMQR

C. KPSU D. NSWX

81. The Wahabi leader, who was arrested in charge of Sedition during 19th century:

A. Muhammad Zafar

B. Ghazzan Khan

C. Mubarak Ali

D. Salman Khan

82. Match the following :

Education Institute	**District**
(*a*) I. I. I. T.	(*i*) Rohtak
(*b*) I. I. M.	(*ii*) Sonipat
(*c*) N.I. D.	(*iii*) Punchkula
(*d*) N. I. F. T.	(*iv*) Kurukshetra

Choose the ***correct*** code :

	(*a*)	(*b*)	(*c*)	(*d*)
A.	(*ii*)	(*i*)	(*iii*)	(*iv*)
B.	(*ii*)	(*i*)	(*iv*)	(*iii*)
C.	(*iv*)	(*i*)	(*iii*)	(*ii*)
D.	(*i*)	(*ii*)	(*iii*)	(*iv*)

83. How many Wildlife Sanctuaries are there in Jhajjar district?

A. Two B. Three

C. One D. Four

84. How many Tahsils are there in Haryana ?

A. 71 B. 93

C. 76 D. 68

85. The area of Haryana, which was considered under the sphere of influence of Bhadanakas during the Pre-medieval period :

A. Rewari

B. Ambala

C. Panipat

D. Kurukshetra

86. Consider the following statements about Lala Murlidhar :

(*a*) He practiced Law at Ambala.

(*b*) He attended the first session of Congress held at Bombay.

Which of the above statement/statements is/are true ?

A. Only (*a*) is true.

B. Only (*b*) is true.

C. Neither (*a*) nor (*b*) is true.

D. Both (*a*) and (*b*) are true.

87. Consider the following statements about KMP Expressway :

(*a*) It is also known as Western Peripheral Expressway.

(*b*) Five new cities will be developed along with the KMP Expressway.

Which of the above statement/s is/are true?

A. Only (*a*) is true.

B. Only (*b*) is true.

C. Neither (*a*) nor (*b*) is true.

D. Both (*a*) and (*b*) are true.

88. Who among the following athletes won the Gold in Men's 800 m. race at Asian Games—2018?

A. Jinson Johnson

B. Manjit Singh

C. Arpinder Singh

D. Rakesh Kumar

89. Where the Vulture Conservation and Breeding Center situated?

A. Kairu B. Morni

C. Zhabua D. Pinjore

90. Which of the following districts has the lowest urban population?

A. Mewat B. Mahendragarh

C. Jind D. Sirsa

PART-IV

Social Studies

Directions: *Answer the following questions by selecting the* ***most appropriate*** *option.*

91. The year, in which Gandhiji was arrested for the charge of sedition :

A. 1920 B. 1934
C. 1922 D. 1944

92. Who has given the idea of 'Complex Equality'?

A. Milton Friedman
B. Michael Walzer
C. Isaiah Berlin
D. F. A. Hayek

93. What is the meaning of Per Capita Income?

A. NNP × Population
B. NNP + Population
C. Population ÷ NNP
D. Total Capital ÷ NNP

94. In India sex ratio refers to the numbers of females per .... males.

A. 100 B. 1,000
C. 10,000 D. 1,00,000

95. Who is the "lender of the last resort" in India?

A. SBI B. RBI
C. NABARD D. SEBI

96. The royal cavalry of Shivaji was called :

A. Bargir B. Risala
C. Silahdar D. Dabeer

97. Arrange the following events in chronological order :

(*i*) Shimla Conference to discuss Wavell Plan
(*ii*) Mutiny of Royal Indian Navy
(*iii*) Arrival of Cabinet Mission
(*iv*) The 'Direct Action Day' observed by Muslim League

A. (*iv*), (*iii*), (*ii*), (*i*)
B. (*i*), (*iii*), (*ii*), (*iv*)
C. (*i*), (*ii*), (*iii*), (*iv*)
D. (*i*) (*iv*), (*iii*), (*ii*)

98. The Separate Electorate was first introduced in India by :

A. Indian Councils Act, 1892
B. Indian Councils Act, 1909
C. Government of India Act, 1919
D. Government of India Act, 1935

99. 'Bardoli Chheerha' are local storms occurring in :

A. Tripura
B. Jammu and Kashmir
C. Karnataka
D. Assam

100. Arrange the following events of the struggle of 1857 in chronological order :

(*a*) Uprising in Meerut
(*b*) Uprising in Lucknow
(*c*) Uprising in Jhansi
(*d*) Uprising in Nasirabad

A. (*d*), (*a*), (*c*), (*b*)
B. (*a*), (*d*), (*b*), (*c*)
C. (*c*), (*b*), (*a*), (*d*)
D. (*b*), (*c*), (*d*), (*a*)

101. Which of the following Iron and Steel Plant has been developed with Russian Collaboration?

A. Vizag Steel Plant
B. Rourkela Steel Plant
C. Bhilai Steel Plant
D. Durgapur Steel Plant

102. Karewas are:

A. Glacial deposits
B. Tropical grasslands
C. A tribe of Jammu and Kashmir
D. A local wind of Himachal Pradesh

103. Kalahandi and Sambalpur are leading producers of:

A. Iron-ore B. Bauxite
C. Mica D. Gold

104. Which one of the following is ***not*** correctly matched?

Article of the Indian Constitution		Provision
A. 76	–	Attorney-General of India
B. 148	–	Comptroller and Auditor General of India
C. 324	–	Election Commission of India
D. 337	–	National Commission for Scheduled Castes

105. Which of the following is ***not*** correctly matched?

Inventor		Agricultural Inventions
A. Jethroo Tull	–	Seed Drill
B. Charles Townshend	–	Rotation of Crops
C. Robert Bakewell	–	Technique to improve breeds of live-stock
D. Arthur Young	–	Chemical Fertilizer

106. The male and female literacy rate of India as per Census 2011 (Final data) is :
A. 80.89 – 64.64
B. 81.89 – 63.64
C. 80.69 – 64.24
D. 81.89 – 63.63

107. Which year is known as year of great division for India's population?
A. 1921 B. 1931
C. 1951 D. 1991

108. Which of the following are the characteristics of Liberal Democracy?
I. More than one political parties freely competing for political power.
II. Political offices not confined to any privileged class.
III. Periodic election based on universal adult franchise.
IV. Dependent Judiciary.

Correct option is :
A. I, II and III
B. I, II and IV
C. I, III and IV
D. II, III and IV

109. Which of the following are the characteristics of Federal Government?
I. Supremacy of the Constitution.
II. Distribution of powers between the Federal Centre and the federating units.
III. Presence of Bi-cameral Federal legislature.

Correct option is :
A. I and II B. II and III
C. I, II and III D. I and III

110. Which of the following pair is incorrect?
A. Cyclones — Indian Ocean
B. Willy-Willies — Western Australia
C. Typhoons — East Atlantic Ocean
D. Hurricane — Atlantic Ocean

111. Which of the following thinkers are related to 'Elite Theory of Democracy'?
I. Schumpeter
II. Pareto
III. Mosca
IV. David Truman

Correct option is :
A. I, II and III B. II, III and IV
C. I, III and IV D. III and IV

112. In which type of unemployment a person is apparently employed but his contribution to the production is almost nil?
A. Chronic B. Disguised
C. Structural D. Seasonal

113. ICAR stands for :
A. Indian Council of Agro Research
B. Indian Committee of Agriculture Review
C. Indian Commercial and Agro Research
D. Indian Council of Agriculture Research

114. The Indian coastal plains along the Bay of Bengal are called as :
A. Coromandel & Northern Sarkar
B. Coromandel & Malabar
C. Northern Sarkar & Konkan
D. Malabar & Kannad

115. Doon Valleys of Himalaya are situated between :
A. Greater Himalaya & Lesser Himalaya
B. Greater Himalaya & Karakoram Mountains
C. Lesser Himalaya & Shivalik Mountains
D. Lesser Himalaya & Karakoram Mountains

116. In which General Election did the Congress Party lost majority in the Parliament for the first time?
A. 1967 B. 1977
C. 1980 D. None of these

117. Which of the following is ***not*** a constituent of Human Development Index (HDI)?
A. Per Capita Income (on the basis of Gross National Income)
B. Life expectancy at birth
C. Gross Enrolment Rate
D. Health and Nutrition

118. 'SAIL' stands for :
A. Steel Authority of India Limited
B. Small Agricultural Industry Limited
C. South Asian Investment Limited
D. None of these

119. The terminology 'one dimensional man' related to which thinker?
A. Habermas
B. Herbert Marcuse
C. Erich Fromm
D. Althusser

120. Which one of the following thinkers believes that Nationalism is an expression of cultural and social mechanism peculiar to modernity, such as modern communications?
A. Benedict Anderson
B. Earnest Gellner
C. Karl Deutsch
D. Hobsbawm

121. The inner planets are :
A. Satellites of planets

B. Gaseous planets
C. Planets between Sun and Earth only
D. Planets between Sun and Belt of Asteroids

122. Aphelion is :
A. When the earth is nearest from the moon.
B. When the earth is nearest from the sun.
C. When the earth is farthest from the moon.
D. When the earth is farthest from the sun.

123. Which of the following statements are ***correct*** in context to 'ASEAN'?
I. It was created on 8 August, 1967.
II. Indonesia, Malaysia, Philippines, Singapore and Thailand are its founding members.
III. At present there are 10 member countries of 'ASEAN'.

Correct option is :
A. I and II
B. I and III
C. II and III
D. I, II and III

124. Which of the following is ***not*** an intrusive volcanic landform?
A. Batholith
B. Lacolith
C. Caldera
D. Phacolith

125. Speaker of the Lok Sabha addresses his/her resignation to :
A. President of India
B. Chief Justice of India
C. Deputy Speaker of Lok Sabha
D. Vice President of India

126. Socialist Economy is a :
A. Planned Economy
B. Price Determined Economy
C. Mixed Economy
D. Profit Oriented Economy

127. UNFCCC (United Nations Framework Convention on Climate Change) enters into force from :
A. 10 May, 1992
B. 5 June, 1992
C. 5 June, 1994
D. 21 March, 1994

128. Which one of the following books has ***not*** been written by John Rawls?
A. A Theory of Justice
B. The Law of Peoples
C. Political Liberalism
D. Capitalism and Freedom

129. Which of the following pair is incorrect ?

Gases		Percentage of Volume
A. Nitrogen	–	78.08
B. Carbon dioxide	–	0.0036
C. Oxygen	–	20.95
D. Argon	–	0.93

130. A horizontal demand curve implies that the elasticity of demand is:
A. equal to one
B. less than one
C. zero
D. infinite

131. "I may not agree what you say but I shall die for your right to say it." Who made this statement?
A. J.J. Rousseau B. Voltaire
C. J. S. Mill D. John Locke

132. Who were 'Banjara' in Medieval India?
A. Transporter of goods such as gram
B. A warrior community
C. Dancers and Musician
D. A Muslim community

133. Al-Biruni's 'Kitab-ul-Hind' is written in which of the following language?
A. Persian B. Arabic
C. Turkish D. Urdu

134. What was the condition of Indian Agriculture Sector before independence?
A. Sustainable development
B. Self-dependent
C. Advanced
D. Stagnation

135. The force exerted by rotation of the earth is known as:
A. Nuclear Force
B. Spring Force
C. Coriolis
D. Gravitational

136. The famous sculpture 'Descent of Ganga' is found at:
A. Badami B. Amaravati
C. Mahabalipuram D. Kanchi

137. Which one is **not** a mathematical mean in the following?
A. Mode B. Mean
C. G.M. D. H.M.

138. The Sufi Saint whose Dargah is situated in Ajodhan:
A. Sheikh Kutubuddin Bakhtiyar Kaki
B. Sheikh Fariduddin ganj-i-Shakar
C. Sheikh Nasiruddin
D. Sheikh Nizamuddin

139. The three components of maps are:
A. Distance, direction and symbol
B. Distance, size and temperature
C. Direction, shape and pressure
D. Symbol, mass and speed

140. Which among the following Gupta rulers maternally related to Lichhavis?
A. Shrigupta
B. Ghatotkachgupta
C. Samudragupta
D. Chandragupta-I

141. Which one of the following is a variable cost in the short run?
A. Payment of rent on building
B. Cost of raw materials
C. Cost of equipment
D. Interest payment on past borrowings

142. What is the full form of "FERA"?
A. Finance and Export Regulation Act
B. Foreign Exchange Regulation Act
C. Foreign Export Revaluation Association
D. Funds Exchange Regulation Association

143. Which Article of the Constitution of India is related to the procedure for impeachment of the President ?
A. 58 B. 59
C. 60 D. 61

144. Which of the following statements is ***not*** true about Dancing Girl Statuette of Indus Valley Civilization?
A. It was found in Mohan-jo-Daro.
B. It is sculpted in bronze.
C. There are more than two dozens bangles in the left arm of the Dancing Girl.
D. The height of this statuette is 2 feet.

145. Which of the following Stupa is built in white stone?
A. Sanchi
B. Bharhut
C. Amaravati
D. Sarnath

146. Which one of the following pair is **not** correctly matched in context to Cold War?

Year		Event
A. 1947	–	Truman Doctrine
B. 1954	–	Creation of SEATO
C. 1955	–	Creation of Baghdad Pact
D. 1957	–	Intervention of USSR in Hungary

147. When was the National Green Tribunal Act implemented for the purpose of environmental protection?
A. August, 2008
B. October, 2010
C. September, 2010
D. June, 2005

148. Asthenosphere is:
A. Lower portion of Mantle
B. Upper portion of Mantle
C. Lower portion of Crust
D. Upper portion of Crust

149. All of the following are determinants of demand, except :
A. Px
B. Py
C. Quantity Supplied
D. Income

150. 'Long Walk to Freedom' is the Autobiography of :
A. Winnie Mandela
B. Aung San Suu Kyi
C. Nelson Mandela
D. Barak Obama

Answers

1	**2**	**3**	**4**	**5**	**6**	**7**	**8**	**9**	**10**
D	B	D	A	A	D	C	C	A	A
11	**12**	**13**	**14**	**15**	**16**	**17**	**18**	**19**	**20**
A	D	C	B	A	C	D	D	C	C
21	**22**	**23**	**24**	**25**	**26**	**27**	**28**	**29**	**30**
D	B	B	B	B	D	D	C	B	C
31	**32**	**33**	**34**	**35**	**36**	**37**	**38**	**39**	**40**
A	A	C	D	B	A,D	C	C	C	B
41	**42**	**43**	**44**	**45**	**46**	**47**	**48**	**49**	**50**
A	A	A	A	A	B	B	A	C	A
51	**52**	**53**	**54**	**55**	**56**	**57**	**58**	**59**	**60**
A	D	A	D	C	C	B	A	C	B

61	62	63	64	65	66	67	68	69	70
C	B	B	C	B	C	D	C,D	D	C
71	**72**	**73**	**74**	**75**	**76**	**77**	**78**	**79**	**80**
*	A	B	C	D	D	C	B	D	C
81	**82**	**83**	**84**	**85**	**86**	**87**	**88**	**89**	**90**
A	B	A	B	A	D	D	B	D	A
91	**92**	**93**	**94**	**95**	**96**	**97**	**98**	**99**	**100**
C	B	B	B	B	A	C	B	D	B
101	**102**	**103**	**104**	**105**	**106**	**107**	**108**	**109**	**110**
C	A	B	D	D	A	A	A	C	C
111	**112**	**113**	**114**	**115**	**116**	**117**	**118**	**119**	**120**
A	B	D	A	C	B	D	A	B	C
121	**122**	**123**	**124**	**125**	**126**	**127**	**128**	**129**	**130**
D	D	D	C	C	A	D	D	B	D
131	**132**	**133**	**134**	**135**	**136**	**137**	**138**	**139**	**140**
B	A	B	D	C	C	A	B	A	C
141	**142**	**143**	**144**	**145**	**146**	**147**	**148**	**149**	**150**
B	B	D	D	C	D	B	B	C	C

Previous Paper (Solved)

Haryana Teacher Eligibility Test (HTET)

TGT Social Studies (Level-2), Exam 2017*

PART-I

Child Development and Pedagogy

Directions: *Answer the following questions by selecting the **most appropriate** option.*

1. Which of the following is ***not*** a subordinate law given in 'trial and error'?
A. Law of Multiple response
B. Law of Attitude
C. Law of Exercise
D. Law of Response by analogy

2. According to Piaget, the age range of the substage 'mental representation', of the sensory motor stage is:
A. Birth to 1 month
B. 4 to 8 months
C. 8 to 12 months
D. 18 months to 2 years

3. The psychologist who tried to develop a learning theory using principles of topology (A branch of Mathematics) is:
A. Kurt Lewin B. Sigmund Freud
C. William James D. Skinner

4. Which of the following is ***not*** an example of children with special needs as per RPWD Act, 2016?
A. Acid attack victims
B. Cerebral palsy
C. Children with visual impairment
D. None of these

5. Testing used during instruction to aid in planning and diagnosis is known as:
A. Formative Assessment
B. Summative Assessment
C. Normative Assessment
D. None of these

6. The teacher said Rekha that she is not allowed to participate in Game period as she has not completed her home work. It is an example of:
A. Negative reinforcement
B. Punishment
C. Positive reinforcement
D. Tangible reward

7. The ability of classification develops at:
A. Sensory motor stage
B. Preoperational stage
C. Concrete operational stage
D. None of the above

8. Which type of teaching material is most effective for a child with visual impairment?
A. Video based B. Visual material
C. Tactile based D. None of these

9. Modelling is the concept given by:
A. Albert Bandura B. J.B. Watson
C. Freud D. Vygotsky

10. Which of the following has viewed the child as 'Tabula-Rasa' (Blank-Slate)?
A. Freud B. Piaget
C. Skinner D. John Locke

11. Which of the following theory viewed cognitive development as a socially mediated process?
A. Socio Cultural Theory
B. Social Learning Theory
C. Psycho Sexual Theory
D. Sign Learning Theory

12. A three year old boy says, "The sun is angry'. It is an example of:
A. Animism B. Egocentrism
C. Criticism D. Intuition

13. Which of the following is ***not*** a type of Intelligence as given by Gardner?
A. Musical intelligence
B. Spatial intelligence
C. Interpersonal intelligence
D. Analytical intelligence

14. "TEACCH" programme is mostly used to teach children with:
A. Hearing impairment
B. Gifted students
C. Intellectual disability
D. Autism

*Exam held on 24-12-2017.

15. Which of the following studied moral development in children?
A. Kohlberg B. Piaget
C. Both A and B D. None of the above

16. Providing salary to the teacher at the end of every month, which schedule of reinforcement it reflects?
A. Fixed ratio B. Variable ratio
C. Fixed interval D. Variable interval

17. Who proposed that all children have language acquisition device?
A. Piaget B. Chomsky
C. Vygotsky D. Dan Slobin

18. Who proposed Advanced Organizer Model of teaching?
A. Bruner B. Pavlov
C. Ausubel D. Piaget

19. Multiple Intelligence theory was proposed by:
A. Alfred Binet B. Jean Piaget
C. Harward Gardner D. Jensen

20. According to Freud the age range of 'Oral stage' of psycho-sexual development is:
A. Birth to one year
B. Birth to two years
C. Birth to three years
D. None of these

21. The long-term memory for 'how to do things' is known as:
A. Procedural memory B. Episodic memory
C. Immediate memory D. Sensory memory

22. The triarchic theory of successful intelligence was given by:
A. Spearman B. Binet
C. Thorndike D. Sternberg

23. The law which is ***not*** a part of Gestalt views of learning is:
A. Law of similarity B. Law of proximity
C. Law of closure D. Law of use

24. After occurrence of a desirable behaviour, the teacher says 'very good' to the child. She has used:
A. Primary reinforcer
B. Secondary reinforcer
C. Negative reinforcement
D. None of the above

25. According to Ecological system theory, which system includes 'values'?
A. Micro system B. Macro system
C. Meso system D. Exo system

26. Using our current 'schemes' to interpret the external world is known as:
A. Assimilation B. Accommodation
C. Organization D. None of these

27. Which of the following is ***not*** an example of acquired motive?
A. Attitude B. Interest
C. Curiosity D. Hunger

28. Which of the following is an example of Developmental Disorder?
A. Blindness B. Hearing impairment
C. Intellectual disability D. Leprosy

29. Which part of the brain supports grammatical processing and language production?
A. Broca's area B. Frontal lobe
C. Perietal lobe D. Occipital lobe

30. Programmed learning is based on the work of:
A. Skinner B. Piaget
C. Pavlov D. Bandura

PART-II

भाषा-I: हिन्दी

निर्देश: *निम्नलिखित प्रश्नों के उत्तर देने के लिए* ***सबसे उचित*** *विकल्प चुनिए।*

31. कौन-सा शब्द उर्दू उपसर्ग से निर्मित है?
A. खुशबू B. स्वयंसिद्ध
C. अधकच्चा D. निहत्था

32. ***अशुद्ध*** विलोम युग्म को पहचानिए :
A. आध्यात्मिक-आधिदैविक B. स्मरण-विस्मरण
C. हेय-स्तुत्य D. वृद्धि-क्षय

33. किस विकल्प में वर्तनी की दृष्टि से ***अशुद्ध*** शब्द है?
A. दवाईयाँ B. पौलस्त्य
C. आभिजात्य D. आपराधिक

34. किस विकल्प में संधि नियम का उल्लंघन होने के कारण ***अशुद्ध*** शब्द बना है?
A. अभिषेक B. निषेध
C. अनुशंगी D. सुषुप्ति

35. किस विकल्प में ऊनतावाचक तद्धित प्रत्यय है?
A. बहूटी B. बहिनापा
C. दूधैल D. चुड़िहारा

36. *"कोमल गात, मृदुल बसंत, हरे-हरे ये पात"*
—उक्त पंक्ति में प्रयुक्त पदों में से कौन-सा पद विशेषण ***नहीं*** है?
A. मृदुल B. गात
C. हरे-हरे D. कोमल

37. निम्न में से किस विकल्प में कर्मधारय का उदाहरण है?
A. सूरकृत B. नीलगगन
C. आजीवन D. रामोपासक

38. कौन-सा विकल्प लिंग सम्बन्धिनी ***अशुद्धि*** से युक्त है?
A. पापिनी स्त्री B. बुद्धिमती भार्या
C. गुणवान कन्या D. प्रभावशालिनी भाषा

39. निम्न में से कौन-सा शब्द 'योगरूढ़' है?
A. अहिंसा B. पाशविक
C. मुख्यमंत्री D. चक्षु:श्रवा

40. किस शब्द में विसर्ग संधि का प्रयोग ***नहीं*** हुआ है?
A. यशोदा B. पयोद
C. तमोगुण D. महोदधि

41. किस विकल्प में 'नामधातु' क्रिया है?
A. धड़धड़ाहट B. खिलवाना
C. उठना D. गरमाना

42. 'परुष' का समानार्थक (पर्याय) शब्द है :
A. कठोर B. पुरुष
C. परख D. प्रणाली

43. 'आप भला तो जग भला' वाक्य किस सर्वनाम का उदाहरण बनेगा?
A. संबंधवाचक सर्वनाम B. निजवाचक सर्वनाम
C. निश्चयवाचक सर्वनाम D. पुरुषवाचक सर्वनाम

44. कौन-सा शब्द स्त्रीलिंग बोधक ***नहीं*** है?
A. मृत्यु B. ऋतु
C. रेणु D. तालु

45. निम्न कथनों में से कौन-सा कथन ***असत्य*** है?
A. 'ड्' उत्क्षिप्त व्यंजन है।
B. 'स्' संघर्षी व्यंजन है।
C. 'द्' स्पर्शी व्यंजन है।
D. 'र्' पार्श्विक वर्ण है।

PART-II

Language-II : English

Directions: *Answer the following questions by selecting the* ***most appropriate*** *option.*

46. 'Dancing is her hobby.'
The underlined word is used as a:
A. verb B. gerund
C. participle D adjective

47. Choose the most appropriate modal for the blank:
She .... swim for hours at the age of eight.
A. can B. may
C. might D. could

48. "The girl who is wearing a red ribbon is my sister."
The underlined words are a:
A. Noun Clause B. Adjective Clause
C. Adverb Clause D. None of the above

49. Choose the most appropriate form of indirect speech for the given sentence:
He said to her, "you are a very reasonable person."
A. He said to her she is a very reasonable person.
B. He told her that she was a very reasonable person.
C. He told to her that he is a very reasonable person.
D. He said to her that she is a very reasonable person.

50. Fill in the blank with the appropriate preposition.
He lost all his property because of his addiction .... drinking and gambling.
A. with B. in
C. to D. of

51. "Business falls off during summer months."
The underlined phrasal verb means:
A. to decline B. to grow
C. to increase D. to disappear

52. Fill in the blank with the appropriate option:
"I paid the bill but the cashier did not give the ...."
A. receipt B. receive
C. receiving D. received

53. 'She could not figure out the theme of the play clearly.'
The underlined phrasal verb means:
A. comprehend B. examine
C. enjoy D. draw

54. Fill in the blank by choosing the correct option.
"Asha and I .... on M.G. Road when we saw an old man walking slowly."
A. were shopping B. have been shopping
C. had been shopping D. shopping

55. Choose the correct Passive Construction for the sentence given:
"Mrs. Sharma knows me."
A. I am known by Mrs. Sharma.
B. I was known by Mrs. Sharma.
C. I am known to Mrs. Sharma.
D. I have known to Mrs. Sharma.

56. Choose the correct word for the following expression:

One who is present everywhere

A. Omnipotent
B. Omniscient
C. Omnipresent
D. Omnission

57. Choose a suitable connector for the blank from the options given:

"My father burnt his hand .... he was lighting a candle."

A. but B. while
C. because D. since

58. "Maharana Pratap fought bravely and won the war." The underlined word in the sentence has been used as a:

A. Noun B. Verb
C. Adverb D. Adjective

59. 'Agreement' is a noun with 'ment' as a suffix. Which of the following options will become a noun if we add the suffix 'ment' to it?

A. amuse B. extort
C. correct D. colour

60. Choose the word which is spelt correctly:

A. comittee B. committe
C. committee D. commitee

PART-III

General Studies : Quantitative Aptitude, Reasoning Ability and GK & Awareness

Directions: *Answer the following questions by selecting the most appropriate option.*

61. If income of A is 20% less than income of B. How much percentage is B's income more than income of A?

A. 20% B. 25%
C. $16\frac{2}{3}\%$ D. $33\frac{1}{3}\%$

62. How many 9's are there which are followed by 9 in given series?

9879902999031992796569781967899290

A. 2 B. 4
C. 5 D. 6

63. $\frac{3}{7}$th part of a bucket can be filled in one minute. Rest part of the bucket can be filled in:

A. $\frac{7}{3}$ minutes B. 21 minutes
C. $\frac{4}{7}$ minute D. $\frac{4}{3}$ minutes

64. A number, when divided by 8, 12 and 15, gives always remainder 5. Then number is:

A. 9505 B. 9605
C. 9705 D. 9805

65. Find the smallest number such that if it is added to sum of squares of 9 and 10, then complete square is obtained:

A. 0 B. 3
C. 8 D. 15

66. $13\frac{1}{2}-\left[4\frac{1}{2}-\left\{3-\left(2-\frac{1}{2}\right)\right\}\right]$ is equal to:

A. $9\frac{1}{2}$ B. $10\frac{1}{2}$
C. $10\frac{3}{4}$ D. $13\frac{1}{2}$

67. Average of eight numbers is 12. If each number is increased by 2, then average of new numbers is:

A. 13 B. 12
C. 15 D. 14

68. How many numbers are there from 1 to 100 which are completely divisible by 7?

A. 9 B. 11
C. 17 D. 14

69. Which of the following fraction is greater than 1/3?

A. $\frac{27}{82}$ B. $\frac{20}{61}$
C. $\frac{16}{45}$ D. $\frac{51}{154}$

70. Find the smallest number such that by multiplying it with 24, a complete square number is obtained:

A. 2 B. 3
C. 4 D. 6

71. Find the odd-one:

A. Oxygen
B. Ice
C. Water
D. Steam

72. The number of triangles shown in the figure is:

A. 6
B. 8
C. 10
D. 12

73. If GRASP is coded as INOPQ, BROWN is coded as RNSTU, then SPARROW will be coded as:

A. PQONNST
B. PQONNOT
C. POQNNSU
D. PQONNSU

74. **Statements :** I. A triangle has 3 angles.
II. A square has 4 angles.

Conclusion : A polygon has many angles.

Then which of the following is ***correct***?

A. Conclusion is correct.
B. Conclusion is wrong.
C. Conclusion is not logical.
D. None of these

75. In given figure, circle represents rich people, rectangle represents hardworking and triangle represents rural people. Then rural people who are hardworking but poor, are indicated by:

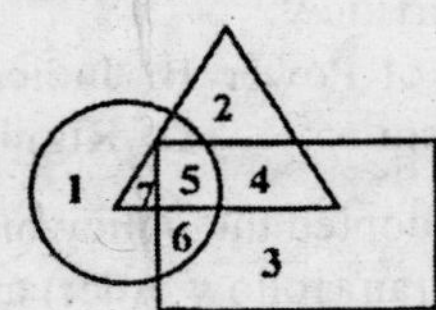

A. 5
B. 7
C. 4
D. 6

76. The maximum possible number of Sundays in 3 consecutive calendar months is:

A. 14
B. 15
C. 13
D. 12

77. A is brother of B, B is wife of C, C is son of D and D is wife of E. What is E to B?

A. Son-in-law
B. Father-in-law
C. Brother-in-law
D. Mother-in-law

78. There are seven numbers. Average of first four numbers is 4. Average of last four numbers is also 4. Average of all seven numbers is 3. Find the fourth number:

A. 4
B. 3
C. 11
D. 7

79. Find the missing number in given square:

5	25	18
15	10	12
20	5	?

A. 15
B. 10
C. 20
D. 25

80. Find the missing term of the series:
2, 7, 17, 32, ?, 77

A. 47
B. 52
C. 57
D. 62

81. The Deputy Speaker of 13th Legislative Assembly of Haryana is:

A. Kuldeep Sharma
B. Kanwar Pal
C. R.K. Nandal
D. Santosh Yadav

82. The river of Haryana, which originates from Rajasthan, is:

A. Markanda
B. Sahibi
C. Ghaggar
D. Saraswati

83. 'The Technological Institute of Textile and Science' is situated at:

A. Gurugram
B. Bhiwani
C. Rohtak
D. Panchkula

84. As per the Census-2011, the population density of Haryana is (in per square k.m.):

A. 478
B. 573
C. 385
D. 325

85. The first Nuclear Power Project of Haryana is being set-up at:

A. Gorakhpur
B. Kakroi
C. Sampla
D. Yamunanagar

86. Where has the Haryana government organised Pravasi Haryana Divas in 2017?

A. Ashoka University, Sonipat
B. Kingdom of Dream, Gurugram
C. Pinjore Garden, Panchkula
D. Vigyan Bhawan, New Delhi

87. The Math (Monastery), which was rejuvenated and chosen as main center by Baba Mastnath, was:

A. Kansrati
B. Asthal Bohar
C. Pehwa
D. Jalandhar

88. The tomb of Bu Ali Shah is situated at:

A. Hissar
B. Yamunanagar
C. Panipat
D. Jind

89. In which of the following locations, a National Park is situated?

A. Sultanpur
B. Bhindawas
C. Nahan
D. Abubshahar

90. The partner Nation in 31st Surajkund International Crafts Mela was:

A. Egypt
B. China
C. Thailand
D. Japan

PART-IV

Social Studies

Directions: *Answer the following questions by selecting the* ***most appropriate*** *option.*

91. The legend of Satyakam Jabal is mentioned in:
A. Jabal Upanishad
B. Brihadaranyaka Upanishad
C. Chhandogya Upanishad
D. Kathopanishad

92. Using the codes given below, identify the Vice-President/s of India's Constituent Assembly:
(*a*) B. N. Rau
(*b*) H. C. Mookerjee
(*c*) V. T. Krishnamachari
(*d*) G. V. Mavalankar
A. (*b*) and (*d*) B. (*a*) and (*c*)
C. only (*b*) D. (*b*) and (*c*)

93. The mid-Atlantic ridge is an example of:
A. Divergent plate boundary
B. Convergent plate boundary
C. Conservative plate boundary
D. Continent-Ocean convergence boundary

94. 'Kayal' are a distinguished feature of which of the following coast of India?
A. Kutch-Kathiawar B. Coromandal
C. Konkan D. Malabar

95. 'Milpa' is a shifting cultivation practised in:
A. Thailand B. Indonesia
C. Mexico D. North East India

96. If Marginal Rate of Technical Substitution (MRTS) is constant, then Production Possibility Curve will be:
A. downward sloping concave
B. downward sloping convex
C. downward sloping straight line
D. horizontal line parallel to X-axis

97. Secularism in Indian Constitution does ***not*** include:
A. No official religion of the state
B. Doctrine of Benevolent neutrality
C. Separation of state and religion
D. Doctrine of Principled Distance

98. Marginal propensity to save (Δ = change, y = income and s = saving):
A. $\Delta y/\Delta s$ B. y/s
C. $\Delta s/\Delta y$ D. s/y

99. In which of the following river, 'Majuli river island' is situated?
A. Brahmaputra B. Kaveri
C. Chambal D. Jhelum

100. Inter Tropical Convergence Zone (ITCZ) is located at:
A. Polar region B. Equatorial region
C. Temperate region D. None of these

101. The Gupta temple which is ***not*** situated in Madhya Pradesh?
A. Vishnu Temple of Tigawa
B. Shiv Temple of Bhumara
C. Dashavatara Temple of Deogarh
D. Bhitargaon Temple

102. When price of a good falls from ₹ 20 per unit to ₹ 15 per unit, its demand rises by 25 per cent. Calculate price elasticity of demand. (by percentage method)
A. 0.88 B. 1.0
C. 1.25 D. 0.33

103. The Harappan used to procure tin from:
A. Afghanistan B. Gujarat
C. Karnataka D. Rajasthan

104. Which one of the following is ***not*** exclusively a federal characteristic?
A. Distribution of Power B. Judicial review
C. Bi-Cameralism D. Rigid Constitution

105. Samudragupta adopted the policy of Sarvakardan (pay tribute), Agyakaran (follow order) and Pranamagaman (bow to him) with ruler of:
A. Kamarupa B. Kanchi
C. Vengi D. Abhira

106. Personal Bias is possible under:
A. Random sampling B. Purposive sampling
C. Stratified sampling D. Systematic sampling

107. Match the following:

Neolithic Site	***Salient feature***
(*a*) Burzahom	(*i*) Earliest Neolithic Site
(*b*) Mahagara	(*ii*) Ash Mound
(*c*) Utnoor	(*iii*) Rice Cultivation
(*d*) Mehargarh	(*iv*) Pit Dwelling

Code:
A. (*a*) - (*iv*), (*b*) - (*ii*), (*c*) - (*iii*), (*d*) - (*i*)
B. (*a*) - (*ii*), (*b*) - (*iv*), (*c*) - (*iii*), (*d*) - (*i*)
C. (*a*) - (*i*), (*b*) - (*ii*), (*c*) - (*iii*), (*d*) - (*iv*)
D. (*a*) - (*iv*), (*b*) - (*iii*), (*c*) - (*ii*), (*d*) - (*i*)

108. Among the following, what is ***not*** included in the concept of 'Equality'?
A. Protective Discrimination
B. Homogeneity
C. Reasonable classification
D. Equal opportunity

109. In order to correct the situation of deflation:
A. Securities are purchased by the commercial banks.
B. Securities are under possession by the commercial banks.
C. Securities are purchased by the central bank.
D. Securities are sold by the central bank.

110. The place, where Ashokan inscription has been found:
A. Ujjain B. Patliputra
C. Taxila D. Sanchi

111. Marginal revenue of a firm is constant throughout under ....
A. Perfect competition
B. Monopoly
C. Monopolistic competition
D. Oligopoly

112. The principle source of 'Indo-Greek' history is:
A. Buddhist Text B. Coins
C. Epigraph D. Travelogues

113. Which of the following is ***incorrect***?
A. $GDP_{MP} = NDP_{MP}$ + Depreciation
B. $GNP_{FC} = GNP_{MP}$ + Net indirect taxes
C. $NNP_{MP} = NDP_{MP}$ + Net factor income from abroad
D. $NDP_{FC} = GDP_{FC}$ – Depreciation

114. Which of the following Seismic waves are similar to sound waves?
A. L-waves B. S-waves
C. P-waves D. T-waves

115. As a consequence of the 42nd Constitution Amendment Act (1976), the following three terms were inserted in the preamble of the Constitution:
A. Socialist, Secular, Integrity
B. Socialist, Republic, Integrity
C. Secular, Democratic, Sovereign
D. Sovereign, Secular, Integrity

116. The map focus on specific information is called:
A. Political map B. Thematic map
C. Physical map D. Global map

117. Identify the terminology, which is ***not*** related to Feminism?
A. The Personal is the Political
B. Distinction between Sex and Gender
C. Patriarchy as a Power Structure
D. Will to Power

118. Which among the following states of India is ***not*** 'land locked'?
A. Jharkhand B. Chhattisgarh
C. Madhya Pradesh D. Karnataka

119. The interest elasticity of demand for money in liquidity trap is:
A. Zero B. Unity
C. Infinite D. Between zero and one

120. Identify the group of countries, in which democratic governments have been established during 1975 to 2000?
A. Russia, South Africa, Vietnam, Slovakia
B. Turkey, Laos, Albania, Hungary
C. Zimbabwe, Spain, Iran, Egypt
D. Italy, Greece, Poland, Latvia

121. Match List-I with List-II and select the correct answer by using the codes given below:

List-I ***(Name of State)***	***List-II*** ***(Year of Formation)***
(*a*) Gujarat	(*i*) 1966
(*b*) Jharkhand	(*ii*) 1960
(*c*) Haryana	(*iii*) 2000
(*d*) Sikkim	(*iv*) 1987
	(*v*) 1975

Codes:
A. (*a*) - (*ii*), (*b*) - (*iii*), (*c*) - (*iv*), (*d*) - (*v*)
B. (*a*) - (*i*), (*b*) - (*iii*), (*c*) - (*ii*), (*d*) - (*iv*)
C. (*a*) - (*ii*), (*b*) - (*iii*), (*c*) - (*i*), (*d*) - (*v*)
D. (*a*) - (*iv*), (*b*) - (*ii*), (*c*) - (*i*), (*d*) - (*iii*)

122. The cost curve which is a rectangular hyperbola is:
A. TFC curve B. TVC curve
C. AFC curve D. AVC curve

123. 'Jet Stream' blows from:
A. West to East B. East to West
C. South to North D. North to South

124. 'Megalopolis' term was given by:
A. Grifith Taylor B. Jean Gottman
C. Von Thunen D. Lewis Mumford

125. The 'Entrepot' port for Asia is:
A. Singapore B. Bangkok
C. Manila D. Kolkata

126. Among the following, what is ***not*** in conformity with the Idea of Democracy?
A. Rule of Law
B. Periodic Elections
C. Majoritarianism
D. Charter of Rights for citizens

127. In the distribution of subjects between the Union and the States, Cyber law belongs to:
A. Union list B. State list
C. Concurrent list D. Residuary subjects

128. Politics of which state is polarized along Vokkaliga-Lingayat castes?
A. Tamil Nadu B. Karnataka
C. Andhra Pradesh D. Kerala

129. Identify the ***incorrect*** statement about Mahalwari Land Revenue System:
A. The land revenue settlement was done with the entire village or mahal.
B. It was implemented in Doab area of Ganga-Yamuna and some parts of Central India.

C. The demand of revenue was to determine periodically.
D. Mahalwari system was devised by Alexander Reed.

130. Identify the ***incorrect*** pair of political party and its founder leader:
A. Jan Sangh — Shyama Prasad Mukherjee
B. Praja Socialist Party — N.G. Ranga
C. Independent Labour Party — Bhim Rao Ambedkar
D. Congress Socialist Party — Acharya Narendra Dev

131. The theme of Amir 'Khusrow's work 'Qiran-us-Sadain' is:
A. Reconciliation meeting of Kaiqubad and Bughra Khan
B. Military expeditions of Alauddin Khilaji
C. Gospels of Nizamuddin Auliya
D. Deval Rani - Khizra Khan episode

132. The turning point of human history which is associated with 'Fertile Crescent' (Part of West Asia):
A. Origin of Homo Sapiens
B. Beginning of Cultivation
C. Discovery of Iron
D. Emergence of Christianity

133. What does 'Jat' denote in Mansabdari system?
(*i*) Rank (*ii*) Salary
(*iii*) Military responsibility (*iv*) Social Status
Choose the ***correct*** code:
A. (*i*) & (*iii*) B. (*i*) & (*iv*)
C. (*i*) & (*ii*) D. (*i*), (*ii*), (*iii*) & (*iv*)

134. To meets the needs of the present generation without compromising the needs of future generation is called:
A. Economic Development
B. Sustainable Development
C. Social Development
D. Economic Growth

135. Identify the incorrect pair of Right and the related Fundamental Right in the Indian Constitution:
A. Right to Education – Right to Freedom
B. Freedom of Conscience – Right to Freedom of Religion
C. Right to Speedy Trial – Right to Constitutional Remedies
D. Right of Minorities – Cultural and Educational Right

136. The food item, which was ***not*** introduced in India during Medieval Period:
A. Pumpkin B. Potato
C. Tomato D. Red Chilli

137. According to census 2011, the Male literacy rate of India is:
A. 75.3% B. 77.1%
C. 80.9% D. 88.8%

138. Which concept is broadest in Foreign Trade Accounts?
A. Balance of Payment B. Balance of Trade
C. Capital Account D. Current Account

139. Rate of inflation is equal to:
[A = Price Index]
A. $\frac{A_1}{A_2 + A_1} \times 100$ B. $\frac{A_2 + A_1}{A_1} \times 100$
C. $\frac{A_1}{A_2 - A_1} \times 100$ D. $\frac{A_2 - A_1}{A_1} \times 100$

140. The 'Boer' war is associated with:
A. Colonialism in Asia B. Colonialism in Africa
C. European History D. History of U.S.A.

141. The programme of economic reforms in India was started on:
A. 24 July, 1991 B. 1 July, 1991
C. 1 January, 1991 D. 24 April, 1991

142. Which of the following coined the term 'geography'?
A. Humboldt B. Aristotle
C. Eratosthenes D. Blache

143. The Saint, which is related to "Veerashaiva Sect"?
A. Haridas Thakur B. Kanak Das
C. Allam Prabhu D. Appar

144. In Indian parliament, the total number of nominated members are:
A. 10 B. 12
C. 14 D. 16

145. Which of the following 18th century state is ***not*** considered as "Inheritor State"?
A. Awadh B. Kerala
C. Hyderabad D. Bengal

146. According to census 2011 schedule caste to total population is found maximum in which state of India?
A. Himachal Pradesh B. Punjab
C. Uttar Pradesh D. West Bengal

147. The Dinesh Goswami Committee was concerned with:
A. De-nationalisation of Banks
B. Electoral reforms
C. Steps to put down insurgency in the north east
D. The problem of the chakmas

148. The condition when the earth is closest to the sun is known as:
A. Apogee B. Apehelion
C. Perigee D. Perihelion

149. Primary Deficit is equal to:
A. Revenue deficit – interest payment
B. Budget deficit – interest payment
C. Fiscal deficit – interest payment
D. Monetary deficit – interest payment

150. As per census 2011 (Final Data), the sex ratio in Rural India is:
A. 926 B. 949
C. 940 D. 919

Answers

1	2	3	4	5	6	7	8	9	10
C	D	A	D	A	B	C	C	A	D
11	**12**	**13**	**14**	**15**	**16**	**17**	**18**	**19**	**20**
A	A	D	D	C	C	B	C	C	A
21	**22**	**23**	**24**	**25**	**26**	**27**	**28**	**29**	**30**
A	D	D	B	B	A	D	C	A	A
31	**32**	**33**	**34**	**35**	**36**	**37**	**38**	**39**	**40**
A	A	A	C	A	B	B	C	D	D
41	**42**	**43**	**44**	**45**	**46**	**47**	**48**	**49**	**50**
D	A	B	D	D	B	D	B	B	C
51	**52**	**53**	**54**	**55**	**56**	**57**	**58**	**59**	**60**
A	A	A	A	C	C	B	C	A	C
61	**62**	**63**	**64**	**65**	**66**	**67**	**68**	**69**	**70**
B	C	D	B	D	B	D	D	C	D
71	**72**	**73**	**74**	**75**	**76**	**77**	**78**	**79**	**80**
A	C	A	A	C	A	B	C	B	B
81	**82**	**83**	**84**	**85**	**86**	**87**	**88**	**89**	**90**
D	B	B	B	A	B	B	C	A	A
91	**92**	**93**	**94**	**95**	**96**	**97**	**98**	**99**	**100**
C	D	A	D	C	C	C	C	A	B
101	**102**	**103**	**104**	**105**	**106**	**107**	**108**	**109**	**110**
C & D	B	A	B & C	A	B	D	B	C	D
111	**112**	**113**	**114**	**115**	**116**	**117**	**118**	**119**	**120**
A	B	B	C	A	B	D	D	C	A
121	**122**	**123**	**124**	**125**	**126**	**127**	**128**	**129**	**130**
C	C	A	B	A	C	D	B	D	B
131	**132**	**133**	**134**	**135**	**136**	**137**	**138**	**139**	**140**
A	B	C	B	C	A	C	A	D	B
141	**142**	**143**	**144**	**145**	**146**	**147**	**148**	**149**	**150**
A	C	C	C	B	B	B	D	C	B

Explanatory Answers

61. Let B's income = ₹ 100

Then, A's income = ₹ 80

B's income more than A's income

$$= \frac{100-80}{80} \times 100 = \frac{20}{80} \times 100 = 25\%.$$

63. $\frac{3}{7}$ part filled in 1 minute

1 part filled in $\frac{7}{3}$ minutes

$$\text{Rest part } \left(1-\frac{3}{7}\right) = \frac{4}{7}$$

$$\frac{4}{7}\text{th part filled} = \frac{1}{\left(\frac{3}{7}\right)} \times \frac{4}{7}$$

$$= \frac{7}{3} \times \frac{4}{7} = \frac{4}{3} \text{ minutes.}$$

64. LCM (8, 12, 15) = 120

Check the option,

(*a*) 9505 ÷ 120

Remainder = 25

(*b*) 9605 ÷ 120

Remainder = 5

∴ 9605 is the number which gives remainder 5 after dividing [illegible] 12 and 15.

65. Let the number = x

According to question,

$$= (9)^2 + (10)^2 + x$$
$$= 81 + 100 + x$$
$$= 181 + x$$

Nearest square number of 181 is 196

$$\therefore \quad x = 196 - 181 = 15.$$

67. We know that,

If each number is increased by x, then their average will also increase by x.

$\therefore$ Average of new number = 12 + 2 = 14.

66. $13\frac{1}{2}-\left[4\frac{1}{2}-\left\{3-\left(2-\frac{1}{2}\right)\right\}\right]$

$= \frac{27}{2}-\left[\frac{9}{2}-\left\{3-\frac{3}{2}\right\}\right]$

$= \frac{27}{2}-\left[\frac{9}{2}-\frac{3}{2}\right] = \frac{27}{2}-3 = 10\frac{1}{2}.$

68. 1 to 100, Numbers which are divisible by 7

7, 14, 21, 28, 35, 42, 49, 56, 63, 70, 77, 84, 91, 98

$\therefore$ Total number = 14.

69. $\because \quad \frac{1}{3} = 0.333$

(*a*) $\frac{27}{82} = 0.329$

(*b*) $\frac{20}{61} = 0.327$

(*c*) $\frac{16}{45} = 0.355$

(*d*) $\frac{51}{154} = 0.331$

$\therefore \quad \frac{16}{45}$ is greater than $\frac{1}{3}$.

70. 24 × 6 = 144

which is a square number of 12

$\therefore$ 6 is the smallest number such that by multiplying it with 24, we obtain a square number.

71. Except (A), all others are the three stage of water while oxygen is a gas.

72.

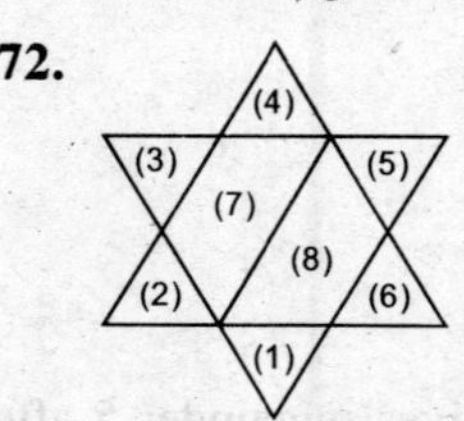

Total triangles = 8 + 2 = 10.

73. As,

G	R	A	S	P		B	R	O	W	N
↓	↓	↓	↓	↓		↓	↓	↓	↓	↓
I	N	O	P	Q		R	N	S	T	U

Similarly,

S	P	A	R	R	O	W
↓	↓	↓	↓	↓	↓	↓
P	Q	O	N	N	S	T

76. In Calendar year 2017

October Month's total days = 31

Sundays in October = 5 (1, 8, 15, 22, 29)

November Month's total days = 30

Sundays in November = 4 (5, 12, 19, 26)

December Month's total days = 31

Sundays in December = 5 (3, 10, 17, 24, 31)

Total Sundays in 3 months = 5 + 4 + 5

= 14.

This happens first sunday falls on the 1st of any of three month.

77.

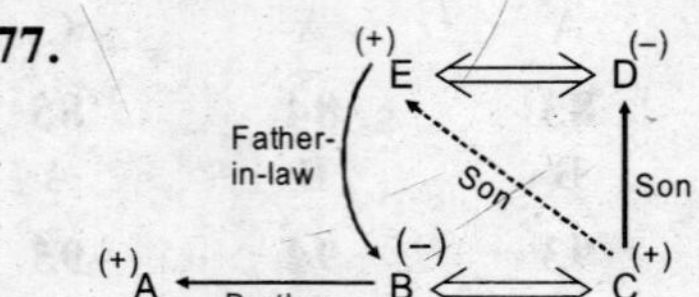

78. Fourth Number = (4 × 4 + 4 × 4) – 7 × 3

= (16 + 16) – 21

= 32 – 21 = 11.

79. Column I ⇒ 5 + 15 + 20 = 40

Column II ⇒ 25 + 10 + 5 = 40

Column III ⇒ 18 + 12 + ? = 40

30 + ? = 40

? = 10

80. 2 7 17 32 [52] 77

+ 5, + 10, + 15, + 20, + 25

82. The **Sahibi river,** also called the **Sabi River,** is an ephemeral, rain-fed river flowing through Rajasthan, Haryana and Delhi states in India. It drains into Yamuna at Delhi, where its channelled course is also called the Najafgarh drain, which also serves as Najafgarh drain bird sanctuary. Sahibi is a seasonal river which is 120 km long and flows from Aravalli hills in Rajasthan to Haryana, of which 100 km is in Haryana.

83. The Technological Institute of Textile and Sciences (TIT&S), founded in 1943, offers engineering programs and postgraduate programs. The institute is located in Birla Colony, opposite Bhiwani railway station. It is one of the oldest colleges in India. The Technical College established in 1943 was initially affiliated to the Department of Industrial Training, Punjab for 3-year Diploma course in Spinning Technology and

Weaving Technology. TITS remained a part of the Birla Education Trust up to 31 March, 1985. From 1 April, 1985 it was separated from the Trust and an independent Society known as "The Technological Institute of Textiles" was formed to manage it which was registered under the West Bengal Societies Registration Act 1961. To reflect the expanded instructional facilities and new courses the Society was rechristened as "The Technological Institute of Textile & Sciences".

85. Nuclear Power Corp of India Ltd (NPCIL) has selected Gorakhpur village (around 175 km from Delhi) in Fatehabad district of Haryana to set up the states first 4 × 700 mw nuclear power plant. The foundation stone of the 2800 Megawatt nuclear power plant was laid on 13 January, 2014. The first phase of the project will have an installed capacity of 1400 MW and is expected to be completed by 2021.

86. On 10-11 January 2017; the first-ever Pravasi Haryana Divas—2017 was celebrated in Kingdom of Dreams, Gurugram, Haryana. Haryana Chief Minister Manohar Lal Khattar inaugurated the event. The objective of the Pravasi Haryana Divas is to recognize the achievements of NRIs and PIOs of Haryana as well as those persons from Haryana who are now settled in other States of India and to harness their energies in the future development of Haryana.

87. Shri Baba Mast Nath Math, Asthal Bohar is the oldest and most popular place of Nath Sect belonging to Kanphada Yogis. This is the main Tapasthali (Place of Worship) of Nath Yogi and is situated 5 kms away from Rohtak city and 1 km away from M.D. University Campus on Delhi-Rohtak National Highway No. 10. The Math has been the centre and live-wire of ancient civilization and has been doing Yeo-man services for the benefit of mankind. Shri Baba Mast Nath Ji rejuvenated the Math Ashtal Bohar in 18th Century. His able pupils have been rightfully performing the duties and responsibilities of a Mahent. Late Mahent Shreo Nath Yogi (Ex-Health Minister for Haryana Govt.) the most able and active in series of pupils had raised many institutions in the sweet memory of his Guru Baba Mast Nath Ji, so has done his immediate follower and present incumbent to the Gaddi, Mahent Chand Nath Yogi.

88. Shaikh Sharafuddeen Bu Ali Qalandar Panipati also called Bu Ali Qalandar (1209-1324 CE probably born at Panipat, Haryana) in India was a Sufi saint of the Chisti order. His dargah (mausoleum) in the town of Panipat is a place of pilgrimage.

The dargah (mausoleum or shrine), mosque and enclosure at the Qalandar Chowk in Panipat were constructed by Mahabat Khan, a general in the service of the Mughal Emperor Jahangir. Mahabat Khan's own tomb in red sandstone is adjacent to the saint's mausoleum. The tombs of Hakim Mukaram Khan and the Urdu poet Maulana Altaf Hussain Hali are also located within the enclosure. A nearby structure is the tomb of the last Lodi dynasty ruler of Delhi, Ibrahim Lodi, killed in the First Battle of Panipat (1526).

89. Sultanpur Bird Sanctuary is a very popular national park located in Gurgaon district in Haryana State. Sultanpur is located 40 kilometres (25 mi) from Dhaula Kuan in Delhi and 15 kilometres (9.3 mi) from Gurgaon on the Gurgaon-Farrukhnagar Road. This Bird Sanctuary, ideal for birding and bird watchers, is best visited in winters when a large number of migratory birds come here.

Among approximately 1,800 migratory bird species out of total 10,000 species of birds in the world, nearly 370 species migrate to India due to seasonal changes, including 175 long-distance migration species that use the Central Asian Flyway route which also include Amur falcons, Egyptian vultures, plovers, ducks, storks, ibises, flamingoes, jacanas, pochards and sociable lapwing. Among these approximately 250 species of Birds are found at Sultanpur Bird Sanctuary. Some of them are resident, while others come from distant regions like Siberia, Europe and Afghanistan.

90. Egypt was the Partner Nation during the Surajkund International Crafts Mela. Hosted jointly by the Haryana government and the Surajkund Mela Authority, in collaboration with the union ministries of Tourism, Textiles, Culture and External Affairs, the Surajkund Mela showcased some of the most exquisite handloom, handicraft and culture diversity of India and other countries. "For the first time, Egypt had the honour of becoming the Partner Nation during the much-admired festival... Egypt had always been keen to interconnect with India on a cultural, people-to-people level, especially when it come to preserving and disseminating cultural heritage across the globe.

The Mela showcased the richness and diversity of the handicrafts, handlooms and the cultural heritage of India. The idea of hosting the Mela is to recreate a pristine rural ambience for foreign and domestic tourists, tell the patrons of arts and crafts of the skills involved in creative arts, to introduce craftspersons directly to the buyers, and to identify, nurture and preserve the languishing crafts of the country.

93. Divergent boundaries (Constructive) occur where two plates slide apart from each other. At zones of ocean-to-ocean rifting, divergent boundaries form by seafloor spreading, allowing for the formation of new ocean basin.

The North American and Eurasian Plates are moving away from each other along the line of the Mid Atlantic Ridge. The Ridge extends into the South

Atlantic Ocean between the South American and African Plates. It is a divergent tectonic plate or constructive plate boundary located along the floor of the Atlantic Ocean, and part of the longest mountain range in the world.

94. The western coastal plains are narrow in the middle and get broader towards north and south. The rivers flowing through this coastal plain do not form any delta. The Malabar coast has got certain distinguishing features in the form of 'Kayals' (backwaters), which are used for fishing, inland navigation and also due to its special attraction for tourists. Every year the famous Nehru Trophy Vallamkali (boat race) is held in Punnamada Kayal in Kerala.

95. Milpa is a crop-growing system used throughout Mesoamerica. It has been most extensively described in the Yucatán peninsula area of Mexico.

Milpa agriculture is a form of the traditional 'slash and burn' agriculture. The natural vegetation is cut and then let to dry out before it is burned. The ash is then incorporated into the soil as fertilizer.

99. Majuli is a large river island in the Brahmaputra river, in the Indian state of Assam. Majuli had a total area of 1,250 square kilometres (483 sq mi), but having lost significantly to erosion it has an area of only 421.65 square kilometers.

100. The Inter Tropical Convergence Zone, or ITCZ, is a belt of low pressure which circles the Earth generally near the equator where the trade winds of the Northern and Southern Hemispheres come together. It is characterised by convective activity which generates often vigorous thunderstorms over large areas. It is most active over continental land masses by day and relatively less active over the oceans.

103. The current evidence indicates that the Harappans got tin from scattered deposits available in Afghanistan. It is strongly suggested that Shortugai, a trading outpost of the IVC in Northern Afghanistan, might have had connections to the import of lapis lazuli, tin and camels into the cities of the IVC.

105. The frontier states in the east and the north which accepted Samudragupta's suzerainty were ruled by kings. The names of these states were Samatata (which formed a part of Bengal on the sea-shore), Devaka (or the Naogaon district of Assam), Kamarupa (which comprised a part of Assam including Gauhati), Nepal and Kartripura (which was situated in the Kumaun, Garhwal and Rohilkhand regions).

107. **Burzahom** in the Valley of Kashmir, where deep pit dwellings are associated with ground stone axes, bone tools, and gray burnished pottery.

Almost contemporaneous with Koldihawa, the site of **Mahagara** has yielded some bone implements along with a tool kit of mesolithic and neolithic tools made of materials such as chalcedony, agate, quartz and basalt. This site has also reported a cattle pen, which indicates the domestication of cattle. The pottery used by the neolithic folk was handmade and poorly fired; with straw and rice husk being used as tempering agents. The principal pottery type is the corded or cordimpressed ware though sometimes incised designs are also seen.

Utnur excavations have shown cattle hoof prints in the ash. The Budhidal excavations showed the presence of a habitation that was directly associated with ash mounds.

Mehrgarh is the site of the earliest known agrarian settlements in the South Asian subcontinent and lies to the west of the Indus River. The archaeological site of Mehrgarh consist of a number of low archaeological mounds in the Kachi plain, close to the mouth of the Bolan Pass.

110. **Sanchi Stupa** is a pillar of finely polished sandstone, one of the Pillars of Ashoka, was also erected on the side of the main Torana gateway. The bottom part of the pillar still stands. The upper parts of the pillar are at the nearby Sanchi Archaeological Museum. The capital consists in four lions, which probably supported a Wheel of Law, as also suggested by later illustrations among the Sanchi reliefs. The pillar has an Ashokan inscription (Schism Edict) and an inscription in the ornamental Sankha Lipi from the Gupta period.

112. The History of the Indo-Greek Kingdom covers a period from the 2nd century BCE to the beginning of the 1st century CE in northern and northwestern India. There were over 30 Indo-Greek kings, often in competition on different territories. Many of them are only known through their coins.

115. As a consequence of the 42nd constitution amendment act (1976) the three terms were inserted in the preamble of the Constitution : Socialist, Secular, Integrity. It is, therefore, proposed to amend the Constitution to spell out expressly the high ideals of socialism, secularism and the integrity of the nation, to make the directive principles more comprehensive and give them precedence over those fundamental rights which have been allowed to be relied upon to frustrate socio-economic reforms for implementing the directive principles.

123. **Jet Streams** are fast flowing, narrow, meandering air currents in the atmospheres of some planets, including Earth. The jet stream is a core of strong winds around 5 to 7 miles above the Earth's surface, blowing from west to east.

Previous Paper (Solved)

Haryana Teacher Eligibility Test (HTET)

TGT Social Studies (Level-2) Exam 2015*

Child Development and Pedagogy

Directions: *Answer the following questions by selecting the* ***most appropriate*** *option.*

1. Sixteen years old Neeraj is attempting to develop a sense of himself as a separate, self-governing individual. He is developing:

A. hatred for rules B. autonomy
C. teenage arrogance D. maturity

2. The habit of telling lie of children may be improved by:

A. Punishing them
B. Giving lecture on the bad effects of telling a lie
C. Giving examples of children who speak truth
D. Awarding children who speak truth

3. According to Stanley Hall the period of great stress and storm is:

A. Adulthood B. Childhood
C. Adolescence D. Infancy

4. Creative answers require:

A. Open ended answer type questions
B. Content based questions
C. Closed answer type questions
D. Direct questions

5. Which of the following factor influences personality development of a child?

A. Hereditary
B. Physical environment
C. Social environment
D. All of the above

6. Which law of Thorndike indicates the importance of award and punishment in learning?

A. Law of readiness B. Law of effect
C. Law of exercise D. All of the above

7. Which of the following is *not* developed in adolescence?

A. Ego-centralism
B. Interests
C. Reasoning power
D. Ability of observation

8. What effort will you make for bringing change in the behaviour of a problematic child?

A. Make effort to bring change in child's environment and attitude.
B. Try to improve by punishing the child.
C. Will not pay attention to him/her.
D. Will seat him in the front row in the class.

9. Which of the following is *not* considered as exceptional type of children?

A. Slow learners
B. Creative children
C. Physically handicapped
D. Resourceful children

10. To check rising anger in the learner, the teacher should:

A. give protection to all his interests though undue.
B. not interfere in the child's everyday affairs.
C. give him more work to provide him no time to get angry.
D. see that he gets very favourable treatment in the classroom.

11. Which of the following factors will *not* help in improving the memory of a child?

A. Repetition and practice
B. Taking help from rhythm
C. Proper grouping of subject-matter
D. Theory of motivated forgetting

12. Generally the following characteristic of physical development of girls and boys are observed

A. Development is equal in both at the same age.
B. Boys are two years ahead in physical development.
C. Girls are two-three years ahead in physical development.
D. Girls are five years back than boys.

13. What is *not* important to keep mental health of the students?

A. Provisions of co-curricular activities
B. Revision of the syllabus
C. Allowing freedom of expression
D. Paying attention to difference in interests

* Exam held on 15 November, 2015

14. Which of the following is a problem related to teaching-learning?
A. Problem related to understanding of subject-matter
B. Indiscipline in classroom
C. Copying in examination
D. Reaching late in class

15. A child first learns moving his hand, then fingers and then hand and fingers together. Which principle of growth and development is represented by this example?
A. Principle of continuity
B. Principle of integration
C. Principle of general to specific
D. Principle of individual differences

16. Observing a child while playing in school ground is an observation of:
A. Formal B. Informal
C. Participant D. None of the above

17. Which of the following plays an important role in mental growth and development?
A. Learning
B. Maturation
C. Both Learning and Maturation
D. Social Norms

18. Which of the following is ***not*** a personal factor affecting social development of a child?
A. Peer group
B. Health
C. Emotions
D. Intelligence

19. Peer pressure has its highest effect during:
A. Early childhood
B. Middle childhood
C. Early adolescence
D. Later adolescence

20. Following is influenced by maximum utilization of senses by students:
A. Teaching process
B. Learning process
C. Learning product
D. Learning product and process

21. Which of the following is ***not*** a characteristic related to mental development?
A. Instinct of curiosity in abundance
B. Tendency of rote learning
C. Abundant creativity
D. Cooperative attitude

22. Learning by practice is a modification of:
A. Motivation
B. Behaviour
C. Basic instinct
D. Drive

23. Which of the following statements is ***incorrect*** with reference to adolescence?
A. Many new internal and external changes are observed.
B. This age is highly emotional.
C. Intellect tries to reach to its extreme limit.
D. Self-consciousness is reduced.

24. Earlier psychology was a part of:
A. Philosophy
B. Ethics
C. Logic
D. Physics

25. Which of the following statements is ***not*** correct?
A. Creativity is originality in any art.
B. Thinking is not required for creativity.
C. Creativity is a new consequence of a work performed.
D. Creativity must have utility for society or for any group.

26. A teacher has to be resourceful. It means:
A. He should have enough money and property.
B. He should have contacts with higher authorities.
C. He should have adequate knowledge to solve problems of his students.
D. He should have good reputation among students.

27. Method for identifying gifted children is:
A. Observation
B. Intelligence test
C. Personality test
D. All of the above

28. Which statement is ***wrong*** in the context of personality?
A. Personality is unique and specific.
B. Personality is a joint product of heredity and environment.
C. Personality spreads over the sub-conscious and unconscious behaviour of the person.
D. Personality is limited only to the appearance of a person.

29. The concentration and creativity is related to which type of development?
A. Social development
B. Moral development
C. Intellectual development
D. Emotional development

30. If a student asks a wrong question in the class, then what will you do?
A. Scold the student
B. Correct the question with the help of other students
C. Will indicate the mistake by giving example
D. Will explain the affect on the answer due to wrong question

English Language

Directions: *Answer the following questions by selecting the **most appropriate** option.*

31. I must remember my key.
What does the underlined auxiliary 'must' suggest ?
A. Necessity B. Determination
C. Promise D. Obligation

32. Which of the following sentences is ***correct***?
A. He reached the station before the train started.
B. I arrived at the station after the train started.
C. He was seeing the sea.
D. The nightingale as well as the cuckoo is a singing bird.

33. Choose the ***mis-spelt*** word:
A. Simlie B. Singular
C. Sieve D. Siege

34. When learners are involved in real communication, their natural strategies for language acquisition will be used, and this will allow them to learn to use the language.
Which approach/method of teaching English is based on the above idea?
A. Audio-lingual method
B. Direct method
C. Communicative approach
D. Grammar-Translation method

35. Choose the ***correct*** indirect form of the following sentence:
I said to my friend, 'I don't know the way. Do you?'
A. I told my friend that I did not know the way and asked if he did.
B. I said to my friend that I do not know the way and asked if he knows.
C. I confessed my ignorance of the way to my friend and asked him if he knew the way.
D. I told my friend that I do not know the way and asked him if he knew the way.

36. Choose the ***correct*** one word for 'incapable of being wiped out or effaced':
A. Irrevocable B. Ineligible
C. Indelible D. Invincible

37. Choose the ***correct*** passive construction of the following sentence:
We made him complete the work.
A. We forced him to complete the work.
B. He was made to complete the work.
C. He has been made to complete the work.
D. He is being made to complete the work by us.

38. As he was not there, I spoke to his brother.
The underlined is an example of:
A. Adverb Clause of Time
B. Adverb Clause of Place
C. Adverb Clause of Condition
D. Adverb Clause of Reason

39. Identify the ***pattern*** of the following sentence:
Nothing will make him repent.
A. SVO B. SV
C. SVOC D. SVC

40. He lay all night on his sleepless pillow.
The underlined is an example of:
A. Hyperbole B. Synecdoche
C. Transferred Epithet D. None of the above

41. The moral law is above the civil.
The underlined word in the above sentence is a/an:
A. Adverb B. Preposition
C. Adjective D. Noun

42. Which of the following sentences is ***not true*** about Communicative Language Teaching?
A. Teachers in communicative classrooms will find themselves talking less and listening more.
B. The teacher sets up the exercise, but because the students' participation is the goal, the teacher must step back and observe.
C. The classroom during a communicative class is quiet.
D. Students gain confidence in using the target language in general.

Directions (Q. Nos. 43 & 44): *Which part of the given sentences has an **error**?*

43. We are looking (A)/ for a sight (B)/ for the new (C)/ School building. (D).

44. The fort at Chittor (A)/ is perhaps (B)/ most famous (C)/ than the Golconda fort (D).

45. The idiom 'know the ropes' means:
A. To feel awkward and useless
B. To understand the procedures and details involved in something
C. To put someone in a difficult and dangerous situation
D. Concede defeat

Directions (Q. Nos. 46 to 50): *Fill in the blanks in the following sentences by the most suitable option:*

46. When it started to rain, the children took shelter in a .... hut.
A. close B. nearly
C. near D. nearby

47. I'm going to buy .... bread.
A. a B. the
C. some D. None of the above

48. Vanya speaks English .... No wonder she won a prize in the Elocution Contest.
A. frankly and freely
B. graciously and profusely
C. awkwardly and stiffly
D. fluently and correctly

49. Sahil read the letter .... carefully the second time to make sure he hadn't missed any detail.
A. much
B. many
C. more
D. most

50. He .... a lot of letters yesterday.
A. had written
B. had been writing
C. wrote
D. has written

Directions (Q. Nos. 51 to 56): *Read the following passage and answer the questions by choosing the most appropriate option:*

A traveller who studies the menu on a transatlantic liner or, indeed, in some American hotels has a paralyzing sensation. There is so much to eat – far more than he can possibly digest. One sometimes has the same feeling about education, which also offers an enormous bill of fare. Almost any dish can be found in it, from Greek to stenography, from music to economics. How are we to choose from the bewildering profusion? What dishes are we to order if we wish not merely to fill ourselves up, but to get the nourishment necessary to a healthy life, to become really educated people?

That question cannot be answered without asking and answering another—what is education for? If that problem were suddenly put to pupils in school, or to students in college, or even to parents, I doubt if all of them could, on the spur of the moment, give a clear and convincing reply. Most of us are educated because our parents wish it, or because attendance at school is a habit of our society, or because it is compulsory, or because it is apparently necessary to succeed in the world. But these, though at the moment they may be conclusive reasons for desiring education or, at any rate, submitting to it, will not by themselves secure our getting from it what it has to give; and if we go to schools or colleges with no more definite reasons at the back of our minds, we are likely to rise from our meal there replete perhaps but ill-nourished.

Whether we are teachers or students, we ought to get firmly in our minds the idea that whatever else may come by the way, education will be incomplete and unsatisfactory if it fails to give a clear view of what is first-rate in the subject studied. Otherwise we may have got some knowledge, but we shall not have got education.

51. How does education offer an enormous bill of fare?
A. There is a lot to eat.
B. There are a lot of dishes available.
C. It should be properly digested.
D. There are a variety of courses to choose from.

52. What according to the writer is education for?
A. To please one's parents.
B. It is compulsory to attend school.
C. It is necessary to succeed in the world.
D. To know the first-rate in the subject that we study.

53. Which of the following sentences is ***not said*** by the writer?
A. There is a bewildering profusion of courses to choose from.
B. We should not order dishes only to fill ourselves up but to get proper nourishment for a healthy life.
C. We should attend school to pass exams and to secure degrees.
D. Education will be complete and satisfactory if it gives a clear view of what is best in the course/subject studied.

54. Which of the following is ***not*** a synonym of 'profusion'?
A. Abundance
B. Plenitude
C. Plethora
D. Limited

55. Which of the following is a synonym of 'replete'?
A. Sated
B. Starved
C. Deprived
D. None of the above

56. Which of the following seems to be the most likely purpose of writing this passage?
A. To discuss the utility of knowledge.
B. To describe the variety of food available in American hotels.
C. To guide the students to get proper nourishment.
D. To motivate readers to pursue excellence in their chosen area of interest.

Directions (Q. Nos. 57 & 58): *Replace the underlined group of words by the most suitable option:*

57. Jamsetji Nusserwanji Tata was a clever and perceptive businessman.
A. Dense
B. Astute
C. Naïve
D. Gullible

58. This place has been officially marked as a conservation area, and any kind of building is forbidden here.
A. Designated
B. Designed
C. Selected
D. Identified

59. Since Rahul was five years old, swimming has been his passion.
The underlined word in the above sentence is a/an
A. Present Participle
B. Gerund
C. Infinitive
D. None of the above

60. Which of the following sentences is ***incorrect***?
A. Either you or I am wrong.
B. He sold all his furniture.
C. The luggage was packed.
D. One should do his duty well.

हिन्दी भाषा

निर्देशः *निम्नलिखित प्रश्नों के उत्तर देने के लिए* **सबसे उचित** *विकल्प चुनिए।*

61. नीचे दिए शब्दों में से किसकी वर्तनी शुद्ध है?
A. जाग्रति B. पूज्यानीया
C. अन्तर्ध्यान D. अभ्यारण्य

62. 'जिसके पास कुछ न हो' उसके लिए उपयुक्त शब्द है :
A. अभावग्रस्त B. अकिंचन
C. दीनहीन D. महादीन

63. निम्नलिखित में से क्रिया-विशेषण है :
A. अँधेरा B. धीरे-धीरे
C. चाल-चलन D. सौंदर्य

64. 'निर्दय' का विलोम शब्द है :
A. सहृदय B. सहृय
C. सभय D. सदय

65. 'अनश्वर' शब्द के लिए एक वाक्य है :
A. नष्ट होने वाला
B. ईश्वर को न मानने वाला
C. नष्ट न होने वाला
D. जो इन्द्रियों के द्वारा न जाना जा सके

66. 'अखरोट' शब्द का तत्सम रूप है :
A. अक्षवाट B. अक्षोट
C. अक्षरोट D. अषरोट

67. निम्नलिखित में से कौन-सा प्रकम्पित वर्ण है?
A. र B. ल
C. य D. व

68. 'प्रत्युत्पन्नमति' में कौन-सा उपसर्ग है?
A. प्रत्य B. प्रत्
C. प्रति D. प्रत्यु

69. निम्नलिखित वाक्यों में से अपादान कारक का उदाहरण कौन-सा है?
A. राधा घर से निकली।
B. सीता गीता से अच्छा गाती है।
C. मुझे आपसे बहुत डर लगता है।
D. उपर्युक्त सभी

70. 'तत् + शंकर' संधि विच्छेद से बनने वाला शब्द है :
A. तच्छंकर B. तत्शंकर
C. तच्शंकर D. तत्संकर

71. 'स्थावर' का विलोम है :
A. जंगल B. संपत्ति
C. जंगम D. स्थापना

72. ये फल उसके लिए है। इस वाक्य में रेखांकित अंश है :
A. अन्यपुरुष, एकवचन, संप्रदान
B. मध्यमपुरुष, बहुवचन, कर्ता
C. मध्यमपुरुष, एकवचन, संप्रदान
D. उत्तमपुरुष, एकवचन, संप्रदान

73. 'सव्यसाची' शब्द के लिए एक वाक्य है :
A. सदा सत्य बोलने वाला
B. बाएँ हाथ से कार्य करने वाला
C. जिसने बहुत कुछ सुना हो
D. अपनी इच्छा के अनुसार आचरण करने वाला

74. 'वह श्रेष्ठ उपासक है' में विशेष्य है :
A. वह B. श्रेष्ठ
C. उपासक D. है

75. इनमें से किस वाक्य में 'पूर्वकालिक' क्रिया का प्रयोग हुआ है?
A. ठोकर लगते ही लड़का बेहोश हो गया।
B. विद्यार्थी पढ़ेंगे तो पास होंगे।
C. श्याम दूध पीकर घूमने जाता है।
D. अध्यापक बच्चों को प्रतिदिन हिंदी पढ़ाता है।

76 निम्नलिखित में से कौन-से शब्द अपने विभाजन के पश्चात् अन्य अर्थ में प्रचलित हो जाते हैं?
A. सार्थक B. योगरूढ़
C. रूढ़ D. यौगिक

77. 'गुरु के समीप रहकर शिक्षा ग्रहण करने वाला' के लिए एक शब्द है :
A. गुरुकुलवासी B. छात्रावासी
C. अन्तेवासी D. आश्रमवासी

78. 'उतर गई लोई तो क्या करेगा कोई' कहावत का सही अर्थ है :
A. कंगले को किसी हानि की आशंका नहीं होती
B. गंभीर रोगी की चिकित्सा संभव नहीं होती
C. खोई हुई प्रतिष्ठा वापस नहीं मिल सकती
D. बेशर्म हो चुके व्यक्ति को इज्जत गँवा देने का भय नहीं रहता

79. कृदंत प्रत्यय किसके साथ जुड़ते हैं?
A. संज्ञा B. सर्वनाम
C. धातु D. विशेषण

80. 'जनार्दन' किसका पर्यायवाची है?
A. राम B. कृष्ण
C. विष्णु D. ब्रह्म

81. "शबरी प्रतिदिन राम की प्रतीक्षा करती थी।" वाक्य का सही भेद है :
A. संदेहार्थक B. विधानार्थक
C. प्रश्नार्थक D. आज्ञार्थक

82. 'सावधानी' शब्द में कौन-सा प्रत्यय है?
A. नी B. ई
C. इ D. आनी

83. 'सियार' का तत्सम क्या है?
A. शृंगार
B. स्यार
C. श्यालक
D. शृगाल

84. 'पित्राज्ञा' शब्द का सही संधि-विच्छेद है :
A. पित्र + आज्ञा
B. पित्रा + आज्ञा
C. पितृ + आज्ञा
D. उपर्युक्त सभी

85. निम्नलिखित में से किस शब्द में एक प्रत्यय लगा हुआ है?
A. सागर
B. नगर
C. अगर
D. जादूगर

86. मुखावयवों के निकट आने से संघर्ष के पश्चात् प्रकट होने वाली ध्वनि कौन-सी है?
A. स्पर्श
B. अंतस्थ
C. वर्त्स्य
D. ऊष्म

87. 'षट्पद' का पर्यायवाची है
A. तितली
B. भ्रमर
C. मकड़ी
D. केकड़ा

88. एक उद्देश्य एवं एक विधेय से मिलकर बनने वाला वाक्य क्या कहलाता है?
A. संयुक्त वाक्य
B. साधारण वाक्य
C. मिश्र वाक्य
D. आज्ञार्थक

89. 'देहलता' इस सामासिक पद में कौन-सा समास है?
A. कर्मधारय
B. द्विगु
C. अव्ययीभाव
D. द्वन्द्व

90. *शुद्ध* वर्तनी का चयन कीजिए :
A. अहुण्य
B. अक्षुण्य
C. अक्षुण्ण
D. अक्ष्णुण

Subject Specific—Social Studies

Directions: *Answer the following questions by selecting the **most appropriate** option.*

91. In June, 1789 A.D., the Third Estate and National Assembly in France was led by :
A. Danton
B. Robespierre
C. Mirabeau
D. Marat

92. Which of the following is non-ferrous metal?
A. Manganese
B. Cobalt
C. Steel
D. Lead

93. The Indian coastal plains along the Bay of Bengal are called as :
A. Coromandel & Northern Sarkar
B. Coromandel & Malabar
C. Northern Sarkar & Konkan
D. Malabar & Kannad

94. Birsa Munda was the resident of :
A. Calcutta
B. Patna
C. Chhota Nagpur
D. Munger

95. The first English Factory was started in India at :
A. Madras
B. Hugali
C. Bombay
D. Surat

96. Which of the following political parties is ***not*** in the category of National Party?
A. Shiv Sena
B. Bhartiya Janta Party
C. Indian National Congress
D. Bahujan Samaj Party

97. Which amongst the following was ***not*** the Nazi Programme announced by Hitler?
A. To have the treaty of Versailles amended
B. To recover the lost German territories
C. To restore the old German glory
D. To enable the German women equal to men

98. The Indian Monsoon is called 'South-West Monsoon', because :
A. Monsoon winds run through North-East to South-West direction.
B. Monsoon winds run through South-West to North-East direction.
C. Monsoon hits South-West part of India in the beginning.
D. None of the above

99. According to Plate Tectonic Theory, the formation of Himalayan mountains took place from the compression of the materials of which sea?
A. Indian Ocean
B. Tethys Sea
C. Caspian Sea
D. Mediterranean Sea

100. The country, where Buddhism was ***not*** propagated :
A. Thailand
B. Sri Lanka
C. Indonesia
D. Greece

101. In which Session of the Indian National Congress decision was taken for the Non-Cooperation Movement?
A. Ahmedabad
B. Bombay
C. Nagpur
D. Patna

102. Who founded Depressed Classes Association in 1930 A.D.?
A. Dr. B.R. Ambedkar
B. Mahatma Gandhi
C. Jyotiba Phule
D. Maulana Azad

103. Techniques adopted by pressure groups are:
(*i*) Propaganda
(*ii*) Lobbying
(*iii*) Demonstration
Choose the ***right*** answer :
A. (*i*) and (*ii*)
B. (*i*) and (*iii*)
C. (*ii*) and (*iii*)
D. (*i*), (*ii*) and (*iii*)

104. Which of the following objectives can be achieved through a multipurpose hydroelectricity project?
(*a*) Hydroelectricity
(*b*) Canal irrigation
(*c*) Flood control
(*d*) Water sports development
(*e*) Potable water supply
Choose the ***correct*** answer :
A. (*a*), (*b*), (*d*) and (*e*) B. (*a*), (*b*), (*c*) and (*e*)
C. (*a*), (*b*) and (*e*) D. (*a*), (*b*), (*c*), (*d*) and (*e*)

105. "Vellanvagai" was the kind of land referred in the Chola inscriptions, it denotes :
A. land granted to the Brahmins
B. land given to the schools
C. land given to the temples
D. land of the Farmer other than Brahmin

106. Which of the following is a tidal forest?
A. Conical forest
B. Mangrove forest
C. Tropical deciduous forest
D. Tropical rain forest

107. According to the Constitution, Prime Minister is :
A. Head of the States
B. Head of the Union Council of Ministers
C. Head of the Union Government
D. Head of the Union Administration

108. When the 'Indigo Revolt' took place in Bengal?
A. March, 1859 B. May, 1857
C. April, 1776 D. March, 1880

109. Shershah defeated Humayun in the battle of :
A. Chausa (1539) B. Chanderi (1528)
C. Golkunda (1687) D. Dohariya (1532)

110. Which is ***not*** the aim of a political party?
A. To propagate own ideology
B. The spiritual development of the people
C. To form the public opinion
D. Aspiration to form the government

111. Doon Valleys of Himalaya are situated between :
A. Greater Himalaya & Lesser Himalaya
B. Greater Himalaya & Karakoram Mountains
C. Lesser Himalaya & Shivalik Mountains
D. Lesser Himalaya & Karakoram Mountains

112. The British Governor General who adopted the policy of 'Paramountcy', was :
A. Warren Hastings B. Lord Auckland
C. Lord Cornwallis D. Lord Hastings

113. Amongst the neighbouring countries which countries are having longest and shortest international boundaries respectively with India?
A. China & Bhutan
B. Bangladesh & Bhutan
C. China & Afghanistan
D. Bangladesh & Afghanistan

114. The First Cotton Textile Mill was established in India at :
A. Surat (1700) B. Murshidabad (1765)
C. Ahmedabad (1919) D. Bombay (1854)

115. In the history of Indian census, in which decade the population growth of India was recorded highest?
A. 1951-1961 B. 1961-1971
C. 1971-1981 D. 1981-1991

116. B.C.E. is used with the dates in history; it means :
A. Before Christian Empire
B. Before Common Era
C. Before Christ Entiti
D. Before Century Era

117. Chauhan ruler who defeated Muhammad Ghori in 1191, was :
A. Ajayraj B. Arnoraj
C. Prithviraj-III D. Hariraj

118. El-nino is a :
A. A warm current of Indian Ocean
B. A warm air of Indian Ocean
C. A warm current of South Pacific Ocean
D. A warm air of South Pacific Ocean

119. Who was the editor of the weekly magazine Bengal Gazette started in 1780 A.D.?
A. James Augustus Hickey
B. William Bolts
C. Gangadhar Bhattacharya
D. Raja Ram Mohan Roy

120. According to the targets of the National Population Policy-2000, in which year Indian population will achieve the status of stable population?
A. 2015 B. 2025
C. 2035 D. 2045

121. Which Article of the Constitution makes special provisions for Jammu and Kashmir?
A. Article 368 B. Article 370
C. Article 369 D. Article 371

122. Inflation is caused by :
A. increase in supply of goods
B. increase in cash with the Government
C. decrease in money supply
D. increase in money supply

123. Constitution of India describes India as a :
A. Union of States B. Voluntary Federation
C. Confederation D. Federation

124. In which General Election did the Congress Party lost majority in the Parliament for the first time?
A. 1967 B. 1977
C. 1980 D. None of these

125. Cheque can be issued against :
A. demand deposits in bank
B. fixed deposits in bank
C. without deposits in bank
D. fixed deposits in post office

126. The First Session of the Constitutional Assembly was held on :
A. 9 December, 1946 B. 11 December, 1946
C. 3 June, 1947 D. 26 January, 1946

127. The Right which is legal but not Constitutional :
A. Freedom to move freely
B. Right to property
C. Right against exploitation
D. Right to minorities to establish educational institutions

128. Among the following, which soil is having very high moisture retention capacity?
A. Desert soil B. Alluvial soil
C. Black soil D. Mountain soil

129. Which one of the following is ***not*** renewable resource?
A. Geothermal energy B. Tidal energy
C. Hydro-electricity D. Fossil fuel

130. Which of the following is revenue expenditure of the Government?
A. Payment of interest
B. Purchase of building
C. Purchase of machine
D. Loans to State Government

131. During recent years the GDP in India from different sectors is received in the following descending order :
A. Agriculture, manufacturing and tertiary sector
B. Manufacturing, agriculture and tertiary sector
C. Tertiary sector, manufacturing and agriculture sector
D. Tertiary sector, agriculture and manufacturing sector

132. Budget is a statement of :
A. income and expenditure
B. purchase and sales of goods
C. prices of commodities
D. expected income and expected expenditure

133. Which of the following is ***not*** a constituent of Human Development Index (HDI)?
A. Per Capita Income (on the basis of Gross National Income)
B. Life expectancy at birth
C. Gross Enrolment Rate
D. Health and Nutrition

134. Who was the main Indian thinker of Democratic Socialism?
A. Pandit Nehru B. M.N. Roy
C. S.A. Dange D. None of the above

135. The maximum number of members that the Legislative Assembly of a State in India can have :
A. 400 B. 450
C. 500 D. 600

136. National income in India is estimated by :
A. Planning Commission
B. Indian Statistical Institute
C. Central Statistical Organisation
D. National Sample Survey

137. Agenda-21 was declared in :
A. First Earth Summit, 1992
B. Second Earth Summit, 2002
C. Third Earth Summit, 2012
D. First World Climate Summit, 1979

138. According to census-2011 the density of population and sex ratio respectively in India are :
A. 382, 943 B. 380, 930
C. 424, 830 D. 390, 935

139. One-third (1/3) members of Rajya Sabha retire :
A. Every year B. Every two years
C. Every three years D. Never retire

140. Which Government of India Act profoundly influenced the making of Indian Constitution?
A. Government of India Act, 1909
B. Government of India Act, 1919
C. Government of India Act, 1935
D. Government of India Act, 1947

141. Find out the ***odd*** :
A. State Bank of India B. Canara Bank
C. HDFC Bank D. Central Bank of India

142. Species which are confined to some particular areas usually isolated by geographical barriers are known as :
A. Endangered Species B. Extinct Species
C. Rare Species D. Endemic Species

143. The Finance Commission in India is :
A. an autonomous body B. an advisory body
C. a constitutional body D. a statutory body

144. Which of the following is ***not*** decided by the Reserve Bank of India?
A. Bank Rate B. Repo Rate
C. Reverse Repo Rate D. Income Tax Rates

145. According to census-2011 the population in the age group of 0-6 years in India is approximately
A. 14 crores B. 16 crores
C. 18 crores D. 12 crores

146. The Fundamental Right which ***cannot*** be suspended even during emergency is :
A. Freedom of assembling peacefully
B. Freedom to reside
C. Protection of life and personal liberty
D. Right to freedom of religion

147. Impeachment proceeding against the President for violation of the Constitution can be initiated in :
A. Either House of Parliament
B. The Lok Sabha
C. The Rajya Sabha
D. Supreme Court

148. In an economy, the sectors are classified into public and private on the basis of :
A. working conditions
B. nature of economic activities
C. ownership of enterprises
D. All of the above

149. Which of the following is ***not*** the function of Reserve Bank of India?
A. Issue of notes
B. Banker to the government
C. Clearing house function
D. Loan provider to the public

150. There is an increase in real national income, when :
A. prices of essential goods increase.
B. savings of the people increase.
C. supply of money in the economy increases.
D. total production in the economy increases.

ANSWERS

1	2	3	4	5	6	7	8	9	10
B	D	C	A	D	B	A	A	D	B
11	**12**	**13**	**14**	**15**	**16**	**17**	**18**	**19**	**20**
D	C	B	A	B	B	C	A	D	D
21	**22**	**23**	**24**	**25**	**26**	**27**	**28**	**29**	**30**
D	B	D	A	B	C	D	D	C	C
31	**32**	**33**	**34**	**35**	**36**	**37**	**38**	**39**	**40**
A	D	A	C	A	C	B	D	C	C
41	**42**	**43**	**44**	**45**	**46**	**47**	**48**	**49**	**50**
B	C	B	C	B	D	C	D	C	C
51	**52**	**53**	**54**	**55**	**56**	**57**	**58**	**59**	**60**
D	D	C	D	A	D	B	A	B	D
61	**62**	**63**	**64**	**65**	**66**	**67**	**68**	**69**	**70**
A	B	B	D	C	B	A	C	D	A
71	**72**	**73**	**74**	**75**	**76**	**77**	**78**	**79**	**80**
C	A	B	C	C	B	C	D	C	C
81	**82**	**83**	**84**	**85**	**86**	**87**	**88**	**89**	**90**
B	B	D	C	D	D	B	B	A	C
91	**92**	**93**	**94**	**95**	**96**	**97**	**98**	**99**	**100**
C	D	A	C	D	A	D	B	B	D
101	**102**	**103**	**104**	**105**	**106**	**107**	**108**	**109**	**110**
C	A	D	D	D	B	B	A	A	B
111	**112**	**113**	**114**	**115**	**116**	**117**	**118**	**119**	**120**
C	D	D	D	B	B	C	C	A	D
121	**122**	**123**	**124**	**125**	**126**	**127**	**128**	**129**	**130**
B	D	A	B	A	A	B	C	D	A
131	**132**	**133**	**134**	**135**	**136**	**137**	**138**	**139**	**140**
C	D	D	A	C	C	A	A	B	C
141	**142**	**143**	**144**	**145**	**146**	**147**	**148**	**149**	**150**
C	D	C	D	B	C	A	C	D	D

Previous Paper (Solved)

Haryana Teacher Eligibility Test (HTET)

TGT Social Studies (Level-2) Exam 2014

Child Development and Pedagogy

Direction: *Answer the following questions by selecting the **most appropriate** option.*

1. The desire of a person "to earn name and fame in life" is
A. Intrinsic motive
B. Extrinsic motive
C. Physiological motive
D. Psychological motive

2. The teaching method, in which two or more teachers make a plan of the subjects co-operatively, carry it out, & always evaluate its effect on the students periodically, is called
A. Audio-visual teaching
B. Team teaching
C. Visual teaching
D. Individual teaching

3. In a classroom a teacher is using student centered approach for teaching. The method is ***not*** suitable for
A. Group discussion
B. Project method
C. Demonstration
D. Question-answer

4. Evaluation in science
A. should consist entirely of objective tests in order to be strictly scientific
B. should come only in the end of pupils' activities
C. should be an integral part of all activities
D. should include only content & concepts, & omit process and attitude

5. The stage of human development which is called 'golden age' is
A. Infancy B. Childhood
C. Adolescence D. Adulthood

6. The most important quality of a good teacher is
A. Sound knowledge of subject-matter
B. Good communication skills
C. Concern for students welfare
D. Effective leadership qualities

7. The characteristic which is ***not*** limited with co-operative situation is
A. Face to face interaction
B. Individual accountability
C. Emphasis on tasks
D. Teacher centered

8. While teaching in lower classes, a teacher should prefer
A. Lecture method B. Assignment
C. Story telling D. Group discussion

9. A good school is one
A. which emphasizes on the feeling of strong competition
B. where every child feels happy & learns individually without co-operating with one another
C. which could understand social stratification of child & makes the class environment progressive & inspired
D. which emphasizes on rote memorization of ideal answers

10. The stages of cognitive development according to Piaget is followed by
A. Sensory motor period - concrete operational period - preoperational period - formal operational period
B. Sensory motor period - preoperational period - concrete operational period - formal operational period
C. Preoperational period - sensory motor period - concrete operational period - formal operational period
D. Preoperational period - sensory motor period - formal operational period - concrete operational period

11. What is ***wrong*** about heredity in following statements?
A. Heredity determines the sex of the child
B. It contributes significantly towards physical constitution
C. It contributes towards the birth of twins
D. It includes interests, attitudes, likes, dislikes and emotional state of mind

12. The statement, "we have people amongst us, some who are tall & some who are short, & some are fair and some others are dark, some people are strong & some others are weak" is based on the established principle of
A. Intelligence and sex differences
B. Intelligence and racial differences
C. Individual dissimilarity
D. Individual advancement

13. Impairment is disturbance at
A. Bodily level B. Functional level
C. Social level D. Educational level

14. Irfan breaks toys and dismantles them to explore their components. What would you do?
A. Never let Irfan play with toys
B. Always keep a close watch
C. Encourage his inquistive nature and channelise his energy
D. Make him understand that toys should not be broken

15. Which is ***wrong*** in the process of development of thinking power?
A. Adequacy of knowledge and experiences
B. Adequate motivation
C. Adequate freedom & flexibility
D. Less intelligence and wisdom

16. The 'emotional' aspect of behaviour falls in
A. Cognitive domain of learning
B. Affective domain of learning
C. Conative domain of learning
D. Psychological domain of learning

17. When learning in one area helps in the learning of another area, is called
A. Positive transfer of learning
B. Negative transfer of learning
C. Zero transfer of learning
D. Absolute transfer of learning

18. It is difficult for teachers to assess pupils' readiness for a learning task because
A. All the elements of readiness do not mature at same time
B. Many elements of readiness are not outwardly visible
C. Parents force their children to achieve
D. Teachers are poor in judging pupils' overt behaviour

19. The term 'emotional revolution' is closely associated with
A. Infancy B. Childhood
C. Adolescence D. Adulthood

20. Which is ***incorrect*** about creativity?
A. Creativity and intelligence always go hand in hand
B. Creativity is flexible
C. Creativity is universal concept
D. Creativity carries ego involvement

21. The field theory of psychology was given by
A. Kurt Lewin B. C.T. Morgan
C. Leon Festinger D. Henry Goddard

22. The theory of 'multiple intelligence' was developed by
A. Alfred Binet B. Howard Gardner
C. Francis Galton D. B.S. Bloom

23. Constructivism as a theory
A. focuses on the role of imitation
B. emphasizes the role of the learner in constructing his own view of the word
C. emphasizes on memorizing information & testing through recall
D. emphasizes on the dominant role of the teacher

24. Which of the following is ***not*** an appropriate tool for formative assessment?
A. Assignment B. Oral questions
C. Term test D. Quiz & games

25. The stages of cognitive development according to Jean Piaget is known as pre-conceptual period is related to
A. Sensory motor stage
B. Concrete operations stage
C. Pre-operational stage
D. Formal operations stage

26. Which of the following is ***not*** a sign of reading difficulty among young learners?
A. Difficulty in letter and word recognition
B. Difficulty in reading speed and fluency
C. Difficulty in understanding words and ideas
D. Difficulty in spelling consistency

27. Enrichment programmes are needed for
A. Slow learner
B. Gifted children
C. Average children
D. Children with physical disability

28. Intelligence includes
A. Divergent thinking B. Convergent thinking
C. Critical thinking D. Reflective thinking

29. Thinking is essentially
A. A conative activity
B. An affective behaviour
C. A cognitive activity
D. A psychomotor process

30. Which statement is ***wrong*** about inclusive school setting?
A. Develops feeling of equality
B. Develops positive self-esteem
C. Develops inferiority complex within the children with special need
D. Boost the moral of special children

English Language

Directions: *Answer the following questions by selecting the most* ***appropriate*** *option.*

31. Choose the ***mis-spelt*** word
A. peace
B. piece
C. peirce
D. piety

32. Choose the ***correct*** passive construction of the sentence: 'Someone sells tickets at the box office'.
A. Tickets are sold at the box office.
B. Tickets are being sold at the box office.
C. Tickets were sold at the box office by somebody.
D. At the box office, tickets were sold by somebody.

33. Manoj is one of the only students who .... passed the exam.
A. have
B. has
C. had
D. would have

34. How can language be best acquired?
A. Reading, writing, speaking, listening
B. Listening, speaking, reading, writing
C. Writing, reading, listening, speaking
D. Speaking, listening, reading, writing

35. Which of the following is ***not*** a characteristic of a slow learner?
A. Limited vocabulary
B. Short attention span
C. Abstract thinking
D. Limited range of interests

36. Passengers must switch off their mobile phones. What does the underlined auxiliary 'must' suggest?
A. expectation
B. compulsion
C. obligation
D. none of the above

37. The English Language Teaching Method that refrains from using the learners native language and just uses the target language is
A. The audio-lingual method
B. The grammar translation method
C. Communicative language teaching
D. The direct method

38. Choose the ***correct*** indirect form of the sentence: The policeman said, "Please move this car."
A. The policeman commanded me to move the car.
B. The policeman requested me to move the car.
C. The policeman suggested that I move the car.
D. The policeman advised me to move the car.

Directions (Q. Nos. 39 & 40): *Replace the underlined words by the* ***most suitable*** *option.*

39. "No, no", she cried, "You must not say such grossly irreverent things – you must not even think them."
A. sacrilegious B. pious
C. respectful D. religious

40. The street bazaar was a changing and enjoyable mixture of colours, smells and sounds.
A. telescope B. kaleidoscope
C. stethoscope D. microscope

41. Which of the following means— 'a drop in the ocean'
A. is a small problem that will probably get larger
B. something so small that it won't make any noticeable difference
C. every small contribution helps
D. None of the above

Directions (Q. Nos. 42 to 50): *Fill in the blanks by the most appropriate word in the following sentences:*

42. As a child, she .... dream of living in a castle.
A. is used to B. used to
C. will D. got used to

43. Don't .... me you've lost your keys again.
A. say B. tell
C. speak D. inform

44. I gave him a punch on .... nose.
A. the B. to
C. a D. an

45. .... people prefer tea to coffee.
A. A great deal of B. Plenty of
C. Much D. A lot of

46. The board at the ration shop announced. "We have .... rice. Wait till the next stock."
A. run down
B. run away
C. run over
D. run out of

47. The gallery has over 1,000 paintings. These .... during the last 100 years.
A. have collected
B. have been collected
C. had been collected
D. had collected

48. If you had worked hard, you ....
A. will pass
B. would pass
C. would have passed
D. had been pass

49. In 2004, ... a doctor?

A. you was B. was you
C. were you D. did you be

50. Bread and butter .... a wholesome food.

A. is B. are
C. was D. were

Directions (Q. Nos. 51 to 57): *Read the following passage and answer the questions that follow by selecting the* ***most appropriate*** *option.*

If you were to ask 20 people the meaning of physical fitness, you would get 20 different answers. Fitness is all things to all people, a precious commodity which enables us to live our lives to the full yet is really cherished only when it begins to fade away. To an older person, it might be the feeling of youthful vigour, to an athlete the capacity to run a mile in four minutes, to a stenographer ability to type for eight hours at a stretch without developing aching shoulder muscles. To a coach it is something which comes with training, to a physician it is a functional state of the body defined in technical terms.

It is all these things, and more. It is strength, flexibility, agility, power, speed, and muscular and cardiovascular endurance. It is the ability to enjoy our daily lives and to achieve our goals without undue fatigue or stress. It is having a reserve of physical stamina and strength for safety and the enjoyment of leisure activities. It is protection against degenerative diseases, and feeling physically youthful even when we are growing old.

Fitness is active, not passive. Yet recent decades have seen a quantum leap in the number of devices which help us to avoid effort and movement, the two key ingredients in physical fitness. We can no longer take fitness for granted, as could people of an earlier era, because the automatic movements which should maintain it—walking, carrying, pushing, running, jumping, digging, lifting —are gradually becoming unnecessary. We don't have to get to our feet to change television programs.

It's only human to take advantage of short cuts. But even though many of us are beginning to recognize the need to combat the rising toll of degenerative diseases and the decrease in capacity for activities which require effort, all too often we still look for a button to push. We want to get fit without having to work at it and without making changes in our life styles. This is not possible.

51. The statement that 'Fitness is all things to all people' implies that

A. everybody regards fitness to be the absolute good.
B. everybody includes everything under the concept of fitness.
C. everyone has his/her own definition of fitness.
D. there is an agreed comprehensive meaning of fitness

52. (*i*) Recent developments have vastly decreased the need for physical effort and movement.

(*ii*) Resorting to short cuts is against human nature.

A. Statement (*i*) is true
B. Statement (*ii*) is true
C. Both (*i*) and (*ii*) statements are true
D. Both (*i*) and (*ii*) statements are false

53. 'Fitness is active, not passive' means

A. We can take fitness for granted
B. We should avoid effort and movement
C. We can resort to short cuts
D. We cannot be sedentary

54. 'Take for granted' means

A. To value someone or something too lightly
B. To appreciate the value of something
C. Both A and B are correct
D. Both A and B are incorrect

55. The word 'vigour' means

A. weakness
B. lethargy
C. vitality
D. frailty

56. According to the passage, what has negatively affected our physical fitness?

A. Walking, carrying, pushing, running, jumping, digging, lifting
B. A quantum leap in the number of devices which help us to avoid effort and movement
C. Both A and B are correct
D. Both A and B are incorrect

57. 'All too often we still look for a button to push' means

A. We love to do physical work
B. We get on to our feet to change television programs
C. We accept the need for fitness and make it a personal commitment
D. We want to get fit without having to work at it and without making changes to our life styles

Directions (Q. Nos. 58 and 59): *Choose the* ***correct*** *prefix to build the word. The meaning of the word is given.*

58. .... beat = positive and enthusiastic.

A. up B. out
C. down D. over

59. .... hold = look at or see something or somebody.

A. with B. up
C. over D. be

60. As we got older we just grew apart. The underlined word in the sentence mean

A. natured
B. developed a strong bond
C. stayed at a distance
D. stopped having a close relationship

हिन्दी भाषा

निर्देशः *निम्नलिखित प्रश्नों के उत्तर देने के लिए **सबसे उचित** विकल्प चुनिए।*

61. 'दुष्ट अपनी दुष्टता नहीं छोड़ता' के लिए उचित लोकोक्ति है
A. खिसियानी बिल्ली खंभा नोचे
B. गंगा गए तो गंगादास, जमुना गए तो जमुनादास
C. कबहुँ निरामिष होय न कागा
D. जिस पत्तल में खाना, उसी में छेद करना

62. किस शब्द में 'ल' प्रत्यय रूप में ***नहीं*** आया है?
A. कुशल B. मृदुल
C. विमल D. रोमल

63. "पंडित दूध पीता है।" इस वाक्य में कारक है
A. कर्म, करण B. संप्रदान, संबंध
C. कर्ता, कर्म D. कोई नहीं

64. रंगमंच पर पर्दे के पीछे का स्थान कहलाता है
A. नैऋत्य B. नेपथ्य
C. प्रेक्षागृह D. अलिंद

65. किस शब्द का संधि-विच्छेद सही ***नहीं*** है?
A. प्र + ऊढ़ = प्रौढ़
B. नी + ऊन = न्यून
C. अंबु + ऊर्मि = अंबूर्मि
D. शची + इंद्र = शचींद्र

66. निम्न में से किस शब्द में बहुव्रीहि समास है?
A. चौराहा B. पंसेरी
C. शताब्दी D. पंजाब

67. निम्न में से सकर्मक क्रिया है
A. हँसना B. पढ़ना
C. सोना D. रोना

68. 'अनजान सुजान, सदा कल्यान' लोकोक्ति का भावार्थ है
A. अनजान और सुजान के साथ सदैव लाभ मिलता है
B. भोला-भाला ज्ञानी कल्याणकारक होता है
C. मूर्ख और ज्ञानी दोनों मजे में रहते हैं
D. मूर्ख स्वयं को ज्ञानी समझकर नुकसान कराता है

69. 'ज्ञ' को वर्णमाला में माना जाता है
A. संयुक्त व्यंजन
B. स्वर संधि
C. अनुस्वार
D. व्यंजन

70. निम्न में से कौन-सा वर्ण स्पर्श संघर्षी है?
A. झ B. श
C. ट D. ह

71. कौन-सा शब्द 'ईन' प्रत्यय के योग से ***नहीं*** बना है?
A. मनोहारिन B. नमकीन
C. युगीन D. ग्रामीण

72. अधोलिखित शब्दयुग्म का **सही** अर्थ विकल्प चुनिएः
अनुलंब – अनुलग्न
A. ऊर्ध्वाकार – समय के अनुसार
B. ऊपरी – जुड़ा हुआ
C. अनिश्चित – किसी के साथ जुड़ा हुआ
D. लम्बाई के अनुसार – शुभकाल

73. 'इन्द्र' के पर्यायवाची शब्दों का समूह है
A. वैनतेय, चन्द्रमौलि, सुरपति, देवराज
B. मधवा, पुरन्दर, शचीपति, वासव
C. सुरपति, पुरन्दर, उपेन्द्र, अंशुमाली
D. वैनतेय, मधवा, सुरपति, वासव

74. 'कवि' शब्द में संज्ञा है
A. व्यक्तिवाचक B. जातिवाचक
C. द्रव्यवाचक D. कोई नहीं

75. विसर्ग सन्धि का उदाहरण है
A. अतएव B. विस्मरण
C. उच्चारण D. विसर्ग

76. प्रत्येक पाठ के प्रारंभ में होना चाहिए
A. पाठ का सार B. परिशिष्ट
C. प्रस्तावना D. अभ्यास

77. 'कनक' शब्द का अर्थ-समूह चुनिए
A. वृक्ष, स्वर्ण, धतूरा B. स्वर्ण, धतूरा, गेहूँ
C. स्त्री, पलाश, आभूषण D. कोई नहीं

78. भाषा प्रवाह तथा अभिव्यक्ति कौशल के मूल्यांकन का उपयुक्त तरीका है
A. लिखित परीक्षाएँ B. वस्तुनिष्ठ परीक्षण
C. मौखिक वार्तालाप D. उपर्युक्त में से कोई नहीं

79. 'प्राक्तन' शब्द में उपसर्ग एवं मूल शब्द का **सही** विकल्प है
A. प्रा + तन B. प्राक् + तन
C. पर् + तन D. प्रा + कतन

80. विद्यार्थियों में भाषा की रुचि का विकास करने का उपयुक्त उपाय है
A. विद्यार्थियों के व्याकरण के ज्ञान को बढ़ाना
B. विद्यार्थियों को पाठ्यपुस्तकें पढ़वाना
C. विद्यार्थियों को मौखिक रूप से अधिकाधिक समझाना
D. उपर्युक्त सभी

81. भाषा अधिगम में प्रायः कठिनाई नहीं आती
A. संकोची स्वभाव
B. आत्म विश्वास की कमी
C. मानसिक अस्वस्थता
D. मानसिक स्वस्थता

82. निम्न में ***शुद्ध*** रूप से लिखा वाक्य है
A. किसी आदमी को भेज दो।
B. हम तो अवश्य ही जाएँगे।
C. तब शायद यह काम अवश्य हो जाएगा।
D. कृपया आने का अनुग्रह करें।

83. शब्दकोश में निम्न में से सर्वप्रथम आने वाला शब्द है
A. प्याऊ
B. प्रकंप
C. प्लवन
D. प्रकीर्ण

84. वर्तनी की दृष्टि से ***शुद्ध*** शब्द है
A. इक्षा
B. आव्हान
C. शृंगार
D. प्रत्यूष

निर्देश (प्र. सं. 85 से 88) : *निम्नलिखित गद्यांश को पढ़कर दिए गए प्रश्नों के उत्तर* ***सबसे उचित*** *विकल्प को चुनकर दीजिए :*

वर्तमान मेरे लिए और मुझ जैसे बहुत से और लोगों के लिए मध्ययुगीनता, भयंकर गरीबी एवं दुर्गति और मध्यवर्ग की कुछ-कुछ सतही आधुनिकता का विचित्र मिश्रण है। मैं अपने वर्ग और अपनी किस्म के लोगों का प्रशंसक नहीं था, फिर भी भारतीय संघर्ष में नेतृत्व के लिए मैं निश्चित रूप से मध्यवर्ग की ओर देखता था। यह मध्यवर्ग स्वयं को बंदी और सीमाओं में जकड़ा हुआ महसूस करता था और खुद तरक्की और विकास करना चाहता था। अंग्रेजी शासन के ढाँचे के भीतर ऐसा न कर पाने के कारण उसके भीतर विद्रोह की चेतना पनपी। लेकिन यह चेतना उस ढाँचे के खिलाफ नहीं जाती थी जिसने हमें रौंद दिया था। ये उस ढाँचे को बनाए रखना चाहते थे और अंग्रेजों को हटाकर उसका संचालन करना चाहते थे। ये मध्यवर्ग के लोग इस हद तक इस ढाँचे की पैदाइश थे कि उसे चुनौती देना या उसे उखाड़ फेंकने का प्रयास करना इनके बस की बात नहीं थी।

85. लेखक किस वर्ग से संबंधित है?
A. सामंत वर्ग
B. मध्यवर्ग
C. निम्न वर्ग
D. उपर्युक्त में से कोई नहीं

86. मध्यवर्ग में विद्रोही चेतना का कारण था
A. मध्यवर्ग साम्राज्यवाद विरोधी था
B. मध्यवर्ग राष्ट्रवादी था
C. मध्यवर्ग अंग्रेजों को विस्थापित करके शासन संचालन चाहता था
D. उपर्युक्त सभी

87. गद्यांश में आए भारतीय संघर्ष का संदर्भ है
A. भारत का स्वतंत्रता संघर्ष
B. चीन के विरुद्ध संघर्ष
C. पाकिस्तान के विरुद्ध संघर्ष
D. महाशक्तियों के विरुद्ध संघर्ष

88. निम्न में से कौन-सा सामाजिक वर्ग ब्रिटिश शासन प्रणाली की उपज था?
A. उच्च वर्ग
B. सामंत वर्ग
C. किसान
D. मध्यवर्ग

89. भाषा शिक्षण का आदर्श वातावरण है
A. विद्यार्थियों को अभिशक्ति के भरपूर अवसर
B. भाषागत शुद्धता पर अत्यधिक बल
C. अध्यापक का एकालाप
D. दृश्य-श्रव्य सामग्री का प्रचुर उपयोग

90. भाषा शिक्षक को एक बहु-सांस्कृतिक कक्षा में किस बात पर बल देना चाहिए?
A. बच्चों को भाषा प्रयोग के अधिक से अधिक अवसर देना
B. पाठ्यपुस्तक के प्रत्येक पाठ को भली-भांति समझाना
C. बच्चों को व्याकरण सिखाना
D. स्वयं द्वारा भाषा का शुद्ध प्रयोग करना

Subject Specific—Social Studies

Direction: *Answer the following questions by selecting the* ***most appropriate*** *option.*

91. The prominent nihilist thinker in Russia was
A. Turgnev
B. Lenin
C. Tolstoy
D. Prince Koptikin

92. In which sector, industries are included?
A. Primary sector
B. Secondary sector
C. Service sector
D. None of the above

93. When did Parliament passed the Consumer Protection Act?
A. 15th December, 1985
B. 24th December, 1986
C. 15th March, 1985
D. 24th December 1987

94. In which census decade the decadal population growth of India was recorded highest?
A. 1951-61
B. 1961-71
C. 1971-81
D. 1981-91

95. In agricultural production, Food grains include
A. Only cereals
B. Cereals and pulses
C. Cereals and oilseeds
D. Pulses and oilseeds

96. Match List-I with List-II:

List-I	**List-II**
(*a*) Surendranath Banerjee	1. Hind Swaraj
(*b*) Dada Bhai Naoroji	2. The Indian Struggle
(*c*) Subhash Chandra Bose	3. Poverty and Unbritish rule in India
(*d*) Mahatma Gandhi	4. A Nation in Making

	(*a*)	(*b*)	(*c*)	(*d*)
A.	4	3	2	1
B.	1	2	3	4
C.	2	3	4	1
D.	3	4	1	2

97. In India the Apex body for agriculture loan is
A. Reserve Bank of India
B. State Bank of India
C. State Cooperative Bank
D. National Bank for agriculture and Rural Development

98. The Governor of Reserve Bank of India is
A. Dr. D. Subbarao
B. Bimal Jalan
C. C. Rangrajan
D. Raghuram Rajan

99. Which amongst the following are known as 'Bretonwoods twins'?
A. I.M.F. and W.T.O.
B. World Bank and I.M.F.
C. W.T.O. and W.L.O.
D. W.L.O. and I.F.O.

100. Consider the following statements:
(*i*) Mahatma Gandhi NREGA was enacted by government of India in 2005.
(*ii*) It provides 100 days guaranteed employment in every financial year to adults of rural household.
Among these which statement is ***correct***?
A. (*i*) only
B. (*ii*) only
C. (*i*) and (*ii*) both
D. None

101. Coins in India are minted by
A. Reserve Bank of India
B. State Bank of India
C. Government of India
D. Planning Commission

102. The film made by Dada Saheb Falke in 1913 was
A. C.I.D.
B. Hanging Garden
C. Raja Harishchandra
D. Guest House

103. The commodity on which India spends largest amount to import is?
A. Iron and Steel
B. Food Grains
C. Crude Oil
D. Gold and Silver

104. The pioneer of humanism was
A. Boccaccio
B. Dante
C. Petrarch
D. Bacon

105. The financial year in India starts from
A. January
B. April
C. June
D. October

106. In economic terminology the final production of goods and services valued at market prices during a year of a nation is known as
A. Gross Domestic Product
B. Gross National Product
C. National Income
D. Net National Product

107. One of the founders of Swarajya Party was
A. Madan Mohan Malviya
B. Moti Lal Nehru
C. Rajendra Prasad
D. Lala Lajpat Roy

108. Who amongst the following was the contemporary ruler of Akbar?
A. Queen Victoria of British
B. Shah Abbas I of Persia
C. Catherine the great of Russia
D. None of the above

109. The type of unemployment, in agriculture sector in India is
A. Structural
B. Frictional
C. Open
D. Seasonal

110. Which of the following statements is/are ***correct*** about Reserve Bank of India?
A. It is a Nationalised Bank
B. It is the Central Bank of India
C. It was established in 1935
D. All of the above

111. Which one of the following is an example of Block Mountain?
A. Nilgiri Mountain
B. Aravalli Mountain
C. Satpura Mountain
D. Sahyadri Mountain

112. A personal account can ***not*** be opened in
A. A Cooperative Bank
B. A Scheduled Bank
C. The Reserve Bank of India
D. A Private Bank

113. The reason in difference between GNP and GDP is
A. Gross Foreign Investment
B. Net Foreign Investment
C. Net Exports
D. Net Factor Income from abroad

114. The incident of Chauri-Chaura is associated with
A. Non-cooperation Movement
B. Civil Disobedience Movement
C. Quit India Movement
D. Revolutionary Movement

115. The religious tax collected by French Church prior to 1789, was
A. Taille B. Gebul
C. Tithe D. Corvee

116. Who was the first Surveyor General of Archaeological Survey of India?
A. Sir William Jones
B. James Prinsep
C. James Fergusson
D. Alexander Cunningham

117. The components of Human Development Index are
A. Life expectancy, per capita GDP and sex ratio
B. Sex ratio, educational attainment and pure drinking water
C. Life expectancy, per capita GDP and educational attainment
D. Per capita GDP, infrastructure and sex ratio

118. Among the agro-based industries in India which one is the second largest industry after cotton textile?
A. Jute Industry B. Silk Industry
C. Woollen Textile D. Sugar Industry

119. In which states and union territories the sex ratio is in favour of Females (2011)?
A. Kerala & Puducherry
B. Kerala, Puducherry & Lakshadweep
C. Puducherry & Tamil Nadu
D. Tamil Nadu & Lakshadweep

120. Project Tiger was started in
A. 1973 B. 1975
C. 1976 D. 1977

121. Which one of the following is a national political party?
A. Bahujan Samaj Party
B. Communist Party (Marxist)
C. Nationalist Congress Party
D. All of the above

122. Which one of the following is ***not*** correctly matched?
A. Cornwallis – Permanent Settlement
B. William Bentinck – Abolition of Sati Act
C. Lytton – Vernacular Press Act
D. Ripon – Rowlatt Act

123. 180° Longitude is known as
A. Prime Meridian
B. International Date Line
C. Greenwich Line
D. Equator

124. Vembanad is
A. A Sea Port
B. Lagoon Lake
C. Mountain peak
D. Multipurpose project

125. The feature which applies to pressure groups but not to political parties is
A. fielding of candidates for contesting election
B. objective of safeguarding the interest of whole society
C. Membership is exclusive
D. Do not participate directly in political process

126. From which date the model code of conduct is enforced in elections?
A. From the date of notification
B. From the last date of filling the nomination
C. From the last date of withdrawal of candidatures
D. From the date of announcement of election schedule by the Election Commission

127. Karn Prayag is the confluence of
A. Bhagirathi & Alakhnanda
B. Bhagirathi & Pinder
C. Dholi Ganga & Alakhnanda
D. Alakhnanda & Pinder

128. How many members can be nominated in Rajya Sabha by the President?
A. 10 B. 12
C. 17 D. 15

129. Which one of the following means "by what authority"?
A. Habeas corpus B. Quo warranto
C. Certiorari D. Mandamus

130. Which soil is found in the areas of excessive leaching due to heavy rainfall?
A. Black B. Laterite
C. Alluvial D. Mountain

131. The Right which is a legal but not a fundamental one?
A. Freedom to move freely
B. Right against exploitation
C. Right to minorities to establish educational institutions
D. Right to property

132. Which amongst the following states sends highest number of parliamentarians in Lok Sabha?
A. Maharashtra B. Bihar
C. Andhra Pradesh D. Tamil Nadu

133. Where the first, second & third Earth Summits took place in 1992, 2002 & 2012 respectively?
A. Johannesburg, Doha, Rio De Janeiro
B. Rio De Janeiro, Johannesburg, Doha
C. Rio De Janeiro, Kyoto, Johannesburg
D. Rio De Janeiro, Johannesburg, Rio De Janeiro

134. Which of the following is ***not*** a session of Lok Sabha?
A. Budget session
B. Summer session
C. Winter session
D. Monsoon session

135. Aurangzeb spent nearly 25 years in Deccan, because
A. He was totally free from North India
B. He wanted to shift his capital in South
C. He wanted to check Maratha expansion
D. He was not secured in his own capital

136. Which amongst the following statement is/are ***correct*** about IMF?
(*i*) There are 188 member countries in IMF.
(*ii*) It is a specialised agency of United Nations.
(*iii*) In IMF member states do not have equal voting rights.
(*iv*) It gives loan and technical advice to member countries in the balance of payment crisis.
A. (*i*), (*ii*)
B. (*i*), (*iii*)
C. (*i*), (*ii*), (*iii*) and (*iv*)
D. (*i*), (*iv*)

137. Which amongst the following was ***not*** a Constituent Assembly Member?
A. G. Durgabai Deshmukh
B. Mrs. Hansa Mehta
C. Mrs. Renuka Ray
D. Vijaylaxmi Pandit

138. Which of the following crops had shown the maximum production increase after the beginning of Green Revolution in 1960?
A. Wheat & Rice
B. Oil seeds
C. Pulses
D. All of the above

139. On which plate margins maximum volcanoes & earthquakes occur?
A. Destructive Plate Margins
B. Constructive Plate Margins
C. Conservative Plate Margins
D. None of the above

140. The constitutional schedule which contain the list of recognised languages of India is
A. 7th Schedule
B. 8th Schedule
C. 9th Schedule
D. 10th Schedule

141. Mangla oil well is located in
A. Haryana
B. Rajasthan
C. Goa
D. Assam

142. The newspaper, which upheld the nationalist cause during India's struggle for freedom was
A. The Leader
B. The Civil & Military Gazette
C. Dawn
D. The Statesman

143. In Haryana, a Gram Sabha consists of
A. Elected members of Village Panchayat
B. Members of Panchayat Samiti
C. Registered voters of the village/villages in the Panchayat circle
D. All residents of the village/villages in the Panchayat circle

144. Arrange the following Delhi Sultans in chronological order:
(*i*) Qutub-ud-din Aibak
(*ii*) Iltutmish
(*iii*) Razia
(*iv*) Nasir-ud-din Mahmud
Choose ***correct*** answer
A. (*i*), (*ii*), (*iii*), (*iv*)
B. (*i*), (*iv*), (*ii*), (*iii*)
C. (*ii*), (*i*), (*iii*), (*iv*)
D. (*i*), (*ii*), (*iv*), (*iii*)

145. In Indonesia the "slash and burn agriculture" is called as
A. Jhoom
B. Roke
C. Milpa
D. Ladang

146. The retreating monsoon in Indian subcontinent is known as
A. South-West Monsoon
B. South-East Monsoon
C. North-East Monsoon
D. North-West Monsoon

147. The theory which gave birth to the French Revolution and the Revolution in America is
A. Legal theory of rights
B. Theory of natural rights
C. Social welfare theory
D. Historical theory of rights

148. Which of the following forest type cover the maximum area on Indian land?
A. Tropical rain forest
B. Tropical Deciduous forest
C. Mountain forest
D. Mangrove forest

149. The provision of social security is the fundamental principle of
A. Laissez Faire Theory
B. Theory of Welfare State
C. Pluralistic Theory
D. Evolutionary Theory

150. The Asiatic Society of Bengal was founded by
A. Sir James Grant
B. Max Mullor
C. Sir William Jones
D. Macaulay

ANSWERS

1	**2**	**3**	**4**	**5**	**6**	**7**	**8**	**9**	**10**
A	B	C	C	B	A & B	D	C	C	B
11	**12**	**13**	**14**	**15**	**16**	**17**	**18**	**19**	**20**
D	C	B	C	D	B	A	A	C	A
21	**22**	**23**	**24**	**25**	**26**	**27**	**28**	**29**	**30**
A	B	B	A	C	B	B	B	C	C
31	**32**	**33**	**34**	**35**	**36**	**37**	**38**	**39**	**40**
C	A	B	B	C	C	D	B	A	B
41	**42**	**43**	**44**	**45**	**46**	**47**	**48**	**49**	**50**
B	B	B	A	D	D	B	C	C	A
51	**52**	**53**	**54**	**55**	**56**	**57**	**58**	**59**	**60**
C	A	D	A	C	B	D	A	D	D
61	**62**	**63**	**64**	**65**	**66**	**67**	**68**	**69**	**70**
C	C	C	B	B	D	B	C	A	A
71	**72**	**73**	**74**	**75**	**76**	**77**	**78**	**79**	**80**
A	C	B	B	A	C	B	C	B	C
81	**82**	**83**	**84**	**85**	**86**	**87**	**88**	**89**	**90**
D	A	A	D	B	C	A	D	A	A
91	**92**	**93**	**94**	**95**	**96**	**97**	**98**	**99**	**100**
D	B	B	B	B	A	D	D	B	C
101	**102**	**103**	**104**	**105**	**106**	**107**	**108**	**109**	**110**
C	C	C	C	B	A	B	B	D	D
111	**112**	**113**	**114**	**115**	**116**	**117**	**118**	**119**	**120**
C	C	D	A	C	D	C	D	A	A
121	**122**	**123**	**124**	**125**	**126**	**127**	**128**	**129**	**130**
D	D	B	B	D	D	D	B	B	B
131	**132**	**133**	**134**	**135**	**136**	**137**	**138**	**139**	**140**
D	A	D	B	C	C	D	A	A	B
141	**142**	**143**	**144**	**145**	**146**	**147**	**148**	**149**	**150**
B	A	C	A	D	C	B	B	B	C

Previous Paper (Solved)

Haryana Teacher Eligibility Test (HTET)

TGT Social Studies (Level-2) Exam 2011

Child Development and Pedagogy

Directions: *Answer the following questions by selecting the* ***most appropriate*** *option.*

1. Teaching becomes much more effective provided:
A. Students are given autonomy and control to work on their own
B. Students learning is directed and controlled by the teacher
C. Teacher plays a central role in explaining the facts
D. Teacher directs learning

2. Teaching becomes effective provided:
A. Direct instruction is used in the classroom
B. Teacher directed methods are used in the classroom
C. Both teacher directed methods and direct instruction are used
D. Learner centered instruction and interactive methods are used

3. A good classroom teacher:
A. Nurtures learner's natural curiosity
B. Encourages learners to engage in dialogue
C. Involves learners in real world situations
D. All of the above

4. Characteristic of creativity is:
A. Originality
B. Fluency
C. Flexibility
D. All of the above

5. Students have following characteristics for learning and teaching:
A. Activeness in learning
B. Students have abilities to learn
C. Students construct knowledge through self activity in relation to new experiences
D. All of the above

6. A slow learner needs:
A. extra help
B. special help
C. no help
D. some help

7. If a student gives wrong answer to a question put up by you. You will:
A. put up another question so that he himself realises that his answer was wrong
B. tell him why his answer was wrong
C. ask some other student to answer
D. tell the correct answer

8. Teaching is defined as:
A. Facilitation of learning
B. Transmission of knowledge by teachers and its reception by the students
C. Reading the textbooks
D. Transmission of knowledge by teachers

9. Which one of the following is a level of teaching?
A. Reflective
B. Interactive
C. Projective
D. Summative

10. Teachers need to practise the following teaching methods:
A. Lecture method
B. Interactive methods
C. Narratives
D. None of the above

11. Counselling to students is most useful for:
A. Enhancing their knowledge
B. Developing their skills
C. Developing self confidence in them
D. Making them worldly successful

12. Multigrade teaching is that where in:
A. A student can pass more than one class at a time
B. A teacher has to teach the students of more than one class at the same time
C. There is no point in classwise teaching
D. All of the above

13. The role of the teacher is:
A. communicating knowledge
B. maintaining discipline among students

C. creating a learner centered, activity based, interactive learning
D. All of the above

14. Teachers should do while teaching:
A. Transmit knowledge verbally
B. Encourage inquiry
C. Teach through textbook in the classroom
D. None of the above

15. You can help a talented child by:
A. Paying more attention to him
B. Giving him more books
C. Spending more time on him
D. Giving enriched learning experiences

16. According to Prof. Jean Piaget, the mental development of 0-14 years age group occurs in four stages. Name the stage of development for 7-14 years age group:
A. Sensori motor stage
B. Pre-operational stage
C. Concrete operational stage
D. Formal operational stage

17. As a teacher, how would you deal with those students sitting in the backseats and talking to each other?
A. By ignoring them
B. Ask them to keep quiet or leave the class
C. Get them out from the class
D. Ask them why they are not paying attention

18. Most objective method for measuring personality of a child is:
A. Projective method
B. Interview method
C. Questionnaire method
D. Sociometry method

19. Education system in India is:
A. Preparing students for life
B. Preparing for employment
C. Preparing for vocational courses
D. Preparing for examination

20. In a class, a naughty child disturbs the students. Which method should a teacher adopt to know the problem of the child?
A. Survey method
B. Case study method
C. Experimental method
D. Observation method

21. Oral guidance is less effective in:
A. Teaching concepts
B. Teaching skills
C. Teaching facts
D. None of the above

22. An emotionally stable student:
A. maintains cordial interrelationship with classmates
B. does not interact effectively with other classmates
C. does not contribute any new ideas
D. does not respect the ideas given by other classmates

23. The role of a teacher is:
A. Transferring information
B. Providing knowledge
C. Giving training in skills
D. Facilitating of knowledge construction

24. You can gain attention of your class through:
A. Speaking loudly
B. Writing on Black Board
C. Drawing diagrams
D. Stimulus Variation

25. For adaptive and positive behavior, a student needs following life skills:
A. Effective interpersonal communication
B. Decision making ability
C. Coping with emotions and stress
D. All of the above

26. If a student asks a question of which you don't have answer. What will you do? You will:
A. tell the student that his question is senseless
B. try to avoid
C. explore the answer of the question and convey him next day
D. rebuke the student for asking unnecessary questions

27. A reflective teacher creates classroom situation for
A. Listening the lecture
B. Taking notes from the lecture of the teacher
C. Maintaining classroom discipline
D. Promoting interaction between students and the teacher

28. The aim of education should be:
A. To develop vocational skills in the students
B. To develop social awareness in the students
C. To prepare the students for examination
D. To prepare the students for practical life

29. It is necessary for a teacher to know to guide a student:
A. His learning difficulty
B. His personality
C. Environment of his home
D. All of the above

30. Which of the following is the nature of educational psychology?
A. Art B. Science
C. Positive Science D. None of the above

हिन्दी भाषा

निर्देश (प्रश्न संख्या 31 से 35 तक): *निम्नलिखित गद्यांश को पढ़कर दिए गए प्रश्नों के उत्तर सबसे उचित विकल्प चुनकर दीजिए।*

लोकगीत अपनी लोच, ताजगी और लोकप्रियता में शास्त्रीय संगीत से भिन्न हैं। लोकगीत सीधे जनता के संगीत हैं। घर, गाँव और नगर की जनता के गीत हैं ये। इनके लिए साधना की जरूरत नहीं होती। त्योहारों और विशेष अवसरों पर ये गाए जाते हैं।

एक समय था जब शास्त्रीय संगीत के सामने इनको हेय समझा जाता था। अभी हाल तक इनकी बड़ी उपेक्षा की जाती थी। पर इधर साधारण जनता की ओर जो लोगों की नजर फिरी है तो साहित्य और कला के क्षेत्र में भी परिवर्तन हुआ है। अनेक लोगों ने विविध बोलियों के लोक-साहित्य और लोकगीतों के संग्रह पर कमर बाँधी है और इस प्रकार के अनेक संग्रह अब तक प्रकाशित भी हो गए हैं।

वास्तविक लोकगीत देश के गाँवों और देहातों में है। इनका संबंध देहात की जनता से है। चैता, कजरी, बारहमासा, सावन आदि मिर्जापुर, बनारस और उत्तर प्रदेश के पूरबी और बिहार के पश्चिमी जिलों में गाए जाते हैं। बाउल और भतियाली बंगाल के लोकगीत हैं। हीर-राँझा, सोहनी-महीवाल संबंधी गीत पंजाबी में और ढोला-मारू आदि के गीत राजस्थानी में बड़े चाव से गाए जाते हैं।

31. 'देहात की जनता' का तात्पर्य है :
A. कस्बे का जनसमुदाय B. ग्रामीण जनसमुदाय
C. शहरी जनसमुदाय D. आदिवासी जनसमुदाय

32. 'कजरी' गायी जाती है :
A. उत्तर प्रदेश में B. आसाम में
C. गुजरात में D. राजस्थान में

33. 'नजर फिरी है' का तात्पर्य है :
A. उपेक्षा करना B. दृष्टिकोण में परिवर्तन आना
C. अवलोकन करना D. कुदृष्टि डालना

34. जनता का संगीत है :
A. लोकगीत B. फिल्म संगीत
C. शास्त्रीय संगीत D. पाश्चात्य संगीत

35. 'बाउल' कहाँ का लोक संगीत है?
A. गुजरात B. उत्तर प्रदेश
C. बिहार D. बंगाल

36. 'तृ' की ध्वनियाँ हैं :
A. त् + ऋ B. त + र
C. त् + ऋ + अ D. त्र + अ

37. निम्न में से कौन-सा समूह 'विष्णु' के पर्यायवाची शब्दों का है?
A. सुदेश, चक्रपाणि, चतुर्भुज, फणीश
B. चक्रपाणि, चतुर्भुज, शेषशायी, गरुड़ध्वज
C. शेखर, शशांक, दामोदर, विठ्ठल
D. महीधर, वैनतेय, वासव, देवराज

38. निम्न में से तद्भव शब्द है :
A. कुमार B. कुक्कुर
C. काजल D. कोण

39. निम्न में से शुद्ध शब्द पहचानिए :
A. सहानुभूती B. अश्रू
C. अनुपातिक D. ऐतिहासिक

40. 'पतझड़' में समास है :
A. करण तत्पुरुष B. कर्म तत्पुरुष
C. बहुव्रीहि D. द्वन्द्व

41. 'हँसना' कैसी क्रिया है?
A. सकर्मक क्रिया B. अकर्मक क्रिया
C. संयुक्त क्रिया D. प्रेरणार्थक क्रिया

42. ''जो पहले कभी नहीं हुआ हो'' कहलाता है :
A. अद्भुत B. अप्रत्याशित
C. अनुपम D. अभूतपूर्व

43. निम्न में से सघोष वर्ण है :
A. अ B. क
C. ख D. च

44. 'हृषीकेश' की संधि है :
A. हृषी + केश B. ऋषी + केश
C. हृषीक + ईश D. ऋषी + ईश

45. टिकाऊ में प्रत्यय है :
A. ऊ B. आऊ
C. वू D. उक

46. शब्दकोश में निम्न शब्दों का सही क्रम बताइए :
A. विश्व, विश्वंभरा, विश्वस्त, विश्वास
B. विश्वस्त, विश्व, विश्वंभरा, विश्वास
C. विश्वंभरा, विश्वस्त, विश्व, विश्वास
D. विश्वंभरा, विश्व, विश्वस्त, विश्वास

निर्देश (प्रश्न संख्या 47 से 51 तक): *निम्नलिखित गद्यांश को पढ़कर दिए गए प्रश्नों के उत्तर सबसे उचित विकल्प चुनकर दीजिए।*

मोर के सिर की कलगी और सघन, ऊँची तथा चमकीली हो गई। चोंच अधिक बंकिम और पैनी हो गई, गोल आँखों में इंद्रनी की नीलाभ द्युति झलकने लगी। लंबी नील-हरित ग्रीवा की हर भंगिमा में धूपछाँही तरंगें उठने-गिरने लगी। दक्षिण-वाम दोनों पंखों में सलेटी और सफेद आलेखन स्पष्ट होने लगे। पूँछ लंबी हुई और उसके पंखों पर चंद्रिकाओं के इंद्रधनुषी रंग उद्दीप्त हो उठे। रंग-रहित पैरों को गरवीली गति ने एक नयी गरिमा से रंजित कर दिया। उसका गरदन ऊँची कर देखना, विशेष भंगिमा के साथ उसे नीची कर दाना चुगना, पानी पीना, टेढ़ी कर शब्द सुनना आदि क्रियाओं में जो सुकुमारता और सौंदर्य था, उसका अनुभव देखकर ही किया जा सकता है। गति का चित्र नहीं आँका जा सकता।

मोरनी का विकास मोर के समान चमत्कारिक तो नहीं हुआ–परंतु अपनी लंबी धूपछाँही गरदन, हवा में चंचल कलगी, पंखों की श्याम-श्वेत पत्रलेखा, मंथर गति आदि से वह भी मोर की उपयुक्त सहचारिणी होने का प्रमाण देने लगी।

47. प्रस्तुत गद्यांश है :
A. एक शब्दचित्र B. एक निबंध
C. एक रिपोर्ताज D. एक कहानी

48. 'रंजित' का तात्पर्य है :
A. रंगयुक्त B. आवेश युक्त
C. शोभा युक्त D. इनमें से कोई नहीं

49. मंथर गति होती है :
A. तेज गति B. धीमी गति
C. लय युक्त गति D. टेढ़ी गति

50. बंकिम का तात्पर्य है :
A. टेढ़ा B. सुंदर
C. तीखा D. कठोर

51. किसकी क्रियाओं में सुकुमारता व सौंदर्य था?
A. मोर की B. मोरनी की
C. तोते की D. लेखिका की

52. शब्द युग्म अवर-अपर का सही अर्थ है?
A. अतिरिक्त – निम्न B. निम्न – अन्य
C. उच्च – निम्न D. निम्न – उच्च

53. 'किसी वस्तु को गलत समझ लेना' है :
A. सन्देह B. संशय
C. भ्रान्ति D. अज्ञान

54. 'पण्डित' से बनी भाववाचक संज्ञा है :
A. पाण्डित्य B. पंडिताईन
C. पठन D. ये सभी

55. 'मुद्रा' शब्द का अर्थ समूह चुनिए :
A. मोहर, छाप, सिक्का, अँगूठी
B. चेहरे का भाव, छाप, अँगूठी, प्रति
C. नाम, लिखना, सिक्का, छापाखाना
D. चोट, छापा, धन, स्टाम्प

56. 'मरने की इच्छा' के लिए एक शब्द है :
A. मृत्युकांक्षी B. मुमुर्षा
C. मरणेच्छु D. मरणासन्न

57. निम्नलिखित में से एक अनेकार्थी शब्द 'खग' से संबंधित नहीं है, उसको चुनिए।
A. मन B. तीर
C. पक्षी D. आकाश

58. निम्न में से तत्सम शब्द है :
A. अगम B. अमिय
C. आंवला D. आशिष

59. निम्न में से कौन शब्द हमेशा बहुवचन में प्रयुक्त होता है?
A. हस्ताक्षर B. समाचारपत्र
C. चिड़िया D. तिजोरी

60. 'त्यक्त' शब्द का सही विलोम है :
A. गृहीत B. त्याज्य
C. तुच्छ D. प्रिय

English Language

61. Choose the correct word for the blank:
You can park the car on .... side of the road.
A. either B. none
C. both D. neither

62. Choose the correct meaning of:
'A beverage'
A. something red B. an alcoholic drink
C. any drink D. soft drink

63. Choose *one word* for the words underlined:
When her dog died she cried very hard for half an hour.
A. howl B. screamed
C. sobbed D. drowned

64. Kashmir is .... between India & Pakistan.
A. an apple of eye B. an apple of discord
C. an apple of fight D. None of the above

65. The Solitary Reaper is a melancholy song. Here, the word melancholy means:
A. expressing joy B. expressing sadness
C. expressing humour D. expressing anger

Directions (Q. No. 66 to 75) : *Read the passage given below and answer the questions that follow by selecting the **most appropriate** option.*

A completely uneducated farmer's work is far more important than that of a professor. We can live without education, but we die if we have no food. If no one cleaned our streets and took the rubbish away from the house, we should get terrible diseases in our towns. In countries, where there are no servants, because every one is ashamed of doing house work, the professor have to waste much of their time doing house work.

In fact, when we say that all of us must be educated, we mean that all of us must be educated in such a way that firstly, each of us can do what every job is suited to his ability and brain and secondly that we can realize that all jobs are necessary to society and that it is very bad to be ashamed of one's work or to scorn some one else's. Only such type of education can be called valuable to society.

66. If no one cleans our streets we should:
A. be unclean B. be unhappy
C. get diseases D. get dirty

67. Only such type of education can be called valuable. Such type of education refers to:
A. that which enables us to do any thing
B. that which enables us to scorn some one else's work
C. that which develops dislike in us
D. that which enables us to do any work and not to hate any work

68. Which word in the passage is one word for 'one who is a university teacher'?
A. teacher B. professor
C. educationist D. lecturer

69. A completely uneducated farmer's work is more important than:
A. that of a businessman
B. that of a professor
C. that of an artist
D. that of an advocate

70. Professors, in some countries waste their time because:
A. they have to do house work
B. they have to teach lower classes
C. they have to help the students
D. they have to wait for train

71. Which word in the passage is the ***opposite*** of 'like'?
A. terrible B. ashamed
C. scorn D. dislike

72. According to this passage, what is very bad?
A. to be ashamed of one's work
B. to scorn some one else's work
C. both A and B
D. not to do work suited to our ability

73. Which word in the passage means 'waste material'?
A. uneducated B. ashamed
C. rubbish D. None of these

74. We can live without:
A. food B. education
C. playing D. doing exercise

75. What should we realize? We should realize that:
A. each of us can do farming
B. all jobs are necessary to society
C. all of us cannot get education
D. all of us should not do house work

76. The word 'Oasis' means:
A. a garden full of flowers
B. a palace surrounded by trees
C. a green patch in a desert
D. a barren piece of land

77. The passive form of 'He knows her' is:
A. She knows him
B. She is known to him
C. She has known to him
D. She has been known to him

78. Choose the correct ***conjunction*** for the blank:
He is witty .... vulgar.
A. that B. because
C. though D. so

79. Choose the correctly punctuated sentence:
A. What a day. B. What a day?
C. What, a day? D. What a day!

80. The phrase—'to look into' means:
A. to examine B. to search
C. to exercise D. to take care of

81. 'To imitate' someone means to:
A. copy someone
B. tease someone
C. make someone angry
D. please someone

82. Choose the correct ***preposition*** for the blank:
I mix up the butter .... I bake the cake.
A. before B. after
C. to D. None of the above

83. Choose the correct ***indirect*** form of:
Ravi said, "Guests have taken their lunch".
A. Ravi said that guests had taken their lunch.
B. Ravi said that guests have taken their lunch.
C. Ravi said that guests had to take their lunch.
D. Ravi said that guests are taking their lunch.

84. Choose the correct ***preposition*** for the blank:
There is a bench .... the lamp post.
A. through B. over
C. along D. beside

85. Choose the correct ***article*** for the blank:
Please help me clean my .... apartment.
A. a B. an
C. the D. Zero article

86. Choose the correct ***opposite*** word for the underlined word:
Her nephew isn't ugly.
A. beautiful B. handsome
C. large D. heavy

87. Choose the ***plural*** of the word given in bracket:

Scientists are always studying the .... (phenomenon) of nature.

A. phenomenons B. phenomenones
C. phenomena D. phenomenas

88. Meaning of the word 'prophecy' is:

A. proverb B. old saying
C. prediction D. None of the above

89. Choose the most natural order of the following words:

what's that bag/? in small

A. What's small in that bag?
B. Small whats in that bag?
C. What's in that small bag?
D. All of the above

90. Choose the correct ***tense*** of the underlined verb phrase:

Kavita said that she had been waiting for me for two hours when I arrived.

A. simple past
B. past perfect continuous
C. past perfect
D. present perfect continuous

Subject Specific—Social Studies

91. Who is responsible for maintaining the land record?

A. Patwari B. Tahsildaar
C. Numbardaar D. None of the above

92. In which province Raiyatwari revenue system was implemented?

A. Bombay province B. Bengal province
C. Madras province D. Central province

93. In which Article of Indian Constitution the 'Right to life and personal liberty' has been described?

A. Article 12 B. Article 21
C. Article 22 D. Article 20

94. The duration for Election Campaign decided by the Election Commission in India, is:

A. 3 weeks B. 2 weeks
C. 1 weeks D. None of the above

95. The maximum limit of expenditure allowed by the Election Commission in India to contestant for the parliament and legislative assembly elections should not exceed:

A. 25 lac and 10 lac B. 10 lac and 25 lac
C. 30 lac and 15 lac D. 15 lac and 30 lac

96. The reason behind the growth of nationalism in Europe was:

A. Inspirational influence of French revolution
B. Impact of Napolean's administrative reform
C. Origin of middle class
D. All of the above

97. How many Lok Sabha seats are there in Haryana?

A. 10 B. 15
C. 20 D. 25

98. National Archives is situated in:

A. Mumbai B. Kolkata
C. New Delhi D. Pune

99. In which of the following pair of cities the 'fire alters' have been found?

A. Kalibangan — Lothal
B. Mohan-Jo-Daro — Harappa
C. Dhaulavira — Lothal
D. Amari — Kotdiji

100. Match the following:

A. Pt. Motilal Nehru	(*i*) Member of Constituent Assembly
B. B.R. Ambedkar	(*ii*) President of Constituent Assembly
C. Rajendra Prasad	(*iii*) President of Drafting Committee
D. Sarojini Naidu	(*iv*) Formed the Constitution Resolution in 1928

101. The Chairman of Public Account Committee of Parliament is:

A. Pranab Mukherjee B. Sushma Swaraj
C. Lalkrishna Advani D. Murli Manohar Joshi

102. What do you mean by 'Patent'?

A. Exclusive rights on property
B. Exclusive rights on education
C. Exclusive rights on any ideas or inventions
D. Exclusive rights on right to information

103. Which among the foilowing was ***not*** the consequence Industrialization?

A. Urbanization B. Mass production
C. Colonization D. Blind nationalism

104. The battle of Buxar took place in:

A. 1674 B. 1746
C. 1774 D. 1764

105. The first ever compilation of Jain religious text took place at:

A. Amravati B. Vallabhai
C. Prayag D. Ujjain

106. Who was the architect of New Delhi?

A. Charles Correa B. Edward Lutyens
C. Le Corbusier D. None of the above

107. Which among the following countries is ***not*** a part of the 'Balkan region'?
A. Romania B. Bulgaria
C. Greece D. Italy

108. The word "Democracy" is taken from which language?
A. Spanish B. French
C. Greek D. Dutch

109. Who was the first Vice-President of India?
A. Dr. Sarvapalli Radhakrishnan
B. Varahagiri Venkata Giri
C. Dr. Zakir Hussain
D. B.D. Jatti

110. Indo-China was the Colony of:
A. Italy B. Germany
C. France D. England

111. Article 368 relates to:
A. Emergency
B. Election of President
C. Amendment to the Constitution
D. Fundamental Rights

112. The Parliament of India comprises of:
A. Loksabha, Rajyasabha and Council of Ministers
B. Loksabha, Rajyasabha and Prime Minister
C. Loksabha and Rajyasabha
D. Loksabha, Rajyasabha and President

113. The subject matter of Buddhist scripture 'Vinay Pitak' is:
A. Religious Sermon
B. The life sketch of Buddha
C. Rules for Monks
D. None of the above

114. Which one of the following is ***not*** a 'Fundamental Right'?
A. Right to strike
B. Right against exploitation
C. Right to equality
D. Right to freedom of religion

115. Who among the following is ***not*** related with the unification of Italy?
A. Mazzini B. Garibaldi
C. Cavour D. Mussolini

116. "Indian National Congress" was established in:
A. 1885 B. 1889
C. 1887 D. 1881

117. Sidhu and Kanhu are related to:
A. Munda uprising
B. Santhal uprising
C. Bheel uprising
D. Koya uprising

118. In which State the Mid Day Meal scheme was first introduced?
A. Tamil Nadu
B. Andhra Pradesh
C. Haryana
D. Punjab

119. Which of the following dynasties built grand gardens in medieval India?
A. Mughal B. Tuglaq
C. Khilaji D. Sayyad

120. Who was the inventor of Printing Press in Europe?
A. Guttenberg
B. Caxton
C. Remington
D. None of the above

121. .... Unemployment is when people appear to be employed but actually they are not.
A. Open B. Seasonal
C. Disguised D. Structural

122. Lines that are drawn on the Globe parallel to the equator are called:
A. Tropics B. Longitudes
C. Latitudes D. Meridians

123. The largest rail-route of the world is:
A. Trans Siberian Railway
B. Trans Arabian Railway
C. Trans European Railway
D. Trans Asian Railway

124. India constitutes ....% in the total Geographical Area of the world.
A. 2.4 B. 3.5
C. 3.2 D. 3.7

125. The largest Commercial Bank of the country is:
A. Reserve Bank of India
B. State Bank of India
C. ICICI Bank
D. IDBI

126. Which State in India has the largest coastline?
A. Orissa
B. Andhra Pradesh
C. Gujarat
D. Kerala

127. 'Sarva Siksha Abhiyan' is a step towards providing elementary education to all children in the age group of:
A. Six to Fourteen
B. Eight to Ten
C. Ten to Twelve
D. Four to Fifteen

128. Himalaya and Alps are:
A. Fold Mountain
B. Block Mountain.
C. Volcanic Mountain
D. None of the above

129. The earth rotates:
A. East to West
B. West to East
C. North to South
D. South to North

130. Which among the following is ***not*** an inner planets?
A. Mercury B. Venus
C. Earth D. Jupiter

131. Which among the following is a conventional source of energy?
A. Hydro energy B. Solar energy
C. Wind energy D. Tidal energy

132. 'Gir National Park' is located in:
A. Rajasthan B. Gujarat
C. Maharashtra D. Assam

133. In which part of India is 'Jhoom cultivation' practiced?
A. Western Ghats
B. Southern India
C. Middle India
D. North Eastern India

134. 'Chinook' is:
A. Cold wind blowing in winter
B. Warm wind blowing in winter
C. Cold wind blowing in summer
D. Warm wind blowing in summer

135. Which is the Central Bank of India?
A. Reserve Bank of India
B. State Bank of India
C. Central Co-operative Bank
D. Central Bank of India

136. The period of 12th Five Year Plan is:
A. 2009-2014 B. 2012-2017
C. 2011-2016 D. 2010-2015

137. The East-West breadth of India is:
A. 3214 Km B. 3516 Km
C. 5200 Km D. 2933 Km

138. 'Bugyal' means:
A. Grass land situated in mountains
B. Arid forest
C. Desert region
D. None of the above

139. What is the sex ratio in India according to the census 2011?
A. 933 B. 920
C. 861 D. 940

140. Which among the following mountain range separates Asia from Europe?
A. Andes B. Himalaya
C. Eural D. Pyrenees

141. The Vice-President who assumes the office of the President in case of vacancy due to death holds it for:
A. The unexpired term
B. A year
C. Six months at most
D. Till the date when newly elected President assumes office

142. The 'Decadal growth' in Indian population according to census 2011 is:
A. 21.02% B. 17.64%
C. 19.5% D. 19.6%

143. The Service Tax in India is:
A. Direct Tax
B. Indirect Tax
C. Increasing Tax
D. Decreasing Tax

144. Which option is ***not*** correct in the following?
A. Kalapakkam — Tamil Nadu
B. Tarapur — Rajasthan
C. Narora -- Uttar Pradesh
D. Kaiga — Karnataka

145. The country, having longest International border with India is:
A. Bangladesh B. China
C. Myanmar D. Pakistan

146. Kerala has low infant mortality rate because of:
A. better educational facilities
B. adequate provision of basic health
C. better employment opportunities
D. All of the above

147. Which is the largest river among the following?
A. Ganges B. Brahmaputra
C. Yamuna D. Chambal

148. The fifth largest planet is:
A. Mars B. Venus
C. Earth D. Saturn

149. Human Development Report published by UNDP Compares countries on the basis of:
A. Education level of the citizen
B. Their health status
C. Country's per capita income
D. All of the above

150. 'Equinox' means:
A. Equal day and night on the entire Earth
B. Shortest day in the Northern hemisphere
C. Shortest day in the Southern hemisphere
D. None of the above

ANSWERS

1	2	3	4	5	6	7	8	9	10
A	D	D	D	D	A	A	A	A	B
11	**12**	**13**	**14**	**15**	**16**	**17**	**18**	**19**	**20**
C	B	C	B	D	C	D	D	D	B
21	**22**	**23**	**24**	**25**	**26**	**27**	**28**	**29**	**30**
B	A	D	D	D	C	D	D	D	C
31	**32**	**33**	**34**	**35**	**36**	**37**	**38**	**39**	**40**
B	A	B	A	D	A	B	C	D	C
41	**42**	**43**	**44**	**45**	**46**	**47**	**48**	**49**	**50**
B	D	A	C	B	D	A	C	B	B
51	**52**	**53**	**54**	**55**	**56**	**57**	**58**	**59**	**60**
A	B	C	A	A	B	A	D	A	A
61	**62**	**63**	**64**	**65**	**66**	**67**	**68**	**69**	**70**
A	C	C	B	B	C	D	B	B	A
71	**72**	**73**	**74**	**75**	**76**	**77**	**78**	**79**	**80**
C	C	C	B	B	C	B	C	D	A
81	**82**	**83**	**84**	**85**	**86**	**87**	**88**	**89**	**90**
A	A	A	D	D	B	C	C	C	B
91	**92**	**93**	**94**	**95**	**96**	**97**	**98**	**99**	**100**
A	C	B	B	A	D	A	C	A	A
101	**102**	**103**	**104**	**105**	**106**	**107**	**108**	**109**	**110**
D	C	D	D	B	B	D	C	A	C
111	**112**	**113**	**114**	**115**	**116**	**117**	**118**	**119**	**120**
C	D	C	A	D	A	B	A	A	A
121	**122**	**123**	**124**	**125**	**126**	**127**	**128**	**129**	**130**
C	C	A	A	B	C	A	A	B	D
131	**132**	**133**	**134**	**135**	**136**	**137**	**138**	**139**	**140**
A	B	D	B	A	B	D	A	D	C
141	**142**	**143**	**144**	**145**	**146**	**147**	**148**	**149**	**150**
D	B	B	B	A	D	B	C	D	A

Child Development & Pedagogy

CHILD DEVELOPMENT

CONCEPT OF DEVELOPMENT

Development refers to interaction of a person with his environmental surroundings whose after product is to increase:

- The strength
- The degree of differentiation
- The organization of personality

Development refers to those effects upon the person's cognitive and emotional systems which strengthen one or more abilities of the person in the desired manner. Thus, development is the qualitative changes in the organism. Environment has very important role to play in the process of development.

Three Concepts of Development

1. *Development is maturation :* According to **Arnold Gessell**, the role of physical changes is very important in development. The development from infancy to adolescence is governed by physical changes. When physical growth of the particular stage gets matured only then development in that stage is possible. For example, a growing nervous system changes systematically and automatically and this results in predictable changes in bones and muscles. Thus major changes in the organism are based on maturation.

   According to Gessell, there is internal programming toward physical and cognitive growth and each year is characterized by certain behavioural changes. Development is always guided and controlled by these changes.

2. *Development is learning :* According to **Baer**, "development is the behavioural changes which require programming and programming requires time but not enough of it to call it age."

   Programming here means the sequence of learning which may happen naturally or it may be arranged in the life of an individual with the help of the environment. Thus, according to this definition, development is genetic and environmental both. Whatever we learn in the process of our life is related to development of us.

3. *Development is the synthesis of abilities :* According to **Jean Piaget**, there are four basic elements that take part in the process of development and development is the result of synthesis of all these elements. They are given below:

I. Maturation	An automatic and innate process
II. Social transmission	Learning through language, schooling or training given by parents
III. Experiences	Obtained from the outer environment informally
IV. Equilibration	Whatever is learnt or gained internally or externally is equilibrated here.

STAGES OF DEVELOPMENT

From infancy to adulthood human being undergoes the following stages of development.

1	Infancy	-	0-2 years
2	Early childhood	-	3-6 years
3	Later childhood	-	7-12 years
4	Adolescence	-	13-17 years
5	Adulthood	-	18-25 years

At each stage of human development, certain physical, intellectual, language, emotional and social changes occur which may be similar or entirely different from the preceding age. We will describe all these stages one by one.

Dimensions (Areas) of Development

Before coming to the stages of development it is better to know what the physical, intellectual, emotional and social development are:

1. **Physical development :** Important characteristics of physical growth and development are given below:
   - Physical growth is curvilinear not steady or regular. Rapid growth is followed by slow growth and then again rapid growth may be there.
   - Different parts (organs) of the body have its own unique way of development. Whatever changes we see in hands and legs cannot be seen in heart or lung.
   - Physical growth and development is affected by climatic conditions. For example, cold countries have more favourable conditions of growth and development than hot or humid countries.
   - Heredity fixes a limit of physical growth and development. The descendents of five feeted man is not supposed to have a height of more than 6 feet or 5½ feet.
   - Physical growth is very rapid in the infancy and in the later childhood. It is again fast in the start of adolescence.

Dimensions of Physical Growth : Important dimensions of physical growth and development are as follows:

(i) Height : A new born baby is 19-20 inches in length at the time of birth. As soon as the baby grows, his height also increases.

(ii) Weight : Human baby has a weight of 2.5 kg. –3.5 kg. at the time of birth. Girl babies are generally lighter than male babies here. When a baby becomes an adult he acquires a weight of 55 kg. at the height 5.5 feet. The weight of boys are generally higher than girls due to increased height. If height is more, weight will also be high.

(iii) Body proportion : Some organs of the body are more developed at the time of birth than others. But as soon as the baby grows and reaches to the period of adulthood, proportionate change and growth are seen. For example, head is already somewhat developed at the time of birth but it grows less proportionately than other parts of body.

(iv) Internal organs : Internal organs of the body also develop with age. As the child grows, the heart beat which is 100-120 per minute in infancy, becomes regular and normal, *i.e.*, 72 times per minute. Respiration also becomes slower, deeper and regular, food takes longer time to pass the digestive tract, the body temperature becomes stable and so on and all this happens due to growth and development of the internal organs of the body. This increase in efficiency enables the older children and adults to adapt to the environmental changes.

It is pitutory gland which is responsible for growth in the early years of life. Sex gland is also activated under the influence of this gland, and influence the pitutory gland as well. If sex hormones did not restrain the function of pitutory gland the human being would become a giant.

2. **Motor development :** Motor development includes movement of hands, lags, mouth and other related muscles of the body. Important features of motor development are as follows:
   - Motor development occurs in those structures which lie nearest to the main axis especially near the vaist, thighs, legs etc. The child learns to control the muscles of his arms earlier than those of fingers.
   - Bilateral to unilateral trend in the coordination and control of muscles is seen. The child first uses both of his hands then he gradually learns to use only one hand in specialized manner.
   - From general to specific trend in motor development is seen.
   - An orderly sequence of motor development is also seen. **Hurlock** found that motor development in the head region takes place first, followed by the motor development of arms, hands, legs, etc. This trend is not reversed any how.
   - If motor development of the child is delayed by any reason, his emotional and social development will also be delayed or disturbed.

3. **Intellectual development :** Intellectual development includes attending, perceiving, observing, thinking, recalling, analyzing, evaluating, problem solving and the development of language and concepts. These aspects of mind grow and change with age. Generally these activities of mind are inter related. Important features of intellectual development are as follows:

- Mental development is a continuous but steady process and all activities of mind are inter-related also.
- As long as the experiences of the child increase, his mental horizon expands. He learns not only to differentiate but to integrate different elements of the physical as well as meta-physical world.
- Factors affecting mental development are maturation and learning.
- Mental activities are guided and controlled by nervous system. Brain which is an important part of nervous system plays the key role in the mental development of the child.
- Sensation and perception are the primary aspects of mental activities. In fact, mental activities start from these two aspects. Sensation is the first step to knowledge which is accompanied by perception.
- Perceptual experience leads to concept formation. Concept formation takes place on the basis of general and common qualities of an object, e.g., concept of "book" is developed after seeing so many things like books and then we say that books are for reading. Thus, concept is developed on the basis of common qualities of an object. It involves discrimination and generalization both.
- Concept of an object or idea changes with the change in experiences for example, cold season of December may have different meaning for the people of Kolkata and Srinagar due to difference of experiences.
- Child's concepts change with the increase in his age. For example, a small child may develop a unique concept of ghost. But when he becomes an adult, his concept of ghost changes.

4. **Language development :** Language development is actually the verbalization of concepts which is learnt by imitation (hearing). If child is deaf, his language development will be zero. Important features of language development are given below.
   - Language is a tool to be used for all types of communication. Without proper language development, no communication from one person to the other is possible.
   - Language is used as a tool in acquiring knowledge. When knowledge increases, vocabulary also increases.
   - Language development starts with mere names of objects or events and when it reaches at its peak it develops ideas into universal concepts.
   - Growth and maturity of speech is an important aspect of language development. Four needs of the child motivates him to learn speech.

Desire to secure information more and more (Interrogative sentences).

(*a*) Desire to give commands or to do requests (Imperative sentences).

(*b*) Desire to come into social relationship with others.

(*c*) Desire to express feelings and thoughts (Exclamatory and Assertive sentences)

- There are spurts or rest in the speech development. It is not constant throughout life. Sometimes it is very rapid and sometimes very slow.
- The development of thinking moves from simple to complex and from the concrete to the abstract.
- An individual stops growing intellectually upto the age of 20 years in general.

5. **Emotional development :** Emotion is a strong feeling that is so strong that it can be observed overtly. There are **four qualities of emotional experiences:**
   - Every emotional experience involves feeling
   - Every emotional experience is accompanied by marked physiological changes
   - An emotional experience includes an impulse towards some kind of action, ie, overt response is seen
   - Emotion involves awareness or perception of what it is or what it might be that causes these impulses and feelings

Important features of emotional development are as follows :

(*a*) Emotions start immediately after birth. For example, an infant shows fear, anger, love etc, though his emotions are not clear at this age, according to Sherman.

(*b*) Children's emotions are very intense as compared to adults. As they grow they begin to exercise restraint over their emotions. They learn to modify and hide their emotions also.

(*c*) Child's emotions last only for a few minutes and then it ends all of a sudden. The transitory nature of the child's emotions lies in a rapid shift from one emotion to another. When he shows anger, he at the next moment smiles.

(d) In the beginning, the emotional expression is diffused and generalized. It becomes stable, differentiated, selective, moderate and graded as the child grows older.

(e) Emotional development is also determined by the socio-economic background of the child. If a child belongs to a cultured family, he will show more emotional maturity.

(f) Emotional development is affected by the physical development of the child also. For example, if a child is physically weak due to malnutrition or diseases, his emotions will be less stable and less subtle.

6. **Social development :** Human baby is the only organism in the world that takes maximum and longer time to be socially and economically self dependent. He needs help from others more than any other creature. This dependence of the child on others helps him to learn how to interact with others in diverse situations. The more a person is healthy in his social interactions, the more he is said to be socially developed. Important features of social development are as follows:

- Social development starts with the process of socialization, a process which enables a child to acquire his social status according to his age. It is the process of socialization that helps the child to learn social traditions, customs and culture.
- The child increases his social circles gradually. These circles increase further when the child grows with age. It makes very difficult for the child to adjust with different types of people in the society. Thus, social development is actually an adjustment training.
- Social development means to share joy and sorrows with others, to work as a member of a group, to cooperate with others and to develop social perception for the purpose of developing belongingness with the rest of the society.
- The end points of social development is social maturity, ie, to adapt successfully to the social environment without frustration. A socially matured person is one who is fair in his dealing, courteous in his behaviour and honest in his character. His sense of responsibility, his self confidence, and his leadership quality make him distinct from others. He confirms what is acceptable to others and denies what is antagonistic to him.

Lifespan and Development

(A) **Infancy and development :** Various dimensions of development during the period of infancy are given below.

1. **Physical development :** This period is marked by following characteristics of physical development.

(i) Physical development is very rapid during this period. For example size increases ten inches upto second year. Weight also becomes almost double at the age 4½ months, i.e., from 3 kg at birth to almost 6 kg. At the age of 4½ month.

(ii) Though sex organs are totally undeveloped and inactive during this period, yet a tendency to sexual development is seen in the second year of life. Child actually passes through three stages of sexual development. First stage, the stage of self love belongs to infancy. Here the child derives pleasure from his body, by sucking his thumbs of hand or legs or by touching his sex organs. The other two stages- homosexual or hetero sexual belong to early childhood.

(iii) At the time of birth, boys are heavier than girls. 7% weight loss is seen in the first seven days then the baby start to gain weight.

(iv) Study shows that boys are on the average heavier than girls at all age levels except from 11-14 years of age in which girls are found heavier than boys.

(v) Head is more developed than other parts of the body at birth. It grows proportionately at lesser speed than other parts of the body. At 6 years, the child gains 90% of the adult size of head.

(vi) Facial skeleton is found larger in proportion to cranium from birth to seven years of age.

(vii) Nose is proportionately small and flat on the face in the first four years. It gains full size at the age of 13 or 14.

(viii) Trunk is found heavy during the period of infancy. It along with legs lengthens gradually.

(ix) At birth, the weight of the brain is one fourth of an adult brain. It is one half by the age of 9 months and three fourth by the age of two years.

(x) In the first year of the baby the heart beat is very irregular and its speed is very high. As the child grows, the heart beat becomes regular and slower. Other physical changes are given below.

- Food takes longer time to pass through the digestive tract and to reach the intestines.
- Urine bladder can retain urine for a longer period of time.
- Body temperature becomes more stable.
- Composition of blood does not change.

(xi) The weight becomes almost three times the birth weight at the end of first year. By the age of 2, it becomes 3½ times the birth weight.

2. Nervous system :

(i) Nerve cells attain maturity during this period

(ii) Brain also grows rapidly and its size and weight increases

(iii) Improvement in the functioning and structure of sensory organs is seen. Thus, by the end of this period the child is able to perform all the functions of seeing, hearing, smelling, tasting and touching properly.

3. Motor development :

(i) Co-ordination and control of bodily movements are seen.

(ii) The child starts grasping objects in the fourth month of his life.

(iii) He sits in the sixth month. He crawls in the seventh or eighth month. He stands with the help of support in the ninth month and in the 12th month he begins to walk slowly without support.

(iv) Running begins in the second year of his life

(v) Greater muscular involvement is seen during infancy

4. Language development :

(i) It starts with vocalization in the form of cries or explosive sounds. This vocalization may be described as pre speech form.

(ii) The child only cries at the time of birth to express his emotions or desires. This crying is used even in the second year of life to express desires and needs.

(iii) He begins to utter few words by the end of the first year like mama, dada etc. Some unintelligible words spoken by the child may be seen in the seventh or eighth month.

(iv) Language development properly begins in the beginning of the second year. The rate of language development becomes rapid at the age of 1.5 years and the child crames any new learnt word just in order to retain it in his mind.

(v) By the end of two years he begins to speak proper but short sentences, though grammatical mistakes may be there.

5. Intellectual development :

(i) No clear cut sign of intellectual development is seen during infancy. His capacity to grasp new words is totally based on rote memory, though his cramming is without reason or intellect.

(ii) He lacks abstract understanding. His understanding is exclusively restricted to concrete materials but he thinks that heavier is one which is bigger in size. Thus, a plastic ball of bigger size is heavier than a metal ball of smaller size for the child.

(iii) Sign of creativity is seen at the end of the 2nd year. The infant often engages himself in collecting many articles.

(iv) This is a period of make belief. When he attains the age of 2, he believes in what he is told by his elders.

(v) A baby perceives an unfamiliar object as a form or as a figure. He has an innate tendency to organize his sense field and to perceive the object as a whole but this perception lacks definiteness.

6. Social development :

(i) He learns social skills in the company of his mother and fathers. When he is responded by them he learns how to respond to others. Thus, he learns all his social experiences from his family members in the first year but in the second year his horizon expands to his neighbourhood.

(ii) By the end of two years he begins to take the notice of other infants and plays with them.

(iii) He totally depends upon his family members for the fulfillment of his social, psychological and physical needs.

(iv) He expects that every body around him should love him and care him. When this expectation is not fulfilled he becomes irritated and cries.

(v) The baby becomes aware of other persons around him at the age of one month. In the second month, he smiles in response to the attentions of adults and he is able to distinguish his mother and other women. In the third month he waves his hands and legs when he is talked to. In the fourth month, he makes anticipatory adjustment to being lifted by someone. In the fifth month, he attends to the human face and looks in the direction of the person who leaves him. He smiles in response to the person who speaks and plays with him. In the sixth month, he reacts differently to

smiling and scolding and shows negative responses to strangers. In the ninth month, he tries to imitate the speech of others. He copies simple acts and gestures of others after observation in the tenth month. In the 12th month, he can refrain from doing things when he is forbidden to do so.

In the second year of life he exhibits fear and dislike for strangers by crying or withdrawing. When the baby attains the age of 18 months, he shows negativism in the form of stubborn resistance to the demands of adults.

(vi) In the first two years, the child's play is self centred. He does not like to be interfered by other children or adults. He plays in his own way. He is generally non-cooperative and has to be handled with patience and tacts. In short, the baby is socially underdeveloped.

(vii) Hurlock has presented the social development taking place during first two years of infancy as under :

1. First month	Understand human and other voices
2. Second month	Recognizes human voices and greets with smile
3. Third month	Recognizes mother and distresses on her being away
4. Fourth month	Recognizes human faces
5. Fifth month	Understands the tone of voices i.e. love and hate
6. Sixth or Seventh month	Welcomes the known with smile
7. 8th or 9th month	Plays with his own shadow
8. 24th month	Participates in elder's work

7. Emotional development:

(i) He is completely egocentric and selfish. When he reaches the age of 2, he even does not want to share his toys.

(ii) He is irritated and cries when he is chided by his family members.

(iii) His emotions are intense, frequent and totally unstable though emotional reactions become distinct in the beginning of the second year. These emotions are spontaneous and he can not control them.

(iv) He cannot hide his feelings thus, his entire emotions are in the overt form.

(v) Emotions of anger, fear, disgust, elation, love and affections are seen. For example, when he is loved by his mother, he shows his affection by his activities. Similarly, when he is not attended by his family members, he feels disgusted. He also feels pleasure in the company of his mother or his father.

(vi) A number of psychologists are of the view that infants are able to undergo emotional experiences. Emotions of fear, anger, joy, hate etc. are seen in them even in the first year.

(vii) During the period of infancy only those conditions arouse emotional responses which affect the child's immediate needs and well being, but when the child grows, his spectrum increases and he becomes responsive to a number of stimuli.

(viii) It has been noticed that babies and children show their pronounced emotional disturbance just before eating, sleeping, or waking up. For example, when a baby wakes up after sleep, he cries whether he is hungry or not.

(ix) Intellectually dull children are less emotionally disturbed than the normal children.

(x) Infants show smiling response to any human face whether familiar or stranger between eight and twenty weeks of age. Negative responses to strangers starts after 20 weeks of age and continues upto 40 weeks.

(B) Early childhood and development : Various dimensions of development during the period of early childhood (3-6 years) are as follows:

1. Physical and motor development :

(i) He acquires many motor skills like catching, throwing, running, jumping, climbing, using simple tools, riding a tricycle etc.

(ii) Growth in outer parts of the body especially height, weight, formation of muscles etc. is not as fast as it was during infancy. The child, however begins to assume the body proportion of an adult.

(iii) The growth of legs is rapid and it acquires about half of an adult size. The growth of head is, however, very slow and that of trunk is medium.

(iv) The height of a three years old child is 38 inches on an average though Indian children may be slightly lower than this size. Similarly, the weight should also be 33 pounds at the age of three. By the age of five years, the average weight of children is 43 pounds and average height for boys is 43 inches.

Motor	2 years	3 years	4 and 5 years
Development	Walks without help, jumps, runs	Skips, hops	Free and active movement responds to music
Fine motor coordination	Copying	Can match shapes, sees similarities and differences	Can name colours
Perceptual	Identifies self, matches colours	Can fit nuts, boxes	Matches shapes and colours, distinguishes names
Vocalization	200 words, uses few words	900 words, follows commands	Can repeat 4 digits-2000 to 3000 words, can define familiar words
Adaptive behaviour	Bowel control	Builds blocks, can draw a man	4 digits, draws body with details

(v) Muscles develop at a very rapid speed due to excess involvement of the child in motor activities.

(vi) The rate of heart beat and pulse slow down and blood pressure goes up steadily.

(vii) By the age of 5-6 the child acquires 90% of the adult weight of brain. Nerve fibres in the brain areas also come to almost maturity by the end of the period of early childhood. It should be noted that the growth of brain and nerve fibres is very rapid from birth to four years.

(viii) Self feeding, self dressing, self bathing, combing the hair, brushing the teeth, playing with toys, using pencils for writing or sketching etc are also seen during this period.

2. Intellectual development :

(i) Perceptual development begins from mass movement to differentiation. Norms for perceptual development is given in the callout table.

(ii) The child perceives those things quickly and clearly which are concerned with his mental set and interest.

(iii) The child begins to explore his social environment and acquire new experiences at the age of three.

(iv) By the age of six, the child develops clear perception of size, shape, colour, time and distance. He does not consider all bigger objects as heavier too.

(v) The child begins to form concepts of physical and social reality. For example, he does not do any thing against the wishes of his family members. If he does so, he hides the same.

(vi) The child starts learning many materials by rote memorization. His capacity to retain learnt material increases.

(vii) Imagination begins to grow and creativity is seen. He manipulates or breaks his toys to understand its mechanism. But his thinking process is restricted to concrete objects only.

(viii) Span of attention increases from 7 minutes to 20 minutes.

(ix) His curiosity forces him to explore the environment. He asks so many questions from his elders for this purpose.

(x) The child is now able to use symbols in language and mathematics.

(xi) The child develops a lot of concepts during this period but many of his concepts cannot be verbalized by him due to limited vocabulary.

(xii) During this period, children's concepts of spatial relations, distance and depth are vague. This makes the children awkward in their behaviour. For example they calculate height and distance wrongly.

(xiii) By the age of five, they are able to distinguish between past, present and future, ie, between yesterday, tomorrow and day after tomorrow etc.

(xiv) The concepts of number and quantity also become clear to them. According to Piaget, children acquire concept of number even before they are able to count.

(xv) Children's social concepts are influenced by the nature of inter-personal relationship.

(xvi) This stage is also called the stage of fantasy. The child takes shelter into his imaginary world in order to escape the harsh realities of his world at home and neighbourhood. If he is given more chance to interact with people, his social concepts will be rich.

3. Language development

(i) The child has to master four major tasks in the process of learning to speak properly.

- Comprehension of the speech of others
- Building a vocabulary
- Using and combining words into sentences
- Pronouncing the words correctly

By the end of the period of early childhood, the child is able to master all these four tasks.

(ii) Language development of a child actually begins from birth cry. When he is responded by his mother after crying, he comes to understand the meaning and importance of crying.

(iii) A ten month old child is able to use one or two words only but by the end of the first year his vocabulary increases to four, as **Smith** has observed. By the end of 2nd year, he can use 272 words. In the third year, his vocabulary increase to 896. when he attains the age of four, he can use 1560 words and at the age of 6 he can use 2562 words as Smith has observed.

(iv) Language development of children is not uniform. It depends upon better socio-economic environment at home, better schooling and independent living of the child.

4. Social development:

(i) Feeling of autonomy develops in children. They try to explore and manipulate their environment independently.

(ii) The child learns how to behave, talk and interact with the family members and neighbourhood.

(iii) The child may be frustrated if social atmosphere of the neighbourhood is not similar to that of the atmosphere at home.

(iv) The child's play no longer remains a solitary play after the age of three. The child selects his playmates and develops casual friendship with them. He learns cooperation, competition, sympathy, jealousy, teasing, bullying, quarrelling, etc. in the company of his playmates.

(v) Imitation, timidity, shyness, desire for possession etc. are other forms of social behaviour that develop during this period.

(vi) The child who is resistive upto the age of three years becomes cooperative and friendly and seeks approval of adults upto the age of four years. That is why he does not object to exchange his toys with his best friends.

(vii) At the age of 5-6 he begins to pride about his parents and boast about other members of his family after six.

(viii) Most of the children want to dominate in their respective groups at the age of six. Thus group leader changes every time in the group. In this way, the child learns how to adjust in the society in varied situations.

(ix) Children of both sexes play together without any discrimination.

(x) They also take part in those games which involve physical energy and motor activity like hide and seek.

(xi) They take interest in fairy tales and animal stories in which they want that someone should win in the fighting. They are very much interested to know which animal is stronger and strongest out of so many at the age of 4-5.

(xii) Negativism increases during this period. It is believed that the more a child is frustrated by the interference of adults, the more negativistic his behaviour will be.

(xiii) Girls have been found more dominating than boys in social and group situations.

5. Emotional development : Contributions of emotions are very much recognized in the personal and social adjustment of the individuals. Important features of emotional development during this period are given below.

(i) Emotions of the child are exhibited only for a very short period. It means that child shifts from one emotion to another very rapidly. For example, if a three or four years old child who is weeping loudly is given a toffee, he will become pleased at once.

(ii) Emotions of children are intense irrespective of the intensity of the stimulus. A very simple stimulus can create a very intense emotional experience.

(iii) Children are helpless to hide their emotions and they express them by different activities like crying, throwing objects, nail biting, bullying, thumb sucking and speech difficulties. Emotions of hope, disappointment, fear, anxiety, shame, jealousy, hatred etc. are expressed during this period in different ways.

(iv) He is still guided by his innate tendencies and instincts.

(v) His moral behaviour is also guided by his emotions-pleasure and pain.

(vi) Emotions of submission and elation are alternately seen in the child.

(vii) At the age of five his emotions begin to organize into sentiment. The most primitive sentiment is his love for his own self and his love for his toys. Due to this reason, this stage is also called "Narcissism autoerotism" or self love. This word **narcissism** has been derived from Greek language which means falling in love with one self.

(viii) The child also develops a deep sentiment of affection for his parents. At the age of 6-7 it is very painful for the child to see his/her father or mother ailing. Here Freud is of the opinion that girl is very much attached to her father and boy feels more attachment to his mother. Former is called Elektra complex and later is called Oedipus complex.

(ix) The child begins to show "moodiness" expressed in sulking and bad emotions at the age of four. This emotion reaches to its peak during the period of adolescence.

(x) Most of the emotional responses are learned by children by imitating parents and other family members. Thus, emotions are innate but emotional responses are innate and learnt both.

Educational Implications of the Period of Early Childhood

Early childhood is basically a pre-school period. The formal education of the child begins when he attains the age of five so, sixth year of life of the child is very important from point of view of educating the child. Since success of education of this period will depend on the pre-school education, so, the whole period from 3-6 becomes very important. Following strategies must be adopted by the school to develop the child educationally.

(i) The teacher in the school should first see whether the child has proper physical and motor development. Regular medical and health check up programme should be organized in the school for this purpose.

(ii) Parents should also be consulted if teacher finds some problem in the physical or motor development of the child.

(iii) It is the teacher who will first notice the physical or motor problems of the child. Hence, he should know the norms of physical and social development of children. On the basis of his very report, the child will be sent to the doctor for further diagnosis and investigation.

(iv) Various types of games and play activities should be organized in the school according to the age of children and they should be motivated to participate in those activities.

(v) The child is very active physically during this period. He mostly takes part in those activities, which involve muscular movement. Seeing this, he should be given rich diet to eat. If child is not getting proper nutrition, he will not gain height or weight properly.

(vi) This is a period of taking shift from dependence to self help, so child should be given more and more freedom to do in whatever manner he likes and to manipulate his environment in his own way.

(vii) This is a period of rapid intellectual growth. Hence, he should be sent to pre-primary school for learning through plays.

(viii) He should also be taught religious and moral principles so that he may become an acceptable member of the society.

(ix) He should be given freedom to manipulate objects so that he may develop his creative potentials.

(x) The teacher should narrate the stories of animals before such children. It will develop their vocabulary and imaginative power.

(xi) The child can concentrate for a longer period. Hence, the teacher can teach him any thing systematically. Even mathematics can be taught to him because he can understand symbols.

(xii) Efforts should be made to increase the vocabulary of the child as much as possible so that he can verbalize all the concepts that he knows.

(xiii) In order to save the child from frustration, he should not be interfered by the adults or parents.

(xiv) The child can increase his vocabulary mostly by hearing, so, he should be talked more and more. Better environment created at home means better language development.

(xv) Group activities are most suitable for such children. They should be given chance to get involve in such activities. Through these activities they would learn competition, cooperation, sympathy and the like feeling.

(xvi) The child seeks approval of adults. Adults should not be miserly in giving such approvals. They should rather love him.

(xvii) Girls and boys can be educated in a co-setting. This arrangement will create no administrative problem.

(xviii) If the child disobeys the parents they should not mind it. It is a natural phenomenon and will come down in the later childhood.

(xix) Girls should be preferred to be given the role of group leaders.

(xx) A teacher can control intense emotions of the child by his loving behaviour.

(xxi) Since children of this age can not hide their emotions, it is very easier for the teacher to deal these children effectively.

(xxii) Early childhood is a period in which the child can be emotionally attached to any body who loves him. The emotional attachment with parents may be generalized and extended to teachers in the school. A teacher can exploit this tendency and get the students involved in so many types of tasks.

(C) Later childhood and development : This is the period between the age of 6-12 years. At the end of this period, puberty symptoms begin to grow and the period of adolescence starts. This period is marked by **pseudo maturity** and excellence in different fields. As far as sexual maturity is concerned, it remains completely dormant during this period, but this sex emerges with a great force at the end of this period. Because of the dormant nature of sex, this stage is also called **latency period**. Various dimensions of development during this period are given below.

1. Physical development :

(i) Steady and slow but uniform growth in the external as well as internal organs are seen.

(ii) Milk teeth are replaced by permanent set.

(iii) Auscification of bones takes place due to increase in height and weight.

(iv) Refinement in motor skills are seen.

(v) The child is physically restless during this period. He finds himself engaged in one activity or the other.

(vi) The brain acquires the size of an adult.

(vii) It is the period of best health of the individual during his whole life. During this period children never get tired. They burn their calories in physical activities and eat to the maximum level possible.

(viii) Girls are ahead of boys by two years in height and weight physiologically. Girls at the age of 11 are ahead of boys by at least one year.

(ix) Shedding of milk teeth and growth of permanent teeth change the shape of mouth, like flattening of forehead, sharpening nose and broadening of the chest.

(x) Important physical characteristics of this period are increased manual dexterity, high muscular strength, increased resistance to fatigue, increased endurance for play activities and so on.

2. Intellectual development :

(i) The child develops the powers of observation, reasoning and abstract thinking.

(ii) He can accumulate huge amount of knowledge in his mind. He can derive information and pleasure from books.

(iii) His perceptual ability, memory, and application of mental powers become keener.

(iv) The IQ of the child becomes stable and determines his IQ level in future. In short, it is a period of intellectual maturity.

(v) Boys love adventure and fairy tales and girls love mild form of romance and biographies.

(vi) The child begins to admire things and people around him and he begins to imitate the behaviour of those people who he likes.

(vii) The child begins to make clear distinction between himself and the outer world. He starts working on reality principles according to Freud.

(viii) The concept of natural laws becomes fully developed at the end of this period.

(ix) Capacity of logical thinking and power of reasoning increases.

(x) Interest in science fictions and stories reaches at its peak by the end of later childhood.

(xi) Courage and loyalty both increase simultaneously.

(xii) The child starts day dreaming and he defeats his rivals in his imaginative plays.

(xiii) The early imaginary fears are disappeared by the end of 12 years.

(xiv) When a child attains the age of ten, he shows high ability of generalization.

(xv) Children of this age are concerned with immediate cause and effect relationship and current happening. They live in the realm of present and don't care for future.

(xvi) The child begins to understand conceptual problem very well. He can analyse it and can give suggestions for its solutions.

(xvii) The physical growth is slow and steady during this period but intellectual growth and the functioning of mind are very rapid during this period.

(xviii) The child develops clear concepts of length, breath, time and distance.

3. Sexual development :

(i) From this angle this stage of the child is called latency period. Generally sexual energy at this age remains dormant but it becomes very active immediately after the age of 12 years.

(ii) Indifferent and antagonistic attitude towards the opposite sex are seen by the age of 10-11. As a result of this attitude, boys do not like to mix up with girls and girls are antagonistic to mix up with boys. Due to this reason upper primary education (from VIth –VIIIth) in co educational setting is not suited in school.

4. Emotional development :

(i) Rapid shift from one type of emotion to another is not seen and the child learns how to control his emotions in a variety of social situations. For example, he avoids weeping in the company of his friends.

(ii) Emotional responses of the child become less diffused and undifferentiated, ie, intensity of emotions is reduced.

(iii) Emotions are expressed even in the absence of concrete materials.

(iv) Fear of animals, ghosts, loneliness and high place that was found in the early childhood, no longer persists in the later childhood.

(v) Certain new fear appear during this stage like fear of failing in the attempt such as games examinations, etc, fear of supernatural objects, such as heaven or hell etc and fear of being ridiculed etc.

(vi) The child gets angry if he is thwarted, teased or prejudiced. If he is compared with other children wrongly, he is interfered in his activities or he is ridiculed by elders, all these things will make the child angry.

(vii) If child thinks that some other children are being favoured by elders, he again gets angry. He becomes jealous of those children who are favoured. Emotion of jealousy is found in girls more than in boys.

(viii) All emotions like joy, love, curiosity, grief and affection appear during this stage in a stable manner. The child can hide his emotions. He expresses only those emotions which are approved socially.

(ix) Emotions are structured into sentiments. Various types of sentiments like religious, moral, patriotic and aesthetic sentiments develop during this period.

(x) Complex of superiority develops during this period. Boys consider themselves superior to girls.

5. Social development :

(i) He loves to play in groups and shares his toys with other children. Team spirit and group loyalties are commonly seen in such children in a more matured form.

(ii) Social horizon of the child increases to neighbourhood and school and he looses the shackles of his family ties. He becomes independent of his parents and does many things against their wishes.

(iii) He wants to become hero or leader in the group in the same way as we see in the period of early childrenhood.

(iv) He cares himself more than others. His self centred behaviour sometimes gives rise to rivalries and aggression.

(v) He accepts social norms. He feels pride to be ruled by public opinions. He is so much attached with his group that he can defy even the orders of his parents if they do not match with the norms of the group to which the child belongs. This tendency in children continues upto the age of 17-18.

(vi) Social development of the child mostly takes place in the play ground. The child mostly takes interest in those games which require stiff competition like football, hockey, kabaddi and kho kho.

(vii) Girls mostly prefer indoor games but if they are exposed to outdoor games they enjoy more than boys. Badminton, tennis and skipping are their favorite games.

(viii) When something wrong happens, boys indulge into physical combat and girls into verbal fights or pulling each others hairs. The behaviour of the child is largely influenced by the group to which child belongs.

(ix) The age from 10-12 is referred to gang age when children take much interest in gang activities and adhere to gang loyalties. That is why we see that every child in the age group of 10-12 necessarily joins a group and follows its rules and regulations strictly.

(x) Sex differentiation becomes sharp,i.e., girls play with girls only. The child does not like to play with girls during this period.

He accepts only those girls in his group which are very energetic and courageous.

(xi) It is the period of peak unruliness in schools and homes especially when child is thwarted by his peers and relatives. Here, the child rejects many of the standards set by the adults or his family members and tries to live an independent life in his own circle.

(xii) Some delinquent acts like bullying, stealing, gang activities etc begin at the end of this period.

(xiii) Boys are more rebellion than girls and their groups or gangs are more organized than girls.

(xiv) Because of the excess involvement of boys and girls in their respective groups, this period is particularly known as gang age period.

6. Moral development:

(i) When the child attains the age of six, his capacity to understand relationship increases. He accepts lawful and unlawful social matters, though his concept of right and wrong may be different from his peers.

(ii) At the age of 8 he moves from specific response to generalized response and thus his concepts become more generalized. For example, he comes to realize that stealing of any thing is bad whether it be the matter of money or books.

(iii) During the period of later childhood morality is defined as performing good acts and maintaining the conventional social order. Children of this age are not deficient of this respect in any way.

(iv) At the age of 11-12, moral behaviour is oriented towards authority and maintaining the status quo which is considered to be a primary value. When the child changes his group loyalties, moral values may also change. It is because their conduct is mostly governed by the mores of his group.

(v) The development of right and wrong concepts begins at home in the period of early childhood, but it actually matures in the group. That is why we see that the child may float the authority of his parents but he may not go against the wishes of his gang. Such moral behaviour is dangerous only when the group is not following social and moral norms properly.

Educational Implications of the Period of Later Childhood

(i) Suitable freedom should be given to children to develop physically, emotionally and intellectually.

(ii) These children like games, sports and group activities very much. School should organize such activities and should make them an indispensable part of the curriculum.

(iii) A teacher should not try to compare boys with girls. It is because girls feel themselves superior to boys and vice versa. If a teacher does not follow this maxim, it will create hatred for girls in the minds of boys.

(iv) Most of the lessons should be taught to children of this age through group activities.

(v) A teacher must be democratic in dealing such children. If anything is imposed on them irrationally, they will not follow it.

(vi) It is also necessary for the teacher to express faith in such children. He should not suspect the integrity and honesty of these children without reason.

(vii) Many desirable behaviours come to light during this period. Such behaviours should be reinforced regularly.

(viii) Children should be allowed to go to neighbourhood to learn community experiences. Remember that only school experiences are not enough.

(ix) The parents should not take the gang activities of their sons and daughters with anger. The only thing that is needed is that the gang should be good in behaviour.

(x) Certain hobbies are developed during this period. They should be encouraged by teachers and parents.

(xi) Interest and liking of boys and girls differ. Hence, they should be assigned different types of works according to their liking.

(xii) Children should be motivated to take rich diet in order to develop their muscles and bones.

(xiii) Child is never at rest during this period. So, a teacher should always get them involve in certain activities—physical or mental. If child is free, he may be destructive and problematic for the family.

(xiv) If a teacher knows the norm of physical growth of these boys and girls, he can guide them accordingly in the class. If the child is not growing on a satisfactory line, the

teacher can report to the parents of the child.

(xv) If a teacher is successful in developing reading habits as a part of their routine activity in students, they can accumulate huge amount of information and knowledge.

(xvi) The teacher should take the child to the laboratory for observation and experimentation. Lab work must start at the age of 12.

(xvii) Children of this age should be taught stories full of adventure and romance.

(xviii) The tendency of hero worshiping in such children should be exploited by the teacher.

(xix) Power of reasoning of the child should be utilized in understanding religion and mytnology.

(xx) Parents should not forbid the child from doing a particular thing in a straight forward manner. They should give reason to the child why it should not be done.

(xxi) The child should be given chance to generalize laws and principles as mush as possible.

(xxii) Children of this age do not care much for their tomorrow. Hence, whatever good is done by them should be reinforced immediately.

(xxiii) At the age of ten, girls do not like to mix up with boys and vice versa. So, a teacher should guide them separately and co-education at the junior level is not recommended at all.

(xxiv) Children can hide any of their emotions at this age. So, a teacher should not study them in hurry and draw conclusion about the child.

(xxv) The behaviour of the teacher should be completely unbiased. He should not discriminate any child on any ground. Biased attitude and discrimination make the child angry.

(xxvi) The child should be given opportunity to lead at least one group in any curricular or co-curricular activities.

(xxvii) Religious and moral educations should properly begin at this stage.

(xxviii) Gang activities of children should not be discouraged by the teacher. Such activities are essential for self expression and exposure.

THEORIES OF CHILD DEVELOPMENT

Theories of child development can be classified into three broad categories. The first is psycho analytic theory propounded by Sigmund Freud and his associates. This theory gives much importance to unconscious motivation developed especially in the early period's of life and it determines the personality of the individual in the later parts of life also. The second is behaviouristic theory of child development which lays stress on the connection between stimulus and response. The major advantage of this category of theories is that it can be experimented and verified in clinical setting and thus these theories are more scientific in nature. The last category is cognitive theory of child development. It is a molar approach of explanation of human development and it takes the total situation facing the mind into account. It lays stress on perception and its organization responsible for learning and development.

Some of these theories are being described below:

1. **Psychoanalytic Theory (Freud) :** According to this theory, every child passes through five stages of psycho-sexual development. These stages are given below.

(a) *Oral stage:* At this stage focus of pleasure is mouth. When child sucks milk from the breast of her mother, he not only quenches his hunger but also gets pleasure by the excitement of mouth.

(b) *Anal stage :* When child attains the age of two the focus of pleasure shifts from mouth to anus. The child obtains pleasure from the activities related to anus during this period. That is why defecating is enjoying for the child.

(c) *Phallic stage :* This period starts at the age of three and lasts at the age of six. Here the focus of pleasure shifts from anus to sexual organs like pennis or vagina. That is why habit of masturbation is common in children. Two special complexes also develop during this period (1) Oedipus complex-here the male child wants his mother more but finds his father as a powerful rival. He wants to destroy this rival but he is unable to do so. (2) Elektra complex-Here female child comes closer to her father and hates her mother.

(d) *Latency stage :* During this period all earlier forms of sexual activities are stopped. The child takes interest in learning skills and in the development of social and religious values. This stage helps the child to develop his super ego on the basis of his ego.

(e) *Genital stage :* The focus of pleasure shifts to the member of the opposite sex by using genital organs here. This stage starts after 13 years.

2. Ericksons' Theory of Psychosocial Stages : Erickson has proposed another theory of stages of child development. He divides stages of development into eight phases marked by specific developmental characteristics. The stages are as follows :

S.No.	STAGE	PSYCHOSOCIAL CRISES
1	Birth to first year	Trust Vs mistrust
2	1 to 2 years	Autonomy Vs shame, doubt
3	3 to 5 years	Initiative Vs Guilt
4	6 to 12 years	Industry Vs inferiority
5	Adolescence	Identity Vs identity diffusion
6	Early adult period	Intimacy Vs Isolation
7	Young and middle adult	Generativity Vs self-absorption
8	Later adult period	Integrity Vs despair

A brief explanation of these stages are given below:

(i) The infant develops a sense of trust in himself as well as in the environment. This trust is developed when he finds others at the beck and call of his physiological needs. Contrary to this, if his needs are not fulfilled by the people around him, he aches and cries. As a result, he loses his faith in the people around him.

(ii) When the child attains the age of 1.5 years, he develops the sense of autonomy in him. He does not want help from others. If parents give them reasonable freedom, it will develop confidence in them. Children who are not given such freedom to explore the environment, develop suspicion and doubt about their abilities. When they perform a task they become shy and hesitant. They are afraid of their mistakes which can bring about shame for them.

(iii) At the age of three, rapid growth of children in all dimensions is seen. At this age, the child starts to take initiatives on various tasks. The social horizon of the child begins to spread from home to neighbourhood and then to school. At this age, children also begin to develop the sense of right or wrong. Feeling of guilt is developed when they do not follow moral principles and codes given by their parents and teachers.

(iv) Fourth stage of development in the life of a child starts at age of six and comes to an end just before adolescence. During this period child utilizes his energies for self improvement and for the conquest of the outer world. He shows his industry and hard labour in all directions with special emphasis to motor field. The child wants to understand different mechanisms of the world through his toys and other usable articles. If the above opportunities are not given to him and the child is still treated as a child of low mind, it develops inferiority complex in him.

(v) When the child attains the age of thirteen he begins to fight for his identity in his group. He wants to become a leader in various activities and through this he wants to gain popularity among girls. Contrary to this if he is completely disregarded in the group to which he belongs, his identity is diffused.

(vi) Adulthood period starts at the age of 17. In the early years of adulthood, the individual wants to increase his social circle as large as possible. If he is amiable by nature, he is liked by others and if he is selfish, self centred or intolerant or he is hated by others especially by the girls, he starts to live in isolation. Many tragic songs and dramas are written during this period.

(vii) In the middle years of adulthood, generativity is seen. The individual exposes himself through any outstanding efforts in any field. He wants to live for others. That is why he is very much interested to see a better and disciplined world around him. The condition of self absorption is seen when an individual does not receive any encouragement for his tasks from anywhere.

(viii) Last stage is known for the integrity of the person to his profession, group, organization and institution to which he belongs. When justice is not maintained or an individual is not paid and recognized according to his efforts, his integrity is turned into despair.

3. Robert Sears' Development Theory: This theory represents the behavioural approach to the study of child development. According to Robert Sears learning experiences of the child are the result of stimulus-response associations that may result either classical or operant conditioning procedures . Thus according to this theory, development is a process of observable social interaction. The more there is social interaction, the more there is learning which is enhanced by reinforcement also.

There are three broad phases of human development according to this theory which are given below-

(a) *Phase (I) Rudimentary behaviour :* Initial behavioural training starts during this period. The period of this stage is birth to sixteen months of age. During this period the infant is activated by his innate needs of hunger, thirst, motor movement, defecation etc. These needs create tension in him and in order to reduce this tension, the infant is motivated for action. When action of the infant is reinforced by positive response, his needs are satisfied. The infant is very much selfish in his behaviour in the beginning and does not care for any social world. But when social world (parents and relatives) fulfills his needs and infant is reinforced for his action of say crying learning takes place which makes the learner more learned and goal directed.

Since, the infant here depends on someone else for the gratification of needs, the development becomes a process of social interaction. It is a type of operant behaviour here. The social environment in which the child is born greatly influences the development of the child. If child is not reinforced by anybody, *i.e*, his needs are not fulfilled, no development will be there. Socio-economic condition of the family, birth order of the child, his sex, the education or profession of his parents etc., affect the development of the child.

In other words, we can say that the first phase of the child's development interlinks the biological endowments (innate abilities) of the child with his social environment. The more the social environment is conducive to the fulfillment of biological needs of the child, the more learning and development will be there.

(b) *Phase II (Secondary behaviour) :* When child is reinforced by his parents and other members of the family, and the child's biological needs are gratified, he comes to develop secondary behaviour system, *i.e.*, he has to respond to others. If his response is fine he will be motivated. If response of the child is not upto the mark, it will be corrected by others and thus the process of development of correct secondary behaviour goes on.

The secondary behaviour of children starts by imitation. If model to be imitated is good, behaviour of the child will also be fine. The secondary behaviour of children should also be reinforced by parents and others and use of punishment as a technique should be avoided as much as possible because it can create behaviour problems in the child.

During this phase when the child begins to fulfil his needs himself by learning some new behaviour, his dependency on others decreases with age till the child is grown up fully and becomes an independent member of the society.

(c) *Phase III (Behaviour motivated) :* After the age of 11-12 the social boundary of the child expands a lot. The child comes in contact with other parents and their sons and with many people in his school and thus his process of socialization is accelerated. His dependency on others is reduced further but some new dependency in the school increases also. If child is given approval by his parents and other persons of the society that his behaviour is fine, he motivated to repeat that behaviour again and thus the process of development expands.

As the number of environmental **reinforcers** increases, the child comes to identify those persons well who satisfy his needs and he accepts those people as his model.

4. **Bandura's Theory of Development :** He gives equal importance to reward and punishment in the development of behaviour. Thus Bandura is mainly concerned with the social development of the individual. He believed that responses which are reinforced are more likely to recur than those responses of children which are not reinforced. Behaviour is learned either through conditioning or observational learning. In early childhood many behaviours of children are not approved by parents. Children are rather punished for the execution of such behaviour. Due to this fear, children are conditioned not to repeat that behaviour even in the later periods of life. Thus reward and punishment both are necessary for the moral and social development of the child.

   Observation (imitation) is the second mechanism responsible for learning (or acquisition of behaviour. The child creates some models in his mind or he is impressed by the behaviour of some people and accepts them as his model. These models are imitated by the child. Imitation follows certain principles such as competency, social status, power and similarity of the model with the imitator.

5. **Jean Piaget's Theory of Development :** He has explained his theory in the context of cognitive (mental) development of the child. Before coming to various stages of

development according to this theory it is better to know various related concepts to understand the theory in detail. These concept are given below:

1. **The schema :** The concept of schema is applied to the sensory motor behaviour of the infant. The infant does various activities such as sucking milk from the mother's breast, looking at the objects of the environment and pointing at it and in the process he tries to comprehend and conceptualize the objects, animals or space. This process of conceptualization depends on the sequence of behaviour employed by the infant to adapt to his environment. This is called schema which is not the same in all the individuals. Basic structure, is however the same. Although a particular scheme derives its name from the sequence of behaviour which the schema denotes yet some internal organizational disposition is there to enable the sequence to adapt itself to a number of conditions. As the development of the individual takes place, each schema is enlarged, modified and co-ordinated with other schemas. In this way, more complex schemas are formed.

   The sensory motor scheme develops out of reflex behaviour of the infant. When this behaviour is repeated by the infant many times and is responded by others, it is internalized and is gradually converted into cognitive schema. For example, in northern India when a child says mum and is given water by the parents the child conceptualizes mum as water. Many such defects are corrected in the later stage of life.

   Piaget believes that schemed a (cognitive structure) exists in primiive form even at conception and develops progressively with age.

2. **Assimilation and accommodation :** The schemas which are acquired in infancy period are practiced and modified in the later stages of life. This process of practice and change is called assimilation and accommodation by the cognitive field theorists. These assimilation and accumulation processes go hand in hand. For example, during infancy when infant acquires grasping schema he pick up objects and grasps them. This grasping of objects is called assimilation. But if that particular object is too big or too small to grasp it., the child changes his schema in order to manage the new situation. It is called accommodation.

   The cognitive structure (schema) changes from one stage to another by the process of equilibration. Through this process the child tries to adapt to his changing environment every time to maintain equilibrium between him and the environment.

PRINCIPLES OF DEVELOPMENT

1. *Development is a product of interaction :* Development is a process which is the result of constant interchange of energy within the organism and his environment. Thus hereditary forces interact with environmental forces and the process of development goes further. These two forces are so closely interacted that it is very difficult to isolate the contribution of either of them. The contribution of gene may be 10% as compared to 90% contribution of environment in the process of development.

2. *Development follows an orderly sequence :* The rate of growth and development is different in different individuals depending upon a number of factors but it does follow an orderly sequence in all the individuals. The psychologists have reported three important directional trends in the process of development:

   (a) *Cephaulo caudal :* Development starts from head and proceed toward heel. We see that development of head of a child is well advanced as compared to other parts of the body.

   (b) *Proximodigital :* Development starts from the central part of the body. Then it spread to other outer or more distant parts of the body. We see that an infant uses his shoulders and elbows first to reach an object and then he uses his fingers and wrists.

   (c) *Locomotion :* Locomotion develops in a sequence in all the individuals belonging to different cultures of the world. The rate of development for different infants may be different but every infant wili have to pass through these stages at all cost. For example, an infant first learns to crawl, then to sit, then to stand and finally to walk. No infant can walk directly in the first stage.

3. *Development is a continuous process :* Development is a continuous process which begins from the time of conception in the womb of the mother and continues till death. But this process is not always smooth or gradual. Ups and downs are most of the time seen in every stage of development. There are spurts in physical growth and psychological functioning. Sharp growth rate is seen at the time of spurts. For example, a sharp increase in height and weight in the early adolescent period, a fast rise in vocabulary during pre-school period, sudden improvement in problem solving abilities during adolescence and so on.

4. *Development goes from bilateral to unilateral trend :* Infants up to the age of 2.5 years use both of their hands with equal ease. Then they learn to use any of their hands preferably. Similarly, in the beginning of cycle learning we use both the hands to control it but when we become fully experts in cycle learning we can control the cycle single handedly. Thus, development is a process of specialization also.

5. *Inter-relationship of different aspects of development:* Different aspects of development are interdependent and inter related. For example child's social behaviour is interrelated with his physical development. If child is physically handicapped, his emotional development may also be slow with aggressive development in some emotions. Similarly, if social development of an individual is poor, his mental or physical development will also be slow.

6. *Development is individualized process :* All individuals develop in their own way depending on their genetic characteristics and the training received from the environment. Thus, each child has his own rate of physical, social, mental or emotional development. If we observe ten years old children in a society, we find that there are great differences in their height, weight, sociability, emotional expressions and learning readiness. Similarly, the rate of growth is very high during infancy or pre-adolescent period as compared to other periods of life. Thus, rate of growth also changes with the change in stages of life.

7. *Development is positive and negative both :* Up to a certain period of human's life all the faculties of the individual develop but after that retardation starts specially after the age of 70. Physical and emotional retardations are seen during this age with zero social development. Mental development still continues but it too ultimately starts diminishing with the increase in age. Death is nothing but the collapse of all these processes of development.

8. *Development is cumulative :* Development is a cumulative process. Certain changes impress the observer and it looks as these changes are sudden but actually they are not sudden. They are the cumulative effect of all the changes in the individual. The child climbs the steps of the development one by one and then he reaches the zenith. The child first of all learns the words, then he learns the phrases, then sentences and finally he comes to know how the stories or essays are written. Thus, each change in the child is the culmination of his prior growth and experiences.

9. *Development proceed from general to specific:* In all types of development we find the principle of mass differentiation and integration. At the time of birth, the world is like big blooming confusion for the child. Then by and by his behaviours are refined and become goal directed responses.

10. *Rate of development differs with sex :* There is slight difference in the process of development between boys and girls. Girls mature earlier than boys at least emotionally. Girls are taller and heavier than boys in pre adolescence period but by the end of this period boys surpass them.

Dimensions of Growth and Development

1. *Physical growth and development :* It refers to strengthening of body and muscles with better proficiency and coordination of motor organs, if a person is able to do heavy work with ease, if he is able to do the task in lesser time, if he is able to do the task with accuracy and if he is able to do the task with neatness and beauty, then it is said that physical growth and development of the person is satisfactory.

2. *Social growth and development :* It refers to improvement and refinement of behaviour of an individual in social situations. If a person is stable in his behaviour even in adverse situations, if the behaviour of the person is fully acceptable to the society and if he is able to influence the society by his behaviour, then it is said that the social growth and development of the person is satisfactory.

3. *Emotional growth and development :* It refers to the accuracy of responses that an individual will exhibit under the influence of his emotions. These exhibited responses will be real as well. For example, if anger is not exhibited at the abuse given by any other person, it means that emotional growth and development is not satisfactory. Expressing sorrow at losses but not so much sorrow as it is beyond control is emotional maturity. If a person gets angry at his insults but he fully controls his anger according to the situation, then it is said that his emotional growth and development is satisfactory. Same is the case with other emotions also.
4. *Intellectual growth and development :* It refers to the ability to draw out conclusion from jumbled informations and to apply the inferences to real life situations in order to make the life happy and meaningful. If a person normally does what he is expected to do, if he is able to mould the situation in his own favour, if he is able to manipulate the situation against the other and if he is not backward in any way in mental operations, then it is said that his mental growth and development is satisfactory.
5. *Language growth and development :* Language is means of expressing, thinking and action. Had we not been given this power, we would not have been able to interact with others and our social existence was not possible. Language may be verbal and non verbal both. Human being uses both types of languages at a time to inform others about his thinking and behaviour and to be informed about their thinking and behaviour. Thus, language development refers to the ability of a person to convince the people what he thinks right.

Factors Affecting Growth and Development

Many factors affect to these dimensions of growth and development. Some of them affect mental or social growth and development and some factors affect all of them. Important such factors are given below:

1. *Proper Diet :* There is direct relationship between nutrition and physical growth. If diet is not taken according to the physical activities, physical growth will be retarded which will in turn affect the social, mental and emotional growth and development also.
2. *Exercise :* Physical exercise on regular basis will also improve physical growth and development. If a person is slow in his physical activities, his health might be worsened. The more an organ of the body is used, the more it will become strong.
3. *Sanitation and hygiene :* A disease free body is likely to grow more freely. This is possible only when the person is following the norms of hygiene and live in a good sanitary condition. It will save the person from communicable diseases.
4. *Genetic factors :* Genes play very important role in the process of growth and development. Nobody can surpass his genetic characteristics. If a person belongs to a race which is genetically short in height he can not increase his height by taking nutritious food and doing exercises.
5. *Recognition in the society :* If the individuality of a person is recognized in the society and he is given full freedom to grow his potentialities, his physical as well as social growth and development will be maximum. Unnecessary restrictions imposed on a person hampers the process of growth and development.
6. *Sociability :* Social relations also affect growth and development of a person. If a person is discarded by the society and people are biased against him, he will get less chance of socialization. As a result, his social horizon will be limited which will reduce his social learning. This will deteriorate the social growth and development. In that case the person will get less chance of exposure in the society. It will reduce his physical development also. As far as language development is concerned, sociability is a must.
7. *Training :* Growth and development is science in itself. If proper training on scientific lines is given to the individual, he is likely to grow and develop by leaps and bounds. Physical and health education serves this purpose.
8. *Games and sports :* Games and sports are necessary for all types of growth and development. They release pent up feeling of the person on one hand and give more chance of physical activities on the other. They are an important source of recreation as well. All these things are very conducive to physical, social and emotional growth and development.
9. *Protection :* A person must feel secure in the society only then his growth and development will be natural and spontaneous. If an

individual is living in a surcharged atmosphere and his life and property is always in danger, he will develop negative thinking. Negative attitude towards life and society is an enemy of growth and development in general.

10. *Manipulation of the environment :* If a person is given full enhance to manipulate the environment, his thinking will expand. It will have a positive bearing on his mental and emotional development.

11. *Free exchange of ideas :* Language development takes place only when a person is exposed in the society. In such an environment free exchange of ideas takes place. It increase word power of a person.

12. *Self contentment :* Human desires have no ends. If first desire of the wants is satisfied, another desire replaces the first, thus man always becomes slave of desires. It creates a tension in the mind of man. On the other, if a man is fully contended with what he has, he becomes tension free. It can improve his process of growth and development to a great extent.

HEREDITY AND ITS INFLUENCE

All that which we inherit from our parents, grandparents, great grandparents and so on as a free gift is called heredity. It is of two types: (i) Biological heredity and (ii) *Social heredity*

· Biological heredity is that which a person inherits from his forefathers in the forms of chromosomes and genes.

Social heredity means all that one generation receives from the preceding generation in the form of social traditions customs and skills.

Person belonging to Rajput race is generally found muscular with strong and wide bones. It is an example of biological heredity. And the son of a carpenter is also likely to be an expert carpenter. It is an example of social heredity.

We will talk in this part only about biological heredity which is determined by genes. These genes are located in chromosomes. A person inherits chromosomes from his forefathers. With the transfer of these chromosomes genes are also transferred which are actually the carrier of heredity. Sex of an individual is also determined by genes. In order to know how traits are fixed by genes, we must first of all know the principles of heredity.

Principles of Heredity

There are two principles in this regard :

(a) *Principle of resemblance* : This principle states that like begets like. A cat can only give birth to a kitten, a human can only give birth to a baby and so on. According to this principle children generally resemble their parents or relatives.

(b) *Principle of Variability* : Many children do not resemble their parents. There are many instances where intelligent parents have dull children or ugly parents have beautiful children. This variation is universal in nature. That is why we see every individual unique in certain respect. This is called principle of variability of inheritance.

Mechanism of Heredity

When human sperm and egg unite, they are fertilized into zygote. Each zygote has 23 pairs of chromosomes. Every egg in the body contains the same number of chromosomes. The number of chromosomes in a given species are same but different species have different number of chromosomes.

For example, all humans contain 46 chromosomes. Half of them come from mother and half of them come from father. Within the chromosomes there are thousands of minute particles called genes. They are actually the carriers of hereditary traits from one generation to another.

Chromosomes are made up of long organic molecules whose main substance is deoxyribo nucleic acid (DNA). It is found in the chromosomes as two long strands periodically connected by chemical bonds.

Our heredity information is not found in the two long strands of DNA but in their order of appearance between the two strands of DNA. One pair of chromosomes is related to sex (gender) also. Females have two x chromosomes and males have an x and a y chromosome. If sperm of x chromosomes unite with the egg of y chromosomes, then the child will be a girl. If on the other hand, the sperm of y unite with the egg of x chromosomes, then the offspring will be a male child.

The story of hereditary influence will not be complete without knowing the influence of genes on our traits. It is because traits are determined exclusively by genes.

Genes are of two types **(i) dominant and (ii) recessive**. We inherit the same qualities of our parents because of dominant genes. If same characteristics are not inherited it means that recessive gene is active there. If marriages between blood relations take place, the recessive genes are developed which can cause many deformities in the body, i.e., offspring may become physically or mentally handicapped.

Law of Inheritance

Gregor Mendel (1866) discovered the law of inheritance in hybrid peas growing in the garden of an Austrain monastery. His law was found applicable to animals also. His law can be summarized as under.

"If a man who is homozygous for blue eyes marries a woman who is homozygous for brown eyes, the children of the couple will have brown eyes only" (Homozygous condition is that condition in which information concerning a given characteristic differ in the paired gene position)

If a homozygous man marries to a heterozygous woman the distribution of children from the couple will be such that one fourth of them will be homozygous for brown eyes, one half of them, will he heterozygous and one fourth of them will be homozygous for blue eyes.

By this law, Mendel concluded that all genetic informations come to the individual in units rather than in graduated series. In other words, we receive from our ancestors genes controlling the development of specific unitary characteristics not a composite of traits called tendencies.

The second conclusion that can be drawn from this law is that characteristics of men do not remain constant. They tend to vary continuously along a dimension of genes.

Some Studies on Influence of Heredity

How great the role of inheritance is in shaping the personality of an individual by the process of growth and development can be understood by the following studies:

1. **Galton :** He was the first psychologist who conducted studies on the nature and extent of genetic influences in man. He studied 997 eminent British people and found that there were 322 people out of 997 who were also distinguished. He also studied 997 average people and found that only one of them was eminent. He thus concluded that eminent men were found in families which have already one eminent member at least. He also found that decreased instances of imminence were seen when eminent people decreased their relationship with eminent persons. Thus, according to him eminence is inherited from generation to generation.

   He also studied some people of U.S.A. who were given better educational facilities and compared them with the eminent people of U.K. who were given average educational facilities. He found that people of USA were not better performed than that of UK.

2. **Goddard (1914) :** He studied a Kalikak family of USA. Martia Kalikak who was a soldier in the American revolution, developed illegal sexual relation with a feeble-minded lady and an illegitimate child was born. 480 descendents were traced from the family tree of this illegitimate boy. Out of them 143 were feeble-minded, 291 were borderline normal and only 46 were found normal in intelligence.

   After the revolution when Mr. Kalikak married a normal lady a legitimate child was born. 496 descendents were traced from the family tree of this boy. All of them except two were found normal or above normal in intelligence and they became teachers, lawyers, businessmen etc. This study proves that intelligence is inherited from one generation to the next.

   These two studies show that heredity plays an important role in determining the traits. But the conclusions derived from these two studies can not be fully relied upon because of the following reasons.

   (i) They do not distinguish between biological and social inheritance. Their studies combine these two factors. So, it is very difficult to isolate the contribution of gene in shaping the personality.

   (ii) Testing material used in these studies was not perfect and the survey is also unsystematic and unreliable.

   (iii) The researchers were already biased in favour of hereditary factors. So, their conclusions can not be relied upon.

3. **Kellogg and Kellogg :** In order to study the relative influence of heredity and environment they conducted a systematic research by taking their own son and a chimpanzee. Their respective ages were 10 months and 7.5 months. Both of them were brought up in the same environment with similar type of facilities given to them. Their behaviours were systematically studied at regular intervals. It was found that in the beginning the chimpanzee surpassed the son in motor skills of jumping, running, climbing, etc. Chimpanzee also learned some social skills such as eating with spoon and drinking from a glass, but he could learn 93 words only. But later on, the son caught him up in all areas of development except physical strength.

   This study shows that heredity sets a limit for maximum development which can not be improved even by providing the best environment.

ENVIRONMENT AND ITS INFLUENCE

Environment here means social and cultural environment especially. Physical environment also becomes the part of social environment when it is used in the learning process. When an individual lives in a society, in a family, he learns many things from the social and cultural environment. These learnings bring about certain changes in his behaviour. Some of these changes may be of permanent nature. These permanent changes become the part and parcel of his habits. When these habits are converted into values after maturity, they become the representative traits of the individual. Individual is now recognized with these traits.

Influence of Environment in Shaping the Personality

The role or contribution of environment is no less than that of the heredity. In fact human being is a by product of heredity and environment both. The importance of environment in the process of growth and development can be understood by the following example.

A missionary in (Midnapur) Bihar found two children who were taken by wolves in early children hood. These children were reared in the company of wolves in beast environment. They learned to walk on four feet, ate raw flesh and verbalized like wolves. These children were brought back from the forest and kept in a hospital. One of them died next day and the other could hardly learn elementary things. This study shows that if suitable environment is not provided to a person, his genetic qualities will not flourish at all.

On the basis of studies on heredity and environment with regard to growth and development following conclusions can be drawn:

1. Heredity and environment both play combined role in the development of personality of an individual.
2. Heredity does not determine any trait of the personality in isolation. It only provides a base and then environment develops the trait.
3. Subjective traits of the individual like physique, colour of skin, resistance level of the body etc are determined by the hereditary factors. Certain diseases are also inherited because of low resistability of the body of the individual.
4. Bad environment can surpass good inheritance but good environment is not a substitute for poor heredity. It means heredity sets a limit for the maximum development. Even good training and experiences will not enable the person to cross this limit. On the other hand, even good man by genes can be made corrupt in a bad environment.
5. Training and experiences can improve the traits of an individual to a great extent. Even intelligence level can be improved to some extent.

Environmental Factors Affecting Growth and Development

Environmental influences begin since the time of conception of the child into the womb of his mother. Mental, physical and emotional conditions of mother, also influence the development of foetus in the womb. When child opens his eyes in the physical world, he immediately comes in contact with the environment. Since he takes birth in a society, he is also influenced by a number of social and cultural factors. The impact of some of these factors on his growth and development is given below:

1. **Physical factors of the environment :** Physical and geographical conditions of the environment play an important role in shaping the personality of an individual. People living in deserts, hilly areas and plains have great difference in their body strength, height, structure, mode of living, habits etc. Climate of the region also affects the behaviour, body built and resistance to fight the environmental forces. For example, people living in Siberian region can tolerate lower degree of temperature than those who live in Indian sub continent. Personality traits are also determined by these environmental factors, for example, people living in African continent are more aggressive and get easily annoyed than those living in North America.
2. **Family of the individual :** Personality of an individual develops fully only when interaction between biological inheritance and environmental forces take place. Home is the first place of these interactions. Whatever early changes take place in the nature and pattern of personality formation in the initial life of an individual at home, they are generally upheld in the whole life. In the family, child comes in contact with his parents, grandparents, uncles, aunties and cousins. These people give full recognition to the child. They also respond him keeping his likes and dislikes. Several empirical evidences support that childhood experiences are decisive determinants of his personality in later life. For example, if a child is deprived of family love and other facilities, he may grow into

either an aggressive or totally submissive person in future. Margarets Ribble in 1944 started a series of investigations on the effects of some psychological deprivations in infancy. She studied 600 children in this regard and concluded that lack of adequate cuddling and other close physical contact with some friendly adults can impose serious handicaps on the growing infants.

Each and every characteristic of the family affects the personality of the child in future. We are taking here one more example of morale of the family. A low morale home does not present a good model before the child for imitation. Stort in 1939 on the basis of a questionnaire administered on 1800 adolescents concluded three things given below-

- Children coming from homes where good morale pattern dominated were better adjusted, more independent in thinking and action and more satisfactorily related to their parents than those who were average in this dimension.
- Adolescents who came from discarded and nagging families were poorly adjusted in the society.
- Economic factors also influence the development of personality. Poverty of parents and lack of money even to fulfil legitimate needs of their children led to certain kinds of frustrations in adolescents.

3. **School :** School is a miniature society in itself. Here individual stays for almost six hours daily in the early quarter period of his life. His personality is shaped by the school in the following ways.
   - School poses new problems before the child to be acquired and new models for imitation.
   - School provides new knowledge and expands the horizon of the child. These behavioural changes determine the pattern and direction of growth and development.
   - Social interaction with teachers, classmates and peers is possible in schools. These interaction also shape the personality of the individual.
4. **Teacher :** Teacher can play a very crucial role in shaping the personality of the individual. The way the teacher behaves and handles his students and the personality traits exhibited by him have an important effect on the future personality of students. He influences a child in the following ways.
   - The way the teacher carries out his role in the class will affect the emotional climate of the classroom. An authoritarian teacher will establish an autocratic climate and a democratic teacher will create a permissive climate in the classroom. Autocratic climate will tend to create aggression and bostility among students. If climate is democratic, it will develop constructive, thoughtful and cooperative behaviour among students. All good personality traits can be developed by democratic climate in the class. Because of this reason democratic dealing is preferred to autocratic dealing. The more a teacher is democratic in his attitude and behaviour, the more his students will be accommodative to others.
   - Studies have shown that children who repeatedly fail in the class are likely to be cruel, selfish, unfriendly, unhappy, impolite, boastful and quarrelsome. Thus, teacher tries to reduce the occurrence of failures in the class by his dedicated efforts.
   - Whatever model of character is presented by the teacher in the class, it is immediately copied down by the students. If teacher has ideal traits in him, students, are also likely to be idealistic.
5. **Language :** Language is the medium by which the society is structured and experiences of the race are transmitted from generation to generation. The child learns the languages of the society. He learns many experiences and knowledge by these languages. He also communicates the other members of the society by these languages. Thus, by these processes he becomes an integral part of the social environment.
6. **Social roles :** The word role has been derived from the theatre world. In theatres the actors play the role of different characters as the situation demands. Worlds is also a stage and human beings are just actors who play their respective roles. Man is a social animal. He comes in contact with different people in the society. As a result he has to play the role of a father, son, brother, friend, student etc. throughout his life at various stages of his development. Social roles are the process by which an individual interacts with other members of the society. Thus, social roles are the collection of behaviour and relevant attitudes towards others. These roles are learned by individuals through observation and imitation.

7. **Self concept :** Self concepts are the means by which we create our unique image and identity in the society. Self concept in the child is initiated by physical awareness. The other means of developing self concept are how we maintain our social status, how we dress ourselves and how we speak and respond to others. Self concept influences our personality development in two ways. The first is that if people hold us in high esteem, we feel exalted. And the second is that if others hold negative attitude towards us, it creates the feeling of worthlessness and it may lead to self defence or withdrawl from the social situation. If self concept is fully developed in an individual his rate of growth and development will be high.
8. **Identification :** Identification is the process by which we imitate the physical, social or mental characteristics of our model. When a boy identifies himself with his father by coping father's behaviour it means that he wants to be like him. If identifying models are solid physically, mentally or socially, the identification process will also be solid and healthy.
9. **Living standard :** Physical and mental health of a person is directly related to his living standard. If he is getting nutritious food and sufficient amount of time for sports and exercise, his rate of development will be high. People of developed countries are found very advanced because of this reason.
10. **Cultural heritage :** Every society is identified by its cultural heritage which is transmitted from one generation to the next. The transmission of cultural heritage may also be termed as social heredity. The personality of an individual is gradually shaped by the culture he is born in.

E.R. Tyler defined culture in the following words. "It is that complex whole which includes knowledge, beliefs, morals law, customs and many other capabilities (skills) and habits acquired by man as a member of society."

Thus, culture refers to total life activities of a society. Whatever a person learns from the society by the process of interaction is called culture. In other words, what the people think, feel and do constitute the culture of a society. Biological inheritance is more or less the same all over the world but whatever differences are seen in the process of growth and development of personality among individuals it is because of the differences of social inheritance (culture). We can easily identify people reared in different cultures by the personality patterns they possess. English, Africans, Arabs and Indians can be identified by their cultural background more than by their biological heredity.

No single culture dominates in big countries. Sub cultures within the culture is also seen which brings about social conflicts. This conflict distorts the personality of individuals as well. Culture or sub cultures are silent educators and they mould the personality of individuals very silently.

The influence of cultural forces is so powerful that if three identical twins of a Hindu family are reared in three different cultures such as houses of Muslims, Christians and jews, the impact of their respective cultures will produce three distinct type of personality. These twins will not have any thing of their original Hindu culture.

The influence of culture can also be understood by the following words:

"Culture regulates our lives at every turn. From the moment we are born until we die, whether we are conscious of it or not, constant pressure on us forces us to follow certain types of behaviour that other men have created for us".

Culture influences the personality development of an individual in the following ways:

- Ideas, values, beliefs, customs and traditions are internationalized through the process of learning. A child who takes birth in a particular culture is reared in that very culture. He learns ideas, beliefs, values, customs etc. of his society and thus he acquires distinctive personality characteristics in the process.
- Various cultures are propagated by various institutions. When individual takes part in these activities actively or in a passive manner, he gets attached to these cultural institutions. Thus, his culture is institutionalized. This is the **second stage of culture formation**. When culture of a region reaches this stage it becomes very difficult to wipe it out by other cultures.

PIAGET'S STAGES OF COGNITIVE DEVELOPMENT

According to him, there is an orderly sequence of stages in cognitive development. Thus progression from one stage to another is always fixed. The child can not adopt the strategies of a later stage at an early stage of development. It is because he must have to acquire and exercise the strategies and schemas of earlier stages. For example, in order to understand words, the child must know letters first or we can not teach Electronic Physics to a child of primary class.

Ausbel commenting upon the development stages of Piaget writes "Piaget's stages are identifiable, sequential phases in an orderly progression of development that are qualitatively discriminable from adjacent phases and generally characteristic of most members of a broadly defined age range".

The stages of cognitive development are related in the sense that they represent forms of adaptation, but these forms are qualitatively different, that is the adaptive functions are transformed as the child moves from one stage to the next. This theory of development is quite different from the theory of associationists who emphasize the gradual accumulation of responses.

Important stages of Piaget's theory of mental development are given below.

I. Period of sensorimotor adaptation (from 0-2 years): The infant starts this stage by his reflex activities and then he reaches to the stage of sensorimotor schemes by practice and accommodation. The intellectual development at this stage is marked by the following characteristics.

(a) *Object concept formation :* Objects exist in the mind of an adult whether they are present before the person or not. But in the psychological world of a child, only those objects exist which have a psychological presence for the child, ie, he can look and touch it. As soon as they are removed from the eyes of the child, they cease to exist for the child. When the child experiences the same object repeatedly, he develops the concept of permanence of objects. This concept is developed in the first year of life. When this type of structure is formed in the mind, practice of concepts is started by the child.

(b) *Coordinated space :* Spatial world at first is totally uncoordinated for the child. Each sensory modality has its own space. By the end of two years, the child develops the concepts which are marked by the coordination among different objects and between objects and body of the child

(c) *Objectified causalty :* The concept of cause and effect relationship is established when action of the child brings about an effect. Then this effect is taken as the cause of that event.

(d) *Objectification of time :* By the end of two years the child is also able to objectify time.

II. Period of symbolic and preconceptual thought (2-4 years): Ideas begin to develop in the mind of the child at the third year. By imitation and observation, he demonstrates that he is capable of extending his physical world to metaphysics. He begins to use symbols in the 4th year. Now he can represent the environment in the absence of perceptual cues only on the basis of ideas.

III. Period of intuitive thought (4-8 years): At this stage the child can use various concepts in different situations, *i.e.*, he is able to generalize his past and present experiences. His thoughts are not based on logical reasoning. It is rather governed by intution. The child can talk about this and that momentary static condition in a separate manner but he can not properly integrate various sets of conditions into an integrated whole due to lack of logical weakness, *i.e.*, logical coherence is not found here. For example, a child can write fine sentences representing various topics but he can not write a compact essay.

IV. The period of concrete operation (8-12 years): Here the child is able to direct his attention away from the static condition, ie, he can accommodate with all the successive changes taking place in the system. It means that he can reorganize his future on the basis of his past experience as well as trends at present. Reasoning power of the child is well developed during this period. Some examples of what a child can do are handling and manipulating the numbers in various ways by various operations, arrangement of objects and materials into various groups and sub groups, ordering of objects according to one or more attributes and so on. Piaget has described a term "grouping" for this stage of cognitive development.

This period also shows some logical inconsistency in the thinking of the child. Piaget has coined a term "syncretism" for this defect. Despite this, beginning of abstract operation is seen during this stage.

V. Period of formal (abstract) operation (12-18 years): During this period, the thought process of the child becomes systematic, consistent and reasonably well integrated. Reality guides the contemplation process of the child. The formal operation of thinking starts with the formulation of hypothesis, (deductive reasoning) and reaches at its peak when hypothesis is tested by experiments, ie, inductive reasoning. At this stage, the boy can manipulate any abstract idea in his own way and form new idea entirely different from the old one. His wisdom lies in the expertise administration of the unforeseen. Whenever an adolescent faces any problem with the help of formal operation of thought he identifies various relevant variables which may be helpful in the solution of that problem and then all these variables are manipulated by him.

Thus, development of formal operation capacity enables the adolescent to transfer understanding from one situation to another and to evaluate the results on the basis of its pros and cons. Physical (concrete) objects are never required for thinking (operation) during this period. The thought process is completely abstract here.

KOHLBERG'S THEORY OF DEVELOPMENT

According to him moral development of the child proceeds in sequential but distinctive stages. These stages are given below:

(a) **Stage-I :** In the early years of a child's life (from zero-four years) the physical consequences of an action determines its goodness or badness. If fire burns the child, he does not touch it. The child is ego-centric and standards of morality are external here.

(b) **Stage-II :** The child gives importance to his own point of view, (his self) and is able to take account of other's roles insofar as he can use them in his own way. This is a period of make belief. Right action is what which satisfies the needs of the child. The role of others is also important in the sense that a child does only what can bring approval of others. Thus, only that behaviour is moral which can satisfy not only self needs of the child but it must please others also.

(c) **Stage-III :** At this stage the child adopts the view pints of others on the basis of their consequences. He does not question the views of others. The child considers only that thing as right which are considered as right by others. Thus, the child is totally conformist to the standard of the society.

(d) **Stage-IV:** At this stage, the child is able to make any moral decision on his own without caring for the thinking of others. Though he considers laws and regulations set by the society as the essence of morality, yet he develops his own principles of morality on various occasions. Thus, he is a non-conformist to the norms of the society to a great extent.

(e) **Stage-V :** Standards and norms are more internalized here. The adolescents examine various view points prepared by different societies and recognize them. They think that the laws prepared by their own society are correct. Other societies may have good moral principles that must be adopted after careful appraisal.

(f) **Stage-VI :** This is the last stage of moral development according to Kohlberg. Here the universality of the view points of the individual is seen. He formulates his own universal moral principles which he thinks that all societies should adhere to it. True understanding of right and wrong is developed at this stage.

HAVIGHURST'S THEORY OF DEVELOPMENT

According to him at each stage of development, there are certain tasks, skills and understanding that must be completed before a person can proceed to a higher level of development.

Havighurst Says –

"At or about a certain period in the life of the individual, successful achievement leads to his happiness and to success with later tasks, while failure leads to unhappiness in the individual, disapproval by society and difficulty with later tasks".

LIST OF DEVELOPMENT TASKS GIVEN BY HAVIGHURST

S.No.	Birth to 6 years	6 to 12 years
1	Learning to walk	Learning physical skills, ordinary games.
2	Learning to take solid food	Building wholesome attitudes towards oneself as a growing organism
3	Learning to talk	Learning to get along with age mates
4	Learning to control the elimination of body wastes.	Learning an appropriate masculine or feminine role.
5	Learning sex differences	Developing fundamental skills in reading, writing and calculating.

6	Achieving physiological stability	Developing concepts necessary for everyday living
7	Forming simple concepts of social and physical reality	Developing the ability of manipulating the ideas and concepts.
8	Learning to relate oneself emotionally to parents, siblings and other people	Achieving personal independence
9	Learning to distinguish right and wrong and developing a conscience	Developing attitudes towards social groups and institutions

COMPARISON OF THREE CATEGORIES OF THEORIES

S. No.	Psycho analytic	Behaviouristic	Cognitive
1	Feeling is important here	Stimulus and behaviour of others are important here	Thinking is all responsible for development
2	In order to acquire moral principles, parental -values are internalized	Moral values are adopted from either models or they are acquired by conditioning	Moral principles are acquired automatically with age, ie, mental development
3	Super ego, a moral conduct is formed at the age of five	Learning of morality is a life long process	Super ego is formed during the period of adolescence
4	Moral values are not free from culture	Same	Moral values are universal
5	Parents and relatives are agents of socialization	Adults and peers who give reinforcement are the main agents of socialization	People of the matured age are the agents of socialization

VYGOTSKY'S SOCIOCULTURAL THEORY

Both Jean Piaget and Lev Vygotsky believed that children build knowledge through experiences. Piaget believed this happened through exploration with hands-on activities. Vygotsky, on the other hand, believed that children learn through social and cultural experiences. Interactions with peers and adults help children in this process. While interacting with others, children learn the customs, values, beliefs, and language of their culture. For this reason, families and teachers should provide plently of social interaction for young children.

Vygotsky believed language is an important tool for thought and plays a key role in cognitive development. He introduced the term ***private speech***, or self-talk. This refers to when children ''think out loud''. After learning language, children engage in this self-talk to help guide their activity and develop their thinking. Generally, self-talk continues until children reach school age.

One of Vygotsky's most important contributions was the *zone of **proximal development*** (ZPD). This concept presents learning as a scale. One end of the scale or ''zone'' includes the tasks that are within the child's current development level. The other end of the scale includes tasks too difficult for children to accomplish, even with help. In the middle are the tasks children cannot accomplish alone. These are achieved with help from another knowledgeable peer or adult. The term used for this assistance is ***scaffolding***. Just as a painter needs a structure on which to stand and point a building, scaffolding provides the structure for learning to occur. For example, a teacher could scaffold a child's learning while constructing a puzzle. The teacher might demonstrate how a piece fits or provide clues regarding colour, shape or size. The ''zone'' is constantly changing. In contrast to Piaget, Vygotsky believed that learning was not limited by stage or maturation. Children move forward in their cognitive development with the right social interaction and guided learning.

CONCEPTS OF CHILD-CENTERED AND PROGRESSIVE EDUCATION

Child-Centered Education

Child-centered education is the idea that the needs and desires of the child should take precedence in structuring the learning day. The whole idea is that learning should be fun and engaging for the child, and is most likely to be that way if the child is incharge of the learning experience, rather than the adult parent or teacher.

Child-centered education is most characterised by learning 'centers' in a classroom that promote hands-on, active participation by the child. There may be magnifying glasses and bug slides in the science center, books and puppets that could be used to re-tell the stories in the language arts center, and wood blocks and shapes in the math center. The children are free to manipulate the objects in these centers. It is the process, the activity, the experience, that is valuable, not the facts, ideas, concepts or skills.

It is a relatively new approach to education. For centuries past, adults defined what education should be and children were the ones who did the adjusting. Education was considered work, not play.

Then came the softening influences of child psychologist Jean-Jacques Rousseau, as well as Dr. Marria Montessori, John Dewey, Jean Piaget and Lev Vygotsky, who all contended that a child's self-esteem and self-concept should be built up in order to create a better learner. Soon, the colleges of education were promoting child-centered education instead of instructionally centered education.

Role of Learner in Child-Centered Education

Learners are active as opposed to passive recipients of knowledge. Learners may assume a decision-making role in the classroom. Learners often decide what is to be learned, through which activities and at what pace. Learners can also produce materials and provide activities for the classroom.

Role of Teacher in Child-Centered Education

To put this approach into practice, teachers need to help students set achievable goals; they encourage students to assess themselves and their peers; help them to work co-operatively in groups and ensure that they know how to make use of all the available resources for learning.

Progressive Education

During most of the twentieth century, the term 'progressive education' has been used to describe ideas and practices that aim to make schools more effective agencies of a democratic society. Although there are numerous differences of style and emphasis among progressive educators, they share the conviction that democracy means active participation by all citizens in social, political and economic decisions that will affect their lives. The education of engaged citizens, according to this perspective, involves two essential elements: (1) respect for diversity, meaning that each individual should be recognised for his or her own abilities, interests, ideas, needs, and cultural identity, and (2) the development of critical, socially engaged intelligence, which enables individuals to understand and participate effectively in the affairs of their community in a collaborative effort to achieve a common good. These elements of progressive education have been termed 'child-centered' and 'social reconstruction' approaches, and while in extreme forms they have sometimes been separated, in the thought of John Dewey and other major theorists they are seen as being necessarily related to each other.

The term 'progressive' arose from a period (roughly 1890–1920) during which many Americans took a more careful look at the political and social effects of vast concentrations of corporate power and private wealth. Dewey, in particular, saw that with the decline of local community life and small scale enterprise, young people were losing valuable opportunities to learn the arts of democratic participation, and he concluded that education would need to make up for this loss. In his Laboratory School at the University of Chicago, where he worked between 1896 and 1904, Dewey tested ideas he shared with leading school reformers such as Francis W. Parker and Ella Flagg Young. Between 1899 and 1916 he circulated his ideas in works such as The School and Society, The Child and the Curriculum, Schools of Tomorrow, and Democracy and Education, and through numerous lectures and articles. During these years other experimental schools were established around the country, and in 1919 the Progressive Education Association was founded, aiming at ''reforming the entire school system of America''.

Therefore, progressive education is a reaction against the traditional style of teaching which teaches facts largely at the expense of understanding what is being taught. According to **John French,** ''The progressive school teaches the child to think for himself instead of passively accepting stereotyped ideas. It keeps always in mind that each child is different from every other, and that what makes an educated person useful in his particular walk of life, what makes him interesting, what makes him an individual, is not his resemblance to other people, but his differences''.

Philosophies and Practices of Progressive Education

1. Curriculum is strongly influenced by what the children are interested in, and is child-centered rather than adult driven.
2. Learning is 'hands-on', experiential and the emphasis is on process rather than product children are 'learning to learn'.
3. Children learn through integrated, theme-based units or inquiry projects and the 'theme' often emerges from the children.
4. Assessment is authentic and holistic. Children are well known by their teachers and peers. There are no tests or letter grades. Instead, narrative reports are written about children

that cover all aspects of their development: social, emotional, personal, physical and intellectual level.

5. Classes are usually of mixed ages and no ability grouping is used. Children are able to work at their own pace and cross-age friendships are encouraged.
6. Progressive education practices a developmental approach which holds that each child is a unique being unfolding and developing at their own pace according to a specific pattern. At each stage of development there are things that can be learned and things that should not be learned. Respecting a child's development is central to progressive education.

Types of Progressive Education

1. **Humanistic :** The humanistic form of progressive education focuses on the humanities, arts and social sciences. Its emphasis is on the individual child and not the curriculum. This type of progressivism aims to build a well-rounded individual with highly developed critical thinking and reasoning skills. The children learn think for themselves instead of accepting everything teachers tell them. Social development and interaction among the students are seen as valuable learning techniques.
2. **Constructivism :** Constructivism is a type of child-centered progressivism. It focuses on the child's creativity and learning abilities. Teachers should build the curriculum around the requirements and interests of the child. It maintains that education should consider children's developmental stages. Swiss psychologist **Jean Piaget** influenced the theories of constructivist education. Experiential learning, or learning by doing, allows students to construct their own knowledge.
3. **Montessori :** Italian doctor Marria Montessori started the Montessori progressive educational system. She developed her teaching theories by clinical observation and analysis of how children learn. Her method of education focused on how children naturally learn, all by themselves, without the help of adults. Maria Montessori concluded that children teach themselves, and it's the job of teachers to facilitate this process, not dominate it. Montessori teachers provide a sensory-rich environment and hands-on activities.

CRITICAL PERSPECTIVE OF THE CONSTRUCT OF INTELLIGENCE

Introduction

The most important variable that affects schooling or performance on a job is intelligence. Psychologists have interpreted the term intelligence in different ways and there is no consensus among them on the term even so far. In psychology this term is treated as a construct whose structure is different in different individuals.

The vagueness of the term arises due to the fact that intelligence is not a concrete material. It is rather abstraction from the behaviour of the individual which is indirectly inferred and elaborated as an adjective.

The dictionary meaning of term "intelligence" is the capacity to acquire and apply knowledge. **Boring** defines intelligence as intelligence is what an intelligence test measures.

Definitions of Intelligence

Several psychologists have classified and defined intelligence in several ways. Some of them are given below:

1. Vernon's Classification of Intelligence

(a) *Biological Approach:* Man is an organism among millions living on earth. Environment works as a foe for him. Intelligence is the capacity to adapt to the environment or new situations of life at every moment.

This definition of intelligence can be criticized on the ground that there have been many intelligent and renowned persons who were ill adapted to their social and physical environment. Besides, if we want to study individual differences in a society, this definition serves no practical purpose.

(b) *Psychological Approach :* According to psychologists intelligence is the relative effects of heredity and environment both. An English psychologist, **C. Burt** defined intelligence as the innate general cognitive ability.

In support of psychological definitions of intelligence **Hebb** and **R.B. Catell** distinguished two kinds of intelligence. The first is intelligence "A" which is Fluid intelligence and which is related to genetic potentialities or innate qualities of the individual's nervous system. Second is intelligence "B" which is crystalised "intelligence" and which is related to experiences, learning and environmental factors. These two types of intelligence in normal circumstances so much overlap on each other that they are practically indistinguishable.

(c) *Operational Approach :* These definitions help us to understand the concept of intelligence in clear and definite terms. In this approach scientific terms are first of all defined operationally and then observations are conducted with reference to these terms. For example, in order to determine a child's IQ, we first administer a test of a specific kind. Then we observe his performance on the test and finally draw certain conclusions in the context of the pre-determined objectives.

2. Freeman's Classification

(a) *Ability of adjustment :* An individual is intelligent to the extent to which he is able to adjust to new situations and problems of life. The more a person is intelligent, the more he is able to adapt to his environment in antagonistic conditions. The person who is low in intelligence has less capacity to adjust to the new situations of life.

(b) *Ability of learning :* Learning ability is also an index of intelligence. The more a person is intelligent, the more he will be able to learn new things.

(c) *Ability to carry on abstract thinking :* This category of definitions of intelligence is related to the effective use of concepts and symbols in dealing with situations and solving the problems through the use of verbal and numerical symbols. According to **Terman**, an individual is intelligent to the extent he is able to carry on abstract thinking.

3. E.L. Thorndike's Classification

(a) *Concrete intelligence :* The intellectual ability in relation to concrete materials is called concrete intelligence. It is the ability of a person to comprehend the actual situations and react to them adequately. This kind of intelligence is measured by using performance tests or picture tests in which the subject manipulates the concrete materials.

(b) *Abstract intelligence :* It is the ability to respond to words, letters, numbers or symbols. This type of intelligence is required in all academic activities in schools or outside the schools. The highest level of abstract intelligence is manifested in the thoughts of philosophers or in the inventions of scientists and mathematicians.

(c) *Social intelligence :* It is the ability of an individual to react to social situations of life. It is the ability to understand others and to react to them in such a manner that they may not feel unjust attitude regarding them.

4. Intelligence as a Global Capacity

A comprehensive definitions of intelligence : **Stoddard** (1943) and **Wechsler** (1944) have defined intelligence in the following words :

"Intelligence is the aggregate or the global capacity of the individual to act purposefully, to think rationally and to deal with the environment effectively".

Stoddard further elaborated that intelligence is the capacity of a person to undertake such activities which are: (*i*) difficult (*ii*) complex (*iii*) abstract (*iv*) economical (*v*) goal directed (*vi*) valuable from social view points (*vii*) original. These activities demand concentration of energy and a resistance to emotional forces.

Characteristics of Intelligence

From the above definitions of intelligence, we can draw the following characteristics of intelligence:

(*i*) Intelligence is the composite of several intellectual skills, such as thinking, doing, reasoning, dealing, learning etc.

(*ii*) Intelligence is displayed by the behaviour of the individual as a whole and intelligent behaviour is always goal directed.

(*iii*) Intelligence is the ability to adjust to abnormal and challenging situations of life.

(*iv*) Intelligence is not related to ordinary tasks of life. It is always related to extra ordinary manipulation.

(*v*) Wechsler has included the concepts of drive and incentive which are implied in his statement. "To act purposefully" and "to deal effectively". But many psychologists are of the view that drive and incentive are non-intellectual traits of personality and if they are included in a test of mental ability, more confusions will be created thereof.

(*vi*) There are seven fundamental elements of intelligence according to **Stoddard.** Intelligent person can undertake difficult and abstract tasks with ease. He can manipulate and deal the abstract ideas and concepts efficiently. Similarly, economy refers to the rate at which a mental task is done or a problem is solved. If "A" solves a problem sooner than 'B' then 'A' will be considered more intelligent than 'B'. The term social value indicates whether a mental task performed by a person is in accordance with the socially desirable and acceptable norms or not. The last term original refers to a person's, ability to discover something new and different, *i.e.*, this term is directly related to creative potential of a person. Discovery of some new facts and principles and inventions of new concrete materials by the scientists are few examples of originality.

Stoddard's definition of intelligence has been criticized on two grounds :

(a) It includes social values in intelligence, *i.e.*, intelligent task must be socially desirable. Psychologists criticize this point by saying that social value is a subjective phenomenon, *i.e.*, what is desirable for me, may not be necessarily desirable for others. So, there is no scope of subjectivity in an objective intelligence test.

(b) He has included two conditions of intelligent behaviour in his definition. First is concentration of energy and second is resistance to emotional forces. Psychologists say that these elements are non-intellectual traits and hence they should not be included in mental abilities at any cost.

Theories of Intelligence

1. Faculty theory of intelligence:

This is the oldest theory of intelligence given during the period of pre-experimental psychology. According to this theory mind is made up of different faculties like reasoning, logic, memory, imagination and discrimination. These faculties are independent of each other and can be developed by rigorous mental exercises of the difficult subject-matter.

This theory does not take the hereditary factors of intelligence into account and thus this theory was discarded by the later psychologists who believed that we can never improve the intellectual capacity of a person if he is mentally slow by birth.

2. Unifactor theory:

According to Alfred Binet (1916) intelligence is a general intellectual ability which is made up of several discrete abilities. These abilities include

(i) to reason well with abstract material

(ii) to comprehend well

(iii) to have a clear direction of thoughts

(iv) to relate thinking with the attainment of a desirable end and

(v) to be self-critical.

All these abilities combined together is called general mental ability. Thus, intelligence is a single but complex mental process which can be measured by different kinds of materials designed for the purpose.

3. Two factors theory:

This theory was developed by an English psychologist, **Charles Spearman** in 1904. According to him, intellectual abilities consist of two factors, general ability known as 'G' factors and specific abilities known as 'S' factors.

Characteristics of G factors

(i) It is universal inborn ability.

(ii) It is general mental energy.

(iii) It is constant, *i.e.*, it remains the same in all the individuals and does not change with time.

(iv) The amount of G differs from person to person depending on his genes.

(v) It is used in every life activity.

(vi) Greater the amount of G in an individual, larger is the chance of his success in life.

Characteristics of 'S' factors

(i) It is learnt and hence acquired in the environment.

(ii) It varies from activity to activity in the same individual.

(iii) The amount of S also differs from person to person due to his accessibility to learning situations.

(iv) 'S' factors are related to the specific activity. A low correlation between two or more functions or activities indicates the presence of 'S' factor involved in the activity. A person can be expert only in one or few activities because of the specific factors involved in the activity.

According to Spearman, out of these two factors 'G' factor is more important and thus it is an important measure of intelligence. So, any intelligence test should measure only 'G' factor because it provides most important basis of predicting a person's behaviour in different situations. Raven's Progressive Matrices and Catell's Culture Fair Test both measure 'G' factor.

Spearman has explained his theory with the help of a tetrad equation which is given below :

rap × rbq – raq × rbp = 0

Here,

a = opposites

b = discrimination

p = completion

q = cancellation

Thus, rap means correlation between opposites and completions, rbq means correlation between cancellation and discrimination, raq means correlation between opposite and cancellation and rbp means correlation between discrimination and completion. This theory can also be explained with the help of a diagram given below :

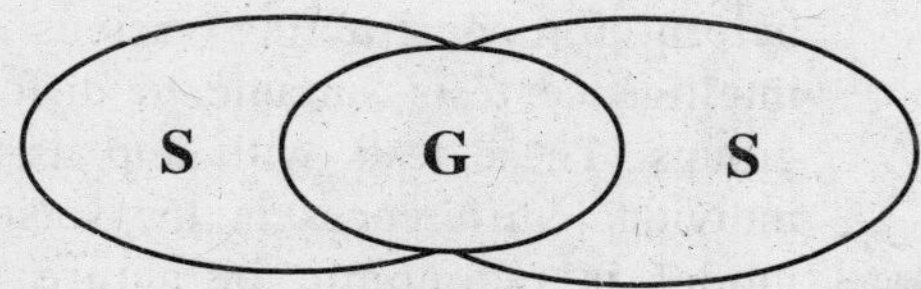

4. Multi-factors theory :

This theory was developed by an American psychologist, **E.L. Thorndike.** He opposed the theory of general intelligence by saying that there are specific stimuli and specific mental responses. Intelligence is nothing more than a potential specific connections between these stimuli and responses. Differences of intelligence among people are due to the different number of such connections in the neurological system. This theory is also called **atomistic theory** of intelligence. There are **four attributes of intelligence** according to him:

(a) *Level :* It refers to the difficulty of a task that can be removed by using intelligence. If different tasks are arranged in increasing difficulty order, then the height that a person can attain determines his level of intelligence. It is a kind of power test.

(b) *Range :* It refers to the number of tasks of the same difficulty value that a person can do in a certain period of time. Theoretically, an individual possessing a certain level of intelligence should be able to solve the whole range of tasks at a given level. It is a kind of speed test.

Range and level can not be completely isolated from each other. We can not measure range without altitude (level) and vice versa.

(c) *Area :* It refers to the total numbers of situations at each level to which the individual is able to respond. Area is the summation of all ranges at each level of intelligence. Area = Level × Range.

(d) *Speed :* It refers to the rapidity with which an individual can respond to a test items. Speed and level are positively correlated. It is different from range in the sense that no specific time is given here to complete a task.

Every intelligence test should consist of these four attributes.

5. Group factor structure of intelligence (PMA Test) :

This theory was developed by **L.L. Thurstone.** According to him, intelligence is not an expression of general factor but a combination of group of traits. They are intermediate factors, *i.e.*, they are not so universal as 'G' factor and they are not so specific as 'S' factor. This primary group of factors give the common mental abilities, a functional cohesiveness and then constitute a group. Another group of common mental abilities is said to have another primary factor and so on. In this way, there are a number of groups of mental abilities each of which has its own primary factors. On the basis of factor analysis of these groups, Thurstone identified the following seven group factors which are termed as primary mental abilities (PMA).

1. Number factor (N) : It is the ability to do numerical calculations rapidly and accurately.
2. Verbal factor (V) : They are related to the operations involving verbal comprehension.
3. Space factor (S) : It is related to the tasks in which subject manipulates an object imaginary in space.
4. Word fluency factor (W) : It is involved to the situation when the subject is asked to think of isolated words at a fast rate.
5. Reasoning factors (R) : It is used in those tasks that require the subject to discover a rule or principles involved in series or groups of letters.
6. Rote memory (M) : It is the ability to memorize a fact quickly.
7. Perceptual speed (P) : It is the ability to note perceptual (visual) details rapidly.

The point to be noted here is that these seven abilities are significantly correlated with each other.

6. Structure of intelligence (SI) model :

This model was given by **J.P. Guilford** in 1966 in the University of California on the basis of factor analysis of many tests. According to him human mind is composed of at least three dimensions—operations, contents and products, and each dimension of intellect is sufficiently distinct which can be detected by factor analysis. These three dimensions of mind are given below:

(A) **Operations :** Operations can be divided into five major groups of intellectual abilities.

- **Cognition :** It includes discovery, recognition of informations and new understanding of the facts.
- **Memory :** It is the ability to recognize or recall previously learnt material.
- **Divergent thinking :** This operation is closely associated with creative potential. It refers to the ability to search out and think in a novel out of track way.
- **Convergent thinking :** It refers to the generation of information from given information and drawing conclusion from the given facts.

- **Evaluation :** It is the ability to make judgement on the basis of merits and demerits of a phenomenon. Here, value judgement on knowledge and thoughts is placed after critically examining them.

(B) **Contents :** Five kinds of contents are involved here. Operations are performed on these contents.

- **Figural content :** It is the concrete material perceived through the senses. Visual materials have three properties, size, form and colour.
- **Auditory content :** It includes nature and characteristics of sound perceived.
- **Symbolic content :** It includes letters, digits and other conventional signs usually organised in general pattern.
- **Semantic content :** It refers to those verbal meanings, ideas and concepts for which no examples are necessary.
- **Behavioural content :** It includes knowledge regarding other persons.

(C) **Products :** When five operations are applied to five types of contents, six kinds of products are made.

- **Units :** It refers to the production of a single word, definition or isolated bits of informations.
- **Classes :** It refers to the production of a concept.
- **Relations :** It refers to the production of any form of relationship, such as, analogy, opposite or similar ones.
- **System :** It refers to the production of internally consistent set of classification of various forms.
- **Transformation :** It refers to the production of changes in meaning, organisation or some other arrangement.
- **Implication :** It refers to the production of such information which is beyond the data given.

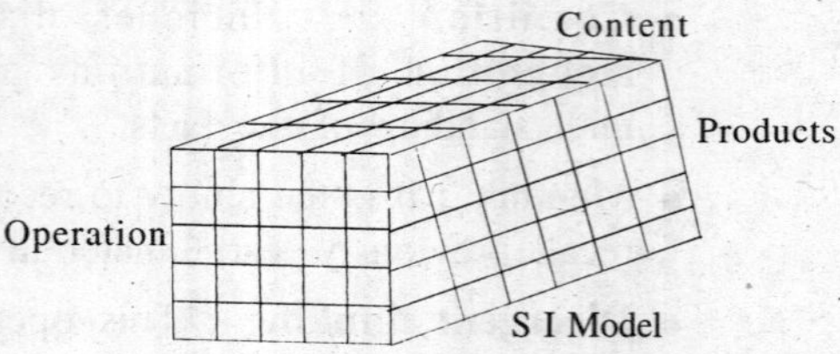

S I Model

On the basis of the model given above it can be stated that there are $5 \times 5 \times 6 = 150$ factors involved in intelligent acts.

Educational Implication of the Model

(a) **In psychology :** This model is very much helpful for constructing various types of intelligence tests suitable to different age groups. These tests will help us to study individual differences in the society. This model is taxonomic in nature and has discovered many abilities which were not known before. If test maker has included items representing contents and operations, he can see whether products are same or different. Conversely, if products are shown by the subject through the test, the test maker can find out the content and operation and match them with the items given in the test.

(b) **In vocational testing :** This model shows that there are 150 intellectual abilities. This model predicts five kinds of mental abilities classified as content. This means that different kinds of test items are needed in vocational testing. Six types of products are also tested on the basis of items representing the products. For example, if a person is able to deal with items of figural contents, he can deal with machines, operators, engineers etc. and any or all of the six types of products can be made by him, such as, he can define a machine or any operator. He can give clear concept about how a machine is operated and so on.

(c) **In the field of education :** Conventionally, learner was considered to be a kind of stimulus response device. Once the stimulus is given to him, he will respond but the new conception of the learner in the light of SI model is that of electronic computer which not only stores information but uses that information to generate new information either by divergent or convergent thinking.

Thus, this model gives the idea that learning is not merely the association of informations but it is the discovery of information as well. Model suggests that in order to understand human learning and higher mental processes of thinking, some drastic modifications are to be made in our theory of curriculum construction and pedagogy of instruction.

Similarly, education is no longer considered to be the training of mind. Now, main emphasis on education is given to the learning of specific skills and modification of behaviour and all these materials are not taught merely for the purpose of training the mind of humans.

7. Two Level Process Theory of Intelligence :

This theory was developed by **Jensen** in 1968. According to him intelligence is a combination of two levels of processes. One is associative intelligence and the other is abstract intelligence. Associative intelligence includes those kinds of tests that depend upon memory and simple verbal association. Abstract intelligence includes those factors as concept learning, thinking, problem solving skills, multiple discrimination, principle learning etc.

8. Burt and Vernon's Hierarchy Theory :

Burt (1940) separated four factors of intelligence by using statistical techniques :

- General factors (common to all traits)
- Group factors (common to some of the traits)
- Specific factors (limited to few traits)
- Error factors (limited to a particular trait when it is measured)

When human mind is put at the top, there will be 5 level hierarchical model of intelligence where general factors will come next to intelligence and error factors will come in the last.

Vernon, on the other hand, suggested that intelligence tests measure an overall factor G as well as two other mental abilities. First are related to verbal, numerical and educational. Second are related to practical, mechanical, spatial and physical. These two major factors can be divided into minor group factors. These minor factors can further be divided into various specific factors and so on.

MEASUREMENT OF INTELLIGENCE

Historical development of mental testing can be divided into three periods for the purpose of convenience.

(A) Pre-Binet Period :

In the 19th century, there was a good deal of interest in the field of psychophysics in which attempts were made to develop general rule of sensory judgement. The functioning of sensory reactions of the typical individuals is actually studied in psycho-physics. Method of limits procedure was used here to measure the extent to which people were able to differentiate between stimuli. But the limitation of these experiments was that accurate generalization of the result was not possible.

Francis Galton was the first psychologist who took interest in studying whether individual characteristics are acquired or inherited. For this purpose, he studied the lives of prominent English men and in his book "Hereditary Genius" he demonstrated that personal characteristics, (mental and physical) of men are inherited. He developed a series of tests to measure these characteristics. It was the starting point of mental measurement.

The first laboratory of experimental psychology was established by **Wundt** in 1879 in Leiping. He employed two methods to test vision, hearing, reaction time and psychosomatic problems—*(i)* psycho-physical method *(ii)* Introspection method. He also developed mental tests which could measure the keenness of vision and hearing, muscular strength, reaction time and other sensory motor functions of body.

Many of **Galton's** ideas were brought to USA by an American psychologist **J.M. Catell.** Like **Galton** he also believed that intellectual functions can best be measured by the reaction time and sensory discrimination tests.

In the last quarter of the 19th century, many psychological laboratories came into existence and studies of individual differences in mental abilities started.

The word "**Mental Test**" was first used by Catell in 1890 but his tests were actually tests of sensory discrimination, speed of motor responses and the like.

Thus, upto this period mental ability was identified as sensory acuity of an individual. The correlation between mental abilities and academic achievements was not known at the time.

Drawbacks of this period:

- Psychologists were unable to identify and define the nature of intelligence. Keenness of sensory motor reactions were related to intelligence.
- They were unable to measure the complex functions of the body.
- Intelligence tests developed during this period were measuring other than intelligence.

(B) Binet Period :

An important incident led the people to think about mental measurement during this period. In the beginning of the 20th century in France, a large number of students failed in the examination. For this teachers and students blamed each other. Seeing this, superintendent of public instruction appointed a committee to device some techniques to screen out slow learners in the schools. Binet and Simon were among members of the committee. They developed a variety of paper pencil tests in their psychological laboratory established in 1889, to administer them on children of different ages. Through these tests Binet tried to measure more complex mental functions such as power of judgement and reasoning, memory, arithmetic ability, etc.

An important contribution of Binet and Simon is that they categorised their tests in terms of age levels by administering their test items to children of different ages. In this way, an age scale of intelligence was also developed. For example, if an item was correctly answered by majority of seven years old children but only few six years old children could respond it correctly, then this item was reserved for seven years old children. In this way, Binet and Simon developed separate tests for different ages.

Similarly, if an item suited to eight years old child was correctly answered by a child of 6 years and if the same trend was shown by the six years old child in most of the cases of a test, then the mental age of the child was considered to be eight years not six years, though his chronological age is six years only. Thus, the concept of mental age was also introduced by Binet and Simon for the first time in the history of mental testing and with the help of this concept we could assess the intellectual ability of a person. Some of the tests developed during this period are given below:

Binet-Simon Scale

The first scale of Binet-Simon was published in 1905. This scale consisted of 30 items arranged in increasing order of difficulty. This scale was a crude measure of intelligence of school going children.

In order to remove some of its defects they revised their scale in 1908. It was the first age based scale and it created a lot of interest among the psychologists across the world. The items in the tests were grouped according to the appropriate age levels from 3 to 13 years.

Some items for three years age

- Point to your nose, eyes and mouth.
- Repeat two digits 3, 5.
- Repeat sentences of six syllables.
- Enumerate objects in a picture.
- Give family names.

Some items of eight years age

- Read a passage and remember two lines.
- Add up the value of five coins.
- Name four colours.
- Count reverse from 20 to zero.
- Give differences between two objects.

1908 revision of Binet-Simon Scale was adopted by many psychologists of America, Switzerland and Germany and many suggestions were given by them for the improvement of the scale. Binet-Simon accepted their suggestions and revised their scale again in 1911.

Some sample items of 1911 scale are given below:

(A) Age = 8 years

- Gives difference between two objects.
- Counts reverse from 20 to zero.
- Points out omissions from unfinished pictures.
- Tells the dates correctly.
- Repeats the digits.

(B) Age = 10 years

- Arranges five blocks in order of increasing weights.
- Reproduces two geometric designs by using memory.
- Criticizes absurd statements.
- Comprehends and answers difficult questions.
- Uses three given words in two sentences.

Main Features of Binet-Simon Scale

(i) They are really scales, *i.e.*, items of the tests are arranged in the increasing difficulty order. Easiest items are put in the beginning and the most difficult item is put in the last. Thus, these scales measure the level or aptitude of an examinee and not their speed.

(ii) These tests measure the general abilities of intelligence instead of specific abilities.

(iii) They can also measure the mental growth of the subject because they are arranged according to different ages from 3 to 14 years.

(iv) They are administered on subjects individually.

(v) Their system of scoring is tied to age norms. A child's performance on the scale will be compared to that of children of his own age.

L.M. Terman's revision of Binet–Simon Scale: L.M. Terman of **Stanford** University revised this scale in 1916 to adapt to American situations. He introduced one new concept which was intelligence Quotient (IQ) in his revision. His scale consisted of 90 items ranging from 3 to 14 years of age. Some items of this scale are given below:

Age = 7 years

- Knows number of fingers on both hands.
- Describes pictures.
- Repeats five digits.
- Gives differences between paired objects.
- Ties a bowknot.

1937 Revision of Binet-Simon Scale : Terman along with his associate Merill revised 1916 scale again in 1937. This revision had two equivalent forms L and M. The number of items in the test was raised to 129 in each L M. forms. A new change was also introduced in the test which was the calculation of chronological age. Upto 13 years CA was taken to be as original but after 13 years CA was computed in the following manner.

At 14 years = 13 yrs+2/3 of 14th year = 13 2/3 years.

At 15 years = 13+2/3 of 2 years = 14 1/3 years.

At 16 years = 13+2/3 of 3 years = 15 years.

Besides, 16 years was taken to be the last age for calculation of IQ. After that, CA was taken to be constant.

LM form revision of 1960 : Binet-Simon scale was last revised in 1960 in which items of both L and M forms were included in the scale. This revision has a range of 2 years of mental age scores to 22 years and 11 months of mental age score. This form of the test measures abilities from 7 categories namely, language, memory, reasoning, social intelligence, conceptual phenomenon, numerical, reasoning and visual motor. Test items are in the form of words, objects and pictures and the responses given by the examinees are in the form of drawing, calculating, writing and speaking. Administration of the test requires one full hour. In this revision intelligence is expressed in terms of standard scores of the deviation IQ.

Wechsler Scale : This scale may be considered an improvement over Binet-Simon scale as it can measure the intelligence of adults very effectively. David Wechsler developed this scale in 1939. This scale was developed in two equivalent forms, each form consisted of ten subtests of which five tests were verbal and five were non-verbal or performance type. This scale was revised in 1955 and was renamed as Wechsler Adult Intelligence Scale (WAIS). It comprised of 11 sub tests of which six were verbal and five were non-verbal. This scale is used on persons above 16 years of age upto 64 and administration time of the scale is one hour. The detail of these 11 subtests are given below:

(a) Verbal subtests :

1. *Information* : 29 questions are given here to test the recall of knowledge concerning wide varieties of information.
2. *Comprehension* : 14 questions are given here to test understanding of knowledge concerning a particular subject or event.
3. *Arithmetic* : 14 questions are given here to test numerical ability. These questions are solved orally without using paper and pencil at all.
4. *Similarity* : 13 questions are given here to measure abstract verbal reasoning. Examinees are required here to compare two objects and find out the relationship between them.
5. *Digit span* : Memory for digits are measured here. In the first half, the examinee is asked to repeat in the same order, three to nine digits presented in the forward directions and in the second half, the digits are repeated in a backward direction.
6. *Vocabulary* : 40 words of increasing difficulty value are presented before the examinees here and they are asked to tell the meaning of these words.

(b) Non-verbal or performance subtests:

1. *Digit symbol* : Nine digits each with different digit symbols are given to the examinees here and they are asked to give the right code for each digits or symbols.
2. *Picture completion* : This subtest measures the ability of the examinees to analyse the parts from the whole. Examinees are given 21 cards containing incomplete pictures and they are asked to fill the missing part of each picture.
3. *Block design* : Its purpose is to measure the ability to analyse the complex whole. There are only 7 designs in these blocks which have red, white and red-white sides. Examinees are asked to produce a given design with the help of these blocks.
4. *Picture arrangement* : Its purpose is to measure the ability to identify the whole from the parts. Here six set of pictures are given to the examinees and they are asked to arrange them in an order which tells a meaningful story.
5. *Object assembly* : Its purpose is to measure the ability to synthesise the whole with the help of parts. Here examinees are given some puzzle pictures each representing some parts of the human body and they are asked to assemble them in the form of a complete man.

Speed and accuracy factors are also scored in Arithmetic, digit symbol, block design, picture arrangement and object assembly. Raw scores of each subject are converted into normalized standard scores with a mean of 10 and SD of 3. This makes the scores of each sub tests comparable. Separate IQ for verbal and non-verbal subtest forms is calculated by adding up the respective subtests of the two forms and if we add up scores on all the 11 subtests, we obtain total scale score. These standard scores are expressed in the form of deviation IQ with a mean of 100 and SD of 15.

Wechsler developed another scale known as Wechsler intelligence Scale for Children in 1949 to test the intelligence of children from 5 to 15 years of age. It also takes one hour to administer, though there are 12 subtests in this scale. Maze test is the only test which is extra in WISC. Maze subtest has eight mazes to be traced by the examinee with a pencil. These mazes are given in increasing order of difficulty.

The scoring system of both the tests WAIS and WISC are the same. Here also the total scores are converted into deviation IQ with a mean of 100 and SD of 15.

Advantages of Wechsler Scales

(i) Though Binet's scale and Wechsler's scale both are individual scales, yet the later can be

administered on small groups of children and adults.

(ii) Wechsler's scale is easier to administer than Binet's Scale and its scoring is also less complex than the former.

(iii) Wechsler has prepared separate scales for children and adults Binet's scale does not possess this advantage.

Other differences of Wechsler Scales and Stanford Binet Scale

(i) In Wechsler scale, items are not grouped in terms of mental age as is the case of Stanford-Binet scale. Points are given here for all correct responses. Thus, WAIS or WISC is a point scale.

(ii) In Stanford-Binet scale items are interpreted in terms of different age levels of the examinees but in WAIS or WISC similar types of items are grouped together to form subtests.

(iii) WAIS has separate age norms for adults but in SB Scale all the individuals above 18 are treated in a similar manner as far as computation of IQ is concerned. Thus, people of all age levels are treated as 18 years of age after 18.

(iv) In SB tests items are varied, unrelated and upgraded but in WAIS and WISC tests, items are graded according to various range of ages.

(v) SB scale is internally standardized and rigid but WAIS is externally standardized and flexible.

(vi) SB scale refers to qualitative evaluation while WAIS refers to quantitative evaluation.

(vii) Slight chance of statistical treatment is possible in SB scale but WAIS is fully subject to all statistical analysis.

(c) Post Binet period :

This period is particularly known for testing intelligence in groups and thus group test of intelligence became popular during this periods.

A group test is one that can be given to a number of subjects at a time by a single examiner. This type of test came into being during first World War for the purpose of classifying soldiers for various jobs in accordance with their mental abilities. Army Alpha and Army Beta, two tests were developed during this period. Army Alpha is a verbal group test of intelligence meant for literate people. Army beta is a non-verbal group test of intelligence meant for illiterate persons.

We will discuss here some more group test of intelligence :

1. **Catell's Culture Fair Test :** This test was developed by RB Catell and was published by IPAT (Institute for Personality and Ability Testing) in 1961. The test has three scales and can be administered on children and adults both.

   Scale I meant for 4-8 years
   Scale II meant for 8-15 years
   Scale III meant for 15 years and above

   This test measures the general intelligence factor and takes 30-60 minutes to administer. The test has been prepared in such a manner that previously learnt skill or knowledge does not help the examinee to score more on this test. That is why, it is said to be independent of school achievement, social advantages and environmental influences.

2. **Large Thorndike's Intelligence Test :** This test is meant for primary and secondary school children graded into five different levels. The purpose of the test is to measure verbal comprehension, numerical skill and reasoning abilities. Test has verbal as well as non-verbal items. Only non-verbals items are, however, included at the lower levels. The administration of the test takes 30 minutes in all.

3. **Raven Progressive Matrices Test :** This test was developed in England. It consists of geometric figures and designs. The subjects find out the relationship between figures and select appropriate parts for completion of each pattern of relations.

Classification of Intelligence Test

(A) Classification from the point of view of administration

1. **Individual intelligence test :** An individual intelligence test is one which is administered to only one person at a time. Binet-Simon is an example.

2. **Group intelligence test :** A group intelligence test is one which can be administered to more than one persons at a time. Army Alpha and Army Beta are two examples of such tests.

Some general characteristics of group intelligence tests are as follows :

(i) They have been developed on the assumption that intelligence is a general capacity and can be measured by sampling a variety of mental activities.

(ii) In group tests the similar types of items are pooled together in different subtests.

(iii) Every group test is standardized for a special range of ages or school grades.

(iv) Construction of individual test is also very difficult and costly as compared to group tests.

Their scoring and standardization is also time consuming process.

(v) It is very difficult to establish rapport between the examiner and the examinees and hence examinees can not be motivated properly in group tests of intelligence. These two limitations are not seen in individual tests.

(vi) Group tests are superior to individual tests in the sense that norms established here are more dependable than that of individual tests. It is because these norms are calculated on the basis of a very large sample.

(vii) Individual test provides qualitative performance of the individual while group tests are mostly point scale and express the performance in quantities.

(B) Classification from the point of view of nature of items of the test

1. **Verbal test :** Verbal test of intelligence is one in which instructions and items are produced before the examinees through the written language. So, examinees must be literate to take these tests. Mohsin's General intelligence Test, Joshi's General Mental Ability test and Jalota's Group General Mental Ability Test are some examples of verbal tests of intelligence of Indian origin.

2. **Non-verbal test :** A non-verbal test is one which requires the use of language only to impart instructions. The examinees are asked to manipulate the test materials in their own way. Since language is not needed to respond to items here, it can be administered to illiterate persons as well. They are also culturally free and hence they can be applied to any situation representing any culture. Test items are usually of figured relation type. Army Beta is a good example of non-language test.

3. **Performance test :** A performance test is one in which a subject has to perform some thing or to manipulate some concrete materials without much use of the language ability. Non-verbal and performance tests are useful for the following groups of people:

   (a) *Deaf and Dumb :* Those children who cannot hear or speak can be tested with the help of performance test.

   (b) *Illiterates :* Verbal test of intelligence is useless for those who cannot read or write. Performance test is useful for them.

   (c) *Shy children :* Many withdrawn children are hesitant to express before others. Performance and non-verbal test of intelligence will suit them very much.

   (d) *Educationally deficient children :* Verbal test of intelligence generally measure learning along with intelligence. If children are educationally poor, they will perform poorly on intelligence test too and thus they will be wrongly declared as children of below average intelligence. Such a problem can be overcome by using performance test or non-verbal intelligence test.

   (e) *Useful for children of other culture :* A particular culture dominates in every verbal intelligence test and thus the test can not be adopted by other cultures. Due to free from culture, performance test is suitable for these foreign students.

Some performance tests of intelligence are given below :

(a) Pintner Paterson Scale : This is the first systematic performance test. This scale was standardized in 1917. It consists of 15 subtests.

(b) Goodenough Drawing Test : This scale was developed by Florence Goodenough in 1926. Here child is asked to draw the picture of a man as best as possible without any time limit. This is especially useful for those children who are suspected to be mentally retarted.

Weaknesses of performance test :

- Here the subject can score high due to practice effect and chance success is more frequent than verbal tests. Because of this reason, reliability coefficient is very low.
- They fail to distinguish between gifted and average children due to limited scope of these tests.
- These scales fail to test fine mental abilities such as, ability to make abstraction or concept formation or evaluation abilities of mind.

Interpretation of Intelligence Test Scores : Intelligence test scores can be interpreted in the following three ways:

1. **Mental age :** This concept was first introduced by **Afred Binet** of France in 1908. It refers to a score that is determined by comparing a child's score with the scores obtained by younger or older children in the norming group. Here a child's score is compared with the average score of his own age. For example, if a 9-year-old child scores 60 on an intelligence test and suppose mental age norms for that scale are as follows:

   Mental age of 8 years = 60
   Mental age of 9 years = 70
   Mental age of 10 years = 80

Then, in that case, mental age of the child will be considered as 8 years instead of 9 though his chronological age is 9 years.

Similarly, if another child of 8 years obtains a score of 80, then his mental age will be 10 years, though his chronological age is 8 years only.

Thus, we can say that the mean performance of each age level becomes the mental age for that age level.

2. **Intelligent Quotient (IQ) :** IQ is also based on the concept of mental age. It is the ratio of mental age to the chronological age multiplied by 100.

$$IQ = \frac{MA}{CA} \times 100.$$

Suppose, the mental age of a 10-year-old child is 12 years on the basis of his scores on an intelligence test, his IQ will be

$$\frac{12}{10} \times 100 = 120.$$

Similarly, if mental age of a person is nine years two months and his age is 12 years 6 months, then his IQ will be

$$\frac{110}{150} \times 100 = 73.3.$$

General classification of persons in terms of IQ

IQ	Classification
140 and above	Genius
130-140	Very superior
120-130	Superior
110-120	Bright
90-110	Average
80-90	Dull
70-80	Borderline
Below 70	Mentally retarded.

Shortcomings of IQ: Some of the main short comings of IQ are as follows:

(i) It is a well-known fact that after 18 years, the mental age of a person tends to stabilize. Thus, if IQ is calculated after this age, the result will be misleading, *i.e.*, a person will be less intelligent if he grows in age.

(ii) Variability of IQ scores from one test to another is not the same. As a result IQ scores for different tests would not be directly comparable.

(iii) It has also been found that variability in IQ scores for the different age levels on the same test is not the same. In that case IQ scores would be a misleading index because it would indicate that a person's IQ may increase or decrease as he grows in age. An example will illustrate this point.

Age	IQ	SD
9 years old child	120	12
7 years old child	120	9

Here IQ of 120 of both the children is not the same due to difference in SD.

3. **Deviation IQ :** Now-a-days IQ ratio is converted into a normalized standard score with a fixed mean of 100 and SD of 15. This is known as DIQ. This fixed mean and SD remain constant through all the age levels. It means that if a child's score is 1 SD above the mean his DIQ will be 100 + 15 = 115. Similarly, if his score is 1 SD below the mean his DIQ will be 100 – 15 = 85 and so on. Thus, with the help of these **DIQ** scores inter age comparison is also possible.

Uses of Intelligence Test

Intelligence tests can be applied in the following situations.

1. **Measurement of general learning abilities:** Intelligence and achievement in schools are highly correlated. If a person is high on an intelligence test, he is expected to score high on school achievements also. Conversely if a person scores high on an intelligence test and still his school achievement is very poor, we can find out other reasons for his educational backwardness.
2. **Assessment of individual differences and categorization :** With the help of intelligence tests we can categories a particular class into several convenient groups and plan our instructional strategies accordingly. Thus, intelligence testing is very useful for educational guidance.
3. **Exact definition of mental retardation is possible :** It is said that those who are below 70 in IQ are retarded but to what extent they are mentally retarded can further be studied with the help of higher screening. We may define the three groups of mentally retarted in the following ways.

Category	IQ level
Morons	45-69
Imbeciles	25-45
Idiots	Below 25

4. **Identification of gifted children :** Gifted children are the treasure of the society. They must be identified in the earlier stages of their

lives so that they can be fully guided and helped for their better advancement which is directly related to the advancement of the society as well. Intelligence testing will help the concerned organisations to chalk out plans in the desired manner.

5. **Vocational guidance :** Some children are very forward in verbal abilities and some are superior in non-verbal abilities. This identification is possible only with the help of intelligence tests. Since academic subjects need verbal intelligence and technical subjects need non-verbal or performing abilities, hence children may be guided accordingly.
6. **Screening :** In today's age of competition and rush, screening has become a necessity. Every school has limited seats of admission and it has to select only those students who can raise the academic level of the school high and get name for it. Same is the case with appointments in jobs. For all these purposes, intelligence testing is a must.
7. **Study of mental growth :** Mental abilities develop in a sequential order onward. We can use intelligence tests for studying the trends of mental development of individuals. Intelligence tests have made it clear that mental development of children is a steady consistent process from year-to-year till the age of 25. Intelligence tests show that mind does not develop rapidly in the period of adolescence like the physical and emotional development, but in childhood, it develops rapidly.

Limitations of Intelligence Tests

1. Generally intelligence test shows what a person can do at a certain point of time. These abilities are tested on the basis of certain items included in the test. In order to make the results dependable, a proper size of the sample must be selected for standardization of the test.
2. Some people may be fatigued earlier than others when take a test. This extent of fatigue may reduce their scores and hence intelligence testing will not be accurate. So scores should be taken with caution.
3. No intelligence test is fully free from cultural influences. So, home or school background may affect the intelligence test scores of subjects.
4. Administration of the test also affects the scores of subjects. If proper rapport is there between the examiner and the examinee. IQ scores may be high. On the other hand, if children are frightened with the testing situation as is case of slow learners they will perform poorly on the test.
5. Taking intelligence scores in absolute form is misleading. Intelligence tests do not reveal all the mental abilities in most of the cases. So, intelligence test must be supplemented with clinical setting and case history method to collect detailed information about a subject as is done in clinics by physician who does not entirely believe in physical investigations. He rather takes the help of clinical diagnosis before giving remedial treatment to the patients.

THOUGHT AND LANGUAGE

In this section we examines the relationship between language and thought: that language determines thought, that thought determines language, and that thought and language have different origins. Let us examine these three viewpoints in some detail.

Language as Determinant of Thought

In Hindi and other Indian languages we use a number of different words for various kinship relationships. We have different terms for mother's brother, father's elder brother, father's younger brother, mother's sister's husband, father's sister's husband and so on. An English person uses just one word *uncle* to describe all these kinship relationships. In the English language there are dozens of words for colours whereas some tribal languages have only two to four colour terms. Do such differences matter for how we think? Does an Indian child find it easier to think about and differentiate between various kinship relationships compared to her English-speaking counterpart? Does our thinking process depend on how we describe it in our language?

Benjamin Lee Whorf was of the view that language determines the contents of thought. This view is known as **linguistic relativity hypothesis**. In its strong version, this hypothesis holds what and how individuals can possibly think is determined by the language and linguistic categories they use **(linguistic determinism).** Experimental evidence, however, maintains that it is possible to have the same level or quality of thoughts in all languages depending upon the availability of linguistic categories and structures. Some thoughts may be easier in one language compared to another.

Thought as Determinant of Language

The noted Swiss psychologist, Jean Piaget believed that thought not only determines language, but also precedes it. Piaget argued that children form an internal representation of the world through thinking. For example, when children see something and later copy it (a process called imitation), thinking does take place, which does not involve language. A child's observation of other's behaviour and imitation of the same behaviour, no doubt involves thinking but not language. Language is just one of the vehicles of thinking. As actions become internalised, language may affect children's range of symbolic thinking but is not necessary for the origins of thought. Piaget believed that though language can be taught to children, understanding of the words require knowledge of the underlying concepts (*i.e.* thinking). Thus, thought is basic, and necessary if language is to be understood.

Different Origins of Language and Thought

The Russian psychologist, Lev Vyogotsky, argued that thoughts and language develop in a child separately until about two years of age, when they merge. Before two years thought is preverbal and is experienced more in action (Piaget's sensory motor stage). The child's utterances are more automotic reflexes—crying when uncomfortable—than thought-based. Around two years of age, the child expresses thought verbally and her/his speech reflects rationality. Now children are able to manipulate thoughts using soundless speech. He believed that during this period the development of language and thinking become interdependent; the development of conceptual thinking depends upon the quality of inner speech and vice versa. Thought is used without language when the vehicle of thinking is non-verbal such as visual or movement-related. Language is used without thought when expressing feelings or exchanging pleasantries, for example ''Good morning! How are you?'' ''Very well, I am fine''. When the two functions overlap, they can be used together to produce verbal thought and rational speech.

Development of Language

Language is a complex system and unique to human beings. Psychologists have tried to teach sign language, use of symbols to chimpanzees, dolphins, parrots, etc. But it is observed that, human language is more complex, creative, and spontaneous than the system of communication other animals can learn. There is also a great deal of **regularity** with which children all over the world seem to be learning the language or languages to which they are exposed. When we compare individual children, we find that they differ a great deal in the rate of their language development as well as in how they go about it. But when we take a general view of children's acquisition of language all over the world we find some *predictable pattern* in which children proceed from almost no use of language to the point of becoming competent language users. Language develops through some of the stages discussed below.

Newborn babies and young infants make a variety of sounds, which gradually get modified to resemble words. The first sound produced by babies is crying. Initial crying is undifferentiated and similar across various situations. Gradually, the pattern of crying varies in its pitch and intensity to signify different states such as hunger, pain, and sleepiness, etc. These differentiated crying sounds gradually become more meaningful *cooing sounds* (like 'aaa', 'uuu', etc). usually to express happiness.

At around six months of age children enter the *babbling* stage. Babbling involves prolonged repetition of a variety of consonants and vowel sounds (for example, da—, aa—, ba—). By about nine months of age these sounds get elaborated to strings of some sound combinations, such as 'dadadadadada' into repetitive patterns called *echolalia.* While the early babblings are random or accidental in nature, the later babblings seem to be imitative of adult voices. Children show some understanding of a few words by the time they are six months old. Around the first birthday (the exact age varies from child-to-child) most children enter the *one-word-stage.* Their first word usually contains one syllable—*ma or da*, for instance. Gradually they move to one or more words which are combined to form whole sentences or phrases. So they are called *holophrases*. When they are 18 to 20 months of age, children enter a *two-word stage* and begin to use two words together. The two-word stage exemplifies *telegraphic speech.* Like telegrams (got admission, send money) it contains mostly nouns and verbs. Close to their third birthday, *i.e.* beyond two-and-a-half years, children's language development gets focused on rules of the language they hear.

How is language acquired? You must be wondering: ''How do we learn to speak?'' As with many other topics in psychology, the questions of whether a behaviour develops as a result of inherited characteristics (nature) or from the effects of learning (nurture) has been raised with regard to language. Most psychologists accept that both nature and nurture are important in language acquisition.

Behaviourist B.F. Skinner believed we learn language the same way as animals learn to pick keys or press bars. Language development, for the behaviourists follow the learning principles, such as association (the sight of bottle with the word 'bottle'), imitation (adults use of word ''bottle''), and reinforcement (smiles and hugs when the child says something right). There is also evidence that children produce sounds that are appropriate to a language of the parent or care-giver and are reinforced for having done so. The principle of shaping leads to successive approximation of the desired responses so that the child eventually speaks as well as the adult. Regional differences in pronunciation and phrasing illustrate how different patterns are reinforced in different areas.

Linguist Noam Chomsky put forth the innate proposition of development of language. For him the *rate at which children acquire words and grammar* without being taught can not be explained only by learning principles. Children also *create all sorts of sentences* they have never heard and, therefore, could not be imitating. Children throughout the world seem to have a *critical period*—a period when learning must occur if it is to occur successfully—for learning language. Children across the world also go through the same stages of language development. Chomsky believes language development is just like physical maturation given adequate care, it ''just happens to the child''. Children are born with ''universal grammar''. They readily learn the grammar of whatever language they hear.

Skinner's emphasis on learning explains why infants acquire the language they hear and how they add new words to their vocabularies. Chomsky's emphasis on our built-in readiness to learn grammar helps explain why children acquire language so readily without direct teaching.

GENDER AS A SOCIAL CONSTRUCT; GENDER ROLES, GENDER-BIAS AND EDUCATIONAL PRACTICE

Gender refers to the social distinctions between boys and girls and men and women that are socially constructed rather than biologically determined. These distinctions are reflected in the roles that boys and girls play in society and the status that they occupy within it. Gender roles tend to be dynamic. They vary from one culture and time period to another and are characterized by unequal power relationships.

Ending gender bias and discrimination is crucial to the empowerment of women and girls and to the achievement of gender equality in education. Applying a gender perspective helps to make differences in power relations visible. It also helps us to see more clearly the needs and rights of girls and boys in particular geographical, cultural and economic contexts.

The ultimate goal is to eliminate gender biases and discriminatory practices and policies, both overt and covert. This is at the heart of gender analysis. Gender analysis should therefore be a prerequisite for identifying and understanding problems as they relate to education, and especially to the continued exclusion of girls from quality schooling. Gender analysis guides the process of finding viable and sustainable solutions to the problems of access, quality and learning achievement.

Gender analysis of what learners bring to education (including early childhood socialization, feeding and health access, cultural heritage and language), the content of education, teaching and learning processes, learning environments and learning outcomes help to highlight bad (and good) educational practices and policies. This analysis, in turn, should form the basis for educational interventions that are sensitive to both gender and human rights.

Gender Bias in Teaching

A common response from teachers when asked about gender inequity in classrooms is that they treat all their students the same. There are two problems with this statement. First, students are diverse and have different learning issues, thus treating all students in the same way means that some students will have a better learning experience than their peers. Second, teachers may be ignoring their unconscious gender biases towards their students, their schools and themselves. If ignored, these gender biases, which may have developed from cultural norms, may lead to bias in the classroom.

Gender bias occurs when people make assumptions regarding behaviours, abilities or preferences of others based upon their gender. Because there are strong gender role stereotypes for masculinity and femininity, students who do not match them can encounter problems with teachers and with their peers. For example, the expectation is that boys naturally exhibit boisterous, unruly behaviour, are academically able, rational, and socially uncommunicative, whereas girls are quiet, polite, and studious. Girls are also expected to possess better social skills than boys and to excel at reading and the language arts. So girls who present discipline problems for teachers, or quiet, studious boys, may encounter a lack of understanding from peers and teachers. Within the classroom, these biases unfold in students' practices and teachers' acceptance of certain behaviours from one student or another based upon the students' gender. Also, bias due to a person's gender is not mutually exclusive of other social categories such as race, ethnicity, class, religion, and language. For example, some teachers may perceive African American or other Black girls as loud and uncontrollable because the girls do not exhibit the feminine behaviours associated with White women, such as quiet, self-effacing and malleable.

Gender bias can occur within subject areas and school activities. For example, in subjects such as mathematics and the sciences, there are different participation patterns for girls and boys. Gender bias promulgates a myth that boys are naturally better at mathematics and science than girls. The implications are that if girls succeed in these subjects it is due to their hard work, not their intelligence, whereas boys' success is credited to their natural talent. There are some signs that gender bias in schools may be decreasing in some areas. The percentage of girls participating in science has increased and achieved parity with boys in biology, chemistry and algebra. However, subjects that are prerequisites for college majors such as engineering or physics remain dominated by men. Only 25% of high school students enrolled in physics are female. Moreover, there has been little increase in the percentage of women in engineering programs.

Males are also more likely than females to be in remedial programs and students' race also impacts these patterns. For example, African American males are more likely than White or female peers to enroll in remedial reading and mathematics courses. And non-White students have a higher representation in vocational and noncollege preparatory courses than their White peers. Teachers are critical components in challenging gender bias in schooling, but they also can be major contributors to it as well, through their pedagogical practices, curriculum choices, and assessment strategies.

Gender Bias in Teachers

Teachers' unconscious gender biases can produce stereo-typic expectations for students' success and participation in the classroom. Teachers view male students' domination of the classroom and their time as typical masculine behaviour. However, these biases have consequences for the students and the classroom climate. More than two decades ago, researchers identified and named groups of students who dominated the teacher's time and the classroom resources as ''target students'' (Tobin & Gallagher, 1987). Target students were typically white and male. They answered most of the teacher's questions and also asked most of the questions. This behaviour pattern was particularly insidious in mathematics and science classrooms because teachers did not expect girls to have competent knowledge in these subject areas. Classroom observations documented that target students typically called out answers to the teacher's questions, thus denying other students the opportunity to engage in dialogue with the teacher or get to grips with the subject matter. Furthermore, because boys are perceived as having natural talent in science, teachers asked boys harder and more complicated questions than girls. If girls attempted to answer more difficult questions than boys and faltered, teachers often repeated the question and asked that another student, typically a boy, provide the answer. However, if a boy failed to answer correctly, teachers reframed the question or broke it into a series of simpler questions that could help the student find the answer. Teachers' unconscious stereotyped gender bias that boys are smarter than girls, especially in mathematics and the sciences, meant they were willing to work with boys to reach the answer because they perceived boys were capable of achieving that goal but girls were not. Conversely, teachers of subjects perceived as feminine will spend more time engaged with girls.

Teachers' gendered perceptions of students' ability is also reflected in the type of praise and expectations they have of their students. Teachers often give girls less meaningful and less critical praise than boys. Boys' work is described as unique or brilliant, while girls' work is often undervalued, critically ignored and praised for its appearance. This aspect of teachers' behaviour is particularly detrimental to girls because it means they do not receive feedback on their work that could help them develop deeper understandings of concepts (Liu, 2006).

Teachers also use target students to maintain the tempo and pace of classroom instruction. For example, in a lecture or whole class discussion when a teacher is posing questions to the class, he or she may encourage target students to call out answers in order to keep the lesson moving, rather than wait for the other students to process the question and provide an answer. This short ''wait time'' may be detrimental to learning. More than three decades ago, researchers found that if teachers waited three to five seconds before accepting a student's answer, more students became engaged in the classroom and also improved their understanding of the content. Moreover, the longer wait time meant that teachers began to ask more cognitively challenging questions. However, the existence of target students in classes who often call out answers without direction from teachers meant that fewer students, especially girls, engaged in the lessons. In the absence of proactive teacher intervention, these patterns in which males dominate classroom interactions also occur in mixed-gender, small groups.

Target students dominate classroom interactions and exchanges at all education levels. In the early 2000s, researchers identified these same patterns of engagement in a professional development program for science teachers. When alerted to the invasive behaviours of the male teachers in the cohort, faculty began using overt breaching strategies to stop the target students calling out answers, dominating the human and materials resources of the classroom, and showing disrespect to their peers (Martin Milne & Scantlebury, 2006).

Teachers' gender bias towards students can also extend to their response to students who challenge their authority. Such risk-taking behaviour in boys is expected and at times praised, but assertiveness in girls is viewed negatively and labelled unfeminine. Similarly, boys who do not exhibit stereotypic masculine behaviours may be ridiculed (Renold, 2006).

Teachers use gender expectations as a means of maintaining classroom control. For example, teachers will seat undisciplined boys next to girls as a classroom management strategy. Further, teachers use the gendered expectation that girls' nurturing characteristics will lead them to place others' needs before their own. In other words, teachers often ask girls to assume mothering roles towards students who have fallen behind with learning because of inattentiveness, absenteeism through truancy, or in-school disciplinary procedures, and often those students are male.

Effects of Gender Bias

Gender bias can impact students' attitudes towards learning and their engagement with the subject. If affected by gender bias, girls will tend to believe that any success they have is due to hard work rather than any innate talent or intelligence. Boys may be encouraged to believe that success in science and mathematics should come easily to them because of their gender. Some males report dropping out of college science and mathematics programs because they no longer perceive these subjects as easy. Overall, teachers have lower expectations for girls' academic success compared to boys, and their attitudes are shown through the type and quality of the student-teacher interaction. The type and quality of critique teachers give their students can also have an impact. Teachers' comments on girls' work focuses on its appearance but with boys' work teachers focus on the content. Girls often do not receive substantive comments or criticism from teachers from which they could improve their ability to learn. During the many hours spent in classrooms, girls receive less time and attention from teachers than their male peers. Teachers usually ask girls easier questions than they ask boys. Typically, girls receive fewer opportunities to engage in classroom discourse, use equipment and assert their knowledge in classrooms.

Reducing Gender Bias

Gender bias in education is a series of microinequities whose impact is cumulative and often ignored. Girls are rewarded and praised for compliant behaviour. Teachers do not challenge girls with questions and rarely offer criticisms of their works. Teachers can reduce and challenge gender bias through an examination of their pedagogical practices and by posing simple questions about their practices. For example, which students do they frequently interact with? Are target students evident in their classroom? If so, how does the teacher deal with those students? What questioning techniques does the teacher use to engage students? Does the teacher ask complicated questions to girls as well as boys? Does the teacher use a variety of pedagogical and assessment practices? Which students are engaged with the curriculum?

Another way of reducing gender bias would be for teachers to videotape their classes and review their interactions with the students. Or they could invite a colleague to watch their teaching and record which students are being asked questions and what type of questions. However, teachers must also prepare for the consequences of changing their practices. Girls are conditioned to receiving less of the teacher's attention, and they do not usually cause discipline problems if they are not receiving their fair share, but boys can react negatively to losing the teacher's attention, causing disruption to lessons and becoming discipline problems. Moreover, research has also shown that boys avoid written work and often have poor communication skills when asked to work in singlesex groups.

However, the gains in reducing gender bias in education may disappear with the requirements of high-stakes testing required by No Child Left Behind (NCLB). NCLB requires that states report academic achievement data in most social categories, except gender (Kahle, 2004). This may result in less attention being placed on gender bias and less data that might reveal it. Continued monitoring of gender bias is necessary to minimize its impact on students' opportunities for learning and achievement.

INDIVIDUAL DIFFERENCES AMONG LEARNERS

It is not unusual to find a wide range of differences among students in a class or a group. These differences are invariably identified in terms of student's characteristics such as physical (appearance, height, size, sex, colour, etc.), demographic (age, caste, socio-economic status, etc.) and cognitive behaviour (thinking, remembering, problem solving, creating idea, etc.). The differences that exist among students due to physical, demographic, affective behaviour and cognitive behaviour characteristics are referred to as individual differences.

Differences due to physical and demographic characteristics are conspicuous and easy to identify. However, the differences that exist in the way they solve problem in Mathematics or in their ability to interpret and explain ideas are not easily visible but are identified through their performance. Let us examine, for instance, the answers given by Bitto and

Neha, two students of the same class to the following proverb.

Interpret the saying, ''Pen is mighter than the sword''.

Bitto's Interpretation

It means that writing had always been able to influence mankind more than any amount of sheer physical strength; writing undoubtedly makes a more lasting impact in the minds of the people than any form of physical demonstration. In the case of the latter the impact might be forceful though less lasting. Great thinkers, writers and philosophers have from time immemovial been able to hold sway over the minds of the people by means of their profound knowledge through their writings. For example, Socrates won the wrath of a powerful state, because of his great ability to hold spellbound the young through his discourses. Similarly, the writing of Voltaire and Rousseau inspired the French to rise up in revolt.

Neha's Interpretation

It is a common proverb which simply means that through writing it is possible to win more victories than by using physical force and weapons. When any good book is read it is possible to retain in our memory the message it contains. On the other hand, success achieved through physical might is not for mankind.

The above illustration reflects the differences between Bitto and Neha in their interpretation of the proverb. While Bitto delves deep in her interpretation, Neha states only the meaning.

According to Skinner, individual differences in learner behaviours are the result of the organism's genetic endowment and reinforcement. Thus, Skinner believed that defective genetic endowment and/or defective reinforcement contingencies in an individual's experience result in a failure to acquire a variety of learned behaviours.

The process of an individual's mental activities such as remembering, analysing, interpreting, reasoning, problem solving and thinking are cognitive domain behaviours and are essential for learning and achievement. How we think, what and how we remember, how we solve problem and how we create ideas are cognitive domain behaviours and individuals differ by these behaviours. Such differences are often identified by psychologists in terms of intelligence, aptitude, creating and academic achievement.

Individual differences are crucial for teachers who are responsible for guiding all forms of learning. In fact, many educators would suggest that the primary role of teachers is to provide education to meet the individual differences and to develop student cognitive process.

Do Individuals Differ in Intelligence?

Well, they do differ. But how? Differences are due to the differences in the level of general intellectual ability and the underlying cognitive process among individuals.

How do we identify differences in intelligence?

Using suitable intelligence tests we can measure and identify the difference. An intelligence test may contain sub-tests (sub-sections) and each sub-test represents a different set of ability. The scores obtained in all sub-tests are added up to obtain a single score to represent the general ability of the student. Thus, the single score obtained for each individual in a test is expressed in terms of **intelligence quotient** (IQ). IQ is a measure of intelligence and is defined as the ratio of mental age (average age of children who give correct responses/answers in an intelligence test) to the chronological age (actual age) multiplied by 100 (to avoid fraction). Thus mental age is:

$$IQ = \frac{\text{Mental age}}{\text{Chronological age}} \times 100$$

IQ scores help us estimate individual differences by categorising individuals on the basis of their IQs. These differences have important consequences for learning and performance. Let us examine the different categories of students based on their intelligence level.

Gifted : Those students who possess IQs of 130 or above are called gifted students. They are superior in intelligence and have high ability to reason. As compared to other children, they can perform academic activities grasping concepts, memorising, perceiving, seeing relationships, generalising, dealing with abstract ideas, critical thinking and solving problems more effectively and quickly. They have a broad attention span that permits concentration and the ability for a high level of academic performance. They take initiative in intellectual work and follow complex directions. Such individuals are small in number as compared to normal or average children. Normal groups have those children whose IQs range from 90 to 110 and they are able to profit from regular school programmes with varying degrees of effort.

Disabled : There are children with **disability** due to low level to intellectual functioning or specific learning deficits. Children with low level or below-average intellectual functioning are called mentally retarded. The children with inadequate level of intelligence are impaired in their ability to learn and to adapt to the demands of society. Mentally retarded children are of different categories. They can be:

- **Border line** (IQ ranges 90-70) and **educable mentally retarded** (IQ ranges 70-50) children can perform academic activities but are slow in their learning. Special instructional strategies can help them to profit from learning activities. They can take care of themselves and live independently as adults.
- **Trainable mentally retarded** (IQ ranges 50-35) are capable of learning only certain rudimentary literacy materials and simple occupational skills. They possess some ability to take care of their personal needs and can be trained in daily living skills. Such children require special classes or schools to study in.
- **Severely retarded** (IQ below 35) have quite limited adaptive behaviour and are never found in school. They are dependent on their families for their personal needs.

Children with specific learning defects are called learning disabled group. They are normal to above-average on intelligence but have difficulties in one or more psychological processes involved in understanding or in using language or numbers (written or spoken). The difficulties manifest in their ability to listen, think, speak, read, write, spell or do mathematical calculations. These difficulties are identified as **aphasia** (difficulty in grasping spoken language), **dylesia** (difficulty in reading), **hyperlexia** (little or no comprehension), **dyscalculia** (difficulty in doing arithmetic) and **dysgraphia** (difficulty in writing). Some are hyperactive in the sense that they are excessively active inattentive and behave impulsively. They follow instructions poorly and do not often complete the assigned tasks.

Instructional Strategies for Handling Individual Differences

- Organise instruction for the development of cognitive process.
- Use existing cognitive level as base.
- Strengthen memory.
- Formulate level specific instructional strategy.
- Use individual meeting.
- Provide instructions to overcome learning disability.

Do Individuals Differ in Aptitude?

Yes, they do differ. An individual may have a mechanical aptitude, another may have an aptitude for mathematics or yet another may have an aptitude for language, music or athletics. Such differences are due to the differences in the combination of abilities related to the cognitive processes, and the sensory and psychomotor components. For instance, when we talk of mechanical aptitude, we may deal with ability for spatial relations, ability to acquire information on mechanical matters and ability to comprehend mechanical relations, besides sensory and psychomotor abilities. Similarly, when we discuss aptitude in music, we may identify ability for musical memory, pitch discrimination, loudness discrimination, time discrimination and judgement of rhythm. Likewise, abilities required for science or mathematics are different and each requires a separate set of abilities.

The differences in aptitude can be identified using aptitude tests. Aptitude tests for areas such as mechanical skills, mathematics, science, language, music and graphic art can be used to identify the aptitude of students in each area of performance. You might have heard of the use of aptitude tests in medicine, engineering, business management, law or teacher training for selection of students for studies in the respective fields. The aptitude test, in fact, provides a measure of the candidates promise or teachability in a field of study, say, medicine. In other words, the test would tell whether the candidate possesses the required aptitude or readiness to profit from studies in the concerned field of study.

Instructional Strategy for Handling Individual Differences

The suggested approach for handling individual differences is **adaptive instructional system**. In this approach at least two alternative instructional treatments are needed to ensure academic success. Which is the most appropriate instructional treatment for the student depends upon his or her existing level of aptitude (learning readiness). Students with high aptitude may choose unstructured instructional strategy. With minimum guidance from teacher, they may be encouraged to learn through the discovery oriented approach. You may use the inductive process but instructional treatment is essentially learner-centered.

In contrast, highly structured instructional treatment for low aptitude learners is designed in small units through sequential steps and feedback. Frequent summary and review with simplified illustration, analogy and precise explanation of concepts and principles to be learned will facilitate progressive learning. Periodic achievement and aptitude assessments and comparison of these scores with the aptitude scores obtained at the start of instruction would tell the degree to which each learner in the specific treatment group has achieved.

However, for those who are unable to profit from either of the alternative treatments presented above, **compensatory aptitude training** is suggested. This consists of directed reading skill, study habits, self-learning skills, note taking and related activities. The main aim of compensatory aptitude training is to develop readiness for entry into structured treatment. Periodic monitoring should be formulated to identify the students who reach the required level for entry into alternative treatment.

Do Learners Differ in their Academic Achievements?

They do differ, but how? We have seen that those who possess appropriate pre-requisite knowledge learn more effectively than those who lack such knowledge. Differences in pre-requisite knowledge possessed by students create differences in the attainment of knowledge. Further, knowledge is attained progressively. Progressive differences in knowledge attainment leads to cumulative differences in knowledge attainment and this form of differences is often called **Mathew Effect.** It means that academically rich get richer and those who are poor continue to be poor. Thus, differences in pre-requisites and cumulative knowledge lead to differences in the knowledge possessed by the students likewise, they also differ in their capabilities to manipulate the knowledge in a given situation and the differences are identified in terms of the abilities to apply, analyse, synthesise and evaluate knowledge. In fact, ability is an essential condition for learning and the abilities related to intelligence, aptitude and creativity are important for academic achievement. We have seen the instructional strategies for meeting the differences in intelligence, aptitude and creativity through classroom situations. It means that differences in intelligence, aptitude and creativity do create differences in academic achievement.

The differences in academic achievement can be identified using an achievement test in the concerned subject. However, if the achievement test contains only knowledge level items (questions), it tells only knowledge level differences. On the other hand, if it contains items (questions) on knowledge and capabilities—comprehension, application, analysis, synthesis and evaluation—the various levels of differences can be identified. Besides, the total marks, each level-wise total is needed to identify the strengths and weaknesses of every student as well as the differences among students. As a teacher, if you know the strengths and weaknesses of your students in a subject, you may be able to adopt appropriate instructional strategies to suit their strenghts and weaknesses in that subject.

Apart from these achievement differences are quite often identified in terms of categories of achievers by classifying students as high, average and low achievers. Though there is no strict cut-off points, these categories can be created using marks. High achievers are those who possess higher level of knowledge and capabilities (say, with marks 66% and above) than the rest and those who possess average level of knowledge and capabilities (say, with marks 36% to 65%) are called average achievers. On the other extreme, you may find learners with low level knowledge and capabilities (with 35% and below marks). They are called low achievers. If you are interested in identifying the high, average and low achievers in a subject, say Science or language, the categories are created using the marks obtained in the concerned subject. However, categories can also be created based on the overall achievement in a class.

As a teacher, you may be curious to know the strategies for meeting the achievement differences in your classroom or the challenges posed by the strengths and weaknesses of the students in teaching-learning situations. Let us discuss important instructional strategies.

What are Instructional Strategies?

Let us discuss the major strategies to cope up with the differences in academic achievement.

- Provide appropriate pre-requisites to organise and learn new information.
- Use visual aids.
- Use analogy, example and illustration.
- Ensure learner's active involvement in learning.
- Periodic assessment.

EVALUATION AND ASSESSMENT

Evaluation

Evaluation, particularly educational evaluation is a series of activities designed to measure the effectiveness of the teaching-learning systems as a whole. According to Mary Thorpe (1980), ''Evaluation is the collection, analysis and interpretation of information about any aspect of a programme of education.'' Teaching-learning process is a continuous activity. It needs to be evaluated from beginning to end. Evaluation during the learning process (continuous assessment), often termed as ''formative evaluation'', is important for learners and teachers alike.

The bases of evaluation are learning objectives, performance standards and achievement tests on the one hand, and learners' and experts' opinions on the other. Evaluation helps to build an educational programme, assess its achievement and improve upon its effectiveness. It also provides valuable feedback on the design, development and implementation of the programme. It is, of course, an important component of the teaching-learning process. It helps in making the value judgement, determining educational status, or measuring achievement of learners.

The scope of evaluation in schools extents to almost all the areas of learner's personality development. It includes both scholastic and non-scholastic areas. It reveals the strengths and weaknesses of the learners, so that the learners have better opportunity to understand and improve themselves.

Evaluation is helpful to teachers also. It provides feedback to them to reshape their teaching strategies according to the needs of the learners. Evaluation in education in general and in distance education in particular becomes imperative to know as to what extent the goals of education have been achieved.

Thus, evaluation is not merely assigning grades to learners. It is a continuous process of acquiring and processing information in order to improve one's learning and to assess decisions made in designing an instructional system. If we analyse the above statement we easily notice that it has three important implications for the entire teaching-learning system. They are as follows:

1. Evaluation is a continuous process and not a one time performance measurement, effected at the end of a course/programme. It starts at the stage of curriculum development and continues until the instruction ends.
2. Evaluation process is goal-directed. It is aimed at finding ways and means to improve learning and thereby to achieve learning objectives more effectively and more efficiently.
3. Evaluation requires the use of accurate and appropriate measuring instructions to collect information for taking decisions about the quality and operation of education.

It is clear that in designing an effective learning system, one of the earliest steps we need to take is to prepare a comprehensive evaluation plan, which should be developed soon after the learning objectives have been formulated. This practice will help us to:

- determine whether the objectives are attainable or need revisions before we start designing the instructional system;
- collect data/information in a form that suits our purposes adequately and at a time when it is available, otherwise the opportunity to collect specific information may be lost; and
- have sufficient time to test the effectiveness of a design.

Continuous and Comprehensive Evaluation (CCE)

Continuous and Comprehensive Evaluation (CCE) refers to a system of school based evaluation of a student that covers all aspects of a student development. It is a developmental process of student which emphasizes on two fold objectives. These objectives are continuity in evaluation and assessment of broad based learning and behaviourial outcomes on the other.

The term **'continuous'** is meant to emphasise that evaluation of identified aspects of students **'growth and development'** is a continuous process rather than an event, built into the total teaching-learning process and spread over the entire span of academic session. It means regularity of assessment, frequency of unit testing, diagnosis of learning gaps, use of corrective measures, retesting and feedback of evidence to teachers and students for their self evaluation.

The second term **'comprehensive'** means that the scheme attempts to cover both the scholastic and the co-scholastic aspects of the students' growth and development. Since abilities, attitudes and aptitudes can manifest themselves in forms other than the written word, the term refers to application of variety of tools and techniques (both testing and non-testing) and aims at assessing a learner's development in areas of learning, like:

- Knowledge
- Understanding
- Applying
- Analyzing
- Evaluating
- Creating

Objectives of CCE

- To help develop cognitive, psychomotor and affective skills.
- To lay emphasis on thought process and de-emphasise memorization.
- To make evaluation an integral part of teaching-learning process.
- To use evaluation for improvement of students achievement and teaching-learning strategies on the basis of regular diagnosis followed by remedial instructions.
- To use evaluation as a quality control device to maintain desired standard of performance.
- To determine social utility, desirability or effectiveness of a programme and take appropriate decisions about the learner, the process of learning and the learning environment.
- To make the process of teaching and learning a learner-centered activity.

Features of CCE

- The **'continuous'** aspect of CCE takes care of **'continual'** and **'periodicity'** aspect of evaluation.

- Continual means assessment of students in the beginning of instructions (placement evaluation) and assessment during the instructional process (**formative evaluation**) done informally using multiple techniques of evaluation.
- Periodicity means assessment of performance done frequently at the end of unit/term (**summative evaluation**).
- The **'comprehensive'** component of CCE takes care of assessment of all round development of the child's personality. It includes assessment in **Scholastic as well as Co-Scholastic** aspects of the pupil's growth.
- Scholastic aspects include curricular areas or subject specific areas, whereas Co-Scholastic aspects include Life Skills, Co-Curricular Activities, Attitudes and Values.
- Assessment in Scholastic areas is done informally and formally using multiple techniques of evaluation continually and periodically. The diagnostic evaluation takes place at the end of unit/term test. The causes of poor performance in some units are diagnosed using diagnostic tests. These are followed with appropriate interventions followed by retesting.
- Assessment in Co-Scholastic areas is done using multiple techniques on the basis of identified criteria, while assessment in Life Skills is done on the basis of Indicators of Assessment and Checklists.

Functions of CCE

- It helps the teacher to organize effective teaching strategies.
- Continuous evaluation helps in regular assessment to the extent and degree of Learner's progress (ability and achievement with reference to specific Scholastic and Co-Scholastic areas).
- Continuous evaluation serves to diagnose weaknesses and permits the teacher to ascertain an individual learner's strengths and weaknesses and her needs. It provides immediate feedback to the teacher, who can then decide whether a particular unit or concept needs a discussion again in the whole class or whether a few individuals are in need of remedial instruction.
- By continuous evaluation, children can know their strengths and weaknesses. It provides the child a realistic self assessment of how he/she studies. It can motivate children to develop good study habits, to correct errors, and to direct their activities towards the achievement of desired goals. It helps a learner to determine the areas of instruction in where more emphasis is required.
- Continuous and comprehensive evaluation identifies areas of aptitude and interest. It helps in identifying changes in attitudes and value systems.
- It helps in making decisions for the future, regarding choice of subjects, courses and careers.
- It provides information/reports on the progress of students in Scholastic and Co-Scholastic areas and thus helps in predicting the future success of the learner.

Continuous evaluation helps in bringing awareness of the achievement to the child, teachers and parents from time-to-time. They can look into the probable cause of the fall in performance if any, and may take remedial measures of instruction in which more emphasis is required. Many times, because of some personal reasons, family problems or adjustment problems, the children start neglecting their studies, resulting in sudden drop in their performance. If the teacher, child and parents do not notice the sudden drop in the performance of the child in academics, it could result in a permanent deficiency in the childs' learning.

The major emphasis of CCE is on the continuous growth of students ensuring their intellectual, emotional, physical, cultural and social development and therefore, it will not be merely limited to assessment of learner's scholastic attainments. CCE uses assessment as a means of motivating learners to provide feedback and follow up work to improve upon the learning in the classroom and to present a comprehensive picture of a learner's profile. It is this that has led to the emergence of the concept of **School Based Continuous and Comprehensive Evaluation.**

Scholastic and Co-Scholastic Assessment

In order to have Continuous and Comprehensive Evaluation, both Scholastic and Co-Scholastic aspects need to be given due recognition. Such a holistic assessment requires maintaining an ongoing and comprehensive profile for each learner that is honest, encouraging and discreet. While teachers frequently reflect, plan and implement remedial strategies, the child's ability to retain and articulate what has been learned over a period of time also requires periodic assessment. These assessments can take many forms but all of them should be as comprehensive and discreet as possible. **Weekly**, **fortnightly**, or **quarterly** reviews (depending on the learning area), that do not openly compare one learner with another are generally recommended. The objective is to promote and enhance not just learning and retention among children, but their soft skills as well.

Scholastic Assessment

The objectives of the Scholastic domain are:-

- Desirable behaviour related to the learner's knowledge, understanding, application, evaluation, analysis and the ability to apply it in an unfamiliar situation.
- To improve the teaching learning process.
- Assessment should be both **Formative** and **Summative**.

Summative and Formative Assessment

Assessment is often divided into formative and summative categories for the purpose of considering different objectives for assessment practices.

Summative Assessment

Summative assessment is intended to measure learning outcomes and report those outcomes to students, parents and administrators. In an educational setting, it generally occurs at the conclusion of a class, course, semester or academic year. In the context of a course summative assessments are typically used to assign students a course grade. It is also referred to in a learning context as **''assessment of learning''.** **Performance-based assessment** is similar to summative assessment, as it focuses on achievement. A well-defined task is identified and students are asked to create, produce, or do something, often in settings that involve real-world application of knowledge and skills. Proficiency is demonstrated by providing an extended response. Performance formats are further differentiated into products and performances. The performance may result in a product, such as a painting, portfolio, paper, or exhibition, or it may consist of a performance, such as a speech, athletic skill, musical recital, or reading.

Definitions of Summative Assessment

- ''Good summative assessments—tests and other graded evaluations—must be demonstrably reliable, valid, and free of bias'' (Angelo and Cross, 1993).
- '...assessment (that) has increasingly been used to sum up learning' (Black and William, 1999).
- '...looks at past achievements ... adds procedures or tests to existing work ... involves only marking and feedback grades to student ... is separated from teaching ... is carried out at intervals when achievement has to be summarized and reported.' (Harlen, 1998).

Features of Summative Assessment

- Assessment of learning.
- Generally taken by students at the end of a unit or semester to demonstrate the **''sum''** of what they have or have not learned.
- Summative assessment methods are the most traditional way of evaluating student work.

Formative Assessment

Formative assessment is generally carried out throughout a course or project. In an educational setting, formative assessment is used by teachers to consider approaches to teaching and next steps for individual learners and the class, and would not necessarily be used for grading purposes. Formative assessment, also referred to as **''educative assessment''** or **''assessment for learning'',** is used to aid learning. Assessment for learning is defined as ''all those activities undertaken by teachers and/or students, which provide information to be used as feedback to modify the teaching and learning activities in which they are engaged'' (Black and William 2004).

Definitions of Formative Assessment

- '... often means no more than that the assessment is carried out frequently and is planned at the same time as teaching'. (Black and William, 1999)
- '... provides feedback which leads to students recognizing the (learning) gap and closing it ... it is forward looking ...' (Harlen, 1998).
- '... includes both feedback and self-monitoring'. (Sadler, 1989)
- '... is used essentially to get a feedback into the teaching and learning process.' (Tunstall and Gipps, 1996)

Features of Formative Assessment

- Is diagnostic and remedial.
- Makes provision for effective feedback.
- Provides a platform for the active involvement of students in their own learning.
- Enables teachers to adjust teaching to take account of the results of assessment.
- Recognizes the profound influence assessment has on the motivation and self-esteem of students, both of which are crucial influences on learning.
- Recognizes the need for students to be able to assess themselves and understand how to improve.
- Builds on students' prior knowledge and experience in designing what is taught.
- Incorporates varied learning styles to decide how and what to teach.
- Encourages students to understand the criteria that will be used to judge their work.

- Offers an opportunity to students to improve their work after they get the feedback.
- Helps student to support their peer group and vice-versa.

A common form of formative assessment is **"diagnostic assessment"**. Diagnostic assessment measures a student's current knowledge and skills for the purpose of identifying a suitable program of learning. **"Self-assessment"** is a form of diagnostic assessment which involves students assessing themselves. **"Forward-looking assessment"** asks those being assessed to consider themselves in hypothetical future situations.

Co-Scholastic Assessment

The desirable behaviour related to learner's life skills, attitudes, interests, values, co-curricular activities and physical health are described as skills to be acquired in co-scholastic domain.

The process of assessing the students' progress in achieving objectives related to scholastic and co-scholastic domain is called comprehensive evaluation. It has been observed that usually under the scholastic domain such as knowledge and understanding of the facts, concepts, principles etc. of a subject are assessed. The Co-Scholastic elements are either altogether excluded from the evaluation process or they are not given adequate attention. For making the evaluation comprehensive, both Scholastic and Co-Scholastic aspects should be given importance. Simple and manageable means of assessment of Co-Scholastic aspects of growth must be included in the comprehensive evaluation scheme.

Comprehensive evaluation would necessitate the use of a variety of tools and techniques. This will be so because both different and specific areas of learner's growth can be evaluated through certain special techniques.

School Based CCE

School based Evaluation is held at school level unlike external examination conducted by the Boards of School Education. This is done by the teachers according to the schedule developed by the school and guidelines given by the Board. Though this evaluation has been done at school level all along, certain shortcomings have crept into this system. These shortcomings can be attributed to various factors. The basic factor is the misconception of teachers regarding the place of evaluation and its importance in the educational process. The other factor has been the imitation of the practice of external examination which is generally held at the end of the session.

In the School Based System of evaluation, the focus on the purpose of assessment has changed. Now, it includes readiness testing, screening of development, evaluation of performance in cognitive, affective and psychomotor domains more frequently, systematically and effectively.

In other words, School Based Evaluation is child-centred, school-centred and multidimensional evaluation. Hence, in its true spirit, it triggers an all round development of the learner. It encourages all kinds of learning in life both inside the school as well as outside it. It is child-centered as it attempts to consider the learner as a unique entity for its individual pattern of development. It builds on individual child's abilities, progress and development in achieving already set goals and objectives of education as an individual and not just his/her position in relation to other learners.

Further, this evaluation helps a learner to use his/her potential in a better manner and also provides insight to the teachers to discover the methods which may be helpful to the individual learner in resolving his/her problems and difficulties.

Besides being ***child-centred,*** this evaluation is ***school-centred*** as well. It means that no outside agency interferes in this evaluation process. It is entirely school based and done by the teacher. The teacher is trusted and given full responsibility of evaluating students with the brief that the teacher knows best about his/her students.

School Based Evaluation is ***multidimensional.*** Its multidimensional nature is reflected in recognizing and taking care of learners' social, emotional, physical, intellectual and other areas of development which are interrelated and cannot be considered in isolation. It also calls for the use of multiple techniques and tools of evaluation.

Aim of School Based CCE

- Elimination of chance element and subjectivity (as far as possible), de-emphasis on memorization, encouraging comprehensive evaluation incorporating both Scholastic and Co-Scholastic aspects of learners development.
- Continuous evaluation spread over the total span of the instructional time as an integral built-in aspect of the total teaching-learning process.
- Functional and meaningful declaration of results for effective use by teachers, students, parents and the society.
- Wider uses of test results for purposes not merely of the assessment of levels of pupils' achievements and proficiencies, but mainly for their improvement, thorough diagnosis and remedial/enrichment programmes.

- Improvement in the mechanics of conducting examinations for realizing a number of other allied purposes.
- Introduction of concomitant changes in instructional materials and methodology.
- Introduction of the semester system.
- The use of grades in place of marks in determining and declaring the level of pupil performance and proficiency.

Its Characteristics

School Based Evaluation has the following characteristics:

- Is broader, more comprehensive and continuous than traditional system.
- Aims primarily to help learners for systematic learning and development.
- Takes care of the needs of the learner as responsible citizens of the future.
- Is more transparent, futuristic and provides more scope for association among learners, teachers and parents.

School based evaluation provides opportunities to teachers to **know the following about their learners:**

- What they learn?
- How they learn?
- What type of difficulties/limitations they face in working in tandem?
- What do the children think?
- What do the children feel?
- What are their interests and dispositions?

The focus has shifted to developing a deep learning environment. There is a paradigm shift in the pedagogy and competencies from 'controlling' to 'enriching' to 'empowering' schools.

Traditional Schooling	Enriching Schooling	Empowering Schooling
• Teacher centred	• Student centred	• Experience centred
• Subjects and classes-teacher directed	• Self directed	• Virtual authenticity
• Sorting and ranking individuals	• Continuous assessment	• Multi literacies
Competency:	**Competency:**	**Competency:**
• Memory	• Critical thinking	• Risk taking
• Competitive	• Collaborative	• Ethical
	• Creative	• Interactive

Implementing School Based Assessment would mean:

- Elimination of chance element and subjectivity (as far as possible), de-emphasis of memorization, encouraging Comprehensive evaluation incorporating both scholastic and co-scholastic aspects of learners development.
- Continuous evaluation spread over the total span of the instructional time as an integral built-in aspect of the total teaching-learning process.
- Functional and meaningful declaration of results for effective use by teachers, students, parents and the society.
- Wider uses of test results for purposes not merely of the assessment of levels of pupils' achievements and proficiencies, but mainly for its improvement, through diagnosis and remedial/enrichment programmes.
- Improvements in the mechanics of conducting examinations for realizing a number of other allied purposes.
- Introduction of concomitant changes in instructional materials and methodology.
- Introduction of the semester system from the secondary stage onwards.
- The use of grades in place of marks in determining and declaring the level of pupil performance and proficiency.

The above goals are relevant for both external examination and evaluation in schools.

Shortcoming of Traditional External Examination

- It is a one shot examination at the end of a year at the terminal stage of schooling.
- It mainly evaluates only the scholastic aspects of learning of the students.
- It does not evaluate all the abilities of the children. On the basis of marks obtained in written examination the students are declared pass or fail and further classified into predetermined divisions.

- Pass and fail system causes frustration and is inhumane because the failed candidates come to feel that they are good for nothing.
- Co-scholastic areas are almost totally ignored and have no place in the currently prevalent scheme of education and evaluation.
- The practice of testing of untaught content also reflects poor learning achievement.
- Only limited techniques of evaluation without potential for judging a student are being used.
- The aim of evaluation is to improve learner's quality which is not served by external examination.
- The current practice of awarding marks suffers from many discrepancies due to variety of errors.
- The varied ranges of obtained scores of students in different subjects create the problem in declaring reliable results.
- Analysis and interpretation of test results is not done in a scientific way.

School Based Continuous and Comprehensive Evaluation System should be Established to:

- reduce stress on children.
- make evaluation comprehensive and regular.
- provide space for the teacher for creative teaching.
- provide a tool of diagnosis and remediation.
- produce learners with greater skills.

Four Assessment Paradigms

Assessment *of* Learning

The 'assessment **of** learning' is defined as a process whereby someone attempts to describe and quantify the knowledge, attitudes or skills possessed by another. Teacher direction is paramount and the student has little involvement in the design or implementation of the assessment process in these circumstances.

- Teacher designs learning
- Teacher collects evidence
- Teacher judges what has been learnt (and what has not been learnt)

Assessment *for* Learning

The 'assessment **for** learning' involves increased level of student autonomy, but not without teacher guidance and collaboration. The assessment **for** learning is sometimes seen as being akin to 'formative assessment'. There is more emphasis towards giving useful advice to the student and less emphasis on the giving of marks and the grading function.

- Teacher designs learning
- Teacher designs assessment with feedback to student
- Teacher judges what has been learnt (student develops insight into what has not)

Assessment *as* Learning

The 'assessment **as** learning' is perhaps more connected with diagnostic assessment and can be constructed with more of an emphasis on peer learning. Assessment **as** learning generates opportunities for self assessment and peer assessment. Students take on increased responsibility to generate quality information about their learning and that of others.

- Teacher and student co-construct learning
- Teacher and student co-construct assessment
- Teacher and student co-construct learning progress map

Assessment **for** learning and assessment **as** learning activities should be deeply embedded in teaching and learning and be the source of interactive feedback, allowing students to adjust, re-think and re-learn.

Assessment *in* Learning

The 'assessment **in** learning' places the question at the centre of teaching and learning. It deflects the teaching from its focus on a 'correct answer' to a focus on 'a fertile question'. Through enquiry students engage in processes that generates feedback about their learning, which come from multiple sources and activities. It contributes to the construction of other learning activities, line of enquiry and the generation of other questions.

- Student as the centre of learning
- Student monitors, assesses and reflects on learning
- Student initiates demonstration of learning (to self and others)
- Teacher as coach and mentor.

Teachers and students need to understand the purpose of each assessment strategy. The overall assessment 'package' being used by learners and teachers should accurately capture, generate and use meaningful learning information to generate deep learning and understanding.

ASSESSING LEARNERS

Any meaningful report on the quality and extent of a child's learning needs to be comprehensive. We need a curriculum whose creativity, innovativeness, and development of the whole being, the hallmark of a good education makes uniform tests that assess memorised facts and textbook-based learning obsolete. We need to redefine and seek new parameters for and ways of evaluation and feedback. In addition to the learner's achievements in specific subject areas that lend themselves to testing easily, assessment would need to encompass attitudes to learning, interest, and the ability to learn independently.

ASSESSMENT IN THE COURSE OF TEACHING

Preparing report cards is a way for the teacher to think about each individual child and review what she/he has learnt during the term, and what she/he needs to work on and improve. To be able to write such report cards, teachers would need to think about each individual child, and hence pay attention to them during their everyday teaching and interaction. One does not need special tests for this; learning activities themselves provide the basis for such ongoing observational and qualitative assessments of children. Maintaining a daily diary based on observation helps in continuous and comprehensive evaluation. An extract from the diary of a teacher for a week notes the following: "Kiran enjoyed his work. He took an instant liking to the books that were informative and brief. He says that he likes simple and clear language. In noting down facts, he goes for short answers. He says that it helps him understand things easily. He favours a practical approach." Similarly, keeping samples and notes of the child's work at different stages provides both the teacher and the learner herself or himself with a systematic record of his/her learning progress.

The belief that assessment must lead to finding learning difficulties to then be remediated is often very impractical and not founded on a sound understanding of pedagogic practice. Problems regarding conceptual development cannot and do not wait for formal tests in order to be detected. A teacher can, in the course of teaching itself, come to know of such problems by asking questions that make children think or by giving them small assignments. She can then attend to them in the process of teaching—by ensuring that her planning is flexible and responsive to the learners and their learning.

CURRICULAR AREAS THAT CANNOT BE 'TESTED FOR MARKS'

Each area of the curriculum may not lend itself to being 'tested'; it may even be antithetical to the nature of learning in the curricular area. This includes areas such as work, health, yoga, physical education, music and art. While the skill-based component of physical education and yoga could be tested, the health aspect needs continuous and qualitative assessments. Currently, this has the effect of making these subjects and activities 'less important' in the curriculum; these areas are inadequately provided for in terms of material resources and curricular planning, and marked by a lack of seriousness. Further, the time allocated for them is also frequently sacrificed to accommodate special classes. This is a serious compromise with parts of the curriculum that have deep educational significance and potential.

Even if 'marks' cannot be given, children can be assessed for their development in these areas. Participation, interest, and level of involvement, and the extent to which abilities and skills have been honed, are some markers that can help teachers to gauge the benefits of what children learn and gain through such activities. Asking children to self-report on their learning can also provide teachers with insight into children's educational progress and give them feedback on improving curriculum or pedagogy.

DESIGN AND CONDUCT OF ASSESSMENT

Assessments and examinations must be credible, and based on valid ways of gauging learning.

As long as examinations and tests assess children's ability to remember and recall textbook knowledge, all attempts to redirect the curriculum towards learning will be thwarted. First, tests in knowledge-based subject areas must be able to gauge what children have learnt, and their ability to use this knowledge for problem solving and application in the real world. In addition, they must also be able to test the processes of thinking to gauge if the learner has also learnt where to find information, how to use new information, and to analyse and evaluate the same.

The types of questions that are set for assessment need to go beyond what is given in the book. Often children's learning is restricted as teachers do not accept their answers if they are different from what is presented in the guidebooks.

Questions that are open-ended and challenging could also be used. Designing good test items and questions is an art, and teachers should spend time thinking about and devising such questions. The interest and ability of teachers to design good questions can be promoted through district—or state-level competitions. All question papers must be designed graded for difficulty in order to permit all children to experience a level of success, and to gain confidence in their ability to answer and solve problems.

Trying to devise a good and effective open-book examination can be a challenge that we must try to take up in our curricular efforts at all levels of school. This would require teachers and examination setters to emphasise the interpretation and application of learning over the arguments and facts that can be located in the book. There have been successful demonstrations that such examinations can be carried out on a large scale, and that teachers can themselves be trusted with moderating the results of such examinations. In this way, the assessment of projects and lab work can also be made credible and sound.

It is important that after receiving their corrected papers, children rewrite the answers and that these are again reviewed by teachers to ensure that children have learnt and gained something out of the ordeal.

Competition is motivating, but it is an extrinsic rather than intrinsic form of motivation. It is, of course, much easier to establish and to manipulate, and therefore frequently resorted to by teachers and school systems as a way creating and nurturing the drive for excellence. Schools begin 'ranking' children as early as their pre-primary years as a way of inculcating in them a competitive spirit. Such a competitive drive has several negative side effects on learning, often superficial learning is sufficient to create and maintain impressions, and over time students lose their ability to take initiative or do things for the fulfilment of one's own interest; hence, areas that cannot be 'marked' are neglected. This has unhealthy consequences for classroom culture, making children individualistic and unsuited to team work. There is an absurd and unnecessary importance given to term examinations, often accompanied by extreme arrangements of invigilation and secrecy. While the physical and psychological effects of this may not be readily visible until middle school, they frequently lead to high levels of stress in children, and cause early burnout. Schools and teachers need to ask themselves whether there is really much to be gained out of such practices and to what extent learning requires such systems of marking and ranking.

SELF-ASSESSMENT AND FEEDBACK

The role of assessment is to gauge the progress that both learner and teacher have made towards achieving the aims that have been set and appraising how this could be done better. Opportunity for feedback, leading to revision and improvement of performance, should constantly be available, without exams and evaluations being used as a threat to study.

Grading and correction carried out in the presence of students and providing feedback on the answers they get right and wrong, and why. Asking children about why they answered what they did assists teachers in going beyond the written answer to engage with children's thinking. Such processes also take away the frightening judgemental quality of marks obtained in a test, and enable children to understand and focus on their mistakes and learn through these mistakes. Sometimes head teachers object, claiming that correction in the presence of the child reduces 'objectivity'. This is a misplaced concern for 'objectivity', stemming from a competitive system that believes in judging children. Such a concern for 'objectivity' is misplaced in evaluation, which is consistent with educational goals.

Not only learning outcomes but also learning experiences themselves must be evaluated. Learners happily comment on the totality of their experience. Exercises, both individual and collective, can be designed to enable them to reflect on and assess their learning experiences. Such experiences also provide them with self-regulatory capabilities essential for 'learning to learn'. Such information is also valuable feedback to the teacher, and can be used to modify the learning system as a whole.

Every classroom interaction with children requires their evaluation of their own work, and a discussion with them about what should be tested and the ways of finding out whether the competencies are being developed or not. Even very young children are able to give correct assessments of what they can or cannot do well. The role of teaching is to provide an opportunity to each child to learn to the best of his or her ability and provide learning experiences that develop cognitive qualities, physical well-being and athletic qualities, as also affective and aesthetic qualities.

Report cards need to present to children and parents a comprehensive and holistic view of the child's development in many fields. Teachers must be able to say things about each child/student, that conveys to them a sense of individualised attention, reaffirms a positive self-image, and communicates personal goals for them to work towards. Whether it is marks or grades that are reported, a qualitative statement by the teacher is necessary to support the assessment. Only through such a relationship with each child can any teacher succeed in influencing him/her, and contributing to his/her learning. Along with the teacher assessing each child, each student could also assess himself or herself and include this self-assessment in the report card.

Currently, many report cards carry information on subject areas and have nothing to say about other aspects of the child's development, including health, physical fitness and abilities in games, social skills, and abilities in art and craft. Qualitative statements about these aspects of children's education and development would provide a more holistic assessment of educational concerns.

AREAS THAT REQUIRE FRESH THINKING

There are many areas of the curriculum that can be assessed but for which we still do not have reliable and efficient instruments. This includes assessing learning that is carried out in groups, and learning in areas such as theatre, work and craft where skills and competencies develop over longer time scales and require careful observation.

Continuous and comprehensive evaluation has frequently been cited as the only meaningful kind of evaluation. This also requires much more careful thinking through about when it is to be employed in a system effectively. Such evaluation places a lot of demand on teachers' time and ability to maintain meticulous records if it is to be meaningfully executed and if it is to have any reliability as an assessment. If this simply increases stress on children by reducing all their activities into items for assessment, or making them experience the teacher's 'power', then it defeats the purpose of education. Unless a system is adequately geared for such assessment, it is better for teachers to engage in more limited forms of evaluation, but incorporating into them more features that will make the assessment a meaningful record of learning.

Finally, there is a need to evolve and maintain credibility in assessment so that they perform their function of providing feedback in a meaningful way.

ASSESSMENT AT DIFFERENT STAGES

ECCE and Classes I and II of the Elementary Stage: At this stage, assessment must be purely qualitative judgements of children's activities in various domains and an assessment of the status of their health and physical development, based on observations through everyday interactions. On no account should they be made to take any form of test, oral or written.

Class III to Class VIII of the Elementary Stage: A variety of methods may be used, including oral and written tests and observations. Children should be aware that they are being assessed, but this must be seen by them as a part of the teaching process and not as a fearful constant threat. Grades or marks along with qualitative judgements of achievement and areas requiring attention are essential at this stage. Children's own self-evaluation can also be a part of the report card from Class V onwards. Rather than examinations, there could be short tests from time-to-time, which are criterion based. Term-wise examinations could be commenced from Class VII onwards when children are more psychologically ready to study large chunks of material and, to spend a few hours in an examination room, working at answering questions. Again, the progress card must indicate general observations on health and nutrition, specific observations on the overall progress of the learner, and information and advice for the parents.

Class IX to Class XII of the Secondary and Higher Secondary Stages: Assessment may be based more on tests, examinations and project reports for the knowledge-based areas of the curriculum, along with self-assessment. Other areas would be assessed through observation and also through self-evaluation.

Reports could include much more analysis about the students, various skill/knowledge areas and percentiles, etc. This would assist them by pointing out the areas of study that they need to focus on, and also help them by providing a basis for further choices that they make regarding what to study thereafter.

CONCEPT OF INCLUSIVE EDUCATION & UNDERSTANDING CHILDREN WITH SPECIAL NEEDS

CONCEPT OF INCLUSIVE EDUCATION

Every child is special for his/her parent and, every child has a special need for love, acceptance and a feeling of belongingness. Here, we call **children with special needs** to those who are "different" from their cohorts. They are born equal with some limitations and with the help of inclusion be able to actively participate as equal citizens in all aspects of society and community life. Thus, children with special needs refer to "all those children who require adaptations to the normal process of education due to problems of vision, hearing, movement, learning and intellect." In other words, these children have some kind of **disability**.

Inclusive Education denotes that all children irrespective of their strengths and weaknesses will be part of the mainstream education. Thus, inclusive education means, "the act of ensuring that all children despite their differences, receive the opportunity of being part of the same classroom as other children of their age, and in the process get the opportunity to being exposed to the curriculum to their optimal potential."

EDUCATIONAL PROVISIONS FOR CHILDREN WITH SPECIAL NEEDS

The last two decades of the 19th century has witnessed the knowledge and processes of educating the disabled children through Christian Missionaries. The first school for the deaf was established in Mumbai in 1883 and the first school for the blind in Amritsar in 1887. At that time, it was believed that children with disabilities could not be educated alongwith normal children. Therefore, education to disabled children was offered through special school. This trend continued early sixties of the last century with the help of some international agencies who developed programme of integrated education. Here, children disabilities were placed in regular school so that they could study alongwith their non-disabled 'peers". The integrated education adopts various models for service deliver. Presently the emphasis is on the need to provide education for all in appropriate environment with inclusive philosophy through inclusive education.

INTEGRATED EDUCATION FOR THE DISABLED CHILDREN (IEDC)

With the development of science and technology and improvement in Medical Services and Aggressive neo-natal intervention has ensured that a large number of babies who would earlier have not survived but often with different abilities. The number of differently abled children is on the increasing trend but it is not possible to create the required number of special schools throughout the country to meet this challenge due to the high cost and also due to the fact that the population is so scattered. The best alternative under these situations is to make use of the infrastructural facilities already present in terms of regular schools and integrate children into the mainstream of education.

Consequent on the success of international institutions in introducing differently abled children in regular schools, the planning commission, Govt. of India, in 1971 includes in its plan a programme for integrated education. In 1974, the Union Government introduced a scheme called "Integrated Schools" to do just this. This scheme was later revised and a plan of action formulated. The important aims of IEDC includes:

- Provide educational opportunity to differently abled children in regular schools.
- Facilitate retention of differently abled in the school system.

- Integrate children from special school to common schools.

The scope of the scheme of IEDC includes pre-school training, counselling for the parents, and special training in skills for all kinds of differently abled children. It provides facilities in the form of books, stationary, uniforms and allowances for transport, reader and escort etc.

Project Integrated Education for the Disabled (PIED)

This scheme was launched by MHRD Govt. of India in collaboration with UNICEF in 1987 to strengthen the integration of differently abled into regular schools. Under this scheme, a cluster instead of individual school is given importance. This scheme is an improvement over the special schools in one or many ways and provides a way towards universalisation of elementary education and Education for All including for differently abled children.

Assumption About Integrated Education

Integrated education assumes a process of bringing disabled children into mainstream schools, where the system remains the same. As per the system, the child is the problem. So, it is essential to change the child where the resources are focused on the individual child. The failure is due to the child's problem; he is not able, not ready, not good enough to cope up with the system.

In integrated education; it is the children with disabilities who are seen as the problem, who must be "fixed", "changed" & "adapted" to suit the existing regular, mainstream school. It is the disabled child who is seen as a square peg in a round table. The system remains the same. The onus for successful integration therefore, is on the disabled child.

Assumption About Inclusive Education

Assumptions of inclusive education is opposite to integrated education. Inclusive education assumes that changes the system to fit the child. It is essential to addresses all types of individual needs, not just disability. Teachers and schools are held responsible for children's learning. It focuses on flexibility of curriculum, teacher training and change in environmental. Failure is the problem with the system not with the child. It is quite essential to assumes that all children can learn and that all children need their learning to be supported in diverse ways.

In this model of inclusive education, it is not the child, but the education system, which is seen as a problem. Therefore, it is the system (with all its components) with should be changed, modified & made flexible enough to accommodate the diverse needs of all learners, including children with disabilities. The onus for success is therefore on the flexibility of the system. It focuses on the environment, as the "disabling" cause because it fails to provide appropriate access to equal opportunities for all persons to participate fully in social life.

Though integrated education of differently abled children has gained momentum all over the country since 1974, there are some other possibilities too for these children to get education. For example, the NIOS (National Institute of Open Schooling) offers education which have the advantage of being specially adopted to the needs of every child as well as aimed at giving the child every opportunity to progress at his/her pace. Another example is alternative schooling and community-based rehabilitation programmes.

EDUCATION FOR A COHESIVE SOCIETY

Despite more than half a century of independence, India is struggling for freedom from various kinds of biases and imbalances such as rural/urban, rich/poor, and differences on the basis of caste, religion, ideology, gender etc. Education can play a very significant role in minimising and finally eliminating these differences by providing equality of access to quality education and opportunity.

Equality of opportunity means ensuring that every individual receives suitable education at a pace and through methods suited to his/her being. Children of the disadvantaged, and socially discriminated groups and also those suffering from specific challenges must be paid special attention.

Provision for equal opportunity to all not only in access, but also in the conditions for success is a precondition for the promotion of equality. The curriculum must create an awareness of the inherent equality of all with a view to removing prejudices and complexes transmitted through the social environment and the factor of birth.

EDUCATION OF GIRLS

Equality among sexes is a fundamental right under the constitution of India. The state, however, also has the right to exercise positive protective discrimination in favour of the disadvantaged population groups including women. Emphasis in education has moved from 'Equality of Educational Opportunity' (NPE, 1968) to 'Education for Women's Equality and Empowerment' (1986). As a result, the curricular and training strategies for the education of girls now demand more attention. Besides, making education accessible to more and more girls, especially rural girls, removing all gender discrimination and gender bias in school curriculum, textbooks and the process of transaction is absolutely necessary. There is a need to develop and implement gender inclusive and gender sensitive curricular strategies to nurture a generation of girls and boys who are equally competent and are sensitive to one another, and grow up in a caring and sharing mode as equals, and not as adversaries.

EDUCATION OF LEARNERS FROM DISADVANTAGED GROUPS

For achieving a cohesive society it would be essential to respond to specific educational needs of learners from different sections of the society with special emphasis on the Scheduled Castes, the Scheduled Tribes and the other socially and economically disadvantaged groups. In order to do so, there is a need for integrating the socio-cultural perspectives partly by showing concern for their linguistic specificities and pedagogic requirements. Implications of the multilingual and multicultural environment shall have to be taken care of through specifically devised methodology. Contextualisation of curriculum shall have to be effected through curricular materials. The fundamental rights of the disadvantaged groups have to be consciously incorporated in the curriculum. Even the problem of educating the migrating population shall have to be handled through specific condensed educational programmes based on the main ingredients of the national curriculum.

EDUCATION OF THE GIFTED AND TALENTED

An educational system has the dual role of promoting equality as well as excellence. Education is increasingly called upon to liberate all the creative potentialities of human consciousness. Man essentially fulfils himself in and through creation. It is in the context of this, that education of gifted and talented children assumes great importance. A curricular programme while on the one hand should identify such children, on the other it should also nurture their diverse creative abilities by paying them special attention. It is also important that the identification and nurturance begins right from the earliest stage of education. Moreover, the task of identifying the gifted and talented must be accomplished on the basis of a broad conceptualisation of the process from multiple perspectives rather than as a search for a unitary human attribute. Not only their IQ (Intelligence Quotient) but also their EQ (Emotional Quotient) and SQ (Spiritual Quotient) ought to be assessed.

NATIONAL LEVEL POLICY AND LEGISLATION

Kothari Commission (1964-66)

The Kothari Commission first suggested that the education of handicapped children has to be organised not merely on humanitarian grounds, but also an aspects of utility. The commission emphasised that the education of children with disability should be "an inseparable part of the general education system. The commission also specifically emphasised that the education of children with disability should be "an inseparable part of the general education system. The commission also specifically emphasised. the importance of integrated education in meeting this target as it is cost effective and useful in developing mutual understanding between children with and without disabilities.

National Policy on Education (1986)

The National Policy on Education was adopted by Indian Parliament in 1986. The policy emphasized the removal of disparities, and ensuring equalisation of educational opportunity under its para education of the disabled.

National Policies for Persons with Disabilities (2006)

This recognises that persons with disabilities are valuable human resources for the country and seek to create an environment that provides them equal opportunities, protection of their rights and full participation in society.

Persons with Disabilities (Equal Opportunities, Protection of Rights & Full Participation) Act, 1995

Landmark legislation in the history of special education in India is the persons with Disabilities Act, 1995. This comprehensive Act covers seven disabilities, namely blindness, low vision, hearing impaired, loco-motor impaired, mental retardation, leprosy cured and mental illness.

The Rehabilitation Council of India (RCI) Act, 1992

This Act was passed in 1992 for the purpose of constituting the Rehabilitation Professionals and for maintenance of a Central Rehabilitation Register. It was amended by Rehabilitation Council of India (Amendment) Act, 2000 to provide for monitoring the training of rehabilitation professionals and personal, promoting research in rehabilitation and special education as additional objectives of the council.

LEARNING AND PEDAGOGY

LEARNING

A considerable change in the behaviour of the organism is called learning. When organism comes in contact with his environment certain necessary adjustment in the behaviour is needed. This adjustment in behaviour is the result of acquision of various habits, skills, attitudes and knowledge which is actually learning in simple term

Thus, learning means change in response or behaviour (modification, elimination or acquisition of responses involving some degree of performance) caused partly or wholly by conscious or unconscious experiences. This learning does not include physiological changes such as fatigue, temporary sensory resistance or non functioning even after continued stimulation.

Definition of Learning

It is very difficult to give a universally acceptable definition of learning because psychologists have defined the concept from different angles on the basis of their experiments. The common feature among these definitions is that learning in psychology has the status of a construct which means an idea or image that can not be directly observed like electrons or genes but they are inferred from the behaviour of the organism.

Melvin H Marx has defined learning in the following words;

"Learning is a relatively enduring change in behaviour which is a function of prior behaviour (usually called practice)

Explanation : According to the definition given above learning has three attributes:

1. Learning is a some what permanent change in behaviour. Changes occurred due to illness, fatigue, maturation or the consumption of intoxicants is not learning.
2. Learning is not directly observable. It is inferred from the behaviour of the organism in the form of construct.
3. Learning is a function of practice and experience. Experiences adds learning and practice gives it an enduring nature.

Some other **definitions** of learning are given below;

"Learning is modification of behaviour through experiences." **— Gates**

"Learning involves the acquisition of habit knowledge and attitudes". **—Crow and Crow**

"Learning is any change in behaviour resulting from behaviour." **—Guilford**

"Learning includes both acquisition and retention." **—Skinner**

"Any activity can be called learning so far as it develops the individual (in any respect good or bad) and makes him after behaviour and experiences different from what that would otherwise have been." **—Woodworth**

"The term learning covers every modification in behaviour to meet environmental requirement". **—Gardner Murply**

"Learning is the process by which behaviour (in the broader sense) is originated or changed through practice or training." **—Kingsley and Garry**

"Learning is the acquisition of new behaviour or the strengthening or weakening of old behaviour as a result of experience." **—Henry P. Smith**

"Learning is an episode in which a motivated individual attempts to adapt his behaviour so as to succeed in a situation which he perceives as requiring action to attain a goal."

— **Presey, Robinson & Horrocks**

"Learning is the process by which an activity originates or is changed through reacting to an encountered situation, provided that the characteristics of the changes in activity can not be explained on the basis of native response tendencies maturation or temporary state of the organism (e.g. fatigue or drugs etc.)

—**Milgard**

Characteristics of Learning

On the basis of the meaning and definitions given above following characteristics of learning can be derived:

1. **Learning is a relatively permanent change in behaviour :** Temporary changes in behaviour brought about due to some accidents or consuming any drugs is not learning at all. Learning is a relatively permanent change in behaviour. It is in this context we can say that reading some selected material to pass an examination is not learning. It is because learnt material is forgotten immediately after the exam.
2. **Learning is a progress or growth of the organism :** Learning is a fundamental need of life. Without it, no progress or growth is possible. This process of growth is unending also. One achievement of the organism motivates him to go for further achievement and thus excellence in many cases is achieved.
3. **Learning is a life long process :** An organism needs learning (behavioural change) at every moment of life to adjust to new situations at every moment. He can not sit idle at any time. Situations all the time force him for the acquisition of new learning.
4. **Learning is not directly observable :** How much learning has taken place in an organism can not be directly observed. It is inferred from his behaviour which is manifested by some activities, mental or physical.
5. **Learning is the result of experiences :** Experiences are gained at every moment of life. Learning is the other name of these experiences.
6. **Learning is a goal directed process :** Learning is a purposeful activity. It is a goal directed process. Learning which is the result of unconscious efforts of the individual is not learning in actual sense.
7. **Learning is retained through practice :** Practice or exercise is a must to retain learning. If practice is not made, learning will be forgotten and the nature of learning will no longer remain permanent. Thus, learning is acquisition and retention both.
8. **Learning reinforces further learning :** Learning definitely gives satisfaction to the individual which further motivates him for higher level of learning. Similarly, learning which is accompanied by reinforcement is more likely to become permanent and motivating for further learning.
9. **Learning is motivated by adjustment :** Man has to adjust himself according to the new environment. In this way learning is an adjustment.
10. **Learning is aroused by individual and social needs :** Learning depends upon our social needs, problems, desires, and ideals. There are certain persons who learn very fast whereas others are slow in learning. It should be noticed that social environment affects learning. It is impossible to learn in the absence of environment.
11. **Learning is transferable :** It means that learning may change place but the quantum of change in the place may be different. Change in the place is caused by techniques, ideals and the process. Change of place takes place from one field of education to the other field and from one class to other class.
12. **Learning is a process not a product :** Learning is a product for public at large but a psychologist considers it a process which has got the following four shapes-Need, Goal, adjustment and change.
13. **Improvement in the behaviour through learning :** When man reacts to the environment there is progressive modification of behaviour through learning. That is why, learning is known as improvement.
14. **Learning is active and creative :** Learning is active and creative i.e. learning depends upon the active involvement of the learner. It is said that if the learner is not self active, he cannot learn.

    It is, therefore, said that learning is the result of active involvement and experience from the sender and the receiver both.
15. **Learning is universal :** Humans are not the only organism that learn ie, react to the environment for adjustment. Animals also go through the process of learning though their speed of learning may be slower than humans.

Learning differentiated from Some Concepts

1. **Learning and instinct :** Some behaviour of every organism is reflexive or inborn, eg, breathing, breast feeding etc. All such activities take place without the process of learning. As we move to lower animals reflexes or instincts are seen more and more in their behaviour. The least example of instincts are found in humans. These instincts are not the result of any learning or experiences. They are relatively invariant in form and are reliably elicited or released by a particular and usually very simple stimulus (R Habber 1966) Thus learning is not needed for instincts or reflexive behaviour.
2. **Learning and maturation :** Maturation means physiological development of the individual according to the norms of a particular age. Learning and maturation are very closely related in the sense that for a successful learning, a definite level of maturation is a must. Thus learning is induced by maturation. For example, we can not teach quantum mechanics to a six year old child due to lack of maturation.

   Maturation on the other hand, is qualitative changes in the organism which are not induced by learning. Maturation is an increase in competency and adaptability according to Baldwin.

   Thus, we see that maturation is purely an internal process in the organism and learning is an external process more than an internal change in the behaviour of the organism. Learning and training should start only when a child must have reached an appropriate level of maturation. Maturation is actually the readiness for an activity due to physiological preparation.
3. **Leaning and cramming :** Cramming does not bring about any change in the behaviour of a student. So, cramming can never be called as learning. Despite this fact, in order to make a durable or permanent change in the behaviour of an organism, cramming will be very much helpful.
4. **Learning and acquisition of knowledge :** Acquisition of knowledge and skills is generally termed as learning but if that change of behaviour in the organism is not applied in any situation in any manner, mere accumulation of facts and information is not learning in real sense.
5. **Learning and education :** As the meaning of education suggested by the Good's dictionary of education, education is the aggregate of all the processes, by means of which a persons develops his abilities, attitudes and other forms of behaviour of positive value in the society in which the organism lives. Learning is also a process of change in the behaviour of the organism but this change may be of positive and negative value both.

Mental Process Involved in Learning

Learning may be the result of conditioning of behaviour but following mental processes are also involved in learning:

1. **Direction :** The person must be directed to the process of learning. It means that he must be full attentive to the process. He must have a clear cut goal for learning and he must take full interest to achieve that goal.
2. **Interpretation :** Learning needs perception, reaction to the stimuli and then concepts formation. The organism must realize all these relations in his mind.
3. **Selection :** So many stimuli or experiences may be there before the organism at the time of learning. He selects and recalls only those stimuli and experiences which are relevant to the situation.
4. **Insight :** When organism comes across a number of stimuli and experiences, he tries to find out various types of relationship among them. An insight helps him to reach the correct relationship.
5. **Creation :** When learning takes place, certain new mental pattern is formed which forces the organism to think and act in a new way.
6. **Criticism :** When an organism learns something (his behaviour is changed) he does not accept it so easily. he evaluates all workable solutions in his mind before putting it into application or practice.

TYPES OF LEARNING

Different criteria of classification of learning are given below:

(A) Learning according to the development of body organs

Such type of learning can broadly be classified into two categories:

1. **Motor learning :** It involves motor and muscular parts of the body. Motor learning is

also of two types sensory motor and perceptual motor. Sensory motor learning is related to the acquisition of simple habits through sense organs. Learning of skills in nursery school play ground is a good example of sensory motor learning.

Perceptual motor learning is related to the acquisition of social habits and complex motor skills. Dancing, cycling, handwriting, typing, swimming, driving, playing a musical instrument, etc, are some examples of perceptual motor learning. It is very much objective in nature.

2. **Ideational learning :** In this type of learning, muscular or motor activity is not needed. It is related to the acquisition of concepts, ideas and mental associations. This type of learning is mostly subjective in nature.

Ideational learning can also be classified into the following categories.

(i) Perceptual learning which mostly comes through senses (direct experiences with the objects). Learning through concrete materials, learning through written or spoken symbols,, drawing a picture, nature study and sight seeing are some examples of perceptual learning

(ii) Conceptual learning is the other name of abstract learning. It is related to the acquisition of concepts and abstract ideas.

(iii) Associative learning is learned incidentally or by connecting two different types of learning. Prescribed sequence is followed while linking one information with the other.

(iv) Imaginative learning is the process by which things of the past, present and future are given a definite form. It involves the acquisition of images and understanding of things beyond the normal range of sensory experiences.

(B) Learning according to the domains of behaviour involved

Domains of human behaviour are three, cognitive, affective, and psychomotor so, learning can also be classified into these three categories.

1. **Cognitive learning :** It is related to the acquisition of knowledge, understanding of concepts, inter-relationship of various concepts and ideas etc. This type of learning is 90% emphasized in the classroom. Here only mind is brought into action. When this type of learning is well developed, a learner is able to generalize and evaluate concepts as well as personal experiences.

2. **Attitudinal learning :** Attitudes, values and social systems are also learnt by the individual. This type of learning begins with the feeling of belongingness of a person to his group. How a person should react to others in various types of emotional situations is the result of this type of learning.

3. **Skill learning and habit formation :** Motor behaviour of the individual along with feeling is involved here. Practice is an important aspect of this type of learning. Reading, writing, playing a certain game or doing some physical job with perfection is the result of this type of learning.

(C) Gagne's classification of learning

Gagne has classified learning into eight categories in a hierarchical order as given below.

1. **Signal learning :** This is called classical conditioning learning developed by Russian psychologist Pavlov. In this learning unconditioning stimulus (food) and conditioned stimulus, (sound of the bell are paired together and presented to a dog a number of times. Due to this paring sound of the bell (conditioned) stimulus also forces the dog to elicit the response (to salivate) This secretion of saliva by the sound of the bell is called conditioning. Sound of the bell works as signal here.

2. **Stimulus-response learning (operant conditioning) :** This study of operant conditioning started with the work of E.L. Thorndike He placed a hungry cat in a box and dish of food was kept outside. When cat manipulated the lever of the box correctly, it opened and cat could get food. Here manipulation of lever as a response is instrumental in producing the reward (food) here hence, this learning is also called instrumental conditioning. Instrumental conditioning is more flexible than classical one in the sense that responses are conditioned here to a variety of efforts. Such experiments were conducted and improved further by Skinner to explain operant nature of behaviour in a set form with the help of reinforcement.

3. **Chain learning :** Chaining means connection between S-R is formed in sequence Chaining is of two types, motor and verbal. Using remote controller to switch on or off a T V is an example of motor sequence and greeting a guest at home is an example of verbal sequence.

In verbal chaining, two or more previously learned verbal sequences in stimulus response form are chained. If first member or the second member word of the sequence comes, the other member will automatically come, such as mummy daddy, chhola bhatora, old, young etc. Opposite words are also used in the sequence to form a chain.

In motor chaining, a number of related activities are tied in such a sequence that one activity will necessarily be followed by the other. Driving a car or weaving cloth on a handloom are best examples of motor chain. The driver of a car comes to the next activity taking the gear into neutral position immediately after applying the brakes. This second activity is chained in a sequence.

It must be noted here that a chain can not be established unless the organism is capable of linking various acts in a sequence.

4. **Verbal associate learning :** In this type of learning verbal language is also used along with showing an object, ie, seeing is associated with a word. For example, we show an object to a child and say that it is monkey. Next time when the child will see an object exactly or almost similar to the object previously seen by him, he will name it as monkey.

Two types of chaining are involved here:

(i) Observing S-R connection that connects the appearance of the object and distinguishes it from other objects, i.e., the child distinguishes the object before him from the other objects not similar to it.

(ii) When object is clearly distinguished from the other objects it becomes next stimulus for the child and when the child say it is monkey, it is the second response. Thus, a connection between S-R is formed

In order to make this type of learning a success, the following points must be kept in mind:

(i) Verbal units must be presented in a proper sequence, *i.e.*, one chain must come after the other and the whole chain at a time.

(ii) Learner must be active enough to make responses required by every chain.

(iii) Cues may be used to facilitate verbal association.

(iv) Span of retention power of the individual determines the length of the chain. There is however, a limit of these verbal chains. Unlimited number of chains can not be retained at all.

(v) There must be provision for the confirmation of correct responses in the learning situation.

5. **Learning by discrimination :** When specific behaviour is shown to only one given stimulus and other stimuli are totally excluded it is called discrimination. This type of learning is seen from the beginning of life of the organism. An infant does not consider all women having breast or feeding him by their breast as mothers. Only one out of so many is her mother and that is well discriminated. The child discriminates a feeding bottle and other bottles, the child of the home and the child outside the home etc. thus, a relatively higher mental operation is involved in discrimination.

The concept opposite to discrimination is generalization. When after conditioning to a particular stimulus, other similar stimuli also cause to elicit same response, the process is called stimulus generalization. The point to be noted here is that without perfection in stimulus generalization, nobody will be able to learn by discrimination.

Fine discrimination takes place only out of the process of stimulus generalization. Initially the infant accepts every woman as mummy but when he does not get required response from every one, he narrows down the spirit of generalization and recognizes his real mummy on the basis of her responses.

Discrimination is also not similar to the word of differentiation. In discrimination, emphasis is placed on stimulus side, but in differentiation, emphasis is placed on the response side. In discrimination, we eliminate the unwanted responses to the other stimuli through selective reinforcement but in differenciation, we develop a very specific type of response on the basis of the stimuli presented through selective reinforcement after examining a number of related responses too.

6. **Concept learning :** Concept is developed on the basis of common characteristics of an object. When we identify an object or an idea on the basis of its common properties, which a class of objects share in common not specific to other objects or ideas, it is called concept learning. The properties of shape, size, colour, form, nature etc are used to discriminate an object from other objects of the same class. For example, trees are many but the concept of a mango tree is applied to a tree which has some very specific property.

Concept learning is the pre-requisite for learning a law or principle. Learning of abstract concept is more difficult than concrete concepts ;because discrimination is done here on the basis of ideation only.

7. **Learning of principles :** Learning of principles or laws takes place only after concept learning. It is because regular and constant relationship between two or more concepts is established in a principle. Knowledge of so many principles and laws are necessary to function properly in the environment and to save our time in repeated experimentations. Most of the learning obtained in schools is concentrated to laws, principles, systems etc.

8. **Problem solving :** It is the highest stage of learning in the hierarchy. When an individual has learned all laws and principles, he evaluates them from the point of view of utility or facticity. This evaluation helps him to solve various problems of life.

IMPORTANCE OF LEANING FOR TEACHERS

Learning is important for a teacher in the following ways:

1. A teacher can adopt learning centred approach of teaching such as, activity programme, project method, problem solving method etc., and avoid teaching centred approach. Former is autonomous process and later is a burden on students.
2. A teacher can use the whole and part learning methods alternately to benefit the poor and talented students equally in the class.
3. Verbalization on the part of the teacher along with other motor activity can explain and clarify the concepts and remove the difficulties of students. Cue is also used by the teacher in the class.
4. A teacher will not bank upon memorization from the very beginning of teaching. Desired change of behaviour is not related to memorization,
5. A teacher can keep the maturity level and inborn capacity of students in mind for effective learning.
6. A teacher can provide varied experiences to students in such a way that they can identify similarities and differences in objects, situations and concepts. This approach of learning will facilitate learning in the class.
7. The primary objective of schooling is to bring about desirable changes in the behaviour of learners through the process of learning. A teacher must know all these approaches and operations of learning and their relative significance. A teacher can adopt a better teaching strategy in the class only after knowing different approaches and operations of teaching.
8. A teacher can accommodate his teaching according to the individual differences of students only after knowing the process and theories of learning.
9. An important contribution of leaning psychology is that it has propounded and popularized the concept of motivation and its uses on scientific lines. We are now in a better position to use different techniques to motivate the students for verbal, mental or motor activity. The teacher can motivate the students in the class according to their age levels.
10. A teacher can know various procedures of remembering and forgetting and he can utilize various techniques of learning to minimize the share of forgetting in the class. He can help the students to transfer skills and informations acquired in the classroom to daily life situations outside the school and vice versa.
11. Modern psychology of learning lays much stree on social psychology of leaning and group dynamics. A teacher can improve social learning environment of the class by putting various theories and procedures of learning into practice.

THEORIES OF LEARNING

We may categories all these theories of learning into two groups.

1. Laboratory psychologists' theories of association or connection (S-R theories)
2. Cognitive field theories or gestalt psychology of learning. S-R theories of learning can further be classified into two categories as under

(A) S-R theories without Reinforcement	(B) S-R theories with reinforcement
1. Pavlov's conditioning theory	Thorndike's theory
2. Watson's learning theory	Hull's theory
3. Guthrie's learning theory	Skinner's theory

As far as field theories are concerned there are three important theories which are given below:

1. Gestalt theory of learning
2. Lewin's theory of leaning
3. Tolman's sign gestalt theory of learning

HOW CHILDREN THINK AND LEARN

Children learn from anything and everything they see and act upon. They have learnt a lot before they join school, and they continue to learn outside the school hours. If we believe that children learn only in school, it is because of what we wrongly regard as learning. When a child spends hours on trying to solve a Jigsaw puzzle (say), he/she is often reprimanded by adults for wasting study time. Little do the grown-ups realise that it is through such interesting games that this child may be increasing his/her understanding of shapes and size. And, this learning is taking place outside the school hours, without formal instruction. A curriculum built upon assumptions about children's learning, that ignore this aspect, is also responsible for children losing interest in mathematics or in any formal learning.

From the time a child is born, his/her interaction with the world around his/her starts. He/she perceives things around his/her, and gradually makes sense of them. He/she slowly begins to recognise people and objects, relate more and more to the environment, and observe things through the senses of touch, sight, taste, smell and sound. There are **four different stages** of learning or development that each child goes through.

Sensorimotor

This is from the ages of birth to about two years old. During this time the child's primary mode of learning occurs through the five senses. He/she learns to experience environment. The child touches things, holds, looks, listens, tastes, feels, bangs, and shakes everything in sight. When the child adds motor skills such as creeping, crawling and walking, his/her environment expands by leaps and bounds. The child is now exploring their environment with both senses and the ability to get around.

Preoperational

This is the stages between ages two and seven. During this stage the child is busy gathering information or learning, and then trying to figure out ways that they can used what they have learned to begin solving problems.

During this stage of his/her life child will be thinking in specifics and will find it very difficult to get generalise anything. This is the time when a child learns by asking questions. The child generally will not want a real answer to his question at this point. When he asks why do we have grass .... He simply wants to know that it is for him to play in. No technical answers for know. The child in this age group judges everything on the 'me' basis—How does it affect me? Do I like it?

Concrete Operations Period

This is the period of time when child is between the ages of seven to ten. This is a wonderful age as this is when children begin to manipulate data mentally. They take the information at hand and begin to define, compare and contrast it. They, however, still think concretely.

The concrete operational child is capable of logical thought. This child still learns through their senses, but no longer relies on only them to teach him. He now thinks as well. A good teacher for this age group would start each lesson at a concrete level and then more toward a generalised level. The child, during this period, is very literal in their thinking.

Formal Operations Period

The period begins at about age eleven. At this time the child will break through the barrier of literalism and more on to thinking in more abstract terms. He no longer restricts thinking to time and space. This child now starts to reflect, hypothesize and theorize. In the formal operation period, children need to develop cognitive abilities. The following is a list of six simple categories of cognitive abilities. The following is a list of six simple categories of cognitive abilities:

1. **Knowledge of facts and principals:** This is the direct recall of facts and principals. **Examples:** memorisation of dates, name, definition, vocabulary words.
2. **Comprehension:** Understanding of facts and ideas.
3. **Application:** Needs to know, rules, principles, and procedures and how to use them.
4. **Analysis:** Breaking down concepts into parts.
5. **Synthesis:** Putting together information or ideas.
6. **Evaluation:** Judging the value of information.

BASIC PROCESSES OF TEACHING AND LEARNING

Teaching-learning process is the heart of education. On it depends the fulfilment of the aims & objectives of education. It is the most powerful instrument of education to bring about desired changes in the students. Teaching learning are related terms. In teaching-learning process, the teacher, the learner, the curriculum & other variables are organised in a systematic way to attain some pre-determined goal.

Essential Aspects of the Teaching-learning Process

According to Diana Laurillard, there are four aspects of the teaching-learning process:

1. **Discussion**—between the teacher and learner.
2. **Interaction**—between the learner and some aspect of the world defined by the teacher.
3. **Adaptation**—of the world by the teacher and action by the learner.
4. **Reflection**—on the learner's performance by both teacher and learner.

According to **Burton** in the figure above

1. Teaching can become effective only by relating it to process of learning.
2. Teaching objective cannot be realised without being related to learning situation.
3. We may create and use teaching aids to create some appropriate learning situation.
4. The strategies and devices of teaching may be selected in such a manner that the optimal objectives of learning area achieved.
5. To understand principles, goals, objectives of education in right perspective.
6. Appropriate learning situation condition may be created for congenial and effective teaching.

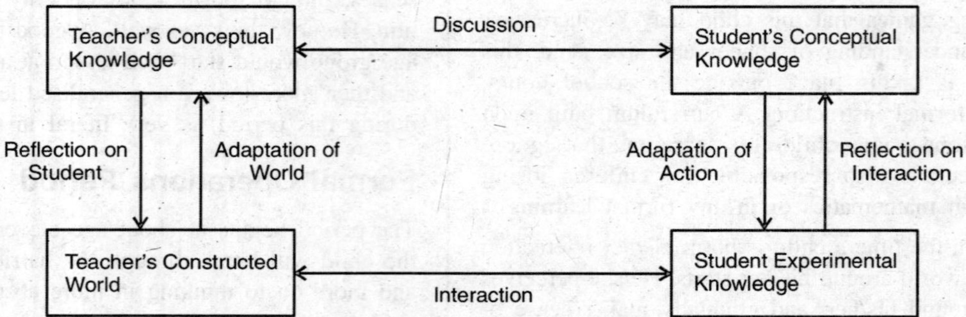

Fig. 1: *Essential aspects of the ideal teaching-learning process*

Approaches to Learning Theories

Aspect	Behaviourist	Cognitivist	Humanist
Learning theorists	Thorndike, Pavlov, Watson, Guthrie, Hull, Tolman, Skinner	Koffka, Kohler, Lewin, Piaget, Ausubel, Bruner, Gagne	Maslow, Rogers
View of the learning process	Change in behaviour	Internal mental process (including insight, information processing, memory, perception)	A personal act to fulfil potential
Locus of learning	Stimuli in external environment	Internal cognitive structuring	Affective and cognitive needs
Purpose in education	Produce behavioural change in desired direction	Develop capacity and skills to learn better	Become self-actualized autonomous
Educator's role	Arranges environment to elicit desired response	Structures content of learning activity	Facilitates development of the whole person
Manifestations in adult learning	Behavioural objectives	Cognitive development	Andragogy
	Competency-based education	Intelligence, learning and memory as function of age	Self-directed learning
	Skill development and training	Learning how to learn	

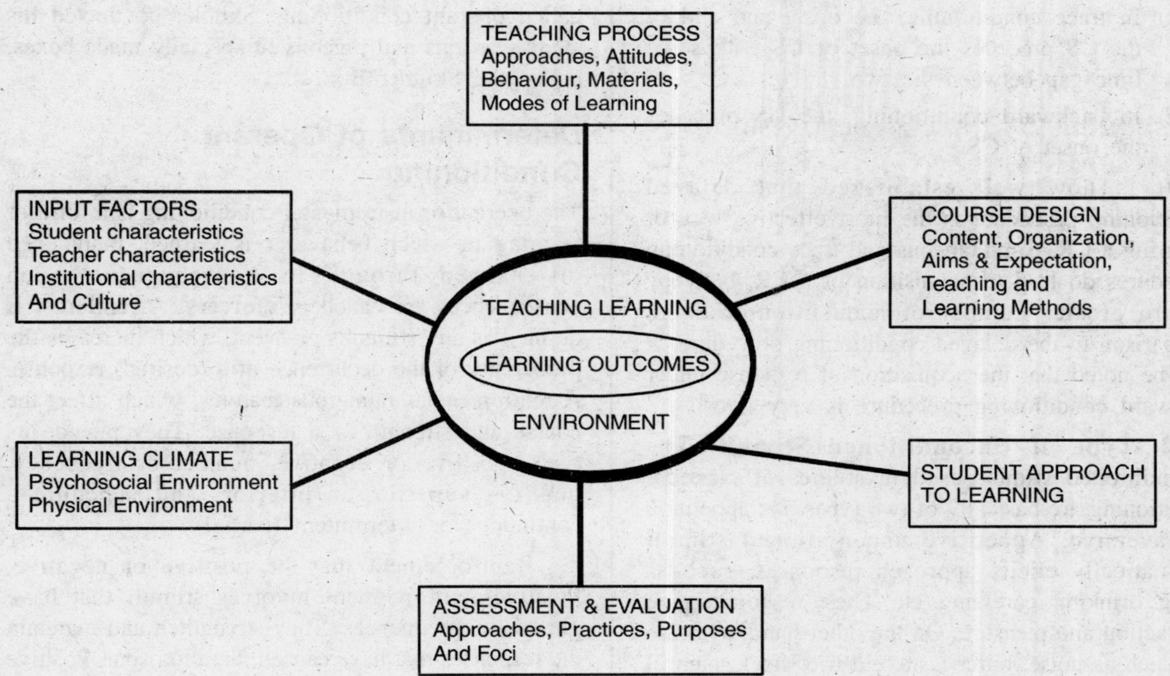

Fig. 2: *Teaching-Learning Environment*

PARADIGMS OF LEARNING

Learning takes place in many ways. There are some methods that are used in acquisition of simple responses while other methods are used in the acquisition of complex responses. The simplest kind of learning is called conditioning. Two types of conditioning have been identified. The first one is called classical conditioning and the second instrumental/operant conditioning. In addition, we have observational learning, cognitive learning, verbal learning, concept learning and skill learning.

Classical Conditioning

This type of learning was first investigated by Ivan P. Pavlov. Like many great scientific advances, classical conditioning was discovered accidentally. The nineteenth-century Russian physiologist Ivan Pavlov was looking at salivation in dogs in response to being fed, when he noticed that his dogs would begin to salivate whenever he entered the room, even when he was not bringing them food. However, when Pavlov discovered that any object or event which the dogs learnt to associate with food (such as the food bowl) would trigger the same response, he realised that he had made an important scientific discovery, and he devoted the rest of his career to studying this type of learning.

Classical conditioning is 'classical' in that it is the first systematic study of basic laws of learning. Classical conditioning involves learning to associate an unconditioned stimulus that already brings about a particular response (*i.e.* a reflex) with a new (conditioned) stimulus, so that the new stimulus brings about the same response. The unconditioned stimulus (or UCS) is the object or event that originally produces the reflexive/natural response.

Once the neutral stimulus has become associated with the unconditioned stimulus, it becomes a conditioned stimulus (CS). The conditioned response (CR) is the response to the conditioned stimulus. Thus, learning situation in classical conditioning is one of S-S learning in which one stimulus becomes a signal of another stimulus.

Determinants of Classical Conditioning

How quickly and strongly acquisition of a response occurs in classical conditioning depends on several factors. Some of the major factors influencing learning a CR are described below:

1. Time Relations between Stimuli: The classical conditioning procedures, discussed below, are basically of four types based on the time relations between the onset of conditioned stimulus (CS) and unconditioned stimulus (US). The first three are called forward conditioning procedures, and the fourth one is called backward conditioning procedure. The basic experimental arrangements of these procedures are as follows:

(*a*) When the CS and US are presented together, it is called simultaneous conditioning.

(*b*) In delayed conditioning, the onset of CS precedes the onset of US. The CS ends before the end of the US.

(*c*) In trace conditioning, the onset and end of the CS precedes the onset of US with some time gap between the two.

(*d*) In backward conditioning, the US precedes the onset of CS.

It is now well established that delayed conditioning procedure is the most effective way of acquiring a CR. Simultaneous and trace conditioning procedures do lead to acquisition of a CR, but they require greater number of acquisition trials in comparison to the delayed conditioning procedure. It may be noted that the acquisition of response under backward conditioning procedure is very rare.

2. Type of Unconditioned Stimuli: The unconditioned stimuli used in studies of classical conditioning are basically of two types, *i.e.* appetitive and aversive. Appetitive unconditioned stimuli automatically elicits approach responses, such as eating, drinking, caressing, etc. These responses give satisfaction and pleasure. On the other hand, aversive US, such as noise, bitter taste, electric shock, painful injections, etc. are painful, harmful, and elicit avoidance and escape responses. It has been found that appetitive classical conditioning is slower and requires greater number of acquisition trials, but aversive classical conditioning is established in one, two or three trials depending on the intensity of the aversive US.

3. Intensity of Conditioned Stimuli: This influences the course of both appetitive and aversive classical conditioning. More intense conditioned stimuli are more effective in accelerating the acquisition of conditioned responses. It means that the more intense the conditioned stimulus, the fewer are the number of acquisition trials needed for conditioning.

Operant/Instrumental Conditioning

B.F. Skinner is regarded as the father of operant conditioning, but his work was based on **Thorndike's law of effect.** In the late nineteenth century, psychologist Edward Thorndike proposed the law of effect. The law of effect states that any behaviour that has good consequences will tend to be repeated, and any behaviour that has bad consequences will tend to be avoided. In the 1930s, B.F. Skinner, extended this idea and began to study operant conditioning. Operant conditioning is a type of learning in which responses come to be controlled by their consequences.

Operants are those behaviours or responses, which are emitted by animals and human beings voluntarily and are under their control. The term operant is used because the organism operates on the environment. Conditioning of operant behaviour is called operant conditioning. Skinner conducted his studies on rats and pigeons in specially made boxes, called the Skinner Box.

Determinants of Operant Conditioning

The operant or instrumental conditioning is a form of learning in which behaviour is learned, maintained or changed through its consequences. Such consequences are called **reinforcers**. A reinforcer is defined as any stimulus or event, which increases the probability of the occurrence of a (desired) response. A reinforcer has numerous features, which affect the course and strength of a response. They include its type—positive or negative, number or frequency, quality—superior or inferior, and schedule—continuous or intermittent (partial).

Reinforcement may be positive or negative. Positive reinforcement involves stimuli that have pleasant consequences. They strengthen and maintain the responses that have caused them to occur. Positive reinforcers satisfy needs, which include food, water, medals, praise, money, status, information, etc. Negative reinforcers involve unpleasant and painful stimuli. Responses that lead organisms to get rid of painful stimuli or avoid and escape from them provide negative reinforcement. Thus, negative reinforcement leads to learning of avoidance and escape responses. For instance, one learns to put on woollen clothes, burn firewood or use electric heaters to avoid the unpleasant cold weather. One learns to move away from dangerous stimuli because they provide negative reinforcement. It may be noted that negative reinforcement is not punishment. Use of punishment reduces or suppresses the response while a negative reinforcer increases the probability of avoidance or escape response. For instance, drivers and co-drivers wear their seat belts to avoid getting injured in case of an accident or to avoid being fined by the traffic police.

Classical and Operant Conditioning : Differences

1. In classical conditioning, the responses are under the control of some stimulus because they are reflexes, automatically elicited by the appropriate stimuli. Such stimuli are selected as US and responses elicited by them as UR. Thus Pavlovian conditioning, in which US elicits responses, is often called respondent conditioning.
   In instrumental conditioning, responses are under the control of the organism and are voluntary responses or 'operants'. Thus, in the two forms of conditioning different types of responses are conditioned.

2. In classical conditioning, the CS and US are well-defined, but in operant conditioning CS is not defined. It can be inferred but is not directly known.
3. In classical conditioning, the experimenter controls the occurrence of US, while in operant conditioning the occurrence of the reinforcer is under the control of the organism that is learning. Thus, for US in classical conditioning the organism remains passive, while in operant conditioning the subject has to be active in order to be reinforced.
4. In the two forms of conditioning, the technical terms used to characterise the experimental proceedings are different. Moreover what is called reinforcer in operant conditioning is called US in classical conditioning. An US has two functions. In the beginning, it elicits the response and also reinforces the response to be associated and elicited later on by the CS.

OBSERVATIONAL LEARNING

The other form of learning takes place by observing others. Earlier this form of learning was called **imitation**. Bandura and his colleagues in a series of experimental studies investigated observational learning in detail. In this kind of learning, human beings learn social behaviours, therefore, it is sometimes called **social learning**. In many situations individuals do not know how to behave. They observe others and emulate their behaviour. This form of learning is called **modelling**.

Examples of observational learning abound in our social life. Fashion designers employ tall, pretty, and gracious young girls and tall, smart, and well-built young boys for popularising clothes of different designs and fabrics. People observe them on televised fashion shows and advertisements in magazines and newspapers. They imitate these models. Observing superiors and likeable persons and then emulating their behaviour in a novel social situation is a common experience.

The children observe adults' behaviours, at home and during social ceremonies and functions. They enact adults in their plays and games. For instance, young children play games of marriage ceremonies, birthday parties, thief and policeman, house keeping, etc. Actually they enact in their games what they observe in society, on television, and read in books.

Children learn most of the social behaviours by observing and emulating adults. The way to put on clothes, dress one's hair, and conduct oneself in society are learned through observing others. It has also been shown that children learn and develop various personality characteristics through observational learning. Aggressiveness, prosocial behaviour, courtesy, politeness, diligence, and indolence are acquired by this method of learning.

COGNITIVE LEARNING

Some psychologists view learning in terms of cognitive processes that underlie it. They have developed approaches that focus on such processes that occur during learning rather than concentrating solely on S-R and S-S connections. Thus, in cognitive learning, there is a change in what the learner knows rather than what he/she does. This form of learning shows up in insight learning and latent learning.

Insight Learning

Kohler demonstrated a model of learning which could not be readily explained by conditioning. He performed a series of experiments with chimpanzees that involved solving complex problems. Kohler placed chimpanzees in an enclosed play area where food was kept out of their reach. Tools such as poles and boxes were placed in the enclosure. The chimpanzees rapidly learned how to use a box to stand on or a pole to move the food in their direction. In this experiment, learning did not occur as a result of trial and error and reinforcement, but came about in sudden flashes of insight. The chimpanzees would roam about the enclosure for some time and then suddenly would stand on a box, grab a pole and strike a banana, which was out of normal reach above the enclosure. The chimpanzee exhibited what Kohler called insight learning—the process by which the solution to a problem suddenly becomes clear.

In a normal experiment on insight learning, a problem is presented, followed by a period of time when no apparent progress is made and finally a solution suddenly emerges. In insight learning, sudden solution is the rule. Once the solution has appeared, it can be repeated immediately the next time the problem is confronted. Thus, it is clear that what is learned is not a specific set of conditioned associations between stimuli and responses but a cognitive relationship between a means and an end. As a result, insight learning can be generalised to other similar problem situations.

Latent Learning

Another type of cognitive learning is known as latent learning. In latent learning, a new behaviour is learned but not demonstrated until reinforcement is provided for displaying it. Tolman made an early contribution to the concept of latent learning. To have an idea of latent learning, we may briefly understand his experiment. Tolman put two groups of rats in a maze and gave them an opportunity to explore. In one group, rats found food at the end of the maze and soon learned to make their way rapidly through the maze. On the other hand, rats in the second group were not rewarded and showed no apparent signs of learning. But later, when these rats were reinforced, they ran through the maze as efficiently as the rewarded group.

Tolman contended that the unrewarded rats had learned the layout of the maze early in their explorations. They just never displayed their latent learning until the reinforcement was provided. Instead, the rats developed a cognitive map of the maze, *i.e.* a mental representation of the spatial locations and directions, which they needed to reach their goal.

LEARNING AS A SOCIAL ACTIVITY

Learning is a social activity. Our learning is intimately associated with our connection with other human beings, our teachers, our peers, our family as well as casual acquaintances, including the people before us or next to us. We are more likely to be successful in our efforts to educate, if we recognise this principle rather than try to avoid it. Much of traditional education, as Dewey pointed out, is directed towards isolating the learner from all social interaction, and towards seeing education as a one-on-one relationship between the learner and the objective material to be learned. In contrast, progressive education (to continue to use Dewey's formulation) recognizes the social aspect of learning and uses conversations interaction with others, and the application of knowledge as an integral aspect of learning.

SOCIAL CONTEXT OF LEARNING

Social Learning theory

Social learning theory focuses on the learning that occurs within a social context. It considers that people learn from one another, including such concepts as observational learning, imitation, and modelling. Among others **Albert Bandura** is considered the leading proponent of this theory.

General Principles of Social Learning Theory Follows:

1. People can learn by observing the behaviour is of others and the outcomes of those behaviours.
2. Learning can occur without a change in behaviour. Behaviourists say that learning has to be represented by a permanent change in behaviour, in contrast social learning theorists say that because people can learn through observation alone, their learning may not necessarily be shown in their performance. Learning may or may not result in a behaviour change.
3. Cognition plays a role in learning. Over the last 40 years social learning theory has become increasingly cognitive in its interpretation of human learning. Awareness and expectations of future reinforcements or punishments can have a major effect on the behaviours that people exhibit.
4. Social learning theory can be considered a bridge or a transition between behaviourist learning theories and cognitive learning theories.

How the Environment Reinforces and Punishes Modelling:

People are often reinforced for modelling the behaviour of others. Bandura suggested that the environment also reinforces modelling. This is in several possible ways:

1. The observer is reinforced by the model. For example, a student who changes dress to fit in with a certain group of students has a strong likelihood of being accepted and thus reinforced by that group.
2. The observer is reinforced by a third person. The observer might be modelling the actions of someone else, for example, an outstanding class leader or student. The teacher notices this and compliments and praises the observer for modelling such behaviour thus reinforcing that behaviour.
3. The imitated behaviour itself leads to reinforcing consequences. Many behaviours that we learn from others produce satisfying or reinforcing results. For example, a student in my multimedia class could observe how the extra work a classmate does is fun. This student in turn would do the same extra work and also receive enjoyment.
4. Consequences of the model's behaviour affect the observers behaviour vicariously. This is known as vicarious reinforcement. This is where in the model is reinforced for a response and then the observer shows an increase in that same response. Bandura illustrated this by having students watch a film of a model hitting a inflated clown doll. One group of children saw the model being praised for such action. Without being reinforced, the group of children began to also hit the doll.

Contemporary Social Learning Perspective of Reinforcement and Punishment

1. Contemporary theory proposes that both reinforcement and punishment have indirect effects on learning. They are not the sole or main cause.
2. Reinforcement and punishment influence the extent to which an individual exhibits a behaviour that has been learned.
3. The expectation of reinforcement influences cognitive processes that promote learning. Therefore, attention pays a critical role in learning. And attention is influenced by the expectation of reinforcement. An example would be, where the teacher tells a group of students that what they will study next is not on the test. Students will not pay attention, because they do not expect to know the information for a test.

Cognitive Factors in Social Learning

Social learning theory has cognitive factors as well as behaviourist factors (actually operant factors).

1. **Learning without performance:** Bandura makes a distinction between learning through observation and the actual imitation of what has been learned.
2. **Cognitive processing during learning:** Social learning theorists contend that attention is a critical factor in learning.
3. **Expectations:** As a result of being reinforced, people form expectations about the consequences that future behaviours are likely to bring. They expect certain behaviours to bring reinforcements and others to bring punishment. The learner needs to be aware however, of the response reinforcements and response punishment. Reinforcement increases a response only when the learner is aware of that connection.
4. **Reciprocal causation:** Bandura proposed that behaviour can influence both the environment and the person. In fact each of these three variables, the person, the behaviour, and the environment can have an influence on each other.
5. **Modelling:** There are different types of models. There is the live model, and actual person demonstrating the behaviour. There can also be a symbolic model, which can be a person or action portrayed in some other medium, such as television, videotape, computer programs.

Behaviours that can be learned through modelling:

Many behaviours can be learned, at least partly, through modelling. Examples that can be cited are, students can watch parents read, students can watch the demonstrations of mathematics problems, or seen someone acting bravely and a fearful situation. Aggression can be learned through models. Much research indicate that children become more aggressive when they observed aggressive or violent models. Moral thinking and moral behaviour are influenced by observation and modelling. This includes moral judgments regarding right and wrong which can in part, develop through modelling.

Conditions Necessary for Effective Modelling to Occur:

Bandura mentions four conditions that are necessary before an individual can successfully model the behaviour of someone else:

1. **Attention:** the person must first pay attention to the model.
2. **Retention:** the observer must be able to remember the behaviour that has been observed. One way of increasing this is using the technique of rehearsal.
3. **Motor reproduction:** the third condition is the ability to replicate the behaviour that the model has just demonstrated. This means that the observer has to be able to replicate the action, which could be a problem with a learner who is not ready developmentally to replicate the action. For example, little children have difficulty doing complex physical motion.
4. **Motivation:** the final necessary ingredient for modelling to occur is motivation, learners must want to demonstrate what they have learned. Remember that since these four conditions vary among individuals, different people will reproduce the same behaviour differently.

Effects of Modelling on Behaviour:

Modelling teaches new behaviours.

Modelling influences the frequency of previously learned behaviours.

Modelling may encourage previously forbidden behaviours.

Modelling increases the frequency of similar behaviours. For example, a student might see a friend excel in basketball and he tries to excel in football because he is not tall enough for basketball.

Educational implications of social learning theory:

Social learning theory has numerous implications for classroom use.

1. Students often learn a great deal simply by observing other people.
2. Describing the consequences of behaviour is can effectively increase the appropriate behaviours and decrease inappropriate ones. This can involve discussing with learners about the rewards and consequences of various behaviours.
3. Modelling provides an alternative to shaping for teaching new behaviours. Instead of using shaping, which is operant conditioning, modelling can provide a faster, more efficient means for teaching new behaviour. To promote effective modelling a teacher must make sure that the four essential conditions exist; attention, retention, motor reproduction, and motivation.
4. Teachers and parents must model appropriate behaviours and take care that they do not model inappropriate behaviours.
5. Teachers should expose students to a variety of other models. This technique is especially important to break down traditional stereotypes.
6. Students must believe that they are capable of accomplishing school tasks. Thus, it is very important to develop a sense of self-efficacy for students. Teachers can promote such self-efficacy by having students receive confidence-building messages, watch others be successful, and experience success on their own.
7. Teachers should help students set realistic expectations for their academic accomplishments. In general in my class that means making sure that expectations are not set too low. I want to realistically challenge my students. However, sometimes the task is beyond a student's ability, example would be the cancer group.
8. Self-regulation techniques provide an effective method for improving student behaviour.

PLANNING FOR PROBLEM SOLVING

A curriculum that accommodates a variety of developmental levels as well as individual differences in young children sets the stage for problem solving. Choices, decision-making, and a curriculum framework that integrates learning, such as Katz and Chard's project method, are especially appropriate for young learners. The project approach facilitates cooperative learning and promotes diverse ideas. Donna Ogle's K-W-L (what you KNOW, what you WANT to know, and what you have LEARNED) is another method of organizing work that promotes problem solving. Themes, units, webbing, and the KWL method are all ways of organizing curriculum that can support problem solving. Beginning with the needs and interests of the children, problem solving develops from meaningful experiences important to the children. The teacher-designed curriculum provides the classroom basis for these experiences.

For example, a second grade investigation of waste materials from a classroom led one group of young children to explore the topic in an integrated way. Reading, writing, counting, measuring, interviews of community people, and science experiments were planned, initiated and reported. Solutions to many problems posed during the investigation were tried out and some were found to be successful. Through group work, individuals were able to participate and communicate as cognitive and social needs were met. Each child, at individual levels and in individual ways, was successful within the group experience. Problem solving empowers children.

Providing for Problem Solving

Problem solving is a skill that can be learned and must be practiced. It is facilitated by a classroom schedule that provides for integrated learning in large blocks of time, space for ongoing group projects, and many open-ended materials. The teacher provides the time, space, and materials necessary for in-depth learning.

1. Time: Teachers can provide for problem solving by enlarging blocks of learning time during the school day. Because making choices, discussing decisions, and evaluating mistakes takes time, large time blocks best suit the problem-solving process. It is important that children know they have time to identify and solve problems.

2. Space: Projects and group meetings may require an assessment of classroom space. Moving desks and tables together facilitates communication and cooperation in the classroom. Once the teacher has observed the patterns of traffic in the classroom, equipment can be moved or eliminated to promote problem solving.

3. Materials: The open-ended materials that are needed for the construction and concrete solving of problems should be safe, durable, and varied. Well-marked storage units should be easily accessible to children, and materials should be available for ongoing exploration and manipulation. Access to a variety of materials encourages children to use materials in new and diverse ways. This freedom promotes problem solving.

The Problem-Solving Model

Individuals or groups can solve problems. Group problem solving is important to young children because many diverse ideas are generated. Both individual and group processes should be included in the early childhood classroom. Becoming skillful at problem solving is based on the understanding and use of sequenced steps. These steps are:

1. Identifying the problem,
2. Brainstorming a variety of solutions,
3. Choosing one solution and trying it out, and
4. Evaluating what has happened.

Choosing Good Problems

Goffin provides teachers with guiding questions that will help them identify appropriate problems for young children. Some of these are:

1. Is the problem meaningful and interesting?
2. Can the problem be solved at a variety of levels?
3. Must a new decision be made?
4. Can the actions be evaluated?

Problem solving is a way to make sense of the environment and, in fact, control it. The process allows children in an increasingly diverse world to be active participants and to implement changes. By including problem solving in the early childhood classroom, we equip children with a life-long skill that is useful in all areas of learning.

Obstacles to Solving Problems

Two major obstacles to solving a problem are mental set and lack of motivation.

Mental Set

Mental set is a tendency of a person to solve problems by following already tried mental operations or steps. Prior success with a particular strategy would sometimes help in solving a new problem. However, this tendency also creates a mental rigidity that obstructs the problem solver to think of any new rules or strategies. Thus, while in some situations mental set can enhance the quality and speed of problem solving, in other situations it hinders problem solving. You might have experienced this while solving mathematical problems. After completing a couple of questions, you form an idea of the steps that are required to solve these questions and subsequently you go on following the same steps, until a point where you fail. At this point you may experience difficulty in avoiding the already used steps. Those steps would interfere in your thought for new strategies. However, in day-to-day activities we often rely on past experiences with similar or related problems.

Like mental set, **functional fixedness** in problem solving occurs when people fail to solve a problem because they are fixed on a thing's usual function. If you have ever used a hardbound book to hammer a nail, then you have overcome functional fixedness.

Lack of Motivation

People might be great at solving problems, but all their skills and talents are of no use if they are not motivated. Sometimes people give up easily when they encounter a problem or failure in implementing the first step. Therefore, there is a need to persist in their effort to find a solution.

ALTERNATIVE CONCEPTIONS OF LEARNING

When teachers provide instruction on concepts in various subjects, they are teaching students who already have some pre-instructional knowledge about the topic. Student knowledge, however, can be erroneous, illogical or misinformed. These erroneous understandings are termed alternative conceptions or misconceptions (or intuitive theories). Alternative conceptions (misconceptions) are not unusual. In fact, they are a normal part of the learning process. We quite naturally form ideas from our everyday experience, but obviously not all the ideas we develop are correct with respect to the most current evidence and scholarship in a given discipline. Moreover, some concepts in different content areas are simply very difficult to grasp. They may be very abstract, counterintuitive or quite complex. Hence, our understanding of them is flawed. In addition, things we have already learned are sometimes unhelpful in learning new concepts/theories. This occurs when the new concept or theory is inconsistent with previously learned material. Accordingly, as noted, it is very typical for students (and adults) to have misconceptions in different domains (content knowledge areas). Indeed, researchers have found that there is a common set of alternative conceptions (misconceptions) that most students typically exhibit. There is one class of alternative theories (or misconceptions) that is very deeply entrenched. These are "ontological misconceptions," which relate to ontological beliefs (*i.e.*, beliefs about the fundamental categories and properties of the world).

Alternative conceptions (misconceptions) can impede learning for several reasons. First, students generally are unaware that the knowledge they have is wrong. Moreover, misconceptions can be very entrenched in student thinking. In addition, new experiences are interpreted through these erroneous understandings, thereby interfering with being able to correctly grasp new information. Also, alternative conceptions (misconceptions) tend to be very resistant to instruction because learning entails replacing or radically reorganizing student knowledge. Hence, conceptual change has to occur for learning to happen. This puts teachers in the very challenging position of needing to bring about significant conceptual change in student knowledge. Generally, ordinary forms of instruction, such as lectures, labs, discovery learning, or simply reading texts, are not very successful at overcoming student misconceptions. For all these reasons, misconceptions can be hard nuts for teachers to crack. However, several instructional strategies have been found to be effective in achieving conceptual change and helping students leave their alternative conceptions behind and learn correct concepts or theories.

Instructional strategies that can lead to change in students' alternative conceptions (misconceptions) and to learning of new concepts and theories

1. Present new concepts or theories that you are teaching in such a way that students see as plausible, high-quality, intelligible and generative.
2. Use students' correct conceptions and build on those by creating a bridge of examples to the new concept or theory that students are having trouble learning due to misconceptions they hold.
3. Use model-ased reasoning, which helps students construct new representations that vary from their intuitive theories.
4. Use diverse instruction, wherein you present a few examples that challenge multiple assumptions, rather than a larger number of examples that challenge just one assumption.
5. Help students become aware of (raise student metacognition about) their own alternative conceptions (misconceptions).
6. Present students with experiences that cause cognitive conflict in students' minds. Experiences (as in strategy 3 above) that can cause cognitive conflict are ones that get students to consider their erroneous (misconception) knowledge side-by-side with, or at the same time as, the correct concept or theory.
7. Engage in Interactive Conceptual Instruction (ICI).
8. Develop students' epistemological thinking, which incorporates beliefs and theories about the nature of knowledge and the nature of learning, in ways that will facilitate conceptual change. The more naive students' beliefs are about knowledge and learning, the less likely they are to revise their misconceptions.
9. Help students "self-repair" their misconceptions.
10. Once students have overcome their alternative conceptions (misconceptions).

Presenting new concepts or theories

In presenting new concepts or theories, teachers should be sure to show these theories or concepts as:

1. Plausible: The new information should be shown to be consistent with other knowledge and able to explain the available data. Learners must see how the new conception (theory) is consistent with other knowledge and a good explanation of the data.

2. High quality: Of course, the theory/concept to be taught is of high quality from a scientific point of view, since it is a correct theory. However, the presented theory should take a better account of the data than what students currently have available to them. For example, the instructor should deal with the problem from the perspective of the students (*e.g.*, students for whom a "flat earth" theory provides a better account of the data available than does a "spherical earth" theory). Hence, the quality of the new theory must be considered along with the kind of data that students know about.

3. Intelligible: Teachers should do what they can to increase the intelligibility of the new theory. Learners must be able to grasp how the new conception works. To increase intelligibility, teachers can use methods such as use of:

(*a*) analogies,

(*b*) models, and

(*c*) direct exposition.

4. Generative/fruitful: Teachers should show that the new concept/theory can be extended to open up new areas of inquiry. Learners must be able to extend the new conception to new areas of inquiry. Teachers might accomplish this by illustrating the application of the new concept/theory to a range of problems. These problems can include familiar ones and new ones.

UNDERSTANDING CHILDREN'S 'ERRORS' AS SIGNIFICANT STEPS IN THE LEARNING PROCESS

The legacy of Jean Piaget to the world of early childhood education is that he fundamentally altered the view of how a child learns. And a teacher, he believed, was more than a transmitter of knowledge she was also an essential observer and guide to helping children build their own knowledge.

As a university graduate, Swiss-born Piaget got a routine job in Paris standardizing Binet-Simon IQ tests, where the emphasis was on children getting the right answers. Piaget observed that many children of the same ages gave the same kinds of incorrect answers. What could be learned from this?

Piaget interviewed many hundreds of children and concluded that children who are allowed to make mistakes often go on to discover their errors and correct them, or find new solutions. In this process, children build their own way of learning. From children's errors, teachers can obtain insights into the child's view of the world and can tell where guidance is needed. They can provide appropriate materials, ask encouraging questions, and allow the child to construct his own knowledge.

Piaget's continued interactions with young children became part of his life-long research. After reading about a child who thought that the sun and moon followed him wherever he went, Piaget wanted to find out if all young children had a similar belief. He found that many did indeed believe this. Piaget went on to explore children's countless "why" questions, such as, "Why is the sun round?" or "Why is grass green?" He concluded that children do not think like adults. Their thought processes have their own distinct order and special logic. Children are not "empty vessels to be filled with knowledge" (as traditional pedagogical theory had it). They are "active builders of knowledge-little scientists who construct their own theories of the world."

COGNITION & EMOTIONS

What is Cognition?

Cognition is the ability to preceive, memorise, reason and understand. These abilities change with age. As the child grows, her thinking becomes more mature and efficient. Therefore, cognition can simply be defined as the process of acquiring, processing, organising and using knowledge. The development of cognition means development of all these abilities. A child's thinking changes as result of both age (maturation) and increased experiences.

Major Cognitive Characteristics of Children

Infancy

It is interesting to see the number of changes that take place in the first two years. Children at this stage are very active learners. Even when it seems the child is only lying and looking at nothing (e.g. 2 month old) she is actually looking at and trying to understand the things around her.

The first two years children begin by exploring their own bodies and move to the outside objects. Children at 2/3 months discover their thumb or hand or occasionally their own foot. These fascinate them they try to play with them. For a two month old a toy is not as satisfying as her/his own thumb in her/his mouth. Gradually, by about six months, children begin to play with objects outside the body. This could be the toy, the sheet, the bottle, etc. Later, by two years they can even indulge in pretend play [example doctor-doctor, house-house, etc.].

What children also achieve by two years is the understanding of object permanance. **Object permanance is the understanding that things exist even if you can not see them.** Let us take an example. If you show a five month old a toy she gets excited. If you hide the toy the child soon forgets that any toy even existed. This is because she thinks out of sight is out of mind. Do the same thing with a 1½ year old and you will find the child is either looking for it or asks you to find it. This is because she knows the toy exists even if she can not see it. This understanding, that things exist even if you can not see them, is called object permanance.

The other major development that happens by two years is that children begin to learn the symbols. What are symbols? A two year old can convey her thoughts and desires through language. All these are essential processes of cognition.

Early Childhood

This is a period when the childs mastery in use of symbols increases. We can observe this in the everyday behaviour and activities of the child, *i.e.* in what she plays, her language etc. Gradually her representations of objects become more flexible and less self centred. A one year old while playing does not need a toy phone to pretend speaking on the phone. She can use any object. This is indicative of flexibility in thinking. Gradually, children also start directing play between dolls, *e.g.,* one doll is the mother and the other doll the child. This is indicative of the child moving away from self to becoming less self centred.

Children at this stage also believe that all objects have feelings like human beings. That is why you will often see the child feeding her teddy bear.

Children at this stage can also focus on only one aspect of a situation and can not go back. Let us now take an example. You offer cola to a 4 yr old in a tall glass. You then change your mind and pour the coke from the tall glass to a short glass and give it to the child. You will find the child will say I want the big glass. This is because she can only focus on one aspect (height) at a time. Also, she is not able to go back mentally and realise that in the process of pouring from big to small glass, no cola was taken away.

Similarly, take two plates and put in one 6 pieces of chocolate spreadout and in the other make a tower of 6 pieces of chocolate. You will find the child thinking the spread out chocolate is more. This is because the child can only focus on one aspect at a time. This limitation seriously restricts the problem solving and logical thinking abilities of the child.

It also indicates the child's inability to understand that another point of view different from her own can exist, *e.g.,* you often find children responding to your question by nodding their heads, even if they are not in the same room as you. This is because they do not see another's point of view.

Middle Childhood

During this period, children begin to understand that another view point can exist. They are also able to focus on more than one aspect of a situation and go back and forth on their thinking. This makes their thinking more logical and efficient. However, children are only comfortable with concrete ideas/objects. It means, something that is real for them, *i.e.,* either something they have seen, *e.g.,* a house or something is in front of them, a plant or something linked to what they know, *e.g.,* blue like the sky. They are not able to think about abstract ideas, *e.g.,* what would happen if everyone could fly?

Emotion

Emotions, put simply, are feelings. In infants we can see these very clearly in the form of joy, anger and fear. These are similar to the emotions that adults have.

1. **The variety of emotions increases with age:** The basic emotions of joy, fear, anger are visible in infants. Gradually, as a sense of self develops; children begin to relate with people around them and value their opinions. Then we can see the emotion like pride, shame, sympathy, guilt also developing in them.
2. **The expression of emotion also changes with age:** Emotions are both innate and learnt. The instinctive response to a stimulus is innate but how to express that feeling is learnt, *e.g.* taking away of a toy makes the child angry (innate) but instead crying she is encouraged to ask for it back (learnt). Frustration tolerance increases with age. As children grow older, their responses change in both as well as instinctive method of expression, *e.g.,* when 2 year old falls downs she cries loudly and later forgets quickly. A 6 year old on the other hand, may not cry but forgets far less easily.
3. **The triggers or cause of emotions change with age:** The stimuli that elicit emotion also change with age, *e.g.,* an infant may cry on hearing the loud explosion of a cracker but a middle childhood child may laugh. Sucking a thumb may give great joy to an infant but provides no pleasure to a child is middle childhood.
4. **The coping techniques change with age:** Methods of coping with frustration and stress change with age. While a younger child may cry, or cling to the adult, an older child is likely to suppress the emotion.

Factors Affecting Emotional Development

If we look round in our environment, we will find that people differ in the emotions they experience and express. Some are happy, some are angry, some moody, some helpful. What then affects our emotional development?

1. **Parenting style:** Democratic parenting where induction is used as a method of disciplining allows for more mature emotional development and also for development of personal behaviour.
2. **Role model:** There are two factors which influence what a child ultimately learns:
   (i) How adults and others in the child's environment handle their emotions.
   (ii) How successful is the emotional expression in achieving their needs.
3. **Violence in the child's environment:** The kind of behaviour the child see in the community (*e.g.* during riots) or on TV will affect her expressions of emotions.
4. **Cultural norms:** Emotional expressions are learnt from the environment. It is the environment that tells us how to react in a situation (*e.g.* some people feel the emotion of fear when a black cat crosses their path). It is also the environment that tells us the acceptable way of expressing ones emotions (*e.g.* in many families it is unacceptable for boys to express their distress by crying). Therefore, our cultural beliefs and values also influence our emotional development.

MOTIVATION AND LEARNING

Definition of Motivation

1. **J.P. Guilford :** Motivation is any internal factor or conditions that needs to initiate or sustain an activity.
2. **B.F. Skinner :** Motivation in school learning involves arousing, persisting, sustaining and directing desirable behaviour .

3. **Lowell :** Motivation is psycho-physiological and internal process initiated by some needs which led to activity and which will satisfy those needs.
4. **Thompson :** Motivation is the act of stimulating interest in the pupils (individuals) where there is no such interest.
5. **Woodworth :** Motivation is the state of the individual which disposes him of certain behaviour for seeking goals.

Nature and Characteristics of Motivation

On the basis of above definitions following nature and characteristics of motivation are established:

1. Motivation is such a psychological factor which is controlled by physical conditions. This is an internal process. When this process becomes active in the body of an organism, he starts activity. This very process furthers the activity and directs the activity as well. As soon as the process stops activity also stops immediately.
2. In school environment motivation arouses the behaviour of pupils, directs it and helps the pupils to persist on it. A teacher can make any thing do by the students in the class by it.
3. A person is motivated to do an activity only when he is driven by any internal need for that job. When study becomes the need of the pupil, he is motivated to study. If this need is not there in him, it is created by the teacher from outside. This need gets satisfied at the fulfillment of the activity. The same job is performed by all sports and games coach in fields and playgrounds.
4. Need of life depends upon the objectives of life. If the student has fixed the objective of scoring 80% marks in the examination, this objective works as a need for him. Thus, teacher, by making the aimless students sensitive to objectives of life, motivates them to do better and better.
5. Motivation is an art of increasing the interest of students. Students can not be motivated to teaching learning process just by arousing their interest without creating the needs.

In conclusion we can say that need is the main factor behind motivation. Other factors are interest, objectives of life, curiosity, intelligence etc.

Needs : The feeling of want of something is called need. Condition of restlessness continues until the need is fulfilled. Man manifests any specific type of behaviour because of this very tension.

Maslow's Hierarchy of Human Needs

Abraham Maslow explained the theories of motivation in 1954 in the perspective of needs. He classified human needs in five levels in a continuum of pyramid. He termed the physiological, safety and belongingness needs as lower level needs and esteem and self-actualization needs as higher level needs.

1. **Physiological needs:** These primary needs are created in an individual by nature. Needs of air, water, food, defecation etc. are such needs. Unless these needs of the individual are satisfied, he can not even think of higher level needs. Meaning thereby, we can not motivate a hungry or thirsty pupil for learning in the class. If a child does not have even resources to fulfil these needs, he can defer these needs by his will power but only for a short duration, but ultimately these needs will have any how to be fulfilled.
2. **Safety needs:** After fulfilling the physiological needs an organism wants to be protected in the environment from his enemies whether they are his fellow being or the fury of the environment in the form of heat, cold, rain etc. In the school situation a child wants that he should not be teased by any body. If the school is unable to protect the child, the child can never be motivated for learning.
3. **Needs of belongingness:** Having the above two needs been fulfilled an individual wants to be associated with others. He wants love, affection and friendship from his fellow beings. In order to satisfy these very needs child participates in different types of programmes in the school. In order to draw the attention and love of his teachers, he fulfills the home works given to him. Those teachers who fail to satisfy these needs of their pupils, they cannot motivate them for learning as well.
4. **Esteem needs :** After the lower level of needs being fulfilled, an organism wants respects and recognition in the society. For this purpose he exhibits some extra ordinary performance on certain affairs. The organism wants some powers in his hand to use it in the society. For example, he wants to become monitor of the class or captain of football or cricket team. In order to motivate such students for learning, it is necessary that such needs of these students must be fulfilled to the maximum level possible.
5. **Needs of self actualization :** An individual comes to recognise his strengths and weakness fully before coming to this last level of needs.

On the basis of potentialities he wants to do such an extra-ordinary work so that he may acquire the top place in the eyes of the people. For example, talented students after a period of time come to know that they can top the class. In order to achieve this target they try their best. If a teacher fails to recognise the abilities of these students and does not respond properly at their achievement, these students lag behind their actual level of performance.

It is clear from the above classification that there are five groups of people found in every society. The first group gets satisfied only at the fulfillment of its first level needs and does not care for the next. Second group can be satisfied only at fulfilling the two levels of needs. The next two groups are smaller than these. They can be motivated only when their higher levels of needs are fulfilled. The last group is actually never contended. It always tries its best to excel more and more.

Types of Motivation

1. **Extrinsic Motivation :** In such type of motivation efforts are made to create such environment from outside that individual starts taking interest in the task. For example, if a student does not take interest in teaching learning process because of his hunger, thirst or lack of safety, first of all, these needs of the students are satisfied. Important other extrinsic motivations are reward and punishment, praise and blame, success and failure, competition and cooperation, and so on.
2. **Intrinsic Motivation :** These motivations are related to subject matter or activities of the students. This motivation stresses to fulfil the higher level of needs such as esteem or self actualization needs. Such type of individuals can hardly be motivated by extrinsic motivation. Here efforts are made to create such an environment from within the individual that higher performance becomes his needs and objective of life. Unless and until these needs are fulfilled, he never sits idle. Knowledge of progress, novelty in the procedure, and higher aspiration level, goals, etc, are important intrinsic motivating factors.
3. **External Internal Motivation :** This is the joint technique of motivation and is applied simultaneously on the individual.

Techniques of Motivation

Important extrinsic and intrinsic techniques of motivation are as follows:

1. Reward and Punishment

Student endeavours to do the best in order to get reward. He becomes pleased when he is given reward and greater enthusiasm on the part of the student is shown. Following things must be kept in mind while giving reward to an individual.

(a) The nature or amount of reward should be according to the level of performance. Additional reward is always fatal for the future progress of an individual.

(b) Individual must know the importance of reward. If reward is given to so many individuals at a time, the reward loses its validity.

(c) Reward should not be traditional or a routine activity. Different types of rewards should be given at different occasions.

(d) Reward should have some monetary or social value.

As far as punishment is concerned its fear leads an individual not to do unwanted jobs. The child comes to the class with full preparation in order to avoid punishment. Following things must be kept in mind before assigning any punishment:

(a) Punishment should not be regular. Such punishment can make the children habitual to punishment.

(b) Punishment should not be so severe. Such punishment can create hatred in the minds of children towards the whole system.

(c) Punishment should be given keeping in view the mental and physical resistance of children.

(d) Punishment should be judiciously distributed to all guilty persons.

Researches have made it clear that reward is better technique of motivation than punishment. Punishment is fatal to the psychological development of the organism also. So, punishment should be avoided as much as possible.

2. Praise and Blame

When a child is praised at his successes, he is overjoyed. As a result he works better than before. Following points must be kept in view while using praise as a technique of motivation:

(a) If an organism is praised at every big or small successes randomly, he will be addicted to listening the words of praise.

As a result no new behaviour is created due to praise.

(b) Weaker children should be praised even at their small bits of successes while talented children should be praised only when they have really done something very unique.

(c) Praise technique should be applied according to changing ratio schedule, i.e., sometimes, it should be used and sometimes not and the subject must not know at what time this is to be given.

As far as blame is concerned, students are directly blamed for their failures and they are made ashamed. But excess use of blame as a technique of motivation may frustrate the child. Following points must be kept in mind before blaming the students on their failures:

(a) Positive efforts of a child must be praised first before blaming him on his failure.

(b) Students should not be solely made responsible for their failure. Other related factors and conditions must also be included in the list of factors causing failures in life.

(c) The language of the blame should not be insulting for students. The self respect of every individual must be recognised.

3. Success and Failure

Success creates self confidence among individuals and possibility of more successes increases. Teacher creates such an environment in the class in which all the barriers in the way of success are removed.

Failure can also work as a source of motivation. Especially the talented students accepts the failure as a challenge for them. In order to use this technique in the classroom situation, the teacher presents such problems in the class which students are unable to solve. The bright students accept this challenge for future and thus they are motivated for work.

4. Competition and Cooperation

The feeling of competition is universal in humans. In the classroom situations weak students compare themselves with their own group and bright students compare their achievements with that of bright group of students. In this way the whole class is motivated. In games and sports too, competitions works as the best motivator. Every sports person does harder and harder efforts to raise his performance level. Such type of competition is called individual competition. Team competition also works as a good motivating force. These two types of competitive feelings are aroused by the teacher in the class in order to motivate the pupils.

The utility of cooperation as a technique of motivation is very limited. Here. Students are asked to work with mutual cooperation so that every one in the group may get opportunity to develop. Project method of teaching is a good example of this technique.

5. Knowledge of Progress

It is a traditional method of motivating the students that they are regularly told about their progress on the basis of formative evaluations. When they come to know about their achievements, they work harder to raise this level due to the feedback obtained from the knowledge of their progress. Teacher and sports teacher should regularly evaluate the achievement of students and students should be informed immediately about this. If any delay is made in evaluation or its reporting, the teachers will not be able to give any feedback to his students. For this purpose, regular tests should be conducted in the class and they should be evaluated with no delay. If evaluation and its reporting takes much time, students forget their mistakes or actual activities and, as a result, they do not get any feedback from these.

6. Novelty

Researches have proved that monotony makes a man bored. In order to motivate such persons in their task novelty and change in the approach is essential. In the class room situation a teacher brings about novelty in his method of teaching at regular intervals. This makes the students come across to new experiences at every movement. Level of students must be kept in view while introducing novelty in the situation so that this novelty may not work as a bouncer.

7. Aspiration Level

Level of aspiration has a direct relationship with the objectives of life. An individual can achieve the objectives of his life when his aspiration level is high. A teacher tries to raise this level as much high as possible but it is always matched with the mental or physical potentialities of the pupils. If this level of aspiration is higher than physical or mental level, student will get frustrated at their successive failures. Contrary to this if this level is lower than the physical or mental level, it will reduce the activities of students and they will develop inferiority complex.

THEORIES OF MOTIVATION

1. Instinct Theory

This theory of motivation was propounded by an English psychologist **Mc Dougall**. He pleaded that every human being has some innate powers or instincts. These instincts work as motives also and influence our behaviour. Under the influence of these instincts relationship between the object and the individual is established. Sentiments are aroused as a result of this. These sentiments organise an individual's emotional life and bring about stability in his behaviour. Thus, sentiments are an important factor behind the force of motivation. He explained the importance of self respect regarding sentiments. An individual's character is evaluated in terms of the stability of his self respect. If organisation of moral sentiments is more stable than the sentiments regarding the self respect, the character of the person will be strong.

2. Psychoanalytic Theory : (By Freud, Young and Adler)

According to them conscious plays main role in controlling an individuals' behaviour. As against unconscious mind there is the role of repression. Repression is the elimination of painful and unhealthy experiences from the conscious mind. Thus, repression is a defense mechanism with the help of which an individual tries to adjust partially. This repression is necessary because as child grows, many of his needs and feelings are disliked by the people which were earlier liked. When these needs are eliminated from the conscious mind, they are collected into unconscious mind and affect human behaviour indirectly. Sometimes these repressed needs come to the conscious level also when they receive any stimulus from outside. Thus, according to these psychologists, human behaviour is influenced by such motives also about which he is totally unaware.

3. Maslow's Need Theory

This theory has already been explained under the head of Maslow's Hierarchy of needs.

4. Social Theory

This theory is of two type :

(a) **Cultural Pattern Theory** (by **Mead & Benedict**) **:** According to this theory, behaviour of a person is influenced by the respective culture in which he lives. For example, individuals of those castes which have strict controlling system on their members become foolish, dry and short tempered when they grow. On the contrary, the castes in which children are behaved affectionately, they manifest considerate behaviour when they grow. Thus, behaviour is very much influenced by the pattern of rearing of a person. In the classroom situation, a teacher can motivate his students by his own behaviour.

(b) **Field Theory** (by **Kurt Levin**) **:** According to this theory, the behaviour of an individual is not determined by his qualities or personality traits but all those forces which act between an individual and his environment. Thus, there is a close relationship between an individual and his environment. In the class room situation a child can be motivated by creating an environment suitable to the child.

5. Drive Theory

This theory is somewhat similar to need theory of Maslow. According to this theory an individual is driven to act when certain biological needs create some inner tension which is called drive. Thus drive is the primary cause of motivation.

The drawback of this theory is that it is helpless to explain why an individual, in the absence of inner drive behaves in a particular situation due to the effect of his environment as is explained by the social theory of motivation.

6. Incentive Theory

According to this theory, external incentives such as rewards, monetary benefits, promotion in the social status etc. can also motivate an individual to act in a certain direction.

7. Expectancy Theory

According to this theory an individual is not actually getting any reward or monetary benefits but the expectation of getting such a reward or benefits can motivate him to do the job in the best manner possible. In the field of games, a sportsman can be motivated to perform his best by giving him some incentive not at present but in the future.

8. Learning of behaviour Theory (Clark Hall)

According to this theory an individual's behaviour depends on the satisfaction or dissatisfaction of his needs. When his needs are satisfied, his psychological tensions are reduced and he retains the reaction of his learnt behaviour. When his organic needs are satisfied, he learns to link the social conditions with his primary needs and retains that particular behaviour.

9. Motivation Hygiene Theory (Fredrick Herzberg)

This theory was indoctrinated in the field of industry and commerce first. Herzberg interviewed farmers, account officers, nurses and house wives in Pistbarg University in 1966 and propounded this theory.

According to this theory motives enhance the efficiency by providing comforts and satisfactions to the pupils. Motives keep them delighted by increasing their achievement on one hand and pupils get satisfied by their motives on the other. This in turn enriches learning. Since the effect of motives are positive and persists for a longer period of time, as a result motives develop the following feelings in the pupils:

(a) Achievement
(b) Recognition
(c) Responsibility
(d) Advancement
(e) Personal growth

The above feeling are directly affected by hygiene factors. They are given below :

(a) Methods of supervision
(b) Condition of work
(c) Inter-personal relations
(d) Social policy and administration
(e) Status
(f) Security

If level of these factors is low, the individual becomes unhappy, and as a result, learning outcome will fall. It can also develop negative attitude among the learner. The learner can be motivated by raising the level of these six hygiene factors.

This theory has direct application in the field of education and sports along with other field of life. Performance of students of government schools is low only because of low level of some of hygiene factors. If organizational climate of the school is made good, it will automatically increase the achievement of pupils.

10. Operant Conditioning Model of Motivation

This model was presented by Skinner. It suggests that behaviour would change by the consequence of that very behaviour. If the result of a particular behaviour is satisfactory, it will be automatically reinforced and repeated in future. Reinforcement is given from outside also for the recurrence of desired behaviour.

Thus, this model does not give importance to the inner motivation of the individual. It ignores drives and needs of learners as well. Level of aspiration is also ignored by this model. This model is rather based on the observable and measurable overt behavioural responses which are modified slowly by giving proper reinforcement.

According to this model the desirable behaviours are first identified. Then conditions are created for the occurrence of these behaviours. And finally, once they occur, reinforcement is given for the recurrence of these behaviours.

Techniques of motivation and students' needs, teaching objectives and learning structures

Need (lower needs)	Teaching structure	Teaching objectives	Techniques of motivation (Extrinsic)
1. Physiological	1. Signal learning	1. Knowledge	1. Reward
2. Safety	2. Chain learning	2. Comprehension or understanding	2. Praise and reward
3. Belongingness (higher needs)	3. Multiple discrimination learning	3.Above + Analysis	3. Success and failure (extrinsic and intrinsic)
4. Esteem	4. Cocept learning	4.Application	4. Competition and cooperation
5. Self actualization	5. Principle learning	5.Creativity	5. Knowledge of result 6. Novelty 7. Level of aspiration 8. Self-motivation

Techniques of motivation and students' needs : The teacher should first of all find out the needs of his student's *i.e.*, at what level of needs the students are. Only then the teacher can give intrinsic or extrinsic motivation to his students. It is also likely that students do not have the capacity to think beyond the third level of Maslow's needs. In that case the teacher should create the other two needs in his students by telling the students about the goals of life and its related difficulties.

These very needs will motivate the students for effort and desired behaviour will be seen in future.

Motivation techniques and learning objectives

While selecting suitable techniques of motivation the teacher keeps this fact into account what learning objectives he had formulated in the beginning. Thus, a teacher takes 6 × 3 = 18 objectives into account while selecting motivation techniques. We will discuss these three domains of objectives in relation to motivation techniques below :

(a) *Cognitive Domain Objectives :* If teacher has restricted his objectives to the level of application only, then for realising these three levels of objectives, a composite techniques of motivation may be proved to be successful. But if the objectives are extended to analysis, synthesis or evaluation, motivation techniques will not work much. The teacher will rather have to take the help of teaching strategies and tactics such as self study, problem solving group discussion, symposium and seminars etc.

(b) *Affective objectives :* Lower level of affective objectives like receiving, responding and valuing etc, can be achieved by using techniques of motivation. But techniques of motivation are not very much helpful for achieving higher level of objectives and in that case, the teacher should use strategies of teaching like self study, brain storming , CAI etc. more than motivation techniques.

(c) *Psychomotor objectives :* Techniques of motivation are most helpful for realising objectives of psychomotor domain and extrinsic techniques are more powerful than intrinsic techniques here.

Motivation and Learning Structure

Various techniques of motivation should also he selected according to different structures of learning. These five structures are given here:

(a) **Signal learning** : Stimulus and responses are directly connected here. Extrinsic techniques of motivation are most suitable here.

(b) **Chain learning** : Chain is formed between stimuli and responses here. Environment is especially significant here so, extrinsic techniques are most suitable in chain learning.

(c) **Multiple discrimination learning** : So many stimuli are presented before the students simultaneously here and they respond to these stimuli on the basis of similarities and differences. Environment and content both are important here. In this type of learning structure, both types of motivation techniques are useful.

(d) **Concept learning** : In such type of learning content and its presentation are given preference here. Therefore, only intrinsic techniques of motivation are useful here.

(e) **Principle learning** : In this structure, various concepts are presented in the form of chain here. When this is done, they take the form of laws or principles. It means that only content is important here. So, only intrinsic techniques of motivation is useful here.

FACTORS CONTRIBUTING TO LEARNING

Introduction

Learning, can be considered as the process by which skills, attitudes, knowledge and concepts are acquired, understood, applied and extended. All human beings, whether grown ups or children engage in the process of learning, either consciously, sub-consciously or subliminally. It is through learning that their competence and ability to function in their environment get enhanced. It is important to understand that while we learn some ideas and concepts through instruction or teaching, we also learn through our feelings and experiences. Feelings and experiences are a tangible part of our lives and these greatly influence what we learn, how we learn and why we learn.

Learning has been considered partly a cognitive process and partly a social and affective one. It qualifies as a cognitive process because it involves the functions of attention, perception, reasoning, analysis, drawing of conclusions, making interpretations and giving meaning to the observed phenomena. All of these are mental processes which relate to the intellectual functions of the individual. Learning is a social and affective process, as the societal and cultural context in which we function and the feelings and experiences which we have, greatly influence our ideas, concepts, images and understanding of the world. These constitute inner subjective interpretations and represent our own unique, personalized constructions of the specific universe of functioning. Our knowledge, ideas, concepts, attitudes, beliefs and the skills which we acquire are a consequence of these combined processes.

CLASSIFICATION OF FACTORS: PERSONAL & ENVIRONMENT

To understand how we categorise the factors affecting learning, let us begin by considering the following examples:

- Ravi is sixteen year old and wants to please his mother by getting good results in his board examinations. He is so eager to please her, that he spends long hours of concentrated time and energy on his studies. He consciously tries to control other sources of distraction in his life and reduces the time spent on watching television, playing games and chatting with his friends.

- Rita Williams wants to be a famous tennis player. To achieve her goal, she practices tennis whenever she can, even though she gets no encouragement from her family. She makes it a point to watch tennis matches and maintain a good rapport with her sports teacher.
- Yuvraj is a good student, but lately he has been scoring very low marks at school. He is not able to concentrate or pay attention and his class work and home assignments reflect a very poor quality. Sources revealed that his parents fight a lot with each other and are about to get divorced.
- Arti and Kavita are two sisters. Arti is very good at art and craft and can sketch just about anything she sees. Kavita has a ear for music. She knows most songs and can sing them even if she has heard them only once. Both of them spend hours together pursuing their respective interest areas.
- Sayeeda is tall, attractive and has a very good figure. She wants to be a model or an air-hostess and nurtures this secretly as her dream. She is too scared to share her wishes with her family, since she belongs to an orthodox family, where girls at best can pursue teaching as a career. When she tries telling her mother what she wants, she is firmly told that she can only do her B.Ed and can go to the coaching classes for these.

The above cited examples illustrate that learning is a universal phenomenon mediated by a number of factors, both personal and environmental in nature. The dictum "everybody learns" is as true as its corollary, *i.e.*, everybody learns in accordance with his/her unique, individualized blend of personal and environmental factors. For example, in case of Ravi, the desire to please his mother, striving to do well in his board exams and managing his life situations appropriately constitute the key factors which influence him. For Rita Williams, it is her intrinsic desire to be a good tennis player which is paramount. She is not deterred by the lack of family support and continues to make efforts to promote her love for tennis on her own and fulfil her desire to be successful.

In case of Yuvraj, in spite of his innate capacity to study and perform well, his lack of achievement can be attributed to the emotional insecurity stemming from his parents' divorce. As far as Arti and Kavita are concerned, their special interests and talent in art and music respectively, seem to guide their activities.

For Sayeeda, the home environment and family culture and values determine her professional choice. Her own inner interests, desires and wishes are not to be taken into cognizance.

In all the examples cited, we can find evidence of both personal and environmental factors influencing the process of learning. Learning can thus be defined as a function of the interaction of personal and environmental factors.

$$L = f\,(EF \times PF)$$

L = learning; f = function; EF = environmental factors; PF = personal factors.

Personal factors are the intra individual factors like motivation, interests, abilities etc which predispose an individual towards learning as in the case of Rita Williams, Arti and Kavita. Environmental factors on the other hand, are those contextual factors which highlight the role of the environment in learning, such as the socio-emotional, societal and cultural factors as seen in the case of Yuvraj and Sayeeda. Although the two factors represent different categories, they operate in a common system. The environmental factors provide the context within which the personal factors, operate. The learner and the learning process can only be completely understood with reference to the interaction of both environmental and personal factors. This may be diagrammatically represented as follows:

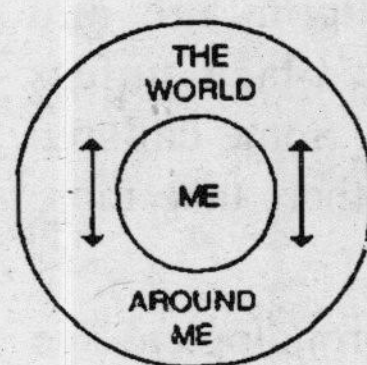

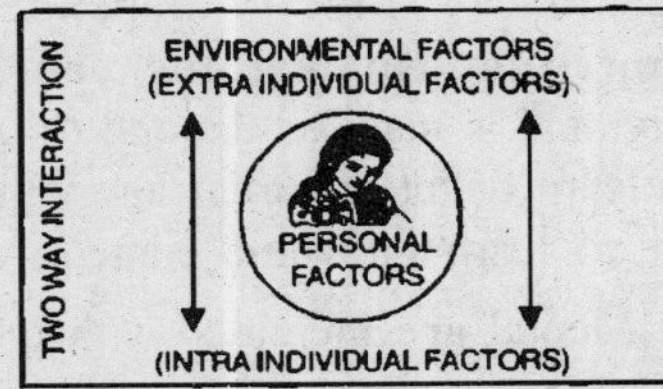

Fig: *Factors affecting learning*

Personal Factors Influencing Learning

The process of learning is influenced by a variety of personal factors. A thorough knowledge of these factors will prove very helpful for teachers and parents in understanding and guiding their children's learning. Some of the personal factors that influence the learning process may be classified as under : sensation and perception, fatigue and boredom, maturation, emotional condition, needs, interests, motivation, attention, intelligence, aptitude, attitude, etc. Let us discuss the important personal factors in the following sub-sections.

Sensation and Perception

Apart from the general health of the students, sensation and perception are the psychological factors which help in learning. Sensation is at the core of perception. There are five sense organs *i.e.*, skin, ears, tongue, eyes and nose. These sense organs are the gateways of knowledge and help in perception of various stimuli in the environment. Any defect in any of the sense organs will affect learning and hence acquisition of knowledge. For example, defects of vision such as myopia, hypermetropia, astigmatism, etc., cause headaches, nausia and general disinclination to study. A blind person depends upon the sense of touch or skin for learning and thus acquires knowledge and skills, as he can not visualise the objects. The stimuli are preceived and assimilated, and hence learnt through various sense organs. In this way we can say that sensation and perception is the bases of knowledge and learning.

Fatigue and Boredom

It is virtually boredom or lassitude rather than fatigue which bothers the students. The difference between the two is that fatigue is mental or physical tiredness which decreases in efficiency and competency to work. Boredom, on the other hand, is a lack of desire on an aversion to work. Such an aversion makes one feel fatigued without being actually fatigued. Studying seldom causes fatigue. It is mainly boredom which, besides causing the impression of fatigue, decreases student efficiency in learning.

Age and Maturation

Learning is directly dependent upon age and maturation. No learning can take place unless individual is matured enough to learn. Some children can learn better at earlier age while others take more time to learn the same content.

Mental age increases with the chronological age and ceases at about the age of sixteen years. Increase in age means intellectual maturation which helps in solving difficult problems. The principle of maturation warns us against enforcing learning on a child when he is not mature enough to learn the specific skills. Teachers should explain this principle to parents who are over ambitious or over enthusiastic in sending their children to school at the very early age.

Emotional Conditions

Desirable emotional conditions enhance the quality and speed of learning. Happiness, joy and satisfaction are always favourable for any type of learning. Adverse emotional conditons, on the other hand, hinder learning. Many studies have established the fact that emotional strain, stress, tensions, disturbances, etc., are extremely inimical to scholastic pursuits.

Needs

A need is the lack of something which, if provided, would facilitate child's usual behaviour. The lack of something is experienced by the child. The child then tries to perform that activity which culminates in the satisfaction of the need. Thus, the needs are associated with goals. Among human beings, the needs are realtively permanent tendencies which seek satisfaction in achieving certain specific goals. When these goals are achieved, the particular need is satisfied or met for the time being, but it recurs sooner or later and energises further activity. The needs in human beings can be physiological such as need for oxygen, food, water, etc. They may be social such as the need for affection, recognition, self-regard, etc. Social needs are however, quite different from physiological needs. Social needs might originate after physiological needs are satisfied. These needs have a complex structure and dominate the individual's behaviour.

There is not equal urgency in the satisfaction of all needs. Some have to be satisfied before others can manifest themselves.

In schools, children are not expected to do any intellectual thinking unless their physiological needs are satisfied. Poor, starved children may concentrate less on attainment of knowledge than on food. Similarly, very cold or hot classrooms or over-crowded seats will not be conducive to good learning. Likewise the need for safety, love and esteem, all act as powerful motives in the learning situations. If the child is afraid of the teacher or feels unsafe while in the school on account of too much beating or some other form of punishment, no learning can take place. Similarly, his needs for warmth and affection are very stimulating and hence results in effective learning.

Interests

Various types of interests of the students can be exploited to facilitate their learning. The interests during early infancy are mostly limited and short lived. As the child grows older his interests diversify and stabilize. You, a school teacher, should have thorough knowledge of children's interests. You can eliminate much drudgery, monotony and boredom from the school work if you make your instruction lively and stimulating and arouse student interest in it.

Once the students' interest is aroused in an activity you should expend more effort on it. No learning can be achieved without proper expenditure of effort on it. Students can even overcome distraction, fatigue and boredom if they feel interested in your instruction and class activities. It has often been found that, in most cases, fatigue in reality is loss of interest in the learning activity. Interest, should be exploited to yield results of greater quantity and quality learning in school.

Life is so exciting that many interesting things and activities often clamor to attract our attention.

Children frequently face the dilemma of mutually conflicting interests. Immediate interests often seem to be clashing with the remoter ones. A student might be in a quandary at least for the time being when his interest in sports impels him towards the play-field and his interest in studies force him to concentrate on books.

In such cases of conflicting interests a lot of hesitancy, wastage, frustration and unhappiness is bound to follow. What is needed is education at home and school which helps/trains children to achieve a healthy balance in their interests. They should be trained to budget their time in such a manner as to pay a reasonable attention to various interests, scholastic, athletic, social etc., within the time at their disposal.

Motivation

Motivation is the heart of the learning process. It generates the will in an individual to do something. Adequate motivation not only engages the student in an activity which results in learning, but also sustains and directs learning. Two types of motivation are commonly recognised. These are: intrinsic and extrinsic motivation.

Intelligence

Intelligence as expressed by an I.Q. score on an intelligence test is positively related to learning. Generally, students with higher I.Q. learn rapidly. However, higher I.Q. in itself is no guarantee for rapid learning, since other factors such as needs, interest, motivation, etc., of the students and the methods used for learning are also important.

Aptitude

A student who possesses appropriate aptitude for a particular subject of study or skill, will learn better and retain it for a longer time. On the other hand, he will require relatively longer time to study a subject for which he lacks natural aptitude. He is liable to forget it soon besides feeling bored and unhappy all the time while learning it. Hence, it is extremely desirable to analyse the aptitude of students before prescribing courses of study for them.

Attitude

The learning process is also influenced considerably by the attitude of the student. If he is alert, attentive and interested in the material to be learnt, he is bound to have a favourable attitude towards it. Such an attitude will enable him to tackle the learning situation economically, pleasantly and effectively. Conversely, if he is inattentive and is uninterested in the material his attitude is bound to be unfavourable. This will hinder the smooth learning of the material in hand besides involving undue strain and tension in the learner.

Environmental Factors

Environmental influences begin since the time of the conception of the child in the womb of the mother. Mother's mental, physical and emotional conditions influence the development of foetus in the womb. The external environment starts from the time of birth of the child. It (external environment) refers to the surroundings which prevail in home, school and locality. At these places, the child interacts with members of the family, teachers, classmates or peers and neighbours and establishes relationship with them. The relationship with the members of the society, and the surroundings may affect the development of the child and also the way he learns. Some of the environmental factors are discussed as follows:

Surrounding : Natural, Social and Cultural

As the title of the sub-section indicates, we shall discuss here natural, social and cultural environment the child interacts with and get influenced.

Natural surrounding covers the climatic and atmospheric condition. These conditions affect learning directly. It has been found that high temperature and humidity reduces mental efficiency. For a limited time, humidity and high temperature can be tolerated but prolonged humidity and high temperature become unbearable and decrease mental efficiency. The intellectual productivity and creativeness of people living in hot regions are much low. Likewise, the morning time is always better for mastering difficult tasks. Mental efficiency decreases due to increased humidity and temperature. Studies on the academic progress of evening school students shows losses of efficiency varying from one to six per cent.

Social surrounding includes especially the environment of home, school and locality. Physical conditions at home such as large family, small family, (specific place of the study), insufficient ventilation, improper lighting, uncomfortable temperature, noisy home environment due to use of radio, TV, etc., noisy neighbourhood, constant visits by friends or relatives, etc., influence the intellectual learning of the student. The socio-emotional factors such as child rearing practices, reward and punishment, scope for freedom and independence in activities and decision making, play and study facilities, ambitions and aspirations of the parents, disorganisation and discord among birth positions such as eldest, youngest or single child have their definite influence on learning. For example, a student who comes from a very poor family and never had any intellectual stimulation at home remains dull and unresponsive in the class. In some societies there is a strong sex bias. Girls are directly or indirectly told that education is not meant for them. In the middle class families, on the other hand, parents are rather over-ambitious. They wish their children to make quick academic progress, grow-up and find a respectable vocation preferably a white collar job. Such children, therefore get sufficient incentive from their families. This, of course, is most favourable to scholastic learning, although an overdose of family emphasis on acquiring academic excellence might affect the child's mental and physical health adversely. Similarly, school activities, study facilities and teaching methods and behaviour of teachers, principals and non-teaching staff have an impact upon learning. If the school atmosphere is unconducive, it adversely affects the learning process. Locality also has an influence on a child. If the locality is bad, the learning will be ineffective to some extent.

Cultural demands and social expectations also influence learning. The spirit of culture is reflected in its social and educational institutions. Children's learning, therefore, is greatly determined by the demands and expectations of their culture. Thus, for instance, in an industrialized culture the emphasis mostly centres mechanical sciences and preparing children for highly mechanised vocations. In an agriculture based community, on the other hand, the educational process focusses on preparing its members for those skills which are suited to the needs of an agrarian community.

The philosophical elements of culture also influence the spirit of children's learning. Children in a democratic culture tend to acquire democrative and values and attitudes. A feudal, aristocratic or dictatorial culture, on the other hand, promotes autocratic modes of thought and behaviour.

Relationship with Teacher, Parents and Peers

The teacher is an important constituent in the instructional process. She/he plays an important role in shaping the behaviour of students. The way he teaches and manages the students has an affect on their learning. An authoritarian teacher will create an aggression and hostility among students while a democratic teacher will create a participatory climate for learning. The democratic environment leads students to constructive, thoughtful and cooperative behaviour. Generally, students learn better in a democratic set up because they like democratic procedures. The teacher is no more an instructor or the director of learning in a democratic set up. She/he helps his/her students in their learning. The teachers no more dominate the scene, they can get better results by decentralizing authority, increasing independence of students. They can attend to the comments and questions of the students. They can encourage students to participate in learning activities in and outside the class. There should be more emphasis on activity-centred classroom where student's active participation in the teaching-learning process is encouraged and the teacher acts as a guide to promote learning.

Relationship with parents plays a vital role in the learning process of the student. If the child-parents relationship is based on mutual respect and faith, it can provide the child a congenial atmosphere which in turn can facilitate his/her learning. A distorted and unhealthy environment, on the other hand, adversely affects the learning of the student. The upward mobility brings resistance on the part of the student to learn. Students in such families find themselves unable to cope up. A subtle but powerful influence on the growing child arises from his/her position among the children in the family. The parents of the first born expect the child to act like miniature adults and hence the first-born are found to encounter a variety of expectations and stresses. Whereas parents tend to be more relaxed in their do's and dont's with the last-born. Factors like traumatic events at home, separation or death can also precipitate learning problems in the normal child.

A healthy peer group relationship also plays an important role in learning. Student-student relationship in the classroom, school, society, etc., create a particular type of emotional climate. The climate solely depends upon their relationships. A sound relationships provides a tension free environment to the student to learn more and to compete in the class. If the relationship among peers is not good, it adversely affects their learning. Therefore, to improve the classroom learning climate, free discussion should be there. You should help your students understand each other in formal or informal meetings. They should be encouraged to meet each other and their teachers freely. If any mis-understanding is created or developed, it should be immediately clarified so as to maintain the healthy climate and cordial relationship among peers.

Mass Media Influence on Learning

Today, mass media is all pervaive and omnipresent. Our day-to-day life is inundated with the presence of mass media. We can access mass media through television, radio and print. If, some years ago, radio and print were the main tools of mass communication, television seems to have taken over the place now.

Mass media is informative and influence the thinking of people. It creates a learning environment. Mass media is not controlled by a single agency and what it represents is neither organized learning (as in schools) nor the immediate reality surrounding you (as in home and community). Mass media offers a wide range of information and reality far removed from immediate reality. The informal learning environment created by mass media is intense and far reaching in impact than any other informal learning environment.

Learning through print medium presupposes the ability to read alike. Hence, its reach as an informal learning agency is limited. Radio is more effective than print as the listener requires only comprehension skill. The advent of twenty four hours television channels have redefined the role of mass media as an agency of informal learning. Television is more powerful and effective than radio and print as it exercises greater influence on the viewers through visual images.

Both radio and television appeal to literates and illiterates alike. The mass media-is not an agency of organized learning. However, the mass media is sometimes used by state agencies to effect purposeful and specific learning at a mass level. For example, the family planning, pulse polio, and HIV/AIDS programmes on mass media sponsored by the state are intended to bring about behaviour modification among the masses.

For children who have access to the mass media, especially the television, it becomes an additional and supportive source of learning in the context of organized learning. Children who are exposed to the mass media are well informsd and that often facilitate their reddiness for new learning in the organized learning context. However, learning through the mass media, especially the television is not always positive or constnictive learning. Through television viewing, children often pick up values that are not in conformity with the values of the family, school, or community. Thus, television or any other mass media teaches academic and cognitive skills and social behaviours but it can have both positive and negative influences on children.

These days television and radio are used as supportive agencies in imparting organized learning. For example, the Indira Gandhl National Open University utilizes the electronic media (television and radio) for teaching-learning purposes. We can say that the electronic media is used for creating a virtual learning environment. Through interactive radio counselling students sitting across the country are able to tune in to listen to their teachers and interact with them. Teleconferencing creates interactive virtual classroom. The virtual learning environment created on television or computer is found effective due to the presence of visual images and the use of multimedia. Then, there are noninteractive virtual learning environments, like the telecast of UGC's country-wideclassrooms. Decades ago when television was a rarity, the government of India used All India Radio to educate the Indian fanners about the technological advances in farming to bring in India's Green Revolution. Thus, mass media can play a significant role in formal and non-formal learning.

MULTIPLE CHOICE QUESTIONS

1. According to Piaget, during the first stage of development (birth to about 2 years age), a child learns best
   (*a*) by thinking in an abstract fashion
   (*b*) by applying newly acquired knowledge of language
   (*c*) by using the senses
   (*d*) by comprehending neutral words
2. The most intense and crucial socialization takes place
   (*a*) during early childhood
   (*b*) during adulthood
   (*c*) throughout the life of a person
   (*d*) during adolescence
3. Heredity is considered as a .... social structure.
   (*a*) dynamic (*b*) static
   (*c*) primary (*d*) secondary
4. Theory of learning which totally and only depends on '*observable behaviour*' is associated with .... theory of learning.
   (*a*) Behaviourist (*b*) Constructivist
   (*c*) Cognitivist (*d*) Developmental
5. Which of the following does ***not*** reflect 'teaching for understanding'?
   (*a*) Help students see similarities and differences and generate analogies
   (*b*) Enable students to memorize isolated facts and procedures
   (*c*) Ask students to explain a phenomenon or a concept in their own words
   (*d*) Teach students to provide examples to illustrate how a law works
6. Which of the following is ***not*** a characteristic feature of intrinsically motivated children?
   (*a*) They display a high level of energy while working
   (*b*) They like challenging tasks
   (*c*) They always succeed
   (*d*) They enjoy doing their work
7. A teacher wants the gifted children of her class to achieve their potential. Which of the following should she ***not*** do to achieve her objective?
   (*a*) Segregate them from their peers for special attention
   (*b*) Challenge them to enhance their creativity
   (*c*) Teach them to enjoy non-academic activities
   (*d*) Teach them to manage stress
8. Which of the following is ***not*** a sign of reading difficulty among young learners? Difficulty in
   (*a*) understanding words and ideas
   (*b*) spelling consistency
   (*c*) letter and word recognition
   (*d*) reading speed and fluency
9. 'Self-regulation' of learners refers to
   (*a*) rules and regulations made by the student body
   (*b*) self-discipline and control
   (*c*) their ability to monitor their own learning
   (*d*) creating regulations for student behaviour
10. Which of the following statements ***cannot*** be considered as a feature of 'learning'?
    (*a*) Study of behaviour is learning
    (*b*) Unlearning is also a part of learning
    (*c*) Learning is a process that mediates behaviour
    (*d*) Learning is something that occurs as a result of certain experiences
11. Constructivism as a theory
    (*a*) emphasises on memorising information and testing through recall
    (*b*) emphasises on the dominant role of the teacher
    (*c*) focuses on the role of imitation
    (*d*) emphasises the role of the learner in constructing his own view of the world
12. A creative learner refers to one who is
    (*a*) capable of scoring consistently good marks in tests
    (*b*) good at lateral thinking and problem solving
    (*c*) very talented in drawing and painting
    (*d*) highly intelligent
13. Development of concepts is primarily a part of
    (*a*) physical development
    (*b*) social development
    (*c*) emotional development
    (*d*) intellectual development

14. Individual learners differ from each other in
(*a*) sequence of development
(*b*) general capacity for development
(*c*) principles of growth and development
(*d*) rate of development

15. The statement : 'An important precondition for the proper development of a child is ensuring her/his healthy physical development'
(*a*) is true because physical development occupies the topmost place in the sequence of development
(*b*) is true because physical development is interrelated with other domains of development
(*c*) is untrue as physical development does not affect other domains of development in any way
(*d*) may be incorrect as development varies from individual to individual

16. Irfan breaks toys and dismantles them to explore their components. What would you do?
(*a*) Encourage his inquisitive nature and channelise his energy
(*b*) Make him understand that toys should not be broken
(*c*) Never let Irfan play with toys
(*d*) Always keep a close watch

17. Understanding the principles of development of a child helps a teacher in
(*a*) rationalizing why the learner ought to be taught
(*b*) effectively catering to the different learning styles of learners
(*c*) identifying the social status of the learner
(*d*) identifying the economic background of the learner

18. Every learner is unique means that
(*a*) A common curriculum for all learners is not possible
(*b*) It is impossible to develop the potential of learners in a heterogeneous class
(*c*) No two learners are alike in their abilities, interests and talents
(*d*) Learners do not have any common qualities, nor do they share common goals

19. The statement 'Men are generally more intelligent than women'
(*a*) shows gender bias
(*b*) is true for different domains of intelligence
(*c*) is ture
(*d*) may be true

20. Christina took her class for a field trip and after coming back, she discussed the trip with her students. It may be connotated as
(*a*) Learning for Assessment
(*b*) Learning of Assessment
(*c*) Assessment of Learning
(*d*) Assessment for Learning

21. Human development is based on certain principles. Which of the following is ***not*** a principle of human development?
(*a*) General to Specific
(*b*) Reversible
(*c*) Continuity
(*d*) Sequentiality

22. Centrally sponsored scheme of Integrated Education for disabled children aims at providing educational opportunities to children with disabilities in
(*a*) Open schools
(*b*) Blind Relief Association schools
(*c*) Regular schools
(*d*) Special schools

23. Which of the following statements is true about 'learning'?
(*a*) Learning is not affected by emotional factors at any stage of learning.
(*b*) Learning is fundamentally a mental activity.
(*c*) Errors made by children indicate that no learning has taken place.
(*d*) Learning is effective in an environment that is emotionally positive and satisfying for the learners.

24. The main purpose of assessment should be
(*a*) to decide if a student should be promoted to the next class
(*b*) to diagnose and remedy gaps in learning
(*c*) to point out the errors of the learners
(*d*) to measure the achievement of learners

25. Helping learners recapitulate or recall what they have already learnt is important because
(*a*) it is an effective way of revising old lessons
(*b*) it enhances the memory of learners thereby strengthening learning
(*c*) it is a convenient beginning for any classroom instruction
(*d*) relating new information to prior knowledge enhances learning

26. Creative answers require
(*a*) open-ended questions
(*b*) a highly disciplined classroom
(*c*) direct teaching and direct questions
(*d*) content-based questions

27. Learners should ***not*** be encouraged to
(*a*) participate in as many co-curricular activities as possible
(*b*) memorize all the answers to questions which the teacher may ask
(*c*) ask as many questions as possible both inside and outside the class

(*d*) actively interact with other learners in group work

28. Which of the following is ***not*** an appropriate tool for Formative Assessment?
(*a*) Term test (*b*) Quiz and games
(*c*) Assignment (*d*) Oral questions

29. Diagnosis of the gaps in the learning of students should be followed by
(*a*) systematic revision of all lessons
(*b*) reporting the findings to learners and parents
(*c*) appropriate remedial measures
(*d*) intensive drill and practice

30. Multilingual character of Indian society should be seen as
(*a*) a challenge to teacher's capacity to motivate students to learn
(*b*) a factor that makes school life a complex experience for the learners
(*c*) a hindrance in teaching-learning process
(*d*) a resource for enrichment of school life

31. Which of the following statements regarding personality traits is correct?
(*a*) Traits of personality can not be developed in isolation without taking the help of environment
(*b*) Subjective traits of the individual are determined by genetic factors
(*c*) Bad environment can surpass good inheritance but good environment is not a substitute for poor heredity
(*d*) All of these

32. Which of the following characteristics denote infancy period?
(*a*) Physical growth is curvilinear
(*b*) Physical growth is rapid
(*c*) Head grows at relatively slower rate as compared to other parts of the body
(*d*) All of these

33. Which of the following is not the characteristic of infancy period?
(*a*) From bilateral to unilateral trend in motor organs
(*b*) From general to specific trend in motor organs
(*c*) Emotional/social development is not associated with motor development
(*d*) Steady mental development

34. Which of the following illustrates conceptual development?
(*a*) Perception is the beginning of concept formation
(*b*) Concept changes with changes in experiences
(*c*) Concept changes with age
(*d*) All of these

35. There is one thing common in language and physical development what is that?
(*a*) Spurts of development at different ages
(*b*) Dependence on experience
(*c*) Dependence on training
(*d*) None of these

36. Which of the following characteristics is not associated with emotional development?
(*a*) Emotion is accompanied by physiological changes
(*b*) Emotions start immediately after birth
(*c*) Intense form of emotions are seen during early childhood period
(*d*) Emotions are unrelated to physical development

37. The child acquires about three fourth of the brain weight by the age of
(*a*) 2½ years (*b*) 2 years
(*c*) 6 years (*d*) 8 years

38. Social development of an infant depends on
(*a*) his chance of interaction with others
(*b*) love and affection shown to the child
(*c*) the extent to which he is able to attract the attention of others
(*d*) all of the above

39. In which of the following stages the child looks self centred?
(*a*) Infancy (*b*) Early childhood
(*c*) Adolescence (*d*) Adulthood

40. In the period of infancy, emotions are
(*a*) intense, frequent and unstable
(*b*) like an open book(overt)
(*c*) need based
(*d*) all of these

41. Which of the following organs of the body shows rapid growth in infancy?
(*a*) growth of hands (*b*) growth of head
(*c*) growth of legs (*d*) growth of fingers

42. In normal learning environment, forgetting is caused
(*a*) due to back of practice for a long time
(*b*) due to the interference of other learnt material
(*c*) due to lack of consolidation of memory traces
(*d*) all of these

43. Clear conception of size, weight, colour, time etc., is seen at the age of
(*a*) six (*b*) four
(*c*) four and half (*d*) five

44. Which of the following is not the characteristics of intellectual development of early childhood?
(*a*) increased span of attention
(*b*) exploration of the environment
(*c*) ability to verbalize all known concepts
(*d*) ability to distinguish past, present and future

45. Social development by the end of early childhood is marked by
(a) the feeling of autonomy
(b) the end of solitary plays
(c) the temperament of co-operation and friendliness
(d) all of these

46. Fictional world of the child starts at the age of
(a) 5-6 (b) 6-8
(c) 3-4 (d) 4-5

47. Girls are more dominating than boys in social situations in which of the following periods?
(a) pre-adolescent period
(b) early childhood period
(c) both of these
(d) none of these

48. In the period of early childhood, child is
(a) helpless to hide his emotions
(b) seen shifting his emotions very rapidly and frequently
(c) guided by his innate tendencies and instincts
(d) all of these

49. A nursery teacher should organize
(a) group games in the school
(b) those games which involve motor organs of the body
(c) those games which help the child to manipulate the environment
(d) all of these

50. Later childhood is called latency period because
(a) creative potentials are dormant
(b) sex remains dormant
(c) it is a period of inactivity
(d) all of these

51. Physical development of later childhood is marked by
(a) Auscification of bones
(b) Permanent teeth
(c) Excessive motor activity
(d) All of these

52. Girls surpass boys physically in
(a) infancy
(b) later childhood
(c) early childhood
(d) adolescence

53. The period of later childhood is marked by
(a) intellectual maturity
(b) high muscular energy
(c) hero worship
(d) all of these

54. Which of the following is not the characteristics of intellectual development of later childhood?
(a) High interest in science fiction
(b) Increased logical power
(c) Careful for future
(d) End of imaginary fears

55. Children are very much hateful or indifferent to opposite sex at the age of
(a) 11-12 (b) 13-14
(c) 10-11 (d) 15-16

56. Period of later childhood is marked by
(a) slow and steady physical growth
(b) stability in emotions
(c) anger against injustice
(d) all of these

57. At the end of later childhood period, the child
(a) feels himself superior to girls
(b) becomes independent of his family
(c) wants to become hero
(d) all of these

58. The best place of social development for a 12 years old child is
(a) neighbourhood
(b) family
(c) playground
(d) school

59. Group activities and group loyalties are at its peak at the age of
(a) 10-12 (b) 13-15
(c) 8-10 (d) 18-20

60. A teacher should not let a 12 years old child any time free because
(a) child is always interested to get involve in physical or mental activities
(b) spurts of creativity are seen at this age
(c) child is frustrated
(d) all of these

61. Elektra complex refers to
(a) daughter comes closer to the father
(b) son comes closer to the mother
(c) inferiority complex in the presence of girls
(d) none of these

62. According to Freud, super ego is properly developed during
(a) latency period (b) anal period
(c) phallic period (d) none of these

63. Development is a process of observable social interaction. This is the opinion of
(a) Erikson (b) Skinner
(c) Robert Sears (d) None of these

64. The secondary behaviour of the child according to Robert Sears starts with
(a) reinforcement (b) imitation
(c) modelling (d) none of these

65. The period of sensory motor adoptation of Piaget is
(a) 0-2 years (b) 1-3 years
(c) 3-5 years (d) 4-6 years

66. The child adopts the view points of others on the basis of consequences of these views in the
(*a*) third stage of Kohlberg's theory
(*b*) second stage of Kohlberg's theory
(*c*) fourth stage of Kohlberg's theory
(*d*) fifth stage of Kohlberg's theory

67. Which of the following is not the view point of cognitive theories of development?
(*a*) moral principles are acquired automatically with age
(*b*) super ego is formed during the period of adolescence
(*c*) Moral values are determined by culture
(*d*) Mural principles are universal

68. Organization of sensory experiences about a particular object is called
(*a*) percepts (*b*) reasoning
(*c*) concept (*d*) none of these

69. The concept building in a person depends on
(*a*) the age and maturity of the person
(*b*) past experiences of the learner
(*c*) intelligence of the learner
(*d*) all of these

70. Agreement on a concept is possible because
(*a*) concepts are subjective
(*b*) concepts are objective
(*c*) concepts are hierarchical
(*d*) b and c both

71. Which of the following statements about concepts is correct?
(*a*) Some concepts are more powerful than others
(*b*) All concepts are universal
(*c*) Concepts are differentiated on the basis of their attributes
(*d*) None of these

72. Which is the highest level of concept formation?
(*a*) formal level (*b*) sensory level
(*c*) concrete level (*d*) none of these

73. How many steps of problem solving has been given by Gates?
(*a*) Six (*b*) Seven
(*c*) Five (*d*) Ten

74. Freeman considers intelligence as an ability
(*a*) to adjust in an adverse situation
(*b*) to learn better and faster
(*c*) to manipulate abstract materials
(*d*) all of these

75. Single factor theory of intelligence was given by
(*a*) Alfred Binet (*b*) Thorndike
(*c*) Freeman (*d*) None of them

76. Which of the following is not the characteristics of 'S' factor according to Spearman ?
(*a*) It is the acquired capacity of the individual
(*b*) Specialization in only one trade is possible
(*c*) It varies from activity to activity in the same individual
(*d*) Individuals differ only in 'S' factor of intelligence

77. In multifactor theory, range is related to
(*a*) Number of tasks that a person can do in a limited period of time
(*b*) Difficulty level of items
(*c*) General intelligence of learners
(*d*) None of these

78. SI model of intelligence was given by I P Guilford in
(*a*) 1911 (*b*) 1904
(*c*) 1966 (*d*) 1975

79. Hierarchy theory of intelligence was given by
(*a*) Jenson
(*b*) Thorndike
(*c*) Burt and Vernon
(*d*) None of them

80. In the pre-Binet period, intelligence was considered as
(*a*) Sensory acuity of the individual
(*b*) Verbal ability of the individual
(*c*) Associative ability of the individual
(*d*) All of these

81. An age scale of intelligence was first developed by
(*a*) Spearman (*b*) Terman
(*c*) Binet-Simon (*d*) None of them

82. Binet-Simon scale of intelligence measures
(*a*) General mental abilities not specific ones.
(*b*) Mental growth of the individual over a period of time
(*c*) The aptitude or level of an examinee not their speed
(*d*) All of these

83. WAIS came into being in
(*a*) 1939 (*b*) 1955
(*c*) 1960 (*d*) 1964

84. Wechsler developed an intelligence test for children in
(*a*) 1939 (*b*) 1949
(*c*) 1955 (*d*) 1956

85. Cell's culture fair test of intelligence was developed in
(*a*) 1960 (*b*) 1961
(*c*) 1965 (*d*) 1955

86. Non-verbal test of intelligence is suitable for
(*a*) deaf and dumb
(*b*) illiterates
(*c*) backward children
(*d*) all of these

87. Intelligence testing is useful for knowing
(*a*) individual difference
(*b*) mental retardation

(*c*) educational backwardness
(*d*) all of these

88. Scores on intelligence tests can not be fully relied on because
(*a*) fatigue level can influence the performance
(*b*) cultural factors can influence the score
(*c*) they generally do not reveal all the mental abilities of a person
(*d*) all of these

89. Who among the following psychologists is of the view that a learner can be motivated by satisfying his needs?
(*a*) Henry Murray (*b*) Abraham Maslow
(*c*) Both of these (*d*) None of these

90. Permanent change in behaviour brought about by experience or training is called.
(*a*) Learning (*b*) Motivation
(*c*) Assimilation (*d*) None of these

91. The book "**Theory of Motivation**" has been written by
(*a*) K B Madson (*b*) Maslow
(*c*) Murray (*d*) None of them

92. Motivated behaviour of a person is
(*a*) Well directed and well guided towards the goal
(*b*) Agitated until the goal is achieved
(*c*) Both of these
(*d*) None of these

93. Factors affecting motivations are
(*a*) Physiological factors only
(*b*) Psychological factors only
(*c*) Psycho-social factors
(*d*) All of these

94. Process of motivation is affected by all except
(*a*) Habits
(*b*) Mental sets and values
(*c*) Physical factors
(*d*) None of these

95. Which of the following does not come under the category of social motives?
(*a*) Prestige and Status
(*b*) Social approval
(*c*) Personal goal
(*d*) Money hoarding

96. Our action and behaviour is motivated by the desire for getting pleasure and avoiding pain. This is the opinion of
(*a*) Thomas Hobbes (*b*) Descartes
(*c*) Kant (*d*) John Locke

97. Fundamental instincts of humans are inherited rather than acquired. These instincts are the spring of human behaviour. The above opinion was held by
(*a*) Charles Darwin (*b*) Mc Dougall
(*c*) Both of these (*d*) None of these

98. Instinct theory of behaviour was rejected by psychologists on which of the following grounds?
(*a*) Adult behaviour is guided by experience and learning also. It is not always guided by instinct
(*b*) Human behaviour is affected by the cultural factors also
(*c*) Human being is a rational animal. He is not supposed to be directed by instincts only
(*d*) All of these

99. Central motive state was explained by
(*a*) Morgan
(*b*) Mc Dougall
(*c*) Murray
(*d*) None of them

100. Abraham Maslow was basically a
(*a*) Pragmatist (*b*) Humanist
(*c*) Realist (*d*) All of them

101. A self actualized person is one who
(*a*) Does not accept restrictions imposed by the society
(*b*) Always seeks perfection
(*c*) Is very good in inter personal relationship with others
(*d*) All of these

102. The theory of achievement motivation was developed by Mc Clelland of Harward University in
(*a*) 1949 (*b*) 1951
(*c*) 1965 (*d*) 1944

103. Achievement motive in a child can be developed by
(*a*) Proper guidance and high expectation from the child
(*b*) Telling the stories of great men to the child
(*c*) Setting a realistic goal for the child
(*d*) All of these

104. Which of the following is not a characteristic of learning?
(*a*) Learning is a relatively permanent change in behaviour
(*b*) Learning is a growth of the organism
(*c*) Learning is directly observed
(*d*) Learning is a goal directed process

105. In the beginning of life, the baby is guided by
(*a*) maturation
(*b*) instincts
(*c*) learning
(*d*) none of these

106. Accumulation of knowledge or facts becomes learning when
(*a*) It is applied in real life situation
(*b*) It is done by the learner himself
(*c*) It is provided by the teacher
(*d*) None of these

107. Dancing, driving, writing etc are the examples of
(*a*) Mechanical learning
(*b*) Perceptual motor learning
(*c*) Psychomotor learning
(*d*) both (*b*) and (*c*)

108. In Gagne's hierarchy, learning has been divided into
(*a*) eight parts (*b*) nine parts
(*c*) seven parts (*d*) none of the above

109. Match the following:

(A)	**(B)**
(*i*) Classical conditioning	1. Kohler
(*ii*) Drive reduction	2. Hull
(*iii*) Sign gestalt	3. Pavlov
(*iv*) Learning by insight	4. Tolman

	(*i*)	(*ii*)	(*iii*)	(*iv*)
(*a*)	1	2	3	4
(*b*)	3	2	4	1
(*c*)	2	1	3	4
(*d*)	4	3	2	1

110. Reflexes are of two types according to Pavlov. They are physiological and
(*a*) Psychic (*b*) Neural
(*c*) Mental (*d*) None of these

111. In classical conditioning, extinction will take place when
(*a*) Organism is poor in generalization
(*b*) CS is given without UCS for a long time
(*c*) CS > UCS
(*d*) None of these

112. Backward conditioning will take place when
(*a*) UCS is presented prior to CS
(*b*) CS is presented prior to UCS
(*c*) Reward is not given to the organism
(*d*) None of these

113. When connection is not established between a CS and CR, due to any factor, that is called
(*a*) Spontaneous recovery
(*b*) Extinction
(*c*) Inhibition
(*d*) None of these

114. When a child responds to all women who wear black suit because of the black suit of her mother, it is the example of
(*a*) internal inhibition
(*b*) generalization
(*c*) assimilation
(*d*) all of these

115. Which of the following is not a behaviourist?
(*a*) Watson
(*b*) Skinner
(*c*) Pavlov
(*d*) Lewin

116. Learning according to Watson is
(*a*) the shifting of old responses to the new stimuli
(*b*) the result of connection between S-R formed in the brain
(*c*) both of these
(*d*) none of these

117. Which of the following points differentiates the theories of Watson and Guthrie?
(*a*) law of contiguity
(*b*) law of recency
(*c*) generalization
(*d*) law of frequency

118. In operant conditioning reward works as motives but in Guthrie's theory motives are
(*a*) Stimuli given to the learner
(*b*) Actions done by the learner
(*c*) Both of these
(*d*) None of these

119. We forget something not by disuse but by other learning. This is the theory of
(*a*) contiguity
(*b*) trial and error
(*c*) learning by insight
(*d*) perception

120. Which of the following is not an essential requirement for trial and error learning?
(*a*) Drive
(*b*) Barrier
(*c*) Chance success
(*d*) Selective movement of the organism

121. According to the law of trial and error, learning occurs when
(*a*) it is satisfying for the learner
(*b*) bond between S-R is strengthened by the repeated use
(*c*) drive is there in the learner to act
(*d*) all of these

122. Which of the following facilitates learning according to Thorndike?
(*a*) Transfer of training
(*b*) Mental set of the learner
(*c*) Law of contiguity
(*d*) All of these

123. In Hull's theory, for learning to occur, the S-R connection must be associated with the
(*a*) cognitive field of the learner
(*b*) diminution of the need
(*c*) both of these
(*d*) none of these

124. Reinforcement in Skinner's theory is similar to drive reduction in which theory
(*a*) Hull's theory
(*b*) Guthrie's theory
(*c*) Lewin's theory
(*d*) None of these

125. Which of the following theories is most quantitatively measurable?
(*a*) Pavlov's
(*b*) Skinner's
(*c*) Hull's
(*d*) None of these

126. In drive reduction theory, the effective stimulus in learning is the trace. It is formed
(*a*) in the brain
(*b*) by the bond of S-R
(*c*) in the nervous system
(*d*) none of these

127. In drive reduction theory, habit formation is a function of
(*a*) stimulus potential
(*b*) stimulus generalization
(*c*) reaction potential
(*d*) all of these

128. Hull may be considered superior to other S-R Theorists in the sense that he was able to measure
(*a*) latency of response
(*b*) reinforcement potential
(*c*) both of these
(*d*) none of these

129. Which of the following points differentiates Skinner from other S-R theorists?
(*a*) His operant conditioning (type R learning)
(*b*) His schedule of reinforcement
(*c*) His way of shaping behaviour
(*d*) All of these

130. Skinner's theory is more objective in nature than the others because
(*a*) operant behaviour is external
(*b*) reflexes never have zero strength
(*c*) reinforcement is followed by responses
(*d*) all of these

131. Aversive stimuli in operant conditioning means
(*a*) individual will not do a particular act because of fear of such stimuli
(*b*) individual will not do a particular act because of the disapproval from others
(*c*) both of these
(*d*) none of these

132. In Skinner's theory, reinforcement is given to the learner when
(*a*) his response is 100% correct
(*b*) his response is closer to the correct behaviour
(*c*) both of these
(*d*) none of these

133. Which of the following statements regarding S-R theories is not correct?
(*a*) Man behaves like a machine
(*b*) Behaviour is overt and can be objectively measured
(*c*) Learning proceeds from simple to complex
(*d*) Things are perceived in the context of figure ground *i.e.*, in relation to other things

134. Which of the following statements regarding field theories are correct?
(*a*) Learning is not additive
(*b*) Molar approach of behaviour is followed here
(*c*) Interaction between organism and the environment is essential for learning
(*d*) All of these

135. Operant conditioning is different from respondent conditioning in which of the following points
(*a*) In OC reinforcement is given after the response is made
(*b*) In operant conditioning, behaviour is controlled by central nervous system
(*c*) A chain of responses is needed for shaping the behaviour (learning)
(*d*) All of these

136. Thorndike and Skinner do not differ at all in
(*a*) the law of effect
(*b*) law of readiness
(*c*) law of contiguity
(*d*) all of these

137. According to gestalt psychologists, behaviour can not be quantified because
(*a*) it is always changeable
(*b*) it is governed by the configuration produced in the mind
(*c*) it is rarely overt
(*d*) all of these

138. Law of pragnanz is the other name of the law of
(*a*) continuity
(*b*) closure
(*c*) contiguity
(*d*) none of these

139. How does the law of similarity work according to field theorists?
(*a*) Similar ideas and experiences get associated to form a whole
(*b*) Similar objects or experiences are easily learnt
(*c*) Both of these
(*d*) None of these

140. Learning by insight looks similar to some extent to which of the following theories?
(*a*) Need reduction theory
(*b*) R type of learning
(*c*) Trial and error theory
(*d*) None of the above

141. The other name of conditioned reflexes is
(*a*) psychic reflexes
(*b*) motor reflexes

(c) physiological reflexes
(d) none of the above

142. According to Renzuli, a gifted child is one
(a) Who possesses above average ability in almost every field
(b) Who is committed to task and highly motivated
(c) Who is definitely creative
(d) All of these

143. Gifted and talented children must be identified as early as possible because
(a) If their potentials are not developed by proper guidance of the teacher, it is a loss of the society
(b) They are likely to create problems for others, if they are not given work according to their ability
(c) Ordinary level of curriculum will not suit to these children
(d) All of these

144. Achievement test can be a good indicator of intellectual power if
(a) It is conducted immediately after the teaching is over
(b) A student shows good performance consistently on different achievement test
(c) Both of these
(d) None of these

145. Which of the following skills does not require high intellectual ability?
(a) Technical skills
(b) Mechanical skills
(c) Teaching skills
(d) Management skills

146. Cognitive abilities related to giftedness are all except
(a) High comprehensive and analytical abilities
(b) High level of verbal intelligence
(c) High retention power
(d) None of these

147. A superior child is advanced to a normal child by at least
(a) 2½ years
(b) Four years
(c) 1 years
(d) 1½ years

148. A gifted child is
(a) realistic in his approach
(b) highly interested in solving social problems
(c) more frequently chosen by his age mates and peers
(d) all of these

149. Which of the following enrichment programmes is suitable for gifted children in the school?
(a) Mathematics or Science Olympiad
(b) Challenging home assignments
(c) Map work during studies
(d) All of these

150. Which of the following does not come under the category of acceleration for gifted children?
(a) Skipping of classes
(b) Early admission
(c) Extra laboratory work
(d) Organizing summer camps

151. Under achievers are those who
(a) Score low on intelligence tests
(b) Achieve low in the class consistently despite their superior intelligence
(c) Are unable to correspond their achievement to the level of their innate abilities
(d) Both (b) and (c)

152. Which of the following conditions must be satisfied in order to designate a person mentally retarded?
(a) Sub-normal intellectual functioning
(b) Very poor adaptive ability
(c) Dependability on others
(d) All of these

153. The best measure of identifying mildly mentally retarded is
(a) Administration of standardized intelligence test
(b) Administration of behaviour test
(c) Administration of adjustment test
(d) A combination of all

154. Physical trauma during pregnancy may cause
(a) Mental retardation
(b) Blindness
(c) Deafness
(d) All of these

155. All of the following may cause mental retardation except
(a) Blood incompatibility
(b) Action of toxic agent
(c) Radio-activity
(d) None of these

156. Which of the following is an important postnatal cause of mental retardation?
(a) Brain injury
(b) Infection
(c) Severe malnutrition
(d) All of these

157. Dullers do not differ from normal children in
(a) Physical characteristics
(b) Level of social expectancy
(c) Both of these
(d) None of these

158. Which of the following things is not required for educating mildly mentally retarded children?
(a) Regular counseling
(b) Remedial teaching

(c) Modification in the curriculum
(d) Regular evaluation

159. Teaching of which of the following skills is not suitable to borderline cases?
(a) Electric fitting
(b) Repairing of electric or electronic equipments
(c) Oratory skills
(d) Activity based skills

160. IQ range of morons are in the range of
(a) 60-90 (b) 50-75
(c) 60-80 (d) 30-50

161. Morons are slow in
(a) Physical growth
(b) Thinking and planning
(c) Taking initiative
(d) All of these

162. Unsatisfactory relation of a mentally retarded child with the environment is technically called
(a) Autism
(b) Maladjustment
(c) Pseudo-dullness
(d) None of these

163. All of the following are characteristics of morons except
(a) They are restricted to unskilled or semi skilled occupations
(b) They are likely to be delinquent more easily
(c) They have stronger sex drives than the normals
(d) They are educable upto normal level but at a slower rate

164. Which of the following modifications in the curriculum is needed for morons?
(a) Activity based curriculum
(b) Skill dominated curriculum
(c) Emphasis on social training
(d) All of these

165. Which of the following things can not be taught to Imbeciles?
(a) Self help skills
(b) Unskilled job to be performed under supervision
(c) Writing skills
(d) Social skills

166. In which of the following cases divergent thinking is required?
(a) Attempting a multiple choice items
(b) Writing an essay
(c) Doing a research activity
(d) Both (a) and (c)

167. Which of the following tests is similar to Guilford's test of cognitive abilities?
(a) Word association test
(b) Things test
(c) Hidden shapes test
(d) None of these

168. In Hidden shapes test of creativity, which of the following things is used?
(a) Pictures
(b) Words
(c) Things
(d) None of them

169. A creative child in the class can not be satisfied unless
(a) He is given freedom to manipulate ideas or things
(b) He is allowed to ask questions in his own way
(c) Both of these
(d) None of these

170. A creative child is one who
(a) Is ideationally productive and unconventional
(b) Does not stick to social and religious norms in a hard manner
(c) Is all the time restless to do something uncommon and unique
(d) All of these

171. For the development of creative potential of a child, the teacher should
(a) Allow him to be critical to ideas and people
(b) Give them chance of problem solving
(c) Both of these
(d) None of these

172. New ideas (Eureka) suddenly comes in the minds of the creative children in the stage of
(a) Preparation
(b) Illumination
(c) Revision
(d) Incubation

173. The technique to foster creativity in children is
(a) Brain storming
(b) Problem solving
(c) Both of these
(d) None of these

174. A teacher can foster creativity in children by
(a) Developing confidence in them
(b) Giving them opportunity to express
(c) Both of these
(d) None of these

175. Learning disabled children are
(a) Deficient in using potentials
(b) Low in intelligence
(c) Slow in activity
(d) None of these

176. Learning disabled children perform very poorly in
(a) academic areas
(b) technical areas

(c) both of these
(d) none of these

177. Problem of learning disability is more complex than that of other disabilities because
(a) Its causes can not be easily ascertained by applying usual tests
(b) It is associated to behaviour problems
(c) Both of these
(d) None of these

178. Educationally, learning disabled look similar to
(a) dullers
(b) backward children
(c) both of these
(d) none of these

179. In which of the following physical characteristics learning disabled children differ from the normal ones?
(a) They are all the time clumsy and awkward
(b) Poor coordination of motor abilities
(c) Height, weight and health
(d) All of these

180. Which of the following methods is most suitable for learning disabled children?
(a) Behaviour guidance method
(b) Remedial teaching
(c) Brain storming
(d) None of them

181. In order to improve work habits of learning disabled what should be done?
(a) Unattending behaviour should be penalized
(b) Close monitoring of the behaviour is needed
(c) Cues and prompt should be given
(d) All of these

182. Those who are normal in intelligence but slow in academic achievement due to psycho-social reasons are called
(a) Backward children
(b) Gifted under achievers
(c) Both of these
(d) None of these

183. Consistent low achievement leads to low intelligence because
(a) 50% intellectual ability is expressed in verbal form
(b) Learning develops thinking and reasoning power
(c) Both of these
(d) None of these

184. Which of the following situations may lead to educational backwardness?
(a) Sensory impairment
(b) Motor disability
(c) Long diseases and health problems.
(d) All of these

185. Emotional disturbances may lead to educational backwardness because
(a) Proper emotional development is necessary for social interactions
(b) Emotions will develop intellectual power, *i.e.*, emotional intelligence
(c) Both of these
(d) None of these

186. Which of the following factors will not lead to educational backwardness?
(a) Poor socio economic status of the family
(b) Poor educational environment of the school
(c) Occupation of the family
(d) Poor emotional climate of the family

187. Which of the following is an important cause of educational backwardness at primary level of education in India?
(a) Poor school organisation
(b) Lack of accountability
(c) Attitude of the masses towards education
(d) All of these

188. Which of the following measures should be adopted by the teacher to check educational backwardness?
(a) Continuous evaluation and regular feedback
(b) Remedial teaching
(c) Adjustment and behaviour training
(d) All of these

189. Teaching by small steps and frequent short assignment techniques are useful for
(a) Slow learners
(b) Learning disabled
(c) Educationally backward children
(d) Children of all types of disabilities

190. Special schools are required for backward children when
(a) Backwardness is due to any serious physical handicap
(b) The size of population of backward children in the society is very large as is the case of Gujarat where the achievement of students in mathematics is always seen very low
(c) Both of these
(d) None of these

191. Which of the following should be considered the most important quality of a teacher at primary level?
(a) Patience and perseverance
(b) Competence in methods of teaching and knowledge of subjects
(c) Competence to teach in highly standardised language
(d) Eagerness to teach

192. A teacher, because of his/her democratic nature, allows students to sit all over the class. Some sit together and discuss or do group reading. Some

sit quietly and read themselves. A parent does not like it. Which of the following may be the best way to handle the situation?
(*a*) Parents should request the principal to change the section of their ward
(*b*) Parents should show trust in the teacher and discuss the problem with the teacher
(*c*) Parents should take away the child from that school
(*d*) Parents should complain against the teacher to the principal

193. The stage in which a child begins to think logically about objects and events is known as
(*a*) Formal operational stage
(*b*) Pre-operational stage
(*c*) Concrete operational stage
(*d*) Sensori-motor stage

194. 'Mind mapping' refers to
(*a*) a plan of action for an adventure
(*b*) drawing the picture of a mind
(*c*) researching the functioning of the mind
(*d*) a technique to enhance comprehension

195. The best way, specially at primary level, to address the learning difficulties of students is to use
(*a*) expensive and glossy support material
(*b*) easy and interesting textbooks
(*c*) story-telling method
(*d*) a variety of teaching methods suited to the disability

196. Which of the following will foster creativity among learners?
(*a*) Providing opportunities to question and to nurture the innate talents of every learner
(*b*) Emphasizing achievement goals from the beginning of school life
(*c*) Coaching students for good marks in examination
(*d*) Teaching the students the practical value of good education

197. According to Piaget, at which of the following stages does a child begin to think logically about abstract propositions?
(*a*) Formal operational stage (11 years and up)
(*b*) Sensori-motor stage (Birth–02 years)
(*c*) Pre-operational stage (02–07 years)
(*d*) Concrete operational stage (07–11 years)

198. Learning can be enriched if
(*a*) more and more teaching aids are used in the class
(*b*) teachers use different types of lectures and explanation
(*c*) due attention is paid to periodic tests in the class
(*d*) situations from the real world are brought into the class in which students interact with each other and the teahcer facilitates

199. Which of the following statements ***cannot*** be considered as a feature of the process of learning?
(*a*) Learning is a comprehensive process
(*b*) Learning is goal-oriented
(*c*) Unlearning is also a learning process
(*d*) Educational institutions are the only place where learning takes place

200. A student of V-grade with 'visual deficiency' should be
(*a*) helped with his/her routine-work by parents and friends
(*b*) treated normally in the classroom and provided support through Audio CDs
(*c*) given special treatment in the classroom
(*d*) excused to do a lower level of work

201. Which of the following is ***not*** related to the socio-psychological needs of the child?
(*a*) Need for emotional security
(*b*) Regular elimination of waste products from the body
(*c*) Need for company
(*d*) Need for appreciation or social approval

202. Which is the place where the child's 'cognitive' development is defined in the best way?
(*a*) School and classroom environment
(*b*) Auditorium
(*c*) Home
(*d*) Playground

203. .... is considered a sign of motivated teaching.
(*a*) Remedial work given by the teacher
(*b*) Questioning by students
(*c*) Pin drop silence in the class
(*d*) Maximum attendance in the class

204. Which of the following is ***not*** a sign of an intelligent young child?
(*a*) One who has the ability to communicate fluently and appropriately
(*b*) One who carries on thinking in an abstract manner
(*c*) One who can adjust oneself in a new environment
(*d*) One who has the ability to cram long essays very quickly

205. "Children actively construct their understanding of the world" is a statement attributed to
(*a*) Pavlov (*b*) Kohlberg
(*c*) Skinner (*d*) Piaget

206. Kritika who does ***not*** talk much at home, talks a lot at school. It shows that
(*a*) teachers demand that children should talk a lot at school
(*b*) she does not like her home at all
(*c*) her thoughts get ackrowledged at school
(*d*) the school provides opportunities to children to talk a lot

207. A teacher should make an attempt to understand the potentialities of her/his students. Which of the following fields is related to this objective?
(*a*) Social Philosophy
(*b*) Media – Psychology
(*c*) Educational Psychology
(*d*) Educational Sociology

208. Motivation, in the process of learning,
(*a*) differentiates new learning from old learning
(*b*) makes learners think unidirectionally
(*c*) creates interest for learning among young learners
(*d*) sharpens the memory of learners

209. The term 'curriculum' in the field of education refers to
(*a*) overall programme of the school which students experience on a day-to-day basis
(*b*) evaluation process
(*c*) text-material to be used in the class
(*d*) methods of teaching and the content to be taught

210. At lower classes, play-way method of teaching is based on
(*a*) principles of methods of teaching
(*b*) psychological principles of development and growth
(*c*) sociological principles of teaching
(*d*) theory of physical education programmes

211. "A young child responds to a new situation on the basis of the response made by him/her in a similar situation as in the past." This is related to
(*a*) 'Law of Effect' of learning
(*b*) 'Law of Attitude' of learning process
(*c*) 'Law of Readiness' of learning
(*d*) 'Law of Analogy' of learning

212. .... is ***not*** considered a sign of 'being gifted'.
(*a*) Fighting with others
(*b*) Novelty in expression
(*c*) Curiosity
(*d*) Creative ideas

213. Education of children with special needs should be provided
(*a*) by methods developed for special children in special schools
(*b*) in special schools
(*c*) by special teachers in special schools
(*d*) along with other normal children

214. To make assessment a 'useful and interesting' process, one should be careful about
(*a*) labelling students as intelligent or average learners
(*b*) using a variety of ways to collect information about the student's learning across the scholastic and co-scholastic boundaries
(*c*) using technical language to give feedback
(*d*) making comparisons between different students

215. 'Dyslexia' is associated with
(*a*) Mathematical disorder
(*b*) Reading disorder
(*c*) Behavioural disorder
(*d*) Mental disorder

216. Parents should play a .... role in the learning process of young children.
(*a*) proactive
(*b*) sympathetic
(*c*) neutral
(*d*) negative

217. "Development is a never ending process." This idea is associated with
(*a*) Principle of continuity
(*b*) Principle of integration
(*c*) Principle of interaction
(*d*) Principle of interrelation

218. The 'insight theory of learning' is promoted by
(*a*) Pavlov
(*b*) Jean Piaget
(*c*) Vygotsky
(*d*) 'Gestalt' theorists

219. In which of the following stages do children become active members of their peer group?
(*a*) Adulthood
(*b*) Early childhood
(*c*) Childhood
(*d*) Adolescence

220. Four distinct stages of children's intellectual development are identified by
(*a*) Erikson (*b*) Skinner
(*c*) Piaget (*d*) Kohlberg

221. Mass media, cinema and library are passive agencies of education because
(*a*) learner can not react to the feedback system of these agencies directly
(*b*) they provide informal education
(*c*) they can not come closer to the educant
(*d*) all of these

222. Education of a child really begins
(*a*) Once he takes birth
(*b*) Once he attains the age of three
(*c*) Once he is admitted to post nursery schools
(*d*) Once he learns to speak

223. Family is the original social institution from which all other institutions emerged, who said this
(*a*) Brown (*b*) Ballard
(*c*) Machiver (*d*) None of them

224. Which of the following is not the primary function of schools
(*a*) reorganization and reconstruction of Human experiences

(b) all-round development of the child
(c) to make the children self reliant
(d) advancement of culture

225. In a democratic country, school should reflect
(a) National aspirations
(b) Community related local aspirations
(c) Both of these
(d) None of these

226. The best teacher in a village school is he who
(a) carries community experiences to the class room
(b) prepares instructional programmes in the interest of the community
(c) carries classroom experiences to the community
(d) all of these

227. Universalisation of education is the concept adopted by
(a) modern state (b) democratic state
(c) totalitarian state (d) religious state

228. Secular education in India means
(a) an education opposed to religion
(b) an education indifferent to religion
(c) an education emphasizing equality of religions
(d) none of these

229. School works as a social sub system for
(a) transmission of culture
(b) preservation of culture
(c) advancement of culture
(d) all of these

230. "Society is nothing but a process of interaction among people." Who said this?
(a) Lapier (b) Cuber
(c) Reuter (d) Payne

231. The best model of schooling is
(a) Close interaction between education of society
(b) Self reliant society by education
(c) Reflection of openness by schools
(d) All of these

232. Special provisions have been made for socially and educationally backward classes of the nation under article
(a) 29 (b) 31
(c) 15 (d) 19

233. Religious education is prohibited in government schools and colleges under Article
(a) 29 (b) 28 (1)
(c) 39 (2) (d) 15 (a)

234. Religious and linguistic minorities shall have the right to establish and administer their own educational institutions under Article
(a) 30(1) (b) 31(2)
(c) 40 (d) 41

235. Article 351 is about
(a) education of tribals
(b) promotion of Hindi
(c) promotion of secularism
(d) English as official language

236. Status of central university is given to any educational institution under union list of
(a) Entry 65 (b) Entry 63
(c) Entry 66 (d) None of these

237. Entry 25 of concurrent list states about
(a) vocational and technical training of labour
(b) the education of working class
(c) the education of disabled
(d) none of the above

238. Education in the mother tongue at primary stage to children belonging to linguistic minorities has been mentioned in Article
(a) 250 (b) 350
(c) 349 (d) 351

239. Educational and economic interests of SCs and STs have been safeguarded under Article
(a) 46 (b) 45(a)
(c) 351 (d) 52

240. Education of union territories is administered by the central government under Article
(a) 350 (b) 229
(c) 239 (d) 50

241. Education was transferred from state list of subjects to concurrent list in
(a) 1976 (b) 1972
(c) 1980 (d) 1950

242. Which of the following statements about growth and development is not correct?
(a) Growth generally refers to quantitative changes while development refers to qualitative changes
(b) Growth is a function of the environment
(c) Growth is not possible without development and vice versa
(d) Growth is determined by intrinsic and genetic factors of the organism

243. The limit of growth is fixed by
(a) internal factors of the organism
(b) nutrition and exercise
(c) both of these
(d) none of these

244. Development is
(a) Maturation
(b) Learning
(c) Synthesis of abilities
(d) All of these

245. Development takes place when
(a) environmental forces work on the organism
(b) environmental forces interact with the hereditary forces in an organism

(c) both of these
(d) none of these

246. Which of the following statements about development is correct?
(a) Process of development can be improved by exercise and nutrition
(b) Development may be positive and negative both
(c) Development proceeds from general to specific
(d) All of these

247. The son of a goldsmith becomes an expert goldsmith. It is an example of a
(a) biological heredity
(b) social heredity
(c) transfer of instinct
(d) none of these

248. All humans contain .... chromosomes.
(a) 26 (b) 36
(c) 46 (d) 42

249. DNA test helps us to know
(a) the genetic traits of a person
(b) nature of personality and its composition
(c) both of these
(d) none of these

250. The law of inheritance was discovered by Gregor Mendel in
(a) 1866 (b) 1911
(c) 1888 (d) 1920

251. Everything which influences child's development is categorised under the 'Environment' other than 'Heredity.' This statement is given by
(a) Boring (b) Woodworth
(c) Douglas (d) Holland

252. During infancy which of the following aspect of development is not completed?
(a) Moral Development
(b) Emotional Development
(c) Social Development
(d) Language Development

253. A teacher who has given the responsibility of 'Infant education,' he must pay attention on
(a) The education must be child-centred
(b) The education must be mother-centred
(c) The education must be sport-centred
(d) The education must be school-centred

254. Which one of the following stage of child's development is popularly nicknamed as Mysterious period of the life?
(a) Infancy (b) Childhood
(c) Adolescence (d) Adulthood

255. Which one of the following is the defect of language development in children?
(a) Stammering (b) Talktiveness
(c) Scribbled writing (d) Reserve nature

256. The major change occurs in adolescent period is
(a) In voice
(b) In Bodily shape and organs
(c) In gestures and manners
(d) In all the above

257. In adolescent girls the following abilities are much better in comparison than the adolescent boys
(a) Language Abilities
(b) Functional Abilities
(c) Thinking Abilities
(d) Scientific Abilities

258. The psychologist who has given much importance to individual difference in children is
(a) Galton (b) Young
(c) Freud (d) Robert

259. In which age-group a child can differentiate between the anger and affection?
(a) In infancy (b) In childhood
(c) In adolescence (d) In adulthood

260. The chief social behaviour of infancy is
(a) Birth of group-feelings
(b) Exchange of toys
(c) Imitation of approved nouns
(d) All the above

261. The nearest emotion of distress which is developed after three months of the age in children
(a) Anger (b) Hate
(c) Fear (d) All the above

262. The best controlling powers of emotionally are displayed by
(a) Gifted children
(b) Mentally retarded
(c) Physically powerful children
(d) The children having escaping tendencies from work

263. Which one of the following does not having maximum development during adolescent stage?
(a) Intellectual abilities
(b) Mental abilities
(c) Interest-related abilities
(d) All of the above

264. In order to develop group-feelings among children, the provision in education required as
(a) The co-operative games and sports in school
(b) The group activities like dance, music and drama
(c) The mass drills and physical exercises on the games field
(d) All the above

265. It is said that in childhood, the children should be exposed to adventurous stories of great historical journeys which may develop the quality of

(*a*) Elimination of fear syndrome
(*b*) Discipline and obedience
(*c*) Delightfulness
(*d*) Enthusiasm and motivation

266. In early childhood, the children should be given education through

(*a*) Toys and games (*b*) Paper-Pencil
(*c*) Models (*d*) Plants

267. Which one of the following is not associated with the social development in childhood?

(*a*) Gang formation
(*b*) Formation of sex-groups
(*c*) Desire for social acceptance in children
(*d*) Attraction towards girls in boys

268. According to Piagent, infants in the sensorimotor thought stage cannot

(*a*) use sensory (*b*) use motor actions
(*c*) form symbolic (*d*) display reflexes

269. According to Piaget, the imaginary audience and the personal fable are both parts of

(*a*) intuitive (*b*) object
(*c*) conservation (*d*) adolescent

270. What is the term that Erikson coined?

(*a*) Oedipus Complex
(*b*) Self-fulfilling Prophecy
(*c*) Identity Crisis
(*d*) Positive Reinforcement

271. The two main personality differences identified by Eysenck are

(*a*) extroversion/introversion and neuroticism/stability
(*b*) pessimism/optimism and sufficiency/insecurity
(*c*) extroversion/introversion and shrewdness/insecurity
(*d*) neuroticism/stability and optimism/pessimism

272. Erik Erikson's theory is a good example of the .... approach.

(*a*) proactive (*b*) idiographic
(*c*) nomothetic (*d*) psychoanalytic

273. Attitudes are .... throughout life and are embodied our socialization process.

(*a*) constant (*b*) seen
(*c*) rigid (*d*) learned

274. Who is called as father of Conditioning?

(*a*) Pavlov (*b*) Koffka
(*c*) Wertheimer (*d*) Skinner

275. Which of the following concept in the basic element of conditioned Response?

(*a*) Associative Reflex
(*b*) Association Response
(*c*) Stimulus effect
(*d*) Latercy Response

276. When a child is asked that chocolate is not given to you, if you are telling-a-lie. This conditioning is an example of

(*a*) Non-reinforced training
(*b*) Discriminatory punishment training
(*c*) Escape training
(*d*) Discriminatory training

277. The meaning of the word conditioning is

(*a*) Relationship between the stimuli
(*b*) Substitution of organism behaviour with another behaviour
(*c*) Accommodation with new stimuli
(*d*) Learning through exercise

278. Which one of the following is not associated with Classical conditioning?

(*a*) Contemporary conditioning
(*b*) Delayed conditioning
(*c*) Trace conditioning
(*d*) Non-reinforced conditioning

279. Instrumental conditioning is also called as

(*a*) S-type conditioning
(*b*) Q-type conditioning
(*c*) C-type conditioning
(*d*) R-type conditioning

280. In which type of conditioning the reward is depend on the response?

(*a*) Classical conditioning
(*b*) Instrumental conditioning
(*c*) Respondents behaviour
(*d*) Operant behaviour

281. The ability of the learner to utilize or apply the acquired knowledge or skills in school to solve problems in similar or related situations at some future date is known as

(*a*) Knowledge acquisition
(*b*) Reinforcement
(*c*) Motivation
(*d*) Transfer of learning

282. In the learning of sciences and math's, scientifically their is no difference in performance as a result of gender. Which of the following influence gender based performance?

(*a*) Culture (*b*) Attitude
(*c*) Stereotyping (*d*) Race

283. Learning is best defined as a process that involves:

(*a*) Two stimuli being paired that produce a conditioned response over time
(*b*) An organism interacting with its environment, becoming changed by

experience, and thereby modifying subsequent behaviours
(c) An organism interacting with its environment through autoshaping and conditioning
(d) An organism responding to its environment based on reinforcement or punishment for behaviours

284. The basic understanding of the relationship between unconditoned response (UR) and conditioned response (CR) included which of the following ideas?
(a) The UR and Cr are not always the same response
(b) Organisms come to generally behave toward conditioned stimulus as they do unconditioned stimulus
(c) Stimulus substitution
(d) The UR and Cr are always the same response

285. Which of the following is accurate in relation to the law of effect?
(a) The law of effect relates to Pavlov's proposal that reward will strengthen the connection between the response that proceeded it and any stimuli present when it is delivere(d)
(b) In modern terminology, Thorndike's 'satisfiers' and 'annoyers' are called enforcers and punishers
(c) In the law of effect, a stimulus-response (S-R) association is learne(d)
(d) It is generally thought that the likelihood of an animal responding in a particular way cannot be controlled by the consequence of that response.

286. Which of the following statements applies to instrumental learning?
(a) Instrumental learning is the process by which an animal learns about the relationship between its behaviour and the consequence of that behaviour.
(b) Instrumentally trained responses are not entirely elicited by identifiable stimuli.
(c) Instrumental learning allows the animal to control the occurrence of environmental events.
(d) All of the above

287. Generally the construct of Personality can be defined in terms of
(a) Biological Approaches
(b) Psycho-sexual Approaches
(c) Psycho-physical Approaches
(d) Bio-chemical Approaches

288. The consistent and distinct style of behavioural tendencies are called as
(a) Habit (b) Trait
(c) Learning (d) Instinct

289. The personal changes that occur among the students through socialization can be judged through
(a) Inter-personal relationship among the specialised groups of the students
(b) The activities of the student
(c) Collecting the information from the parents
(d) Asking to the students

290. Co-operation is the fundamental basis of inter-personal relations which means
(a) It is self-centred in the early development of the children
(b) It is society-centred which is expressed in interpersonal relationship
(c) It can be learned through imitation and suggestibility
(d) It is voluntary in nature and can not be imposed

291. Personality is the sum total of all reactions which a person exhibits
(a) In context of environment
(b) In context of a person
(c) In context of society
(d) In context of himself

292. According to Sri Aurobindo, the basic elements of personality can be sequentially arranged as under
(a) Physical-Emotional-Intellectual-Spiritual-Super Mental
(b) Physical-Intellectual-Super Mental
(c) Physical-Intelecutual-Spiritual
(d) Physical-Emotional-Spiritual

293. Which of the following statements is correct in relation to values?
(a) Value is the dimension of arriving at an aim
(b) Value is a process which activated by a stimulus
(c) Value is a feeling which form through acts
(d) All the above

294. The need of the development of interest is felt in children
(a) They are playful in nature which leads them towards the development of constructive tendencies
(b) The interests make children's feelings more mature
(c) The interests enrich children's instincts
(d) All the above

295. The propounder of the Single factor theory of intelligence was
(a) Alfred Binet (b) Charles Spearman
(c) Burt (d) Guilford

296. Which of intelligence is accepted (recognised) by Trorndike?
(a) Simple-factor theory

(*b*) Bi-factor theory
(*c*) Multi-factor theory
(*d*) Three-dimensional theory

297. The two-factor theory of intelligence has been put forth by
(*a*) Burt and Vernon (*b*) Terman
(*c*) Spearman (*d*) Skinner

298. The factor which is most important in influencing the intellectual development of the individual is
(*a*) Family environment
(*b*) School environment
(*c*) Neighbourhood
(*d*) Cultural environment

299. The most important school related factor influencing child's intelligence is
(*a*) Curriculum
(*b*) Discipline
(*c*) Curriculum Activities
(*d*) All the above

300. Verbal intelligence tests are the better option for
(*a*) Literate persons (*b*) Illiterate persons
(*c*) Small children (*d*) Special children

ANSWERS

1	2	3	4	5	6	7	8	9	10
(*c*)	(*d*)	(*b*)	(*a*)	(*b*)	(*c*)	(*a*)	(*a*)	(*c*)	(*a*)
11	**12**	**13**	**14**	**15**	**16**	**17**	**18**	**19**	**20**
(*d*)	(*b*)	(*d*)	(*d*)	(*b*)	(*a*)	(*b*)	(*c*)	(*a*)	(*c*)
21	**22**	**23**	**24**	**25**	**26**	**27**	**28**	**29**	**30**
(*b*)	(*c*)	(*d*)	(*d*)	(*d*)	(*a*)	(*b*)	(*a*)	(*c*)	(*d*)
31	**32**	**33**	**34**	**35**	**36**	**37**	**38**	**39**	**40**
(*d*)	(*d*)	(*c*)	(*d*)	(*a*)	(*d*)	(*b*)	(*d*)	(*a*)	(*d*)
41	**42**	**43**	**44**	**45**	**46**	**47**	**48**	**49**	**50**
(*c*)	(*d*)	(*a*)	(*c*)	(*d*)	(*a*)	(*c*)	(*d*)	(*d*)	(*b*)
51	**52**	**53**	**54**	**55**	**56**	**57**	**58**	**59**	**60**
(*d*)	(*b*)	(*d*)	(*c*)	(*a*)	(*d*)	(*d*)	(*c*)	(*a*)	(*a*)
61	**62**	**63**	**64**	**65**	**66**	**67**	**68**	**69**	**70**
(*a*)	(*a*)	(*c*)	(*b*)	(*a*)	(*a*)	(*c*)	(*a*)	(*d*)	(*d*)
71	**72**	**73**	**74**	**75**	**76**	**77**	**78**	**79**	**80**
(*b*)	(*a*)	(*c*)	(*d*)	(*a*)	(*d*)	(*a*)	(*c*)	(*c*)	(*a*)
81	**82**	**83**	**84**	**85**	**86**	**87**	**88**	**89**	**90**
(*c*)	(*d*)	(*b*)	(*b*)	(*b*)	(*d*)	(*d*)	(*d*)	(*c*)	(*a*)
91	**92**	**93**	**94**	**95**	**96**	**97**	**98**	**99**	**100**
(*a*)	(*c*)	(*d*)	(*d*)	(*c*)	(*a*)	(*c*)	(*d*)	(*a*)	(*b*)
101	**102**	**103**	**104**	**105**	**106**	**107**	**108**	**109**	**110**
(*d*)	(*b*)	(*d*)	(*c*)	(*b*)	(*a*)	(*d*)	(*a*)	(*b*)	(*a*)
111	**112**	**113**	**114**	**115**	**116**	**117**	**118**	**119**	**120**
(*b*)	(*a*)	(*c*)	(*b*)	(*d*)	(*c*)	(*d*)	(*a*)	(*a*)	(*d*)
121	**122**	**123**	**124**	**125**	**126**	**127**	**128**	**129**	**130**
(*d*)	(*d*)	(*b*)	(*a*)	(*c*)	(*c*)	(*a*)	(*a*)	(*d*)	(*a*)
131	**132**	**133**	**134**	**135**	**136**	**137**	**138**	**139**	**140**
(*a*)	(*c*)	(*d*)	(*d*)	(*d*)	(*a*)	(*b*)	(*b*)	(*a*)	(*c*)
141	**142**	**143**	**144**	**145**	**146**	**147**	**148**	**149**	**150**
(*a*)	(*d*)	(*d*)	(*c*)	(*a*)	(*d*)	(*a*)	(*d*)	(*d*)	(*c*)
151	**152**	**153**	**154**	**155**	**156**	**157**	**158**	**159**	**160**
(*d*)	(*d*)	(*d*)	(*d*)	(*d*)	(*d*)	(*c*)	(*c*)	(*c*)	(*b*)
161	**162**	**163**	**164**	**165**	**166**	**167**	**168**	**169**	**170**
(*d*)	(*a*)	(*d*)	(*d*)	(*d*)	(*d*)	(*b*)	(*a*)	(*c*)	(*a*)

171	**172**	**173**	**174**	**175**	**176**	**177**	**178**	**179**	**180**
(*c*)	(*b*)	(*c*)	(*c*)	(*d*)	(*a*)	(*a*)	(*b*)	(*b*)	(*a*)
181	**182**	**183**	**184**	**185**	**186**	**187**	**188**	**189**	**190**
(*d*)	(*a*)	(*c*)	(*d*)	(*c*)	(*c*)	(*d*)	(*d*)	(*d*)	(*c*)
191	**192**	**193**	**194**	**195**	**196**	**197**	**198**	**199**	**200**
(*a*)	(*b*)	(*a*)	(*d*)	(*d*)	(*a*)	(*d*)	(*d*)	(*d*)	(*b*)
201	**202**	**203**	**204**	**205**	**206**	**207**	**208**	**209**	**210**
(*b*)	(*a*)	(*b*)	(*d*)	(*d*)	(*c*)	(*c*)	(*c*)	(*a*)	(*b*)
211	**212**	**213**	**214**	**215**	**216**	**217**	**218**	**219**	**220**
(*a*)	(*a*)	(*d*)	(*d*)	(*b*)	(*a*)	(*a*)	(*d*)	(*d*)	(*c*)
221	**222**	**223**	**224**	**225**	**226**	**227**	**228**	**229**	**230**
(*a*)	(*a*)	(*b*)	(*d*)	(*c*)	(*d*)	(*a*)	(*c*)	(*d*)	(*c*)
231	**232**	**233**	**234**	**235**	**236**	**237**	**238**	**239**	**240**
(*a*)	(*c*)	(*b*)	(*a*)	(*b*)	(*b*)	(*a*)	(*b*)	(*a*)	(*c*)
241	**242**	**243**	**244**	**245**	**246**	**247**	**248**	**249**	**250**
(*a*)	(*b*)	(*a*)	(*d*)	(*c*)	(*d*)	(*b*)	(*c*)	(*c*)	(*a*)
251	**252**	**253**	**254**	**255**	**256**	**257**	**258**	**259**	**260**
(*a*)	(*a*)	(*c*)	(*b*)	(*a*)	(*d*)	(*a*)	(*a*)	(*a*)	(*d*)
261	**262**	**263**	**264**	**265**	**266**	**267**	**268**	**269**	**270**
(*d*)	(*a*)	(*d*)	(*d*)	(*d*)	(*a*)	(*d*)	(*c*)	(*d*)	(*c*)
271	**272**	**273**	**274**	**275**	**276**	**277**	**278**	**279**	**280**
(*a*)	(*b*)	(*d*)	(*a*)	(*a*)	(*a*)	(*a*)	(*d*)	(*a*)	(*d*)
281	**282**	**283**	**284**	**285**	**286**	**287**	**288**	**289**	**290**
(*d*)	(*b*)	(*b*)	(*b*)	(*a*)	(*b*)	(*d*)	(*c*)	(*a*)	(*b*)
291	**292**	**293**	**294**	**295**	**296**	**297**	**298**	**299**	**300**
(*a*)	(*a*)	(*d*)	(*d*)	(*a*)	(*c*)	(*c*)	(*a*)	(*d*)	(*a*)

SOCIAL SCIENCE

- History
- Democratic Politics
- Geography
- Economics

HISTORY

Ancient India

INDUS VALLEY CIVILIZATION

The Indus Valley Civilization or The Harappan culture was the most extensive of the ancient civilizations in area, including not only the Indus plain (the Punjab and Sind), but also northern Rajasthan and the region of Kathiawar in western India. It was essentially a city culture.

Common Characteristic Features

The most important feature is the systematic town planning on the lines of the 'grid system', that is streets and lanes cutting across one another almost at right angles, thus dividing the city into several rectangular blocks. At Harappa, Mahan-jo-daro and Kalibangan, this consists of two distinct elements: on the west a 'citadel' mound built on a high podium of mud brick, with a long axis running north to south, and to the east a lower town consisting of the main residential areas.

Another important feature is the large scale use of standardised burnt bricks in almost all kinds of constructions and total absence of stone buildings. The width of each brick was twice its height, and its length twice as large as its width (7.5 × 15 × 30 cm or 10 × 20 × 40 cm). The bricks were mainly made in an open mould, but for special purposes, such as bathroom, sawn bricks were used, and wells constructed with wedge-shaped moulded bricks. Hammer dressed limestone slabs are occasionally found covering bricks drains. Timber was used for the flat roofs.

Another unique feature was the underground drainage system connecting all houses to the street drains which were covered with either bricks or stone slabs and equipped with manholes.

The citadel was defined by wall and on it were constructed the public buildings such as religious buildings, granaries, residences of the ruling class etc. Below this citadel was the town proper, consisting of the houses of the commoners. Houses stood on both sides of the streets. Houses generally had side entrances and there were no windows facing the main streets.

An average house had besides kitchen and baths, four to six living rooms, large houses with thirty rooms and staircases suggest that there were large two or three storeyed buildings. Most of the houses had wells within them. There were also arrangement for street lighting.

Town Planning

The first thing that strikes us with regard to Harappan culture is the town planning and urbanisation. Mohenjo-daro, Harappa, Lothal or Sutkagendor were built on similar plan. To the west of each was a citadel built on a high platform. It was defended by wall and on it were constructed the public buildings. Below this citadel was the town proper. Everywhere, the main streets ran from north to south and other streets ran at right angles to the main streets. Houses, residential or others, stood on both sides of the streets. Both at Harappa and Mohenjo-daro, houses were built of kiln-burnt bricks. At Lothal and Kalibangan, residential houses were made of sun-dried bricks. The drains, wells and bathing platforms were made of kiln-burnt bricks. An average house had, besides kitchen and bath, four to six living rooms. Large houses with thirty rooms and staircases suggest that there were large two or three storyed buildings. Most of the houses had wells within them and a drainage system carried the waste water to the main underground drain of the street. There were also public baths with wells. The covered drains of the streets had soak-pits and manholes for clearing. There were also arrangements for street lighting.

VEDIC CULTURE

With the arrival of Aryans, a new era began in India. That is called Vedic Age. The Vedic Age has been divided into two parts-The Early Vedic Age or Rigvedic Age and the Later Vedic Age. The Rigvedic era belongs from (1500-1000 B.C.). Historians and scholars have expressed different opinions regarding the original home land of the Aryans. They did not live in cities. Different scholars have different opinion regarding the home land of Aryans. India, Central Asia, South Russia, Plateau of Pamir, Scandinavia, Germany, Austria, Hungary etc., have been alternatively suggested as the original home of the Aryans by scholars who have tried to justify their respective contentions on the basis of history, philology, archaeological discoveries. But the majority of scholars have thought that the original home land of Aryans was from Poland and South Russia to Central Asia.

RIGVEDIC PERIOD

The only source of the Early Vedic Age is the Rigveda. Most of the hymns of the Rigveda were composed between the period 1500-1000 B.C.

The Aryans called their state as the Rashtra. Political organisation was based on patriarchal family. The State was divided into *Grama, Vis* and *Jana.* The relationship between all three divisions was not stated clearly. Grama was the smallest unit and gramani was the Lord of Grama. The lord of Vis was called Vispati and Gopa was the protector of Jana. The prevailing form of government among the Rig-Vedic tribes was monarchical.

Kingship was usually hereditary. The foremost duty of the king was the protection of the tribe and the tribal territory. He fought against external enemies. The king had no right over the land but he had the right to disown anybody from it. The plough land and the domestic animals were regarded the personal property of the farmer and the pasture-land was the property of the village.

Bhag, Sulk and Bali were the taxes collected by the king. The land revenue was 1/10 to l/6 of the production. The king was assisted by a number of functional areas like purohit, senani etc. Senani was the leader of army. The army was divided into two parts. One part included foot soldiers later called patti and the other part were called Rathis who fought from chariots. The main weapons were bow, arrows, spears, lancess and strings.

There was no regular court for Justice. Justice was provided by the king and assisted by purohits. Punishment were also given. It may be turned out of the state, fined, put to physical torture or put to death. There were two popular assemblies to assist the king in administration. Majority of historians believe that one assembly is known as *Samiti* and the other was *Sabha.* Samiti was the assembly of larger group of people while Sabha was the council of elders. The powers of these assemblies were not defined but these were quite influential during the early Vedic Age.

LATER VEDIC PERIOD

The period between B.C. 1000 and B.C. 600 is generally known as Later Vedic period. This age is also called as the Epic Age because the two great epics Ramayana and Mahabharata were written during this period. The Aryans during this period moved to the Gangetic Valley.

The Gangetic Valley or Aryavartha became the centre of political activity. Kingdoms like Kosala, Videha, Kuru,Magadha, Kasi, Avanti and Panchala came into existence. The position of the king was considerably high. Sabha and Samiti did not stand in his way. Kingship became hereditary. The kings were in charge of defense and maintaining law and order of their kingdoms. They built vast empires. They tried to extend their territories. Therefore frequent wars were fought. Rituals and sacrifices such as Rajasuya, Ashvamedha, Vajapeya and Yagas were performed by the kings.

Kings assumed titles like Ekrat, Samrat and Sariahaurna. Village administration was looked after by the village councils. Taxes like Sulk and Bhaga were collected from the people. The revenue was spent for the benefit of the subjects.

EARLY STATES

MAHAJANPADAS

In the later Vedic period, the tribal organisations changed its identity and gradually shifted to the territorial identity, and the area of settlement were now regarded as *janapadas* or states. In transition from tribe to monarchy, they lost the essential democratic pattern of the tribe but retained the idea of government through an assembly representing the tribes. These states consisted of either a single tribe such as the *Shakyas*, *Kolias*, *Mallas* etc. or a confederacy of tribes such as the *Vrijis*, *Yadavas*, *Parchala* etc.

The people in the lower Ganges Valley and Delta, which were outside the Aryan pale, were regarded as *Mlecchas*. There was, therefore, a strong consciousness of the pure land of the Aryans called *Aryavarta*. Each *janapada* tried to dominate and subjugate other *janapadas* to become *Mahajanapadas*.

According to *Anguttara Nikaya*, there were about sixteen *Mahajanapadas* in the sixth century BC. Their capitals and locations are given in a table on the 16 *Mahajanapadas*.

Important Republics

The kings in these states had the supreme authority. The *Mahajanapadas* of Vrijji, Malla, Kuru, Panchal and Kamboj were republican states and so were other smaller states like Lichhavi, Shakya, Koliya, Bhagga, and Moriya. These republican states had a *Gana-parishad* or an Assembly of senior and responsible citizens. This *Gana-Parishad* had the supreme authority in the state. All the administrative decisions were taken by this *Parishad*. Again, the republics were basically of two types: (*a*) the republics comprising a single tribe like those of the Sakyas, the Kolias and the Mallas, and (*b*) the republics comprising a number of tribes or the republics of confederacy like the Vrijjis.

RISE OF MAGADH

The Haryankas : Magadha came into prominence under the leadership of **Bimbisara** (542-493 BC), who belonged to the ***Haryanka dynasty***. He strengthened his position by marriage alliances. He took three wives. His first wife was the daughter of the king of Kosala and the sister of Prasenajit. His second wife Chellana was a *Lichchhavi* Princess from Vaishali, and his third wife was the daughter of the chief of the Madra clan of Punjab. Marriage relations with the different princely families gave enormous diplomatic prestige and paved the way the expansion of Magadha westward and northward.

The earliest capital of Magadha was at Rajgir, which was called Girivraja at that time. It was surrounded by five hills, the openings in which were closed by stone walls on all sides. This made Rajgir impregnable.

Bimbisar was succeeded by his son **Ajatasatru** (492-460 BC). Ajatasatru killed his father and seized the throne for himself. Throughout his reign, he pursued an aggressive policy of expansion.

Ajatasatru was succeeded by **Udayin** (460-444 BC). His reign is important because he built the fort upon the confluence of the Ganga and Son at Patna. This was done because Patna lay in the centre of the Magadhan kingdom.

The Sisunagas : Udayin was succeeded by the dynasty of ***Sisunagas***, who temporarily shifted the capital to Vaishali. Their greatest achievement was the destruction of the power of Avanti with its capital at Ujjain. This brought to an end the 100 years old rivalry between Magadha and Avanti.

The Nandas : The *Sisunagas* were succeeded by the *Nandas*, who proved to be the most powerful rulers of Magadha. So great was their power that Alexander, who invaded Punjab at that time, did not dare to move towards the east. The Nandas added to the Magadhan power by conquering Kalinga from where they brought an image of the Jina as a victory trophy. All this took place in the reign of **Mahapadma Nanda**. He claimed to be *ekarat,* the sole sovereign who destroyed all the other ruling princes.

The Nandas were the first non-kshatriya rulers. The last Nanda ruler was defeated by Chandragupta Maurya who founded the Maurya Empire.

ALEXANDER'S INVASION

- Alexander marched to India through the Khyber Pass in 326 B.C.
- He was bravely checked by the local chieftains despite the fact that they had no chance of success.
- He was even checked by the queens of the vanquished and dead chiefs.
- His advance was checked on the bank of the Beas because of the mutiny of his soldiers.
- In 325 B.C., he began his homeward journey.
- In 324 B.C., he reached Susa in Persia and died the next year.
- The Greek invasion of India opened the trade route between north-west India and Western Asia.
- Eastwards trade went through the Ganga delta to the coast of Northern Burma and south along the east coast.
- Guilds (*Shreni*) came into existence.
- Money was introduced. Punch-marked coins in gold and silver and of copper cast have been discovered.
- Introduction of money facilitated the trade.

JAINISM AND BUDDHISM

JAINISM

The Founder : Rishabha, who was the father of king Bharata, the first *chakravarti* king of India, founded Jainism. The *Vishnu Purana* and *Bhagavat Purana* describe Rishabha as an incarnation of Narayana.

Risabha was succeeded by 23 other *Tirthankaras.* Parsvanatha (850 BC) was the 23rd *Tirthankara.* Jainism became a major religion under Vardhamana Mahavira, the 24th Tirthankara.

According to Jainism, the Tirthankaras descended on earth from time to time to guide the masses.

Vardhamana Mahavira : Vardhamana Mahavira was born in 540 BC in a village (Kundagrama) near Vaishali. His father was the head of a famous kshatriya clan (Inatrika), and his mother a Lichachhavi princess. They were also connected with the royal family of Magadha. In the beginning Mahavira led the life of a householder, but in the search for truth, he abandoned the world at the age of thirty and became an ascetic. He kept on wandering for twelve years from place to place. During the course of his long journey, it is said, he never changed his clothes for twelve years, and abandoned them altogether when he attained perfect knowledge or *kaivalya* at the age of 42. Through *kaivalya,* he conquered misery and happiness. Because of this conquest, he is known as Mahavira or the great hero or *jina,* i.e., the conqueror, and his followers are known as *Jainas*. He propagated his religion for thirty years, and his mission took him to Kosala, Magadha, Mithila, Champa, etc. He passed away at the age of 72 in 468 BC at a place called Pavapuri near modern Rajgir in Bihar.

Teachings : Jainism taught five doctrines: (i) do not commit violence, (ii) do not speak a lie, (iii) do not steal, (iv) do not acquire property, and (v) observe continence (*brahmacharya*). It is said that only the fifth doctrine was added by Mahavira, the other four being taken over by him from Prasavanath.

Jainism recognized the existence of the gods but placed them lower than the *jina.* It did not condemn the varna system. According to Mahavira, a person is born in a high or in a lower varna in consequence of the sins or the virtues acquired by him in the previous birth. In his opinion, through pure and meritorious life, members of the lower castes can attain liberation.

Jainism rejected the authority of the *Vedas* and *Vedic* retrials. It did not believe in the existence of God, but it believed in *Karma* and the transmigration of soul (Nirvana).

BUDDHISM

Gautama Buddha : Gautama Buddha or Siddhartha was a contemporary of Mahavira. He was born in 563 BC in a Shakya (kshatriya) family in Lumbini near Kapilavastu, which is situated on the foothills of Nepal. Gautama's father (Shudhodana) seems to have been the elected ruler of Kapilavastu, and headed the republican clan of the Shakyas. His mother (Mahamaya) was a princess from the Kosalan dynasty. From his early childhood, Gautama showed a meditative bent of mind. **Alara Kama** was his teacher of meditation. His charioteer was **Channa**, while his horse's name was **Kanthaks**. He was married early, but married life did not interest him. At the age of 29, he left home. He kept on, wandering for about seven years and then attained knowledge at the age of 35 at Bodh Gaya under a *pipal* tree, From this time onwards, he began to be called the Buddha or **The Enlightened.**

Gautama Buddha delivered his first sermons at Sarnath in Banaras. Gautama Buddha passed away at the age of 80 in 483 BC at a place called Kusinagar, identical with the village called Kasia in the district of Deoria in eastern Uttar Pradesh.

Teachings : Buddha said that the world is full of sorrows and people suffer on account of desires. If desires are conquered, *nirvana* will be attained. He recommended an **eight-fold path** (*astangika marga*) for the elimination of human misery. It comprised : Right Observation, Right Determination, Right Speech, Right Action, Right Livelihood, Right Exercise, Right Memory and Right Meditation. Buddha also laid down a code of conduct for his followers. The main items in this social conduct are: (i) do not covet the property of others, (ii) do not commit violence, (iii) do not use intoxicants, (iv) do not tell a lie, and (v) do not indulge in corrupt practices.

Buddha (The Entightened), ***Dhamma*** (The Doctrine) and ***Sangha*** (The order) are **three jewels of Buddhism**.

Buddhism does not recognize the existence of god and soul (*atman*). It particularly won the support of the lower orders as it attacked the varna system. Women also were admitted to the *sangha* and thus, brought at a par with men.

MAURYA AGE

The Maurya Empire was the first and one of the greatest empires that were established on Indian soil. Chandra Gupta Maurya was the first ruler who unified enitre Indian under one political unit. About Mauryan rulers we have epigraphical sources, literary sources, foreign accounts and materials obtained from archaelogical excavations. The Arthasashtra of Kautilya gives its detailed information about the administrative system of the Mauryan Empire.

Chandragupta Maurya (321-293 BC)

The Maurya dynasty was founded by Chandragupta

Maurya. He took advantage of the growing weakness and unpopularity of the Nandas in the last days of their rule. With the help of Chanakya, who is known as Kautilya, he overthrew the Nandas and established the rule of the Maurya dynasty.

Chandragupta built up a vast empire which included not only Bihar and good portions of Bengal, but also western and north-western India, and the Deccan. Leaving Kerala, Tamil Nadu and parts of north-eastern India, the Mauryas ruled over the whole of the subcontinent. In the north-west, they held sway over certain areas which were not included even in the British empire.

Bindusara (293-273 BC)

He was son of Chandragupta and was known as *Amitraghta* (slayer of foes) by the Greek writers. He continued his friendly links with the Syrian King Antiochus I and is stated to have requested him for a present of figs and wine together with a sophist. Antiochus sent figs and wine but replied that Greek philosophers were not for export. He received a Greek ambassador, Daimachos, from Antiochus I. Pliny tells that Ptolemy II Philadelphus of Egypt sent an envoy, Dionysios, to Bindusara's court.

Ashoka (273-232 BC)

Ashoka was the third and the greatest of the Mauryan rulers. He occupies a high position not only in the history of India but in the world history also. He was coronated four years after the death of his father, Bindusara (273BC). The gap is interpreted differently by different historians.

Ashoka's Dhamma: There was a great difference between Ashoka's personal religion and the religion he preached. His personal religion was, of course, Buddhism as he frankly admitted in the *Bhabru Edict* that he believed in the principles of Buddhism. In several of his edicts, in the capacity of the defender of the faith, he prescribed rules of punishment for those *Bhikshus* (monks) who violated the principles of Buddhism. He undertook journeys to the holy places of Buddhism and also called a Buddhist Council to meet in his time. However, the greatness of the Ashoka lies in the fact that he never thrusted his own religion upon anyone else. The *Dhamma* he placed before the world to follow was not pure Buddhism but it was the essence of all religions.

He appointed a new class of officers called *dharmayuktas, dharma-mahamatras* and *stri-adhyaksha* for the moral and spiritual uplift of the subjects.

KANVA DYNASTY

The last Sunga ruler was put to death by Vasudev Kanva, who ruled for about nine years. The dynasty lasted for about 45 years. The other rulers of the dynasty were Bhumiputra, Narayana and Susharma.

SATAVAHANAS

King Simuka established Satavahana dynasty in the Andhra region. Their empire, at one time, was expanded in a large Deccan area. Paithan, Vaijayanti and Amaravati were famous towns of that time.

1. The Satavahana kings being Brahmans felt strongly to revive Brahmanism. They were also zealous to revive the Varna Ashrama system.
2. The religious notions, during the Satavahana period were quite considerate and tolerant.
3. During Satavahana period Buddhism flourished. The Buddhist religion contributed significantly in the domain of art.

LATER MAURYAN AGE

BACTRIANS

- Demetrius, the Greek ruler of Bactria invaded Afghanistan and Punjab and occupied them. From Taxila, he sent two of his Commanders, Appolodotus and Menander for further conquests.
- Menander extended his rule up to Mathura and from there he made attempts to capture Pataliputra. But he was stopped by the army of Vasumitra, the grandson of Pushyamitra Sunga.
- Menander was also known as Milinda and the capital of his kingdom was Sakala (Sialcot). He evinced much interest in Buddhism and his dialogues with the Buddhist monk Nagasena was compiled in the Pali work, Milindapanho (Questions of Milinda).
- A Greek ambassador Heliodorus became a Vaishnavite and erected the Garuda Pillar at Besnagar(Vidisha).

SAKAS

- The Sakas or the Scythians attacked Bactria and Parthia and captured them from the Greek rulers.
- The founder the Saka rule in India in the first century B.C. was Maues.
- The most famous Saka ruler in India was Rudradaman I. His achievements are highlighted in his Junagarh inscription.

KUSHANAS

- The Kushanas were a branch of Yuchi tribe, whose original home was central Asia.
- The founder of the Kushana dynasty was Kujula Kadphises or Kadphises I.
- Wima Kadphises or Kadphises II conquered the whole of northwestern India as far as Mathura. He issued gold coins with high-sounding titles like the 'Lord of the Whole World'.

Kanishka (78–120 A.D.)

- Kanishka was the most important ruler of the Kushana dynasty. His capital was **Purushapura** or **Peshawar**. He constructed a city called **Kanishkapuram.**
- He was the founder of the Saka era which starts from 78 A.D.
- According to Kalhana, Kanishka invaded Kashmir and occupied it.
- Kanishka had convened the **Fourth** Buddhist Council at **Kundalvana** in Kashmir. Many Buddhist monks like **Vasumitra, Nagarjuna** and **Parsva** attended it. **Ashwagosha** presided over the council. He wrote **Buddha Charita**.
- **Vasumitra** wrote the great **Mahavibhasha. Nagarjuna** wrote the book titled, **Madhyamika Sutra.**
- Kanishka patronised **Charaka.**
- **Charaka** wrote the **Charaka Samhita**. It deals with medicine. Another medical scholar **Susruta** also belonged to Kanishka's time. He has written the **Susruta Samhita**. It is devoted to surgery.
- In the age of Kanishka the Mahayana Buddhism came into vogue.
- A new school of sculpture developed during Kanishka's time. It is called **Gandhara Sculpture**.

GUPTA AGE

The Early Guptas

Srigupta and his son Ghatotkachagupta were non-entities assuming the simple title of maharaja. As it is not known definitely where these Gupta kings ruled and whether they owed allegiance to any paramount soverign, it is better to leave undecided the status of the first two Gupta kings.

Chandragupta-I (320-335 AD)

The third ruler Chandragupta-I, the son and successor at Ghatotkacha, was definitely a strong ruler whose hands were sought by the Lichchhavis who gave their princess Kumardevi in marriage to him. This matrimonial alliance with this ancient historic family no doubt enhanced the status of the obscure Guptas. The Lichchhavi territory of north Bihar and the adjoining principality over which the Guptas ruled were united under Chandragupta and the latter was able to extend his dominion over Avadh as well as Magadha, and along the Ganges as far as Prayaga or Allahabad. Chandragupta-I is usually regarded as the founder of the Gupta era, which commenced on 26 February, A.D. 320 to commemorate his accession or coronation–an era which continued in parts of India for several centuries.

Samudragupta (335-375 AD)

Chandragupta-I was succeeded by his son Samudragupta, who became the ruler after subduing his rival, Kacha, an obscure prince of the dynasty. The Allahabad Pillar Inscription, written by Harisena, gives a detailed account of the conquests of his royal master. This account contains a long list of states, kings and tribes which were conquered and brought under various degrees of subjugation.

Chandragupta-II (380-415 AD)

Samdura Gupta was succeeded by his son Chandragupta-II, surnamed Vikramaditya. But according to some scholars, the immediate successor of Samudra Gupta was his son Ramagupta, the elder brother of Chandragupta-II. A drama Chandraguptam, by Visakhadatta, mentions that Ramagupta agreed to surrender his queen Dhruvadevi to the infatuation of a Saka Chief (Basana) who had invaded his kingdom. The honour of the queen was saved by Chandragupta, younger brother of Ramagupta, who killed the Saka chief, usurped the throne and married the widow. This story with slight variations is referred to in Bana's Harshacharita, Rajasekhara's Kavyamimamsa and some Rashtrakuta inscriptions of the 9th and 10th centuries. However, the historicity of Ramagupta is a matter of great doubt as neither the contemporary inscriptions nor the coins mention any king of this name.

LATER GUPTAS

EMERGENCE OF REGIONAL STATES (NORTH AND SOUTH INDIA)

North India

Prathiharas

- **Nagabhatta** I founded this dynasty. **Kanuaj** was their capital.
- The most famous king of the Prathiharas was king **Mihira Bhoja**. He ruled from 836 A.D. to 885 A.D.
- **Mihira Bhoja's son Mahendrapal** was also equally great and powerful. Under his rule, the Prathihara empire reached its zenith. His court poet and dramatist **Rajashekara** wrote **Bala Ramayana, Bala Bharatha** and a few more works in Sanskrit.

Chauhans

- Another branch of the Rajputs was the **Chauhans of Ajmer**.
- This kingdom was founded at the end of the 8th century A.D. The famous king of this dynasty was **Visaldeva**. He captured Delhi from the **Tomaras**.
- The last and the most powerful king of this dynasty was **Prithviraj Chauhan**. He defeated Muhammad of Ghor in the **First Battle of Tarain** in 1191 A.D. But in the next year Prithviraj was defeated and killed by Muhammed of Ghor in the Second **Battle of Tarain**.

Chandelas

- The **Chandelas** had ruled the region called **Bundelkhand**.
- The important rulers of this dynasty were **Dhanga** and **Kirtivarman**.
- The famous **Vishnu Temple** was built by **Yashovarman** at **Khajuraho** in 955 A.D. He made **Mahoba** his capital. Two other temples of this period are the **Parshwanath Jain** temple and the **Kandariya Mahadeva** temple at **Khajuraho**.
- The last ruler of this dynasty was defeated by **Qutb-ud-din Aibak**. And thus came the end of the Chandella rule in Bundelkhand.

Paramaras

- **Upendra** was the **founder** of this dynasty.
- The most important king of this dynasty was **Bhoja** (1010 A.D.- 1055 A.D.). He dug a very big lake (more than 250 square miles). It is situated to the South East of Bhopal.

Palas of Bengal

- **Gopala** (A.D. 765-A.D.769) was the first ruler of the Pala Dynasty of Bengal.
- **Gopala** was succeeded by **Dharmapala** (A.D.769-A.D.815). He ruled Bengal for nearly four decades. He was a follower of Buddhism. He founded the **University of Vikramasila**.

South India

Pallavas

- The Pallavas established their kingdom in Tondaimandalam with its capital at Kanchipuram. Their rule continued till Tondaimandalam was captured and annexed by the Imperial Cholas in the beginning of the 10th century A.D.
- The early Pallava rulers from 250 A.D. to 350 A.D. issued their charters in Prakrit. Important among them were Sivaskandavarman and Vijayaskandavarman.
- Other great Pallava rulers were Mahendravarman I, Narasimhavarman I, and Narasimhavarman II.
- The Pallavas introduced the art of excavating temples from the rock. In fact, the Dravidian style of temple architecture began with the Pallava rule.
- Mahendravarman I introduced the rock-cut temples. This style of Pallava temples are seen at places like Mandagappattu, Mahendravadi, Mamandur, Dalavanur, Tiruchirappalli, Vallam, Siyamangalam and Tirukalukkunram.

Chalukyas (543 – 755 A.D.)

- Pulakesin I was the founder of the Chalukya dynasty. He established a small kingdom with Vatapi or Badami as its capital.
- **Pulakesin II** was the contemporary of Harsha Vardhana.
- There was a battle between Harsha and Pulakesin II on the banks of the river **Narmadha**. Pulakesin II defeated Harsha.
- The Chalukyas were great patrons of art. They developed the vesara style in the building of structural temples.
- The structural temples of the Chalukyas exist at Aihole, Badami and Pattadakal (**Virupaksha temple**). Cave temple architecture was also famous under the Chalukyas. Their cave temples are found in Ajanta, Ellora and Nasik.

Rashtrakutas (755 – 975 A.D.)

- Dantidurga was the founder of the Rashtrakuta dynasty. He defeated the Gurjaras and captured Malwa from them. Then, he annexed the Chalukya kingdom by defeating Kirtivarman II. Thus, the Rashtrakutas became a paramount power in the Deccan.
- Dantidurga was succeeded by Krishna I.
- Krishna I built the magnificent rock-cut monolithic Kailasa temple at Ellora.
- The art and architecture of the Rashtrakutas were found at Ellora and Elephanta.

Cholas

- Cholas became prominent in the ninth century and established an empire comprising the major portion of South India. Their capital was Tanjore.
- The founder of the Chola kingdom was Vijayalaya.
- The most powerful Chola kings were Rajaraja I and his son Rajendra I. Rajaraja ruled from A.D. 985 to A.D 1012. He had conquered the neighbouring Pandya kingdoms and extended his conquest upto to the Northern part of Ceylon.
- Rajendra I assumed a number of titles, the most famous being Mudikondan, Gangaikondan, Kadaram Kondan and Pandita Cholan.
- Rajendra III was the last Chola king who was defeated by Jatavarman Sundarapandya II. The Chola country was absorbed into the Pandya Empire.
- The Dravidian style of art and architecture reached its perfection under the Cholas.
- The chief feature of the Chola temple is the vimana.
- Raja Raja Chola built the famous **Brahadeeswara temple** at **Tanjore**. It is also known as the **Big temple**.
- **Rajendra I** founded a new capital at **Gangaikonda Cholapuram** in 1025 A.D . He also built a temple at this place.
- The bronzes of the Chola period are world-famous. The bronze statues of Nataraja or dancing Siva are master pieces.

Medieval India

SULTANS OF DELHI

- The Muslim invasions into India had ultimately resulted in the establishment of Delhi Sultanate which existed from A.D. 1206 to 1526.
- The five dynasties which ruled Delhi were :
  1. The Slave dynasty 1206-1290
  2. The Khilji dynasty 1290-1320
  3. The Tughlaq dynasty 1320-1414
  4. The Sayyid dynasty 1414-1451
  5. The Lodi dynasty 1451-1526

SLAVE DYNASTY

- The Slave dynasty was also called Mamluk dynasty. Mamluk was the Quranic term for slave.
- The Slave dynasty ruled Delhi from A.D. 1206 to 1290. In fact, three dynasties were established during this period. They were-
  1. Qutbi dynasty (1206-1211) founded by Qutbuddin Aibak.
  2. First Ilbari dynasty (1211- 1266) founded by Iltutmish.
  3. Second Ilbari dynasty (1266-1290) founded by Balban.

Qutb-ud-din Aibak

- **Qutb-ud-din Aibak** was the first Sultan of Delhi.
- Qutbuddin Aibak was a slave of Muhammad Ghori, who made him the Governor of his Indian possessions.
- After the death of Ghori in 1206, Aibak declared his independence. He assumed the title Sultan and made Lahore his capital.
- Muslim writers call Aibak *Lakh Baksh* or giver of lakhs because he gave liberal donations to them.
- Aibak died of injuries received in a fall from his horse while playing **chaugan** (Polo) in 1210.

Iltutmish

- Iltutmish belonged to the Ilbari tribe and hence his dynasty was named as Ilbari dynasty.
- He shifted his capital from Lahore to Delhi.
- He received the mansur, the letter of recognition, from the Abbasid Caliph in 1229 by which he became the legal sovereign ruler of India.
- He patronized many scholars and a number Sufi saints came to India during his reign. Minhaj-us-Siraj, Taj-ud-din., Nizam-ul-mulk Muhammad Janaidi, Malik Qutb-ud-din Hasan and Fakhrul-Mulk Isami were his contemporary scholars who added grandeur to his court.

Raziya

- She was the first and last Muslim lady who sat on the throne of Delhi.
- She appointed an Abyssinian slave Yakuth as Master of the Royal Horses.
- In 1240, Altunia, the governor of Bhatinda revolted against her. She went in person to suppress the revolt but Altunia killed Yakuth and took Raziya prisoner.

Ghiyas-ud-din Balban

- Ghiyas-ud-din Balban, who was also known as Ulugh Khan, served as Naib or regent to Sultan Nasiruddin Mahmud.

- Balban introduced rigorous court discipline and new customs such as prostration and kissing the Sultan's feet to prove his superiority over the nobles.
- He also introduced the Persian festival of *Nauroz* to impress the nobles and people with his wealth and power.
- He established a separate military department - *diwan-i-arz* – and reorganized the army.

KHILJI DYNASTY

Jalaluddin Khilji

- The founder of the Khilji dynasty was Jalaluddin Khilji.
- The important event of Jalaluddin's reign was the attack on Devagiri in the Deccan. His nephew and son-in-law **Ala-ud-din Khilji** plundered **Devagiri** and defeated its ruler **Ramachandra Deva** and returned to Kara. During the reception there, Alauddin Khilji treacherously murdered his father-in-law Jalaluddin Khilji and usurped the throne of Delhi.

Alauddin Khilji

- **Ala-ud-din Khilji** was the greatest ruler of the Khilji Dynasty.
- He was the first Muslim ruler to extend his empire right upto Rameshwaram in the South.
- The Sultan had built a new city called **Siri** near Delhi.
- **Amir Khusrau** the great Persian poet, patronised by Balban, continued to live in Alauddin Khilji's court also.
- He introduced the system of *dagh* (branding of horses) and prepared *huliya* (descriptive list of soldiers).
- Alauddin Khilji maintained a large permanent standing army and paid them in cash from the royal treasury.
- The introduction of paying salaries in cash to the soldiers led to price regulations popularly called as Market Reforms.

TUGHLAQ DYNASTY

Ghiyas-ud-din Tughlaq

- Ghiyas-ud-din Tughlaq was the founder of the Tughlaq dynasty.
- Ghiyas-ud-din laid the foundation for Tughlaqabad near Delhi.
- Ghiyas-ud-din Tughlaq's son Ulugh Khan killed his father and ascended the throne with the title Muhammad bin Tughlaq in 1325.

Muhammad bin Tughlaq

- Muhammad bin Tughlaq was the only Delhi Sultan who had received a comprehensive literary, religious and philosophical education.
- To have the capital at the centre of the empire and safe from the Mongol raids, Tughlaq chose Devagiri as his new capital in A.D. 1327.The Sultan renamed the new capital **Daulatabad.**
- In 1329-30, Muhammad bin Tughlaq introduced a token currency.
- A separate department for agriculture, *Diwan-i- Kohi* was established.
- Muhammad bin Tughlaq died in 1351.

Firoz Shah Tughlaq

- **Firuz Shah Tughlaq** became Sultan after the death of Muhammad-bin-Tughlaq in A.D. 1351.
- He appointed *Khan-i-Jahan* Maqbal, a Telugu Brahmin convert as wazir (prime minister).
- He was the first Sultan to impose irrigation tax.
- **Firuz Shah Tughlaq** constructed many canals for irrigation. The longest canal was about 200 kilometres from Sutlej to Hansi. Another canal was between Yamuna and Hissar.
- A new department called *Diwan-i-Khairat* was created to take care of orphans and widows.
- He had built new towns of **Firozabad, Jaunpur, Hissar** and **Firozpur**.

Invasion of Timur

- **Timur,** the Turkish chief of Central Asia, was a great conqueror. Taking advantage of India's weakness, he had entered India in A.D. 1398. At that time, Nasiruddin Mahmud was the ruler.
- When Timur entered Delhi there was no opposition and he sacked Delhi for three days murdering thousands of people and looting enormous wealth.
- **Timur** withdrew from India in 1399 and his invasion in fact delivered a death blow to the Tughlaq dynasty.

SAYYID DYNASTY

- Before his departure from India, Timur appointed Khizr Khan as governor of Multan. He captured Delhi and founded the Sayyid dynasty in 1414.
- **Mubarak Shah, Mohammed Shah** and **Alam Shah** were some of the other important noteworthy rulers of Sayyid Dynasty.
- Muhammad Shah died in 1445 and was succeeded by his son Alam Shah (1445-1451)

the weakest of the Sayyid princes. He handed over the throne to Bahlol Lodi and retired to Badaun.

LODIS

- The Lodis, who succeeded Sayyids, were Afghans.
- Bahlol Lodi was the first Afghan ruler while his predecessors were all Turks. He died in 1489 and was succeeded by his son, Sikandar Lodi.
- In 1504, Sikandar Lodi founded the city of Agra and transferred his capital from **Delhi** to **Agra**.
- Sikander was the greatest of the Lodi Kings.
- On Sikandar Lodi's death in A.D. 1517, his son **Ibrahim Lodi** unanimously became the Sultan of Delhi.
- Ibrahim Lodi failed to get the support of Afghan nobles.
- A powerful Afghan noble, **Daulatkhan Lodi**, invited **Babar**, the ruler of Afghanistan, to invade India and overthrow Ibrahim Lodi.
- Babar marched against Delhi and defeated and killed Ibrahim Lodi in the first battle of Panipat (1526).

VIJAYANAGAR AND BAHMANI KINGDOM

THE VIJAYANAGAR KINGDOM (1350-1564 A.D.)

The origin of the kingdom of Vijayanagar is still a matter of controversy. According to tradition, the kingdom was founded by the five sons of Sangama of whom the two most prominent were Harihara and Bukka who reverted to Hinduism after having been converted to Islam. They were encouraged in their enterprise by two scholars, Madhava Vidyaratna and his brother Sayana. According to Father Heras, this kingdom was founded by the Hoysala King, Vira Bailala III. However, it seems certain that the kingdom owed its origin to a reaction to the devastating Muslim raids which threatened to overwhelm the Hindu civilisation in southern India. The capital of the kingdom was Hastinavati (Hampi).

Reasons for Growth of Vijayanagar Empire

- Growth in agriculture and trade in the territories of Karnataka.
- Chola state was finished. The re-emergence of powerful chieftainships over portions of Tamil country outside of Cholamandalam firmly established independent bases of competitive power.
- Early Vijayanagar expansion came at the expense of great Hindu kingdoms such as the Hoysala states of Karnataka and the Reddi kingdom of Kondavidu in Andhra.
- These northern warriors drew resources from the newly overrun areas by way of tributes.
- Small warriors of *nayakas* were the leading political figures in the Vijayanagar states and European sources refer to the acquisition and shifting of some part of the resources commanded by them to the capital city in the form of tribute.

Vijayanagar Dynasties

Dynasty	Founder	Period
Sangama	Harihara and Bukka	1336-1485
Saluva	Saluva Narsimha	1485-1505
Tuluva	Veer Narsimha	1505-1570
Aravidu	Trumala	1570-mid 17th Century

THE BAHMANI KINGDOM (1347-1526 A.D.)

The Bahmani kingdom was founded in 1347 by Hasan Gangu who revolted and proclaimed his independence, from the Sultanate. He assumed the title of *Alauddin Bahmani* (Also Bahman Shah). Gulbarga was his capital. He divided his kingdom into four *Tarafs* (provinces) and placed each one under a Tarafdar (Governor). He was succeeded by Muhammad Shah I (1358-73) whose reign was chiefly occupied in waging savage wars against Vijayanagar and Warangal. Some of the other notable rulers of the dynasty were Firoz Shah (1397-1422) who twice defeated Vijayanagar but was ultimately defeated at Pangul; Ahmad Shah (1422-33) who conquered warangal and shifted the capital to Bidar and who was also known as Wali on account of his association with a sufi, Gesu Daraz; Humayun (1451-61) famous for his minister, Khwaja Mahmud Gawan; Muhammad Shah III (1463-82) whose reign saw Mahmud Gawan expand the Kingdom as never before. In his campaign against Vijaynagar in 1481, he even reached and plundered Kanchi. He overran Dabhol and Goa on the western coast. However, Gawan was a Persian by birth and hence disliked by the 'Deccani' chiefs who were native. The Deccani party conspired against him and got him executed in 1481.

Gradually, the Bahmani Kingdom declined in power till in 1526, Amir Barid usurped the throne. Thus the dynasty came to end. Five independent kingdoms rose on the ruins of the Bahmani kingdom, namely Berar, Bidar, Ahmednagar, Golconda and Bijapur.

Berar

It was the first province to break loose from the Bahmani Kingdom when in 1484, Fathulla, the governor of Gowilgarh, revolted against Mahmud Bahmani. The dynasty he founded was called the Imad Shahi dynasty because he borne the title of Imadoul-Mulk. His capital was at Elichpur. The dynasty lasted for about 90 years until 1574 when it was annexed by Ahmednagar.

Bidar

The kingdom comprised the territory around the Bahmani capital. Qasim Barid, a former minister of Mahmud Gawan, had become its de facto ruler as early as 1492. But he and his successor hesitated from assuming formal ranks until 1527. The dynasty lasted till 1619 when, it was annexed by Bijapur.

Ahmednagar

In 1490, Malik Ahmad, the governor of Junmar, successfully revolted and established himself as an independent sovereign. He founded the city of Ahmednagar and along with, the Nizam Shahi dynasty. Frequently embroiled in wars with Bijapur and Golkonda, it formed a Subha of Akbar's Empire and was finally annexed to the Mughal in 1637 under Shahjahan.

Golkonda

Founded the last of all (1518), the Golkonda kingdom comprised the ruins of the Kakatiya principality of Warangal and was extensive, fertile and rich in territory. It was founded in 1518 by a Turkish officer, Sultan Quli Qutub Shah, who was appointed the Governor of Golkonda by Mahmud Gawan. He moved the capital from Warangal to Golkonda. Initially, in spite of the incessant warfare that waged between Bijapur and Ahmednagar, it enjoyed a comparative seclusion. Gradually, however, Golkonda too got embroiled in the Deccan politics, fought serious war against Bijapur and in 1565 joined the Muslim confederacy against the Vijayanagar kingdom.

Like Bijapur, Golkonda too became a famous centre of art and architecture and is famous for its tombs which were made of granite. Golkonda fort and Charminar are its famous examples of architecture. The state was finally annexed to the Mughal Empire by Aurangzeb in 1687.

Bijapur

Out of the five kingdoms of the Deccan Sultanate, Bijapur was the most important. It was founded by Yusuf Adil Shah, who waged wars against Vijayanagar and his neighbours but his great achievement was the recovery of Goa from the Portuguese commander, Albuquerque, though the Portuguese retook it in 1510. He was succeeded by his minor son, Ismail Shah, who recovered Raichur Doab from Vijayanagar. During the reign of Ibrahim Adil Shah, the kingdoms of Golkonda, Bidar and Ahmednagar attacked Bijapur but it was well defended by its able minister Asad Khan. Ibrahim died in 1557 and was succeeded by his son, Ali Adil Shah. Ibrahim Adil Shah II (1579-1626) was perhaps the greatest of the Adil Shah kings. He was a good administrator and introduced a very efficient system of revenue settlement. He was tolerant of all creeds and faiths. He kept friendly relations with the Portugese and allowed them to preach Christianity in his dominions.

Bahmani Kingdoms

Kingdom	Year	Founder	Dynasty	Annexation
Berar	1484	Fataullah Imad	Imad Shahi Shah	1574 (Ahmednagar)
Bijapur	1489	Yusuf Adil Khan	Adil Shahi	1686 (Aurangzeb)
Ahmednagar	1490	Malik Ahmad	Nizam Shahi	1633 (Shahjahan)
Golkonda	1512-1581	Quli Shah	Qutab Shahi	1687 (Aurangzeb)
Bidar	1526-1527	Amir Ali Barid	Barid Shahi	1618 (Bijapur)

RELIGIOUS MOVEMENT

The exchange of ideas between Hindus and Muslims resulted in the development of two popular movements. *The Bhakti movement in the Hindus* and *the sufi movement/sufism in the Islam.*

BHAKTI MOVEMENT

The term Bhakti means single minded devotion to one god. *The god may have a form (Saguna) or may be even formless (Nirguna)*. The Saguna Bhakti worshipped their gods in the various incarnations of god. The followers of *Nirguna* Bhakti do not believe in idol worship. To them god is omnipresent. Yet, both believed in the Upanishadic philosophy of *Advaita* (Non-duality of god).

Nirguna Bhakti and their Exponents

(*i*) **Kabir:** Kabir, a Muslim weaver, was one of the greatest pupils of Ramananda. According to tradition, he was the abandoned child of a Brahmin widow. He grew up as the foster-child of the weaver Niru and his wife. He flourished, most probably, in the end of the fourteenth and early fifteenth century. He composed beautiful verses in Hindi which are still familiar in Northern India. His followers are called *Kabirpanthis* meaning, 'the travellers in the path of Kabir' and Kabir himself was claimed to be '*at once the child of Allah and of Ram*'. When he died both Muslims and Hindus claimed his corpse. The story goes that when they raised the shroud covering the corpse, they found nothing but a heap of flowers. The Hindus took half and cremated it at Varanasi; the Muslim buried the other half near Gorkhpur.

(*ii*) **Guru Nanak:** Nanak was born in a Khatri family on 1469 at Talwandi in the Lahore district. He spent his life preaching the gospel of tolerance. In order to put an end to the religious conflicts he laid stress on moral virtues. " Religious consistent not in mere words" said Nanak; he who looks on all men as equal is religious. Religion consistent not in wandering to tombs or places of cremation, or sitting in attitudes of contemplation. Religion consistent not in wandering in foreign countries, or in bathing at places of pilgrimage. Abide pure amidst the impurities of the world, thus shall they find the way to religion."

(*iii*) **Namadeva:** Namdeva was born in 1270, he was a *Nirguna Upasaka*. Some of his abhangas are included in Guru Granth Sahib.

(*iv*) **Ramananda:** Ramananda was a Bhakti saint in the North, who was a great devotee of Sri Rama. He opened his doors to all-upper castes, untouchables, Muslims etc. Kabir thereby, come across him and was greatly influenced.

Ten Sikh Gurus

(*i*) Guru Nanak (1496-1539)
(*ii*) Guru Angad (1539-1552)
(*iii*) Guru Amardas (1552-1574)
(*iv*) Guru Ram Das (1574-1581)
(*v*) Guru Arjun Dev (1581-1606)
(*vi*) Guru Har Gobind (1606-1644)
(*vii*) Guru Har Rai (1645-1661)
(*viii*) Guru Har Kishan (1661-1664)
(*ix*) Guru Tegh Bahadur (1664-1675)
(*x*) Guru Gobind Singh (1675-1708)

SUFI MOVEMENT

Sufism represents the spiritual and mystical dimensions of Islam. The term *Sufi* probably came from the Arabic word Sof (wool). This was perhaps due to the result of the old ascetic practice of wearing only a coarse woollen garment.

This movement was first born in Iran when some of the religious scholars and liberal thinkers in that country realised that there was little difference among the various beliefs like the Shia and the Sunni sects. In the realm of ideas, it marks the end of the domination of the Mutazila or rationalist philosophy, and the rise of orthodox schools base on the *Quran* and *Hadis (Traditions* of the Prophet and his companions) and of the *Sufi* mystic orders.

The Sufi silsilas were named after the name or surname of the founder of the particular order. Such as Chishti, Suhrawardi, Naqshbandi etc.

Chishti Silsila: The Chishti order was founded by *Khwaja Abdal Chisti* in Herat, it was brought to India by *Khwaja Moin-ud-din Chisti* (1142-1236). He arrived at Lahore in 1161 AD and settled at Ajmer in about 1206. However, the most famous of Chishti saints were *Nizamuddin Auliya* and *Nasiruddin Chirag-i-Delhi*. Auliya was generally known as *Mahbub-i-Ilahi* (beloved of God). They made themselves popular by adopting musical recitation called *Saint* to create mood of nearness to god.

Suhrawardi Silsila: It was founded by *Sheikh Shihabuddin Suhrawardi*. The credit of organising it goes to *Shaikh Bahauddin Zakariya*. Its main centre was Multan. Saints of this order had big jagirs and had closed contact with the state.

Firdausi Silsila: *Sheikh Badruddin of Samark* first moved to Bihar and became the most influential mystic order. Its most distinguished saints was *Sheikh Shamasuddin Yahya Munair* who believed in pantheistic monoism.

Shattari Silsila: It was founded in India by *Shah Abdullah Shattan*. However, it gained in popularity under *Sheikh Muhammad Ghauth* of Gwalior. Among his disciples were the famous musician *Tansen*. The shattari saints sought to synthesize Hindu and mystical Muslim thoughts to practice.

Qadiri Silsila: *Shah Niamatullah Qadri* was probably the first notable saint of this order to enter India but it was *Syed Muhammad Jilani* who organised it on effective basis. *Dara Shikoh*, the eldest son of Shahjahan was follower of this order.

Naqshbandi Silsila: This Silsila was introduced in India by *Khwaja Baqi Billah* during the later years, of Akbar's reign. It attained a position of great importance in India under the leadership of *Sheikh Ahmad Sirhindi*. He was opposed to pantheistic philosophy *Wahadat-ul-Wajud* and propounded the theory of *wahadat-ul-shudud*.

Mahadawi Movement: It was initiated by *Syed Muhammad Mahadi* of Jaunpur. He concentrated his energies on regeneration of people.

Raushaniyah Movement: The movement owed its origin to *Miyan Bayazid Ansari*, a native of Jalandhar. He emphasised inter-organisation of religious rites and inspired his followers with the ideal of ascetic self-denial.

MUGHAL EMPIRE

Babar

- Babar was the founder of the Mughal Empire in India. His original name was Zahiruddin Muhammad. He was related to Timur from his father's side and to Chengaz Khan through his mother.
- **Daulat Khan Lodi,** the Governor of Lahore, openly invited Babar to invade India.
- On 21st April 1526 the first Battle of Panipat took place between Babar and Ibrahim Lodi, who was killed in the battle. Babar's success was due his cavalry and artillery.
- Artillery was used for the first time in the battle of Panipat.
- Babar defeated **Rana Sanga** of **Mewar** in the battle of **Kanwah** in A.D. 1527. Babur assumed the title Ghazi.
- Babar died at Agra in 1530 at the age of forty seven.

Humayun

- Humayun succeeded to the throne of Delhi in A.D. 1530.
- **Sher Shah** defeated Humayun at **Chausa** in A.D. 1539 and again at **Kanauj** in A.D. 1540.
- After losing his kingdom, Humayun became an exile for the next fifteen years.
- He married **Hamida Banu Begam** who gave birth to Akbar at **Amarkot** in A.D.1542.
- In 1555, Humayun defeated the Afghans and recovered the Mughal throne. After six months, he died in 1556 due to his fall from the staircase of his library.

Sher Shah Suri

- The founder of the Sur dynasty was Sher Shah, whose original name was Farid.
- Sher Shah became the ruler of Delhi in 1540.
- Sher Shah introduced new silver coins called "Dam" and they were in circulation till 1835.
- He built a new city on the banks of the river Yamuna near Delhi. Now the old fort called Purana Quila and its mosque is alone surviving.
- He built a Mausoleum at Sasaram, which is considered as one of the master pieces of Indian architecture.

Akbar

- When Akbar ascended the throne in A.D. 1556 he was only 14 years old. His guardian **Bairam Khan** served him as a faithful minister and tutor.
- Bairam Khan, along with Akbar met Hemu in the second Battle of Panipat in 1556. Hemu was initially successful, but lost his consciousness after an arrow hit him. Akbar killed him.
- Akbar abolished the pilgrim tax and in 1564, he abolished jiziya.
- Akbar evolved a new faith called **Din-i-Illahi** or **Divine Faith**. However, his new faith proved to be a failure.
- The land revenue system of Akbar was called Zabti or Bandobast system. It was further improved by Raja Todar Mal. It was known as Dahsala System.

Jahangir

- Jahangir's **'Memoirs'** or **Tuzuk-i-Jahangiri** - (an autobiography of Jahangir) gives an account of his reign.
- He enjoyed a reputation for Justice. He had fixed a big bell with a golden chain. It was hung at the gates of his royal palace. Anyone could pull the chain and ask for justice.
- Jahangir's eldest son, **Khusrau**, rebelled against him. He was arrested and put into prison. **Guru Arjun Dev,** the **fifth Sikh Guru,** who assisted him was killed for refusal to pay a fine.

- During Jahangir's reign **Captain William Hawkins** and **Sir Thomas Roe** visited his court.
- Sir Thomas Roe secured permission from Jahangir in A.D. 1615 to trade at Surat.
- Jahangir died in A.D. 1627.

Shahjahan

- The reign of Shah Jahan is generally considered as the Golden Age of the Mughal period.
- Shah Jahan is called as the Prince of Builders. He had built the Jama Masjid & Red Fort in Delhi and Taj Mahal in Agra.
- The Taj Mahal is the most famous building of Shahjahan. It is located at Agra on the banks of the river Yamuna. Shahjahan built it in memory of his beloved wife Mumtaj Mahal.

Aurangazeb

- Aurangazeb was the last great Mughal ruler. He ascended the throne after killing his three brothers Dara, Shuja and Murad in a fratricidal war.
- Aurangazeb defeated Sikandar Shah of Bijapur and annexed his kingdom. Then, he proceeded against Golkonda and eliminated the Kutb Shahi dynasty. It was also annexed by him.
- Aurangazeb forbade music in the Mughal court. He discontinued the practice of Jarokhadarshan. He also discontinued the celebration of Dasarah and royal astronomers and astrologers were also dismissed from service.
- In 1679, he reimposed jiziya and pilgrim tax.
- Aurangazeb was also against the Sikhs and he executed the ninth Sikh Guru Tegh Bahadur. This had resulted in the transformation of Sikhs into a warring community. The tenth Sikh Guru, Guru Govind Singh built up a powerful army called the Khalsa to drive the Mughals out of India.
- Aurangazeb died in A.D.1707.

Mughal Administration

- Akbar borrowed Sher Shah's administrative features. So, Sher Shah is regarded as the forerunner of Akbar's administration.
- The empire was divided into 15 provinces during Akbar's rule. They were called Subas.
- The head of a Suba was called Subedar. He was responsible for the civil and military duties.
- The Diwan was in charge of Subas' finance.
- The provinces were divided into Sarkars or districts. Faujdar was the civil and military head of the district. Each Sarkar was administered by a number of officers.
- The Sarkar was further divided into Parganas. Shiqdar, Amil and Fotadar were the officers who were in-charge of the Parganas.
- The lowest unit in Mughal administration was the village.
- The Mughal army consisted of infantry, artillery and elephantry, but no navy.
- Akbar introduced the Mansabdari system, and it was followed by his successors.
- Mansab means Rank or place. There was a grade of Mansabdars. It ranged from owners of 10 to 10,000 horses. Besides the horses, they had to maintain foot soldiers also.
- Raja Todar Mal, the famous revenue minister, worked under Akbar. He also worked under Sher Shah, the forerunner of Akbar.
- Akbar introduced the Zabti system.

Modern India

THE ESTABLISHMENT OF COMPANY POWER

The Portuguese

On his arrival at Calicut, Vasco-da-Gama was received by its Hindu ruler, known by the title of Zamorin. The arrival of Vasco da Gama led to the establishment of trading stations at Calicut.

Vasco-da-Gama established a factory at Cochin in 1502. He was followed by Alfonso de Albuquerque in 1503. In 1505, the Portuguese decided to appoint a governor to look after their Indian affairs. Francisco de Almeida became the first governor. Albuquerque succeeded him in 1509. Albuquerque was the real founder of the Portuguese empire in the east.

After Albuquerque, the Portuguese began to decline and in the end, they were left only with Goa, Diu and Daman, which they retained till 1961.

The Dutch

The lucrative trade which prospered the Portuguese merchants compelled the jealous Dutch to get direct access to the spice markets in South-East Asia. After undertaking a series of voyages since 1596, they set up a small commercial organisation, named the **United East India Company** in 1602.

- **Formation of the Company :** The Dutch East India Company was formed in March, 1602, by a Charter of the Dutch Parliament,
- **Establishment of Factories:** The Dutch set up factories at Masulipatam (1605), Pulicat (1610), Surat (1616), Bimilipatam (1641), K.Arikal (1645), Chinsura (1653), Kasimbazar, Barangore, Patna, Balasore, Negapatam (all in 1658) and Cochin (1663).
- Pulicat was their main centre in India till 1690, after which Negapatam replaced it.

The French

In the middle of the seventeenth century Louis XIV's finance minister Colbert formed a **French East India Company** named **Compagnie des Indes Orientales** in 1664. Louis XIV provided the Company with an interest-free loan of 3 million livre. The Company was thus, created and financed by the State. After initial attempts made to colonise Madagascar had proved a failure, the Company undertook a fresh expedition in 1667 under the command of Francis Caron accompanied by Marcara, a native of Ispahan reached India and set up the first French factory at Surat in 1668. The second factory was set up at Masulipatnam in 1669. A factory was also developed at Chandernagar (Bengal) between 1690 and 1692. Two major French trading posts in India were Pondicherry, established in 1674 by Francis Martin, and Chandernagar.

In 1693, the newly built French factory at Pondicherry was captured by the Dutch but by the Treaty of Ryswick between the European powers, there was restoration of mutual conquests and the Dutch returned Pondicherry to the French in 1697.

When Dupleix become Governor of Pondicherry, there was a change in the character and objective of the French Company motive of imperial expansion replaced their former commercial motive. This naturally opened a new chapter in the Anglo-French conflict in India.

The English

On 31st December, 1600, Queen Elizabeth granted a Charter to the Company named 'The Governor and Company of Merchants of London Trading in the East Indies' the rights to carry on trade with all countries of the East. This company is commonly known as the English East India Company.

For a few years, the English East India Company confined its activities to the spice trade with Java, Sumatra and the Moluccas. But in 1608 **Captain William Hawkins** came to the court of Jehangir with a letter from James I, king of England, requesting permission for the English merchants to establish in India. But due to vehement opposition of the Portuguese and the Surat merchants, Emperor Jehangir had to change his mind and Hawkin's mission failed. Next year, Jehangir issued a *farman* permitting the English to establish a factory permanently at Surat. In 1615, a British mission under Sir Thomas Roe succeeded in obtaining *firmans* from the Mughal court confirming free trade without liability to pay inland toll. In 1632, the English obtained from the Sultan of Golconda the *Golden farman* granting them the right to trade throughout the kingdom of Golconda on payment of a fixed customs duty of 500 *pagodas* per year. This *farman* was renewed in 1634.

The Company obtained from the Nawab Shuja-ud-din a *farman* in 1651 granting the English the right to carry on their trade on payment of a fixed duty of Rs. 3,000 per year.

British Success in Bengal

The Nawab of Bengal, during the middle of 18th century, was, for all practical purposes, an independent ruler though he nominally acknowledged the supremacy of Mughal king. However, Bengal lacked any political strength or stability. Utilising the opportunity, the English Company not only strengthened themselves but also interfered in Bengal politics. Nawab Sirajud-dulah, realising the danger of English power, captured their Calcutta Fort. English got reinforcement from Madras and regained Calcutta Fort. In the Battle of Plassey in 1757, Englishmen, getting the support from Siraj-ud-dullah's commander-in-chief Mir Jafar, defeated Bengal's army. This battle marked the beginning of the establishment of British power in India. Subsequently, the English Company became all powerful, with Nawab Mir Jafar being a puppet only. The Company made unreasonable demands, leaving Nawab's treasury empty. Mir Qasim, the successor of Mir Jafar, realised the desperate position and took steps to strengthen his position. English angered at it, defeated him in a battle, forcing him to take refuge in Awadh. The combined forces of Nawabs of Awadh and Bengal and Mughal Emperor Shah Alam fought war against British forces in Buxar but were defeated. The Battle of Buxar in 1764 proved to be a turning point in Indian history as Britishers got right to collect revenue in Bengal, Bihar and Orissa and. were left with no potential enemy in the Gangetic plains of India.

THE REVOLT OF 1857

The Revolt of 1857, a watershed in the history of British rule in India, shook the very foundation of the British empire in India. It changed the character of British rule, marking the end of the rule of the East India Company and bringing British India directly under the British Crown.

Causes of the Revolt

As about the nature of the rebellion, there is also considerable controversy regarding its actual causes. Historians, both British and Indian, have over emphasised the importance of military grievances and the greased cartridges affair. But recent research has established beyond doubt that the "greased cartridge" was not the only cause nor even the most important. On the contrary, there were a variety of causes—political, social, religious and economic—which combined to produce the rebellion.

Political Causes: The British policy of annexations had disturbed the political equilibrium in the country. The indiscriminate application of the "Doctrine of Lapse" by Lord Dalhousie had caused widespread discontent. The overthrow of Nawab Wajid Ali Shah of Awadh, annexation of several Hindu principalities and forfeiture on the ex-Peshwa's pension had alarmed the Princely States. The annexation of Princely States was not a blow to the princely families alone, but to their dependent subjects as well.

Administrative and Economic Causes: The annexation of Indian states produced startling economic and social consequences under the British rule. Not only was the Indian aristocracy deprived of power and position, but all high posts, civil and military, were reserved for the Europeans. Racial discrimination was evident everywhere.

The administrative machinery of the East India Company was inefficient and inadequate. The land revenue policy was most unpopular. Many districts in the newly annexed states were in permanent revolt. Many taluqdars (hereditary landlords) were deprived of their position and resources. Large estates were confiscated and auctioned off. Thus the new land revenue settlements made by the East India Company in the newly annexed states, made the aristocracy poor without benefiting the peasantry, who fell into the clutches of unprincipled money-lenders and groaned under the weight of heavy assessments and excessive duties. The judicial system that the Company introduced in India became an instrument of oppression.

Social and Religious Causes: The Traditional Indian social system and culture appeared to be in danger under the reformist zeal of the British administrators. The sway of leaders of orthodoxy both maulvis and pandits regarding common law in matters of succession, inheritance, etc. was challenged. The missionaries were given ample facilities for the propagation of Christianity. The Religious Disabilities Act of 1856 modified Hindu customs; a change in religion did not debar a son from inheriting the property of his heathen father. The Indian mind was getting increasingly convinced that the English were conspiring to convert them into Christianity.

Military Causes: There was widespread discontent amongst the Indian soldiers serving in the British army, in which the majority of the soldiers and junior officers were Indians. The Indian soldiers resented their low pay and poor prospects of promotion. Campaigns in strange lands outside the boundaries of India were unpopular with them, on account of the great hardships involved. Indian soldiers serving overseas were either not given overseas allowances (bhatta) at all or paid much lower than the European soldiers serving in the British army, which was one of the major causes of discontent among Indian soldiers.

Suppression of the Revolt

The rebel leaders could not consolidate their initial gains, while the Governor General, Lord Canning took all possible steps to gather the forces from Bombay, Madras, Calcutta and Punjab to quell the rebellion. On July 16, 1857 Bithur and Kanpur were captured from Nana Saheb, who probably escaped to Nepal. Nana Saheb's Prime Minister Tantia Tope with his soldiers then joined Rani Lakshmibai at Jhansi. On September 20, 1857, the British troops captured Delhi. Bahadur Shah II surrendered to the English on the sole condition that his life should be spared. Thereupon he, along with his favourite Queen Begum Zinnat Mahal and her son, were made captives in the palace of the fort. On September 2, three young sons of Bahadur Shah II were shot dead publicly. Emperor Bahadur Shah was tried by a court martial, found guilty and sentenced to imprisonment for life. He was exiled to Rangoon with his queen Zinnat Mahal, and died after four years, on November 7, 1862.

By the end of 1859 all the great leaders of the Revolt, such as Kunwar Singh, the Ruhela leader Khan Bahadur Khan of Bareilly, Maulvi Ahmadullah of Awadh, Tantia Tope etc. were dead and Begum Hazrat Mahal and Nana Saheb had escaped to Nepal leading to the restoration of the British authority in India fully and firmly.

SOCIAL AND RELIGIOUS MOVEMENT

In the 19th century the emancipation of women and dalit became a matter of prime concern for the socio-religious reformers. Women then were shamelessly exploited, kept backward and were victims of many degrading customs like Sati, female infanticide, purdah, child marriage, polygamy, etc.

In the view of the reformers, as long as women, constituting roughly one-half of the population, remained exploited and backward, society could not advance. Women's status was, therefore, the most important symbol of social change. By the second half of the 19th century British India was bristling with the activity of reform groups which focused attention on women-related issues. Their activities provided a stimulus and the atmosphere to improve the lot of the Indian women. Name of the some pioneers who contributed for the emancipation of women are as follow :

Raja Rammohan Roy : Raja Rammohan Roy was a man of extraordinary intellect. He fought vehemently against the custom of *sati* prevalent in the contemporary society. In 1815, Rammohan founded the *Atmiya Sabha.* On 20th August 1828, he founded the *Brahmo Samaj.*

The *Brahmo Samaj* led a crusade against *sati*, polygamy, child-marriage, caste-system, *purdah* system, untouchability, use of intoxicants etc. The leaders of Brahmo Samaj also worked for the welfare of peasants, liberty of press, social legislation. The *Brahmo Samaj* participated in building up national sentiment by glorifying the Indian culture.

Ishwar Chandra Vidyasagar : Ishwar Chandra Vidyasagar (1820-91) was another reformer in Bengal who championed female education. He was an impassioned supporter of widow remarriage and vehement opponent of polygamy. He urged the British to pass legislation enabling Hindu widows to remarry and prohibiting polygamy. He submitted petitions to this effect to the Indian Legislative Council and to the British Government. Vidyasagar's effort led to the passing of the Hindu Widow Remarriage Act in 1856. To promote female education, Vidyasagar opened a number of schools for girls in Bengal and was closely associated with the Hindu Kanya Vidyalaya founded by J.E.D. Bethune.

Kandukuri Virasalingam Pantulu : Kandukuri Virasalingam Pantulu (1848-1919), a Telugu Brahmin of Madras Presidency, was the earliest champion in South India of women's emancipation. He published

Viveka Vardhani (Journal to Promote Enlightenment), opened his first girls' school in 1874 and made widow remarriage and female education the key points of his programme for social reform.

Mahadev Govind Ranade : Mahadev Govind Ranade (1842-1901) and his wife Ramabai also contributed greatly to the cause of women. In 1869, Ranade joined the Widow Remarriage Association and encouraged widow remarriage and female education and opposed child marriage. He founded the National Social Conference, which became a pre-eminent institution for social reform. The role of Pandita Ramabai (1858-1922) was remarkable as a pioneer in women's education and a rebel champion of women's rights. She founded the ***Sharda Sadan***, a school for widows, in Bombay and at Mukti, near Pune. Her greatest legacy was her effort, the first in India, to educate widows.

Swami Vivekananda : At the turn of the century, Swami Vivekananda argued that women could become a powerful regenerative force.

Swami Dayanand Saraswati : Swami Dayanand Saraswati, the founder of the Arya Samaj, encouraged female education and widow remarriage and condemned the customs he regarded as degrading to women, such as child marriage, dowry and polygamy.

Behramji Malabari : The Parsi social reformer, Behramji Malabari, captured the attention of the British people with his articles in ***The Times*** (of London) on the evils of child marriage and the tragedy of enforced widowhood for young women.

Dhondo Keshav Karve : The greatest champion of the cause of women's emancipation was Dhondo Keshav Karve (1858-1962), who worked the longest for this cause. Karve encouraged widow remarriage. He founded the female school and widow homes in Pune. The curriculum in his schools was designed to make young widows employable and self-sufficient. Karve believed that "widows needed an education that would make them economically independent and enable them to think for themselves". He also founded the first Indian women's university in 1916.

Some Associations for Women

Movements for the emancipation of women and spread of education among women led to the establishment of a number of associations formed for women, which became the medium for the expression of women's opinion. Some of these important associations were as under:

The Bharat Mahila Parishad: was a part of the National Social Conference to provide a forum for the discussion of social issues.

The Arya Mahila Samaj: was founded by Ramabai, wife of Justice Ranade, to provide a support network for newly educated women.

The Bharat Stree Mahamandal: was founded by Sarladevi Chaudhurani at Allahabad in 1910. It was the first permanent association of Indian women to promote their common interests. The Mahamandal's leaders regarded purdah as the main stumbling-block to female education and defined women's issues such as female education, child marriage and women's status in the family.

The Women's Indian Association: was founded by an Irish feminist and theosophist. Dorothy Jinarajadasa, in 1915, with its membership open to both Indians and Europeans. Annie Besant became its first President. The principal work of the WIA was educational and its branches were encouraged to set up adult classes for literacy, sewing and first aid. The WIA was politically active from the beginning and in 1917, it sent a delegation to the Secretary of State, Montagu, to grant franchise for women. The WIA also set up widow homes. Its journal, ***Stri Dharma***, carried news of events of interest to women, reports from its branches, and articles on women's condition.

The National Council of Women for India: was an all-India organisation established in 1925, which was affiliated to the International Council of Women. Mehribai Tata (wife of Dorab Tata) played a key role in its advancement. But on account of its elitist nature, the Council failed to grow and became a vital national organisation.

THE NATIONALIST MOVEMENT

Allan Octavian Hume (A.O. Hume), a retired British member of the Indian Civil Service who had settled at Simla, founded the Indian National Union the fore runner of the Indian National Congress, in 1884. After touring Calcutta, Bombay and Madras (Kolkata, Mumbai and Chennai), Hume announced that a conference of the Indian National Union would be held at Pune in December, which would be composed of educated delegates from all parts of the three presidencies. But cholera having broken out at Pune, the venue of the conference was shifted to Tejpal Sanskrit Pathsala, Bombay. The first session of the Indian National Union was held on December 28, 1885. At the suggestion of Dadabhai Naoroji the name of the organisation was changed to Indian National Congress (INC). Womesh Chandra Banerjee, a leading lawyer of Calcutta (Kolkata), was elected its president.

Early Political Associations

- The British Indian Association — 1851, Bengal
- The Bombay Association — 1852
- East India Association — 1856, London
- Madras Native Association 1852
- Poona Sarvojanik Sabha — 1870
- The Madras Mahajana Sabha — 1884

Indian National Movement (1905-1916)

- The period from 1905 was known as the era of extremism in the Indian National Movement.
- The important extremist leaders were Lala Lajpat Rai, Bal Gangadhar Tilak, Bipin Chandra Pal and Aurobindo Ghosh.

Causes for the Rise of Extremism

1. The failure of the Moderates to win any notable success other than the expansion of the legislative councils by the Indian Councils Act (1892).
2. The economic conditions of the people became worse.
3. The Russo-Japanese war of 1904-05 in which Japan defeated the European power Russia. This encouraged Indians to fight against the European nation, Britain.
4. The immediate cause for the rise of extremism was the reactionary rule of Lord Curzon:
   - He passed the Calcutta Corporation Act, (1899) reducing the Indian control of this local body.
   - The Universities Act (1904) reduced the elected members in the University bodies. It also reduced the autonomy of the universities and made them government departments.
   - The Sedition Act and the Official Secrets Act reduced the freedoms of all people.
   - His worst measure was the Partition of Bengal (1905).

- Bal Gangadhar Tilak is regarded as the real founder of the popular anti-British movement in India. He was known as **'Lokamanya'**. He attacked the British through his weeklies *The Mahratta* and the *Kesari*.
- Tilak set up the Home Rule League in 1916 at Poona and declared "Swaraj is my birth-right and I will have it."

Partition of Bengal and the Rise of Extremism

- The partition of Bengal in 1905 provided a spark for the rise of extremism in the Indian National Movement.
- Curzon's real motives behind this partition were:
  - To break the growing strength of Bengali nationalism since Bengal was the base of Indian nationalism.
  - To divide the Hindus and Muslims in Bengal.
  - To show the enormous power of the British Government in doing whatever it liked.
- The anti-partition movement culminated into the Swadeshi Movement and spread to other parts of India.

Swadeshi Movement

- The Swadeshi Movement involved programmes like the boycott of government service, courts, schools and colleges and of foreign goods, promotion of Swadeshi goods, Promotion of National Education through the establishment of national schools and colleges. It was both a political and economic movement.

Formation of the Muslim League (1906)

- In December 1906, Muslim delegates from all over India met at Dacca for the Muslim Educational Conference.
- Taking advantage of this occasion, Nawab Salimullah of Dacca proposed the setting up of an organisation to look after the Muslim interests. The proposal was accepted.
- The All-India Muslim League was finally set up on December 30, 1906.

Minto-Morley Reforms – 1909

- Minto, the Viceroy and Morley, the Secretary of State for India jointly proposed reforms to the Indian Councils. An Act, called the **Indian Councils Act or the Minto-Morley Reforms Act** was passed in 1909.
- It introduced reforms in the functioning of the Indian Councils. It increased the number of elected members in the Councils.
- A separate communal electorate was introduced for the Muslims.

The Lucknow Pact (1916)

- During the 1916 Congress session at Lucknow two major events occurred. The divided Congress became united. An understanding for joint action against the British was reached between the Congress and the Muslim League and it was called the Lucknow Pact.
- It was at this session Jawaharlal Nehru met Gandhiji for the first time.
- The signing of the Lucknow Pact by the Congress and the Muslim League in 1916

marked an important step in the Hindu-Muslim unity.

The Home Rule Movement (1916)

- Two Home Rule Leagues were established, one by B.G. Tilak at Poona in April 1916 and the other by Mrs. Annie Besant at Madras in September 1916.
- The aim of the Movement was to get self-government for India within the British Empire. It believed freedom was the natural right of all nations.
- While Tilak's Movement concentrated on Maharashtra, Annie Besant's Movement covered the rest of the country.

Montague – Chelmsford Reforms Act, 1919

- **Montague,** the Secretary of State for India and **Chelmsford,** the Viceroy of India were jointly responsible for passing of this Act in the British Parliament.
- By this Act separate electorates were given to three other communities – **Christians, Anglo Indians** and **the Sikhs.**
- It introduced Dyarchy in the Province. More Indians entered the Legislative bodies.
- Mrs. Annie Besant described this Act as ungenerous for England to offer and unworthy for India to accept.

Revolutionary Movements

- The revolutionaries were not satisfied with the methods of both the moderates and extremists. Hence, they started many revolutionary secret organizations.
- In Bengal, Anusilan Samiti and Jugantar were established. In Maharashtra Savarkar brothers had set up Abhinava Bharat. In the Madras Presidency, Bharathmatha Association was started by Nilakanta Bramachari.
- In Punjab, Ajit Singh set up a secret society to spread revolutionary ideas among the youth.
- In London, at India House, Shyamji Krishna Verma gathered young Indian nationalists like Madan Lal Dhingra, Savarkar, V.V.S. Iyer and T.S.S. Rajan.
- Lala Hardyal set up the 'Ghadar Party' in USA to organise revolutionary activities from outside India.

Rowlatt Act (1919)

- In 1917, a committee was set up under the presidentship of Sir Sydney Rowlatt to look into the militant Nationalist activities. On the basis of its report the Rowlatt Act was passed in March 1919 by the Central Legislative Council. As per this Act, any person could be arrested on the basis of suspicion. No appeal or petition could be filed against such arrests.
- This Act was called the Black Act and it was widely opposed. An all-India hartal was organized on 6 April 1919. Meetings were held all over the country. Mahatma Gandhi was arrested near Delhi. Two prominent leaders of Punjab, Dr. Satya Pal and Dr. Saifuddin Kitchlew, were arrested in Amritsar.

Jallianwala Bagh Massacre (13 April, 1919)

- The Jallianwala Bagh Massacre took place on 13 April 1919 and it remained a turning point in the history of India's freedom movement.
- On 13th April, the Baisakhi day (harvest festival), a public meeting was organized at the Jallianwala Bagh (garden). Gen. Dyer marched in and without any warning opened fire on the crowd. The firing continued for about 10 to 15 minutes and it stopped only after the ammunition exhausted.

Khilafat Movement

- The chief cause of the Khilafat Movement was the defeat of Turkey in the First World War.The harsh terms of the Treaty of Sevres (1920) was felt by the Muslims as a great insult to them.
- The whole movement was based on the Muslim belief that the Caliph (the Sultan of Turkey) was the religious head of the Muslims all over the world. The Muslims in India were upset over the British attitude against Turkey and launched the Khilafat Movement.
- Maulana Abul Kalam Azad, M.A. Ansari, Saifuddin Kitchlew and the Ali brothers were the prominent leaders of this movement.
- A Khilafat Committee had been formed and on 19th October 1919, the whole country had observed the Khilafat day. On 23 November, a joint conference of the Hindus and the Muslims had also been held under the chairmanship of Mahatma Gandhi.

Non-Co-operation Movement (1920-1922)

- Mahatma Gandhi announced his plan to begin Non-Cooperation with the government as a sequel to the Rowlatt Act, Jallianwala Bagh massacre and the Khilafat Movement. It was approved by the Indian National Congress at the Nagpur session in December, 1920.
- The Congress observed the Non-Co-operation movement in 1920. The main aim of this movement was to attain Swaraj through non–violent and peaceful means.

- The programmes of the Non-Co-operation Movement were:
  - Surrender of titles and honorary positions.
  - Resignation of membership from the local bodies.
  - Boycott of elections held under the provisions of the 1919 Act.
  - Boycott of government functions.
  - Boycott of courts, government schools and colleges.
  - Boycott of foreign goods.
  - Establishment of national schools, colleges and private panchayat courts.
  - Popularizing swadeshi goods and khadi.
- National schools such as the Kashi Vidyapeeth, the Bihar Vidyapeeth and the Jamia Millia Islamia were set up.
- On 5th February an angry mob set fire to the police station at Chauri Chaura and twenty two police men were burnt to death.

Swaraj Party

- Leaders like Motilal Nehru and Chittranjan Das formed a separate group within the Congress known as the Swaraj Party on 1 January 1923.
- The Swarajists wanted to contest the council elections and wreck the government from within. Elections to Legislative Councils were held in November 1923. In this, the **Swaraj Party** gained impressive successes. In the Central Legislative Council Motilal Nehru became the leader of the party whereas in Bengal the party was headed by C.R. Das.

Simon Commission (1927)

- The Act of 1919 included a provision for its review after a lapse of ten years. However, the review commission was appointed by the British Government two years earlier of its schedule in 1927. It came to be known as Simon Commission after the name of its chairman, Sir John Simon.
- All its seven members were Englishmen. As there was no Indian member in it, the Commission faced a lot of criticism even before its landing in India. Almost all the political parties including the Congress decided to oppose the Commission.
- The report of the Simon Commission was published in May 1930.

Nehru Report (1928)

- The Secretary of State, Lord Birkenhead, challenged the Indians to produce a Constitution that would be acceptable to all. The challenge was accepted by the Congress, which convened an all party meeting on 28 February 1928.
- A committee consisting of eight was constituted to draw up a blueprint for the future Constitution of India. It was headed by Motilal Nehru. The Report published by this Committee came to be known as the **Nehru Report**.

Lahore Session (1929)

- On Dec. 19, 1929, under the Presidentship of J.L. Nehru, the INC, as its Lahore session, declared *Poorna Swaraj* (Complete Independence) as its ultimate goal.
- On Dec. 31, 1929, the newly adopted tricolour flag was unfurled and Jan. 26. 26, 1930 was fixed as the First Independence Day, which was to be celebrated every year.

Civil Disobedience Movement (1930-1934)

- In December 1929,the annual session of the Congress was held at Lahore. During this session presided over by Jawaharlal Nehru the Congress passed the **Poorna Swaraj** resolution.
- The Congress had observed January 26, 1930 as the Day of Independence. Since then January 26th had been observed as a day of independence every year. The same date later became the Republic Day when the Indian Constitution was enforced in 1950.
- On 12th March 1930, Gandhi began his famous March to Dandi with his chosen 79 followers to break the salt laws. He reached the coast of Dandi on 5 April 1930 after marching a distance of 200 miles and on 6 April formally launched the Civil Disobedience Movement by breaking the salt laws.

Round Table Conference

- The first Round Table Conference was held in November 1930 at London and it was boycotted it by the Congress.
- On 8 March 1931 the **Gandhi-Irwin Pact** was signed. As per this pact, Mahatma Gandhi agreed to suspend the Civil-Disobedience Movement and participate in the Second-Round Table Conference.
- In September 1931, the Second Round Table Conference was held at London. Mahatma Gandhi participated in the Conference but returned to India disappointed as no agreement could be reached on the demand of complete independence and on the communal question.
- In January 1932, the Civil-Disobedience Movement was resumed. The government responded to it by arresting Mahatma Gandhi

and Sardar Patel and by reimposing the ban on the Congress party.

Poona Pact (1932)

- On 16 August 1932 the British Prime Minister Ramsay MacDonald made an announcement, which came to be as the **Communal Award**. According to this award, the depressed classes were considered as a separate community and as such provisions were made for separate electorates for them.
- Mahatma Gandhi protested against the Communal Award and went on a fast unto death in the Yeravada jail on 20 September 1932. Finally, an agreement was reached between Dr. Ambedkar and Gandhi. This agreement came to be called as the **Poona Pact**. The British Government also approved of it. Accordingly, 148 seats in different Provincial Legislatures were reserved for the Depressed Classes in place of 71 as provided in the Communal Award.

The Government of India Act 1935

- The Government of India Act was passed in 1935. It was based on the **Simon Commission** report and the proposals of the three Round Table Conferences.
- It introduced the following changes. This act(1) Introduced provincial autonomy, (2) Abolished dyarchy in the provinces, (3) Established federal Government at the Centre, (4) Provided for the establishment of a federal court to decide the conflicts between the provinces and the centre and (5) Provided for the establishment of a Federal Reserve Bank.

Cripps Mission (1942)

- The British Government in its effort to secure Indian co-operation in the Second World War sent Sir Stafford Cripps to India on 23 March 1942. This is known as **Cripps Mission**.
- The main recommendations of Cripps were:
  - ➢ The promise of Dominion Status to India,
  - ➢ Protection of minorities,
  - ➢ Setting up of a Constituent Assembly in which there would be representatives from the Princely States along with those of the British Provinces,
  - ➢ There would be provision for any Province of British India not prepared to accept this Constitution, either to retain its present constitutional position or frame a constitution of its own.
- Gandhi called Cripp's proposals as a **"Post-dated Cheque"**.

Quit India Movement (1942-1944)

- The All India Congress Committee met at Bombay on 8 August 1942 and passed the famous **Quit India Resolution**. On the same day, Gandhi gave his call of **'do or die'**.
- On 8th and 9th August 1942, the government arrested all the prominent leaders of the Congress. Mahatma Gandhi was kept in prison at Poona. Pandit Jawaharlal Nehru, Abul Kalam Azad, and other leaders were imprisoned in the Ahamednagar Fort.
- Quit India Movement was the final attempt for country's freedom.

Naval Mutiny (1945)

- A revolt took place in *HMS Talwar* on Feb. 18, 1945 in Bombay due to racial discrimination, unpalatable food and abuse after the rarrest of B.C. Dutta who had written 'British Quit India' on the wall.
- Next day, *HMS Hindustan* in Karachi also revolted.
- Soon the revolt spread to other places also. Im Bombay, the mutineers hoisted the tricolour on their ship masts together with a portrait of S.C. Bose and shouted Jai Hind those belonging to the Inidna National Army.
- It was suppressed after persuasion by the Indian leaders.

Indian National Army

- On 2 July 1943, Subhash Chandra Bose reached Singapore and gave the rousing war cry of **'Dilli Chalo'**. He was made the President of Indian Independence League and soon became the supreme commander of the **Indian National Army**.He gave the country the slogan of **Jai Hind**.
- The Indian National Army marched towards Imphal after registering its victory over Kohima. After Japan's surrender in 1945, the INA failed in its efforts.
- The trial of the soldiers of INA was held at Red Fort in Delhi. Pandit Jawaharlal Nehru, Bhulabhai Desai and Tej Bahadur Sapru fought the case on behalf of the soldiers.

Cabinet Mission (1946)

- After the Second World War, Lord Atlee became the Prime Minister of England.
- On 15 March, 1946 Lord Atlee made a historic announcement in which the right to self-determination and the framing of a Constitution for India were conceded. Consequently, three members of the British Cabinet - Pathick Lawrence, Sir Stafford Cripps and A. V. Alexander - were sent to India. This is known as the **Cabinet Mission**.

- The Cabinet Mission put forward a plan for solution of the constitutional problem. Provision was made for three groups of provinces to possess their separate constitutions. The Cabinet Mission also proposed the formation of a Union of India, comprising both the British India and the Princely States. The Union would remain in charge of only foreign affairs, defence and communications leaving the residuary powers to be vested in the provinces. A proposal was envisaged for setting up an Interim Government, which would remain in office till a new government was elected on the basis of the new Constitution framed by the Constituent Assembly. Both the Muslim League and the Congress accepted the plan.

Mountbatten Plan (1947)

- On 20 February 1947, Prime Minister Atlee announced in the House of Commons the definite intention of the British Government to transfer power to responsible Indian hands by a date not later than June 1948.
- Lord Mountbatten armed with vast powers became India's Viceroy on 24 March 1947. The partition of India and the creation of Pakistan appeared inevitable to him.
- After extensive consultation Lord Mountbatten put forth the plan of partition of India on **3 June 1947.** The Congress and the Muslim League ultimately approved the **Mountbatten Plan.**

Indian Independence Act 1947

- The salient features of this Act were:
  - The partition of the country into India and Pakistan would come into effect from 15 August 1947.
  - The British Government would transfer all powers to these two Dominions.
  - A Boundary Commission would demarcate the boundaries of the provinces of the Punjab and Bengal.
  - The Act provided for the transfer of power to the Constituent Assemblies of the two Dominions, which will have full authority to frame their respective Constitutions.
- **C. Rajagopalachari** became the first and last Indian Governor-General of India. When India became a Republic on 26 January 1950 **Dr. Rajendra Prasad** became the first President of our country.

World History

RENAISSANCE

Renaissance means rebirth. It was initially used to describe revival of interest in the learning of older civilizations of Greece and Rome. Knowledge of their achievements led to a series of new developments in the field of art, literature, religion, science and politics. Renaissance began in Italy in the 16th century. Its main emphasis was on freedom of the individual, inalienable rights of the individual and respecting the dignity of man. It stressed on the limitless potentialities of man rejected religious asceticism and withdrawal from the world. It aimed at providing happiness to man. The emphasis shifted from divinity to humanity, i.e., human being. The Renaissance era gave rise to quest for knowledge, especially history and literature. The effects of Renaissance were development of humanism, nationalism, spread of education, growth in trade and commerce, exposure of myths and establishment of reasoning. Some of the greatest achievements were made in painting, sculpture and architecture. Leonardo da Vinci, Michael Angelo and Raphael were famous artists of that time. Dante was a great poet of that time while Machiavelli, a diplomat, historian and political philosopher wrote about sta:tecraft. As the Renaissance spread throughout Europe, it took on a more religious character, paving the way for Reformation. Moreover, during the period, Europeans began to look for sea route to Asia, with Columbus reaching Central America in 1492 and Vasco-da-Gama in India in 1498.

REFORMATION

The key event of the 16th century in Europe was the Reformation, a movement to reform the Catholic church. It began in Germany and then spread throughout northern Europe. Martin Luther, a German theologian and religious transformer set alight widespread discontent against the Church. New Protestant Church belonging to reformers sprang up, with the aim of following only the teachings of the Bible, and getting rid of church traditions. Several powerful kings and princes supported the reformers like John Calvin, Olrich Zwingli and others. Although the Catholic church responded by introducing reforms from within, violent conflicts between Catholics and Protestants erupted. In 1534, King Henry VIII took the help of the English church because the Pope would not let him divorce his first wife. Though Queen Mary tried to restore Church's authority in England, getting the nickname "Bloody Mary" due to execution of Protestants, the Catholics were reduced to minority in England.

ENGLISH REVOLUTION OF 1688

England was ruled by despotic rulers in the first half of 17th century — James I and Charles I. They believed that they were appointed by God, not answerable to Parliament or people. The dispute ,between the King and Parliament led to civil war in England in 1642. James I was defeated and executed. In 1660, Charles II was appointed king on the condition that he will not interfere in religious affairs of the people and rule with consultation with Parliament. However, James II followed his father's footsteps and tried to breakaway from Parliament's supervision and gave more powers to Catholics in the Protestant dominated country. This led to revolt by the people who invited the Dutch Protestant King William to come to England. James II fled to France. Williams and daughters of James II, Mary were declared joint Monarchs. The revolution has been described as glorious due to lack of bloodshed. The revolution led to end of divine rights of Kings, acceptance of the authority of the Parliament, independent judiciary, freedom of Press and supremacy of Protestants in England.

AMERICAN WAR OF INDEPENDENCE

With the rise of Capitalism and industrial revolution in Europe, the demand for raw materials, cheap labour and markets grew. European kings encouraged exploration of new areas which were subsequently colonized. In 1492, Columbus had discovered West Indies and later America was found. By the middle of 18th century, a large part of North America had come under England's occupation. Landless peasants, Protestants and others started living in this area. English Parliament put severe restrictions on the American colonies, politically as well as economically. Colonies were forbidden to start certain industries and heavy duties were imposed. The imposition of stamp duty in 1765 aroused violent resentment among Americans and there were uprisings, besides boycott of English goods. Though English Parliament agreed to revoke stamp duty, it later imposed tax on tea to assert their right to levy taxes. Several colonies refused to unload the tea and in 1773, a group of people boarded a ship in Boston and threw tea into water. The incident is called "Boston Tea Party". Subsequently, in 1775, English troops fought with local troops. On July 4, 1776, the Declaration of Independence was adopted by American leaders. It said all men are created equal; People have a right to set up their own government and the colonies have right to be free and independent states. The war between English and American forces intensified with other European countries favouring the colonial forces. The English forces surrendered in 1781 and in 1783, England recognized the independence of its 13 former colonies.

England, despite being a powerful nation, lost against the local troops due to distance constraints, help by other European nations to American leaders, good leadership of the war of Americans and lack of coordination among English Generals.

The independence of America was an important event in the world history. For the first time, a federal Government, democratic in character, was sworn in under the written constitution. The event was a great setback to England. It served as an example to other revolutionaries of the world and the French Revolution followed a few years later.

FRENCH REVOLUTION

France was a strong and powerful state in the 18th century. However, internally there were problems. A small section of people owned most of the land and occupied all senior administrative and army positions. There was a large number of peasants who lived under miserable conditions. In between was the middle class, which was educated and sometimes rich, yet did not have social status or political rights. There were a large number of thinkers in France who advocated rationalism, democracy and attacked clergy. Moreover, the wars abroad and large patronage brought the King to the point of bankruptcy. A stand off between the royal forces and protestors led to the fall of Bastille prison on July 14, 1789. A new constitution was adopted, declaring equality, liberty and fraternity for everyone. The privileged class people tied to other countries to sought their help and France was involved in wars with its neighbouring countries. However, a new order had been established in France and it reached new heights under the leadership of Napolean Bonaparte.

INDUSTRIAL REVOLUTION

In middle ages, the occupation of majority of the population in Europe was Agriculture and whatever trade was undertaken, was done on barter system: However, discoveries and new inventions, spread of education and new ideas led to development of methods and machineries that could produce faster, better and cheaper goods. The industrial revolution began in England because of availability of coal and iron, availability of labour, peaceful atmosphere and availability of good Navy to carry new methods to England and finished goods to the markets. However, it spread to other European nations as well because colonies were being established in Asia and Africa and cheap raw material and labour was easily available. These were good markets for ready material and the businessmen supported the scientists and engineers to do more research. The profits made from selling goods were ploughed back into the industry, leading to more development. The development of mechanical and electrical energy and establishment of big industries also helped the revolution. It led to large scale changes in textiles, iron extraction, mining, transportation, communication, agriculture and energy. The industrial revolution also had some adverse impacts as small farmers and industries were wiped off. It led to exploitation of poor, ladies, children and people of colonies; unemployment, wars for colonies, urbanization and increase in crimes. The positive impact was improvement in life-styles, increase in national income, increase in agricultural output and enactment of legislations for workers' welfare.

COLONIALISM

To sustain the growth of their industries, European nations needed raw material, cheep labour and ready markets. Asian and African nations were their easy targets. Moreover, for strategic, religious and military reasons, it was found useful by Europeans to have as many colonies as possible. However, these European nations fought among themselves several times to take control over colonies. The colonies were economically exploited by the Europeans and their social and political setup demolished. Their cultures were spoiled -and their inhabitants were tortured. The positive aspect of colonialism was spread of education, scientific temperament, nationalism, good administration and development of infrastructure in these colonies. Some of the colonies and colonisers were as follows:

- **Colonies of Belgium:** Congo
- **Colonies of England:** Cape Colony, Bechuanaland, Rhodesia, Natal, Transvaal, Orange Free State, Gold Coast, Nigeria, Egypt, Sudan, India, Canada, New Zealand, Australia
- **Colonies of France:** Algeria, Tunisia, Senegal, Moracco, Somaliland, Mada gascar, Cambodia, Parts of India, Laos
- **Colonies of Holland:** Malaya Islands, Indonesia
- **Colonies of Germany:** Tanganika, Cameroon
- **Colonies of Portugal:** Angola, Goa in India
- **Colonies of Italy:** Eriterea, Syria, parts of Somaliland, Libya
- **Colonies of Russia:** Afghanistan, Persia, Manchuria, Korea

NATIONALISM

The spirit of love for the nation got prominent in the 18th century. It began in Europe and then spread to Asia and Africa. Several countries became independent consequently:

(a) **Spain:** Democratic government established in 1870

(b) **Greece:** Got independence from Turkey in 1829

(c) **Belgium:** Got independence from Holland in 1930

(d) **Poland:** People of Warsaw revolted against Russian rule in 1848

(e) **Australia:** Democratic Constitution accepted in 1867

(f) **Balkon States:** Serbia, Romania and Montanegro got liberated from Turkey in 1855

(g) **Italy:** Unification of Italy completed in 1871 with the efforts of Mazzini and Garibaldi

(h) **Germany:** Unification of Germany completed in 1870 with the efforts of Bismarck

(i) **China:** Dr Sun-Yat-Sen led a successful movement in establishing a democracy in 1911 but in 1949, a Communist government was set up under Mao-Tse-Tung

(j) **Turkey:** Mustafa Kamal Pasha established democracy in 1923, after ousting the forces of Italy, France and Greece

(k) **Iran:** Feudalism ended in 1925 and Sardar Raza Khan became King

(l) **Syria:** Syrians opposed French forces and became independent in 1936

(m) **Palestine:** After England's departure, Jews declared an independent nation by name 'Israel'

(n) **Afghanistan:** Rebellion in 1926 forced the British to free it

(o) **Egypt:** Movement under the leadership of Jagalul Pasha led to independence in 1936; Suez Canal nationalised in 1956 leading to end of European interference

(p) **Indonesia:** It was a colony of Holland but went under Japan's control during Second World War. However, after the end of war, Indonesia became independent in 1949

(q) **Malaysia:** People there opposed the British rule and it got independence in 1957

(r) **Ghana:** Got independence in 1957

(s) **Algeria:** National Movement got momentum during Second World War and independence came in 1963

(t) **Kenya:** "Mao-Mao" movement led to its independence in 1965

In 1960, Congo and Mali became independent while in 1961, Sierre Lone, Somalia, in 1962 Jamaica, Rwanda, Trinidad, Tobago, Uganda and in 1965,

Zanzibar became independent. East Timor(2002) is the latest country to join the independent nations.

RUSSIAN REVOLUTION

In 1917, the monarchs of Russia Czars were overthrown and the world's first communist state was set up by Bolshaviks under the leadership of Lenin. The revolution was sparked by Russia's crippling defeat in the first world war, the resultant hardship at home and the inability of the king to cope up with this. Riots and strikes spread throughout the country. The removal of the Czar was an easy job but Bolsheviks were opposed by nationalists, non-Russians, democrats and military dictators but by 1920, the Communist government was firmly in the seat.

FIRST-WORLD WAR

Rivalry between European nations over the issue of colonies and political dominations led to tension that had been building up since late 19th century. Germany was a late entrant into the race for colonies and hence resented the expansion of French and British empire. France had been defeated completely by Germans in 1870. In Balkan area, Russia and Austria-Hungary had deep suspicion about each other. Britain had been traditional rival of France but fearing the might of German navy, both the countries agreed to cooperate in case of an attack. Moreover, German economy had made tremendous progress, leaving Britain and France far behind. The Ottoman Empire, comprising Turkey had occupied areas in Balkan but in 1912 they became independent after fighting a war. The precipitating matter for the first world war was the assassination of Archduke Francis Ferdinand, heir to the throne of Austria-Hungary in Sarajevo. Austria, suspecting Serb hand, declared war on Serbia. Russia declared support for Serbia. Germany declared war on Russia and France while Britain declared war on Germany. A large number of new weapons, like aircrafts, tanks, submarines and poison gas were used in the war. America entered into the war in 1917, siding with France and Britain. Russia withdrew from the war in 1918, after the revolution at home. All the colonies in the world took part in the war as per their ruler's intention. The war ended in 1918 with Bulgaria, Germany, Turkey and Austria-Hungary surrendering.

SECOND WORLD WAR

The Second World War, like the first, started in Europe and assumed the character of a world war. In Germany, the Nazi forces under the leadership of Adolf Hitler, had come into power, exploiting Germany's humiliation at defeat in the first world war and signing of an unjust treaty after the war. The League of Nations set up after the first world war did not prove effective in dealing with the problems of that period. Fascist forces had taken over in Italy while Japan was pursuing policies of expansion and militarism. Britain, France, USA initially overlooked the German invasion and avoided Russia's call to form alliance to check the aggression, but finally they had to come under an umbrella of Allied Power to check the advance of Axis powers which included Germany, Italy, Japan and their satellites. Allied powers included Britain, France, Russia, USA, China, Australia, Belgium etc. The war started on September 1, 1939 when Germany attacked Poland. This was followed by attacks on Norway, Denmark, Belgium and Holland. France surrendered in June, 1940. A year later, Germany attacked Soviet Union, Japan attacked American naval base of Pearl Harbour in Hawai in December, 1941 bringing in USA into war. By the middle of 1942, Axis forces had reached their peak but then their decline began. In all fronts, Germany and Italy suffered setbacks and they surrendered in May 1945. But Japan had to be attacked by nuclear bombs twice before being subjected to surrender.

REUNIFICATION OF GERMANY

Mikhail Gorbachev's tenure as the President of Soviet Union was period of weakening of Communist forces all over the world. The East Germany Communist regime collapsed in late 1989, as waves of East Germans took advantage of ending of travel restrictions between Hungary and Austria to leave their country. About 2 lakh East Germans left for the West and on November 9, 1989, the Berlin Wall was breached and within a weak, 3 million East Germans crossed over. The Politburo and Central Committee of Communist Party resigned within weeks. In 1990, the action of reunification got unprecedented momentum and on October 3, 1990, the two states became one country. Two months later, a united Germany voted in the first nationwide elections since 1932.

Multiple Choice Questions

1. Indus Valley Civilisation people did not probably know about the use of:
A. cow B. bull
C. horse D. dog

2. Among the four Vedas, the first one was:
A. Rig Veda B. Sama Veda
C. Yajur Veda D. Atharva Veda

3. The Ramayana was written by:
A. Ved Vyas B. Tulsidas
C. Dronacharya D. Valmiki

4. Vardhman Mahavir was the ...... Tirthankar of Jainism.
A. first B. second
C. third D. twenty fourth

5. The forces of Alexander and Porus fought on the banks of river:
A. Ravi B. Jhelum
C. Sutlej D. Indus

6. At the time of Alexander's invasion, Magadha was being ruled by:
A. Nanda Kings B. Gupta Kings
C. Maurya Kings D. Vardhana King

7. The Satavahans ruled mostly in:
A. Avadh B. Andhra
C. Central India D. Magadh

8. Ashoka belonged to:
A. Gupta dynasty B. Maurya dynasty
C. Kushan dynasty D. Saka dynasty

9. Vikramaditya was the name given to:
A. Chandragupta Maurya
B. Bindusar
C. Chandragupta II
D. Samudragupta

10. Harshavardhana, the last great Hindu King of Northem India ruled in the:
A. 2nd century AD B. 4th century AD
C. 7th century AD D. 10th century AD

11. The slave dynasty was established by:
A. Balban B. Iltutmish
C. Razia Begum D. Outb-ud-din Aibak

12. Razia Begum was the daughter of:
A. Iltutmish
B. Balban
C. Alauddin Khilji
D. Ghayasuddin Tughlak

13. Tughlaq dynasty occupied Delhi throne after decline of:
A. Lodhi dynasty B. Khilji dynasty
C. Slave dynasty D. Suri dynasty

14. The King, known for transferring the capital from Delhi to Daulatabad was:
A. Firoz Tughlaq
B. Ghyasuddin Tughlaq
C. Muhammad Tughlaq
D. Muhammad Bin Oasim

15. In the first battle of Panipat, Babar fought against:
A. Sher Shah Suri B. Firoz Tughlaq
C. Humayun D. Ibrahim Lodhi

16. Fatehpur Sikri has been built by:
A. Babur B. Aurangzeb
C. Akbar D. Jahangir

17. Khurram was the original name of:
A. Akbar B. Jahangir
C. Shahjahan D. Shah Alam

18. Din-i-Ilahi was launched by:
A. Akbar B. Humayun
C. Babur D. Jahangir

19. Sher Shah defeated which Mughal King:
A. Babur B. Humayun
C. Akbar D. Aurangzeb

20. The last Mughal King was:
A. Shah Alam
B. Muhammad Shah Rangeela
C. Bahadur Shah Zafar
D. Dost Muhammad

21. Which battle proved crucial in giving foothold to the British in India?
A. Battle of Plassey
B. Battle of Buxar

C. Third Battle of Panipat
D. Battle of Mysore

22. Sati was abolished by:
A. Lord Comwallis B. Lord Clive
C. Lord Wellesley D. Lord Bentinck

23. The partition of Bengal was carried out by:
A. Lord Minto B. Lord Curzon
C. Lord Canning D. Lord Ripon

24. At the time of independence, the Governor General of India was:
A. Lord Mountbatten
B. Lord Wavell
C. Rajgopalachari
D. Lord Linlithgow

25. Krishnadeva Rai was the great:
A. Chola King
B. Pallava King
C. Rashtrakuta King
D. King of Vijayanagar empire

26. The Sikh guru to be beheaded by Mughal King was:
A. Guru Gobind Singh
B. Guru Tegh Bahadur
C. Guru Angad Dev
D. Guru Arjan

27. Who was not involved in 1857 rebellion:
A. Nana Saheb B. Kunwar Singh
C. Ranjit Singh D. Rani Jhansi

28. People of Ongese tribe live in:
A. Andaman Islands B. Bihar
C. Nilgiri hills D. Meghalaya

29. Rajput King Rana Pratap fought the Mughal forces in the:
A. Battle of Khanwah
B. Battle of Haldighati
C. Battle of Thanesar
D. Battle of Wandiwash

30. Chand Bibi is known for:
A. Participating in 1857 revolt
B. Social religious reforms process
C. Valiantly fighting the Mughal forces
D. None of the above

31. Simon Commission came to India in:
A. 1927 B. 1928
C. 1929 D. 1930

32. The Congress split among the extremists and the moderates in:
A. 1906 B. 1915
C. 1907 D. 1927

33. Chauri-Chaura incident led to the suspension of:
A. Civil Disobedience Movement
B. Quit India Movement
C. Khilafat Agitation
D. Non-Cooperation Movement

34. The Congress participated in which Round Table Conference:
A. First only B. Second only
C. First and Third D. All three

35. At the time of Indian independence, Britain was being ruled by:
A. Labour party B. Conservative party
C. Liberal party D. National government

36. Delhi was made capital by the British govemment in:
A. 1892 B. 1905.
C. 1911 D. 1927

37. Permanent settlement of Bengal was introduced in:
A. 1757 B. 1763
C. 1793 D. 1858

38. The first President of the Congress was:
A. A.O. Hume B. S.N. Banerjee
C. D.B. Naoroji D. W.C. Banerjee

39. The Grand Trunk Road was built by:
A. Chandragupta B. Sher Shah Suri
C. Jahangir D. Lord Bentinck

40. Balban belonged to:
A. Khilji dynasty B. Tughlaq dynasty
C. Slave dynasty D. Suri dynasty

41. Which among the following was not a Rajput dynasty?
A. Solankis B. Rashtrakutas
C. Chauhans D. Chandelas

42. Aryabhatta was the famous:
A. Gupta King
B. astronomer and mathematician
C. poet
D. spy

43. Hieun Tsang came to India during the reign of:
A. Ashok B. Chandragupta
C. Skandagupta D. Harshavardhana

44. Who among the following was an expert in medicine?
A. Banabhatta B. Ashvaghosha
C. Charaka D. Satkarni

45. The favourite pastime of the early Aryans was:
A. chariot racing B. playing dice
C. painting D. dancing and music

46. Poet Amir Khusro lived during the reign of:
A. Balban B. Qutub-ud-din Aibak
B. Iltutmish D. Alau-din Khilji

47. Chinese pilgrim Fa-hien visited India during:
A. 3rd century BC B. 4th century BC
C. 5th century AD D. 4th century AD

48. Sufi saints mostly belonged to:
A. Islam B. Hinduism
C. Christianity D. Buddhism

49. Who among the following is known as the Indian Napoleon?
A. Chandragupta Maurya
B. Samudragupta
C. Chandragupta Vikramaditya
D. Bindusar

50. The Bahmani Kingdom existed in the:
A. 13th century B. 14th century
C. 15th century D. 16th century

51. English was made medium of higher education in India by:
A. Lord Mayo B. Lord Chelmsford
C. Lord Rippon D. Lord Bentinck

52. First Indian to be Governor-General was:
A. C. Rajagopalachari
B. Pt. Nehru
C. Sardar Patel
D. Rajendra Prasad

53. Nadir Shah invaded and sacked Delhi in the year:
A. 1645 B. 1695
C. 1739 D. 1752

54. Brahmo Samaj was founded by:
A. Devendranath Tagore
B. A.O. Hume
C. Dayanand Saraswati
D. Raja Ram Mohan Roy

55. The battle of Wandiwash was fought between:
A. the English and the French
B. the English and Tipu Sultan
C. the English and the Dutch
D. the English and the Mughal emperor

56. The reign of which Mugal emperor is called the golden age of the Mughal dynasty?
A. Humayun B. Akbar
C. Shahjahan D. Aurangzeb

57. Banaras Hindu University was founded by:
A. C.R. Das
B. Pt. J.L. Nehru
C. Madan Mohan Malviya
D. Vivekananda

58. Gandhara School of Art flourished during:
A. Ashoka
B. Kanishka
C. Chandragupta Maurya
D. Samudragupta

59. Treaty of Seringapatam was signed between:
A. Tipu Sultan and Nawab of Hyderabad
B. Tipu Sultan and the French
C. Tipu Sultan and the English
D. Tipu Sultan and Hyder Ali

60. Which of the following happened first?
A. Simon Commission
B. Jallianwala Bagh tragedy
C. Resolution of Purna Swaraj
D. Non-Cooperation Movement

61. The first woman President of the Congress was:
A. Annie Besant
B. Sarojini Naidu
C. Indira Gandhi
D. Vijaya Lakshmi Pandit

62. Who among the following was an extremist leader in the early phase of the Congress?
A. Dadabhai Naoroji
B. Gopal Krishna Gokhale
C. C. Rajgopalachari
D. Bal Gangadhar Tilak

63. The main aim of the Swaraj party was:
A. to launch Non-Cooperation Movement
B. to support the extremist
C. to take part in the legislative council meetings and voice the problems of India and the Indians
D. Boycott the foreign goods

64. "Delhi Chalo" was the slogan of:
A. Bhagat Singh
B. Subhash Chandra Bose
C. Mahatma Gandhi
D. Lala Lajpat Rai

65. 'Sardar' was the title given to Vallabh Bhai Patel by:
A. Mahatma Gandhi
B. the British government
C. M.L. Nehru
D. G.K. Gokhale

66. Annual festivals in memory of Shivaji and Lord Ganesha were started by:
A. G.K. Gokhale B. A.A. Pandurang
C. B.R. Ambedkar D. B.G. Tilak

67. 'Champaran Movement' was meant for:
A. securing rights of lower castes
B. separate electorate of Muslims
C. solving problems of Indian farmers
D. protest against the government's education policy

68. Who among the following died due to hunger strike in prison?
A. Lala Lajpat Rai B. Sukhdev
C. Jatin Das D. Mangal Pandey

69. The Non-Cooperation Movement was suspended in:
A. 1921 B. 1922
C. 1929 D. 1930

70. Lala Lajpat Rai suffered fatal injuries while protesting against:
A. Cripps Mission
B. Simon Commission
C. Cabinet Commission
D. Bengal Partition

71. The Quit India Movement was launched in:
A. 1939 B. 1941
C. 1942 D. 1945

72. Muslim League for the first time gave a call for a separate state in:
A. 1916 B. 1929
C. 1937 D. 1940

73. Gandhiji launched his first mass movement in India in:
A. Champaran B. Wardha
C. Sabarmati D. Bardoli

SOCIAL SCIENCE

74. Kuka Movement was started by:
A. the Congress B. the Muslim League
C. the Army D. the Sikhs

75. The Home Rule Movement was started by:
A. Mrs Annie Besant
B. Mahatma Gandhi
C. G.K. Gokhale
D. MA Jinnah

76. The first use to which wheel was put appears to be:
A. chariot B. pottery
C. ornament D. none of the above

77. Which metal was found first?
A. Bronze B. Brass
C. Iron D. Copper

78. Which city does not belong to Harappa Civilization?
A. Lothal B. Mohan-jo-daro
C. Memphis D. Banavali

79. Pharaohs belonged to which civilization?
A. Egypt B. Mesopotamian
C. Chinese D. Harappan

80. Chinese calendar was based on:
A. Solar
B. Lunar
C. Solar and Lunar both
D. Movement of stars

81. Shvetamber sect belongs to:
A. Jainism B. Buddhism
C. Islam D. Hinduism

82. Napolean was finally arrested after the battle of:
A. Borodino B. Leipzig
C. Waterloo D. Austerlitz

83. Which country was not among the Allied powers in World War I?
A. Belgium B. Bulgaria
C. Britain D. France

84. Rasputin was a:
A. Spanish explorer
B. French King
C. British General
D. Russian monk

85. 'Adi Granth' the sacred book of Sikhism was compiled by:
A. Guru Arjun
B. Guru Hargovind
C. Guru Tegh Bahadur
D. Guru Ramdas

86. The Iran-Iraq war ended in:
A. 1984 B. 1987
C. 1991 D. 1992

87. Zulus are natives of:
A. North Pole B. South Pole
C. South Africa D. Persia

88. Who is described as a man of blood and iron?
A. Bismark
B. Woodrow Wilson
C. Louis XIV
D. Garibaldi

89. The turning point in American Independence War was:
A. Boston tea party
B. Battle of Gettysberg
C. Battle of Trafalgar
D. Battle of Verdum

90. Shintoism is popular in:
A. China B. India
C. America D. Japan

91. Protestant movement was started by:
A. St. Augustine
B. Martin Luther
C. Martin Luther King
D. Pope John V

92. The "Fall of Bastille" is linked to:
A. American War of Independence
B. Russian Revolution
C. French Revolution
D. Chinese Revolution

93. United States of America at the time of independence had:
A. 13 colonies
B. 26 colonies
C. 50 colonies
D. 52 colonies

94. The writer of Declaration of American Independence was:
A. Milton B. Harrington
C. Locke D. Jefferson

95. Which great artist does not belong to renaissance age?
A. Raphael
B. Piccaso
C. Leonardo da Vinci
D. Michaelangelo

96. The Incas civilization existed in:
A. Africa B. South America
C. Central America D. North America

97. Jerusalem is not a sacred place for the followers of:
A. Christianity
B. Islam
C. Zoroastrianism
D. Judaism

98. Saxon dynasty ruled in:
A. Germany B. France
C. England D. Italy

99. Germany's attack on which country sparked the second world war?
A. Poland B. Austria
C. Czechoslovakia D. Russia

100. Gunpowder was discovered by:
A. Egyptians B. Indians
C. Chinse D. Assyrians

ANSWERS

1	2	3	4	5	6	7	8	9	10
A	A	D	D	B	A	B	B	C	C
11	**12**	**13**	**14**	**15**	**16**	**17**	**18**	**19**	**20**
D	A	B	C	D	C	C	A	B	C
21	**22**	**23**	**24**	**25**	**26**	**27**	**28**	**29**	**30**
A	D	B	A	D	B	C	A	B	C
31	**32**	**33**	**34**	**35**	**36**	**37**	**38**	**39**	**40**
B	C	D	B	A	C	C	D	B	C
41	**42**	**43**	**44**	**45**	**46**	**47**	**48**	**49**	**50**
B	B	D	C	A	D	C	A	B	B
51	**52**	**53**	**54**	**55**	**56**	**57**	**58**	**59**	**60**
D	A	C	D	A	C	C	B	C	B
61	**62**	**63**	**64**	**65**	**66**	**67**	**68**	**69**	**70**
A	D	C	B	A	D	C	C	B	B
71	**72**	**73**	**74**	**75**	**76**	**77**	**78**	**79**	**80**
C	D	A	D	A	B	D	C	A	C
81	**82**	**83**	**84**	**85**	**86**	**87**	**88**	**89**	**90**
A	C	B	D	A	B	C	A	B	D
91	**92**	**93**	**94**	**95**	**96**	**97**	**98**	**99**	**100**
B	C	A	D	B	B	C	C	A	C

DEMOCRATIC POLITICS

DIVERSITY AND DEMOCRACY

DIVERSITY

Diversity, one of the buzzwords of the early twenty-first century, has become a concept that has multiple meanings to different groups of people. Although dictionaries usually define diversity by using terms like "variety," "difference," or "dissimilarity." Social scientists usually talk about diversity in at least four different ways.

1. Counting diversity refers to empirically enumerating differences within a given population. Using this definition, social scientists take a particular population and simply count the members according to specific criteria, often including race, gender, and ethnicity. In addition, it is possible to take a particular unit within a society like a school, workplace, or government and compare its race, ethnic, or gender distribution to that of the general population. Often, suspicious questions are raised the farther the diversity of a subunit differs from that of the larger population.
2. Culture diversity refers to the importance of understanding and appreciating the cultural differences between race, ethnic, and gender groups. Since members of one culture often view others in relationship to their own standards, social scientists using the culture diversity definition would argue that it is important to show that differences do not have to be evaluated along a good-bad or moral-immoral scale. With greater tolerance and understanding, the argument goes, different cultural groups can coexist with one another in the same society.
3. Good-for-business diversity refers to the belief that businesses will be more profitable and government agencies and not-for-profit corporations will be more efficient with diverse labour forces. According to this approach, members of particular cultural groups are more effective than non-group members in dealing with their own groups so it is in the interests of organizations to diversify workers and managers.
4. Conflict diversity refers to understanding how different groups exist in a hierarchy of inequality in terms of power, privilege, and wealth. According to this definition,dominant groups oppress subordinate groups in many societies and it is important for social scientists to understand the nature of this oppression in order to help attain a more egalitarian society.

In the real world, above mentioned approaches often overlap. However, people using different approaches often ask different types of questions.

A social scientist with a counting diversity perspective might compare the black and Hispanic distribution in the police department with the distribution in the city. Typically, blacks and Hispanics would be underrepresented in the police department and even more highly underrepresented at the upper levels of the department.

A culture diversity scholar, on the other hand, would be more concerned with how the police understand the black and Hispanic communities since this also affects their actions. Do the predominantly white police interpret certain types of speech and clothing as threatening when it is simply part of the black and Hispanic subculture? Do they act in ways that inadvertently disrespect members of the community, thus causing even more tension? Being more sensitive to black and Hispanic cultural values might make the job of the police easier.

The good-for-business perspective would argue that the police would be more effective if they had more black and Hispanic officers who would be more likely to be familiar with the culture of those communities. In addition, members of the community might not be so hostile if the police were seen as some of their own.

Finally, culture conflict social scientists would argue that the police represent the interests of the dominant group: wealthy, white men in business and politics. The police represent the property rights of the dominant group and enforce the laws that they have enacted. Black and Hispanic police officers enforce the same unfair laws as their white colleagues, although they may do it more humanely. The goal is not just to have a more representative and culturally sensitive police force. The goal is to change the laws in order to have a more equitable society.

Concerns about diversity, however it is defined, also intersect with policies like affirmative action. Employment-based affirmative action is based on comparing the racial distribution of employees in a given workplace with the racial distribution of the pool of workers who are qualified for a specific job. This is counting diversity. In the United States, employers with $50,000 in federal contracts and fifty or more employees are required to make a "good faith effort" to achieve a representative labour force; that is, they must try. Formal hiring quotas, where employers are legally obligated to hire a certain percentage of underrepresented workers, are more difficult to justify. In India, on the other hand, these hiring quotas are used much more extensively.

In higher education, both counting diversity and a version of culture diversity are involved. According to the 2003 Grutter and Gratz decisions of the U.S. Supreme Court, affirmative action in college admissions is constitutional because it is in the educational interests of all students to be exposed to a diversity of views on campus. Racial diversity is one way to enhance the diversity of views. However, strict numerical comparisons and formulas cannot be used. Instead, "holistic" assessments of each candidate must take place in order to achieve an undefined "critical mass" of each student group. Since white and Asian students are overrepresented in American higher education, these critical mass guidelines refer mainly to underrepresented minorities like blacks, Hispanics, and Native Americans. A good-for-business perspective is also involved since the court noted that law schools and, to a lesser extent, all of higher education train future leaders who should be selected from all racial groups.

Neither affirmative action in employment nor in higher education reflects the conflict diversity perspective since the role and structure of higher education and the economy is not questioned. The relative power of workers and their bosses/managers is not addressed. The purpose of higher education is not addressed. All that is addressed is the racial characteristics of those who occupy various positions. When reading an article about diversity, it is critical to understand which approach the author is using.

DEMOCRACY

Meaning and Definition

In the dictionary definition, democracy "is government by the people in which the supreme power is vested in the people and exercised directly by them or by their elected agents under a free electoral system." In the words of Abraham Lincoln, democracy is a government "of the people, by the people, and for the people." There is no clear – cut, universal definition of democracy. Most definitions of democracy focus on qualities, procedures, and institutions. There are many types of democracy and their varied practices produce similarly varied effects.

The word 'democracy' itself means 'rule by the people. "A democracy is a system where people can change their rulers in a peaceful manner and the government is given the right to rule because the people say it may.

Types of Democracy

Democracies fall into two categories: Direct and Indirect.

Direct Democracy

In a direct democracy, all citizens, without the intermediary of elected or appointed officials, can participate in making public decisions. Such a system is clearly only practical with relatively small numbers of people in a community organization to tribal council, for example, or the local unit of a labor union, where members can meet in a single room to discuss issues and arrive at decisions by consensus or majority vote.

Ancient Athens, the world's first democracy, managed to practice direct democracy with an assembly of as many as 5,000 to 6,000 persons. In Switzerland direct democracy is followed even at the national level.

Indirect Democracy

Everyone has the right to take part in the government of his country, directly or though freely chosen representatives. The will of the people shall be the basis of the authority of government; this shall be expressed in periodic and genuine election that shall be held by universal and equal suffrage and shall be held by secret vote or the equivalent free voting procedures.

India is the best example of a representative democracy. Voting is one of the mechanisms that guides a democratic state and keeps its leaders on track, and it serves to let the leadership know how they have performed.

During elections, citizens vote for the candidate for their choice. Elected leader represent "the people" and govern for a set period of office. Representatives are chosen through elections based on the constituency or proportional representation system, or on a combination of the two.

Merits of Democracy

1. The participation of the individual members in the government facilitates to enlist their sympathy and co-operation to the success of the government.
2. It is an effective form to educate the public about political, economic and social affairs.
3. It is helpful to promote patriotism among the people and prevents occurrence of violent revolutions.
4. It helps to make progress and development and enables changes to take place in a peaceful manner.
5. It ensures to the people freedom of speech, conscience, assembly and action.
6. It guarantees liberty and equality, which are necessary for human development.

Demerits of Democracy

1. It sometimes leads to establish the majority view over the minority view.
2. Party leaders and political office holders in government control the citizens and the members of the party.
3. It does not encourage individuals to give their opinions.
4. It is a very expensive form of government because elections have to be conducted periodically to various office.
5. It is difficult to prevent corruption and malpractices.
6. It is also known as government by amateurs and lead to domination of masses.

THE CONSTITUTION

The Indian Constitution is a systematic outgrowth of following factors.

1. India's subjection to colonial rule and struggle for independence.
2. The ideological and intellectual inputs provided by stalwarts like Gandhi, Nehru, Ambedkar, Rajendra Prasad and others.
3. Socio-economic milieu of Indian society.
4. Liberal democratic ideas of representative government, adult franchise, elected institutions etc. which was more pragmatic and commensurate with Indian ethos.

Apart from the above cited factors many factors have contributed to affect the constitutional provisions and it would be far from truth to accept that Indian Constitution is still in the process of evolution.

SOURCES OF CONSTITUTIONAL PROVISIONS

Great Britain	: Parliamentary form of Government, process of law making, institution of speaker, writ jurisdiction.
America	: Federal structure, supremacy of the constitution, independent judiciary, Judicial review, impeachment, process of ratification of Constitutional amendments by state Legislatures, Fundamental Rights.
Ireland	: Directive Principles, Method of the election of President, nomination of members in the Rajya Sabha.
Canada	: Definition of Indian Federation as an Union of State and giving residuary power to the Union.
Australia	: Concurrent List Article 245-258.
Japan	: Article-21 Procedure established by law.
Germany	: Emergency provisions.
USSR	: Fundamental Duties
South Africa	: Constitutional Amendments

BASIC FEATURES OF THE CONSTITUTION

The Constitution of a country is the legal document with the help of which a country's affairs are managed. It is a combination of many factors, viz., history, values, traditions, ethos, socio-political milieu and alike. It is a document which establishes the doctrine of limited government and promotes democratic rule. Indian constitution drafted and enacted after a period of struggle and deliberation is among the longest in the world. Though most of it is taken from the Government of India Act 1935, the Indian framers gave it a twist so as to be an instrument of socio-economic justice without compromising the aspect of security, good governance and other aspects.

The following are the basic features of Indian Constitution.

1. One of the longest document in the world. Originally it contained 395 Articles and 8 schedule.
2. Indian Constitution is a written Constitution like American, Canadian and French Constitution.
3. India has a federal system with unitary bias. The desire and commitment to preserve the unity without compromising the issue of development of different regions, made this choice inevitable.
4. Independent and impartial judiciary is hallmark of Indian Constitution.
5. Novel features like fundamental rights, fundamental duties and directive principles of state policy in a single document.
6. Parliamentary system of government.
7. Compromise between Parliamentary supremacy and Judicial Review.
8. A democratic Republic, head of the state is elected indirectly. He/she is not hereditary.
9. A mix of rigid and flexible elements the constitution amendment procedure as moderate enough to address the needs of change. But, is also strict in the sense that crucial provisions need special majority.
10. Citizenship is single, everybody fulfilling certain qualification is entitled for citizenship of the country, not of a particular state.

FUNDAMENTAL RIGHTS

The Constitution of India is committed to a fundamental change in the social order so as to ensure more human life of people. Fundamental Rights are classified as:

1. Right to Equality
2. Right to Freedom
3. Right against Exploitation
4. Right to freedom of Religion
5. Cultural and educational rights
6. Right to Constitutional Remedies

The Original Constitution provided for the Right to property but it has been abolished by the 44th Amendment.

Recently, Right to primary education has been included in Part three under Article 21 A.

1. **Right to Equality :** Article 14 to 18 deals with the Right to Equality.
   Article 14, says that "the state shall not deny to any person equality before the law or the equal protection of the laws within the territory of India.
   - **Equality Before Law :** It is an expression of English common law and is somewhat negative concept implying absence of special privilege on grounds of birth, caste, creed, colour or sex.
     Equality before law is second corrollary from Dicey's concept of the "rule of law." It implies that no one is above the law of land. It is the law no one is supreme. However, exceptions are granted to the office of President and Governor.
   - **Equal Protection of the Law :** It is of American origin and is a more positive concept implying equality of treatment in equal circumstances.

   It provides for protective discrimination.
2. **Right to Freedom :** Article 19 to 22 deals with the Right to Freedom.
   Article 19(1) includes six freedoms.
   (*a*) Freedom of Speech and Expression.
   (*b*) Freedom of Assembly.
   (*c*) Freedom of Association.
   (*d*) Freedom of Movement.
   (*e*) Freedom of Residence and settlement.
   (*f*) Freedom of profession, occupation, trade and business.
   (*g*) included freedom 'to acquire hold and dispose of property' which has been abolished by the 44th Amendment.

   Freedom of the Press is included under Article 19(1)(a).
   Article 20 provides protection against arbitrary and excessive punishment to any person who commits an offence. It can not be suspended during the period of emergency.
   Article 21 guarantees right to life and personal liberty. It says that "No person shall be deprived of his life or personal liberty except according to the procedure established by law."
   It is the most important Article which has been hailed as backbone of Part III and Part IV of the Constitution by the Supreme Court. It can never be suspended.
   Article 21 is the bedrock from which many rights have been inferred by the Supreme Court.
   Article 22 provides protection against arbitrary arrest and detention. It includes
   - informing the detainee of the cause of his arrest.
   - allowing him to consult and be defended by a legal practitioner of his choice.
   - producing him before a nearest magistrate within the period of 24 hours.
3. **Right against Exploitation :** There are two Articles : 23 and 24 under it.
   Article 23 : it seeks to ban traffic in human beings, begar or any form of forced Labour.

Article 24 it prohibits employment of children below the age of 14 years in any factory or mine or any hazardous condition.

4. **Right to Freedom of Religion :** it includes four rights under Article 25, 26, 27, 28.
   Article 25 entitles everyone the freedom of conscience and the right to process, practice and propagate a religion of one's choice.
   Article 26 grants right to religious denominations to
   - establish institutions for practice or propagating their religion.
   - manage its own affairs in matters of religion.
   - passes and dispose of their immovable property.

   Article 27 provides for exempting religious institutions from paying taxes to state for religious purposes.
   Article 28 deals with religious instruction to be imparted in educational institutions.
   - No religious instruction can be provided in institutions owned and administered by the state.
   - Religious instruction may be imparted but pupil may not be compelled to attend them in institutions recognized by the state and receiving aid out of state funds.
   - Religious instructions can be imparted and people can be compelled to attend them in educational institutions administered by state established by a religious endowment or religious trust.
5. **Cultural and Educational Rights :** It includes Articles 29 and 30.
   Article 29 provides for criteria for determination of minority.
   Article 30 provides that all minorities shall have the right to establish and administer educational institution of their choice.
6. **Right to Constitutional Remedies :** It has only one Article 32. In the words of Dr. Ambedkar Article 32 is fundamental of all Fundamental Rights. This right makes it constitutionally obligatory on the part of the Supreme Court to enforce the Fundamental Rights.
   It includes five kinds of writ jurisdiction adopted from England.

- Habeas Corpus
- Mandamus
- Certeorari
- Prohibition
- Quo Warranto

''Habeas Corpus'' is in the nature of an order calling upon the person who has detained another to produce the latter before the court. It literally means 'to have a body.' In addition to aggrieved person; other individual or organization can head for its enforcement.

''Mandamus'' means command. It is issued to command a person or a body to do what is his or its duty to do. It is a discretionary remedy at the hands of HC and an aggrieved person can approach the court. It can be issued against public offices as well as inferior courts and judicial bodies.

''Prohibition'' issued to an inferior court to keep within limits of their jurisdiction. It is a matter of right for which only aggrieved person can approach the Court.

''Quo Warranto'' issued to enquire into the legality of the claim of a public office. It asks 'What is your authority.' Its intention is to see that unlawful claimant does not usurp a public office.

''Certeorari'' issued to quash orders passed in excess of jurisdiction of a court.

FUNDAMENTAL DUTIES

In ancient times, it was felt that if everyone performs his duties, then the rights would automatically be safeguarded.

There was no provision of Fundamental Duties in the original Constitution. The Constitution (Forty Second Amendment) Act, 1976 added part IVA and a new Article 51A to the Constitution. It gives a list of 11 Fundamental Duties. They are as follows :

1. To abide by the Constitution and respect its ideals and institutions, the National flag and the National Anthem.
2. To cherish and follow the noble ideals which inspired our national struggle for freedom.
3. To uphold and proved the sovereignty, unity and integrity of India.
4. To defend the country and render national service when called upon to do so.
5. To promote harmony and spirit of common brotherhood amongst all the people of India transcending religious, linguistic and regional or sectional diversities, to renounce practices derogatory to the dignity of women.
6. To value and preserve the rich heritage of our composite culture.
7. To protect and improve the natural environment including forests, lakes, rivers and wild life and to have compassion for living creatures.
8. To develop the scientific temper, humanism and the spirit of inquiry and reform.
9. To safeguard public property and to abjure violence.
10. To strive towards excellence in all spheres of individual and collective activity so that the nation constantly rises to higher levels of endeavour of achievement.
11. Every citizen to offer opportunities for education to his child the age of 6-14 years.

DIRECTIVE PRINCIPLES OF STATE POLICY

The Directive Principles of State Policy mentioned in Part IV of the Constitution contain 15 Articles (36-51). They are one of the many novel elements of the Constitution which have been adopted from the Irish Constitution. They are in the nature of certain ideals the state should strive for. They give certain directions to executive and the legislature. They give certain unforcible rights which the state shall aim at securing by its various policies. These features have undergone evolution and represent context and experience of India. They are a combination of socialist ideals, Gandhian perception, Western liberalism and the ideals of India's freedom struggle.

Provisions

The various articles on Directive Principles are as follows.

Article 38 instructs the state to promote the welfare of people by securing and protecting a social order in which justice (socio-economic and political) shall inform all the institutions of national life.

Article 39(a) it talks about state's role in providing adequate means of livelihood to all its citizens.

Article 39(b) provides for state's direction for equitable distribution of resources.

Article 39(c) provides for prevention of concentration of wealth in fewer hands.

Artcile 39(d) provides for equal pay for equal work, for both; men and women.

Article 39(a) provides for equal justice and free legal Aid.

Article 40 says that the state shall organize village Panchayats as units of self-government.

Article 41 provides for right to work, public assistance in case of unemployment, old age, sickness and disablement keeping in view the limitations of economic resources.

Article 43 provides for living wages for worker and a decent standard of life, leisure and social and cultural opportunities for people.

Article 43(a) provides for participation of workers in the management of industry and other undertakings. It has been added by 42nd Amendment.

Article 44 provides for a Uniform Civil Code applicable to the entire country.

Article 45 provides free and compulsory education to children till 14 years of age. It has now been made a fundamental right under Article 21A.

Article 46 provides for protection of educational and economic interests of weaker sections of the society and in particular, of the scheduled castes and scheduled tribes.

Article 47 provides for prohibition of consumption of intoxicating liquor and to raise the level of nutrition and five improvement of public health.

Article 48 provides for preserving and improving the breeds and prohibiting the slaughter of cows, calves and other milks and draught cattles.

Article 48A added by 42nd Amendment, provides for protection and improvement of the environment and to safeguard the forests and wild life of the country.

Article 49 provides for protection of monuments of historical and national importance.

Article 50 provides for separation of judiciary from executive.

Article 51 provides for promotion of international peace and security.

Significance of Directive Principles of State Policy

Firstly, they are intended to usher an egalitarian order, once the limitations or resources is overcome and state is competent enough to fulfil them. For, most of the directives are resource consuming.

Secondly, they have exercised an important check on the government. Rightly remarked by Ambedkar that the directives 'can be the best election manifesto.'

Thirdly, they guide both, the government and the people in the realm of politics and society. They have significant educative value.

Fourthly, they emphasize the goal of welfare state and social justice that are warranted in Indian polity and keep check on elitist or populist measures.

PARLIAMENT AND UNION GOVERNMENT

The Constitution of India adopts a Parliamentary form of government like the British Westminster model. However, it is not sovereign in the British sense. Instead, it was expected to suit the requirements of federal polity and acts as an instrument of governance, change and social transformation. It is specifically outlined in Part V of the Constitution from Article 79-123.

The Indian Parliament or the Union Legislature in India consists of the President and the two houses viz, the Lok Sabha and the Rajya Sabha. Unlike the Presidential system that is promised on the principle of separation of powers, the Parliamentary system envisage a scheme of interrelationship between executive and legislative branch of government.

Composition

1. The President.
2. The Lok Sabha or the Lower House or the House of People.
3. The Rajya Sabha or the upper house or council of state.

Functions

1. To enact laws for the administration of the country.
2. To reflect federal sentiment of the Indian polity.
3. To exercise control over the government and ensure limited government.
4. To provide forum for deliberation on issues concerning affairs of the polity.
5. To integrate the polity by providing membership to the representatives.

THE LOK SABHA

Composition : The members of Lok Sabha are elected directly by people from their respective constituencies. Under the provision of the constitution.

- Lok Sabha at present consists of 543 members elected from States and Union Territories.
- 2 members were nominated from the Anglo-Indian community by the President, but by the 104th amendment of the constitution this provision have been abolished.

Term : The term of Lok Sabha is of 5 years from the date appointed for its first meeting. It may be dissolved before the expiration of its full term by the President if the government loses the confidence of the Lower House and there are no other alternative to form the government.

The term of Lok Sabha can be extended (not necessarily).

When a proclamation of emergency is in force, for a period not exceeding one year at a time and not exceeding a period of six months after the proclamation of Emergency cease to operate.

Qualifications : To be a member of the Lok Sabha a person should be

- an Indian Citizen
- Completed 25 years of age

Disqualifications : A member of the Lok Sabha can be disqualified if the person

- holds any office of profit under the Govern-ment of India or the State.
- is of unsound mind and stands so declared by a competent court.
- is an undischarged insolvent
- is not a citizen of India, or has voluntarily acquired the citizenship of a foreign state.
- is to be disqualified by or under any law made by Parliament.

Sessions : The Lok Sabha is to meet at least twice a year and the interval between two consecutive sessions shall be less than 6 months.

A special session of the Lok Sabha can be called if a notice in writing signed by not less than one-tenth of members of the Lok Sabha is given to the Speaker.

When such a notice is given to the President he must summon the session within 14 days.

Speaker

The Speaker is the presiding officer of the Lok Sabha who is elected from amongst the members by a simple majority. His office is an office of much dignity, honour and prestige.

Election : Governed by Article 93. Under the influence of convention that has developed in India, a candidate of the ruling party is elected unopposed to the post of speaker of Lok Sabha.

Removal : Article 94. A speaker can be removed only by a resolution passed by effective majority after 14 days notice of moving of such a resolution has been given.

Powers and Functions of Speaker

The speaker is endowed with a wide range of powers. His powers are

1. To see that there is decorum and discipline in the House.
2. To decide who shall hold the floor and speak in deliberations of the House.
3. To safeguard the rights and privileges of the members of the House.
4. To put the motion of the vote to announce the result. He does not vote but in case of a tie, he casts his vote.
5. To act as administrative head of the Lok Sabha Secretariat.
6. To accept resignations sent by members of Lok Sabha.
7. To protect the House from unnecessary executive intrusion.
8. To allot time for each item on the agenda of the House.

Some of his special powers are:

9. To certify whether a particular Bill is a money Bill or not (Article 110).
10. To preside over joint sitting of both the houses of the Parliament.
11. To admit a vote of no-confidence against the Government.

Parliamentary Privileges

Certain privileges and immunities are granted to members of the Parliament to enable them to work freely and efficiently. They are as follows :

1. Freedom of speech.
2. Freedom from arrest in civil cases for duration of session of Parliament and 40 days before and after.
3. To summon any person to produce documents or to answer charges for contempt of the house.
4. Right to exclude outsiders from the proceedings of the house.
5. Power to punish for breach of privileges committed, mode or outside the Parliament.
6. Right to regulate its own internal proceedings without interference from any executive or judicial authority.

THE RAJYA SABHA

Also called Upper House or Council of States.

Composition : Article 80 of the Constitution outlines that

- Not more than 238 representatives to be sent from States and Union Territories.
- Twelve members to be nominated by the President having special knowledge or practical experience in the field of science, art, literature and social service.

However, the Parliament by law has fixed the total strength of Rajya Sabha to be not more than 245 (233 elected + 12 nominated).

Term : The Rajya Sabha is a permanent body, not subject to dissolution. The term of the members of the house is six years. Nearly one-third of the members of the Rajya Sabha retire after every two years.

Method of Election : Except for a few members (twelve) who are nominated by the President, the members are elected indirectly by proportional representation by means of single transferrable vote. They are elected by an electoral college consisting of elected members of the state Legislative Assemblies. Union Territories elect through the same method by special electoral college.

Qualification : A person seeking membership of Rajya Sabha must be 30 years of age.

THE PRESIDENT

The Constitution makers of India adopted a Parliamentary form of Government based on British westminster model. But, unlike the British model, they opted for a chosen head of state elected indirectly for five years. He occupies a position of pre-eminence in the institutional set of the country and regarded as first citizen of the country.

Qualification : A person should be

1. a citizen of India.
2. must not be less than 35 years.
3. must be qualified to be elected as member of Lok Sabha.
4. must not hold any office of profit under the state.

Election : According to Article 54, the President shall be elected by a electoral college. The election of President is held in accordance with system of proportional representation by means of single transferable vote.

Term : The term of President's office is five years from the date on which he enters upon his office. However, he is eligible for re-eiection.

Resignation : President may resign his office by writing under his hand addressed to the Vice-President.

Impeachment : The President may be impeached for 'violation of the Constitution' in accordance with the provisions in Article 61 of the Constitution.

Procedure for Impeachments : A motion seeking removal of the President can be introduced in either house of the Parliament by giving a notice signed by not less than 1/4 of the total strength of the house. The resolution can be moved after a fourteen days notice is served on him.

If the house passes the resolution by not less than 2/3rd of the total strength of the house, the matter is to be referred to the other house which will investigate the charges.

The President however, has the right to defend himself in the other house either by himself or through an attorney. If the second house also passes the resolution by majority of not less than 2/3rd of the total strength of the house, the President is considered removed from his office from the date of passing of such resolution.

Powers and Functions of the President

The Parliamentary form of government depends on principles and practices wherein the President is the formal executive and council of minister headed by the Prime Minister is the real executive. All the actions of government are undertaken in the name of President but only on the advice of ministers chosen by him. According to Article 53 of the Constitution ''executive powers of the Union shall be vested in the hands of the President who shall exercise it either directly or through officers subordinate to him in accordance with the provisions of the Constitution.''

The powers of the President can be broadly categorized as :

1. **Executive Power :** All executive actions are taken in his name. He has power to appoint the Prime Minister, other ministers of the Government of India, Attorney General for India, the Comptroller and Auditor General of India, the Judges of the Supreme Court, the Judges of High Court of States, the Governors of State, Members of Union and Joint Public Service Commission, the members of Finance Commission, the Chief Election Commissioner and members of election commission.
   The President shall also have the power to remove ministers, Attorney General, judge of Supreme Court or High Court or Election Commissioner on the advice of Parliament, Chairman and member of Public Service Commission on the report of Supreme Court.
2. **Legislative Power :** President is an integral part of Indian Parliament. In this respect
   - he can prorogue or summon the houses of Parliament, dissolve the Lok Sabha and summon the Joint session of the two houses of Parliament in case of a deadlock.
   - he gives his assent to all bills passed by the Parliament to become a law.
   - he addresses either or both houses of Parliament, at the first session of the lower house after each general election and at the commencement of first session each year.
   - he has power to send messages to either house of Parliament which the House must consider.
   - he has power to nominate not more than 12 members to the Rajya Sabha.
   - he has power to promulgate an ordinance when the Parliament is not in the session (Article 123). Presidential ordinance has the same force and effect as an Act of Parliament.
   - he has power to declare his assent to a bill declare that he withholds his assent return the bill for reconsideration (not money bill)
   - The Governor of a state may reserve a bill for President assent, but it is obligatory when the Bill derogates the power of High Court. In cases where a state bill is reserved for Presidential assent, he can declare that he withhold his assent or can give assent.
3. **Military Power :** The President is the Commander-in-Chief of the Defence forces. However, the exercise of his power is to be regulated by law of the Parliament.
4. **Judicial Power :** The President is accorded the power to grant pardon, reprieve, respite, remission of punishment in cases of (a) Court Martial (b) offences against laws made under the Union and Concurrent lists (c) death sentences. He also appoints judges of the Supreme Court and High Courts through an integrated consultative process.
5. **Diplomatic Power :** As the highest constitutional dignitary, the President appoints ambassadors to foreign countries and receives diplomatic delegates of foreign countries.
6. **Financial Power :** It is President who causes to laid before the Parliament, the annual budget. Money Bill can be introduced only with his prior recommendation.
7. **Emergency Power :** President is assigned three kinds of emergency powers under Article 352, 356 and 360.

THE JUDICIARY

Article 233-237: provides for a single, unified, hierarchically organised judiciary.

One court exercises administrative control over court below and judges of one hierarchy getting elevated and appointed as judges of courts above.

SUPREME COURT

The Constitution makers of India adopted the concept of Supreme Court from the United States of America. However, unlike the U.S.A., the Supreme Court in India is not the sovereign body. It is endowed with vast powers and functions including the power of judicial review. In the last 75 years of its working, the court has helped in strengthening democracy, protecting people's right and checked authoritarianism. It is vested with administrative powers over courts lying below it. Indian constitution provides for a single integrated judiciary with the Supreme Court, at the top of hierarchy.

Composition

The Supreme Court at present consists of Chief Justice and 33 other Judges. In 1950, it had only eight Judges. Parliament was, however, authorised to change the number of its Judges. On account of the increase in its work load, the strength of the Supreme Court judges has been raised from time to time. In 1956, the Parliament passed the Supreme Court

Number of Judges Act, which raised the total strength to 11. In 1960, the Supreme Court number of Judges Amendment Act was passed further raising the strength of the Court Judges to 14 including the Chief Justice. Its strength was further increased to 18 in 1977, 26 in 1986 and 31 in 2008. In 2019 it was increased from 31 to 34.

Appointment : Article 124 a judge of the Supreme Court is appointed by the President in consultation with such of the judges of the Supreme Court and of the High Court in the States as the President may deem necessary for the purpose. In the Case of appointment of a Judge other than the Chief Justice, the Chief Justice of India must be consulted. In practice, the appointment of the Chief Justice of India as well as of the other judges of the Supreme Court is recommended by the Home Ministry and after the matter has been examined by the Appointments Committee of the Indian Cabinet and the decision receives the blessings of the Prime Ministers, it is formalised by the Indian President.

Salary : Provided in Second Schedule

Chief Justice	:	2,80,000
Other Judges	:	2,50,000 (same of CAG)

Qualifications : A person shall not be qualified for appointment as a Judge of the Supreme Court unless he is a citizen of India and :

(a) has been for at least five years a Judge of a High Court or of two or more such courts in succession; or

(b) has been worked for at least ten years as an advocate of a High Court or of two or more such courts in succession; or

(c) is, in the opinion of the President, a distinguished jurist.

The inclusion of the last provision which would enable the President to appoint a distinguished jurist on the Supreme Court, even if he did not qualify by a specified number of years of practices at the Bar, was intended to open a wider field of choice.

Tenure

No minimum age is prescribed for appointment as a Judge of the Supreme Court, nor any fixed period office. Once appointed, a Judge of the Supreme Court may cease to be so, on any one of the following grounds (other than death); (a) on attaining the age of 65 years; (b) on resigning his office by writing addressed to the President; (c) on being removed by the President upon an address to that effect being passed by a special majority of each House of Parliament.

Independence of Supreme Court

To ensure the independence of Supreme Court following steps have been undertaken

- Appointment of judges by the President in consultation with CJI and such other judges as he may deem fit.
- Fixed tenure and removal only on ground of proved misbehaviour or incapacity and address by both houses of Parliament by special majority.
- The terms and conditions of Service of a judge can be varied to his disadvantage after his appointment (Article 125).
- The Salaries and allowances of the judges as well as of the staff are charged on the consolidated fund of India and not subjected to vote in Parliament (Art 146).
- No discussion can take place in the Parliament, with respect to conduct of any judge in the discharge of his duties except when a resolution for his removal is under consideration (Article 121).
- No person who has held office as a judge of the Supreme Court can plead or act in any court or before any authority within the territory of India.

Court of Record : Article 129 provides The Supreme Court shall be a Court of record and shall have all powers of such a Court, including the power to punish for contempt itself. A Court of record obviously is one where the acts and Judicial proceedings are kept for memory and testimony. As a court of record the Supreme Court has power to punish those who are adjudged as guilty of contempt of court. The Court has taken up the cases for their contempt.

Jurisdiction of the Supreme Court

Indian Supreme Court enjoys a number of powers evident in its jurisdiction. They are of following kinds

1. Original
2. Writ
3. Appellate
4. Advisory
5. Revisory

1. **Original Jurisdiction :** Article 131 of Indian Constitution provides for original jurisdiction that deals with disputes (i) between the Government of India and one or more States, (ii) between the Government of India and any State or States on the one side and one or more other States on the other, or (iii) between two or more states. However, disputes arising out of the provisions of treaties with the former Indian States or to which any such State is a party are excluded from the Original Jurisdiction of the Supreme Court.
2. **Writ Jurisdiction :** Supreme Court enjoys powers under Article 32 for the enforcement of Fundamental Rights. It is exercised in the nature of writs, viz; Habeas Corpus, Mandamas, Certeorari, Quo Warranto and Prohibition.

3. **Appellate Jurisdiction :** The Supreme Court is the highest court of appeal in all Civil, Criminal and Constitutional cases. Moreover, under "special leave to Appeal" provided in Article 136; the Supreme Court has discretionary powers to take cases from High Courts.

   Article 134 of the Constitution for the first time provides for an appeal to the Supreme Court from any judgement, final order or sentence in a criminal proceeding of a High Court, as of right, in two specified classes of cases—(a) where the High Court has on an appeal reversed an order of acquital of an accused person and sentenced him to death; (b) where the High Court has withdrawn for trial before itself any case from any Court subordinate to its authority and has in such trial convicted the accused and sentenced him to death. In these two classes of cases relating to a sentence of death by the High Court, appeal lies to the Supreme Court as of right.

   Moreover, an appeal may lie to the Supreme Court in any criminal case if the High Court certifies that the case is a fit one for appeal to the Supreme Court.

4. **Advisory Jurisdiction :** Under Article 143 of the Constitution, President can seek advisory opinion of the Supreme Court when it appeals to him that a question of law or fact has arisen, or is likely to arise, which is of such a nature and of such public importance that it is expedient to obtain the opinion of the Supreme Court upon it. The President is not bound to accept the opinion of the Supreme Court. The Court is not bound to give its advice.

5. **Revisory Jurisdiction :** Under Article 137 the Supreme Court can revise its own judgement, order or direction. Besides, Article 138 and Article 139 provides that Parliament by law can extend the jurisdiction of the Supreme Court.

Judicial Review

Judicial review is the power of Supreme Court and High Court to declare a law as unconstitutional and void if it is inconsistent with one or more provisions of the constitution to the extent of such inconsistency.

Under this it can examine legislature enactments and their constitutionality.

It can examine the validity of any order of the executive or any law of the legislature.

It is the Supreme Court to declare what the provisions of the Constitution mean.

The Supreme Court has power to review any judgement or order made by it earlier.

The power of judicial review is more implicit and traceable to Article 82, 226 and also under Article 13.

HIGH COURTS

The Constitution provides for a High Court for every State. However, the Parliament can provide for one High Court for two or more States. The Parliament can provide for a separate High Court for a Union Territory or include a Union Territory in the jurisdiction of a High Court of a State.

Each High Court has a Chief Justice and several judges whose number is decided by the President. The State Governor is consulted in their appointment. In the appointment of other judges, Chief Justice of the High Court is also consulted. The judges hold office upto the age of 62. The salaries and allowances of the judges once fixed cannot be changed to their disadvantage except in financial emergency. Their salaries are charged to the consolidated fund of India.

The Government can appoint additional and acting judges, if required. The President has the powers to transfer a judge from one High Court to the other. This provision in the Constitution was made to ensure impartiality and unbiasedness by the judges. However, these transfers cannot be used as punishments. Effective consultation with the Chief Justice of Supreme Court is essential before ordering the transfer.

Qualification

The qualifications required for judges of a High Court are: (*i*) He must be a citizen of India; (*ii*) He must have held a judicial office in India, or must have practised as an advocate of a High Court for at least 10 years. A High Court judge can resign before the retirement age of 62 years or can be promoted to Supreme Court. He can also be removed from his office by the President on an address presented to him by the Parliament after having passed it in each house by a majority of its total membership as well as by two-thirds of those present and voting. The only ground on which such an address can be passed by the Parliament is either proven misbehaviour or incapacity.

Jurisdiction

Ordinarily, the jurisdiction of a High Court of a State or of a Union Territory is coterminus with the territorial limits of that State or Union Territory. However, the Parliament has powers to extend the jurisdiction of one High Court to an adjoining State or Union Territory. Usually, High Courts are courts of appeal and their area of original jurisdiction is limited. In the presidency towns of Kolkata, Mumbai and Chennai, High Courts had some original jurisdiction, *e.g.,* they could hear the cases, involving Christians and Parsis. After the independence also, these High Courts have retained these powers. Cases, involving marriage laws, divorce, inheritance or contempt of

High Court can be directly taken to the High Court.

Otherwise, High Courts have wide powers in appeal cases. In the criminal cases, an appeal against the Session Court judgement can be made in a High Court. In civil cases, an appeal can go to the High Court if the amount involved in the case exceeds the limits. In the economic offences, appeals against tribunal can be made in the High Courts. High Courts have power to issue writs, for the enforcement of fundamental rights and other purposes. High Courts have the power to transfer cases either to themselves or from one court to another. If a case involves interpretation of Constitution, High Court can transfer the case to itself. High Court acts as a court of record. Its decisions are published and can be referred to. It can sentence anyone for the contempt of Court.

High Courts have superintendence over all courts and tribunals throughout the territories in relation to which it exercises jurisdiction except military courts. This is a wide power because it includes all courts or tribunals whether an appeal against its decision lies to the High Court or not. High Courts can intervene and revise the decisions where it feels gross injustice or non-exercise or abuse of jurisdiction. High Courts have administrative control over the subordinate judiciary in the State which includes district judges, judges of city civil courts as well as Metropolitan magistrates and members of the judicial service of the State. This control is exercised in the manner of appointments, posting, promotion and administrative controls. They can make and issue general rules and prescribe forms for regulating the practice and proceedings of lower courts. They can transfer case from the court to the other.

STATE GOVERNMENT

THE GOVERNOR

The Constitution provides for a Governor as the **head of the executive** at the state level. But, for a long time the institutional functioning was determined by one party dominant system. A major change occurred after the **fourth General Elections in 1967**. In a number of States, the party in power was different from that of the Union. There occurred fragmentation of political parties and emergence of new regional parties. Unpredictable realignments of political parties and groups took place for the purpose of forming Government. The Governors were called upon to exercise their discretionary powers more frequently. The manner in which they exercised those functions direct affect impact on Union-State relations.

The state executive consists of a Governor with a council of ministers with Chief Minister at its head.

Powers of The Governor

1. **Executive :** All the executive functions in the state are carried on in the name of the Governor. He appoints the Chief Minister and on his advice appoints other Ministers and distribute portfolios among them.

   He also appoints Advocate-General, Chairman and members of State public service commission. Members of the state public service commission cannot be removed by him, they can be removed only by the President on the report of the Supreme Court on reference made by the President.

   He is entitled to be consulted by the President in the matter of appointment of Judges of State High Court. He can nominate 1/6 part of the total members of the Legislative Council.

   In the states of **Jharkhand, Chattisgarh, Madhya Pradesh and Odisha, it is the special responsibility** of the Governor to see that a Minister is placed in charge of tribal welfare.

   In Assam, the Governor is given certain **special powers** with respect to the administration of the tribal areas provided in the sixth schedule of the Constitution. In fact, all executive actions of the government are taken in his name.
2. **Legislative :** Governor is an integral part of the state legislature. Governor of state enjoys extensive legislative powers. He summons either or both Houses of the State Legislature to meet at a time and at a place as he thinks fit. The only condition is that six months shall not intervene between its last sitting in one session and the date appointed for its first sitting in the next session. He may prorogue either House or dissolve the Legislative Assembly. He may address either House and may send messages to it. It is provided that the Houses to which he send message will consider any matter required by the message to be taken into consideration. The Governor addresses the House or the Houses on the commencement of the first session after general election and at the commencement of the first session on each year. When a bill has been passed by a House or Houses, it must be presented to the Governor. The Governor shall declare that he assents to it or that he withholds his assent or that he reserves the bill for the consideration of the

President. The Governor may return a Non-Money bill with a message for reconsideration. He may suggest amendments. The House or Houses must consider his suggestions without delay. If the bill is passed again by the House or Houses without amendment, he cannot with hold his assent.

3. **Judicial : Article 161** empowers Governor to grant pardons, reprieves, respites or remission of punishment or to suspend or commute the sentence of death to any person convicted of any offence against which executive power of state extends. He has **no power to pardon in case of defence of death**. But has the power to suspend, remit a sentence of death. He is entitled to be consulted by the president in appointment of Judges of State High Court.
4. **Emergency :** Governor has the power to make a report to the President whenever he is satisfied that a situation has arisen in which Government of the state cannot be carried on in accordance with the provisions of the constitution [Article 356]. But this power has often been misused as Rajiv Dhawan has indicated.
5. **Financial :** He causes the annual financial statement to be laid before state legislature and reconmmends for introducing money Bill. No demand for grants can be made except on the recommendation of the Governor.

Ordinance Making Power

The Governor can promulgate ordinance only when houses are not in the session. It is not a discretionary power. Ordinance cease to have effect at the expiry of six weeks from the date of reassembly, unless disapproved earlier. He himself is competent to withdraw the ordinance at any time.

Ordinance making power is co-extensive with legislative power of State Legislature. If the provisions of ordinance are repugnant with a union law relating a concurrent subject, the Governor's ordinance will prevail notwithstanding repugnancy, if the ordinance had been made in pursuance of the instructions of the President.

STATE LEGISLATURE

Every state has a legislature consisting of the Governor and the Legislative Assembly. Some states have the second chamber, called Legislative Council.

Legislative Assembly

- It consists of not more than 500 or less than 60.
- Assembly of Mizoram and Goa have 40 members each, while Puduherry has 30 and Sikkim has 32 only.
- The member must be 25 years of age.
- Term of the Assembly is 5 year.
- To be elected to Legislative Council or Legislative Assembly, a person must be a elector for any seat in Legislative Assembly in the state.

As regards disqualifications of members, the decision of Governor in consultation with the election commission shall be final.

Constitution provides for joint sitting for only one purpose at the state level : When the Governor adresses the legislature at the beginning of Budget session or immediately after the general election.

Legislative Council

- It exists in six states, viz; Bihar, Karnataka, Andhra Pradesh, Telangana, Maharashtra and U.P.
- Under **Article 169**, the Parliament by law, can provide for the creation of Legislative Council in a state or abolition if it exists, provided the Legislative Assembly of the state passes a resolution to that effect (by a majority of the total membership of the Assembly and by a majority of not less than two-thirds of the members present and voting).
- Its total members not to exceed 1/3 of Legislative Assembly.
- The total membership in no case be less than 40.
- Composition

  1/3 elected by Vidhan Sabha

  1/3 elected by Local bodies

  1/12 elected by graduates of three years standing

  1/12 elected by teachers school & colleges

  1/6 elected by Governor (also from co-operative)

  Thus 5/6 elected indirectly elected 1/6 nominated.
- To become, a member a person must be 30 years age.

LOCAL GOVERNMENT

The term 'Panchayati Raj' in India signifies the system of rural local self-government. It is created in all the states in India by the acts of the state legislatures to establish democracy at the grass roots level. It is entrusted with the duties and responsibilities in the field of rural development. It was constitutionalised through the 73rd Constitutional Amendment Act of 1992. At the central level, the Ministry of Rural Development looks after the matters relating to the Panchayati Raj bodies.

In the scheme of division of powers between the centre and the states in the Indian federal system, the item of *'Local Government'* is given to the states. Thus the fifth entry of the State List of the seventh schedule to the constitution of India deals with 'local government'.

Balwantray Mehta Committee

In January 1957, the Government of India appointed a committee to examine the working of the Community Development Programme (1952) and the National Extension Service (1953) and to suggest measures for their better working. The chairman of this committee was Balwantray G. Mehta. The committee submitted its report in November 1957 and recommended the establishment of the scheme of 'democratic decentralisation' which ultimately came to the known as panchayati raj. The specific recommendations made by it are:

1. Establishment of three-tier Panchayati Raj System—Gram Panchayat at the village level, Panchayat Samiti at the block level, and Zila Parishad at the district level. These tiers should be organically linked through a device of indirect elections.
2. The village Panchayat should be constituted with directly elected representatives, whereas the Panchayat Samiti and Zila Parishad should be constituted with indirectly elected members.
3. All planning and developmental activities should be entrusted to these bodies.
4. The Panchayat Samiti should be the executive body while the Zila Parishad should be the advisory, coordinating and supervisory body.
5. The District Collector should be the chairman of the Zila Parishad.
6. There should be a genuine transfer of power and responsibility to these democratic bodies.
7. Adequate resources should be transferred to these bodies to enable them to discharge their functions and fulfil their responsibilities.

RURAL LOCAL GOVERNMENT

73rd Amendment Act of 1992

This act has added Part-IX to the Constitution of India. It is entitled as 'The Panchayats' and consists of provisions from articles 243 to 243-O. In addition, the Act has also added Eleventh schedule to the Constitution. It contains 29 functional items of the Panchayats and deals wih Article 243-G.

The salient features of the Act are:

1. **Gram Sabha:** The Act provides for a Gram Sabha as the foundation of the Panchayati Raj system. It is a body consisting of persons registered in the electoral rolls of a village comprised within the area of Panchayat at the village level.
2. **Three-Tier System:** The Act provides for a three-tier system of Panchayati Raj in every state, that is Panchayats at the village, intermediate, and district levels. The Act defines all these terms in the following manner.
   (*i*) Panchayat means an institution (by whatever name called) of self-government for rural areas.
   (*ii*) Village means, a village specified by the Governor by public notification to be a village for this purpose, and includes a group of villages so specified.
   (*iii*) Intermediate level means a level between the village and district levels specified by the Governor by public notification for this purpose.
   (*iv*) District means a district in a state.

   Thus, the Act brings about uniformity in the structure of Panchayati Raj throughout the country. However a state having a population not exceeding 20 lakhs may not constitute panchayats at the intermediate level.
3. **Election of Members and Chairpersons:** All the members of Panchayats at the village, intermediate and district levels shall be elected directly by the people. Further, the chairperson of Panchayats at the intermediate and district levels shall be elected indirectly—by and from amongst the elected members of. However, the chairperson of a Panchayat at the village level shall be elected in such manner as the state legislature determines.
4. **Reservation of seats:** The Act provides for the reservation of seats for scheduled castes and scheduled tribes in every Panchayat in proportion of their population to the total population in the Panchayat area. Further, the state legislature shall provide for the reservation of offices of chairpersons in the Panchayat at the village or any other level for the SC and ST. The Act provides for the reservation of not less than one-third of the total number of seats for women. Further, not less than one-third of the total number of offices of chairpersons in the Panchayat at each level shall be reserved for women.

   The Act also authorises the legislature of a state to make any provision for reservation of seats in any Panchayat or offices of chairperson in the Panchayat at any level in favour of backward classes.

5. **Duration of Panchayats:** The Act provides for a five-year term of office to the Panchayat at every level. However, it can be dissolved before the completion of its term. Further, fresh election to constitute a Panchayat shall be completed *(i)* before the expiry of its duration of five years; or *(ii)* in case of dissolution, before the expiry of a period of six months from the date of its dissolution.
6. **Disqualifications:** A person shall be disqualified for being chosen as or for being a member of Panchayat if he is so disqualified *(i)* under any law for the time being in force for the purposes of elections to the legislature of the state concerned, or *(ii)* under any law made by the state legislature. However, no person shall be disqualified on the ground that he is less than 25 years of age if he has attained the age of 21 years. Further, all questions of disqualifications shall be referred to such authority as the state legislature determines.
7. **Powers and Functions:** The state legislature may endow the Panchayats, with such powers and authority as may be necessary to enable them to function as institutions of self-government. Such a scheme may contain provisions for the devolution of powers and responsibilities upon Panchayats at the appropriate level with respect to *(i)* the preparation of plans for economic development and social justice; *(ii)* the implementation of schemes for economic development and social justice as may be entrusted to them, including those in relation to the 29 matters listed in the Eleventh Schedule.
8. **Finances:** The state legislature may *(i)* authorise a Panchayat to levy, collect and appropriate taxes, duties, tolls and fees; *(ii)* assign to a Panchayat taxes, duties, tolls end fees levied and collected by the state government; *(iii)* provide for making grants-in-aid to the Panchayats from the Consolidated Fund of the state; and *(iv)* provide for constitution of funds crediting all moneys of the panchayats.

URBAN LOCAL GOVERNMENT

The term *'Urban Local Government'* in India signifies the governance of an urban area by the people through their elected representatives. The jurisdiction of an urban local government is limited to a specific urban area which is demarcated for this purpose by the state government.

There are eight types of urban local governments in India-Municipal Corporation, Municipality, Notified Area Committee, Town Area Committee, Cantonment Board, Township, Port Trust and Special Purpose Agency. The system of urban government was constitutionalised through the 74th constitutional Amendment Act of 1992. At the central level, the subject of 'urban local government' is dealt with by the following three ministries.

1. Ministry of Urban Development created as a separate ministry in 1985.
2. Ministry of Defence in the case of cantonment boards.
3. Ministry of Home Affairs in the case of Union Territories.

Historical Perspective

The institutions of urban local government originated and developed in modern India during the period of British rule. The major events in this context are:

(i) In 1687, the first municipal corporation in India was set up at Madras.

(ii) In 1726, the municipal corporations were set up in Bombay and Calcutta.

(iii) Lord Mayo's Resolution of 1870 on financial decentralisation visualised the development of local self-government institutions.

(iv) Lord Ripon's Resolution of 1882 has been hailed as the 'Magna carta' of local self-government. He is called as the father of local-self government in India.

(v) The Royal Commission on decentralisation was appointed in 1907 and it submitted its report in 1909. Its chairman was Hobhouse.

(vi) Under the dyarchical scheme introduced in Provinces by the Government of India Act of 1919, local self-government became a transferred subject under the charge of a responsible Indian minister.

(vii) In 1924, the Cantonments Act was passed by the Central legislature.

(viii) Under the provincial autonomy scheme introduced by the Government of India Act of 1935, local self-government was declared a provincial subject.

74th Amendment Act of 1992

This Act has added Part IX-A to the Constitution of India. It is entitled as "The Municipalities' and consists of provisions from articles 243-P to 243-ZG. In addition, the Act has also added Twelfth Schedule to the Constitution. It contains 18 functional items of municipalities and deals with Article 243-W.

The Act gave constitutional status to the municipalities. It has brought them under the purview of justiciable part of the constitution. In other words, state governments are under constitutional obligation to adopt the new system of municipalities in accordance with the provisions of the Act.

The Act aims at revitalising and strengthening the urban governments so that they function effectively as units of local government.

The salient features of the Act are:

1. **Three Types of Municipalities:** The Act provides for the constitution of the following three types of municipalities in every state.
   (*a*) A Nagar Panchayat (by whatever name called) for a transitional area, that is, an area in transition from a rural area to an urban area.
   (*b*) A Municipality for a smaller urban area.
   (*c*) A Municipal Corporation for a larger urban area.

   A transitional area, a smaller urban area or a larger urban area means such area as the Governor may specify by public notification for this purpose with regard to the following factors.
   (*a*) Population of the area
   (*b*) Density of population
   (*c*) Revenue generated for local administration
   (*d*) Percentage of employment in non-agricultural activities
   (*e*) Economic importance or such other factors as the Governor may deem fit.
2. **Composition:** All the members of a municipality shall be elected directly by the people of the municipal area. For this purpose, each municipal area shall be divided int territorial constituencies to be known as wards. The state legislature may provide the manner of election of the chairperson of a municipality. It may also provide for the representation of the following persons in a municipality.
   (*i*) Persons having special knowledge or experience in municipal administration without the right to vote in the meetings of municipality.
   (*ii*) The members of the Lok Sabha and the state legislative Assembly representing constituencies which comprise wholly or partly the municipal area.
   (*iii*) The members of the Rajya Sabha and the state legislative council registered as electors with the municipal area.
   (*iv*) The chairpersons of committees (other than wards committees).
3. **Wards Committees:** There shall be constituted a wards committee, consisting of one or more wards, within the territorial area of a municipality having population of three lakhs or more. The state legislature may make provision with respect to the composition and the territorial area of a wards committee and the manner in which the seats in a wards committee shall be filled. It may also make any provision for the constitution of committees in addition to the wards committees.
4. **Reservation of Seats:** The Act provides for the reservation of seats for the scheduled castes and the scheduled tribes in every municipality in propor-tion of their population to the total population in the municipal area. Further, it provides for the reservation of not less than one-third of the total number of seats for women (including the number of seats reserved for women belonging to the SCs and the STs). The state legislature may provide for the manner of reservation of offices of chairpersons in the municipalities for the SCs, the STs and the women. It may also make any provision for the reservation of seats in any municipality or offices of chairpersons in municipalities in favour of backward classes.
5. **Duration of Municipalities:** The Act provides for a five-year term of office for every municipality. However, it can be dissolved before the completion of its term. Further, the fresh election to constitute a municipality shall be completed (*i*) before the expiry of its duration of five years; or (*ii*) in case of dissolution, before the expiry of a period of six months from the date of its dissolution.
6. **Disqualifications:** A person shall be disqualified for being chosen as or for being a member of a municipality if he is so disqualified
   (*i*) under any law for the time being in force for the purposes of elections to the legislature of the state concerned; or
   (*ii*) under any law made by the state legislature.

   However, no person shall be disqualified on the ground that he is less than 25 years of age if he has attained the age of 21 years. Further, all questions of disqualifications shall be referred to such authority as the state legislature determines.
7. **State Election Commission:** The superintendence, direction and control of the preparation of electoral rolls and the conduct of all elections of the municipalities shall be vested in the State Election Commission.
8. **Powers and Functions:** The state legislature may endow the municipalities with such powers and authority as may be necessary to enable them to function as institutions of self-government. Such a scheme may contain provisions for the devolution of powers and responsibilities upon municipalities at the appropriate level with respect to (*i*) the preparation of plans for economic development and social justice; (*ii*) the implementation of schemes for economic development and social justice as may be entrusted to them including

those in relation to the 18 matters listed in the Twelfth Schedule.

9. **Finances:** The state legislature may (*i*) authorise a municipality to levy, collect and appropriate taxes, duties, tolls and fees; (*ii*) assign to a muicipality taxes, duties, tolls and fees levied and collected by state government; (*iii*) provide for making grants-in-aid to the municipalities from the Consolidated Found of the state; and (*iv*) provide for constitution of funds for crediting all moneys of the municipalities.

SOCIAL JUSTICE AND THE MARGINALISED

WOMEN

After a brief spell of equality of sexes in the vedic period, there began deterioration in status of women. During the medieval age purdah became a custom among muslim and sati became prevalent among Hindus. Patriarchal norms were expressed through cultural metaphors. British system of education together with liberal sentiments led to reformist movement. Organization and persons took cognizance of injustices meted out to women. Social legislation, viz. Abolition of Sati (1829) Widow Remarriage Act (1856), Civil Marriage Act (1872) were important steps in this regard. The Nationalist Movement and Gandhiji's call dragged women into the mainstream of Indian politics. **All India Women's Conference** was organized in 1927.

After independence a number of steps were taken to ensure equality and dignity of women and free them from the clutches of unjustified subjugation. These include :

Constitutional Provisions

Article 14 : provides that the state shall not delay to any person equality before the law or equal protection of law.

Article 15 : prohibits discrimination on grounds such as caste, religion and sex.

Article 16 : provides for equality of opportunity in matters relating to public employment.

Article 16(4) : empowers the state to make special provisions for women and children.

These provisions are justifiable.

Article 39(a) : equal right to and adequate means of livelihood.

Article 39(c) : equal pay for equal work for both; men and women.

Article 42 : make provisions for just and human conditions of work and maternity relief.

42 Amendment Part IV A Article 51A imposes a **fundamental duty to renounce practices derogatory to the dignity of women.**

The 73rd and 74th Amendment Act heralded a new era by reserving 1/3 seats at all levels of rural and urban local self government for women.

Enactments

Special Marriage Act 1954

Hindu Marriage Act 1955

Hindu Maintenance and Adoption Act 1956

Dowry Prohibition Act 1961

Equal Remuneration Act 1976

Child Marriage Restraint (Amendment) Act 1978

Dowry Prohibition (Amendment) Act 1984.

Judiciary has also been active as shown in the Shah Bano case (1982)

The Protection of Women from Domestic Violence Act, 2005 came into force on October 26, 2006.

Other Measures

Social Welfare Board was constituted in 1953 to grant aid, promote welfare and development services for women.

In 1985 a separate department of women and child development was set up at the centre.

In 1986 National Policy on Education outlined several features for women's education.

In 1987 programme of support to training cum employment for women was started.

In 1990 Parliament enacted a law to create National Commission for women. It came into existence in 1992.

In 1995 Indira Mahila Yojna was started with the aim of organizing women at grassroots level.

In 2001 National Policy for Empowerment of women was launched.

National Commission for Women

- Statutory body created in 1992
- Consists of a Chairman nominated by the Government.
- There are 5 other members and a member secretary.
- It is vested with power of civil court.

Functions

1. To investigate and examine all matters relating to safeguards for women.

2. Make recommendation for effective implementation of safeguards.
3. Review the existing provision of the Constitution.
4. Call for special studies or investigations into specific problems.

How to Empower

- Widening the ambit of women's participation in public institutions and bringing them directly into the mainstream to enjoy the benefits of society.
- Universalizing existing developmental programmes to include women.
- To promote gender sensitiveness by proactive measures like one child norm (providing free education to the lone girl child).
- To invest in sectors where women could be a better performer.
- Skilling women through training and workshops.
- Insuring credit facilities.
- Creating legal awareness through producing book, pamphlets and media campaign.
- Ensure equal access to quality education for girls.
- Provide scholarships, mentorship, and support for women in higher education.
- Promote literacy and vocational training in rural or marginalised communities.
- Ensure equal pay for equal work.
- Support women entrepreneurs with credit, training and markets.
- Provide maternity benefits and safe working environments.
- Encourage workplace leadership and representation.
- Enforce laws against gender-based violence, harassment and discrimination.
- Encourage women's participation in politics and governance.
- Reform property, inheritance and family laws that disadvantage women.
- Promote women's leadership in community, business and government roles.
- Support women's organisations, media platforms and advocacy groups.
- Challenge stereotypes that silence or belittle women's contributions.
- Challenge gender stereotypes in media and education.
- Engage men and boys as allies in promoting gender equality.
- Celebrate women's achievements in history, art, science and leadership.
- Ensure access to quality healthcare, including reproductive rights.
- Provide safe spaces and support systems for survivors of violence.

DALITS

The category 'Dalits' includes the castes who fall outside the Varna system. They are also called by various names; such as outcastes, untouchables or achhuts. They are marginalised sections whose major source of frustration relates to individual behaviour, norms of the society and state apparatus. Though their position has improved due to constitutional provisions, welfare policies and positive discrimination measures, a firm commitment is required to hinder the hindrances in ensuring equality.

Constitutional Provisions

1. **Article 341** deals with the criteria for identification of scheduled castes.
2. **Article 342** deals with Scheduled Tribes.
3. **Article 17** abolished practice of untouchability in any form.
4. **Articles 14, 15 ,16 and 16(4)** place them in equal position with other members and entrust state to make special provisions.
5. **Article 38** enjoins the state to promote the welfare of people by ensuring justice in society.
6. **Article 46** entrusts the state to promote the educational and economic interests of scheduled caste.
7. 65th Amendment Act, 1990 provided for **National Commission** for SCs and STs. But, recently there has been bifurcation of the commission to deal exclusively with one category.

Legal Enactments

1. Untouchability offences Act 1995.
2. Protection of Civil Rights Act 1975.
3. SC and ST (Prevention of Atrocities) Act 1989.

Development Measures

1. Book Bank Scheme
2. Girls Hostel and Boys Hostel Schemes
3. Coaching
4. Scheduled Caste Development Corporation
5. Separate plan of Action for Primitive Tribe
6. Tribal sub plan strategy to provide legal and administrative support and promote their development.

Multiple Choice Questions

1. The Constitution of India was adopted on:
A. 15 August, 1947
B. 26 January, 1950
C. 26 November, 1949
D. 15 August, 1950

2. Who administers the oaths of office to the Vice-President?
A. Chief Justice of India
B. President of India
C. Speaker of the Lok Sabha
D. Attorney-General of India

3. Who among the following is not appointed by the President?
A. Chairman of UPSC
B. Governor of State
C. Judge of a High Court
D. Vice-President

4. The President can dissolve the Lok Sabha before expiry of its term, on the advice of:
A. Prime Minister
B. Speaker
C. Vice-President
D. Election Commissioner

5. A presidential ordinance remains in force for:
A. three months B. one month
C. six months D. till it is revoked

6. The idea of Fundamental Duties is derived from:
A. Russian Constitution
B. British Constitution
C. American Constitution
D. German Constitution

7. The Fundamental Right, which cannot be suspended even during an emergency is:
A. Right to equality
B. Right to freedom of expression
C. Right to movement
D. Right to life

8. Whether the bill in the Parliament, is a money bill or not, is decided by:
A. Prime Minister
B. Speaker
C. President
D. Comptroller and Auditor General

9. Which of the following is presided over by a non-member:
A. Lok Sabha
B. Rajya Sabha
C. Vidhan Sabha
D. Joint sitting of Lok Sabha and Rajya Sabha

10. For the Union Territories, not having legislatures of their own, laws are enacted by:
A. Parliament B. President
C. Administrators D. Union Law Ministry

11. Arunachal Pradesh was granted statehood in:
A. 1972 B. 1984
C. 1985 D. 1987

12. The official language of Jammu and Kashmir is:
A. Dogri B. Kashmiri
C. Urdu D. Hindustani

13. The minimum age to qualify for the membership of Rajya Sabha is:
A. 18 years B. 21 years
C. 25 years D. 30 years

14. A minister, who is not a member of either house of the Parliament must get himself elected within:
A. a year B. six months
C. three months D. two months

15. By convention, the Governor of a state generally belongs to:
A. ruling party in the state
B. opposition party of the state
C. IAS cadre of the state
D. some other state

16. The world 'secular' in the Preamble of the Indian Constitution was incorporated by the:
A. 42nd amendment
B. 62nd amendment

C. 44th amendment
D. 41st amendment

17. Constitution describes India as a:
A. Federation of states
B. Quasi-federation
C. Union of states
D. Dominion of free states

18. Which of the following article cannot be amended by simple majority?
A. Creation of new states
B. Procedure of election of the President
C. Official language of the Union
D. Quorum in the Parliament

19. Constitution provides residual powers to the:
A. Union Government
B. State Government
C. President
D. Supreme Court

20. President of India has immunity from:
A. Civil proceedings during the term of office
B. Criminal proceedings during the term of office
C. Civil and criminal proceedings during the term of office
D. Civil and criminal proceedings after the retirement

21. Minimum age to qualify for the President's post is:
A. 21 years B. 25 years
C. 30 years D. 35 years

22. The constitutional amendment which made Sikkim a state of India was:
A. 34th B. 35th
C. 36th D. 37th

23. State legislatures are not allowed to discuss:
A. conduct of speaker
B. conduct of any High Court judge
C. autonomy issue
D. taxation

24. Reservation of seats for Scheduled Castes/Tribes was initially provided till:
A. 1955 B. 1960
C. 1970 D. 1980

25. In case of unavailability of the President and Vice-President, the duties of the President are discharged by:
A. Prime Minister
B. Speaker of the Lok Sabha
C. Senior-most Cabinet Minister
D. Chief Justice of India

26. Which Fundamental Right can be described as the soul and heart of the Constitution:
A. Right to equality
B. Right to prosperity
C. Right to constitutional remedies
D. Right to freedom of speech

27. Ordinances are promulgated by:
A. Prime Minister
B. Lok Sabha Speaker
C. President
D. Rajya Sabha Chairman

28. Indian states have been constituted on the basis of:
A. geographical continuity
B. language
C. administrative convenience
D. economic conditions

29. The Chief Election Commissioner can be removed by:
A. Prime Minister
B. President
C. Supreme Court's Chief Justice
D. Parliament

30. Speaker of the Lok Sabha can only:
A. adjourn the house
B. prorogue the house
C. summon the house
D. dissolve the house

31. Membership of state assembly range from:
A. 30 to 300 B. 40 to 400
C. 50 to 600 D. 60 to 500

32. Salaries of Supreme Court judges are drawn from:
A. Law Ministry Grants
B. Consolidated Fund of India
C. Home Ministry Grants
D. Parliamentary Grants

33. The need of establish Panchayati Raj institutions is prescribed in:
A. Directive Principles
B. Fundamental Rights
C. Preamble
D. Seventh Schedule

34. Which Constitutional amendment curtailed the power of judicial review by the Supreme Court?
A. 24th amendment
B. 42nd amendment
C. 43rd amendment
D. 44th amendment

35. The quorum in Lok Sabha is:
A. 50
B. 55
C. one-fourth of the strength
D. one-tenth of the strength

36. The disagreement between Lok Sabha and Rajya Sabha is solved by:
A. setting up Joint Select Committee
B. dissolving Lok Sabha
C. setting up adjudication committee
D. calling a joint session

37. The seventh schedule consists of:
A. List of national languages
B. List of oaths and affirmations
C. List of subjects
D. List of States and Union Territories

38. Provisions of disqualification on ground of defection are listed in:
A. second schedule B. fourth schedule
C. eighth schedule D. tenth schedule

39. The Union Territories get representation in:
A. only Lok Sabha
B. only Rajya Sabha
C. both Lok Sabha and Rajya Sabha
D. neither Lok Sabha nor Rajya Sabha

40. If Lok Sabha and Rajya Sabha disagree on a constitutional amendment bill:
A. the bill lapses
B. a joint sitting is called
C. Lok Sabha's decision prevails
D. Rajya Sabha's decision prevails

41. The Preamble of the Constitution was amended by:
A. 1st amendment B. 26th amendment
C. 42nd amendment D. 44th amendment

42. Eighth General Elections were held in:
A. 1980 B. 1985
C. 1989 D. 1991

43. The retirement age for Supreme Court judges is:
A. 58 years B. 60 years
C. 62 years D. 65 years

44. One can be disqualified from voting, only on the grounds of:
A. Age B. Sex
C. Religion D. Education

45. Governors of states are:
A. appointed by Chief Ministers
B. appointed by the President
C. elected by members of Legislative Assembly
D. elected by people

46. First General elections in the country were held in:
A. 1948 B. 1950
C. 1949 D. 1952

47. A total of ...... members can be nominated by the President of Rajya Sabha.
A. 6 B. 12
C. 15 D. 18

48. The Union executive is responsible to:
A. Lok Sabha B. Rajya Sabha
C. President D. Supreme Court

49. Attorney-General of India is appointed by:
A. UPSC B. President
C. Prime Minister D. Lok Sabha Speaker

50. Time gap between two sessions of Parliament cannot exceed:
A. 3 months B. 6 months
C. 1 year D. no fixed gap

51. Supreme Commander of defence forces is:
A. Army Chief B. Defence Minister
C. Prime Minister D. President

52. Which of the following is not a state?
A. Mizoram B. Manipur
C. Puducherry D. Arunachal Pradesh

53. India is a republic because:
A. every adult can take part in elections
B. executive is responsible to legislature
C. elected representatives can be recalled
D. President is elected for a fixed term

54. Article 356 deals with:
A. National emergency
B. Constitutional emergency
C. Financial emergency
D. Fundamental Rights during emergency

55. The only President to be elected twice is:
A. Rajendra Prasad
B. Radhakrishnan
C. V.V. Giri
D. Neelam Sanjeeva Reddy

56. Vice-President can submit his resignation to:
A. President
B. Prime Minister
C. Chief Justice of India
D. Deputy Chairman of Rajya Sabha

57. Which two words were added to Preamble of Constitution by amendment?
A. Secular democratic
B. Democratic republic
C. Secular socialist
D. Republic socialist

58. The Chairman of the drafting committee of the Constitution was:
A. Rajendra Prasad B. Jawaharlal Nehru
C. B.R. Ambedkar D. Sardar Patel

59. The Fundamental Rights are:
A. only available to citizens
B. only a few are available to citizens
C. none is available to non-citizens
D. only a few are available to non-citizens

60. Which one is not a national duty?
A. Respect the Constitution
B. Respect the President
C. Defend the country
D. Protect natural environment

61. Which one of the following is not a writ, issued by Supreme Court?
A. Prohibition B. Habeas Corpus
C. Certiorari D. Suo-Moto

62. Which one is not a Directive Principle?
A. Equal pay for equal work
B. Prevention of cow slaughter
C. Pollution control
D. Promotion of international peace

63. Governments try to follow Directive Principles because:
A. Legislatures can pass no-confidence motion on the issue

B. they represent the demands and aspirations of people
C. courts can pass injunctions, if not accepted
D. President can dismiss Government

64. Which Directive Principle has been fully implemented in the country?
A. Setting up village Panchayats as the unit of self-Government
B. Securing the Uniform Civil Code throughout the country
C. Prohibition of the use of intoxicants
D. Providing adequate means of livelihood for all citizens

65. Which house of Parliament can create All-India Services?
A. Lok Sabha
B. Rajya Sabha
C. Either house
D. Joint sitting of both houses

66. Two houses of the Parliament enjoy equal powers with regard to:
A. Money Bill
B. Election of President
C. Removal of Government
D. Creation of All India Services

67. The Committee which looks after the financial matters of the Government is:
A. Business Advisory Committee
B. Committee on Government Assurances
C. Privilege Committee
D. Public Accounts Committee

68. Lok Sabha cannot be addressed by:
A. Vice-President
B. Attorney-General
C. Minister, not a member of Lok Sabha
D. Speaker

69. President does not appoint:
A. Prime Minister
B. Lok Sabha Speaker
C. Election Commissioner
D. Comptroller and Auditor-General

70. Prime Minister of India, at the time of appointment, need not be:
A. citizen of India
B. above 25 years of age
C. Member of Parliament
D. of sound mind

71. The Prime Minister, who could not face the Parliament even once, was:
A. V.P. Singh B. Charan Singh
C. Morarji Desai D. Deve Gowda

72. Among the judicial powers, the President can not:
A. grant pardon B. grant reprieve
C. grant amnesty D. grant change of court

73. National emergency can not be imposed in case of:
A. Armed rebellion
B. Political crisis
C. Internal aggression
D. War

74. Constitutional emergency can be renewed upto:
A. six months B. two years
C. three years D. indefinitely

75. Vice-President is ex-officio:
A. Member of Rajya Sabha
B. Chairman of Rajya Sabha
C. Member of Lok Sabha
D. Speaker of Lok Sabha

76. Governor can consult the President, in regard to:
A. Appointment of Chief Minister
B. Money bill
C. Non-money bill
D. Dissolving assembly

77. The resolution to abolish or create legislative council should be:
A. approved by two-third of majority of assembly members voting
B. approved by two-third majority of total strength of assembly
C. approved by a simple majority of assembly members voting
D. approved by a simple majority and forwarded by the Governor

78. Which of the following High Court has jurisdiction over a Union Territory?
A. Calcutta B. Patna
C. Karnataka D. Allahabad

79. Which state does not have its High Court at the Capital?
A. Andhra Pradesh B. Kerala
C. Bihar D. Maharashtra

80. Tax not imposed by the Central Government is:
A. Income tax B. Corporation tax
C. Professional tax D. Capital gains tax

81. Official language of the Union is:
A. Hindi in Devanagri script
B. Hindi in Roman script
C. English in Roman script
D. Hindi and English

82. The first constitutional amendment related to:
A. Preamble
B. Directive Principles
C. Fundamental Duties
D. Ninth Schedule

83. The number of schedules in the Constitution is:
A. 395 B. 100
C. 12 D. 8

84. Indian citizenship cannot be terminated by:
A. Renunciation B. Termination
C. Deprivation D. Imprisonment

85. Supreme Court comes to the rescue of Fundamental Rights, if:
A. Executive violates
B. Legislature violates
C. An individual violates
D. either of the above

86. The residuary power of making law vests with:
A. Centre
B. State
C. Both of them
D. Supreme Court decides

87. Finance Commission is constituted by:
A. Parliament B. President
C. Prime Minister D. Lok Sabha Speaker

88. Which of the following is not a state subject?
A. Administration of justice
B. Agriculture
C. Audit and Accounts
D. Public health

89. The dispute relating to the election of the President is referred to:
A. Election Commissioner
B. Supreme Court
C. Parliament
D. Parliament and State assemblies

90. In the absence of the Prime Minister, cabinet meetings are presided over by:
A. Defence Minister
B. Home Minister
C. Finance Minister
D. Prime Minister decides

ANSWERS

1	2	3	4	5	6	7	8	9	10
C	B	D	A	C	A	D	B	B	A
11	**12**	**13**	**14**	**15**	**16**	**17**	**18**	**19**	**20**
D	C	D	B	D	A	C	B	A	B
21	**22**	**23**	**24**	**25**	**26**	**27**	**28**	**29**	**30**
D	C	B	B	D	C	C	B	D	A
31	**32**	**33**	**34**	**35**	**36**	**37**	**38**	**39**	**40**
D	B	A	B	D	D	C	D	C	A
41	**42**	**43**	**44**	**45**	**46**	**47**	**48**	**49**	**50**
C	B	D	A	B	D	B	A	B	B
51	**52**	**53**	**54**	**55**	**56**	**57**	**58**	**59**	**60**
D	C	D	B	A	A	C	C	D	B
61	**62**	**63**	**64**	**65**	**66**	**67**	**68**	**69**	**70**
D	C	B	A	B	B	D	A	B	C
71	**72**	**73**	**74**	**75**	**76**	**77**	**78**	**79**	**80**
B	D	B	C	B	C	A	A	B	C
81	**82**	**83**	**84**	**85**	**86**	**87**	**88**	**89**	**90**
A	D	C	D	D	A	B	C	B	D

World Geography

THE SOLAR SYSTEM

The solar system is a group of celestial bodies comprising the sun and the large number of bodies that are bound gravitationally to the sun and revolve around it.

THE SUN

The sun is the star at the centre of the solar system. It is the nearest star to the earth. The next nearest star, Alpha Centauri, is more than 4.0×10^{13} km away. The general statistics of the sun is as:

Diameter	1.392×10^6 km
Volume	1.304×10^6 times the volume of earth
Temperature	6000ºC at surface and 15 million degree C at the centre
Relative Density	1.4
Gravitational Pull	28 times the gravitational pull of the earth

The outermost part of sun's atmosphere is called corona. The visible surface of the sun and source of the adsorption spectrum is called *Photosphere* which is characteristic of the most stars. The stratum of sun's atmosphere immediately above the photosphere and below is *Chromosphere*. The whole body of the sun is gaseous in form. The gas is mostly hydrogen, which accounts 70% of its mass. The remainder is made up of 28% helium and 2% all other heavier elements from lithium to uranium. The generation of solar energy comes from thermo-nuclear reactions.

The dark spot in the Sun is called sunspot which appears dark by contrast with the solar surface, because they have a somewhat lower temperature of about 4500º K. The number of sunspot are found to vary from year to year with a period of about 11 years. This periodicity is known as Sunspot-cycle.

THE EARTH

The earth is a member of a group of celestial bodies which comprises the sun and Eight planets, Mercury, Venus, Earth, Mars, Jupiter, Saturn, Uranus and Neptune. Planets have no light of their own and all of them, except Venus and Uranus rotate upon their axis from west to east. Venus and Uranus rotate upon their axis from east to west. Many satellites are revolving around their respective planets. Thousands of comets and billions of meteoroids are there in the space. The Earth has only one satellite the moon while Mercury and Venus have none. The average distance of the earth from the sun is 1.496×10^8 km. The earth is the third nearest planet to the sun and is the fifth largest planet.

The Earth: Facts and Figures	
Mass of Earth	5.880×10^{21} tons
Density of Earth	5.517 times that of water
Volume of Earth	1.083×10^{11} cubic km
Equatorial Circumference	4.007×10^4 km
Polar Diameter	12, 714 km
Equatorial Diameter	12756 km
Polar or Meridional Circumference	4.0×10^4 km

Estimated Age	At least 4600 million years
Land Surface	148,951,000 sq km
Water Surface	361,150,000 sq km (71 per cent of total area
Highest Point of the land surface	Mt. Everest (8,848 metres)
Lowest point of the land surface	Shores of the Dead Sea (396 metres below the sea level)
Greatest Ocean Depth	Mariana Trench, East of Philippines (11,033 metres below the sea level)

Shape of the Earth

The earth is an oblate spheroid and not a true sphere because it is flattened at the poles and bulges out at the equator. The polar diameter of the earth is 42 km shorter than the equatorial diameter, therefore the earth oblate.

Motion of the Earth

The earth spins like a top on its axis completing one rotation every 24 hours and revolves around the sun once in 365.25 days. While the daily rotation, *i.e.*, spin of the earth causes day and night, the revolution is responsible for the change of the seasons. The earth is a non-luminous sphere, emitting no light of its own. The part of the earth's surface which is towards the sun at any time is lit, while the remaining past, on the other side of the earth, is dark. The earth rotates from west to east. That is why the sun, the moon and the stars appears to us to be moving in the opposite direction.

Effect of Rotation

The daily axial rotation of the earth causes:

(i) Formation of day and night
(ii) Difference in Longitude and Time
(iii) Change in direction of winds and currents
(iv) Tides occur twice a day

Effect of Revolution

The earth revolves around the sun in a vast elliptical orbit. One such revolution takes about 365.25 days. One ordinary year contains 365 days, and to make up for the difference, every fourth year which is called a Leap Year, is calculated as 366 days. The change of seasons is mainly due to the revolution.

- **21st June:** At this time it is summer in the Northern Hemisphere and winter in the Southern Hemisphere. The midday sun shines vertically over the Tropic of Cancer.
- **22nd December:** At this time it is winter in the Northern Hemisphere and summer in the Southern Hemisphere. The midday sun shines vertically over the Tropic of Capricorn.

Equinoxes

On 21st March and 23rd September the season is either spring or Autumn. These days, days and nights are equal everywhere. Sun's rays fall vertically on the equator. These two position of the earth are called Equinoxes due to the equal length of the days and nights.

Inclination of the Earth's Axis

The earth's polar axis is not vertical but inclined and it make an angle of 66½° with the plane of the elliptic and is tilted 33½° from a line perpendicular to the plane in which the earth's orbit and the sun lie. The plane is imagined to be horizontal and to pass through the centre of globe. As a result of the inclination of the axis of the earth and its elliptical orbit around the sun, the earth attains four critical position in respect of the sun. On 21st June, the earth is so located in its orbit that the north polar end of its axis leans at the maximum angle of 23½° towards the sun, *i.e.*, the Tropic of Cancer receives the vertical rays of the sun. This condition is known as summer solstice, the longest day in the norther hemisphere. On 22nd December the earth is in an equivalent but opposite position in its orbit, *i.e.*, the Tropic of Capricorn receives the vertical rays of the sun. This condition is the winter solstice, the longest day in the southern hemisphere. Equinoxes occur when the earth's axis makes 90° angle with a line drawn to the sun, *i.e.*, the equator receives the vertical rays of the sun and day and night are equal. The vernal equinox occurs on 21st March and autumnal equinox on 23rd September. At the time of winter solstice the sun is not visible to a person on the north pole and during the summer solstice, the sun is not visible to a person on the south pole.

Latitude and Longitude

Lines of latitude and longitude are drawn on a map to locate position of the place on the surface of the earth. The latitude of place is defined as its distance north or south of the equator, measured as an angle. Latitudes are thus lines drawn parallel to the equator which is at 0° and they are counted up to 90° north and south, the two poles. The longitudes show the distance of a point east or west of the Prime Meridian which is at 0° and passes through Greenwich village near London in U.K. There are 360° Longitude and all the longitudinal lines join the poles. The longitude of a place can be defined as its distance east or west the meridian of Greenwich, measured as an angle.

Tropics

Tropics are literally the turning points. They refer to those parallels where the sun is imagined to stop its movement and turn about northward or southward, as the case may be. They are the 23° North parallel or Tropic of Cancer and 23½° South parallel or Tropic of Capricorn. Both are imaginary lines.

- **Local Time:** The system in which we measure time is based on the concept of the solar day. The time when the sun's altitude is the highest at that place, the shadow of a vertical rod fixed in the ground is the shortest. If at this time we set our watch at 12 O'clock. It will indicate local time.
- **Standard Time:** If every place were to are its own local time that would cause confusion in administration and other activities. So the local time of a place generally in the middle of the country, is used everywhere in that country as the Standard Time of that country and is taken in to be uniform throughout Standard Time of India is the local time of a place near Allahabad situated at 82½° E longitude.

  However, in bigger countries like Russia, America etc, it is not possible to have a single standard time for the whole country. Therefore, a number of standard times are chosen which are applicable for a limited region.

THE MOON

Moon is the only natural satellite of the earth. It has diameter of about 3,480 km and has a mass of 1/81 that of the earth. The moon's period of revolution with reference to the sun is about 29.53 days. This period is called a synodic month. Moon also rotates on its own axis. The time taken by the moon to complete one rotation on its axis in 27.32 days. This fact has an important bearing upon the earth-moon relationship. Consequent to this relationship, we always see the same face of the moon from the earth. Only 59% of the moon's surface is directly visible from earth.

- **Eclipses:** Eclipses are caused by the fact that light travels in a straight line, producing clearly well defined shadows of objects in its path. When the earth comes between the moon and the sun, and it shuts off the light of the sun from falling upon the moon and this is called *Lunar Eclipse*. When the moon comes directly between the sun and the earth it obstructs light of the sun from falling upon the earth and this is called Solar Eclipse. Solar and Lunar eclipses do not occur every month because the moon's path around the earth is at an angle to the path of the earth around the sun. Sometimes only, the bodies fall in a line, producing an eclipse.

ATMOSPHERE

Atmosphere is the thin gaseous envelope surrounding and protecting the earth. It contains about 5.0×10^2 tonnes of gases a small amount of water vapour and some dust particle. The dry air of the atmosphere comprises of nitrogen 78.09%, oxygen 20.95%, and argon 0.93%. Besides, there are minute proportions of other gases, including carbon dioxide, helium, methane, hydrogen, ozone, neon, xenon, etc. The amount of carbon dioxide varies from place to place being greatest around the cities and smallest in the countryside.

The atmosphere is essential for life on earth. Oxygen and carbon dioxide in the atmosphere are necessary for animal and plant life. The ozone layer in the stratosphere protects life on earth by absorbing most of the sun's harmful radiation.

ATMOSPHERIC LAYERS

The atmosphere has been divided into subspheres according to the general characteristics of temperature variations. The different atmospheric layers are:

(i) **Troposphere:** It is the nearest to the earth's surface and extends to a distance of about 13 km. In Troposphere, generally, the temperature decreases as height increases. It is the densest of all layers and contains water vapours, moistures and dust. It also profoundly influences earth's climate since 80% of the mass of air comprising the entire atmosphere is concentrated in this zone.

(ii) **Tropopause:** It refers to the boundary region which separates troposphere from the adjoining atmospheric layer known as stratosphere.

(iii) **Stratosphere:** It is a region of uniform temperature extending from an altitude of about 11 km above the earth to a height of nearly 30 km. It is free from water vapour, clouds and dust. The upper part of stratosphere has plenty of ozone which affords protection to human beings on the earth against the fatal effects of solar ultraviolet radiations.

(iv) **Mesosphere:** It is a very cold region above the ozone rich layer of stratosphere.

(v) **Ionosphere:** It comes immediately above mesosphere, extends from about 50 km to 500 km above the earth. It includes the thermosphere and exosphere. The region contains ionised or electrically charged air and reflects radio waves facilitating wireless communication between distant places. The ionised air also protect those on earth from the falling meteorites, most of which are made to burn out at this region.

(vi) **Thermosphere:** It constitutes the middle layer of ionosphere and has a temperature of 100° C.

(vii) **Exosphere:** It is the uppermost region of the atmosphere, where the air density is so low that an air molecule moving rapidly straight upward is more than 50% likely to escape from the atmosphere instead of hitting other molecules.

Weather: It refers to conditions of temperature wind, humidity, rainfall at a given time and place.

Climate: It refers to the average weather conditions of a region as a whole over a comparatively long period of time.

PRECIPITATION

The term precipitation refers to falling of water snow or hail from the clouds and results when condensation is occurring rapidly with in a cloud. The most common form of precipitation is rain and is formed when many cloud droplets coalesce into drops too large to remain suspended in the air. Sometimes the raindrops freeze before reaching the ground, then the precipitation occurs in form of pellets, called sleet. Precipitation can be orographic, conventional or cyclonic in nature. When the air is caused to rise upwards due to cyclonic circulation. The resulting precipitation is said to be of the cyclonic type.

- **Clouds:** Clouds are huge collection of water-vapours. They are formed by very minute suspended water particles present in the air. When there is very low temperature, they are formed by huge collection of very small crystal like structure of snow.

  Clouds are of different type and they can be classified on the basis of their form and altitude. On the basis of form clouds are known as stratiform or layered types, and cumuliform or massive type. According to the altitudes, clouds are called cirrus and the combination of these two lead to the cirrocumulus, cirrostratus.

- **Fog:** When moist air meets cold surface of earth, some of the water vapours condense on the particles of dust in air. This cloud of condensed vapour is called fog.

- **Mist:** Like fog, it is also formed on account of the fall of temperature of air. Here the droplet of water formed on account of condensation are heavier than those of the fog, therefore, mist is always seen close to the earth and does not rise up so high as the fog.

- **Dew:** At night, the earth may frequently become cooler than the air above it. This causes water vapour contained in the air to get condensed and deposited on the cooled surface. This is known as dew. Dew is more likely to occur on clear and calm nights.

- **Rainfall:** When the rain-laden clouds rise up, they expand and become cooler. They also become cooler because they are moving away from hotter region. The cooling of the air resulting in the precipitation of rain etc. It may be due to relief, convention and cyclone.

  As we ascend a hill or a mountain temperature decreases. If, then, a wind blowing from the sea and saturated with water vapour comes to a mountain, it is forced to rise. On rising the clouds reach thinner layers of air and consequently it expands. Expansion produces cooling. The moisture in the clouds is then condensed and falls as rain. Such rains are called the relief rains.

  When air is heated, it tends to rise up. As it rises, it is cooled and rain falls even though there are no mountains nearby. The air at the Equator is intensely heated almost each day and hence it rises each day, causing rain each afternoon. This rising of the wind when heated is called convection, and the rain that is so caused is called the convectional rain.

  A cyclones has a low pressure at the centre, and it brings rainy or stormy weather. The rain brought about by a cyclone is called the cyclonic rain.

WINDS

Air moving from one direction to another horizontally is known as winds. It is air in motion and is caused by difference in pressure. Wind blows from region of high pressure to a region of low pressure. Due to earth's rotation on its axis from west to east, all winds are deflected to the right in the northern hemisphere and to the left in the southern hemisphere. There are certain identifiable wind systems in the world:

1. The low pressure region round the equator, is calm usually and is called doldrum. Although there are no regular winds there, violent squalls and thunderstorms are frequent which come from high pressure areas north and south of the equator.
2. **Trade Winds:** As the temperature at equators is high, the air becomes hot and rises up. The air moves northwards and southwards and descends near 30°N and 30°S, causing high pressure. The wind then blows from here towards the equator and this is called trade wind. They are named so because trading ships take advantage of the direction of these winds.
3. **Westerlies:** These are also called anti-trade winds as they blow from about 40°N to the Arctic circle and from about 35°S to the Antarctic circle

throughout the year. They derive their name from the direction in which they blow. In the northern hemisphere, they blow in the south-westerly direction and in the north-westerly direction in the southern hemisphere.

4. **Polar winds:** They blow from the high pressure area around the poles towards the temperate regions. Since they rise from the colder regions, they are extremely cold.
5. **Periodical Winds:** They blow in one direction at a particular time or during a particular season. Monsoons and land and sea breezes belong to this category. In India, South-west monsoon blow in summer and North-east in winter.
6. **Variable winds:** They are irregular winds like cyclones and anti-cyclones which originate due to local factors.

Cyclones and Anticyclones

Cyclones is wind rotating round the centre of minimum of low barometric pressure. The wind rush inwards from all direction. Due to the inclination of earth's axis and the rotation of the earth, in northern hemisphere the winds circulates in an anticlockwise direction and in the southern hemisphere in clockwise direction.

Anticyclone refers to the region in which the atmospheric is high, with the highest point at the centre. In this situation the winds blow spirally outwards from the centre, clockwise in northern hemisphere and anticlockwise in southern hemisphere. In summer anti-cyclones are associated with warm and sunny conditions, in winter they imply frost and fog as well as sunshine.

HYDROSPHERE

Hydrosphere is the name given to the masses of water that cover about 70.8% of the surface of the earth. The great stretches of salt water called oceans and seas. Pacific ocean, which is the largest among the ocean sprawls over an area of about 1.65×10^8 sq. km an area which is more than total combined area of all the continents. The average depth of oceans is about 4 km.

The water in the oceans totals over 1,300 million cubic km which is more than 97% of world's total water. The balance of water resources are contributed by glaciers, ice and snow, fresh water lakes, rivers and the underground water.

The oceans occupy the deep hollows of the earth's crust. The floor of the ocean beds are covered with ridges and valleys. The raised parts of the ocean floor are called ridges. The valley are called deeps or trenches. The most famous ridge is the Mid Atlantic Ridge and the most famous trenches include the Tuscarora Deep and Mariana Trench.

All the oceans of the world are interconnected. Antarctica is entirely surrounded by a great stretch of water called the southern ocean. From there stretch northwards, the three most oceans — the Indian, Pacific and Atlantic Oceans. The fifth ocean is the Arctic ocean which surrounds the North pole.

The Ocean Floor

The bottom of oceans is not as smooth as it is presented to be. It can categorised into four parts:

1. **Continental Shelf:** It is the seaward extension of the continent and is a shallows platform with a variable width of a few miles in the north-west pacific coast to over 100 miles near north-west Europe. They are of great significance because shallow water enables sunlight to penetrate and help growth of planktons. This helps in large growth of fishes in the area near the banks.
2. **Continental Slope:** The continental shelf abruptly starts declining and showing large slopes.
3. **Ocean Trough:** They are deep sea plains which are undulating with an average depth of 3000 organic deposits. They have extensive submerged plateaus, ridges, trenches, basins and oceanic islands.
4. **Ocean Deeps:** They are long, narrow and deep trenches, often plunging upto 30,000 feet.

Salinity

A number of minerals which are held in solution in the sea water have great importance. As a result of large concentration of minerals, like sodium sulphate, sodium chloride, magnesium chloride and calcium chloride etc., sea water is salty to taste. The proportion of dissolved salts to pure water is called Salinity. It varies from place to place in the oceans. The average figure being 35 gm per 1000 cc. Usually salinity is higher where the addition of fresh water is less and evaporation is high and vice-versa. Chlorine is the most abundant element causing salinity in sea water.

Waves and Current

Wave is a disturbance on the surface of a liquid body e.g. a sea or a lake. Wave is mainly caused by the wind which heaps up the water. Along coasts, waves are destructive agents of erosion.

Currents are those powerful movements of the ocean that proceed regularly, constantly and in definite direction. The movement of these current is clearly visible on the surface of the water and may be called gushing streams of water over the otherwise calm surface of the ocean. Hence streams of water move with a greater velocity than their counterparts do on the surface of the earth. They modify the climate of a coastal region. The warm Gulf stream brings in ice-free winter conditions along the south eastern coast of USA. Winds passing over warm current pick up moisture and bring rain. Japan, British Isles etc. receive rainfall in this manner. Kalahari and Atacama deserts are drier than they would be because of cold Peruvian current. The meeting of cold and warm current causes dense fog which is dangerous for navigation. However, at the meeting place, growth of the fishes gets enhanced due to abundance of nutrients.

LITHOSPHERE

The Lithosphere refers to the top crust of the earth on which our continents countries and the ocean basins rest. The lithosphere has a thickness between 38 to 52 km in the continental regions, but becomes thin between 7 to 13 km under the ocean beds. In the high mountain regions, its thickness is estimated at about 65 km. It includes both the land mass as well as the ocean floors, generally it is used to denote only the land surface which occupies a little less than 30% of total area of the earth.

INTERIOR STRUCTURE OF THE EARTH

The interior structure of the earth is based on the seismic waves, as they travel through the earth. The centre of the earth is occupied by the core, about 3500 km in radius. The outer part of the core is believed to have the properties of a liquid and the innermost part of the core may be called solid. The core is the densest part of the earth and is known as nife. Outside the core lies the mantle, a layer about 2925 km thick, composed of minerals in a solid state. The rocks in this layer may be in glassy state. The topmost portion of earth, the crust is the land mass comprising soil, sand and rock. In fact all the sand and much of the soil that we have has come to us from ancient rocks that crumbled down under the impact of heat of the sun and the cool of the rain, a process that has gone on for thousands years.

PLAIN

A plain is defined as an area with gently sloping land and very low local relief. It can be classified as peneplain, flood plain, delta plain, alluvial plain, coastal plain, lacustrine plain, karst plain and glacial plain etc.

The combined action of weathering and streams on land makes peneplain. The deposition of material by rivers makes flood plains, delta plains and alluvial plains. Coastal plains are those parts of the continental shelf which have been uplifted. Lacustrine plains are old lake beds and are made up of sediments deposited by rivers. Karst plains are formed in limestone areas mainly by the agency of underground water. Glacial plains are formed through glacial erosion and deposition.

PLATEAUS

It can be classified as intermontane, piedmont and continental. Intermontane plateaus are formed in association with mountains and are enclosed by them *e.g.* the Tibetan plateau. Piedmont plateaus lie between mountains on one side and the sea on the other *e.g.* the Patagonian plateau in South America. Continental plateau rise abruptly from the seas or low lands and are extensive e.g. the Indian plateau and Greenland.

MOUNTAINS

Mountains are masses of land considerably higher than the surrounding areas, higher than a hill, and with fairly steep slopes. They are classified as fold mountain, block mountains, volcanic mountains, and residual mountains.

As the molten centrosphere cooled and contracted, the crust at several places became crumpled, *i.e.*, full of wrinkles or folds. The elevated parts became mountains termed as fold mountains and the intervening depressions are known as valleys. The great mountain chains of the world like, the Himalayas, the Alps, Andes and the Rockies have been formed by this process.

If there are two parallel vertical faults in the earth's crust, the contraction of the inner molten rock to matter causes the parts on either side of the middle block of the rock to subside. This process causes the formation of a Block Mountain.

Volcanic mountains results from volcanic eruptions and the outflow of lava. The Fujiyama of Japan is an example of volcanic mountains. Sometimes, the mountains are carved out as a result of erosion of plateaus and high plains by various agents of erosion. These are known as residual mountains *e.g.* the Highlands of Scotland and the Sieroas of Central Spain.

The sinking down of the part of the earth's crust between two parallel vertical faults forms a Rift Valley. It is U-shaped, whereas a Fold Valley is V-shaped. The Red Sea, Dead Sea and Narmada Valley in India are example of rift valleys.

ROCKS

Rocks are the main materials composing the earth's crust. Rocks are composed of minerals. Minerals are natural inorganic substance each with a fairly definite chemical composition and recognisable crystal form, colour, hardness, lustre, texture and other physical characteristics. Rocks of the earth are grouped in three principal classes — Igneous, Sedimentary and Metamorphic.

Rocks which are solidified directly from molten materials are called igneous rocks. These rocks are crystalline in nature and make up nearly 85 per cent of the earth's crust. Granites, Basalt are examples of Igneous rocks. Sedimentary rocks are formed in layers on beds of rivers, lakes and seas. They are formed over a long period of time and natural factors like Streams, Rivers, Glaciers or Wind etc. play an important role in their formation. They often contain fossils of plants, animals and other micro-organisms. Sandstone, Shale, Clay, Rock salts, Gypsum, Potash and Nitrates are examples of Sedimentary rocks. Metamorphic rocks are literally rocks which have changed their form. In course of time, the original form of these rock is changed owing to excessive heat and great pressure, like clay changing into slate. Granite changes into gneiss, limestone into marble, sandstone into quartzite and coal into graphite.

VOLCANO

It is an opening in the earth's crust through which lava is ejected. The thrown up lava forms a conical hill with a funnel-shaped hollow called Crater at its top. Crater is the mouth of a volcano. It is usually cup-shaped and serves as the vent for the lava to erupt. Volcanoes which are no longer active are called extinct volcanoes. A volcano which is only sleeping and may become active is called a dormat volcano. The volcanoes which erupt frequently are called active volcanoes. Mt Etna in Italy is an example of active volcano while Fujiyama in Japan and Chimborazo in Andes are examples of dormant and extinct volcanoes respectively. The eruption of lava from a volcano can be of explosive type or quiet type.

There are several thousands volcanoes in the world. They are distributed in several belts across the continents. The most important belt runs right round the Pacific ocean. Another, rather less important, runs from Iceland just touching the British Isles, through the Azones across the Atlantic to the West-Indies with a branch running through the Mediterranean sea.

EARTHQUAKES

It is the shaking of the earth's crust sometimes accompanied by a permanent elevation or depression, but often no lasting effect is visible on the surface except the damage done by shaking. The main cause of earthquakes are due to sudden cooling and contraction of the earth's surface, coming into activity of some dormant volcanos, and due to internal heat, sometimes water changes into steam, expands and this causes an earthquake. Earthquakes occur in almost every part of the world. They are very common in volcanic districts, and where the earth's crust is weak. The most active region is a belt surrounding the Pacific ocean which includes western coasts of North and South America, the eastern coast of Asia, New Zealand and the islands of the South-east Pacific. In India, the North-East region and Shivalik range of Himalayas are more susceptible of earthquakes though Plateau has also experienced it sometimes. The intensity of an earthquake is measured on Richter-Scale by an instrument seismograph. An earthquake that originates in or near the sea, causing gigantic waves, is called Tsunami.

MAIN NATURAL REGIONS OF THE WORLD

A natural region is a geographical unit which contains countries or parts of countries, where the condition of temperature, rainfall and cultivated vegetation and consequently human activity are almost uniform.

(i) **Hot Deserts:** They are situated near the tropics between 20° and 30° in the West of the land masses. These occupy about one-fourth of the land surface of the earth. The climate of the region is mostly hot and dry. The Sahara, Arabia, West Rajasthan and Sindh deserts are included in this region. Gold, silver, copper and diamonds are available in these deserts.

(ii) **Tropical Grasslands:** Agriculture and cattle-rearing are the chief occupations, and wool, skins and hides the chief commercial products of this region.

(iii) **Monsoon Region:** It lies mostly in the south-east of Asia and includes portions of Australia, Africa and America. Hence the climate is hot and moist in summer and warm and dry in winter. Natural vegetation is forests.

(iv) **Equatorial Region:** These regions have dense forests of evergreen trees but they are not suitable for human habitation. Some medicinal forest products are gathered.

(v) **Mediterranean Region:** This region lies around the Mediterranean sea and on both sides of the equator, in the west of the land masses and between 30° and 45° north and south of equator. The climate is hot in summer and wet in winter. It is famous for fruit trees like olive, vine, lemon almonds, etc.

(vi) **Cool Temperate Region:** On the western margins of continents. In these regions cereals are grown, cattle are raised for dairy product and fishing is also important. In the eastern margins coniferous forests provide soft wood. Lumbering, fishing and farming are important.

(vii) **Polar Tundra Regions:** Too cold for most human activity. Only mineral extraction can attract a large concentration of people in the future. Gold and oil are found in Alaska, and nickel in Siberia.

(viii) **Siberian Type Region:** It includes Siberia, north Europe, specially north Russia, Finland, Scandinavian countries, etc. Here winters are very severe. Natural vegetation is coniferous forests. Wheat, potatoes, etc are grown in summer.

(ix) **China Type Region:** It lies in the east of land masses between 30° and 45° degree. Here summers are warm and moist and winters are very cold. Natural vegetation is forests.

(x) **British Type:** It includes the area of British Columbia, North-West Europe including British Isles, South Chile, Tasmania and South Islands of New Zealand. The countries in this region are industrially advanced, and agriculture is carried on by scientific method. People on the whole are engaged in different industries.

PATTERN OF CLIMATE

Different regions of the world have different climates and the factor for this variation is presence of different temperature, winds, precipitation and their interaction with the surface of the earth. The hottest and wettest regions of the world are found along the equators. The areas located near Tropic of Capricorn usually have dry climates, except for small area of Australia, Africa and South America. There is more climate variation along the Tropic of Cancer. The climate of a region is an important factor in the lifestyle of people, crop pattern, housing pattern and economic pattern. The main types of climates are as follows:

(a) Equatorial Climate: This type of climate is found in the area lying in a belt stretching about 5° on both sides of the equator. The temperature is high all round the year and does not vary much. Rainfall is large and continues for the whole year, making the climate sultry. The Amazon and Congo basins, East and West Indies, the Malay Peninsula and Andaman and Nicobar show this type of climate.

(b) Desert Climate: As the sand heats up quickly and losses heat also fast, the highest temperatures in the world are found in the regions affected by desert climate. The nights are very cold. The hot deserts, occupy lowlands along the Tropics of Cancer and Capricorn. Sahara, Thar and deserts of Arabia, Australia, South Africa (Kalahari) and South America (Atacama) are examples of such deserts. However, cold deserts are also found in plateaus outside the tropics. They show very low temperatures, particularly during winter. Gobi (Central Asia), Colorado (North America) and deserts of Iran belong to this climate.

(c) Mediterranean Climate: The climate in areas around the Mediterranean sea is known by the sea. The region lies between latitudes 30° and 45°. The area is hot and dry in summer but moist and mild weather is observed during winter. This type of climate is also prevalent on western sides of North and South America, South Africa and South of Australia.

(d) Temperate Maritime Climate: This type of climate is prevalent in North-West Europe, West Canada, South Chile and New Zealand. The area gets rain throughout the year but compared to tropical regions, the quantum is usually less.

(e) Continental Climate: This type of climate is found in regions far away from the oceans. Due to lack of moderating influence of seas, the summers are very hot and winters are very cold. Rains fall mostly in spring and early summer but quantity is not much. The grasslands where this climate occurs are the Prairies of Canada and USA, the Steppes of Russia, Pampas of South America, Downs of Australia and Veldt of South Africa.

(f) Monsoon Climate: The areas which receives rain in summer due to monsoon, show this type of climate. It is characterised by three seasons — the cold season with a little rain from November to February, the summer from March to June and finally rainy season from late June to October. The summers are hot. The climate is prevalent in northern hemisphere around the Indian ocean area like India, Myanmar etc. North-West Australia and parts of the Africa also show the climate.

(g) Cold Forest Climate: The summers are cool and winter are colder with moisture coming down as snow and not as rain. The area is known for coniferous trees, and occurs in Northern parts of America, Europe and Asia.

(h) Tropical Climate: This climate is found on either side of the equatorial belt and is well developed in Africa. Rainfall is heavier during summer and winter remains dry.

(i) Alpine Climate: The climate has been named after the mountain chain of Europe, the Alps. The climate changes as the height of mountain increases and becomes colder. Due to low density of air, the climate is different from other snow bound areas of Arctic or Antarctica.

(j) Arctic Climate: The winters here are very long and very cold. The summers are very short. The climate is prevalent in the Arctic and Antarctica circles.

On the South and North poles, permanent ice and snow exists and these are called Polar Caps. They receive very little sunlight. During winter, no sunlight touches either pole while in summer, much of the light reaching the poles is reflected into space by the glare of the snow. The North Pole lies on a frozen sea, the Arctic Ocean while the South Pole sits upon the continent of Antarctica, covered by a layer of ice and snow at least a mile deep.

Indian Geography

India, the largest country in the Indian sub-continent, lies in South Asia between latitude 8°4' north and 37°6' north and from longitude 68°7' east to 97°25' east. The Tropic of Cancer passes right through the centre cutting the country into two halves. The territories of India's mainland extend for 3,214 km between the extremes of north and south and 2,933 km in east-west extreme point. The total length of the mainland coastline is nearly 6,100 km and the land frontier about 15,200 km. With an area of about 32,87,263 sq. km, India is the seventh largest country in the world accounting for about 2.4% of total world area.

India's neighbours in the north are China, Nepal and Bhutan, in the East are Myanmar, Bangladesh, in the West is Pakistan and in the South is Sri Lanka. Indian states bordering with Pakistan are Jammu and Kashmir, Punjab, Rajasthan and Gujarat and with Bangladesh are West Bengal, Assam, Meghalaya and Tripura.

PHYSICAL FEATURES

The Himalayas form India's northern boundary beyond which lie China, Nepal and Bhutan, which also border India in the north and north-east covering a portion of Himalayan region. A series of mountain ranges in the east separates India from Myanmar. In the East, lies Bangladesh bounded by the Indian States of West Bengal, Assam, Meghalaya, Tripura and Mizoram. In the north-west, Pakistan and Afghanistan border on India. In the South, the Gulf of Mannar and the Palk Strait separate India from Sri Lanka. The Andaman and Nicobar Islands in the Bay of Bengal and the Lakshadweep Islands in the Arabian Sea are parts of the territory of India. India can be divided into three natural region:

The Himalayas

The Himalayas are one of the youngest mountain ranges in the world. They form the northern boundary of India, extending from Jammu and Kashmir in the west to Assam, Manipur and Mizoram in the east. The total length of this chain is about 5000 km of which about 2500 km stretches in the form of an arc along the border. The Himalayas comprise a number of almost parallel ranges. The main range rises to an average elevation of 6000 meter above mean sea level. This is the birth place of multitude of glaciers some of which are among the longest in the world. These are called Himadri or Greater Himalayas. The average height is 6,100 metres above mean sea level. It is snow-bound throughout the year. It contains the world's highest peaks, e.g., Mt Everest (8,848 m), Kanchenjunga (8,598 m), Dhaulagiri (8,166 m) and Nanga Parbat (8,126 m).

These ranges have passes through them which are sometimes blocked by ice. Some important passes are Zojila in Ladakh, Bara Lacha La and Shipki La in Himachal Pradesh, Thag La and Lipu Lekh pass in Uttarakhand and Jelep La in Sikkim. The lesser Himalaya lying south of the main range is the middle range with an average height between 2600 and 4600 m. The lesser Himalaya does not support any glaciers, as its altitude is below the snowline. They have a width of 60 to 80 km. They are known as the Himachal range and have numerous hill stations like Nainital, Mussoorie, Ranikhet etc. Pir Panjal is the most important range of lesser Himalayas. The outer Himalaya comprises the mountain range that lies between the lesser Himalaya and the plain of India. It has an average elevation of 1000-1300 meters. These are also called Siwaliks, with width varying from 50 km in the west and 15 km in the east. They are made up mostly of tertiary sediments brought by various rivers.

North of the main range lies the Trans-Himalayas or Tibet-Himalayas. This range acts as a watershed between rivers flowing to the north and those flowing to the south. There are also some minor ranges in the

Himalayan System. They include the Karakoram (highest Peak — K2) and Zanskar ranges in the west and the Pathkoi, Lushai and Garo ranges in the east.

Aravalli range in the north-western India is one of the oldest mountain system in the world. The present Aravalli range is only a remnant of the gigantic system that existed in prehistoric times with several of its summits rising above the snowline and nourishing glaciers of stupendous magnitude which in turn fed many great rivers.

The Punjab Himalayas extended over 562 km between rivers Indus and Sutlej. The Kumaun Himalayas extend further east for 320 km from the Sutlej to river Kali. The Nepal Himalayas cover a distance of about 800 km from the river Kali to river Teesta. The highest peaks of the Himalayas extend east of the Teesta up to the Brahmaputra over about 750 km.

The Plain of Ganga

This plain is about 2400 km in length and 240 to 320 km broad and formed by the basin of three distinct river systems the Indus, the Ganga and the Brahmaputra. These rivers have deposited soil which originates due to friction with the mountains. They include an area of 7 lakh square km, one of the largest among the plains of the world. They are widest in Punjab-Haryana and narrowest in Bihar. The older alluvium deposited higher than the level of flood plain is called bhangar whereas the newer alluvium forming the flood plain is called Khadar. It extends from West-Bengal to Punjab. They are one of the most *densely* populated area on the earth. Soil is very fertile and climate very healthy. This plain is very productive.

The Peninsular Plateau

The peninsular plateau is the name given to the area spreading south of the Indo-Gangetic plain and flanked by sea on three sides. The Deccan plateau is shaped like a triangle with its base in the north. The River Narmada, which flows through a rift valley, divides the region into two parts: the Malva plateau in the north and the Deccan Trap in the south. Most of the rock in the plateau region are very old and are of igneous type.

The Peninsular Deccan Plateau from the Vindhya mountain to Cape Comorin, is a table land 300 to 1000 meters above sea level. It resembles a triangle in shape with the Eastern Ghat and the Western Ghats as the two sides of the triangle. It is uneven and rocky. The Mahanadi, Godavari, Krishna, Narmada and Tapti are the chief rivers.

The western ghats or Sahyadris are a continuous chain of range that commence in Maharashtra and run parallel to the west coast upto Kanyakumari. The continuity is disturbed by a few gaps. Dodabetta peak (2,637 m) in Tamil Nadu is the largest in western ghats. The eastern ghats form a chain of a discontinuous range broken up by numerous river valleys and called by different names in different area. They are Nallamalla hills and Palkonda hills in Andhra Pradesh; Javadi hills, Pachimalai, Gondumalai and Bilgiri range hills in Tamil Nadu.

The Western Ghats are connected to the Eastern Ghats by the Nilgiri Hills. South of these are the Annamalai which are separated from the former by the Palghat Pass. Two branches of the Annamalai Hills are known as the Palani Hills and the Yelagiri Hills. Many rivers of the Western Ghats make waterfalls. The Sivasamudram Fall, the Gokak Fall and the Mahatma Gandhi Fall are important waterfalls in this area.

Coastal Plains

In between the ghats and coasts on eastern as well as western side, there exists plains. The western plains are narrower than the eastern plains. The eastern coastal plain consists of river deltas formed by Mahanadi, Godavari, Krishna and Cauvery interspersed with the lakes, namely Chilka (between Godavari and Mahanadi), Kolleru (Godavari and Krishna) and Pulicat (North of Chennai). The western plains are formed by alluvial plains in Gujarat which continues as Konkan plains in the south. The comparatively narrow plains in Kerala has numerous lagoons and splits along it. A lagoon is a shallow stretch of water which is partly or completely separated from the sea by a narrow strip of land and a split is a narrow low lying area of sand.

Besides, there are 247 Indian islands of which 204 lie in the Bay of Bengal and remaining in the Arabian sea. The western islands are called Lakshdweeps and eastern ones are Andamans and Nicobars.

RIVER SYSTEMS

The Himalayan Rivers

The great river water system of Northern India are Indus, Ganga and Brahmputra. The most important river system is the Indus system. The Rivers Indus dominates this system and is joined by the rivers Shyoke, Shigar and Gilgit in Jammu and Kashmir. The important tributaries, including the Jhelum, Chenab, Ravi, Beas and Sutlej join it after entering Pakistan. The second major system is of the Ganga river. The Ganga, the head stream is constituted of two major rivers — Bhagirathi and Alaknanda, which combine at Dev Prayag to form the Ganga. The Yamuna which joins the Ganga at Allahabad, is the major tributary. Other tributaries of Ganga include Ghaghara, Sone, Gandak, Kosi and Damodar. The important tributaries of the Yamuna include the

Chambal, Betwa and Ken. The Brahmaputra is the third major system in the north. The head stream of the Brahmaputra rises in Tibet, where it is called Tsangpo, and enters Indian territory under the name of Dihang. The Subansiri, Kameng, Dharsiri, Manas and Teesta are the major rivers, joining it from the north and Bushi, Dihing, Disang and Kopoli join it from the south. The Lohit is also an important tributary of the Brahmaputra.

The Deccan Rivers

The rivers of the Deccan are different from those of Northern India. They rise in the hills of the plateau and are fed only by monsoon rains. The most important of these rivers are Mahanadi, Godawari, Krishna and Cauvery. They become dry when there are no monsoon rain. Mahanadi, Godavari, Krishna and Cauvery are east flowing rivers and form large deltas before getting merged in the sea. On the other hand, the west flowing rivers — Narmada, Tapti and Sarasvati run through valleys and form estuaries instead of deltas.

CLIMATE

India is nearer to the Equator and its position at the head of the Indian Ocean are two main factors that influence the climate. On the whole, the Climate of India is of the monsoon type and India is termed as a monsoon country, the climate is far from uniform, with variations being spatial as well as temporal. At one extreme are the highly humid areas in the north-east, where total amount of rainfall exceeds 1000 cm. At the other extreme are areas like the Thar Desert and the cold desert area in the Laddakh region which receive less than 10 cm of precipitation most years. Likewise, the higher reaches of the Himalayas are characterised by very low temperatures while areas in central and southern India touch very high temperature in summer. The climate is also determined by latitude of place. The tropic of cancer divides the country into two, the temperate half in the north and tropical half in the south. Himalayas play an important role in climate determination by acting as meteorological barrier. They give the country tropical character by maintaining high temperature uniformly throughout the year. They block the South-West monsoon and bring about rainfall.

An important feature of the monsoon is the complete reversal of winds which leads to the alternation of seasons. On the basis of monsoon variations, the year is divided into four seasons which are more observable in northern parts of the country.

(*i*) Winter season — December to February
(*ii*) Summer season — March to May
(*iii*) Rainy season — June to September
(*iv*) Autumn season — October to November

The Winter season, starts in December and the cold weather season becomes fully established in January and the temperature distribution over India shows a marked decline as one moves from south to north. The days are bright and sunny, however occasionally disturbed by the western disturbances which bring light rainfall and severe cold waves.

The Summer season comes between March and May with rising temperatures and decreasing air pressure as the belt of intense heat shift from south to north. By the end of May, low pressure trough is developed which occasionally attracts the moisture laden winds, while coming into contact with the hot dryland winds which cause pre-monsoon rains.

The Rainy season comes by early June. The low pressure area over north-western plains becomes highly intense to attract the south-west rain bearing winds which approach suddenly with thunder and lightning. Within almost one month time, these winds over-run almost the entire country. The south-west monsoons originate from the Indian ocean and blow over the land mass of India from June to September. Due to the intense summer heat a low pressure area is formed the northern plains of India. But the oceanic region has a low temperature and a high pressure centre. Consequently, air starts moving from the high pressure area of the Indian ocean towards the low pressure area over the land mass of India in the form of rain bearing monsoon winds.

The Autumn season starts by mid September leaving the land moist and the atmosphere humid. The weather during this season is characterised by the high day temperature, clear sky and pleasant nights.

Climatic Regions of India

India has several climatic regions:

(a) ***Tropical rain forest:*** This type of climate is found in the West Coastal Plains, on western ghats and in Assam. The temperatures are high throughout the year. South-West monsoon bring heavy rains and squally winds. Dense forests, tea and coffee plantations and spices are grown in the region.

(b) ***Tropical Savanna:*** This type of climate is found in Peninsula except in the leeside of the Sahyadris. It is marked by long dry weather in winter and early summer. The temperature is high even during winter and goes up in summer. The rainfall varies from 75 to 160 cm, mostly received from south-west monsoon except in Tamil Nadu. A variety of crops are raised.

(c) ***Tropical Semi-arid Steppe:*** This type of climate is found in the rain shadow belt from Maharashtra to Tamil Nadu on the leeside of the western ghats and Cardamom hills. The rainfall is scanty, usually less than 75 cm. High average temperatures are recorded. The region is suitable only for dry farming and livestock rearing though it also suffers from recurring droughts.

(d) ***Tropical and Sub-tropical Steppe:*** This type of climate is found in area stretching from Punjab to Kutch, forming the transition from the humid Ganga plains in the east and Thar desert in the west. The rainfall varies from 30 to 63 cm. The temperature varies from about 10ºC in winter to around 40ºC in summer. Scanty and low rainfall in the region permits only dry farming besides cattle and sheep rearing.

(e) ***Tropical desert:*** Western part of Rajasthan and a large region of Kutch in Gujarat form Thar desert which experiences tropical desert climate. The average rainfall is about 30 cm which occurs in the form of cloud bursts between July and September. High temperatures are recorded during summers with hot, dry winds blowing throughout the day. Winters are cold with temperatures going below freezing point. Dry farming and cattle rearing are common in the area.

(f) ***Humid Sub-tropical with dry weather:*** This type of climate is found in areas south of Himalayas from Punjab to Assam and in east of Aravalli ranges. The annual rainfall in the area varies from 60 cm in the west to more than 250 cm in the east. Rainfall is received during south-west monsoon season. Winters are cold and dry while summers are hot. As the temperature and rainfall changes, the crop variation is large.

(g) ***Mountain climate:*** The mountains, at 6,000 m above sea level, expe-rience this type of climate. The climate is dry and cold. As we go eastwards, the rainfall increases. On the southern slopes, there is heavy rainfall and temperature here is comparatively large due to protection from chilly winds coming north. In places like Laddakh, where south-west monsoon winds fail to reach, vegetation is sparse and stunted. Dense forests exist in lower slopes of the Himachal and Siwaliks range.

Monsoon in India

Monsoons are periodic winds which blow from sea to land for six months in summer and from land to sea for six months in winter. Monsoon winds prevail over India at different seasons.

(a) ***South-West Monsoon:*** These are rain-bearing winds prevailing from end-May to the end of September. During summer, the sun's rays fall vertically on the Tropic of Cancer making the Indian Plains intensely hot but the rays fall obliquely over the Indian Ocean during the period. The land is hotter than the sea, and it causes building up of low pressure on the land and high pressure on the sea. The winds blow from high to low pressure, *i.e.*, from sea to the land. Thus, the wind is moist and when they hit a mountain the rainfall is observed. Due to rotation of the earth, the monsoon winds blowing over India deflect to the right after crossing the equator and become south-west winds. India depends on these winds mostly for rainfall. From June to September, India gets 90% of its rainfall.

(b) ***North-East Monsoon:*** As the sun moves southwards, its rays start falling vertically on Tropic of Capricorn. The air over the Indian Ocean becomes hot and light, causing low pressure zone. As the sun's rays are falling obliquely on the plains of India during the months of October to January, the air over the plains becomes cold and heavy and there is a high pressure zone. The winds blow from plains to the sea while crossing the equator, they deflect to the left and are known as north-east monsoons. They bring about 10% of total rain in India, particularly in Tamil Nadu.

SOILS

The soils of India can be classified on the basis of several criteria. Indian Agricultural Research Institute (IARI) Delhi divides soils into eight groups.

(i) **Alluvial Soil:** The largest and the most important group is alluvial soil, which cover about 24% of India's land surface. This type of soil is composed of sediments deposited by the mighty rivers in the interior parts of India and by the sea wave in the coastal areas of the country. The Great Plains of India running from Punjab to Assam possess rich alluvial soil. It is also found in Narmada and Tapti valleys in Madhya Pradesh and Orissa, Godavari valley in Andhra Pradesh and Cauvery valley in Tamil Nadu. It also occurs in the deltas of Mahanadi, Godavari, Krishna and Cauvery rivers. Alluvial soils are generally deficient in nitrogen and humus and thus need repeated use of fertilizers. Such soils are suitable for growing all types of cereals, pulses, sugarcane, vegetables, oilseeds etc.

(ii) **Black Soil:** The second major group is black soil. Ideal for the cultivation of cotton crop, it is frequently referred to as black cotton soil and covers large tracts of the Deccan plateau. This soil is also classified as Chernozem though locally known as regur soil. It covers large areas in Maharashtra, Gujarat, Madhya Pradesh, Karnataka, Andhra Pradesh and in Tamil Nadu. The black colour is due to the presence of compounds of iron and aluminium. The soil is sticky when wet and its level of fertility is well known. Possessing high moisture retention capacity, black soil does not require much irrigation.

(iii) **Red Soil:** The red soil, the third major group occurs mostly in the southern peninsula and extends up to Jhansi in the north, Kutch in the west and Rajmahal Hills in the east. This soil is made up of crystalline and metamorphic rocks and is rich in ferromagnese minerals and soluble salts but is deficient in nitrogen and humus and thus needs fertilisers. It has a light texture and a porous structure. Red soil is most suited to growth of rice, ragi, tobacco and vegetables.

(iv) **Laterite Soil:** Laterites and lateritic soil are the fourth group formed through the process of laterisation. They contain iron oxides which import a red to the soil. The soil occurs in the higher reaches of the Sahyadris, Eastern Ghats, Rajmahal Hills and other higher areas in the peninsular region. It can also be found on the lower lands in parts of Maharashtra, Karnataka and in many parts of Kerala, as well as pockets of Orissa, West Bengal and Assam Generally poor in nitrogen and mineral salts due to heavy leaching, it is suitable for rice and ragi cultivation if manured.

(v) **Forest Soil:** Forest soil is rich in organic matter and humus. It is found in the Himalayas and other mountain regions of the north, higher summit of the Sahyadris, Eastern Ghats, Karnataka, Tamil Nadu, Kerala, Manipur, Jammu and Kashmir and Himachal Pradesh. Crops like tea, coffee, spices and tropical fruits are grown on this type of soil.

(vi) **Arid and Desert Soil:** It is found in north western India. It covers the entire area west of the Aravalli's in Rajasthan and parts of Haryana, Punjab and Gujarat. It is rich in phosphates but poor in nitrogen and proves quite fertile if irrigated.

(vii) **Saline and Alkaline Soil:** Soils in many parts of the arid and semi-arid areas of Rajasthan, Punjab, Haryana and Uttar Pradesh. Bihar have saline and alkaline effervescences mainly of sodium, calcium and magnesium. These soil are called reh or kallar or usar and are infertile. The salts are usually confined to the upper layers and soil can be reclaimed by improving drainage.

(viii) **Peaty and other Organic Soils:** Peaty soils contain large accumulations of humus, organic matter and soluble salts. These soils are highly saline and are deficient phosphorus and potash. Marshy soil occurs in regions of Orissa, West-Bengal and Tamil Nadu. They are also found in central and north Bihar and in Almora district of U.P.

NATURAL VEGETATION IN INDIA

The natural vegetation in India is largely of tropical type but there is a variation with respect to species and growth of plants, due to changes in temperature and rainfall condition. Variation in soil gives rise to variation in forests. The forest cover in India has been on decline because of clearing for the purpose of cultivation and industrialisation. Forests are unequally distributed in the country, with Punjab, Haryana, Rajasthan and Gujarat having less than 10 per cent of forest coverage. The low coverage here is primarily due to scanty rainfall. The natural vegetation is of following types:

1. ***Tropical Wet Evergreen and Semi-Evergreen Forests:*** They are found where the rainfall is more than 250 cm. Such forests exist in Assam, North-Eastern States, Andaman and Nicobar Islands and the West Coast. These forests provide timber, firewood and bamboo. The products of tropical evergreen forests are used in paper and match factories, plywood and tea processing industries. Due to dense nature of these forests, transport facility is problem, thereby protecting the wealth from exploitation. Timber varieties are Ebony, Paan, Ironwood, and Rosewood.

2. ***Tropical Moist and Dry Deciduous Forests:*** The deciduous forests are also called monsoon forests. They are found between the Himalayas, the Thar and the Western Ghats. They grow in areas with a rainfall of 100 to 200 cm annually. They are economically most important as commercially valuable species are grown here in large number. They can be exploited easily. The important trees are Sal, Teak, Sandalwood, Shisham, Mahua, Khair. The moist deciduous forests grow in Orissa, eastern Madhya Pradesh, Chhota Nagpur plateau and a strip along the Siwaliks where rainfall is large. The trees are large sized with a denser undergrowth than in wet evergreen forests. They shed their leaves during spring and early summer. Dry deciduous forests occur in area with rainfall 100 to 150 cm. The variety of trees is almost the same as the moist one but the growth is stunted and trees are widely spaced.

3. ***Tidal Forests:*** They occur along the seaward fringes, channels and islands of the deltas of Ganga, Mahanadi, Godavari and Krishna. The Sunderbans delta is known for tidal forests. The trees are used to growth in mud and silt. The water may be fresh or brackish. Mangrove, Sundari, Pines, Cane and Palms are the common varieties of tidal forests.
4. ***Tropical Dry Evergreen Forests:*** They are found in coastal Tamil Nadu where retreating monsoon gives about 100 cm of rainfall.
5. ***Tropical Thorn Forests:*** They are found in the north and north-western parts of the country and on the beside of the Sahyadris. The rainfall is about 75 cm. The vegetation is of open stunted nature degenerating into desert type in the Thar desert. Khair, Babul, Neem, Pipal and Khardhari are some important trees.
6. ***Montane Sub-tropical and Temperate Types:*** They occur mostly on the hills of South India. Wet hill forests are found in Nilgiri and Palani hills at a height of 1000 to 1500 metres while wet temperature forests are found above 1500 m on these hills. Magnolia, Laurel, Elm, Cinchona, Wattle and Eucalyptus are common trees.
7. ***Vegetation in the Himalayan Region:*** The vegetation on the Himalayas vary with the altitude and temperature. Wet hill forests comprise dense and high trees and are found in the eastern Himalayas at a height of 1000 to 2000 metre. Evergreen oak, Chestnut, and beech grow in these forests. Sub-tropical pine forests grow in western Himalayas at a height of 1000 to 2000 metre. Chir, a variety of pine is common here which is used for making railway sleepers and construction work. Sub-tropical dry evergreen forests appear in the Himalayan foothills of Kashmir where the rainfall is between 50 and 100 cm. Wild olives and acacia are important species of the region. Moist temperate forests cover the range where the rainfall is 100 to 250 cm and altitude 1500 to 3700 metre. Oak, Laurel, Chestnut, Pine, Cedar, Silverfir, Spruce and Deodar are common trees. In the dry temperate forests, the rainfall is less than 100 cm and trees commonly grown are Deodar, Birch, Oak, and Elm. In the Himalayas between 2800 and 3600 m, a dense and stunted growth of Silver fir, Juniper, Pine and Birch is found. The dwarfish growth gives the trees a shrubby appearance. They are called Alpine forests.

WILDLIFE SANCTUARIES AND NATIONAL PARKS

India is rich in flora and fauna. However, due to increasing population and industrial and commercial activities, there has been acute pressure on forests. The Government has taken several steps to check the sharp fall in the number of these species. Among the measures are declaration of certain habitats as national parks and sanctuaries. 106 national parks and 573 sanctuaries have been established till June 2025, important ones being given below:

Assam: Kaziranga National Park (know for one-horn Rhinoceroses); Manas Sanctuary.

Jharkhand: Hazaribagh National Park; Palamau Reserve.

Gujarat: Valvadar National Park, Bhavnagar; Marine National Park, Gulf of Kutch; Gir Forests.

Himachal Pradesh: Rohla National Park; Motichur Sanctuary.

Jammu & Kashmir: Dachigam Sanctuary.

Karnataka: Bandipur National Park; Bannargheta National Park, Bangalore; Nagorhole National Park, Coorg; Ranganthitto Bird Sanctuary.

Kerala: Eravikulam Rajmallay National Park, Idduki; Periyar Game Sanc-tuary.

Madhya Pradesh: Kanha National Park; Bandhavgarh National Park, Shahdol; Shivpuri National Park.

Maharashtra: Taloba National Park, Chandrapur; Panch National Park, Nagpur; Borivali National Park, Mumbai; Nawagaon National Park, Bandara; Melghat National Park.

Manipur: Reibul Lamjao National Park.

Odisha: Simlipal.

Rajasthan: Sarsika Sanctuary; Ghana Bird Sanctuary, Bharatpur.

Sikkim: Khangchandzenda National Park, Gangtok.

Tamil Nadu: Vedanthangal Bird Sanctuary; Guindy National Park, Chennai; Mudumalai Sanctuary; Kalakad-Munden Thurai Reserve.

Uttar Pradesh: Chandraprabha Sanctuary; Dudhwa National Park, Lakhimpur.

West Bengal: Jaldapara Sanctuary; Sunderbans.

Uttarakhand: Corbett National Park; Nainital

A 'National Park' is a relatively large area of land kept by the national government for its people to enjoy, because of its natural beauty. They are given the status by their law making bodies. Forestry, settlement or trespassing are not allowed. They protect the entire ecosystem.

A 'Wild Life Sanctuary' is a place for preservation and protection of animals and plants in the natural state. Forestry activities are permitted and human settlements for original inhabitants or tribal people is allowed.

A 'Game Sanctuary' is a place for protecting wild animals and birds that are hunted or caught for sport or for food. These resorts are developed to prevent poaching, stealing and hunting without permission.

Biosphere reserves

They are multi-purpose protected areas to preserve the genetic diversity in representative eco-systems. The major objectives of setting up these reserves are to conserve diversity and integrity of plants, animals and micro-organisms; to promote research on ecological conservation and other environmental aspects; and to provide facilities for education, awareness and training. So far, 18 biosphere reserves have been set up, Important are—(1) Nilgiri; (2) Nanda Devi; (3) Nokrek; (4) Great Nicobar; (5) Gulf of Mannar; (6) Manas; (7) Sunderbans; and (8) Similipal.

Project Tiger

This is one of the premier conservation efforts of the country that was taken up in 1973 to protect one of the magnificient species of the land. Under the scheme, 58 Tiger Reserves are notified all over the country to provide natural environment to the animal and rule out poaching. A Global Tiger Forum has been set up for Tiger range countries and India playing a lead role has hosted its interim secretariat.

After success of Project Tiger, Project Elephant was taken up to ensure long-term survival of identified viable populations of elephants in their natural habitats.

AGRICULTURE IN INDIA

"Agriculture is the art or technique of raising plant life from the soil for the use of mankind. The object of agriculture is to raise and fruitful crops and plants".

Agriculture is the mainstay of the people of India; about 49 per cent of the people of India are dependent upon it

Agricultural crops of India may be divided into food crops and non-food crops.

Food Crops

- **Rice:** It is the chief food crop of India. The chief rice-growing states are West-Bengal, U.P., Punjab, Andhra Pradesh, Tamil Nadu and Bihar. It is also grown in several other parts of India. Due to Japanese method of rice cultivation the production of rice has increased, but even then India is not anywhere near the world productivity. Rice is grown in areas where abundant water is available. Northern states of Punjab and Haryana took up rice cultivation after the establishment of irrigation facilities.
- **Wheat:** It is second in importance to rice in India. It is the staple food of the people of Punjab, Haryana and U.P. It is largely grown in U.P., M.P., Punjab, Haryana and Rajasthan. Total area under wheat in the Indian Union is over 10 million hectares. A new type of Mexican wheat has been introduced and this has led to increased yield (four to five times) per acre. Punjab and Haryana have increased their wheat production considerably on account of better seeds what is grown during the winter season.
- **Millets (Jowar and Bajra):** It is largely grown in Tamil Nadu, Maharashtra, Gujarat, M.P., U.P., Haryana and the dry areas of Andhra Pradesh. It forms the staple food of the poor. It thrives best in hot and dry climate with moderate rainfall at intervals.
- **Barley:** It is used as food grain and also for preparing beer. The main barley growing states are U.P., Punjab and Haryana.
- **Maize:** It grows more or less all over India but chiefly in Karnataka, Madhya Pradesh, Andhra Pradesh, Bihar, U.P., Punjab, Rajasthan, Maharashtra and Gujarat.
- **Pulses:** They are grown in different parts of India, especially in M.P., Maharashtra, Punjab, U.P., West Bengal, and Gujarat. At present over 30 million hectares are used for growing pulses and gram in the Indian Union, and the total yield is about 26.06 million tons. The per capita availability of pulses has been gradually declining on account of the serious shortfalls in production.
- **Sugarcane:** India is one of the biggest cane producing country in the world. It is grown nearly in all the states of the Indian Union, but mostly in U.P., Maharashtra, Karnataka, Bihar and A.P. Production of sugar in India has been fluctuating very widely from year to year. As on 31st August, 2024 there were more than 700 installed sugar factories in the country against 138 during 1950-51. In 2023-24 the sugarcane production was 453.2 million tonnes. India has to import sugar in some years on account of a shortfall in production, while in some years, we are in search of export markets, when the production suddenly jumps to dizzy heights. Sugar industry is the second important industry of India, textile being the first.

Non-Food Crops or Cash Crops

- **Tea:** India is the second largest tea producing country in the world. It is mainly grown in

Assam, West Bengal, the Nilgiris, Kerala, Dehra Dun (Uttarakhand) and Kangra Valley. At present, India supplies more than 40 per cent of the world's trade in tea.

- **Coffee:** It requires a warm moist climate, and height of 1500 ft. to 2500 ft. It is largely grown in Karnataka, Kerala and Tamil Nadu. Half the annual production of coffee is consumed in India and the other half is exported to U.K., Germany, Holland, Belgium, Australia and Iraq. Coffee is gradually emerging as one of our major exchange earners.
- **Tobacco:** India occupies a dominant place as a tobacco producing country in the world; U.S.A. comes first. It is mainly produced in A.P., Bihar, U.P., Tamil Nadu, Karnataka, Maharashtra, Gujarat and in some parts of Punjab.
- **Oilseeds:** India is one of the biggest oilseed producing countries. They are grown chiefly in Rajasthan, M.P., Gujarat, Bihar, Odisha, U.P., Maharashtra, Andhra Pradesh and Punjab. There is an acute shortage of edible oils in India.
- **Cotton:** Maharashtra, Gujarat, M.P., Tamil Nadu and Andhra Pradesh are the chief producers. Before the partition, India was self-sufficient in cotton and exported a part of it. But after the partition, it had to import cotton to meet the growing requirements of the textiles mills.
- **Jute:** It is chiefly grown in West Bengal, Assam, Bihar, Odisha and some parts of U.P., India is almost self-sufficient in the production of raw jute; Bangladesh is the largest exporter of raw jute. The jute mills are mostly situated near Kolkata.
- **Rubber:** It is mainly grown in Tamil Nadu, Karnataka and Kerala. Indian Union produces nearly 7,00,000 tons annualy. Rubber industry is fast developing in this country. Kerala produces 95% of rubber in India. Production of rubber has been undertaken in Tripura and the results have been encouraging.
- **Silk:** In India, silk is produced in Karnataka, West Bengal, Bihar, Assam and Kashmir. The silkworm is fed on mulberry leaves, or on the leaves of castor plant and it produces cocoons which, when boiled, give us the silk thread.
- **Hemp:** Russia is the largest producer of hemp (a type of fibre); Italy, the U.S.A., India and China come next.
- **Wool:** It is obtained from the hilly tracts of Punjab, U.P., and Kashmir and also from Tamil Nadu and Rajasthan; Kalimpong (Bengal) is a main wool collecting centre.
- **Coconut:** Production of coconut in India comes from Karnataka, Kerala, Maharashtra, Gujarat and Tamil Nadu.

MINERALS

Nature has been very kind to India in term of endowment of mineral resources. Of the various minerals found in India, the most important are coal, manganese, ilmenite, mica, iron ore and salt. India is the world's main source of supply of manganese, mica, monazite and zircon.

- **Coal & Lignites:** Coal is our largest available mineral resource and presently India ranks third in the world after China and USA in the realm of coal production. The main centres of coal in India are the West Bengal-Jharkhand region, Madhya Pradesh, Maharashtra, Odisha and Andhra regions. Bulk of the coal production comes from Bengal-Jharkhand coal fields. They contribute 60 to 65% of the total production. The total known geological reserves of all types of coal in gondwana and tertiary coal-fields stands estimated at 378.21 billion tonnes as on April 1, 2023. The reserves of lignite has been estimated at around 47.37 billion tonnes April 2023 out of which the major contributor is the lignite basins of Tamil Nadu.
- **Fluorspar:** The total resources of fluorite in the country is estimated at 18.2 million tonnes. This mineral is mainly available in Gujarat, Chhattisgarh, Rajasthan and Maharashtra. The total resources of fluorspar is about 18.2 million tonnes.
- **Manganese:** Its maximum deposit is found in Karnataka. Besides, Odisha, Maharastra and Goa also possess relatively larger deposits of manganese. Some deposits are also found in Andhra Pradesh, Jharkhand, Rajasthan, Gujarat and West Bengal.
- **Copper:** Singhbhum Copper Belt (Jharkhand); Darjeeling (West Bengal), Agnigundla (Andhra Pradesh) and Khetri (Rajasthan) and Malanjkhand (M.P.) are known for copper deposits.
- **Gold:** Kolar goldfields are in the state of Karnataka. These mines were nationalised in 1956. Gold deposits have been located in Chittoor and Anantapur districts of Andhra Pradesh.
- **Mica:** The important mica bearing pegmatite occurs in Andhra Pradesh, Jharkhand, Bihar, Rajasthan. The total reserves of the mica in the country are placed at 5,32,237 tonnes.

Its maximum deposit is found in Andhra Pradesh, Rajasthan and Jharkhand.

- **Ilmenite:** India is its largest producer. It is the whitest of all substances; it is found in the 'black sand' on the beaches near Cape Comorin, the southernmost point of India.
- **Petroleum:** Digboi, Badarpur, Masimpur and Palhara fields of Assam, Ankleshwar, Moran, Mumbai High and Palanpur (Gujarat).
- Drilling was carried on in Jawalamukhi (Punjab) but only natural gas deposits were found. It was also carried on in Jaisalmer (Rajasthan) for the exploration of oil and natural gas. Oil has been struck at Cambay, Ankaleshwar and Kalol (Gujarat), Naharkatiya, Rudrasagar, Sibsagar and Moran (Assam). Efforts are being made to locate oil in the offshore region of the Gulf of Cambay. Sagar Samrat, a big ship equipped with drilling machinery, has been purchased from Japan for this purpose. In February, 1974, vast deposits of oil and natural gas were located at Mumbai High. Oil is likely to be found in Bakultala in West Bengal, Tripura and Arunachal Pradesh.
- **Refining:** The present refining capacity in the country as on 1st April, 2024 was 256.8 Million Metric Tonnes Per Annum (MMTPA). Out of 22 refineries operating in the country, 18 are in public sector, 3 are in private sector and one is in JV (Joint venture) of Public Sector. Out of 18 Public Sector refineries, 9 are owned by Indian Oil Corporation Ltd. (IOCL), 2 each by Chennai Petroleum Corporation Limited (a subsidiary of IOCL), Hindustan Petroleum Corporation Limited (HPCL), Bharat Petroleum Corporation Limited (BPCL) and Oil & Natural Gas Corporation Limited (ONGC). Numaligarh Refinery Limited (a subsidiary of BPCL) and Mangalore Refinery & Petrochemicals Limited have one each.
- **Iron:** India has a very high grade iron ore. These ores are available in Odisha (Keonjhar, Talcher, Bonai and Mayurbhanj), Jharkhand (Singbhum district), Chhattisgarh, Madhya Pradesh, Karnataka and Maharashtra. India is the second largest producer of crude steel only after China. India is also the second largest consumer of steel. However, its per capita total finished steel consumption was around 74.7 kg during FY20 as against the global average of 229 kg. Further, the capacity utilization in crude steel plants continues to be low. Kudremukh iron ore deposits were developed primarily for export to Iron.
- **Salt:** It is obtained from the Sambhar Lake (Rajasthan). It is also obtained by the evaporation of sea water, especially near Kutch, Tamil Nadu, Mumbai, Kathiawar Coasts of India. Rock Salt is found in Mandi (Himachal Pradesh). India is self-sufficient in salt; rather it export, this commodity.
- **Monazite:** Found in sandy beaches of Kerala. India supplies 88% of world needs. Due to its thorium content, it is used for the generation of nuclear energy.
- **Bauxite:** Bauxite is a main source of metal like aluminium. India stands fifth in the world in having deposits of bauxite resources. The areas of bauxite deposits in India are : Andhra Pradesh, Jharkhand, Goa, Gujarat, J&K, Karnataka, Kerala, Madhya Pradesh, Maharashtra, Odisha, Rajasthan, Tamil Nadu and Uttar Pradesh. Major reserves are concentrated in the East Coast bauxite deposits of Odisha and Andhra Pradesh.
- **Silver:** A small quantity of silver is obtained from Kolar mines (Karnataka) and also from Manbhum (Jharkhand).
- **Gypsum:** Most of its deposits are found in Rajasthan, Tamil Nadu, Jammu & Kashmir, Himachal Pradesh and Uttar Pradesh. Some deposits are also found in Gujarat. Rajasthan is the main producer of Gypsum followed by Jammu & Kashmir.
- **Graphite:** Jammu & Kashmir, Jharkhand, Madhya Pradesh and Tamil Nadu. Odisha is the main producing state of graphite.
- **Magnesite:** Uttarakhand, Tamil Nadu, Karnataka and Rajasthan.
- **Zinc:** It is obtained from Zawar mines near Udaipur (Rajasthan), Maharashtra
- **Asbestos:** It is extensively used in the manufacture of special type of cement, for lining in the automobile industry and for heat insulation. Deposits occur in Andhra Pradesh, Jharkhand and Karnataka.
- **Minerals for Atomic Energy — Uranium:** At present the minerals containing uranium are used for the generation of atomic energy. Uranium is chiefly mined in Zaire. In India Uranium is found in Jharkhand (Jaduguda mines).
- **Thorium:** It is the potential atomic fuel of the future. The chief ore of thorium is the mineral monazite, which occurs in the sands on Kerala and Tamil Nadu coast.
- **Beryllium:** Though not radioactive, it is of great importance in the atomic energy development because of its property of slowing down neutrons without absorbing them. It is thus extensively used as a moderator in atomic piles. The deposits in India are in Rajasthan, Jharkhand and Andhra Pradesh.
- **Kyanite:** It is used in ceramic industries. The deposits are found in Singbhum district (Jharkhand), Mayurbhanj district (Odisha) and Nellore district (Andhra).

- **Zircon:** The rare metal is used in atomic energy and in alloy metallurgy. It is found in the beach sands on Malabar and Coromandel coasts.
- **White Marble:** Obtained from Makrana mines (Rajasthan) and from Jabalpur (M.P.).
- **Diamonds:** Available in Kimberley mines (South Africa), Ghana and Congo. In India, diamonds are available in Panna mines (M.P.). India has produced some famous historical diamonds like the Kohinoor.

INDUSTRIES

- **Cotton Textile Industry:** The origin of the cotton textile industry, the largest single industry in the country, dates back to 1818 when the first cotton mill was established at Fort Gloster near Kolkata. There are now over 800 mills in the country — and over 24 lakh looms. Maharashtra, Gujarat, Tamil Nadu, U.P., West Bengal, M.P., Karnataka, Kerala and Delhi are the chief centres of this industry.

  Mumbai is especially suited for this industry because of: (1) Abundant supply of raw materials. (2) Black soil of Mumbai is good for cotton. (3) A large supply of cheap labour. (4) Cheap electric power is available. (5) There is a good harbour to export the textiles. (6) Climate is moist.

  South India (Coimbatore, Madurai and Chennai); Madhya Pradesh (Akola has a number of cotton mills) and Delhi specialise in the production of coarse cloth.
- **Jute Industry:** Raw Jute was almost the monopoly of Bangladesh for few years, but now, India is providing raw jute from West Bengal, Bihar, Assam, Orissa and U.P. Most of the requirements of jute mills are met by local production.

  Almost all the jute mills are concentrated in Calcutta. The reasons are that (i) the soil of Bengal is suitable for jute; (ii) availability of coal; (iii) a large supply of cheap labour and water required for the Industry; (iv) the port of Calcutta can easily export all the jute goods.
- **Sugar Industry:** The sugar industry ranks second amongst the major agro-industries in India. Dual pricing has been introduced for sugar. Under this policy, 65 per cent of the total production of the factories is procured by government as levy sugar at controlled prices and the balance 35 per cent is allowed to be sold in the open market without any price control. U.P., and Bihar are regarded as sugar belts — Kanpur, Gorakhpur, Lucknow, Bareilly (U.P.), Champaran, Muzaffarpur, Bhagalpur and Dalmianagar (Bihar). Other sugar centres are Coimbatore in Tamil Nadu and Amritsar and Phagwara in the Punjab. Sugar mills have been set up in Maharashtra also.
- **Silk Industry:** Mysore, Murshidabad and Srinagar produce raw silk. This industry is mainly confined to these area.
- **Woollen Industry:** Kanpur, Dhariwal, Mumbai, Panipat, Ludhiana.
- **Blankets:** Amritsar, Srinagar, Bangalore, Agra, Mirzapur and Kanpur.
- **Shawls:** Kashmir.
- **Iron and Steel:** Jameshdpur (Jharkhand); Burnpur (W. Bengal); Bhadrawati (Karnataka); Bhilai (Chhatisgarh); Rourkela (Orissa); Durgapur (West Bengal), Bokaro (Jharkhand); and Vishakhapatnam (A.P.). The earliest successful attempt to manufacture iron and steel by modern methods was made in the country in 1874. But the first efforts at large-scale production got underway when Tata Iron and Steel Company (TISCO) was set up at Jamshedpur in 1907. This was followed by the establishment of the Indian Iron and Steel Company (IISCO) at Burnpur in 1919. The first unit in the public sector, now known as the Visvesvaraya Iron and Steel Works Ltd., started functioning at Bhadravati in 1923.

TRANSPORTATION

Railways

The first train in India was started on a small rail route of 34 kilometres between Bombay and Thane on April 16, 1,853. Indian Railways is one of the world's largest rail networks with 69,181 Route kilometres of route lengths as on March 31, 2024. Out of this Broad Gauge (BG) constitutes 66,820 route kilometres (96.58%), Metre Gauge (MG) 1,159 route kilometres (1.67%) and Narrow Gauge (NG) 1,202 route kilometres (1.73%). Indian Railways' network is the second railways in Asia and the fourth biggest railways in the world. [US (25,0000 km); China (1,00,000 km); Russia (85,500 kms)]. About 90% (62,253 km) of the route kilometres, has been electrified. Indian railways is the world's eighth largest employer, with more than 1.190 million employees as of March 2024.

First Double-decker Train Runs on Wheel in India

India's first double-decker fully air-conditioned train has been put on the wheels. The them Railway Minister Mr. Dinesh Trivedi started it with green flag between Howrah and Dhanbad on Oct. 1, 2011. This train, having 9 coaches, consists seven double decker coaches. These coaches has been made in Kapurthala

Coach Factory. The maximum speed of this train between Howarah and Dhanbad has been fixed at 110 km per hour.

Konkan Railway Project

The Konkan Railway project consisting of the 760 km long broad gauge line from Roha (150 km south of Mumbai) to Mangalore has been completed. The construction of this line is a big technical feat as it has 1,998 bridges and 73 tunnels, with the longest tunnel and the tallest viaduct in Asia. This new line has substantially reduced the journey time between Mumbai and Mangalore, Mumbai and Cochin and Mumbai and Goa. This line will largely benefit the Konkan Region.

Uni-Gauge Project

In a bid to get rid of a multi-gauge system in favour of uniform gauge systems, Indian Railway in 1992, had decided to get rid of multi-gauge system in favour of uniform gauge systems. This is being done by gradually converting railway lines of other gauges to broad gauge in a planned manner. It has already converted more than 10,000 km of track to broad gauge in the last 10 years and work is still in progress.

Railway Zones

The network of railways is divided into zones. These zones are headed by a General Manager, who is responsible to the Railway Board for operation, maintenance and financial matters. The zones with their headquarters are as follows :

Name of the Zones		Headquarters
1. Northern Railway	–	New Delhi
2. Western Railway	–	Church gate Mumbai
3. South Central Railway	–	Secunderabad
4. South Eastern Railway	–	Kolkata
5. Central Railway	–	Mumbai CST
6. Southern Railway	–	Chennai
7. North-Eastern Railway	–	Gorakhpur
8. Eastern Railway	–	Kotkata
9. North-East Frontier Railway	–	Maligaon (Guwahati)
10. East-Central Railway	–	Hajipur
11. North Western Railway	–	Jaipur
12. East-Coast Railway	–	Bhubaneshwar
13. North-Central Railway	–	Prayagraj
14. South-Western Railway	–	Hubli
15. Western-Central Railway	–	Jabalpur
16. South-East Central Railway	–	Bilaspur
17. Kolkata Metro	–	Kolkata
18. South Coast Railway	–	Vishakhapatnam (Proposed)

Roads

The Indian road network, the largest in the world aggregating 63.45 lakh km consists of 1,46,195 km of National Highways, 1,79,535 km of State Highways and about 60,19,723 km of Other District and Rural Roads. The National Highways account for about 2.08% of the total road network but carry as much as 40% of the total road traffic in the country.

Roads are classified into six classes according to their importance : 1. Golden Quadrilateral Super Highways, 2. National Highways, 3. State Highways, 4. Border Roads, 5. Major District Roads, and 6. Rural Roads including other district roads.

1. Golden Quadrilateral Super Highways

The government has launched a major road development project linking Delhi-Kolkata-Chennai-Mumbai and Delhi by six-lane Super Highways. The North-South corridors linking Srinagar (Jammu & Kashmir) and Kanyakumari (Tamil Nadu), and East-West Corridor connecting Silcher (Assam) and Porbander (Gujarat) are part of this project. The major objective of these Super Highways is to reduce the time and distance between the mega cities of India. These highway projects are being impliemented by the National Highway Authority of India (NHAI).

2. National Highways

National Highways link extreme parts of the country. These are the primary road systems and are laid and maintained by the Central Public Works Department (CPWD). A number of major National Highways run in North-South and East-West directions. The historical Sher-Shah Suri Marg is between Delhi and Amritsar. National Highway 44 (NH44) is the longest-running major North-South National Highway in India. It starts from Srinagar and terminates in Kanyakumari.

3. State Highways

Roads linking a state capital with different district headquarters are known as State Highways. These roads are constructed and maintained by the State Public Works Department (PWD) in State and Union Territories.

Air Transport

The scheduled civil air transport in India commenced during 1929-30 when the British, French and the Dutch extended their services to and beyond India. The first internal air service was established between Karachi and Chennai via Mumbai in 1922. By the beginning of the Second World War, major cities like Karachi, Lahore, Delhi, Mumbai, Kolkata and Chennai had scheduled air services operated by private companies. At the time of independence, there were four companies. By 1951, from more private companies were operating air services. The Air Transport Enquiry Committee setup in 1950 recommended the merger of these eight companies into a corporation. Under the Air Corporation Act 1953, the Indian Airlines Corporation was set up to operate all internal civil air services and Air India International was constituted for managing international air transport.

The Governement ended the monopoly of Indian Airlines and Air India on the scheduled operations by repealing the Air Corporation Act, 1953. There are at present ten scheduled airlines operating on the domestic network rendering the passengers a wide choice of flights.

Apart from this, more than 40 companies are holding non-scheduled operators permit. The policy on domestic air transport service was approved in April 1997 according to which barriers to entry and exit from this sector have been removed.

The main trunk routes having high density of traffic are operated by Air Bus and Boeing aircraft. The remote areas are served by smaller aircraft. A third airline—Vayudoot—was incorporated as private limited company in January 1981. The Pawan Hans Limited was set up in October 1985 to provide transport services for short distances.

Airport Authority of India (AAI) provides for safe efficient air traffic and aeronautical communication services in the India Air Space.

Privatization of Air India

On January 27, 2022 the Government of India successfully handed over Air India to the Tata Group, nearly 69 years after it was taken from TATAs. The Tata Group, as part of the deal are also handed over the Air India express and a 50% stake in the ground handling arm of Air India SATS. Air India will be the third airline brand in Tata's stable as the conglomerate holds a majority interest in Air Asia India and Vistara. Tata Group chairman N. Chandrashekhar witnessed the formal transfer of the Air India to Tata Group. The Government of India on October 8, 2021 had announced the sale of the national carrier to its original developer–the salt-to-software conglomerate Tata Group at an enterprise value of ₹ 18,000 crore. This is the first major privatisation step in about two decades.

Some Important International Airports are :

Mumbai (Chhatrapati Shivaji International Airport). **Delhi** (Indira Gandhi International Airport). **Kolkata** (Subhash Chandra Bose I.A.), **Chennai** (Meenambakkam I.A.), **Trivendrum** (Thiruvananthpuram) **Ahmedabad** (Sardar Vallabh Bhai Patel Airport), **Cochin** (Needumbassery I.A.), **Goa** (Dabolim I.A.), **Guwahati** (Lokpriya Gopinath Bardoloi I.A.), **Hyderabad** (Rajiv Gandhi I.A.), **Amritsar** (Sri Guru Ram Dass Jee International Airport) **Bengaluru** (Kempegowda International Airport). Civeli Aviation Training College (Prayagraj) provides training on various operational areas.

National Institute of Aviation Management and Research (NIAMAR) at Delhi is managed by AAI.

Indira Gandhi Rastriya Udan Academy at Fursat Ganj in U.P is an autonomous body under Ministry of Civil Aviation. It imparts training.

Water Transport

India has a vast coastline of about 7,515 km and over two million sq. km of Exclusive Economic Zone (EEZ). The entire coastline is studded with 13 major ports handle about 15,000 Cargo vessels per annum. In terms of cargo handling, Mumbai is the biggest port in India.

Major Ports

There are 12 major ports and 200 minor working ports in the country. Major ports are the direct responsibility of the Central Government while minor ports including intermediate ports fall in the concurrent list of the Constitution and are managed and administered by the respective maritime state government.

Marmagaon, Kandla, Bombay, New Manglore and Cochin are the major ports on the west coast. A new major port at Nhava Sheva off Bombay is highly developed. On the east coast, Tuticorin, Chennai, Vishakhapatnam, Paradip, Ennore, and Kolkata-Haldia are the major ports.

1. **Mumbai :** It is the biggest port in the country. It is a natural harbour and handles more than one-fifth of the total traffic of the ports. The bulk of the total traffic consists of petroleum products and dry cargo.
2. **Shyama Prasad Mukherjee (Kolkata) :** It is a riverine port handling diversified commodities. It is the largest terminal port in South Asia. Haldia dock-system is a fully equipped containerised berth. Its mechanised dock system with provision for deep draft vessels downstream of Kolkata supplements the facilities already available at Kolkata port. It mainly handles coal, petroleum products and dry cargo.
3. **Kochi :** It is a natural harbour on the west coast. It largely handles petroleum products, fertilisers, raw materials and general cargo.
4. **Deendayal (Kandla) :** It is a tidal port having a free trade zone. It largely handles petroleum products and fertilizers. Foodgrains, cotton, cement and edible oils are also handled.
5. **Chennai :** It is one of the oldest ports on the east coast and caters to traffic in iron ore, petroleum products and dry cargo.
6. **New Mangaluru :** On the west coast, it was declared a major port in 1947. Facilities have been developed at this port for the export of Kudremukh iron granite stone. dry cargo is also handled at this port.

7. **Mormugao (Goa) :** It enjoys the second position in total traffic tonnage, bulk of which is iron ore for export.
8. **Paradip :** In Odisha, it mainly handles iron ore, coal and general cargo.
9. **V.O. Chidambaranar (Tuticorin) :** On the east coast, it was declared a major port in 1947. It handles mainly salt, coal, edible oils, foodgrains, fertilizers, petroleum products and dry cargo.
10. **Vishakhapatnam :** It is the deepest landlocked and protected port where an outer harbour has been developed for exporting mainly iron ore to Japan. Crude oil, petroleum products, coal and dry cargo are also handled.
11. **Jawaharlal Nehru Port (Nhava Sheva) :** Jawaharlal Nehru Port is India's biggest and most modern seaport near Mumbai. This port has large berthing facilities, latest traffic and cargo handling equipment and most modern operational techniques.
12. **Kamarajar Port Limited (Ennore) :** Kamarajar Port Limited (KPL), the 12th major port under the Ministry of Shipping was commissioned in 2001, primarily as a coal port dedicated to handling thermal coal requirements of Tamil Nadu Electricity Board (TNEB). KPL has the distinction of being the only corporate port amongst the major ports administered by the central government.

Inland Waterways

India has over 14,500 km of navigable waterways. Considering the inherent advantages of Inland Water Transport (IWT) mode namely; fuel efficiency, environment friendlines, cost effectiveness and decongestion of road and rail networks, particularly for movement to bulk goods, hazardous good and over dimensional approach. Inland Waterways Authority of India (IWAI) was set up in 1986 for regulation and development of inland waterways for the purpose of shipping and navigation. IWAI is primarily responsible for development, maintenance and regulation of national waterways.

Following five waterways have so far been declared as national waterways:

- Allahabad-Haldia stretch (1620 km) of the Ganga-Bhagirathi-Hooghly river system (NW-1) in 1986.
- Sadiya-Dhubri stretch (891 km) of Brahmaputra river (NW-2) in 1988).
- Kottapuram-Kollam stretch of West Coast Canal along with Champakara Canal and Udyogmandal Canal (205 km) (NW-3) in 1993.
- Kakinada-Puducherry stretch of Canal and Kalurelly Tank, stretches of river Godavari and Krishna (1928 km) in 2008.
- Talcher-Dhamra stretch of river Brahmani, Geonkhali Charbatia stretch of East Coast Canel, Charbatia-Dhamra stretch of Matai river along with Mahanadi delta river system (585 km) in 2008. (NW-5)
- Lakhipur to Bhanga of River Barak, NW-6, proposed in 2013, total length 121 km.

Pipelines

Pipelines transport network is a new arrival on the transportation map of India. In the past, these were used to transport water to cities and industries. Now, these are used for transporting crude oil, petroleum products and natural gas from oil and natural gas fields to refineries, fertilizer factories and big thermal power plants.

Solids can also be transported through a pipeline when converted into slurry. The far inland locations of refineries like Barauni, Mathura, Panipat and gas based fertilizer plants could be thought of only because of pipelines.

Initial cost of laying pipelines is high but subsequent running costs are minimal. It rules out trans-shipment losses or delays. There are three important network of pipeline transportation in the country.

- From oil field in upper Assam to Kanpur (Uttar Pradesh), via Guwahati, Barauni and Prayagraj. It has branches from Barauni to Haldia, via Rajbandh to Maurigram and Guwahati to Siliguri. From Salaya in Gujarat to Jalandhar in Punjab, via Viramgam, Mathura, Delhi and Sonipat. It has branches to connect Koyali (near Vododara in Gujarat) Chakshu and other places.
- **Gas pipeline** from Hazira in Gujarat connects Jagdishpur in Uttar Pradesh, via Vijaipur in Madhya Pradesh. It has branch to Kota in Rajasthan, Shahjahanpur, Babrala and other places in Uttar Pradesh.

Multiple Choice Questions

1. Which is the biggest planet?
   A. Venus B. Mars
   C. Mercury D. Jupiter
2. Which is the smallest continent in the world?
   A. Australia B. Africa
   C. South America D. Europe
3. Which is the lowest body of water in the world?
   A. Black Sea B. Dead Sea
   C. Adriatic Sea D. Red Sea
4. In which state the famous Kamakhya Temple is situated?
   A. West Bengal B. Gujarat
   C. Uttar Pradesh D. Assam
5. Which is the largest island sea in the world?
   A. Caribbean Sea B. Mediterranean Sea
   C. Red Sea D. Beaufort Sea
6. Which is the largest continent of the world?
   A. Asia B. Africa
   C. Australia D. North America
7. Name the highest peak in the Indian sub-continent:
   A. Nanda Devi B. Everest
   C. Trishul D. Kanchanjunga
8. Which is the largest island in the world?
   A. New Guinea B. Brneo
   C. Madagascar D. Greenland
9. Which of the following is not a peak of the Himalayas?
   A. Mount Koyo B. Kanchenjunga
   C. Dhaulagiri D. Makalu
10. Which is the biggest ocean?
    A. Pacific Ocean B. Atlantic Ocean
    C. Antarctic Ocean D. Indian Ocean
11. Which is the largest peninsula in the world?
    A. Pacific B. Arabia
    C. Bangladesh D. Africa
12. Which is the largest Archipelago in the world?
    A. Indonesia B. Malaysia
    C. New Zealand D. Malta
13. Which is the deepest ocean in the world?
    A. Arctic B. Atlantic
    C. Pacific D. Indian
14. The State producing maximum vegetables in India is:
    A. West Bengal B. Uttar Pradesh
    C. Punjab D. Maharashtra
15. What does the 17th Parallel line separate?
    A. South and North America
    B. North and South Korea
    C. South and North Yemen
    D. South and North Vietnam
16. Which continent/portion of the world is uninhabited?
    A. Antarctica B. Rajasthan
    C. Australia D. Gobi
17. Land of the Golden Fleece is:
    A. Bhutan B. Japan
    C. Canada D. Australia
18. Which mountains are called 'the Blue Mountains?
    A. Nilgiri Mountains B. The Alps
    C. Mount Everest D. The Himalayas
19. Name the countries which lie on either side of Durand Line?
    A. India and Pakistan
    B. Indian and Bangladesh
    C. Afghanistan and Pakistan
    D. Iran and Iraq
20. Which is the largest lake in the world?
    A. Caspian (C.I.S., Iran)
    B. Lake Huron (Canada, U.S.)
    C. Nyanza (Tanzania-Kenya)
    D. Lake Superior (U.S.A. Canada)
21. Name the countries which lie on either side of MacMohan Line?
    A. South Vietnam and North Vietnam
    B. India and China
    C. India and Ceylon
    D. France and Germany

22. Which is the largest Gulf in the world?
A. Gulf of Aqaba B. Gulf of Bengal
C. Gulf of Mexico D. Gulf of Aden

23. Which country is called the "Land of Morning Calm"?
A. Sweden B. Netherlands
C. Norway D. Korea

24. Which is called the Dark Continent?
A. Africa B. Australia
C. Greenland D. South America

25. What does the 38th Parallel Line separate?
A. India from Bangladesh
B. India from China
C. North Korea from South Korea
D. India from Pakistan

26. The Panama Canal connects:
A. The Pacific and Atlantic Oceans
B. The Pacific and Arctic Oceans
C. The Atlantic and Arctic Oceans
D. The Atlantic and Indian Oceans

27. What is the habitable portion of the world land area?
A. Less than 35%
B. Less than half of it
C. 50%
D. About 75%

28. Which one of the following ocean current is not a cold ocean current?
A. Canary Current
B. California Current
C. Kuroshio Current
D. Oyashio Current

29. The Regur soil is also known as:
A. Red soil B. Black soil
C. Yellow soil D. Alluvial soil

30. Rome is the:
A. Eternal city B. Forbidden city
C. City of palaces D. Cleanest city

31. The capital of Israel is:
A. Palestine B. Tel Aviv
C. Vatican D. Jerusalem

32. The City of Seven Hills is:
A. Rome B. Athens
C. Cairo D. Tokyo

33. Laplands is a group of countries located in:
A. Europe B. Australia
C. Asia D. America

34. Zanzibar is called:
A. Island of cloves B. Eternal city
C. Holy land D. Land of spices

35. The Himalayas constitute the natural boundary between :
A. China and India
B. China and Afghanistan
C. India and Nepal
D. India and Myanmar

36. Hermit Kingdom is:
A. Korea B. Palestine
C. Rome D. Haridwar

37. The highest of all the plateaus in the world is the:
A. Deccan Plateau B. Bolivian Plateau
C. Tibetan Plateau D. Colombian Plateau

38. Eternal City is:
A. Kolkata B. Rome
C. Athens D. Bangkok

39. The city of Khartoum is situated on the banks of:
A. Hudson B. Nile
C. Tiber D. Seine

40. In which continent some of its parts are over 1500 miles from the sea and in which the hottest as well as the coldest climates of the world are to be found:
A. America B. Asia
C. Europe D. Australia

41. Paris is situated on the river:
A. Tibea B. Seine
C. Danube D. None of the above

42. Name the place where Blue and White Nile Rivers effect a confluence:
A. Cairo
B. Constantinople (except Greenland)
C. Khartoum
D. Teheran

43. The basin of Godavari River does not lie in which of the following states?
A. Odisha B. Chhattisgarh
C. Gujarat D. Madhya Pradesh

44. Australia is the:
A. only continent in the Southern Hemisphere
B. island continent
C. smallest continent
D. all the above points are true

45. Name the place where Rhine and Spree rivers meet in Europe:
A. Lyons B. Paris
C. Hamburg D. Berlin

46. Moscow is situated on the bank of:
A. Moskva B. Spree
C. Volga D. Tagus

47. The country Congo is in the ..... continent:
A. European B. Australian
C. Asian D. African

48. China's Sorrow is:
A. Lin Piao B. Sinkiang
C. Hwang-ho D. I'sang Ho

49. Sugar Bowl of the world is:
A. Manila B. Japan
C. Cuba D. Havana

50. The City of Palaces is:
A. Peru B. Rome
C. Kolkata D. Bangkok

SOCIAL SCIENCE

51. The highest peak in Europe is:
A. Mont Blanc B. Andes
C. Monte Rosa D. Elburz

52. Land of the Rising Sun is:
A. Japan B. Norway
C. Assam D.Myanmar

53. Where was electricity supply first introduced in India?
A. Darjeeling B. Kolkata
C. Mumbai D. Delhi

54. Name the largest island in the world:
A. New Guinea B. Greenland
C. Madagascar D. Great Britain

55. Land of the Midnight Sun is:
A. Japan B. Myanmar
C. Norway D. Manipur

56. The longest river in the world is:
A. Nile B. Amazon
C. Yangtze D. Missouri-Mississippi

57. The Island Continent is:
A. Asia B. America
C. Africa D. Australia

58. Suez Canal joins:
A. London to Paris
B. Tokyo to Osaka
C. Mediterranean to the Red Sea
D. Rangoon to Philippines

59. The Radcliffe Line was drawn on 15th August, 1947 between:
A. India and Myanmar (Burma)
B. Pakistan and China
C. Pakistan and India
D. Pakistan and Nepal

60. New York is situated on the river bank of:
A. Rhine B. Thames
C. Hudson D. Amazon

61. Which place is called the land of Golden Fleece?
A. Australia B. Cuba
C. Austria D. Myanmar

62. Kiel is a:
A. renowned explorer
B. American antelope
C. big American sea bird
D. shipping canal between London and Baltic Sea

63. USA consists of so many States:
A. 30 B. 50
C. 20 D. 40

64. The Turan Type of Regions have the climate of extremes because:
A. These lie in the interior ports of the continent
B. These have either too much or too less rain
C. These are either on hills or near the deserts
D. None of the above

65. Which country tops in the mining of gold:
A. U.S.A. B. Canada
C. China D. India

66. The largest Fresh water lake is:
A. Lake Superior B. Caspian Sea
C. Lake Baikal D. Hind Sea

67. ..... is the most important occupation of the people in the Monsoon Lands:
A. Forestry B. Agriculture
C. Industry D. Mining

68. There is the great variations of vegetation in the Monsoon Region because of:
A. It depends on nearness to forests, oceans, mountains
B. Variation in the amount of rainfall in different places
C. The effect of rainfall is different in different regions.
D. None of the above

69. In the Amur Valley of the Russia ..... is the most important economic activity:
A. agriculture B. animal rearing
C. mining D. industry

70. Which is the Land of White Elephants?
A. Korea B. Japan
C. Thailand D. Tanzania

71. The most important occupation of the people in the Turan Type of Regions is .....
A. agriculture
B. cattle and animal rearing
C. mountaineering
D. industry

72. Which is the City of Magnificent Buildings?
A. Tokyo B. New York
C. Washington D. Rome

73. In the West European Type of Regions, the summer temperature hardly exceeds ..... °C.
A. 10°C B. 16°C
C. 7°C D. 8°C

74. The extensive treeless tracts of North America, which are covered with tall coarse grass, are called:
A. Savanna B. Tundras
C. Pampas D. Prairies

75. ....., ... and ..... are the important animal products of the Iran Type of Regions.
A. Skins and hides
B. Meat canning and export
C. Wool, meat and skins
D. Wool and hides

76. Which is the largest country of the world (in area)?
A. U.S.A. B. Russia
C. China D. Canada

77. The main natural regions of the world are:
A. Hot, Polar, Arctic and Antarctic
B. Forests, deserts. sea, ocean
C. Tropical Regions, Warm Temperate Region, Cool Temperate Regions, Polar Regions
D. None of these

78. The second highest peak in the world is:
A. Kanchanjunga B. K-2
C. Himalayas D. Andes

79. Which state in the world occupies the smallest area:
A. Bermuda B. Peru
C. Monaco D. Vatican

80. The source of the origin of river Narmada is:
A. Amarkantak B. Bhedaghat
C. Brahmagiri D. Mahabaleshwar

81. The Toda tribes are the original inhabitants of:
A. Aravali Hills B. Satpura Hills
C. Nilgiri Hills D. Guru Shikhar

82. Korba is famous for
I. Thermal power plant
II. Aluminium plant
III. Hydroelectric power plant
The correct answer out of these is
A. I only B. II only
C. I and II only D. I, II and III

83. India's biggest multi-purpose river valley scheme is
A. Kosi B. Hirakud
C. Bhakra Nangal D. Nagarjunasagar

84. Match the following columns:

(*a*) Spain	1. Madrid
(*b*) Finland	2. Oslo
(*c*) Lebanon	3. Helsinki
(*d*) Norway	4. Beirut

	(*a*)	(*b*)	(*c*)	(*d*)
A.	1	3	4	2
B.	1	4	3	2
C.	4	1	2	3
D.	2	1	4	3

85. Arrange the following states in the descending order of their respective population?
1. West Bengal
2. Uttarakhand
3. Maharashtra
A. 1, 2, 3 B. 3, 1, 2
C. 2, 3, 1 D. 1, 3, 2

86. From which of the following places is Kathmandu nearest by air route?
A. Patna B. Gorakhpur
C. Varansi D. Kolkata

87. Chota Nagpur region in Jharkhand is famous for:
A. oil refinery B. fertile soil
C. lac industry D. textiles

88. Which of the following pairs is correct?
A. Bhilai—Bihar
B. Bokaro—Madhya Pradesh
C. Durgapur—Karnataka
D. Rourkela—Orissa

89. The state where Shipki-la pass is located:
A. Sikkim
B. Arunachal Pradesh
C. Himachal Pradesh
D. Meghalaya

90. Khetri is famous for
A. copper complex
B. gold fields
C. aluminium complex
D. fertilisers

91. Savana grasslands are found in—
A. Australia
B. East Asia
C. South America
D. Africa

92. Which of the following ports is not a major port in India?
A. Marmugao
B. Cochin
C. Kozhikode
D. Kandla

93. Which of the following is associated with the creation of a Third World news agency?
A. NAMEDIA
B. CHOGM
C. COMECON
D. NAM

94. Which of the following ports has a free trade zone?
A. Kandla B. Cochin
C. Chennai D. Tuticorin

95. Approximately how many kilometres are represented by 1° of latitude?
A. 421 km B. 111 km
C. 91 km D. 211 km

96. Which state in India has the largest area?
A. Assam B. Uttar Pradesh
C. West Bengal D. Rajasthan

97. Which of the following winds cause rainfall in Tamil Nadu?
A. Cyclonic winds in the Bay of Bengal
B. South-West monsoons
C. North-East monsoons
D. North-West monsoons

98. 'Aeroflot' is the name of the airline of:
A. Germany B. Thailand
C. Indonesia D. Russia

99. The water of which of the following seas is most saline?
A. Black Sea B. Dead Sea
C. Baltic Sea D. Red Sea

100. Beirut is the capital of:
A. Libya B. Lebanon
C. Jordan D. Syria

ANSWERS

1	2	3	4	5	6	7	8	9	10
D	A	B	D	B	A	B	D	A	A
11	**12**	**13**	**14**	**15**	**16**	**17**	**18**	**19**	**20**
B	A	C	A	D	A	D	A	C	A
21	**22**	**23**	**24**	**25**	**26**	**27**	**28**	**29**	**30**
B	C	D	A	C	A	B	C	B	A
31	**32**	**33**	**34**	**35**	**36**	**37**	**38**	**39**	**40**
D	A	A	A	A	A	C	B	B	B
41	**42**	**43**	**44**	**45**	**46**	**47**	**48**	**49**	**50**
B	B	C	D	A	A	D	C	C	A
51	**52**	**53**	**54**	**55**	**56**	**57**	**58**	**59**	**60**
D	A	A	B	C	A	D	C	C	C
61	**62**	**63**	**64**	**65**	**66**	**67**	**68**	**69**	**70**
A	D	B	A	C	A	B	B	A	C
71	**72**	**73**	**74**	**75**	**76**	**77**	**78**	**79**	**80**
B	C	B	D	C	B	C	B	D	A
81	**82**	**83**	**84**	**85**	**86**	**87**	**88**	**89**	**90**
C	A	C	A	B	A	C	D	C	A
91	**92**	**93**	**94**	**95**	**96**	**97**	**98**	**99**	**100**
D	C	A	A	B	D	D	D	B	B

ECONOMICS

MICRO AND MACRO ECONOMICS

The Subject-matter of economics has been divided into two Parts—**Microeconomics** and **Macroeconomics. Ragner Frisch** was the first to use the terms "micro" and "macro" in economics in **1933.** The term microeconomics is derived from the Greek word **mikros,** meaning **"small"** and the term macroeconomics is derived from the Greek word **makros,** meaning **"large"**. Thus micro economics related to the study of individual economic units while the latter is a study of the economy as a whole.

Micro Economics

Microeconomics is the study of economic actions and behaviour of individual units and small groups. In the other words, in microeconomics we make a microscopic study of the economy. The determination of equilibrium output of the firm or industry, the wage of a particular type of labour, the price of a particular commodity are some of the fields of microeconomics theory. Thus the theory of product pricing and the theory of factor pricing (or the theory of distribution) fall within the domain of microeconomics. The whole content of microeconomic theory is presented in the following chart :

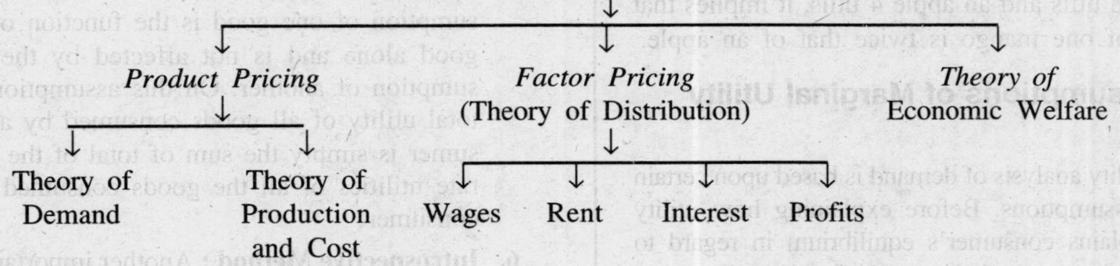

Macro Economics

Macroeconomics is the study of aggregates or averages covering the entire economy, such as total employment, the national product or income, the general price level of the economy. Therefore, macroeconomics is also known as **aggregative economics.** Macroeconomics analyses and establishes the functional relationship between these large aggregates. Thus **Professor Boulding** says, "Macroeconomics deals not with individuals quantities as such but with the aggregates of these quantities; not with individual incomes but with the national income; not with individual prices but with the price level; not with individual outputs but with the national output."

Macroeconomics is also known as the theory of income and employment, or simply income analysis. It is concerned with the problems of unemployment, economic fluctuations, inflation or deflation, international trade and economic growth.

We have now stated, in brief, all aspects of macroeconomic theory. These various aspects of macroeconomic theory are shown, in the following chart :

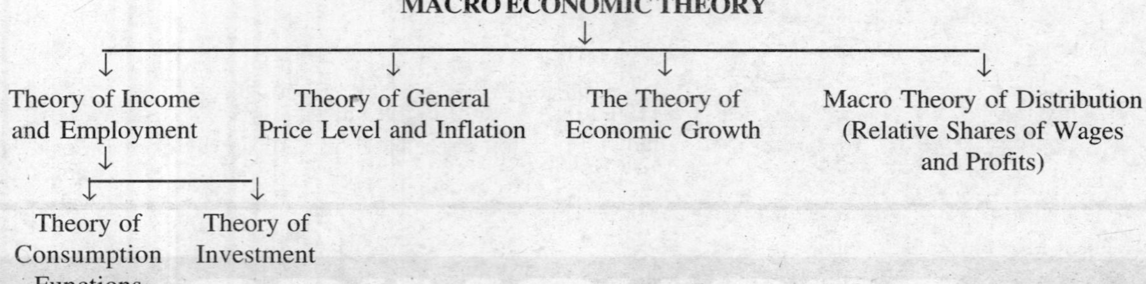

CONSUMER DEMAND THEORY

There are two basic approaches to the study of consumer demand theory. The first, or **classical approach,** involves the use of measurable marginal utility (satisfaction). It is generally called the **Cardinal utility approach.** The second, or indifference curve approach, is generally called the **ordinal approach.**

MARGINAL UTILITY ANALYSIS

Marginal utility analysis is the oldest theory of demand which provides an explanation of Consumer's demand for a product and it derives the law of demand which establishes an inverse relationship between price and quantity demanded of the product. Though marginal utility approach to the theory of demand is very old, its final shape emerged at the hands of **Marshall.** Marginal utility analysis is based on the concept of **Cardinal approach** which assumes that utility is measurable and additive. It is expressed as a quantity measured in hypothetical units which are called **'utils'.** If a consumer imagines that one mango has 8 utils and an apple 4 utils, it implies that the utility of one mango is twice that of an apple.

Basic Assumptions of Marginal Utility Analysis

Marginal utility analysis of demand is based upon certain important assumptions. Before explaining how utility analysis explains consumer's equilibrium in regard to the demand for goods, it is essential to describe those basic assumptions on which the whole utility analysis rests. The following are the main assumptions.

1. **Rationality :** The consumer is rational. He aims at the maximisation of his utility subject to the constraint imposed by his given income.
2. **Cardinal Utility :** The utility of each commodity is measurable. Utility is a Cardinal concept. The most convenient measure is money. The utility is measured by the monetary units that the consumer is prepared to pay for another unit of the commodity.
3. **Constant Marginal Utility of Money :** Another important assumption of the marginal utility analysis is that the marginal utility of money remains constant even though the quantity of money with consumer is diminished by the successive purchases made by him. It is assumed that while marginal utility of a commodity varies with the quantity of the commodity purchased, the marginal utility of money remains throughout the same as the quantity of the good purchased varies. This assumption becomes necessary because the marginal utility of a commodity is measured in terms of money.
4. **Diminishing Marginal Utility :** The utility gained from successive units of a commodity diminishes. In other words, the marginal utility of a commodity diminishes as the consumer acquires large quantities of it. This is the axion of **diminishing marginal utility.**
5. **Utilities are Independent :** Marginal utility analysis assumes that the utilities of different commodities are independent of one another. That is, the utility of one commodity does not in any way affect that of another. In other words, the satisfaction derived from the consumption of one good is the function of that good alone and is not affected by the consumption of another. On this assumption, the total utility of all goods consumed by a consumer is simply the sum of total of the separate utilities of all the goods consumed by a consumer.
6. **Introspective Method :** Another important hypothesis of the marginal utility analysis is the use of introspective method in judging the behaviour of marginal utility. "Introspection is the ability of the observer to reconstruct events which go on in the mind of another person with the help of self-observation. This form of comprehension may be just guess work or intuition or the result of long-lasting experience."

TOTAL UTILITY AND MARGINAL UTILITY

When a consumer purchases a good, he obtains satisfaction from the possession of that good. That is, he derives utility from the possession of the good. When the consumer buys apples he receives them in units, 1, 2, 3, 4, etc. 2 apples have more utility than 1, 3 more utility than 2, and 4 more than 3. The units of apples which the consumer chooses are in a descending order of their utilities. In his estimation, the first apple is the best out of the lot available to him and thus gives him the highest satisfaction, measured as 20 utils. The second apple will naturally be the second best with lesser amount of utility than the first, and has 15 utils. The third apple has 10 utils and the fourth 5 utils. In our illustration, the total utility of two apples is 35 = 20 + 15 utils, of three apples is 45 = 20 + 15 + 10 utils, and of four apples is 50 = 20 + 15 + 10 + 5. **Marginal utility is the addition made to total utility by having an additional unit of the commodity.** The total utility of the two apples is 35 utils. When the consumer consumes the third apple, the total utility becomes 45 utils. Thus, marginal utility of the third apple is 10 utils (45 – 35). In other words, marginal utility is defined as the change in total utility resulting from a unit change in the consumption of the good in question per unit of time.

Algebraically, the marginal utility (MU) of n units of a commodity is the total utility (TU) of n units minus the total utility of $(n - 1)$. Thus,

$$MU_n = TU_n - TU_{n-1}$$

The relation between the total and marginal utility is explained with the help of following table.

TABLE

Units of Apple	TU in Utils	MU in Utils
0	0	0
1	20	20
2	35	15
3	45	10
4	50	5
5	50	0
6	45	– 5
7	35	– 10

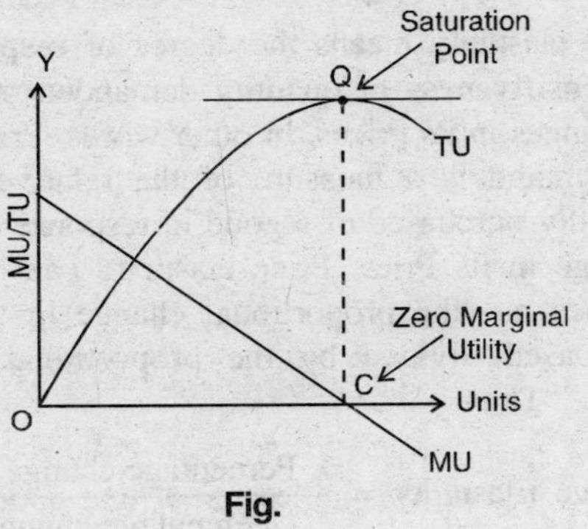

Fig.

So long as total utility is increasing, marginal utility is decreasing upto the 4th unit. When total utility is maximum (at the fifth unit), marginal utility is zero. It is the point of **Satiety (Saturation)** for the consumer. When total utility is decreasing, marginal utility is negative.

LAW OF DIMINISHING MARGINAL UTILITY

Satisfaction of human wants follows some very importants laws and one of them is the Law of Diminishing Marginal utility. **Hermann Heinrich Gossen** was the first to formulate this law in 1854 though the name was given by Marshall. **Javons** called it **Gossen's First Law.** Gossen stated it thus. "The magnitude of one and the same satisfaction, when we continue to enjoy it without interruption, continually decreases until satisfaction is reached." According to this law the marginal utility of a good diminishes as an individual consumes more units of a good. In other words, as a consumer takes more units of a good, the extra utility or satisfaction that he derives from an extra unit of the good goes on falling. It should be carefully noted that it is the marginal utility and not the total utility that declines with the increase in the consumption of a good. The law of diminishing marginal utility means that the total utility increases but at a decreasing rate.

Marshall states the Law thus : "The additional benefits which a person derives from a given increase of his stock of a thing diminishes with every increase in the stock that he already has."

This Law is based upon two important facts. **Firstly,** while the total wants of a man are virtually unlimited, each single want is satiable. Therefore, as an individual consumes more and more units of a good, intensity of his want for the good goes on falling and a point is reached where the individual no longer wants any more units of the good. That is **when Saturation Point is reached marginal utility of a good becomes zero.** The second fact on which the law of diminishing marginal utility is based is that the different goods are not perfect substitutes for each other in the satisfaction of various particular wants. When an individual consumes more and more units of a good, the intensity of his particular want for the good diminishes but if the units of that good could be devoted to the satisfaction of other wants and yielded as much satisfaction as they did initially in the satisfaction of the first want, marginal utility of the good would not have diminished.

The significance of the diminishing marginal utility of a good for the theory of demand is that the quantity demanded of a good rises as the price falls and **vice-versa.** Thus it is because of the diminishing marginal utility that the demand curve slopes downward.

Law of diminishing marginal utility is a universal law and applies to all objects of desire including money. But, it is worth mentioning that marginal utility of money is generally never zero or negative. Money represents purchasing power over all other goods, that is, a man can satisfy all his material wants if he possesses enough money. Since man's total wants are practically unlimited, therefore the marginal utility of money tc him never falls to zero.

DEMAND

Demand is a function of price, income, price of related goods and tastes and is expressed as

$$D = f(p, y, pr, t).$$

When income, prices of related goods and tastes are given, the demand function is

$$D = f(p).$$

It shows quantities of a commodity purchased at given prices. Demand is also related to a period of time. In the **Marshallian analysis,** the other determinants of demand are taken as given and constant.

Types of Demand

Three kinds of demands may be distinguished :

(a) Price Demand

(b) Income Demand

(c) Cross Demand

Price Demand : Price demand refers to the various quantities of a commodity or service that a consumer or service that a consumer would purchase at a given time in a market at various hypothetical prices. It is assumed that other things, such as consumer's income, his tastes and prices of inter-related goods, remain unchanged.

The demand of the individual consumer is called **Individual Demand** and the total demand of all the consumers combined for the commodity or service is called **Industry Demand.** The total demand for the product of an individual firm at various prices is known as firm's demand or **Individual Seller's Demand.**

Income Demand : The income demand refers to the various qualities of goods and services which would be purchased by the consumers at various levels of incomes. Here we assume that the price of the commodity or service as well as the prices of inter-related goods and the tastes and desires of consumers do not change.

Cross Demand : The cross demand means the quantities of a good or service which will be purchase with reference to change in price not of this good but of other inter-related goods. These goods are either substitutes or complementary goods. A change in the price of tea, for instance, will affect the demand for coffee.

Law of Demand

This law expresses a relationship between the quantity demanded and its price. It may be defined in Marshall's words as "the amount demanded increase with a fall in price, and diminishes with a rise in price." Thus it expresses an inverse relation between price and demand. The inverse price-demand relationship is based on **other things remaining equal.** This phrase points towards certain important assumption on which this law is based.

These assumptions are :

(i) There is no change in the tastes and preferences of the consumer;

(ii) The income of the consumer remains constant;

(iii) There is no change in customs;

(iv) There should not be any change in the prices of other products;

(v) There should not be any change in the quality of the product;

(vi) The habits of the consumers should remain unchanged.

Given these conditions, the law of demand operates. If there is change even in one of these conditions, it will stop operating.

Elasticity of Demand

It is price elasticity of demand which is usually referred to as elasticity of demand. But, besides price elasticity of demand, there are various other concepts of demand elasticity. Demand for a good is determined by its price, incomes of the people, prices of related goods etc. Quantity demanded of a good will change as a result of a change in the size of any of these determinants of demand. The concept of elasticity of demand therefore refers to the **degree of responsiveness** of quantity demanded of a good to a change in its price, income or prices of related goods. Accordingly, there are three kinds of demand elasticity–

1. Price Elasticity
2. Income Elasticity
3. Cross Elasticity

Price Elasticity of Demand

Price elasticity means the degree of **responsive-ness** or **sensitiveness** of quantity demanded of a good to a changes in its prices. In other words, Price elasticity of demand is a measure of the relative change in quantity purchased of a good in response to a relative change in its Price. Price elasticity can be precisely defined as "the proportional change in the quantity purchased divided by the proportional change in price." Thus

$$\text{Price Elasticity} = -\frac{\text{Percentage change in quantity}}{\text{Percentage change in price}}$$

Cross Elasticity of Demand

The change in the demand for one good in response to the change in price of the other good represents the cross elasticity of demand of one good for the other. In other words, the cross elasticity of demand is the relation between percentage change in the quantity demanded of a good to the percentage in the price of a related good.

Income Elasticity

The responsiveness of demand to changes in income is termed **income elasticity of demand.** It shows how the quantity demanded will change when the income of the purchaser changes, the price of the commodity remaining the same, it may be defined thus : The Income Elasticity of demand for a good is the ratio of the percentage change in the amount spent on the commodity to a percentage change in the consumer's income price of commodity remaining constant. Thus,

$$\text{Income Elasticity} = \frac{\text{Percentage change in quantity demanded}}{\text{Percentage change in income}}$$

CONSUMER'S SURPLUS

Concept of consumer's surplus is a very important concept in economic theory especially in welfare economics. The concept of consumer's surplus was first of all evolved by **Dr. Alfred Marshall,** who maintained that it can be measured in monetary units, and is equal to the difference between the amount of money that a consumer actually pays to buy a certain quantity of a commodity X, and the amount that he would be willing to pay for this quantity rather than do without it.

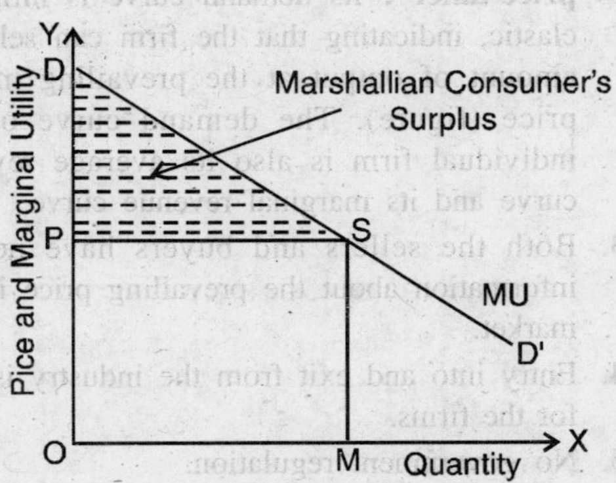

Fig.: *Marshall's Measure of Consumer's Surplus*

The concept of consumer surplus is important not only in economic theory but also in economic policies, such as taxation by the Government and price policy pursued by the monopolistic seller of a product. The essence of the concept of consumer's surplus is that a consumer derives extra satisfaction from the purchases he daily makes over the price he actually pays for them. **Marshall** defines the consumer's surplus in the following words :

"Excess of the price which a consumer would be willing to pay, rather than go without a thing over that which he actually does pay, is the economic measure of this surplus satisfaction ... it may be called consumer's surplus."

The amount of money which a person is prepared to pay for a good indicates the amount of utility he derives from that good, the greater the amount of money he is willing to pay, the greater the satisfaction or utility he will obtain from it. Therefore, the marginal utility of a unit of a good determines the price a consumer will be prepared to pay for that unit. The total utility which a person will get from a good will be given by sum of marginal utilities (ΣMU) of the units of the good purchased and the total price which he will actually pay is equal to the price per unit multiplied by the number of units purchased. Thus,

Consumer's Surplus = What a consumer is prepared to pay minus what he actually pays.

$= \Sigma \text{ MU} - (\text{Price} \times \text{Number of units purchased})$

CONSUMER'S EQUILIBRIUM

A consumer is in equilibrium when given his tastes, and prices of the two goods, he spends a given money income on the purchase of two goods in such a way as to get the maximum satisfaction. In the indifference curve technique the consumer's equilibrium is discussed in respect of the purchases of two goods by the consumer.

The indifference curve analysis of consumer's equilibrium is based on the following assumptions :

1. The consumer has a given indifference map exhibiting his scale of preferences for various combinations of two goods, X and Y.
2. He has a fixed amount of money to spend on the two goods. He has to spend whole of his given money on the two goods.
3. Prices of the goods are given and constant for him. He cannot influence the prices of the goods by buying more or less of them.
4. Goods are homogeneous and divisible.

LAWS OF PRODUCTION

The laws of production describe the technically possible ways of increasing the level of production. Output may increase in various ways.

Output can be increased by changing all factors or production. Clearly this is possible only in the long-run. Thus **the laws of returns to scale** refer to the long-run analysis of production.

In the short run output may be increased by using more of the variable factor, while capital (and possibly other factors as well) are kept constant. The marginal product of the variable factor will decline eventually as more and more quantities of this factor are combined with the other constant factors. The expansion of output with one factor constant is described by the **law of diminishing returns** of the variable factor, which is often referred to as the **law of variable proportions.**

Laws of Returns to Scale

In the long run expansion of output may be achieved by varying all factors. In the long run all factors are variable. The laws of returns to scale refer to the effects of scale relationships.

In the long run output may be increased by changing **all factors by the same proportion,** or by different proportions. Traditional theory of production concentrates on the first case, that is, the study of output as all inputs change by the **same proportion. The term 'return to scale' refers to the changes in output as all factors change by the same proportion.**

THE CONCEPT OF REVENUE

The term 'revenue' refers to the receipts obtained by a firm from the sale of certain quantities of a commodity at various prices. The revenue concept relates to total revenue, average revenue and marginal revenue.

Total Revenue : Total revenue refers to the total amount of money that the firm receives from the sale of its products. Thus, the total revenue is obviously equal to the quantity sold multiplied by the selling price of the commodity, *i.e.,*

$$TR = P.Q.$$

where

TR = total revenue

P = price per unit

Q = quantity

Average Revenue : Average revenue can be obtained by dividing by the total revenue by the number of units sold. Thus,

$$\text{average revenue} = \frac{\text{total revenue}}{\text{total output sold}}$$

$$\text{or,} \quad AR = \frac{TR}{Q} = \frac{P.Q}{Q} = P$$

Thus, average revenue is the price of commodity. It follows from this that the curve which relates average revenue to output is identical with the demand curve that relates price to output.

Marginal Revenue : Marginal revenue is the net revenue earned by selling on additional unit of the product. In other words, marginal revenue is the addition made to the total revenue by selling one more unit of the good. Putting it in algebraic expression marginal revenue is the addition made to total revenue by selling *n* units of a product instead of (*n* – 1) where *n* is any given number. Therefore,

Marginal Revenue = difference in total revenue in increasing sales from (*n* – 1) units to *n* units

$$MR_n = TR_n - TR_{n-1}$$

If TR stands for total revenue and Q stands for output, then marginal revenue (MR) can be expressed as follows :

$$MR = \frac{d(TR)}{dQ}$$

$\frac{d(TR)}{dQ}$ indicates the slope of the total revenue curve. Thus if the total revenue curve is given to us, we can find out marginal revenue at various levels of output by measuring the slopes at the corresponding points on the total revenue curve.

PERFECT COMPETITION

Perfect competition is a market structure characterised by a complete absence of rivalry among the individual firms. In other words, perfect competition implies no rivalry among firms.

Assumptions

The model of perfect competition is based on the following assumptions.

1. There are a large number of firms producing and selling a product.
2. The product of all firms is homogeneous. The assumptions of large numbers of sellers and of product homogeneity imply that the individual firm in perfect competition is a **price-taker :** Its demand curve is infinitely elastic, indicating that the firm can sell any amount of output at the prevailing market price (figure). The demand curve of the individual firm is also its average revenue curve and its marginal revenue curve.
3. Both the sellers and buyers have perfect information about the prevailing price in the market.
4. Entry into and exit from the industry is free for the firms.
5. No government regulation.
6. Perfect mobility of factors of production.

Equilibrium of the Firm in the Short Run

The firm is in equilibrium when it maximises its profits (π), defined as the difference between the total cost and total revenue.

$$\pi = TR - TC$$

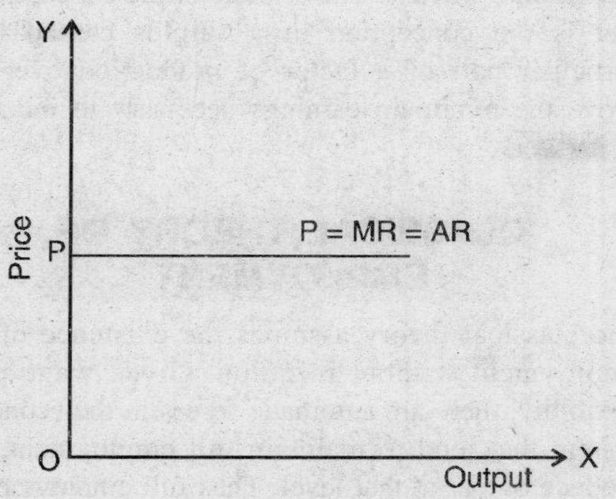

Fig.: *Perfect Competition'*

Given that the normal rate of profit is included in the cost items of the firm, π is the profit above the normal rate of return on capital and the remuneration for the risk-bearing function of the entrepreneur. The firm is in equilibrium when it produces the output that maximises that difference between total receipt and total costs. The equilibrium of the firm may be shown graphically in two ways. Either by using the TR and TC curves, or the MR and MC curves.

MONOPOLY

Monopoly is a market structure in which there is a single seller, there are no close substitutes for the commodity it produces and there are barriers to entry. Two points are worth noting in this definition. *Firstly*, there must be a single producer or seller of a product if there is to be monopoly. A *second condition* which is essential for a firm to be called monopolist is that no *close substitutes* for the product of that firm should be available.

We can express the second condtion of monopoly in terms of *cross elasticity of demand* also. Cross elsticity of demand shows a change in the demand for a good as a result of change in the price of another good. Therefore, if there is to be monopoly *the cross elasticity of demand between the product of the monopolist and the product of any other producer must be very small.*

The above two conditions ensure that the monopolist can set the price of his product and can pursue an independent price policy. Power to influence price is very essence of monopoly. From this it must not be gathered that the monopolist is so powerful that he can dictate the price as wel as the amount sold. Monopolist can do one of these things only; either he can fix the price leaving the amount sold to the consumers, or he can fix the quantity he wants to produce and sell and leave the price to be determined by the demand of the consumers.

UTILITY MAXIMISATION

Williamson has developed the utility maximisation hypothesis as against profit maximisation. Like Baumol's sales maximisation theory, it is one of the managerial theories. It is also known as the **'managerial discretion theory.'**

In large modern firms, shareholders and managers are two separate groups. The former want the maximum return on their investment and hence the maximisation of profits. The managers, on the other hand, have consideration other than profit maximisation in their utility functions. Thus the managers are interested not only in their own emoluments but also in the size of their staff and expenditure on them. Thus Williamson's theory is related to the maximisation of the manager's utility which is a function of the expenditure on staff and emoluments and discretionary funds.

To pursue his goal of utility maximisation, the manager directs the firms's resources in three ways:

First, the manager desires to expand his staff and to increase their salaries. "More staff are valued because they lead to the manager getting more salary, more prestige and more security." **Second,** to maximise his utility, the manager indulges in "feather bedding" such as pretty secretaries, company cars, too many company phones, 'perks' for employees etc. Such expenditures are characterised as **'management slack'** by Williamson. **Third,** the manager likes to set up "discretionary funds" for making investments to advance or promote company projects that are close to his heart Discretionary funds (or profits or investments) are what remains with the manager after paying taxes, and dividends to shareholders in order to retain effective control of the firm.

CONCEPTS OF PRODUCTIVITY

Average Physical Productivity is the total production divided by the number of units of a factor employed.

Average Productivity of a factor

$$= \frac{\text{Total Output}}{\text{Total Number of units of a factor}}$$

Marginal physical productivity of a factor is the increase in total output caused by employing an additional unit of the factor, quantity of other factors remaining fixed.

$$MP_L = \frac{dX}{dL} \quad \text{and} \quad MP_K = \frac{dX}{dK}$$

Where

MP_L = marginal productivity of labour

MP_K = marginal productivity of capital

dX = change in output

dL = change in labour

dK = change in capital.

Marginal Revenue Product (MRP)

Marginal Revenue Product is the increment in the total value product caused by employing an additional unit of a factor, the expenditure on other factors remaining unchanged. In other words, marginal revenue product is the marginal physical product of the factor multiplied by the marginal revenue.

$$MRP = MPP \times MR$$

THE THEORY OF RENT

Rent as an economic surplus, as used by modern economists means the earning of a factor of production in excess of the minimum amount necessary to keep it in its present use. It is not a differential surplus, the difference between the superior and the inferior grades of lands as **Ricardo** meant by rent. Moreover, it accrues not to land alone, but to all other factor services.

Ricardian Theory of Rent

David Ricardo was a brilliant 19th century economist of England who propounded a systematic theory of rent which is in many ways the basis of the modern concept of rent.

Ricardo defined rent as follows: **"Rent is that portion of the produce of earth which is paid to the land lord for the use of the original and indestructible powers of the soil."** It should be noticed that land rent, according to Ricardian definition, is a payment for the use of only land and is different from contractual rent which includes.

- According to Ricardo, marginal land earns no rent.
- In Ricardian Theory, rent is not price determining. In fact, in this theory rent is price determined, that is, it is price which determines rent. To quote Ricardo, **"Corn is not high because a rent is paid, but a rent is paid because corn is high."**

Modern Theory of Rent

Modern theory of rent does not confine itself to the determination of the reward of only land as a factor of production. Rent according to the modern sense can arise in respect of any factor of product ion. It is a surplus payment in excess of transfer earnings of that factor. **Transfer earnings means the amount of money which any particular unit of a factor could earn in its next best alternative use.** In other words, economic rent in such a case is the difference between the present earnings and transfer earnings. **In Joan Robinson's words,** "The essence of the conception of rent is the conception of a surplus earned by a particular part of a factor of production over and above the minimum earnings necessary to induce it to its work."

CLASSICAL THEORY OF EMPLOYMENT

The classical theory assumes the existence of full employment without inflation. Given wage-price flexibility, there are automatic forces in the economic system that tend to maintain full employment, and produce output at that level. Thus full employment is ragarded as a normal situation and any deviation from this level is something abnormal which automatically tends towards full employment. The classical theory of output and employment is based on the following assumptions:

1. There is the existence of full employment without inflation.
2. There is perfect competition in labour and product markets.
3. There is a closed *laissez faire* capitalist economy without foreign trade.
4. Labour is homogenous.
5. Total output of the economy is divided between consumption and investment expenditures.
6. The quantity of money is given.
7. Wages and prices are flexible.
8. Money wages and real wages are directly related and proportional.
9. Capital stock and technological knowledge are given in the short run.

DETERMINATION OF NATIONAL INCOME : KEYNESIAN THEORY

The Keynesian theory is relevant in the context of the **short run** only since the stock of capital, techniques of production, efficiency of labour, the size of population, forms of business organisation have been assumed to remain constant in this theory. Therefore, in the Keynesian theory which deals with the short run, the level of income of the country will change as a result of changes in the level of labour employment. Thus, in an advanced capitalist economy in the short-run, income is a function of employment. Infact, both income and employment go together. The higher the level of employment; the higher the level of income. As level of employment is determined by aggregate demand and aggregate supply, the level of income is also determined by aggregate demand and aggregate supply.

Aggregate Supply

Equilibrium level of national income in the short run depends upon aggregate demand and aggregate supply. The aggregate supply depends on physical or technical conditions of production which do not change in the short-run. Since Keynes assumes the aggregate supply to be stable, he concentrates his entire attention upon the aggregate demand to fight depression and unemployment.

Aggregate Demand

Aggregate demand is determined by consump-tion demand and investment demand. Therefore,

Aggregate Demand = Consumption Demand + Investment Demand

$$AD = C + I$$

Where AD = aggregate demand

C = consumption demand

I = investment demand

Equilibrium Level of Income

The equilibrium level of national income is determined at a point where the aggregate demand function intersects the aggregate supply function.

NATIONAL INCOME ANALYSIS

There are various concepts of national income which we shall study one by one.

1. Gross National product (GNP)

Gross National product is defined as the total market value of all final goods and services produced in a year. Two things must be noted in regard to gross national product. *First,* it measures the market value of annual output. In other words, GNP is a *monetary measure.*

Secondly, for calculating gross national product accurately, all goods and services produced in any given year must be counted once, and not more than once.

2. GNP at Factor Cost

GNP at factor cost is the sum of the money value of the income produced by and accruing to the various factors of production in one year in a country.

GNP at market prices, always includes indirect taxes levied by the government on goods which raise their prices. But GNP at factor cost is the income which the factors of production receive in return for their services alone. It is the cost of production. Thus GNP at market prices is always higher than GNP at factor cost.

3. Gross Domestic Product (GDP)

GDP = GNP – Net Foreign Investment

Net Foreign Investment = Export – Import

(X – M)

$\therefore$ GDP = GNP – (X– M)

4. Net National Product (NNP)

GNP includes the value of total output of consumption goods and investment goods. But the process of production uses up a certain amount of fixed capital. Some fixed equipment wears out, its other components are damaged or destroyed, and still other some rendered obsolete through technological changes. All this process is termed depreciation or capital consumption allowance. In order to arrive at NNP, we deduct depreciation from GNP. The word 'net' refers to the exclusion of that part of total output which represents depreciation.

NNP = GNP – Depreciation

5. NNP at Market Prices

Net National Product at Market prices is the net value of final goods and services evaluated at market prices in the course of one year in a country. If we deduct depreciation from GNP at market prices, we get NNP at market prices. Thus NNP at Market Prices = GNP at Market Prices – Depreciation.

6. NNP at Factor Cost

Net National Product at factor cost is the net output evaluated at factor prices. It includes income earned by factors of production through participation in the production process such as wages and salaries, rates, profits, etc. It is also called *National Income.* This measure differs from NNP at market prices in that indirect taxes are deducted and subsidies are added to NNP at market prices in order to arrive at NNP at factor cost. Thus

NNP ar factor cost = NNP at Market Prices – Indirect Taxes + Subsidies.

= GNP at Market Prices – Depreciation – Indirect Taxes + Subsidies.

7. NDP at Factor Cost

Net Domestic Product at factor cost is arrived by making adjustments for net indirect taxes *i.e.* indirect taxes and subsidies in the Net Domestic Product at market prices. The market prices contain an element of indirect taxes which though paid out by the buyers in the form of Product Prices, do not accrue to the production units.

Hence to find out factor incomes, we deduct the indirect taxes from the Net Domestic Product at market prices. Like wise, we add subsidies to the Net Domestic Product at market prices because these subsidies form the factor incomes though they are not a part of the market prices. Thus,

Net Domestic Product at Factor Cost = Net Domestic Product at Market Prices – Indirect Taxes + Subsidies.

8. Per Capita Income

The average income of the people of a country in a particular year is called Per Capital Income for that year. This concept also refers to the measurement of income at current prices and at constant prices. For instance, in order to find out the per capital income for 2001, at current prices, the national income of a country is divided by the population of the country in that year

$$\text{Per Capita Income for 2001} = \frac{\text{National income for 2001}}{\text{population in 2001}}$$

CHARACTERISTICS OF INDIAN ECONOMY

India's economy is in the stage of developing, *i.e.*, in transition from under-developed to developed. Each person in India was earning on income of just $2182.18 per year in 2023-24. This compares poorly with rich countries (Germany: $49,530, Japan: $42,870, USA: $58,030 France: $42,380, and China: $15,500) or even the low income countries (Egypt: $11,110). Even in terms of Gross National Product, our share in the world economy was only 1.1 % in 2016 though the population's share was 17.7%. Indian economy is characterised by:

1. **Low Per Capita Income:** India's per capita income is very low.
2. **High Population Growth:** India is passing through the phase of large birth rate and low death rate. Population is increasing at nearly 1.64% per annum. In Japan, the growth rate is 0.4%, 0% in Switzerland, 0% in Germany, - 0.1 % in Denmark, 0.8% in Australia and 0% in South Korea.
3. **Widespread Unemployment:** Under employment, Unemployment and disguised unemployment is widespread in India.
4. **Predominance of Agriculture:** About 14.4% of the national income comes from the primary sector. However, 49% of the population is employed in the sector.
5. **Inequalities in Income Distribution:** Richest 8% in rural India take away 46% of the total income while poorest 39% get only 5%.
6. **Poor Quality of Human Capital:** India fares poorly in terms of the Human Development Index. Poor quality of human capital manifests itself from low life expectancy at birth (68.45 years), population with access to safe water (75%), women literacy rate (64.6%) and mean years of schooling (2.4).
7. **Inadequate Capital Formation:** Rate of investment in India is only 28 to 34% of the GDP, as compared to more in developed countries. This rate is insufficient for India as a large investment is needed to offset the population growth itself.
8. **Technical Backwardness:** India spends only a small amount on research and development activities. The expenditure in the private sector also is very meagre.
9. **Infrastructural Inadequacies:** Transport, power, communication network, financial system are not sufficiently developed.
10. **Dualistic Economy:** Coexistence of a traditional low-productivity sector with a modern high-productivity sector.
11. **Lack of Foreign Trade Orientation:** Since Indian population is large, a large produce is consumed at the domestic markets itself. Moreover, due to poor quality consciousness, India is a small player in foreign trade.
12. **Unfavourable Social Value Structure:** Indians are divided on the basis of language, caste, religion and region, thus fragmenting the social structure of the country.
13. **Market Imperfections:** Indian market is imperfect, based towards the rich and prosperous. Limited market information availability, formation of pressure groups and use of strong arm tactics creates imperfections.
14. **Vicious Circles:** People are poor because they are unemployed. They are unemployed because they are illiterate, ill-trained and ill-equipped. This is a vicious circle which seems to have no end.

PLANNING IN INDIA

Leaders of Indian National Movement were greatly impressed by the planned economic growth of the Soviet Union. In the 1931 Karachi session of the Indian National Congress, a resolution was passed, stressing the nationalisation of key and basic industries. In 1937, the Congress appointed a National Planning Committee with Mr Jawaharlal Nehru as its chairman. At the Government level, a planning department was set up by the British Viceroy in 1945. However, after the independence, the need for planned development was acutely felt. An executive resolution was passed in March, 1950 to set up the Planning Commission. The directive principles of state policy of the Constitution also emphasise the need of planning.

NITI AAYOG

65-year-old Planning Commission has been dissolved and a new institution named NITI Aayog has been constituted by the National Democratic Alliance (NDA) government. Like Planning Commission the newly established NITI Aayog is also be chaired by the Prime Minister. NITI Aayog or National Institution for Transforming India serves as a government think tank and is meant to reflect changes required in India's governance structures and provide a more active role for the state governments in achieving national objectives. The newly constituted institution provides governments at the central and state levels with strategic and technical advice across the spectrum of policy making. As per official declaration, this institution includes matters of national and international import on the economic front, dissemination of best practices from within the country as well as from the nations, the infusion of new policy ideas and specific issue-based support. NITI Aayog is headed by the Prime Minister, who is its chairperson. The Prime Minister appoints a vice-chairperson and a chief executive officer (CEO). The CEO is appointed for a fixed tenure; who has a secretary-level position. The organization have full-time members and up to two part-time members from leading universities, research organizations and other relevant institutions. It also has up to four ex-officio members from the Union council of ministers who are nominated by the Prime Minister. While this is the full-time organizational structure, the new institution comprises a governing council which includes state chief ministers and lieutenant governors of Union Territories.

The NITI Aayog works towards the following main objectives :

(*i*) To evolve a shared vision of national development priorities, sectors and strategies with the active involvement of States in the light of national objectives.

(ii) To foster cooperative federalism through structured support initiatives and mechanisms with the States on a continuous basis, recognizing that strong States make a strong nation.

(iii) To develop mechanisms to formulate credible plans at the village level and aggregate these progressively at higher levels of government.

(iv) To ensure, on areas that are specifically referred to it, that the interests of national security are incorporated in economic strategy and policy.

(v) To offer a platform for resolution of inter-sectoral and inter-departmental issues in order to accelerate the implementation of the development agenda.

(vi) To focus on technology upgradation and capacity building for implementation of programmes and initiatives.

INDIAN AGRICULTURE

Role of Agriculture in Indian Economy

1. **Share of Agriculture in National Income :** Agriculture is an important sector of the economy. Though the share of agriculture in national income has come down since the inception of planning era in the economy but still it has substantial share in GDP. The share of agriculture and allied sectors in Gross Value Added (GVA) of the country at current prices was 18.4 per cent for the year 2022-23.
2. **Important Contribution to Employment :** Due to lack of industrialisation and no significant development in service sector, these sectors have contributed very less in employment generation. So, agriculture is the largest employment providing sector in the economy. Agriculture sector, provides employment to 49% of country's work force.
3. **Important Source of Industrial Development:** It provides raw materials to various industries and other agro-based industries. Cotton and Jute textile indus-tries, sugar, vanaspati industry etc. are directly depen-dent on agriculture. This highlights the importance of agriculture in industrial development of the nation.
4. **Importance in International Trade :** India's foreign trade is deeply associated with agriculture sector. Value of agriculture exports to total exports of the country was 10.32 per cent in 2023-24.

LAND REFORMS

Land reforms are institutional changes that make the tenurial system more favourable to the actual tillers and attempt to adjust the size of farms at the operationally viable level. The scope of land reforms includes abolition of intermediaries, tenancy reforms and ceiling on land holdings; consolidation of subdivided and fragmented land holdings; and cooperative farming.

Land reforms are important as they provide incentives and encouragement to the actual tillers by providing a congenial climate and hence act as a costless method of increasing production.

Abolition of Intermediaries

The actual abolition of intermediaries started in 1948 with the enactment of legislation in Madras (Chennai). Intermediary tenural systems like Zamindari, Jagirdari, Inamdari etc, which prevailed over 40% of the country were abolished. Waste and fallow land distributed to the landless.

Tenancy Reforms

Measures of tenancy reforms pertain to—

1. regulation of rent
2. security of tenure
3. conferment of ownership on tenants

Various states have passed necessary legislation for the regulation of rent, but owing to the weak position of the tenants and prevalence of wide spread hunger for land, the rent-regulating law is more breached than complied with. Experience of the implementation of Zamindari abolition showed that, on the plea of resumption for personal cultivation, evictions of tenants took place on a massive scale. During the second plan, the states framed provisions for resumption broadly on the following three different patterns:

(i) All tenants have been given full security of tenure, without giving owners the right of personal cultivation.

(ii) Owners have been given the right to retain a limited area, however, subject to the condition that a minimum area is left with the tenant.

(iii) A limit has been placed on the extent of land, which a land owner may retain, but the tenant is not entitled to retain minimum area for cultivation in all cases.

Ceiling on Land Holding

Land ceiling laws were first enacted in the 50s and 60s. It was further revised in 1972. Family ceilings were lowered to 5 hectares for irrigated land with two crops, 7.5 hectares for irrigated land with one crop and 12 hectares for other lands. The Benami Transactions ordinance, 1988 also makes "benami" transaction illegal. It is an important step towards land reform.

The land reforms policies have been formulated in the right direction but the basic purpose of introducing land reforms has been adversely affected because of various shortcomings in the legislation, lack of political will for implementation of various laws and programmes, absence of pressure from below because the poor agricultural workers and peasants are passive, unorganised and inarticulate, luke-warm and often apathetic attitude of bureaucracy, absence of upto-date land records and legal hurdles in the way of implementation of land reforms.

NEW INDUSTRIAL POLICY (1991)

The Congress Government led by Mr. Narasimha Rao announced the new industrial policy in July 1991. The main aim of the new industrial policy was:

(*i*) to unshackle the Indian industrial economy from the cobwebs of unnecessary bureaucratic control,

(*ii*) to introduce liberalisation with a view to integrate the Indian economy with the world economy,

(*iii*) to remove restrictions on direct foreign investment as also to free the domestic entrepreneur from the restrictions of MRTP Act, and

(*iv*) the policy aimed to shed the load of the public enterprises which have shown a very low rate of return or were incurring losses over the years.

All these reforms of industrial policy led the government to take a series of initiatives in respect of policies in the following areas:

(*a*) Industrial Licensing

(*b*) Foreign Investment

(*c*) Foreign Technology Policy

(*d*) Public Sector Policy

(*e*) MRTP Act.

Abolition of Industrial Licensing

Industrial licensing policy in India has been governed by the Industries (Development and Regulation) Act, 1951. Industrial licensing policy and procedures have been liberalised considerably from time to time. Yet, the industrial licensing policy has all along been resented to by the entrepreneurs as it led to unnecessary governmental interference, delays in investment decisions and bureaucratic red-tapism, curruption etc. Not only this, the industrial licensing policy was also unable to achieve the objectives laid down for it by the government. On account of these considerations, and in order to liberalise the economy and to enable the entrepreneurs to make investment decisions on the basis of their own commercial judgement, the 1991 industrial policy abolished industrial licensing for all but 18 industries. The 18 industries for which licensing was kept necessary were—coal and lignite; petroleum (other than crude) and its distillation products; distillation and brewing of alcoholic drinks; sugar; animal fats and oils; cigars and cigarettes; asbestos and asbestos based products; plywood and other wood based products; raw hides and skins and leathers; tanned or dressed furskins;

motor cars; paper and news print; electronic aerospace and defence equipment; industrial explosives; hazardous chemicals; drugs and pharmaceuticals; entertainment electronics; and white goods (domestic refrigerators, washing machines, air conditioners, etc.). With the passage of time, most of these industries have also been delicensed. As of now, licensing is compulsory for only 5 industries. These are alcohol, cigarettes, hazardous chemicals, defence equipment and industrial explosives.

Public Sector's Role Diluted

The 1956 Resolution had reserved 17 industries for the public sector. The 1991 industrial policy reduced this number to 8 :

1. arms and ammunition,
2. atomic energy,
3. coal and lignite,
4. mineral oils,
5. mining of iron ore, manganese ore, chrome ore, gypsum, sulphur, gold and diamond,
6. mining of copper, lead, zinc, tin, molybdenum and wolfarm
7. minerals specified in the schedule to the atomic energy (control of production and order), 1953 and
8. rail transport.

In 1993, items (5) and (6) were deleted from the reserved list. In 1998-99, items (3) and (4) were also taken out from the reserved list. On May 9, 2001, the government opened up arms and ammunition sector also to the private sector. This now leaves only 3 industries reserved exclusively for the public sector.

The new industrial policy also states that the government will undertake review of the existing public enterprises in low technology, small scale and non-strategic areas as also when there is low or nil social consideration or public purpose. Sick units will be referred to the Board for Industrial and Financial Reconstruction (or a similar body) for advice about rehabilitation and reconstruction. For enterprises remaining in the public sector, it is stated that they will be provided a much greater degree of management autonomy through the system of MOU (memorandum of understanding).

The government has also announced its intention to offer a part of government share holding in the public sector enterprises to mutual funds, financial institutions, the general public and the workers. A beginning in this direction was made in 1991-92 itself by divesting part of the equities of selected public sector enterprises. The new industrial policy indicates the government's intention to invite a greater degree of participation by the private sector in important areas of the economy.

POVERTY AND UNEMPLOYMENT IN INDIA

Poverty is a social phenomenon in which a section of society is unable to fulfil even its basic necessities of life. The term 'Poverty' has been defined in different societies in a different way but all of them are conditioned by the version of minimum or good life to be obtained in society. For instance, the concept of poverty in USA would be significantly different from that in India because the ability to afford a higher living standard is much higher in the United States.

Several economists and organisations have given different estimates of poverty. Most of them estimated the number of persons below the poverty line on the basis of an average calorie intake of 2250 per capita per day. According to the report of 'Task Force on Minimum Needs and Effective Consumption Demand'— an expert group of planning commission, defined poverty line on a nutritional norm of per capita daily intake of 2400 calories in rural areas and 2100 calories for urban areas. A person who fails to obtain this minimum level of calories is treated as being below the poverty line.

The expert committee set up by the Planning Commission under C. Rangarajan former chairperson of Prime Minister's Economic Advisory Council, has redefined the poverty line. According to the report of the committee, the new poverty line should be ₹ 32 in rural areas and ₹ 47 in urban areas. The earlier poverty line figure was ₹ 27 for rural India and ₹ 33 for Urban India.

	No. of Rural poor	No. of Urban poor	Total	Percent of poor
Rangarajan Committee	260.5 million	102.5 million	363 million	29.5
Tendulkar Committee	216.5 million	52.8 million	269 million	21.9%
Difference	44 million	49.7 million	93.7 million	

The Rangarajan report has added 93.7 million more to the list of the poor assessed as per the Suresh Tendulkar Committee formula. Now the total number of poor has reached 363 million from 269 million in 2011-12.

This raise in the poverty line income bar means 93.7 million more people are now below poverty line (BPL).

Various Employment Programmes in India

S. N.	Programmes	Year of beginning	Objectives
1.	Community Development Programme (CDP)	1952	Overall development of rural areas with people's participation
2.	Food for Work Programme	1977-78	Providing foodgrains to labour for the works of development
3.	Antyodaya Yojana	1977-78	To make the poorest families of the village economically independent (only in Rajasthan State)
4.	Training Rural Youth for Self-Employment (TRYSEM)	Aug., 15, 1979	Programme of training rural youth for self-employment
5.	Integrated Rural Development Programme (IRDP)	Oct., 2, 1980	All-round development of the rural poor through a programme of asset endowment for self-employment
6.	National Rural Employment Programme (NREP)	1980	To provide profitable employment opportunities to the rural poor
7.	Development of Women and Children in Rural Areas (DWCRA)	Sept., 1982	To provide suitable opportunities of self-employment to the women belonging to the rural families who are living below the poverty line
8.	Rural Landless Employment Guarantee Programme (RLEGP)	Aug., 15, 1983	For providing employment to landless farmers and labourers
9.	Self-Employment to the Educated Unemployed Youth (SEEUY)	1983-84	To provide financial and technical assistance for self-employment
10.	Self-Employment Programme for the Urban Poor (SEPUP)	Sept., 1986	To provide self-employment to urban poor through provision of subsidy and bank credit
11.	Swarna Jayanti Shahari Rozgar Yojana (SJSRY)	Dec., 1997	To provide gainful employment to urban unemployed and under employed poor through self-employment or wage employment
12.	Pradhan Mantri Gramodaya Yojana	2000	To fulfil basic requirements in rural areas
13.	Antyodaya Anna Yojana	Dec., 25, 2000	To provide food security to poor
14.	Pradhan Mantri Gram Sadak Yojana (PMGSY)	Dec., 25, 2000	To line all villages with pucca road
15.	Mahatama Gandhi National Rural Employment Guarantee Act	Feb., 2, 2006	To Provide at least 100 days wage employment in rural areas
16.	Atal Pension Yojana	1 June 2015	To provide old age income security to workers in unorganised sector.
17.	Pradhan Mantri Suraksha Bima Yojana	1 June 2015	To provide insurance in case of death or accident.
18.	Pradhan Mantri Jeevan Jyoti Yojana	1 June 2015	To provide life insurance cover for death due to any reason.
19.	Pradhan Mantri Garib Kalyan Yojanaye (PMGKY)	April 2015	Implement the pro-poor welfare schemes in more effective way and reaches out to more poor population across the country.
20.	Startup India, Standup India	16 Jan. 2016	To provide support to all start-up businesses in all aspects of doing business in India.
21.	Pradhan Mantri Jan Aushadhi Yojana (PMJAY)	March 2016	Provides Drugs/Medicines at affordable cost across the country.
22.	Atmanirbhar Bharat Abhiyan	May, 2020	Economic Stimulus relief package announced for the poor to overcome difficulties caused by Coronavirus.
23.	SMILE	2022	Support for Marginalised Individuals for Livelihood and Enterprises.
24.	PM Vishwakarma Scheme	Sep. 17, 2023	This scheme supports artisans and Craftsmen engaged in 18 traditional crafts.
25.	Pradhan Mantri Vidyalakshmi Yojana	2024	A new Central Sector scheme that seeks to provide financial support to meritorious students.
26.	Prime Minister Dhan Dhaanya Krishi Yojana	2025	It aims to enhance agricultural productivity.

POPULATION IN INDIA

India and many other Third World countries are now passing through the phase of population explosion. It is being argued that this situation has arisen because economic development in these countries has failed to maintain pace with population growth. The thrust of this argument is that since rapid growth of population causes poverty and proves to be a barrier to development, these countries should take care of their population growth if they seriously wish to solve their poverty problem and put their economy on the path of economic development.

Size and Growth

India's population as on 1 March 2011 stood at 121.08 million (623 million males and 587 million females). India accounts for a meagre 2.4 per cent of the world surface area of 135.79 million sq km. Yet, it supports and sustains a whopping 17.5 per cent of the world population.

The population of India, which at the turn of the twentieth century was around 238.4 million, increased to reach 1028 million at the dawn of the twenty-first century. The population of India as recorded at each decennial census from 1901 has grown steadily except for a decrease during 1911-21.

The per cent decadal growth of population in the inter-censal period 2001-11 varies from a low of –0.6 in Nagaland to a very high 27.9 in Meghalaya.

Population Density

It is defined as the number of persons per sq km. The population density of India in 2011 was 382 per sq km. The density of population was increased in all States and Union Territories between 2001 and 2011. Among major states, Bihar is the most thickly populated state with a population density of 1106 in 2011. West Bangal is now the second highest densely populated state pushing Kerala to the third place.

Sex Ratio

Sex ratio, defined as the number of females per thousand males. The sex ratio in the country had always remained unfavourable to females. It was 72 at the beginning of the 20th century and thereafter showed continuous decline until 1941.

Literacy

For the purpose of census 2011, a person aged seven and above, who can both read and write with understanding in any language, is treated as literate. A person, who can only read but cannot write, is not literate. In the censuses prior to 1991, children below five years of age were necessarily treated as illiterates.

The results of 2011 census reveal that there has been an increase in literacy in the country. The literacy rate in the country is 73.0 per cent, 80.9 for males and 64.6 for females.

Kerala retained its position by being on top with a 94.0 per cent literacy rate, closely followed by Mizoram (91.3 per cent) and Tripura (87.2 per cent). Bihar with a literacy rate of 61.8 per cent ranks last in the country preceded by Arunachal Pradesh (65.4 per cent) and Rajasthan (66.1 per cent). Kerala also occupies the top spot in the country both in male literacy with 96.1 per cent and female literacy with 92.1 per cent. On the contrary, Bihar has recorded the lowest literacy rates in case of males (71.2 per cent) and Rajasthan in females (52.1 per cent).

Multiple Choice Questions

1. The law of Demand refers to
   A. Price-supply relationship
   B. Price-cost relationship
   C. Price-demand relationship
   D. Price-income relationship
2. In a typical demand schedule, quantity demanded
   A. Varies directly with price
   B. Varies proportionately with price
   C. Varies inversely with price
   D. Is independent of price
3. Normally when price per unit of a good falls, its
   A. Quantity demanded increases
   B. Quantity demanded decreases
   C. Quantity demanded remains constant
   D. None of these happens
4. A fall in the price of a commodity leads to
   A. A shift in demand
   B. A fall in demand
   C. A rise in consumers real income
   D. A fall in the consumers real income
5. Market demand for any good is a function of the
   A. Price per unit of the good
   B. Price per unit of other goods
   C. Income of consumers
   D. All of the above
6. A typical demand curve cannot be
   A. Convex to the origin
   B. A straight line parallel to y-axis
   C. A straight line parallel to x-axis
   D. Rising upwards to the right
7. When the law of demand operates the demand curve
   A. Slopes downward from left to right
   B. Slopes upward from left to right
   C. Slopes upward from right to left
   D. Parallel to horizontal axis
8. Which one of the following is true increase of normal goods?
   A. When Price increases, demand decreases
   B. When Price increases, demand also increases
   C. When Price remains constant, demand falls down
   D. When Price falls down, demand remains constant
9. An exceptional demand curve is one that slopes:
   A. Upwards to the right
   B. Down wards to the right
   C. Upwards to the left
   D. Horizontally
10. When there is decrease in demand the demand curve–
    A. Moves downwards towards the axis
    B. Moves upwards away from the axis
    C. Remains unchanged
    D. None of the above
11. Two goods have to be consumed simultaneously are
    A. Identical B. Complementary
    C. Substitutes D. None of these
12. Which of the following pairs of commodities is an example of substitutes
    A. Coffee and milk
    B. Diamond and Cow
    C. Pen and ink
    D. Mustard oil and coconut oil
13. Bread and butter, lamb and mint sauce, illustrate the type of inter related demand known as
    A. Rival demand
    B. Composite demand
    C. Competitive demand
    D. Joint demand
14. 'Change in quantity demanded' refers to
    A. Upward shift of the demand curve
    B. Downward shift of the demand curve
    C. Movement on the same demand curve
    D. None of these
15. An increase in demand can result from
    A. A decline in market price
    B. An increase in income

C. A reduction in the price of substitutes
D. An increase in the price of complements

16. If the price of coffee suddenly shoots up, ceteris paribus, the demand for Tea is expected to—
A. Move rightward along the original demand curve
B. Increase
C. Remain unaffected
D. Decrease

17. In the case of Giffen good like bajra, a fall in its price tends to—
A. Make the demand remain constant
B. Reduce the demand
C. Increase the demand
D. Change demand in an abnormal way

18. Market demand is
A. The sum of all individual demands
B. Demand at prevailing average prices
C. Ability to pay the price asked
D. Demand in a perfectly free market

19. A negative income elasticity of demand for a commodity indicates that as income falls the amount of the commodity purchased
A. Rises
B. Falls
C. Remains unchanged
D. Any of the above

20. When with a change in price the total outlay on a commodity remains constant, it is a case of
A. Perfect elasticity B. Perfect inelasticity
C. Unit elasticity D. Zero elasticity

21. Cross elasticity of complementary goods is
A. Negative B. Zero
C. High D. Infinite

22. Elasticity of demand is equal to unity while marginal revenue is
A. Positive B. Zero
C. Negative D. Indeterminate

23. When the income elasticity of demand is greater than unity, the commodity is
A. A necessity
B. A luxury
C. An inferior good
D. A non-related good

24. Marginal utility (MU) curve is always
A. Rising
B. Falling
C. Parallel to x-axis
D. Parallel to y-axis

25. The total utility is maximum when
A. M.U. is zero
B. A.U. is the highest
C. M.U. is the highest
D. M.U. is equal to A.U.

26. The price which a consumer would be willing to pay for a commodity equals to his
A. Total utility
B. Marginal utility
C. Average utility
D. Does not have any relation to any one of these

27. Consumer's surplus is the highest in the case of
A. Necessities
B. Comforts
C. Luxuries
D. Conventional necessities

28. The market period supply curve for perishable commodities is—
A. Relatively inelastic
B. Perfectly inelastic
C. Relatively elastic
D. Perfectly elastic

29. Supply of a commodity is a
A. Stock concept
B. A flow concept
C. Both stock and flow concept
D. None of these

30. "Production" may be defined as an act of—
A. Creating utility
B. Earning profit
C. Destroying utility
D. Providing services

31. All money costs can be regarded as:
A. Social costs B. Opportunity costs
C. Explicit costs D. Real costs

32. The real aim of production is
A. To create material goods
B. To eliminate poverty
C. To satisfy peoples wants
D. To provide basic necessities

33. In perfect competition, there is a process of
A. Free entry but restricted exit of the firms
B. Free entry and free exit of the firms
C. Restricted entry and exit of the firms
D. Semi-free exit but absolute free entry

34. The difference between gross domestic product and net domestic product equals
A. Transfer payments
B. Depreciation cost
C. Indirect taxes
D. Subsidies

35. The best method of computing national income is
A. Product Method
B. Income Method
C. Expenditure Method
D. Combination of income and production method

36. The National income is equal to
A. GNP – Subsides – Taxes
B. NNP – Indirect Taxes + Subsidies
C. NNP – Direct Taxes + Subsides
D. GNP – Subsidies + Taxes

37. Which state has maximum branches of public sector commercial banks?
A. U.P. B. Maharashtra
C. Karnataka D. Gujarat

38. In which plan phase of industrialisation was initiated?
A. Fourth B. Third
C. Second D. First

39. Which is the first Export Processing Zone declared as Free Trade Zone in India?
A. Santacruz B. Kandla
C. Falta D. Noida

40. Which institution is known as 'soft loan window' of World Bank?
A. IFC
B. IDA
C. IMF
D. Indian Development Forum

41. 'Backwash Effect' was firstly introduced by—
A. Gunnar Myrdal B. Peter Suderland
C. Arthur Dunkel D. Kindelberger

42. Meera Seth Committee was related to—
A. Development of Handlooms
B. Sex-differentiation in employment
C. Abolition of Child Labour
D. Welfare of working women

43. 'SAPTA' is related to—
A. Education B. Trade
C. Security D. Environment

44. National Income estimates in India is prepared by—
A. NITI Aayog
B. RBI
C. Finance Ministry
D. C.S.O.

45. Scheduled bank is that bank which is—
A. Nationalised
B. Not–nationalised
C. Based at foreign country
D. Included in the second schedule of R.B.F

46. The definition of small scale industry in India is based an—
A. Sales of a unit
B. Investment in machines and equipments
C. Market coverage
D. Export capacity

47. Which one of the following committees was set up to review the concept of poverty line?
A. S. Chakravarty Committee
B. K.N. Wanchoo Committee
C. D.T. Lakdawala Committee
D. R.C. Dutt Committee

48. The book 'Politics with Charkha' is written by—
A. Ashok Mehta
B. J.B. Kriplani
C. K.G. Mashruwala
D. Morarji Desai

49. CAPART is related with—
A. Assisting and evaluating rural welfare programmes
B. Computer hardware
C. Consultant service of export promotion
D. Controlling pollution in big industries

50. White revolution refers to:
A. Cement industry B. Dairying
C. Cotton industry D. None of these

51. Which of the following does not grant any tax rebate?
A. National Saving Certificate
B. Indira Vikas Patra
C. National Saving Scheme
D. Public Provident Fund

52. Who is the Chairman of 16th Finance Commission?
A. C. Rangrajan B. Arvind Pangariya
C. L.K. Jha D. None of these

53. SEBI was established in—
A. 1993 B. 1992
C. 1988 D. 1990

54. Asian Development Bank has opened its Residential Office in—
A. New Delhi B. Kolkata
C. Mumbai D. Bangalore

55. Chairman of Tax Reform Committee was—
A. Pranab Mukherjee B. K.P. Narsimham
C. S. Janakiraman D. Raja Chelliah

56. SAIL was established in—
A. 1974 B. 1984
C. 1990 D. 1964

57. Rural women can avail the benefit of Mahila Samriddhi Yojana if they open their account in–
A. Rural Post Offices
B. Commercial Banks
C. Rural Development Bank
D. Any of the above

58. Pradhan Mantri Gram Sadak Yojana (PMGSY) was launched in—
A. 2000 B. 1999
C. 2001 D. 2004

59. The Headquarter of CAPART is situated at—
A. Mumbai B. Kolkata
C. New Delhi D. Bangalore

60. The main security guard of International Trade is–
A. IMF B. World Bank
C. WTO D. IFC

61. 'Closed Economy' is that economy in which—
A. Only export takes place
B. Money supply is fully controlled
C. Deficit financing takes place
D. Neither export nor import takes place

62. National Rural Development Institute is situated at—
A. Shimla B. Hyderabad
C. Patna D. New Delhi

63. The Headquarter of World Bank is situated at—
A. Manila B. Washington D.C.
C. New York D. Geneva

64. Which of the rate is not determined of RBI?
A. Bank Rate B. CRR
C. SLR D. PLR

65. The main foodgrains of India is—
A. Rice B. Wheat
C. Sugarcane D. Maize

66. Which district of Hindi speaking belt has firstly been declared as fully literate?
A. Narsinghpur (M.P.)
B. Palampur (H.P.)
C. Jhunjhanu (Rajasthan)
D. Palamu (Jharkhand)

67. Which sector has the maximum quantum of disguised unemployment in India?
A. Agriculture B. Industry
C. Trade D. Transport

68. 'Food for work programme' was renamed as—
A. RLEGP B. IRDP
C. NREP D. MNP

69. India has emerged in the world as the
A. Second Largest Steel Producer
B. Third Largest Steel Producer
C. Fourth Largest Steel Producer
D. None of these

70. The goods can be taxed heavily to earn additional revenue if they are—
A. Highly elastic B. Unit elastic
C. Perfectly elastic D. Inelastic

71. Scheduled Bank is that bank which is—
A. Nationalised
B. Not nationalised
C. Based at foreign country
D. Included in the second schedule of RBI

72. Which fertilizer is mostly consumed in India?
A. N
B. P
C. K
D. All are used in equal ratio

73. Who is the Chairman of NDC?
A. Finance Minister B. Prime Minister
C. Planning Minister D. Lok Sabha Speaker

74. The field given to Rangarajan Committee was—
A. Modernisation of Cloth Industry
B. To probe Share scam
C. To probe Sugar scam
D. To suggest measures for controlling BOP deficit

75. VAT is imposed—
A. Directly on consumer
B. On final stage of production
C. On first stage of production
D. On all stages between production and final sale

76. Kutir Jyoti scheme is associated with—
A. Promoting cottage industry in villages
B. Promoting employment among rural unemployed youth
C. Providing electricity to rural families living below the poverty line
D. All of these

77. OTCEI is—
A. Atomic submarine of China
B. Economic policy of USA
C. A Indian Share Market
D. A defence research organisation

78. Which is the most liquid measure of money supply?
A. M_1 B. M_2
C. M_3 D. M_4

79. M_3 measure of money supply does not include—
A. Cash with public
B. Demand deposits with Post offices
C. Demand deposits with Banks
D. Time deposits with Banks

80. NITI Aayog was constituted in–
A. 2013 B. 2014
C. 2015 D. 2016

81. Gresham's Law is related to—
A. Consumption and Demand
B. Supply and Demand
C. Circulation of Money
D. Deficit Financing

82. Kelkar Committee report is related to—
A. Tax Reforms
B. Financial Sector Reforms
C. Trade Reforms
D. Administrative Reforms

83. What is 'Super 301'?
A. A name of modern computer
B. A new variety of Rice
C. American trade law
D. American treatment name for Aids

84. When development in economy takes place the share of tertiary sector in National Income?
A. Declines
B. Increases
C. Remains constant
D. First rises and then falls

85. Plan expenditure in India is met by—
A. Internal debt and other resources
B. Assistance from Aid India Club
C. Assistance from IMF
D. Assistance from OECD countries

86. Population Density means—
A. No. of persons living per sq. km.
B. No. of persons living per kilometre
C. Ratio of population living below poverty line to total population
D. No. of persons in a village

87. Which tax is collected by Panchayat?
A. Sales Tax B. Custom Duty
C. Land Revenue D. Tax on local fairs

88. Centralised planning was first adopted in the economy of—
A. Russia B. Poland
C. China D. India

89. Which among the following states is a leading industrialised state?
A. West Bengal B. Odisha
C. Maharashtra D. Madhya Pradesh

90. Which of the following state has been announced as 'a state of total organic farming'?
A. Sikkim B. Karnataka
C. Kerala D. Punjab

91. Indian Green Revolution is the most successful in—
A. Wheat and Potato B. Jwar and Oil Seeds
C. Wheat and Rice D. Tea and Coffee

92. Economic Planning is in—
A. Union list B. State list
C. Concurrent list D. Not any specified list

93. Which types of tax helps in reducing disparities of income?
A. Proportionate tax B. Progressive tax
C. Regressive tax D. All of these

94. 'Golden Handshake Scheme' is associated with—
A. Inviting foreign companies
B. Private investment in public enterprises
C. Establishing joint enterprises
D. Voluntary retirement

95. Which is not a part of new economic reforms in India?
A. Globalisation B. Centralisation
C. Privatisation D. Liberalisation

96. The official exchange rate of Indian rupee is associated with
A. Pound Sterling
B. Dollar
C. SDR
D. A basket of selected currencies

97. As a result of Green Revolution which foodgrains had a reduced percentage in total foodgrain production?
A. Wheat B. Rice
C. Cereals and Pulses D. None of these

98. Corporate Tax is imposed by—
A. State Government
B. Local Government
C. Central Government
D. Both Centre and State Government

99. MRTP is related to—
A. Monopoly and trade restrictions
B. Inflation control
C. Transport control
D. Foreign Exchange Regulations

100. The basis of determining dearness allowance to employee in India is—
A. National Income
B. Consumer Price Index
C. Standard of Living
D. Per Capita Income

ANSWERS

1	2	3	4	5	6	7	8	9	10
C	C	A	B	D	D	A	A	A	A
11	12	13	14	15	16	17	18	19	20
B	D	D	C	B	B	B	A	A	C
21	22	23	24	25	26	27	28	29	30
A	B	B	B	A	D	A	B	B	A
31	32	33	34	35	36	37	38	39	40
C	C	B	B	D	B	A	C	A	B
41	42	43	44	45	46	47	48	49	50
A	A	B	D	D	B	C	B	A	B
51	52	53	54	55	56	57	58	59	60
B	B	C	A	D	A	A	A	C	C
61	62	63	64	65	66	67	68	69	70
D	B	B	D	A	A	A	C	B	D
71	72	73	74	75	76	77	78	79	80
D	A	B	D	D	C	C	A	B	C
81	82	83	84	85	86	87	88	89	90
C	A	C	B	A	A	D	A	C	A
91	92	93	94	95	96	97	98	99	100
C	C	B	D	B	D	C	C	A	B

English Language

1

Comprehension Passages

ENGLISH LANGUAGE COMPREHENSION

The objective of language comprehension test is to ascertain the ability of the candidates to understand the passage properly.

Therefore candidates are required to take notice of the following points:

1. Read the full passage very attentively and intelligently.
2. Try to comprehend the gist of it.
3. Make a mental note of all the important details and points given in the passage.
4. Read the passage for the second time in case you have not been able to understand it satisfactorily.
5. Divide the time proportionately for all the passages.
6. Answer the questions on the basis of facts, as given in the paragraph.
7. Don't waste much time in answering the questions of any one passage.
8. Check all the answers once again, very carefully, to see whether any question is left unanswered by mistake.

MODEL QUESTIONS (FOR PRACTICE)

Directions: *Each of the following passages is followed by five questions. Read the passage carefully and then answer the questions that follow each. For each question, four probable answers A, B, C and D are given. Only one out of these is correct. Choose the correct answer.*

PASSAGE-1

The use of words like 'welcome', 'thank you', 'please', etc., at the right moment reflects a polite nature. The civic sense also lies within the scope of good manners. We should not shout or talk loudly in public places like hospitals and libraries and create disturbance. We should not cheat people or make fun of them. Cleanliness is also necessary. We must not throw the waste on roads and make use of dustbins. We should not harm the public property as it belongs to all of us. While in a queue, discipline should be maintained. We must give fair chance to others.

1. Expressions like 'welcome' 'thank you' and 'please' reflect
   A. happiness B. discipline
   C. civic sense D. polite nature
2. While in a library, we should
   A. respect others B. avoid arguments
   C. talk in low tone D. be courteous
3. A public property belongs to
   A. nobody B. all of us
   C. government D. one who maintains it
4. Discipline is
   A. the rule of proper conduct or action
   B. the rule of road sense
   C. making use of dustbins
   D. forming a queue
5. The most appropriate title for this passage would be
   A. Polite Nature B. Courtesy
   C. Good Manners D. Civic Sense

PASSAGE-2

There is an old proverb 'Early to bed and early to rise makes a man healthy and wise.' I am in the habit of getting up early in the morning and have formed the habit of taking long morning walks in the past two years. It is a light exercise and best for physical fitness. The morning air which is fresh and pure is beneficial for the lungs. The early rays of the rising sun are good for healthy skin. 'Health is wealth' and doctors also recommend morning walk to their patients for gaining sound health and freshness of energy.

1. What is good for lungs?
   A. Sunrays B. Fresh air
   C. Sound sleep D. Light exercise
2. What is a light exercise?
   A. Early to bed B. Early to rise
   C. Morning walk D. Gaining sound health
3. What is good for skin?
   A. Fresh air B. Morning air
   C. Morning walk D. Rising sun's rays
4. What is best for physical fitness?
   A. Light exercise B. Long morning walk
   C. Early to rise D. Fresh and pure air
5. Long morning walk
   A. bring sound sleep
   B. ensures physical fitness
   C. ensures healthy skin
   D. keeps healthy, wealthy and wise

PASSAGE-3

Mahatma Gandhi lived a splendid long life and has set great moral standards before us. He showed to the world the true way to peace. He wished to see India prosper but he became a martyr for the noble cause of Hindu-Muslim unity at the time of partition when a religious fanatic, Nathuram Godse, shot him dead on January 30, 1948. His last words were 'Hey Ram'. He lived and died for his country and countryman.

1. Mahatma Gandhi showed the world the true way to
A. prosperity B. love
C. truth D. peace

2. Mahatma Gandhi became a martyr for the noble cause of
A. truth B. non-violence
C. freedom of India D. Hindu-Muslim unity

3. Mahatma Gandhi was shot dead
A. before India achieved independence
B. by a mad man
C. by an intolerant religious person
D. by a non-religious person

4. Mahatma Gandhi set great moral standards. It means
A. he was a great religious teacher
B. he was a great moralist
C. he made India morally stronger
D. moral was everything to him

5. Gandhiji lived and died for his country and countryman. It means
A. he was born in India and died in India
B. he was a patriot
C. he was a great moralist
D. he sacrified his life for India and her people

PASSAGE-4

On one hot day a crow felt very thirsty. He flew from one place to another in search of water. After long hours of labour he found a pitcher. Eagerly, he perched on the mouth of the pitcher. He found that the water was at the bottom of the vessel. He tried his best to dip his beak but did not succeed. He did not know what to do. Suddenly some pebbles lying nearby gave him an idea. One by one he dropped the pebbles with his beak into the pitcher. The level of water slowly came up to the mouth of the pitcher. The crow then drank the water and quenched his thirst.

1. The crow found a pitcher
A. as it flew
B. after many hours of labour
C. full of water
D. which was empty

2. What is the moral of the passage?
A. No pains, no gains
B. God helps those who help themselves
C. Necessity is the mother of invention
D. Try and try again, you will succeed at last

3. The crow flew from place to place
A. in search of pitcher B. in search of pebbles
C. in search of water D. in search of a vessel

4. The pitcher, the crow found
A. was full of water
B. was dry
C. had little water in the bottom
D. had water up to its mouth

5. As the crow dropped pebbles into the pitcher, what happend?
A. The pitcher broke down
B. The water leaked one of the pitcher
C. The level of water into the pitcher rose up slowly
D. Water level immediately rose to the mouth of the pitcher

PASSAGE-5

Once upon a time a crane and a fox lived in a forest. They were good friend. One day the fox invited the crane to a feast. He made a tasty food and served it before the crane on a plate. The crane could not eat anything because of the long beak. But the fox licked all his food. The crane felt insulted. He decided to teach the fox a lesson. Next day he invited the fox. He prepared the same tasty food and placed it in front of the fox inside a narrow glass. The crane ate easily while the fox looked on. Now, it was the fox's turn to remain hungry.

1: What is the moral of the passage?
A. Beware of the wicked
B. One good turn deserves another
C. Be contented with what you have
D. Tit for tat

2. The crane could not eat tasty food because the
A. food was served in a shallow plate
B. food was very hot
C. food was served in a long jar
D. crane was not hungry

3. The fox had to remain hungry because
A. the food served was not enough in quantity
B. the food was served inside a narrow glass
C. the food served was not tasty
D. the food was all liquid

4. Why did the crane feel insulted?
A. Because he was invited to feast but he could not eat anything
B. Because the food was served in a shallow plate and he could not eat
C. Because the food was too hot
D. Because the fox gulped all the food quickly

5. The crane successfully taught a lesson to the fox when he invited the fox to a feast and served the food
A. in a narrow glass B. in a large plate
C. in a broken plate D. in a long jar

PASSAGE-6

The family set down at the table and began to talk about the summer holidays. They had to decide a place to visit during the vacation. Should they go to their village or to a hill station? The parents preferred the village while the children wished to go the hill station. After few moments of discussion the elders decided to visit both the places. First they shall go to the village for a week and then stay at the hill station for the remaining days. For the first time the family shall be together during the holidays. The children were happy with the holiday plan.

1. The purpose for which the family set down at the table was
A. to decide a place to visit during the vacation
B. to educate the children how to carry articles during a visit to a hill station
C. to decide the date when they should start their journey
D. to tell the children that they will visit a hill station during this vacation

2. The final plan was to visit
A. their village
B. a hill station
C. their village as well as a hill station
D. their home town

3. The final decision was made by
A. the boys B. the girls
C. the women D. the elders

4. They decided first to go to their village and stay there for
A. a day B. a week
C. ten days D. a fortnight

5. Why were children happy?
A. Because a hill station was included in their holiday plan
B. Because a visit to their village was excluded from their holiday plan
C. Because their choice prevailed
D. Because they were going all alone to the hill station

PASSAGE-7

Once Govind intended to go on pilgrimage with his family. He asked Mirind to accompany. But for his trade's reason, he did not go with him. So Govind thought it safe to leave the box of his jewellery with him, as it was dangerous to leave it in a lone house or take it on the journey. So he went to him with the box. He took him to a lonely place under a tree and handed it over to him. He told Mirind, "Keep it safe with you. I shall return from the journey after six month then I shall take it back from you." Mirind said, "Don't worry, I shall keep it as safe as own."

1. Govind intended to go
A. for a business trip
B. to a hill station
C. on a long journey to a sacred place
D. to his home town for a long period

2. Why did Govind leave his box of jewellery with Mirind?
A. Because it was not safe to take the box with him on a long journey
B. Because Mirind was his fast friend
C. Because the box was very heavy
D. Because his house was unsafe

3. Why did Govind take Mirind to a lonely place?
A. To tell him that the box contained valuable jewellery
B. So that no third person could see box
C. To show him what was within the box
D. To tell him that the box will remain with him

4. Where did Govind hand over the box of jewellery to Mirind?
A. At Mirind's house
B. At his own house
C. In a lonely place
D. In a lonely place under a tree

5. It was not safe to leave the box in a lone house. Here the word 'lone house' means
A. a house in a deserted place
B. a house where none lives
C. a house without door and lock
D. a house near the forest

PASSAGE-8

Zahir-ud-din Babar was the first Mughal emperor of India. A descendent of Timur on father's side and Changez Khan on his mother's side, Babar was a brave warrior. After defeating Ibrahim Lodhi in the First Battle of Panipat in 1526 he entered Delhi and soon gained control over Agra. After many more battles with Rajputs he extended his empire over Punjab, Uttar Pradesh and north Bihar. He died at a young age of 48 years in 1530 at his capital Agra without getting much time to consolidate his victories.

1. Zahir-ud-din Babar was the first
A. Muslim ruler of India B. Mughal ruler of India
C. Afghan ruler of India D. Turk ruler of India

2. Babar was born in the years
A. 1480 B. 1482
C. 1492 D. 1962

3. Babar first occupied
A. Punjab B. Agra
C. Delhi D. Panipat

4. Babar was a brave warrior. Here brave warrior means
A. courageous soldier B. a kind hearted soldier
C. a clever fighter D. a victorious general

5. Babar extended his empire over Punjab and Uttar Pradesh after many more battles with the
A. Afghans B. Rajputs
C. Mughals D. Lodhies

PASSAGE-9

Our National Flag is tricolour. It has three equal horizontal strips. The strip at the top is saffron, in the middle is white and at the bottom is green. The ratio of width to length of the flag is 2 : 3. In the centre of the white strip is a wheel in navy blue. The wheel represents the *chakra.* Its design is similar to the wheel which appears on the abacus of the Sarnath Lion Capital of Ashoka. Its diameter approximates to the width of the white strip. The wheel has 24 spokes. It was adopted by Constituent Assembly on July 22, 1947. We love our national flag. We respect it. We are ready to sacrifice our life to protect its honour. It represents the nation. So it is a symbol of national honour.

1. In our national flag the wheel is located in the centre of

A. saffron strip B. white strip
C. green strip D. blue strip

2. In our national flag which of the strips is at the bottom in our national flag

A. blue C. saffron
B. white D. green

3. Why do we love our national flag?

A. Because it is tricolour
B. Because it has three strips
C. Because it has a wheel at the centre
D. Because it is a symbol of national honour

4. Our national flag was approved by

A. President
B. Lok Sabha
C. Parliament
D. Constituent Assembly

5. The diameter approximates to the width of the white strip. Here the word 'approximates' means

A. is more or less equal
B. is exactly equal
C. is not equal
D. is related

PASSAGE-10

Distance in large cities are long. All the people do not have their own means of transport. They have to depend upon the state or private buses. The number of bus users is very large. Every bus stop is, therefore, crowded. The number of buses is not adequate. Thus people suffer the torture of long wait at the bus stop. Some bus stops are quite orderly. People form queues and get into the buses turn by turn. However, often this order is forgotten and confusion spreads when the bus comes and the law of jungle prevails.

1. Why are the bus stops crowded?

A. Because they are small is size
B. Because the number of passengers is very large
C. Because they are situated at some busy centre
D. Because people do not form queues

2. Long wait at the bus stop is the result of

A. over-crowding in the buses
B. late running of buses
C. shortage of buses
D. slow speed of buses

3. Some bus stops are quite orderly where

A. there is no crowd
B. the number of buses is adequate
C. people do not have to wait for long
D. people form queues and enter the buses one by one

4. Most of the people who travel by buses are

A. non-working
B. do not have their own vehicles
C. have to go a long distance
D. live in large cities

5. What happens when people do not have their own transport?

A. They have to wait for a bus at a bus stop
B. They have to depend upon the state or private buses
C. They have to travel long distances
D. They form queues and get into buses one by one

ANSWERS

	1	2	3	4	5
Passage 1.	D	C	B	A	C
Passage 2.	B	C	D	B	B
Passage 3.	D	D	C	B	D
Passage 4.	B	C	C	C	C
Passage 5.	D	A	B	B	A
Passage 6.	A	C	D	B	A
Passage 7.	C	A	B	D	B
Passage 8.	B	B	C	A	B
Passage 9.	B	D	D	D	A
Passage 10.	B	C	D	B	B

●●●

2

English Grammar

PARTS OF SPEECH

Part of speech	Definition or Function	Examples
Noun	Name of a person, place, animal, quality or thing	Ram, boy, dog pen, sun, Delhi, truth, honesty
Pronoun	Used in place of a noun	I, you, he she, they
Articles & Determiners	Points out indefinite and definite nouns	a, an, the, few, some
Adjective	Describes a noun or pronoun	big, honest, wooden valuable, quiet, deep, soft, narrow
Adverb	Describes a verb, an adjective or another adverb	silently, widely, softly, quietly, very, carefully
Verb	Tells about action or state of something or someone	is, am, was, have, do, like, walk, work, make, throw, tell
Conjuction	Joins words, clauses or sentences	and, but, when, yet, while, else
Preposition	Links a noun or pronoun to another word	at, to, after, on for, under, over, with
Interjection	Expresses sudden feelings or emotions	Ah!, Alas!, oh!, ouch!, hi!, well!, Hurrah!

NOUNS

A word which denotes a person, a thing, an animal or a place is said to be a noun.

There are two noun numbers in English — the *Singular* and the *Plural*.

Singular Numbers : A noun that denotes one person or one thing, is said to be in the Singular number. For example — book, pencil, bird, dog, hen etc. are in singular number.

Plural Number : A noun that denotes more than one person or one thing is said to be in plural number. For example — boys, pens, lions, girls, men etc. are in plural number.

REMEMBER

Singular	*Plural*	*Singular*	*Plural*
Cat	Cats	Book	Books
Pen	Pens	Room	Rooms
Tree	Trees	Bus	Buses
Bush	Bushes	Box	Boxes
Glass	Glasses	Dish	Dishes
Judge	Judges	Tax	Taxes
Watch	Watches	Calf	Calves
Thief	Thieves	Knife	Knives
Scarf	Scarves	Wife	Wives
Leaf	Leaves	Wolf	Wolves
Half	Halves	Monarch	Monarchs
Roof	Roofs	Hoof	Hoofs
Gulf	Gulfs	Staff	Staffs
Radio	Radios	Bamboo	Bamboos
Folio	Folios	Hero	Heroes
Volcano	Volcanoes	Mango	Mangoes
Potato	Potatoes	Photo	Photos
Piano	Pianos	Baby	Babies
Fly	Flies	Country	Countries
Lady	Ladies	Boy	Boys
Monkey	Monkeys	Ox	Oxen
Child	Children	Man	Men
Woman	Women	Tooth	Teeth
Axis	Axes	Basis	Bases
Foot	Feet	Goose	Geese
Englishman	Englishmen	Radius	Radii
Vertex	Vertices	Stimulus	Stimuli

1. Note the plurals of the following nouns:

Singular	*Plural*	*Singular*	*Plural*
copy	copies	cry	cries
baby	babies	duty	duties
body	bodies	country	countries
family	families	diary	diaries
fly	flies	fairy	fairies
city	cities	spy	spies
army	armies	storey	storeys
bay	bays	monkey	monkeys

2. The following nouns do not undergo any change in plural form, in general.

Singular	*Plural*	*Singular*	*Plural*
deer	deer	sheep	sheep
thousand	thousand	pair	pair
hundred	hundred	score	score
dozen	dozen	gross	gross

Note: We can write—

(*a*) thousands of men; (*b*) two pairs of shoes; (*c*) dozens of mangoes; (*d*) scores of people etc. But—

(*a*) two thousand rupees; (*b*) three hundred men; (*c*) five dozen eggs, etc.

3. The following nouns are usually used in plural forms. They take a plural verb after them—

eatables	fetters	surroundings
riches	alms	spectacles
trousers	pants	scissors
premises	thanks	annals
congratulations	goods	shorts
tongs	pains	arms
breeches	(for troubles)	

4. The following are the nouns which are plural in appearance but are usually used in singular number. They are followed by a singular verb—

news	politics	physics
mathematics	economics	ethics
politics	classics	gallows
statistics	athletics	innings
mechanics	summons	mumps

5. Collective nouns often used as plurals—

public	police	cattle
audience	clergy	folk
people	poultry	nation
elite	gentry	glitterati

6. The nouns that are usually used in singular forms—

advice	hair	rice
fuel	alphabet	machinery
offspring	issue	furniture
mischief	stationery	luggage
bedding	information	abuse

7. Material nouns are always used in singular number—

gold	copper	milk
water	silk	wool

Note: They may be used in plural with a different meaning. copper coins (coppers), chains or fetters (irons), cans made of tin (tins).

GENDERS

The difference in sex is denoted by Gender in grammar. The various genders are as follows :

1. **Masculine Gender :** A noun that denotes a male is said to be of the masculine gender, as man, uncle, ox, boy etc.
2. **Feminine Gender :** A noun that denotes a female is said to be of feminine gender, as woman, aunt, princess, cow etc.
3. **Common Gender :** Nouns which denote both males and females are said to be of the common gender, as friend, cousin, person, parent, baby etc.
4. **Neuter Gender :** A noun that denotes the name of object without life is said to be of neuter gender, as file, table, pencil.

REMEMBER

Masculine	*Feminine*
Boy	Girl
Son	Daughter
Brother	Sister
Murderer	Murderess
Sorcerer	Sorceress
Son-in-law	Daughter-in-law
Father-in-law	Mother-in-law
Man-servant	Maid-servant
Land-lord	Land-lady
Bachelor	Maid
Gentleman	Lady
Monk	Nun
Earl	Countess
Lad	Lass
Sir	Madam
Duke	Dutchess
Emperor	Empress
Milk-man	Milk-maid
Pea-cock	Pea-hen
Step-father	Step-mother
Hero	Heroine
Viceroy	Vicerine
Mr.	Mrs.
Governor	Governess
Master	Mistress
Wizard	Witch
Heir	Heiress
Host	Hostess
Lion	Lioness
Mayor	Mayoress
Actor	Actress
Buck	Doe
Colt	Filly
Dog	Bitch
Horse	Mare
Count	Countess
Hunter	Huntress
Prince	Princess
Abbot	Abbess
God	Goddess
Author	Authoress
Ox	Cow
Widower	Widow
Grand-father	Grand-mother
He-goat	She-goat
Milk-man	Milk-woman
Bridegroom	Bride
Tiger	Tigress
Priest	Priestess
Poet	Poetess
Shepherd	Shepherdess
Nephew	Niece
Stag	Hind

PRONOUNS

The repetition of a noun in a sentence or a set of sentences is really boring. So, instead of repeating the noun, we can use a word (for that noun) called the pronoun.
"A pronoun is a word that we use instead of a noun".

Example:
This is *Sachin. He* plays cricket.
Note: *He* is the pronoun used in place of *Sachin.*

Kinds of Pronouns

1. **Personal pronouns :** A pronoun which is used instead of the name of a person is known as a 'Personal Pronoun'. A list of the 'Personal pronouns' is listed below :
   I, my, mine, me, we (First Person)
   You, your, yours (Second Person)
   He, his, him, she, her, hers, it,
   its, they, their, theirs, them (Third Person)
2. **Demonstrative, Indefinite and Distributive Pronouns :**
   (a) Demonstrative Pronouns : Pronouns used to point out the objects to which they refer are called Demonstrative Pronouns.
   Examples :
   (i) *This* is a present from my uncle.
   (ii) *These* are merely excuses.
   (iii) Bembay mangoes are better than *those* of Bangaluru.
   (b) Indefinite Pronouns : All pronouns which refer to persons or things in a general way and do not refer to any particular person or thing are called Indefinite Pronouns.
   Examples :
   (i) *Somebody* has stolen my watch.
   (ii) *Few* escaped unhurt.
   (iii) Did you ask *anybody* to come?
   (c) Distributive Pronouns : Each, either, neither are called distributive pronouns because they refer to persons or things one at a time. For this reason they are always singular and followed by the verb in singular.
   Examples :
   (i) *Each* of the men received a reward.
   (ii) *These* men received *each* a reward.
   (iii) *Either* of you can go.
3. **Relative Pronouns :** A relative pronoun refers or relates to some noun going before, which is called its Antecedent.
   Examples :
   (i) I met Hari *who* used to live here.
   (ii) I have found the pen *which* I had lost.
   (iii) Here is the book *that* you lent me.
4. **Interrogative Pronouns :** These pronouns, are used for asking questions.
   Examples :
   (i) *Whose* book is this?
   (ii) *What* will all the neighbours say?
   (iii) *Which* do you prefer, tea or coffee?
   Note : Interrogative pronouns can also be used in asking indirect questions. Consider the following examples :
   (i) I asked *who* was speaking.
   (ii) Tell me *what* you have done.
   (iii) Say *which* you would like best.

Behaviour of the Pronouns

1. If three pronouns are used together in the same sentence they are arranged in the following order :

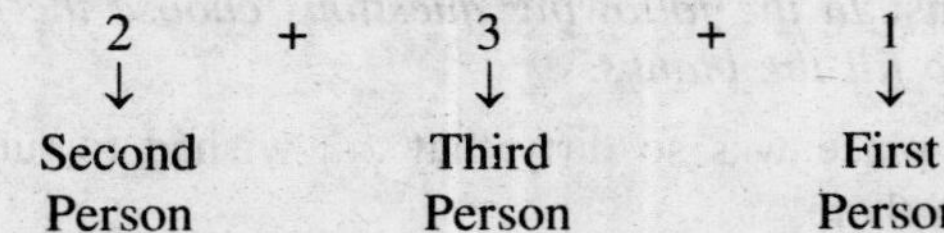

   Examples :
   I, you and he must help *that* poor man. (Incorrect)
   You, he and I must help *that* poor man. Correct)
2. When two or more singular nouns are joined by and, the pronoun used for them should be plural.
   Examples :
   Mohan and Sohan are friends. *They* play football. *They* live at Lajpat Nagar.
3. But if these nouns joined by and refer to the same person or thing, the pronoun used should be singular.
   Examples :
   (i) Delhi, the beautiful city and the capital of India, is famous for *its* historical monuments.
   (ii) The manager and owner of the firm expressed *his* views on the demands of the workers.
4. When two nouns are used with as well as, the pronoun agrees with the first subject.
   Examples :
   (a) Mohan as well as his friends is doing *his* work.
   (b) The students as well as their teachers are doing *their* work.
5. When two singular nouns joined by 'and' are preceded by *each* or *every,* the pronoun used must be singular and should agree in gender with the second noun.
   Examples :
   (a) Every man and every woman will do *her* best for the nation.
   (b) Each boy and each girl went to *her* house.
6. When two nouns are joined by using 'with', the pronoun agrees with the noun coming before 'with'.
   Examples :
   (a) The boy with *his* parents has gone to see a movie.
   (b) The children with *their* parents have gone to picnic.
7. When two different nouns are joined by either.......... or; neither .... nor, the pronoun is used according to the number and gender of the second noun.

Examples :

(a) Either your sister or you have done *your* work.

(b) Neither the students nor the teacher was in *his* class.

8. The pronoun coming after '*than*' must be in the same case as that coming before '*than*'.

Examples :

(a) She plays better than *me*. (Incorrect)
She plays better than *I*. (Correct)

(b) His elder brother is more intelligent than *him*. (Incorrect)
His elder brother is more intelligent than *he*. (Correct)

9. 'Many a' always takes a singular pronoun and singular verb.

Example :

Many a soldier has met *his* death in the battle field.

10. 'Who', 'Whose', 'Whom' are used only for persons.

Examples :

(a) *Who* is knocking at the door?

(b) *Whose* pen is this?

(c) *What* do you want?

11. 'Which' is used for things.

Example : *Which* game do you like?

MULTIPLE CHOICE QUESTIONS

Directions: *In the following questions choose the correct options to fill the blanks.*

1. The place was so dirty that ..... wished to run away from there.
A. everybody B. anybody
C. few D. some

2. ..... was there to help me.
A. Somebody B. Anything
C. Anybody D. Nobody

3. Is there .... to eat?
A. some B. something
C. any D. few

4. ..... of the students were making a great noise.
A. Anyone B. Somebody
C. Many D. Nobody

5. ..... of the students can solve this sum.
A. Someone B. Anybody
C. Somebody D. None

6. . .... of us should try our best to make India a heaven.
A. Any B. Somebody
C. Anybody D. All

7. ...... of us do not know the real meaning of our lives.
A. Any B. Something
C. Several D. Many

8. My .... black.
A. hairs are B. hair is
C. hairs shall D. hair will

9. She saw two .... on the last Sunday.
A. thiefs B. theifs
C. thieves D. theives

10. My sister is a ....
A. bacheloress B. bachelor
C. unmaried D. spinster

11. One is supposed to do ....
A. our duty B. their duty
C. one's duty D. his duty

12. Take anything .... you want.
A. that B. which
C. than D. then

13. I cannot tolerate ....
A. separated you B. your separation
C. separation from you D. you separated

14. He is .... faithful partner.
A. Yours B. You
C. Your D. Your's

15. Ajay is more smart than ....
A. her B. hers
C. herself D. she

16. Vivek works harder than ....
A. me B. I
C. her D. his

17. They should help ....
A. the poor people B. the poor
C. the poor persons D. the poor peoples

18. .... are mad.
A. All his sons B. His all sons
C. Sons all his D. All sons his

19. The poor fellow .... to fate.
A. resigned B. resigned himself
C. resigned itself D. resigned themselves

20. Nobody will help you but ....
A. I B. me
C. ours D. his

21. It is a good chance, You must avail ...... this opportunity.
A. of B. yourself of
C. for D. from

22. The person who is elected .... my relative.
A. is B. he is
C. his D. him

23. He made ....
A. yours mention B. mention of you
C. mention for you D. mention about you

24. .... I know, he is quite faithful.
A. As far as B. So far as
C. So far this D. So far so

25. It is a duty of a person to take .... for his family.
A. pain B. pains
C. pain-killers D. pained

26. She does not love .... husband.
A. his B. her
C. its D. their

27. Let .... work together.
A. him and me B. he and I
C. he and him D. I and me

28. Copper, Silver and Gold ....
A. each will do B. either will do
C. any one will do D. any will do

29. Jessica and Roma are very irregular .... habits.
A. in her B. in their
C. in its D. in every

30. One likes to enjoy .... who was a great poet.
A. The sonnets of Shakespeare
B. Shakespeare's sonnets
C. Sonnets
D. Shakespeare

ANSWERS

1	2	3	4	5	6	7	8	9	10
A	D	B	C	D	D	D	B	C	D
11	12	13	14	15	16	17	18	19	20
C	A	C	C	D	B	B	A	B	B
21	22	23	24	25	26	27	28	29	30
B	A	B	A	B	B	A	C	B	A

ARTICLES

The family of the articles has only three members. They are : A, An and The. However, they fall under two groups :

(a) Definite Article *(b)* Indefinite Article

'The' is known as definite article whereas 'a' and 'an' are known as indefinite articles.

Use of the Definite Article 'The'

'The' is used before

1. The superlative degree :
He is the ablest man of the town.
(ablest is a superlative degree)
2. The name of states, countries etc. having a descriptive name :
(i) The J & K is a small state. (J & K is a descriptive name)
(ii) He lives in the U.S.A. (U.S.A. is a descriptive name)
(But the Delhi and the America are wrong because neither Delhi nor America is a descriptive name)
3. The names of the scriptures :
The Gita is a holy book. (Gita is a scripture)
4. Name of newspapers :
The Tribune is published from Chandigarh.
5. Name of rivers, canals, seas, oceans, bays, gulfs, groups of islands etc. :
(i) The Ganga is a holy river.
(ii) The Indian Ocean is the deepest ocean.
(iii) The Persian Gulf is a narrow gulf.
6. The name of famous buildings :
The Taj is one of the best buildings in India.
7. The names of nationals, sects and communities:
(i) The English defeated the Germans in the World War.
(ii) The rich should help the poor.
(iii) The Hindus believe in the caste system.
8. Proper nouns used as common nouns :
(i) Kalidas is the Shakespeare of India.
(ii) Delhi is the London of India.
9. Famous historical events :
The Industrial Revolution changed the face of England.
10. The directions and the celestial bodies:
The sun rises in the east.
11. Titles : Akbar, the Great was loved by his subjects.

Do not use 'the'

1. Before languages :
The English is an international language. (Incorrect)
English is an international language. (Correct)
2. Before the names of games :
The hockey is a popular game. (Incorrect)
Hockey is a popular game. (Correct)

Use of the Indefinite Articles 'A' and 'An'

'A' is used before :

1. All singular common nouns beginning with a consonant :
(i) A boy sings a song.
(ii) A black and a white cow were grazing in the field.
2. If a word begins with a vowel but gives the sound of a consonant, 'a' should be used before it :
(i) He was helped in his work by a European.
(ii) He is a one-eyed man.
(iii) It is a useful work.

'An' is used as follows :

1. All singular common nouns beginning with a vowel (*i.e.*, a, e, i, o, u) :
   (i) He is an artist. (ii) He is an old man. (iii) I intend to buy an umbrella.
2. If a word starts with a consonant but gives the sound of a vowel, "an" should be used before it :
   (i) Brutus is an honourable man.
   (ii) He is an honour to his profession.
   (iii) He is an L.L.B.

Demonstratives, that, these and those

1. The demonstrative adjectives and pronouns are for objects nearby the speaker:
   this (singular) those (plural)
   and for objects far away from the speaker.
   That (singular) those (plural)
2. Demonstratives are the only adjectives that agree in number with their nouns.
   That hat is nice.
   Those hats are nice.
3. When there is the idea of selection, the pronoun "one" (or "ones") often follows the demonstrative.
   I want a book. I'll get this (one).
   If the demonstrative is followed by an adjective, "one"(or "ones") must be used.
   I want a book. I'll get this big one.

MULTIPLE CHOICE QUESTIONS

Directions: *In the following questions choose the correct options to fill the blanks.*

1. .... will have to be paid for this material.
A. Half rupee B. Half a rupee
C. A half rupee D. An half rupee

2. .... is taking keen interest in India.
A. The USA B. USA
C. An USA D. A USA

3. Only .... can save our country.
A. the Hitler B. a Hitler
C. Hitler D. an Hitler

4. I can run for ....
A. hundred miles B. the hundred miles
C. a hundred miles D. an hundred miles.

5. .... man-eater has been killed.
A. The B. A
C. An D. Either A or B

6. What .... fine idea!
A. the B. an
C. a D. No article

7. .... earth is moving around the sun.
A. An B. A
C. The D. No article

8. This is .... first example while I got.
A. the B. a
C. an D. No article

9. This is .... house which was built during earthquake.
A. a B. an
C. the D. No article

10. .... America is a rich country.
A. The B. An
C. A D. No article

11. .... U.S.A. is a developed country.
A. A B. An
C. The D. No article

12. .... Bible is a holy book.
A. A B. The
C. An D. No article

13. .... rich should help the poor.
A. The B. A
C. An D. No article

14. .... Gold is a costly metal.
A. The B. A
C. An D. No article

15. Kalidas is .... Shakespeare of India.
A. a B. an
C. the D. No article

16. I cannot do .... difficult work.
A. a such B. the such
C. such the D. such a

17. How foolish .... plan it is!
A. a B. an
C. the D. No article

18. An ink is .... useful article.
A. an B. a
C. the D. No article

19. There are .... husband and wife.
A. a B. an
C. the D. No article

20. He is learning .... French
A. the B. a
C. an D. No article

ANSWERS

1	2	3	4	5	6	7	8	9	10
B	A	B	C	D	C	C	A	C	D
11	**12**	**13**	**14**	**15**	**16**	**17**	**18**	**19**	**20**
C	B	A	D	C	D	A	B	D	D

ADJECTIVES & ADVERBS

An Adjective is a word which adds something to the meaning of a noun or a pronoun.

Mridula is an *intelligent* girl. He has a *black* goat.
He is a *brilliant* student. She is a *clever* girl.
It is a *beautiful* picture.

In the sentences given above, the words in italics are adjectives.

An Adverb is a word which qualifies the meaning of a Verb, an Adjective or another Adverb.

(*i*) He talks *slowly*.
(*ii*) He is a *very* good student.
(*iii*) He talks *very* slowly.

In sentence (*i*), *slowly* qualifies the verb *talks.*
In sentence (*ii*), *very* qualifies the adjective *good.*
In sentence (*iii*), *very* qualifies the adverb *slowly.*

Adjectives have three degrees of comparison :

1. **Positive Degree :** It expresses the common form of an adjective.
   Example :
   Ram is a *tall* boy.
   In the above sentence *tall* is an adjective and expresses the common form.
2. **Comparative Degree :** It expresses the more of the same form.
   Example :
   Ram is *taller* than Mahesh.
   In the above sentence *taller* is an adjective that expresses the more of the common form of the adjective *tall*.

"When and How to Use" Comparative Degree?

(a) Comparative Degree is used when two persons or two groups of persons or things are compared.
Examples :
(a)He is *wiser* than his younger brother.
(b)This glass is *cleaner* than the other.

(b) When two different qualities in the same person are compared, more is used instead of 'er' to form the comparative. The formula used in this case should be :
More + Positive Degree
She is *fairer* than polite. (Incorrect)
She is *more fair* than polite. (Correct)

(c) When selection of one out of two persons or things is meant, the degree of comparison is followed by of and *the* is used before it.
Example :
Zia is abler of *the* two sisters.

(d) If two comparatives are used in the same sentence to impress upon an idea, both should be preceded by the definite article.
Examples :
(i) The higher you go, the cooler it is.
(ii) The more we get, the more we desire.

(e) When one person or thing is compared with another of the same kind, other is used after the comparative degree. In such sentences other is normally preceded by any or all.
Examples :
(i) Kalidas is greater than any dramatist.
(Incorrect)
Kalidas is greater than any other dramatist.
(Correct)
(ii) Lead is heavier than all metals.
(Incorrect)
Lead is heavier than all other metals.
(Correct)

(f) Senior, junior, superior, inferior, prior, anterior (earlier than) and posterior (later than) are always followed by 'to'.
Examples :
(i) Ram is senior *to* Mohan by three years.
(ii) That pen is inferior *to* that.
(iii) He is junior *to* me in rank.
(iv) This event was posterior *to* that.

Note: Never use *than* after the above mentioned adjectives.

Important Information

(a) 'Preferable' is also used as an adjective of the comparative degree. As such, it is always followed by *to* and not *a*.
Death is preferable than dishonour. (Incorrect)
Death is preferable *to* dishonour. (Correct)

(b) To intensify the Degree of comparison, we use *far* or *much* before the comparative.
Examples :
(i) This book is *far* better than that.
(ii) His performance was *much* better than Mohan's.
Warning : Always avoid the use of double comparatives.
Don't say : Ram is more cleverer than his younger brother.
Say: Ram is cleverer than his younger brother.

3. **Superlative Degree :** It expresses the most of the common form of an adjective.
   Example :
   He is the ablest man of the town.

How and when to use the Superlative Degree?

(a) The Superlative Degree is used when more than two persons or things are compared.

(b) The Superlative Degree is generally preceded by 'the' and followed by 'of' in most of the cases or otherwise.

(c) When an adjective of the superlative degree is preceded by a Possessive Adjective or a Noun in the Possessive case, 'the' should not be used before it.
Example :
Which is Kalidas' best play?

It will be a blunder to use 'the' before the Superlative Degree in such cases.

Don't say : Which is Kalidas' the best play.

(d) To intensify the degree of comparison, *by far* is used before the superlative degree.

Example :

India is *by far* the most beautiful country of the world.

Note: Always avoid the use of double superlatives.

Don't say : He is the most strongest boy in the class.

Say : He is the strongest boy in the class.

Use of some Important Adjectives

1. (a) '**Some**' is used as follows :
   (i) With countable nouns where it means— a little, a small quantity.
   (ii) In a question which shows some request.

   Examples :
   (i) There is some water in the bottle.
   (ii) Some of the students were absent yesterday.
   (iii) Will you have some milk?
   (iv) Will you buy some fruit for me?

   (b) **'Any'** is used as follows :
   (i) In negative sentences.
   (ii) In interrogative sentences.
   (iii) After 'Hardly', 'Scarcely' and 'Barely'.
   (iv) After 'If'.

   Examples :
   (i) There is not any sugar in the pot.
   (ii) We haven't any rice in the house.
   (iii) I have hardly any money.
   (iv) There are scarcely any plants in this field.
   (v) If there is any danger, blow the whistle.

2. (a) **Older :** Older (and oldest) are used for persons animals and things. But 'Older' and 'Oldest' refer to the persons who do not belong to the same family.

   Examples :
   (i) Radha is older than Shyama.
   (ii) John is the oldest member of the staff.
   'Older' and 'Oldest' refer to the persons who do not belong to the same family.

   (b) **Elder** (and **eldest**) are used in respect of the members of the same family like sons, daughters, brothers, sisters.

   Examples :
   (i) My elder sister is a lecturer.
   (ii) Meenakshi is the eldest of the three sisters.

   Note :
   (i) 'Elder' is not followed by 'than'.
   (ii) 'Elder' and 'Eldest' cannot be used for things.

3. (a) **'Few'** is negative and is the opposite of 'Many'. It means 'not many'.
   (b) **'A few'** is positive and means 'some at least'. It is the opposite of 'None'.
   (c) **'The few'** means 'minority' and suggests 'whether there is'.

   Examples :
   (i) We have few holidays in school.
   (ii) Only a few boys will fail in the examination.
   (iii) The few poems that he wrote are very popular.

4. (a) **Further** means 'something additional'.
   (b) **Farther** means 'a greater distance'.

   Examples :
   (i) Further discussion will be held in the office of the principal.
   (ii) Amritsar is farther from Delhi than Ambala.

5. (a) **Little** is negative. It means, 'not much', or 'hardly any'.
   (b) **A little** is positive. It means 'some quantity'.
   (c) **The little** denotes quantity. It means, 'not much but all that is, or whatever quantity there is'.

   Examples :
   (i) There is little hope of his success.
   (ii) He knows a little of everything.
   (iii) I have spent the little money I had.
   (iv) The little knowledge of shoe-making proved very useful to me.

6. (a) **'Much'** expresses 'quantity'.
   (b) **'Many'** expresses 'number'.
   (c) **'Many a'**—'Singular noun' and 'Singular verb' are used with 'many a'.

   Examples :
   (i) There is not *much* water in the jug.
   (ii) *Many* boys are absent today.
   (iii) *Many* a battle has been fought on the soil of India.

7. (a) **'Less'** denotes 'in a small degree'.
   (b) **'Fewer'** denotes 'number'.

   Examples :
   (i) He devotes less time to his studies.
   (ii) There are no fewer than ten chairs in this room.

8. (a) **'Each'** is used for a single number of 'two persons' or 'things'.
   (b) **'Every'** is used for a single number of 'many persons' or 'things'.

   Examples :
   (i) Each boy must take part in games.
   (ii) There are only two poets. Each poet recited his poem.
   (iii) Every man dies in this world.
   (iv) Every man is expected to do his duty.

9. (a) **'Either'** means one of the two or both.
   (b) **'Neither'** is negative of the either.

   Examples :
   (i) You may buy either of these two chairs.
   (ii) Neither of them could speak on the stage.

10. (a) **'Later'** expresses 'late in time'.
    (b) **'Latter'** means 'second in position or order'.

    Examples :
    (i) My father reached later than I expected.
    (ii) The latter position was better than the former.

Use of some Important Adverbs

1. (a) Also, too, enough:
   (i) He taught English. Also, he edited the school magazine
   (ii) He is a writer and also he is a painter.
   (iii) He is too obstinate to listen to any reason.
   (iv) This is too difficult a piece for the junior students.
   (v) Sarla was kind enough to help the poor.
   (vi) He is brave enough to help the truth.
   Note: 'Too' is used in a negative sense, but enough is used in a positive sense.

   (b) Fairly and rather: Both suggest the meaning 'moderately'. But, mainly 'fairly' is used with the words that denote a positive meaning and rather is used with the words that denote a negative meaning:
   (i) Rita did fairly well in that competition, but her performance was rather poor in sports.
   (ii) Mona is fairly rich, but she is rather stingy.
   Note: 'Rather' can also be used in a positive sense.
   (i) This is a rather interesting job.
   (ii) That boy is rather smart.

   (c) Hardly, barely, scarcely: These words mostly convey the negative suggestions and are almost similar.
   (i) I have hardly any strength now.
   (ii) There was barely any supply to the township,
   (iii) There were scarcely a hundred guests present.
   Note: With slight variance in the meaning, the words given above convey the idea of 'very little', 'not enough', 'lack of quantity and number'.

   (d) Yet, Still: These adverbs can often be used to connect the sentence units:
   (i) He has been defeated many times in the contest; still he wants to be a competitor.
   (ii) Mona was sick; yet she went on doing her work.

   (e) Alone:
   (i) He alone (none else) is capable of handling that fire,
   (ii) He hunted all alone in the forest. (not in any company)

Special Note:

(a) Apart from their conventional positions the adverbs might be used in different positions with different meanings and angles.
   (i) He had only four books.
   (ii) John only contacted his friend in need.
   (iii) He greeted me only.
   (iv) Only he greeted me there.

(b) Inversion: Some adverbs can be inverted *i.e.* placed in the beginning of the sentence and then be followed by an interrogative form. The most common of these adverb are: so, seldom, never, nowhere, under no circumstances, hardly, scarcely etc.
   (i) So big was the bus that it could not enter the narrow lane.
   (ii) Hardly had he reached the station when he received the message.

MULTIPLE CHOICE QUESTIONS

Directions: *In the following questions choose the correct options to fill the blanks.*

1. The girl whom you met is the .... sister of Ravi.
A. eldest B. elder
C. older D. oldest

2. The historical place is ....
A. seeing worth B. worthy of seeing
C. worth seeing D. worthy seeing

3. These flowers smell ....
A. sweet B. sweetly
C. more sweetly D. sweetest

4. .... aspirant cannot pass the entrance examination.
A. Each B. Every
C. All D. No

5. Harivansh Rai .... second Shakespeare.
A. is a B. is
C. is the D. is an

6. .... student in the class got prizes.
A. Each and every B. Every and each
C. Every D. Never

7. It is .... picture than the one we saw last Monday.
A. interesting B. much interesting
C. more interesting D. most interesting

8. She is clever ....
A. that her mother is B. as her mother is
C. to her mother is D. than her mother is

9. They will get ....
A. Red, green and black paper
B. Red, green black paper
C. Red and green and black paper
D. Red green black paper

10. Health is .... wealth.
A. preferable to B. more preferable than
C. more preferable to D. most preferable then

11. .... water that was in the jug evaporated.
A. Little B. The little
C. Small D. A small

12. He has not sung .... songs.
A. much B. most
C. more D. many

13. Srishti has searched .... office.
A. whole the B. the whole
C. a whole D. some whole

14. Premchand was .... best and .... famous writer.
A. a, the most B. the, a most
C. the, more D. the, the most

15. William Shakespeare is famous as ....
A. a poet and a dramatist
B. a poet and dramatist
C. the poet and the dramatist
D. a poet and the dramatist

16. What does .... leader suggest?
A. other B. another
C. others D. anothers

17. He .... money.
A. has few B. have few
C. has little D. have little

18. The .... boys are rewarded.
A. first two B. two first
C. firsts two D. two's first

19. He is .... brave.
A. stronger than
B. stronger then
C. more strong then
D. more strong than

20. No sooner said ....
A. so done B. and done
C. then done D. but done

21. She returned .... than I had thought.
A. quickly B. more quicker
C. more quickly D. quicker

22. He is .... foolish person.
A. rather the B. a rather
C. rather a D. rather

23. This pen .... rupees.
A. costs twenty B. twenty costs only
C. costs only twenty D. only costs twenty

24. It is .... pride.
A. nothing else but B. nothing else than
C. else nothing than D. but

25. This tea is .... to drink.
A. too hot B. very hot
C. enough hot D. much hot

ANSWERS

1	2	3	4	5	6	7	8	9	10
A	C	A	B	A	C	C	C	A	A
11	**12**	**13**	**14**	**15**	**16**	**17**	**18**	**19**	**20**
B	D	B	D	B	B	C	A	D	C
21	**22**	**23**	**24**	**25**					
C	C	C	A	A					

DETERMINERS

Determiners are actually Adjectives. They are always followed by nouns.

Determiners are of the following kinds:

1. **Demonstrative Determiners :** this, that, these, those
2. **Possessive Determiners :** my, our, your, his, her, its, their
3. **Quantitative Determiners :** some, any, much, enough, sufficient, whole, a little, the little, little, all, both
4. **Numerical Determiners:** a few, some, few, the few, any, several, many, no, etc.
   One, two, three ... (Cardinals)
   First, second, third ... (Ordinals)
5. **Distributive Determiners:** either, neither
6. **Articles: Indefinite:** a, an, **Definite:** the

MULTIPLE CHOICE QUESTIONS

Directions: *In the following questions choose the correct options to fill the blanks.*

1. Give me .... rice.
A. some B. few
C. a few D. any

2. ...... sheep grazing on the slope of the hill had gone away.
A. Any B. The few
C. This D. Much

3. Have you got .... magazines to read?
A. all B. much
C. some D. little

4. I have .... money that I want to spend on shares.
A. any B. much
C. less D. some

5. There is .... owl on the branch of the tree.
A. a B. the
C. an D. some

6. My brother is .... MBA.
A. a B. an
C. the D. any

7. Have you got .... cheese?
A. some B. many
C. a few D. few

8. No, I have not got .... cheese.
A. many B. few
C. any D. some

9. There is only .... milk left in the bottle.
A. enough B. few
C. much D. a little

10. There is .... hope of his recovery.
A. any B. little
C. many D. few

11. .... dogs were barking at the strangers.
A. Some B. Any
C. Much D. Less

12. The girl bought her father .... juice.
A. few B. some
C. any D. many

13. You should take .... honey everyday.
A. any B. many
C. a little D. a few

14. .... boy was punished by the teacher.
A. Either B. All
C. Any D. Many

15. .... girl was asked to join the army.
A. None B. Neither
C. All D. Any

16. .... water in the jug has been drunk by Mohan.
A. The little B. The few
C. A few D. Few

17. I shall play .... piano at the party.
A. some B. any
C. the D. few

18. .... labourers were found dead in the mine.
A. Any B. Fewer
C. Many D. Less

19. Could I borrow .... umbrella?
A. our B. your
C. yours D. my

20. My brother is standing in the .... row.
A. any B. many
C. some D. first

ANSWERS

1	2	3	4	5	6	7	8	9	10
A	B	C	D	C	B	A	C	D	B
11	**12**	**13**	**14**	**15**	**16**	**17**	**18**	**19**	**20**
A	B	C	A	B	A	C	C	B	D

THE VERB

A Verb is a word that tells something about the action or state of or happenning to a person or thing.

A Verb tells the following:

1. What a person or thing does.
   Sachin goes to school daily.
   The bell *rang* loudly.
   Many birds fly in the sky.
   She *sang* a song.
2. What a person or thing is.
   India *is* the biggest democracy in the world.
   Ram Mehar *is* very rich.
   They *are* happy.
3. What is done to a person or thing.
   You *are liked* by all.
   Two thieves *were arrested*.
   Four students *were punished* by the teacher.
4. What happens to a person or thing.
   His maternal uncle *died* last week.
   Two ships *sank* yesterday.
   Leaves *turn* yellow in autumn.
5. What a person or thing has, had, and so on.
   I *have* a new car.
   He *had* a scooter last year.
   He *has* several cows and goats.

It goes without saying that a verb is the most important part of a sentence. No sentence is complete without a Verb.

Important Information

1. If two or more singular nouns are joined by 'and' the verb used will be plural.
   Example:
   (i) He and I were going to the market.
   (ii) Ram and Mohan are friends.
2. If two singular nouns joined by 'and' points out to the same thing or person, the verb used must be singular.
   Example:
   (i) Rice and curry is the favourite food of the Punjabis.
   (ii) The Collector and District Magistrate is away.
3. In case two subjects are joined by 'as well as' the verb agrees with the first subject.
   Example :
   (i) Kanta as well as her children is playing.
   (ii) Children as well as their mother are playing.
   In the case of first sentence the verb (is) agrees with Kanta and in the case of second sentence the verb (are) agrees with the children.
4. 'Neither', 'Either', 'Every', 'Each', 'Everyone', and 'Many a' are followed by a singular verb.
   Example :
   (i) Either of the plans is to be adopted.
   (ii) Neither of the two brothers is sure to pass.
   (iii) Every student is expected to be obedient.
   (iv) Everyone of them desires this.
   (v) Many a person is drowned in the sea.

5. If two subjects are joined by 'Either .... or' / 'Neither .... nor', the verb agrees with the subject near to it.

   Example :

   (i) Either my brother or I am to do this work.

   (ii) Neither he nor they are prepared to do this work.

6. 'A great many' is always followed by a 'plural noun' and a 'plural verb'. For example :

   A great many students have been declared successful.

7. Similarly if two subjects are joined by 'with', 'together with', 'no less than', in addition to 'and not', etc. the verb agrees with the first subject.

   Example :

   (i) The boy with his parents has arrived.

   (ii) He, no less than I, is to blame.

8. Nouns, plural in form, but singular in meaning, take a singular verb.

   Example :

   This news was broadcast from television yesterday.

MULTIPLE CHOICE QUESTIONS

Directions: *In the following questions choose the correct options to fill the blanks.*

1. The bus with all its passengers .... lost.
A. were B. was
C. are D. would

2. You as well as I .... responsible for this work.
A. am B. are
C. was D. is

3. Raghava like all his companions .... a spoiled child.
A. are B. were
C. is D. will be

4. Pen and ink .... required for me.
A. are B. were
C. is D. has required

5. Every girl and every boy .... attended the seminar.
A. have B. has
C. is D. are

6. Not only she but all her sisters ...... been married.
A. has B. have
C. is D. are

7. There .... nothing but miseries in life.
A. is B. are
C. were D. will be

8. Neither prose nor poem .... given.
A. were B. was
C. has D. have

9. Either he or I .... wrong.
A. is B. are
C. am D. were

10. Either Sulekha or Rekha .... coming here.
A. are B. is
C. were D. have

11. .... the child or his parents to blame?
A. Is B. Are
C. Were D. Has

12. You and I .... neighbours.
A. am B. are
C. was D. has

13. The house with all its belongings ..... sold away.
A. were B. are
C. was D. must

14. Either water or juice .... required.
A. is B. are
C. were D. has

15. There were not as many tables as .... required.
A. was B. were
C. is D. are

16. They each .... a book.
A. have B. are
C. has D. is

17. He and I .... class friends.
A. is B. am
C. was D. are

18. She as well as I .... guilty.
A. is B. are
C. am D. must be

19. Purushottam .... not read more on this chapter.
A. needs
B. has been need
C. need
D. had been need

20. He came .... to his aunt.
A. run B. running
C. to run D. in run

ANSWERS

1	2	3	4	5	6	7	8	9	10
B	B	C	C	B	B	A	B	C	B
11	**12**	**13**	**14**	**15**	**16**	**17**	**18**	**19**	**20**
A	B	C	A	B	C	D	A	C	B

CONJUNCTIONS

A conjunction is a word which connects words, clauses or sentences.

Look at the following sentences.

(i) He bought apples *and* mangoes.

(ii) God made the country *and* man made the town.

(iii) The door was open *but* there was no one in the house.

(iv) He knows that I am here *and* that I want to see him.

In the sentence (i), *and* connects two words—*apples* and *mangoes.*

In the sentence (ii), *and* connects two sentences—*God made the country* and *man made the town.*

In the sentence (iii), *but* connects two sentences— *The door was open* and *there was no one in the house.*

In the sentence (iv), *and* connects two clauses—*that I am here* and *that I want to see him.*

The main coordinating conjunctions are:

and, but, for, or, nor, also, either ..... or, neither ..... nor.

There are some conjunctions which are used in pairs. They are:

either .... or, ... neither .... nor, both .... and, though .... yet, whether .... or, not only .... but also.

Example: *Either* take it *or* leave it.

It is *neither* useful *nor* ornamental.

They *both* like *and* respect me.

Though he is suffering from high fever, *yet* he does not cry.

He does not care *whether* you go *or* stay.

He is *not only* doltish, *but also* obstinate.

The conjunctions which are used in pairs in this way, are called correlative conjunctions, or merely correlatives.

Use of Important Conjunctions

1. **As soon as :** As soon as denotes simultaneous time.

   Example : As soon as he saw his enemy, he took to his heels.

2. **No sooner .... than :**

   (a) 'No sooner' is always followed by 'than'.

   (b) Please remember that 'No sooner' is always followed by do/does/did. As such only first form of the verb should be used after the subject.

   Example :

   No sooner did he see his enemy than he took to his heels.

3. **Hardly :** Hardly is followed by when.

   Examples :

   (i) Hardly had I left the house when it started raining.

   (ii) We had hardly come into the room when his father began chastising him.

   Note :

   A. Hardly is never followed by than.

   B. 'Scarcely' can also be used in the sense and manner of 'Hardly'.

4. **Lest :** Lest is used in the sense of so that .... not. It is always followed by should. Lest is negative in sense. Hence 'not' should never be used with it.

   Example :

   Work hard lest you should fail.

   Note : 'Lest' is always followed by 'should' and not 'may'.

5. **Unless :** Unless expresses condition. It is also used in the negative sense. Use of 'not' is not allowed with unless because unless is already in the negative sense.

   Example :

   Unless you labour hard you will not pass.

6. **Until :** 'Until' expresses time. It means 'till not'.

   Example : Wait here until I return.

   Note : Until is in the negative sense. So 'not' should not be used with it. Example :

   Wait here until I do not return. (Incorrect)

   Wait here until I return. (Correct)

7. **As well as :** When two subjects are joined by 'as well as', the verb always agrees with the first subject.

   Examples :

   (i) The teacher as well as students is playing.

   (ii) Students as well as the teacher are playing.

   Note : 'Both' and 'as well as' cannot be used together in the same sentence.

   Examples :

   Both Sita as well as Kanta are beautiful. (Incorrect)

   Sita as well as Kanta is beautiful. (Correct)

   Both Sita and Kanta are beautiful. (Correct)

8. **As if :** 'As if' is used in the sense of pretension. While using 'as if' in a sentence, we should see that even the third person singular subject gets 'were'.

   Example : He talks as if he were mad.

9. **Till :** Till expresses time. Till is always used in the affirmative.

   Example :

   We did not come back till sunset.

10. **Rather than :** 'Rather than' is used in the sense of 'preference'. 'Rather' is always followed by 'than'.

    Example :

    I would rather die than submit.

11. **As long as/so long as :** Both express time during which an action or event takes place.

    Example :

    As long as there is life, there is hope.

12. **However :** It is both a subordinate and co-ordinate clause.

    Examples :

    (a) Mala worked hard, she however, failed.

    (b) However hard he may work, he cannot pass.

13. **Such as :** 'Such as' gives us the sense of 'like'. Such is always followed by 'as'.

    Example :

    Life is such a puzzle as cannot be solved.

MULTIPLE CHOICE QUESTIONS

Directions: *In the following questions choose the correct options to fill the blanks.*

1. Neither he .... his friend is good.
A. or B. and
C. but D. nor

2. The officer asked the peon .... why he was late.
A. that B. if
C. but D. No word needed

3. Both Ajay .... Vijay are intelligent.
A. or B. nor
C. and D. No word needed

4. No Sooner did the thief see the public .... he ran away.
A. then B. and
C. but D. than

5. Abhinav .... his brothers was going to Mumbai.
A. but
B. yet
C. No word needed
D. together with

6. He behaves .... he were the captain of the team.
A. as if B. as
C. No word needed D. that

7. Either Rupali .... Sonali is going to attend the meeting.
A. and B. but
C. nor D. or

8. Neither Nirmal .... Ashwinee is going to listen the speech.
A. and B. but
C. nor D. or

9. Ravi .... Prakash are going to Kolkata.
A. or B. nor
C. but D. and

10. Rice .... curry is my usual breakfast.
A. and B. but
C. then D. than

11. Hardly had he left .... his brother came.
A. then B. than
C. when D. that

12. I would rather have a copy .... a book.
A. then B. than
C. when D. that

13. He is no other .... my friend.
A. then B. than
C. when D. but

14. He saw a snake ....he awoke.
A. then B. when
C. than D. No word needed

15. Ten years have passed .... my grandmother died.
A. since B. when
C. then D. than

16. She is .... good .... bad.
A. either, not B. neither, or
C. neither, nor D. neither, than

17. The cellphone is both cheap .... best.
A. than B. and
C. then D. or

18. No sooner did the rogue see the police .... he disappeared.
A. then B. than
C. so D. because

19. Srishti will go .... Sanju goes.
A. if B. than
C. then D. although

20. She is wise .... timid.
A. and B. yet
C. but D. however

21. Make hay .... the sun shines.
A. though B. while
C. after D. before

22. He is so weak .... he cannot walk.
A. but B. that
C. then D. so

23. Although he is rich, ... he is unhappy.
A. but B. yet
C. so D. still

24. Wait here ...... I come back.
A. till B. until
C. before D. after

25. He is my friend .... I shall help him.
A. so B. hence
C. that is why D. therefore

26. He must go away .... he will be beaten.
A. otherwise B. and
C. or D. else

27. God loves good men .... good men love God.
A. and B. or
C. that D. those

28. He was late .... he was not punished.
A. but B. yet
C. still D. therefore

29. Walk slowly ...., you may fall.
A. and B. or
C. so D. otherwise

30. Work hard, ... you will fail.
A. and B. or
C. otherwise D. else

ANSWERS

1	2	3	4	5	6	7	8	9	10
D	D	C	D	D	A	D	C	D	A
11	12	13	14	15	16	17	18	19	20
C	B	B	B	A	C	B	B	A	C
21	22	23	24	25	26	27	28	29	30
B	B	B	A	B	C	A	C	D	D

PREPOSITIONS

A *Preposition* is a word which is placed before a noun or a pronoun to show its relation to some other word in the sentence.

1. I saw a goat *in* the field.
2. I am fond *of* hot coffee.

In sentence 1, the word *in* shows the relation between two things—*goat* and *field.*

In sentence 2, the word *of* shows the relation between the attribute expressed by the adjective *found* and *tea.*

The words *in* and *of* are here used as prepositions.

The noun or pronoun which is used with a preposition is called its object. The noun or pronoun is in the objective case. It is governed by the preposition. Now it is absolutely clear that in sentence 1, the noun *field* is in the objective case. The word *field* is governed by the preposition *in.*

A preposition may have two or more objects.

The road runs over *hill* and *plain.*

Here, the words *hill* and *plain* are used as objects.

Use of Important Prepositions

1. Among, Between

'**Among**' is used for more than two persons or things; '**Between**' is used only for two.

Examples :

(i) Distribute these sweets *among* the poor students of the class.

(ii) Distribute these books *between* Ram and Shyam.

2. Among, In

'**Among**' is used before collective plural nouns. '**In**' is used before collective singular nouns.

Examples :

(i) I found him standing *among* the crowd.

(ii) I saw him in the crowd.

3. Beside, Besides

'**Beside**' means 'by the side of'. '**Besides**' means 'in addition to'.

Examples :

(i) The daughter was sitting *beside* her mother.

(ii) *Besides* his relatives, he invited his friends also.

4. In, Within

'**In**' means at the expiry of a period of time in future, '**Within**' means before the expiry of a period of time in any tense.

Examples :

(i) She will return *in* a week.

(ii) I shall finish my work *within* a weak.

5. On, Upon

'**On**' is used for things at rest; '**Upon**' is used for things in motion.

Examples :

(i) He is sitting *on* the floor.

(ii) The dog sprang *upon* the table.

6. By, With

'**By**' denotes the agent or doer, '**With**' denotes the instrument with which anything is done.

Examples :

(i) The bird was killed *by* the hunter with an arrow.

(ii) He beat the dog *with* a stick.

(iii) I shall reach here *by* five o'clock.

7. After, In

'**After**' means at the end of a period of time in the past. '**In**' means at the end of a period of time in future.

Examples :

(i) I shall return your book *in* a week.

(ii) He returned the book *after* a week.

8. For, From, Since

'**For**' is used before a noun denoting a period of time with all the tenses. '**From**' is used before a noun or phrase denoting a point of time, it is used in all the tenses. '**Since**' is used before a noun or phrase denoting some point of time and is always produced by a verb in the perfect continuous tense or third form of a verb.

Examples :

(i) We have been playing cards *for* two hours.

(ii) She stayed with her uncle *from* the 15th of March to the 15th of May.

(iii) I have been reading this book *since* morning.

9. Above, Over

'**Above**' means 'higher from', **Over** is used in the following four senses :

(i) In the sense of 'above' :
At noon, the sun is *over* our heads.

(ii) In the sense of 'beyond' :
I cannot get *over* my disappointment.

(iii) In the sense of 'Superiority' :
God *over* all blesses for ever more.

(iv) In the sense of 'Conclusion' :
It is all *over* with me.

10. At, Towards

'**At**' denotes the idea of aim, '**Towards**' denotes the idea of destination.

Examples :

(i) He threw the stone *at* the cat.

(ii) He went *towards* the house.

11. At, In, On

'At' is used as follows :

(i) '**At**' is used with small towns and villages. **Examples:**

(a) He was born *at* Sonepat.

(b) He lives *at* village Bangra. (Bangra is a village)

(ii) '**At**' is used before a noun denoting a definite point of time.

Example :

He called on me *at* 9 p.m. yesterday.

'In' is used as follows :

(iii) '**In**' is used with the names of big cities, provinces and countries.

Examples :

(a) His father lives *in* England.

(b) His younger brother lives *in* Calcutta.

(iv) '**In**' is used before the names of months and years.

Example :

His elder sister was born *in* 1972 *in* the month of May.

'**On**' is used with dates and names of days. **Examples:**

(a) I joined college *on* the 26th April.

(b) He will leave for Kolkata *on* Wednesday next.

Important Information

1. '**In**' is also used in the following phrases :
   In the morning; In the evening, In winter, In summer.
2. '**In**' also denotes a place inside anything.
   He travelled *in* a crowded bus.
3. '**At**' is used in the following phrases :
   At home, *At* the station, *At* work, *At* play.

12. Below, Beneath

Below means 'of lower level in position, dignity and expectation' etc. *Beneath* means 'under'.

Examples :

(i) It is *below* my dignity to talk to her.

(ii) They rested *beneath* the shade of a tree.

13. In, Into, To

'**In**' expresses Rest or Motion inside anything. '**Into**' expresses Motion towards the inside of anything or change from one medium to another. '**To**' denotes motion from one place to another.

Examples :

(i) The boys are *in* the room.

(ii) Translate this passage from English *into* Hindi.

(iii) Every morning he goes *to* the temple.

14. Till, By, Of, Off

- 'Till' means upto or not earlier than.
- 'By' means not later than.
- 'Of' shows cause, source, separation, quality, contents, possession, apposition, point of reference, space in time etc.
- 'Off' shows separation at a near distance, and detached condition.

Consider the following examples:

(i) I shall work *till* 5 a.m.

(ii) Madhu died *of* cancer.

(iii) The nib *of* the pen is made *of* gold.

(iv) He presented me a bottle *of* perfume.

(v) Our principal is a man *of* principle.

(vi) He lived in the house *of* his friend.

(vii) *By* this time tomorrow, I'll have finished my job.

(viii) My house is *off* the road.

(ix) The book fell *off* the table.

MULTIPLE CHOICE QUESTIONS

Directions: *Tick the correct preposition for the blank in each of the following sentences.*

1. He applied ...... the manager.
A. for B. to
C. with D. by

2. Trust ...... God and do the right.
A. in B. for
C. to D. with

3. She is worthy ...... a prize.
A. with B. for
C. to D. of

4. Mr. Gomes has no taste ...... music.
A. of B. for
C. with D. to

5. You are hard ...... hearing.
A. at B. of
C. with D. for

6. He is sure ...... his success
A. for B. with
C. on D. of

7. Preeti was warned ...... the danger ahead.
A. for B. at
C. of D. about

8. I am thankful ...... you for a good advice.
A. for B. with
C. to D. of

9. Deepak would not surrender ...... the police.
A. with B. to
C. for D. on

10. The small plant in your lawn is very sensitive ...... touch.
A. on B. with
C. to D. about

11. Divya was sure to succeed ..... the examination.
A. for B. in
C. to D. with

12. Geeta was jealous ...... Ravina's beauty.
A. to B. with
C. for D. of

13. He was ignorant ..... what was happening there.
A. for B. of
C. to D. with

14. Your pen is inferior ...... mine.
A. than B. with
C. from D. to

15. Reenu is no match ...... Meenu.
A. to B. for
C. with D. upon

16. It is necessary ...... you to apply for this job.
A. on B. with
C. for D. to

17. Be loyal ...... your country.
A. for B. to
C. on D. with

18. Mukesh is junior ...... me.
A. than B. to
C. from D. of

19. Deepika was innocent ..... the crime.
A. of B. with
C. from D. to

20. I am desirous.... joining the Indian cricket team.
A. for B. of
C. to D. on

ANSWERS

1	2	3	4	5	6	7	8	9	10
B	A	D	B	B	D	D	D	B	D
11	12	13	14	15	16	17	18	19	20
B	D	B	D	B	D	B	B	A	B

SYNONYMS

A synonym is a word which conveys a meaning similar to the given word.

REMEMBER

Words	*Synonyms*
Add	Increase
Adequate	Enough
Adjust	Adapt
All	Aggregate
Allow	Permit
Abode	Dwelling
Apt	Proper
Assess	Appraise
Accuse	Calumniate
Abashed	Timid
Annoy	Displease
Ample	Enough, Sufficient
Amplify	Increase
Apathetic	Unenthusiastic
Accost	Address
Authentic	True
Adjust	Fit
Approve	Assent, Allow, Accept
Adapt	Conform
Adversary	Opponent, Rival, Competitor
Beat	Whack
Benign	Kind
Breeze	Zephyr
Baffle	Puzzle
Booty	Spoil

Words	*Synonyms*
Beauty	Charm
Beast	Animal
Bandit	Robber
Blaze	Shine
Bond	Tie
Bend	Twist
Bate	Diminish
Beg	Plead
Barbaric	Wild, Savage
Bashful	Shy, Reserved
Begin	Start
Blend	Mix, Mingle
Bizarre	Funny
Below	Under
Bedevil	Confuse
Bemoan	Lament
Babble	Nonsense
Blame	Fault
Behaviour	Demeanour
Call	Accost
Copy	Imitate
Close	Shut
Caress	Love
Camp	Stay
Connect	Attach
Cut	Injure, Curtail
Cling	Stick
Conical	Funny
Convey	Carry
Conspicuous	Prominent
Cheerful	Happy, Pleasant

Words	Synonyms
Curtail	Decrease
Cheerless	Sad, Dejected
Curious	Strange
Circumstance	Factor, Situation, Condition
Competent	Capable
Congruent	Overlapping
Cope	Deal, Endure
Confident	Sure
Complex	Intricate
Cajole	Coax, Flatter
Cunning	Crafty
Delectable	Joyful, Delightful
Devilish	Diabolical
Delicate	Soft
Devil	Fiend
Delay	Postpone
Dislike	Repugnance
Destroy	Ruin
Dwell	Live, Dilate
Declare	Pronounce
Drunk	Flushed
Deficient	Lacking
Damn	Condemn, Curse
Decrease	Diminish
Destruction	Devastation
Efficient	Competent
Ethnic	Racial
Enthral	Enslave
Earnest	Serious
Envious	Jealous
Ending	Final
Egg	Incite
Extempore	At once
Extensive	Far-ranging
Extra	Surplus
Existence	Life
Exceed	Overstep
Enormous	Vast
Excessive	Superfluous
Free	Unhindered
Frigid	Cold
Feed	Cater
Fame	Reputation
Frame	Make
First	Initial
Frighten	Terrorise, Intimidate
Fervent	Fervid
Fall	Decline
Feeble	Frail
Fickle	Changeable
Finish	Conclude
Fraud	Deception
Forgiving	Placable

Words	Synonyms
Grow	Develop
Greed	Avidity
Greet	Welcome
Grave	Serious
Group	Constellation
Given	Bestowed
Gratitude	Thankfulness
Have	Possess
Hire	Rent
Hit	Strike
Handsome	Beautiful
Hinder	Prevent
Heap	Pile
Hope	Expect
Hard	Harsh
Help	Aid
Hymn	Song
Henpecked	Enslaved
Hoodwink	Mystify, Cheat
Humble	Polite, Urbane, Modest
Harass	Vex, Trouble
Impart	Instil
Intact	Untouched
Instal	Establish
Indict	Impeach
Imitate	Ape
Instigate	Incite
Initiate	Start, Introduce
Inimical	Unfriendly
Insufferable	Intolerable
Impartiality	Justice
Jolly	Merry
Joyful	Delectable
Join	Conjoin
Kind	Benign
Kill	Murder
Kindred	Similar
Kinship	Relationship
Keen	Sharp
Knowledge	Scholarship
Lazy	Slothful
Large	Substantial, Gargantuan
Listless	Careless, Lackadaisical
Lax	Loose
Little	Small
Lifelike	Realistic
Lofty	High
Lenient	Soft, Gentle
Lacking	Deficient, Wanting
Lessen	Decrease
Middleclass	Bourgeois
Mitigate	Lessen, Abate
Modesty	Humility, Lowliness

Words	Synonyms
Mix	Mingle, Blend
Mixture	Mingling
Mixed	Assorted
Modify	Decrease
Mean	Imply
Multifarious	Varied
Miscarry	Abort
Note	Notice
Noble	Stately
Native	Indigenous
Needful	Necessary
Notify	Declare
Nervous	Shaky, Tremulous, Timid
Natural	Spontaneous
Near	Close
Normal	Natural
Offend	Displease
Oppress	Persecute, Tyrannize
Opponent	Adversary
Obstruct	Hinder, Check
Offence	Fault
Offender	Villain
Overstep	Exceed
Overlapping	Congruent
Occult	Mystic
Profane	Unholy
Patience	Forbearance
Pornographic	Obscene
Plenitude	Abundance
Prominent	Important
Prodigal	Spender
Procrastinate	Postpone
Promote	Develop, Honour
Persecute	Tyrannise
Profess	Claim
Pliant	Flexible
Plebian	Common
Polished	Sophisticated
Quake	Shake
Quit	Leave
Queer	Eccentric
Quell	Suppress
Quantify	Allot
Reply	Answer
Relinquish	Retire
Read	Peruse
Relation	Reference
Render	Do
Remainder	Residuals
Repeat	Reiterate
Repentant	Contrite
Retaliative	Retaliatory
Rumour	Hearsay
Reveal	Divulge

Words	Synonyms
Ritualistic	Ceremonious
Soft	Delicate
Sort	Kind, Choose, Select
Selfish	Egoistic
Sensual	Earthly
Suppress	Quell, Check
Stimulate	Provoke
Tasteless	Insipid
Travel	Journey
True	Authentic, Faithful, Truthful
Turbulence	Turmoil
Tragedy	Calamity
Tasteful	Tasty, Delicious
Touching	Painful
Thankful	Grateful
Tremendous	Great, Huge
Tough	Strong
Terminate	Conclude, End
Theory	Doctrine
Tell	Relate
Tremble	Shake, Shiver
Urge	Spur
Unbeaten	Unsubdued
Use	Utilize, Practise
Underhand	Unfair, Undue
Unfair	Unjust
Unravel	Reveal, Divulge
Unimportant	Common
Unconcerned	Apathetic
Unimitated	Inimitable
Unfortunate	Unlucky
Understand	Perceive, Comprehend
Vain	Proud, Haughty, Conceited, Shameless
Vale	Valley, Dale, Dell
Vice	Fault
Virtue	Quality
Veracity	Reality
Value	Price, Prize
Vex	Tease
Vibrate	Quiver, Shake
Violent	Excessive
Vivid	Clear, Lucid
Victory	Triumph
Vulgar	Indecent
Virtuous	Honest
Variegated	Varied, Multifarious
Well	Good
Yell	Cry, Shout
Yonder	There
Yearn	Wish, Desire
Yoke	Slavery
Zest	Earnestness, Enthusiasm
Zealous	Earnest

ANTONYMS

A antonym is a word which conveys a meaning opposite to the given word.

REMEMBER

Words	*Antonyms*
Abhor	Love
Abnormal	Normal
Able	Unable
Acceptable	Unacceptable
Adequate	Inadequate
Amusing	Boring
Angry	Calm
Apex	Bottom
Attract	Repel
Bad	Good
Barren	Fertile
Beautiful	Ugly
Bitter	Sweet
Brave	Cowardly
Brief	Lengthy
Bright	Dull
Calm	Violent
Careful	Careless
Clear	Vague, Cloudy
Cold	Hot
Cruel	Kind
Dear	Cheap
Deep	Shallow
Difficult	Easy
Direct	Indirect
Dishonest	Honest
Disobey	Obey
Encourage	Discourage
Enormous	Tiny
Excellent	Bad
Expensive	Cheap
Eat	Fast
Fair	Unfair
Fake	Authentic
False	True
Famous	Notorious
Fool	Genius
Generous	Miserly
Genius	Fool
Genuine	Unauthentic
Gigantic	Tiny
Glad	Depressed
Good	Bad
Great	Little
Happy	Sad
Hard	Soft
Hate	Love
Honest	Dishonest
Idle	Busy

Words	*Antonyms*
Immoral	Moral
Include	Exclude
Incorrect	Correct
Intelligent	Unintelligent
Kind	Cruel
Like	Dislike
Long	Short
Lucid	Vague
Major	Minor
Naive	Experienced
Nadir	Apex
Neat	Clumsy
Obedient	Disobedient
Obscure	Clear
Oppose	Support
Optimistic	Pessimistic
Out	In
Patience	Impatience
Peaceful	Belligerent
Pious	Impious
Polite	Impolite
Potent	Impotent
Prominent	Unimportant
Proper	Improper
Pure	Impure
Quick	Slow
Quiet	Disturbance
Real	False, Unreal
Reject	Select, Choose
Reliable	Unreliable
Respect	Disrespect
Right	Wrong
Robust	Feeble, Weak
Sad	Happy
Secret	Open
Sensible	Insensible
Severe	Mild
Sharp	Blunt
Simple	Complex
Sociable	Unsociable
Tall	Short
Tidy	Untidy
Uncanny	Canny
Violent	Calm
Vivid	Vague
Strong	Weak
Big	Small
Easy	Difficult
Fast	Slow
High	Low
Catchy	Unattractive
Ugly	Handsome, Beautiful, Tidy
Tasty	Insipid
Sonorous	Harsh

MULTIPLE CHOICE QUESTIONS

Directions (Qs. 1 to 20): *In the following questions choose the word which best expresses the meaning of the given word.*

1. ABSURD
A. Foolish B. Simple
C. Courageous D. Silly

2. ABANDON
A. Lose B. Profit
C. Vacate D. Foil

3. CAJOLE
A. Pause B. Lenient
C. Blast D. Lure

4. COMBAT
A. Fight B. Conflict
C. Shoot D. Quarrel

5. LAMENT
A. Condone B. Console
C. Complain D. Contribution

6. DEBACLE
A. Disgrace B. Defeat
C. Collapse D. Decline

7. SHIVER
A. Fear B. Tremble
C. Shake D. Ache

8. TORTURE
A. Terror B. Harassment
C. Torment D. Tranquility

9. LAUDABLE
A. Lovable B. Commendable
C. Profitable D. Oblivious

10. FIXED
A. Sterile B. Static
C. Stubborn D. Parennial

11. QUEER
A. Unfamiliar B. Cute
C. Curious D. Strange

12. SUFFICIENT
A. Fit B. Proper
C. Adequate D. Vast

13. GLOSS
A. Brightness B. Soothing
C. Rubbing D. Miracle

14. LONGING
A. Prune B. Apathy
C. Curtail D. Craving

15. JEER
A. Applaud B. Magnanimity
C. Avoid D. Scoff

16. ZENITH
A. Minimum B. Nadir
C. Plant D. Peak

17. GARB
A. Distort B. Dress
C. Trivial D. Rage

18. ABHOR
A. Rude B. Reconcile
C. Crave D. Detest

19. YIELD
A. Shum B. Incisive
C. Retain D. Surrender

20. YOKE
A. Twist B. Release
C. Link D. Extra

Directions (Qs. 21 to 26): *In the following questions choose the word which best expresses the opposite of the given word.*

21. TRAGIC
A. Dramatic B. Strong
C. Gentle D. Comic

22. ORAL
A. Verbal B. Sane
C. Minor D. Written

23. ADMIRE
A. Hate B. Unlike
C. Dislike D. Enough

24. VIOLENT
A. Gentle B. Savage
C. Haughty D. Decline

25. ADVERSITY
A. Windfall B. Inprosperity
C. Prosperity D. Slave

26. GENUINE
A. Spurious B. Obscure
C. Countless D. Apathetic

ANSWERS

1	2	3	4	5	6	7	8	9	10
D	C	D	A	C	C	B	C	B	B
11	12	13	14	15	16	17	18	19	20
D	C	A	D	D	D	B	D	D	C
21	22	23	24	25	26				
D	D	C	A	C	A				

●●●

3

Sentence Completion

It is such an exercise which starts with the primary schools and continues in the highest level of competitive examinations. One must practise it regularly to score well.

Directions (Qs. 1 to 15): *Pick out the most effective word(s) from the given words to fill in the blanks to make the sentence meaningfully complete.*

1. The student ...... that book from the library to study at home.
A. issued B. borrowed
C. hired D. lent

2. I wish I ...... a king.
A. was B. am
C. should be D. were

3. He ...... to listen to my arguments and walked away.
A. denied B. disliked
C. objected D. refused

4. The flow of blood was so ...... that the patient died.
A. intense B. adequate
C. profuse D. extensive

5. When I met her yesterday, it was the first time I ...... her since Christmas.
A. saw B. have seen
C. had seen D. have been seing

6. Can you pay ...... all these articles?
A. for B. of
C. off D. out

7. I ...... you to be at the party this evening.
A. expect B. hope
C. look forward to D. desire

8. ...... being a handicapped person, he is very cooperative and self-reliant.
A. Because B. Although
C. Since D. Despite

9. The child broke ...... from his mother and ran towards the painting.
A. away B. after
C. down D. with

10. With his ...... income, he finds it difficult to live a comfortable life.
A. brief
B. sufficient
C. meagre
D. huge

11. He could ...... a lot of money in such a short time by using his intelligence and working hard.
A. spend
B. spoil
C. exchange
D. accumulate

12. Though the brothers are twins, they look ......
A. alike B. handsome
C. indifferent D. different

13. Unfavourable weather conditions can ..... illness.
A. cure B. detect
C. treat D. enhance

14. No sooner did the bell ring, ... the actor started singing.
A. when B. than
C. after D. before

15. If I ...... realised it, I would not have acted on his advice.
A. was B. had
C. were D. have

Directions (Qs. 16 to 25): *In each question, an incomplete statement (Stem) followed by four fillers is given. Pick out the best one which can complete the incomplete stem correctly and meaningfully.*

16. Unless you work harder you will fail, means .....
A. if you fail you will work harder.
B. you must at least plan well than you will not fail.
C. hardly you will fail if you do not desire so.
D. if you do not put more efforts, then you will fail.

17. Even if it rains I shall come, means .....
A. if I come it will not rain.
B. if it rains I shall not come.
C. I will certainly come whether it rains or not.
D. whenever there is rain I shall come.

18. Dinesh is as stupid as he is lazy means .....
A. Dinesh is stupid because he is lazy.
B. Dinesh is lazy because he is stupid.
C. Dinesh is either stupid or lazy.
D. Dinesh is equally stupid and lazy.

19. He is so lazy that he .....
A. cannot depend on others for getting his work done.
B. cannot delay the schedule of completing the work.
C. can seldom complete his work on time.
D. dislike to postpone the work that he undertakes to do.

20. He always stammers in public meetings, but his today's speech .....
A. was fairly audible to everyone present in the hall.
B. was not received satisfactorily.
C. could not be understood properly.
D. was free from that defect.

21. In order to raise the company's profit, the employees.....
A. demanded two additional increments.
B. decided to go on paid holidays.
C. requested the management to implement new welfare schemes.
D. offered to work overtime without any compensation.

22. Although, he is reputed for making very candid statements, ...
A. his today's speech was not fairly audible.
B. his promises had always been realistic.
C. his speech was very interesting.
D. his today's statements were very ambiguous.

23. I felt somewhat more relaxed .....
A. but tense as compared to earlier.
B. and tense as compared to earlier.
C. as there was already no tension at all.
D. and tension-free as compared to earlier.

24. With great efforts his son succeeded in convincing him not to donate his entire wealth to an orphanage ....
A. and lead the life of a wealthy merchant.
B. but to a home for the forsaken children.
C. and make an orphan of himself.
D. as the orphanage needed a lot of donations.

25. Even though it is a very large house, ...
A. there is a lot of space available in it for children.
B. there is hardly any space available for children.
C. there is no dearth of space for children.
D. the servants take a long time to clean it.

ANSWERS

1	**2**	**3**	**4**	**5**	**6**	**7**	**8**	**9**	**10**
B	D	D	C	C	A	A	D	A	C
11	**12**	**13**	**14**	**15**	**16**	**17**	**18**	**19**	**20**
D	D	D	B	B	D	C	D	C	D
21	**22**	**23**	**24**	**25**					
D	D	D	C	B					

●●●

4

Spotting Errors

The most common errors in English are of spellings, grammar and usage of words. By regular practice, the errors can be easily spotted and minimised.

MULTIPLE CHOICE QUESTIONS

Directions: *In the following questions some of the sentences have errors and some are correct. Find out which part of a sentence has an error, the number of that part is your answer. If a sentence is free from errors, then your answer is D i.e., No error.*

1. (A) Either Ram or/(B) you is responsible/(C) for this action./(D) No error.

2. (A) The student flatly denied/(B) that he had copied/(C) in the examination hall./(D) No error.

3. (A) By the time you arrive tomorrow/(B) I have finished/(C) my work./(D) No error.

4. (A) The captain with the members of his team/(B) are returning/(C) after a fortnight./(D) No error.

5. (A) After returning from/(B) an all-India tour/(C) I had to describe about it./(D) No error.

6. (A) The teacher asked his students/(B) if they had gone through/(C) either of the three chapters included in the prescribed text./(D) No error.

7. (A) Do you know/(B) how old were you/(C) when you came here?/(D) No error.

8. (A) Beware of/(B) a fair-weather friend/(C) who is neither a friend in need nor a friend indeed./(D) No error.

9. (A) Copernicus proved/(B) that Earth/(C) moves round the Sun./(D) No error.

10. (A) The property/(B) was divided/(C) among the two brothers./(D) No error.

11. (A) I am quite certain/(B) that the lady is not only greedy/(C) but miserly./(D) No error.

12. (A) The brilliant success in the examination/(B) as well as his record in sports/(C) deserves high praise./(D) No error.

13. (A) I cannot find/(B) where has he gone/(C) though I have tried may best./(D) No error.

14. (A) If I was/(B) the Prime Minister of India/(C) I would work wonders/(D) No error.

15. (A) If it weren't/(B) for you,/(C) I wouldn't be alive today./(D) No error.

16. (A) He looked like a lion/(B) baulked from/(C) its prey./(D) No error.

17. (A) Widespread flooding/(B) is affecting/(C) large areas of the villages./(D) No error.

18. (A) If we really set to/(B) we can get the whole house/(C) cleaned in an afternoon./(D) No error.

ANSWERS

1	2	3	4	5	6	7	8	9	10
B	D	B	B	C	C	D	D	B	C
11	**12**	**13**	**14**	**15**	**16**	**17**	**18**	**19**	**20**
C	D	B	A	C	C	C	A	A	C

EXPLANATORY ANSWERS

1. Replace 'is' by 'are'.
2. No error.
3. Replace 'have' by 'would have'.
4. Replace 'are' by 'is'.
5. Replace 'had to describe' by 'described'.
6. Replace 'either' by 'any'.
7. No error.
8. No error.
9. Omit 'that'.
10. Replace 'among' by 'between'.
11. Add 'also'.
12. No error.
13. Replace 'has he' by 'he has'.
14. Replace 'was' by 'were'.
15. Replace 'wouldn't be' by 'would not have been'.
16. Replace 'its' by 'his'.
17. Replace 'areas' by 'area'.
18. Replace 'set to' by 'set on'.

●●●

5

One Word Substitution

There are many single words in English language which can be perfectly used for a number of words. These words help in expressing ideas in a short and correct manner for the right occasion. Such words not only increase the vocabulary but also enable you to economise in the use of words to a great extent.

Multiple Word Expression	*Substitution*
One who always looks towards the bright side of things	Optimist
One who always looks towards the dark side of things	Pessimist
The time when one develops from a child into an adult	Adolescence
The process of growing more plants in order to form a forest.	Afforestation
The science which deals with farming	Agriculture
From some other country or place etc.	Alien
A term, etc. giving more than one meaning	Ambiguous
A vehicle which is used to carry sick persons	Ambulance
An animal which can live both in water and on land	Amphibian
A lawless situation when there is no government	Anarchy
Belonging to the history of thousands of years old	Ancient
Once a year	Annual
A very old object but still valuable	Antique
Words of opposite meanings	Antonyms
Words of similar meanings	Synonyms
Signatures of a famous person	Autograph
A government led by one person with absolute authority	Autocracy
A written work of one's own life history	Autobiography
A person who has never been married	Bachelor
A person usually having no hair on his head	Bald
A place where one can deposit money and get interest	Bank
A person who cuts our hair	Barber
A building/group of buildings where soldiers live	Barracks
A person who makes buns and biscuits	Baker
A person who lives by asking people for food and money without doing any useful job	Beggar
The crime of having married to two persons at the same time	Bigamy
The branch of science which deals with the study of plants	Botany
Able to speak two languages	Bilingual
Able to speak more than two languages	Polyglot
The branch of science which deals with the living organisms	Biology
A powerful snow storm	Blizzard
A great successful book or movie	Blockbuster
A short news on the radio or TV	Bulletin
A system in which the most important works are organised by the government officials	Bureaucracy
A person who has no vision in his eyes	Blind
A page or a series of pages on which the information of days, weeks, months, etc. is given	Calendar
A person who eats human flesh	Cannibal
A complete list of items often arranged alphabetically	Catalogue
A sudden disaster	Catastrophe
A period of 100 years	Century

Multiple Word Expression	*Substitution*
A branch of science which deals with chemicals	Chemistry
A printed leaf usually issued by banks that we sign to carry certain financial deal	Cheque
A person who makes or mends shoes	Cobbler
A group of people who has been chosen by others to make decisions on their own	Committee
A building in which nuns live	Convent
An animal which feeds on other animals	Carnivorous
A person who does criticism	Critic
A person who cannot hear	Deaf
A condition in which one loses a lot of water from one's body because of vomiting, etc.	Dehydration
A system of government in which the people cast their votes to elect their leaders	Democracy
The study of skin problems	Dermatology
A long piece of land covered with sand	Desert
The art of managing relationships between countries	Diplomacy
A piece of information about the words in a book form	Dictionary
A piece of information about the telephone numbers of the people in a book from	Directory
A person in charge of a newspapers, magazine etc.	Editor
A person who thinks he is better than the others	Egoist
To leave your country and settle in some other country	Emigrate
A book or series of books giving almost all knowledge about an area or some persons etc.	Encyclopaedia
Study of insects	Entomology
Time when day and night are of the same duration	Equinox
To sell things out of the country	Export
To purchase things from some other country	Import
A plant or animal no longer in existence	Extinct
A situation when there is a shortage of food for a long period of time	Famine
An amount of money that we pay for some action or services	Fee
Related to women	Feminine
An animal strong and aggressive	Ferocious
A piece of land where plants grow easily from the soil that is favourable to them	Fertile
A work of literature having some imaginary events	Fiction
A large amount of water covering certain area	Flood
A person who sells flowers	Florist
A religious ceremony for burying or cremating a dead person	Funeral
A substance which kills fungus	Fungicide
A person studying or having studied the diseases and the related things of female reproductory system	Gynaecologist
The murder of the person of the same group race or country	Genocide
A substance which kills germs	Germicide
A situation in which many people die because of fire during war	Holocaust
The act of killing a person deliberately	Homicide
A word having the pronunciation as the other one does but it differs in meaning	Homophone
A word having the same spelling as the other one does but it is pronounced in some other way	Homonym
A person who is attracted towards the person of the same sex	Homosexual
Go across and parallel to the ground	Horizontal
A substance which kills the insects	Insecticide
That cannot be corrected	Incorrigible
That cannot be defeated	Invincible
That cannot be eaten	Inedible
That cannot be seen	Invisible
A place in a school or college where books are kept for the benefit of students, teachers etc.	Library
A place in a school or college where scientific experiments are performed	Laboratory

Multiple Word Expression	*Substitution*
An official who is a judge in the lowest court	Magistrate
A piece of music or a book before it is printed	Manuscript
Related to men	Masculine
One who believes in the existence of God	A theist
One who does not believe in the existence of good	An atheist
That can be believed	Credible
That cannot be believed	Incredible
That which dissolves in a solvent	Soluble
That which does not dissolves in a solvent	Insoluble
Hard writing that can be read	Legible
Hard writing that cannot be read	Illegible
A person who does jobs beneficial to mankind	Philanthropist
A person who goes on foot	Pedestrian
A person who fights for his own country	Patriot
An act of killing oneself	Suicide
A woman whose husband is dead	Widow
A man whose wife is dead	Widower
A person who eats vegetarian and non-vegetarian diets	Omnivorous
Something which is everywhere at the same time	Omnipresent
One who knows everything	Omniscient
A child who does not have parents	Orphan
An award etc. given after the death of the person	Posthumous
The place where animals are kept for amusement and to increase the knowledge of the public	Zoo
The science which deals with the study of animals	Zoology

MULTIPLE CHOICE QUESTIONS

Directions: *In questions given below, out of the four alternatives, choose the one which can be substituted for the given words/sentences.*

1. Something that relates to everyone in the world
A. General B. Common
C. Usual D. Universal

2. An expression of mild disapproval
A. Warning B. Denigration
C. Impertinence D. Reproof

3. One who is not easily pleased by anything
A. Maiden B. Medieval
C. Precarious D. Fastidious

4. Murder of a king
A. Infanticide B. Matricide
C. Genocide D. Regicide

5. A remedy for all diseases
A. Stoic B. Marvel
C. Panacea D. Recompense

6. A dramatic performance
A. Mask B. Mosque
C. Masque D. Mascot

7. Study of birds
A. Orology B. Optology
C. Ophthalmology D. Ornithology

8. Ready to believe
A. Credulous B. Credible
C. Creditable D. Incredible

9. Incapable of being seen through
A. Ductile B. Opaque
C. Obsolete D. Potable

10. One who eats everything
A. Omnivorous B. Omniscient
C. Irresistible D. Insolvent

11. A place where bees are kept is called
A. An apiary B. A mole
C. A hive D. A sanctuary

12. One who cannot be corrected
A. Incurable B. Incorrigible
C. Hardened D. Invulnerable

13. One who is in charge of a museum
A. Curator B. Supervisor
C. Caretaker D. Warden

14. Continuing fight between parties, families, clans, etc.
A. Enmity B. Feud
C. Quarrel D. Skirmish

15. A voice loud enough to be heard
A. Audible B. Applaudable
C. Laudable D. Oral

16. A paper written by hand
A. Handicraft B. Manuscript
C. Handiwork D. Thesis

17. Habitually silent or talking little
A. Serville B. Unequivocal
C. Taciturn D. Synoptic

18. To slap with a flat object
A. Chop B. Hew
C. Gnaw D. Swat

19. A person who speaks many languages
A. Linguist B. Monolingual
C. Polyglot D. Bilingual

20. A light sailing-boat built specially for racing
A. Canoe B. Yacht
C. Frigate D. Dinghy

21. A fixed orbit in space in relation to earth
A. Geological B. Geo-synchronous
C. Geo-centric D. Geo-stationary

22. A style in which a writer makes a display of his knowledge
A. Pedantic B. Verbose
C. Pompous D. Ornate

23. A religious discourse
A. Preach B. Stanza
C. Sanctorum D. Sermon

24. A place that provides refuge
A. Asylum B. Sanatorium
C. Shelter D. Orphanage

25. Detailed plan of a journey
A. Travelogue B. Travelkit
C. Schedule D. Itinerary

26. A person who insists on something
A. Disciplinarian B. Stickler
C. Instantaneous D. Boaster

27. A drawing on transparent paper
A. Red print B. Blue print
C. Negative D. Transparency

28. One who believes that all things and events in life are predetermined is a
A. Fatalist B. Puritan
C. Egoist D. Tyrant

29. A school boy who cuts classes frequently is a
A. Defeatist B. Sycophant
C. Truant D. Martinet

30. The act of violating the sanctity of the church is
A. Blasphemy B. Heresy
C. Sacrilege D. Desecration

31. A place where monks live as a secluded community
A. Cathedral B. Diocese
C. Convent D. Monastery

32. One who is fond of fighting
A. Bellicose B. Aggressive
C. Belligerent D. Militant

33. Tending to move away from the centre or axis
A. Centrifugal B. Centripetal
C. Axiomatic D. Awry

34. Words inscribed on tomb
A. Epitome B. Epistle
C. Epilogue D. Epitaph

35. Leave or remove from a place considered dangerous
A. Evade B. Evacuate
C. Avoid D. Exterminate

36. Original inhabitants of a country
A. Abroge B. Aborger
C. Aborgory D. Aborigins

37. Government by the officials
A. Theocracy B. Plutocracy
C. Bureaucracy D. Democracy

38. Incapable of being exhausted
A. Inexhaustible B. Inaexhaustible
C. Exhaustable D. Non-tired

39. A person of good understanding, knowledge and reasoning power
A. Expert B. Intellectual
C. Snob D. Literate

40. One absorbed in his own thoughts and feelings rather than in things outside
A. Scholar B. Recluse
C. Introvert D. Intellectual

ANSWERS

1	2	3	4	5	6	7	8	9	10
D	D	D	D	C	C	D	A	B	A
11	**12**	**13**	**14**	**15**	**16**	**17**	**18**	**19**	**20**
A	B	A	B	A	B	C	D	A	B
21	**22**	**23**	**24**	**25**	**26**	**27**	**28**	**29**	**30**
D	A	D	A	D	B	D	A	C	C
31	**32**	**33**	**34**	**35**	**36**	**37**	**38**	**39**	**40**
D	A	A	D	B	B	C	A	B	C

●●●

6

Spelling Errors

There are thousands of words in English language. It is difficult to remember the spellings and meanings of all at once. Try to learn as many as you can. Use a dictionary regularly.

Directions: *Find the correctly spelt words.*

1. A. Damage B. Dammage C. Damaige D. Dammege

2. A. Efficiant B. Effecient C. Efficient D. Eficient

3. A. Schedule B. Schdule C. Schedale D. Schedeule

4. A. Occurad B. Occurred C. Ocurred D. Occured

5. A. Grieff B. Grief C. Grieef D. Grrief

6. A. Guarantee B. Garuntee C. Guaruntee D. Gaurantee

7. A. Meddicine B. Medicine C. Medicene D. Medicinne

8. A. Benefeted B. Benefitted C. Benifited D. Benefited

9. A. Acommodation B. Acomodation C. Accomodation D. Accommodation

10. A. Querrelsome B. Quarrelsame C. Quarrelsome D. Querralsome

11. A. Sympathetic B. Smypathetic C. Sympothetic D. Sympethetic

12. A. Prograssive B. Progressive C. Progresive D. Prograsive

13. A. Uncivilized B. Uncevilized C. Uncivillized D. Uncevelized

14. A. Extravagant B. Extreragent C. Extreregant D. Extravegent

15. A. Missunderstood B. Miesunderstood C. Misunderstood D. Misunderstod

16. A. Belligerent B. Beligirent C. Belligarant D. Belligerrent

17. A. Astonished B. Astronished C. Astoneshed D. Asstonished

18. A. Sincerely B. Sencerely C. Sincerelly D. Sincerrely

19. A. Rigourous B. Rigerous C. Rigorous D. Regerous

20. A. Satellite B. Sattellite C. Satelite D. Sattelite

21. A. Pesanger B. Passenger C. Pessenger D. Pasanger

22. A. Humurous B. Humorous C. Humoreus D. Humorrous

23. A. Exeggerate B. Exaggerate C. Exadgerate D. Exagerate

24. A. Fariegn B. Forein C. Foriegn D. Foreign

25. A. Excesive B. Excessive C. Exccessive D. Exccesive

26. A. Forcaust B. Forcast C. Forecast D. Forecaste

27. A. Paralleted B. Paralelled C. Parralleled D. Parallelled

28. A. Ocasion B. Occassion C. Occasion D. Ocassion

29. A. Boquet B. Bouquet C. Bouquete D. Bouquette

30. A. Chettering B. Chaterring C. Chattering D. Chatering

31. A. Discourage B. Disscourage C. Discourege D. Discaurage

32. A. Curageous B. Courageous C. Courrageous D. Couregeous

33. A. Abandon B. Abanddon C. Abendon D. Abbandon

34. A. Embarassment B. Emberrassement C. Embarrassment D. Embbaresment

35. A. Eccintric B. Eccentrie C. Eccentric D. Eccintrie

36. A. Occasional B. Occassional C. Occesional D. Occessional

37. A. Querrel B. Querral C. Quarrel D. Quarel

38. A. Contrebution B. Contribution C. Contributtion D. Conterbution

39. A. Desgrace B. Disgrece
C. Disgrice D. Disgrace

40. A. Harassment B. Herassment
C. Harasment D. Harassmient

41. A. Imaginative B. Imeginative
C. Imagenative D. Imaginetive

42. A. Suficient B. Suficiant
C. Sufficient D. Sufficiant

43. A. Adequate B. Edequate
C. Adaquete D. Edaquete

44. A. Experienced B. Experianced
C. Experienced D. Experrienced

45. A. Flatering B. Fletering
C. Flattering D. Fletaring

46. A. Cuttiveted B. Culltrivated
C. Cultivated D. Caltivated

47. A. Praiceworthy B. Peiseworthy
C. Praiseworthy D. Praisaworthy

48. A. Profesional B. Professionel
C. Professional D. Profissional

49. A. Ameteur B. Amateur
C. Amataur D. Amateor

50. A. Unfevourable B. Unfevaurable
C. Unfavourable D. Unfivourable

ANSWERS

1	2	3	4	5	6	7	8	9	10
A	C	A	B	B	A	B	B	D	C
11	**12**	**13**	**14**	**15**	**16**	**17**	**18**	**19**	**20**
A	B	A	A	C	A	A	A	C	A
21	**22**	**23**	**24**	**25**	**26**	**27**	**28**	**29**	**30**
B	B	B	D	B	C	A	C	B	C
31	**32**	**33**	**34**	**35**	**36**	**37**	**38**	**39**	**40**
A	B	A	C	C	A	C	B	D	A
41	**42**	**43**	**44**	**45**	**46**	**47**	**48**	**49**	**50**
A	C	A	C	A	C	C	C	B	C

●●●

हिंदी

व्याकरण

व्याकरण वह शास्त्र है जिसके द्वारा किसी भी भाषा के शब्दों और वाक्यों के शुद्ध स्वरूपों एवं शुद्ध प्रयोगों का ज्ञान कराया जाता है।

व्याकरण के चार अंग हैं : (i) वर्ण विचार (ii) शब्द विचार (iii) पद विचार और (iv) वाक्य विचार

भाषा : भाषा अभिव्यक्ति का एक ऐसा साधन है जिसके द्वारा मनुष्य अपने विचारों को दूसरों पर प्रकट कर सकता है और दूसरों के विचार जान सकता है। भाषा के दो रूप हैं–(i) मौखिक और (ii) लिखित।

बोली : भाषा का क्षेत्रीय रूप बोली कहलाता है।

लिपि : किसी भी भाषा के लिखने की विधि को लिपि कहते हैं।

वर्ण : हिन्दी भाषा में प्रयुक्त सबसे छोटी ध्वनि वर्ण कहलाती है। जैसे–अ, आ, ई, क्, ख्, आदि

वर्णमाला : वर्णों के समुदाय को वर्णमाला कहते हैं। हिन्दी वर्णमाला में 44 वर्ण हैं। जिनमें 11 स्वर तथा 33 व्यंजन हैं।

स्वरवर्ण : उन वर्णों को कहते हैं, जिनका उच्चारण बिना किसी दूसरे वर्ण की सहायता से होता है। हिन्दी में 11 स्वर हैं–अ, आ, इ, ई, उ, ऊ, ए, ऐ, ओ, औ, ऋ।

व्यंजन वर्ण : उन वर्णों को कहते हैं, जिनका उच्चारण स्वर वर्णों की सहायता के बिना नहीं हो सकता है। इनकी संख्या 33 है–

क ख ग घ ड़ च छ ज झ ञ ट् ठ

ड ढ़ ण त थ द ध न प फ ब भ

म य र ल व श ष स ह।

वर्ण : एक या अधिक वर्णों से बनी हुई स्वतन्त्र सार्थक ध्वनि शब्द कहलाती है।

शब्दों को तत्सम, तद्भव, देशज और विदेशी भागों में बाँटा जाता है।

तत्सम : जो शब्द संस्कृत भाषा से हिन्दी में बिना किसी परिवर्तन के लिए जाते हैं वे तत्सम कहलाते हैं, जैसे– अग्नि, क्षेत्र, मित्र, नासिका आदि।

तद्भव : उन शब्दों को कहते हैं, जो संस्कृत से ही लिए गए हैं, परन्तु हिन्दी में आने पर जिनका रूप बदल गया है। जैसे–आग, खेत, रात आदि।

देशज : उन शब्दों को कहते हैं, जो बोलचाल तथा देश की अन्य भाषाओं से लिए गए हैं। जैसे–कटोरा, झंझत, डिबिया, लोटा आदि।

विदेशज या विदेशी : उन शब्दों को कहते हैं, जो किसी विदेशी भाषा से आए हैं। जैसे–स्कूल, कार, कमरा, खुदा, जोश, सरकार आदि।

शब्द सम्पदा

तत्सम शब्दों के तद्भव रूप

तत्सम	तद्भव	तत्सम	तद्भव
अग्नि	आग	अद्य	आज
अष्ट	आठ	अक्षि	आँख
अर्ध	आधा	अस्थि	हड्डी
अश्रु	आँसू	आम्र	आम
ग्राम	गाँव	गर्दभ	गधा
गृघ्र	गीध	गौर	गोरा
गह	घर	घट	घड़ा
धातु	धात	धृत	घी
लक्ष	लाख	सप्त	सात
त्वम्	तुम	दुग्ध	दूध
रत्न	रतन	वर्ष	बरस
भक्त	भगत	मर्कट	बन्दर
रात्रि	रात	उलूक	उल्लू
अन्धकार	अन्धेरा	क्षीर	खीर
निद्रा	नींद	पृष्ठ	पीठ
ज्येष्ठ	जेठ	स्वर्ण	सोना
श्वास	साँस	काक	काग
कार्य	काज	कर्ण	कान

तत्सम	तद्भव	तत्सम	तद्भव
पाद	पाँव	हस्त	हाथ
नासिका	नाक	कंटक	काँटा
दश	दस	दधि	दही
दीप	दीया	निद्रा	नींद
नव	नौ	पत्र	पत्ता
प्रस्तर	पत्थर	जिह्वा	जीभ
हस्ती	हाथी	दन्त	दाँत
क्षेत्र	खेत	नृत्य	नाच
सूचिका	सूई	स्वर्णकार	सुनार
लोक	लोग	पर्यड़्क	पलंग
स्वप्न	सपना	कातर	कायर
पुत्र	पूत	मानव	मनुष्य
शत	सौ	पुष्प	फूल
पक्व	पक्का	कृषक	किसान
कर्म	कार्य	आम्र	आम
कर्ण	कान	अष्ट	आठ
घंटिका	घंटी	चन्द्र	चन्द
यव	जौ	धूम्र	धुआँ

विराम चिह्न

विराम का अर्थ रुकना। अपने विचारों को ठीक ढंग से प्रकट करने के पढ़ते अथवा लिखते समय हमें कुछ रुकना पड़ता है। इस प्रकार के रुकने को विराम कहते हैं।

प्रत्येक-विराम के लिए अलग-अलग चिह्न हैं–

पूर्ण विराम	[।]
अल्प विराम	[,]
अर्ध विराम	[;]
प्रश्न बोधक	[?]
विस्मयादि बोधक	[!]
योजक	[–]
उद्धरण	[" "]

कारक

कारक शब्द उस रूप को कहते हैं, जिससे संज्ञा या सर्वनाम वाक्य के साथ सम्बन्ध जाना जाता है। जैसे–शीला कलम **से** लिखती है।

यह सीमा **की** पुस्तक है।

कारक के भेद विभक्ति चिह्नों सहित

कारक	**विभक्ति**
कर्त्ता	ने
कर्म	को
करण	से
सम्प्रदान	के लिए
अपादान	से
सम्बन्ध	का, के, की
अधिकरण	में, पर
सम्बोधन	हे, अरे!

पर्यायवाची शब्द

जिन शब्दों से एक समान अर्थ का बोध होता है, उन्हें पर्यायवाची या समानार्थी शब्द कहते हैं।

कुछ पर्यायवाची शब्दों के उदाहरण निम्नलिखित हैं–

आग – अग्नि, अनल, पावक, हुताशन, ज्वाला।
आकाश – नभ, आसमान, गगन, लोभ।
असुर – राक्षस, दानव, निशाचर, दैत्य।
अमृत – अभिय, पीयूष, सुधा, सोम।
अन्धकार – अन्धेरा, तिमिर, तम, तमिस्त्र।
आँख – नेत्र, नयन, लोचन, चक्षु, दृग।
कमल – जलज, पंकज, नीरज, राजीव।
इन्द्र – सुरपति, देवेन्द्र, सुरेन्द्र, देवेश।
ईश्वर – प्रभु, भगवान, जगदीश, दीनबन्धु।
पक्षी – खग, विहग, चिड़िया, नभचर।
बादल – घन, जलधर, वारिद, नीरद।
गंगा – सुरसरि, जाह्नवी, त्रिपथगा, देवनदी, विष्णुपदी।
चन्द्रमा – शशि, मयंक, निशाकर, सुधाकर, सुधांशु, सोम हिमांशु, राकेश।
जल – पानी, नीर, लोभ, अम्बु, सलिल, क्षीर, वारि।
फूल – पुष्प, कुसुम, सुमन, प्रसून, सारंग।
पृथ्वी – भू, भूमि, धरा, वसुन्धरा, वसुधा, धरती क्षमा, लोक।
कपड़ा – पट, वस्त्र, चीर, अम्बर, दुकूल।
घर – गृह, गेह, निकेतन, आलय, निलय, भवन, शाला, धाम, सदन।
जंगल – वन, कानन, अरण्य, विपिन।
तालाब – सरोवर, ताल, जलाशय, तड़ाग।
दिन – दिवस, वासर, वार।
पहाड़ – गिरि, पर्वत, गूधर, नग, महीधर, मेरू।
पत्थर – पहाड़, प्रस्तर, पाहन।
पवन – वायु, समीर, हवा, मारुत, अनिल।
पुत्र – सुत, तनय, पूत, आत्मज।
बिजली – तड़ित, चपला, दामिनी।
वृक्ष – तरू, रूख, विटप, पेड़।
मनुष्य – नर, मानव, मनुज, आदमी।
हाथी – करि, हस्ती, गज।
मित्र – सखा, मीत, सहचर, दोस्त।
राजा – नरेश, नृप, महीप, भूप।
समुद्र – सागर, सिन्धु, जलधि, नीरधि।
सरस्वती – शारदा, वागेश्वरी, भारती, महाश्वेता।
साँप – पन्नग, सर्प, विषधर, अहि, व्याल।
सूर्य – दिनकर, दिवाकर, रवि, भानु, भास्कर।
स्त्री – नारी, महिला, दारा, वामा।
शरीर – देह, तन, काया, गात, बदन।
गणेश – गजानन, गणपति, विनायक, एकदन्त, गजवदन लम्बोदर, विघ्न नाशक।
घोड़ा – तुरंग, बाजि, हय, अश्व, घोटक।
युद्ध – समर, रण, संग्राम।
सिंह – केसरी, मृगराज, केहरी।
शत्रु – अरि, रिपु, बैरी।
विष्णु – हरि, कमलेश, रमापति, चक्रपाणि, केशव, माधव, पीताम्बर।
कोष – खजाना, भण्डार, निधि।
धन – दौलत, द्रव्य, मुद्रा।

तलवार – कृपाण, असि, खड्ग।
अंग – भाग, हिस्सा, अवयव।
चोर – तस्कर, दस्यु, रजनीचर।
पत्नी – भार्या, दारा, गृहिणी।
पुत्र – तनय, सुत, लड़का, बेटा।
पुत्री – तनया, सुता, लड़की, बेटी।
माता – जननी, अम्बा, अम्बिका, अम्मा, माँ, धात्री।
मोर – शिखी, नीलकण्ठ, मयूर।
मृत्यु – मौत, काल, देहान्त।
रक्त – रुधिर, शोणित, खून, लहू।
विष – जहर, हलाहल, गरल।
सोना – कंचन, स्वर्ण, कनक।
हृदय – उर, छाती, वक्ष, वक्षस्थल, हिय, हिया।
सभा – अधिवेशन, परिषद्, बैठक, महासभा, समागम, समिति, सम्मेलन।
यमुना – कालिन्दी, कृष्णा, जमुना, रविसुता तरणि-तनुजा।

विलोम-शब्द

शब्दों के अपने निश्चित अर्थ होते हैं। उन अर्थों के विपरीत अर्थ देने वाले शब्द को विलोम-शब्द कहते हैं।

शब्द	विलोम	शब्द	विलोम
अमृत	विष	उदार	संकीर्ण
अनुकूल	प्रतिकूल	अनुराग	विराग
आदि	अन्त	उत्थान	पतन
इच्छा	अनिच्छा	उचित	अनुचित
अल्पायु	दीर्घायु	अनुज	अग्रज
उन्नति	अवनति	आकाश	पाताल
अधिक	न्यून	आयात	निर्यात
एक	अनेक	अन्धकार	प्रकाश
अर्थ	अनर्थ	उदय	अस्त
परकीया	स्वकीया	जड़	चेतन
जय	पराजय	अनिवार्य	वैकल्पिक
नकद	उधार	अपेक्षा	उपेक्षा
उपस्थित	अनुपस्थित	आदर	अनादर
अन्धेरा	उजाला	अपना	पराया
उत्तम	अधम	आय	व्यय
सुपुत्र	कुपुत्र	स्वाधीन	पराधीन
आहार	निराहार	कठोर	कोमल
दाता	याचक	दोषी	निर्दोषि
खेद	प्रसन्नता	धनी	निर्धन
निकट	दूर	चर	अचर
देव	दानव	खरा	खोटा
गरीब	अमीर	प्रेम	घृणा
जीवन	मृत्यु	बुरा	भला
सजीव	निर्जीव	मित्र	शत्रु
सुगन्ध	दुर्गन्ध	मौखिक	लिखित
संक्षेप	विस्तार	कटु	मधुर
आरम्भ	अन्त	कड़वा	मीठा
कृतज्ञ	कृतघ्न	दिन	रात
साक्षर	निरक्षर	पवित्र	अपवित्र
पाप	पुण्य	जल	थल
धीर	अधीर	निर्मल	मलिन

शब्द	विलोम	शब्द	विलोम
गुण	अवगुण	नश्वर	अनश्वर
निन्दा	स्तुति	भारी	हल्का
मनुष्यता	पशुता	सरस	नीरस
मान	अपमान	क्रय	विक्रय
धर्म	अधर्म	गहरा	उथला
गुरु	शिष्य	पक्ष	विपक्ष
जन्म	मृत्यु	बन्धन	मुक्ति
यश	अपयश	ज्ञान	अज्ञान
आदर	अनादर	पूर्ण	अपूर्ण
सफल	असफल	शान्त	अशान्त
कीर्ति	अपकीर्ति	वादी	प्रतिवादी
आस्तिक	नास्तिक	स्वदेश	परदेश
सज्जन	दुर्जन	राग	द्वेष
ऊसर	उर्वर	उदार	कृपण
अगला	पिछला	अगम	सुगम
अग्नि	जल	अति	अल्प
अर्थ	अनर्थ	अतल	वितल
अत्यधिक	स्वल्प	अधः	उपरि
अधिकतम	न्यूनतम	अतिवृष्टि	अनावृष्टि
अनाथ	सनाथ	ईश्वर	जीव
अनुलोम	विलोम	अर्पण	ग्रहण
अवनि	अम्बर	अस्त	उदय
आकर्षण	विकर्षण	आगे	पीछे
आजाद	गुलाम	आदान	प्रदान
आधुनिक	प्राचीन	आना	जाना
आय	व्यय	आयात	निर्यात
आवश्यक	अनावश्यक	आशा	निराशा
आस्था	अनास्था	इहलोक	परलोक
उच्च	निम्न	उत्थान	पतन
उपकार	अपकार	उपयोग	दुरुपयोग
एकता	अनेकता	कल	आज
कृत्रिम	प्राकृत	कृष्ण	शुक्ल
कपूत	सपूत	कोमल	कठोर
गगन	धरा	ज्ञान	अज्ञान

लिंग

लिंग का अर्थ है 'चिह्न'। लिंग शब्द उस चिह्न को कहते हैं जिससे वस्तु के पुरुष या स्त्री होने की कल्पना हो। लिंग दो प्रकार के होते हैं—(1) पुल्लिंग (2) स्त्रीलिंग

पुल्लिंग—पुल्लिंग संज्ञा के उस रूप को कहते हैं जिससे उसके पुरुष होने का ज्ञान होता है। जैसे—राम, श्याम, घोड़ा, हाथी, कुत्ता आदि।

स्त्रीलिंग—स्त्रीलिंग संज्ञा के उस रूप को कहते हैं जिससे उसके स्त्री होने का ज्ञान हो। जैसे—भैंस, गाय, बकरी, सीता, रमा इत्यादि।

पुल्लिंग	स्त्रीलिंग	पुल्लिंग	स्त्रीलिंग
इन्द्र	इन्द्राणी	मेहतर	मेहतरानी
नौकर	नौकरानी	जेठ	जेठानी
देवर	देवरानी	सेठ	सेठानी
पण्डित	पण्डिताइन	ओझा	ओझाइन
बनिया	बनियाइन	दुबे	दुबाइन
हलवाई	हलवाइन	चौबे	चौबाइन
गुरु	गुरुआइन	लड़का	लड़की
दास	दासी	कबूतर	कबूतरी
हिरण	हिरणी	क्षत्रिय	क्षत्राणी
मुगल	मुगलानी	हिन्दू	हिन्दुआनी
चौधरी	चौधरानी	भव	भवानी
लाला	ललाइन	पण्डा	पण्डाइन
ठाकुर	ठकुराइन	बाबू	बबुआइन
घोड़ा	घोड़ी	गूँगा	गूँगी
बच्चा	बच्ची	चाचा	चाची
बकरा	बकरी	मामा	मामी
मुर्गा	मुर्गी	साला	साली
चींटा	चींटी	रस्सा	रस्सी
देव	देवी	ब्राह्मण	ब्राह्मणी
बेटा	बेटी	बूढ़ा	बुढ़िया
चूहा	चुहिया	डिब्बा	डिबिया
गुड्डा	गुड़िया	कुम्हार	कुम्हारिन
सुनार	सुनारिन	नाती	नातिन
जुलाहा	जुलाहिन	दर्जी	दर्जिन
पापी	पापिन	हाथी	हथिनी

पुल्लिंग	स्त्रीलिंग	पुल्लिंग	स्त्रीलिंग
पिता	माता	बैल	गाय
कवि	कवयित्री	विधुर	विधवा
बाप	माँ	बादशाह	बेगम
नर	मादा	मर्द	औरत
युवक	युवती	वर	वधू
सम्राट्	सम्राज्ञी	साढू	साली
फूफा	बुआ	पुत्र	पुत्री
पहाड़	पहाड़ी	गोप	गोपी
गधा	गधी	तरुण	तरुणी
नर्तक	नर्तकी	बेटा	बिटिया
बछड़ा	बछिया	चिड़ा	चिड़िया
बन्दर	बन्दरिया	कुत्ता	कुतिया
नाई	नाइन	धोबी	धोबिन
ग्वाला	ग्वालिन	भंगी	भंगिन
स्वामी	स्वामिनी	विद्वान्	विदुषी
साधु	साध्वी	पुरुष	स्त्री
पति	पत्नी	वीर	वीरांगना
साहब	मेम	सास	ससुर
मियाँ	बीबी	राजा	रानी
बिलाड़	बिल्ली	अनुज	अनुजा
छात्र	छात्रा	महोदय	महोदया
प्रिय	प्रिया	मामा	मामी
लोटा	लुटिया	मोर	मोरनी
शेर	शेरनी	जाट	जाटिन
डाक्टर	डाक्टरनी	मालिक	मालकिन
माली	मालिन	बाघ	बाघिन
हाथी	हथिनी	स्वामी	स्वामिनी
बालक	बालिका	धनवान	धनवती
धावक	धाविका	नेता	नेत्री
गुणवान	गुणवती	नर	मादा
अभिनेता	अभिनेत्री	प्राचार्य	प्राचार्या
प्रबन्धकर्ता	प्रबन्धकर्ती	दाता	दात्री
ननदोई	ननद	अध्यापक	अध्यापिका

वचन

शब्द के जिस रूप से उसके एक अथवा अनेक होने का बोध हो, उसे वचन कहते हैं।

हिन्दी में दो वचन होते हैं—

(1) एकवचन और (2) बहुवचन

एकवचन—शब्द के जिस रूप से एक ही वस्तु का बोध हो, उसे एकवचन कहते हैं। जैसे—लड़का, गाय, बकरी, घोड़ा, राम, सीता आदि।

बहुवचन—शब्द के जिस रूप से अनेकता का बोध हो उसे बहुवचन कहते हैं। जैसे—लड़के, कपड़े, गायें आदि।

एकवचन	बहुवचन	एकवचन	बहुवचन
लड़का	लड़के	कौवा	कौवे
बेटा	बेटे	कमरा	कमरे
कपड़ा	कपड़े	बहन	बहनें
चीज	चीजें	गधा	गधे
रुपया	रुपये	घोड़ा	घोड़े
नहर	नहरें	रात	रातें
बात	बातें	सड़क	सड़कें
दाना	दाने	लोटा	लोटे
पैसा	पैसे	पुस्तक	पुस्तकें
कन्या	कन्याएँ	वधू	वधुएँ
नारी	नारियाँ	लड़की	लड़कियाँ
मुर्गा	मुर्गे	घण्टा	घण्टे
गद्दा	गद्दे	हीरा	हीरे
बच्चा	बच्चे	प्याला	प्याले
छाता	छाते	गाय	गायें
कथा	कथाएँ	कविता	कविताएँ
बहू	बहुएँ	टोपी	टोपियाँ
नाली	नालियाँ	बेटा	बेटे
ताला	ताले	जूता	जूते

एकवचन	बहुवचन	एकवचन	बहुवचन
डिबिया	डिबियाँ	नाक	नाकें
पूँछ	पूँछें	मूँछ	मूँछें
चिड़िया	चिड़ियाँ	सरिता	सरिताएँ
बालिका	बालिकाएँ	चाभी	चाभियाँ
कहानी	कहानियाँ	दरवाजा	दरवाजे
कलम	कलमें	कुटिया	कुटियाँ
रानी	रानियाँ	नाई	नाइयों
माता	माताएँ	बाल	बालों
हाथ	हाथों	मुख	मुख
कोट	कोट	दाँत	दाँतों
नाखून	नाखूनों	पैर	पैरों
बैल	बैलों	माली	मालियों
राजा	राजाओं	पिता	पिता
चन्द्रमा	चन्द्रमा	कवि	कवियों
मुनि	मुनियों	कौआ	कौए
छात्रा	छात्राएँ	सेना	सेनाएँ
दिशा	दिशाएँ	गुड़िया	गुड़ियाँ
मेज	मेजें	भैंस	भैंसें
अंगूर	अंगूरों	समुद्र	समुद्र

अनेक शब्दों के लिए एक शब्द

जिसकी कोई उपमा न हो : **अनुपम**
तेज बुद्धि वाला : **कुशाग्रबुद्धि**
कल्पना से परे हो : **कल्पनातीत**
जो उपकार नहीं मानता है : **कृतघ्न**
जो उपकार मानता है : **कृतज्ञ**
किसी की हँसी उड़ाना : **उपहास**
ऊपर कहा हुआ : **उपर्युक्त**
ऊपर लिखा हुआ : **उपरलिखित**
जिस पर उपकार किया गया हो : **उपकृत**
इतिहास का ज्ञाता : **इतिहासज्ञ**
आलोचना करने वाला : **आलोचक**
ईश्वर में आस्था रखने वाला : **आस्तिक**
बिना वेतन का : **अवैतनिक**
जो कहा न जा सके : **अकथनीय**
जो गिना न जा सके : **अगणित**
जिसका कोई शत्रु ही न जन्मा हो : **अजातशत्रु**
जिसके समान कोई दूसरा न हो : **अद्वितीय**
जो परिचित न हो : **अपरिचित**
आकाश में उड़ने वाला : **नभचर**
जो टुकड़े-टुकड़े हो गया हो : **खण्डित**

मछली की तरह आँखों वाली : **मीनाक्षी**
मयूर की तरह आँखों वाली : **मयूराक्षी**
बच्चों के लिए काम की वस्तु : **बालोपयोगी**
जिसकी बहुत अधिक चर्चा हो : **बहुचर्चित**
जिस स्त्री को कभी सन्तान न हुई हो : **बन्ध्या (बाँझ)**
फेन से भरा हुआ : **फेनिल**
प्रिय बोलने वाली स्त्री : **प्रियम्वदा**
जिसकी उपमा न हो : **निरुपम**
जो थोड़ी देर पहले पैदा हुआ हो : **नवजात**
जिसका कोई आधार न हो : **निराधार**
नगर में वास करने वाला : **नागरिक**
रात में घूमने वाला : **निशाचर**
ईश्वर में विश्वास न रखने वाला : **नास्तिक**
माँस न खाने वाला : **निरामिष**
बिल्कुल बर्बाद हो गया : **ध्वस्त**
जिसकी धर्म में निष्ठा हो : **धर्मनिष्ठ**
देखने योग्य : **दर्शनीय**
बहुत तेज चलने वाला : **द्रुतगामी**
जो किसी पक्ष में न रहे : **तटस्थ**
तत्त्व को जानने वाला : **तत्त्वज्ञ**

तप करने वाला : **तपस्वी**
जिसे देखकर डर लगे : **डरावना**
जो जन्म से अन्ध हो : **जन्मान्ध**
जीने की प्रबल इच्छा : **जिजीविषा**
जिसने इन्द्रियों को जीत लिया हो : **जितेन्द्रिय**
चिन्ता में डूबा हुआ : **चिन्तित**
जो बहुत समय तक ठहरे : **चिरस्थायी**
जिसकी चार भुजाएँ हों : **चतुर्भुज**
जिसके हाथ में चक्र हों : **चक्रपाणि**
जिससे घृणा की जाए : **घृणित**
जिसे गुप्त रखा जाए : **गोपनीय**
गणित ज्ञाता : **गणितज्ञ**
आकाश को चूमने वाला : **गगनचुम्बी**
जिसका आदि न हो : **अनादि**
जो कुछ न जानता हो : **अज्ञ**
जो अनुकरण करने योग्य हो : **अनुकरणीय**
जिसका अन्त न हो : **अनन्त**
जो कभी न मरे : **अमर**
जो कम बोलता हो : **अल्पभाषी**
जिसका इलाज न हो : **लाइलाज**
जिसका कोई नाथ न हो : **अनाथ**
कम जानने वाला : **अल्पज्ञ**
जहाँ जाना सम्भव न हो : **अगम**
बड़ा भाई : **अग्रज**
कम खाने वाला : **अल्पाहारी**
जो बात पहले कभी न हुई हो : **अभूतपूर्व**
दूसरों के पीछे चलने वाला : **अनुचर**
जो पहले न पढ़ा हो : **अपठित**
जिसके आर-पार दिखाई देता हो : **पारदर्शी**
आज्ञा पालन करने वाला : **आज्ञाकारी**
काम से जी चुराने वाला : **कामचोर**
प्रतिदिन होने वाला : **दैनिक**
जिसका कोई अर्थ न हो : **निरर्थक**
हाथ से लिखा हुआ : **हस्तलिखित**
आँखों के सामने होने वाला : **प्रत्यक्ष**
जिसका आचरण अच्छा हो : **सदाचारी**
वह पुरुष जिसकी पत्नी मर गई हो : **विधुर**
वह स्त्री जिसका पति मर गया हो : **विधवा**
जिसका रूप अच्छा न हो : **कुरूप**
सदा सत्य बोलने वाला : **सत्यवादी**
बड़ी इमारत के टूटे-फूटे भाग : **खण्डहर**
प्रशंसा के योग्य : **प्रशंसनीय**

जहाँ अनाथ रहते हों : **अनाथालय**
प्रत्येक मास होने वाला : **मासिक**
जहाँ पानी के जहाज आकर रुकते हैं : **बन्दरगाह**
प्रत्येक सप्ताह होने वाला : **साप्ताहिक**
प्रत्येक वर्ष होने वाला : **वार्षिक**
जो कठिनाई से मिले : **दुर्लभ**
जिसका आकार हो : **साकार**
जिसका आकार न हो : **निराकार**
जो कभी बूढ़ा न हो : **अजर**
बहुत बोलने वाला : **वाचाल**
पृथ्वी पर रहने वाला : **थलचर**
जल में रहने वाला : **जलचर**
नभ में विचरण करने वाला : **नभचर**
जल-थल दोनों में रहने वाला : **उभयचर**
जिसमें रस न हो : **नीरस**
पढ़ने वाला : **पाठक**
जो भाषण देता हो : **वक्ता**
जो साथ में पढ़ता हो : **सहपाठी**
जिसके नीचे रेखा खींची हो : **रेखांकित**
जानने की इच्छा रखने वाला : **जिज्ञासु**
जिसकी कोई सन्तान न हो : **निःसन्तान**
जिसका कोई मूल्य न हो : **अमूल्य**
जो वन में घूमता हो : **वनचर**
जो इस लोक के बाहर की बात हो : **अलौकिक**
जो इस लोक की बात हो : **लौकिक**
जिसका सम्बन्ध पश्चिम से हो : **पाश्चात्य**
जो स्थिर रहे : **स्थावर**
दुःखान्त नाटक : **त्रासदी**
ज्ञान देने वाली : **ज्ञानदा**
भूत, वर्तमान भविष्य को देखने वाला : **त्रिकालदर्शी**
जो क्षमा के योग्य हो : **क्षम्य**
हिंसा करने वाला : **हिंसक**
हित चाहने वाला : **हितैषी**
सब कुछ जानने वाला : **सर्वज्ञ**
जो स्वयं पैदा हुआ हो : **स्वयंभू**
जो शरण में आया हो : **शरणागत**
जिसका वर्णन न किया जा सके : **वर्णनातीत**
व्याकरण जानने वाला : **वैयाकरण**
रचना करने वाला : **रचयिता**
खून से रंगा हुआ : **रक्तरंजित**
अत्यन्त सुन्दर स्त्री : **रूपसी**
कीर्तिमान पुरुष : **यशस्वी**

महत्त्वपूर्ण शब्दों की भाववाचक संज्ञा

शब्द	भाववाचक संज्ञा	शब्द	भाववाचक संज्ञा
दास	दासता	क्षत्रिय	क्षत्रियत्व
पशु	पशुता	बालक	बालकपन
बन्धु	बन्धुत्व	मित्र	मित्रता
बूढ़ा	बुढ़ापा	सती	सतीत्व
सेवक	सेवा	शिशु	शैशव
अपना	अपनत्व	पराया	परायापन
पण्डित	पाण्डित्य	पुरुष	पुरुषत्व
ब्राह्मण	ब्राह्मणत्व	बच्चा	बचपन
प्रभु	प्रभुता	नारी	नारीत्व
देव	देवत्व	लड़का	लड़कपन
मनुष्य	मनुष्यता	दानव	दानवता
निज	निजता	स्व	स्वत्व

शब्द	भाववाचक संज्ञा	शब्द	भाववाचक संज्ञा
अहं	अहंकार	अपना	अपनापन
व्यक्ति	व्यक्तित्व	मीठा	मिठास
गरीब	गरीबी	सफल	सफलता
बुरा	बुराई	स्वस्थ	स्वास्थ्य
सरल	सरलता	कंजुस	कंजुसी
कमजोर	कमजोरी	हरा	हरियाली
गर्म	गर्मी	मोटा	मोटाई
चालाक	चालाकी	गम्भीर	गम्भीरता
पढ़ना	पढ़ाई	लिखना	लिखाई
थकना	थकावट	लिखना	लिखावट
लूटना	लूट	लड़ना	लड़ाई
हँसना	हँसी	आप	अपनत्व

महत्त्वपूर्ण शब्दों के विशेषण

शब्द	विशेषण	शब्द	विशेषण
अंक	अंकित	अर्थ	आर्थिक
इतिहास	ऐतिहासिक	उदासी	उदास
कलंक	कलंकित	कुसुम	कुसुमित
जटा	जटिल	भार	भारी
बनारस	बनारसी	बाजार	बाजारू
प्यास	प्यासा	पुराण	पौराणिक
पंक	पंकित	पक्ष	पाक्षिक
धन	धनी	दो	दूसरा
तीन	तीसरा	झगड़ा	झगड़ालू
ठण्ड	ठण्डा	जाति	जातीय
काँटा	कँटीला	विदेश	विदेशी
रोज	रोजाना	भूगोल	भौगोलिक
पीड़ा	पीड़ित	पुत्र	पुत्रवान
आलस्य	आलसी	अंतर	आंतरिक
ईर्ष्या	ईर्ष्यालु	कर्म	कर्मठ
करुणा	कारुणिक	कृपा	कृपालु
गुण	गुणी	जल	जलमय
जीव	जैविक	तट	तटस्थ
तर्क	तार्किक	धर्म	धार्मिक
नमक	नमकीन	पत्थर	पथरीला
पल्लव	पल्लवित	पान	पनवाड़ी
मुख	मुखर	मिठास	मीठा
मास	मासिक	मद	मादक
रक्त	रक्तिम	रस	रसीला

शब्द	विशेषण	शब्द	विशेषण
वन	वन्य	विष्णु	वैष्णव
शहर	शहरी	तप	तपस्वी
जापान	जापानी	तेज	तेजस्वी
तत्त्व	तात्त्विक	दया	दयालु
देव	दैविक	निंदा	निंदक
नव	नवीन	पोषण	पोषक
पेट	पेटू	पाप	पापी
पूजा	पूज्य	भूख	भूखा
फेन	फेनिल	भारत	भारतीय
माया	मायावी	रंग	रंगीन
विष	विषैला	श्री	श्रीमान
सुर	सुरीला	विवाह	वैवाहिक
आदर	आदरणीय	ऋण	ऋणी
किताब	किताबी	क्रम	क्रमिक
ग्राम	ग्रामीण	घर	घरेलू
चतुर	चतुरता	जहर	जहरीला
सप्ताह	साप्ताहिक	अनुभव	अनुभवी
ओज	ओजस्वी	कल्पना	काल्पनिक
कुल	कुलीन	गाँव	गँवार
चमक	चमकीला	चाचा	चचेरा
दीन	दीनता	नगर	नागरिक
नागपुर	नागपुरी	परिवार	पारिवारिक
पुष्प	पुष्पित	पिता	पैतृक
फ्रांस	फ्रांसीसी	बाहर	बाहरी

शब्द	विशेषण	शब्द	विशेषण	शब्द	विशेषण	शब्द	विशेषण
भय	भयभीत	मधु	मधुर	गाना	गायक	बेचना	बिकाऊ
मौन	मौनी	मन	मानसिक	भागना	भगोड़ा	वन्द	वन्दनीय
मानव	मानवीय	रक्षा	रक्षक	चलना	चलती	घूमना	घुमक्कड़
रघु	राघव	रोग	रोगी	चलना	चालू	मरना	मरियल
वर्ष	वार्षिक	शक्ति	शक्तिशाली	भूलना	भुलक्कड़	पीछे	पिछला
श्रम	श्रमिक	अंत	अंतिम	भीतर	भीतरी	नीचे	निम्न
कागज	कागजी	मर्म	मार्मिक	अणु	आणविक	अधिकार	आधिकारिक
शब्द	शाब्दिक	अज्ञान	अज्ञानी	अनुभव	अनुभवी	अन्याय	अन्यायी
गुलाब	गुलाबी	प्रकृति	प्राकृतिक	अपमान	अपमानित	अभ्यास	अभ्यासी
परिचय	परिचित	पूजा	पुजारी	अवश्य	आवश्यक	आदि	आदिम
रोग	रोगी	ग्राम	ग्रामीण	आयु	आयुष्मान्	उदय	उदित
सुगंध	सुगंधित	मैं	मेरा	उपज	उपजाऊ	एकता	एक
जो	जैसा	आप	आप-सा	अंत	अंतिम	कुल	कुलीन
तुम	तुम्हारा	कौन	कैसा	खर्च	खर्चीला	खून	खूनी
वह	वैसा	पढ़ना	पढ़ाकू	गुण	गुणी		

श्रुतिसम भिन्नार्थक शब्द

शब्द	अर्थ	शब्द	अर्थ
आदि	आरम्भ	आदी	अभ्यस्त
कुल	वंश	कूल	किनारा
अरि	शत्रु	अरी	सम्बोधन
अगम	दुर्गम	आगम	शास्त्र
अयश	अपकीर्ति	अयस्क	लोहा
अपेक्षा	चाहना, तुलना में	उपेक्षा	निरादर
अनिल	हवा	अनल	आग
अवधि	काल, समय	अवधी	अवध की भाषा
आयात	बाहर से आना	आयत	एक आकृति
चिर	पुराना	चीर	कपड़ा
तनु	पतला	तनू	पुत्र, गाय
तरंग	लहर	तुरंग	घोड़ा
दारा	स्त्री	द्वार	दरवाजा
दूत	संदेशवाहक	द्यूत	जुआ
जलद	बादल	जलज	कमल
प्रदीप	दीपक	प्रतीप	उल्टा
प्रसाद	कृपा	प्रासाद	महल
पास	निकट	पाश	बन्धन
द्विप	हाथी	द्वीप	टापू
देव	देवता	दैव	भाग्य
नीर	जल	नीड़	घोंसला
पवन	वायु	पावन	पवित्र

शब्द	अर्थ	शब्द	अर्थ
बन्द	खुला नहीं	बद	बुरा
पथ	रास्ता	पथ्य	रोगी का भोजन
पुर	नगर	पूर	बाढ़
भवन	महल	भुवन	संसार
लक्ष्य	उद्देश्य	लक्ष	लाख
सर	तालाब	शर	बाण
सर्ग	अध्याय	स्वर्ग	एक लोक
कर्म	कार्य	क्रम	सिलसिला
चिता	शव जलाने के लिए लकड़ियों का ढेर	चीता	बाघ
शव	लाश	शब	रात
शस्त्र	हथियार	शास्त्र	ग्रन्थ
श्रवण	सुनना	श्रमण	बौद्ध संन्यासी
मत	विचार	मत्त	मस्त
शोक	दुःख	शौक	चाव
ग्रह	नक्षत्र	गृह	घर
कपट	धोखा	कपाट	दरवाजा
उपयुक्त	ठीक	उपर्युक्त	ऊपर कहा गया
सुत	बेटा	सूत	धागा
शूर	वीर	सूर	अंधा
श्याम	कृष्ण	शाम	संध्या
दिन	वार	दीन	गरीब
कटिबद्ध	तैयार रहना	करबद्ध	हाथ जोड़ना

अनेकार्थक शब्द

शब्द	विभिन्न अर्थ
अंक	संख्या, गोद
अक्षर	वर्ण, ईश्वर
पानी	जल, प्रतिष्ठा
अचल	पवर्त, स्थिर
आम	फल, सामान्य
अंबर	वस्त्र, आकाश
अवस्था	आयु, दशा
उत्तर	दिशा, जबाव
विधि	तरीका, भाग्य
कर	हाथ, टैक्स
कनक	सोना, धतुरा
गुरु	श्रेष्ठ, शिक्षक
हान	भारी हथौड़ा, बादल
जड़	मूर्ख, मूल
कल	मशीन, आनेवाला कल, चैन
सुर	देवता, स्वर

शब्द	विभिन्न अर्थ
द्विज	पक्षी, ब्राह्मण
तीर	किनारा, बाण
प्रकृति	स्वभाव, कुदरत
पत्र	चिट्ठी, पत्र
पद	पैर, उपाधि
फल	परिणाम, फल
तनु	पतला, कोमल
वर्ण	रंग, जाति
हल	समाधान, खेत जोतने का साधन
अशोक	राजा, वृक्ष
आभीर	अहीर, एक राग
एकाक्ष	काना, कौआ
खल	दुष्ट, खलिहान
घट	घड़ा, हृदय
जलज	कमल, मछली
हेम	सोना, जल

सामान्य अशुद्धियाँ

अशुद्ध	शुद्ध	अशुद्ध	शुद्ध
दुनियां	दुनिया	श्रीमति	श्रीमती
सामिग्री	सामग्री	वापिस	वापस
प्रदर्शिनी	प्रदर्शनी	द्वारिका	द्वारका
ऊत्थान	उत्थान	दुसरा	दूसरा
प्रशाद	प्रसाद	अमावश्या	अमावस्या
बसंत	वसंत	बर्ष	वर्ष
विना	बिना	बन	वन
दाइत्व	दायित्व	सम्वाद	संवाद
कुन्डली	कुण्डली	मॉसिक	मानसिक
कन्ठ	कण्ठ	अगामी	आगामी
सप्ताहिक	साप्ताहिक	संसारिक	सांसारिक
आधीन	अधीन	हस्ताक्षेप	हस्तक्षेप
बरात	बारात	क्षत्रीय	क्षत्रिय
तिथी	तिथि	कालीदास	कालिदास
पुर्ती	पूर्ति	अतिथी	अतिथि
नीती	नीति	ग्रहणी	गृहिणी
क्यूँ	क्यों	साधू	साधु
वधु	वधू	रेणू	रेणु
नुपुर	नूपुर	निर्वान	निर्वाण
जादु	जादू	द्रश्य	दृश्य

अशुद्ध	शुद्ध	अशुद्ध	शुद्ध
अनुग्रहीत	अनुगृहीत	बृज	ब्रज
बनस्पति	वनस्पति	श्राप	शाप
सैना	सेना	सेनिक	सैनिक
इतिहासिक	ऐतिहासिक	प्रथक	पृथक
सम्पति	सम्पत्ति	कृतघन	कृतघ्न
बिमारी	बीमारी	व्यक्तिक	वैयक्तिक
वितीत	व्यतीत	निस्वार्थ	निःस्वार्थ
परिस्थित	परिस्थिति	रचियता	रचयिता
मैथिलिशरण	मैथिलीशरण	आर्शिवाद	आशीर्वाद
निरिक्षण	निरीक्षण	पत्नि	पत्नी
शताब्दि	शताब्दी	लड़ायी	लड़ाई
स्थाई	स्थायी	लिखायी	लिखाई
अलोकिक	अलौकिक	कृप्या	कृपया
गंवार	गँवार	असोक	अशोक
दुस्कर	दुष्कर	मूल्यावान	मूल्यवान्
नवम्	नवम	क्षात्र	छात्र
छमा	क्षमा	प्रन्तु	परन्तु
प्रीक्षा	परीक्षा	मरयादा	मर्यादा
दुदर्शा	दुर्दशा	विषेश	विशेष
उज्वल	उज्ज्वल	आल्हाद	आहलाद्

अशुद्ध	शुद्ध	अशुद्ध	शुद्ध
महत्व	महत्त्व	उपलक्ष	उपलक्ष्य
लीये	लिये	पिओ	पियो
हुये	हुए	कवित्री	कवयित्री
प्रमात्मा	परमात्मा	घनिष्ट	घनिष्ठ
यथेष्ठ	यथेष्ट	पियास	प्यास
व्यस्क	वयस्क	त्यौहार	त्योहार
मुसलिम	मुस्लिम	ऐैनक	ऐनक
नोकरी	नौकरी	कल्यान	कल्याण
पाणी	पानी	आसा	आशा
हुदय	हृदय	घ्रणा	घृणा
श्रंगार	शृंगार	हिन्दुस्थान	हिन्दुस्तान
प्रशन	प्रश्न	ग्यान	ज्ञान
अन्धेरा	अँधेरा	पेड	पेड़
महयान्हन	मध्यान्ह	मेंहदी	मेहंदी
शमशान	श्मशान	चिन्ह	चिह्न
कुंज	कुञ्ज	ग्रहस्थ	गृहस्थ
अजोध्या	अयोध्या	अनधिकार	अनाधिकार
अनिष्ठा	अनिष्ट	अनुकुल	अनुकूल
अनुसंगिक	आनुषंगिक	अनुशरण	अनुसरण
अभिसेक	अभिषेक	अरमाण	अरमान
अहिल्या	अहल्या	आदरनीय	आदरणीय
आविस्कार	आविष्कार	उँचाई	ऊँचाई
उत्तरदाई	उत्तरदायी	उपर	ऊपर
उपरोक्त	उपर्युक्त	उश्रृंखल	उच्छृंखल
कलस	कलश	कल्यान	कल्याण
गनित	गणित	जबाब	जवाब
तत्व	तत्त्व	तलाब	तालाब
तिरष्कार	तिरस्कार	त्रिवार्षिक	त्रैवार्षिक
दिपिका	दीपिका	देहिक	दैहिक
द्वन्द	द्वन्द्व	नरायन	नारायण
निरव	नीरव	निरोग	नीरोग
पुष्टी	पुष्टि	पुस्प	पुष्प
पेत्रिक	पैतृक	प्रनय	प्रणय

अशुद्ध	शुद्ध	अशुद्ध	शुद्ध
प्रनाम	प्रणाम	प्रयाप्त	पर्याप्त
प्रसंशा	प्रशंसा	प्रांगन	प्रांगण
प्रान	प्राण	पृष्ट	पृष्ठ
ब्रत	व्रत	भगीरथी	भागीरथी
भरथ	भरत	भष्म	भस्म
मंत्रीमंडल	मंत्रिमण्डल	रसायण	रसायन
राज्यमहल	राजमहल	रामायन	रामायण
वनोवास	वनवास	वानी	वाणी
वाल्मीकी	वाल्मीकि	वास्प	वाष्प
व्योहार	व्यवहार	सन्यासी	संन्यासी
सम्राज	साम्राज्य	सविनयपूर्वक	सविनय
सिंदुर	सिंदूर	स्त्रवण	श्रवण
हरीश्चन्द्र	हरिश्चन्द्र	हिन्दु	हिन्दू
हिन्दूस्तान	हिन्दुस्तान	बुद्धिवान	बुद्धिमान्
भाग्यमान	भाग्यवान	विद्धान	विद्वान्
श्रीमान	श्रीमान्	आंख	आँख
ऊंट	ऊँट	कंगना	कँगना
गँगा	गंगा	गांधी	गाँधी
जांच	जाँच	तांगा	ताँगा
दांत	दाँत	मंहगा	महँगा
मांस	माँस	मुंह	मुँह
सांप	साँप	सांस	साँस
हुँकार	हुंकार	निर्पेक्ष	निरपेक्ष
भाष्कर	भास्कर	सन्मुख	सम्मुख
माताहीन	मातृहीन	विद्यार्थि	विद्यार्थी
गुणि	गुणी	द्वैवार्षिक	द्विवार्षिक
पूज्यनीय	पूजनीय	अकाश	आकाश
इद	ईद	इसलाम	इस्लाम
ऐैसा	ऐसा	दोसरा	दूसरा
पुत्रि	पुत्री	प्रस्तूत	प्रस्तुत
हरयाली	हरियाली	दिवाली	दीवाली
राष्ट्रिय	राष्ट्रीय	एकहरा	इकहरा
एतबार	इतबार		

वाक्यगत अशुद्धियाँ

अशुद्ध	शुद्ध
हम अच्छी भाषण दिए थे।	हमने अच्छा भाषण दिया था।
आप खाए कि नहीं?	आपने खाया कि नहीं?
वह मुझे देखा तो घबरा गया।	उसने मुझे देखा तो घबरा गया।
मैं किताब पढ़ा हूँ।	मैंने किताब पढ़ी है।
मैं सारी पुस्तक पढ़ डाली।	मैंने सारी पुस्तक पढ़ डाली।
सीता भात खायी।	सीता ने भात खाया।

अशुद्ध	शुद्ध
राम रोटी खाया।	राम ने रोटी खायी।
लड़की ने दही गिरा दी।	लड़की ने दही गिरा दिया।
शुद्ध गाय की घी दो।	गाय का शुद्ध घी दो।
तुम, मैं और वह चलेगा।	तुम, वह और मैं चलूँगा।
राम और सीता आयी थी।	राम और सीता आए थे।
भाई-बहन जा रही हैं।	भाई-बहन जा रहे हैं।

अशुद्ध	शुद्ध
वह लड़की को बुलाओ।	उस लड़की को बुलाओ।
मेरे लिए पढ़ता हूँ।	अपने लिए पढ़ता हूँ।
सीता राम की आज्ञाकारी पत्नी थी।	सीता राम की आज्ञाकारिणी पत्नी थीं।
देरी न करना।	देर न करना।
उसे मृत्युदण्ड की सजा मिली।	उसे मृत्युदण्ड मिला।
हमारे शिक्षक प्रश्न पूछते हैं।	हमारे शिक्षक प्रश्न करते हैं।
कै बजे? तीन बजा।	कितना बजा? तीन बजे।
उसका प्राण उड़ गया।	उसके प्राण उड़ गये।
मैंने आँख से देखा।	मैंने आँखों से देखा।
अपन को पढ़ना है।	मुझे पढ़ना है।
पुस्तक फट गया।	पुस्तक फट गई है।
घोड़ी तेज दौड़ता है।	घोड़ी तेज दौड़ती है।
मेरा प्रणम स्वीकार करो।	मेरा प्रणाम स्वीकार करो।
दो बालक खेलता है।	दो बालक खेलते हैं।

अशुद्ध	शुद्ध
ये सब मेरा पुस्तक है।	ये सब मेरी पुस्तकें हैं।
सूरज पूरब में उगते हैं।	सूरज पूर्व में उगता है।
वह लौट आए।	वे लौट आए।
वहाँ अनेकों लोग थे।	वहाँ अनेक लोग थे।
मेरे को मत मारो।	मुझे मत मारो।
मोहन ने पत्र को पढ़ा।	मोहन ने पत्र पढ़ा।
पुस्तक पर नहीं लिखो।	पुस्तक पर मत लिखो।
वह सज्जन पुरुष है।	वह सज्जन है।
आप हमारे घर आओ।	आप हमारे घर आइए।
हम आपसे कुछ कहे थे।	हमने आपसे कुछ कहा था।
मकान की दायीं ओर सड़क है।	मकान के दायीं ओर सड़क है।
पिताजी घर नहीं हैं।	पिताजी घर पर नहीं हैं।
घर पर सब कुशल हैं।	घर में सब कुशल हैं।
उसे भारी दुःख हुआ।	उसे बहुत दुःख हुआ।
सड़क में मत खेलो।	सड़क पर मत खेलो।

मुहावरे तथा लोकोक्तियाँ

- अँगूठी का नगीना–अत्यन्त महत्त्वपूर्ण।
- अंधा दरबार–न्यायहीन स्थान।
- अंधेर नगरी–न्याय का अभाव।
- अक्ल का दुश्मन–मूर्ख।
- अक्ल का दुम–मूर्ख।
- आँख का तारा–अतिप्रिय।
- ईद का चाँद–बहुत दिनों के बाद दिखाई देना।
- कछुआ चाल–धीमी गति।
- काला नाग–दुष्ट आदमी।
- किताबी कीड़ा–सदैव कुछ-न-कुछ पढ़ना।
- किस्मत का मारा–भाग्य का मन्द।
- कोल्हू का बैल–बहुत कठिन परिश्रम करनेवाला।
- कोड़ी का तीन–तुच्छ।
- खाली हाथ–पैसे का अभाव।
- गाजर-मूली–अशक्त।
- गुलर का फूल–दुर्लभ वस्तु।
- गोबर-गणेश–निरामूर्ख।
- घर का उजाला–कुल-दीपक।
- घड़ियाली आँसू–बनावटी शोक।
- चलता-पुरजा–चालाक।
- चाँद का टुकड़ा–परम सुन्दर वस्तु या व्यक्ति।
- चाँदी का जूता–रिश्वत।
- चार दिन की चाँदनी–थोड़े समय का सुख।
- जलती आँख–क्रोधाभिभूत।
- जीभ का पतला–लालची।
- टेढ़ी खीर–विकट काम।
- ठिकाने की बात–न्यायसंगत बात।
- अढ़ाई दिन की हुकूमत–थोड़े समय का ऐश्वर्य।
- तकदीर का सिकन्दर–भाग्य का बलवान्।
- थाली का बैंगन–मत बदलते रहना।
- दाँत कटी रोटी–घनिष्ठता।
- दाहिना हाथ–सहायक।
- दिल का बादशाह–बहुत बड़ा उदार।
- दूध का दूध और पानी का पानी–उचित न्याय।
- दूध का धोआ–निर्दोष।
- दो दिन का मेहमान–बहुत थोड़े समय ठहरने वाला।
- धरती का फूल–ऐसा व्यक्ति जो हाल में अमीर हुआ है।
- धोबी का कुत्ता–निकम्मा।
- नसीब का मारा–बुरे दिन देखनेवाला।
- निन्यानबे का फेरा–धन बढ़ाने की चिन्ता।
- पत्थर का कलेजा–हर दुःख सहने की शक्ति।
- पत्थर की लकीर–चिरस्थायी सदा सत्य।
- फूलों की सेज–आनन्ददायक कार्य।
- बगुला-भगत–कपटी व्यक्ति।

- बच्चों का खेल–साधारण काम।
- बलि का बकरा–निःसहाय व्यक्ति।
- बरसाती बादल–अस्थायी।
- बात का पक्का–सत्यवादी।
- बायें हाथ का खेल–सरल काम।
- बिन बादल बरसात–असमय लाभ।
- बे-पेंदी का लोटा–बे ठिकाने का आदमी।
- भागीरथ प्रयत्न–अत्यधिक परिश्रम।
- भीष्म प्रतिज्ञा–दृढ़ संकल्प।
- मक्खी चूस–कंजूस।
- मिट्टी के मोल–बहुत सस्ता।
- मोटा असामी–मूर्ख मालदार।
- राम कहानी–आत्मवृतान्त।
- लँगोटिया यार– बचपन का मित्र।
- हवाई महल–कोरी कल्पना।
- आँख लगना–नींद आना।
- आँख खुलना–होश में आना।
- आँखें दिखाना–क्रोध से घूरना।
- आँसू पोंछना–धैर्य बँधाना।
- अन्धे की लकड़ी–एकमात्र सहारा।
- कान भरना–चुगली करना।
- कान पर जूँ न रेंगना–कोई असर न होना।
- नाक कटना–प्रतिष्ठा खत्म होना।
- नाक रगड़ना–दीनता दिखाना।
- नाकों चने चबवाना–खूब सताना।
- मुँह की खाना–बुरी तरह हारना।
- आस्तीन का साँप–विश्वासघाती मित्र।
- कन्धे से कन्धा मिलाना–पूरा सहयोग करना।
- ईंट से ईंट बजाना–पूरी तरह नष्ट कर देना।
- नौ दो ग्यारह होना–भाग जाना।
- दाँत खट्टे करना–बुरी तरह हराना।
- हाथ मलना–पछताना।
- खून का प्यासा–जानी दुश्मन।
- घी के दिए जलाना–खुशी मनाना।
- चार चाँद लगाना–प्रतिष्ठा बढ़ाना।
- तीन तेरह होना–अलग-अलग होना।
- पानी फेर देना–नाश कर देना।
- गाल बजाना–डींगे मारना।
- जान से हाथ धो बैठना–मारा जाना।
- पानी-पानी होना–बहुत लज्जित होना।
- फूला न समाना–बहुत प्रसन्न होना।
- अपना उल्लू सीधा करना–अपना मतलब निकालना।
- आँखें चुरा लेना–अनदेखा कर देना।
- अन्धे की लाठी–एकमात्र सहारा।
- आसमान पर चढ़ना–बहुत अभिमान करना।
- आँखें खुलना–होश आना।
- चोरी और सीना जोरी–दोषी होकर धमकाना।
- आग में घी डालना–क्रोध को भड़काना।
- अँगुली पर नचाना– अच्छी तरह वश में करना।
- एक आँख से देखना–समान दृष्टि से देखना।
- एक ही थैले के चट्टे-बट्टे–एक जैसे।
- ओखली में सिर देना–जान-बूझकर आपत्ति मोल लेना।
- कलेजा मुँह को आना–बहुत दुःखी होना।
- कफन बाँधकर चलना–मौत से न घबराना।
- काँटे बिछाना–बाधा डालना।
- कलेजा ठण्डा होना–सन्तोष होना।
- कमर कसना–तैयार होना।
- खून खौलना–जोश में आना।
- खाक छानना–मारे-मारे फिरना।
- गागर में सागर भरना–थोड़े शब्दों में बहुत कुछ कह देना।
- घाव पर नमक छिड़कना–दुखी को अधिक दुखी करना।
- घी के दिए जलाना–खुशी मनाना।
- घोड़े बेचकर सोना–गहरी नींद में सोना।
- चल बसना–परलोक सिधारना।
- छठी का दूध याद आना–भारी संकट में पड़ना।
- छाती पर साँप लोटना–बहुत ईर्ष्या होना।
- जमीन पर पैर न रखना–अधिक घमण्ड होना।
- झक मारना–व्यर्थ समय खोना।
- टेढ़ी खीर–कठिन काम।
- डींग मारना–अपनी झूठी प्रशंसा करना।
- डूब मरना–बहुत लज्जित होना।
- तलवे चाटना–चापलूसी करना।
- ताक में रहना–मौका ढूँढ़ते रहना।
- दंग रह जाना–आश्चर्य में पड़ जाना।
- दाल न गलना–वश न चलना।
- दाल में काला होना–संदेह होना।
- पीठ दिखाना–हारकर भागना।
- मुँह तोड़ उत्तर देना–खरा उत्तर देना।

वस्तुनिष्ठ प्रश्न

अभ्यास-1

निर्देशः *नीचे प्रत्येक शुद्ध शब्द की वर्तनी के लिए चार विकल्प दिए गए हैं। आपको सही विकल्प का चयन करना है।*

1. A. ऋषि B. ऋषी C. रिषी D. ऋसि

2. A. विषेसन B. विशेषण C. विसेशन D. विशेशन

3. A. दुशासन B. दुसाशन C. दूशाषण D. दुःशासन

4. A. संस्कृति B. संसकृति C. संष्कृति D. संस्कृती

5. A. दूनियां B. दुनियां C. दुनिया D. दूनिआ

6. A. टिपनी B. टिप्पणि C. टिप्पणी D. टिप्पनी

7. A. शाषण B. साशन C. शासन D. शाशन

8. A. किसमस B. किरसमस C. क्रिसमुस D. कृसमस

9. A. अनुग्रहित B. अनुग्रहीत C. अनुगृहीत D. अनुग्रहित

10. A. पराकम B. प्राक्रम C. पराक्रम D. प्राकर्म

11. A. नायका B. नाइका C. नाइक D. नायिका

12. A. समरिधी B. समद्धी C. समृद्धि D. समरिद्धि

13. A. युधिष्ठर B. यूधिष्ठर C. युधिष्ठिर D. युधिष्टर

14. A. वाल्मीकि B. बाल्मीकि C. बालमीकि D. बाल्मिक

15. A. परलोकिक B. प्रलौकिक C. पारलौकिक D. परलौकिक

16. A. त्रितीय B. तर्तीय C. तृतीय D. तिरतीय

17. A. व्योहार B. व्यौहार C. व्यवहार D. ब्यवहार

18. A. अहिल्या B. अहल्या C. अहिलया D. अहीलया

19. A. आदरनीय B. आदरणीय C. आदरनीया D. आदरणीया

20. A. आर्द B. आद्र C. आर्द्र D. आर्दृ

21. A. आधीन B. अधिन C. अधीन D. अधीम

22. A. आविस्कार B. आविष्कार C. आवीस्कार D. आविश्कार

23. A. आसा B. आषा C. आशा D. अशा

24. A. उज्वल B. उजज्ज्वल C. उजज्वल D. उज्ज्वल

25. A. उन्नती B. उन्नित C. उन्नति D. उन्नती

26. A. कलस B. कलष C. कलश D. कलशा

27. A. गनीत B. गनित C. गणीत D. गणित

28. A. तलाव B. तालाव C. तलाब D. तालाब

29. A. दुष्ट B. दूष्ट C. दुस्त D. दुश्त

30. A. निरोग B. निररोग C. नीरोग D. नीरोगी

उत्तरमाला

1. A	**2.** B	**3.** D	**4.** A	**5.** C
6. C	**7.** C	**8.** C	**9.** C	**10.** C
11. D	**12.** C	**13.** C	**14.** A	**15.** C
16. C	**17.** C	**18.** B	**19.** B	**20.** C
21. C	**22.** B	**23.** C	**24.** D	**25.** C
26. C	**27.** D	**28.** D	**29.** A	**30.** C

अभ्यास-2

निर्देशः *नीचे कुछ शब्द दिए गए हैं। प्रत्येक के पर्यायवाची के चार विकल्प दिए गए हैं। इनमें से एक विकल्प सही पर्यायवाची है, उसका चयन कीजिए :*

1. अग्नि
A. अनिल B. अनल C. गर्म D. ताप

2. अमृत
A. पीयूष B. गरल C. सरस D. जीवनदायनी

3. आँख
A. लोचन B. आस्थि
C. वदन D. जलज

4. आकाश
A. अनन्त B. पाताल
C. वितल D. तल

5. कपड़ा
A. परिधान B. पटिका
C. पीताम्बर D. लँहगा

6. कमल
A. सरोज B. सरोवर
C. पंक D. पुष्प

7. गंगा
A. पाताल नदी B. हिमनदी
C. भागीरथ D. त्रिपथगा

8. चाँद
A. मयंक B. भानु
C. दिनकर D. रवि

9. नदी
A. सरिता B. प्रवाह
C. धारा D. जलधर

10. पर्वत
A. पत्थर B. चट्टान
C. शिखर D. मेरू

11. पवन
A. अनिल B. अनल
C. अग D. विहग

12. पति
A. साजन B. प्रिया
C. भार्या D. दारा

13. पानी
A. मही B. मेदिनी
C. अम्बु D. तरणी

14. पुत्र
A. आत्मज B. तनया
C. सुता D. आत्मजा

15. पुत्री
A. सुता B. सुत
C. आत्मज D. नन्दन

16. फूल
A. बहार B. मधु
C. माधव D. सुमन

17. वृक्ष
A. विटप B. अम्र
C. प्रसून D. रसा

18. बादल
A. अज B. व्यामोह
C. नीरद D. मधुप

19. बिजली
A. चंचला B. खटका
C. त्रास D. संत्रास

20. माता
A. धात्री B. धरणी
C. धरित्री D. श्यामा

21. घोषणा
A. आवाज B. पुकारना
C. ऐलान D. ललकारना

22. उत्कर्ष
A. आकर्षण B. विकर्षण
C. उन्नति D. निष्कर्ष

23. उदय
A. अन्त B. विकास
C. प्रगट D. व्यस्त

24. दक्ष
A. निपुण B. समर्थ
C. कर्मठ D. मेहनती

25. संवाद
A. विवाद B. झगड़ा
C. सम्बोधन D. वार्तालाप

उत्तरमाला

1. B	**2.** A	**3.** A	**4.** A	**5.** A
6. A	**7.** D	**8.** A	**9.** A	**10.** D
11. A	**12.** A	**13.** C	**14.** A	**15.** A
16. D	**17.** A	**18.** C	**19.** A	**20.** A
21. C	**22.** C	**23.** C	**24.** A	**25.** D

अभ्यास-3

निर्देशः *नीचे चार-चार शब्दों के समूह दिए गए हैं। प्रत्येक समूह में एक शब्द बेमेल है तथा शेष तीन शब्द पर्यायवाची हैं, आपको उस शब्द का चयन करना है, जो बेमेल है :*

1. A. तम B. अंधकार
C. तिमिर D. अंश

2. A. अनल B. आग
C. दहन D. तमिस्रा

3. A. अतुल B. अद्वितीय
C. अनुपम D. शुष्मा

4. A. अहं B. अहंकार
C. दर्प D. निराला

5. A. पता B. खोज
C. जाँच D. शोध

6. A. गरल B. पीयूष
C. सुधा D. सोम

7. A. कानन B. जंगल
C. पादप D. वन

8. A. अश्व B. गज
C. घोड़ा D. तुरंग

9. A. दानव B. मानव
C. दैत्य D. राक्षस

10. A. आँख B. चक्षु
C. नयन D. मुख

11. A. अन्तरिक्ष B. वसुन्धरा
C. आसमान D. गगन

12. A. इच्छा B. अभिलाषा
C. कामना D. प्रयोजन

13. A. कपड़ा B. चीर
C. वसन D. पोशाक

14. A. अब्ज B. कमल
C. राजीव D. आम्र

15. A. कोयल B. पिक
C. काग D. वनप्रिय

16. A. गंगा B. देवनदी
C. गोदावरी D. भागीरथी

17. A. गणेश B. एकदन्त
C. देवराज D. गणपति

18. A. घर B. निलय
C. निकेतन D. झोपड़ी

19. A. चाँद B. हिमांशु
C. विनायक D. सुधांशु

20. A. नदी B. तरणी
C. तटिनी D. सरिता

21. A. पक्षी B. चिड़िया
C. सुमन D. विहग

22. A. पवन B. अचला
C. वात D. वायु

23. A. समीर B. पृथ्वी
C. भू D. भूमि

24. A. पानी B. समीर
C. अम्बु D. जल

25. A. पुत्र B. तनया
C. तनय D. सुत

26. A. पुत्र B. तनया
C. सुता D. कन्या

27. A. गृहिणी B. आदमी
C. पुरुष D. नर

28. A. मधु B. फूल
C. पुष्प D. सुमन

29. A. माधव B. तरु
C. पेड़ D. वृक्ष

30. A. माता B. अम्बु
C. अम्मा D. जननी

उत्तरमाला

1. D	**2.** D	**3.** D	**4.** D	**5.** A
6. A	**7.** C	**8.** B	**9.** B	**10.** D
11. B	**12.** D	**13.** D	**14.** D	**15.** C
16. C	**17.** C	**18.** D	**19.** C	**20.** B
21. C	**22.** B	**23.** A	**24.** B	**25.** B
26. A	**27.** A	**28.** A	**29.** A	**30.** B

अभ्यास-4

निर्देशः *गहरे काले शब्द के विलोम शब्द का चयन कीजिए:*

1. उसे हर काम में **सफलता** मिल रही है।
A. असफलता B. सफल
C. कुशलता D. निपुणता

2. कभी किसी की **निन्दा** नहीं करनी चाहिए।
A. गुणगान B. स्तुति
C. प्रशंसा D. यशोगान

3. आलस्य व्यक्ति का सबसे बड़ा **दुश्मन** है।
A. शत्रु B. घातक
C. मित्र D. सहायक

4. वे बुढ़ापे से **दुखी** हैं।
A. अप्रसन्न B. सुखी
C. खुश D. नाराज

5. यहाँ उसकी **चतुराई** नहीं चली।
A. चालाकी B. बहादुरी
C. निपुणता D. मूर्खता

6. शहद की **मिठास** कम नहीं होती।
A. मीठा B. तीखा
C. कड़वा D. खट्टा

7. साहसी के **साहस** को देखकर मैं चकित रह गया।
A. हिम्मत B. बहादुरी
C. निडर D. भय

8. फिल्मोत्सव में सर्वश्रेष्ठ **अभिनेता** को पुरस्कार प्रदान किया गया।
A. हीरोइन B. नेत्री
C. मीनाक्षी D. अभिनेत्री

9. नाटक में नायक और **नायिका** की भूमिका महत्वपूर्ण होती हैः
A. हीरो B. नायक
C. नेत्र D. नेता

10. कवि-सम्मेलन में एक कवि और एक **कवयित्री** को आमंत्रित किया गया था।
A. लेखक B. सम्पादक
C. नेता D. कवि

11. विद्यालय के वार्षिकोत्सव के लिए नेता और एक **नेत्री** को आमंत्रित किया गया।
A. अभिनेता B. विद्वान्
C. विदुषी D. नेता

12. मोहन बहुत **चतुर** है।
A. निपुण B. तेज
C. सुस्त D. मूर्ख

13. सोहन अब पूर्ण **स्वस्थ** है।
A. प्रसन्न B. खुश
C. अस्वस्थ D. अप्रसन्न

14. पक्षी **आकाश** में उड़ते हैं :
A. गगन B. नभ
C. धरती D. पाताल

15. वह विद्यालय में देर से आया और **अनुपस्थित** हो गया।
A. पूर्व B. उपस्थित
C. प्रवेश D. समयपूर्व

16. **बालक** चाँद की ओर देख रहा है।
A. बालिका B. लड़का
C. बच्चा D. बच्ची

17. मैं उसके विचार से बिल्कुल **सहमत** नहीं हूँ।
A. समर्थन B. सहमति
C. असहमत D. प्रशंसक

18. उसकी हालत **अधिक** खराब है।
A. बहुत B. कम
C. ठीक D. कुशल

19. **धर्म** की सर्वत्र विजय होती हैः
A. अधर्म B. ज्ञान
C. भक्ति D. ईमानदारी

20. अच्छे चरित्र के बिना जीवन **निरर्थक** हैः
A. व्यर्थ B. अर्थपूर्ण
C. सार्थक D. कुशल

21. **ईमानदारी** बड़ी दुर्लभ वस्तु हैः
A. सच्चाई B. भलाई
C. बेइमानी D. परोपकारी

22. एवरेस्ट संसार का सबसे **ऊँचा** पर्वत हैः
A. नीचा B. वितल
C. पाताल D. मध्यम

23. वह विश्वास के **योग्य** नहीं हैः
A. काबिल B. विश्वासी
C. अयोग्य D. बेकार

24. क्या वह इतना **मूर्ख** है?
A. चालाक B. विद्वान्
C. बुद्धिमान D. धूर्त

25. कितना सुहावना **दृश्य** है!
A. अदृश्य B. दर्शनीय
C. सुन्दर D. व्यर्थ

उत्तरमाला

1. A	**2.** C	**3.** C	**4.** B	**5.** D
6. C	**7.** D	**8.** D	**9.** B	**10.** D
11. D	**12.** D	**13.** C	**14.** D	**15.** B
16. A	**17.** C	**18.** B	**19.** A	**20.** C
21. C	**22.** A	**23.** C	**24.** C	**25.** A

अभ्यास-5

निर्देशः नीचे प्रत्येक **काले गहरे शब्द** के चार विलोम दिए गए हैं। इनमें सही विलोम का चयन कीजिए :

1. **अग्नि**
A. आग B. अनल
C. दहन D. जल

2. **अग्रज**
A. अनुज B. भ्राता
C. भाई D. अम्बा

3. **अच्छा**
A. बुरा B. खराब
C. गंदा D. भ्रष्ट

4. **अंत**
A. प्रारम्भ B. समाप्त
C. शेष D. अल्प

5. **अचल**
A. विचल B. वितल
C. सजल D. चल

6. अति

A. अधिक B. बहुत
C. अल्प D. कम

7. अत्यधिक

A. अल्प B. अधिक
C. स्वल्प D. न्यूनतम

8. अंधकार

A. अंधेरा B. प्रकाश
C. रात्रि D. दिन

9. अतिवृष्टि

A. अनावृष्टि B. वृष्टि
C. वर्षा D. वर्षण

10. अनाथ

A. नाथ B. स्वामी
C. मासिक D. सनाथ

11. अनुकूल

A. मनोकूल B. प्रतिकूल
C. अनुकरण D. मनस्वी

12. अनुराग

A. राग B. विराग
C. विग्रह D. स्नेह

13. अन्त

A. श्री गणेश B. आदि
C. शुरुआत D. समाप्त

14. अपना

A. अपनत्व B. पराया
C. मित्र D. शत्रु

15. अपमान

A. मान B. सम्मान
C. वर्तमान D. स्वाभिमान

16. अपेक्षा

A. इच्छा B. स्वेच्छा
C. प्रविच्छा D. उपेक्षा

17. अमर

A. मर्त्य B. मृत्यु
C. सुधा D. गरल

18. अल्पायु

A. चिरायु B. उमरदराज
C. नश्वर D. सनातन

19. अस्त

A. उदय B. विकास
C. निर्माण D. सृष्टि

20. आकर्षण

A. प्रतिकर्षण B. विकर्षण
C. सम्मोहन D. विरत

21. आकाश

A. गगन B. नभ
C. वसुन्धरा D. पाताल

22. आगे

A. पीछे B. पूर्व
C. पृष्ट D. पृष्ठ

23. आजाद

A. स्वतंत्र B. स्वतंत्रतता
C. परतंत्र D. गुलाम

24. आदान

A. आयात B. निर्यात
C. प्रदान D. निदान

25. आधुनिक

A. अर्वाचीन B. नूतन
C. प्राचीन D. वर्तमान

उत्तरमाला

1. D	**2.** A	**3.** A	**4.** A	**5.** D
6. D	**7.** C	**8.** B	**9.** A	**10.** D
11. B	**12.** B	**13.** A	**14.** B	**15.** B
16. D	**17.** A	**18.** A	**19.** A	**20.** B
21. D	**22.** A	**23.** D	**24.** C	**25.** C

अभ्यास-6

निर्देशः *नीचे कुछ शब्द दिए गए हैं प्रत्येक शब्द के चार वैकल्पिक अर्थ दिए गए हैं। सही अर्थ का चयन कीजिए :*

1. सुरक्षित

A. कुशल B. घटना
C. दुर्घटना D. बचाव

2. प्रतिभाशाली

A. सज्जन B. कुशाग्र
C. विद्वान् D. वैभवशाली

3. आत्मसमर्पण

A. अपने आप को सौंपना B. समर्पण
C. अर्पण D. त्यागज

4. सिद्धहस्त

A. निपुण B. कर्मठ
C. मेहनती D. परिश्रमी

5. सुशोभित

A. मजेदार B. सुस्वागतम्
C. अच्छा D. शोभा पाना

6. स्वादिष्ट

A. मजेदार B. बेकार
C. मीठा D. तीखा

7. स्वावलम्बी
A. निर्भर B. परालंबी
C. आत्मनिर्भर D. अतिथि

8. उपकरण
A. साधन B. युक्ति
C. यंत्र D. मशीन

9. कीमत
A. क्रय B. विक्रय
C. मूल्य D. बिक्री

10. संगठन
A. एकता B. अनेकता
C. समूह D. संस्था

11. विपत्ति
A. दुख B. विपदा
C. मुसीबत D. सुख

12. तृण
A. तिनका B. धूल
C. धूप D. लकड़ी

13. आश्चर्य
A. निरीक्षण B. दृष्टिगोचर
C. हैरानी D. थकावट

14. हार्दिक
A. हृदय से B. शरीर से
C. मन से D. मस्तिष्क से

15. नियति
A. भाग्य B. किनारा
C. समय D. पवित्र

16. सुगन्धित
A. दुर्गन्ध B. खुशबू वाला
C. फूल D. कमल

17. उत्साह
A. होश B. हवास
C. जोश D. हिम्मत

18. सहयोग
A. मिलन सार B. मेहनती
C. परोपकारी D. आपसी सहायता

19. मुसीबत
A. विपत्ति B. सुशोभित
C. सहायता D. मदद

20. निरक्षर
A. साक्षर B. दर्शनीय
C. पठनीय D. अनपढ़

21. उपवन
A. वन B. तीर
C. जंगल D. बाग

22. मेघ
A. बादल B. पंकज
C. राजीव D. मेघनाद

23. आधुनिक
A. प्राचीन B. पुरातन
C. भूतकाल D. आज का

24. तीर
A. वाण B. धनुष
C. किनारा D. नदी

25. परीक्षण
A. जाँच B. पड़ताल
C. परीक्षा D. इम्तहान

26. अभिवादन
A. नमस्ते B. प्रणाम
C. बधाई D. शुभकामना

27. सर्वत्र
A. नश्वर B. सजीव
C. ईश्वर D. सभी जगह

28. हलवाहा
A. चरवाहा B. किसान
C. मजदूर D. हल चलाने वाला

29. शिखर
A. पर्वत B. पहाड़
C. टीला D. चोटी

30. भयानक
A. डरावना B. भयभीत
C. डरना D. खूँखार

उत्तरमाला

1. D	**2.** B	**3.** A	**4.** A	**5.** D
6. A	**7.** C	**8.** C	**9.** C	**10.** A
11. C	**12.** A	**13.** C	**14.** A	**15.** A
16. B	**17.** C	**18.** D	**19.** A	**20.** D
21. D	**22.** A	**23.** D	**24.** A	**25.** A
26. B	**27.** D	**28.** D	**29.** D	**30.** A

अभ्यास-7

निर्देशः *नीचे कुछ शब्द दिए जा रहे हैं। प्रत्येक शब्द के* **उपसर्ग** *के सन्दर्भ में चार विकल्प दिए गए हैं। आपको सही विकल्प का चयन करना है :*

1. अलबत्ता
A. अ B. अल
C. लब D. त्ता

2. अलगरज
A. अल B. लग
C. गर D. रज

3. कमसिन
A. क B. कम
C. सि D. सिन

4. अनमोल
A. अ B. अन
C. मो D. मोल

5. अनजान
A. अ B. अन
C. जा D. जान

6. अनपढ़
A. अ B. पढ़
C. प D. अन

7. अधखिला
A. अ B. अध
C. ला D. खिला

8. अधजला
A. अ B. ज
C. अध D. ला

9. अधपका
A. अ B. अध
C. पका D. का

10. अघखिला
A. अ B. अघ
C. खिला D. ला

11. उन्नीस
A. उन B. उन्
C. नीस D. स

12. उनसठ
A. उ B. उन
C. सठ D. ठ

13. दुकाल
A. द B. दुक
C. दु D. काल

14. दुबला
A. दब B. दुब
C. ला D. दु

15. निकम्मा
A. नि B. निक
C. कम्मा D. मा

16. निर्लज्ज
A. निर B. निल
C. नि D. लज्ज

17. बिनब्याहा
A. बि B. बिन
C. ब्याहा D. हा

18. भरपेट
A. भर B. पेट
C. पे D. ट

19. भरपाई
A. भ B. र
C. पा D. भर

20. कुपात्र
A. कु B. कुप
C. पा D. पात्र

21. सुजान
A. सु B. सुज
C. सुजा D. जान

22. गैर कानूनी
A. गै B. गैर
C. कानु D. नुनी

23. गैरसरकारी
A. गैर B. सर
C. का D. कारी

24. अपमान
A. अ B. अप
C. मा D. मान

25. अनुशासन
A. अ B. शासन
C. सन D. अनु

26. अविनीत
A. अवि B. अ
C. नी D. नीत

27. अभिमान
A. अभि B. अ
C. मा D. मान

28. अभियान
A. अ B. मान
C. यान D. अभि

29. अध्ययन
A. अध् B. अधि
C. यन D. न

30. निश्चल
A. नि B. निर
C. निस D. चल

उत्तरमाला

1. B	**2.** A	**3.** B	**4.** B	**5.** B
6. D	**7.** B	**8.** C	**9.** B	**10.** B
11. A	**12.** B	**13.** C	**14.** D	**15.** B
16. A	**17.** B	**18.** A	**19.** D	**20.** A
21. A	**22.** B	**23.** A	**24.** B	**25.** D
26. B	**27.** A	**28.** D	**29.** B	**30.** A

अभ्यास-8

निर्देशः *निम्नलिखित शब्दों में प्रयुक्त प्रत्यय सम्बन्धी चार विकल्प दिए गए हैं, सही विकल्प का चयन कीजिए :*

1. भलाई
A. ई B. लाई
C. आई D. भला

2. चतुराई
A. चतु B. रा
C. ई D. आई

3. भूखा
A. भू B. भूख
C. खा D. आ

4. भिड़न्त
A. भिड् B. भि
C. न्त D. अन्त

5. प्यासा
A. आस B. सा
C. आसा D. सा

6. बिकाऊ
A. बिक B. काऊ
C. आऊ D. ऊ

7. तैराक
A. तै B. तैर
C. राक D. आक

8. सन्नाटा
A. सन् B. सन्ना
C. नाटा D. आटा

9. लोहार
A. लोह B. आरा
C. आरी D. आर

10. मिलान
A. आना B. आने
C. आनी D. आन

11. चढ़ाव
A. चढ़ B. चढ़ा
C. आव D. व

12. लगाव
A. लग B. अव
C. आव D. गाव

13. लिखावट
A. लिख B. लिखा
C. वट D. आवट

14. मिलावट
A. मिल B. वट
C. आवट D. ट

15. मिठास
A. मिठ B. ठास
C. आस D. स

16. चिकनाहट
A. चिक B. नाट्ट
C. हट D. आहट

17. सड़ियल
A. सड़ B. यल
C. ड़ियल D. इयल

18. मरियल
A. मर B. यल
C. मरि D. इयल

19. गड़रिया
A. गड़ B. इया
C. रिया D. या

20. सजीला
A. ईला B. इला
C. ला D. स

21. लुटेरा
A. लुट B. एरा
C. ऐरा D. रा

22. लठैत
A. ए B. ऐ
C. ऐत D. त

23. भगोड़ा
A. ओ B. ओड़ा
C. ड़ा D. भगो

24. खपत
A. ख B. प
C. त D. पत

25. जीवट
A. व B. अट
C. जीव D. जी

उत्तरमाला

1. C	**2.** D	**3.** D	**4.** D	**5.** D
6. C	**7.** D	**8.** D	**9.** D	**10.** D
11. C	**12.** C	**13.** D	**14.** C	**15.** C
16. D	**17.** D	**18.** D	**19.** B	**20.** A
21. B	**22.** C	**23.** B	**24.** C	**25.** B

अभ्यास-9

निर्देशः *नीचे कुछ मुहावरे दिए गए हैं। प्रत्येक के अर्थ के लिए चार विकल्प दिए गए हैं। आपको सही विकल्प का चयन करना है :*

1. अक्ल पर पत्थर पड़ना
A. बुद्धि काम न करना B. दुविधा होना
C. संकट में होना D. परेशान होना

2. अपना उल्लू सीधा करना
A. अवसर देखना B. काम निकालना
C. मतलब साधना D. मूर्ख बनाना

3. अपने मुँह मियाँ-मिट्ठू बनना
A. मिठाई खाना B. प्रशंसा करना
C. निंदा करना D. अपनी प्रशंसा स्वयं करना

4. अपने पाँव पर आप कुल्हाड़ी मारना
A. हानि पहुँचाना B. खेद होना
C. अपना पैर काटना D. अपनी हानि स्वयं करना

5. आँखें चुरा लेना
A. भाग जाना B. छिप जाना
C. अनदेखा करना D. मिल जाना

6. अक्ल का दुश्मन
A. मित्र होना B. शत्रु होना
C. महामूर्ख D. महाविद्वान्

7. अंधे की लाठी
A. एक मात्र सहारा B. मित्र होना
C. शत्रु होना D. दुख पहुँचाना

8. आकाश-पाताल एक करना
A. भाग-दौड़ करना B. परेशान होना
C. थक जाना D. कठिन परिश्रम करना

9. घड़ों पानी पड़ना
A. लज्जित होना B. तुच्छ समझना
C. लाभ होना D. थकावट

10. अगर-मगर करना
A. नुकसान करना B. बहाने बनाना
C. बदनाम करना D. कपट करना

11. मुँह की खाना
A. गिर जाना B. हार जाना
C. भाग जाना D. व्यर्थ होना

12. आस्तीन का साँप होना
A. शत्रु B. मित्र
C. कपटी मित्र D. दयालु

13. एक आँख से देखना
A. बुरा व्यवहार B. समान व्यवहार
C. कपट करना D. लज्जित होना

14. बाल-बाँका न होना
A. घायल होना B. साफ बच जाना
C. क्रोधित होना D. स्वस्थ होना

15. दाँतों तले उँगली दबाना
A. उँगली काटना B. चिंतित हो जाना
C. चकित रह जाना D. प्रसन्न हो जाना

16. जान के लाले पड़ना
A. मरने का खतरा होना B. भाग जाना
C. हार जाना D. मुश्किल में पड़ना

17. बोली मारना
A. ताना देना B. सताना
C. मजाक करना D. याद दिलाना

18. अंधों में काना राजा
A. मूर्खों में अल्पज्ञ को विद्वान् माना जाना
B. सबको मूर्ख समझना
C. अत्यधिक महत्त्वपूर्ण
D. काना राजा

19. अक्ल के घोड़े दौड़ाना
A. बुद्धि लड़ाना
B. कल्पना करना
C. तरह-तरह के उपाय सोचना
D. ज्ञान-प्राप्त करना

20. पानी उतर जाना
A. शर्म करना B. लज्जित न होना
C. भाग जाना D. इज्जत करना

21. तीन-पाँच करना
A. तितर-बितर करना
B. वचन देकर फिर जाना
C. घुमा-फिरा कर बातें करना
D. परेशान करना

22. हथियार डाल देना
A. हार जाना B. जीत जाना
C. धोखा देना D. विजय होना

23. आँख खुलना
A. होश में आना B. अत्यन्त प्यार होना
C. उल्टा काम करना D. क्रोध करना

24. कमर सीधी करना
A. थक जाना B. थकावट दूर करना
C. काम करना D. परिश्रम करना

25. पगड़ी रखना
A. चैन की सांस लेना B. अपमान करना
C. दया की भीख माँगना D. अपमान होना

26. लोहा मानना
A. संघर्ष करना B. विजय होना
C. श्रेष्ठता स्वीकार करना D. खुशामद करना

27. काठ मार जाना
A. दुःखी होना B. चुप होना
C. सफल होना D. मर जाना

28. चाँद पर थूकना
A. अपमान करना
B. बढ़कर बातें करना
C. महान पुरुष पर लांछन लगाना
D. महत्त्वाकांक्षी होना

29. उगल देना
A. अपराध स्वीकार कर लेना
B. सच बोलना
C. उल्टी करना
D. अनपच होना

30. हाथ मलना
A. पश्चाताप करना B. सर्दी मिटाना
C. दुख करना D. तैयार होना

उत्तरमाला

1. A	**2.** C	**3.** D	**4.** D	**5.** C
6. C	**7.** A	**8.** D	**9.** A	**10.** B
11. B	**12.** C	**13.** B	**14.** B	**15.** C
16. D	**17.** A	**18.** A	**19.** A	**20.** B
21. C	**22.** A	**23.** A	**24.** B	**25.** C
26. C	**27.** B	**28.** C	**29.** A	**30.** A

अभ्यास-10

निर्देशः *नीचे कुछ वाक्य खण्ड दिए गए हैं, पूरे वाक्य खण्ड के लिए एक शब्द का चयन कीजिए।*

1. जिसका आदि न हो
A. अनंत B. अमर
C. शाश्वत D. अनादि

2. जो कुछ न जानता हो
A. मूर्ख B. महामूर्ख
C. ज्ञानी D. अज्ञ

3. जो अनुकरण करने योग्य हो
A. अनुकरणीय B. अद्वितीय
C. आदरणीय D. अगम

4. जिसका अंत न हो
A. अनंत B. अनादि
C. आदि D. परलोक

5. जो कभी न मरे
A. मर्त्य B. मुर्त्त
C. अर्मुत्त D. अमर

6. जिसके समान दूसरा न हो
A. अनुकूल B. प्रतिकूल
C. कृतज्ञ D. अद्वितीय

7. जो कम बोलता हो
A. मृदुभाषी B. वाचाल
C. अल्पभाषी D. अल्पज्ञ

8. जिसका इलाज न हो
A. मरणशील B. अमरत्व
C. बिमारी D. लाइलाज

9. जिस का विश्वास न किया जा सके
A. विश्वसनीय B. अविश्वसनीय
C. विश्वासी D. धूर्त्त

10. जिसका कोई नाथ न हो
A. सनाथ B. स्वामी
C. नाथ D. अनाथ

11. कम जानने वाला
A. अल्पज्ञ B. अज्ञ
C. विद् D. विद्वान

12. जहाँ जाना संभव न हो
A. दुर्गम B. अगम
C. तल D. वितल

13. कम खाने वाला
A. बहुभोजी B. पेटु
C. कंजूस D. अल्पाहारी

14. जो बात पहले कभी न हुई हो
A. भूतपूर्व B. अभूतपूर्व
C. प्राचीन D. अर्वाचीन

15. जिस स्त्री के सन्तान न हों
A. बाँझ B. कुलटा
C. पतिता D. विधवा

16. जो कहा न जा सके
A. अकथनीय B. अकथ्य
C. करणीय D. सम्भव

17. एहसान न मानने वाला
A. कृतज्ञ B. कृतघ्न
C. आस्तिक D. विश्वासी

18. जिसने देश के साथ विश्वासघात किया हो
A. विश्वासघाती B. द्रोही
C. आतंकवादी D. देश द्रोही

19. जिसने राष्ट्र के हित में अपना जीवन बलिदान कर दिया हो
A. देशभक्त B. शहीद
C. राष्ट्रभूत D. भारतपुत्र

20. वह जमीन जिसमें कुछ भी पैदा न हो
A. ऊसर B. बंजर
C. उर्वर D. पथरीला

21. वह वस्तु जिसकी चाह हो
A. श्रेष्ठ B. आवश्यक
C. इच्छित D. अभीष्ट

22. दूसरों के पीछे चलने वाला
A. अनुयायी B. अनुज
C. अनुचर D. अनुकरणीय

23. जो पहले न पढ़ा हो
A. पठित B. अपठित
C. पठनीय D. अपठनीय

24. जिसके आर-पार दिखाई देता हो
A. अपारदर्शी B. गम्य
C. अगम्य D. पारदर्शी

25. आज्ञा पालन करने वाला
A. शिष्य B. शिष्या
C. अनुचर D. आज्ञाकारी

26. काम से जी चुराने वाला
A. कामचोर B. आलसी
C. कर्मठ D. परिश्रमी

27. प्रतिदिन होने वाला
A. दैनिक B. शाश्वत
C. सनातन D. अमर

28. जिसका कोई अर्थ न हो
A. सार्थक B. निरर्थक
C. आर्थिक D. अनार्थिक

29. उपकार मानने वाला
A. कृतज्ञ B. कृतघ्न
C. विश्वासी D. अनुयायी

30. हाथ से लिखा हुआ
A. पठनीय B. अपठनीय
C. स्पष्ट D. हस्तलिखित

उत्तरमाला

1. D	**2.** D	**3.** A	**4.** A	**5.** D
6. D	**7.** C	**8.** D	**9.** B	**10.** D
11. A	**12.** A	**13.** D	**14.** B	**15.** A
16. A	**17.** B	**18.** D	**19.** B	**20.** A
21. C	**22.** C	**23.** B	**24.** D	**25.** D
26. A	**27.** A	**28.** B	**29.** A	**30.** D

अभ्यास-11

निर्देशः *नीचे कुछ संज्ञा शब्द दिए जा रहे हैं। प्रत्येक के संज्ञा-भेद के लिए चार विकल्प दिए गये है। सही विकल्प का चयन कीजिए :*

1. तुलसीदास
A. जातिवाचक B. भाववाचक
C. व्यक्तिवाचक D. समूहवाचक

2. यमुना
A. व्यक्तिवाचक B. जातिवाचक
C. समूहवाचक D. भाववाचक

3. बच्चा
A. जातिवाचक B. समूहवाचक
C. भाववाचक D. व्यक्तिवाचक

4. मानवता
A. भाववाचक B. जातिवाचक
C. द्रव्यवाचक D. समूहवाचक

5. हिमालय
A. व्यक्तिवाचक B. जातिवाचक
C. भाववाचक D. समूहवाचक

6. भारत
A. जातिवाचक B. भाववाचक
C. व्यक्तिवाचक D. समूहवाचक

7. एशिया
A. व्यक्तिवाचक B. भाववाचक
C. द्रव्यवाचक D. समूहवाचक

8. महाराष्ट्र
A. जातिवाचक B. व्यक्तिवाचक
C. समूहवाचक D. द्रव्यवाचक

9. सूर सागर
A. व्यक्तिवाचक B. भाववाचक
C. द्रव्यवाचक D. समूहवाचक

10. सोमवार
A. जातिवाचक B. व्यक्तिवाचक
C. द्रव्यवाचक D. समूहवाचक

11. खटमल
A. जातिवाचक B. व्यक्तिवाचक
C. द्रव्यवाचक D. समूहवाचक

12. मैना
A. जातिवाचक B. व्यक्तिवाचक
C. द्रव्यवाचक D. समूहवाचक

13. चाँदी
A. द्रव्यवाचक B. समूहवाचक
C. भाववाचक D. व्यक्तिवाचक

14. अच्छाई
A. भाववाचक B. समूहवाचक
C. जातिवाचक D. व्यक्तिवाचक

15. पीतल
A. द्रव्यवाचक B. भाववाचक
C. व्यक्तिवाचक D. जातिवाचक

16. वीरता
A. भाववाचक B. जातिवाचक
C. द्रव्यवाचक D. समूहवाचक

17. रूस
A. जातिवाचक B. व्यक्तिवाचक
C. भाववाचक D. द्रव्यवाचक

18. लम्बाई

A. भाववाचक B. समूहवाचक
C. द्रव्यवाचक D. व्यक्तिवाचक

19. दल

A. जातिवाचक B. व्यक्तिवाचक
C. समूहवाचक D. द्रव्यवाचक

20. मार्च

A. समूहवाचक B. व्यक्तिवाचक
C. द्रव्यवाचक D. जातिवाचक

21. झुण्ड

A. समूहवाचक B. जातिवाचक
C. व्यक्तिवाचक D. द्रव्यवाचक

22. टोली

A. जातिवाचक B. व्यक्तिवाचक
C. समूहवाचक D. द्रव्यवाचक

23. सुभाष चौक

A. जातिवाचक B. समूहवाचक
C. व्यक्तिवाचक D. भाववाचक

24. संघ

A. जातिवाचक B. द्रव्यवाचक
C. समूहवाचक D. भाववाचक

25. गिरोह

A. समूहवाचक B. द्रव्यवाचक
C. जातिवाचक D. भाववाचक

उत्तरमाला

1. C	**2.** A	**3.** A	**4.** A	**5.** A
6. C	**7.** A	**8.** B	**9.** A	**10.** B
11. A	**12.** A	**13.** A	**14.** A	**15.** A
16. A	**17.** B	**18.** A	**19.** C	**20.** B
21. A	**22.** C	**23.** C	**24.** C	**25.** A

अभ्यास-12

निर्देश: *नीचे दिए गए वाक्य में रिक्त स्थान है। प्रत्येक वाक्य के नीचे कारक चिह्न दिए गए हैं। रिक्त स्थान की पूर्ति के लिए उपयुक्त कारक चिह्न का चयन कीजिए :*

1. निम्नलिखित शब्दों........अर्थ बताइए

A. का B. के
C. से D. पर

2. सरकार मुझे नौकरी........मत निकालिए

A. पर B. में
C. से D. को

3. इस कथन........पुष्टि कीजिए

A. को B. से
C. की D. ने

4. छात्र-छात्राएँ राष्ट्र........सम्पत्ति और उसके भावी कर्णधार होते हैं

A. के B. की
C. को D. में

5. प्रत्येक प्रश्न........चार सम्भावित उत्तर दिए गए हैं

A. के लिए B. में
C. के D. से

6. माता बच्चे........पढ़ाती है

A. को B. के
C. की D. से

7. गुरुजी........सबसे छोटे लड़के को एक नारंगी दी

A. ने B. को
C. से D. के लिए

8. मोहन सोहन से मिलने........गया है

A. से B. के
C. को D. के लिए

9. उसने कलम........लिखा

A. के B. में
C. पर D. से

10. मैं ड्राइवर........गाड़ी चलवाता हूँ

A. के B. पर
C. में D. से

11. शिक्षक छात्रों........पुस्तक पढ़वाते हैं

A. के लिए B. मैं
C. पर D. से

12. मैंने दाढ़ी........उसे मुसलमान समझ लिया

A. से B. के
C. को D. के लिए

13. श्याम अपने भाई हरि........आम लाया है

A. के B. के लिए
C. का D. पर

14. मोहन घर........आता है

A. में B. पर
C. से D. का

15. उसे पाँच दिनों........मूर्च्छा आया करती है

A. पर B. से
C. के D. को

16. मेधावी छात्र परीक्षा........चोरी नहीं करते

A. में B. पर
C. से D. के लिए

उत्तरमाला

1. A	**2.** C	**3.** C	**4.** B	**5.** C
6. A	**7.** A	**8.** D	**9.** D	**10.** D
11. D	**12.** A	**13.** B	**14.** C	**15.** B
16. D				

गद्यांश (अपठित-बोध)

गद्यांश 1

यदि हम निरन्तर प्रयत्न करेंगे तो निश्चय ही अपने सभी लक्ष्यों को प्राप्त कर लेंगे, किन्तु प्रायः देखा जाता है कि अधिक आशावादी लोग थोड़ा सा प्रयत्न करके अधिक फल की कामना करने लगते हैं और मनोवांछित फल प्राप्त न होने पर निराश हो जाते हैं। अतः जीवन में सफलता प्राप्त करने के लिए परिस्थितियों के समक्ष घुटने न टेकें, बल्कि दृढ़ता से उनका मुकाबला करें। याद रखें, जितना कठोर हमारा परिश्रम होगा उसका फल भी उतना ही मीठा होगा।

उपर्युक्त गद्यांश को ध्यानपूर्वक पढ़ें और निम्न प्रश्नों के उत्तर के लिए सही विकल्प को चुनें:

1. फल न मिलने पर कौन निराश हो जाते हैं?
   A. आशावादी लोग B. कम आशावादी लोग
   C. अधिक आशावादी लोग D. निराशावादी लोग
2. लक्ष्य प्राप्ति के लिए क्या किया जाना चाहिए?
   A. फल की कामना B. हिम्मत से मुकाबला
   C. निरन्तर प्रयत्न D. परिस्थितियों से मुकाबला
3. आशावादी शब्द का विलोम शब्द है:
   A. निराश B. निराशावादी
   B. दुखी D. अप्रसन्न
4. मनोवांछित शब्द का क्या अर्थ है?
   A. इच्छित B. परीक्षित
   C. लाभदायक D. मन को खुश करने वाले
5. परिश्रम शब्द का अर्थ है:
   A. साहस B. हिम्मत
   C. काम D. कठिन मेहनत

गद्यांश 2

पन्द्रह अगस्त 1947 को हमारा देश स्वतंत्र हुआ। स्वतन्त्रता प्राप्ति के बाद विश्व के दूसरे देशों के साथ भारत के राजनयिक एवं सांस्कृतिक सम्बन्ध जुड़े। पर्यटकों के साथ-साथ राजनीतिज्ञों और साहित्यकारों को भी विदेश यात्रा के पर्याप्त अवसर मिले। विभिन्न प्रकार की छात्रवृत्तियों के माध्यम से बहुत से लोग विदेशों में पढ़ने गए। बहुत से लोगों ने विदेशों में उपलब्ध आजीविका के अवसरों का लाभ उठाया। इन सबके परिणामस्वरूप प्रचुर मात्रा में यात्रावृत्तांत लिखे गए। विदेश-विषयक यात्रावृतांत्तों में रूस और स्वदेश-विषयक यात्रावृतांत्तों में लेखकों की दृष्टि कश्मीर से कन्याकुमारी तक व्याप्त हुई।

उपर्युक्त गद्यांश को ध्यानपूर्वक पढ़ें और निम्नलिखित प्रश्नों के उत्तर के लिए सही विकल्प को चुनें:

1. भारत कब स्वतंत्र हुआ?
   A. 15 अगस्त 1947 B. 15 अगस्त 1946
   C. 15 अगस्त 1948 D. 15 अगस्त 1949
2. स्वतंत्र भारत के अन्य देशों के साथ किस प्रकार के संबंध जुड़े?
   A. राजनीतिक
   B. राजनयिक
   C. धार्मिक
   D. राजनयिक एवं सांस्कृतिक
3. आजीविका का क्या अर्थ है?
   A. उपार्जन B. वेतन
   C. मेहनत D. रोजगार
4. यात्रा-वृत्तांत का क्या अर्थ है?
   A. भ्रमण B. पर्यटन
   C. सफरनामा D. विदेशभ्रमण
5. स्वतंत्र का विलोम शब्द है:
   A. परतंत्र B. आजाद
   C. गुलामी D. मुक्ति

गद्यांश 3

युवा वर्ग का मस्तिष्क नई-नई बातों की ओर ज्यादा तेज दौड़ता है। उसमें अन्य वर्ग के व्यक्तियों से अधिक आवेश और शक्ति होती है। इस अवस्था में यदि सही शिक्षा और उचित मार्ग-दर्शन न मिले तो यही शक्ति प्रेरणा और निर्माण के स्थान पर विनाश की ओर ले जाती है। बिगड़ने और बनने की यही आयु होती है। दुर्भाग्य से हमारे देश में शिक्षा पद्धति केवल उपाधि बाँटने का काम ही करती है। एक सम्पूर्ण व्यक्तित्वपूर्ण मनुष्य बनाना आज की शिक्षा पद्धति के लिए मुश्किल है।

उपर्युक्त गद्यांश को ध्यानपूर्वक पढ़ें और निम्नलिखित प्रश्नों के उत्तर के लिए सही विकल्प को चुनें।

1. निर्माण का विलोम शब्द क्या हैं?
   A. रचना B. बनावट
   C. विनाश D. सृजन
2. मार्ग-दर्शन का क्या अर्थ है?
   A. उपाधि B. रास्ता
   C. उद्देश्य D. रास्ता दिखलाना
3. शक्ति विनाश की ओर कब अग्रसर होती है?
   A. अधिक आवेश और शक्ति के अभाव में
   B. सही शिक्षा और उचित मार्ग दर्शन के अभाव में
   C. दुर्भाग्यपूर्ण शिक्षा पद्धति के कारण
   D. इनमें से कोई नहीं
4. हमारे देश की शिक्षा पद्धति क्या कार्य करती है?
   A. मार्ग-दर्शन B. शक्ति प्रेरणा
   C. उपाधि देना D. उपर्युक्त सभी
5. दुर्भाग्य का विपरीत शब्द है:
   A. भाग्य B. सौभाग्य
   C. भाग्यशाली D. भाग्यवान

गद्यांश 4

भिखारी की भाँति गिड़गिड़ाना प्रेम की भाषा नहीं है। यहाँ तक कि मुक्ति के लिए भगवान् की उपासना करना भी अधम उपासना में गिना जाता है। प्रेम कोई पुरस्कार नहीं चाहता। प्रेम सर्वथा प्रेम के लिए ही होता है। भक्त इसलिए प्रेम करता है कि बिना प्रेम किए वह रह ही नहीं सकता। जब तुम किसी मनोहर प्राकृतिक दृश्य को देखकर उस पर मोहित हो जाते हो तो तुम किसी फल की याचना नहीं करते और न वह दृश्य ही तुमसे कुछ माँगता है। फिर भी उस दृश्य का दर्शन तुम्हारे मन को आनंद से भर देता है।

उपर्युक्त गद्यांश को ध्यानपूर्वक पढ़ें और निम्नलिखित प्रश्नों के उत्तर के लिए सही विकल्प का चयन करें:

1. प्रेम का उद्देश्य क्या होता है?
   A. मुक्ति B. उपासना
   C. भक्ति D. प्रेम
2. मुक्ति का अर्थ है:
   A. आजादी B. स्वतंत्रता
   C. परतंत्र D. निर्वाण
3. कैसी उपासना अधम मानी गई है?
   A. प्रेम की उपासना B. भगवान की उपासना
   C. मुक्ति की उपासना D. भक्ति की उपासना
4. मनोहर शब्द हैं:
   A. विशेषण B. संज्ञा
   C. सर्वनाम D. अव्यय
5. प्राकृतिक शब्द का अर्थ है:
   A. ईश्वरीय B. मानव संबंधी
   C. प्रकृति संबंधी D. प्रेम संबंधी

गद्यांश 5

कुछ लोग भाग्यवादी होते हैं और सब-कुछ भाग्य के सहारे छोड़कर कर्म से विरत हो जाते हैं। ऐसे लोग समाज के लिए बोझ हैं। वे कभी कोई बड़ा काम नहीं कर पाते। बड़ी-बड़ी खोज, बड़े-बड़े आविष्कार और बड़े-बड़े निर्माण कार्य कर्मशील लोगों के द्वारा ही संभव हो सके हैं। हम अपनी बुद्धि और प्रतिभा तथा कार्य-क्षमता के बल पर सही मार्ग पर चल सकते हैं, किन्तु बिना कठिन श्रम के अपने लक्ष्य तक नहीं पहुँच सकते। कठिन परिश्रम करने के बाद पाई गई सफलता हमारे मन को अलौकिक आनंद से भर देती है। यदि हम अपने कार्य में अपेक्षित श्रम नहीं करते तो हमारा मन ग्लानि का अनुभव करता है।

उपर्युक्त गद्यांश को ध्यानपूर्वक पढ़ें और निम्नलिखित प्रश्नों के उत्तर के लिए सही विकल्प चुनें:

1. "आविष्कार" शब्द का अर्थ है :
   A. अनुसंधान B. खोज
   C. निर्माण D. विनाश
2. **अलौकिक** शब्द का क्या अर्थ है?
   A. संसारिक B. भौतिक
   C. अमानुषी D. प्राकृतिक
3. सफलता का विलोम क्या है?
   A. सफल B. असफल
   C. सफलतापूर्वक D. असफलता
4. परिश्रम करने और न करने से हमारे जीवन पर क्या प्रभाव पड़ता है?
   A. लोग भाग्यवादी बन जाते हैं
   B. कर्म से विरत हो जाते हैं
   C. मन में ग्लानि का अनुभव होता है
   D. इनमें से कोई नहीं
5. किस प्रकार के लोग समाज के लिए बोझ हैं?
   A. भाग्यवादी B. कर्मठ
   C. परिश्रमी D. प्रतिभाशाली

गद्यांश 6

वैदिक काल से हिमालय के पहाड़ बहुत पवित्र माने जाते हैं। इसमें कोई सन्देह नहीं कि हिमालय के पहाड़ों का दृश्य अति सुन्दर है। उसकी विशालता को देखकर मन में आनन्द और कृतज्ञता की लहर उठती है। ऐसा लगता है कि यह विशाल सृष्टि प्रभु की अनुपम देन है। सारी सृष्टि के प्रति समभाव जाग्रत होता है। वस्तुतः यह दृष्टि कोरी कल्पनात्मक या आध्यात्मिक नहीं है। देखा जाए तो सारे भारत की जलवायु का समतोल करने वाले यह हिमालय के पहाड़ हैं, विशेषकर उत्तरी भारत को वर्षा और पानी देने वाले ये ही हैं। गंगोत्री, यमुनोत्री, बद्री, केदार को तीर्थ माना जाता है, जो व्यर्थ कल्पना नहीं है। उन स्थानों से निकलने वाली पवित्र नदियाँ ही वास्तव में हमारी प्राणदात्री रही हैं।

उपर्युक्त गद्यांश को ध्यानपूर्वक पढ़ें और निम्नलिखित प्रश्नों के उत्तर के लिए सही विकल्प चुनें :

1. हिमालय के पर्वत बहुत पवित्र कब से माने जाते हैं?
   A. पाषाण काल से B. वैदिक काल से
   C. प्राचीन काल से D. आधुनिक काल से
2. विशालता शब्द है :
   A. जातिवाचक B. भाववाचक
   C. विशेषण D. सर्वनाम
3. भारत की जलवायु को समतोल कौन करता है?
   A. गंगोत्री B. यमुनोत्री
   C. केदार D. हिमालय
4. सृष्टि का समानार्थक शब्द है :
   A. सृजन B. रचना
   C. प्रकृति D. संसार
5. प्राणदात्री का क्या अर्थ है?
   A. गंगोत्री
   B. यमुनोत्री
   C. प्राणसंचार करने वाली
   D. समभाव जाग्रत करने वाली

गद्यांश 7

सच्चा मित्र एक शिक्षक की भाँति होता है। जिस प्रकार शिक्षक अपने छात्र को सन्मार्ग की ही ओर अग्रसर करता है, उसी प्रकार एक सच्चा मित्र अपने मित्र को पाप के गर्त में गिरने से बचाता है। मानव-जीवन अधिक रहस्यपूर्ण है। कभी-कभी जीवन में ऐसे अवसर उपस्थित हो जाते हैं, जब मनुष्य की धर्मबुद्धि नष्ट हो जाती है और उसका मन द्रुत गति से पाप की ओर दौड़ता है। ऐसे समय में मित्र का ही उपदेश अधिक कल्याणकारी सिद्ध होता है। मित्र के उपदेश का जितना प्रभाव हृदय पर पड़ता है, उतना और किसी का नहीं पड़ता है।

उपर्युक्त गद्यांश को ध्यानपूर्वक पढ़ें और निम्नलिखित प्रश्नों के उत्तर के लिए सही विकल्प चुनें :

1. सच्चा मित्र किस प्रकार का होता है?
A. विपत्ति में सहायता देने वाला
B. गलत मार्ग पर चलने से रोकने वाला
C. शिक्षक के भाँति
D. धार्मिक गुरु की तरह

2. सन्मार्ग शब्द का विपरीत शब्द है :
A. अग्रसर B. कुमार्ग
C. सुमार्ग D. मार्गदर्शक

3. व्यक्ति को पाप के गर्त्त में गिरने से कौन बचाता है?
A. शिक्षक B. भाई
C. पिता D. सच्चा मित्र

4. मानव पाप की ओर कब दौड़ता है?
A. जब स्वार्थी बन जाता है
B. जब धर्म-बुद्धि नष्ट हो जाती है
C. जब सच्चामित्र साथ छोड़ देता है
D. जब धनवान बन जाता है

5. उपदेश में कौन-सा उपसर्ग है?
A. उ B. उप
C. दे D. देश

गद्यांश 8

सब तरह के भावों को प्रकट करने की योग्यता रखने वाली और निर्दोष होने पर भी यदि कोई भाषा अपना निज का साहित्य नहीं रखती, तो वह रूपवती भिखारिन की तरह कदापि आदरणीय नहीं हो सकती। उनकी शोभा, उसकी बड़ी सम्पन्नता, उसकी मान-मर्यादा उसके साहित्य पर ही अवलम्बित रहती है। उसके विचारों और राजनैतिक स्थितियों का प्रतिबिम्ब देखने को यदि कहीं मिल सकता है, तो उसके ग्रन्थ साहित्य में मिल सकता है। सामाजिक शक्ति या सजीवता, सामाजिक अशक्ति या निर्जीवता और सामाजिक सभ्यता तथा असभ्यता का निर्णायक एकमात्र साहित्य है।

उपर्युक्त गद्यांश को ध्यानपूर्वक पढ़ें और निम्नलिखित प्रश्नों के उत्तर के लिए सही विकल्प चुनें :

1. साहित्य विहीन भाषा किस प्रकार की होती है?
A. आदरणीय B. भिखारिन
C. रूपवती D. रूपवती भिखारिन

2. रूपवती का पुल्लिंग रूप है:
A. रूपवान B. सुन्दर
C. सुन्दरी D. रूपवत

3. भाषा की मान मर्यादा किस पर निर्भर करती है?
A. लिपि पर B. साहित्यकार पर
C. भक्ति पर D. साहित्य पर

4. ''सम्पन्नता'' शब्द का विपरीत शब्द है:
A. गरीबी B. विपन्न
C. अमीर D. विपन्नता

5. राजनैतिक, सामाजिक शक्ति का दर्शन हमें किसमें मिलता है?
A. समाज B. राज्य
C. नेता D. साहित्य

गद्यांश 9

स्वतंत्र भारत का सम्पूर्ण दायित्व आज विद्यार्थियों के ही ऊपर है, क्योंकि आज जो विद्यार्थी हैं, वे ही कल स्वतंत्र भारत के नागरिक होंगे। भारत की उन्नति, उसका उत्थान उन्हीं की उन्नति और उत्थान पर निर्भर करता है। अतः विद्यार्थियों को चाहिए कि वे अपने भावी जीवन का निर्माण बड़ी सतर्कता और सावधानी के साथ करें। उन्हें प्रत्येक क्षण अपने राष्ट्र, अपने समाज, अपने धर्म, अपनी संस्कृति को अपनी आँखों के सामने रखना चाहिए, जिससे उनके जीवन से राष्ट्र को कुछ बल प्राप्त हो सके। जो विद्यार्थी राष्ट्रीय दृष्टिकोण से अपने जीवन का निर्माण नहीं करते, वे राष्ट्र और समाज के लिए भार-स्वरूप हैं।

उपर्युक्त गद्यांश को ध्यानपूर्वक पढ़ें और निम्नलिखित प्रश्नों के उत्तर के लिए सही विकल्प चुनें :

1. भारत की उन्नति किस पर निर्भर करती है?
A. युवाओं पर B. नेताओं पर
C. साहित्यकारों पर D. विद्यार्थियों पर

2. **उन्नति** का समानार्थक शब्द है :
A. पतन B. उत्थान
C. विकास D. उदय

3. **उत्थान** का विपरीत शब्द है :
A. उदय B. पतन
C. पराजय D. हार

4. किसे अपने जीवन का निर्माण सतर्कता और सावधानी से करना चाहिए?
A. युवाओं को B. नेताओं को
C. बच्चों को D. विद्यार्थियों को

5. धर्म, संस्कृति तथा समाज का रक्षक कौन है?
A. नागरिक B. ग्रामीण
C. विद्यार्थी D. युवा

गद्यांश 10

हास्य एक ऐसा माध्यम है, जो नीरस-जीवन को भी सुखद बना देता है। हास्य का जादू इतना प्रभावशाली होता है कि वह छूत के रोग की तरह चारों ओर फैल जाता है। जिसने कभी हँसना नहीं सीखा, सचमुच उसने जीना नहीं सीखा। सामान्यतः मनुष्य को जीवन में इतनी मुसीबतें झेलनी पड़ती हैं कि वह अपने जीवन को पहाड़ समझने लगता है। ऐसे दूभर जीवन को यदि जीने योग्य बनाना हो तो उसके लिए आवश्यक है कि जीवन में हँसने की गुंजाइश हो। हँसी के सहारे मनुष्य अपने कष्टों को भुलाने का प्रयत्न करता है। संघर्ष, तनाव, व्यस्तता, घुटन यदि आज के जीवन की सहज देन हैं, तो इनसे बचने के लिए यह आवश्यक है कि हम हँसना सीखें।

उपर्युक्त गद्यांश को ध्यानपूर्वक पढ़ें और निम्नलिखित प्रश्नों के उत्तर के लिए सही विकल्प चुनें :

1. नीरस जीवन को कौन सुखद बना देता है?

A. संगीत B. गीत
C. आमोद प्रमोद D. हास्य

2. **नीरस** का संधि विच्छेद है :

A. नी + रस B. नि + रस
C. निः + रस D. नीः + रस

3. किसका जीवन व्यर्थ है?

A. जिसने रोना नहीं सीखा
B. जिसने हँसना नहीं सीखा
C. जिसने गाना नहीं सीखा
D. इनमें से कोई नहीं

4. **हँसना** शब्द है :

A. संज्ञा B. विशेषण
C. क्रिया विशेषण D. क्रिया

5. तनाव और घुटन से बचने के लिए क्या करना चाहिए?

A. रोना चाहिए B. गाना चाहिए
C. हँसना चाहिए D. काम करना चाहिए

गद्यांश 11

किसी पुस्तक को पढ़ने में जल्दी नहीं करनी चाहिए, जो कुछ लेखक कहता है, उसे समझने की चेष्टा करनी चाहिए। प्रत्येक शब्द का अर्थ समझने की चेष्टा करनी चाहिए। यदि लेखक योग्य है, तो दूसरी बार वह पुस्तक और अधिक आनन्द देगी और तीसरी बार और अधिक। प्रत्येक बार अध्ययन करने पर आपको नवीन सुन्दर और नए विचार मिलेंगे और उसे आप जितना ही पढ़ेंगे, उतना ही स्नेह करने लगेंगे। सहस्रों व्यक्तियों ने गीता और रामायण तथा कुरान और बाइबिल को बार-बार पढ़ा है। उनका अनुभव है कि प्रत्येक बार उन्हें नई सूझ और नए विचार मिलते गए। कुछ लोग तो इस बात पर गर्व करते हैं कि उन्होंने अमुक पुस्तक को अनेक बार पढ़ा है, उन्हें कंठस्थ हो गई है।

उपर्युक्त गद्यांश को ध्यानपूर्वक पढ़ें और निम्नलिखित प्रश्नों के उत्तर के लिए सही विकल्प चुनें :

1. किसे समझने की चेष्टा करनी चाहिए?

A. पुस्तक B. रामायण
C. महाभारत D. गीता

2. पुस्तक की सजीवता किस पर निर्भर करती है?

A. लेखक B. प्रकाशक
C. पाठक D. चिन्तक

3. **आनन्द** का विपरीत शब्द है :

A. शोक B. दुख
C. संताप D. खुशी

4. नवीन, सुन्दर और नए विचार हमें कहाँ से प्राप्त होता हैं?

A. पुस्तक को बार-बार पढ़कर
B. सुनकर
C. भाषण से
D. अच्छे व्यक्तियों से मिलने पर

5. **कंठस्थ** शब्द का शब्दार्थ है :

A. कंठ में स्थित B. सुंदर कंठ
C. जबानी याद D. पंडित जी

गद्यांश 12

अहिंसा परम धर्म है और हिंसा आपद् धर्म। मनुष्य बराबर अहिंसा की ओर चलना चाहता है, किन्तु परिस्थितियाँ उससे हिंसा कराती है, अर्थात् परमधर्म की रक्षा के लिए आदमी बराबर आपद्धर्म से काम लेता रहा है। भारत अपनी सेनाओं को विघटित कर दे, तब भी उसका अपमान उससे अधिक होने वाला नहीं, जितना नेफा में हुआ। किन्तु परमधर्म पर टिकने की सामर्थ्य अगर भारत में नहीं है, तो आपद्धर्म पर उसे आना चाहिए। व्यवहारतः आपद्धर्म परमधर्म का विरोधी नहीं, उसका रक्षक है।

उपर्युक्त गद्यांश को ध्यानपूर्वक पढ़ें और निम्नलिखित प्रश्नों के उत्तर के लिए सही विकल्प चुनें :

1. **परमधर्म** का विपरीत शब्द है :

A. महान धर्म B. आपद्धर्म
C. सच्चाधर्म D. इनमें से कोई नहीं

2. आपद्धर्म किसे कहा जाता है?

A. अहिंसा B. सत्याग्रह
C. विपत्ति D. हिंसा

3. मानव से हिंसा कौन करवाती है?

A. लोभ B. स्वार्थ
C. द्वेष D. परिस्थितियाँ

4. **सामर्थ्य** का शब्दार्थ है :

A. संघर्ष B. परिश्रम
C. शक्ति D. पराक्रम

5. **परमधर्म** की रक्षा कौन करता है?

A. अहिंसा B. हिंसा
C. आपदधर्म D. युद्ध

गद्यांश 13

वर्तमान काल विज्ञापन का युग माना जाता है। समाचार-पत्रों के अतिरिक्त रेडियो और टेलीविजन भी विज्ञापन के सफल साधन हैं। विज्ञापन का मूल उद्देश्य उत्पादक और भोक्ता में सीधा सम्पर्क स्थापित करना होता है। जितना अधिक विज्ञापन किसी पदार्थ का होगा, उतनी ही उसकी लोकप्रियता बढ़ेगी। इन विज्ञापनों पर धन तो अधिक व्यय होता है, पर इनसे बिक्री बढ़ जाती है। ग्राहक जब इन आकर्षक विज्ञापनों को देखता है तो वह उस वस्तु-विशेष के प्रति आकृष्ट होकर उसे खरीदने को बाध्य हो जाता है।

उपर्युक्त गद्यांश को ध्यानपूर्वक पढ़ें और निम्नलिखित प्रश्नों के उत्तर के लिए सही विकल्प चुनें :

1. वर्तमान को किसका युग माना जाता है?

A. फैशन B. विज्ञापन
C. संगीत D. धन

2. उत्पादक तथा भोक्ता के बीच कौन संबंध स्थापित करता है?

A. टेलीविजन B. समाचार-पत्र
C. रेडियो D. विज्ञापन

3. वर्तमान शब्द का विपरीत शब्द है :

A. अर्वाचीन B. आधुनिक
C. आजकल D. प्राचीन

4. आकर्षक का शब्दार्थ है :

A. विकर्षक B. सुन्दर
C. मनमोहक D. आश्चर्यजनक

5. भोक्ता किस कारण वस्तुओं को खरीदने के लिए बाध्य हो जाता है?

A. विज्ञापन
B. आकर्षक विज्ञापन
C. लोकप्रियता के कारण
D. आसानी से उपलब्ध होना

गद्यांश 14

लगभग दो सौ वर्ष की गुलामी ने भारत के राष्ट्रीय स्वाभिमान को पैरों से रौंद डाला, हमारी संस्कृति को समाप्त कर दिया, हमारे विश्वासों को हिला दिया और हमारे आत्मविश्वास को चकनाचूर कर दिया, किन्तु अपने इस बूढ़े देश से प्यार करने वाले, इसके एक सामान्य संकेत पर प्राण न्यौछावर करने वाले दीवानों का अभाव न था। एक आवाज उठी और देखते ही देखते राष्ट्र का दबा हुआ आत्माभिमान उन्मत्त हो उठा। इतिहास साक्षी है जाने और अनजाने सहस्त्रों देशभक्त स्वतंत्रता की अनमोल निधि को पाने के लिए शहीद हो गए।

उपर्युक्त गद्यांश को ध्यानपूर्वक पढ़ें और निम्नलिखित प्रश्नों के उत्तर के लिए सही विकल्प चुनें :

1. स्वाभिमान का संधि विच्छेद है:

A. स्वा + भिमान B. स्वः + अभिमान
C. स्व + अभिमान D. स्वा + अभिमान

2. भारत का राष्ट्रीय स्वाभिमान किस कारण समाप्त हो गया था?

A. लम्बे गुलामी से B. निरंकुश शासक से
C. स्वार्थी मानव से D. धर्म के विनाश से

3. आत्मविश्वास का शब्दार्थ है

A. घमण्ड B. गर्व
C. अपने पर विश्वास D. अभिमान

4. भारत की अनमोल निधि को पाने के लिए कौन शहीद हो गए?

A. देशभक्त B. नेता
C. युवा D. युवती

5. अनमोल निधि का शब्दार्थ है:

A. अनन्त खजाना B. अमूल्य खजाना
C. बहुमूल्य D. स्वतंत्रता

गद्यांश 15

दुनिया के विभिन्न देशों के विकास पर विहंगम दृष्टि डालने से यह स्पष्ट हो जाता है कि आज जिस देश ने वैज्ञानिक उपलब्धियों के सहारे अपना औद्योगीकरण कर लिया, उसी को उन्नत देश कहा जाता है। जिस देश में औद्योगीकरण का स्तर नीचा है, वह पिछड़ा हुआ देश कहा जाता है। वैज्ञानिक आविष्कारों और औद्योगीकरण के आधार पर ही किसी देश की प्रगति को आँका जाता रहा है। विज्ञान ने मानव को पूरी तरह बदल दिया है।

उपर्युक्त गद्यांश को ध्यानपूर्वक पढ़ें और निम्नलिखित प्रश्नों के उत्तर के लिए सही विकल्प चुनें :

1. विहंगम दृष्टि का क्या अर्थ है?

A. एक झलक B. गहन दृष्टि
C. गहन चिन्तन D. इनमें से कोई नहीं

2. विकास का विपरीत शब्द है :

A. उत्थान B. उदय
C. पतन D. विनाश

3. वैज्ञानिक शब्द में कौन-सा प्रत्यय हैं?

A. निक B. वै
C. ईक D. इक

4. मानव जीवन को किसने बदल दिया है :

A. विकास B. वैज्ञानिक
C. विज्ञान D. उद्योग

5. किसी भी देश की स्तर को किससे नापा जाता है?

A. उपलब्धियों पर B. औद्योगीकरण से
C. वैज्ञानिकों से D. आविष्कारों से

गद्यांश 16

विश्व का वर्तमान उन्नत रूप मानव-श्रम की ही कहानी कह रहा है। गगन चुंबी अट्टालिकाएँ, लंबी-चौड़ी सड़कें, बड़े-बड़े विशाल नगर आकाश में उड़ते वायुयान तथा मानव-जीवन को सुखी और समृद्ध बनाने में योगदान करने वाले ज्ञान-विज्ञान के अनन्त रूप-ये सभी मनुष्य के श्रम का जयघोष करते हैं। स्पष्ट है कि मनुष्य और उसका शरीर विधाता की अनुपम रचना है जो निश्चय ही महान उद्देश्यों की संपूर्ति के

लिए दिया गया है। इस दुर्लभ तन को यदि हम आलस्य, प्रसाद अथवा घटिया कामों में गँवा देते हैं तो उस विधाता के प्रति अन्याय करते हैं।

उपर्युक्त गद्यांश को ध्यानपूर्वक पढ़ें और निम्नलिखित प्रश्नों के उत्तर के लिए सही विकल्प चुनें :

1. विश्व का वर्तमान रूप किसका उद्योतक है?
   A. चिन्तक का B. नेता का
   C. वैज्ञानिक का D. मानव श्रम
2. **गगन चुंबी अट्टालिकाएँ** का अर्थ है :
   A. आकाश में उड़ने वाला B. आकाश को छूने वाला
   C. बहुमंजिली इमारत D. इनमें से कोई नहीं
3. आकाश का समानार्थक शब्द है :
   A. वसुन्धरा B. धरा
   C. पयोद D. गगन
4. **सुखी** का विपरीत शब्द है :
   A. प्रसन्न B. अप्रसन्न
   C. दुखी D. उदासी
5. विधाता की अनुपम रचना क्या है?
   A. मानव शरीर B. समुद्र
   C. वन D. पृथ्वी

गद्यांश 17

हमारे देश में एक ऐसा भी युग था जब नैतिक और आध्यात्मिक विकास ही जीवन का वास्तविक लक्ष्य माना जाता था। अहिंसा की भावना सर्वोपरि थी। आज पूरा जीवन दर्शन ही बदल गया है। सर्वत्र पैसे की हाय-हाय तथा धन का उपार्जन ही मुख्य ध्येय हो गया है, भले ही धन-उपार्जन के तरीके गलत ही क्यों न हों? इन सबका असर मनुष्य के प्रतिदिन के जीवन पर पड़ रहा है। समाज का वातावरण दूषित हो गया है—

बाह्य वातावरण तो दूषित है ही, आज सब जानते हैं पर्यावरण की समस्याएँ कितनी चिन्तनीय हो उठी है। इन सबके कारण मानसिक और शारीरिक तनाव-खिंचाव और व्याधियाँ पैदा हो रही हैं।

उपर्युक्त गद्यांश को ध्यानपूर्वक पढ़ें और निम्नलिखित प्रश्नों के उत्तर के लिए सही विकल्प चुनें :

1. भारत का प्राचीन आदर्श था :
   A. सत्य और अहिंसा B. नैतिक और आध्यात्मिक विकास
   C. धन उपार्जन D. इनमें से कोई नहीं
2. **अहिंसा** का विपरीत शब्द है :
   A. हिंसा B. सत्याग्रह
   C. विनम्रता D. नैतिकता
3. जीवन दर्शन क्यों बदल गया है?
   A. हिंसा के कारण B. अहिंसा के कारण
   C. धन लिप्सा के कारण D. आध्यात्मिक विकास के कारण
4. समाज का वातावरण दूषित क्यों हो गया है?
   A. शारीरिक तनाव B. मानसिक व्याधियाँ
   C. पर्यावरण की समस्याएँ D. धन उपार्जन के गलत तरीके
5. **पर्यावरण** का शब्दार्थ है:
   A. जलमंडल B. स्थलमंडल
   C. वायुमंडल D. वातावरण

उत्तरमाला

गद्यांश 1

1. C 2. D 3. B 4. A 5. D

गद्यांश 2

1. A 2. D 3. D 4. C 5. A

गद्यांश 3

1. C 2. D 3. B 4. C 5. B

गद्यांश 4

1. D 2. D 3. C 4. A 5. C

गद्यांश 5

1. B 2. D 3. D 4. C 5. A

गद्यांश 6

1. B 2. B 3. D 4. A 5. C

गद्यांश 7

1. C 2. B 3. D 4. B 5. B

गद्यांश 8

1. D 2. A 3. D 4. D 5. D

गद्यांश 9

1. D 2. B 3. B 4. D 5. C

गद्यांश 10

1. D 2. C 3. B 4. D 5. C

गद्यांश 11

1. A 2. A 3. A 4. A 5. C

गद्यांश 12

1. B 2. D 3. D 4. C 5. C

गद्यांश 13

1. B 2. D 3. D 4. C 5. B

गद्यांश 14

1. C 2. A 3. C 4. A 5. B

गद्यांश 15

1. A 2. D 3. C 4. C 5. B

गद्यांश 16

1. D 2. C 3. D 4. C 5. A

गद्यांश 17

1. B 2. A 3. C 4. D 5. D

●●●

QUANTITATIVE APTITUDE

NUMBER SYSTEM

1. There are four numbers A, B, C and D. Average of the first three *i.e.*, A, B and C is 15 and that of B, C and D is 16. If the last number, *i.e.*, D is 19, then the first number is—
A. 15 B. 16
C. 17 D. 18

2. Of the three numbers, the first is twice the second and thrice the third. If the average of three is 22, the three numbers are—
A. 12, 18, 36
B. 18, 12, 36
C. 36, 12, 18
D. 36, 18, 12

3. If a person is standing on the sixth number in the queue from both the ends, the total persons in the queue are—
A. 9 B. 11
C. 12 D. 13

4. A number 'x' when multiplied by 5 and added to three times its own gives 64, the number is—
A. 8 B. 12
C. 14 D. 18

5. A number which when multiplied by 11 is as much above 180 as it was originally below it. The number is—
A. 25 B. 30
C. 40 D. 45

6. The sum of a number and its reciprocal is thrice the difference of the number and its reciprocal. Find the number.
A. $\sqrt{2}$ B. $\sqrt{3}$
C. $\sqrt{5}$ D. $\sqrt{7}$

7. A boy was asked to find $\frac{7}{9}$ of a fraction. He made a mistake of dividing the fraction by $\frac{7}{9}$ and so got an answer which exceeded the correct answer by $\frac{8}{21}$. Find the correct answer.
A. $\frac{2}{3}$ B. $\frac{5}{7}$
C. $\frac{7}{12}$ D. $\frac{7}{15}$

8. There are 408 boys and 312 girls in a school, which are to be divided into equal sections of either boys or girls alone. Find the maximum number of boys or girls that can be placed in a section. Also find the total number of sections thus formed.
A. 10, 20 B. 24, 30
C. 24, 40 D. 30, 30

9. The sum of all possible two-digit number formed from three different one-digit natural numbers, when divided by the sum of the original three numbers is equal to—
A. 11 B. 18
C. 22 D. 36

10. There are four prime numbers written in ascending order. The product of the first three is 385 and that of the last three is 1001. The last number is—
A. 19 B. 17
C. 13 D. 11

11. If the number 357 ★ 25 ★ is divisible by both 3 and 5, then the missing digits in the unit's place and thousandth place respectively are—
A. 0, 4 B. 5, 4
C. 5, 6 D. 0, 6

12. The difference between two numbers is 1365. When the larger number is divided by the smaller one, the quotient is 6 and the remainder is 15. The smaller number is:
A. 360 B. 295
C. 270 D. 240

13. When a number is divided by 31, the remainder is 29. When the same number is divided by 16, what will be the remainder?
A. 15 B. 13
C. 11 D. Data inadequate

14. In dividing a number by 585, a student applied the method of short division. He divided the number successively by 5, 9 and 13 (factor of 585) and got the remainders 4, 8 and 12. If he had divided the number by 585, the remainder would have been:
A. 584 B. 292
C. 144 D. 24

15. When a number divided by 6 leaves a remainder 3. When the square of the same number is divided by 6, the remainder is:
A. 3 B. 2
C. 1 D. zero

ANSWERS

1	2	3	4	5	6	7	8	9	10
B	D	B	A	B	A	C	B	C	C
11	12	13	14	15					
C	C	D	A	A					

EXPLANATORY ANSWERS

1. $\frac{A+B+C}{3} = 15,$

or, $A + B + C = 15 \times 3 = 45$ ... *(i)*

$\frac{B+C+D}{3} = 16,$

or $B + C + D = 48$ .... *(ii)*

$D = 19$

$\therefore$ $B + C + 19 = 48$ or, $B + C = 48 - 19 = 29$

But, $A + B + C = 45$

Putting the value of $B + C = 29$ in the above equation *(i)*, we get $A + 29 = 45$

$\therefore$ $A = 45 - 29 = 16$.

2. Let the third number = x

$\therefore$ First number = $3x$

Second number = $\frac{3x}{2}$

$\therefore \frac{1}{3}\left[x+3x+\frac{3x}{2}\right] = 22 \Rightarrow \frac{11}{2}x = 66$

$\Rightarrow x = \frac{66 \times 2}{11} = 12$ = Third number,

$12 \times 3 = 36$ = First number,

$\frac{12 \times 3}{2} = 18$ = Second number.

3. If the person is standing at sixth number in the queue from both sides, that means there are five persons ahead and five persons behind him. Hence, total number of persons in the queue is $5 + 1 + 5 = 11$.

4. $5 \times x + 3x = 64 \quad \Rightarrow 8x = 64$

$\therefore \quad x = \frac{64}{8} = 8.$

5. Let the number is x

$\therefore \quad 180 - x = 11x - 180$

$\Rightarrow \quad 180 + 180 = 11x + x$

$\Rightarrow \quad 360 = 12x,$

$\Rightarrow \quad x = \frac{360}{12} = 30.$

6. Let the no. = x then its reciprocal = $\frac{1}{x}$

By the question, $\left(x+\frac{1}{x}\right) = 3\left(x-\frac{1}{x}\right)$

$\Rightarrow \quad \frac{x^2+1}{x} = \frac{3(x^2-1)}{x}$

$\Rightarrow \quad x^2 + 1 = 3x^2 - 3$

$\Rightarrow \quad 3x^2 - x^2 = 3 + 1$

$\therefore \quad x = \sqrt{2}.$

7. Let the required fraction = x

then, by the question $x \div \frac{7}{9} - x \times \frac{7}{9} = \frac{8}{21}$

$\Rightarrow \quad x \times \frac{9}{7} - \frac{7x}{9} = \frac{8}{21}$

$\Rightarrow \quad \frac{32x}{63} = \frac{8}{21}$

$\Rightarrow \quad x = \frac{8}{21} \times \frac{63}{32} = \frac{3}{4}$

Hence, the correct answer = $\frac{3}{4} \times \frac{7}{9} = \frac{7}{12}$.

8.

```
312) 408(1
     312
      96) 312 (3
          288
           24) 96 (4
               96
               ×
```

$\therefore$ Maximum number of girls or boys that can be placed in a section = 24 and total number of such

section = $\frac{408}{24} + \frac{312}{24}$

$= 17 + 13 = 30$

9. Let three different one digit natural numbers be x, y and z.

Then, sum of all possible two digits numbers

$= (10x + y) + (10y + x) + (10x + z) + (10z + x) + (10y + z) + (10z + y)$

$= 22x + 22y + 22z = 22(x + y + z)$

Hence, required number = 22.

10. Let four prime numbers be a, b, c and d respectively.

Now, $\frac{abc}{bcd} = \frac{385}{1001}$

$\Rightarrow \quad \frac{c}{d} = \frac{5}{13}$

Hence, $a = 5$ and $d = 13$

11. 357 ★ 25 ★

For divisible by 5, the last digit must be either 0 or 5.

If last digit is 0, then other required digit will be 2 or 5 or 8

Hence, the numbers are (0, 2) or (0, 5) or (0, 8)

If last digit is 5, then other required digit will be 0 or 3 or 6 or 9

Hence, the numbers are (5, 0) or (5, 3) or (5, 6) or (5, 9)

So, correct option is (c).

12. Here, $(x + 1365) = 6x + 15$

$\Rightarrow 5x = 1350$

$\therefore \; x = \frac{1350}{5} = 270$

Hence, the smaller number = 270.

13. The number = $31x + 29$.

Here, given data is inadequate.

14.

5	a
9	$b - 4$
13	$c - 8$
	$1 - 12$

Now, $c = 13 \times 1 + 12 = 25$

$b = 9c + 8 = 9 \times 25 + 8 = 233$

$a = 5b + 4 = 5 \times 233 + 4$

$= 1165 + 4 = 1169$

$1169 = 585 \times 1 + 584$

Hence, required remainder = 584.

15. The number = $6x + 3$

Now, $(6x + 3)^2 = 36x^2 + 36x + 9$

$= (36x^2 + 36x + 6) + 3$

$= 6(6x^2 + 6x + 1) + 3$

Hence, required remainder = 3.

LCM AND HCF

1. The L.C.M. and H.C.F. of two numbers are 4284 and 32 respectively. If one of the numbers is 204, the other is

A. 672 B. 576
C. 676 D. 572

2. Two numbers are in the ratio of 8 : 15. If their H.C.F. is 4, the numbers are

A. 32 and 60 B. 16 and 30
C. 80 and 150 D. 64 and 120

3. The greatest number that will divide 366, 513 and 324 leaving the same remainder in each case is

A. 21 B. 18
C. 27 D. 42

4. The L.C.M. of two numbers is 45 times their H.C.F. If the sum of the L.C.M. and the H.C.F. of these two numbers is 1150 and one of the numbers is 125, then the other number is

A. 256 B. 225
C. 250 D. 255

5. The H.C.F. and the L.C.M. of two numbers are 50 and 250 respectively. On dividing one of these numbers by 2, 50 is obtained as quotient. The numbrs are

A. 100, 125 B. 80, 100
C. 125, 100 D. 200, 250

6. Three bells ring respectively at an interval of 15 seconds, 20 seconds and 24 seconds. If they ring continuously for 12 minutes then how many times, during this period, will they ring together?

A. 2 times B. 6 times
C. 5 times D. 3 times

7. If the sum of two numbers is 55 and the H.C.F. and L.C.M. of these numbers are 5 and 120 respectively. Find the sum of their reciprocals.

A. $\frac{120}{11}$ B. $\frac{11}{120}$

C. $\frac{601}{55}$ D. $\frac{55}{601}$

8. The LCM of two numbers is 48. The numbers are in the ratio of 2 : 3. The sum of the numbers is

A. 64 B. 40
C. 32 D. 28

9. Find the greatest number that will divide 43, 91 and 183 so as to leave the same remainder in each case.

A. 13 B. 9
C. 7 D. 4

10. The greatest possible length which can be used to measure exactly the length 7m, 3m 85cm, 12m 95 cm is

A. 42 cm B. 35 cm
C. 25 cm D. 15 cm

11. A, B and C start at the same time in the same direction to run around a circular park. A completes a round in 252 seconds, B in 308 seconds and C in 198 seconds, all starting at the same point. After what time will they meet again at the starting point?

A. 46 minutes 12 seconds
B. 45 minutes
C. 42 minutes 36 seconds
D. 26 minutes 18 seconds

12. Which of the following has most numbers of divisors?

A. 182 B. 176
C. 101 D. 99

13. Which is of the following is a co-primes?

A. (23, 92) B. (21, 35)
C. (18, 25) D. (16, 62)

14. Let N be the greatest number that will divide 1305, 4665 and 6905, leaving the same remainder in each case. Then find the sum of the digits in N.

A. 8 B. 6
C. 5 D. 4

15. The greatest number which one dividing 1657 and 2037 leaves remainder 6 and 5 respectively, is:

A. 305 B. 235
C. 127 D. 123

ANSWERS

1	2	3	4	5	6	7	8	9	10
A	A	A	B	A	B	B	B	D	B
11	**12**	**13**	**14**	**15**					
A	B	C	D	C					

EXPLANATORY ANSWERS

1. 1st number × 2nd number = LCM × HCF

$\therefore$ 204 × 2nd number = 4284 × 32

$\therefore$ 2nd number $= \frac{4284 \times 32}{204} = 672$

$\therefore$ 2nd number = 672

2. Let the numbers be $8x$ and $15x$

$8x = 2 \times 2 \times 2 \times x$

$15x = 3 \times 5 \times x$

$\therefore$ LCM of $8x$ and $15x = 2 \times 2 \times 2 \times x \times 3 \times 5 = 120x$

Now, 1st number × 2nd number = HCF × LCM

$\Rightarrow$ $8x \times 15x = 4 \times 120x$

$\Rightarrow$ $120x^2 = 4 \times 120x$

$\Rightarrow$ $x = 4$

$\therefore$ Numbers are 8 × 4 = 32 and 15 × 4 = 60

3. Difference between 366 and 513 = 513 – 366 = 147

and difference between 513 and 324 = 513 – 324 = 189

$\therefore$ HCF of 147 and 189

147) 189 (1
147
× 42) 147 (3
126
× 21) 42 (2
42
×

$\therefore$ The required largest number is 21.

4. LCM of the two numbers = 45 × HCF

and LCM + HCF = 1150

$\Rightarrow$ 45 × HCF + HCF = 1150

$\Rightarrow$ HCF(45 + 1) = 1150

$\Rightarrow$ HCF $= \frac{1150}{46} = 25$

$\therefore$ LCM = 45 × 25 = 1125

$\because$ 1st number × 2nd number = LCM × HCF

$\therefore$ 125 × 2nd number = 1125 × 25

$\therefore$ 2nd number $= \frac{1125 \times 25}{125} = 225.$

5. According to the condition of the problem, 50 is obtained on dividing one of the numbers by 2

$\therefore$ One of the numbers = 50 × 2 = 100

Now, 1st number × 2nd number = LCM × HCF

$\therefore$ 100 × 2nd number = 250 × 50

$\therefore$ 2nd number $= \frac{250 \times 50}{100} = 125$

Hence, numbers are 100 and 125.

6. LCM of 15, 20 and 24

5	15, 20, 24
4	3, 4, 24
3	3, 1, 6
	1, 1, 2

LCM = 5 × 4 × 3 × 2 = 120

$\because$ 12 minutes = 12 × 60 = 720 seconds

$\therefore$ Number of times the bells will ring together during 12 minutes

$= \frac{720}{120} = 6$ times.

7. Let the number be x and y.
Then, $x + y = 55$;
$xy = HCF \times LCM = 5 \times 120$
$\therefore$ Sum of their reciprocals
$= \frac{1}{x} + \frac{1}{y} = \frac{x+y}{xy} = \frac{55}{5 \times 120} = \frac{11}{120}$.

8. Let the two numbers be $2x$ and $3x$;
their LCM = $6x$
Now, $6x = 48$ $\therefore$ $x = 8$
Hence, the numbers are $2 \times 8,\ 3 \times 8 = 16, 24$
Their sum = 16 + 24 = 40.

9. 2240) 3360 (1
2240
1120) 2240 (2
2240
×

1120) 5600 (5
5600
×

Hence, N = HCF of 3360, 2240 and 5600 = 1120
Sum of digits in N = 1 + 1 + 2 + 0 = 4.

10. 7m = 700 cm;
3m 85 = 385 cm;
12m 95cm = 1295 cm

385) 700 (1
385
315) 385 (1
315
70) 315 (4
280
35) 70 (2
70
×

35) 1295 (37
105
245
245
×

Hence, required length = HCF of 700 cm, 385 cm, 1295 cm = 35 cm.

11.

2	252,	308,	198
2	126,	154,	99
3	63,	77,	99
3	21,	77,	33
7	7,	77,	11
11	1,	11,	11
	1,	1,	1

Hence, LCM = 2 × 2 × 3 × 3 × 7 × 11 = 2772
Hence, A, B, C will meet again at the starting point after 2772 sec. = 46 min 12 sec.

12. ***Numbers*** ***Their divisors***

182 → 1, 2, 7, 13, 14, 26, 91 and 182
176 → 1, 2, 4, 8, 16, 22, 44, 88 and 176
101 → 1 and 101
99 → 1, 3, 9, 11, 33 and 99

Therefore, 176 has the most number of divisors.

13. HCF of 23 and 92 = 23
HCF of 21 and 35 = 7
HCF of 18 and 25 = 1
HCF of 16 and 62 = 2
Hence, 18 and 25 are co-prime numbers.

14. N = HCF of (4665 – 1305), (6905 – 4665) and (6905 – 1305)
= HCF of 3360, 2240 and 5600 = 112
Sum of digit of 1 + 1 + 2 = 4.

15. Required number = HCF of (1657 – 6) and (2037 – 5)
= HCF of 1651 and 2032 = 127.

1651) 2032 (1
1651
381) 1651 (4
1524
127) 381 (3
381
×

AVERAGE

1. One-third of a certain journey was covered at the rate of 25 km per hour, one-fourth at the rate of 30 km per hour and the rest at the 50 km per hour. What is the average speed per hour for whole journey?

A. $33\frac{1}{3}$ kmph B. $44\frac{1}{4}$ kmph
C. $22\frac{1}{2}$ kmph D. 33 kmph

2. A batsman has a certain average of runs for 16 innings. In the 17th innings, he makes a score of 85 runs thereby increasing his average by 3. What is the average after the 17th inning?

A. 33 runs B. 34 runs
C. 37 runs D. 36 runs

3. The average of 6 observations is 12. A new seventh observation is included and the new average is decreased by 1. The seventh observation is

A. 1 B. 3
C. 5 D. 6

4. The average age of 30 students in a class is 12 years. The average age of a group of 5 of the students is 10 years and that of another group of 5 of them is 14 years. The average age of the remaining students is
A. 8 years B. 10 years
C. 12 years D. 14 years

5. Out of the three given numbers, the first number is twice the second and thrice the third. If the average of three numbers is 121, what is the difference between the first and third number?
A. 144 B. 77
C. 99 D. 132

6. If the average marks of three batches of 55, 60 and 45 students is 50, 55 and 60, then average marks of all the students is:
A. 55 B. 54
C. 54.68 D. 55.68

7. The average of 8 numbers is 20. The average of first two numbers is $15\frac{1}{2}$ and that of the next three is $21\frac{1}{3}$. If the sixth number is less than the seventh and eighth numbers by 4 and 7 respectively, then the eighth number is:
A. 27 B. 25
C. 22 D. 18

8. A pupil's marks were wrongly entered as 83 instead of 63. Due to that the average marks for the class got increased by half. What is the number of pupils in the class?
A. 73 B. 40
C. 40 D. 10

9. A cricketer whose bowling average is 12.4 runs per wicket takes 5 wickets for 26 runs and thereby decreases his average by 0.4. The number of wickets taken by him till the last match was:
A. 85 B. 80
C. 72 D. 64

10. The average weight of a class of 24 students is 35 kg. If the weight of the teacher is included, the average rises by 400 g. What is the weight of the teacher?
A. 55 kg B. 53 kg
C. 50 kg D. 45 kg

11. Nine men went to a hotel. Eight of them spent Rs. 3 for each over their meals and the ninth spent Rs. 2 more than the average expenditure of all the nine. What is the total money spent by them?
A. Rs. 29.25 B. Rs. 29.50
C. Rs. 29 D. Rs. 30

12. The average age of 24 students in a class is 10. If the teacher's age is included, the average increases by one. The age of the teacher is
A. 25 B. 30
C. 35 D. 40

13. The average of 5 consecutive even numbers A, B, C, D and E is 34. What is the product of B and D?
A. 1152 B. 1368
C. 1224 D. 1088

14. The average of 50 numbers is 30. If two numbers, 35 and 40 are discarded, then the average of the remaining numbers is nearly:
A. 29.68 B. 29.27
C. 28.78 D. 28.32

15. The average monthly salary of 20 employees of an organisation is Rs. 1500. If the manager's salary is added, then the average salary increases by Rs. 100. Find the manager's monthly salary?
A. Rs. 4800 B. Rs. 3600
C. Rs. 2400 D. Rs. 2000

ANSWERS

1	2	3	4	5	6	7	8	9	10
A	C	C	C	D	C	B	B	A	D
11	**12**	**13**	**14**	**15**					
A	C	A	A	B					

EXPLANATORY ANSWERS

1. Let the total distance covered during journey = 60 km

$\frac{1}{3}$ of the distance covered during journey

$= 60 \times \frac{1}{3} = 20$ km

$\frac{1}{4}$ of the distance covered during journey

$= \frac{1}{4} \times 60 = 15$ km

$\therefore$ The distance covered during the rest of journey = $60 - (20 + 15) = 25$ km

Time taken to cover 20 km at 25 km/h

$= \frac{20}{25}$ hours $= \frac{4}{5}$ hour

Time taken to cover 15 km at 30 km/h

$= \frac{15}{30}$ hours $= \frac{1}{2}$ hour

Time taken to cover 25 km at 50 km/h

$= \frac{25}{50}$ hours $= \frac{1}{2}$ hour

Total time taken $= \frac{4}{5} + \frac{1}{2} + \frac{1}{2}$

$= \frac{9}{5}$ hours

Hence average speed per hour $= 60 \div \frac{9}{5}$

$= \frac{60 \times 5}{9} = \frac{100}{3}$ km/h

$= 33\frac{1}{3}$ km/h

2. Average increase in the score of 17 innings
= 3 runs
Total increase in the score of 17 innings
= 3 × 17 = 51 runs
∴ His average of 16 innings = 85 – 51
= 34 runs
Hence, average after the 17th innings
= 34 + 3 = 37 runs

3. Seventh observation = (7 × 11 – 6 × 12) = 5

4. Let, the required average age be x
Then, $5 \times 10 + 5 \times 14 + 20 \times x = 30 \times 12$
$\Rightarrow \quad 20x = 360 - 120$
$\Rightarrow \quad 20x = 240$
$\Rightarrow \quad x = 12$

5. Let the three numbers be x, $\frac{x}{2}$ and $\frac{x}{3}$ respectively,

Now, $\frac{1}{3}\left(x + \frac{x}{2} + \frac{x}{3}\right) = 121$

$\Rightarrow \frac{11x}{6} = 121 \times 3$

$\therefore \; x = \frac{121 \times 3 \times 6}{11} = 198$

Hence, required difference $= x - \frac{x}{3} = \frac{2x}{3}$

$= \frac{2}{3} \times 198 = 132$

6. Required average Marks

$= \frac{55 \times 50 + 60 \times 55 + 45 \times 60}{55 + 60 + 45} = \frac{8750}{160} = 54.68$

7. Let the sixth, seventh and eighth numbers are x, x + 4 and x + 7.
Sum of last three numbers

$= 8 \times 20 - (2 \times \frac{31}{2} + 3 \times \frac{64}{3})$

$\Rightarrow x + x + 4 + x + 7 = 160 - 95$
$\Rightarrow 3x + 11 = 65$
$\Rightarrow 3x = 54 \qquad \therefore x = 18$
New eighth number = $x + 7 = 18 + 7 = 25$

8. Let the total number of pupils in the class be x; then,

$\frac{83 - 63}{x} = \frac{1}{2} \quad \Rightarrow \frac{20}{x} = \frac{1}{2} \qquad \therefore x = 40$

9. Let the number of wickets taken by him be x till the last match.

Then, $\frac{x \times 12.4 + 26}{x + 5} = 12$

$\Rightarrow 12.4x + 26 = 12x + 60$

$\Rightarrow 0.4x = 34 \quad \therefore \; x = \frac{340}{4} = 85$

10. Let the weight of the teacher be x kgs, then

$\frac{24 \times 35 + x}{25} = 35.4$

$\Rightarrow 840 + x = 885 \qquad \therefore \; x = 45$ kgs

12. Age of the teacher = (25 × 11 – 24 × 10) years
= 35 years

13. Let 5 consecutive even numbers A, B, C, D and E be x, $x + 2$, $x + 4$, $x + 6$ and $x + 8$ respectively.

Now, $\frac{x + x + 2 + x + 4 + x + 6 + x + 8}{5} = 34$

$\Rightarrow 5x + 20 = 170$
$\Rightarrow 5x = 150 \qquad \therefore x = 30$
Then, B = $x + 2 = 30 + 2 = 32$;
D = $x + 6 = 30 + 6 = 36$
Hence, their product = 32 × 36 = 1152

14. The average of remaining 48 numbers

$= \frac{50 \times 30 - (35 + 40)}{48} = \frac{1500 - 75}{48}$

$= \frac{1425}{48} = 29.68$

15. Let manager's salary be Rs. x, then

$\frac{20 \times 1500 + x}{21} = 1600$

$\Rightarrow 30{,}000 + x = 33600$
$\therefore \; x =$ Rs. 3600

PROBLEMS BASED ON AGES

1. The ratio of ages of A and B is 3 : 11. After 3 years the ratio becomes 1 : 3. What are the ages of A and B?
A. 9 years, 33 years
B. 10 years, 40 years
C. 9 years, 27 years
D. None of these

2. Two years ago, the ratio of Ram's and Mohan's age was 3 : 2 and at present 7 : 5. What are their present ages?
A. 14 years, 10 years B. 15 years, 10 years
C. 13 years, 9 years D. None of these

3. The ages of Samir and Saurabh are in the ratio of 8 : 15 respectively. After 9 years the ratio of their ages will be 11 : 18. What is the difference between their ages in years?
A. 20 years B. 21 years
C. 22 years D. 24 years

4. The present age of father is 34 years more than that of his son. 12 years ago, father's age was 18 times the age of his son. The present age of son in years is:
A. 12 B. 14
C. 16 D. 18

5. A mother is 25 years older than her daughter. Five years ago, the age of the mother was 6 times the age of the daughter. What is the present age of mother?
A. 25 years B. 29 years
C. 32 years D. 35 years

6. The difference between the present ages of P and Q is 4 years. The ratio of their ages after 5 years will be 9 : 8. The present age of P is:
A. 24 years B. 30 years
C. 32 years D. None of these

7. Ten years ago, the age of Divya was half of the age of Namrata. If the ratio of present ages of both is 3 : 4, the sum of their present ages is:
A. 35 years B. 30 years
C. 25 years D. 18 years

8. The ratio between the present ages of A and B is 5 : 3 respectively. The ratio between A's age 4 years ago and B's age 4 years hence is 1 : 1. The ratio between A's age 4 years hence and B's age 4 years ago is:
A. 4 : 1 B. 3 : 1
C. 2 : 1 D. 1 : 3

9. Ram got married 8 years ago. His present age is $\frac{6}{5}$ times his age at the time of marriage. Ram's sister was 10 years younger to him at the time of his marriage. What is the present age of Ram's sister?
A. 40 years B. 38 years
C. 36 years D. 32 years

10. A father said to his son, "I was as old as you are at present at the time of your birth." If the father's age is 38 years now. Five years ago the age of son was:
A. 38 years B. 33 years
C. 19 years D. 14 years

ANSWERS

1	2	3	4	5	6	7	8	9	10
A	A	B	B	D	D	A	B	B	D

EXPLANATORY ANSWERS

1. Let the ages of A and B be $3x$ and $11x$ years; then

$$\frac{3x+3}{11x+3}=\frac{1}{3} \quad \Rightarrow \quad 9x + 9 = 11x + 3$$

$\Rightarrow 2x = 6 \quad \therefore \quad x = 3$

Hence, their present age, $3x = 3 \times 3 = 9$ years; $11x = 11 \times 3 = 33$ years

2. Let the present ages of Ram and Mohan are $7x$ and $5x$ years; then

$$\frac{7x-2}{5x-2}=\frac{3}{2} \quad \Rightarrow 14x - 4 = 15x - 6 \therefore x = 2$$

Hence, their present ages : $7 \times 2 = 14$ years and $5 \times 2 = 10$ years

3. Let the present ages of Samir and Saurabh are $8x$ and $15x$ years respectively; then

$$\frac{8x+9}{15x+9}=\frac{11}{18} \quad \Rightarrow \quad 144x + 162 = 165x + 99$$

$\Rightarrow 21x = 63 \quad \therefore \quad x = 3$

Hence, difference of their ages $= 15x - 8x = 7x$
$= 7 \times 3 = 21$ years

4. Let the present ages of father and his son be $x + 34$ and x years respectively; then
$18(x - 12) = x + 34 - 12$
$\Rightarrow 18x - 216 = x + 22$
$\Rightarrow 17x = 238 \quad \therefore x = 14$
Hence, present age of his son = 14 years

5. Let the present ages of mother and her daughter are $(x + 25)$ and x years respectively; then
$6(x - 5) = x + 25 - 5$
$\Rightarrow 6x - 30 = x + 20$
$\Rightarrow 5x = 50 \quad \therefore x = 10$
Hence, the age of the mother = 10 + 25 = 35 years

6. Let the present ages of P and Q be $(x + 4)$ and x years;
then, $\frac{x+4+5}{x+5} = \frac{9}{8} \Rightarrow 8x + 72 = 9x + 45 \quad \therefore x = 27$
Hence, present age of P = 27 + 4 = 31 years

7. Let the present ages of Divya and Namrata are $3x$ and $4x$ years respectively; then
$\frac{3x-10}{4x-10} = \frac{1}{2}$
$\Rightarrow 6x - 20 = 4x - 10$
$\Rightarrow 2x = 10 \quad \therefore x = 5$
Hence, sum of their ages = $3x + 4x = 7x$
$= 7 \times 5 = 35$ years

8. Let the present ages of A and B are $5x$ and $3x$ years respectively; then,
$\frac{5x-4}{3x+4} = 1 \Rightarrow 5x - 4 = 3x + 4$
$\Rightarrow 2x = 8 \quad \therefore x = 4$
Hence, their present ages are 20 years and 12 years.
So, required ratio = $(20 + 4) : (12 - 4)$
$= 24 : 8 = 3 : 1$

9. Let the present age of Ram be x years; then
$\frac{x}{x-8} = \frac{6}{5} \Rightarrow 5x = 6x - 48$
$\therefore x = 48$
Hence, present age of Ram's sister
= 48 – 10 = 38 years.

10. Let the age of father was x years at the time of his son's birth, then present age of father and his son will be $2x$ and x years,
Now, $2x = 38 \quad \therefore x = 19$ years
Hence, 5 years ago the age of son was
19 – 5 = 14 years

CHAIN RULE

1. A fort has provision for 50 days. After 15 days a reinforcement of 150 men arrives and the provision now lasts 25 days. How many men were there in the fort?
A. 300 B. 225
C. 275 D. 200

2. In a fort there is provisions for 40 days for 275 persons. If after 16 days 125 persons leave the fort for how many more days the provisions will last?
A. 35 days B. 44 days
C. 45 days D. 53 days

3. 60 men could complete a work in 250 days. They worked together for 200 days. After that the work had to be stopped for 10 days due to bad weather. How many more men should be engaged to complete the work in time?
A. 20 B. 18
C. 15 D. 10

4. A contractor undertook to complete a project in 90 days and employed 60 men on it. After 60 days, he found that $\frac{3}{4}$ of the work has already been completed. How many men can he discharge so that the project may completed exactly on time?
A. 15 B. 20
C. 30 D. 40

5. A flagstaff 17.5 m high casts a shadow of length 40.25 m. The height of the building, which casts a shadow of length 28.75m under similar condition will be:
A. 21.25 m B. 17.5 m
C. 12.5 m D. 10 m

6. If 5 men or 9 women can do a piece of work in 19 days, then 3 men and 6 women will do the same work in how many days?
A. 21 B. 18
C. 15 D. 12

7. A certain number of men can finish a piece of work in 100 days. If there were 10 men less, it will take 10 days more for the work to be finished. How many men were there originally?
A. 110 B. 100
C. 82 D. 75

8. Some persons can do a piece of work in 12 days. Two times the number of such persons will do half of that work in:

A. 12 days B. 3 days
C. 6 days D. 4 days

9. 2 men and 7 boys can do a piece of work in 14 days; 3 men and 8 boys can do the same in 11 days. Then 8 men and 6 boys can do three times of this work in
A. 30 days B. 4 days
C. 21 days D. 18 days

10. If 3 men or 6 boys, working 7 hours a day can do a piece of work in 10 days; how many days will it take to complete a piece of work twice as large with 6 men and 2 boys working together for 8 hours a day?
A. 9 B. $8\frac{1}{2}$
C. $7\frac{1}{2}$ D. $6\frac{1}{2}$

11. If 15 men can do a certain amount of work in 20 days working 8 hours a day, in how many days will 10 men do three times the work working 6 hours a day?
A. 120 days B. 70 days
C. 100 days D. None of these

12. 40 men consume 60 kgs of rice in 15 days, then in how many days will 30 men consume 12 kgs of rice?
A. 9 days B. $6\frac{1}{4}$ days
C. 4 days D. $3\frac{1}{4}$ days

13. 56 men can complete a piece of work in 24 days. In how many days can 42 men complete the same piece of work?
A. 48 B. 32
C. 20 D. 16

14. Running at the same constant rate, 6 identical machines can produce a total of 270 bottles per minute. At this rate, how many bottles could 10 such machines produce in 4 minutes?
A. 1400 B. 1600
C. 1800 D. 2000

15. 400 persons, working 9 hours a day complete $\frac{1}{4}th$ of the work in 10 days. The number of additional persons, working 8 hours a day, required to complete the remaining work in 20 days, is:
A. 275 B. 250
C. 675 D. 200

ANSWERS

1	2	3	4	5	6	7	8	9	10
B	B	C	B	C	C	A	B	C	C
11	**12**	**13**	**14**	**15**					
A	C	B	C	C					

EXPLANATORY ANSWERS

1. Days Men
35↑ x
25 $x + 150$↓

$$\Rightarrow \frac{x+150}{x} = \frac{35}{25} \quad \Rightarrow 1 + \frac{150}{x} = \frac{35}{25}$$

$$\Rightarrow \frac{150}{x} = \frac{10}{25}$$

$$\therefore x = \frac{25}{10} \times 150 = 375$$

Required number of men = 375 – 150 = 225

2. Persons Days
275↑ 24
150 x↓

$$\Rightarrow \frac{x}{24} = \frac{275}{150} \quad \therefore \quad x = \frac{275}{150} \times 24 = 44 \text{ days}$$

3. Days Men
50↑ 60
40 x↓

$$\Rightarrow \frac{x}{60} = \frac{50}{40} \quad \therefore \quad x = \frac{50}{40} \times 60 = 75 \text{ men}$$

Hence, number of additional men = 75 – 60
= 15

4. Work Days Men
$\frac{3}{4}$ 60 60
$\frac{1}{4}$↓ 30↑ x↓

$$\Rightarrow \frac{x}{60} = \frac{60}{30} \times \frac{1/4}{3/4}$$

$$\therefore \quad x = \frac{60}{30} \times \frac{1}{3} \times 60 = 40 \text{ days}$$

Hence, number of men to be discharged

$= 60 - 40 = 20$

5. Shadow (m) — Object (m)

40.25 ↓ — 17.5 ↓

28.75 — x

$$\Rightarrow \frac{x}{17.5} = \frac{28.75}{40.25}$$

$$\therefore x = \frac{28.75 \times 17.5}{40.25} = 12.5 \text{ m}$$

6. 5 men ≡ 9 women

$$\therefore \text{3 men} = \frac{9}{5} \times 3 = \frac{27}{5} \text{ women}$$

$$\text{Hence, 3 men and 6 women} = \frac{27}{5} + 6$$

$$= \frac{57}{5} \text{ women}$$

Women — Days

9 ↑ — 19 ↓

$\frac{57}{5}$ — x

$$\Rightarrow \frac{x}{19} = \frac{9 \times 5}{57}$$

$$\therefore x = \frac{9 \times 5}{57} \times 19$$

$= 15$ days

7. Days — Men

100 ↑ — x ↓

110 — $x - 10$

$$\Rightarrow \frac{x - 10}{x} = \frac{100}{110}$$

$\Rightarrow 110x - 1100 = 100x$

$\Rightarrow 10x = 1100 \quad \therefore x = 110$

Hence, initially the number of men = 110

8. Work — Persons — Days

1 ↓ — x ↑ — 12 ↓

$\frac{1}{2}$ — $2x$ — a

$$\Rightarrow \frac{a}{12} = \frac{x}{2x} \times \frac{1}{2} \quad \therefore a = \frac{1}{4} \times 12 = 3 \text{ days}$$

9. Here, 14×2 men + 14×7 boys ≡ 11×3 men + 11×8 boys

⇒ 28 men + 98 boys ≡ 33 men + 88 boys

⇒ 5 men = 10 boys

∴ 1 man = 2 boys

Then, 2 men and 7 boys ≡ 4 boys + 7 boys

= 11 boys

& also, 8 men and 6 boys ≡ 16 boys + 6 boys

= 22 boys

Work — Boys — Days

1 ↓ — 11 ↑ — 14 ↓

3 — 22 — x

$$\Rightarrow \frac{x}{14} = \frac{11}{22} \times \frac{3}{1}$$

$$\therefore x = \frac{1}{2} \times 3 \times 14$$

$= 21$ days

12. Men — Rice (kgs) — Days

40 ↑ — 60 ↓ — 15 ↓

30 — 12 — x

$$\Rightarrow \frac{x}{15} = \frac{12}{60} \times \frac{40}{30}$$

$$\therefore x = \frac{12}{60} \times \frac{40}{30} \times 15 = 4 \text{ days}$$

14. Machines — Time (minutes) — Bottles

6 ↓ — 1 ↓ — 270 ↓

10 — 4 — x

$$\Rightarrow \frac{x}{270} = \frac{4}{1} \times \frac{10}{6}$$

$$\therefore x = \frac{4 \times 10}{6} \times 270$$

$= 1800$ bottles

15. Work — Hours — Days — Persons

$\frac{1}{4}$ ↓ — 9 ↑ — 10 ↑ — 400 ↓

$\frac{3}{4}$ — 8 — 20 — x

$$\Rightarrow \frac{x}{400} = \frac{10}{20} \times \frac{9}{8} \times \frac{3/4}{1/4}$$

$$\therefore x = \frac{1}{2} \times \frac{9}{8} \times 3 \times 400 = 675$$

Hence, number of additional persons

$= 675 - 400 = 275$

TIME AND DISTANCE

1. Starting from a point at a speed of 4 km/hr a man reaches at a cerain place and returns back to the point from where he had started journey on bicycle at the speed of 16 km/hr. His average speed during the entire journey will be :
   A. 6.4 km/h B. 8.4 km/h
   C. 5.4 km/h D. 10 km/h
2. A motorist covers a certain distance at a average speed of 48 km/h in 45 minutes. What speed in km/h he must maintain to cover the same distance in 30 minutes?
   A. 66 km/h B. 79 km/h
   C. 80 km/h D. 72 km/h
3. A policeman saw a thief at a distance of 200 m. The policeman and the thief started running at the same time. If the policeman runs at a speed of $4\frac{1}{6}$ m per second and the thief at a speed of $3\frac{1}{3}$ m per second, after what time the policeman will catch the thief?
   A. 12 min B. 10 min
   C. 9 min D. 4 min
4. A monkey wants to climb up a glazed pole. He climbs 12 metres in 1 minute and then he slips back 3 metres in the next minute. If the pole is 63 metre high, how long does he take to climb at the top of the pole?
   A. $11\frac{1}{4}$ min B. $12\frac{1}{2}$ min
   C. $12\frac{3}{4}$ min D. $14\frac{3}{4}$ min
5. The distance between two stations A and B is 300 km. A train leaves the station A with a speed of 40 km/hr. At the same time another train departs from the station B with a speed of 50 km/hr. How much time will these two trains take to cross each other?
   A. 3 hrs 40 min B. 3 hrs 20 min
   C. 2 hrs 20 min D. 3 hrs 45 min
6. Nilesh goes to school from his village at the speed of 4 km/hr and returns from school to village at the speed of 2 km/hr. If he takes 6 hours in all, then what is the distance between the village and the school?
   A. 8 km B. 6 km
   C. 5 km D. 4 km
7. By increasing the speed of the bus by 10 km/hr the time of journey for 72 km is reduced by 36 minutes. What was the original speed of the bus?
   A. 30 km/hr B. 35 km/hr
   C. 40 km/hr D. 45 km/hr
8. A train covers a distance in 50 minutes, if it runs at a speed of 48 km/hr on an average. The speed at which the train must run to reduce the time of journey to 40 minutes will be:
   A. 70 km/hr B. 60 km/hr
   C. 55 km/hr D. 50 km/hr
9. A certain distance is covered by a vehicle at a certain speed. If half of this distance is covered by another vehicle in double the time, the ratio of the speeds of the two vehicles is:
   A. 4 : 1 B. 1 : 4
   C. 2 : 1 D. 1 : 2
10. A is faster than B. A and B each walk 24 km. The sum of their speeds is 7 km/hr and sum of times taken by them is 14 hours. What is the speed of A?
    A. 7 km/hr B. 5 km/hr
    C. 4 km/hr D. 3 km/hr

ANSWERS

1	2	3	4	5	6	7	8	9	10
A	D	D	C	B	A	A	B	A	C

EXPLANATORY ANSWERS

1. Average speed during the entire journey

$$= \frac{2xy}{x+y} = \frac{2 \times 4 \times 16}{4+16} = \frac{8 \times 16}{20} = 6.4 \text{ km/hr.}$$

2. Let required speed be x km/hr; then

$$x \times \frac{1}{2} = 48 \times \frac{3}{4} \quad \therefore \quad x = 48 \times \frac{3}{4} \times 2$$

$$= 72 \text{ km/hr}$$

3. Suppose the policeman will catch the thief after t seconds

then, $\left(\frac{25}{6}-\frac{10}{3}\right)t = 200 \Rightarrow \frac{5}{6}t = 200$

$\therefore t = \frac{200 \times 6}{5} = 240$ sec = 4 min.

4. The monkey climbs 12 metres in 1 minute and then he slips back 3 metres in the next minute

$\therefore$ The monkey climbs in the first 2 minutes $= 12 - 3 = 9$ metres

$\therefore$ In the first 12 minutes the monkey climbs $= 9 \times 6 = 54$ metres

Remaining height of the pole to be covered by the monkey $= 63 - 54 = 9$ metre

$\therefore$ The monkey will climb the height of 9 metres in the 13th minute

$\because$ The monkey climbs 12 metres in 1 minute

$\therefore$ The monkey will climb 9 metres in $\frac{1}{12} \times 9$

$= \frac{3}{4}$ minute

$\therefore$ Time spent in climbing at the top of the pole

$= \left(12 + \frac{3}{4}\right)$ minutes $= 12\frac{3}{4}$ minutes

5. The two trains are moving in the opposite directions

$\therefore$ Relative speed $= 40 + 50 = 90$ km/hr.

$\therefore$ Time taken to cross each other $= \frac{300}{90} = 3\frac{1}{3}$ hours

or, 3 hours 20 minutes.

6. Let x km be the distance between village and the school; then

$\frac{x}{4} + \frac{x}{2} = 6 \quad \Rightarrow \frac{3x}{4} = 6$

$\therefore x = \frac{6 \times 4}{3} = 8$ km

8. Let x km/hr be the required speed of the train; then

$x \times \frac{40}{60} = 48 \times \frac{50}{60}$

$\therefore x = \frac{48 \times 50}{40} = 60$ km/hr

9. Let x km/hr and t hr be the certain speed and certain time.

Then, ratio of their speeds $= \frac{x}{t} : \frac{x}{2 \times 2t} = 1 : \frac{1}{4} = 4 : 1$

10. Let speeds of A and B are x_1 and x_2 km/hr and times taken by them are t_1 and t_2 hrs, then

$x_1 + x_2 = 7$ km/hr ...(i)

$t_1 + t_2 = 14$ hrs ...(ii)

Now, $\frac{24}{x_1} + \frac{24}{x_2} = 14 \Rightarrow \frac{24(x_1 + x_2)}{x_1 x_2} = 14$

$\therefore x_1 x_2 = \frac{24 \times 7}{14} = 12$

Then, $x_1 - x_2 = \sqrt{(x_1 + x_2)^2 - 4x_1 x_2}$

$= \sqrt{(7)^2 - 4 \times 12} = 1$ ...(iii)

Solving *(i)* and *(iii)* we get $x_1 = 4$ km/hr

TIME AND WORK

1. A and B working together complete a work in 35 days. If A takes 60 days to complete it, how long would B alone take to complete it?

A. 64 days B. 72 days
C. 81 days D. 84 days

2. A few children working together can do a piece of work in 18 days. If the number of children employed on the work is made double, how long would they take to complete half of the work?

A. $4\frac{1}{2}$ days B. $2\frac{1}{3}$ days
C. $8\frac{3}{4}$ days D. $6\frac{1}{2}$ days

3. 10 men or 18 boys can do a piece of work in 15 days. In how many days would 25 men and 15 boys complete the same work working together?

A. $5\frac{1}{2}$ days B. $4\frac{1}{2}$ days
C. $6\frac{2}{3}$ days D. $2\frac{1}{3}$ days

4. A cistern is filled by a tap in $3\frac{1}{2}$ hours. Due to a leak in the bottom of the cistern, it takes half an hour longer to fill the cistern. If the cistern is full, how long will it take the leak to empty it?

A. 28 hours B. 29 hours
C. $31\frac{1}{3}$ hours D. 38 hours

5. A is twice as good a workman as B and thrice as good a workman as C. If C alone can do a piece of work in 24 days, how long would the three persons take to finish the work working together?

A. $3\frac{3}{11}$ days B. $4\frac{4}{7}$ days

C. $4\frac{4}{11}$ days D. $3\frac{4}{11}$ days

6. If 3 men and 5 women can do a piece of work in 8 days and 2 men and 7 boys can do the same work in 12 days. Find the number of boys, the work done by whom can equate the work done by 10 women.

A. 19 boys B. 21 boys
C. 23 boys D. 15 boys

7. 8 men alone can complete a piece of work in 12 days. 4 women alone can complete the same piece of work in 48 days and 10 children alone can complete the piece of work in 24 days. In how many days can 10 men, 4 women and 10 children together complete the piece of work?

A. 6 B. 8
C. 10 D. 15

8. A works twice as fast as B. If B can complete a piece of work independently in 12 days. Find in how many days A and B together can complete the work?

A. 8 days B. 6 days
C. 4 days D. 18 days

9. A contractor undertook to complete a project in 90 days and employed 60 men on it. After 60 days, he found that $\frac{3}{4}$ of the work has already been completed. How many men can he discharge so that the project may be completed exactly on time?

A. 15 B. 20
C. 30 D. 40

10. A can do a piece of work in 25 days and B can do it in 20 days. They work together for 5 days and then A goes away. In how many days will B finish the remaining work?

A. 33 days B. 20 days
C. 11 days D. 10 days

ANSWERS

1	2	3	4	5	6	7	8	9	10
D	A	B	A	C	B	A	C	B	C

EXPLANATORY ANSWERS

1. (A + B)'s 1 day's work = $\frac{1}{35}$

and also, A's 1 day's work = $\frac{1}{60}$

Hence, B's 1 day's work = $\frac{1}{35}-\frac{1}{60}=\frac{5}{420}=\frac{1}{84}$

So, B will do the whole work in 84 days.

3. 10 men ≡ 18 boys

25 men ≡ $\frac{18}{10}\times 25 = 45$ boys

Hence, 25 men + 15 boys = 45 + 15 = 60 boys

Now, 18 boys can do a piece of work in 15 days.

Hence, 60 boys will do a piece of work in $\frac{15\times 18}{60}=\frac{9}{2}$ days = $4\frac{1}{2}$ days.

4. In 1 hour $\frac{2}{7}$ cistern is filled by the tap.

Hence, in $\frac{1}{2}$ hour $\frac{2}{14}=\frac{1}{7}$ cistern is filled by the tap.

So, $\frac{1}{7}$ cistern is emptied by the leakage in 4 hours.

So, 1 cistern will be emptied by the leakage in 28 hours.

6. Here, (3 men + 5 women) × 8
≡ (2 men + 7 boys) × 12

⇒ 40 women ≡ 84 boys

∴ 10 women ≡ $\frac{84}{40}\times 10$ = 21 boys

Hence, work done by 10 women
= work done of 21 boys.

7. B's 1 day's work = $\frac{1}{4}-\frac{1}{12}=\frac{2}{12}=\frac{1}{6}$

Hence, B alone will complete the work in 6 days.

8. Ratio of efficiency of A and B = 2 : 1

Then, ratio of their time taking = 1 : 2

Hence, if B can complete the work in 12 days, then A in 6 days.

Now, (A + B)'s 1 day's work = $\frac{1}{6}+\frac{1}{12}=\frac{3}{12}=\frac{1}{4}$

So, A and B together can complete the work in 4 days.

9. After 60 days remaining work = $1-\frac{3}{4}=\frac{1}{4}$

In 60 days $\frac{3}{4}$ work has been done by 60 men

In 30 days $\frac{1}{4}$ work will be done by $60\times\frac{4}{3}\times\frac{1}{4}\times\frac{60}{30}$

= 40 men.

Hence, required number of men = 60 – 40 = 20 (which are to be discharged).

BOATS AND STREAMS

1. A boat goes 6 km upstream and back to the starting point in 2 hours. If the current of the stream runs at the rate of 4 km/hr, find the speed of the boat in still water.

A. 6 km/hr B. 8 km/hr
C. 10 km/hr D. 12 km/hr

2. A boat covers 24 km upstream and 36 km downstream in 6 hours, while it covers 36 km upstream and 24 km downstream in 6½ horus. Find the speed of the current.

A. 2 km/hr B. 4 km/hr
C. 6 km/hr D. 8 km/hr

3. A man can row 5 km/hr in still water and the speed of the stream is 1.5 km/hr. He takes an hour when he travels upstream to a place and back again to the starting point. How far is the place from the starting point?

A. 2.275 km B. 3.5 km
C. 1.5 km D. None of these

4. The speed of a boat in still water is 6 km/hr and the speed of the stream is 1.5 km/hr. A man rows to a place at a distance of 22.5 km and comes back to the starting point. Find the total time taken by him.

A. 8 hours B. 10 hours
C. 12 hours D. 4 hours

5. A boat covers 20 km downstream and 6 km upstream in 3 hours, while it covers 30 km downstream and 12 km upstream in 5 hours. What is the speed of boat in still water?

A. 6 km/hr B. 8 km/hr
C. 10 km/hr D. 12 km/hr.

6. Samir can travel 12 miles downstream in a certain river in 6 hours less than it takes him to travel the same distance upstream. But when he could double his rowing rate for his 24-mile round trip, the downstream 12 miles would then take only one hour less than the upstream 12 miles. Find the speed of the current in miles/hour.

A. $2\frac{2}{3}$ B. $2\frac{1}{3}$
C. $1\frac{2}{3}$ D. $1\frac{1}{3}$

7. A boat takes 6 hours to travel from place M to N downstream and back from N to M upstream. If the speed of the boat in still water is 4 km/hr; what is the distance between two places?

A. 6 kms B. 8 kms
C. 12 kms D. Data inadequate

8. A man can row upstream at 8 km/hr and downstream at 13 km/hr. The speed of the stream is:

A. 2.5 km/hr B. 4.2 km/hr
C. 5 km/hr D. 10.5 km/hr

9. A man's speed with the current is 15 km/hr and the speed of the current is 2.5 km/hr. The man's speed against the current is:

A. 12.5 km/hr B. 10 km/hr
C. 9 km/hr D. 8.5 km/hr

10. A motorboat, whose speed is 15 km/hr in still water goes 30 km downstream and comes back in a total of 4 hours 30 minutes. What is the speed of the stream (in km/hr)?

A. 10 B. 6
C. 5 D. 4

ANSWERS

1	2	3	4	5	6	7	8	9	10
B	A	A	A	B	B	D	A	B	C

EXPLANATORY ANSWERS

1. Let the speed of a boat in still water = x km/hr; then

$$\frac{6}{x-4}+\frac{6}{x+4}=2 \Rightarrow \frac{2x}{x^2-16}=\frac{1}{3}$$

$\Rightarrow x^2 - 6x - 16 = 0$

$\Rightarrow (x - 8)(x + 2) = 0$

Hence, the speed of the boat = 8 km/hr.

2. Let x km/hr and y km/hr be the speeds of the boat in still water and the speed of the current respectively, then

$$\frac{24}{x-y}+\frac{36}{x+y}=6 \Rightarrow \frac{4}{x-y}+\frac{6}{x+y}=1 \quad ...(i)$$

And, $\frac{36}{x-y}+\frac{24}{x+y}=\frac{13}{2}$ ...(ii)

Solving these two equations, we get

$x + y = 12;\ x - y = 8$

Hence, $y=\frac{1}{2}(12-8)=2$ km/hr.

3. Let required distance be x km, then

$$\frac{x}{5-1.5}+\frac{x}{5+1.5}=1 \Rightarrow \frac{x\times 2}{7}+\frac{x\times 2}{13}=1$$

$\Rightarrow 40x = 91 \quad \therefore x = 91/40 = 2.275$ km

4. Required time period $=\frac{22.5}{6+1.5}+\frac{22.5}{6-1.5}$

$=\frac{45}{15}+\frac{45}{9}=8$ hours.

5. Let x km/hr and y km/hr be the speed of boat in still water and speed of current respectively; then

$$\frac{20}{x+y}+\frac{6}{x-y}=3 \quad ...(i)$$

and also, $\frac{30}{x+y}+\frac{12}{x-y}=5$

$$\Rightarrow \frac{15}{x+y}+\frac{6}{x-y}=\frac{5}{2} \quad ...(ii)$$

Solving equations *(i)* & *(ii)*, we get $x + y = 10$ and $x - y = 6$

Since, $x=\frac{1}{2}(10+6)=8$ km/hr.

6. Let x km/hr and y km/hr be the speed of rowing in still water and speed of the current respectively; then

$$\frac{12}{x-y}-\frac{12}{x+y}=6 \Rightarrow \frac{24y}{x^2-y^2}=6$$

$\Rightarrow x^2 = y^2 + 4y$ ...(i)

Again, $\frac{12}{2x-y}-\frac{12}{2x+y}=1$

$$\Rightarrow \frac{24y}{4x^2-y^2}=1 \Rightarrow x^2=\frac{y^2+24y}{4} \quad ...(ii)$$

From equations (i) and (ii), we get

$$y^2+4y=\frac{y^2+24y}{4} \Rightarrow 3y^2=8y$$

$\therefore\ y=\frac{8}{3}=2\frac{1}{3}$ miles/hr.

8. The speed of the stream $=\frac{1}{2}(13-8)=\frac{5}{2}$

$= 2.5$ km/hr.

9. The man's speed in still water

$= 15 - 2.5 = 12.5$ km/hr

Hence, the men's speed against the current

$= 12.5 - 2.5 = 10$ km/hr

10. Let speed of the stream be x km/hr, then

$$\frac{30}{15+x}+\frac{30}{15-x}=4\frac{1}{2} \Rightarrow \frac{30\times 30}{225-x^2}=\frac{9}{2}$$

$\Rightarrow \frac{200}{225-x^2}=1 \Rightarrow x^2 = 225 - 200$

$\Rightarrow x^2 = 25 \quad \therefore x = 5$ km/hr.

ALLIGATION OR MIXTURE

1. A shopkeeper buys 26 kgs of milk @ Rs. 16 per kg. He also buys from another source an inferior quality of milk @ Rs. 10 per kg. How much quantity of the latter should he buy to mix it with the former so that he can sell the mixture @ Rs. 14 per kg without making any loss?

A. 13 kgs B. 12 kgs
C. 14 kgs D. 16 kgs

2. Two vessels A and B contain mixture of milk and water in the ratio 4 : 1 and 9 : 11 respectively. They are mixed in the ratio of 3 : 2. Find the ratio of milk : water in the resulting mixture.

A. 34 : 16 B. 33 : 17
C. 16 : 34 D. 17 : 33

3. A shopkeeper has 50 kgs of rice. He sells a part of it at 20% profit and the rest at 40% profit. If he gains 25% on the whole, find the quantity of each part.

A. 12.5 kgs and 37.5 kgs
B. 37.5 kgs and 12.5 kgs
C. 23.5 kgs and 21.5 kgs
D. 21.5 kgs and 23.5 kgs

4. A man bought a certain quantity of sugar for Rs. 8000. He sells one-fourth of it at 20% loss. At what per cent profit should he sell the remainder stock so as to make an overall profit of 20%?

A. 20% B. 30%
C. 35% D. 40%

5. Rs. 675 was divided among 75 boys and girls. Each boy gets Rs. 20 whereas a girl gets Rs. 5. Find the number of boys and girls.

A. 20, 55 B. 15, 60
C. 25, 50 D. 30, 45

6. A vessel contains mixture of liquids A and B in the ratio 3 : 2. When 20 litres of the mixture is taken out and replaced by 20 litres of liquid B, the ratio changes to 1 : 4. How many litres of liquid A was there initially present in the vessel?

A. 12 litres B. 18 litres
C. 24 litres D. 22 litres

7. A container is full of milk. One-third of milk is taken out of it and replaced by same quantity of water. Then again one-third of the mixture is taken out of it and replaced by the same quantity of water. The process is repeated 4 times. If 16 litres of milk is left in the container at the end of 4th operation, find the capacity of the container.

A. 76 litres B. 81 litres
C. 82 litres D. 85 litres

8. The cost of type-I rice is Rs. 15 per kg and type-II is Rs. 20 per kg. If both type I and type II are mixed in the ratio of 2 : 3, then find the price per kg of the mixed variety.

A. Rs. 19.50 B. Rs. 19
C. Rs. 18.50 D. Rs. 18

9. In what ratio must a grocer mix two varieties of tea worth Rs. 60 a kg and Rs. 65 a kg so that by selling the mixture at Rs. 68.20 a kg he may gain 10%?

A. 4 : 5 B. 3 : 5
C. 3 : 4 D. 3 : 2

10. A vessel contains 80 litres of milk. 16 litres of milk was taken out of the vessel and replaced by water. Then 16 litres of mixture was withdrawn and again replaced by water. The operation was repeated for third time. How much milk is now left in the vessel?

A. 96.40 litres
B. 50.36 litres
C. 40.96 litres
D. 32.76 litres

ANSWERS

1	2	3	4	5	6	7	8	9	10
A	B	B	B	A	B	B	D	D	C

EXPLANATORY ANSWERS

1.

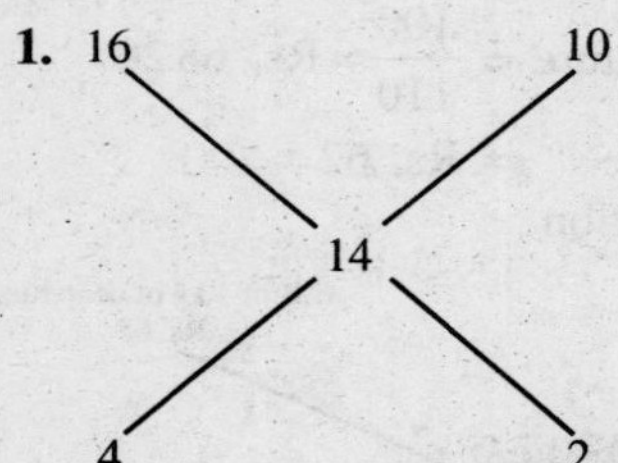

or 2 : 1 $\dfrac{\text{Quantity of milk @ Rs.10 per kg}}{\text{Quantity of milk @ Rs. 16 per kg}} = \dfrac{1}{2}$

So, quantity of milk @ Rs. 10 per kg. $= \dfrac{26}{2} = 13$ kgs.

2. Fraction is *Milk* *Water*

A: $\dfrac{4}{5}$ $\dfrac{1}{5}$

B: $\dfrac{9}{20}$ $\dfrac{11}{20}$

(3A + 2B) = A and B : $\left(\dfrac{12}{5}+\dfrac{9}{10}\right)$ $\left(\dfrac{3}{5}+\dfrac{11}{10}\right)$

$\dfrac{33}{10}$ $\dfrac{17}{10}$

So, Ratio of milk : water in the resulting mixture = 33 : 17.

3.

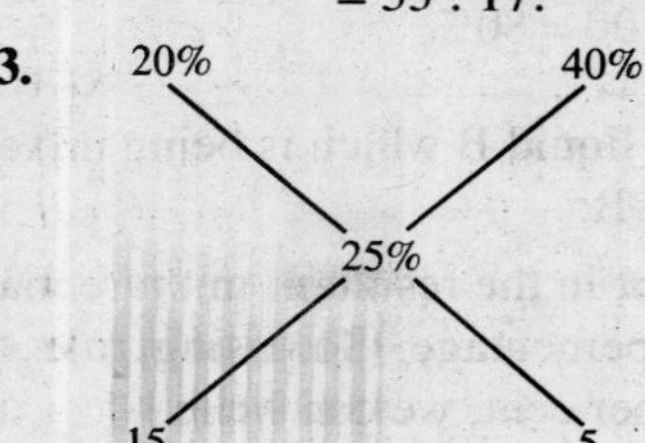

or 3 : 1

Quantity sold at 20% profit = $\frac{3}{3+1} \times 50$

= 37.5 kgs.

Quantity sold at 40% profit = (50 – 37.5)

= 12.5 kgs.

4. Let the remainder stock be sold at x% profit.

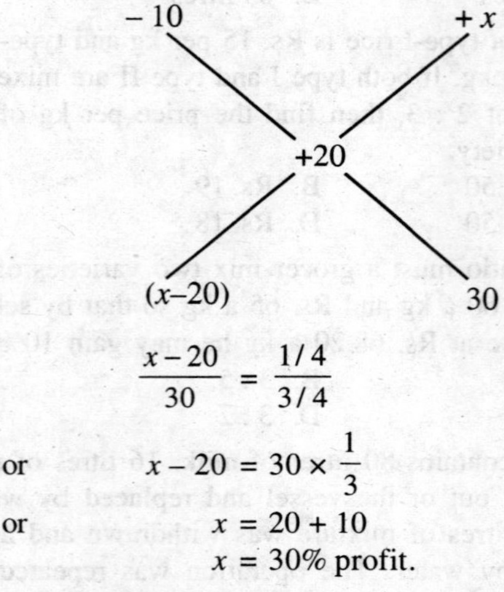

$$\frac{x-20}{30} = \frac{1/4}{3/4}$$

or $x - 20 = 30 \times \frac{1}{3}$

or $x = 20 + 10$

$x = 30\%$ profit.

5. Average money per head (boy or girl)

$$= \text{Rs. } \frac{675}{75} = \text{Rs. } 9$$

(Boys) Rs. 20 (Girls) Rs. 5

(Average) Rs. 9

4 11

Number of boys = $\frac{4}{4+11} \times 75 = 20$

Number of girls = $\frac{11}{4+11} \times 75 = 55.$

6. % of liquid B initially present in the vessel

$$= \frac{2}{3+2} \times 100 = 40\%$$

% of liquid B finally present in the vessel

$$= \frac{4}{1+4} \times 100 = 80\%$$

The second solution is liquid B which is being mixed and it has 100% liquid B.

80% of liquid B present in the resultant mixture may be taken as average percentage. So, using rule of alligation on liquid B per cent, we can write,

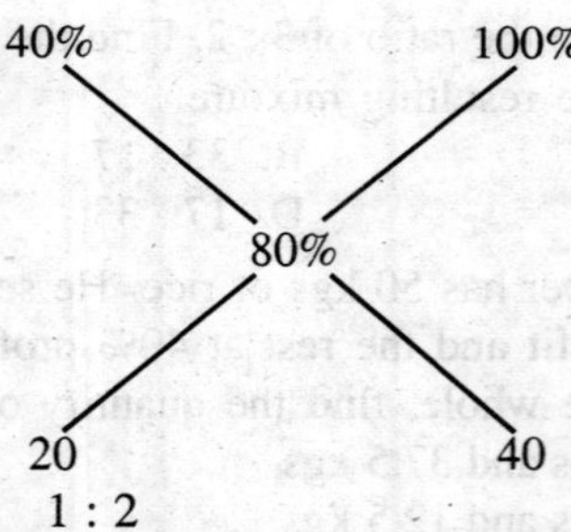

or 1 : 2

The ratio of liquid left in the vessel to liquid B being mixed = 1 : 2

Since the quantity of liquid B being mixed is 20 litres, the quantity of liquid left in the vessel is 10 litres. Therefore, the total quantity of liquid initially present in the vessel

= 10 + 20 = 30 litres

Quantity of liquid A = $\frac{3}{2+3} \times 30 = 18$ litres.

7. Let capacity of the container be x litre; then

$$x(1 - 1/3)^4 = 16 \Rightarrow x\left(\frac{2}{3}\right)^4 = 16$$

$$\Rightarrow x \times \frac{16}{81} = 16 \quad \therefore \quad x = 81 \text{ litres}$$

8. Let the price per kg of mixed variety be Rs. x; then By the rule of alligation,

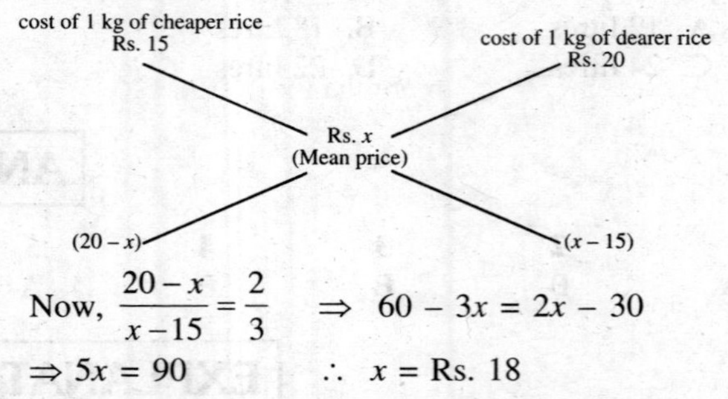

Now, $\frac{20-x}{x-15} = \frac{2}{3} \Rightarrow 60 - 3x = 2x - 30$

$\Rightarrow 5x = 90 \quad \therefore \quad x = \text{Rs. } 18$

9. S.P. of 1 kg mixture = Rs. 68.20, Gain % = 10%

Hence, C.P. of 1 kg mixture = $\frac{100}{110} \times$ Rs. 68.20

= Rs. 62

By the rule of alligation

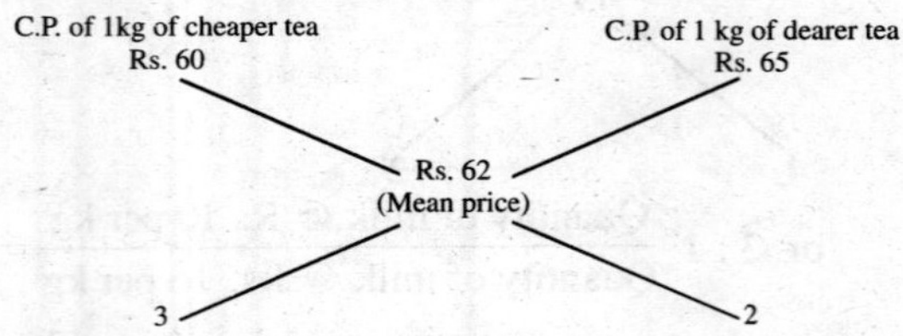

Hence, required ratio = 3 : 2

10. Amount of milk left = $80\left(1 - \frac{16}{80}\right)^3 = 80\left(\frac{4}{5}\right)^3$

$$80 \times \frac{64}{125} = 40.96 \text{ litres.}$$

PERCENTAGE

1. A student who secures 20% marks in an examination fails by 30 marks. Another student who secures 32% gets 42 marks more than those required to pass. The percentage of marks required to pass is:
A. 20 B. 25
C. 28 D. 30

2. In a college election, a candidate secured 62% of the votes and is elected by a majority of 144 votes. The total number of votes polled is:
A. 600 B. 800
C. 925 D. 1200

3. In an organisation, 40% of the employees are matriculates, 50% of the remaining are graduates and the remaining 180 are postgraduates. How many employees are graduates?
A. 360 B. 240
C. 300 D. 180

4. The population of a village is 4500. $\frac{5}{9}$th of them are males and rest females. If 40% of the males are married, then the percentage of married female is :
A. 35 B. 40
C. 50 D. 60

5. A's income is 10% more than B's. How much per cent is B's income is less than A's?
A. 10% B. 7%
C. $9\frac{1}{11}\%$ D. $6\frac{1}{2}\%$

6. If the price of a television set is increased by 25%, then by what percentage should the new price be reduced to bring the price back to original level?
A. 15% B. 20%
C. 25% D. 30%

7. In an election one of the two candidates gets 40% votes and loses by 100 votes. Total number of votes is :
A. 500 B. 400
C. 600 D. 1000

8. The gross income of a person is Rs. 20000. 10% of his income is exempted from income tax and his net income is Rs. 19100. The rate of income tax is :
A. 3% B. 2%
C. 4% D. 5%

9. The owner of a cell phone shop charges his customer 32% more than the cost price. If a customer paid Rs. 6600 for the cell phone, then what was the cost price of the cell phone?
A. Rs. 5000 B. Rs. 5500
C. Rs. 5800 D. Rs. 6100

10. If the cost of pins reduced by Rs. 4 per dozen, 12 more pins can be purchased for Rs. 48. The cost of pins per dozen after reduction is:
A. Rs. 8 B. Rs. 12
C. Rs. 16 D. Rs. 20

11. In an examination 80% of the students passed in Mathematics and 70% passed in English, while 10% students failed in both the subjects. If 360 students passed in both the subjects, find the total number of students who appeared in the examination.
A. 400 B. 600
C. 630 D. 640

12. Electric tax is increased by 20% and its consumption is decreased by 20%. The change in the expenditure is:
A. 4% decrease B. 4% increase
C. 5% decrease D. 5% increase

13. The selling price of certain commodity was reduced by 25%. As a result of it, the sales increased by 30%. What was the effect of it on cash collected by daily sales?
A. 2.5% decrease B. 2.5% increase
C. 5% decrease D. 5% increase

14. The wheat sold by a grocer contained 10% low quality wheat. What quantity of good quality wheat should be added to 150 kgs of wheat so that the percentage of low quality wheat becomes 5%?
A. 50 kgs B. 85 kgs
C. 135 kgs D. 150 kgs

15. Nilam spends 15% of her monthly income on household expenses. She spends 17% of the monthly income in travelling and 6% on medical expenses and saves the rest Rs. 15,500. What is her monthly income?
A. Rs. 20,000 B. Rs. 25,000
C. Rs. 30,000 D. Rs. 35,000

ANSWERS

1	2	3	4	5	6	7	8	9	10
B	A	D	C	C	B	A	D	A	B
11	**12**	**13**	**14**	**15**					
B	A	A	D	B					

EXPLANATORY ANSWERS

1. 20% of $x + 30 = 32\%$ of $x - 42$

$\Rightarrow$ 12% of $x = 72$

$\Rightarrow$ $x = \dfrac{72 \times 100}{12} = 600$

Pass Mark $= 20\%$ of $600 + 30 = 150$

Pass percentage $= \left(\dfrac{150}{600} \times 100\right)\% = 25\%$

2. $(62\%$ of $x - 38\%$ of $x) = 144$

$\Rightarrow 24\%$ of $x = 144 \quad \Rightarrow \quad x = \dfrac{144 \times 100}{24} = 600$

3. Matriculates $= \dfrac{40}{100}x = \dfrac{2x}{5}$

Remaining $= \left(x - \dfrac{2x}{5}\right) = \dfrac{3x}{5}$

Graduates $= \dfrac{50}{100} \times \dfrac{3x}{5} = \dfrac{3x}{10}$

Remaining $= \dfrac{3x}{5} - \dfrac{3x}{10} = \dfrac{3x}{10}$

Now, $\dfrac{3x}{10} = 180 \quad \therefore x = \dfrac{10 \times 180}{3} = 600$

$\therefore$ Graduates $= \dfrac{3 \times 600}{10} = 180.$

4. Males $= \left(\dfrac{5}{9} \times 4500\right) = 2500$

Females $= 2000$

$\therefore$ Married males $= \dfrac{40}{100} \times 2500 = 1000$

and married females $= 1000$

$\therefore$ Percentage of married females

$= \left(\dfrac{1000}{2000} \times 100\right)\% = 50\%.$

5. Required percentage $= \left[\dfrac{10}{(100+10)} \times 100\right]\% = 9\dfrac{1}{11}\%.$

6. Required reduction $= \dfrac{25}{100+25} \times 100 = 20\%.$

7. Out of 100, difference in votes $= (60 - 40) = 20$

20% of $x = 100$

$\therefore x = \dfrac{100 \times 100}{20} = 500.$

8. Gross income = Rs. 20000

Income exempted from income tax = 10% of gross income

$\therefore$ Income on which income tax is chargeable $= (100 - 10\%) = 90\%$ of gross income

$= 20000 \times \dfrac{90}{100} =$ Rs. 18000

$\therefore$ Total income tax paid on

= Rs. 20000 – Rs. 19100 = Rs. 900

$\therefore$ Rate per cent of income tax $= \dfrac{900}{18000} \times 100 = 5\%$

9. Let cost price of the cell phone be Rs. x; then

$x + \dfrac{32}{100} \times x = 6600 \quad \Rightarrow \quad \dfrac{132x}{100} = 6600$

$\therefore x = \dfrac{100 \times 6600}{132} =$ Rs. 5000.

10. Let reduced price by Rs. x per dozen, then

$\dfrac{48}{x} - \dfrac{48}{x+4} = 1 \quad \Rightarrow \quad \dfrac{48 \times 4}{x^2 + 4x} = 1$

$\Rightarrow \quad x^2 + 4x - 192 = 0$

$\Rightarrow (x + 16)(x - 12) = 0$

$\therefore \quad x =$ Rs. 12.

11. Here, percentage of students failed in Mathematics and English be 30% and 20% respectively.

Percentage of students failed either one or both subjects

$= 30 + 20 - 10 = 40\%$

Hence, percentage of pass students $= 100 - 40 = 60\%$

Now, $60\% = 360$

$\therefore 100\% = \dfrac{360}{60} \times 100 = 600.$

12. Let initially electric tax is Rs. 100 and consumption = 100 units

Decrease in consumption

$= 100 \times 100 - 120 \times 80 =$ Rs. 400

Hence, decrease percentage $= \dfrac{400 \times 100}{100 \times 100} = 4\%.$

13. Let the selling price of a commodity be Rs. 100 and number of sales = 100 units

Decrease in daily cash $= 100 \times 100 - 75 \times 130$

= Rs. 250

Hence, decrease percentage $= \dfrac{250 \times 100}{100 \times 100} = 2.5\%.$

14. Let x kg of good wheat be added; then

$\dfrac{10}{100} \times 150 = \dfrac{5}{100}(150 + x)$

$\Rightarrow 150 + x = 300 \quad \therefore \quad x = 150$ kg.

15. Let her monthly income be Rs. x; then

$x - \left(\dfrac{15}{100} \times x + \dfrac{17}{100} \times x + \dfrac{6}{100} \times x\right) = 15{,}500$

$\Rightarrow x - \dfrac{38x}{100} = 15500 \quad \Rightarrow \quad \dfrac{62x}{100} = 15500$

$\therefore \quad x = \dfrac{15500 \times 100}{62} =$ Rs. 25000.

PROFIT AND LOSS

1. Ashok bought 25 kg of rice at the rate of Rs. 6 per kg and 35 kg of rice at the rate of Rs. 7 per kg. He mixed the two and sold the mixture at the rate of Rs. 6.75 per kg. What was his gain or loss in the transaction?

A. Rs. 16 gain B. Rs. 16 loss
C. Rs. 10 gain D. None of these

2. Profit after selling a commodity for Rs. 425 is same as loss after selling it for Rs. 355. The cost of the commodity is :

A. Rs. 285 B. Rs. 390
C. Rs. 295 D. Rs. 400

3. Ram bought 4 dozen apples at Rs. 12 per dozen and 2 dozen at Rs. 16 per dozen. He sold all of them to earn 20%. At what price per dozen did he sell the apples?

A. Rs. 14.40 B. Rs. 16.00
C. Rs. 16.80 D. Rs. 16.20

4. At what price must Kantilal sell a mixture of 80 kg sugar at Rs. 6.75 per kg with 120 kg at Rs. 8 per kg to gain 20%?

A. Rs. 7.50 per kg B. Rs. 8.20 per kg
C. Rs. 8.35 per kg D. Rs. 9 per kg

5. A person bought an article and sold it at a loss of 10%. If he had bought it for 20% less and sold it for Rs. 55 more, he would have had a profit of 40%. The C.P. of the article is :

A. Rs. 200 B. Rs. 225
C. Rs. 250 D. None of these

6. A dealer sold a machine to a shopkeeper at 20% profit. The shopkeeper sold the machine to a customer so as to get 25% profit for himself. The difference between the selling price of the dealer and that of the shopkeeper was found to be Rs. 129. What is the initial price of the machine?

A. Rs. 410 B. Rs. 420
C. Rs. 430 D. Rs. 440

7. A man bought a horse and cart. If he sold the horse at 10% loss and the cart at 20% gain he would not loss anything. If he sold the horse at 5% loss and the cart at 5% gain he would lose Rs. 10 in the bargain. What did he pay for each?

A. Rs. 400, Rs. 200 B. Rs. 300, Rs. 300
C. Rs. 250, Rs. 350 D. Rs. 350, Rs. 250

8. The marked price of a radio is 20% more than its cost price. If a discount of 10% is given on the marked price, the gain percentage is:

A. 8 B. 10
C. 12 D 15

9. A dishonest dealer sells his goods at the cost price and still earns a profit of 60% by underweight. What weight does he use for a kg?

A. 625 gms B. 750 gms
C. 800 gms D. 850 gms

10. A man sells two horses for Rs. 990 each. On one he gains 10% and the other he loses 10%. What is his total percentage of gain or loss in the transaction?

A. 1% gain B. 1% loss
C. 2% gain D. 2% loss

ANSWERS

1	2	3	4	5	6	7	8	9	10
C	B	B	D	C	C	A	A	A	B

EXPLANATORY ANSWERS

1. C.P. of 60 kg mixture = Rs. $(25 \times 6 + 35 \times 7)$
= Rs. 395

S.P. of 60 kg mixtire = Rs. (60×6.75)
= Rs. 405

$\therefore$ Gain = Rs. $(405 - 395)$
= Rs. 10

2. Let C.P. = Rs. x

Then, $425 - x = x - 355 \Rightarrow 2x = 780$

$\therefore$ $x =$ Rs. 390

3. C.P. of 6 dozen apples = Rs. $(12 \times 4 + 16 \times 2)$
= Rs. 80

$\therefore$ S.P. = Rs. $\left(\frac{120}{100} \times 80\right)$
= Rs. 96

$\therefore$ S.P. per dozen = Rs. $\left(\frac{96}{6}\right)$ = Rs. 16

4. C.P. of 1 kg sugar $= \frac{80 \times 6.75 + 120 \times 8}{200}$

$= \text{Rs. } 7.50$

$\therefore$ S.P. of 1 kg = Rs. $\left(\frac{120}{100} \times 7.50\right)$

$= \text{Rs. } 9$ per kg

5. Let, C.P. = Rs. x,

then, S.P. $= \frac{90}{100} \times x = \text{Rs. } \frac{9x}{10}$

Now, when C.P. = Rs. $\frac{80x}{100} = \text{Rs. } \frac{4x}{5}$;

then, S.P. $= \frac{140}{100} \times \frac{4x}{5} = \text{Rs. } \frac{28x}{25}$

But, $\frac{28x}{25} - \frac{9x}{10} = 55 \Rightarrow \frac{11x}{50} = 55$

$\therefore$ $x = \text{Rs. } 250$

6. Let the initial price = Rs. x; then C.P. for dealer

$= \frac{120}{100} \times x = \text{Rs. } \frac{6x}{5}$

Again, C.P. for shopkeeper $= \frac{125}{100} \times \frac{6x}{5}$

$= \text{Rs. } \frac{3x}{2}$

Now, $\frac{3x}{2} - \frac{6x}{5} = 129 \Rightarrow \frac{3x}{10} = 129$

$\therefore\ x = \frac{10 \times 129}{3} = \text{Rs. } 430$

7. Here, 10% C.P. of horse = 20% C.P. of cart; Hence, C.P. of horse = 2 × C.P. of cart;
Let C.P. of cart and horse be Rs. x and Rs. $2x$ respectively; then,

$\frac{5}{100} \times 2x - \frac{5}{100} \times x = 10 \Rightarrow \frac{1}{20}x = 10$

$\therefore x = 200$

Hence, C.P. of a cart = Rs. 200 and C.P. of a horse = 2 × 200 = Rs. 400

8. Let C.P. be Rs. 100; then marked price = Rs. 120

Since, S.P. $= \frac{90}{100} \times 120 = \text{Rs. } 108$

$\therefore$ Profit = 108 – 100 = Rs. 8, Hence, gain = 8%.

9. Required weight $= \frac{100}{160} \times 1000 = 625$ gms.

10. Here, loss % $= \left(\frac{10}{10}\right)^2 = 1\%$.

SIMPLE INTEREST

1. A lent a sum of Rs. 1250 to B at a certain rate of interest for 3 years and a sum of Rs. 1500 to C at the same rate of interest for 2 years. If he was paid total Rs. 258.75 as interest in both cases, find the rate of interest at which money was lent by him.

A. $4\frac{1}{6}\%$ B. $6\frac{1}{4}\%$
C. $2\frac{1}{7}\%$ D. $3\frac{5}{6}\%$

2. A invested Rs. 5000 at a certain rate of simple interest and Rs. 4000 for the same period at 1% higher rate of interest. If the interest in both cases is same, the former rate of interest is :

A. 3% B. 4%
C. 6% D. 5%

3. If a certain sum of money at simple interest amounts to Rs. 1900 in 3 years and to Rs. 2050 in 5 years, the rate per cent per annum is :

A. 4½% B. 3½%
C. 2½% D. 5¼%

4. A certain sum of money lent out on simple interest amounts to Rs. 1760 in 2 years and to Rs. 2000 in 5 years. Find the sum.

A. Rs. 1650 B. Rs. 1500
C. Rs. 1580 D. Rs. 1600

5. Out of the sum of Rs. 1550, a part was lent out at 5% p.a. simple interest and the remaining at 8% p.a. simple interest. If the total interest in both cases after 3 years is Rs. 300, the sum of money lent out at 8% p.a. simple interest was:

A. Rs. 760 B. Rs. 775
C. Rs. 750 D. Rs. 780

6. If simple interest on a certain sum of money for 4 years at 5% p.a. is same as the simple interest on Rs. 840 for 10 years at the rate of 4% p.a., the sum of money is:

A. Rs. 1780 B. Rs. 1660
C. Rs. 1680 D. Rs. 1620

7. What equal instalment of annual payment will discharge a debt which is due as Rs. 848 at the end of 4 years at 4% per annum simple interest?

A. Rs. 200 B. Rs. 212
C. Rs. 225 D. Rs. 250

8. Madhavi lent Rs. 5000 to Kamla for 5 years and Rs. 3000 to Vimla for 4 years. Find the rate of interest, if Madhavi gets an interest of Rs. 600 in the end.

A. 1.62% B. 2.5%
C. 3% D. 4%

9. A sum of money doubles itself in 7 years at simple interest. In how many years it will become four fold?

A. 10 years B. 14 years
C. 21 years D. 35 years

10. An amount doubles itself at the end of 8 years with a certain rate of simple interest. What will be the total simple interest on Rs. 8000 at that rate at the end of 4 years?

A. Rs. 2000 B. Rs. 4000
C. Rs. 6000 D. None of these

ANSWERS

1	2	3	4	5	6	7	8	9	10
D	B	A	D	C	C	A	A	C	B

EXPLANATORY ANSWERS

1. $\frac{1250 \times R \times 3}{100} + \frac{1500 \times R \times 2}{100} = 258.75$

$\Rightarrow 6750\ R = 25875$

$\therefore \quad R = \frac{25875}{6750} = \frac{23}{6} = 3\frac{5}{6}\%$

2. Here, $\frac{5000 \times R \times T}{100} = \frac{4000 \times (R+1) \times T}{100}$

$\Rightarrow 5R = 4R + 4 \quad \therefore \quad R = 4\%$

3. Simple interest for 2 years
= Rs. 2050 – Rs. 1900 = Rs. 150

$\therefore$ Simple interest for 1 year = Rs. $\frac{150}{2}$ = Rs. 75

Since simple interest for 3 years = Rs. 75 × 3
= Rs. 225

$\therefore$ Principal = Rs. 1900 – Rs. 225 = Rs. 1675

Hence, Rate = $\frac{75 \times 100}{1675 \times 1} = 4½\%$

4. Interest for 3 years = Rs. 2000 – Rs. 1760
= Rs. 240

$\therefore$ Interest for 1 year = Rs. $\frac{240}{3}$ = Rs. 80

And interest for 2 years = Rs. 80 × 2 = Rs. 160
$\therefore$ Principal = Rs. 1760 – Rs. 160 = Rs. 1600

5. Let Rs. x and Rs $(1550 - x)$ were lent out at 8% and 5% respectively; then

$$\frac{x \times 8 \times 3}{100} + \frac{(1550 - x) \times 5 \times 3}{100} = 300$$

$\Rightarrow 24x + 23250 - 15x = 30000$

$\Rightarrow 9x = 6750 \quad \therefore \quad x = \frac{6750}{9}$ = Rs. 750

6. Here, $\frac{P \times 5 \times 4}{100} = \frac{840 \times 4 \times 10}{100} \Rightarrow 5P = 8400$

$\therefore \quad P = \frac{8400}{5}$ = Rs. 1680

7. Let equal instalment be Rs. x; then

$$x + \frac{x \times 4 \times 3}{100} + x + \frac{x \times 4 \times 2}{100} + x + \frac{x \times 4 \times 1}{100} + x = 848$$

$\Rightarrow 4x + \frac{24x}{100} = 848 \quad \Rightarrow \quad \frac{106x}{25} = 848$

$\therefore x = \frac{848 \times 25}{106}$ = Rs. 200

8. $\frac{5000 \times R \times 5}{100} + \frac{3000 \times R \times 4}{100} = 600$

$\Rightarrow \quad 250\ R + 120\ R = 600$

$\Rightarrow \quad 370R = 600$

$\therefore \quad R = \frac{600}{370} = 1.62\%$

9. Let principal be Rs. x; then amount = Rs. $2x$, Hence, I = $2x - x$ = Rs. x.

$R = \frac{x \times 100}{x \times 7} = \frac{100}{7}\%$ p.a.

Now, amount = Rs. $4x$; then I = $4x - x$ = Rs. $3x$

Hence, T = $\frac{3x \times 100}{x \times \frac{100}{7}} = \frac{3 \times 100 \times 7}{100}$ = 21 years

10. Let principal = Rs. x; then amount = Rs. $2x$; I = $2x - x$ = Rs. x

$R = \frac{x \times 100}{x \times 8} = \frac{25}{2}\%$

Again, I = $\frac{8000 \times 25 \times 4}{100 \times 2}$ = Rs. 4000

COMPOUND INTEREST

1. The compound interest on a certain sum of money invested for 3 years at 5% per annum is Rs. 1891.50. What will be the simple interest on the same sum at the same rate for 2 years?

A. Rs. 1700 B. Rs. 1200
C. Rs. 1500 D. Rs. 2100

2. A sum of money lent out at a certain rate of simple interest amounts to Rs. 6600 in 2 years and to Rs. 6900 in 3 years. What will be the compound interest on the same sum of money if lent out at the same rate for 2 years?

A. Rs. 605 B. Rs. 715
C. Rs. 615 D. Rs. 595

3. A man deposits Rs. 1200 in a bank on the 1st day of each year. If the bank pays 5% per annum compound interest on deposited sum of money, what will be the amount to his credit on the 10th day of the second year?

A. Rs. 2560 B. Rs. 2460
C. Rs. 2370 D. Rs. 2860

4. If the difference between compound and simple interest on a certain sum of money for 3 years at 5% per annum is Rs. 244, the sum is :

A. Rs. 40000 B. Rs. 25000
C. Rs. 30000 D. Rs. 32000

5. A man purchased a sewing machine for Rs. 5000. If due to sustained use value of this sewing machine depreciates by 6% annually, find its value after 3 years.

A. Rs. 3775.67 B. Rs. 4152.92
C. Rs. 4250.25 D. Rs. 4356.25

6. Find the sum on which the difference between compound and simple interest for 3 years at 10% per annum will be Rs. 868.

A. Rs. 29500 B. Rs. 27625
C. Rs. 28500 D. Rs. 28000

7. Samir invested Rs. 15000 at the rate of interest 10% p.a. for 1 year. If the interest compound six months. What amount will Samir get at the end of the year?

A. Rs. 16,500 B. Rs. 16525.50
C. Rs. 16537.50 D. Rs. 18,150

8. The compound interest on a certain sum for 2 years at 10% per annum is Rs. 525. The simple interest on the same sum for double the time at half the rate per cent per annum is:

A. Rs. 800 B. Rs. 600
C. Rs. 500 D. Rs. 400

9. The least number of complete years in which a sum of money put at 20% compound interest will be more than doubled is:

A. 6 B. 5
C. 4 D. 3

10. On a sum of money, the simple interest for 2 years is Rs. 660, while the compound interest is Rs. 696.30, the rate of interest being the same in both cases. Find the rate of interest.

A. Rs. 12% B. 11%
C. 10% D. 9%

ANSWERS

1	2	3	4	5	6	7	8	9	10
B	C	B	D	B	D	C	C	C	B

EXPLANATORY ANSWERS

1. Here, $1891.50 = P\left[\left(1+\frac{5}{100}\right)^3 - 1\right]$

$\Rightarrow 1891.50 = P\left[\left(\frac{21}{20}\right)^3 - 1\right]$

$\Rightarrow 1891.50 = P\left(\frac{1261}{8000}\right)$

$\therefore P = \frac{1891.50 \times 8000}{1261} = \text{Rs. } 12000$

Now, $\text{S.I.} = \frac{12000 \times 5 \times 2}{100} = \text{Rs. } 1200$

2. Here, 1 year's S.I. = Rs. 6900 – Rs. 6600
= Rs. 300

$\therefore$ 2 year's S.I. = 300 × 2 = Rs. 600

$\therefore$ Principal = Rs. 6600 – Rs. 600
= Rs. 6000

Hence, $\text{Rate} = \frac{600 \times 100}{6000 \times 2} = 5\%$

$\therefore$ C.I. $= 6000\left[\left(1+\frac{5}{100}\right)^2-1\right]$

$= 6000\left[\left(\frac{21}{20}\right)^2-1\right] = \frac{6000\times 41}{400}$ = Rs. 615

3. Required amount $= 1200\left(1+\frac{5}{100}\right) + 1200$

$= 1200 \times \frac{21}{20} + 1200 = 1260 + 1200 =$ Rs. 2460

4. Here, $P\left[\left(1+\frac{5}{100}\right)^3-1\right]-\frac{P\times 5\times 3}{100} = 244$

$\Rightarrow P\times\frac{1261}{8000}-\frac{3P}{20} = 244 \Rightarrow P\times\frac{61}{8000} = 244$

$\therefore P = \frac{244\times 8000}{61}$ = Rs. 32000

5. Here, value of the machine after 3 years

$= 5000\left(1-\frac{6}{100}\right)^3 = 5000\times\frac{47}{50}\times\frac{47}{50}\times\frac{47}{50}$

= Rs. 4152.92.

6. Here, $P\left[\left(1+\frac{10}{100}\right)^3-1\right]-\frac{P\times 10\times 3}{100} = 868$

$\Rightarrow P\times\frac{331}{1000}-\frac{3P}{10} = 868$

$\Rightarrow P\times\frac{31}{1000} = 868 \therefore P = \frac{868\times 1000}{31}$

= Rs. 28000

7. A $= 15000\left(1+\frac{5}{100}\right)^2 = 15000\times\frac{441}{400}$

= Rs. 16537.50

8. Here, $P\left[\left(1+\frac{10}{100}\right)^2-1\right] = 525$

$\Rightarrow P\left[\frac{121}{100}-1\right] = 525 \Rightarrow P\times\frac{21}{100} = 525$

$\therefore P = \frac{525\times 100}{21}$ = Rs. 2500

Hence, required S.I. $= \frac{2500\times 5\times 4}{100}$ = Rs. 500

9. Here, $P\left(1+\frac{20}{100}\right)^n > 2P \Rightarrow \left(\frac{6}{5}\right)^n > 2$

Hence, if $n = 4$ then, $\left(\frac{6}{5}\right)^4 = \frac{1296}{625} > 2$

So, $n = 4$ years

10. Here, S.I. for 1 year = Rs. 330

Since, simple interest of Rs. 330 for 1 year

= 696.30 – 660 = Rs. 36.30

Hence, required rate $= \frac{36.30\times 100}{330\times 1} = \frac{3630}{330} = 11\%$

AREA AND PERIMETER

1. If side of a square is reduced by 50%, its area will be reduced by

A. 50% B. 75%
C. 80% D. 60%

2. If each side of a square is doubled, its area will become

A. double B. four times
C. three times D. eight times

3. Three sides of a triangle are in the ratio of 17 : 15 : 8. If the perimeter of this triangle is 40 m, find its area

A. 50 sq. m. B. 49 sq. m.
C. 60 sq. m. D. 69 sq. m.

4. If the length of a rectangle is increased by 20% and width is decreased by 15%, then its area

A. decreases by 4% B. increases by 2%
C. decreases by 2% D. increases by 3%

5. If the length of a rectangle is increased by 20%, then by how much per cent its breadth must be decreased so as to keep its area unaltered?

A. 25% B. $8\frac{1}{3}\%$
C. $16\frac{2}{3}\%$ D. 20%

6. The ratio of length and breadth of a rectangular plot is 71 : 61 respectively. The area of the plot is 17324 m^2. What is perimeter of the plot?

A. 264 m B. 284 m
C. 528 m D. 614 m

7. If the length and breadth of a rectangular field are increased, the area increases by 50%. If the increase in length was 20%, by what percentage was the breadth increased?

A. 20% B. 25%
C. 30% D. 40%

8. The length and breadth of a varandah is 40 m and 15 m respectively. How many stone slabs of size 6 decimetre × 5 decimetre each are needed in flooring it:

A. 1000 B. 2000
C. 3000 D. 4000

9. The circumference of a circular plot is 396 m. What is the area of the circular plot?

A. 9,446 m^2 B. 9,856 m^2
C. 12,474 m^2 D. 18,634 m^2

10. If the sides of an equilateral triangle are increased by 20%, 30% and 50% respectively to form a new triangle, the increase in the perimeter of the equilateral triangle is:

A. 25% B. $33\frac{1}{3}\%$
C. 50% D. 100%

ANSWERS

1	2	3	4	5	6	7	8	9	10
B	B	C	B	C	C	B	B	C	B

EXPLANATORY ANSWERS

1. Area of the square = x^2 sq. m.

Side of the new square = $x - 50\%$ of $x = \frac{x}{2}$ m

$\therefore$ Area of the new square = $\left(\frac{x}{2}\right)^2 = \frac{x^2}{4}$ sq. m.

$\therefore$ Reduction in area of the square = $x^2 - \frac{x^2}{4}$

$= \frac{3x^2}{4}$ sq. m.

$\therefore$ Percentage reduction = $\frac{3x^2/4}{x^2} \times 100 = 75\%$

2. Area of the square = x^2 sq. m

Now, area of the new square = $(2x)^2 = 4x^2$ sq. m

Hence, it is clear that if side of a square is doubled, its area becomes four times.

3. Suppose sides of the triangle are $17x$ m, $15x$ m and $8x$ metres

$\therefore$ Perimeter = $17x + 15x + 8x = 40x$

Now, $40x = 40$

$\Rightarrow x = 1$ m

Therefore, the sides are $17 \times 1 = 17$ m, $15 \times 1 = 15$ m and $8 \times 1 = 8$ m

$\because (17)^2 = (15)^2 + (8)^2$,

i.e., it is a right angled triangle

$\therefore$ Area of the right angled triangle

$= \frac{1}{2} \times 8 \times 15 = 60$ sq.m.

4. Area of the rectangle = xy sq. metre

Area of the new rectangle = $\frac{120}{100} x \times \frac{85}{100} y$

$= 1.020\, xy$ sq. metre

$\therefore$ Increase in the area = $1.02\, xy - xy = .02\, xy$ sq. m.

$\therefore$ Percentage increase = $\frac{.02xy}{xy} \times 100 = 2\%$

5. Area of the rectangle = xy

On reducing the breadth by A% and increasing the length by 20%

Length of the new rectangle = $\frac{120x}{100} x = 1.2x$

Breadth of the new rectangle = $y - $ A% of $y = y\left(1 - \frac{A}{100}\right)$

$\therefore$ Area of the new rectangle = $1.2x \times y\left(1 - \frac{A}{100}\right)$

Now, $xy = 1.2\, xy\left(1 - \frac{A}{100}\right) \Rightarrow 1 = 1.2\frac{(100 - A)}{100}$

$\Rightarrow 1.2\,A = 120 - 100$

$\therefore A = \frac{20}{1.2} = 16\frac{2}{3}\%$

6. Let length and breadth of a rectangle be $71x$ and $61x$ m; then

$71x \times 61x = 17324 \Rightarrow x^2 = \frac{17324}{71 \times 61} = 4$

$\therefore x = 2$

Hence, length = $71 \times 2 = 142$ m; breadth $= 61 \times 2 = 122$ m

Since, perimeter = $2(142 + 122) = 2 \times 264 = 528$ m

7. Here, $20 + x + \frac{20 \times x}{100} = 50 \Rightarrow x + \frac{x}{5} = 30$

$\Rightarrow \frac{6x}{5} = 30 \qquad \therefore x = \frac{5 \times 30}{6} = 25$

Hence, breadth was increased by 25%

8. Required number of stone slabs = $\frac{40 \times 15}{\frac{6}{10} \times \frac{5}{10}}$

$= \frac{40 \times 15 \times 100}{6 \times 5} = 2000$

VOLUME AND SURFACE AREA

1. If a solid sphere of 3 cm radius is melted and recast into a right circular cone whose base radius is same as that of the sphere, the height of the cone will be

A. 8 cm B. 12 cm
C. 6 cm D. 5 cm

2. Diameter of a roller is 2.4 m and it is 1.68 m long. If it takes 1000 complete revolutions once over to level a field, the area of the field is

A. 12672 sq. m B. 12671 sq. m
C. 12762 sq. m D. 11768 sq. m

3. If each edge of a cube is increased by 10%, then by how much per cent will the surface area of this cube be increased?

A. 21% B. 18%
C. 15% D. 20%

4. Height and base radius of a solid cylinder are 14 m and 4 m respectively. It is melted and recast into a solid cone of the same base radius as that of the cylinder, what will be the height of the cone?

A. 21 m B. 42 m
C. 48 m D. 54 m

5. A room is in the form of a cube of side 10 m. How many bales of cotton can be kept in it if each bale covers 5 cu m space?

A. 100 B. 175
C. 200 D. 225

6. Three cubes having side 2 cm, 3 cm and 4 cm respectively are melted together to form a new cube. The side of the new cube will be

A. 3.526 cm B. 4.628 cm
C. 4.626 cm D. 4.528 cm

7. If base diameter of a cylinder is increased by 50%, then by how much per cent its height must be decreased so as to keep its volume unaltered?

A. 45.56% B. 55.56%
C. 50.16% D. 62.33%

8. The surface area of a cube is 600 sq. m. Its diagonal is

A. $10\sqrt{3}$ cm B. $5\sqrt{3}$ cm
C. $4\sqrt{2}$ cm D. $10\sqrt{2}$ cm

9. The base diameter of a conical tomb is 28 m and its slant height is 50 m. Find the cost of white washing its curved surface at the rate of 80 paise per sq. m?

A. Rs. 1860 B. Rs. 1760
C. Rs. 1950 D. Rs. 1875

10. The volume of a cuboid is 1120 cu cm and its height is 5 cm while the length and the breadth of the cuboid are in the ratio 8 : 7. The length of this cylinder exceeds the breadth by

A. 4 cm B. 2 cm
C. 7 cm D. 5 cm

ANSWERS

1	2	3	4	5	6	7	8	9	10
B	A	A	B	C	C	B	A	B	B

EXPLANATORY ANSWERS

1. Volume of the cone = Volume of the sphere

$\therefore \quad \frac{1}{3}\pi(3)^2 \times h = \frac{4}{3}\pi \times 3^3 \Rightarrow h = 12$ cm

Hence, height of the cone = 12 cm.

2. Surface area of the roller = $2\pi rh$

$= 2 \times \frac{22}{7} \times 1.2 \times 1.68 = 12.672$ sq. m

In one complete revolution, the roller covers 12.672 sq. m.

$\therefore$ It will cover in 1000 revolutions

= 12.672 × 1000 = 12672 sq. m

Hence, area of the field = 12672 sq. m.

3. Percentage increase in the surface area of the cube

$= \left(x + y + \frac{xy}{100}\right)\%$

$= \left(10 + 10 + \frac{10 \times 10}{100}\right)\% = 21\%.$

4. Here,

volume of the cone = Volume of the cylinder

$\Rightarrow \quad \frac{1}{3}\pi r^2 \times \text{height} = \pi r^2 \times 14$

$\therefore \quad$ Height = 14 × 3 = 42 m

Thus, height of the cone = 42 m.

5. Volume of the cubical room $= (10)^3$
$= 1000$ cu m

Number of cotton bales which can be placed in the room

$$= \frac{\text{Volume of the room}}{\text{Volume of each cotton bale}} = \frac{1000}{5} = 200.$$

6. Volume of the new cube $= 2^3 + 3^3 + 4^3$
$= 8 + 27 + 64 = 99$cu cm

$\therefore$ Side of the new cube $= \sqrt[3]{99} = 4.626$ cm.

7. Change in the volume of the cylinder

$$= \left(x+y+(-z)+\frac{xy+y(-z)+(-zx)}{100}+\frac{xy(-z)}{100^2}\right)\%$$

Since volume of the cylinder remains unchanged.

$\therefore$ Change $= 0\%$

Now, $\left(50+50+(-z)+\frac{50\times50-50z-50z}{100}+\frac{50\times50\times(-z)}{100^2}\right)=0$

$\therefore$ $100 - z + 25 - z - .25z = 0$

$\Rightarrow 2.25z = 125 \Rightarrow z = \frac{125}{2.25} = 55.56$

$\therefore$ Height of the cylinder should be decreased by 55.56%.

8. Here, $6 \times (\text{side})^2 = 600$

$\Rightarrow$ $\text{side}^2 = 100$

$\Rightarrow$ $\text{side} = \sqrt{100} = 10$ cm

$\therefore$ Diagonal of the cube$= \sqrt{3} \times \text{side}$

$= \sqrt{3}\times10$

$= 10\sqrt{3}$ cm.

9. Area of the curved surface of the cone

$= \frac{22}{7}\times\frac{28}{2}\times50 = 2200$ sq. m.

$\therefore$ Cost of white washing at 80 paise per sq. m

$= 2200\times\frac{80}{100} =$ Rs. 1760.

10. Suppose the length and the breadth of the cuboid are $8x$ cm and $7x$ cm

$\therefore$ Here, $8x \times 7x \times 5 = 1120$

$\Rightarrow x^2 = \frac{1120}{280} = 4 = (2)^2 \quad \Rightarrow \quad x = 2$

$\therefore$ Length of the cuboid $= 8 \times 2 = 16$ cm

Breadth of the cuboid $= 7 \times 2 = 14$ cm

Hence, it is clear that length of the cuboid exceeds the breadth by 2 cm.

SERIES

Directions (Qs. 1 to 7) : *In the following number series, one of the numbers does not fit into the series. Find the wrong number.*

1. 2, 5, 10, 18, 26, 37, 50
A. 2 B. 5
C. 37 D. 18

2. 3 , 18, 38, 78, 123, 178, 243
A. 123 B. 178
C. 3 D. 38

3. 380, 188, 92, 48, 20, 8, 2
A. 188 B. 92
C. 48 D. 20

4. 5, 11, 23, 47, 96, 191, 383
A. 11 B. 23
C. 47 D. 96

5. 89, 78, 86, 80, 85, 82, 83
A. 78 B. 86
C. 80 D. 85

6. 58, 57, 54, 50, 42, 33, 32
A. 57 B. 54
C. 50 D. 32

7. 2, 20, 27, 44, 64
A. 27 B. 8
C. 20 D. 44

Directions (Qs. 8 to 10) : *Complete the following series.*

8. 1 4 9 16 25 36 49 ....
A. 54 B. 56
C. 64 D. 81

9. 11 13 17 19 23 29 31 37 41 ....
A. 43 B. 47
C. 53 D. 51

10. 3 7 6 5 9 3 12 1 15 ....
A. 18 B. 13
C. –1 D. 3

ANSWERS

1	2	3	4	5	6	7	8	9	10
D	C	C	D	A	C	C	C	A	C

EXPLANATORY ANSWERS

1. 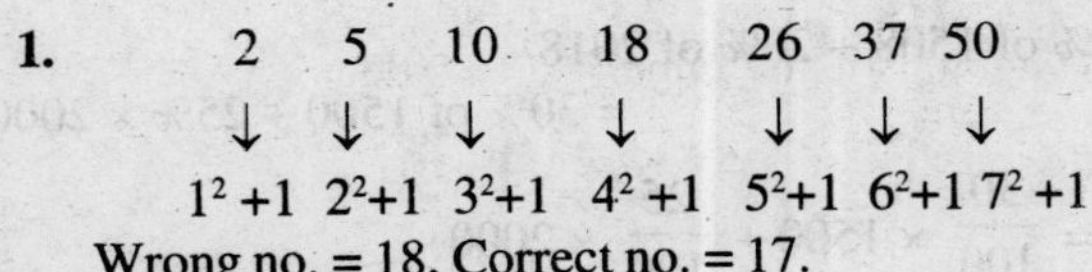

Wrong no. = 18, Correct no. = 17.

2. Only 3 is a prime number.

3. Wrong no. = 48, Correct no. = 44
Each term will be four more than two times the next term.

4. 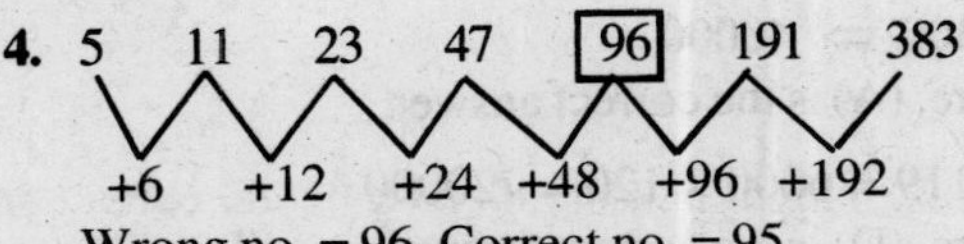

Wrong no. = 96, Correct no. = 95.

5. If 87 is written in place of 78 then tens digit of each term will be 8.

6. 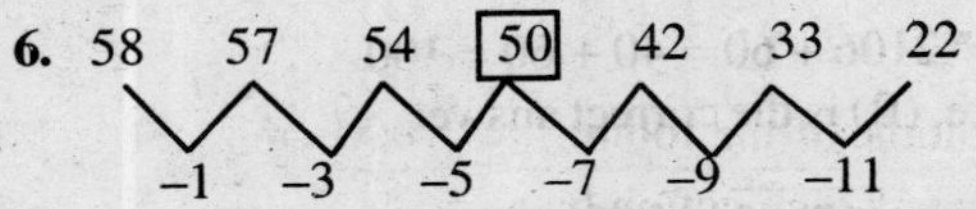

Wrong no. = 50, Correct no. = 49.

7. 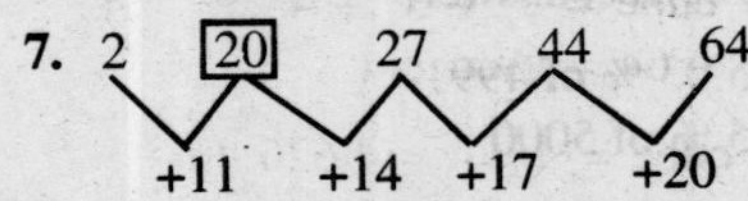

Wrong no. = 20, Correct no. = 13.

8. Numbers are $1^2, 2^2, 3^2, 4^2, 5^2, 6^2, 7^2$.
So, the next number is $8^2 = 64$.

9. Numbers are all primes. The next prime is 43.

10. There are two series, beginning respectively with 3 and 7. In one 3 is added and in another 2 is subtracted. The next number is 1 – 2 = –1.

APPROXIMATE VALUES

1. 85432 ÷ 2106 + 59.5614 = ?
(*a*) 100 (*b*) 60
(*c*) 80 (*d*) 140

2. $\sqrt{67621}$ = ?
(*a*) 320 (*b*) 260
(*c*) 200 (*d*) 280

3. 9.7 % of 5011 + 55.03 % of 4991
(*a*) 5500 (*b*) 7200
(*c*) 6000 (*d*) 4200

4. 730 × 199 = ?
(*a*) 350000 (*b*) 335000
(*c*) 300000 (*d*) 34600

5. .0144 × 0.36 = ?
(*a*) 0.5 (*b*) 0.005
(*c*) 0.05 (*d*) 0.005

6. 31% of 1508 + 26% of 2018
(*a*) 1500 (*b*) 2000
(*c*) 1000 (*d*) 1200

7. 3015 + 13594 + 3738 = ?
(*a*) 40000 (*b*) 36000
(*c*) 42000 (*d*) 46000

8. 6012 × 119 = ?
(*a*) 560000 (*b*) 448000
(*c*) 900000 (*d*) 720000

9. 2712.1563 ÷ 1805.4018 + 3.4982 = ?
(*a*) 9 (*b*) 8
(*c*) 4 (*d*) 5

10. 4182. 365 ÷ 20.886 = ?
(*a*) 300 (*b*) 200
(*c*) 150 (*d*) 250

ANSWERS

1	2	3	4	5	6	7	8	9	10
A	B	D	A	B	C	A	D	D	B

EXPLANATORY ANSWERS

1. $85432 \div 2106 + 60 = 40 + 60 = 100$
Therefore, (B) is the correct answer.

2. $\sqrt{67621} = \sqrt{67600} = 260$
Therefore, (B) is the correct answer.

3. 29.7 % of 5011 + 55.03 % of 4991
= 30 % of 5000 + 55 % of 5000

$= \frac{30}{100} \times 5000 + \frac{55}{100} \times 5000$

$= 1500 + 2750 = 4250 \Rightarrow 4200$
Therefore, (D) is the correct answer.

4. $1730 \times 199 = 1730 \times 200$
$= 346000 \Rightarrow 350000$
Therefore, (B) is the correct answer.

5. $0.0144 \times 0.36 = 0.0140 \times 0.36 = .005040$
$\Rightarrow .005$
Therefore, (B) is the correct answer.

6. 31% of 1508 + 26% of 2018
= 30% of 1500 + 25% × 2000

$= \frac{30}{100} \times 1500 + \frac{25}{100} \times 2000$

$= 450 + 500 = 950 \Rightarrow 1000$
Therefore, (C) is the correct answer.

7. $23015 + 13594 + 3738$
$= 23000 + 13600 + 3700$
$= 40300 \Rightarrow 40000$
Therefore, (A) is the correct answer.

8. $6012 \times 119 = 6000 \times 120 = 720000$
Therefore, (D) is the correct answer.

9. $2712.1563 \div 1805.4018 + 3.4982$
$= 2700 \div 1800 + 3.5 = 1.5 + 3.5 = 5$
Therefore, (D) is the correct answer.

10. $4182.365 \div 20.886 = 4200 \div 21 = 200$
Therefore, (B) is the correct answer.

REASONING ABILITY

SERIES

Directions : *In each of the following series determine the order of the letters. Then from the given options select the one which will complete the given series.*

1. BMK, DLM, FKO, HJQ, ?
A. JIR B. JIT
C. JHS D. JIS

2. A, CD, FGH, ?
A. IJKL B. KLMN
C. JKLM D. LMNO

3. BXJ, ETL, HPN, KLP, ?
A. PHR B. NIR
C. NHR D. MHR

4. PUF, QVG, RWH, ?
A. SXI B. SYZ
C. SXJ D. SVI

5. DEF, HIJ, MNO, ?
A. RTV B. STU
C. PTU D. SRU

Directions : *Which of the following groups of letters will complete the given series?*

6. ab---b-bbaa-
A. babba B. abaab
C. abbab D. baaab

7. aa-ab--aaa-a
A. baaa B. abab
C. aaab D. aabb

8. -baa-aab-a-a
A. baab B. abab
C. aaba D. aabb

9. -a cca-ccca-acccc-aaa
A. ccaa B. acca
C. caac D. caaa

10. c-bbb--abbbb-abbb-
A. abccb B. bacbb
C. aabcb D. abacb

Directions : *In the following questions, select the number(s) from the given options for completing the given series.*

11. 3, 9, 27, 81, 243, ?
A. 486 B. 729
C. 972 D. 359

12. 1, 6, 12, 19, 27, ?
A. 38 B. 35
C. 36 D. 54

13. 2, 6, 14, 30, 62, ?
A. 126 B. 128
C. 120 D. 130

14. 8, 48, 16, 96, 32, ?
A. 192 B. 150
C. 64 D. 288

15. 2, 8, 14, 24, 34, 48, ?
A. 66 B. 62
C. 58 D. 64

Directions : *In the given series find the number which is wrong.*

16. 5, 25, 120, 625, 3125, 15625
A. 15625 B. 625
C. 120 D. 5

17. 4, 8, 11, 22, 18, 36, 24, 50
A. 8 B. 22
C. 36 D. 24

18. 2, 4, 12, 24, 72, 142, 432
A. 432 B. 12
C. 142 D. 72

19. 2, 3, 4, 4, 6, 8, 9, 12, 16
A. 3 B. 9
C. 6 D. 12

20. 97, 91, 86, 83, 79, 77, 76, 76
A. 86 B. 76
C. 91 D. 83

ANSWERS

1	2	3	4	5	6	7	8	9	10
D	C	C	A	B	D	C	B	D	A
11	**12**	**13**	**14**	**15**	**16**	**17**	**18**	**19**	**20**
B	C	A	A	B	C	D	C	B	D

EXPLANATORY ANSWERS

1. The letters in one group correspond to the letters in the next group in the manner +2, –1, +2 respectively.

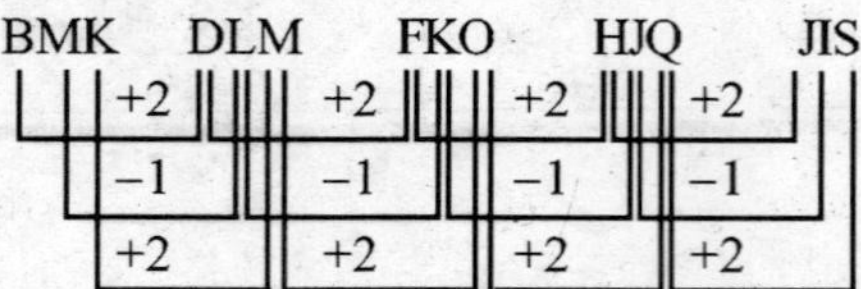

2. The letters are in natural sequence and from one group to the next one letter is dropped. Also the number of letters in groups is increased by one.

A_ CD FGH JKLM

↓ ↓ ↓

B E I

3. The letters in one group correspond to the letters in the next group in the manner +3, – 4, +2 respectively, *i.e.*,

BXJ ETL HPN KLP NHR

+3 +3 +3 +3

–4 –4 –4 –4

+2 +2 +2 +2

4. The three letters in each group are moved one step forward.

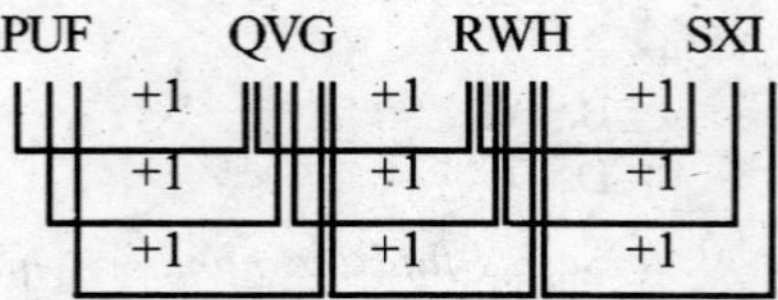

5. The letters are in natural order. The number of letters dropped in between the groups is increased by one at each step.

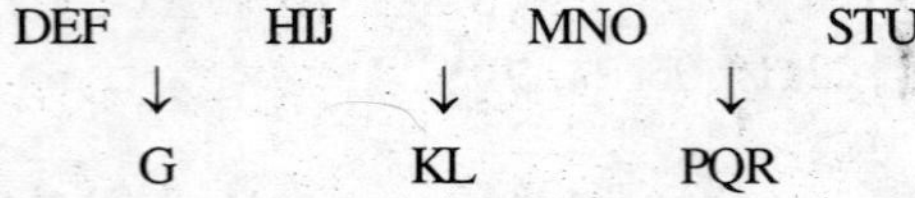

6. The series is abbaab, abbaab

7. The series is aaaaba, aaaaba

8. The series is aba, aba, aba, aba

9. The series is c,a,cc,aa, ccc, aaa, cccc, aaaa

10. The series is cabbbb, cabbbb, cabbbb

11. The numbers in the series are multiplied by 3 to get the next numbers.

12. The difference between the numbers in the series increases by 1, after beginning from 5, *i.e.*,

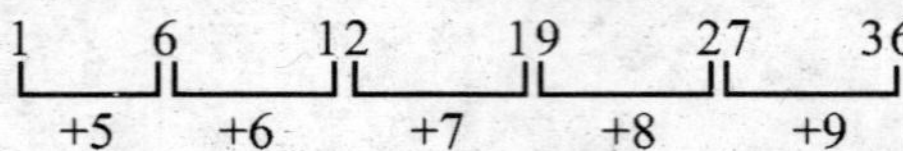

13. The difference between the numbers in the series doubles each time, after beginning from 4, *i.e.*,

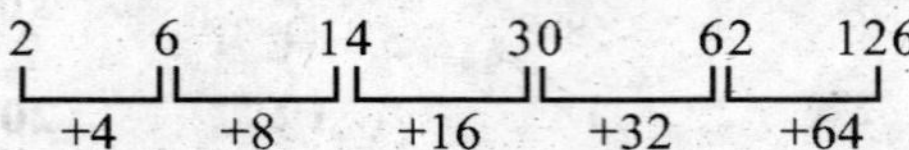

14. *Explanation I* : The sequence in the series is × 6, ÷ 3 which is repeated.

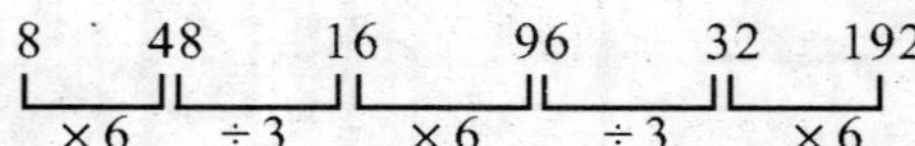

Explanation II : There are two alternate series and the numbers are multiplied by 2.

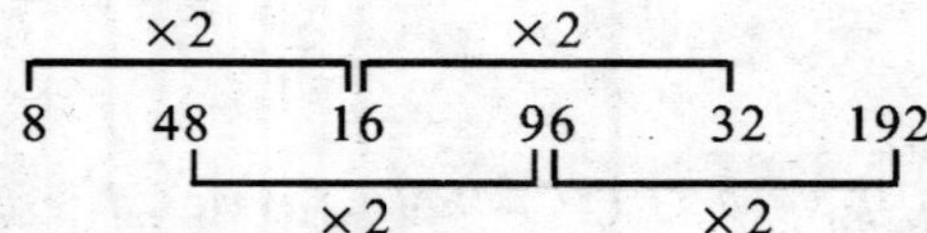

Series I : 8, 16, 32

Series II : 48, 96, 192

15. The sequence in the series is :

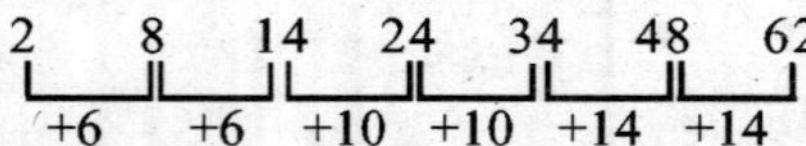

The difference increases by 4 at alternate step.

16. The numbers in the series are multiplied by 5 to get the next number.

∴ 125 should be in place of 120.

17. Two numbers form a pair. The first number increases by 7 for the next pair and the second number is the double of first number.

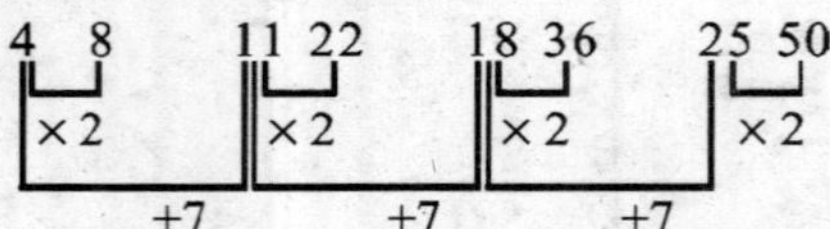

∴ 25 should be in place of 24.

18. There are two alternate series and in each series, the numbers are multiplied by 6 to get the next number.

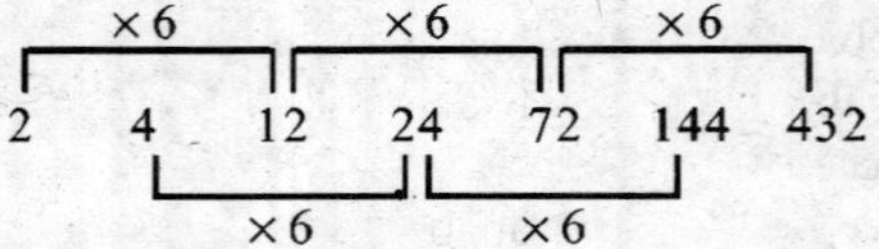

∴ 144 should be in place of 142.

19. There are three alternate series and in each series, the numbers are multiplied by 2 to get the next number.

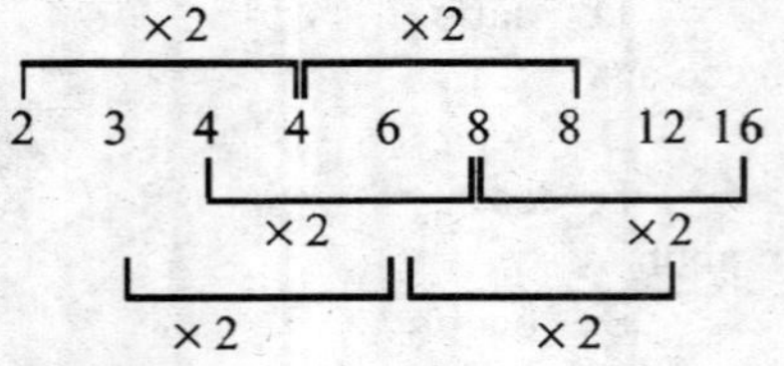

Series I : 2, 4, 8

Series II : 3, 6, 12

Series III : 4, 8, 16

∴ 8 should be in place of 9.

20. The difference between the consecutive numbers in the series decreases by 1 at each step.

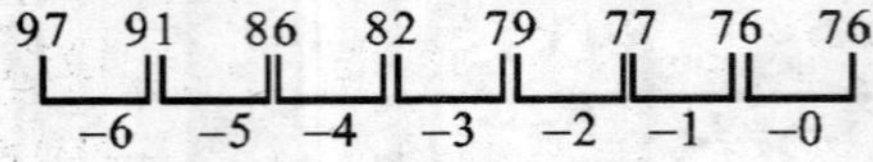

∴ 82 should be in place of 83.

ANALOGIES OR RELATIONSHIPS

Directions : *In the questions given below establish the relationship between the two words. Then from the given options select one which has the same relationship as of the given two words.*

1. ADULT : BABY : : FLOWER : ?
   A. Seed B. Bud
   C. Fruit D. Butterfly
2. WRITER : READER : : PRODUCER : ?
   A. Creator B. Contractor
   C. Creature D. Consumer
3. ENTRANCE : EXIT : : LOYALTY : ?
   A. Treachery B. Patriotism
   C. Fidelity D. Reward
4. MOTHER : MATERNAL : : FATHER : ?
   A. Eternal B. Detrimental
   C. Paternal D. Formidable

Directions : *In the questions given below one term is missing. Based on the relationship of the two given words find the missing term from the given options.*

5. GFC : CFG : : RPJ : ?
   A. JRP B. JPR
   C. PJR D. RJP
6. BCF : DEG : : MNQ : ?
   A. OPR B. PQS
   C. OPP D. QRT
7. NATION : ANITNO : : HUNGRY : ?
   A. HNUGRY B. UNHGYR
   C. YRNGUH D. UHGNYR
8. SSTU : MMNO : : AABC : ?
   A. GGHH B. IJKK
   C. XXYZ D. NOOP

ANSWERS

1	2	3	4	5	6	7	8
B	D	A	C	B	A	D	C

EXPLANATORY ANSWERS

1. The youngone of an adult is a baby and that of a flower is a bud.
2. A writer aims to please the readers by his writings, a producer aims to please the consumers by his products.
3. The related words are opposites.
4. Relations on the mother's side are maternal and on the father's side paternal.
5. The letters of the first group are reversed.

GFC : CFG : : RPJ : JPR

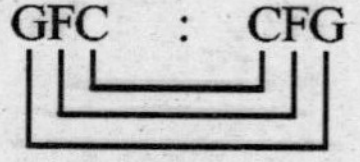
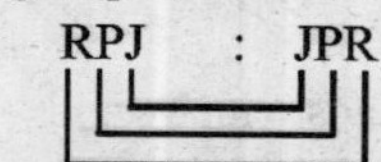

6. The three letters are moved 2, 2 and 1 steps forward respectively.

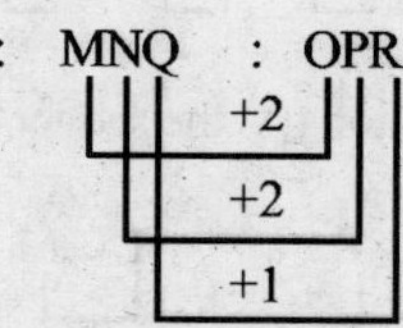

7. The word is divided in sections of two letters and the letters are reversed.

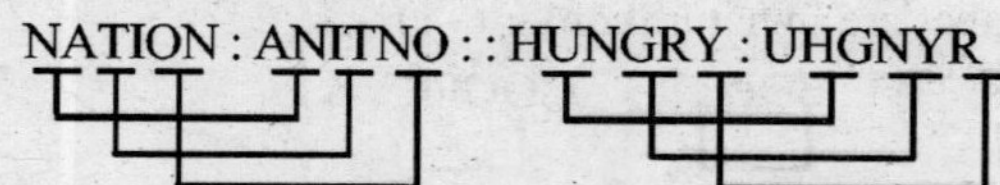

8. The first letter in each group is repeated and followed by two consecutive letters.

ODD ONE OUT

Directions : *Three of the following four in each question are alike in a certain way and so form a group. Select the group of letters that does not belong to that group.*

1. A. ACE B. LOR
   C. GIK D. VXZ
2. A. TSR B. LKJ
   C. PQO D. HGF
3. A. EF LM B. KJ SR
   C. XW HG D. ED YX

4. A. JOPK B. BOPC C. QOPR D. TOPS

5. A. DfH B. MoQ C. UwY D. lnO

6. A. JKkL B. OPpQ C. DEEf D. VWwX

7. A. BdfH B. FHJL C. RTvX D. uVwX

8. A. DFHEG B. TWXUV C. OQSPR D. JLNKM

9. A. FEUV B. DCXW C. BAZY D. HGTS

10. A. UTSR B. XYZW C. ONML D. IHGF

ANSWERS

1	2	3	4	5	6	7	8	9	10
B	C	A	D	D	C	D	B	A	B

EXPLANATORY ANSWERS

1. The sequence in each group is +2. Only option B has sequence in +3, *i.e.,*

ABCDE (+2 +2)   LMNOPQR (+3 +3)

GHIJK (+2 +2)   VWXYZ (+2 +2)

2. The sequence of alphabet in each group is in reverse order. Only option C has sequence in disturbed order.

3. Two consecutive alphabet in each group are in reverse sequence (–1), *i.e.,*

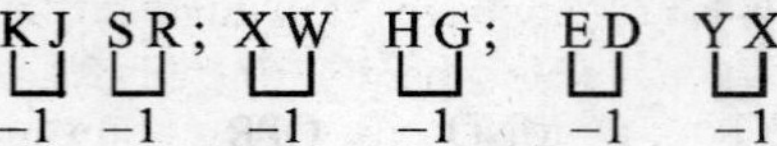

Only in option (A) the sequence is in natural order (+1), *i.e.,*

4. In each group, letters 'OP' are common. The two corner alphabet are in natural order (+1); *i.e.,*

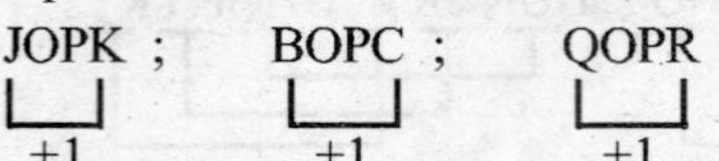

Only in option (D) they are in reverse order (–1); *i.e.,*

5. In other groups, only the alphabet in the centre is of lower case. In this option letter 'L' on the left is also in lower case.

6. In other groups, the third letter which is a repeat of the second alphabet is in lower case.

7. In each group, the sequence of the alphabet, irrespective of the case, is +2; *i.e.,*

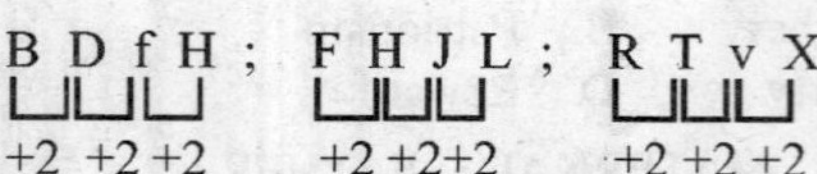

Only in option (D) the sequence is in natural order (+1), *i.e.,*

u V w X (+1 +1 +1)

8. In each group; the alphabet at positions-first, fourth, second, fifth and third, form a natural sequence.

In option (B), the alphabet at positions first, fourth, fifth, second and third, form the natural sequence.

9. In each group, two alphabets in the corner and two alphabets in the centre correspond to their reverse order positioned alphabet. *i.e.,*

natural order → A B C D E F G H I J K L M

reverse order → Z Y X W V U T S R Q P O N

natural order → N O P Q R S T U V W X Y Z

reverse order → M L K J I H G F E D C B A

As such—

D corresponds with W and

C corresponds with X.

B corresponds with Y and

A corresponds with Z.

H corresponds with S and

G corresponds with T.

Similarly,

F should correspond with U and

E should correspond with V;

i.e. letters 'UV' should be written as 'VU'

10. In each group, the alphabet are in reverse order.

In option (B), the order is disturbed.

CODING AND DECODING

Directions : *In the following questions select the right option which indicates the correct code for the word or letter given in the question.*

1. If CHAIR is coded as FKDLU then RAID is coded as:

A. ULGD B. ULKG
C. ULDG D. UDLG

2. If CONDEMN is coded as CNODMEN, then TEACHER is coded as :

A. TEACHER B. TAEECHR
C. TCAEEHR D. TAECEHR

3. In a code language COME is written as XLNV and ABLE as ZYOV. How will MOLLY be written in that code?

A. NLOBO B. NLBOO
C. LNOOB D. NLOOB

4. In a certain code PROFESSION is written as EFORPNOISS. In the same code DICTIONARY will be written as :

A. YRANOITCID B. ITCIDYRANO
C. ITCIDYRNAO D. ITCDIYARNO

5. JUNE is coded as NXPF, how will STAY be coded in the same manner?

A. WWCZ B. WVCZ
C. WWDB D. VWZC

Directions : *In the following questions study the coded patterns and then select the right option from the given alternatives.*

6. In a certain language, (a) 'go ju mi' stands for 'plenty of money'; (b) pao ju go nei vu' for 'money creates lots of problems'; (c) 'kol vu nei' for 'problems create tension'; and (d) 'sol tun ju haw' for 'still money is needed'. Which of the following words stand for 'money'?

A. nei B. ju
C. haw D. go

7. In a certain language, (a) 'FOR' stands for 'old is gold'; (b) 'ROT' stands for 'gold is pure'; (c) 'ROM' stands for 'gold is costly'. How will 'pure old gold is costly' be written?

A. TFROM B. FOTRM
C. FTORM D. TOMRF

8. In a certain code '415' means 'milk is hot'; '18' means 'hot soup'; and '895' means 'soup is tasty'. What number will indicate the word 'tasty'?

A. 9 B. 8
C. 5 D. 4

9. In a certain code '643' means 'she is beautiful', '593' means 'he is handsome', and '567' means 'handsome meets beautiful'. What number will indicate the word 'meets'?

A. 5 B. 3
C. 7 D. 6

10. In a certain code language, (a) 'dugo hui mul zo' stands for 'work is very hard'; (b) 'hui dugo ba ki' for 'Bingo is very smart'; (c) 'nano mul dugo' for 'cake is hard', and (d) 'mul ki qu' for 'smart and hard'. Which of the following words stand for 'Bingo'?

A. jalu B. dugo
C. ki D. ba

ANSWERS

1	2	3	4	5	6	7	8	9	10
D	D	D	B	A	B	A	A	C	D

EXPLANATORY ANSWERS

2. In this word, the second and third letters interchange their places and the fifth and sixth letters do the same. Other letters retain their position.

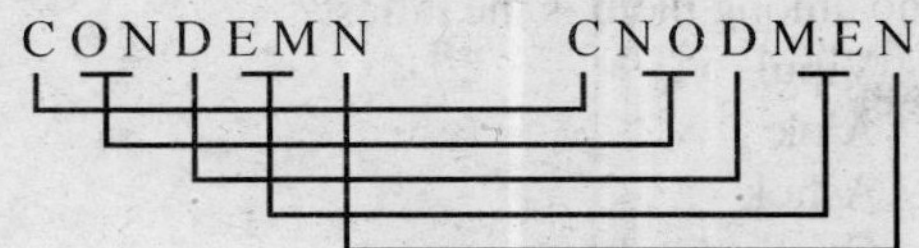

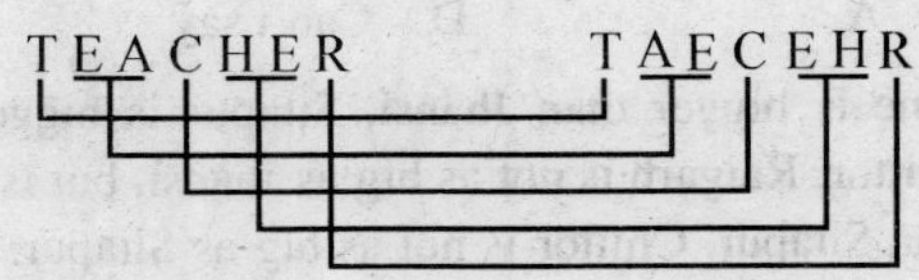

3. The letters of the word are coded by their represented letters in the reverse series.

C O M E → letters in natural series
X L N V → letters in reverse series
↓ ↓ ↓ ↓
3rd15th13th5th → position of letters
A B L E → letters in natural series
Z Y O V → letters in reverse series
↓ ↓ ↓ ↓
1st 2nd12th 5th → position of letters

Similarly,

M O L L Y → letters in natural series
N L O O B → letters in reverse series
↓ ↓ ↓ ↓ ↓
13th 15th 12th 12th 25th → position of letters

4. The word is divided into two equal parts and the letters of each part are written backwards.

Similarly,

5. The word is coded by moving the letters +4, +3, +2, and +1 steps respectively.

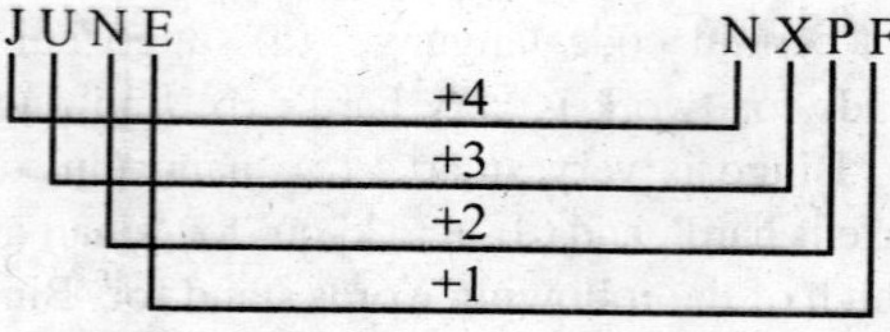

Similarly,

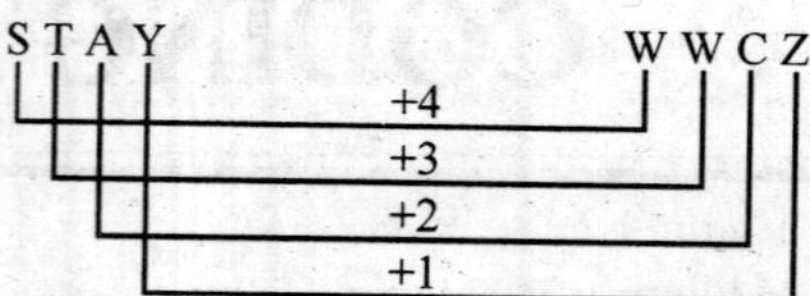

6.

	Code	Sentence
1.	go *ju* mi	plenty of *money*
2.	pao *ju* go nei vu	*money* creates lots of problems
3.	kol vu nei	problems create tension
4.	sol tun *ju* haw	still *money* is needed

In 1st, 2nd and 4th codes and their sentences the word 'ju' is repeated and so is 'money'.

8.

	Code	Sentence
1.	415	milk is hot
2.	18	hot soup
3.	895	soup is *tasty*

From 3rd code and its sentence neither number '9' is repeated nor the word 'tasty'.

9.

	Code	Sentence
1.	643	she is beautiful
2.	593	he is handsome
3.	567	handsome *meets* beautiful

From 3rd code and its sentence, neither number '7' nor the word 'meets' is repeated.

10.

	Code	Sentence
1.	*dugo hui* mul zo	work *is very* hard
2.	*hui dugo* **ba** *ki*	**Bingo** *is very smart*
3.	nano mul *dugo*	cake is *hard*
4.	mul *ki* qu	*smart* and hard

From 2nd code and its sentence, neither 'ba' nor 'Bingo' is repeated.

(Words repeated are in italics)

STATEMENT ANALYSIS

1. Among five friends, A is heavier than B; C is lighter than D; B is lighter than D but heavier than E. Who among them is the heaviest?

A. B
B. C
C. A
D. Can't say

2. Pune is bigger than Jhansi, Sitapur is bigger than Chittor. Raigarh is not as big as Jhansi, but is bigger than Sitapur. Chittor is not as big as Sitapur. Which is the smallest?

A. Jhansi
B. Pune
C. Chittor
D. Sitapur

3. Ajay works more than Ram. Alok works as much as Raju. Pankaj works less than Alok. Ram works more than Alok. Who works the most of all?

A. Ajay
B. Ram
C. Alok
D. Raju

4. Vipul is taller than Hans. Hans is taller than Anand. Alok is taller than Ashok. Ashok is taller than Hans. Who among them is the tallest?

A. Vipul
B. Alok
C. Ashok
D. Cannot be determined

5. Pramod is taller than Gopal. Gopal is shorter than Madhu. To find out who among them is the tallest, which of the following further informations is necessary?
A. Madhu is taller than Gopal.
B. Madhu is shorter than Pramod's brother
C. Pramod is taller than Madhu.
D. Pramod is taller than Madhu's brother.

6. Among five friends P, Q, R, S and T, who is the youngest? To arrive at the answer which of the following information given in the statements (*a*) and (*b*) is sufficient?
(*a*) R is younger than P and T.
(*b*) S is younger than Q.
A. Only (*a*) alone is sufficient
B. Either (*a*) or (*b*) is sufficient
C. Both (*a*) and (*b*) together are needed
D. Both (*a*) and (*b*) together are not sufficient

7. Sushma is richer than Rashmi whereas Anand is richer than Priya. Arun is as rich as Rashmi. Shoba is richer than Sushma.
Which of the following statements is correct according to the above propositions?
A. Rashmi is poorer than Priya.
B. Priya is richer than Arun
C. Arun is poorer than Sushma.
D. Anand is richer than Rashmi

8. A is elder to B while C and D are elder to E who lies between A and B. If C be elder to B, which one of the following statements is necessarily true?
A. E is elder to B
B. A is elder to C
C. C is elder to D
D. D is elder to C

9. Vikram is taller than Rajan but shorter than Annie. Jamal is taller than Annie. Sita is taller than Vikram. Rajan is shorter than Sita. Who is the shortest of all in the group?
A. Sita
B. Rajan
C. Vikram
D. Cannot be determined

10. Suresh is as much older than Kamal as he is younger than Prabodh. Navin is as old as Kamal. Which of the following statements is wrong?
A. Suresh is older than Navin
B. Kamal is younger than Suresh
C. Prabodh is not the oldest
D. Navin is younger than Prabodh

ANSWERS

1	2	3	4	5	6	7	8	9	10
D	C	A	D	C	D	C	A	B	C

EXPLANATORY ANSWERS

1. The five friends in descending order of weight are : A/D, B/C, E or A/D, B, C/E. Either A or D is the heaviest.

2. The order of cities in descending order of size is : Pune, Jhansi, Raigarh, Sitapur, Chittor.

3. On the basis of doing work, the descending order will be : Ajay, Ram, Alok/Raju, Pankaj.

4. On the basis of height, the descending order will be Vipul/Alok, Ashok, Hans, Anand. Either Vipul or Alok is the tallest.

5. According to the information both Pramod and Madhu are taller than Gopal. Option (c) decides who is the tallest.

6. Statements are not inter-related.

7. On the basis of wealth, the descending order will be :
1. Shobha, Sushma, Rashmi/Arun
2. Anand, *and* Priya

(The two statements are not inter-related.)

8. The order in descending seniority will be : A/C/D, E, B.

9. On the basis of height the descending order will be :
Jamal/Sita, Annie, Vikram, Rajan.
or
Jamal, Sita/Annie, Vikram, Rajan.

10. On the basis of age the descending order will be : Prabodh, Suresh, Kamal/Navin.

PLACE ARRANGEMENT

Directions: *In the following questions, understand the arrangement pattern and then select the right answer from the given options :*

1. Five boys are sitting in a row. Raghu is not adjacent to Shyam or Amit. Ajay is not adjacent to Shyam. Raghu is adjacent to Mayank. If Mayank is at the middle in the row, then Ajay is adjacent to whom out of the following?

A. Amit B. Raghu
C. Mayank D. Shyam

2. Mini is to the right of Rajni but to the left of Ananta. Saya is to the right of Mini but to the left of Jaya. Who is on the extreme left if all the girls are facing North?

A. Jaya B. Mini
C. Rajni D. Saya

3. Kittu is in-between Mohan and Sohan. Raju is to the left of Sohan and Shyam is to the right of Mohan. If all of the friends are sitting facing South, then who is on their extreme right?

A. Mohan B. Sohan
C. Kittu D. Shyam

4. A, B, C, D and E are running one behind the other. C is not near E and A is not near D. B is next to A and E is not near D. Who is in the middle?

A. B B. E
C. A D. Cannot be said

5. O, P, Q, R, S and T are standing on a bench according to their height. P is taller than O but shorter than S. Only S is taller than T. R is shorter than P but taller than Q. Who is the shortest?

A. O B. Q
C. P D. Cannot be said

ANSWERS

1	2	3	4	5
B	C	D	A	D

EXPLANATORY ANSWERS

1. The order of sitting is :

Amit, Shyam, Mayank, Ajay, Raghu

or

Ajay, Raghu, Mayank, Amit, Shyam

2. The order in which the girls are positioned is :

Rajni, Mini, Ananta, Saya, Jaya

or

Saya, Jaya, Ananta

or

Saya, Ananta, Jaya

3. The order of sitting while facing South is:

Shyam, Mohan, Kittu, Sohan, Raju.

4. The positions while running behind the other is :

E E
A A
B *or* B
C D
D C

5. In descending order of height, the standing positions are :

S S
T T
P *or* P
R R
O Q
Q O

Either O or Q is the shortest. The information given is not enough to clarify the answer.

DIRECTION SENSE

Directions : *In the following questions, select the right answer from the given options to depict the correct direction/distance.*

1. Kittu walks towards East and then towards South. After walking some distance he turns towards West and then turns to his left. In which direction is he walking now?

A. North B. South
C. East D. West

2. A person is driving towards West. What sequence of directions should he follow so that he is driving towards South?
A. left, right, right
B. right, right, left
C. left, left, left
D. right, right, right

3. Richa drives 8 km to the South, turns left and drives 5 km. Again, she turns left and drives 8 km. How far is she from her starting point?

A. 3 km B. 5 km
C. 8 km D. 13 km

4. Dingi runs 40 km towards North then turns right and runs 50 km. He turns right and runs 30 km, and once again turns right and runs 50 km. How far is he from his starting point?
A. 90 km B. 50 km
C. 10 km D. 5 km

5. Debu walks towards East then towards North and turning 45° right walks for a while and lastly turns towards left. In which direction is he walking now?
A. North B. East
C. South-East D. North-West

ANSWERS

1	2	3	4	5
B	D	B	C	D

EXPLANATORY ANSWERS

1.

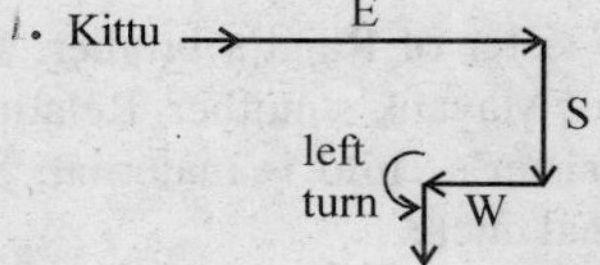

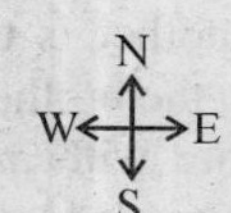

2.

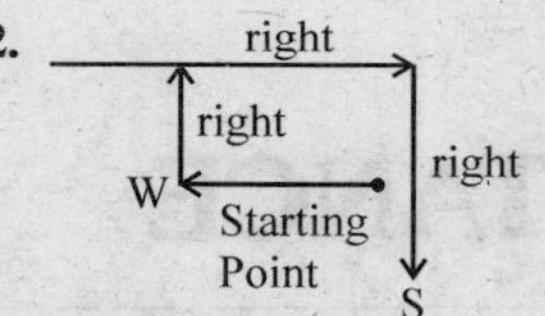

3.

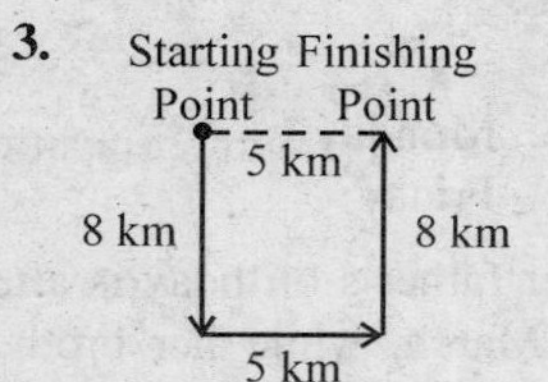

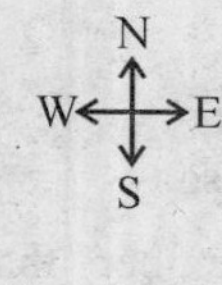

4.

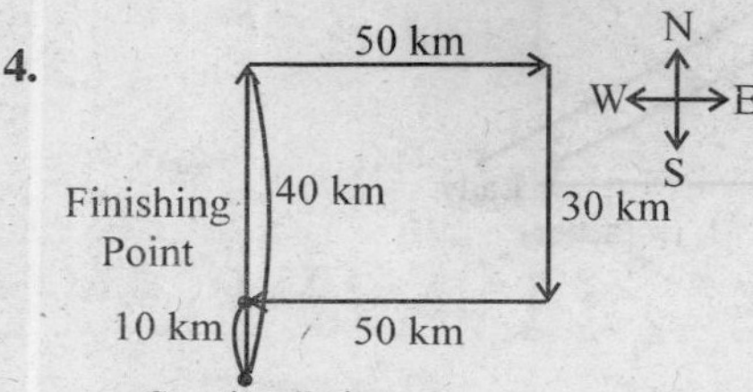

N
W E
S

5.

NW
NE
N
E
Debu's Starting
Point

N
NW NE
W E
SW SE
S

BLOOD RELATIONSHIPS

Directions : *In each of the following questions keenly study the relationship mentioned between the persons, and then from the given options select the right relationship as the answer.*

1. 'A' is the father of 'B' and 'C'. 'B' is the son of 'A' but 'C' is not the son of 'A'. What is 'C's' relation with 'A'?
A. Daughter B. Son
C. Niece D. Nephew

2. A lady said, "The person standing there is my grandfather's only son's daughter". How is the lady related to the standing person?
A. Sister B. Mother
C. Aunt D. Cousin

3. Ravi is the brother of Amit's son's son. What is Amit's relation to Ravi?
A. Cousin B. Father
C. Grandfather D. Son

4. Mayank said, "My mother is the sister of Rajat's brother." What is Rajat's relation with Mayank?
A. Cousin B. Maternal uncle
C. Uncle D. Brother-in-law

5. Introducing Lily, Raghav said, "Her father is my mother's only son". How is Lily related to Raghav?
A. Aunt B. Daughter
C. Mother D. Sister

ANSWERS

1	2	3	4	5
A	A	C	B	B

EXPLANATORY ANSWERS

1. 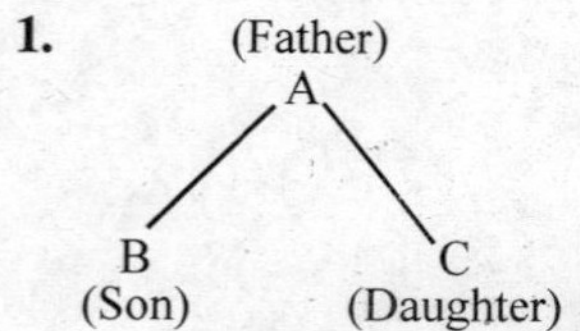

'C' is not the son of 'A', but 'A' is the father of 'C'. So, 'C' is the daughter of 'A'.

2. 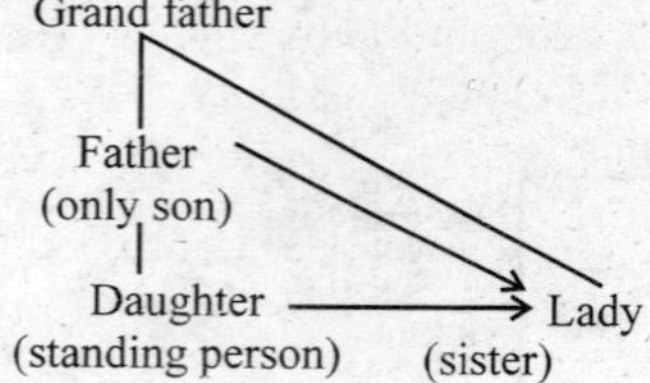

Lady's grandfather's son is lady's father and father's daughter will only be lady's sister.

4. 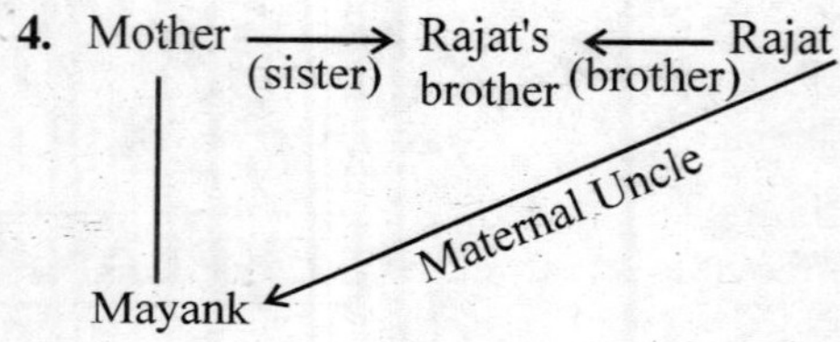

Mayank's mother is the sister of Rajat's brother. So Rajat is also the brother of Mayank's mother. Relation of the brother with his sister's child is maternal. So Rajat is Mayank's maternal uncle.

CALENDAR, CLOCK, TIME, DISTANCE

1. If the day before yesterday was Thursday, when will Sunday be?
A. Tomorrow B. Day after tomorrow
C. Today D. Two days after today

2. There are twenty people working in an office. The first group of five works between 8:00 A.M. and 2:00 PM. The second group of ten works between 10:00 AM to 4:00 PM. And the third group of five works between 12 noon to 6:00 PM. There are three computers in the office which all the employees frequently use. During which of the following hours the computers are likely to be used most?
A. 1:00 PM - 3:00 PM
B. 12 noon - 2:00 PM
C. 2:00 PM - 4:00 PM
D. 10:00 AM - 12 noon

3. If the seventh day of a month is three (3) days earlier than Friday, what day will it be on the nineteenth day of the month?
A. Sunday B. Monday
C. Wednesday D. Friday

4. Radha remembers that her father's birthday is after 16th but before 21st of March, while her brother Mangesh remembers that his father's birthday is before 22nd but after 19th of March. On which date is the birthday of their father?
A. 19th
B. 20th
C. 21st
D. Cannot be determined

5. A man is three (3) years older than his wife and four (4) times as old as his son. If the son attains an age of fifteen (15) years after three (3) years, what is the present age of the mother?
A. 45 years B. 51 years
C. 48 years D. 60 years

6. A clock is so placed that at 12 noon its minute hand points towards north-east. In which direction does its

hour hand point at 1.30 P.M.?

A. East B. West
C. North D. South

7. If in the above question clock is turned through an angle of 135° in an anticlockwise direction, in which direction will its minute hand point at 8.45 P.M.?

A. East B. West
C. North D. South

8. A couple married in 1980 had two children, one in 1982 and the other in 1984. Their combined ages will equal the years of the marriage in?

A. 1986 B. 1985
C. 1987 D. 1988

9. Manoj left home for the bus stop 15 minutes earlier than the usual time. It takes 10 minutes to reach the stop. He reached the stop at 8.40 a.m. What time does he usually leave home for the bus stop?

A. 8.30 a.m. B. 8.55 a.m.
C. 8.45 p.m. D. None of these

10. Mamuni went to the movies nine days ago. She goes to the movies only on Thursday. What day of the week is today?

A. Sunday B. Tuesday
C. Thursday D. Saturday

11. If Thursday was the day after the day before yesterday five days ago, what is the least number of days ago when Sunday was three days before the day after tomorrow?

A. Two days ago B. Three days ago
C. Four days ago D. Five days ago

12. 1.12.91 is the first Sunday. Which is the fourth Tuesday of December 91?

A. 31.12.91 B. 24.12.91
C. 17.12.91 D. 26.12.91

13. If the third day of a month is Monday, which of the following will be the fifth day from 21st of that month?

A. Tuesday B. Monday
C. Wednesday D. Thursday

14. Keshav runs a factory in three shifts of eight hours each with 210 employees. In each shift minimum of 80 employees are required to run the factory effectively. No employee can be allowed to work for more than 16 hours a day. At least how many employees will be required to work for 16 hours every day?

A. 30 B. 60
C. Data inadequate D. None of these

15. If 15 horses eat 15 bags of gram in 15 days, in how many days will one horse eat one bag of grain?

A. 15 days B. 1/15 days
C. 1 day D. 30 days

16. A century leap year is divisible by :

A. 4 B. 16
C. 40 D. 400

17. If the fifth day of a month is Friday, which of the following will be the Seventh day from 10th of that month?

A. Tuesday B. Monday
C. Wednesday D. Thursday

18. Day after tomorrow is my birthday. On the same day next week falls 'Holi'. Today is Monday. What will be the day after 'Holi'?

A. Wednesday B. Thursday
C. Friday D. Saturday

19. A clock shows the time as 3 : 30 p.m. If the minute hand gains 2 minutes every hour, how many minutes will the clock gain by 4 a.m.?

A. 23 Minutes B. 24 Minutes
C. 25 Minutes D. 26 Minutes

20. Two brothers were expected to return home on the same day. Rajat returned 3 days earlier but Rohit returned 4 days later. If Rajat returned on Thursday, what was the expected day when both the brothers were to return home and when did Rohit Return?

A. Wednesday, Sunday
B. Thursday, Monday
C. Sunday, Thursday
D. Monday, Friday

ANSWERS

1	2	3	4	5	6	7	8	9	10
A	B	A	B	A	A	D	A	D	D
11	**12**	**13**	**14**	**15**	**16**	**17**	**18**	**19**	**20**
A	B	C	D	A	D	C	B	C	C

EXPLANATORY ANSWERS

1. Thursday —Day-before-yesterday
Friday —Yesterday
Saturday —Today
Sunday — Tomorrow

2. 1. 5 people work between 8 a.m. to 2 p.m.

2. 10 people work between 10 a.m. to 4 p.m.

3. 5 people work between 12 noon to 6 p.m.

So, computers are used most between 12 noon to 2 p.m.

3. 7th day is 3 days earlier than Friday so, 10th day is Friday, so also is 17th.

∴ 19th day will be 2nd day ahead of Friday, *i.e.*, Sunday.

4. Father's birthday

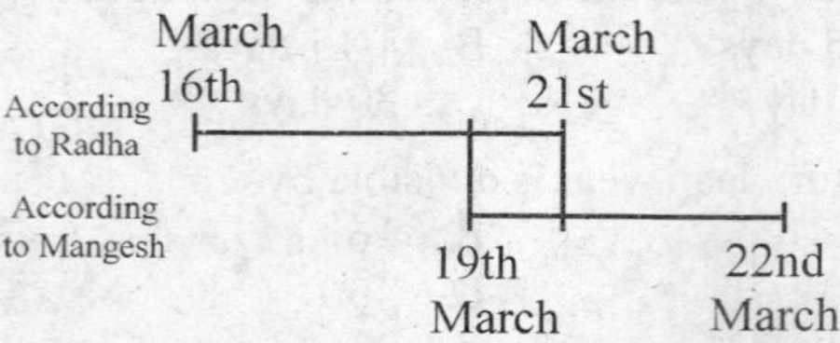

∴ Their father's birthday is on 20th March.

5. Present age of son is 15 – 3 = 12 years. Age of the man is 4 times the age of son, *i.e.*,

12 × 4 = 48 years

Man is 3 years elder to his wife/son's mother.

So Age of the mother is 48 – 3 = 45 years

6.

At 12 noon

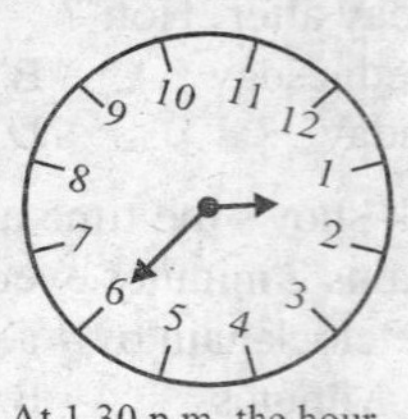

At 1.30 p.m. the hour hand will point towards East.

7.

After rotating the clock in earlier question, its minute hand will point towards South at 8:45 p.m.

8. 1982 — 2 years later — 1st child

1984 — 4 years later — 2nd child

Total age of children — 2 years.

1985 — 5 years later — Total age of children: 4 years.

1986 — 6 years later — Total age of children : 6 years.

9. Manoj reached the bus stop at 8.40 a.m. He left his home at 8:40 – 10 minutes = 8:30 a.m. He left 15 minutes earlier than usual, so his actual time of leaving home is 8:30 am + 15 minutes = 8:45 a.m.

10. Mamuni goes to the movies on Thursday, so nine days ago was Thursday.

∴ Two days ago was also Thursday. So, today is Saturday.

11. Day after the day-before-yesterday five days ago is the 6th day which is Thursday. And so, the 3rd day will be Sunday. Three days before the day-after-tomorrow is Yesterday which is the 1st day of the five days. So, two days ago was Sunday.

12. First Sunday is on 1st December

First Tuesday is on 3rd December

3 weeks later, Fourth Tuesday will be on 3 + (7 × 3) = 24th December.

13. 3rd day of the month is Monday

5th day from 21st is 26th

26 – 3 = 23 days

23 days later, 23/7 leaves 2 days.

So, two days ahead of Monday will be Wednesday.

14. 80 employees are required for double shift.

15. 15 horses eat 15 bags of grain in 15 days

15 horses eat 1 bag of grain in 1 day

1 horse eats 1 bag of grain in 15 days

16. A leap year is divisible by 4 and a century leap year is divisible by 400.

17. Seventh day from 10th is 17th.

5th day is Friday. Next Friday is on 12th, 17 – 12 = 5, 5 days ahead of Friday will be Wednesday. So, 17th is Wednesday.

18. Today is Monday

Day-after-tomorrow is Wednesday

Next week 'Holi' is also on Wednesday

So, Day after Holi is Thursday.

19. Hours between 3:30 p.m. and 4 a.m. are — 12½ hours. Number of minutes gained will be 12½ × 2 = 25 minutes.

20. Rajat returned on Thursday. 3 days later was the day of expected return, *i.e.,* Sunday. Rohit returned 4 days after Sunday, *i.e.,* Thursday.

ROWS AND RANKS

1. In a row of trees, one tree is fifth from either end of the row. How many trees are in the row?
   A. 11 B. 8
   C. 10 D. 9

2. Jaya ranks 5th in a class of 53. What is her rank from the bottom in the class?
   A. 49th B. 48th
   C. 47th D. 50th

3. Mohan ranks twenty-first in a class of sixty-five students. What will be his (Mohan's) rank if the lowest candidate is assigned rank 1?
   A. 44th B. 45th
   C. 46th D. Data inadequate

4. If Rahul finds that he is 12th from the right in a line of boys and 4th from the left, how many boys should be added to the line such that there are 28 boys in the line?
   A. 12 B. 14
   C. 20 D. 13

5. In a row of boys, Rajan is tenth from the right and Suraj is tenth from the left. When Rajan and Suraj interchange their positions, Suraj will be twenty-seventh from the left. Which of the following will be Rajan's position from the right?
   A. Tenth B. Twenty-sixth
   C. Twenty-ninth D. None of these

6. Mahesh and Suresh are ranked 11th and 12th respectively from the top in a class of 41 students. What will be their respective ranks from the bottom?
   A. 32nd and 33rd B. 29th and 30th
   C. 30th and 31st D. 31st and 30th

7. Uma ranked 8th from the top and 37th from bottom in a class. How many students are there in the class?
   A. 47 B. 46
   C. 45 D. None of these

8. In a queue, Sadiq is 14th from the front and Joseph is 17th from the end, while Jane is in between Sadiq and Joseph. If Sadiq be ahead of Joseph and there be 48 persons in the queue, how many persons are there between Sadiq and Jane?
   A. 5 B. 6
   C. 7 D. 8

9. Rohan ranked eleventh from the top and twenty-seventh from the bottom among the students who passed the annual examination in a class. If the number of students who failed in the examination was 12, how many students appeared for the examination?
   A. 48
   B. 49
   C. 50
   D. Cannot be determined

10. Some boys are sitting in a row. P is sitting fourteenth from the left and Q is seventh from the right. If there are four boys between P and Q, how many boys are there in the row?
   A. 19 B. 21
   C. 25 D. 23

ANSWERS

1	2	3	4	5	6	7	8	9	10
D	A	B	D	D	D	D	C	B	C

EXPLANATORY ANSWERS

1. 

Total number of trees in the row are :
(5 + 5) –1 =9

2. 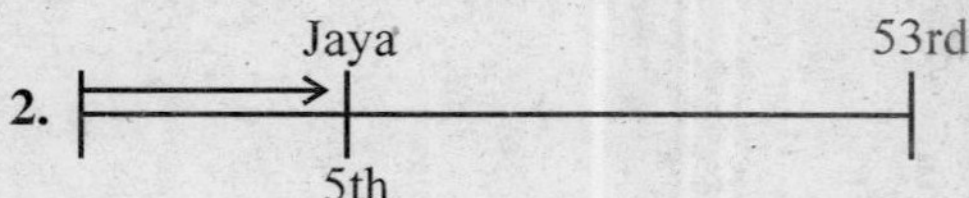

Jaya's rank from the bottom is :
(53 – 5) +1 = 49th.

3. 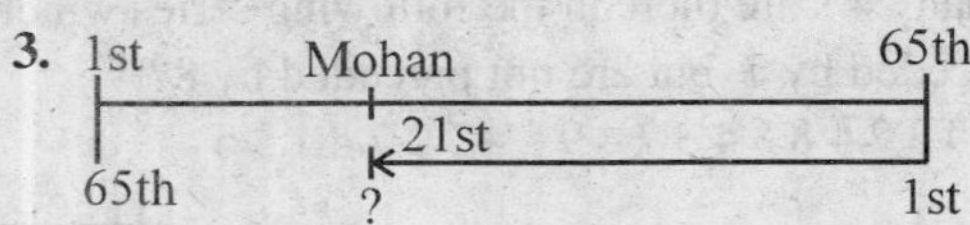

Note : Mohan's rank from the last or the question asked means the same.

Mohan's rank is (65 – 21) +1 = 45th

4.

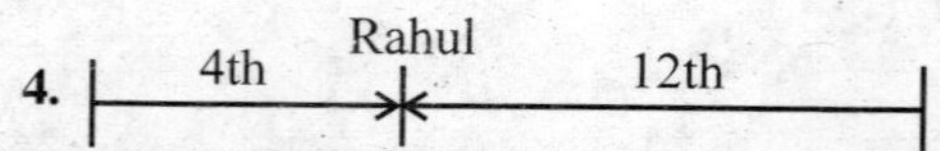

The number of boys in the line are :
(4 + 12) – 1 = 15
To make a line of 28 boys, (28 –15) *i.e.* 13 more boys are needed.

5.

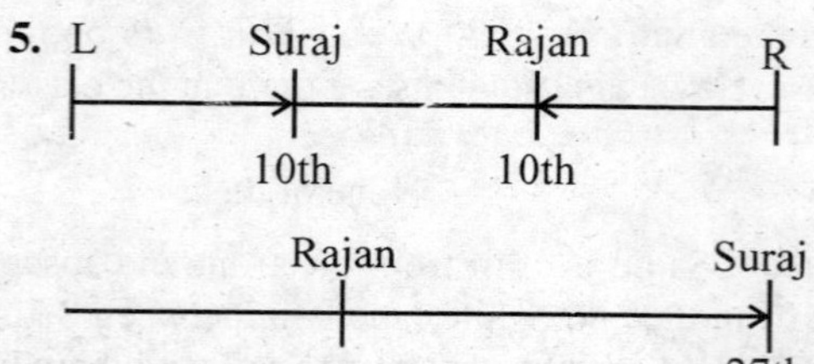

As the position of boys is equal from both ends, Rajan will also be 27th from the right after changing positions.

6.

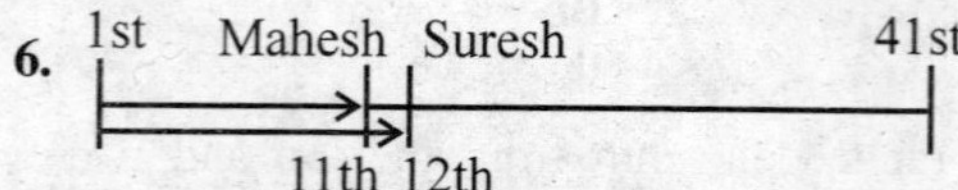

Mahesh's position from bottom is :
(41 – 11) + 1 = 31st
Suresh's position from bottom is :
(41 – 12) +1 = 30th

7.

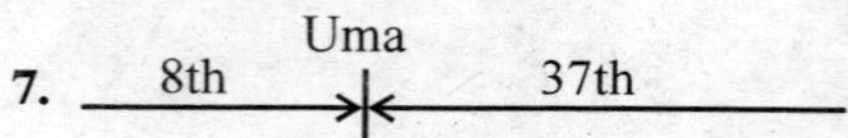

Total number of students in the class are :
(8 + 37) – 1 = 44

8.

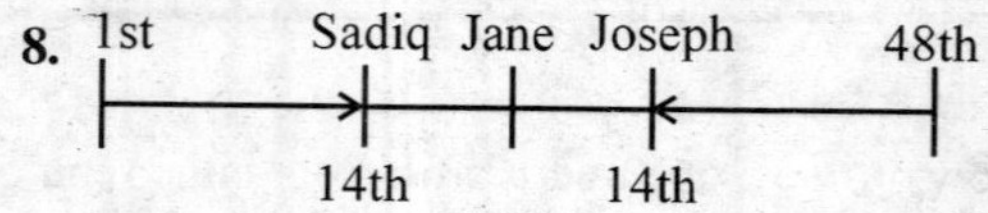

Sadiq's position from last is :
(48 – 14) + 1 = 35th
Number of persons between Sadiq and Joseph are (35 – 17) – 1 = 17
Jane is in-between Sadiq and Joseph *i.e.,* she's at 9th position from both the boys.
∴ there are 8 persons between Sadiq and Jane.
Note : (8 + 8) – 1 = 17

9.

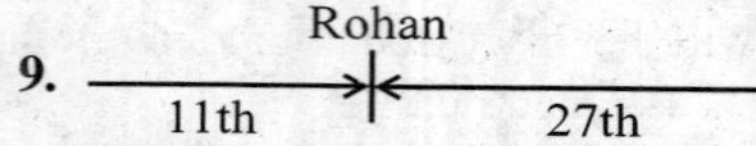

Number of students who passed the examination (11+ 27) – 1 = 37
Those who failed = 12
Total number of students who appeared in the examination = 37 + 12 = 49.

10.

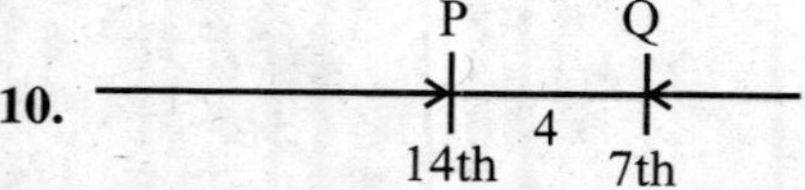

The number of boys in the row are :
(14 + 4 + 7) = 25

NUMBER PROBLEMS

1. How many 6's are there in the following series of numbers which are preceded by 7 but not immediately followed by 9?
6 7 9 5 6 9 7 6 8 7 6 7 8 6 9 4 6 7 7 6 9 5 7 6 3

A. One	B. Two
C. Three	D. Four

2. In a chess tournament each of six players will play every other player exactly once. How many matches will be played during the tournament?

A. 12	B. 15
C. 30	D. 36

3. How many 4's are there in the following series which are preceded by 7, but are not preceded by 8?
3 4 5 7 4 3 7 4 8 5 4 3 7 4 9 8 4 7 2 7 4 1 3 6

A. 1	B. 2
C. 3	D. 4

4. How many even numbers are there in the following series of numbers, each of which is immediately preceded by an odd number, but not immediately followed by an even number?
5 3 4 8 9 7 1 6 5 3 2 9 8 4 3 5

A. Nil	B. 1
C. 2	D. 3

5. If all the numbers from 1 to 51 which are exactly divisible by 3 are arranged in descending order, which of the following numbers will come at the seventh and tenth places from the top?

A. 33 & 27	B. 33 & 21
C. 21 & 30	D. 33 & 24

ANSWERS

1	2	3	4	5
C	B	D	C	D

EXPLANATORY ANSWERS

1. 6795697687678694677695763 (767 marked 1, 876 marked 2, 763 marked 3)

2. When all the players have to play with each other then the method of calculating the number of matches to be played is $\frac{n(n-1)}{2}$ where *'n'* is the number of players playing the match. So, the number of matches played will be :
$(6 \times 5) \div 2 = 30 \div 2 = 15$

3. 3457437485437498472741 36 (74 marked 1, 74 marked 2, 74 marked 3, 74 marked 4)

4. 534897165329843 5 (165 marked 1, 329 marked 2)

5. The numbers divisible by 3 in descending order are :
51, 48, 45, 42, 39, 36, 33, 30 (7th), 27, 24 (10th), 21, 18, 15, 12, 9, 6, 3.

SYMBOL SUBSTITUTION

1. If "+" means "–"; "–" means "×"; "×"means "÷" and "÷" means "+", then
$15 \times 5 \div 10 + 5 - 3 = ?$
A. 9.5 B. 0
C. – 2 D. 24

2. If "+" means "–"; "–" means "×"; "×"means "÷" and "÷" means "+", then
$15 \times 3 \div 15 + 5 - 2 = ?$
A. 0 B. 10
C. 20 D. 6

3. If "+" means "÷"; "×" means "–"; "÷"means "+" and "–" means "×", then
$16 \div 8 \times 6 - 2 + 12 = ?$
A. 22 B. 24
C. 23 D. 20

4. If "+" means "×"; "–" means "÷"; "÷"means "+" and "×" means "–", then what will be the value of $20 \div 40 - 4 \times 5 + 6 = ?$
A. 60 B. 1.67
C. 150 D. 0

5. If "+" means "×"; "–" means "÷"; "×"means "–" and "÷" means "+", then
$5 + 8 - 4 \times 2 \div 9 = ?$
A. 15 B. 13
C. 17 D. 11

ANSWERS

1	2	3	4	5
C	B	C	D	C

EXPLANATORY ANSWERS

1. $15 \div 5 + 10 - 5 \times 3$
$3 + 10 - 15 = -2$

2. $15 \div 3 + 15 - 5 \times 2$
$5 + 15 - 10 = 10$

3. $16 + 8 - 6 \times 2 \div 12$
$16 + 8 - 1 = 23$

4. $20 + 40 \div 4 - 5 \times 6$
$20 + 10 - 30 = 0$

5. $5 \times 8 \div 4 - 2 + 9$
$10 - 2 + 9 = 17$

MISSING NUMBERS

Directions: *In each question given below which one number can be placed at the sign of interrogation?*

1.

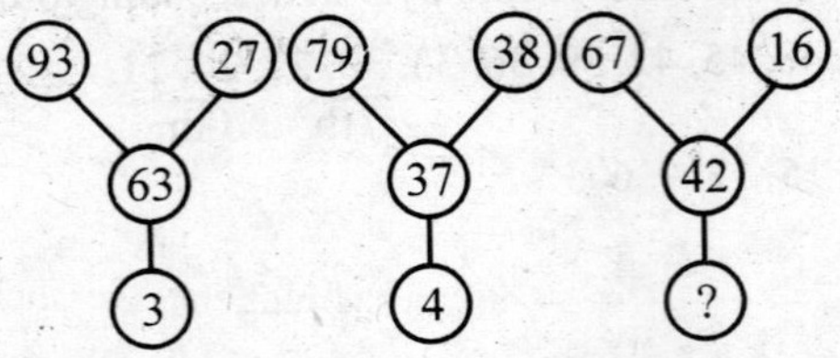

A. 5 B. 6
C. 8 D. 9

2.

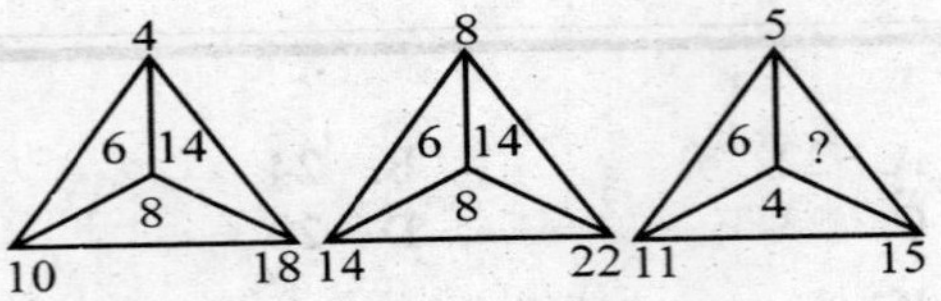

A. 8 B. 14
C. 10 D. 6

3.

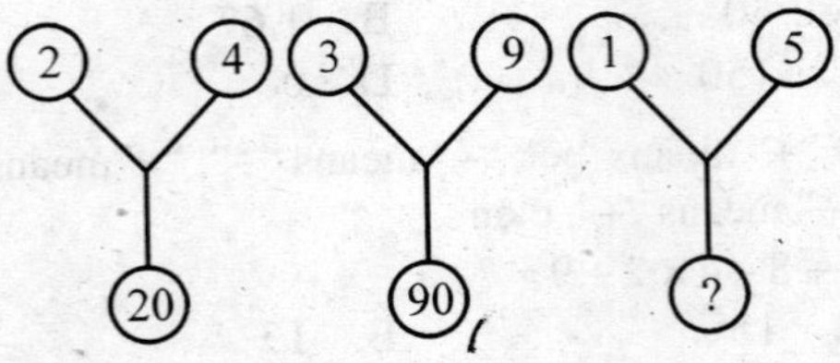

A. 20 B. 25
C. 26 D. 75

4.

27	22	50
13	12	26
9	2	?

A. 12 B. 39
C. 18 D. 24

5.

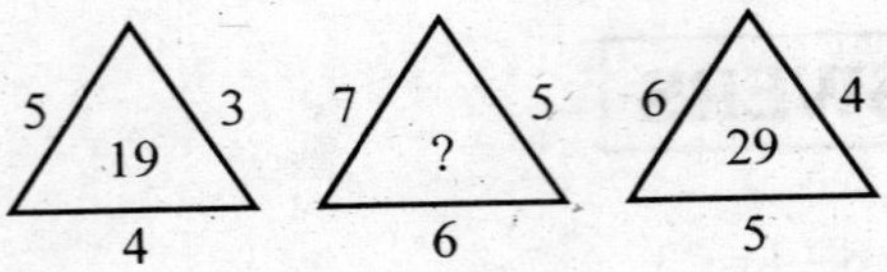

A. 25 B. 47
C. 37 D. 41

6.

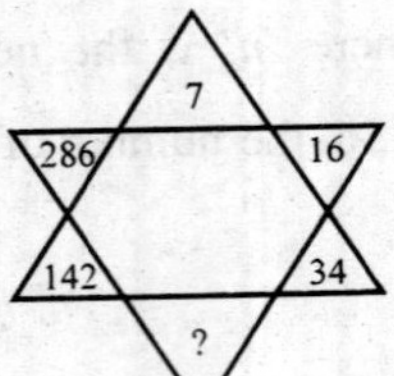

A. 70 B. 68
C. 56 D. 92

7.

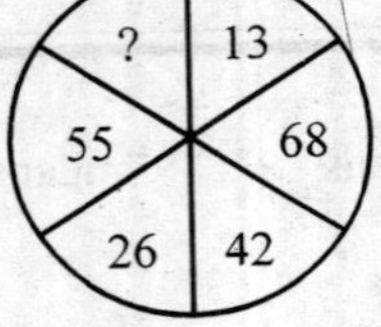

A. 41 B. 37
C. 29 D. 25

8.

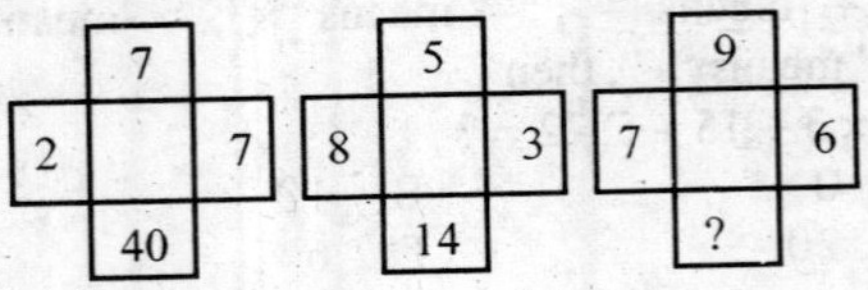

A. 72 B. 68
C. 82 D. 96

9.

42	(21)	22
78	(?)	84
162	(18)	99

A. 12 B. 13
C. 60 D. 72

10.

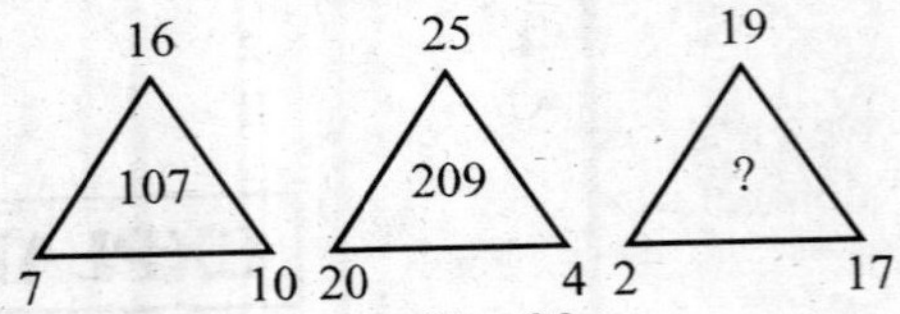

A. 68 B. 93
C. 175 D. 217

ANSWERS

1	2	3	4	5	6	7	8	9	10
D	C	C	A	D	A	C	B	B	A

EXPLANATORY ANSWERS

1. The sum of numbers on right and centre subtracted from the number on the left gives the number at the bottom, *i.e.*,

$93 - (27 + 63) = 3$
$79 - (38 + 37) = 4$

Similarly,
$67 - (16 + 42) = 9$

2. The number inside each triangle is the difference of the numbers at its base *i.e.*
$10 - 4 = 6$, $18 - 4 = 14$ and $18 - 10 = 8$
$14 - 8 = 6$, $22 - 8 = 14$ and $22 - 14 = 8$, similarly
$11 - 5 = 6$, $15 - 5 = 10$ and $15 - 11 = 4$.

3. The sum of squares of two numbers at the top gives the third number below, *i.e.*,
$2^2 + 4^2 = 20$
$3^2 + 9^2 = 90$, similarly
$1^2 + 5^2 = 26$

4. The sum of numbers in 1st and 2nd column plus 1 is the number in the 3rd column, *i.e.*,
$27 + 22 + 1 = 50$
$13 + 12 + 1 = 26$, similarly
$9 + 2 + 1 = 12$

5. The product of numbers on either side of the triangle plus the number at the base is the number inside the triangle, *i.e.*,
$(5 \times 3) + 4 = 19$
$(6 \times 4) + 5 = 29$, similarly
$(7 \times 5) + 6 = 41$

6. Clockwise starting from number 7, the next number is obtained by doubling the number and adding 2, *i.e.*,
$(7 \times 2) + 2 = 16$
$(16 \times 2) + 2 = 34 \ldots$, similarly
$(34 \times 2) + 2 = 70$
$(70 \times 2) + 2 = 142$
$(142 \times 2) + 2 = 286$

7. The difference between the numbers in opposite sectors is 13, *i.e.*,
$26 - 13 = 13$
$68 - 55 = 13$, similarly
The missing number is $42 - 13 = 29$
($42 + 13 = 55$ is not given as option)

8. The number at the bottom is obtained by subtracting the sum of two numbers in the centre grid line from the square of the number at the top, *i.e.*,
$7^2 - (2 + 7) = 40$
$5^2 - (8 + 3) = 14$, similarly
$9^2 - (7 + 6) = 68$

9. The number inside the brackets is obtained by multiplying the number on the left by 2 and then dividing the product by the sum of digits of number on the right, *i.e.*,
$(42 \times 2) \div (2 + 2) = 21$
$(162 \times 2) \div (9 + 9) = 18$, similarly
$(78 \times 2) \div (8 + 4) = 13$

10. Subtracting the sum of squares of two numbers at the base from the square of number at the apex gives the number inside the triangle, *i.e.*,
$16^2 - (7^2 + 10^2) = 107$
$25^2 - (20^2 + 4^2) = 209$, similarly
$19^2 - (2^2 + 17^2) = 68$

ALPHABET PROBLEMS

Directions : *The following questions are based on alphabet series in natural or reverse order and the combinations that can be made by changing the position of alphabet in given words.*

1. Which alphabet comes immediately before the sixth alphabet from the left extreme in alphabetical series?
A. U B. E
C. F D. V

2. Which letter is midway between G and S?
A. L B. N
C. M D. No letter

3. Which letter should be ninth letter to the left of ninth letter from the right if the first half of the alphabet is reversed?
A. I B. D
C. F D. E

4. If the alphabet is in reverse order, which letter will be eighth letter to the left of the seventh letter counting from the right end?
A. O B. P
C. N D. Q

5. What will be the fifth letter to the right of the thirteenth letter from the right?
A. R B. S
C. I D. O

ANSWERS

1	2	3	4	5
B	C	D	A	B

EXPLANATORY ANSWERS

1. 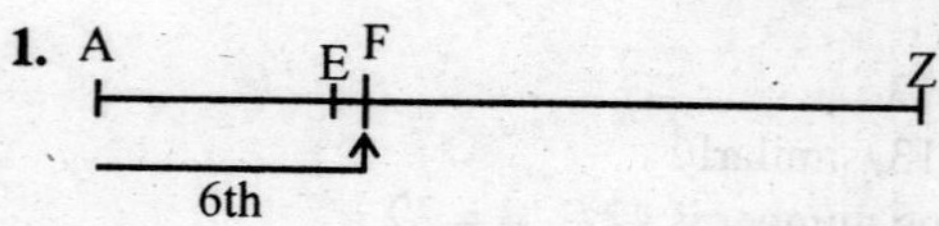

Sixth letter from left is 'F' and letter immediately before 'F' is 'E'.

2. 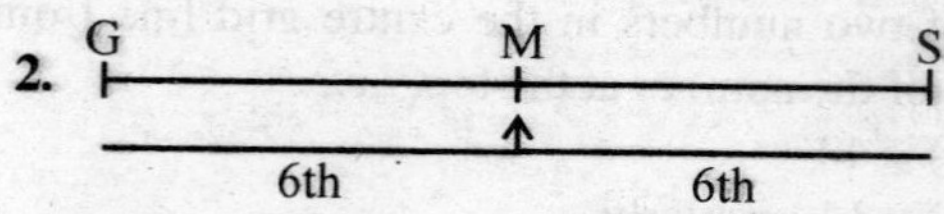

'M' is midway between G and S.

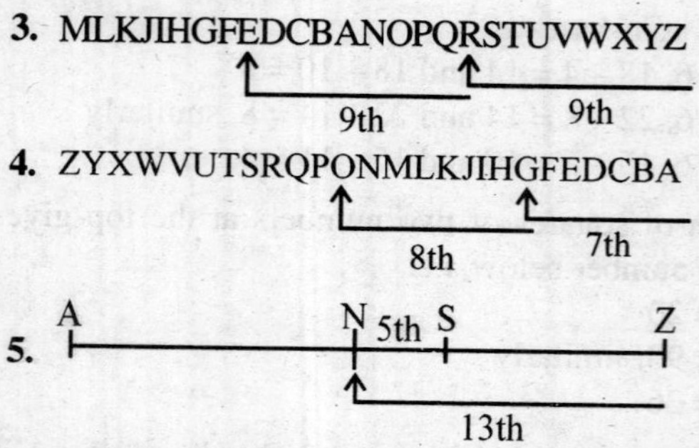

13th letter from right is 'N' and 5th letter to the right of 'N' is 'S'.

NON-VERBAL SERIES

Directions (Q. 1–10) : *In each of the following questions which one of the five answer figures given below should come after the problem figures if the sequence are continued?*

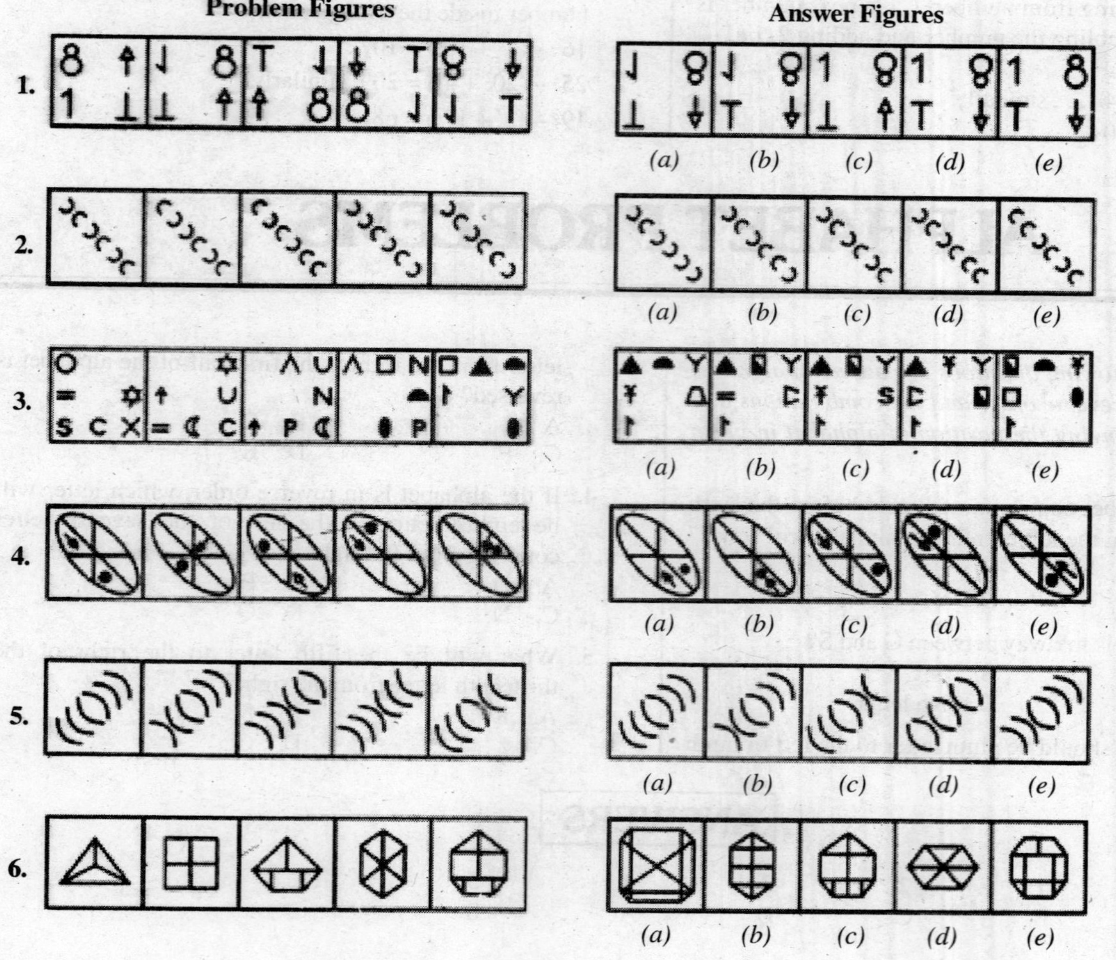

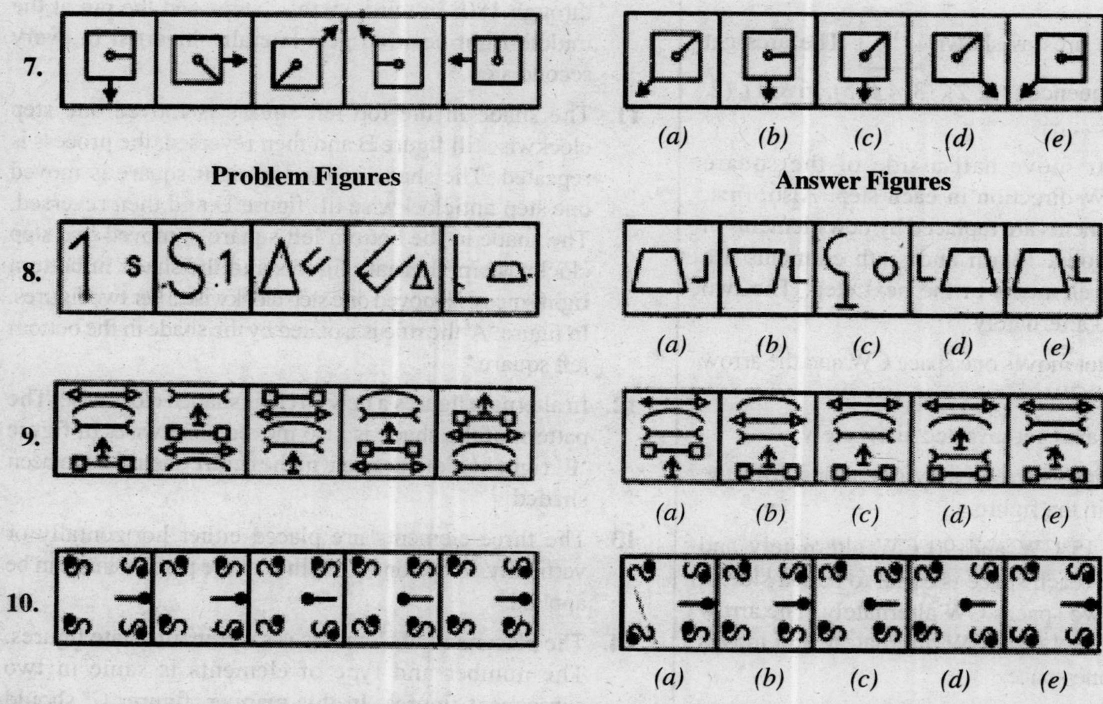

Directions (Q. 11-20) : *In each of these questions, a series begins with an unmarked figure on the extreme left in the row of figures. One and only one of the five lettered figures in the series does not fit into the series. The two unmarked figures, one on the extreme left and the other on the extreme right fit into the series. Take as many aspects into account as possible of the figures in the series and find out the one and only of the five marked figures which does not fit into the series. The letter of that figure is the answer.*

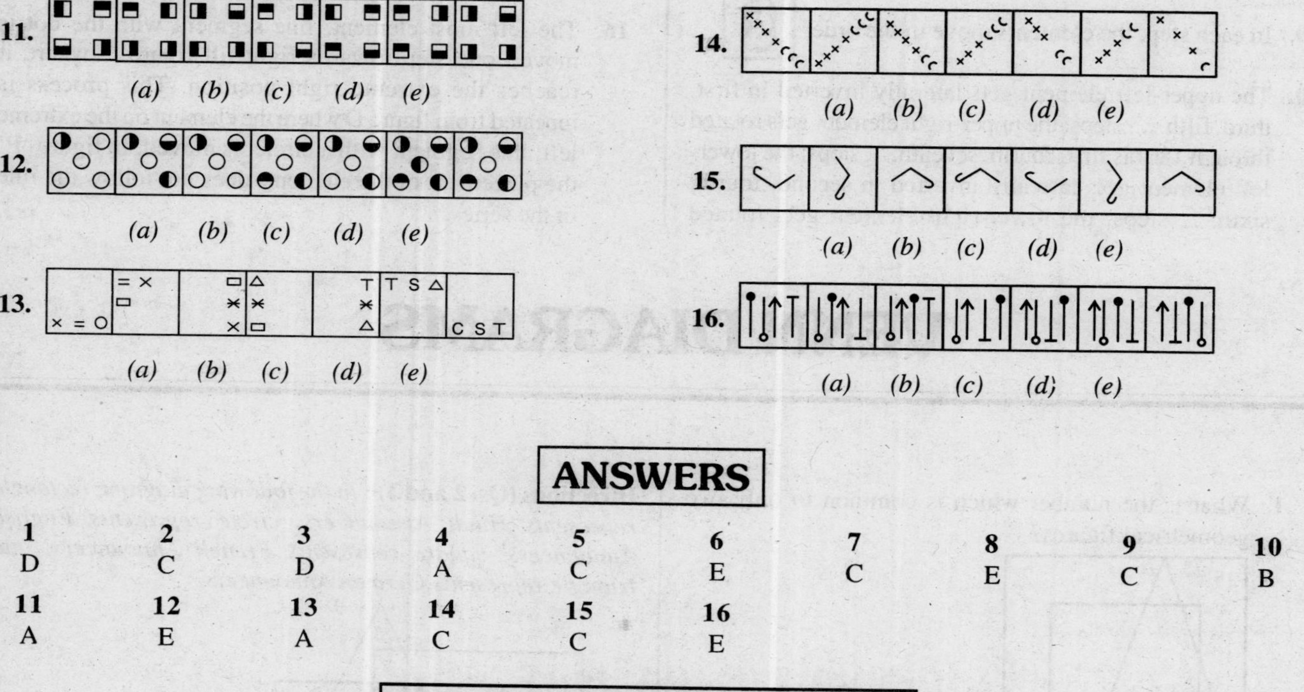

ANSWERS

1	2	3	4	5	6	7	8	9	10
D	C	D	A	C	E	C	E	C	B
11	**12**	**13**	**14**	**15**	**16**				
A	E	A	C	C	E				

EXPLANATORY ANSWERS

1. In each step, all the elements move to the adjacent corner (of the square boundary) in a CW direction and the element that reaches the upper-left corner gets vertically inverted.

2. We can label the arcs as shown [1, 2, 3, 4, 5, 6]. The arcs get inverted in the sequence (1 & 2), (3, 4 & 5), (6 & 1), (2, 3 & 4), (5 & 6), ...

3. All the elements move half-a-side of the square boundary in ACW direction in each step. Also, first, third and fifth elements are replaced by new elements in one step and second, fourth and sixth elements are replaced by new elements in the next step. The two steps are repeated alternately.

4. In each step, the dot moves one space CW and the arrow moves two spaces CW.

5. One arc and four arcs get inverted alternately.

6. The number of parts increases by one along with the number of sides in the figure.

7. The pin rotates 45°CW and 90°CW alternately and moves one space (each space is equal to half-a-side of the square) and two spaces CW alternately. The arrow rotates 90°ACW and 45°ACW alternately and moves two spaces and one space.

8. In one step, the two elements interchange positions and the smaller element gets enlarged while the larger element gets reduced in size. In the next step, the smaller element is replaced by a new small element and the larger element is replaced by a new large element.

9. In each step, the elements move in the order .

10. The upper-left element gets laterally inverted in first, third, fifth. .... steps; the upper-right element gets rotated through 180° is first, fourth, seventh,.... steps; the lower-left element gets laterally inverted in second, fourth, sixth, ... steps; the lower-right element gets rotated through 180° in third, sixth,... steps and the pin at the middle-right position gets laterally inverted in every second step.

11. The shade in the top left square is moved one step clockwise till figure B and then reversed, the process is repeated. The shade in the top right square is moved one step anticlockwise till figure D and then reversed. The shade in the bottom left square is moved one step clockwise in alternate figures and the shade in bottom right square is moved one step clockwise after two figures. In figure 'A' the rule is isolated by the shade in the bottom left square.

12. In alternate figures a new circle is shaded clockwise. The pattern of the shade is also moved clockwise. In figure 'E' right half of the circle in the centre should have been shaded.

13. The three elements are placed either horizontally or vertically. In option 'A' neither of the placements can be applied.

14. The placement of elements is same in alternate figures. The number and type of elements is same in two subsequent figures. In this manner, figure 'C' should have four crosses and two C shapes.

15. *(c)* : The element is moved one step anticlockwise and the arc at one end is turned outside and inside alternately. In figure 'C' the element should be on the right side with the arc turned outside on the top side.

16. The left most element, line segment with the dot is moved one step towards right till figure C where it reaches the extreme right position. This process is repeated from figure D where the element on the extreme left, line segment with a circle, is moved. In figure 'E' the placement of the elements does not follow the rule of the series.

VENN DIAGRAMS

1. What is the number which is common to only two geometrical figures?

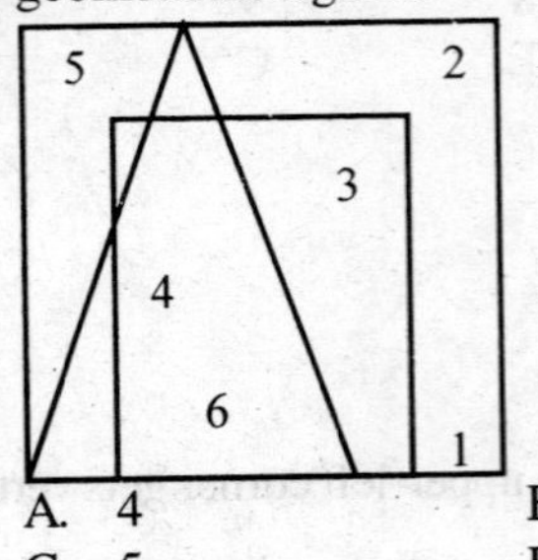

A. 4　　B. 3

C. 5　　D. 2

Directions (Qs. 2 and 3) : *In the following diagram, rectangle represents Hindi Announcers, circle represents English Announcers, square represents French Announcers, and triangle represents German Announcers.*

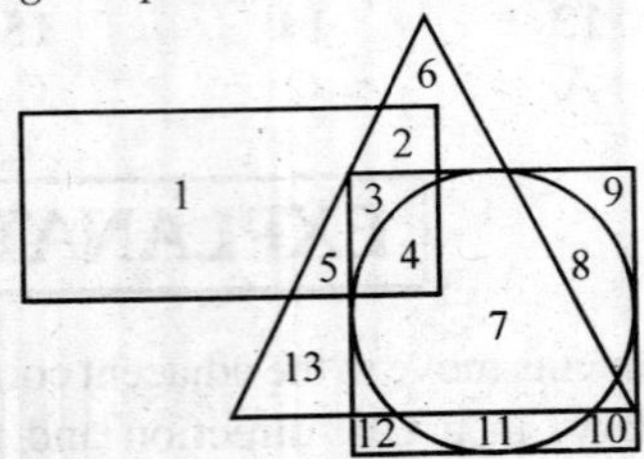

2. Which area represents those announcers who can present programmes in Hindi, French and German only?

A. 1 B. 2
C. 3 D. 4

3 Which area represents those announcers who can present programmes in French and English only?

A. 7 B. 9
C. 11 D. 13

Directions (Qs. 4 and 5) : *Study the diagram to answer these questions.*

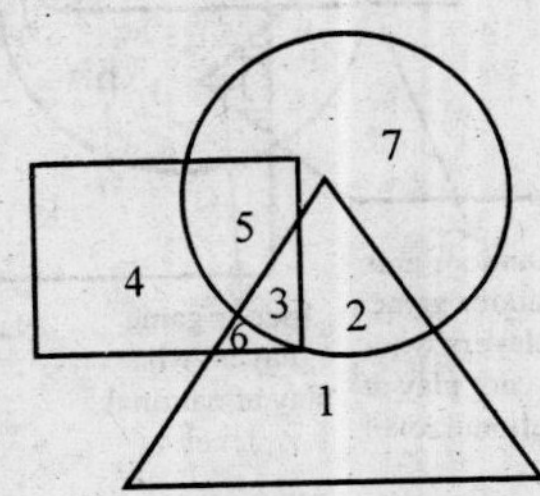

4. Which number is in all the geometrical figures?

A. 5 B. 6
C. 2 D. 3

5. Number 6 is in :

A. Rectangle and triangle
B. Circle and traingle
C. Rectangle and circle
D. Rectangle only

Directions (Qs. 6 to 9) : *In the following diagram*

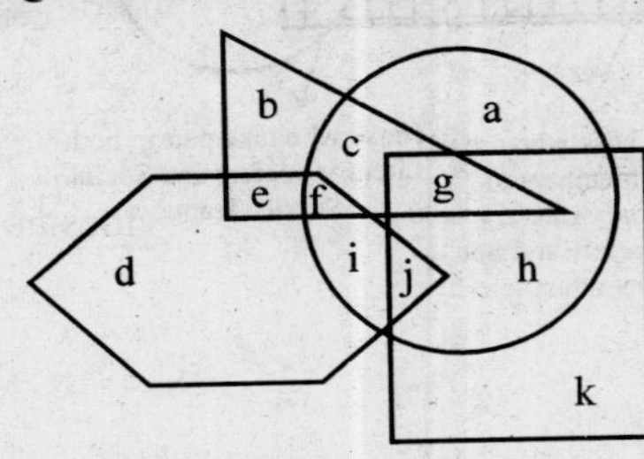

The Circle represents players
The Triangle represents outdoor games
The Hexagon represents indoor games and
The Square represents national level players
Study the diagram and answer the questions given below :

6. The letter in the section representing the players who play indoor games at national level is :

A. f B. i
C. j D. g

7. The letter representing the section of outdoor as well as indoor game players who do not play at the national level is :

A. c B. f
C. e D. i

8. The section representing national level players who do not play either outdoor or indoor games but still come under the category of players is :

A. k B. g
C. c D. h

9. Persons who play outdoor games but do not come under the category of players are represented in the section marked :

A. b B. c
C. a D. d

Directions (Qs. 10 to 13) : *Study the diagram given below.*

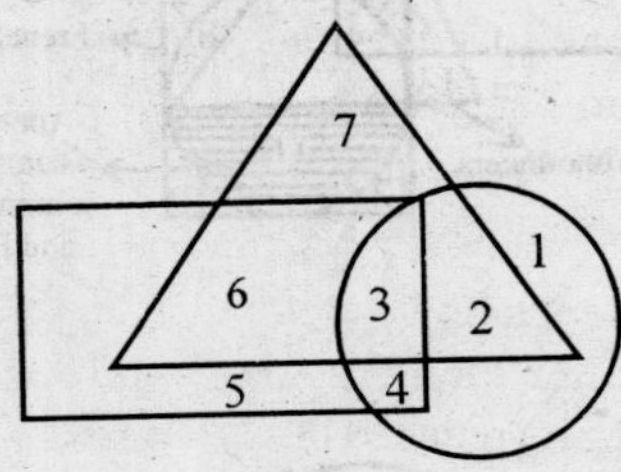

A college provides three different activities, students union represented by triangle, literary society represented by rectangle and social service league represented by circle.

10. Those who take part in both literary society and social service league but not in students union are represented by :

A. 3 & 4 B. 5 & 6
C. 5 & 1 D. 4

11. Those who take part in students union but not in social service league are represented by:

A. 2 & 7 B. 6 & 7
C. 6 D. 7

12. Those students who are members of literary society only and not of any other activity are represented by:

A. 2 B. 5
C. 3 & 4 D. 3

13. Those students who are members of all three groups are represented by :

A. 2 B. 3
C. 4 D. 6

ANSWERS

1	2	3	4	5	6	7	8	9	10
B	C	C	D	A	C	B	D	A	D
11	**12**	**13**							
B	B	B							

EXPLANATORY ANSWERS

1.

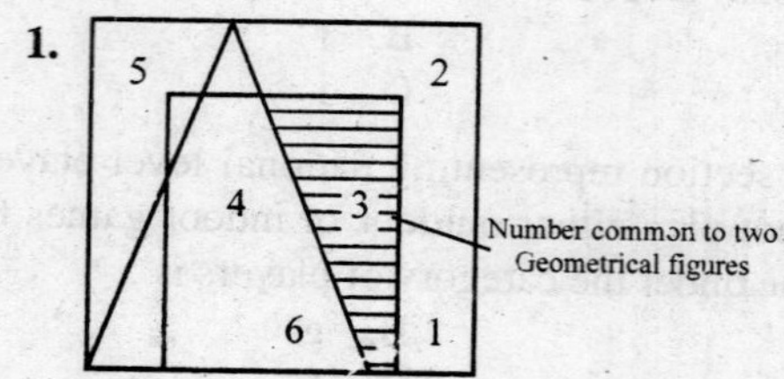

Note : Numbers 4 and 6 are common to all three geometrical figures.

Qs. 2 and 3.

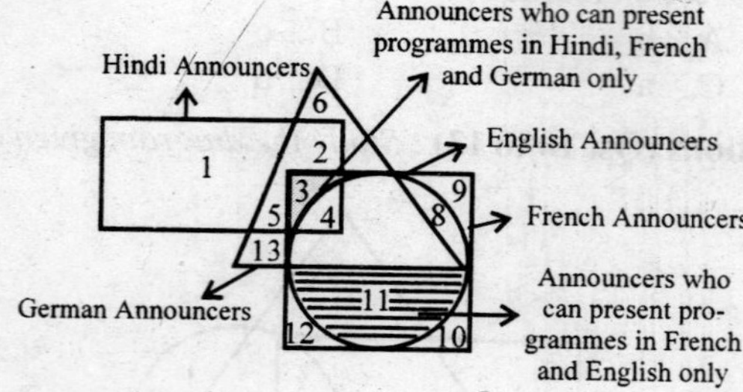

Qs. 4 and 5.

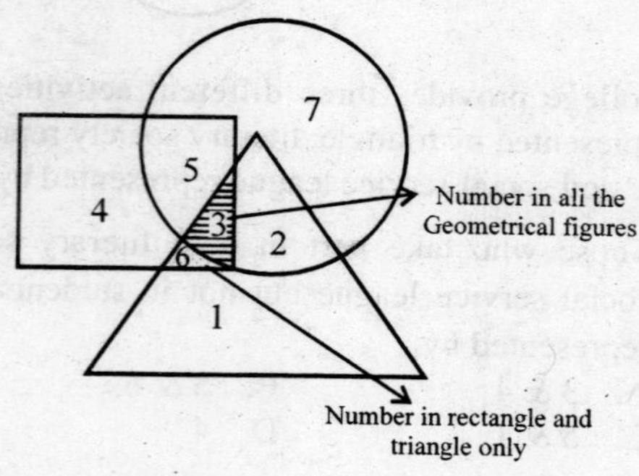

Qs. 6 to 9.

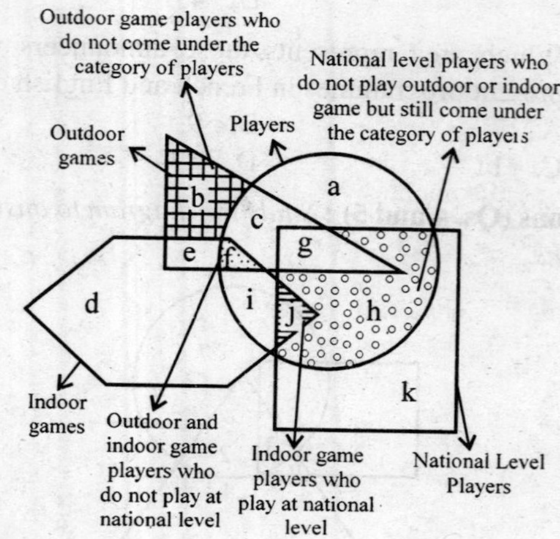

Qs. 10 to 13.

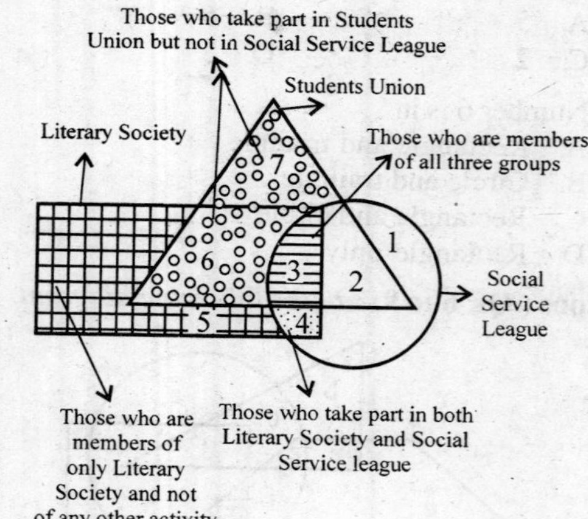

HARYANA

General Knowledge & Awareness

Multiple Choice Questions

1. During the ancient age, modern Haryana state was known as:
(*a*) Brahmavarta (*b*) Brahmarshi region
(*c*) Uttravedi of Brahma (*d*) All of the above

2. Who of the following rulers of Bharata vamsha (descendants of Bharata, according to Rigveda, who were a group of people who lived in the north-west of India) started his campaign from Haryana for establishing his authority in various other Kingdoms of the time?
(*a*) Sudas (*b*) Arjuna
(*c*) Bharata (*d*) Bhishma

3. The famous war of Mahabharata was fought at which of the following places in Haryana?
(*a*) Panipat (*b*) Kurukshetra
(*c*) Jhajjhar (*d*) Ballabh Garh

4. During Mughals, Janapadas of this state were replaced by
(*a*) Gana Sangha (*b*) Gana System
(*c*) Khaps (*d*) Panchayata

5. The territory of modern Haryana was included in which of the following Mahajanapadas of Buddha period?
(*a*) Kuru and Panchala (*b*) Kosala and Vajji
(*c*) Sursena and Avanti (*d*) Asmaka and Vatsa

6. At which of the following places in the state, capital of the Agreyagana was situated?
(*a*) Rewari (*b*) Sirsa
(*c*) Hansi (*d*) Agroha

7. Mahamud Gaznavi attacked on Thanesar in:
(*a*) 1013 AD (*b*) 1014 AD
(*c*) 1016 AD (*d*) 1017 AD

8. Thanesar (now in Haryana) was the capital of which of the following famous rulers of ancient India?
(*a*) Harsha Vardhan
(*b*) Ashoka
(*c*) Chandragupta Vikramaditya
(*d*) Kanishka

9. During the 12th century A.D. who of the following rulers of Chauhan dynasty defeated Tomars of Haryana?
(*a*) Vigraha Raja VI (*b*) Vigrah Raja II
(*c*) Arno Raja (*d*) Prithvi Raj Chauhan

10. When did Sultan Balban of Ghulam dynasty attacked on Mevas of Haryana with a view to establish his authority on Mevas?
(*a*) 1260 AD (*b*) 1265 AD
(*c*) 1266 AD (*d*) 1267 AD

11. Feroz Tughlaq of Tughlaq dynasty built which of the following cities in Haryana?
(*a*) Tohana (*b*) Hansi
(*c*) Siwani (*d*) Fatehabad

12. Timur made an attack on which of the following cities of Haryana?
(*a*) Sirsa (*b*) Fatehabad
(*c*) Hissar (*d*) All of the above

13. The famous battle of 1526 between Babur and Ibrahim Lodi was fought at which of the following places of Haryana?
(*a*) Panipat (*b*) Kurukshetra
(*c*) Tawaru (*d*) Jind

14. Who was the King of Rewari during the reign of famous Mughal Emperor Akbar?
(*a*) Tularam (*b*) Karna Singh
(*c*) Hemachandra (Hemu) (*d*) Phool Singh

15. The famous second battle of Panipat between Akbar and Hemachandra (Hemu) was fought in:
(*a*) 1550 AD (*b*) 1552 AD
(*c*) 1554 AD (*d*) 1556 AD

16. Which of the following famous battle was fought in the state of Haryana between the Marathas and Ahmadshah Abdali?
(*a*) The third battle of Panipat
(*b*) The second battle of Panipat
(*c*) The first battle of Panipat
(*d*) None of these

17. George Thomas built his capital at which of the following places of the state?
(*a*) Raniya (*b*) Tohana
(*c*) The fort of Hansi (*d*) Behram Pur

18. In 1802 AD George Thomas died at which of the following places in Haryana?
(*a*) Mahendragarh (*b*) Behram Pur
(*c*) Narnaul (*d*) Bawal

19. During 1809-10 AD, entire territories of Haryana was under the control of:
(*a*) Marathas (*b*) Satnamies
(*c*) Mughals (*d*) Britishers

20. Modern Haryana state was built on:
(*a*) 1 November, 1966 (*b*) 5 January, 1967
(*c*) 1 November, 1958 (*d*) 15 August, 1947

21. Evidences of Early-Harappan, Mature Harappan and Late Harappan culture have been found at which of the following places in Haryana?
(*a*) Banawali (*b*) Sosawal
(*c*) Mirzapur (*d*) All of the above

22. The period of Aryans of Kuru Vamsha, centuries before the Mahabharata period was marked with the beginning of which of the following ages?
(*a*) Cultivation Age (*b*) Copper Age
(*c*) Iron Age (*d*) Metal Age

23. The essence of the philosophy of Bhagvad Gita preached by Lord Krishna to Arjuna, a noted Commander of the Mahabharata War in the form of a dialogue between the two was delivered at which of the following places of Haryana?
(*a*) Rewari (*b*) Pehwa
(*c*) Kurukshetra (*d*) Panipat

24. During Youdheya period, Haryana was known as:
(*a*) Youdheya confederacy (*b*) Bahudhanyaka region
(*c*) Matsya region (*d*) Gana region

25. The famous pilgrim Hiuen Tsang in his book Si-Yo-ki, has described the prosperity of which of the following cities of Haryana?
(*a*) Sthaneshwar (Thanesmar)
(*b*) Panipat
(*c*) Rohtak
(*d*) Ambala

26. Which of the following treatise provide valuable information about the advancement of trade, art and culture in Haryana during the reign of Tomar Kings?
(*a*) Tahkik-i-Hind (*b*) Harsh Charita
(*c*) Kadambari (*d*) Yashastilak Champu

27. Who was the ruler of the Tawaroo pargana during the invasion of Babur in 1526-27?
(*a*) Hasan Khan (*b*) Mohan Singh Mandhar
(*c*) Faizal Khan (*d*) Jalal Khan

28. During the period of Babur, the Rajput King Mohan Singh Mandhar had its kingdom in Haryana at:
(*a*) Mandhar Pargana of Kaithal
(*b*) Tawaroo
(*c*) Jind
(*d*) Panipat

29. During 1756-57, Haryana was under the control of:
(*a*) Mughals (*b*) Sikhs
(*c*) Marathas (*d*) Satnamies

30. While returning back to his homeland, Ahmad Shah Abdali put the northern part of Haryana (Ambala, Jind, Kurukshetra and Karnal Districts) under the charge of:
(*a*) Mughals
(*b*) Sikhs
(*c*) Jain Khan, the Governor of Sarhind
(*d*) Gen Khan the Governor of Durrani

31. In the sepoy mutiny that broke out in 1857 at Meerut, majority of soldiers who took part in the revolt hailed from which of the following districts of Haryana?
(*a*) Gurugram (*b*) Rohtak
(*c*) Hissar (*d*) All of these

32. Who of the following great warriors of Haryana was the Naib Kotwal of Meerut at the time of Sepoy mutiny:
(*a*) Abdus Samad Khan (*b*) Vikram Singh
(*c*) Rao Krishna Gopal (*d*) Rameshwar Dayal

33. In the battle (for the freedom of India) fought at the village Naseebpur situated near Narnaul, Britishers destroyed which of the following three powers?
(*a*) Rewari, Jhajjhar and Jodhpur
(*b*) Gurugram, Rewari and Jodhpur
(*c*) Jind, Jagadari and Pehwa
(*d*) Panipat, Jhajjhar and Tawaroo

34. In the first Freedom struggle, who of the following Kings of Ballabhgarh led the revolutionary army in Delhi?
(*a*) Raja Karn Singh (*b*) Raja Nahan Singh
(*c*) Raja Suraj Bhan (*d*) Raja Satyapal

35. Which of the following provinces of Haryana extended valuable cooperation to the British army in the revolt of 1857?
(*a*) Bahadurgarh (*b*) Tawaroo
(*c*) Jhajjhar (*d*) Jind

36. In the second Calcutta session of the Indian National Congress held in the year 1886, Haryana was represented by:
(*a*) Pandit Deen Dayal Sharma
(*b*) Lala Murlidhar
(*c*) Bal Mukund Gupta
(*d*) All of these

37. Lala Lajpat Rai had selected which of the following places situated in Haryana as his political and social work-field?
(*a*) Hissar (*b*) Sonipat
(*c*) Gurugram (*d*) Nooh

38. In the fourth session of the Indian National Congress held in 1888 at Allahabad who of the following national leaders represented Hissar?
(*a*) Lala Sultan Singh (*b*) Baldeo Singh
(*c*) Lala Lajpat Rai (*d*) Baini Singh

39. On 8 April, 1919, Gandhiji was arrested from which of the following places of Haryana?
(*a*) Kaithal (*b*) Palwal
(*c*) Gohana (*d*) Ambala

40. When was a conference held at Rohtak presided by Pt. Rambhaj Dutta in which a decision was taken to implement the Non-cooperation movement launched by Gandhiji?
(*a*) January, 1919 (*b*) November, 1919
(*c*) November, 1920 (*d*) September, 1921

41. In the annual session of Congress held at Nagpur, Haryana was represented by :
(*a*) Sardar Buta Singh (*b*) Lala Ugrasen
(*c*) Babu Shyam Lal (*d*) Pt. Neki Ram Sharma

42. On the appeal of Punjab Pradesh Congress, Independence Day was celebrated in entire Haryana on:
(*a*) 12 January, 1932 (*b*) 10 December, 1932
(*c*) 15 August, 1935 (*d*) 26 January, 1932

43. On which day was the Golden Jubilee of Congress celebrated in Haryana?
(*a*) 18 August, 1930 (*b*) 30 January, 1935
(*c*) 28 December, 1935 (*d*) 10 December, 1936

44. Who of the following was the great hero of Haryana who as a member of the INA hoisted the tricoloured flag for the first time on the land of Manipur?
(*a*) Major Pratap Singh (*b*) Major Suraj Mal
(*c*) Darbara Singh (*d*) Bhajan Lal

45. Chaudhary Chhotu Ram started a vigorous campaigns to popularize the Unionist Party in Haryana. In Haryana state this Party was called as:
(*a*) Zamindara League (*b*) Zamindari System
(*c*) Hindu-Muslim (*d*) None of these

46. Publication of which of the following weekly magazine was started by Chaudhary Chhotu Ram in 1916 from Rohtak?
(*a*) Hindu Gazette (*b*) Sikh Gazette
(*c*) Jat Gazette (*d*) None of the above

47. Chaudhary Chhotu Ram alongwith Shri Fazali Hussain set up the Unionist Party in Punjab in:
(*a*) 1919 (*b*) 1921
(*c*) 1922 (*d*) 1923

48. With a view to keep a control on the political activities in Patiala, Jind and Nabha states, a law was enforced in Samvat 1988 Vikrami. What was that law termed as:
(*a*) Hidayat Samvat (*b*) Hizri Samvat
(*c*) Vikram Samvat (*d*) Saka Samvat

49. In 1938, Jind Prajamandal was set up at Sangrur, the capital of Jind by:
(*a*) Rajendra Kumar Jain (*b*) Sadhu Ram
(*c*) Hansraj Rahbar (*d*) Nand Kishore

50. Gandhji was arrested from Palwal on:
(*a*) 5 January, 1919 (*b*) 8 May, 1920
(*c*) 8 April, 1919 (*d*) 17 April, 1921

51. Pt. Deen Dayal Sharma who made a very important contribution in popularizing Sanatan Dharma in whole of the Northern India, hailed from which of the following places of Haryana?
(*a*) Jhajjhar (*b*) Kaithal
(*c*) Hissar (*d*) Jind

52. In the Lahore Session of the Congress in 1892, Hissar was represented by:
(*a*) Balmukund Gupta (*b*) Lala Murlidhar
(*c*) Lala Lajpat Rai (*d*) Pt. Deen Dayal Sharma

53. When was Lala Lajpat Rai and Sardar Ajit Singh were arrested by the British Government and sent to Mandley Jail?
(*a*) In 1907 (*b*) In 1895
(*c*) In 1902 (*d*) In 1896

54. Mahatma Gandhi accompanied with Muhammad Ali and Shaukat Ali arrived Rohtak on:
(*a*) 10 January, 1919 (*b*) 8 October, 1920
(*c*) 1 October, 1920 (*d*) 18 March, 1920

55. The Divisional Political Conference of Ambala Division which was attended by Mahatma Gandhi alongwith Ali brothers, was held at Bhiwani in:
(*a*) March, 1918 (*b*) June, 1920
(*c*) October, 1919 (*d*) October, 1920

56. Even after India became free in 1947, Haryana remained a part of which of the following Indian Provinces?
(*a*) Delhi (*b*) Punjab
(*c*) Uttra Pradesh (*d*) Rajasthan

57. The state Restructuring Commission set up in 1955 by the Government of India had recommended to include which of the following two places in the state of Haryana?
(*a*) Mahendragarh and Jind (*b*) Patiala and Hissar
(*c*) Panipat and Kaithal (*d*) Rohtak and Gurugram

58. The tourist place called 'Tiliyar' is situated in which of the following districts of Haryana?
(*a*) Jind (*b*) Mahendragarh
(*c*) Rohtak (*d*) Kaithal

59. Who was the first Governor of Haryana?
(*a*) Shri Satyapal (*b*) Shri Dharmvir
(*c*) Shri Devilal (*d*) Shri Bansilal

60. Name of the first Non-Congress Chief Minister of Haryana who assumed this office on 24 March, 1967.
(*a*) Chaudhary Bhajan Lal (*b*) Devi Lal
(*c*) Bansi Lal (*d*) Rao Virendra Singh

61. Which of the following Rivers flow from the adjoining areas of Eastern Haryana and Uttar Pradesh?
(*a*) Ganga (*b*) Saraswati
(*c*) Ghaghghar (*d*) Yamuna

62. The main land of Haryana state stretches from 27° 39° N to 30° 55° N latitudes in the North-West of India. It stretches from .... E to .... E longitudes.
(*a*) 74° 28° E to 77° 36° E (*b*) 65° 33° E to 77° 28° E
(*c*) 50° 28° E to 64° 36° E (*d*) 84° 42° E to 89° 41° E

63. Which of the following states is located to the North of Haryana?
(*a*) Uttar Pradesh (*b*) Punjab
(*e*) Himachal Pradesh (*d*) Rajasthan

64. Which of the following states is located to the west of Haryana?
(*a*) Punjab (*b*) Rajasthan
(*c*) Uttar Pradesh (*d*) Himachal Pradesh

65. What is the area of the state of Haryana?
(*a*) 36,154 Sq. km. (*b*) 44,212 Sq. km.
(*c*) 49,105 Sq. km. (*d*) 51,206 Sq. km.

66. Which of the following state is not larger than Haryana by area?
(*a*) Meghalaya (*b*) Bihar
(*c*) Himachal Pradesh (*d*) Punjab

67. Dabwali is a subdivision of which district?
(*a*) Sirsa (*b*) Hissar
(*c*) Rohtak (*d*) Jhajjar

68. The mainland of Haryana is located at the height of .... from the sea level.
(*a*) 700 to 900 ft. (*b*) 750 to 880 ft.
(*c*) 800 to 1000 ft. (*d*) 900 to 1100 ft.

69. Shivalik range is located in which part of Haryana?
(*a*) North-West (*b*) North-East
(*c*) South-West (*d*) South-East

70. Which of the following rivers originate from Shivalik range to flow through the mainland of Haryana?
(*a*) Ghaghghar (*b*) Markanda
(*c*) Tangri (*d*) All of these

71. Which of the following natural parts of Haryana is the largest?
(*a*) the hilly region of the Shivalik
(*b*) the desert of Haryana
(*c*) the mainland of Haryana
(*d*) the dry plains of Aravali range

72. The famous Bibipur and Najafgarh lakes are located in which natural part of Haryana?
(*a*) The Plain
(*b*) The desert
(*c*) Hilly region of the Shivalik
(*d*) The dry plain of Aravali range

73. Which of the following cities of Haryana is not the part of National Capital Region?
(*a*) Sonipat (*b*) Faridabad
(*c*) Hisar (*d*) Gurugram

74. Which part of Haryana experiences maximum rainfall?
(*a*) South-Western Part (*b*) North-Eastern Part
(*c*) North-Western Part (*d*) South-Eastern Part

75. Which of the following parts of Haryana experiences minimum annual rainfall?
(*a*) North-Eastern Part (*b*) South-Eastern Part
(*c*) North-Western Part (*d*) South-Western Part

76. Which type of soil is found on Morney hills of the state?
(*a*) Sandy Soil (*b*) Brownish Soil
(*c*) Laterite Soil (*d*) Sandy Clayee Soil

77. Generally, which type of soil is found in the plains of Haryana?
(*a*) Fertile Soil of Yellow brownish colour
(*b*) Laterite Soil
(*c*) Sandy Soil
(*d*) Sandy Clayee Soil

78. In which of the following districts of Haryana, red chestnut soil is found?
(*a*) Rohtak (*b*) Sirsa
(*c*) Yamuna Nagar (*d*) Bhivani

79. Which of the following rivers of the state of Haryana joins Markanda river near Mulana?
(*a*) Sahibi (*b*) Tangri
(*c*) Krishnawati (*d*) Dohan

80. Which of the following is the oldest and the most important canal of Haryana?
(*a*) Gurugram Canal (*b*) Bhiwani Canal
(*c*) Bhakra Canal (*d*) Western Yamuna Canal

81. Which of the following canals originates from the Yamuna river near Tazewala situated on the Jagadhari-Pona road?
(*a*) Bhakra Canal
(*b*) Western and Eastern Yamuna Canal
(*c*) Jawahar Lal Nehru Canal
(*d*) None of these

82. Jawahar Lal Nehru canal of Haryana originates from:
(*a*) Bhakra Canal (*b*) Bhiwani Canal
(*c*) Gurugram Canal (*d*) Yamuna Canal

83. Which of the following lakes is located in Haryana?
(*a*) Damdama Lake (*b*) Kotla Lake
(*c*) Khalilpur Lake (*d*) All of these

84. Which of the following lakes is situated in Farrukh Nagar block of the state?
(*a*) Sultanpur lake (*b*) Damdama lake
(*c*) Khalilpur lake (*d*) Kotla lake

85. The famous Badkal lake is situated in which of the following districts of Haryana?
(*a*) Gurugram (*b*) Bhivani
(*c*) Faridabad (*d*) Rohtak

86. Which of the following canals of Haryana originates from Yamuna river at Okhla in Delhi?
(*a*) Bhakra Canal (*b*) Gurugram Canal
(*c*) Eastern Yamuna Canal (*d*) None of these

87. Bhakra Canal provides water for irrigation in which of the following districts of Haryana?
(*a*) Sirsa (*b*) Hissar
(*c*) Rohtak (*d*) All of these

88. Which of the following districts of the state gets water for irrigation from Jawahar Lal Nehru Canal?
(*a*) Sirsa (*b*) Rohtak
(*c*) Mahendragarh (*d*) Jind

89. Bhiwani canal originates from which of the following canals?
(*a*) Bhakra Canal (*b*) Gurugram Canal
(*c*) Western Yamuna Canal (*d*) Eastern Yamuna Canal

90. When was the famous Badkal lake of Haryana built?
(*a*) In 1940 (*b*) In 1950
(*c*) In 1974 (*d*) In 1947

91. The famous tourist place 'Tajewala Headworks' is situated in which of the following districts of Haryana?
(*a*) Rohtak (*b*) Faridabad
(*c*) Gurugram (*d*) Yamuna Nagar

92. Haryana has been divided into:
(*a*) 6 Divisions (*b*) 5 Sub Divisions
(*c*) 4 Divisions (*d*) 8 Divisions

93. How many total sub-divisions exist in Haryana state till January, 2025?
(*a*) 60 Sub-Divisions (*b*) 65 Sub-Divisions
(*c*) 68 Sub-Divisions (*d*) 80 Sub-Divisions

94. How many total Tehsils exist in Haryana till January, 2025?
(*a*) 94 (*b*) 68
(*c*) 70 (*d*) 85

95. How many total sub-Tehsils exist in Haryana till January, 2025?
(*a*) 30 (*b*) 31
(*c*) 49 (*d*) 40

96. How many total Blocks exist in Haryana till January, 2025?
(*a*) 95 (*b*) 143
(*c*) 115 (*d*) 119

97. Total number of populated villages in Haryana is:
(*a*) 4,390 (*b*) 4,950
(*c*) 5,845 (*d*) 6,841

98. According to the Census of 2011, the total population of Haryana is:
(*a*) 2,53,51,462 (*b*) 2,40,55,400
(*c*) 2,25,83,912 (*d*) 2,20,45,657

99. Salarganj Gate is situated near which of the following town of Haryana?
(*a*) Rohtak (*b*) Hissar
(*c*) Panipat (*d*) Ambala

100. In terms of area the largest district of Haryana is:
(*a*) Rohtak (*b*) Sirsa
(*c*) Panipat (*d*) Ambala

101. Which of the following minerals is found in abundance in Mahendragarh district of Haryana?
(*a*) Lime stone (*b*) China clay
(*c*) Copper (*d*) All of these

102. At which of the following places in district Rewari, Slate-stone is found in abundance?
(*a*) Kund (*b*) Baval
(*c*) Kusal (*d*) Khol

103. Consider the following statements:
1. Nada Sahib Gurudwara is situated in Ambala.
2. Nada Sahib Gurudwara is situated on the bank of river Ghaggar.

Which of the above statements is/are correct?
(*a*) 2 only (*b*) Both 1 and 2
(*c*) Neither 1 nor 2 (*d*) 1 only

104. At which of the following places in district Bhiwani Granite stones are found?
(*a*) Village Nigana Kalan (*b*) Delheri
(*c*) Riwasa (*d*) All of these

105. When was Shri Krishna Museum established in Kurukshetra?
(*a*) 1987 (*b*) 1970
(*c*) 1989 (*d*) 1995

106. What is the area of the total forest land in Haryana?
(*a*) 1,428 Sq. km. (*b*) 1,614.26 Sq. km.
(*c*) 1,852 Sq. km. (*d*) 1,812 Sq. km.

107. During which of the following years, a comprehensive afforestation scheme 'Greening of Haryana' was started?
(*a*) 1982 - 83 (*b*) 1983 - 86
(*c*) 1989 - 90 (*d*) 1994 - 95

108. Haryana has announced its new Industrial Policy in ....
(*a*) 1995 (*b*) 2011
(*c*) 2005 (*d*) 2002

109. With the aid of the European Union "Haryana Community Development Scheme" (Haryana Samudayiki) was introduced in Haryana in:
(*a*) 1992 - 93 (*b*) 1994 - 95
(*c*) 1996 - 97 (*d*) 1998 - 99

110. Basai wetland is located in which district of Haryana?
(*a*) Gurugram (*b*) Jhajjar
(*c*) Faridabad (*d*) Kurukshetra

111. As per census 2011, literacy of Haryana is:
(*a*) 80.40% (*b*) 65.72%
(*c*) 75.6% (*d*) 68.85%

112. Which of the following tourist place is situated on Samauli Road Panipat?
(*a*) Jyotisar (*b*) Kala Amb
(*c*) Damdama Lake (*d*) King Fisher

113. Which of the following minerals is found in districts Hissar and Karnal?
(*a*) Pig Iron (*b*) Mica
(*c*) Nitre (*d*) Marble

114. Which of the following minerals is found in Rohtak district?
(*a*) Lime (*b*) Copper
(*c*) Manganese (*d*) Mica

115. Which of the following trees are found in abundance in Jind district of Haryana?
(*a*) Rosewood tree (Sesam) (*b*) Acacia tree (Kikar)
(*c*) Safeda (*d*) All of these

116. In the Agricultural University, Hissar 'research on Paddy' was started in:
(*a*) 1966 (*b*) 1970
(*c*) 1974 (*d*) 1989

117. Where is National Cancer Institute situated?
(*a*) Sampla (*b*) Meham
(*c*) Kalanaur (*d*) Badsa

118. Which of the following districts of Haryana is pre-eminent in the production of mushroom (Khumbhi) in India?
(*a*) Ambala (*b*) Sirsa
(*c*) Sonepat (*d*) Yamuna Nagar

119. Which of the following is a major crop produced in Rohtak district of Haryana?
(*a*) Pearl Millet (*b*) Great Millet
(*c*) Sugar cane (*d*) All of these

120. Sugar Mill is located at which of the following places in Kurukshetra?
(*a*) Pehwa (*b*) Shahabad Markanda
(*c*) Ladawa (*d*) Babain

121. Which of the following districts of Haryana is called "a big bowl of paddy" as it has gained world fame in the production of Basmati rice?
(*a*) Hissar (*b*) Kurukshetra
(*c*) Karnal (*d*) Jind

122. Navagrah temple in Haryana is located at ....
(*a*) Kurukshetra (*b*) Kaithal
(*c*) Gurugram (*d*) Faridabad

123. The total installed capacity of energy available to the state till 2023-24 is ....
(*a*) 8,575 MW (*b*) 8,200 MW
(*c*) 14,026.68 MW (*d*) 9,510 MW

124. What was the quantum of production of horticulture crops in Haryana during 2023-24?
(*a*) 41.20 Lakh M.T. (*b*) 85.63 Lakh M.T.
(*c*) 62.15 Lakh M.T. (*d*) 52.25 Lakh M.T.

125. In which of the following districts of Haryana, with a view to check the soil erosion in Shivalik areas, coordinated water flow Development Project is being implemented?
(*a*) Ambala (*b*) Panchkula
(*c*) Yamuna Nagar (*d*) All of these

126. Indira Gandhi Super Thermal Power Project is situated in which district of Haryana?
(*a*) Sirsa (*b*) Hisar
(*c*) Jind (*d*) Jhajjar

127. In the Ambala district of Haryana, canal irrigation system was made available after completion of which of the following irrigation project?
(*a*) Nangal Lift Irrigation Project
(*b*) Hathni Reservoir Barrage Project
(*c*) Jawahar Lal Nehru Irrigation Project
(*d*) Sewani Lift Irrigation Project

128. Which of the following system of irrigation is used in the sandy plains of Haryana?
(*a*) Canal
(*b*) Well
(*c*) With the help of Tubewell-Fountain irrigation
(*d*) Rain water

129. Water from western Yamuna Canal is used for irrigation in which of the following districts of Haryana?
(*a*) Karnal (*b*) Sonepat
(*c*) Rohtak (*d*) All of these

130. Besides Gurugram, in which of the following districts of Haryana water from Gurgaon canal is used for irrigation?
(*a*) Panipat (*b*) Faridabad
(*c*) Sonepat (*d*) Kaithal

131. Hathni Reservoir Barrage Project is related with which of the following districts of Haryana?
(*a*) Yamuna Nagar (*b*) Gurugram
(*c*) Rohtak (*d*) Faridabad

132. Which of the following irrigation projects was launched in Mahendragarh district of Haryana with a view to bring improvement in the field of agriculture?
(*a*) Loharu Lift Irrigation Project
(*b*) Western Yamuna Nagar Scheme
(*c*) J.L.N. Lift Irrigation Project
(*d*) Hathni Reservoir Barrage Project

133. When water was released for the first time from J.L.N. Lift Irrigation Project launched in Mahendragarh district of Haryana?
(*a*) In 1976 (*b*) In 1980
(*c*) In 1982 (*d*) In 1995

134. Which of the following irrigation projects provided irrigation facilities in Swarup Kalauda, Khurl Kalan, Bhikhewala, Kharadwala, Nehra, Fuliya kalan etc. villages of the state?
(*a*) Jhajjhar Lift Irrigation Project
(*b*) Nakhana Irrigation Project
(*c*) Nangal Lift Irrigation Project
(*d*) Jawahar Lal Nehru Lift Irrigation Project

135. Which of the following irrigation schemes was launched for providing irrigation facility in Ahriwal region of Haryana?
(*a*) Rewari Lift Irrigation Scheme
(*b*) Hathni Reservoir Barrage Irrigation Scheme
(*c*) Mewat Lift Irrigation Scheme
(*d*) Bhakra Canal Irrigation Scheme

136. The largest Animal Farm of Haryana is situated at which of the following places?
(*a*) Rohtak (*b*) Hissar
(*c*) Panch Kula (*d*) Jind

137. Which of the following breeds of the Buffalo of Haryana is famous in entire India?
(*a*) Murra (*b*) Tura
(*c*) Puspa (*d*) Chassa

138. At which of the following places of Haryana cooperative milk plant has been set up?
(*a*) Ambala (*b*) Bhivani
(*c*) Jind (*d*) All of the above

139. In the Thanesar town of district Kurukshetra, the building for Poultry disease diagnosis Laboratory was built in:
(*a*) 1980 – 81 (*b*) 1984 – 85
(*c*) 1988 – 89 (*d*) 1995 – 96

140. Besides Nilokheri in Haryana, at which of the following places of the state, training in poultry is imparted?
(*a*) Ambala (*b*) Karnal
(*c*) Hissar (*d*) Kaithal

141. Consider the following statements:
1. Rohtak has a Police Commissionerate located there.
2. Sonipat has a Police Commissionerate located there.

Which of the above statements is/are correct?
(*a*) 2 only (*b*) Both 1 and 2
(*c*) Neither 1 nor 2 (*d*) 1 only

142. Intensive Animal Development project in district Bhivani was launched in:
(*a*) 1966 (*b*) 1970
(*c*) 1972 (*d*) 1978

143. At which place in district Mahendragarh a Semen Bank is located and a liquid Nitrogen Plant has been set-up?
(*a*) Ateli (*b*) Narnaul
(*c*) Nangal Chaudhary (*d*) Mahendragarh

144. In district Bhiwani of Haryana, for diagnosing the diseases in animals the District Village Development Body set up the "Animal Disease Diagnosis Laboratory" in:
(*a*) 1978 (*b*) 1980
(*c*) 1984 (*d*) 1990

145. Haryana gets an average rainfall of ....
(*a*) 100 cms. (*b*) 85 cms.
(*c*) 75 cms. (*d*) 45 cms.

146. The ancient town 'Bery' is situated in which of the following districts of Haryana?
(*a*) Jhajjar (*b*) Yamuna Nagar
(*c*) Karnal (*d*) Kurukshetra

147. Where in Haryana, the National Institute of Fashion Technology is located?
(*a*) Panipat (*b*) Ambala
(*c*) Panchkula (*d*) Kurukshetra

148. The products manufactured by the industrial units of district Yamuna Nagar are exported to which of the following countries?
(*a*) Dubai (*b*) Germany
(*c*) South Africa (*d*) All of the above

149. Saraswati Sugar Mill is located in which of the following districts of Haryana?
(*a*) Rohtak (*b*) Panipat
(*c*) Yamuna Nagar (*d*) Faridabad

150. In Yamuna Nagar, Yanuma Gases Limited was set up in:
(*a*) 1973 (*b*) 1975
(*c*) 1980 (*d*) 1981

151. Yamuna Gases Limited operating in Yamuna Nagar attained a leading position in the production of gases in the year:
(*a*) 1969 (*b*) 1973
(*c*) 1972 (*d*) 1975

152. Bharat Starch Chemical Ltd. was established in Yamuna Nagar in:
(*a*) 1929 (*b*) 1932
(*c*) 1938 (*d*) 1948

153. Before 1947, the Timber Market of Yamuna Nagar was known as:
(*a*) Abdullapur Mandi
(*b*) Sadapur Mandi
(*c*) Yamuna Nagar Mandi
(*d*) Yamuna Pur Mandi

154. Charkhi Dadri was carved out from which district?
(*a*) Bhiwani (*b*) Hissar
(*c*) Sirsa (*d*) Rewari

155. "Bhiwani Textile Mill" in Haryana was established in:
(*a*) 1930 (*b*) 1937
(*c*) 1942 (*d*) 1950

156. In Haryana, where the Vulture Conservation Centre is located?
(*a*) Pinjore (*b*) Jind
(*c*) Mahendragarh (*d*) Ambala

157. The Sahibi river does not flow in which of the following district?
(*a*) Rewari (*b*) Jhajjar
(*c*) Gurugram (*d*) Rohtak

158. Consider the following statements in respect of National Security Guards (NSG):
1. Operational Headquarter of NSG is in Manesar.
2. NSG comes under the control of Union Ministry of Home Affairs.

Which of the above statements is/are correct?
(*a*) 2 only (*b*) Both 1 and 2
(*c*) Neither 1 nor 2 (*d*) 1 only

159. Indian Cement Corporation, A Government of India undertaking, took possession of the factory located at Charkhi-Dadri of Haryana on:
(*a*) 5 April, 1980 (*b*) 23 June, 1981
(*c*) 10 June, 1984 (*d*) 23 June, 1988

160. National Beekeeping and Honey Mission (NBHM) Scheme was started in which year in Haryana?
(*a*) 2017 (*b*) 2018
(*c*) 2019 (*d*) 2020

161. Captive Electricity Plant has been set up in which of the following districts of Haryana?
(*a*) Panipat (*b*) Hissar
(*c*) Rohtak (*d*) Karnal

162. At Baholi of district Panipat which of the following factories has been set up?
(*a*) Cloth Factory
(*b*) Agricultural Implements Factory
(*c*) Oil Refinery
(*d*) Slippers Factory

163. 'Ammonia Plant' has been installed in which of the following districts of Haryana?
(*a*) Panipat (*b*) Kaithal
(*c*) Gurugram (*d*) Karnal

164. District Mahanderagarh ranks first in the state of Haryana in the production of:
(*a*) Rice (*b*) Utensils
(*c*) Mustard (*d*) Bicycle

165. According to the 2011 census sex ratio in the state is ....
(*a*) 787 (*b*) 879
(*c*) 987 (*d*) 973

166. Which of the following industries in Rewari district of Haryana is famous all over India?
(*a*) Shoe Sole Industry
(*b*) Brass Utensil Industry
(*c*) Hero Honda Motor Cycle Factory
(*d*) All of these

167. In addition to Bicycle Factory, which of the following other factories are located in Jind district of Haryana?
(*a*) Utensil Factory (*b*) Textile Factory
(*c*) Sugar Factory (*d*) Leather Shoe Factory

168. According to the 2011 census population density in the state is ....
(*a*) 573 (*b*) 752
(*c*) 482 (*d*) 531

169. Total covered area of the Shri Krishna Museum is:
(*a*) 8764 sq.m. (*b*) 8885 sq.m.
(*c*) 8129 sq.m. (*d*) 8649 sq.m.

170. Which of the following articles manufactured in Karnal district are exported to foreign countries also?
(*a*) Liberty Shoes (*b*) Paint
(*c*) Wooden Furnitures (*d*) Steel Furniture

171. Shahabad Cooperative Sugar Mill in district Kurukshetra was established in:
(*a*) 1976 – 77 (*b*) 1984 – 85
(*c*) 1991 – 92 (*d*) 1994 – 95

172. Which of the following factories have been set up in Faridabad District of Haryana?
(*a*) Tractor Factory (*b*) Refrigerator Factory
(*c*) Rubber Tyre Factory (*d*) All of these

173. In which year the strength of Haryana Assembly was raised to 90?
(*a*) 1977 (*b*) 1967
(*c*) 1971 (*d*) 1985

174. At which of the following places in Haryana Maruti Cars are manufactured?
(*a*) Gurugram (*b*) Ambala
(*c*) Faridabad (*d*) Hissar

175. Which among the following is the highly populated district, as per the 2011 census?
(*a*) Rohtak (*b*) Karnal
(*c*) Gurugram (*d*) Faridabad

176. During which of the following years Government of Haryana decided to confer honour on Freedom Fighters?
(*a*) 1980 (*b*) 1981
(*c*) 1985 (*d*) 1997

177. Which of the following districts of Haryana does not share its boundary with any other state of India?
(*a*) Charkhi Dadri (*b*) Palwal
(*c*) Gurugram (*d*) Jind

178. Skylark Tourist Complex is located at ....
(*a*) Faridabad (*b*) Panipat
(*c*) Karnal (*d*) Rohtak

179. Scheme of granting cash amount, amount payable annually and cash in lieu of land to the soldiers awarded with 'Yuddha Sewa Medal' was discontinued in 1988. This scheme was launched again by the Government of Bansi Lal in:
(*a*) April 1995 (*b*) April 1997
(*c*) April 1996 (*d*) April 1998

180. Chaudhary Devi Lal University in Haryana is located at:
(*a*) Hissar (*b*) Karnal
(*c*) Sirsa (*d*) Panipat

181. Who among the following was not the chief minister of Haryana?
(*a*) Babu Parmanand (*b*) B.D. Gupta
(*c*) Devi Lal (*d*) Hukum Singh

182. National Dairy Research Institute is located at ....
(*a*) Karnal (*b*) Hissar
(*c*) Sirsa (*d*) Rohtak

183. Who was the first governor of Haryana?
(*a*) R.S. Narula (*b*) G.D. Tapse
(*c*) Dharamvir (*d*) B.D. Sharma

184. Hostel for the boys of Scheduled Castes who are engaged in unclean occupation is located at:
(*a*) Karnal (*b*) Faridabad
(*c*) Ambala (*d*) All of these

185. Hostel for the boys of exempted castes is located at :
(*a*) Rohtak (*b*) Jind
(*c*) Faridabad (*d*) Gurugram

186. Legal provisions for ban on liquor were enforced in Haryana on:
(*a*) 1 December, 1991 (*b*) 1 June, 1993
(*c*) 1 July, 1996 (*d*) 1 May, 1997

187. Ban on the sale of liquor was lifted by the state government on:
(*a*) 1 May, 1996 (*b*) 1 May, 1997
(*c*) 1 February, 1996 (*d*) 1 April, 1998

188. Which of the following Child Development Projects is related with the State of Haryana?
(*a*) Coordinated Child Development Project
(*b*) Child Health Project
(*c*) Infant Nutrition Programme
(*d*) Helpless Child Development Project

189. Which of the following schemes are being run for the welfare of the girls belonging to poor families?
(*a*) Paraya Dhan Parayee Beti
(*b*) Apni Beti Paraya Dhan
(*c*) Apni Beti Apna Dhan
(*d*) None of these

190. The total length of National Highway in Haryana till November, 2024 is:
(*a*) 1900 kms. (*b*) 1503 kms.
(*c*) 1800 kms. (*d*) 3391 kms.

191. Each and every village of the State of Haryana became electrified on:
(*a*) 10 June, 1966 (*b*) 25 March, 1971
(*c*) 15 April, 1968 (*d*) 29 November, 1970

192. Aruna is the ancient name of which river?
(*a*) Markanda (*b*) Sahibi
(*c*) Ghaggar (*d*) Yamuna

193. Red Soil is found in ....
(*a*) Rohtak (*b*) Sirsa
(*c*) Karnal (*d*) Bihwani

194. With a view to bring improvement in the availability of electricity in Southern Haryana, a new 50 km long single circuit line has been laid from :
(*a*) Gurugram to Badshahpur
(*b*) Badshahpur to Rewari
(*c*) Faridabad to Rewari
(*d*) Jind to Kaithal

195. Which one of the following pairs is not correctly matched?
(*a*) Surajkund Lake – Kurukshetra
(*b*) Tilyaar Lake – Rohtak
(*c*) Damdama Lake – Gurugram
(*d*) Badkhal Lake – Faridabad

196. Sultanpur Lake is located in which district?
(*a*) Bhiwani (*b*) Mahendragarh
(*c*) Gurugram (*d*) Rewari

197. According to the demands made by farmers, which of the following systems for electricity on the basis of the depth of tubewells has been adopted in the entire state?
(*a*) Stove System
(*b*) Electricity Measurement System
(*c*) Test System
(*d*) None of these

198. Thermal Power Station is located at which of the following places in Haryana?
(*a*) Hissar (*b*) Kaithal
(*c*) Jind (*d*) Faridabad

199. At which of the following places, the Power Plant of 432 MW based on Gas has been installed by NTPC in Haryana?
(*a*) Gurugram (*b*) Faridabad
(*c*) Panipat (*d*) Karnal

200. What is the total length of road in Haryana till November, 2024?
(*a*) 33,453 km (*b*) 24,065 km
(*c*) 25,074 km (*d*) 40,760 km

201. The strength of Legislative Assembly of Haryana is ....
(*a*) 102 (*b*) 110
(*c*) 75 (*d*) 90

202. Where is Nahar Wildlife Sanctuary is situated?
(*a*) Ambala (*b*) Sonipat
(*c*) Rewari (*d*) Yamunanagar

203. When the Public Transport in Haryana was brought under the possession of the Government?
(*a*) In 1972 (*b*) In 1976
(*c*) In 1980 (*d*) In 1985

204. 'Rao Tej Singh Pond' is located in:
(*a*) Panipat (*b*) Sonipat
(*c*) Palwal (*d*) Rewari

205. The Magazine of Haryana Sahitya Academy is:
(*a*) Harigandha (*b*) Haryana Samvad
(*c*) Haryana Sandesh (*d*) Panchajanya

206. While travelling on the National Highway from Delhi to Ferozepur, which of the following important town of Haryana comes on the way:
(*a*) Rohtak (*b*) Sirsa
(*c*) Hissar (*d*) All of these

207. Manu Bhaker of Haryana is related with which sports?
(*a*) Badminton (*b*) Boxing
(*c*) Shooting (*d*) Wrestling

208. Which of the following tourist places is situated at Bahadurgarh in Haryana?
(*a*) Dairango Tourist Place (*b*) Gureya
(*c*) Jal Tarang (*d*) Tiliyar

209. In Haryana, in addition to Hissar, Karnal, Bhiwani, Narnaul and Jind, at which of the following airports metalled run-way has been built?
(*a*) Panipat (*b*) Pinjore
(*c*) Faridabad (*d*) Rewari

210. Where is Tilyar lake is situated?
(*a*) Rohtak (*b*) Gurugram
(*c*) Jind (*d*) Faridabad

211. At which of the following places in Haryana, Heavy Vehicle Driving Training Institute is located?
(*a*) Murthal (*b*) Charkhi-Dadri
(*c*) Ambala (*d*) Tawaroo

212. In Shivalik hills near Pinjore-Kalka in Haryana, utensils have been found which pertain to which of the following ages?
(*a*) Stone Age (*b*) Later Vedic Age
(*c*) Harappan Age (*d*) Early Vedic Age

213. In the treatise named "Avanti Sunderi Katha" Vaivast Manu who is known as the father of human beings is said to be the resident of which of the following places?
(*a*) Panipat (*b*) Rohtak
(*c*) Sthaneshwar (*d*) Panchkula

214. Evidences found from the excavations done at Banwali, Siswal, Kunal, Mirzapur, Daulatpur and Bhagawanpura in the state of Haryana revealed links dating back to:

(*a*) Early Harappan Culture
(*b*) Mature Harappan Culture
(*c*) Late Harappan Culture
(*d*) All of the above phases

215. Who of the following started archaeological survey in Haryana for the first time?
(*a*) Sir John (*b*) Alexander Kaningham
(*c*) Lord Munro (*d*) John Marshall

216. Archaeological Survey in Haryana started in:
(*a*) 1862 (*b*) 1892
(*c*) 1900 (*d*) 1905

217. Under the supervision of Dr. Suraj Bhan, excavations at which of the following places of Haryana brought out very valuable historical evidences?
(*a*) Mithathal (*b*) Dadri
(*c*) Ailanabad (*d*) Safidon

218. From which of the following sites of Haryana, evidences have been found for the first time regarding co-existence of the people of Late Harappan culture and Painted Grey Ware (PGW) culture?
(*a*) Narnaul (*b*) Bhagwanpura
(*c*) Sirsa (*d*) Mahendragarh

219. A great mound pertaining to Harappan culture is situated at which of the following places in district Jind of Haryana?
(*a*) Safidon (*b*) Uchana
(*c*) Narwana (*d*) Rakhigarhi

220. Remains of a Stupa have been found at Chaneti which is situated three kilometers east of Jagadhari. Height of this Stupa is 8 m. Its periphery is:
(*a*) 20 m (*b*) 30 m
(*c*) 45 m (*d*) 50 m

221. Consider the following statements:
1. Sonipat and Jhajjar share border with Delhi.
2. Rohtak does not share border with Delhi.

Which of the above statements is/are correct?
(*a*) 2 only (*b*) Both 1 and 2
(*c*) Neither 1 nor 2 (*d*) 1 only

222. A battle axe type Gold Coin which pertains to the age of Samudra Gupta has been found at which of the following places in Haryana?
(*a*) Kosali (*b*) Rohana
(*c*) Mithathal (*d*) Raniya

223. Which of the following areas of Haryana was under the control of Yudheyas during the 3rd century A.D.?
(*a*) Panipat (*b*) Rohtak
(*c*) Hissar (*d*) Ambala

224. The Gold Coin obtained from Jagadhari pertains to which of the following emperors of the ancient India?
(*a*) Kanishka (*b*) Kumar Gupta
(*c*) Pushyamitra Sunga (*d*) Samudragupta

225. From which of the following places in Haryana, copper coin of the age of Harsha Vardhan has been found which contains an account of Pushyabhuti dynasty of Thanesar?
(*a*) Sonepat (*b*) Sirsa
(*c*) Gurugram (*d*) Kaithal

226. At which of the following places located in district Hissar of Haryana excavations was done by Shri H.L. Srivastava of Archaeo-logical Survey of India?
(*a*) Uklana (*b*) Fatehabad
(*c*) Agroha (*d*) Adampur

227. What is the total number of Primary and Pre Primary Schools in Haryana till 2023-24?
(*a*) 9,872 (*b*) 9,399
(*c*) 11,582 (*d*) 8,780

228. What is the total number of Middle Schools in Haryana till 2023-24?
(*a*) 6,215 (*b*) 2,312
(*c*) 5,640 (*d*) 3,850

229. In Haryana 'Brahma Sarovar' is located in:
(*a*) Palwal (*b*) Kurukshetra
(*c*) Panipat (*d*) Sonipat

230. 'Uchana' is located in:
(*a*) Jind (*b*) Karnal
(*c*) Rohtak (*d*) Faridabad

231. The tenure of nagarpalika, municipality or municipal corporation in Haryana is ....
(*a*) 3 years (*b*) 1 year
(*c*) 4 years (*d*) 5 years

232. What is the area of Sirsa district?
(*a*) 4,277 sq.km (*b*) 5,780 sq.km
(*c*) 3,760 sq.km (*d*) 2,765 sq.km

233. What is the total number of literate people in Haryana?
(*a*) 1,66,25,728 (*b*) 1,65,98,988
(*c*) 1,78,10,882 (*d*) 1,32,58,652

234. The historical monument known as the corridor Chhatta of Rai Mukund Das (Birbal Ka Chhatta) is in:
(*a*) Panipat (*b*) Karnal
(*c*) Kaithal (*d*) Narnaul

235. Navodaya Vidyalaya is situated at which of the following places in the state?
(*a*) Titaram (Kurukshetra) (*b*) Odha (Sirsa)
(*c*) Deorala (Bhiwani) (*d*) All of these

236. During which of the following years Government of Haryana introduced 10+2+3 system of Education in Haryana?
(*a*) 1980 - 81 (*b*) 1976 - 77
(*c*) 1988 - 89 (*d*) 1985 - 86

237. M.D. University is located in which of the following towns of Haryana?
(*a*) Rohtak (*b*) Hissar
(*c*) Faridabad (*d*) Rewari

238. Chaudhary Charan Singh Agricultural University is located in which of the following towns of the state?
(*a*) Jind (*b*) Gurugram
(*c*) Hissar (*d*) Kurukshetra

239. In order to promote Punjabi language in Haryana it has been made the .... language of the state.
(*a*) First (*b*) Second
(*c*) Third (*d*) Fourth

240. Chaudhary Devilal University is located in which of the following towns of Haryana?
(*a*) Kurukshetra (*b*) Hissar
(*c*) Rohtak (*d*) Sirsa

241. In order to give promotion to sports in Haryana, the State Government has launched which of the following important schemes?
(*a*) Providing Grant in aid to the Sports Institutions
(*b*) Training Scheme
(*c*) Sports Stadium
(*d*) All of the above

242. In order to impart training to the players through modern and scientific methods, at which of the following places of Haryana a sports hostel has been set up?
(*a*) Gurugram (*b*) Rohtak
(*c*) Faridabad (*d*) Panipat

243. A sports school is situated at Rai in Sonepat district of Haryana. What is the name of this sports school?
(*a*) Jawahar Lal Nehru Sports School
(*b*) Indira Gandhi Sports School
(*c*) Moti Lal Nehru Sports School
(*d*) Rajiv Gandhi Sports School

244. Kamla Nehru School situated in the premises of Moti Lal Nehru Sports School at Rai in Sonepat district was established in
(*a*) 1970 (*b*) 1974
(*c*) 1982 (*d*) 1986

245. Haryana Shehari Vikas Pradhikaran (HSVP), formerly Haryana Urban Development Authority (HUDA) was constituted in ....
(*a*) 1977 (*b*) 1972
(*c*) 1970 (*d*) 1966

246. Who has variously been described as Plato of Jat Tribes?
(*a*) Suraj Mal (*b*) Churaman
(*c*) Raja Ram Bhajja (*d*) None of these

247. Khoria dance is famous in ....
(*a*) Eastern Haryana (*b*) Western Haryana
(*c*) Central Haryana (*d*) Northern Haryana

248. Which player of Haryana won gold medal in Tokyo Olympics 2020?
(*a*) Bajarang Punia (*b*) Neeraj Chopra
(*c*) Ravi Kumar (*d*) Vijendra Singh

249. The Haryana Shawl is known as ....
(*a*) Phulkari (*b*) Ghagra
(*c*) Iungis (*d*) Bagh

250. The famous story writer of Hindi Shri Vishvambhar Nath Kaushik was born in Haryana at
(*a*) Ambala Cantt (*b*) Sirsa
(*c*) Panchkula (*d*) Rohtak

251. Famous writer of Haryana Pt. Neki Ram Sharma had brought out which of the following papers from Bhiwani?
(*a*) Samvahak (*b*) Sandesh
(*c*) Nivaran (*d*) Vani

252. Who of the following players of Indian Cricket hails from Haryana?
(*a*) Kapil Dev (*b*) Sunil Gavaskar
(*c*) Ajay Jadeja (*d*) Azharuddin

253. The Cricket Test Match in which Kapil Dev of Haryana took 432nd wicket to make a record of taking maximum number of wickets was held on
(*a*) 10 January, 1992 (*b*) 8 December, 1996
(*c*) 8 February, 1994 (*d*) 12 August, 1997

254. Kapil Dev announced to abandon the international cricket on
(*a*) 6 November, 1993 (*b*) 2 November, 1994
(*c*) 18 November, 1997 (*d*) 15 November, 1998

255. Who of the following players of Haryana is not related with Gymnastic?
(*a*) Sunita Sharma (*b*) Sandhya
(*c*) Nirmala Guliya (*d*) Geeta Jutshi

256. Who of the following first ever poet is considered a native poet of Haryana?
(*a*) Goswami Tulsi Das (*b*) Kabir Das
(*c*) Kavi Chandbardai (*d*) Rahim Das

257. Who of the following Muslim Saints of Haryana had made significant contributions in the development of Hindi literature?
(*a*) Shekh-U-Alishaha Kalander
(*b*) Saint Sadullah
(*c*) Shekh Bahauddin Chishti
(*d*) All of these

258. Who of the following first ever poet is not related with Haryana?
(*a*) Virbhan (*b*) Mahatma Haridas
(*c*) Banarsi Das (*d*) Narottam Das

259. Haryana got the status of a full state on
(*a*) 1 November, 1964 (*b*) 10 December, 1965
(*c*) 1 November, 1966 (*d*) 15 June, 1968

260. The capital city of Haryana is
(*a*) Chandigarh (*b*) Rohtak
(*c*) Karnal (*d*) Yamuna Nagar

261. With a view to administrative convenience, Haryana has been divided into
(*a*) Three Divisions (*b*) Six Divisions
(*c*) Five Divisions (*d*) Four Divisions

262. The number of Districts in Haryana is
(*a*) 16 (*b*) 17
(*c*) 18 (*d*) 22

263. The tourist place called Oasis is situated at which of the following places in Haryana?
(*a*) Faridabad (*b*) Bhiwani
(*c*) Uchchhana (*d*) Rewari

264. Which of the following famous tourist place of Haryana is located at a distance of about 20 kms from Delhi?
(*a*) Suraj Kund (*b*) Red Robin
(*c*) Paracot (*d*) Damdama Lake

265. In vast rocky areas extended to the west of Faridabad by the Delhi-Mathura National Highway which of the following tourist place is situated?
(*a*) Damdama Lake (*b*) Badkhal Lake
(*c*) King Fisher (*d*) Dabchik

266. Between the hills of Arawali on Delhi-Alwar road which of the following famous tourist place of Haryana is located?
(*a*) Shama (*b*) Blue-ze
(*c*) Sohana (*d*) Dairangon

267. Who had discovered the Sultanpur Bird Sanctuary of Haryana situated on Gurugram Farrukh Nagar road?
(*a*) Peter Jackson (*b*) Thomar Roe
(*c*) Sir John Marshall (*d*) Robin Hood

268. On the Gurugram-Farrukhabad road which of the following tourist places of Haryana is situated?
(*a*) Dab-bich
(*b*) Sultanpur Bird Sanctuary
(*c*) Oasis
(*d*) Red Robin

269. The Turban worn by male in Haryana is called
(*a*) Khandwa (*b*) Paggada
(*c*) Toda (*d*) Pagari

270. The tourist centre called 'Shama' is situated at which of the following towns of Haryana?
(*a*) Faridabad (*b*) Kaithal
(*c*) Gurugram (*d*) Jind

271. In Haryana, the skirt worn by females from waist to ankle which is without any gusset and made of hand-spun coarse cloth knitted by using four blue and four red threads is called
(*a*) Dharna (*b*) Khara
(*c*) Thara (*d*) Kachara

272. Which of the following ornaments used in the state is not worn around neck?
(*a*) Hansla (*b*) Fool
(*c*) Galshree (*d*) Batan

273. Which of the following ornaments is worn on face and head on the ladies of the state?
(*a*) Singar Patti (*b*) Tagga
(*c*) Bessar (*d*) All of these

274. Which of the following ornaments used in the state is not worn on nose?
(*a*) Nath (*b*) Purli
(*c*) Dhede (*d*) Kokka

275. Which of the following ornaments used in the state is not worn on hands?
(*a*) Pauhchi (*b*) Kandulla
(*c*) Pachhelli (*d*) Bankri

276. According to the augury, which of the following is considered a good omen in the state of Haryana?
(*a*) A pitcher full of water
(*b*) To have a view of a deer
(*c*) A sweeper with a broom in hand
(*d*) All of the above

277. According to the augury, which of the following is considered a bad omen in the state of the Haryana?
(*a*) Empty pitcher
(*b*) To have a view of grass
(*c*) To experience an itching sensation in feet
(*d*) Meeting with a water carrier carrying water.

278. Which of the traditional ornaments is worn by males in Haryana?
(*a*) Goph (*b*) Tagari
(*c*) Nada (*d*) Kadi

279. At which of the following places of religious importance, lakhs of people from all over India go for a religious ritual on the occurrence of solar eclipse?
(*a*) Gurugram (*b*) Kurukshetra
(*c*) Jagadhari (*d*) None of these

280. At Islampur in the district Gurugram, which of the following festivals (Mela) is organised on the ninth day of Bhado (the sixth month of the year according to the Hindu calendar)?
(*a*) Guga Naumi (*b*) Nag Pooja
(*c*) Yamuna Snan (*d*) Shiv Mela

281. In the months of Chait and Aashadh (respectively the opening and the fourth month of the year according to the Hindu caldendar) in district Gurugram of Haryana on every Monday and Tuesday which of the following famous festivals (Melas) is organised?
(*a*) Buddho Mata Ka Mela
(*b*) Shivji Ka Mela
(*c*) Shitla Mata Ka Mela
(*d*) Baba Buddha Ka Mela

282. In which of the following districts of Haryana famous festivals of Ramsarai and Bhuteshwar are organised?
(*a*) Faridabad (*b*) Jind
(*c*) Rohtak (*d*) Jhajjhar

283. In the monastery at Asthal Bohar in Rohtak district of Haryana which of the following festivals (Melas) is organised during the months of February and March?
(*a*) Baba Mastnath Ka Mela
(*b*) Kapal Mochan Ka Mela
(*c*) Devi Mela
(*d*) Pathari Mata Ka Mela

284. Which of the following festivals (Melas) is organised on Kartik-Purnima at Bilaspur situated near Jagadhari?
(*a*) Aadi Badri Mela (*b*) Mela Kali Mai
(*c*) Kapal Mochan Mela (*d*) Panchmukhi Mela

285. At Lakhan Majra in Rohtak district "Gurudwara of Manji Sahib" is situated. Here which of the following festivals (Melas) is organised?
(*a*) Festival of Satya Teej
(*b*) Festival of Mohola Halla
(*c*) Bawan Dwadashi
(*d*) Maanu Mela

286. At Pathri in district Sonepat, on every Wednesday in the months of Chait and Aashadh, which of the following festivals (Melas) is organised?
(*a*) Mata Ka Mela (*b*) Shiva Mela
(*c*) Dehati Mela (*d*) Pathri Mata Ka Mela

287. At Kharak Ramji situated in district Jind, which of the following festivals (Melas) is organised on the day of Holi?
(*a*) Mata Ka Mela
(*b*) Nag Devata Ka Mela
(*c*) Baba Bhalu Nath Ka Mela
(*d*) Mela Sachcha Sauda

288. At Dubaldhan Majra in Rohtak district which of the following festivals (Melas) is organised in the months of February-March?
(*a*) Mela Mata (*b*) Mela Devi
(*c*) Mela Shyamji (*d*) Mela Baba Buddha

289. At Khori in the Gurugram district which of the following festivals (Melas) is organised during the months of April-May?
(*a*) Shah Chokha Khori Mela
(*b*) Shiva Ka Mela
(*c*) Nagpooja Ka Mela
(*d*) Baba Mast Nath Ka Mela

290. At which of the following places in district Sonepat, festival (Mela) of Dera Nagn Balaknath is organised during the months of February-March?
(*a*) Bega (Tehsil Sonepat)
(*b*) Mehripur (Tehsil Sonepat)
(*c*) Rabhara (Tehsil Gohana)
(*d*) Chulkana (Tehsil Sonepat)

291. Which of the following festivals (Melas) is oraganised at Khubadu situated in district Sonepat during the months of February-March?
(*a*) Satakumbha Mela (*b*) Mela Baba Shamakshah
(*c*) Mela Sanjhi (*d*) Devi Mela

292. Which amongst the following is the State Tree of Haryana?
(*a*) Sacred Fig (*b*) Mango Tree
(*c*) Sal Tree (*d*) Banyan Tree

293. At which of the following places in Haryana festival (Mela) of Baba Khedewala is organised on the day of Raksha Bandhan?
(*a*) Naurangabad (*b*) Kaharak Kalan
(*c*) Riwasa (*d*) Tosham

294. On which of the following occasions in the state of Haryana auspicious "Piliya" folk song is sung?
(*a*) In the months of July-August
(*b*) On the occasion of the birth of a male child in the family
(*c*) On the occasion of marriage ceremony
(*d*) In the months of February-March

295. On which of the following occasions, in the state of Haryana folk songs are sung?
(*a*) On the occasion of the birth of a male child in the family
(*b*) In the months of July-August
(*c*) On the occasion of a festival
(*d*) On all of the above occasions

296. In the state, males perform which of the following dances in open field at moon-lit night on flute, scooped gourd (Tumbi), etc.?
(*a*) Dhamal Dance (*b*) Manjeera Dance
(*c*) Loor Dance (*d*) Damru Dance

297. Which of the following dance performances is famous in Mewat area of Haryana which is accompanied with beating huge kettle drum, tambourine and cymbals?
(*a*) Ghora Dance (*b*) Dhamal Dance
(*c*) Manjeera Dance (*d*) Chhathi Dance

298. In Bagar area of Haryana which of the following dance performances is famous that is performed during the festival of Holi?
(*a*) Damru Dance (*b*) Manjeera Dance
(*c*) Ghora Dance (*d*) Loor Dance

299. The Ghora folk dance popular in Haryana is generally performed on which of the following occasions?
(*a*) On the occasion of marriage
(*b*) In the month of February-March
(*c*) On the occasion of birth of a male child in the family
(*d*) In the Month of July-August

300. In Haryana, which of the following dances is performed after the worship of Guggapir in the month of August-September?
(*a*) Dhamal Dance (*b*) Chchari Dance
(*c*) Loor Dance (*d*) Damru Dance

301. Which of the following folk dances is performed by women in the state?
(*a*) Teej Dance (*b*) Dhamal Dance
(*c*) Damru Dance (*d*) Khodiya Dance

302. Which dance is performed by males among the following folk dances practised in the state?
(*a*) Chhatthi dance (*b*) Teej dance
(*c*) Damru dance (*d*) Khodia dance

303. Which of the following folk dances is performed by men and women both in the state?
(*a*) Teej Dance (*b*) Loor Dance
(*c*) Khodiya Dance (*d*) Fag Dance

304. Which of the following Gurudwaras is situated near Pratap Gate in Kaithal town of Haryana?
(*a*) Gurudwara Neem Sahib
(*b*) Gurudwara Nauvi Patshahi
(*c*) Ragdhaar Gurudwara
(*d*) Gurudwara Chhathi Patshahi

305. Gurudwara Manji Sahib is situated in which of the following towns of Haryana?
(*a*) Karnal (*b*) Panipat
(*c*) Kaithal (*d*) Ambala

306. Which place in Haryana is called as "Chhoti Kashi" due to presence of "Navagraha Kunds"?
(*a*) Narnaul (*b*) Kaithal
(*c*) Gurugram (*d*) Kurukshetra

307. At a few distance from Kaithal in Haryana the grave of which of the following great men is situated where every year next dayof Dushera a large festival is organised?
(*a*) Baba Kali Kamli Wale
(*b*) Baba Haridas
(*c*) Baba Ladana
(*d*) Baba Ramdas

308. Which of the following famous places of pilgrimage is situated near Thanesar City Station in district Kurukshetra of Haryana?
(*a*) Brahma Sarovar (*b*) Hatakeshwar
(*c*) Dhosi (*d*) Pundarik Sarovar

309. Which of the following places of pilgrimage is situated on the Kurukshetra-Pehwa road near Kurukshetra Railway Station which is considered as the permanent abode of Lord Vishnu?
(*a*) Brahma Sarovar (*b*) Kaleshwar Tirth
(*c*) Sannihit Sarovar (*d*) Markanday Tirth

310. At which place of piligrimage in Kurukshetra district Shri Krishna had preached Arjuna?
(*a*) Brahm Sarovar (*b*) Kamal Nabh Tirth
(*c*) Prachi Tirth (*d*) Jyotishwar Sarovar

311. When did Maharaja Darbhanga build metalled platform around the Akshya Vat located near the Jyotishwar Sarovar situated in district Kurukshetra?
(*a*) In 1924 (*b*) In 1930
(*c*) In 1932 (*d*) In 1949

312. Who had built the Krishna-Arjuna Rath (Chariot) and the temple of Shankaracharya near the Jyotishwar Sarovar situated in district Kurukshetra?
(*a*) Maharaja Darbhanga
(*b*) Shankaracharya of Kam Koti Peeth
(*c*) King of Kashmir
(*d*) Swami Vishuddhananda Maharaj

313. What is the total length of Jyotishwar Sarovar situated in district Kurukshetra?
(*a*) 1000 ft. (*b*) 1500 ft.
(*c*) 2000 ft. (*d*) 2500 ft.

314. Who was the founder of "Baba Kali Kamli Wale Ka Dera" situated in district Kurukshetra?
(*a*) Swami Ram Tirth
(*b*) Shri Swami Vishuddhananda Maharaja
(*c*) Shankaracharya of Kamkoti Peeth
(*d*) Swami Parmananda Maharaj

315. Gaudiya Math (monastery) related with the period of Bhakti movement in India, is situated in which of the following districts of Haryana?
(*a*) Ambala (*b*) Jind
(*c*) Kurukshetra (*d*) Mahendragarh

316. At which of the following places in district Kurukshetra Baba Laxman Giri Maharaj went into eternal trance?
(*a*) Ban Ganga (*b*) Prachi Tirth
(*c*) Gaudiya Math (*d*) Balmiki Aashram

317. Raj Ghat Gurudwara is situated at which of the following places in Haryana?
(*a*) Kurukshetra (*b*) Yamuna Nagar
(*c*) Kaithal (*d*) Bhiwani

318. Which of the following places of pilgrimage is not situated in district Kurukshetra of Haryana?
(*a*) Kalkeshwar Tirth
(*b*) Prachi Tirth
(*c*) Dhosi Tirth
(*d*) Kuber Tirth

319. Which of the following places of pilgrimage is situated at a distance of 1 km. to the North-West of Kurukshetra University in district Kurukshetra of Haryana?
(*a*) Markandya Tirth
(*b*) Narakatari (Anrak Tirth)
(*c*) Prachi Tirth
(*d*) Kuber Tirth

320. Which of the following important places of pilgrimage is situated at a distance of 25 km to the west of Thanesar in Haryana that is given the same importance by the people of Haryana and adjoining areas as is given to Gaya by the people of Eastern region of India?
(*a*) Pehova (*b*) Panchavati
(*c*) Safeedon (*d*) Pandu-Pindara

321. In which district of Haryana the 'National Institute of Animal Genetics' is located?
(*a*) Hisar (*b*) Yamunanagar
(*c*) Karnal (*d*) Rohtak

322. A place of pilgrimage known as "Panchavati" is situated at which of the following districts of Haryana?
(*a*) Ambala (*b*) Jind
(*c*) Kurukshetra (*d*) Palwal

323. Which of the following is an ancient place of pilgrimage located by Jind-Gohana Road near Jind where a fair is organised every year on Somawati Amavasya?
(*a*) Pandu-Pindara
(*b*) Safeedon
(*c*) Hans Daihar
(*d*) None of the above

324. Temple of Sthaneshwar Mahadeva situated at a distance of a few kilometres from Thanesar was built by which of the following kings prior to Harshavardhan?
(*a*) Pushyabhuti (*b*) Adityavardhan
(*c*) Narvardhan (*d*) Prabhakarvardhan

325. Mahmud Ghaznavi during his return course to Ghazni took away with him from Haryana to Ghazni, statue of which of the ancient temple located in Haryana?
(*a*) Dukh Bhanjaneshwar Temple (Kuruk-shetra)
(*b*) Lord Shiva Temple (Narnaul)
(*c*) Sarveshwar Mahadeva Temple (Kuruk-shetra)
(*d*) Sthaneshwar Mahadeva Temple (Thanesar)

326. Sthaneshwar Temple of Haryana was reconstructed by
(*a*) Maratha Sadashiva Rao
(*b*) Chandra Gupta Vikramaditya
(*c*) Harshavardhan
(*d*) Narvardhan

327. Devikoop (Bhadra Kali Temple) is one of the 51 Shakti Peeths (Seats of goddess personifying divine power) of India. This temple is located at which of the following places in the state?
(*a*) Rohtak (*b*) Kurukshetra
(*c*) Panipat (*d*) Thanesar

328. Which of the following temples is situated near Sannihit Sarovar in Kurukshetra?
(*a*) Narayana Temple
(*b*) Laxmi Narayan Temple
(*c*) Dukh Bhanjaneshwar Temple
(*d*) Birla Mandir

329. Which of the following temples of Kurukshetra was built by the perfect Saint of Giri Sect Baba Shiv Giri Maharaj?
(*a*) Sarveshwar Mahadeva Temple
(*b*) Narayana Temple
(*c*) Laxmi Narayan Temple
(*d*) Dukh Bhanajaneshwar Temple

330. Who had built the famous 'Sarveshwar Mahadeva Temple' of Kurukshetra?
(*a*) Baba Shravan Nath (*b*) Baba Shiva Giri
(*c*) Baba Tarak Nath (*d*) Shri Jugal Kishore Birla

331. Birla Temple situated by the Kurukshetra-Pehova road was built by Shri Jugal Kishore Birla in
(*a*) 1950 (*b*) 1955
(*c*) 1965 (*d*) 1978

332. "Gyarah Rudri Shiva Temple" is situated in which of the following towns of Haryana?
(*a*) Jind (*b*) Panipat
(*c*) Hissar (*d*) Kaithal

333. Maratha General Mangal Raghu Nath Ji had built which of the following temples after the third battle of Panipat?
(*a*) Shiva Temple of Devi Pond
(*b*) Hanuman Temple
(*c*) Devi Temple
(*d*) Rudra Temple

334. In Amin village of Kurukshetra district which one of the following ancient temples is situated?
(*a*) Panchvati Temple
(*b*) Shiva Temple
(*c*) Temple of Aditi
(*d*) Temple of Dauji

335. In Vanchari village situated at a distance of 55 km. from Faridabad, which of the following ancient temples is situated?
(*a*) Temple of Dauji
(*b*) Temple of Aditi
(*c*) Panchvati Temple
(*d*) Temple of Chamunda Devi

336. The famous ancient temple of Mata Sheetala Devi is situated at which of the following places in Haryana?
(*a*) Rewari (*b*) Gurugram
(*c*) Narnaul (*d*) Jind

337. Temple of Mata Sheetala Devi situated at Gurugram was built by Maharaja of Bharatpur in
(*a*) 1620 (*b*) 1645
(*c*) 1648 (*d*) 1650

338. The ancient Shiva temple where the grave of Baba Thandipuri is also located, is situated at which of the following places?
(*a*) Pundrik Tirth (*b*) Gurugram
(*c*) Hissar (*d*) Rohtak

339. Which of the following ancient temples is situated at village Beri of district Jhajjar in Haryana?
(*a*) Old Shiva-Parvati Temple
(*b*) Temple of Mata Sheetala Devi
(*c*) Lal Rudhmal Temple
(*d*) Temple of Dauji

340. The height of the Shivalaya located in Rudhmal temple at village Beri in district Jhajjar of Haryana is
(*a*) 116 ft. (*b*) 122 ft.
(*c*) 132 ft. (*d*) 140 ft.

341. The Shivalaya located in Rudhmal temple at village Beri in district Jhajjar of Haryana was built in
(*a*) 1842 (*b*) 1850
(*c*) 1892 (*d*) 1899

342. The Shivalaya located in Rudhmal temple at village Beri in district Jhajjar was resurrected for the first time in
(*a*) 1943 (*b*) 1945
(*c*) 1950 (*d*) 1953

343. The temple of Chamunda Devi situated at Narnaul was built and resurrected by
(*a*) Raja Parikshit (*b*) Raja Dilip
(*c*) Raja Noorkaran (*d*) Pandavas

344. Chisti sect was established in Haryana by
(*a*) Boo Alishah Kalandar
(*b*) Shekh Farid (Farid-ud-din-Shakarganj)
(*c*) Altaf Hussain
(*d*) Ibrahim Abidullah

345. The eminent saint of Chisti sect Boo Alishah Kalandar made which of the following places the centre of his meditation?
(*a*) Panipat (*b*) Rohtak
(*c*) Sonepat (*d*) Gurugram

346. Dargah of Sufi Saint Altaf Hussain Hali is situated at which of the following places in Haryana?
(*a*) Jhajjhar (*b*) Rewari
(*c*) Panipat (*d*) Rohtak

347. Regarding which of the following Dargahs (tombs of saints which are pilgrimage spots and places of worship) situated at Panipat is believed that bowing heads by believers accomplishes their attending in celebration of Urs of Khwaza of Ajmer?
(*a*) Dargah of Khwaza Shamshuddin Makhdoom Zalaluddin
(*b*) Dargah of Shekh Usman Jindapeer
(*c*) Dargah of Gauss Alishah
(*d*) Dargah of Boo Alishah Kalandar

348. Dargah of which of the following famous saints is situated at village Dharsun which is at a distance of about 10 kms from Narnaul?
(*a*) Hazarat Shah Kalmuddin Hamzapeer Hussain
(*b*) Meer Shah (Baba Shah Khan)
(*c*) Sheikh Nijamuddin
(*d*) Sheikh Junaid

349. At Fatehabad in the courtyard of the tomb of which of the following Sufi saints inscription of Mughal emperor Humayun is engraved on a stone?
(*a*) Mir Taki Khan
(*b*) Mir Junaidi
(*c*) Sheikh Nizamuddin
(*d*) Mir Shah (Baba Shah Khan)

350. Which of the following tombs situated in Haryana has been declared a monument of National importance under the Archaeological Site and Remnant Act, 1958?
(*a*) Sheikh Chehli
(*b*) Boo Alishah Kalandar
(*c*) Sheikh Farid (Farid-ud-din-Shakarganj)
(*d*) Peer Jamal

351. Tomb of Baba Shah Kamal is situated at which of the following places in Haryana?
(*a*) Gohan (*b*) Fatehabad
(*c*) Kaithal (*d*) Rohtak

352. At which one of the following places in the state, tombs of four Sufi-saints (Kutub Sheikh Jamaluddin Ahmad, Kutub Maulana, Basohddin Sufi Qutubuddin Mannawar, Qutub Nuruddin) are located?
(*a*) Karnal (*b*) Hissar
(*c*) Palwal (*d*) Hansi

353. The tomb of who of the following Sufi-saints is situated between Shahabad and Ambala where watch is offered after a desire is fulfilled?
(*a*) Peer Nagauji (*b*) Hamja Peer
(*c*) Peer Naugaja (*d*) Ibrahim Abidullah

354. Which of the following mosques in Rohtak which was previously a temple was turned into a mosque during the reign of Aurangzeb?
(*a*) Qazi Ki Masjid (*b*) Dini Masjid
(*c*) Lal Masjid (*d*) None of these

355. The Lal Masjid situated in Rohtak was built by famous trader Haji Aashiq Ali in
(*a*) 1930 (*b*) 1931
(*c*) 1935 (*d*) 1939

356. Mosque at Sarai Alawardi village in district Gurugram was built during the reign of
(*a*) Babur (*b*) Jahangir
(*c*) Shahjahan (*d*) Alauddin Khilji

357. Which of the following ancient historical Mosques is situated at village Dujana, situated at a distance of 22 km by Jhajjhar road from Rohtak?
(*a*) Lal Masjid (*b*) Qaji Ki Masjid
(*c*) Karim Ji Ki Masjid (*d*) Jama Masjid

358. The famous historic Lal Masjid at Rewari was built during the reign of which of the following Mughal Emperors?
(*a*) Babur (*b*) Humayun
(*c*) Akbar (*d*) Jahangir

359. In addition to Narnaul, Panipat and Ambala, Sufi-saints made which of the following towns of Haryana as a centre of Sufi-sect?
(*a*) Kaithal (*b*) Thanesar
(*c*) Karnal (*d*) Sonepat

360. The majority of Sufi-saints who lived in Haryana for propagating sufi cult belonged to which of the following sects?
(*a*) Chisti (*b*) Nakshbandi
(*c*) Kadari (*d*) All of the above

361. Tomb of famous Sufi-saint Sheikh Chehli which is called as the Tajmahal of Haryana is situated at
(*a*) Hissar (*b*) Fatehabad
(*c*) Thanesar (*d*) Panipat

362. Tomb of which of the following saints is situated at Kalyana village of Charkhi Dadri district where fair is organised on every Wednesday?
(*a*) Peer Mubarak Shah
(*b*) Sheikh Usman Jindapeer
(*c*) Sheikh Nizamuddin
(*d*) Muhammad Afzal

363. Tomb of Meeran Sahib is situated in which of the following towns of Haryana?
(*a*) Ambala (*b*) Panipat
(*c*) Karnal (*d*) Kaithal

364. Where did Lord Krishna delivered his inspirational messages to Arjuna which have been described in "Gita" as a dialogue between the two?
(*a*) Panipat (*b*) Kurukshetra
(*c*) Hodal (*d*) Thanesar

365. Which of the following towns of Haryana was the capital of Shrikantha Janapada during ancient times?
(*a*) Thanesar (*b*) Chandigarh
(*c*) Rohtak (*d*) Gurugram

366. The detailed description of which of the following ancient cities of Haryana is given in the account presented by Chinese pilgrim Huen Tsang?
(*a*) Rohtak (*b*) Ambala
(*c*) Thaneshwar (*d*) Bhiwani

367. Thaneshwar City of this state was at the pinnacle of its glory during
(*a*) Vardhan period (*b*) Gupta period
(*c*) Sunga period (*d*) Maurya period

368. The famous battle between the armies of Babur and Ibrahim Lodi in 1526 was fought at which of the following places in Haryana?
(*a*) Jhajjhar (*b*) Kurukshetra
(*c*) Rohtak (*d*) Panipat

369. Panipat town was given the status of District on
(*a*) 1 January, 1988 (*b*) 1 November, 1989
(*c*) 1 December, 1990 (*d*) 17 June, 1980

370. Rewari district was formed on
(*a*) 10 June, 1977 (*b*) 5 February, 1979
(*c*) 1 November, 1989 (*d*) 17 June, 1980

371. Hissar is the birth place of which of the following famous kings?
(*a*) Shershah Suri (*b*) Akbar
(*c*) Muhammad Tughlaq (*d*) Feroz Tughlaq

372. In which of the following towns has the largest cattle farm of Haryana?
(*a*) Narnaul (*b*) Hissar
(*c*) Panipat (*d*) Karnal

373. In 1354, who of the following famous ruler of the medieval India built the town of Hissar as a fort?
(*a*) Muhammad Tughlaq (*b*) Balban
(*c*) Feroz Tughlaq (*d*) Alauddin Khilji

374. During ancient times, Mahendragarh town of this state was known as
(*a*) Janauva (*b*) Karnpur
(*c*) Mahipgarh (*d*) Kanaud

375. Name the last king of Ballabhgarh who died as a martyr during freedom struggle of 1857.
(*a*) Nahar Singh (*b*) Vijay Singh
(*c*) Pratap Singh (*d*) Mahar Singh

376. Ballabhgarh town is included in which of the following districts of Haryana?
(*a*) Rohtak (*b*) Faridabad
(*c*) Gurugram (*d*) Karnal

377. Narwana Tehsil is situated in which of the following Districts of the state?
(*a*) Sirsa (*b*) Bhiwani
(*c*) Jind (*d*) Fatehabad

378. Grave of the famous Sultana Raziya of Ghulam dynasty is located in which of the following districts of the state?
(*a*) Kaithal (*b*) Gurugram
(*c*) Ambala (*d*) Faridabad

379. Which of the following towns of Haryana is termed as 'a big bowl of paddy' and 'Paris of Haryana'?
(*a*) Rohtak (*b*) Sonepat
(*c*) Faridabad (*d*) Karnal

380. In 1607, Faridabad town was built by
(*a*) Feroz Shah (*b*) Mubarakshah
(*c*) Baba Farid (*d*) Mansub Ali

381. During the Mahabharata period Sirsa was known as
(*a*) Shishira (*b*) Shairishkam
(*c*) Saurish (*d*) Sirisa

382. During ancient times, Gohana town of the state was known as
(*a*) Gawabh Bhawana (*b*) Gadhana
(*c*) Gapat Zamana (*d*) None of these

383. During ancient tines, Bahadurgarh town of the state was known as
(*a*) Bahawalgarh (*b*) Shafirabad
(*c*) Sharfabad (*d*) Balramgarh

384. Britishers confiscated Bahadurgarh from Scindia King and handed it as a Jaghir to the brother of Nawab of Jhajjhar in
(*a*) 1800 AD (*b*) 1801 AD
(*c*) 1805 AD (*d*) 1803 AD

385. Which of the following towns of the state was built by a Rajput named Amba in the 14th century?
(*a*) Jhajjhar (*b*) Rohtak
(*c*) Ambala (*d*) Bhiwani

386. Abdur Rahman Khan who sacrificed his life during freedom struggle, hailed from which of the following towns of Haryana?
(*a*) Kurukshetra (*b*) Jhajjhar
(*c*) Farrukh Nagar (*d*) Rewari

387. Farrukh Nagar was built by which of the following Biloch rulers?
(*a*) Dalel Khan (Faujdar Khan)
(*b*) Shaffuddin Khan
(*c*) Badar Khan
(*d*) Jamaluddin Khan

388. Biloch ruler Dalel Khan (Faujdar Khan) built the town of Farrukh Nagar in the name of which of the following Emperors?
(*a*) Fakhruddin Ahmad (*b*) Farukh Ali
(*c*) Ferozshah Tughlaq (*d*) Farrukh Siyar

389. Great epic Mahabharata was composed by Maharshi Ved Vyas in which of the following towns of Haryana?
(*a*) Panipat (*b*) Rewari
(*c*) Kurukshetra (*d*) Hissar

390. Rise of Vardhan dynasty took place in which of the following towns of Haryana?
(*a*) Thanesar (Sthaneshwar)
(*b*) Rohtak
(*c*) Panipat
(*d*) Kurukshetra

391. In 1556, the famous battle between the forces of Akbar and Hemchandra (Hemu) of Rewari was fought at which of the following places in Haryana?
(*a*) Rewari (*b*) Jind
(*c*) Kurukshetra (*d*) Panipat

392. In 1761 the third battle of Panipat was fought between the forces of
(*a*) Babur and Ibrahim Lodi
(*b*) Akbar and Hemchandra (Hemu)
(*c*) Afghans and Marathas
(*d*) Britishers and Sikhs

393. The town of Panipat was under which of the following districts of Haryana till 31 October, 1989?
(*a*) Rewari (*b*) Ambala
(*c*) Karnal (*d*) Hissar

394. Which of the following districts of the state was included under Gurugram and Mahendragarh districts before 1989?
(*a*) Mahendragarh (*b*) Faridabad
(*c*) Jind (*d*) Rewari

395. Jind was given the status of district in
(*a*) 1966 (*b*) 1972
(*c*) 1968 (*d*) 1975

396. Which of the following districts of Haryana has its headquarters at Narnaul?
(*a*) Hissar (*b*) Faridabad
(*c*) Mahendragarh (*d*) Karnal

397. Who amongst the following did not play for Haryana in Ranji Trophy?
(*a*) Kapil Dev (*b*) Rajinder Goel
(*c*) Sarkar Talwar (*d*) Maninder Singh

398. When Palwal came into existence as the 21st districts of Haryana?
(*a*) 2006 (*b*) 2005
(*c*) 2008 (*d*) 2007

399. During Mahabharat period, which of the following places was given by Raja Yudhishthir to his Guru Dronacharya as a gift?
(*a*) Gurugram village (*b*) Kaithal
(*c*) Hodal (*d*) Sirsa

400. Who was the Collector of Gurugram during the freedom struggle of 1857?
(*a*) Henry (*b*) Sir Helley
(*c*) John Marshall (*d*) Shri Ford

401. In 1858, which of the following districts of Haryana was included in Punjab?
(*a*) Faridabad (*b*) Gurugram
(*c*) Hissar (*d*) Mahendragarh

402. When Faridabad came into existence as the 12th district of Haryana?
(*a*) 15 August, 1970 (*b*) 02 August, 1979
(*c*) 26 January, 1979 (*d*) 8 March, 1982

403. Bahadurgarh town is included in which of the following districts of Haryana?
(*a*) Jhajjar (*b*) Karnal
(*c*) Yamun Nagar (*d*) Faridabad

404. The historical town Gohana is included in which of the following districts of Haryana?
(*a*) Panipat (*b*) Sirsa
(*c*) Sonepat (*d*) Rewari

405. In which year 'Sirsa' became a district?
(*a*) 1980 (*b*) 1975
(*c*) 1990 (*d*) 1995

406. Hodal Sub-division is located in which district of Haryana?
(*a*) Rohtak (*b*) Sonepat
(*c*) Palwal (*d*) Panipat

407. Tosham town of district. Bhiwani was given the status of Sub-Division on
(*a*) 27 April, 1993 (*b*) 10 June, 1995
(*c*) 5 March, 1997 (*d*) 27 April, 1998

408. Which of the following famous temples is situated at historical town "Sadhaura"of district Yamuna Nagar?
(*a*) Manokamna Temple (*b*) Gagarwala Temple
(*c*) Toranwala Temple (*d*) All of these

409. In which of the following historical towns of Yamuna Nagar district, the Gurudwara of Buddhushah is situated which had helped Guru Govind Singh in the battle of Bhagani?
(*a*) Sadhaura (*b*) Radaur
(*c*) Bilaspur (*d*) Chhachhrauli

410. In ancient times Bahadurgarh town of Haryana was called as
(*a*) Charkhabad (*b*) Hasinpur
(*c*) Sharfabad (*d*) Betawabad

411. The historical town of Maham is situated in which of the following districts of the state?
(*a*) Bhiwani (*b*) Rohtak
(*c*) Yamuna Nagar (*d*) Jhajjhar

412. Maham town situated in district Rohtak was rebuilt by a person called Peshora of Kayastha (Baniya) Community in
(*a*) 1266 (*b*) 1295
(*c*) 1298 (*d*) 1299

413. Ailanabad town situated in district Sirsa was earlier known as
(*a*) Ailisabad (*b*) Chavipur
(*c*) Kalisabad (*d*) Khariyal

414. What was the earlier name of the historical town 'Raniyan' situated in district Sirsa?
(*a*) Rajabpur (*b*) Sajupur
(*c*) Rajipur (*d*) Ratipur

415. Which of the following towns situated in district Ambala was built by the King of Sirmour (Himachal Pradesh) Raja Laxmi Narayan?
(*a*) Barara (*b*) Mulana
(*c*) Narayangarh (*d*) Raipur Rani

416. By excavations done in which of the following historical towns of Sonepat district, earthen utensils belonging to Mahabharata period have been found?
(*a*) Rai (*b*) Kheri Gujjar
(*c*) Gankaur (*d*) Gohana

417. Mythological village Aadi Badri is situated in which of the following districts of Haryana?
(*a*) Yamuna Nagar (*b*) Bhiwani
(*c*) Sirsa (*d*) Rewari

418. Which of the following historical villages situated in district Yamuna Nagar is associated with King Santanu of the Mahabharata period?
(*a*) Chhachhrauli (*b*) Aadi Badri
(*c*) Basantar (*d*) None of these

419. At which of the following places Mazaar of Altaf Hussain Hali is located?
(*a*) Sonepat (*b*) Gurugram
(*c*) Panipat (*d*) Jind

420. Which of the following places was made a powerful centre of Afghan chiefs by Ahmadshah Abdali before the third battle of Panipat?
(*a*) Gharauda (*b*) Nilpe Khedi
(*c*) Asangh (*d*) Kunjpura

ANSWERS

1	**2**	**3**	**4**	**5**	**6**	**7**	**8**	**9**	**10**
(*d*)	(*a*)	(*b*)	(*c*)	(*a*)	(*d*)	(*b*)	(*a*)	(*c*)	(*b*)
11	**12**	**13**	**14**	**15**	**16**	**17**	**18**	**19**	**20**
(*d*)	(*d*)	(*a*)	(*c*)	(*d*)	(*a*)	(*c*)	(*b*)	(*d*)	(*a*)
21	**22**	**23**	**24**	**25**	**26**	**27**	**28**	**29**	**30**
(*d*)	(*a*)	(*c*)	(*b*)	(*a*)	(*d*)	(*d*)	(*a*)	(*c*)	(*c*)
31	**32**	**33**	**34**	**35**	**36**	**37**	**38**	**39**	**40**
(*d*)	(*c*)	(*a*)	(*b*)	(*d*)	(*d*)	(*a*)	(*c*)	(*b*)	(*c*)
41	**42**	**43**	**44**	**45**	**46**	**47**	**48**	**49**	**50**
(*d*)	(*a*)	(*c*)	(*b*)	(*a*)	(*c*)	(*d*)	(*a*)	(*c*)	(*c*)
51	**52**	**53**	**54**	**55**	**56**	**57**	**58**	**59**	**60**
(*a*)	(*c*)	(*a*)	(*b*)	(*d*)	(*b*)	(*a*)	(*c*)	(*b*)	(*d*)
61	**62**	**63**	**64**	**65**	**66**	**67**	**68**	**69**	**70**
(*d*)	(*a*)	(*c*)	(*a*)	(*b*)	(*a*)	(*a*)	(*a*)	(*b*)	(*d*)
71	**72**	**73**	**74**	**75**	**76**	**77**	**78**	**79**	**80**
(*c*)	(*a*)	(*c*)	(*b*)	(*d*)	(*c*)	(*a*)	(*c*)	(*b*)	(*d*)
81	**82**	**83**	**84**	**85**	**86**	**87**	**88**	**89**	**90**
(*b*)	(*a*)	(*d*)	(*a*)	(*c*)	(*b*)	(*d*)	(*c*)	(*a*)	(*d*)
91	**92**	**93**	**94**	**95**	**96**	**97**	**98**	**99**	**100**
(*d*)	(*a*)	(*d*)	(*a*)	(*c*)	(*b*)	(*d*)	(*a*)	(*c*)	(*b*)
101	**102**	**103**	**104**	**105**	**106**	**107**	**108**	**109**	**110**
(*d*)	(*a*)	(*a*)	(*d*)	(*a*)	(*b*)	(*c*)	(*b*)	(*d*)	(*a*)
111	**112**	**113**	**114**	**115**	**116**	**117**	**118**	**119**	**120**
(*c*)	(*b*)	(*c*)	(*a*)	(*d*)	(*b*)	(*d*)	(*c*)	(*a*)	(*b*)
121	**122**	**123**	**124**	**125**	**126**	**127**	**128**	**129**	**130**
(*c*)	(*b*)	(*c*)	(*b*)	(*d*)	(*d*)	(*a*)	(*c*)	(*d*)	(*b*)
131	**132**	**133**	**134**	**135**	**136**	**137**	**138**	**139**	**140**
(*a*)	(*c*)	(*a*)	(*b*)	(*a*)	(*b*)	(*a*)	(*d*)	(*c*)	(*b*)
141	**142**	**143**	**144**	**145**	**146**	**147**	**148**	**149**	**150**
(*a*)	(*c*)	(*b*)	(*a*)	(*d*)	(*a*)	(*c*)	(*d*)	(*c*)	(*a*)
151	**152**	**153**	**154**	**155**	**156**	**157**	**158**	**159**	**160**
(*d*)	(*c*)	(*a*)	(*a*)	(*b*)	(*a*)	(*d*)	(*b*)	(*b*)	(*d*)
161	**162**	**163**	**164**	**165**	**166**	**167**	**168**	**169**	**170**
(*a*)	(*c*)	(*a*)	(*c*)	(*b*)	(*d*)	(*c*)	(*a*)	(*b*)	(*a*)

171	172	173	174	175	176	177	178	179	180
(b)	(d)	(a)	(a)	(d)	(b)	(a)	(b)	(b)	(c)
181	**182**	**183**	**184**	**185**	**186**	**187**	**188**	**189**	**190**
(a)	(a)	(c)	(d)	(b)	(c)	(d)	(a)	(c)	(d)
191	**192**	**193**	**194**	**195**	**196**	**197**	**198**	**199**	**200**
(d)	(a)	(b)	(b)	(a)	(c)	(a)	(d)	(b)	(a)
201	**202**	**203**	**204**	**205**	**206**	**207**	**208**	**209**	**210**
(d)	(c)	(a)	(d)	(a)	(d)	(c)	(b)	(b)	(a)
211	**212**	**213**	**214**	**215**	**216**	**217**	**218**	**219**	**220**
(a)	(a)	(c)	(a)	(b)	(a)	(a)	(b)	(d)	(a)
221	**222**	**223**	**224**	**225**	**226**	**227**	**228**	**229**	**230**
(b)	(c)	(b)	(d)	(a)	(c)	(a)	(c)	(b)	(a)
231	**232**	**233**	**234**	**235**	**236**	**237**	**238**	**239**	**240**
(d)	(a)	(b)	(a)	(d)	(d)	(a)	(c)	(b)	(d)
241	**242**	**243**	**244**	**245**	**246**	**247**	**248**	**249**	**250**
(d)	(a)	(c)	(b)	(a)	(a)	(c)	(b)	(a)	(a)
251	**252**	**253**	**254**	**255**	**256**	**257**	**258**	**259**	**260**
(b)	(a)	(c)	(b)	(d)	(c)	(d)	(d)	(c)	(a)
261	**262**	**263**	**264**	**265**	**266**	**267**	**268**	**269**	**270**
(b)	(d)	(c)	(a)	(b)	(c)	(a)	(b)	(a)	(c)
271	**272**	**273**	**274**	**275**	**276**	**277**	**278**	**279**	**280**
(b)	(b)	(d)	(c)	(d)	(d)	(a)	(a)	(b)	(a)
281	**282**	**283**	**284**	**285**	**286**	**287**	**288**	**289**	**290**
(c)	(b)	(a)	(c)	(b)	(d)	(c)	(c)	(a)	(c)
291	**292**	**293**	**294**	**295**	**296**	**297**	**298**	**299**	**300**
(b)	(a)	(a)	(b)	(d)	(a)	(c)	(d)	(a)	(b)
301	**302**	**303**	**304**	**305**	**306**	**307**	**308**	**309**	**310**
(a)	(c)	(d)	(a)	(c)	(b)	(c)	(a)	(c)	(d)
311	**312**	**313**	**314**	**315**	**316**	**317**	**318**	**319**	**320**
(a)	(b)	(a)	(b)	(c)	(d)	(a)	(c)	(b)	(a)
321	**322**	**323**	**324**	**325**	**326**	**327**	**328**	**329**	**330**
(c)	(d)	(a)	(a)	(d)	(a)	(b)	(d)	(c)	(a)
331	**332**	**333**	**334**	**335**	**336**	**337**	**338**	**339**	**340**
(b)	(d)	(a)	(c)	(a)	(b)	(d)	(a)	(c)	(a)
341	**342**	**343**	**344**	**345**	**346**	**347**	**348**	**349**	**350**
(c)	(d)	(c)	(b)	(a)	(c)	(d)	(a)	(d)	(a)
351	**352**	**353**	**354**	**355**	**356**	**357**	**358**	**359**	**360**
(c)	(d)	(c)	(b)	(d)	(d)	(b)	(c)	(b)	(d)
361	**362**	**363**	**364**	**365**	**366**	**367**	**368**	**369**	**370**
(c)	(a)	(c)	(b)	(a)	(c)	(a)	(d)	(b)	(c)
371	**372**	**373**	**374**	**375**	**376**	**377**	**378**	**379**	**380**
(a)	(b)	(c)	(d)	(a)	(b)	(c)	(a)	(d)	(c)
381	**382**	**383**	**384**	**385**	**386**	**387**	**388**	**389**	**390**
(b)	(a)	(c)	(d)	(c)	(b)	(a)	(d)	(c)	(a)
391	**392**	**393**	**394**	**395**	**396**	**397**	**398**	**399**	**400**
(d)	(c)	(c)	(d)	(a)	(c)	(d)	(c)	(a)	(d)
401	**402**	**403**	**404**	**405**	**406**	**407**	**408**	**409**	**410**
(b)	(b)	(a)	(c)	(b)	(c)	(a)	(d)	(a)	(c)
411	**412**	**413**	**414**	**415**	**416**	**417**	**418**	**419**	**420**
(b)	(a)	(d)	(a)	(c)	(b)	(a)	(c)	(c)	(d)

❑ ❑ ❑